T0185358

Lecture Notes in Computer Science 12075

More information about this series at http://www.springer.com/series/7407

Peter Müller (Ed.)

Programming
Languages
and Systems

29th European Symposium on Programming, ESOP 2020
Held as Part of the European Joint Conferences
on Theory and Practice of Software, ETAPS 2020
Dublin, Ireland, April 25–30, 2020
Proceedings

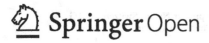 Springer Open

Editor
Peter Müller
ETH Zurich
Zurich, Switzerland

ISSN 0302-9743   ISSN 1611-3349   (electronic)
Lecture Notes in Computer Science
ISBN 978-3-030-44913-1   ISBN 978-3-030-44914-8   (eBook)
https://doi.org/10.1007/978-3-030-44914-8

LNCS Sublibrary: SL1 – Theoretical Computer Science and General Issues

This Springer imprint is published by the registered company Springer Nature Switzerland AG
The registered company address is: Gewerbestrasse 11, 6330 Cham, Switzerland

ETAPS Foreword

Welcome to the 23rd ETAPS! This is the first time that ETAPS took place in Ireland in its beautiful capital Dublin.

ETAPS 2020 was the 23rd instance of the European Joint Conferences on Theory and Practice of Software. ETAPS is an annual federated conference established in 1998, and consists of four conferences: ESOP, FASE, FoSSaCS, and TACAS. Each conference has its own Program Committee (PC) and its own Steering Committee (SC). The conferences cover various aspects of software systems, ranging from theoretical computer science to foundations of programming language developments, analysis tools, and formal approaches to software engineering. Organizing these conferences in a coherent, highly synchronized conference program enables researchers to participate in an exciting event, having the possibility to meet many colleagues working in different directions in the field, and to easily attend talks of different conferences. On the weekend before the main conference, numerous satellite workshops took place that attracted many researchers from all over the globe. Also, for the second time, an ETAPS Mentoring Workshop was organized. This workshop is intended to help students early in the program with advice on research, career, and life in the fields of computing that are covered by the ETAPS conference.

ETAPS 2020 received 424 submissions in total, 129 of which were accepted, yielding an overall acceptance rate of 30.4%. I thank all the authors for their interest in ETAPS, all the reviewers for their reviewing efforts, the PC members for their contributions, and in particular the PC (co-)chairs for their hard work in running this entire intensive process. Last but not least, my congratulations to all authors of the accepted papers!

ETAPS 2020 featured the unifying invited speakers Scott Smolka (Stony Brook University) and Jane Hillston (University of Edinburgh) and the conference-specific invited speakers (ESOP) Işıl Dillig (University of Texas at Austin) and (FASE) Willem Visser (Stellenbosch University). Invited tutorials were provided by Erika Ábrahám (RWTH Aachen University) on the analysis of hybrid systems and Madhusudan Parthasarathy (University of Illinois at Urbana-Champaign) on combining Machine Learning and Formal Methods. On behalf of the ETAPS 2020 attendants, I thank all the speakers for their inspiring and interesting talks!

ETAPS 2020 took place in Dublin, Ireland, and was organized by the University of Limerick and Lero. ETAPS 2020 is further supported by the following associations and societies: ETAPS e.V., EATCS (European Association for Theoretical Computer Science), EAPLS (European Association for Programming Languages and Systems), and EASST (European Association of Software Science and Technology). The local organization team consisted of Tiziana Margaria (general chair, UL and Lero), Vasileios Koutavas (Lero@UCD), Anila Mjeda (Lero@UL), Anthony Ventresque (Lero@UCD), and Petros Stratis (Easy Conferences).

The ETAPS Steering Committee (SC) consists of an Executive Board, and representatives of the individual ETAPS conferences, as well as representatives of EATCS, EAPLS, and EASST. The Executive Board consists of Holger Hermanns (Saarbrücken), Marieke Huisman (chair, Twente), Joost-Pieter Katoen (Aachen and Twente), Jan Kofron (Prague), Gerald Lüttgen (Bamberg), Tarmo Uustalu (Reykjavik and Tallinn), Caterina Urban (Inria, Paris), and Lenore Zuck (Chicago).

Other members of the SC are: Armin Biere (Linz), Jordi Cabot (Barcelona), Jean Goubault-Larrecq (Cachan), Jan-Friso Groote (Eindhoven), Esther Guerra (Madrid), Jurriaan Hage (Utrecht), Reiko Heckel (Leicester), Panagiotis Katsaros (Thessaloniki), Stefan Kiefer (Oxford), Barbara König (Duisburg), Fabrice Kordon (Paris), Jan Kretinsky (Munich), Kim G. Larsen (Aalborg), Tiziana Margaria (Limerick), Peter Müller (Zurich), Catuscia Palamidessi (Palaiseau), Dave Parker (Birmingham), Andrew M. Pitts (Cambridge), Peter Ryan (Luxembourg), Don Sannella (Edinburgh), Bernhard Steffen (Dortmund), Mariëlle Stoelinga (Twente), Gabriele Taentzer (Marburg), Christine Tasson (Paris), Peter Thiemann (Freiburg), Jan Vitek (Prague), Heike Wehrheim (Paderborn), Anton Wijs (Eindhoven), and Nobuko Yoshida (London).

I would like to take this opportunity to thank all speakers, attendants, organizers of the satellite workshops, and Springer for their support. I hope you all enjoyed ETAPS 2020. Finally, a big thanks to Tiziana and her local organization team for all their enormous efforts enabling a fantastic ETAPS in Dublin!

February 2020

Marieke Huisman
ETAPS SC Chair
ETAPS e.V. President

Preface

Welcome to the European Symposium on Programming (ESOP 2020)! The 29th edition of this conference series was initially planned to be held April 27–30, 2020, in Dublin, Ireland, but was then moved to fall 2020 due to the COVID-19 outbreak. ESOP is one of the European Joint Conferences on Theory and Practice of Software (ETAPS). It is devoted to fundamental issues in the specification, design, analysis, and implementation of programming languages and systems.

This volume contains 27 papers, which the Program Committee (PC) selected among 87 submissions. Each submission received between three and six reviews. After an author response period, the papers were discussed electronically among the PC members and external reviewers. The one paper for which the PC chair had a conflict of interest was kindly handled by Sasa Misailovic.

Submissions authored by a PC member were held to slightly higher standards: they received at least four reviews, had an external reviewer, and were accepted only if they were not involved in comparisons of relative merit with other submissions. We accepted two out of four PC submissions.

The final program includes a keynote by Işıl Dillig on "Formal Methods for Evolving Database Applications."

Any conference depends first and foremost on the quality of its submissions. I would like to thank all the authors who submitted their work to ESOP 2020! I am truly impressed by the members of the PC. They produced insightful and constructive reviews, contributed very actively to the online discussions, and were extremely helpful. It was an honor to work with all of you! I am also grateful to the external reviewers, who provided their expert opinions and helped tremendously to reach well-informed decisions. I would like to thank everybody who contributed to the organization of ESOP 2020, especially the ESOP 2020 Steering Committee and its chair Peter Thiemann as well as the ETAPS 2020 Steering Committee and its chair Marieke Huisman, who provided help and guidance on numerous occasions. Finally, I'd like to thank Linard Arquint and Vasileios Koutavas for their help with the proceedings.

February 2020   Peter Müller

Organization

Program Committee

Elvira Albert   Universidad Complutense de Madrid, Spain
Sophia Drossopoulou   Imperial College London, UK
Jean-Christophe Filliatre   LRI, CNRS, France
Arie Gurfinkel   University of Waterloo, Canada
Jan Hoffmann   Carnegie Mellon University, USA
Ranjit Jhala   University of California at San Diego, USA
Woosuk Lee   Hanyang University, South Korea
Rustan Leino   Amazon Web Services, USA
Rupak Majumdar   MPI-SWS, Germany
Roland Meyer   Technische Universität Braunschweig, Germany
Antoine Miné   LIP6, Sorbonne Université, France
Sasa Misailovic   University of Illinois at Urbana-Champaign, USA
Toby Murray   University of Melbourne, Australia
Peter Müller   ETH Zurich, Switzerland
David Naumann   Stevens Institute of Technology, USA
Zvonimir Rakamaric   University of Utah, USA
Francesco Ranzato   University of Padova, Italy
Sukyoung Ryu   KAIST, South Korea
Ilya Sergey   Yale-NUS College and National University
      of Singapore, Singapore
Alexandra Silva   University College London, UK
Nikhil Swamy   Microsoft Research, USA
Sam Tobin-Hochstadt   Indiana University Bloomington, USA
Caterina Urban   Inria Paris, France
Viktor Vafeiadis   MPI-SWS, Germany

Additional Reviewers

Amtoft, Torben
Arenas, Puri
Balabonski, Thibaut
Bernardy, Jean-Philippe
Bierman, Gavin
Blanchet, Bruno
Bonchi, Filippo
Bonelli, Eduardo
Botbol, Vincent
Bourke, Timothy

Brady, Edwin
Brunet, Paul
Caires, Luís
Charguéraud, Arthur
Chini, Peter
Chudnov, Andrey
Correas Fernández, Jesús
Costea, Andreea
Cousot, Patrick
Crole, Roy

Cusumano-Towner, Marco
Dagand, Pierre-Evariste
Dahlqvist, Fredrik
Dang, Hai
Danielsson, Nils Anders
Das, Ankush
Enea, Constantin
Finkbeiner, Bernd
Fromherz, Aymeric
Fuhs, Carsten
Genaim, Samir
Genitrini, Antoine
Ghica, Dan
Gordillo, Pablo
Gordon, Colin S.
Haas, Thomas
Hage, Jurriaan
He, Shaobo
Heljanko, Keijo
Jourdan, Jacques-Henri
Kahn, David
Kang, Jeehoon
Kuderski, Jakub
Lahav, Ori
Laurent, Olivier
Lee, Dongkwon
Lee, Wonyeol
Lesani, Mohsen
Levy, Paul Blain
Lindley, Sam
Martin-Martin, Enrique
Mohan, Anshuman
Mordido, Andreia
Morris, J. Garrett

Muller, Stefan
Ngo, Minh
Oh, Hakjoo
Ouadjaout, Abdelraouf
Ouederni, Meriem
Palamidessi, Catuscia
Pearlmutter, Barak
Peters, Kirstin
Pham, Long
Poli, Federico
Polikarpova, Nadia
Pottier, François
Rival, Xavier
Román-Díez, Guillermo
Sammartino, Matteo
Sasse, Ralf
Scalas, Alceste
Scherer, Gabriel
Sieczkowski, Filip
Sivaramakrishnan, Kc
Staton, Sam
Stutsman, Ryan
Tan, Yong Kiam
van den Brand, Mark
Vákár, Matthijs
Wang, Di
Wang, Meng
Wehrheim, Heike
Weng, Shu-Chun
Wies, Thomas
Wijesekera, Duminda
Wolff, Sebastian
Zufferey, Damien

Formal Methods for Evolving Database Applications
(Abstract of Keynote Talk)

Işıl Dillig

University of Texas at Austin, USA
isil@cs.utexas.edu

Many database applications undergo significant schema changes during their life cycle due to performance or maintainability reasons. Examples of such schema changes include denormalization, splitting a single table into multiple tables, and consolidating multiple tables into a single table. Even though such schema refactorings are quite common in practice, programmers need to spend significant time and effort to re-implement parts of the code base that are affected by the schema change. Furthermore, it is not uncommon to introduce bugs during this code transformation process.

In this talk, I will present our recent work on using formal methods to simplify the schema refactoring process for evolving database applications. Specifically, I will first propose a definition of equivalence between database applications that operate over different schemas. Building on this definition, I will then present a fully automated technique for proving equivalence between a pair of applications. Our verification technique is capable of automatically synthesizing bisimulation invariants between two database applications and uses the inferred bisimulation invariant to automatically prove equivalence.

In the next part of the talk, I will explain how to leverage this verification technique to completely automate the code migration process. Specifically, given an original database application P over schema S and a new schema S', I will discuss a practical program synthesis technique that can be used to generate a new program P' over schema S' such that P and P' are provably equivalent. In particular, I will first present a method for generating a program sketch of the new version; then, I will describe a novel synthesis algorithm that efficiently explores the space of all programs that are in the search space of the generated sketch.

Finally, I will describe experimental results on a suite of schema refactoring benchmarks, including real-world database applications written in Ruby-on-Rails. I will also outline remaining challenges in this area and motivate future research directions relevant to research in programming languages and formal methods.

Contents

Trace-Relating Compiler Correctness and Secure Compilation

Carmine Abate[1]   Roberto Blanco[1]   Ștefan Ciobâcă[2]   Adrian Durier[1]
Deepak Garg[3]   Cătălin Hriţcu[1]   Marco Patrignani[4,5]   Éric Tanter[6,1]   Jérémy Thibault[1]

[1]Inria Paris, France   [2]UAIC Iaşi, Romania   [3]MPI-SWS, Saarbrücken, Germany   [4]Stanford University, Stanford, USA
[5]CISPA, Saarbrücken, Germany   [6]University of Chile, Santiago, Chile

Abstract. Compiler correctness is, in its simplest form, defined as the inclusion of the set of traces of the compiled program into the set of traces of the original program, which is equivalent to the preservation of all trace properties. Here traces collect, for instance, the externally observable events of each execution. This definition requires, however, the set of traces of the source and target languages to be exactly the same, which is not the case when the languages are far apart or when observations are fine-grained. To overcome this issue, we study a generalized compiler correctness definition, which uses source and target traces drawn from potentially different sets and connected by an arbitrary relation. We set out to understand what guarantees this generalized compiler correctness definition gives us when instantiated with a non-trivial relation on traces. When this trace relation is not equality, it is no longer possible to preserve the trace properties of the source program unchanged. Instead, we provide a generic characterization of the target trace property ensured by correctly compiling a program that satisfies a given source property, and dually, of the source trace property one is required to show in order to obtain a certain target property for the compiled code. We show that this view on compiler correctness can naturally account for undefined behavior, resource exhaustion, different source and target values, side-channels, and various abstraction mismatches. Finally, we show that the same generalization also applies to many secure compilation definitions, which characterize the protection of a compiled program against linked adversarial code.

1 Introduction

Compiler correctness is an old idea [37, 40, 41] that has seen a significant revival in recent times. This new wave was started by the creation of the CompCert verified C compiler [33] and continued by the proposal of many significant extensions and variants of CompCert [8, 9, 12, 23, 29, 30, 42, 52, 56, 57, 61] and the success of many other milestone compiler verification projects, including Vellvm [64], Pilsner [45], CakeML [58], CertiCoq [4], etc. Yet, even for these verified compilers, the precise statement of correctness matters. Since proof assistants are used to conduct the verification, an external observer does not have to understand the proofs in order to trust them, but one still has to deeply understand the statement that was proved. And this is true not just for correct compilation, but also for secure compilation, which is the more recent idea that our compilation chains should do more to also ensure security of our programs [3, 26].

Basic Compiler Correctness. The gold standard for compiler correctness is *semantic preservation*, which intuitively says that the semantics of a compiled program (in the target language) is compatible with the semantics of the original program (in the source

P. Müller (Ed.): ESOP 2020, LNCS 12075, pp. 1–28, 2020.
https://doi.org/10.1007/978-3-030-44914-8_1

language). For practical verified compilers, such as CompCert [33] and CakeML [58], semantic preservation is stated extrinsically, by referring to *traces*. In these two settings, a trace is an ordered sequence of events—such as inputs from and outputs to an external environment—that are produced by the execution of a program.

A basic definition of compiler correctness can be given by the set inclusion of the traces of the compiled program into the traces of the original program. Formally [33]:

Definition 1.1 (Basic Compiler Correctness (CC)). *A compiler ↓ is correct iff*
$$\forall \mathsf{W}\ t.\ \mathsf{W}{\downarrow}{\rightsquigarrow}t \Rightarrow \mathsf{W}{\rightsquigarrow}t.$$

This definition says that for any whole[1] source program W, if we compile it (denoted W↓), execute it with respect to the semantics of the target language, and observe a trace t, then the original W can produce *the same* trace t with respect to the semantics of the source language.[2] This definition is simple and easy to understand, since it only references a few familiar concepts: a compiler between a source and a target language, each equipped with a trace-producing semantics (usually nondeterministic).

Beyond Basic Compiler Correctness. This basic compiler correctness definition assumes that any trace produced by a compiled program can be produced by the source program. This is a very strict requirement, and in particular implies that the source and target traces are drawn from the same set and that the same source trace corresponds to a given target trace. These assumptions are often too strong, and hence in practice verified compiler efforts use different formulations of compiler correctness:

CompCert [33] The original compiler correctness theorem of CompCert [33] can be seen as an instance of basic compiler correctness, but it does not provide any guarantees for programs that can exhibit undefined behavior [53]. As allowed by the C standard, such unsafe programs are not even considered to be in the source language, so are not quantified over. This has important practical implications, since undefined behavior often leads to exploitable security vulnerabilities [13, 24, 25] and serious confusion even among experienced C and C++ developers [32, 53, 59, 60]. As such, since 2010, CompCert provides an additional top-level correctness theorem[3] that better accounts for the presence of unsafe programs by providing guarantees for them up to the point when they encounter undefined behavior [53]. This new theorem goes beyond the basic correctness definition above, as a target trace need only correspond to a source trace *up to the occurrence* of undefined behavior in the source trace.

CakeML [58] Compiler correctness for CakeML accounts for memory exhaustion in target executions. Crucially, memory exhaustion events cannot occur in source traces, only in target traces. Hence, dually to CompCert, compiler correctness only requires source and target traces to coincide up to the occurrence of a memory exhaustion event in the target trace.

---

[1] For simplicity, for now we ignore separate compilation and linking, returning to it in §5.

[2] Typesetting convention [47]: we use a blue, sans-serif font for source elements, an orange, bold font for target ones and a *black*, *italic* font for elements common to both languages.

[3] Stated at the top of the CompCert file `driver/Complements.v` and discussed by Regehr [53].

Trace-Relating Compiler Correctness. Generalized formalizations of compiler correctness like the ones above can be naturally expressed as instances of a uniform definition, which we call *trace-relating compiler correctness*. This generalizes basic compiler correctness by (a) considering that source and target traces belong to *possibly distinct* sets Traces_S and Trace_T, and (b) being parameterized by an arbitrary *trace relation* $\sim$.

Definition 1.2 (Trace-Relating Compiler Correctness (CC$^\sim$)). *A compiler $\downarrow$ is correct with respect to a trace relation* $\sim \subseteq \text{Traces}_S \times \text{Trace}_T$ *iff*

$$\forall W.\forall t.\ W\!\downarrow\rightsquigarrow t \Rightarrow \exists s \sim t.\ W\rightsquigarrow s.$$

This definition requires that, for any target trace t produced by the compiled program $W\!\downarrow$, there exist a source trace s that can be produced by the original program W and is *related* to t according to $\sim$ (i.e., $s \sim t$). By choosing the trace relation appropriately, one can recover the different notions of compiler correctness presented above:

Basic CC Take $s \sim t$ to be $s = t$. Trivially, the basic CC of Definition 1.1 is CC$^=$.

CompCert Undefined behavior is modeled in CompCert as a trace-terminating event *Goes_wrong* that can occur in any of its languages (source, target, and all intermediate languages), so for a given phase (or composition thereof), we have $\text{Traces}_S = \text{Trace}_T$. Nevertheless, the relation between source and target traces with which to instantiate CC$^\sim$ to obtain CompCert's current theorem is:

$$s \sim t \quad \equiv \quad s = t \vee (\exists m \leq t.\ s = m \cdot \textit{Goes\_wrong}).$$

A compiler satisfying CC$^\sim$ for this trace relation can turn a source trace ending in undefined behavior $m \cdot$ *Goes_wrong* (where "$\cdot$" is concatenation) either into the same trace in the target (first disjunct), or into a target trace that starts with the prefix m but then continues *arbitrarily* (second disjunct, "$\leq$" is the prefix relation).

CakeML Here, target traces are sequences of symbols from an alphabet Σ_T that has a specific trace-terminating event, $\text{Resource\_limit\_hit}$, which is not available in the source alphabet Σ_S (i.e., $\Sigma_T = \Sigma_S \cup \{\text{Resource\_limit\_hit}\}$). Then, the compiler correctness theorem of CakeML can be obtained by instantiating CC$^\sim$ with the following $\sim$ relation:

$$s \sim t \quad \equiv \quad s = t \vee (\exists m.\ m \leq s.\ t = m \cdot \text{Resource\_limit\_hit}).$$

The resulting CC$^\sim$ instance relates a target trace ending in $\text{Resource\_limit\_hit}$ after executing m to a source trace that first produces m and then continues in a way given by the semantics of the source program.

Beyond undefined behavior and resource exhaustion, there are many other practical uses for CC$^\sim$: in this paper we show that it also accounts for differences between source and target values, for a single source output being turned into a series of target outputs, and for side-channels.

On the flip side, the compiler correctness statement and its implications can be more difficult to understand for CC$^\sim$ than for CC$^=$. The full implications of choosing a particular $\sim$ relation can be subtle. In fact, using a bad relation can make the compiler correctness statement trivial or unexpected. For instance, it should be easy to see that if one uses the total relation, which relates all source traces to all target ones, the CC$^\sim$ property holds for every compiler, yet it might take one a bit more effort to understand that the same is true even for the following relation:

$$s \sim t \quad \equiv \quad \exists W.W\rightsquigarrow s \wedge W\!\downarrow\rightsquigarrow t.$$

Reasoning About Trace Properties. To understand more about a particular $CC^\sim$ instance, we propose to also look at how it preserves *trace properties*—defined as sets of allowed traces [31]—from the source to the target. For instance, it is well known that $CC^=$ is equivalent to the preservation of all trace properties (where $W \models \pi$ reads "W satisfies π" and stands for $\forall t.\ W \leadsto t \Rightarrow t \in \pi$):

$$CC^= \quad \equiv \quad \forall \pi \in 2^{\text{Trace}} \ \forall W.\ W \models \pi \Rightarrow W{\downarrow} \models \pi.$$

However, to the best of our knowledge, similar results have not been formulated for trace relations beyond equality, when it is no longer possible to preserve the trace properties of the source program unchanged. For trace-relating compiler correctness, where source and target traces can be drawn from different sets and related by an arbitrary trace relation, there are two crucial questions to ask:

1. For a source trace property π_S of a program—established for instance by formal verification—what is the strongest target property that any $CC^\sim$ compiler is guaranteed to ensure for the produced target program?

2. For a target trace property π_T, what is the weakest source property we need to show of the original source program to obtain π_T for the result of any $CC^\sim$ compiler?

Far from being mere hypothetical questions, they can help the developer of a verified compiler to better understand the compiler correctness theorem they are proving, and we expect that any user of such a compiler will need to ask either one or the other if they are to make use of that theorem. In this work we provide a simple and natural answer to these questions, for any instance of $CC^\sim$. Building upon a bijection between relations and Galois connections [5, 20, 43], we observe that any trace relation $\sim$ corresponds to two *property mappings* $\tilde{\tau}$ and $\tilde{\sigma}$, which are functions mapping source properties to target ones ($\tilde{\tau}$ standing for "to target") and target properties to source ones ($\tilde{\sigma}$ standing for "to source"):

$$\tilde{\tau}(\pi_S) = \{t \mid \exists s.\ s \sim t \wedge s \in \pi_S\}; \qquad \tilde{\sigma}(\pi_T) = \{s \mid \forall t.\ s \sim t \Rightarrow t \in \pi_T\}.$$

The *existential image* of $\sim$, $\tilde{\tau}$, answers the first question above by mapping a given source property π_S to the target property that contains all target traces for which *there exists a related source trace* that satisfies π_S. Dually, the *universal image* of $\sim$, $\tilde{\sigma}$, answers the second question by mapping a given target property π_T to the source property that contains all source traces for which *all related target traces* satisfy π_T. We introduce two new correct compilation definitions in terms of *trace property preservation* (TP): $TP^{\tilde{\tau}}$ quantifies over all source trace properties and uses $\tilde{\tau}$ to obtain the corresponding target properties. $TP^{\tilde{\sigma}}$ quantifies over all target trace properties and uses $\tilde{\sigma}$ to obtain the corresponding source properties. We prove that these two definitions are equivalent to $CC^\sim$, yielding a novel trinitarian view of compiler correctness (Figure 1).

$$\forall W.\ \forall t.\ W{\downarrow} \leadsto t \Rightarrow \exists s \sim t.\ W \leadsto s$$

$$\text{|||}$$

$$CC^\sim$$

$$\begin{array}{ccc}
\forall \pi_T.\ \forall W.\ W \models \tilde{\sigma}(\pi_T) & & \forall \pi_S.\ \forall W.\ W \models \pi_S \\
\Rightarrow W{\downarrow} \models \pi_T \quad \equiv \quad TP^{\tilde{\sigma}} \longleftrightarrow TP^{\tilde{\tau}} \quad \equiv \quad \Rightarrow W{\downarrow} \models \tilde{\tau}(\pi_S)
\end{array}$$

Fig. 1: The equivalent compiler correctness definitions forming our trinitarian view.

Contributions.

▶ We propose a new trinitarian view of compiler correctness that accounts for non-trivial trace relations. While, as discussed above, specific instances of the $CC^\sim$ definition have already been used in practice, we seem to be the first to propose assessing the meaningfulness of $CC^\sim$ instances in terms of how properties are preserved between the source and the target, and in particular by looking at the property mappings $\tilde\sigma$ and $\tilde\tau$ induced by the trace relation $\sim$. We prove that $CC^\sim$, $TP^{\tilde\sigma}$, and $TP^{\tilde\tau}$ are equivalent for any trace relation (§2.2), as illustrated in Figure 1. In the opposite direction, we show that for every trace relation corresponding to a given Galois connection [20], an analogous equivalence holds. Finally, we extend these results (§2.3) from the preservation of trace properties to the larger class of subset-closed hyperproperties (e.g., noninterference).

▶ We use $CC^\sim$ compilers of various complexities to illustrate that our view on compiler correctness naturally accounts for undefined behavior (§3.1), resource exhaustion (§3.2), different source and target values (§3.3), and differences in the granularity of data and observable events (§3.4). We expect these ideas to apply to any other discrepancies between source and target traces. For each compiler we show how to choose the relation between source and target traces and how the induced property mappings preserve interesting trace properties and subset-closed hyperproperties. We look at the way particular $\tilde\sigma$ and $\tilde\tau$ work on different kinds of properties and how the produced properties can be expressed for different kinds of traces.

▶ We analyze the impact of correct compilation on noninterference [22], showing what can still be preserved (and thus also what is lost) when target observations are finer than source ones, e.g., side-channel observations (§4). We formalize the guarantee obtained by correct compilation of a noninterfering program as *abstract noninterference* [21], a weakening of target noninterference. Dually, we identify a family of declassifications of target noninterference for which source reasoning is possible.

▶ Finally, we show that the trinitarian view also extends to a large class of *secure compilation* definitions [2], formally characterizing the protection of the compiled program against linked adversarial code (§5). For each secure compilation definition we again propose both a property-free characterization in the style of $CC^\sim$, and two characterizations in terms of preserving a class of source or target properties satisfied against arbitrary adversarial contexts. The additional quantification over contexts allows for finer distinctions when considering different property classes, so we study mapping classes not only of trace properties and hyperproperties, but also of relational hyperproperties [2]. An example secure compiler accounting for a target that can produce additional trace events that are not possible in the source illustrates this approach.

The paper closes with discussions of related (§6) and future work (§7). An online appendix contains omitted technical details: https://arxiv.org/abs/1907.05320.

The traces considered in our examples are structured, usually as sequences of events. We notice however that unless explicitly mentioned, all our definitions and results are more general and make no assumption whatsoever about the structure of traces. Most of the theorems formally or informally mentioned in the paper were mechanized in the Coq proof assistant and are marked with ⚓. This development has around 10k lines of code, is described in the online appendix, and is available at the following address: https://github.com/secure-compilation/different_traces.

2   Trace-Relating Compiler Correctness

In this section, we start by generalizing the trace property preservation definitions at the end of the introduction to TP^σ and TP^τ, which depend on two *arbitrary* mappings σ and τ (§2.1). We prove that, whenever σ and τ form a Galois connection, TP^σ and TP^τ are equivalent (Theorem 2.4). We then exploit a bijective correspondence between trace relations and Galois connections to close the trinitarian view (§2.2), with two main benefits: first, it helps us assess the meaningfulness of a given trace relation by looking at the property mappings it induces; second, it allows us to construct new compiler correctness definitions starting from a desired mapping of properties. Finally, we generalize the classic result that compiler correctness (i.e., $\mathsf{CC}^=$) is enough to preserve not just trace properties but also all subset-closed hyperproperties [14]. For this, we show that $\mathsf{CC}^\sim$ is also equivalent to subset-closed hyperproperty preservation, for which we also define both a version in terms of $\tilde{\sigma}$ and a version in terms of $\tilde{\tau}$ (§2.3).

2.1   Property Mappings

As explained in §1, trace-relating compiler correctness $\mathsf{CC}^\sim$, by itself, lacks a crisp description of which trace properties are preserved by compilation. Since even the syntax of traces can differ between source and target, one can either look at trace properties of the source (but then one needs to interpret them in the target), or at trace properties of the target (but then one needs to interpret them in the source). Formally we need two property mappings, $\tau : 2^{\mathsf{Traces}} \to 2^{\mathrm{Trace_T}}$ and $\sigma : 2^{\mathrm{Trace_T}} \to 2^{\mathsf{Traces}}$, which lead us to the following generalization of trace property preservation (TP).

Definition 2.1 (TP^σ and TP^τ). *Given two property mappings, $\tau : 2^{\mathsf{Traces}} \to 2^{\mathrm{Trace_T}}$ and $\sigma : 2^{\mathrm{Trace_T}} \to 2^{\mathsf{Traces}}$, for a compilation chain $\cdot\!\downarrow$ we define:*

$$\mathsf{TP}^\tau \equiv \forall \pi_\mathsf{S}. \forall \mathsf{W}. \mathsf{W} \models \pi_\mathsf{S} \Rightarrow \mathsf{W}{\downarrow} \models \tau(\pi_\mathsf{S}); \quad \mathsf{TP}^\sigma \equiv \forall \pi_\mathrm{T}. \forall \mathsf{W}. \mathsf{W} \models \sigma(\pi_\mathrm{T}) \Rightarrow \mathsf{W}{\downarrow} \models \pi_\mathrm{T}.$$

For an arbitrary source program W, τ interprets a source property π_S as the *target guarantee* for $\mathsf{W}{\downarrow}$. Dually, σ defines a *source obligation* sufficient for the satisfaction of a target property π_T after compilation. Ideally:
- Given π_T, the target interpretation of the source obligation $\sigma(\pi_\mathrm{T})$ should actually guarantee that π_T holds, i.e., $\tau(\sigma(\pi_\mathrm{T})) \subseteq \pi_\mathrm{T}$;
- Dually for π_S, we would not want the source obligation for $\tau(\pi_\mathsf{S})$ to be harder than π_S itself, i.e., $\sigma(\tau(\pi_\mathsf{S})) \supseteq \pi_\mathsf{S}$.

These requirements are satisfied when the two maps form a *Galois connection* between the posets of source and target properties ordered by inclusion. We briefly recall the definition and the characteristic property of Galois connections [16, 38].

Definition 2.2 (Galois connection). *Let $(X, \preceq)$ and $(Y, \sqsubseteq)$ be two posets. A pair of maps, $\alpha : X \to Y, \gamma : Y \to X$ is a Galois connection iff it satisfies the adjunction law: $\forall x \in X. \forall y \in Y. \alpha(x) \sqsubseteq y \iff x \preceq \gamma(y)$. α (resp. γ) is the lower (upper) adjoint or abstraction (concretization) function and Y (X) the abstract (concrete) domain.*

We will often write $\alpha : (X, \preceq) \leftrightarrows (Y, \sqsubseteq) : \gamma$ to denote a Galois connection, or simply $\alpha : X \leftrightarrows Y : \gamma$, or even $\alpha \leftrightarrows \gamma$ when the involved posets are clear from context.

Lemma 2.3 (Characteristic property of Galois connections). *If* $\alpha : (X, \preceq) \leftrightarrows (Y, \sqsubseteq) : \gamma$
is a Galois connection, then α, γ *are monotone and they satisfy these properties:*

$$i) \quad \forall x \in X. \ x \preceq \gamma(\alpha(x)); \qquad\qquad ii) \quad \forall y \in Y. \ \alpha(\gamma(y)) \sqsubseteq y.$$

If X, Y *are complete lattices, then* α *is continuous, i.e.,* $\forall F \subseteq X. \ \alpha(\bigsqcup F) = \bigsqcup \alpha(F).$

If two property mappings, τ and σ, form a Galois connection on trace properties ordered by set inclusion, Lemma 2.3 (with $\alpha = \tau$ and $\gamma = \sigma$) tells us that they satisfy the ideal conditions we discussed above, i.e., $\tau(\sigma(\pi_T)) \subseteq \pi_T$ and $\sigma(\tau(\pi_S)) \supseteq \pi_S$.[4]

The two ideal conditions on τ and σ are sufficient to show the equivalence of the criteria they define, respectively TP^τ and TP^σ.

Theorem 2.4 (TP^τ **and** TP^σ **coincide** ✎). *Let* $\tau : 2^{\mathsf{Traces}} \rightleftarrows 2^{\mathsf{Trace_T}} : \sigma$ *be a Galois connection, with* τ *and* σ *the lower and upper adjoints (resp.). Then* $\mathsf{TP}^\tau \iff \mathsf{TP}^\sigma$.

2.2 Trace Relations and Property Mappings

We now investigate the relation between $\mathsf{CC}^\sim$, TP^τ and TP^σ. We show that for a trace relation and its corresponding Galois connection (Lemma 2.7), the three criteria are equivalent (Theorem 2.8). This equivalence offers interesting insights for both verification and design of a correct compiler. For a $\mathsf{CC}^\sim$ compiler, the equivalence makes explicit both the guarantees one has after compilation ($\tilde{\tau}$) and source proof obligations to ensure the satisfaction of a given target property ($\tilde{\sigma}$). On the other hand, a compiler designer might first determine the target guarantees the compiler itself must provide, i.e., τ, and then prove an equivalent statement, $\mathsf{CC}^\sim$, for which more convenient proof techniques exist in the literature [7, 58].

Definition 2.5 (Existential and Universal Image [20]). *Given any two sets* X *and* Y *and a relation* $\sim \subseteq A \times B$, *define its existential or direct image,* $\tilde{\tau} : 2^X \to 2^Y$ *and its universal image,* $\tilde{\sigma} : 2^Y \to 2^X$ *as follows:*

$$\tilde{\tau} = \lambda \, \pi \in 2^X. \ \{ y \mid \exists x. \ x \sim y \wedge x \in \pi \} \, ; \tilde{\sigma} = \lambda \, \pi \in 2^Y. \ \{ x \mid \forall y. \ x \sim y \Rightarrow y \in \pi \}.$$

When trace relations are considered, the existential and universal images can be used to instantiate Definition 2.1 leading to the trinitarian view already mentioned in §1.

Theorem 2.6 (Trinitarian View ✎**).** *For any trace relation* $\sim$ *and its existential and universal images* $\tilde{\tau}$ *and* $\tilde{\sigma}$, *we have:* $\mathsf{TP}^{\tilde{\tau}} \iff \mathsf{CC}^\sim \iff \mathsf{TP}^{\tilde{\sigma}}$.

This result relies both on Theorem 2.4 and on the fact that the existential and universal images of a trace relation form a Galois connection (✎). Below we further generalize this result (Theorem 2.8) relying on a bijective correspondence between trace relations and Galois connections on properties.

Lemma 2.7 (Trace relations $\cong$ **Galois connections on trace properties).** *The function* $\sim \mapsto \tilde{\tau} \leftrightarrows \tilde{\sigma}$ *that maps a trace relation to its existential and universal images is a bijection between trace relations* $2^{\mathsf{Traces} \times \mathsf{Trace_T}}$ *and Galois connections on trace properties* $2^{\mathsf{Traces}} \leftrightarrows 2^{\mathsf{Trace_T}}$. *Its inverse is* $\tau \leftrightarrows \sigma \mapsto \hat{\sim}$, *where* $\mathsf{s} \hat{\sim} \mathsf{t} \equiv \mathsf{t} \in \tau(\{\mathsf{s}\})$.

---

[4] While target traces are often *"more concrete"* than source ones, trace properties 2^{Trace} (which in Coq we represent as the function type Trace→Prop) are contravariant in Trace and thus target properties correspond to the *abstract domain*.

Proof. Gardiner et al. [20] show that the existential image is a functor from the category of sets and relations to the category of predicate transformers, mapping a set $X \mapsto 2^X$ and a relation $\sim \; \subseteq X \times Y \mapsto \tilde{\tau} : 2^X \to 2^Y$. They also show that such a functor is an isomorphism – hence bijective – when one considers only monotonic predicate transformers that have a – unique – upper adjoint. The universal image of $\sim$, $\tilde{\sigma}$, is the unique adjoint of $\tilde{\tau}$ (⊣), hence $\sim \; \mapsto \tilde{\tau} \leftrightarrows \tilde{\sigma}$ is itself bijective. □

The bijection just introduced allows us to generalize Theorem 2.6 and switch between the three views of compiler correctness described earlier at will.

Theorem 2.8 (Correspondence of Criteria). *For any trace relation $\sim$ and corresponding Galois connection $\tau \leftrightarrows \sigma$, we have:* $\mathsf{TP}^\tau \iff \mathsf{CC}^\sim \iff \mathsf{TP}^\sigma$.

Proof. For a trace relation $\sim$ and the Galois connection $\tilde{\tau} \leftrightarrows \tilde{\sigma}$, the result follows from Theorem 2.6. For a Galois connection $\tau \leftrightarrows \sigma$ and $\hat{\sim}$, use Lemma 2.7 to conclude that the existential and universal images of $\hat{\sim}$ coincide with τ and σ, respectively; the goal then follows from Theorem 2.6. □

We conclude by explicitly noting that sometimes the lifted properties may be trivial: the target guarantee can be the true property (the set of all traces), or the source obligation the false property (the empty set of traces). This might be the case when source observations abstract away too much information (§3.2 presents an example).

2.3 Preservation of Subset-Closed Hyperproperties

A $\mathsf{CC}^=$ compiler ensures the preservation not only of trace properties, but also of all subset-closed hyperproperties, which are known to be preserved by refinement [14]. An example of a subset-closed hyperproperty is *noninterference* [14]; a $\mathsf{CC}^=$ compiler thus guarantees that if W is noninterfering with respect to the inputs and outputs in the trace then so is W↓. To be able to talk about how (hyper)properties such as noninterference are preserved, in this section we propose another trinitarian view involving $\mathsf{CC}^\sim$ and preservation of subset-closed hyperproperties (Theorem 2.11), slightly weakened in that source and target property mappings will need to be closed under subsets.

First, recall that a program satisfies a hyperproperty when its complete set of traces, which from now on we will call its *behavior*, is a member of the hyperproperty [14].

Definition 2.9 (Hyperproperty Satisfaction). *A program W satisfies a hyperproperty H, written $W \models H$, iff $beh(W) \in H$, where $beh(W) = \{t \mid W \leadsto t\}$.*

Hyperproperty preservation is a strong requirement in general. Fortunately, many interesting hyperproperties are *subset-closed* (SCH for short), which simplifies their preservation since it suffices to show that the behaviors of the compiled program refine the behaviors of the source one, which coincides with the statement of $\mathsf{CC}^=$.

To talk about hyperproperty preservation in the trace-relating setting, we need an interpretation of source hyperproperties into the target and vice versa. The one we consider builds on top of the two trace property mappings τ and σ, which are naturally lifted to hyperproperty mappings. This way we are able to extract two hyperproperty mappings from a trace relation similarly to §2.2:

Definition 2.10 (Lifting property mappings to hyperproperty mappings). *Let* τ : $2^{\text{Traces}} \to 2^{\text{Trace}_{\text{T}}}$ *and* σ : $2^{\text{Trace}_{\text{T}}} \to 2^{\text{Traces}}$ *be arbitrary property mappings. The images of* $\text{H}_{\text{S}} \in 2^{2^{\text{Traces}}}, \text{H}_{\text{T}} \in 2^{2^{\text{Trace}_{\text{T}}}}$ *under* τ *and* σ *are, respectively:*

$$\tilde{\tau}(\text{H}_{\text{S}}) = \{\tau(\pi_{\text{S}}) \mid \pi_{\text{S}} \in \text{H}_{\text{S}}\}; \qquad \tilde{\sigma}(\text{H}_{\text{T}}) = \{\sigma(\pi_{\text{T}}) \mid \pi_{\text{T}} \in \text{H}_{\text{T}}\}.$$

Formally we are defining two new mappings, this time on hyperproperties, but by a small abuse of notation we still denote them by τ and σ.

Interestingly, it is not possible to apply the argument used for CC$^{=}$ to show that a CC$^{\sim}$ compiler guarantees $W\!\!\downarrow \models \tilde{\tau}(\text{H}_{\text{S}})$ whenever $W \models \text{H}_{\text{S}}$. This is in fact not true because direct images do not necessarily preserve subset-closure [36, 44]. To fix this we close the image of $\tilde{\tau}$ and $\tilde{\sigma}$ under subsets (denoted as $Cl_{\subseteq}$) and obtain:

Theorem 2.11 (Preservation of Subset-Closed Hyperproperties ⚔). *For any trace relation* $\sim$ *and its existential and universal images lifted to hyperproperties,* $\tilde{\tau}$ *and* $\tilde{\sigma}$, *and for* $Cl_{\subseteq}(H) = \{\pi \mid \exists \pi' \in H. \pi \subseteq \pi'\}$, *we have:*

$$\text{SCHP}^{Cl_{\subseteq} \circ \tilde{\tau}} \iff \text{CC}^{\sim} \iff \text{SCHP}^{Cl_{\subseteq} \circ \tilde{\sigma}}, \text{ where}$$

$$\text{SCHP}^{Cl_{\subseteq} \circ \tilde{\tau}} \equiv \forall W \forall \text{H}_{\text{S}} \in \text{SCH}_{\text{S}}.W \models \text{H}_{\text{S}} \Rightarrow W\!\!\downarrow \models Cl_{\subseteq}(\tilde{\tau}(\text{H}_{\text{S}}));$$

$$\text{SCHP}^{Cl_{\subseteq} \circ \tilde{\sigma}} \equiv \forall W \forall \text{H}_{\text{T}} \in \text{SCH}_{\text{T}}.W \models Cl_{\subseteq}(\tilde{\sigma}(\text{H}_{\text{T}})) \Rightarrow W\!\!\downarrow \models \text{H}_{\text{T}}.$$

Theorem 2.11 makes us aware of the potential loss of precision when interested in preserving subset-closed hyperproperties through compilation. In §4 we focus on a security relevant subset-closed hyperproperty, noninterference, and show that such a loss of precision can be intended as a declassification of noninterference.

3 Instances of Trace-Relating Compiler Correctness

The trace-relating view of compiler correctness above can serve as a unifying framework for studying a range of interesting compilers. This section provides several representative instantiations of the framework: source languages with undefined behavior that compilation can turn into arbitrary target behavior (§3.1), target languages with resource exhaustion that cannot happen in the source (§3.2), changes in the representation of values (§3.3), and differences in the granularity of data and observable events (§3.4).

3.1 Undefined Behavior

We start by expanding upon the discussion of undefined behavior in §1. We first study the model of CompCert, where source and target alphabets are the same, including the event for undefined behavior. The trace relation weakens equality by allowing undefined behavior to be replaced with an arbitrary sequence of events.

Example 3.1 (CompCert-like Undefined Behavior Relation). Source and target traces are sequences of events drawn from Σ, where $Goes\_wrong \in \Sigma$ is a terminal event that represents an undefined behavior. We then use the trace relation from the introduction:

$$s \sim t \quad \equiv \quad s = t \vee \exists m \leq t. s = m \cdot Goes\_wrong.$$

Each trace of a target program produced by a CC$^{\sim}$ compiler is either also a trace of the original source program or it has a finite prefix that the source program also produces, immediately before encountering undefined behavior. As explained in §1, one of the correctness theorems in CompCert can be rephrased as this variant of CC$^{\sim}$.

We proved that the property mappings induced by the relation can be written as (🐓):

$$\tilde{\sigma}(\pi_T) = \{s \mid s{\in}\pi_T \wedge s \neq m{\cdot}Goes\_wrong\} \cup \{m{\cdot}Goes\_wrong \mid \forall t.\, m{\leq}t \implies t{\in}\pi_T\};$$
$$\tilde{\tau}(\pi_S) = \{t \mid t{\in}\pi_S\} \cup \{t \mid \exists m \leq t.\, m{\cdot}Goes\_wrong \in \pi_S\}.$$

These two mappings explain what a $CC^{\sim}$ compiler ensures for the $\sim$ relation above. The target-to-source mapping $\tilde{\sigma}$ states that to prove that a compiled program has a property π_T using source-level reasoning, one has to prove that any trace produced by the source program must either be a target trace satisfying π_T or have undefined behavior, but only provided that *any continuation* of the trace substituted for the undefined behavior satisfies π_T. The source-to-target mapping $\tilde{\tau}$ states that by compiling a program satisfying a property π_S we obtain a program that produces traces that satisfy the same property or that extend a source trace that ends in undefined behavior.

These definitions can help us reason about programs. For instance, $\tilde{\sigma}$ specifies that, to prove that an event does not happen in the target, it is not enough to prove that it does not happen in the source: it is also necessary to prove that the source program is does not have any undefined behavior (second disjunct). Indeed, if it had an undefined behavior, its continuations could exhibit the unwanted event.   ⊡

This relation can be easily generalized to other settings. For instance, consider the setting in which we compile down to a low-level language like machine code. Target traces can now contain new events that cannot occur in the source: indeed, in modern architectures like x86 a compiler typically uses only a fraction of the available instruction set. Some instructions might even perform dangerous operations, such as writing to the hard drive. Formally, the source and target do not have the same events any more. Thus, we consider a source alphabet $\Sigma_S = \Sigma \cup \{Goes\_wrong\}$, and a target alphabet $\Sigma_T = \Sigma \cup \Sigma'$. The trace relation is defined in the same way and we obtain the same property mappings as above, except that since target traces now have more events (some of which may be dangerous), and the arbitrary continuations of target traces get more interesting. For instance, consider a new event that represents writing data on the hard drive, and suppose we want to prove that this event cannot happen for a compiled program. Then, proving this property requires exactly proving that the source program exhibits no undefined behavior [11]. More generally, what one can prove about target-only events can only be either that they cannot appear (because there is no undefined behavior) or that any of them can appear (in the case of undefined behavior).

In §5.2 we study a similar example, showing that even in a safe language linked adversarial contexts can cause dangerous target events that have no source correspondent.

3.2   Resource Exhaustion

Let us return to the discussion about resource exhaustion in §1.

Example 3.2 (Resource Exhaustion). We consider traces made of events drawn from Σ_S in the source, and $\Sigma_T = \Sigma_S \cup \{\text{Resource\_Limit\_Hit}\}$ in the target. Recall the trace relation for resource exhaustion:

$$s \sim t \quad \equiv \quad s = t \vee \exists m \leq s.\ t = m \cdot \text{Resource\_Limit\_Hit}.$$

Formally, this relation is similar to the one for undefined behavior, except this time it is the target trace that is allowed to end early instead of the source trace.

The induced trace property mappings $\tilde{\sigma}$ and $\tilde{\tau}$ are the following (⬥):

$$\tilde{\sigma}(\pi_T) = \{s \mid s \in \pi_T\} \cap \{s \mid \forall m \leq s.\ m \cdot \text{Resource\_Limit\_Hit} \in \pi_T\};$$

$$\tilde{\tau}(\pi_S) = \pi_S \cup \{m \cdot \text{Resource\_Limit\_Hit} \mid \exists s \in \pi_S.\ m \leq s\}.$$

These capture the following intuitions. The target-to-source mapping $\tilde{\sigma}$ states that to prove a property of the compiled program one has to show that the traces of the source program satisfy two conditions: (1) they must also satisfy the target property; and (2) the termination of every one of their prefixes by a resource exhaustion error must be allowed by the target property. This is rather restrictive: any property that prevents resource exhaustion cannot be proved using source-level reasoning. Indeed, if π_T does not allow resource exhaustion, then $\tilde{\sigma}(\pi_T) = \varnothing$. This is to be expected since resource exhaustion is simply not accounted for at the source level. The other mapping $\tilde{\tau}$ states that a compiled program produces traces that either belong to the same properties as the traces of the source program or end early due to resource exhaustion.

In this example, safety properties [31] are mapped (in both directions) to other safety properties (⬥). This can be desirable for a relation: since safety properties are usually easier to reason about, one interested only in safety properties at the target can reason about them using source-level reasoning tools for safety properties.

The compiler correctness theorem in CakeML is an instance of $CC^\sim$ for the $\sim$ relation above. We have also implemented two small compilers that are correct for this relation. The full details can be found in the Coq development in the supplementary materials. The first compiler (⬥) goes from a simple expression language (similar to the one in §3.3 but without inputs) to the same language except that execution is bounded by some amount of fuel: each execution step consumes some amount of fuel and execution immediately halts when it runs out of fuel. The compiler is the identity.

The second compiler (⬥) is more interesting: we proved this $CC^\sim$ instance for a variant of a compiler from a WHILE language to a simple stack machine by Xavier Leroy [35]. We enriched the two languages with outputs and modified the semantics of the stack machine so that it falls into an error state if the stack reaches a certain size. The proof uses a standard forward simulation modified to account for failure.   ⊡

We conclude this subsection by noting that the resource exhaustion relation and the undefined behavior relation from the previous subsection can easily be combined. Indeed, given a relation $\sim_{UB}$ and a relation $\sim_{RE}$ defined as above on the same sets of traces, we can build a new relation $\sim$ that allows both refinement of undefined behavior and resource exhaustion by taking their union: $s \sim t \equiv s \sim_{UB} t \vee s \sim_{RE} t$. A compiler that is $CC^{\sim UB}$ or $CC^{\sim RE}$ is trivially $CC^\sim$, though the converse is not true.

3.3 Different Source and Target Values

We now illustrate trace-relating compilation for a translation mapping source-level booleans to target-level natural numbers. Given the simplicity of this compiler, most of the details of the formalization are deferred to the online appendix.

The source language is a pure, statically typed expression language whose expressions e include naturals n, booleans b, conditionals, arithmetic and relational operations, boolean inputs in_b and natural inputs in_n. A trace s is a list of inputs is paired with a result r, which can be a natural, a boolean, or an error. Well-typed programs never produce error (⬥). Types ty are either N (naturals) or B (booleans); typing is standard. The source language has a standard big-step operational semantics ($e \rightsquigarrow \langle is, r \rangle$) which tells how an expression e generates a trace $\langle is, r \rangle$. The target language is analogous, except that it is untyped, only has naturals n and its only inputs are naturals in_n. The semantics of the target language is also given in big-step style. Since we only have naturals and all expressions operate on them, no error result is possible in the target.

The compiler is homomorphic, translating a source expression to the same target expression; the only differences are natural numbers (and conditionals), as noted below.

$$\mathsf{true}{\downarrow} = 1 \quad \mathsf{in_b}{\downarrow} = \mathsf{in_n} \qquad\qquad e_1 \le e_2{\downarrow} = \text{if } e_1{\downarrow} \le e_2{\downarrow} \text{ then } 1 \text{ else } 0$$

$$\mathsf{false}{\downarrow} = 0 \quad \mathsf{in_n}{\downarrow} = \mathsf{in_n} \quad \text{if } e_1 \text{ then } e_2 \text{ else } e_3{\downarrow} = \text{if } e_1{\downarrow} \le 0 \text{ then } e_3{\downarrow} \text{ else } e_2{\downarrow}$$

When compiling an *if-then-else* the target condition $e_1{\downarrow} \le 0$ is used to check that e_1 is false, and therefore the *then* and *else* branches of the source are swapped in the target.

Relating Traces. We relate basic values (naturals and booleans) in a non-injective fashion as noted below. Then, we extend the relation to lists of inputs pointwise (Rules Empty and Cons) and lift that relation to traces (Rules Nat and Bool).

$$n \sim n \qquad\qquad \mathsf{true} \sim n \text{ if } n > 0 \qquad\qquad \mathsf{false} \sim 0$$

$$\text{(Empty)} \frac{}{\varnothing \sim \varnothing} \qquad \text{(Cons)} \frac{i \sim i \quad is \sim is}{i \cdot is \sim i \cdot is} \qquad \left| \quad \text{(Nat)} \frac{is \sim is \quad n \sim n}{\langle is, n \rangle \sim \langle is, n \rangle} \qquad \text{(Bool)} \frac{is \sim is \quad b \sim n}{\langle is, b \rangle \sim \langle is, n \rangle} \right.$$

Property mappings. The property mappings $\tilde{\sigma}$ and $\tilde{\tau}$ induced by the trace relation $\sim$ defined above capture the intuition behind encoding booleans as naturals:

- the source-to-target mapping allows true to be encoded by any non-zero number;
- the target-to-source mapping requires that 0 be replaceable by *both* 0 and false.

Compiler correctness. With the relation above, the compiler is proven to satisfy $\mathsf{CC}^{\sim}$.

Theorem 3.3 ($\cdot{\downarrow}$ *is correct* ✍). $\cdot{\downarrow}$ *is* $\mathsf{CC}^{\sim}$.

Simulations with different traces. The difficulty in proving Theorem 3.3 arises from the trace-relating compilation setting: For compilation chains that have the same source and target traces, it is customary to prove compiler correctness using a forward simulation (i.e., a simulation between source and target transition system); then, using determinacy [18, 39] of the target language and input totality [19, 63] (aka receptiveness) of the source, this forward simulation is flipped into a backward simulation (a simulation between target and source transition system), as described by Beringer et al. [7], Leroy [34]. This flipping is useful because forward simulations are often much easier to prove (by induction on the transitions of the source) than backward ones, as it is the case here.

We first give the main idea of the flipping proof, when the inputs are the same in the source and the target [7, 34]. We only consider inputs, as it is the most interesting case, since with determinacy, nondeterminism only occurs on inputs. Given a forward simulation $\mathcal{R}$, and a target program W_T that simulates a source program W_S, W_T is able to perform an input iff so is W_S: otherwise, say for instance that W_S performs an output, by forward simulation W_T would also perform an output, which is impossible because of determinacy. By input totality of the source, W_S must be able to perform the exact same input as W_T; using forward simulation and determinacy, the resulting programs must be related.

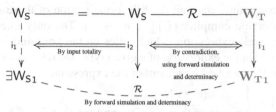

However, our trace relation is not injective (both 0 and false are mapped to 0), therefore these arguments do not apply: not all possible inputs of target programs are accounted for in the forward simulation. We thus have to strengthen the forward simulation assumption, requiring the following additional property to hold, for any source program W_S and target program W_T related by the forward simulation $\mathcal{R}$.

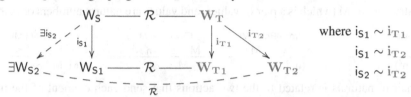

We say that a forward simulation for which this property holds is *flippable*. For our example compiler, a flippable forward simulation works as follows: whenever a boolean input occurs in the source, the target program must perform every strictly positive input n (and not just 1, as suggested by the compiler). Using this property, determinacy of the target, input totality of the source, as well as the fact that any target input has an inverse image through the relation, we can indeed show that the forward simulation can be turned into a backward one: starting from W_S $\mathcal{R}$ W_T and an input i_{T2}, we show that there is i_{S1} and i_{T2} as in the diagram above, using the same arguments as when the inputs are the same; because the simulation is flippable, we can close the diagram, and obtain the existence of an adequate i_{S2}. From this we obtain $CC^{\sim}$.

In fact, we have proven a completely general 'flipping theorem', with this flippable hypothesis on the forward simulation (🦆). We have also shown that if the relation $\sim$ defines a bijection between the inputs of the source and the target, then any forward simulation is flippable, hence reobtaining the usual proof technique [7, 34] as a special case. This flipping theorem is further discussed in the online appendix.

3.4 Abstraction Mismatches

We now consider how to relate traces where a single source action is compiled to multiple target ones. To illustrate this, we take a pure, statically-typed source language that can output (nested) pairs of arbitrary size, and a pure, *untyped* target language where sent values have a fixed size. Concretely, the source is analogous to the language of §3.3, except that it does not have inputs or booleans and it has an expression send e, which can emit a (nested) pair e of values in a single action. That is, given that e reduces to a pair, e.g., $\langle v1, \langle v2, v3 \rangle \rangle$, expression send $\langle v1, \langle v2, v3 \rangle \rangle$ emits action $\langle v1, \langle v2, v3 \rangle \rangle$. That expression is compiled into a sequence of individual sends in the target language send v1 ; send v2 ; send v3, since in the target, send e sends the value that e reduces to, but the language has no pairs.

Due to space constraints we omit the full formalization of these simple languages and of the homomorphic compiler $((\cdot)\!\downarrow \; : \; e \to e)$. The only interesting bit is the compilation of the send $\cdot$ expression, which relies on the gensend $(\cdot)$ function below. That function takes a source expression of a given type and returns a sequence of target send $\cdot$ instructions that send each element of the expression.

$$\text{gensend}\,(\vdash e : \tau) = \begin{cases} \text{send } (\vdash e : N)\!\downarrow & \text{if } \tau = N \\ \text{gensend}\,(\vdash e.1 : \tau'); \text{gensend}\,(\vdash e.2 : \tau'') & \text{if } \tau = \tau' \times \tau'' \end{cases}$$

Relating Traces. We start with the trivial relation between numbers: $n \sim^0 n$, i.e., numbers are related when they are the same. We cannot build a relation between single actions since a single source action is related to multiple target ones. Therefore, we define a relation between a source action M and a target trace t (a list of numbers), inductively on the structure of M (which is a pair of values, and values are natural numbers or pairs).

(Trace-Rel-N-N)
$$\frac{n \sim^0 n \qquad n' \sim^0 n'}{\langle n, n' \rangle \sim n \cdot n'}$$

(Trace-Rel-N-M)
$$\frac{n \sim^0 n \qquad M \sim t}{\langle n, M \rangle \sim n \cdot t}$$

(Trace-Rel-M-N)
$$\frac{M \sim t \qquad n \sim^0 n}{\langle M, n \rangle \sim t \cdot n}$$

(Trace-Rel-M-M)
$$\frac{M \sim t \qquad M' \sim t'}{\langle M, M' \rangle \sim t \cdot t'}$$

A pair of naturals is related to the two actions that send each element of the pair (Rule Trace-Rel-N-N). If a pair is made of sub-pairs, we require all such sub-pairs to be related (Rules Trace-Rel-N-M to Trace-Rel-M-M). We build on these rules to define the $s \sim t$ relation between source and target traces for which the compiler is correct (Theorem 3.4). Trivially, traces are related when they are both empty. Alternatively, given related traces, we can concatenate a source action and a second target trace provided that they are related (Rule Trace-Rel-Single).

(Trace-Rel-Single)
$$\frac{s \sim t \qquad M \sim t'}{s \cdot M \sim t \cdot t'}$$

Theorem 3.4 $((\cdot)\!\downarrow$ **is correct).** $(\cdot)\!\downarrow$ *is* $CC^\sim$.

With our trace relation, the trace property mappings capture the following intuitions:
- The target-to-source mapping states that a source property can reconstruct target action as it sees fit. For example, trace $4 \cdot 6 \cdot 5 \cdot 7$ is related to $\langle 4, 6 \rangle \cdot \langle 5, 7 \rangle$ and $\langle\langle 4, \langle 6, \langle 5, 7 \rangle\rangle\rangle\rangle$ (and many more variations). This gives freedom to the source implementation of a target behavior, which follows from the non-injectivity of $\sim$.[5]
- The source-to-target mapping "forgets" about the way pairs are nested, but is faithful w.r.t. the values v_i contained in a message. Notice that source safety properties are always mapped to target safety properties. For instance, if $\pi_S \in \text{Safety}_S$ prescribes that some bad number is never sent, then $\tilde{\tau}(\pi_S)$ prescribes the same number is never sent in the target and $\tilde{\tau}(\pi_S) \in \text{Safety}_T$. Of course if $\pi_S \in \text{Safety}_S$ prescribes that a particular nested pairing like $\langle 4, \langle 6, \langle 5, 7 \rangle\rangle\rangle$ never happens, then $\tilde{\tau}(\pi_S)$ is still a target safety property, but the trivial one, since $\tilde{\tau}(\pi_S) = \top \in \text{Safety}_T$.

4   Trace-Relating Compilation and Noninterference Preservation

When source and target observations are drawn from the same set, a correct compiler ($CC^=$) is enough to ensure the preservation of all subset-closed hyperproperties, in particular of *noninterference* (NI) [22], as also mentioned at the beginning of §2.3. In the

---

[5] Making $\sim$ injective is a matter of adding open and close parenthesis actions in target traces.

scenario where target observations are strictly more informative than source observations, the best guarantee one may expect from a correct trace-relating compiler ($CC^{\sim}$) is a *weakening* (or *declassification*) of target noninterference that matches the noninterference property satisfied in the source. To formalize this reasoning, this section applies the trinitarian view of trace-relating compilation to the general framework of abstract noninterference (ANI) [21].

We first define NI and explain the issue of preserving source NI via a $CC^{\sim}$ compiler. We then introduce ANI, which allows characterizations of various forms of noninterference, and formulate a general theory of ANI preservation via $CC^{\sim}$. We also study how to deal with cases such as undefined behavior in the target. Finally, we answer the dual question, i.e., which source NI should be satisfied to guarantee that compiled programs are noninterfering with respect to target observers.

Intuitively, NI requires that publicly observable outputs do not reveal information about private inputs. To define this formally, we need a few additions to our setup. We indicate the (disjoint) *input* and *output* projections of a trace t as t° and $t^{\bullet}$ respectively[6]. Denote with $[t]_{low}$ the equivalence class of a trace t, obtained using a standard low-equivalence relation that relates low (public) events only if they are equal, and ingores any difference between private events. Then, NI for source traces can be defined as:

$$\mathsf{NI_S} = \{\pi_S \mid \forall s_1 s_2 \in \pi_S.\ [s_1^{\circ}]_{low} = [s_2^{\circ}]_{low} \Rightarrow [s_1^{\bullet}]_{low} = [s_2^{\bullet}]_{low}\ \}.$$

That is, source NI comprises the sets of traces that have equivalent low output projections as long as their low input projections are equivalent.

Trace-Relating Compilation and Noninterference. When additional observations are possible in the target, it is unclear whether a noninterfering source program is compiled to a noninterfering target program or not, and if so, whether the notion of NI in the target is the expected or desired one. We illustrate this issue considering a scenario where target traces extend source ones by exposing the execution time. While source noninterference $\mathsf{NI_S}$ requires that private inputs do not affect public outputs, $\mathrm{NI_T}$ additionally requires that the execution time is not affected by private inputs.

To model the scenario described, let $\mathsf{Trace_S}$ denote the set of traces in the source, and $\mathrm{Trace_T} = \mathsf{Trace_S} \times \mathbb{N}^{\omega}$ be the set of target traces, where $\mathbb{N}^{\omega} \triangleq \mathbb{N} \cup \{\omega\}$. Target traces have two components: a source trace, and a natural number that denotes the time spent to produce the trace (ω if infinite). Notice that if two source traces s_1, s_2, are low-equivalent then $\{s_1, s_2\} \in \mathsf{NI_S}$ and $\{(s_1, 42), (s_1, 42)\} \in \mathrm{NI_T}$, but $\{(s_1, 42), (s_2, 43)\} \notin \mathrm{NI_T}$ and $\{(s_1, 42), (s_2, 42), (s_1, 43), (s_2, 43)\} \notin \mathrm{NI_T}$.

Consider the following straightforward trace relation, which relates a source trace to any target trace whose first component is equal to it, irrespective of execution time:

$$s \sim t \quad \equiv \quad \exists n.\ t = (s, n).$$

A compiler is $CC^{\sim}$ if any trace that can be exhibited in the target can be simulated in the source in some amount of time. For such a compiler Theorem 2.11 says that if W satisfies $\mathsf{NI_S}$, then $W{\downarrow}$ satisfies $Cl_{\subseteq} \circ \tilde{\tau}(\mathsf{NI_S})$, which however is strictly weaker than $\mathrm{NI_T}$, as it contains, e.g., $\{(s_1, 42), (s_2, 42), (s_1, 43), (s_2, 43)\}$, and one cannot conclude that $W{\downarrow}$ is noninterfering in the target. It is easy to prove that

---

[6] Here we only require the projections to be disjoint. Depending on the scenario and the attacker model the projections might record information such as the ordering of events.

$Cl_{\subseteq} \circ \tilde{\tau}(\mathsf{NI_S}) = Cl_{\subseteq}(\{\,\pi_\mathsf{S} \times \mathbb{N}^\omega \mid \pi_\mathsf{S} \in \mathsf{NI_S}\,\}) = \{\,\pi_\mathsf{S} \times \mathcal{I} \mid \pi_\mathsf{S} \in \mathsf{NI_S} \wedge \mathcal{I} \subseteq \mathbb{N}^\omega\,\}$,
the first equality coming from $\tilde{\tau}(\pi_\mathsf{S}) = \pi_\mathsf{S} \times \mathbb{N}^\omega$, and the second from $\mathsf{NI_S}$ being subset-closed. As we will see, this hyperproperty *can* be characterized as a form of NI, which one might call *timing-insensitive noninterference*, and ensured only against attackers that cannot measure execution time. For this characterization, and to describe different forms of noninterference as well as formally analyze their preservation by a CC~ compiler, we rely on the general framework of *abstract noninterference* [21].

Abstract Noninterference. ANI [21] is a generalization of NI whose formulation relies on abstractions (in abstract interpretation sense [16]) in order to encompass arbitrary variants of NI. ANI is parameterized by an *observer abstraction* ρ, which denotes the distinguishing power of the attacker, and a *selection abstraction* ϕ, which specifies when to check NI, and therefore captures a form of declassification [54].[7] Formally:

$$ANI^\rho_\phi = \{\pi \mid \forall t_1 t_2 \in \pi.\ \phi(t_1^\circ) = \phi(t_2^\circ) \Rightarrow \rho(t_1^\bullet) = \rho(t_2^\bullet)\}.$$

By picking $\phi = \rho = [\cdot]_{low}$, we recover the standard noninterference defined above, where NI must hold for all low inputs (i.e., no declassification of private inputs), and the observational power of the attacker is limited to distinguishing low outputs.

The observational power of the attacker can be weakened by choosing a more liberal relation for ρ. For instance, one may limit the attacker to observe the *parity* of output integer values. Another way to weaken ANI is to use ϕ to specify that noninterference is only required to hold for a subset of low inputs.

To be formally precise, ϕ and ρ are defined over sets of (input and output projections of) traces, so when we write $\phi(t)$ above, this should be understood as a convenience notation for $\phi(\{t\})$. Likewise, $\phi = [\cdot]_{low}$ should be understood as $\phi = \lambda\pi.\bigcup_{t \in \pi}[t]_{low}$, i.e., the powerset lifting of $[\cdot]_{low}$. Additionally, ϕ and ρ are required to be upper-closed operators (*uco*)—i.e., monotonic, idempotent and extensive—on the poset that is the powerset of (input and output projections of) traces ordered by inclusion [21].

Trace-Relating Compilation and ANI for Timing. We can now reformulate our example with observable execution times in the target in terms of ANI. We have $\mathsf{NI_S} = ANI^{\phi_\mathsf{S}}_{\rho_\mathsf{S}}$ with $\phi_\mathsf{S} = \rho_\mathsf{S} = [\cdot]_{low}$. In this case, we can formally describe the hyperproperty that a compiled program W↓ satisfies whenever W satisfies $\mathsf{NI_S}$ as an instance of ANI:

$$Cl_{\subseteq} \circ \tilde{\tau}(\mathsf{NI_S}) = ANI^{\rho_\mathrm{T}}_{\phi_\mathrm{T}},$$

for $\phi_\mathrm{T} = \phi_\mathsf{S}$ and $\rho_\mathrm{T}(\pi_\mathrm{T}) = \{(\mathsf{s}, \mathsf{n}) \mid \exists(\mathsf{s_1}, \mathsf{n_1}) \in \pi_\mathrm{T}.\ [\mathsf{s}^\bullet]_{low} = [\mathsf{s_1}^\bullet]_{low}\}$.
The definition of ϕ_T tells us that the trace relation does not affect the selection abstraction. The definition of ρ_T characterizes an observer that cannot distinguish execution times for noninterfering traces (notice that $\mathsf{n_1}$ in the definition of ρ_T is discarded). For instance, $\rho_\mathrm{T}(\{(\mathsf{s}, \mathsf{n_1})\}) = \rho_\mathrm{T}(\{(\mathsf{s}, \mathsf{n_2})\})$, for any $\mathsf{s}, \mathsf{n_1}, \mathsf{n_2}$. Therefore, in this setting, we know explicitly through ρ_T that a CC~ compiler degrades source noninterference to target *timing-insensitive* noninterference.

Trace-Relating Compilation and ANI in General. While the particular ϕ_T and ρ_T above can be discovered by intuition, we want to know whether there is a systematic way of obtaining them in general. In other words, for *any* trace relation $\sim$ and *any*

---

[7] ANI includes a third parameter η, which describes the maximal input variation that the attacker may control. Here we omit η (i.e., take it to be the identity) in order to simplify the presentation.

notion of source NI, what property is guaranteed on noninterfering source programs by any $CC^\sim$ compiler?

We can now answer this question generally (Theorem 4.1): any source notion of noninterference expressible as an instance of ANI is mapped to a corresponding instance of ANI in the target, whenever source traces are an abstraction of target ones (i.e., when $\sim$ is a total and surjective map). For this result we consider trace relations that can be split into input and output trace relations (denoted as $\sim \triangleq \langle \overset{\circ}{\sim}, \overset{\bullet}{\sim} \rangle$) such that $s \sim t \iff s^\circ \overset{\circ}{\sim} t^\circ \wedge s^\bullet \overset{\bullet}{\sim} t^\bullet$. The trace relation $\sim$ corresponds to a Galois connection between the sets of trace properties $\tilde{\tau} \leftrightarrows \tilde{\sigma}$ as described in §2.2. Similarly, the pair $\overset{\circ}{\sim}$ and $\overset{\bullet}{\sim}$ corresponds to a pair of Galois connections, $\tilde{\tau}^\circ \leftrightarrows \tilde{\sigma}^\circ$ and $\tilde{\tau}^\bullet \leftrightarrows \tilde{\sigma}^\bullet$, between the sets of input and output properties. In the timing example, time is an output so we have $\sim \triangleq \langle =, \overset{\bullet}{\sim} \rangle$ and $\overset{\bullet}{\sim}$ is defined as $s^\bullet \overset{\bullet}{\sim} t^\bullet \equiv \exists n. \, t^\bullet = (s^\bullet, n)$.

Theorem 4.1 (Compiling ANI). *Assume traces of source and target languages are related via* $\sim \subseteq \mathrm{Trace}_S \times \mathrm{Trace}_T$, $\sim \triangleq \langle \overset{\circ}{\sim}, \overset{\bullet}{\sim} \rangle$ *such that* $\overset{\circ}{\sim}$ *and* $\overset{\bullet}{\sim}$ *are both total maps from target to source traces, and* $\overset{\circ}{\sim}$ *is surjective. Assume* $\downarrow$ *is a* $CC^\sim$ *compiler, and* $\phi_S \in uco(2^{\mathrm{Trace}_S^\bullet})$, $\rho_S \in uco(2^{\mathrm{Trace}_S^\circ})$.

If W *satisfies* $ANI_{\phi_S}^{\rho_S}$, *then* $W{\downarrow}$ *satisfies* $ANI_{\phi_T^\#}^{\rho_T^\#}$, *where* $\phi_T^\#$ *and* $\rho_T^\#$ *are defined as:*

$$\phi_T^\# = g^\bullet \circ \phi_S \circ f^\bullet ; \qquad\qquad \rho_T^\# = g^\bullet \circ \rho_S \circ f^\bullet \quad \text{and}$$

$$f^\circ(\pi_T^\circ) = \{s^\circ \mid \exists t^\circ \in \pi_T^\circ. \, s^\circ \overset{\circ}{\sim} t^\circ\} ; \quad g^\circ(\pi_S^\circ) = \{t^\circ \mid \forall s^\circ. \, s^\circ \overset{\circ}{\sim} t^\circ \Rightarrow s^\circ \in \pi_S^\circ\}$$

(and both $f^\bullet$ *and* $g^\bullet$ *are defined analogously).*

For the example above we recover the definitions we justified intuitively, i.e., $\phi_T^\# = g^\bullet \circ \phi_S \circ f^\bullet = \phi_T$ and $\rho_T^\# = g^\bullet \circ \rho_S \circ f^\bullet = \rho_T$. Moreover, we can prove that if $\overset{\bullet}{\sim}$ also is surjective, $ANI_{\phi_T^\#}^{\rho_T^\#} \subseteq Cl_\subseteq \circ \tilde{\tau}(ANI_{\phi_S}^{\rho_S})$. Therefore, the derived guarantee $ANI_{\phi_T^\#}^{\rho_T^\#}$ is at least as strong as the one that follows by just knowing that the compiler $\downarrow$ is $CC^\sim$.

Noninterference and Undefined Behavior. As stated above, Theorem 4.1 does not apply to several scenarios from §3 such as undefined behavior (§3.1), as in those cases the relation $\overset{\bullet}{\sim}$ is not a total map. Nevertheless, we can still exploit our framework to reason about the impact of compilation on noninterference.

Let us consider $\sim \triangleq \langle \overset{\circ}{\sim}, \overset{\bullet}{\sim} \rangle$ where $\overset{\circ}{\sim}$ is any total and surjective map from target to source inputs (e.g., equality) and $\overset{\bullet}{\sim}$ is defined as $s^\bullet \overset{\bullet}{\sim} t^\bullet \equiv s^\bullet = t^\bullet \vee \exists m^\bullet \leq t^\bullet. \, s^\bullet = m^\bullet \cdot Goes\_wrong$. Intuitively, a $CC^\sim$ compiler guarantees that no interference can be observed by a target attacker that cannot exploit undefined behavior to learn private information. This intuition can be made formal by the following theorem.

Theorem 4.2 (Relaxed Compiling ANI). *Relax the assumptions of Theorem 4.1 by allowing* $\overset{\bullet}{\sim}$ *to be any output trace relation. If* W *satisfies* $ANI_{\phi_S}^{\rho_S}$, *then* $W{\downarrow}$ *satisfies* $ANI_{\phi_T^\#}^{\rho_T^\#}$ *where* $\phi_T^\#$ *is defined as in Theorem 4.1, and* $\rho_T^\#$ *is such that:*

$$\forall s \, t. \, s^\bullet \overset{\bullet}{\sim} t^\bullet \Rightarrow \rho_T^\#(t^\bullet) = \rho_T^\#(\tilde{\tau}^\bullet(\rho_S(s^\bullet))).$$

Technically, instead of giving us a *definition* of $\rho_T^\#$, the theorem gives a *property* of it. The property states that, given a target output trace $t^\bullet$, the attacker cannot distinguish it from any other target output traces produced by other possible compilations ($\tilde{\tau}^\bullet$) of the source trace s it relates to, up to the observational power of the source level attacker ρ_S. Therefore, given a source attacker ρ_S, the theorem characterizes a *family* of attackers that cannot observe any interference for a correctly compiled noninterfering program. Notice that the target attacker $\rho_T^{\#} = \lambda\_.\ \top$ satisfies the premise of the theorem, but defines a trivial hyperproperty, so that we cannot prove in general that $ANI^{\rho_T^{\#}}_{\phi_T^{\#}} \subseteq Cl_{\subseteq} \circ \tilde{\tau}(ANI^{\rho_S}_{\phi_S})$. The same $\rho_T^{\#} = \lambda\_.\ \top$ shows that the family of attackers described in Theorem 4.2 is nonempty, and this ensures the existence of a most powerful attacker among them [21], whose explicit characterization we leave for future work.

From Target NI to Source NI. We now explore the dual question: under what hypotheses does trace-relating compiler correctness alone allow target noninterference to be reduced to source noninterference? This is of practical interest, as one would be able to protect from target attackers by ensuring noninterference in the source. This task can be made easier if the source language has some static enforcement mechanism [1, 36].

Let us consider the languages from §3.4 extended with inputting of (pairs of) values. It is easy to show that the compiler described in §3.4 is still $CC^\sim$. Assume that we want to satisfy a given notion of target noninterference after compilation, i.e., $W{\downarrow} \models ANI^{\rho_T}_{\phi_T}$. Recall that the observational power of the target attacker, ρ_T, is expressed as a property of sequences of values. To express the same property (or attacker) in the source, we have to abstract the way pairs of values are nested. For instance, the source attacker should not distinguish $\langle v_1, \langle v_2, v_3 \rangle \rangle$ and $\langle \langle v_1, v_2 \rangle, v_3 \rangle$. In general (i.e., when $\sim$ is not the identity), this argument is valid only when ϕ_T can be represented in the source. More precisely, ϕ_T must consider as equivalent all target inputs that are related to the same source one, because in the source it is not possible to have a finer distinction of inputs. This intuitive correspondence can be formalized as follows:

Theorem 4.3 (Target ANI by source ANI). *Let* $\phi_T \in uco(2^{\mathrm{Trace_T^\circ}})$, $\rho_T \in uco(2^{\mathrm{Trace_T^\bullet}})$ *and* $\stackrel{.}{\sim}$ *a total and surjective map from source outputs to target ones and assume that*

$$\forall s\, t.\ s^\circ \stackrel{.}{\sim} t^\circ \Rightarrow \phi_T(t^\circ) = \phi_T(\tilde{\tau}^\circ(s^\circ)).$$

If $\cdot{\downarrow}$ *is a* $CC^\sim$ *compiler and* W *satisfies* $ANI^{\rho_S^{\#}}_{\phi_S^{\#}}$, *then* $W{\downarrow}$ *satisfies* $ANI^{\rho_T}_{\phi_T}$ *for*

$$\phi_S^{\#} = \tilde{\sigma}^\circ \circ \phi_T \circ \tilde{\tau}^\circ; \qquad\qquad \rho_S^{\#} = \tilde{\sigma}^\bullet \circ \rho_T \circ \tilde{\tau}^\bullet.$$

To wrap up the discussion about noninterference, the results presented in this section formalize and generalize some intuitive facts about compiler correctness and noninterference. Of course, they all place some restrictions on the shape of the noninterference instances that can be considered, because compiler correctness alone is in general not a strong enough criterion for dealing with many security properties [6, 17].

5   Trace-Relating Secure Compilation

So far we have studied compiler correctness criteria for whole, standalone programs. However, in practice, programs do not exist in isolation, but in a context where they interact with other programs, libraries, etc. In many cases, this context cannot be assumed to be benign and could instead behave maliciously to try to disrupt a compiled program.

Hence, in this section we consider the following *secure compilation* scenario: a source program is compiled and linked with an arbitrary target-level context, i.e., one that may not be expressible as the compilation of a source context. Compiler correctness does not address this case, as it does not consider arbitrary target contexts, looking instead at whole programs (empty context [33]) or well-behaved target contexts that behave like source ones (as in compositional compiler correctness [27, 30, 45, 57]).

To account for this scenario, Abate et al. [2] describe several secure compilation criteria based on the preservation of classes of (hyper)properties (e.g., trace properties, safety, hypersafety, hyperproperties, etc.) against arbitrary target contexts. For each of these criteria, they give an equivalent "property-free" criterion, analogous to the equivalence between TP and $CC^=$. For instance, their *robust* trace property preservation criterion (RTP) states that, for any trace property π, if a source *partial* program P plugged into any context C_S satisfies π, then the compiled program P↓ plugged into any target context C_T satisfies π. Their equivalent criterion to RTP is RTC, which states that for any trace produced by the compiled program, when linked with any target context, there is a source context that produces the same trace. Formally (writing $C[P]$ to mean the whole program that results from linking partial program P with context C) they define:

$$RTP \equiv \forall P. \, \forall \pi. \, (\forall C_S. \, \forall t. C_S \, [P] \rightsquigarrow t \Rightarrow t \in \pi) \Rightarrow (\forall C_T. \, \forall t. \, C_T \, [P\!\downarrow] \rightsquigarrow t \Rightarrow t \in \pi);$$

$$RTC \equiv \forall P. \, \forall C_T. \forall t. C_T \, [P\!\downarrow] \rightsquigarrow t \Rightarrow \exists C_S. \, C_S \, [P] \rightsquigarrow t.$$

In the following we adopt the notation $P \models_R \pi$ to mean "P *robustly* satisfies π," i.e., P satisfies π irrespective of the contexts it is linked with. Thus, we write more compactly:

$$RTP \equiv \forall \pi. \, \forall P. \, P \models_R \pi \Rightarrow P\!\downarrow \models_R \pi.$$

All the criteria of Abate et al. [2] share this flavor of stating the existence of some source context that simulates the behavior of any given target context, with some variations depending on the class of (hyper)properties under consideration. All these criteria are stated in a setting where source and target traces are the same. In this section, we extend their result to our trace-relating setting, obtaining trintarian views for secure compilation. Despite the similarities with §2, more challenges show up, in particular when considering the robust preservation of proper sub-classes of trace properties. For example, after application of $\tilde{\sigma}$ or $\tilde{\tau}$, a property may not be safety anymore, a crucial point for the equivalence with the property-free criterion for safety properties by Abate et al. [2]. We solve this by interpreting the class of safety properties as an *abstraction* of the class of all trace properties induced by a closure operator (§5.1). The remaining subsections provide example compilation chains satisfying our trace-relating secure compilation criteria for trace properties (§5.2) and for safety properties hypersafety (§5.3).

5.1   Trace-Relating Secure Compilation: A Spectrum of Trinities

In this subsection we generalize many of the criteria of Abate et al. [2] using the ideas of §2. Before discussing how we solve the challenges for classes such as safety and hypersafety, we show the simple generalization of RTC to the trace-relating setting (RTC~) and its corresponding trinitarian view (Theorem 5.1):

Theorem 5.1 (Trinity for Robust Trace Properties ⚸). *For any trace relation $\sim$ and induced property mappings $\tilde{\tau}$ and $\tilde{\sigma}$, we have:* $RTP^{\tilde{\tau}} \iff RTC^\sim \iff RTP^{\tilde{\sigma}}$, *where*

$$RTC^\sim \equiv \forall P \, \forall C_T \, \forall t. \, C_T \, [P\!\downarrow] \rightsquigarrow t \Rightarrow \exists C_S \, \exists s \sim t. \, C_S \, [P] \rightsquigarrow s;$$

$$RTP^{\tilde{\tau}} \equiv \forall P \, \forall \pi_S \in 2^{\mathsf{Traces}}. \, P \models_R \pi_S \Rightarrow P\!\downarrow \models_R \tilde{\tau}(\pi_S);$$

$$\mathsf{RTP}^{\tilde{\sigma}} \equiv \forall \mathsf{P} \; \forall \pi_\mathrm{T} \in 2^{\mathrm{Trace}_\mathrm{T}} . \; \mathsf{P} \models_\mathsf{R} \tilde{\sigma}(\pi_\mathrm{T}) \Rightarrow \mathsf{P}{\downarrow} \models_\mathsf{R} \pi_\mathrm{T}.$$

Abate et al. [2] propose many more equivalent pairs of criteria, each preserving different classes of (hyper)properties, which we briefly recap now. For trace properties, they also have criteria that preserve safety properties plus their version of liveness properties. For hyperproperties, they have criteria that preserve hypersafety properties, subset-closed hyperproperties, and arbitrary hyperproperties. Finally, they define *relational* hyperproperties, which are relations between the behaviors of multiple programs for expressing, e.g., that a program always runs faster than another. For relational hyperproperties, they have criteria that preserve arbitrary relational properties, relational safety properties, relational hyperproperties and relational subset-closed hyperproperties. Roughly speaking, the security guarantees due to robust preservation of trace properties regard only protecting the integrity of the program from the context, the guarantees of hyperproperties also regard data confidentiality, and the guarantees of relational hyperproperties even regard code confidentiality. Naturally, these stronger guarantees are increasingly harder to enforce and prove.

While we have lifted the most significant criteria from Abate et al. [2] to our trinitarian view, due to space constraints we provide the formal definitions only for the two most interesting criteria. We summarize the generalizations of many other criteria in Figure 2, described at the end. Omitted definitions are available in the online appendix.

Beyond Trace Properties: Robust Safety and Hyperproperty Preservation. We detail robust preservation of safety properties and of arbitrary hyperproperties since they are both relevant from a security point of view and their generalization is interesting.

Theorem 5.2 (Trinity for Robust Safety Properties ✿). *For any trace relation* $\sim$ *and for the induced property mappings* $\tilde{\tau}$ *and* $\tilde{\sigma}$, *we have:*

$$\mathsf{RTP}^{Safe \circ \tilde{\tau}} \iff \mathsf{RSC}^\sim \iff \mathsf{RSP}^{\tilde{\sigma}}, \qquad\qquad where$$

$$\mathsf{RSC}^\sim \equiv \forall \mathsf{P} \; \forall \mathsf{C}_\mathrm{T} \; \forall t \; \forall m \le t.\mathsf{C}_\mathrm{T} \, [\mathsf{P}{\downarrow}]{\rightsquigarrow}t \Rightarrow \exists \mathsf{C}_\mathsf{S} \; \exists t' \ge m \; \exists s \sim t'. \; \mathsf{C}_\mathsf{S} \, [\mathsf{P}]{\rightsquigarrow}s;$$

$$\mathsf{RTP}^{Safe \circ \tilde{\tau}} \equiv \forall \mathsf{P} \forall \pi_\mathsf{S} \in 2^{\mathsf{Traces}} . \mathsf{P} \models_\mathsf{R} \pi_\mathsf{S} \Rightarrow \mathsf{P}{\downarrow} \models_\mathsf{R} (Safe \circ \tilde{\tau})(\pi_\mathsf{S});$$

$$\mathsf{RSP}^{\tilde{\sigma}} \equiv \forall \mathsf{P} \forall \pi_\mathrm{T} \in \mathrm{Safety}_\mathrm{T} . \mathsf{P} \models_\mathsf{R} \tilde{\sigma}(\pi_\mathrm{T}) \Rightarrow \mathsf{P}{\downarrow} \models_\mathsf{R} \pi_\mathrm{T}.$$

There is an interesting asymmetry between the last two characterizations above, which we explain now in more detail. $\mathsf{RSP}^{\tilde{\sigma}}$ quantifies over target safety properties, while $\mathsf{RTP}^{Safe \circ \tilde{\tau}}$ quantifies over *arbitrary* source properties, but imposes the composition of $\tilde{\tau}$ with *Safe*, which maps an arbitrary target property π_T to the target safety property that best over-approximates π_T[8] (an analogous *closure* was needed for subset-closed hyperproperties in Theorem 2.11). More precisely, *Safe* is a closure operator on target properties, with $\mathrm{Safety}_\mathrm{T} = \{ Safe(\pi_\mathrm{T}) \mid \pi_\mathrm{T} \in 2^{\mathrm{Trace}_\mathrm{T}} \}$. The mappings

$$Safe \circ \tilde{\tau} : 2^{\mathsf{Traces}} \leftrightarrows \mathrm{Safety}_\mathrm{T} : \tilde{\sigma}$$

determine a Galois connection between source trace properties and target safety properties, and ensure the equivalence $\mathsf{RTP}^{Safe \circ \tilde{\tau}} \iff \mathsf{RSP}^{\tilde{\sigma}}$ (✿). This argument generalizes to arbitrary closure operators on target properties (✿) and on hyperproperties, as long as the corresponding class is a sub-class of subset-closed hyperproperties, and

---

[8] $Safe(\pi_\mathrm{T}) = \cap \{ S_\mathrm{T} \mid \pi_\mathrm{T} \subseteq S_\mathrm{T} \wedge S_\mathrm{T} \in \mathrm{Safety}_\mathrm{T} \}$ is the topological closure in the topology of Clarkson and Schneider [14], where safety properties coincide with the closed sets.

explains all but one of the asymmetries in Figure 2, the one that concerns the robust preservation of arbitrary hyperproperties:

Theorem 5.3 (Weak Trinity for Robust Hyperproperties ♦). *For a trace relation* $\sim \subseteq \mathsf{Trace_S} \times \mathrm{Trace_T}$ *and induced property mappings* $\tilde{\sigma}$ *and* $\tilde{\tau}$, $\mathsf{RHC}^\sim$ *is equivalent to* $\mathsf{RHP}^{\tilde{\tau}}$; *moreover, if* $\tilde{\tau} \leftrightarrows \tilde{\sigma}$ *is a Galois insertion (i.e.,* $\tilde{\tau} \circ \tilde{\sigma} = id$), $\mathsf{RHC}^\sim$ *implies* $\mathsf{RHP}^{\tilde{\sigma}}$, *while if* $\tilde{\sigma} \leftrightarrows \tilde{\tau}$ *is a Galois reflection (i.e.,* $\tilde{\sigma} \circ \tilde{\tau} = id$), $\mathsf{RHP}^{\tilde{\sigma}}$ *implies* $\mathsf{RHC}^\sim$,

$$\textit{where } \mathsf{RHC}^\sim \equiv \forall P \; \forall \mathrm{C_T} \; \exists \mathsf{C_S} \; \forall t. \; \mathrm{C_T} \, [P{\downarrow}]{\rightsquigarrow}t \iff (\exists s \sim t. \; \mathsf{C_S} \, [P]{\rightsquigarrow}s);$$

$$\mathsf{RHP}^{\tilde{\tau}} \equiv \forall P \; \forall \mathsf{H_S}. \; P \models_\mathsf{R} \mathsf{H_S} \Rightarrow P{\downarrow} \models_\mathrm{R} \tilde{\tau}(\mathsf{H_S});$$

$$\mathsf{RHP}^{\tilde{\sigma}} \equiv \forall P \; \forall \mathrm{H_T}. \; P \models_\mathsf{R} \tilde{\sigma}(\mathrm{H_T}) \Rightarrow P{\downarrow} \models_\mathrm{R} \mathrm{H_T}.$$

This trinity is *weak* since extra hypotheses are needed to prove some implications. While the equivalence $\mathsf{RHC}^\sim \iff \mathsf{RHP}^{\tilde{\tau}}$ holds unconditionally, the other two implications hold only under distinct, stronger assumptions. For $\mathsf{RHP}^{\tilde{\sigma}}$ it is still possible and correct to deduce a source obligation for a given target hyperproperty $\mathrm{H_T}$ when no information is lost in the the the composition $\tilde{\tau} \circ \tilde{\sigma}$ (i.e., the two maps are a Galois *insertion*). On the other hand, $\mathsf{RHP}^{\tilde{\tau}}$ is a consequence of $\mathsf{RHP}^{\tilde{\sigma}}$ when no information is lost in composing in the other direction, $\tilde{\sigma} \circ \tilde{\tau}$ (i.e., the two maps are a Galois *reflection*).

Navigating the Diagram. For a given trace relation $\sim$, Figure 2 orders the generalized criteria according to their relative strength. If a trinity implies another (denoted by $\Rightarrow$), then the former provides stronger security for a compilation chain than the latter.

As mentioned, some property-full criteria regarding proper subclasses (i.e., subset-closed hyperproperties, safety, hypersafety, 2-relational safety and 2-relational hyper-properties) quantify over arbitrary (relational) (hyper)properties and compose $\tilde{\tau}$ with an additional operator. We have already presented the *Safe* operator; other operators are $Cl_{\subseteq}$, *HSafe*, and *2rSafe*, which approximate the image of $\tilde{\tau}$ with a subset-closed hyperproperty, a hypersafety and 2-relational safety respectively.

As a reading aid, when quantifying over arbitrary trace properties we use the shaded blue as background color, we use the red when quantifying over arbitrary subset-closed hyperproperties and green for arbitrary 2-relational properties.

We now describe how to interpret the acronyms in Figure 2. All criteria start with R meaning they refer to robust preservation. Criteria for relational hyperproperties—here only arity 2 is shown—contain 2r. Next, criteria names spell the class of hyperproperties they preserve: H for hyperproperties, SCH for subset-closed hyperproperties, HS for hypersafety, T for trace properties, and S for safety properties. Finally, property-free criteria end with a C while property-full ones involving $\tilde{\sigma}$ and $\tilde{\tau}$ end with P. Thus, *robust* (R) *subset-closed hyperproperty-preserving* (SCH) *compilation* (C) is RSCHC$^\sim$, *robust* (R) *two-relational* (2r) *safety-preserving* (S) *compilation* (C) is R2rSC$^\sim$, etc.

5.2   Instance of Trace-Relating Robust Preservation of Trace Properties

This subsection illustrates trace-relating secure compilation when the target language has strictly more events than the source that target contexts can exploit to break security.

Source and Target Languages. The source and target languages used here are nearly identical expression languages, borrowing from the syntax of the source language of §3.3. Both languages add *sequencing* of expressions, two kinds of *output events*, and

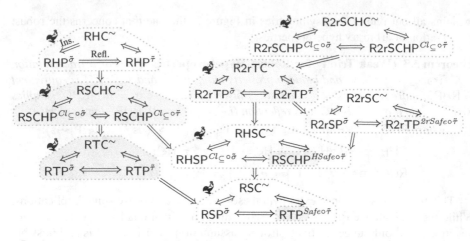

R robust	2r 2-relational	
H hyperproperties	SCH subset-closed hyperproperties	HS hypersafety
T trace properties	S safety properties	
P property-full criterion	C property-free criterion based on σ and τ	

Fig. 2: Hierarchy of trinitarian views of secure compilation criteria preserving classes of hyperproperties and the key to read each acronym. Shorthands 'Ins.' and 'Refl.' stand for Galois Insertion and Reflection. The 🐤 symbol denotes trinities proven in Coq.

the expressions that generate them: out_S n and out_s n usable in source and target, respectively, and out_T n usable only in the target, which is the only difference between source and target. The extra events in the target model the fact that the target language has an increased ability to perform certain operations, some of them potentially dangerous (such as writing to the hard drive), which cannot be performed by the source language, and against which source-level reasoning can therefore offer no protection.

Both languages and compilation chains now deal with partial programs, contexts and linking of those two to produce whole programs. In this setting, a whole program is the combination of a *main expression* to be evaluated and a set of *function definitions* (with distinct names) that can refer to their argument symbolically and can be called by the main expression and by other functions. The set of functions of a whole program is the union of the functions of a partial program and a context; the latter also contains the main expression. The extensions of the typing rules and the operational semantics for whole programs are unsurprising and therefore elided. The trace model also follows closely that of §3.3: it consists of a list of *regular events* (including the new outputs) terminated by a *result event*. Finally, a partial program and a context can be linked into a whole program when their functions satisfy the requirements mentioned above.

Relating Traces. In the present model, source and target traces differ only in the fact that the target draws (regular) events from a strictly larger set than the source, i.e., $\Sigma_T \supset \Sigma_S$. A natural relation between source and target traces essentially maps to a given target trace t the source trace that erases from t those events that exist only at the target level. Let $t|_{\Sigma_S}$ indicate trace t filtered to retain only those elements included in alphabet Σ_S. We define the trace relation as:

$$s \sim t \quad \equiv \quad s = t|_{\Sigma_S}.$$

In the opposite direction, a source trace s is related to many target ones, as any target-only events can be inserted at any point in s. The induced mappings for $\sim$ are:

$$\tilde{\tau}(\pi_S) = \{t \mid \exists s. s = t|_{\Sigma_S} \wedge s \in \pi_S\}; \quad \tilde{\sigma}(\pi_T) = \{s \mid \forall t. s = t|_{\Sigma_S} \Rightarrow t \in \pi_T\}.$$

That is, the target guarantee of a source property is that the target has the same source-level behavior, sprinkled with arbitrary target-level behavior. Conversely, the source-level obligation of a target property is the aggregate of those source traces all of whose target-level enrichments are in the target property.

Since R^S and R^T are very similar, it is simple to prove that the identity compiler $(\cdot\downarrow)$ from R^S to R^T is secure according to the trace relation $\sim$ defined above.

Theorem 5.4 ($\cdot\downarrow$ is Secure ✍). $\cdot\downarrow$ *is* RTC$^\sim$.

5.3 Instances of Trace-Relating Robust Preservation of Safety and Hypersafety

To provide examples of cross-language trace-relations that preserve safety and hyper-safety properties, we show how existing secure compilation results can be interpreted in our framework. This indicates how the more general theory developed here can already be instantiated to encompass existing results, and that existing proof techniques can be used in order to achieve the secure compilation criteria we define.

For the preservation of safety, Patrignani and Garg [50] study a compiler from a typed, concurrent WHILE language to an untyped, concurrent WHILE language with support for memory capabilities. As in §3.3, their source has bools and nats while their target only has nats. Additionally, their source has an ML-like memory (where the domain is locations ℓ) while their target has an assembly-like memory (where the domain is natural numbers n). Their traces consider context-program interactions and as such they are concatenations of call and return actions with parameters, which can include booleans as well as locations. Because of the aforementioned differences, they need a cross-language relation to relate source and target actions.

Besides defining a relation on traces (i.e., an instance of $\sim$), they also define a relation between source and target safety properties. They provide an instantiation of τ that maps all safe source traces to the related target ones. This ensures that no additional target trace is introduced in the target property, and source safety properties are mapped to target safety ones by τ. Their compiler is then proven to generate code that respects τ, so they achieve a variation of RTP$^{Safe \circ \tilde{\tau}}$.

Concerning the preservation of hypersafety, Patrignani and Garg [49] consider compilers in a reactive setting where traces are sequences of input (α?) and output (α!) actions. In their setting, traces are different between source and target, so they define a cross-language relation on actions that is total on the source actions and injective. Additionally, their set of target output actions is strictly larger than the source one, as it includes a special action $\sqrt{}$, which is how compiled code must respond to invalid target inputs (i.e., receiving a bool when a nat was expected). Starting from the relation on actions, they define $\mathbf{TPC}$, which is an instance of what we call τ. Informally, given a set of source traces, $\mathbf{TPC}$ generates all target traces that are related (pointwise) to a source trace. Additionally, it generates all traces with interleavings of undesired inputs α? followed by $\sqrt{}$ as long as removing $\alpha?\sqrt{}$ leaves a trace that relates to the source trace.

TPC preserves hypersafety across languages, i.e., it is an instance of RSCHP$^{HSafe\circ \tilde{\tau}}$ mapping source hypersafety to target hypersafety (and safety to safety).

6 Related Work

We already discussed how our results relate to some existing work in correct compilation [33, 58] and secure compilation [2, 49, 50]. We also already mentioned that most of our definitions and results make no assumptions about the structure of traces. One result that relies on the structure of traces is Theorem 5.2, which involves some *finite prefix* m, suggesting traces should be some sort of sequences of events (or states), as customary when one wants to refer to safety properties [14]. It is however sufficient to fix a topology on properties where safety properties coincide with closed sets [46]. Even for reasoning about safety, hypersafety, or arbitrary hyperproperties, traces can therefore be values, sequences of program states, or of input output events, or even the recently proposed *interaction trees* [62]. In the latter case we believe that the compilation from IMP to ASM proposed by Xia et al. [62] can be seen as an instance of HC$^\sim$, for the relation they call "trace equivalence."

Compilers Where Our Work Could Be Useful. Our work should be broadly applicable to understanding the guarantees provided by many verified compilers. For instance, Wang et al. [61] recently proposed a CompCert variant that compiles all the way down to machine code, and it would be interesting to see if the model at the end of §3.1 applies there too. This and many other verified compilers [12, 29, 42, 56] beyond CakeML [58] deal with resource exhaustion and it would be interesting to also apply the ideas of §3.2 to them. Hur and Dreyer [27] devised a correct compiler from an ML language to assembly using a cross-language logical relation to state their CC theorem. They do not have traces, though were one to add them, the logical relation on values would serve as the basis for the trace relation and therefore their result would attain CC$^\sim$.

Switching to more informative traces capturing the interaction between the program and the context is often used as a proof technique for secure compilation [2, 28, 48]. Most of these results consider a cross-language relation, so they probably could be proved to attain one of the criteria from Figure 2.

Generalizations of Compiler Correctness. The compiler correctness definition of Morris [41] was already general enough to account for trace relations, since it considered a translation between the semantics of the source program and that of the compiled program, which he called "decode" in his diagram, reproduced in Figure 3 (left). And even some of the more recent compiler correctness definitions preserve this kind of flexibility [51]. While CC$^\sim$ can be seen as an instance of a definition by Morris [41], we are not aware of any prior work that investigated the preservation of properties when the "decode translation" is neither the identity nor a bijection, and source properties need to be re-interpreted as target ones and vice versa.

Correct Compilation and Galois Connections. Melton et al. [38] and Sabry and Wadler [55] expressed a strong variant of compiler correctness using the diagram of Figure 3 (right) [38, 55]. They require that compiled programs *parallel* the computation steps of the original source programs, which can be proven showing the existence of a *decompilation* map # that makes the diagram commute, or equivalently, the existence of an adjoint for $\downarrow$ ($W \leq W' \iff W \twoheadrightarrow W'$ for both source and target). The

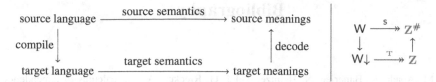

Fig. 3: Morris's [41] (left) and Melton et al.'s [38] and Sabry and Wadler's [55] (right)

"parallel" intuition can be formalized as an instance of $CC^\sim$. Take source and target traces to be finite or infinite sequences of program states (maximal trace semantics [15]), and relate them exactly like Melton et al. [38] and Sabry and Wadler [55].

Translation Validation. Translation validation is an important alternative to proving that all runs of a compiler are correct. A variant of $CC^\sim$ for translation validation can simply be obtained by specializing the definition to a particular W, and one can obtain again the same trinitarian view. Similarly for our other criteria, including our extensions of the secure compilation criteria of Abate et al. [2], which Busi et al. [10] seem to already be considering in the context of translation validation.

7   Conclusion and Future Work

We have extended the property preservation view on compiler correctness to arbitrary trace relations, and believe that this will be useful for understanding the guarantees various compilers provide. An open question is whether, given a compiler, there exists a most precise $\sim$ relation for which this compiler is correct. As mentioned in §1, every compiler is $CC^\sim$ for some $\sim$, but under which conditions is there a most precise relation? In practice, more precision may not always be better though, as it may be at odds with compiler efficiency and may not align with more subjective notions of usefulness, leading to tradeoffs in the selection of suitable relations. Finally, another interesting direction for future work is studying whether using the relation to Galois connections allows to more easily compose trace relations for different purposes, say, for a compiler whose target language has undefined behavior, resource exhaustion, and side-channels. In particular, are there ways to obtain complex relations by combining simpler ones in a way that eases the compiler verification burden?

Acknowledgements. We thank Akram El-Korashy and Amin Timany for participating in an early discussion about this work and the anonymous reviewers for their valuable feedback. This work was in part supported by the European Research Council under ERC Starting Grant SECOMP (715753), by the German Federal Ministry of Education and Research (BMBF) through funding for the CISPA-Stanford Center for Cybersecurity (FKZ: 13N1S0762), by DARPA grant SSITH/HOPE (FA8650-15-C-7558) and by UAIC internal grant 07/2018.

Bibliography

[1] M. Abadi, A. Banerjee, N. Heintze, and J. G. Riecke. A core calculus of dependency. *POPL*, 1999.

[2] C. Abate, R. Blanco, D. Garg, C. Hriţcu, M. Patrignani, and J. Thibault. Journey beyond full abstraction: Exploring robust property preservation for secure compilation. *CSF*, 2019.

[3] A. Ahmed, D. Garg, C. Hriţcu, and F. Piessens. Secure compilation (Dagstuhl Seminar 18201). *Dagstuhl Reports*, 8(5), 2018.

[4] A. Anand, A. Appel, G. Morrisett, Z. Paraskevopoulou, R. Pollack, O. S. Belanger, M. Sozeau, and M. Weaver. CertiCoq: A verified compiler for Coq. CoqPL Workshop, 2017.

[5] K. Backhouse and R. Backhouse. Safety of abstract interpretations for free, via logical relations and Galois connections. *Science of Computer Programming*, 51(1-2), 2004.

[6] G. Barthe, B. Grégoire, and V. Laporte. Secure compilation of side-channel countermeasures: the case of cryptographic "constant-time". *CSF*, 2018.

[7] L. Beringer, G. Stewart, R. Dockins, and A. W. Appel. Verified compilation for shared-memory C. *ESOP*, 2014.

[8] F. Besson, S. Blazy, and P. Wilke. A verified CompCert front-end for a memory model supporting pointer arithmetic and uninitialised data. *Journal of Automated Reasoning*, 62 (4), 2019.

[9] S. Boldo, J. Jourdan, X. Leroy, and G. Melquiond. Verified compilation of floating-point computations. *Journal of Automated Reasoning*, 54(2), 2015.

[10] M. Busi, P. Degano, and L. Galletta. Translation validation for security properties. *CoRR*, abs/1901.05082, 2019.

[11] Q. Cao, L. Beringer, S. Gruetter, J. Dodds, and A. W. Appel. VST-Floyd: A separation logic tool to verify correctness of C programs. *Journal of Automated Reasoning*, 61(1-4), 2018.

[12] Q. Carbonneaux, J. Hoffmann, T. Ramananandro, and Z. Shao. End-to-end verification of stack-space bounds for C programs. *PLDI*, 2014.

[13] C. Cimpanu. Microsoft: 70 percent of all security bugs are memory safety issues. ZDNet, 2019.

[14] M. R. Clarkson and F. B. Schneider. Hyperproperties. *JCS*, 18(6), 2010.

[15] P. Cousot. Constructive design of a hierarchy of semantics of a transition system by abstract interpretation. *TCS*, 277(1-2), 2002.

[16] P. Cousot and R. Cousot. Abstract interpretation: a unified lattice model for static analysis of programs by construction or approximation of fixpoints. *POPL*, 1977.

[17] V. D'Silva, M. Payer, and D. X. Song. The correctness-security gap in compiler optimization. *S&P Workshops*, 2015.

[18] J. Engelfriet. Determinacy implies (observation equivalence = trace equivalence). *TCS*, 36, 1985.

[19] R. Focardi and R. Gorrieri. A taxonomy of security properties for process algebras. *JCS*, 3 (1), 1995.

[20] P. H. Gardiner, C. E. Martin, and O. De Moor. An algebraic construction of predicate transformers. *Science of Computer Programming*, 22(1-2), 1994.

[21] R. Giacobazzi and I. Mastroeni. Abstract non-interference: a unifying framework for weakening information-flow. *ACM Transactions on Privacy and Security*, 21(2), 2018.

[22] J. A. Goguen and J. Meseguer. Security policies and security models. *S&P*, 1982.

[23] R. Gu, Z. Shao, J. Kim, X. N. Wu, J. Koenig, V. Sjöberg, H. Chen, D. Costanzo, and T. Ramananandro. Certified concurrent abstraction layers. *PLDI*, 2018.

[24] I. Haller, Y. Jeon, H. Peng, M. Payer, C. Giuffrida, H. Bos, and E. van der Kouwe. TypeSan: Practical type confusion detection. *CCS*, 2016.

[25] Heartbleed. The Heartbleed bug. http://heartbleed.com/, 2014.

[26] C. Hriţcu, D. Chisnall, D. Garg, and M. Payer. Secure compilation. SIGPLAN PL Perspectives Blog, 2019.

[27] C. Hur and D. Dreyer. A Kripke logical relation between ML and assembly. *POPL*, 2011.

[28] A. Jeffrey and J. Rathke. Java Jr: Fully abstract trace semantics for a core Java language. *ESOP*, 2005.

[29] J. Kang, C. Hur, W. Mansky, D. Garbuzov, S. Zdancewic, and V. Vafeiadis. A formal C memory model supporting integer-pointer casts. *PLDI*, 2015.

[30] J. Kang, Y. Kim, C.-K. Hur, D. Dreyer, and V. Vafeiadis. Lightweight verification of separate compilation. *POPL*, 2016.

[31] L. Lamport and F. B. Schneider. Formal foundation for specification and verification. In *Distributed Systems: Methods and Tools for Specification, An Advanced Course*, 1984.

[32] C. Lattner. What every C programmer should know about undefined behavior #1/3. LLVM Project Blog, 2011.

[33] X. Leroy. Formal verification of a realistic compiler. *CACM*, 52(7), 2009.

[34] X. Leroy. A formally verified compiler back-end. *JAR*, 43(4), 2009.

[35] X. Leroy. The formal verification of compilers (DeepSpec Summer School 2017), 2017.

[36] I. Mastroeni and M. Pasqua. Verifying bounded subset-closed hyperproperties. *SAS*, 2018.

[37] J. McCarthy and J. Painter. Correctness of a compiler for arithmetic expressions. *Mathematical Aspects Of Computer Science 1*, 19 of Proceedings of Symposia in Applied Mathematics, 1967.

[38] A. Melton, D. A. Schmidt, and G. E. Strecker. Galois connections and computer science applications. In *Proceedings of a Tutorial and Workshop on Category Theory and Computer Programming*, 1986.

[39] R. Milner. *A Calculus of Communicating Systems*. Springer-Verlag, Berlin, Heidelberg, 1982.

[40] R. Milner and R. Weyhrauch. Proving compiler correctness in a mechanized logic. In *Proceedings of 7th Annual Machine Intelligence Workshop, volume 7 of Machine Intelligence*, 1972.

[41] F. L. Morris. Advice on structuring compilers and proving them correct. *POPL*, 1973.

[42] E. Mullen, D. Zuniga, Z. Tatlock, and D. Grossman. Verified peephole optimizations for CompCert. *PLDI*, 2016.

[43] D. A. Naumann. A categorical model for higher order imperative programming. *Mathematical Structures in Computer Science*, 8(4), 1998.

[44] D. A. Naumann and M. Ngo. Whither specifications as programs. In *International Symposium on Unifying Theories of Programming*. Springer, 2019.

[45] G. Neis, C. Hur, J. Kaiser, C. McLaughlin, D. Dreyer, and V. Vafeiadis. Pilsner: a compositionally verified compiler for a higher-order imperative language. *ICFP*, 2015.

[46] M. Pasqua and I. Mastroeni. On topologies for (hyper)properties. *CEUR*, 2017.

[47] M. Patrignani. Why should anyone use colours? or, syntax highlighting beyond code snippets, 2020.

[48] M. Patrignani and D. Clarke. Fully abstract trace semantics for protected module architectures. *Computer Languages, Systems & Structures*, 42, 2015.

[49] M. Patrignani and D. Garg. Secure compilation and hyperproperty preservation. *CSF*, 2017.

[50] M. Patrignani and D. Garg. Robustly safe compilation. *ESOP*, 2019.

[51] D. Patterson and A. Ahmed. The next 700 compiler correctness theorems (functional pearl). *PACMPL*, 3(ICFP), 2019.

[52] T. Ramananandro, Z. Shao, S. Weng, J. Koenig, and Y. Fu. A compositional semantics for verified separate compilation and linking. *CPP*, 2015.

[53] J. Regehr. A guide to undefined behavior in C and C++, part 3. Embedded in Academia blog, 2010.

[54] A. Sabelfeld and D. Sands. Dimensions and principles of declassification. *CSFW*, 2005.

[55] A. Sabry and P. Wadler. A reflection on call-by-value. *ACM Transactions on Programming Languages and Systems*, 19(6), 1997.

[56] J. Sevčík, V. Vafeiadis, F. Z. Nardelli, S. Jagannathan, and P. Sewell. CompCertTSO: A verified compiler for relaxed-memory concurrency. *J. ACM*, 60(3), 2013.

[57] G. Stewart, L. Beringer, S. Cuellar, and A. W. Appel. Compositional CompCert. *POPL*, 2015.

[58] Y. K. Tan, M. O. Myreen, R. Kumar, A. Fox, S. Owens, and M. Norrish. The verified CakeML compiler backend. *Journal of Functional Programming*, 29, 2019.

[59] X. Wang, H. Chen, A. Cheung, Z. Jia, N. Zeldovich, and M. F. Kaashoek. Undefined behavior: What happened to my code? *APSYS*, 2012.

[60] X. Wang, N. Zeldovich, M. F. Kaashoek, and A. Solar-Lezama. Towards optimization-safe systems: Analyzing the impact of undefined behavior. *SOSP*, 2013.

[61] Y. Wang, P. Wilke, and Z. Shao. An abstract stack based approach to verified compositional compilation to machine code. *PACMPL*, 3(POPL), 2019.

[62] L. Xia, Y. Zakowski, P. He, C. Hur, G. Malecha, B. C. Pierce, and S. Zdancewic. Interaction trees: representing recursive and impure programs in Coq. *PACMPL*, 4(POPL), 2020.

[63] A. Zakinthinos and E. S. Lee. A general theory of security properties. *S&P*, 1997.

[64] J. Zhao, S. Nagarakatte, M. M. K. Martin, and S. Zdancewic. Formalizing the LLVM intermediate representation for verified program transformations. *POPL*, 2012.

Runners in action

Danel Ahman and Andrej Bauer

Faculty of Mathematics and Physics
University of Ljubljana, Slovenia

Abstract. Runners of algebraic effects, also known as comodels, provide a mathematical model of resource management. We show that they also give rise to a programming concept that models top-level external resources, as well as allows programmers to modularly define their own intermediate "virtual machines". We capture the core ideas of programming with runners in an equational calculus λ_{coop}, which we equip with a sound and coherent denotational semantics that guarantees the linear use of resources and execution of finalisation code. We accompany λ_{coop} with examples of runners in action, provide a prototype language implementation in OCAML, as well as a HASKELL library based on λ_{coop}.

Keywords: Runners, comodels, algebraic effects, resources, finalisation.

1 Introduction

Computational effects, such as exceptions, input-output, state, nondeterminism, and randomness, are an important component of general-purpose programming languages, whether they adopt functional, imperative, object-oriented, or other programming paradigms. Even pure languages exhibit computational effects at the top level, so to speak, by interacting with their external environment.

In modern languages, computational effects are often structured using *monads* [22,23,36], or *algebraic effects and handlers* [12,28,30]. These mechanisms excel at implementation of computational effects within the language itself. For instance, the familiar implementation of mutable state in terms of state-passing functions requires no native state, and can be implemented either as a monad or using handlers. One is naturally drawn to using these techniques also for dealing with actual effects, such as manipulation of native memory and access to hardware. These are represented inside the language as algebraic operations (as in EFF [4]) or a monad (in the style of HASKELL's IO), but treated specially by the language's top-level runtime, which invokes corresponding operating system functionality. While this approach works in practice, it has some unfortunate downsides too, namely *lack of modularity and linearity*, and *excessive generality*.

Lack of modularity is caused by having the external resources hard-coded into the top-level runtime. As a result, changing which resources are available and how they are implemented requires modifications of the language implementation. Additional complications arise when a language supports several operating systems and hardware platforms, each providing their own, different feature set.

© The Author(s) 2020
P. Müller (Ed.): ESOP 2020, LNCS 12075, pp. 29–55, 2020.
https://doi.org/10.1007/978-3-030-44914-8_2

One wishes that the ingenuity of the language implementors were better supported by a more flexible methodology with a sound theoretical footing.

Excessive generality is not as easily discerned, because generality of programming concepts makes a language expressive and useful, such as general algebraic effects and handlers enabling one to implement timeouts, rollbacks, stream redirection [30], async & await [16], and concurrency [9]. However, the flip side of such expressive freedom is the lack of any guarantees about how external resources will actually be used. For instance, consider a simple piece of code, written in EFF-like syntax, which first opens a file, then writes to it, and finally closes it:

```
let fh = open "hello.txt" in write (fh, "Hello, world."); close fh
```

What this program actually does depends on how the operations open, write, and close are handled. For all we know, an enveloping handler may intercept the write operation and discard its continuation, so that close never happens and the file is not properly closed. Telling the programmer not to shoot themselves in the foot by avoiding such handlers is not helpful, because the handler may encounter an external reason for not being able to continue, say a full disk.

Even worse, external resources may be misused accidentally when we combine two handlers, each of which works as intended on its own. For example, if we combine the above code with a non-deterministic choose operation, as in

```
let fh = open "greeting.txt" in
let b = choose () in
if b then write (fh, "hello") else write (fh, "good bye") ; close fh
```

and handle it with the standard non-determinism handler

```
handler { return x → [x], choose () k → return (append (k true) (k false)) }
```

The resulting program attempts to close the file twice, as well as write to it twice, because the continuation k is invoked twice when handling choose. Of course, with enough care all such situations can be dealt with, but that is beside the point. It is worth sacrificing some amount of the generality of algebraic effects and monads in exchange for predictable and safe usage of external computational effects, so long as the vast majority of common use cases are accommodated.

Contributions We address the described issues by showing how to design a programming language based on *runners of algebraic effects*. We review runners in §2 and recast them as a programming construct in §3. In §4, we present λ_{coop}, a calculus that captures the core ideas of programming with runners. We provide a coherent and sound denotational semantics for λ_{coop} in §5, where we also prove that well-typed code is properly finalised. In §6, we show examples of runners in action. The paper is accompanied by a prototype language COOP and a HASKELL library HASKELL-COOP, based on λ_{coop}, see §7. The relationship between λ_{coop} and existing work is addressed in §8, and future possibilities discussed in §9.

The paper is also accompanied by an online appendix (https://arxiv.org/abs/1910.11629) that provides the typing and equational rules we omit in §4.

Runners are *modular* in that they can be used not only to model the top-level interaction with the external environment, but programmers can also use them to define and nest their own intermediate "virtual machines". Our runners are *effectful*: they may handle operations by calling further outer operations, and raise exceptions and send signals, through which exceptional conditions and runtime errors are communicated back to user programs in a safe fashion that preserves linear usage of external resources and ensures their proper finalisation.

We achieve *suitable generality* for handling of external resources by showing how runners provide implementations of algebraic operations together with a natural notion of finalisation, and a strong guarantee that in the absence of external kill signals the finalisation code is executed exactly once (Thm. 7). We argue that for most purposes such discipline is well worth having, and giving up the arbitrariness of effect handlers is an acceptable price to pay. In fact, as will be apparent in the denotational semantics, runners are simply a restricted form of handlers, which apply the continuation at most once in a tail call position.

Runners guarantee *linear usage of resources* not through a linear or uniqueness type system (such as in the CLEAN programming language [15]) or a syntactic discipline governing the application of continuations in handlers, but rather by a design based on the linear state-passing technique studied by Møgelberg and Staton [21]. In this approach, a computational resource may be implemented without restrictions, but is then guaranteed to be used linearly by user code.

2   Algebraic effects, handlers, and runners

We begin with a short overview of the theory of algebraic effects and handlers, as well as runners. To keep focus on how runners give rise to a programming concept, we work naively in set theory. Nevertheless, we use category-theoretic language as appropriate, to make it clear that there are no essential obstacles to extending our work to other settings (we return to this point in §5.1).

2.1   Algebraic effects and handlers

There is by now no lack of material on the algebraic approach to structuring computational effects. For an introductory treatment we refer to [5], while of course also recommend the seminal papers by Plotkin and Power [25,28]. The brief summary given here only recalls the essentials and introduces notation.

An *(algebraic) signature* is given by a set Σ of *operation symbols*, and for each $\mathsf{op} \in \Sigma$ its *operation signature* $\mathsf{op} : A_{\mathsf{op}} \rightsquigarrow B_{\mathsf{op}}$, where A_{op} and B_{op} are called the *parameter* and *arity* set. A Σ-*structure* $\mathcal{M}$ is given by a carrier set $|\mathcal{M}|$, and for each operation symbol $\mathsf{op} \in \Sigma$, a map $\mathsf{op}_{\mathcal{M}} : A_{\mathsf{op}} \times (B_{\mathsf{op}} \Rightarrow |\mathcal{M}|) \to |\mathcal{M}|$, where $\Rightarrow$ is set exponentiation. The *free* Σ-*structure* $\mathrm{Tree}_{\Sigma}(X)$ over a set X is the set of well-founded trees generated inductively by

- $\mathsf{return}\, x \in \mathrm{Tree}_{\Sigma}(X)$, for every $x \in X$, and
- $\mathsf{op}(a, \kappa) \in \mathrm{Tree}_{\Sigma}(X)$, for every $\mathsf{op} \in \Sigma$, $a \in A_{\mathsf{op}}$, and $\kappa : B_{\mathsf{op}} \to \mathrm{Tree}_{\Sigma}(X)$.

We are abusing notation in a slight but standard way, by using op both as the name of an operation and a tree-forming constructor. The elements of $\mathrm{Tree}_\Sigma(X)$ are called *computation trees*: a leaf $\mathrm{return}\, x$ represents a pure computation returning a value x, while $\mathrm{op}(a, \kappa)$ represents an effectful computation that calls op with parameter a and continuation κ, which expects a result from B_{op}.

An *algebraic theory* $\mathcal{T} = (\Sigma_\mathcal{T}, \mathrm{Eq}_\mathcal{T})$ is given by a *signature* $\Sigma_\mathcal{T}$ and a set of *equations* $\mathrm{Eq}_\mathcal{T}$. The equations $\mathrm{Eq}_\mathcal{T}$ express computational behaviour via interactions between operations, and are written in a suitable formalism, e.g., [30]. We explain these by way of examples, as the precise details do not matter for our purposes. Let $\mathbb{0} = \{\,\}$ be the empty set and $\mathbb{1} = \{\star\}$ the standard singleton.

Example 1. Given a set C of possible states, the theory of *C-valued state* has two operations, whose somewhat unusual naming will become clear later on,

$$\mathsf{getenv} : \mathbb{1} \rightsquigarrow C, \qquad \mathsf{setenv} : C \rightsquigarrow \mathbb{1}$$

and the equations (where we elide appearances of $\star$):

$$\mathsf{getenv}(\lambda c.\, \mathsf{setenv}(c, \kappa)) = \kappa, \qquad \mathsf{setenv}(c, \mathsf{getenv}\,\kappa) = \mathsf{setenv}(c, \kappa\, c),$$
$$\mathsf{setenv}(c, \mathsf{setenv}(c', \kappa)) = \mathsf{setenv}(c', \kappa).$$

For example, the second equation states that reading state right after setting it to c gives precisely c. The third equation states that setenv overwrites the state.

Example 2. Given a set of exceptions E, the algebraic theory of *E-many exceptions* is given by a single operation $\mathsf{raise} : E \rightsquigarrow \mathbb{0}$, and no equations.

A $\mathcal{T}$-*model*, also called a $\mathcal{T}$-*algebra*, is a $\Sigma_\mathcal{T}$-structure which satisfies the equations in $\mathrm{Eq}_\mathcal{T}$. The *free* $\mathcal{T}$-*model* over a set X is constructed as the quotient

$$\mathrm{Free}_\mathcal{T}(X) = \mathrm{Tree}_{\Sigma_\mathcal{T}}(X)/\!\sim$$

by the $\Sigma_\mathcal{T}$-congruence $\sim$ generated by $\mathrm{Eq}_\mathcal{T}$. Each $\mathsf{op} \in \Sigma_\mathcal{T}$ is interpreted in the free model as the map $(a, \kappa) \mapsto [\mathsf{op}(a, \kappa)]$, where $[-]$ is the $\sim$-equivalence class. $\mathrm{Free}_\mathcal{T}(-)$ is the functor part of a *monad* on sets, whose *unit* at a set X is

$$X \xrightarrow{\ \mathrm{return}\ } \mathrm{Tree}_{\Sigma_\mathcal{T}}(X) \xrightarrow{\ [-]\ } \mathrm{Free}_\mathcal{T}(X).$$

The *Kleisli extension* for this monad is then the operation which lifts any map $f : X \to \mathrm{Tree}_{\Sigma_\mathcal{T}}(Y)$ to the map $f^\dagger : \mathrm{Free}_{\Sigma_\mathcal{T}}(X) \to \mathrm{Free}_{\Sigma_\mathcal{T}}(Y)$, given by

$$f^\dagger\,[\mathrm{return}\, x] \overset{\mathrm{def}}{=} f\, x, \qquad f^\dagger\,[\mathsf{op}(a, \kappa)] \overset{\mathrm{def}}{=} [\mathsf{op}(a, f^\dagger \circ \kappa)].$$

That is, $f^\dagger$ traverses a computation tree and replaces each leaf $\mathrm{return}\, x$ with $f\, x$.

The preceding construction of free models and the monad may be retrofitted to an algebraic signature Σ, if we construe Σ as an algebraic theory with no equations. In this case $\sim$ is just equality, and so we may omit the quotient and the pesky equivalence classes. Thus the carrier of the free Σ-model is the set of well-founded trees $\mathrm{Tree}_\Sigma(X)$, with the evident monad structure.

A fundamental insight of Plotkin and Power [25,28] was that many computational effects may be adequately described by algebraic theories, with the elements of free models corresponding to effectful computations. For example, the monads induced by the theories from Examples 1 and 2 are respectively isomorphic to the usual *state monad* $\mathsf{St}_C\, X \overset{\text{def}}{=} (C \Rightarrow X \times C)$ and the *exceptions monad* $\mathsf{Exc}_E\, X \overset{\text{def}}{=} X + E$.

Plotkin and Pretnar [30] further observed that the universal property of free models may be used to model a programming concept known as *handlers*. Given a $\mathcal{T}$-model $\mathcal{M}$ and a map $f : X \to |\mathcal{M}|$, the universal property of the free $\mathcal{T}$-model gives us a unique $\mathcal{T}$-homomorphism $f^\ddagger : \mathrm{Free}_\mathcal{T}(X) \to |\mathcal{M}|$ satisfying

$$f^\ddagger\,[\mathsf{return}\,x] = f\,x, \qquad f^\ddagger\,[\mathsf{op}(a, \kappa)] = \mathsf{op}_\mathcal{M}(a, f^\ddagger \circ \kappa).$$

A handler for a theory $\mathcal{T}$ in a language such as EFF amounts to a model $\mathcal{M}$ whose carrier $|\mathcal{M}|$ is the carrier $\mathrm{Free}_{\mathcal{T}'}(Y)$ of the free model for some other theory $\mathcal{T}'$, while the associated handling construct is the induced $\mathcal{T}$-homomorphism $\mathrm{Free}_\mathcal{T}(X) \to \mathrm{Free}_{\mathcal{T}'}(Y)$. Thus handling transforms computations with effects $\mathcal{T}$ to computations with effects $\mathcal{T}'$. There is however no restriction on how a handler implements an operation, in particular, it may use its continuation in an arbitrary fashion. We shall put the universal property of free models to good use as well, while making sure that the continuations are always used affinely.

2.2   Runners

Much like monads, handlers are useful for simulating computational effects, because they allow us to transform $\mathcal{T}$-computations to $\mathcal{T}'$-computations. However, eventually there has to be a "top level" where such transformations cease and actual computational effects happen. For these we need another concept, known as *runners* [35]. Runners are equivalent to the concept of *comodels* [27,31], which are "just models in the opposite category", although one has to apply the motto correctly by using powers and co-powers where seemingly exponentials and products would do. Without getting into the intricacies, let us spell out the definition.

Definition 1. A *runner* $\mathcal{R}$ for a signature Σ is given by a carrier set $|\mathcal{R}|$ together with, for each $\mathsf{op} \in \Sigma$, a *co-operation* $\overline{\mathsf{op}}_\mathcal{R} : A_\mathsf{op} \to (|\mathcal{R}| \Rightarrow B_\mathsf{op} \times |\mathcal{R}|)$.

Runners are usually defined to have co-operations in the equivalent uncurried form $\overline{\mathsf{op}}_\mathcal{R} : A_\mathsf{op} \times |\mathcal{R}| \to B_\mathsf{op} \times |\mathcal{R}|$, but that is less convenient for our purposes.

Runners may be defined more generally for theories $\mathcal{T}$, rather than just signatures, by requiring that the co-operations satisfy $\mathrm{Eq}_\mathcal{T}$. We shall have no use for these, although we expect no obstacles in incorporating them into our work.

A runner tells us what to do when an effectful computation reaches the top-level runtime environment. Think of $|\mathcal{R}|$ as the set of configurations of the runtime environment. Given the current configuration $c \in |\mathcal{R}|$, the operation $\mathsf{op}(a, \kappa)$ is executed as the corresponding co-operation $\overline{\mathsf{op}}_\mathcal{R}\,a\,c$ whose result

$(b, c') \in B_{op} \times |\mathcal{R}|$ gives the result of the operation b and the next runtime configuration c'. The continuation $\kappa\, b$ then proceeds in runtime configuration c'.

It is not too difficult to turn this idea into a mathematical model. For any X, the co-operations induce a Σ-structure $\mathcal{M}$ with $|\mathcal{M}| \overset{\text{def}}{=} \mathsf{St}_{|\mathcal{R}|}X = (|\mathcal{R}| \Rightarrow X \times |\mathcal{R}|)$ and operations $\mathsf{op}_{\mathcal{M}} : A_{op} \times (B_{op} \Rightarrow \mathsf{St}_{|\mathcal{R}|}X) \to \mathsf{St}_{|\mathcal{R}|}X$ given by

$$\mathsf{op}_{\mathcal{M}}(a, \kappa) \overset{\text{def}}{=} \lambda c\,.\, \kappa\, (\pi_1(\overline{\mathsf{op}}_{\mathcal{R}}\, a\, c))\, (\pi_2(\overline{\mathsf{op}}_{\mathcal{R}}\, a\, c)).$$

We may then use the universal property of the free Σ-model to obtain a Σ-homomorphism $\mathsf{r}_X : \mathsf{Tree}_{\Sigma}(X) \to \mathsf{St}_{|\mathcal{R}|}X$ satisfying the equations

$$\mathsf{r}_X(\mathsf{return}\, x) = \lambda c\,.\, (x, c), \qquad\qquad \mathsf{r}_X(\mathsf{op}(a, \kappa)) = \mathsf{op}_{\mathcal{M}}(a, \mathsf{r}_X \circ \kappa).$$

The map r_X precisely captures the idea that a runner *runs computations* by transforming (static) computation trees into state-passing maps. Note how in the above definition of $\mathsf{op}_{\mathcal{M}}$, the continuation κ is used in a controlled way, as it appears precisely once as the head of the outermost application. In terms of programming, this corresponds to linear use in a tail-call position.

Runners are less ad-hoc than they may seem. First, notice that $\mathsf{op}_{\mathcal{M}}$ is just the composition of the co-operation $\overline{\mathsf{op}}_{\mathcal{R}}$ with the state monad's Kleisli extension of the continuation κ, and so is the standard way of turning *generic effects* into Σ-structures [26]. Second, the map r_X is the component at X of a monad morphism $\mathsf{r} : \mathsf{Tree}_{\Sigma}(-) \to \mathsf{St}_{|\mathcal{R}|}$. Møgelberg & Staton [21], as well as Uustalu [35], showed that the passage from a runner $\mathcal{R}$ to the corresponding monad morphism r forms a one-to-one correspondence between the former and the latter.

As defined, runners are too restrictive a model of top-level computation, because the only effect available to co-operations is state, but in practice the runtime environment may also signal errors and perform other effects, by calling its own runtime environment. We are led to the following generalisation.

Definition 2. For a signature Σ and monad T, a *T-runner* $\mathcal{R}$ for Σ, or just an *effectful runner*, is given by, for each $\mathsf{op} \in \Sigma$, a *co-operation* $\overline{\mathsf{op}}_{\mathcal{R}} : A_{op} \to TB_{op}$.

The correspondence between runners and monad morphisms still holds.

Proposition 3. *For a signature Σ and a monad T, the monad morphisms $\mathsf{Tree}_{\Sigma}(-) \to T$ are in one-to-one correspondence with T-runners for Σ.*

Proof. This is an easy generalisation of the correspondence for ordinary runners. Let us fix a signature Σ, and a monad T with unit η and Kleisli extension $-^{\dagger}$.

Let $\mathcal{R}$ be a T-runner for Σ. For any set X, $\mathcal{R}$ induces a Σ-structure $\mathcal{M}$ with $|\mathcal{M}| \overset{\text{def}}{=} TX$ and $\mathsf{op}_{\mathcal{M}} : A_{op} \times (B_{op} \Rightarrow TX) \to TX$ defined as $\mathsf{op}_{\mathcal{M}}(a, \kappa) \overset{\text{def}}{=} \kappa^{\dagger}(\overline{\mathsf{op}}_{\mathcal{R}}\, a)$. As before, the universal property of the free model $\mathsf{Tree}_{\Sigma}(X)$ provides a unique Σ-homomorphism $\mathsf{r}_X : \mathsf{Tree}_{\Sigma}(X) \to TX$, satisfying the equations

$$\mathsf{r}_X(\mathsf{return}\, x) = \eta_X(x), \qquad\qquad \mathsf{r}_X(\mathsf{op}(a, \kappa)) = \mathsf{op}_{\mathcal{M}}(a, \mathsf{r}_X \circ \kappa).$$

The maps r_X collectively give us the desired monad morphism r induced by $\mathcal{R}$.

Conversely, given a monad morphism $\theta : \mathsf{Tree}_{\Sigma}(-) \to T$, we may recover a T-runner $\mathcal{R}$ for Σ by defining the co-operations as $\overline{\mathsf{op}}_{\mathcal{R}}\, a \overset{\text{def}}{=} \theta_{B_{op}}(\mathsf{op}(a, \lambda b\,.\, \mathsf{return}\, b))$. It is not hard to check that we have described a one-to-one correspondence.   □

3 Programming with runners

If ordinary runners are not general enough, the effectful ones are too general: parameterised by arbitrary monads T, they do not combine easily and they lack a clear notion of resource management. Thus, we now engineer more specific monads whose associated runners can be turned into a programming concept. While we give up complete generality, the monads presented below are still quite versatile, as they are parameterised by arbitrary algebraic signatures Σ, and so are extensible and support various combinations of effects.

3.1 The user and kernel monads

Effectful source code running inside a runtime environment is just one example of a more general phenomenon in which effectful computations are enveloped by a layer that provides a supervised access to external resources: a user process is controlled by a kernel, a web page by a browser, an operating system by hardware, or a virtual machine, etc. We shall adopt the parlance of software systems, and refer to the two layers generically as the *user* and *kernel* code. Since the two kinds of code need not, and will not, use the same effects, each will be described by its own algebraic theory and compute in its own monad.

We first address the kernel theory. Specifically, we look for an algebraic theory such that effectful runners for the induced monad satisfy the following desiderata:

1. Runners support management and controlled finalisation of resources.
2. Runners may use further external resources.
3. Runners may signal failure caused by unavoidable circumstances.

The totality of external resources available to user code appears as a stateful external environment, even though it has no direct access to it. Thus, kernel computations should carry state. We achieve this by incorporating into the kernel theory the operations getenv and setenv, and equations for state from Example 1.

Apart from managing state, kernel code should have access to further effects, which may be true external effects, or some outer layer of runners. In either case, we should allow the kernel code to call operations from a given signature Σ.

Because kernel computations ought to be able to signal failure, we should include an exception mechanism. In practice, many programming languages and systems have two flavours of exceptions, variously called recoverable and fatal, checked and unchecked, exceptions and errors, etc. One kind, which we call just *exceptions*, is raised by kernel code when a situation requires special attention by user code. The other kind, which we call *signals*, indicates an unrecoverable condition that prevents normal execution of user code. These correspond precisely to the two standard ways of combining exceptions with state, namely the coproduct and the tensor of algebraic theories [11]. The coproduct simply adjoins exceptions raise : $E \rightsquigarrow \mathbb{0}$ from Example 2 to the theory of state, while the tensor extends the theory of state with signals kill : $S \rightsquigarrow \mathbb{0}$, together with equations

$$\mathsf{getenv}(\lambda c.\,\mathsf{kill}\,s) = \mathsf{kill}\,s, \qquad \mathsf{setenv}(c,\mathsf{kill}\,s) = \mathsf{kill}\,s. \qquad (1)$$

These equations say that a signal discards state, which makes it unrecoverable.

To summarise, the *kernel theory* $\mathcal{K}_{\Sigma,E,S,C}$ contains operations from a signature Σ, as well as state operations getenv : $1 \rightsquigarrow C$, setenv : $C \rightsquigarrow 1$, exceptions raise : $E \rightsquigarrow 0$, and signals kill : $S \rightsquigarrow 0$, with equations for state from Example 1, equations (1) relating state and signals, and for each operation op $\in \Sigma$, equations

$$\mathsf{getenv}(\lambda c.\,\mathsf{op}(a, \kappa\, c)) = \mathsf{op}(a, \lambda b.\,\mathsf{getenv}(\lambda c.\,\kappa\, c\, b)),$$
$$\mathsf{setenv}(c, \mathsf{op}(a, \kappa)) = \mathsf{op}(a, \lambda b.\,\mathsf{setenv}(c, \kappa\, b)),$$

expressing that external operations do not interact with kernel state. It is not difficult to see that $\mathcal{K}_{\Sigma,E,S,C}$ induces, up to isomorphism, the *kernel monad*

$$\mathsf{K}_{\Sigma,E,S,C}X \stackrel{\mathrm{def}}{=} C \Rightarrow \mathrm{Tree}_\Sigma\left(((X + E) \times C) + S\right).$$

How about user code? It can of course call operations from a signature Σ (not necessarily the same as the kernel code), and because we intend it to handle exceptions, it might as well have the ability to raise them. However, user code knows nothing about signals and kernel state. Thus, we choose the *user theory* $\mathcal{U}_{\Sigma,E}$ to be the algebraic theory with operations Σ, exceptions raise : $E \rightsquigarrow 0$, and no equations. This theory induces the *user monad* $\mathsf{U}_{\Sigma,E}X \stackrel{\mathrm{def}}{=} \mathrm{Tree}_\Sigma(X + E)$.

3.2   Runners as a programming construct

In this section, we turn the ideas presented so far into programming constructs. We strive for a realistic result, but when faced with several design options, we prefer simplicity and semantic clarity. We focus here on translating the central concepts, and postpone various details to §4, where we present a full calculus.

We codify the idea of user and kernel computations by having syntactic categories for each of them, as well as one for values. We use letters M, N to indicate user computations, K, L for kernel computations, and V, W for values.

User and kernel code raise exceptions with operation raise, and catch them with exception handlers based on Benton and Kennedy's *exceptional syntax* [7],

$$\mathsf{try}\ M\ \mathsf{with}\ \{\mathsf{return}\ x \mapsto N, \ldots, \mathsf{raise}\ e \mapsto N_e, \ldots\},$$

and analogously for kernel code. The familiar binding construct let $x = M$ in N is simply shorthand for try M with {return $x \mapsto N, \ldots,$ raise $e \mapsto$ raise $e, \ldots$}.

As a programming concept, a runner R takes the form

$$\{(\mathsf{op}\ x \mapsto K_{\mathsf{op}})_{\mathsf{op}\in\Sigma}\}_C,$$

where each K_{op} is a kernel computation, with the variable x bound in K_{op}, so that each clause op $x \mapsto K_{\mathsf{op}}$ determines a co-operation for the kernel monad. The subscript C indicates the type of the state used by the kernel code K_{op}.

The corresponding elimination form is a handling-like construct

$$\mathsf{using}\ R\ @\ V\ \mathsf{run}\ M\ \mathsf{finally}\ F, \tag{2}$$

which uses the co-operations of runner R "at" initial kernel state V to run user code M, and finalises its return value, exceptions, and signals with F, see (3) below. When user code M calls an operation op, the enveloping run construct runs the corresponding co-operation K_{op} of R. While doing so, K_{op} might raise exceptions. But not every exception makes sense for every operation, and so we assign to each operation op a set of exceptions E_{op} which the co-operations implementing it may raise, by augmenting its operation signature with E_{op}, as

$$op : A_{op} \rightsquigarrow B_{op} \,! \, E_{op}.$$

An exception raised by the co-operation K_{op} propagates back to the operation call in the user code. Therefore, an operation call should have not only a continuation $x \,.\, M$ receiving a result, but also continuations N_e, one for each $e \in E_{op}$,

$$op(V, (x \,.\, M), (N_e)_{e \in E_{op}}).$$

If K_{op} returns a value $b \in B_{op}$, the execution proceeds as $M[b/x]$, and as N_e if K_{op} raises an exception $e \in E_{op}$. In examples, we use the generic versions of operations [26], written op V, which pass on return values and re-raise exceptions.

One can pass exceptions back to operation calls also in a language with handlers, such as EFF, by changing the signatures of operations to $A_{op} \rightsquigarrow B_{op} + E_{op}$, and implementing the exception mechanism by hand, so that every operation call is followed by a case distinction on $B_{op} + E_{op}$. One is reminded of how operating system calls communicate errors back to user code as exceptional values.

A co-operation K_{op} may also send a signal, in which case the rest of the user code M is skipped and the control proceeds directly to the corresponding case of the finalisation part F of the run construct (2), whose syntactic form is

$$\{\text{return } x \,@\, c \mapsto N, \dots, \text{raise } e \,@\, c \mapsto N_e, \dots, \text{kill } s \mapsto N_s, \dots\}. \tag{3}$$

Specifically, if M returns a value v, then N is evaluated with x bound to v and c to the final kernel state; if M raises an exception e (either directly or indirectly via a co-operation of R), then N_e is executed, again with c bound to the final kernel state; and if a co-operation of R sends a signal s, then N_s is executed.

Example 4. In anticipation of setting up the complete calculus we show how one can work with files. The language implementors can provide an operation open which opens a file for writing and returns its file handle, an operation close which closes a file handle, and a runner fileIO that implements writing. Let us further suppose that fileIO may raise an exception QuotaExceeded if a write exceeds the user disk quota, and send a signal IOError if an unrecoverable external error occurs. The following code illustrates how to guarantee proper closing of the file:

```
using fileIO @ (open "hello.txt") run
  write "Hello, world."
finally {
  return x @ fh → close fh,
  raise QuotaExceeded @ fh → close fh,
  kill IOError → return () }
```

Notice that the user code does not have direct access to the file handle. Instead, the runner holds it in its state, where it is available to the co-operation that implements write. The finalisation block gets access to the file handle upon successful completion and raised exception, so it can close the file, but when a signal happens the finalisation cannot close the file, nor should it attempt to do so.

We also mention that the code "cheats" by placing the call to open in a position where a value is expected. We should have let-bound the file handle returned by open outside the run construct, which would make it clear that opening the file happens *before* this construct (and that open is *not* handled by the finalisation), but would also expose the file handle. Since there are clear advantages to keeping the file handle inaccessible, a realistic language should accept the above code and hoist computations from value positions automatically.

4   A calculus for programming with runners

Inspired by the semantic notion of runners and the ideas of the previous section, we now present a calculus for programming with co-operations and runners, called λ_{coop}. It is a low-level fine-grain call-by-value calculus [19], and as such could inspire an intermediate language that a high-level language is compiled to.

4.1   Types

The types of λ_{coop} are shown in Fig. 1. The *ground types* contain *base types*, and are closed under finite sums and products. These are used in operation signatures and as types of kernel state. (Allowing arbitrary types in either of these entails substantial complications that can be dealt with but are tangential to our goals.) Ground types can also come with corresponding constant symbols f, each associated with a fixed *constant signature* $f : (A_1, \ldots, A_n) \to B$.

We assume a supply of operation symbols $\mathcal{O}$, exception names $\mathcal{E}$, and signal names $\mathcal{S}$. Each operation symbol $\text{op} \in \mathcal{O}$ is equipped with an *operation signature* $A_{\text{op}} \rightsquigarrow B_{\text{op}} \,!\, E_{\text{op}}$, which specifies its parameter type A_{op} and arity type B_{op}, and the exceptions E_{op} that the corresponding co-operations may raise in runners.

The *value types* extend ground types with two function types, and a type of runners. The *user function type* $X \to Y \,!\, (\Sigma, E)$ classifies functions taking arguments of type X to computations classified by the *user (computation) type* $Y \,!\, (\Sigma, E)$, i.e., those that return values of type Y, and may call operations Σ and raise exceptions E. Similarly, the *kernel function type* $X \to Y \,\natural\, (\Sigma, E, S, C)$ classifies functions taking arguments of type X to computations classified by the *kernel (computation) type* $Y \,\natural\, (\Sigma, E, S, C)$, i.e., those that return values of type Y, and may call operations Σ, raise exceptions E, send signals S, and use state of type C. We note that the ingredients for user and kernel types correspond precisely to the parameters of the user monad $\mathsf{U}_{\Sigma,E}$ and the kernel monad $\mathsf{K}_{\Sigma,E,S,C}$ from §3.1. Finally, the *runner type* $\Sigma \Rightarrow (\Sigma', S, C)$ classifies runners that implement co-operations for the operations Σ as kernel computations which use operations Σ', send signals S, and use state of type C.

Ground type A, B, C ::=	b	base type
	| unit	unit type
	| empty	empty type
	| $A \times B$	product type
	| $A + B$	sum type

Constant signature:	$f : (A_1, \ldots, A_n) \to B$
Signature Σ ::=	$\{op_1, op_2, \ldots, op_n\} \subset \mathcal{O}$
Exception set E ::=	$\{e_1, e_2, \ldots, e_n\} \subset \mathcal{E}$
Signal set S ::=	$\{s_1, s_2, \ldots, s_n\} \subset \mathcal{S}$

| Operation signature: | $op : A_{op} \rightsquigarrow B_{op} \, ! \, E_{op}$ |

Value type X, Y, Z ::=	A	ground type
	| $X \times Y$	product type
	| $X + Y$	sum type
	| $X \to Y \, ! \, \mathcal{U}$	user function type
	| $X \to Y \, \natural \, \mathcal{K}$	kernel function type
	| $\Sigma \Rightarrow (\Sigma', S, C)$	runner type

| User (computation) type: | $X \, ! \, \mathcal{U}$ | where $\mathcal{U} = (\Sigma, E)$ |
| Kernel (computation) type: | $X \, \natural \, \mathcal{K}$ | where $\mathcal{K} = (\Sigma, E, S, C)$ |

Fig. 1. The types of λ_{coop}.

4.2 Values and computations

The syntax of terms is shown in Fig. 2. The usual fine-grain call-by-value strat-ification of terms into pure values and effectful computations is present, except that we further distinguish between *user* and *kernel* computations.

Values Among the values are variables, constants for ground types, and con-structors for sums and products. There are two kinds of functions, for abstracting over user and kernel computations. A *runner* is a value of the form

$$\{(op \, x \mapsto K_{op})_{op \in \Sigma}\}_C.$$

It implements co-operations for operations op as kernel computations K_{op}, with x bound in K_{op}. The type annotation C specifies the type of the state that K_{op} uses. Note that C ranges over ground types, a restriction that allows us to define a naive set-theoretic semantics. We sometimes omit these type annotations.

User and kernel computations The user and kernel computations both have pure computations, function application, exception raising and handling, stan-

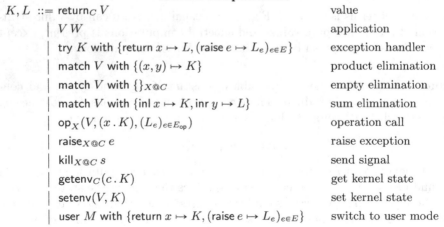

Values

$$V, W ::= x \qquad\qquad \text{variable}$$
$$\mid\ f(V_1, \ldots, V_n) \qquad\qquad \text{ground constant}$$
$$\mid\ () \qquad\qquad \text{unit}$$
$$\mid\ (V, W) \qquad\qquad \text{pair}$$
$$\mid\ \mathsf{inl}_{X,Y}\, V \ \mid\ \mathsf{inr}_{X,Y}\, V \qquad\qquad \text{injection}$$
$$\mid\ \mathsf{fun}\ (x : X) \mapsto M \qquad\qquad \text{user function}$$
$$\mid\ \mathsf{funK}\ (x : X) \mapsto K \qquad\qquad \text{kernel function}$$
$$\mid\ \{(\mathsf{op}\, x \mapsto K_{\mathsf{op}})_{\mathsf{op} \in \Sigma}\}_C \qquad\qquad \text{runner}$$

User computations

$$M, N ::= \mathsf{return}\ V \qquad\qquad \text{value}$$
$$\mid\ V\, W \qquad\qquad \text{application}$$
$$\mid\ \mathsf{try}\ M\ \mathsf{with}\ \{\mathsf{return}\ x \mapsto N, (\mathsf{raise}\ e \mapsto N_e)_{e \in E}\} \qquad\qquad \text{exception handler}$$
$$\mid\ \mathsf{match}\ V\ \mathsf{with}\ \{(x, y) \mapsto M\} \qquad\qquad \text{product elimination}$$
$$\mid\ \mathsf{match}\ V\ \mathsf{with}\ \{\}_X \qquad\qquad \text{empty elimination}$$
$$\mid\ \mathsf{match}\ V\ \mathsf{with}\ \{\mathsf{inl}\ x \mapsto M, \mathsf{inr}\ y \mapsto N\} \qquad\qquad \text{sum elimination}$$
$$\mid\ \mathsf{op}_X(V, (x\,.\,M), (N_e)_{e \in E_{\mathsf{op}}}) \qquad\qquad \text{operation call}$$
$$\mid\ \mathsf{raise}_X\ e \qquad\qquad \text{raise exception}$$
$$\mid\ \mathsf{using}\ V\ @\ W\ \mathsf{run}\ M\ \mathsf{finally}\ F \qquad\qquad \text{running user code}$$
$$\mid\ \mathsf{kernel}\ K\ @\ W\ \mathsf{finally}\ F \qquad\qquad \text{switch to kernel mode}$$

$$F ::= \{\mathsf{return}\ x\ @\ c \mapsto N, (\mathsf{raise}\ e\ @\ c \mapsto N_e)_{e \in E}, (\mathsf{kill}\ s \mapsto N_s)_{s \in S}\}$$

Kernel computations

$$K, L ::= \mathsf{return}_C\ V \qquad\qquad \text{value}$$
$$\mid\ V\, W \qquad\qquad \text{application}$$
$$\mid\ \mathsf{try}\ K\ \mathsf{with}\ \{\mathsf{return}\ x \mapsto L, (\mathsf{raise}\ e \mapsto L_e)_{e \in E}\} \qquad\qquad \text{exception handler}$$
$$\mid\ \mathsf{match}\ V\ \mathsf{with}\ \{(x, y) \mapsto K\} \qquad\qquad \text{product elimination}$$
$$\mid\ \mathsf{match}\ V\ \mathsf{with}\ \{\}_{X@C} \qquad\qquad \text{empty elimination}$$
$$\mid\ \mathsf{match}\ V\ \mathsf{with}\ \{\mathsf{inl}\ x \mapsto K, \mathsf{inr}\ y \mapsto L\} \qquad\qquad \text{sum elimination}$$
$$\mid\ \mathsf{op}_X(V, (x\,.\,K), (L_e)_{e \in E_{\mathsf{op}}}) \qquad\qquad \text{operation call}$$
$$\mid\ \mathsf{raise}_{X@C}\ e \qquad\qquad \text{raise exception}$$
$$\mid\ \mathsf{kill}_{X@C}\ s \qquad\qquad \text{send signal}$$
$$\mid\ \mathsf{getenv}_C(c\,.\,K) \qquad\qquad \text{get kernel state}$$
$$\mid\ \mathsf{setenv}(V, K) \qquad\qquad \text{set kernel state}$$
$$\mid\ \mathsf{user}\ M\ \mathsf{with}\ \{\mathsf{return}\ x \mapsto K, (\mathsf{raise}\ e \mapsto L_e)_{e \in E}\} \qquad\qquad \text{switch to user mode}$$

Fig. 2. Values, user computations, and kernel computations of λ_{coop}.

dard elimination forms, and operation calls. Note that the typing annotations on some of these differ according to their mode. For instance, a user operation call is annotated with the result type X, whereas the annotation $X @ C$ on a kernel operation call also specifies the kernel state type C.

The binding construct $\mathsf{let}_{X!E}\ x = M$ in N is not part of the syntax, but is an abbreviation for $\mathsf{try}\ M$ with $\{\mathsf{return}\ x \mapsto N, (\mathsf{raise}\ e \mapsto \mathsf{raise}_X\ e)_{e \in E}\}$, and there is an analogous one for kernel computations. We often drop the annotation $X!E$.

Some computations are specific to one or the other mode. Only the kernel mode may send a signal with kill, and manipulate state with getenv and setenv, but only the user mode has the run construct from §3.2. Finally, each mode has the ability to "context switch" to the other one. The kernel computation

$$\mathsf{user}\ M\ \mathsf{with}\ \{\mathsf{return}\ x \mapsto K, (\mathsf{raise}\ e \mapsto L_e)_{e \in E}\}$$

runs a user computation M and handles the returned value and leftover exceptions with kernel computations K and L_e. Conversely, the user computation

$$\mathsf{kernel}\ K @ W\ \mathsf{finally}\ \{x @ c \mapsto M, (\mathsf{raise}\ e @ c \mapsto N_e)_{e \in E}, (\mathsf{kill}\ s \mapsto N_s)_{s \in S}\}$$

runs kernel computation K with initial state W, and handles the returned value, and leftover exceptions and signals with user computations M, N_e, and N_s.

4.3   Type system

We equip λ_{coop} with a type system akin to type and effect systems for algebraic effects and handlers [3,7,12]. We are experimenting with resource control, so it makes sense for the type system to tightly control resources. Consequently, our effect system does not allow effects to be implicitly propagated outwards.

In §4.1, we assumed that each operation op $\in \mathcal{O}$ is equipped with some fixed operation signature op : $A_{\mathsf{op}} \rightsquigarrow B_{\mathsf{op}}\ !\ E_{\mathsf{op}}$. We also assumed a fixed constant signature f : $(A_1, \ldots, A_n) \rightarrow B$ for each ground constant f. We consider this information to be part of the type system and say no more about it.

Values, user computations, and kernel computations each have a corresponding *typing judgement* form and a *subtyping relation*, given by

$$\Gamma \vdash V : X, \qquad \Gamma \vdash M : X\,!\,\mathcal{U}, \qquad \Gamma \vdash K : X\,\natural\,\mathcal{K},$$
$$X \sqsubseteq Y, \qquad X\,!\,\mathcal{U} \sqsubseteq Y\,!\,\mathcal{V}, \qquad X\,\natural\,\mathcal{K} \sqsubseteq Y\,\natural\,\mathcal{L},$$

where Γ is a *typing context* $x_1 : X_1, \ldots, x_n : X_n$. The effect information is an over-approximation, i.e., M and K employ *at most* the effects described by $\mathcal{U}$ and $\mathcal{K}$. The complete rules for these judgements are given in the online appendix. We comment here only on the rules that are peculiar to λ_{coop}, see Fig. 3.

Subtyping of ground types SUB-GROUND is trivial, as it relates only equal types. Subtyping of runners SUB-RUNNER and kernel computations SUB-KERNEL requires equality of the kernel state types C and C' because state is used invariantly in the kernel monad. We leave it for future work to replace $C \equiv C'$ with a *lens* [10] from C' to C, i.e., maps $C' \rightarrow C$ and $C' \times C \rightarrow C'$ satisfying state

$$\text{Sub-Ground} \over A \sqsubseteq A$$

$$\text{Sub-Runner}$$
$$\Sigma_1' \subseteq \Sigma_1 \qquad \Sigma_2 \subseteq \Sigma_2' \qquad S \subseteq S' \qquad C \equiv C' \over \Sigma_1 \Rightarrow (\Sigma_2, S, C) \sqsubseteq \Sigma_1' \Rightarrow (\Sigma_2', S', C')$$

$$\text{Sub-Kernel}$$
$$X \sqsubseteq X' \qquad \Sigma \subseteq \Sigma' \qquad E \subseteq E' \qquad S \subseteq S' \qquad C \equiv C' \over X \,\natural\, (\Sigma, E, S, C) \sqsubseteq X' \,\natural\, (\Sigma', E', S', C')$$

$$\text{TyUser-Try}$$
$$\Gamma \vdash M : X \,!\,(\Sigma, E) \qquad \Gamma, x{:}X \vdash N : Y \,!\,(\Sigma, E') \qquad \big(\Gamma \vdash N_e : Y \,!\,(\Sigma, E')\big)_{e \in E} \over \Gamma \vdash \mathsf{try}\ M\ \mathsf{with}\ \{\mathsf{return}\ x \mapsto N, (\mathsf{raise}\ e \mapsto N_e)_{e \in E}\} : Y \,!\,(\Sigma, E')$$

$$\text{TyUser-Run}$$
$$F \equiv \{\mathsf{return}\ x \,@\, c \mapsto N, (\mathsf{raise}\ e \,@\, c \mapsto N_e)_{e \in E}, (\mathsf{kill}\ s \mapsto N_s)_{s \in S}\}$$
$$\Gamma \vdash V : \Sigma \Rightarrow (\Sigma', S, C) \qquad \Gamma \vdash W : C$$
$$\Gamma \vdash M : X \,!\,(\Sigma, E) \qquad \Gamma, x{:}X, c{:}C \vdash N : Y \,!\,(\Sigma', E')$$
$$\big(\Gamma, c{:}C \vdash N_e : Y \,!\,(\Sigma', E')\big)_{e \in E} \qquad \big(\Gamma \vdash N_s : Y \,!\,(\Sigma', E')\big)_{s \in S} \over \Gamma \vdash \mathsf{using}\ V \,@\, W\ \mathsf{run}\ M\ \mathsf{finally}\ F : Y \,!\,(\Sigma', E')$$

$$\text{TyUser-Op}$$
$$\mathcal{U} \equiv (\Sigma, E) \qquad \mathsf{op} \in \Sigma \qquad \Gamma \vdash V : A_{\mathsf{op}}$$
$$\Gamma, x{:}B_{\mathsf{op}} \vdash M : X \,!\,\mathcal{U} \qquad \big(\Gamma \vdash N_e : X \,!\,\mathcal{U}\big)_{e \in E_{\mathsf{op}}} \over \Gamma \vdash \mathsf{op}_X(V, (x\,.\,M), (N_e)_{e \in E_{\mathsf{op}}}) : X \,!\,\mathcal{U}$$

$$\text{TyKernel-Op}$$
$$\mathcal{K} \equiv (\Sigma, E, S, C) \qquad \mathsf{op} \in \Sigma \qquad \Gamma \vdash V : A_{\mathsf{op}}$$
$$\Gamma, x{:}B_{\mathsf{op}} \vdash K : X \,\natural\, \mathcal{K} \qquad \big(\Gamma \vdash L_e : X \,\natural\, \mathcal{K}\big)_{e \in E_{\mathsf{op}}} \over \Gamma \vdash \mathsf{op}_X(V, (x\,.\,K), (L_e)_{e \in E_{\mathsf{op}}}) : X \,\natural\, \mathcal{K}$$

$$\text{TyUser-Kernel}$$
$$F \equiv \{\mathsf{return}\ x \,@\, c \mapsto N, (\mathsf{raise}\ e \,@\, c \mapsto N_e)_{e \in E}, (\mathsf{kill}\ s \mapsto N_s)_{s \in S}\}$$
$$\Gamma \vdash K : X \,\natural\, (\Sigma, E, S, C) \qquad \Gamma \vdash W : C \qquad \Gamma, x{:}X, c{:}C \vdash N : Y \,!\,(\Sigma, E')$$
$$\big(\Gamma, c{:}C \vdash N_e : Y \,!\,(\Sigma, E')\big)_{e \in E} \qquad \big(\Gamma \vdash N_s : Y \,!\,(\Sigma, E')\big)_{s \in S} \over \Gamma \vdash \mathsf{kernel}\ K \,@\, W\ \mathsf{finally}\ F : Y \,!\,(\Sigma, E')$$

$$\text{TyKernel-User}$$
$$\mathcal{K} \equiv (\Sigma, E', S, C) \qquad \Gamma \vdash M : X \,!\,(\Sigma, E)$$
$$\Gamma, x{:}X \vdash K : Y \,\natural\, \mathcal{K} \qquad \big(\Gamma \vdash L_e : Y \,\natural\, \mathcal{K}\big)_{e \in E} \over \Gamma \vdash \mathsf{user}\ M\ \mathsf{with}\ \{\mathsf{return}\ x \mapsto K, (\mathsf{raise}\ e \mapsto L_e)_{e \in E}\} : Y \,\natural\, \mathcal{K}$$

Fig. 3. Selected typing and subtyping rules.

equations analogous to Example 1. It has been observed [24,31] that such a lens in fact amounts to an ordinary runner for C-valued state.

The rules TyUser-Op and TyKernel-Op govern operation calls, where we have a success continuation which receives a value returned by a co-operation, and exceptional continuations which receive exceptions raised by co-operations.

The rule TyUser-Run requires that the runner V implements *all* the operations M can use, meaning that operations are *not* implicitly propagated outside a run block (which is different from how handlers are sometimes implemented). Of course, the co-operations of the runner may call further external operations, as recorded by the signature Σ'. Similarly, we require the finally block F to intercept all exceptions and signals that might be produced by the co-operations of V or the user code M. Such strict control is exercised throughout. For example, in TyUser-Run, TyUser-Kernel, and TyKernel-User we catch all the exceptions and signals that the code might produce. One should judiciously relax these requirements in a language that is presented to the programmer, and allow re-raising and re-sending clauses to be automatically inserted.

4.4 Equational theory

We present λ_{coop} as an *equational calculus*, i.e., the interactions between its components are described by equations. Such a presentation makes it easy to reason about program equivalence. There are three equality judgements

$$\Gamma \vdash V \equiv W : X, \qquad \Gamma \vdash M \equiv N : X \mathbin{!} \mathcal{U}, \qquad \Gamma \vdash K \equiv L : X \mathbin{!} \mathcal{K}.$$

It is presupposed that we only compare well-typed expressions with the indicated types. For the most part, the context and the type annotation on judgements will play no significant role, and so we shall drop them whenever possible.

We comment on the computational equations for constructs characteristic of λ_{coop}, and refer the reader to the online appendix for other equations. When read left-to-right, these equations explain the operational meaning of programs.

Of the three equations for run, the first two specify that returned values and raised exceptions are handled by the corresponding clauses,

$$\mathsf{using}\ V @ W\ \mathsf{run}\ (\mathsf{return}\ V')\ \mathsf{finally}\ F \equiv N[V'/x, W/c],$$

$$\mathsf{using}\ V @ W\ \mathsf{run}\ (\mathsf{raise}_X\ e)\ \mathsf{finally}\ F \equiv N_e[W/c],$$

where $F \stackrel{\mathrm{def}}{=} \{\mathsf{return}\ x @ c \mapsto N, (\mathsf{raise}\ e @ c \mapsto N_e)_{e \in E}, (\mathsf{kill}\ s \mapsto N_s)_{s \in S}\}$. The third equation below relates running an operation op with executing the corresponding co-operation K_{op}, where R stands for the runner $\{(\mathsf{op}\ x \mapsto K_{\mathsf{op}})_{\mathsf{op} \in \Sigma}\}_C$:

$$\mathsf{using}\ R @ W\ \mathsf{run}\ (\mathsf{op}_X(V, (x\,.\,M), (N'_{e'})_{e' \in E_{\mathsf{op}}}))\ \mathsf{finally}\ F \equiv$$
$$\mathsf{kernel}\ K_{\mathsf{op}}[V/x] @ W\ \mathsf{finally}$$
$$\{\mathsf{return}\ x @ c' \mapsto (\mathsf{using}\ R @ c'\ \mathsf{run}\ M\ \mathsf{finally}\ F),$$
$$\big(\mathsf{raise}\ e' @ c' \mapsto (\mathsf{using}\ R @ c'\ \mathsf{run}\ N'_{e'}\ \mathsf{finally}\ F)\big)_{e' \in E_{\mathsf{op}}},$$
$$(\mathsf{kill}\ s \mapsto N_s)_{s \in S}\}$$

Because K_{op} is kernel code, it is executed in kernel mode, whose finally clauses specify what happens afterwards: if K_{op} returns a value, or raises an exception, execution continues with a suitable continuation, with R wrapped around it; and if K_{op} sends a signal, the corresponding finalisation code from F is evaluated.

The next bundle describes how kernel code is executed within user code:

$$\mathsf{kernel}\ (\mathsf{return}_C\ V)\ @\ W\ \mathsf{finally}\ F \equiv N[V/x, W/c],$$
$$\mathsf{kernel}\ (\mathsf{raise}_{X@C}\ e)\ @\ W\ \mathsf{finally}\ F \equiv N_e[W/c],$$
$$\mathsf{kernel}\ (\mathsf{kill}_{X@C}\ s)\ @\ W\ \mathsf{finally}\ F \equiv N_s,$$
$$\mathsf{kernel}\ (\mathsf{getenv}_C(c\,.\,K))\ @\ W\ \mathsf{finally}\ F \equiv \mathsf{kernel}\ K[W/c]\ @\ W\ \mathsf{finally}\ F,$$
$$\mathsf{kernel}\ (\mathsf{setenv}(V, K))\ @\ W\ \mathsf{finally}\ F \equiv \mathsf{kernel}\ K\ @\ V\ \mathsf{finally}\ F.$$

We also have an equation stating that an operation called in kernel mode propagates out to user mode, with its continuations wrapped in kernel mode:

$$\mathsf{kernel}\ \mathsf{op}_X(V, (x\,.\,K), (L_{e'})_{e'\in E})\ @\ W\ \mathsf{finally}\ F \equiv$$
$$\mathsf{op}_X(V, (x\,.\,\mathsf{kernel}\ K\ @\ W\ \mathsf{finally}\ F), (\mathsf{kernel}\ L_{e'}\ @\ W\ \mathsf{finally}\ F)_{e'\in E}).$$

Similar equations govern execution of user computations in kernel mode.

The remaining equations include standard $\beta\eta$-equations for exception handling [7], deconstruction of products and sums, algebraicity equations for operations [33], and the equations of kernel theory from §3.1, describing how getenv and setenv work, and how they interact with signals and other operations.

5 Denotational semantics

We provide a coherent denotational semantics for λ_{coop}, and prove it sound with respect to the equational theory given in §4.4. Having eschewed all forms of recursion, we may afford to work simply over the category of sets and functions, while noting that there is no obstacle to incorporating recursion at all levels and switching to domain theory, similarly to the treatment of effect handlers in [3].

5.1 Semantics of types

The meaning of terms is most naturally defined by structural induction on their typing derivations, which however are not unique in λ_{coop} due to subsumption rules. Thus we must worry about devising a *coherent* semantics, i.e., one in which all derivations of a judgement get the same meaning. We follow prior work on the semantics of effect systems for handlers [3], and proceed by first giving a *skeletal* semantics of λ_{coop} in which derivations are manifestly unique because the effect information is unrefined. We then use the skeletal semantics as the frame upon which rests a refinement-style coherent semantics of the effectful types of λ_{coop}.

The *skeletal* types are like λ_{coop}'s types, but with all effect information erased. In particular, the ground types A, and hence the kernel state types C, do not change as they contain no effect information. The skeletal value types are

$$P, Q ::= A \mid \mathsf{unit} \mid \mathsf{empty} \mid P \times Q \mid P + Q \mid P \to Q! \mid P \to Q\,\raisebox{0.3ex}{\scriptsize $\natural$}\,C \mid \mathsf{runner}\,C.$$

The skeletal versions of the user and kernel types are $P!$ and $P \notdiv C$, respectively. It is best to think of the skeletal types as ML-style types which implicitly over-approximate effect information by "any effect is possible", an idea which is mathematically expressed by their semantics, as explained below.

First of all, the semantics of ground types is straightforward. One only needs to provide sets denoting the base types b, after which the ground types receive the standard set-theoretic meaning, as given in Fig. 4.

Recall that $\mathcal{O}$, $\mathcal{S}$, and $\mathcal{E}$ are the sets of all operations, signals, and exceptions, and that each $\mathsf{op} \in \mathcal{O}$ has a signature $\mathsf{op} : A_{\mathsf{op}} \rightsquigarrow B_{\mathsf{op}} ! E_{\mathsf{op}}$. Let us additionally assume that there is a distinguished operation $\mathtt{\dot{\imath}} \in \mathcal{O}$ with signature $\mathtt{\dot{\imath}} : \mathbb{1} \rightsquigarrow 0!0$ (otherwise we adjoin it to $\mathcal{O}$). It ensures that the denotations of skeletal user and kernel types are *pointed* sets, while operationally $\mathtt{\dot{\imath}}$ indicates a *runtime error*.

Next, we define the *skeletal user and kernel monads* as

$$\mathsf{U}^{\mathsf{s}} X \stackrel{\mathrm{def}}{=} \mathsf{U}_{\mathcal{O},\mathcal{E}} X = \mathrm{Tree}_{\mathcal{O}} (X + \mathcal{E}),$$

$$\mathsf{K}^{\mathsf{s}}_C X \stackrel{\mathrm{def}}{=} \mathsf{K}_{\mathcal{O},\mathcal{E},\mathcal{S},C} X = (C \Rightarrow \mathrm{Tree}_{\mathcal{O}} ((X + \mathcal{E}) \times C + \mathcal{S})),$$

and $\mathsf{Runner}^{\mathsf{s}} C$ as the set of all *skeletal runners* $\mathcal{R}$ *(with state C)*, which are families of co-operations $\{\overline{\mathsf{op}}_{\mathcal{R}} : [\![A_{\mathsf{op}}]\!] \to \mathsf{K}_{\mathcal{O},E_{\mathsf{op}},S,C} [\![B_{\mathsf{op}}]\!]\}_{\mathsf{op} \in \mathcal{O}}$. Note that $\mathsf{K}_{\mathcal{O},E_{\mathsf{op}},S,C}$ is a coproduct [11] of monads $C \Rightarrow \mathrm{Tree}_{\mathcal{O}} (- \times C + \mathcal{S})$ and $\mathsf{Exc}_{E_{\mathsf{op}}}$, and thus the skeletal runners are the effectful runners for the former monad, so long as we read the effectful signatures $\mathsf{op} : A_{\mathsf{op}} \rightsquigarrow B_{\mathsf{op}} ! E_{\mathsf{op}}$ as ordinary algebraic ones $\mathsf{op} : A_{\mathsf{op}} \rightsquigarrow B_{\mathsf{op}} + E_{\mathsf{op}}$. While there is no semantic difference between the two readings, there is one of intention: $\mathsf{K}_{\mathcal{O},E_{\mathsf{op}},S,C}[\![B_{\mathsf{op}}]\!]$ is a kernel computation that (apart from using state and sending signals) returns values of type B_{op} and raises exceptions E_{op}, whereas $C \Rightarrow \mathrm{Tree}_{\mathcal{O}} (([\![B_{\mathsf{op}}]\!] + E_{\mathsf{op}}) \times C + \mathcal{S})$ returns values of type $B_{\mathsf{op}} + E_{\mathsf{op}}$ and raises no exceptions. We prefer the former, as it reflects our treatment of exceptions as a control mechanism rather than exceptional values.

These ingredients suffice for the denotation of skeletal types as sets, as given in Fig. 4. The user and kernel skeletal types are interpreted using the respective skeletal monads, and hence the two function types as Kleisli exponentials.

We proceed with the semantics of effectful types. The *skeleton* of a value type X is the skeletal type X^{s} obtained by removing all effect information, and similarly for user and kernel types, see Fig. 5. We interpret a value type X as a subset $[\![X]\!] \subseteq [\![X^{\mathsf{s}}]\!]$ of the denotation of its skeleton, and similarly for user and computation types. In other words, we treat the effectful types as *refinements* of their skeletons. For this, we define the operation $(X_0, X_1) \Rightarrow (Y_0, Y_1)$, for any $X_0 \subseteq X_1$ and $Y_0 \subseteq Y_1$, as the set of maps $X_1 \to Y_1$ restricted to $X_0 \to Y_0$:

$$(X_0, X_1) \Rightarrow (Y_0, Y_1) \stackrel{\mathrm{def}}{=} \{f : X_1 \to Y_1 \mid \forall x \in X_0 . f(x) \in Y_0\}.$$

Next, observe that the user and the kernel monads preserve subset inclusions, in the sense that $\mathsf{U}_{\Sigma,E} X \subseteq \mathsf{U}_{\Sigma',E'} X'$ and $\mathsf{K}_{\Sigma,E,S,C} X \subseteq \mathsf{K}_{\Sigma',E',S',C} X'$ if $\Sigma \subseteq \Sigma'$, $E \subseteq E'$, $S \subseteq S'$, and $X \subseteq X'$. In particular, we always have $\mathsf{U}_{\Sigma,E} X \subseteq \mathsf{U}^{\mathsf{s}} X$ and $\mathsf{K}_{\Sigma,E,S,C} X \subseteq \mathsf{K}^{\mathsf{s}}_C X$. Finally, let $\mathsf{Runner}_{\Sigma,\Sigma',S} C \subseteq \mathsf{Runner}^{\mathsf{s}} C$ be the subset of those runners $\mathcal{R}$ whose co-operations for Σ factor through $\mathsf{K}_{\Sigma',E_{\mathsf{op}},S,C}$, i.e., $\overline{\mathsf{op}}_{\mathcal{R}} : [\![A_{\mathsf{op}}]\!] \to \mathsf{K}_{\Sigma',E_{\mathsf{op}},S,C} [\![B_{\mathsf{op}}]\!] \subseteq \mathsf{K}_{\mathcal{O},E_{\mathsf{op}},S,C} [\![B_{\mathsf{op}}]\!]$, for each $\mathsf{op} \in \Sigma$.

Ground types

$$[\![b]\!] \stackrel{\text{def}}{=} \cdots \qquad [\![\text{unit}]\!] \stackrel{\text{def}}{=} \mathbb{1} \qquad [\![\text{empty}]\!] \stackrel{\text{def}}{=} \mathbb{0}$$

$$[\![A \times B]\!] \stackrel{\text{def}}{=} [\![A]\!] \times [\![B]\!] \qquad [\![A + B]\!] \stackrel{\text{def}}{=} [\![A]\!] + [\![B]\!]$$

Skeletal types

$$[\![P \times Q]\!] \stackrel{\text{def}}{=} [\![P]\!] \times [\![Q]\!] \qquad [\![P \to Q!]\!] \stackrel{\text{def}}{=} [\![P]\!] \Rightarrow [\![Q!]\!]$$

$$[\![P + Q]\!] \stackrel{\text{def}}{=} [\![P]\!] + [\![Q]\!] \qquad [\![P \to Q \, \natural \, C]\!] \stackrel{\text{def}}{=} [\![P]\!] \Rightarrow [\![Q \, \natural \, C]\!]$$

$$[\![\text{runner } C]\!] \stackrel{\text{def}}{=} \text{Runner}^{\mathsf{s}} [\![C]\!] \qquad [\![P!]\!] \stackrel{\text{def}}{=} \mathsf{U}^{\mathsf{s}}[\![P]\!] \qquad [\![P \, \natural \, C]\!] \stackrel{\text{def}}{=} \mathsf{K}^{\mathsf{s}}_{[\![C]\!]}[\![P]\!]$$

$$[\![x_1 : P_1, \ldots, x_n : P_n]\!] \stackrel{\text{def}}{=} [\![P_1]\!] \times \cdots \times [\![P_n]\!]$$

Fig. 4. Denotations of ground and skeletal types.

Semantics of effectful types is given in Fig. 5. From a category-theoretic viewpoint, it assigns meaning in the category Sub(Set) whose objects are subset inclusions $X_0 \subseteq X_1$ and morphisms from $X_0 \subseteq X_1$ to $Y_0 \subseteq Y_1$ those maps $X_1 \to Y_1$ that restrict to $X_0 \to Y_0$. The interpretations of products, sums, and function types are precisely the corresponding category-theoretic notions $\times$, $+$, and $\Rightarrow$ in Sub(Set). Even better, the pairs of submonads $\mathsf{U}_{\Sigma,E} \subseteq \mathsf{U}^{\mathsf{s}}$ and $\mathsf{K}_{\Sigma,E,S,C} \subseteq \mathsf{K}^{\mathsf{s}}_C$ are the "Sub(Set)-variants" of the user and kernel monads. Such an abstract point of view drives the interpretation of terms, given below, and it additionally suggests how our semantics can be set up on top of a category other than Set. For example, if we replace Set with the category Cpo of ω-complete partial orders, we obtain the domain-theoretic semantics of effect handlers from [3] that models recursion and operations whose signatures contain arbitrary types.

5.2 Semantics of values and computations

To give semantics to λ_{coop}'s terms, we introduce *skeletal typing* judgements

$$\Gamma \vdash^{\mathsf{s}} V : P, \qquad \Gamma \vdash^{\mathsf{s}} M : P!, \qquad \Gamma \vdash^{\mathsf{s}} K : P \, \natural \, C,$$

which assign skeletal types to values and computations. In these judgements, Γ is a *skeletal context* which assigns skeletal types to variables.

The rules for these judgements are obtained from λ_{coop}'s typing rules, by *excluding* subsumption rules and by relaxing restrictions on effects. For example, the skeletal versions of the rules TyVALUE-RUNNER and TyKERNEL-KILL are

$$\frac{\left(\Gamma, x : A_{\text{op}} \vdash^{\mathsf{s}} K_{\text{op}} : B_{\text{op}} \, \natural \, C\right)_{\text{op} \in \Sigma}}{\Gamma \vdash^{\mathsf{s}} \{(\text{op } x \mapsto K_{\text{op}})_{\text{op} \in \Sigma}\}_C : \text{runner } C} \qquad \frac{s \in \mathcal{S}}{\Gamma \vdash^{\mathsf{s}} \text{kill}_{X @ C} \, s : X^{\mathsf{s}} \, \natural \, C}$$

The relationship between effectful and skeletal typing is summarised as follows:

Proposition 5. *(1) Skeletal typing derivations are unique. (2) If $X \sqsubseteq Y$, then $X^{\mathsf{s}} = Y^{\mathsf{s}}$, and analogously for subtyping of user and kernel types. (3) If $\Gamma \vdash V : X$, then $\Gamma^{\mathsf{s}} \vdash^{\mathsf{s}} V : X^{\mathsf{s}}$, and analogously for user and kernel computations.*

Skeletons

$$A^s \overset{\text{def}}{=} A \qquad (\Sigma \Rightarrow (\Sigma', S, C))^s \overset{\text{def}}{=} \text{runner } C \qquad (X \times Y)^s \overset{\text{def}}{=} X^s \times Y^s$$

$$(X \to Y \,!\, \mathcal{U})^s \overset{\text{def}}{=} X^s \to (Y \,!\, \mathcal{U})^s \qquad (X + Y)^s \overset{\text{def}}{=} X^s + Y^s$$

$$(X \to Y \,\natural\, \mathcal{K})^s \overset{\text{def}}{=} X^s \to (Y \,\natural\, \mathcal{K})^s \qquad (X \,!\, \mathcal{U})^s \overset{\text{def}}{=} X^s!$$

$$(x_1 : X_1, \ldots, x_n : X_n)^s \overset{\text{def}}{=} (x_1 : X_1^s, \ldots, x_n : X_n^s) \qquad (X \,\natural\, (\Sigma, E, S, C))^s \overset{\text{def}}{=} X^s \,\natural\, C$$

Denotations

$$[\![A]\!] \overset{\text{def}}{=} [\![A]\!] \qquad\qquad [\![X \times Y]\!] \overset{\text{def}}{=} [\![X]\!] \times [\![X]\!]$$

$$[\![\Sigma \Rightarrow (\Sigma', S, C)]\!] \overset{\text{def}}{=} \text{Runner}_{\Sigma, \Sigma', S} \, [\![C]\!] \qquad [\![X + Y]\!] \overset{\text{def}}{=} [\![X]\!] + [\![X]\!]$$

$$[\![X \to Y \,!\, \mathcal{U}]\!] \overset{\text{def}}{=} ([\![X]\!], [\![X^s]\!]) \Rightarrow ([\![Y \,!\, \mathcal{U}]\!], [\![(Y \,!\, \mathcal{U})^s]\!])$$

$$[\![X \to Y \,\natural\, \mathcal{K}]\!] \overset{\text{def}}{=} ([\![X]\!], [\![X^s]\!]) \Rightarrow ([\![Y \,\natural\, \mathcal{K}]\!], [\![(Y \,\natural\, \mathcal{K})^s]\!])$$

$$[\![X \,!\, (\Sigma, E)]\!] \overset{\text{def}}{=} \mathsf{U}_{\Sigma, E} [\![X]\!] \qquad [\![X \,\natural\, (\Sigma, E, S, C)]\!] \overset{\text{def}}{=} \mathsf{K}_{\Sigma, E, S, [\![C]\!]} [\![X]\!]$$

$$[\![x_1 : X_1, \ldots, x_n : X_n]\!] \overset{\text{def}}{=} [\![X_1]\!] \times \cdots \times [\![X_n]\!]$$

Fig. 5. Skeletons and denotations of types.

Proof. We prove (1) by induction on skeletal typing derivations, and (2) by induction on subtyping derivations. For (1), we further use the occasional type annotations, and the absence of skeletal subsumption rules. For proving (3), suppose that $\mathcal{D}$ is a derivation of $\Gamma \vdash V : X$. We may translate $\mathcal{D}$ to its *skeleton* $\mathcal{D}^s$ deriving $\Gamma^s \vdash^s V : X^s$ by replacing typing rules with matching skeletal ones, skipping subsumption rules due to (2). Computations are treated similarly. □

To ensure semantic coherence, we first define the *skeletal semantics* of skeletal typing judgements, $[\![\Gamma \vdash^s V : P]\!] : [\![\Gamma]\!] \to [\![P]\!]$, $[\![\Gamma \vdash^s M : P!]\!] : [\![\Gamma]\!] \to [\![P!]\!]$, and $[\![\Gamma \vdash^s K : P \natural C]\!] : [\![\Gamma]\!] \to [\![P \natural C]\!]$, by induction on their (unique) derivations.

Provided maps $[\![A_1]\!] \times \cdots \times [\![A_n]\!] \to [\![B]\!]$ denoting ground constants f, values are interpreted in a standard way, using the bi-cartesian closed structure of sets, except for a runner $\{(\text{op } x \mapsto K_{\text{op}})_{\text{op} \in \Sigma}\}_C$, which is interpreted at an environment $\gamma \in [\![\Gamma]\!]$ as the skeletal runner $\{\overline{\text{op}} : [\![A_{\text{op}}]\!] \to \mathsf{K}_{\mathcal{O}, E_{\text{op}}, S, [\![C]\!]} [\![B_{\text{op}}]\!]\}_{\text{op} \in \mathcal{O}}$, given by

$$\overline{\text{op}}\, a \overset{\text{def}}{=} (\text{if op} \in \Sigma \text{ then } \rho([\![\Gamma, x : A_{\text{op}} \vdash^s K_{\text{op}} : B_{\text{op}} \natural C]\!](\gamma, a)) \text{ else } \lightning).$$

Here the map $\rho : \mathsf{K}^s_{[\![C]\!]} [\![B_{\text{op}}]\!] \to \mathsf{K}_{\mathcal{O}, E_{\text{op}}, S, [\![C]\!]} [\![B_{\text{op}}]\!]$ is the skeletal kernel theory homomorphism characterised by the equations

$$\rho(\text{return } b) = \text{return } b, \qquad \rho(\text{op}'(a', \kappa, (\nu_e)_{e \in E_{\text{op}'}})) = \text{op}'(a', \rho \circ \kappa, (\rho(\nu_e))_{e \in E_{\text{op}'}}),$$

$$\rho(\text{getenv } \kappa) = \text{getenv}(\rho \circ \kappa), \qquad \rho(\text{raise } e) = (\text{if } e \in E_{\text{op}} \text{ then raise } e \text{ else } \lightning),$$

$$\rho(\text{setenv}(c, \kappa)) = \text{getenv}(c, \rho \circ \kappa), \qquad \rho(\text{kill } s) = \text{kill } s.$$

The purpose of $\lightning$ in the definition of $\overline{\text{op}}$ is to model a runtime error when the runner is asked to handle an unexpected operation, while ρ makes sure that $\overline{\text{op}}$ raises at most the exceptions E_{op}, as prescribed by the signature of op.

User and kernel computations are interpreted as elements of the corresponding skeletal user and kernel monads. Again, most constructs are interpreted in a standard way: returns as the units of the monads; the operations raise, kill, getenv, setenv, and ops as the corresponding algebraic operations; and match statements as the corresponding semantic elimination forms. The interpretation of exception handling offers no surprises, e.g., as in [30], as long as we follow the strategy of treating unexpected situations with the runtime error $\pm$.

The most interesting part of the interpretation is the semantics of

$$\Gamma \vdash^s (\text{using } V @ W \text{ run } M \text{ finally } F) : Q!, \tag{4}$$

where $F \stackrel{\text{def}}{=} \{\text{return } x @ c \mapsto N, (\text{raise } e @ c \mapsto N_e)_{e \in E}, (\text{kill } s \mapsto N_s)_{s \in S}\}$. At an environment $\gamma \in [\![\Gamma]\!]$, V is interpreted as a skeletal runner with state $[\![C]\!]$, which induces a monad morphism $r : \text{Tree}_{\mathcal{O}}(-) \to ([\![C]\!] \Rightarrow \text{Tree}_{\mathcal{O}}(- \times [\![C]\!] + \mathcal{S}))$, as in the proof of Prop. 3. Let $f : \mathsf{K}^s_{[\![C]\!]}[\![P]\!] \to ([\![C]\!] \Rightarrow \mathsf{U}^s[\![Q]\!])$ be the skeletal kernel theory homomorphism characterised by the equations

$$\begin{aligned}
f(\text{return } p) &= \lambda c \,.\, [\![\Gamma, x : P, c : C \vdash^s N : Q]\!](\gamma, p, c), \\
f(\text{op}(a, \kappa, (\nu_e)_{e \in E_{\text{op}}})) &= \lambda c \,.\, \text{op}(a, \lambda b \,.\, f(\kappa\, b)\, c, (f(\nu_e)\, c)_{e \in E_{\text{op}}}), \\
f(\text{raise } e) &= \lambda c \,.\, (\text{if } e \in E \text{ then } [\![\Gamma, c : C \vdash^s N_e : Q]\!](\gamma, c) \text{ else } \pm), \\
f(\text{kill } s) &= \lambda c \,.\, (\text{if } s \in S \text{ then } [\![\Gamma \vdash^s N_s : Q]\!]\,\gamma \text{ else } \pm), \\
f(\text{getenv } \kappa) &= \lambda c \,.\, f(\kappa\, c)\, c, \qquad f(\text{setenv}(c', \kappa)) = \lambda c \,.\, f\, \kappa\, c'.
\end{aligned} \tag{5}$$

The interpretation of (4) at γ is $f(\mathsf{r}_{[\![P]\!]+\mathcal{E}}([\![\Gamma \vdash^s M : P!]\!]\,\gamma)) ([\![\Gamma \vdash^s W : C]\!]\,\gamma)$, which reads: map the interpretation of M at γ from the skeletal user monad to the skeletal kernel monad using r (which models the operations of M by the cooperations of V), and from there using f to a map $[\![C]\!] \Rightarrow \mathsf{U}^s[\![Q]\!]$, that is then applied to the initial kernel state, namely, the interpretation of W at γ.

We interpret the context switch $\Gamma \vdash^s \text{kernel } K @ W \text{ finally } F : Q!$ at an environment $\gamma \in [\![\Gamma]\!]$ as $f([\![\Gamma \vdash^s K : P \natural C]\!]\,\gamma) ([\![\Gamma \vdash^s W : C]\!]\,\gamma)$, where f is the map (5). Finally, user context switch is interpreted much like exception handling.

We now define coherent semantics of λ_{coop}'s typing derivations by passing through the skeletal semantics. Given a derivation $\mathcal{D}$ of $\Gamma \vdash V : X$, its skeleton $\mathcal{D}^s$ derives $\Gamma^s \vdash^s V : X^s$. We identify the denotation of V with the skeletal one,

$$[\![\![\Gamma \vdash V : X]\!]\!] \stackrel{\text{def}}{=} [\![\Gamma^s \vdash^s V : X^s]\!] : [\![\Gamma^s]\!] \to [\![X^s]\!].$$

All that remains is to check that $[\![\![\Gamma \vdash V : X]\!]\!]$ restricts to $[\![\![\Gamma]\!]\!] \to [\![\![X]\!]\!]$. This is accomplished by induction on $\mathcal{D}$. The only interesting step is subsumption, which relies on a further observation that $X \sqsubseteq Y$ implies $[\![\![X]\!]\!] \subseteq [\![\![Y]\!]\!]$. Typing derivations for user and kernel computations are treated analogously.

5.3   Coherence, soundness, and finalisation theorems

We are now ready to prove a theorem that guarantees execution of finalisation code. But first, let us record the fact that the semantics is coherent and sound.

Theorem 6 (Coherence and soundness). *The denotational semantics of* λ_{coop} *is coherent, and it is sound for the equational theory of* λ_{coop} *from §4.4.*

Proof. Coherence is established by construction: any two derivations of the same typing judgement have the same denotation because they are both (the same) restriction of skeletal semantics. For proving soundness, one just needs to unfold the denotations of the left- and right-hand sides of equations from §4.4, and compare them, where some cases rely on suitable substitution lemmas.   □

To set the stage for the finalisation theorem, let us consider the computation using $V @ W$ run M finally F, well-typed by the rule TyUser-Run from Fig. 3. At an environment $\gamma \in [\![\Gamma]\!]$, the finalisation clauses F are captured semantically by the *finalisation map* $\phi_\gamma : ([\![X]\!] + E) \times [\![C]\!] + S \to [\![Y \,!\, (\Sigma', E')]\!]$, given by

$$\phi_\gamma(\iota_1(\iota_1\, x, c)) \overset{\text{def}}{=} [\![\Gamma, x : X, c : C \vdash N : Y \,!\, (\Sigma', E')]\!](\gamma, x, c),$$

$$\phi_\gamma(\iota_1(\iota_2\, e, c)) \overset{\text{def}}{=} [\![\Gamma, c : C \vdash N_e : Y \,!\, (\Sigma', E')]\!](\gamma, c),$$

$$\phi_\gamma(\iota_2(s)) \overset{\text{def}}{=} [\![\Gamma \vdash N_s : Y \,!\, (\Sigma', E')]\!]\, \gamma.$$

With ϕ in hand, we may formulate the finalisation theorem for λ_{coop}, stating that the semantics of using $V @ W$ run M finally F is a computation tree all of whose branches end with finalisation clauses from F. Thus, unless some enveloping runner sends a signal, finalisation with F is guaranteed to take place.

Theorem 7 (Finalisation). *A well-typed* run *factors through finalisation:*

$$[\![\Gamma \vdash (\text{using } V @ W \text{ run } M \text{ finally } F) : Y \,!\, (\Sigma', E')]\!]\, \gamma = \phi_\gamma^\dagger\, t,$$

for some $t \in \text{Tree}_{\Sigma'}(([\![X]\!] + E) \times [\![C]\!] + S)$.

Proof. We first prove that $f\, u\, c = \phi_\gamma^\dagger(u\, c)$ holds for all $u \in \mathsf{K}_{\Sigma', E, S, [\![C]\!]}[\![X]\!]$ and $c \in [\![C]\!]$, where f is the map (5). The proof proceeds by computational induction on u [29]. The finalisation statement is then just the special case with $u \overset{\text{def}}{=} \mathsf{r}_{[\![X]\!] + E}([\![\Gamma \vdash M : X \,!\, (\Sigma, E)]\!]\, \gamma)$ and $c \overset{\text{def}}{=} [\![\Gamma \vdash W : C]\!]\, \gamma$.   □

6   Runners in action

Let us show examples that demonstrate how runners can be usefully combined to provide flexible resource management. We implemented these and other examples in the language Coop and a library Haskell-Coop, see §7.

To make the code more understandable, we do not adhere strictly to the syntax of λ_{coop}, e.g., we use the generic versions of effects [26], as is customary in programming, and effectful initialisation of kernel state as discussed in §3.2.

Example 8 (Nesting). In Example 4, we considered a runner fileIO for basic file operations. Let us suppose that fileIO is implemented by immediate calls to the operating system. Sometimes, we might prefer to accumulate writes and commit them all at once, which can be accomplished by interposing between fileIO and user code the following runner accIO, which accumulates writes in its state:

```
{ write s' → let s = getenv () in setenv (concat s s') }string
```

By *nesting* the runners, and calling the outer write (the one of fileIO) only in the finalisation code for accIO, the accumulated writes are commited all at once:

```
using fileIO @ (open "hello.txt") run
  using accIO @ (return "") run
    write "Hello, world."; write "Hello, again."
  finally { return x @ s → write s; return x }
finally { return x @ fh → ... , raise QuotaExceeded @ fh → ... , kill IOError → ... }
```

Example 9 (Instrumentation). Above, accIO implements the same signature as fileIO and thus intercepts operations without the user code being aware of it. This kind of invisibility can be more generally used to implement *instrumentation*:

```
using { ..., op x → let c = getenv () in setenv (c+1); op x, ... }int @ (return 0) run
  M
finally { return x @ c → report_cost c; return x, ... }
```

Here the interposed runner implements all operations of some enveloping runner, by simply forwarding them, while also measuring computational cost by counting the total number of operation calls, which is then reported during finalisation.

Example 10 (ML-style references). Continuing with the theme of nested runners, they can also be used to implement abstract and safe interfaces to low-level resources. For instance, suppose we have a low-level implementation of a memory heap that potentially allows unsafe memory access, and we would like to implement ML-style references on top of it. A good first attempt is the runner

```
{ ref x → let h = getenv () in
            let (r,h') = malloc h x in
            setenv h'; return r,
  get r → let h = getenv () in memread h r,
  put (r, x) → let h = getenv () in memset h r x }heap
```

which has the desired interface, but still suffers from three deficiencies that can be addressed with further language support. First, *abstract types* would let us hide the fact that references are just memory locations, so that the user code could never devise invalid references or otherwise misuse them. Second, our simple typing discipline forces all references to hold the same type, but in reality we want them to have different types. This could be achieved through quantification over types in the low-level implementation of the heap, as we have done in the HASKELL-COOP library using HASKELL's forall. Third, user code could hijack a reference and misuse it out of the scope of the runner, which is difficult to prevent. In practice the problem does not occur because, so to speak, the runner for references is at the very top level, from which user code cannot escape.

Example 11 (Monotonic state). Nested runners can also implement access restrictions to resources, with applications in security [8]. For example, we can restrict the references from the previous example to be used *monotonically* by associating a preorder with each reference, which assignments then have to obey. This idea is similar to how monotonic state is implemented in the F* language [2], except that we make dynamic checks where F* statically uses dependent types.

While we could simply modify the previous example, it is better to implement a new runner which is nested inside the previous one, so that we obtain a modular solution that works with *any* runner implementing operations ref, get, and put:

```
{ mref x rel → let r = ref x in
                 let m = getenv () in
                   setenv (add m (r,rel)); return r,
  mget r → get r,
  mput (r, y) → let x = get r in
                  let m = getenv () in
                  match (sel m r) with
                  | inl rel → if (rel x y) then put (r, y)
                                      else raise MonotonicityViolation
                  | inr () → kill NoPreorderFound }map(ref,intRel)
```

The runner's state is a map from references to preorders on integers. The co-operation mref x rel creates a new reference r initialised with x (by calling ref of the outer runner), and then adds the pair (r, rel) to the map stored in the runner's state. Reading is delegated to the outer runner, while assignment first checks that the new state is larger than the old one, according to the associated preorder. If the preorder is respected, the runner proceeds with assignment (again delegated to the outer runner), otherwise it reports a monotonicity violation. We may not assume that every reference has an associated preorder, because user code could pass to mput a reference that was created earlier outside the scope of the runner. If this happens, the runner simply kills the offending user code with a signal.

Example 12 (Pairing). Another form of modularity is achieved by *pairing* runners. Given two runners $\{(op\,x \mapsto K_{op})_{op \in \Sigma_1}\}_{C_1}$ and $\{(op'\,x \mapsto K_{op'})_{op' \in \Sigma_2}\}_{C_2}$, e.g., for state and file operations, we can use them side-by-side by combining them into a single runner with operations $\Sigma_1 + \Sigma_2$ and kernel state $C_1 \times C_2$, as follows (the co-operations op' of the second runner are treated symmetrically):

```
{ op x → let (c,c') = getenv () in
         user
           kernel (Kop x) @ c finally {
               return y @ c'' → return (inl (inl y, c'')),
               (raise e @ c'' → return (inl (inr e, c'')))e∈Eop,
               (kill s → return (inr s))s∈S1}
           with {
               return (inl (inl y, c'')) → setenv (c'', c'); return y,
               return (inl (inr e, c'')) → setenv (c'', c'); raise e,
               return (inr s) → kill s},
  op' x → ... , ... }C1×C2
```

Notice how the inner kernel context switch passes to the co-operation K_{op} only its part of the combined state, and how it returns the result of K_{op} in a reified form (which requires treating exceptions and signals as values). The outer user context switch then receives this reified result, updates the combined state, and forwards the result (return value, exception, or signal) in unreified form.

7   Implementation

We accompany the theoretical development with two implementations of λ_{coop}: a prototype language COOP [6], and a HASKELL library HASKELL-COOP [1].

COOP, implemented in OCAML, demonstrates what a more fully-featured language based on λ_{coop} might look like. It implements a bi-directional variant of λ_{coop}'s type system, extended with type definitions and algebraic datatypes, to provide algorithmic typechecking and type inference. The operational semantics is based on the computation rules of the equational theory from §4.4, but extended with general recursion, pairing of runners from Example 12, and an interface to the OCAML runtime called *containers*—these are essentially top-level runners defined directly in OCAML. They are a modular and systematic way of offering several possible top-level runtime environments to the programmer.

The HASKELL-COOP library is a shallow embedding of λ_{coop} in HASKELL. The implementation closely follows the denotational semantics of λ_{coop}. For instance, user and kernel monads are implemented as corresponding HASKELL monads. Internally, the library uses the FREER monad of Kiselyov [14] to implement free model monads for given signatures of operations. The library also provides a means to run user code via HASKELL's top-level monads. For instance, code that performs input-output operations may be run in HASKELL's IO monad.

HASKELL's advanced features make it possible to use HASKELL-COOP to implement several extensions to examples from §6. For instance, we implement ML-style state that allow references holding arbitrary values (of different types), and state that uses HASKELL's type system to track which references are alive. The library also provides pairing of runners from Example 12, e.g., to combine state and input-output. We also use the library to demonstrate that *ambient functions* from the KOKA language [18] can be implemented with runners by treating their binding and application as co-operations. (These are functions that are bound dynamically but evaluated in the lexical scope of their binding.)

8   Related work

Comodels and (ordinary) runners have been used as a natural model of stateful top-level behaviour. For instance, Plotkin and Power [27] have given a treatment of operational semantics using the tensor product of a model and a comodel. Recently, Katsumata, Rivas, and Uustalu have generalised this interaction of models and comodels to monads and comonads [13]. An early version of EFF [4] implemented *resources*, which were a kind of stateful runners, although they lacked satisfactory theory. Uustalu [35] has pointed out that runners are the additional structure that one has to impose on state to run algebraic effects statefully. Møgelberg and Staton's [21] linear-use state-passing translation also relies on equipping the state with a comodel structure for the effects at hand. Our runners arise when their setup is specialised to a certain Kleisli adjunction.

Our use of kernel state is analogous to the use of parameters in parameter-passing handlers [30]: their return clause also provides a form of finalisation, as the final value of the parameter is available. There is however no guarantee of finalisation happening because handlers need not use the continuation linearly.

The need to tame the excessive generality of handlers, and willingness to give it up in exchange for efficiency and predictability, has recently been recognised by MULTICORE OCAML's implementors, who have observed that in practice most handlers resume continuations precisely once [9]. In exchange for impressive efficiency, they require continuations to be used linearly by default, whereas discarding and copying must be done explicitly, incurring additional cost. Leijen [17] has extended handlers in KOKA with a finally clause, whose semantics ensures that finalisation happens whenever a handler discards its continuation. Leijen also added an initially clause to parameter-passing handlers, which is used to compute the initial value of the parameter before handling, but that gets executed again every time the handler resumes its continuation.

9   Conclusion and future work

We have shown that effectful runners form a mathematically natural and modular model of resources, modelling not only the top level external resources, but allowing programmers to also define their own intermediate "virtual machines". Effectful runners give rise to a bona fide programming concept, an idea we have captured in a small calculus, called λ_{coop}, which we have implemented both as a language and a library. We have given λ_{coop} an algebraically natural denotational semantics, and shown how to program with runners through various examples.

We leave combining runners and general effect handlers for future work. As runners are essentially affine handlers, inspired by MULTICORE OCAML we also plan to investigate efficient compilation for runners. On the theoretical side, by developing semantics in a Sub(Cpo)-enriched setting [32], we plan to support recursion at all levels, and remove the distinction between ground and arbitrary types. Finally, by using proof-relevant subtyping [34] and synthesis of lenses [20], we plan to upgrade subtyping from a simple inclusion to relating types by lenses.

Acknowledgements We thank Daan Leijen for useful discussions about initialisation and finalisation in KOKA, as well as ambient values and ambient functions. We thank Guillaume Munch-Maccagnoni and Matija Pretnar for discussing resources and potential future directions for λ_{coop}. We are also grateful to the participants of the NII Shonan Meeting "Programming and reasoning with algebraic effects and effect handlers" for feedback on an early version of this work.

This project has received funding from the European Union's Horizon 2020 research and innovation programme under the Marie Skłodowska-Curie grant agreement No 834146.

This material is based upon work supported by the Air Force Office of Scientific Research under award number FA9550-17-1-0326.

References

1. Ahman, D.: Library HASKELL-COOP. Available at https://github.com/danelahman/haskell-coop (2019)
2. Ahman, D., Fournet, C., Hritcu, C., Maillard, K., Rastogi, A., Swamy, N.: Recalling a witness: foundations and applications of monotonic state. PACMPL **2**(POPL), 65:1–65:30 (2018)
3. Bauer, A., Pretnar, M.: An effect system for algebraic effects and handlers. Logical Methods in Computer Science **10**(4) (2014)
4. Bauer, A., Pretnar, M.: Programming with algebraic effects and handlers. J. Log. Algebr. Meth. Program. **84**(1), 108–123 (2015)
5. Bauer, A.: What is algebraic about algebraic effects and handlers? CoRR **abs/1807.05923** (2018)
6. Bauer, A.: Programming language COOP. Available at https://github.com/andrejbauer/coop (2019)
7. Benton, N., Kennedy, A.: Exceptional syntax. Journal of Functional Programming **11**(4), 395–410 (2001)
8. Delignat-Lavaud, A., Fournet, C., Kohlweiss, M., Protzenko, J., Rastogi, A., Swamy, N., Zanella-Beguelin, S., Bhargavan, K., Pan, J., Zinzindohoue, J.K.: Implementing and proving the tls 1.3 record layer. In: 2017 IEEE Symp. on Security and Privacy (SP). pp. 463–482 (2017)
9. Dolan, S., Eliopoulos, S., Hillerström, D., Madhavapeddy, A., Sivaramakrishnan, K.C., White, L.: Concurrent system programming with effect handlers. In: Wang, M., Owens, S. (eds.) Trends in Functional Programming. pp. 98–117. Springer International Publishing, Cham (2018)
10. Foster, J.N., Greenwald, M.B., Moore, J.T., Pierce, B.C., Schmitt, A.: Combinators for bidirectional tree transformations: A linguistic approach to the view-update problem. ACM Trans. Program. Lang. Syst. **29**(3) (2007)
11. Hyland, M., Plotkin, G., Power, J.: Combining effects: Sum and tensor. Theor. Comput. Sci. **357**(1–3), 70–99 (2006)
12. Kammar, O., Lindley, S., Oury, N.: Handlers in action. In: Proc. of 18th ACM SIGPLAN Int. Conf. on Functional Programming, ICFP 2013. ACM (2013)
13. Katsumata, S., Rivas, E., Uustalu, T.: Interaction laws of monads and comonads. CoRR **abs/1912.13477** (2019)
14. Kiselyov, O., Ishii, H.: Freer monads, more extensible effects. In: Proc. of 2015 ACM SIGPLAN Symp. on Haskell. pp. 94–105. Haskell '15, ACM (2015)
15. Koopman, P., Fokker, J., Smetsers, S., van Eekelen, M., Plasmeijer, R.: Functional Programming in Clean. University of Nijmegen (1998), draft
16. Leijen, D.: Structured asynchrony with algebraic effects. In: Proceedings of the 2nd ACM SIGPLAN International Workshop on Type-Driven Development, TyDe@ICFP 2017, Oxford, UK, September 3, 2017. pp. 16–29. ACM (2017)
17. Leijen, D.: Algebraic effect handlers with resources and deep finalization. Tech. Rep. MSR-TR-2018-10, Microsoft Research (April 2018)
18. Leijen, D.: Programming with implicit values, functions, and control (or, implicit functions: Dynamic binding with lexical scoping). Tech. Rep. MSR-TR-2019-7, Microsoft Research (March 2019)
19. Levy, P.B.: Call-By-Push-Value: A Functional/Imperative Synthesis, Semantics Structures in Computation, vol. 2. Springer (2004)
20. Miltner, A., Maina, S., Fisher, K., Pierce, B.C., Walker, D., Zdancewic, S.: Synthesizing symmetric lenses. Proc. ACM Program. Lang. **3**(ICFP), 95:1–95:28 (2019)

21. Møgelberg, R.E., Staton, S.: Linear usage of state. Logical Methods in Computer Science **10**(1) (2014)
22. Moggi, E.: Computational lambda-calculus and monads. In: Proc. of 4th Ann. Symp. on Logic in Computer Science, LICS 1989. pp. 14–23. IEEE (1989)
23. Moggi, E.: Notions of computation and monads. Inf. Comput. **93**(1), 55–92 (1991)
24. O'Connor, R.: Functor is to lens as applicative is to biplate: Introducing multiplate. CoRR **abs/1103.2841** (2011)
25. Plotkin, G., Power, J.: Semantics for algebraic operations. In: Proc. of 17th Conf. on the Mathematical Foundations of Programming Semantics, MFPS XVII. ENTCS, vol. 45, pp. 332–345. Elsevier (2001)
26. Plotkin, G., Power, J.: Algebraic operations and generic effects. Appl. Categor. Struct. (1), 69–94 (2003)
27. Plotkin, G., Power, J.: Tensors of comodels and models for operational semantics. In: Proc. of 24th Conf. on Mathematical Foundations of Programming Semantics, MFPS XXIV. ENTCS, vol. 218, pp. 295–311. Elsevier (2008)
28. Plotkin, G.D., Power, J.: Notions of computation determine monads. In: Proc. of 5th Int. Conf. on Foundations of Software Science and Computation Structures, FOSSACS 2002. LNCS, vol. 2303, pp. 342–356. Springer (2002)
29. Plotkin, G.D., Pretnar, M.: A logic for algebraic effects. In: Proc. of 23th Ann. IEEE Symp. on Logic in Computer Science, LICS 2008. pp. 118–129. IEEE (2008)
30. Plotkin, G.D., Pretnar, M.: Handling algebraic effects. Logical Methods in Computer Science **9**(4:23) (2013)
31. Power, J., Shkaravska, O.: From comodels to coalgebras: State and arrays. Electr. Notes Theor. Comput. Sci. **106**, 297–314 (2004)
32. Power, J.: Enriched Lawvere theories. Theory Appl. Categ **6**(7), 83–93 (1999)
33. Pretnar, M.: The Logic and Handling of Algebraic Effects. Ph.D. thesis, School of Informatics, University of Edinburgh (2010)
34. Saleh, A.H., Karachalias, G., Pretnar, M., Schrijvers, T.: Explicit effect subtyping. In: Proc. of 27th European Symposium on Programming, ESOP 2018. pp. 327–354. LNCS, Springer (2018)
35. Uustalu, T.: Stateful runners of effectful computations. Electr. Notes Theor. Comput. Sci. **319**, 403–421 (2015)
36. Wadler, P.: The essence of functional programming. In: Sethi, R. (ed.) Proc. of 19th Ann. ACM SIGPLAN-SIGACT Symp. on Principles of Programming Languages, POPL 1992. pp. 1–14. ACM (1992)

On the Versatility of Open Logical Relations⋆

Continuity, Automatic Differentiation, and a Containment Theorem

Gilles Barthe[1,4], Raphaëlle Crubillé[4], Ugo Dal Lago[2,3], and Francesco Gavazzo[2,3,4]

[1] MPI for Security and Privacy, Bochum, Germany
[2] University of Bologna, Bologna, Italy,
[3] INRIA Sophia Antipolis, Sophia Antipolis, France
[4] IMDEA Software Institute, Madrid, Spain

Abstract. Logical relations are one among the most powerful techniques in the theory of programming languages, and have been used extensively for proving properties of a variety of higher-order calculi. However, there are properties that cannot be immediately proved by means of logical relations, for instance program continuity and differentiability in higher-order languages extended with real-valued functions. Informally, the problem stems from the fact that these properties are naturally expressed on terms of non-ground type (or, equivalently, on open terms of base type), and there is no apparent good definition for a base case (i.e. for closed terms of ground types). To overcome this issue, we study a generalization of the concept of a logical relation, called *open logical relation*, and prove that it can be fruitfully applied in several contexts in which the property of interest is about expressions of first-order type. Our setting is a simply-typed λ-calculus enriched with real numbers and real-valued first-order functions from a given set, such as the one of continuous or differentiable functions. We first prove a containment theorem stating that for any collection of real-valued first-order functions including projection functions and closed under function composition, any well-typed term of first-order type denotes a function belonging to that collection. Then, we show by way of open logical relations the correctness of the core of a recently published algorithm for forward automatic differentiation. Finally, we define a refinement-based type system for local continuity in an extension of our calculus with conditionals, and prove the soundness of the type system using open logical relations.

Keywords: Lambda Calculus · Logical Relations · Continuity Analysis · Automatic Differentiation

⋆ The Second and Fourth Authors are supported by the ANR project 16CE250011 REPAS, the ERC Consolidator Grant DIAPASoN – DLV-818616, and the MIUR PRIN 201784YSZ5 ASPRA.

P. Müller (Ed.): ESOP 2020, LNCS 12075, pp. 56–83, 2020.
https://doi.org/10.1007/978-3-030-44914-8_3

1 Introduction

Logical relations have been extremely successful as a way of proving equivalence between concrete programs as well as correctness of program transformations. In their "unary" version, they also are a formidable tool to prove termination of typable programs, through the so-called *reducibility* technique. The class of programming languages in which these techniques have been instantiated includes not only higher-order calculi with simple types, but also calculi with recursion [3,2,23], various kinds of effects [14,12,25,36,10,11,34], and concurrency [56,13].

Without any aim to be precise, let us see how reducibility works, in the setting of a simply typed calculus. The main idea is to define, by induction on the structure of types, the concept of a well-behaved program, where in the base case one simply makes reference to the underlying notion of observation (e.g. being strong normalizing), while the more interesting case is handled by stipulating that reducible higher-order terms are those which maps reducible terms to reducible terms, this way exploiting the inductive nature of simple types. One can even go beyond the basic setting of simple types, and extend reducibility to, e.g., languages with recursive types [23,2] or even untyped languages [44] by means of techniques such as step-indexing [3].

The same kind of recipe works in a relational setting, where one wants to *compare* programs rather than merely *proving properties* about them. Again, two terms are equivalent at base types if they have the same observable behaviour, while at higher types one wants that equivalent terms are those which maps equivalent arguments to equivalent results.

There are cases, however, in which the property one observes, or the property in which the underlying notion of program equivalence or correctness is based, is formulated for types which are *not* ground (or equivalently, it is formulated for open expressions). As an example, one could be interested in proving that in a higher-order type system all *first-order* expressions compute numerical functions of a specific kind, for example, continuous or derivable ones. We call such properties *first-order properties*[5]. As we will describe in Section 3 below, logical relations do not seem to be applicable *off-the-shelf* to these cases. Informally, this is due to the fact that we cannot start by defining a base case for ground types and then build the relation inductively.

In this paper, we show that logical relations and reducibility can deal with first-order properties in a compositional way without altering their nature. The main idea behind the resulting definition, known as *open logical relations* [59], consists in parameterizing the set of related terms of a certain type (or the underlying reducibility set) on a *ground environment*, this way turning it into a set of pairs of *open terms*. As a consequence, one can define the target first-order property in a natural way.

---

[5] To avoid misunderstandings, we emphasize that we use first-order properties to refer to properties of expressions of first-order types—and not in relation with definability of properties in first-order predicate logic.

Generalizations of logical relations to open terms have been used by several authors, and in several (oftentimes unrelated) contexts (see, for instance, [15,39,47,30,53]). In this paper, we show how open logical relations constitute a powerful technique to systematically prove first-order properties of programs. In this respect, the paper's technical contributions are applications of open logical relations to three distinct problems.

- In Section 4, we use open logical relations to prove a general Containment Theorem. Such a theorem serves as a vehicle to introduce open logical relations but is also of independent interest. The theorem states that given a collection $\mathfrak{F}$ of real-valued functions including projections and closed under function composition, any first-order term of a simply-typed λ-calculus endowed with primitives for real numbers and operators computing functions in $\mathfrak{F}$, computes itself a function in $\mathfrak{F}$. As an instance of such a result, we see that any first-order term in a simply-typed λ-calculus extended with primitives for continuous functions, computes a continuous function. Although the Containment Theorem can be derived from previous results by Lafont [41] (see Section 7), our proof is purely syntactical and consists of a straightforward application of open logical relations.

- In Section 5, we use open logical relations to prove correctness of a core algorithm for forward automatic differentiation of simply-typed terms. The algorithm is a fragment of the one presented in [50]. More specifically, any first-order term is proved to be mapped to another first-order term computing its derivative, in the usual sense of mathematical analysis. This goes beyond the Containment Theorem by dealing with relational properties.

- In Section 6, we consider an extended language with an if-then-else construction. When dealing with continuity, the introduction of conditionals invalidates the Containment Theorem, since conditionals naturally introduce discontinuities. To overcome this deficiency, we introduce a refinement type system ensuring that first-order typable terms are continuous functions on some intended domain, and use open logical relations to prove the soundness of the type system.

Due to space constraints, many details have to be omitted, but can be found in an Extended Version of this work [7].

2   The Playground

In order to facilitate the communication of the main ideas behind open logical relations and their applications, this paper deals with several vehicle calculi. All such calculi can be seen as derived from a unique calculus, denoted by $\Lambda^{\times,\to,\mathbb{R}}$, which thus provides the common ground for our inquiry. The calculus $\Lambda^{\times,\to,\mathbb{R}}$ is obtained by adding to the simply typed λ-calculus with product and arrow types (which we denote by $\Lambda^{\times,\to}$) a ground type $\mathbb{R}$ for real numbers and constants $\underline{r}$ of type $\mathbb{R}$, for each real number r.

Given a collection $\mathfrak{F}$ of real-valued functions, i.e. functions $f : \mathbb{R}^n \to \mathbb{R}$ (with $n \geq 1$), we endow $\Lambda^{\times,\to,\mathbb{R}}$ with an operator $\underline{f}$, for any $f \in \mathfrak{F}$, whose intended meaning is that whenever $t_1, \ldots, t_n$ compute real numbers $r_1, \ldots, r_n$, then $\underline{f}(t_1, \ldots, t_n)$ compute $f(r_1, \ldots, r_n)$. We call the resulting calculus $\Lambda_{\mathfrak{F}}^{\times, \to, \mathbb{R}}$. Depending on the application we are interested in, we will take as $\mathfrak{F}$ specific collections of real-valued functions, such as continuous or differentiable functions.

The syntax and static semantics of $\Lambda_{\mathfrak{F}}^{\times, \to, \mathbb{R}}$ are defined in Figure 1, where $f : \mathbb{R}^n \to \mathbb{R}$ belongs to $\mathfrak{F}$. The static semantics of $\Lambda_{\mathfrak{F}}^{\times, \to, \mathbb{R}}$ is based on judgments of the form $\Gamma \vdash t : \tau$, which have the usual intended meaning. We adopt standard syntactic conventions as in [6], notably the so-called variable convention. In particular, we denote by $FV(t)$ the collection of free variables of t and by $s[t/x]$ the capture-avoiding substitution of the expression t for all free occurrences of x in s.

$$\tau ::= \mathbb{R} \mid \tau \times \tau \mid \tau \to \tau \qquad \qquad \Gamma ::= \cdot \mid x : \tau, \Gamma$$

$$t ::= x \mid \underline{r} \mid \underline{f}(t, \ldots, t) \mid \lambda x.t \mid tt \mid (t, t) \mid t.1 \mid t.2$$

$$\frac{}{\Gamma, x : \tau \vdash x : \tau} \qquad \frac{}{\Gamma \vdash \underline{r} : \mathbb{R}} \qquad \frac{\Gamma \vdash t_1 : \mathbb{R} \quad \cdots \quad \Gamma \vdash t_n : \mathbb{R}}{\Gamma \vdash \underline{f}(t_1, \ldots, t_n) : \mathbb{R}} \qquad \frac{\Gamma, x : \tau_1 \vdash t : \tau_2}{\Gamma \vdash \lambda x.t : \tau_1 \to \tau_2}$$

$$\frac{\Gamma \vdash s : \tau_1 \to \tau_2 \quad \Gamma \vdash t : \tau_1}{\Gamma \vdash st : \tau_2} \qquad \frac{\Gamma \vdash t_1 : \tau \quad \Gamma \vdash t_2 : \sigma}{\Gamma \vdash (t_1, t_2) : \tau \times \sigma} \qquad \frac{\Gamma \vdash t : \tau_1 \times \tau_2}{\Gamma \vdash t.i : \tau_i} \ (i \in \{1, 2\})$$

Fig. 1: Static semantics of $\Lambda_{\mathfrak{F}}^{\times, \to, \mathbb{R}}$.

We do not confine ourselves with a fixed operational semantics (e.g. with a call-by-value operational semantics), but take advantage of the simply-typed nature of $\Lambda_{\mathfrak{F}}^{\times, \to, \mathbb{R}}$ and opt for a set-theoretic denotational semantics. The category of sets and functions being cartesian closed, the denotational semantics of $\Lambda_{\mathfrak{F}}^{\times, \to, \mathbb{R}}$ is standard and associates to any judgment $x_1 : \tau_1, \ldots, x_n : \tau_n \vdash t : \tau$, a function $[\![x_1 : \tau_1, \ldots, x_n : \tau_n \vdash t : \tau]\!] : \prod_i [\![\tau_i]\!] \to [\![\tau]\!]$, where $[\![\tau]\!]$—the *semantics* of τ—is thus defined:

$$[\![\mathbb{R}]\!] = \mathbb{R}; \qquad [\![\tau_1 \to \tau_2]\!] = [\![\tau_2]\!]^{[\![\tau_1]\!]}; \qquad [\![\tau_1 \times \tau_2]\!] = [\![\tau_1]\!] \times [\![\tau_2]\!].$$

Due to space constraints, we omit the definition of $[\![\Gamma \vdash t : \tau]\!]$ and refer the reader to any textbook on the subject (such as [43]).

3 A Fundamental Gap

In this section, we will look informally at a problem which, apparently, cannot be solved using vanilla reducibility or logical relations. This serves both as a motivating example and as a justification of some of the design choices we had to do when designing open logical relations.

Consider the simply-typed λ-calculus $\Lambda^{\times,\to}$, the prototypical example of a well-behaved higher-order functional programming language. As is well known, $\Lambda^{\times,\to}$ is strongly normalizing and the technique of logical relations can be applied on-the-nose. The proof of strong normalization for $\Lambda^{\times,\to}$ is structured around the definition of a family of reducibility sets of *closed* terms $\{Red_\tau\}_\tau$, indexed by types. At any atomic type τ, Red_τ is defined as the set of terms (of type τ) having the property of interest, i.e. as the collection of strongly normalizing terms. The set $Red_{\tau_1\to\tau_2}$, instead, contains those terms which, when applied to a term in Red_{τ_1}, returns a term in Red_{τ_2}. Reducibility sets are *afterwards* generalised to open terms, and finally all typable terms are shown to be reducible.

Let us now consider the calculus $\Lambda_{\mathfrak{F}}^{\times,\to,\mathrm{R}}$, where $\mathfrak{F}$ contains the addition and multiplication functions only. This language has already been considered in the literature, under the name of *higher-order polynomials* [22,40], which are crucial tools in higher-order complexity theory and resource analysis. Now, let us ask ourselves the following question: can we say anything about the nature of those functions $\mathbb{R}^n \to \mathbb{R}$ which are denoted by (closed) terms of type $\mathrm{R}^n \to \mathrm{R}$? Of course, all the polynomials on the real field can be represented, but can we go beyond, thanks to higher-order constructions? The answer is negative: terms of type $\mathrm{R}^n \to \mathrm{R}$ represent all *and only* the polynomials [5,17]. This result is an instance of the general containment theorem mentioned at the end of Section 1.

Let us now focus on proofs of this containment result. It turns out that proofs from the literature are not compositional, and rely on "heavyweight" tools, including strong normalization of $\Lambda^{\times,\to}$ and soundness of the underlying operational semantics. In fact, proving the result using usual reducibility arguments would not be immediate, precisely because there is no obvious choice for the base case. If, for example, we define Red_{R} as the set of terms strongly normalizing to a numeral, $Red_{\mathrm{R}^n\to\mathrm{R}}$ as the set of polynomials, and for any other type as usual, we soon get into troubles: indeed, we would like the two sets of functions

$$Red_{\mathrm{R}\times\mathrm{R}\to\mathrm{R}}; \qquad\qquad Red_{\mathrm{R}\to(\mathrm{R}\to\mathrm{R})};$$

to denote *essentially* the same set of functions, modulo the adjoint between $\mathbb{R}^2 \to \mathbb{R}$ and $\mathbb{R} \to (\mathbb{R} \to \mathbb{R})$. But this is clearly not the case: just consider the function f in $\mathbb{R} \to (\mathbb{R} \to \mathbb{R})$ thus defined:

$$f(x) = \begin{cases} \lambda y.y & \text{if } x \geq 0 \\ \lambda y.y + 1 & \text{if } x < 0. \end{cases}$$

Clearly, f turns any *fixed* real number to a polynomial, but when curried, it is far from being a polynomial. In other words, reducibility seems apparently inadequate to capture situations like the one above, in which the "base case" is not the one of *ground* types, but rather the one of *first-order* types.

Before proceeding any further, it is useful to fix the boundaries of our investigation. We are interested in proving that (the semantics of) programs of first-order type $R^n \to R$ enjoy first-order properties, such as continuity or differentiability, under their standard interpretation in calculus and real analysis. More specifically, our results do not cover notions of continuity and differentiability studied in fields such as (exact) real-number computation [57] or computable analysis [58], which have a strong domain-theoretical flavor, and higher-order generalizations of continuity and differentiability (see, e.g., [26,27,32,29]). We leave for future work the study of open logical relations in these settings. What this paper aims to provide, is a family of *lightweight* techniques that can be used to show that practical properties of interest of real-valued functions are guaranteed to hold when programs are written taking advantage of higher-order constructors. We believe that the three case studies we present in this paper are both a way to point to the practical scenarios we have in mind and of witnessing the versatility of our methodology.

4 Warming Up: A Containment Theorem

In this section we introduce open logical relations in their unary version (i.e. open logical predicates). We do so by proving the following Containment Theorem.

Theorem 1 (Containment Theorem). *Let $\mathfrak{F}$ be a collection of real-valued functions including projections and closed under function composition. Then, any $\Lambda_{\mathfrak{F}}^{\times, \to, R}$ term $x_1 : R, \ldots, x_n : R \vdash t : R$ denotes a function (from $\mathbb{R}^n$ to $\mathbb{R}$) in $\mathfrak{F}$. That is, $[\![x_1 : R, \ldots, x_n : R \vdash t : R]\!] \in \mathfrak{F}$.*

As already remarked in previous sections, notable instances of Theorem 1 are obtained by taking $\mathfrak{F}$ as the collection of continuous functions, or as the collection of polynomials.

Our strategy to prove Theorem 1 consists in defining a logical predicate, denoted by $\mathcal{F}$, ensuring the denotation of programs of a first-order type to be in $\mathfrak{F}$, and hereditary preserving this property at higher-order types. However, $\mathfrak{F}$ being a property of real-valued functions—and the denotation of an *open* term of the form $x_1 : R, \ldots, x_n : R \vdash t : R$ being such a function—we shall work with open terms with free variables of type R and parametrize the candidate logical predicate by types *and* environments Θ containing such variables.

This way, we obtain a family of logical predicates $\mathcal{F}_\tau^\Theta$ acting on terms of the form $\Theta \vdash t : \tau$. As a consequence, when considering the ground type R and an environment $\Theta = x_1 : R, \ldots, x_n : R$, we obtain a predicate $\mathcal{F}_R^\Theta$ on expressions $\Theta \vdash t : R$ which naturally corresponds to functions from $\mathbb{R}^n$ to $\mathbb{R}$, for which belonging to $\mathfrak{F}$ is indeed meaningful.

Definition 1 (Open Logical Predicate). *Let $\Theta = x_1 : R, \ldots, x_n : R$ be a fixed environment. We define the type-indexed family of predicates $\mathcal{F}_\tau^\Theta$ by induction on τ as follows:*

$$t \in \mathcal{F}_R^\Theta \iff (\Theta \vdash t : R \wedge [\![\Theta \vdash t : R]\!] \in \mathfrak{F})$$

$$t \in \mathcal{F}_{\tau_1 \to \tau_2}^\Theta \iff (\Theta \vdash t : \tau_1 \to \tau_2 \wedge \forall s \in \mathcal{F}_{\tau_1}^\Theta. \, ts \in \mathcal{F}_{\tau_2}^\Theta)$$

$$t \in \mathcal{F}_{\tau_1 \times \tau_2}^\Theta \iff (\Theta \vdash t : \tau_1 \times \tau_2 \wedge \forall i \in \{1, 2\}. \, t.i \in \mathcal{F}_{\tau_i}^\Theta).$$

We extend $\mathcal{F}_\tau^\Theta$ to the predicate $\mathcal{F}_\tau^{\Gamma,\Theta}$, where Γ ranges over arbitrary environments (possibly containing variables of type $\mathbb{R}$) as follows:

$$t \in \mathcal{F}_\tau^{\Gamma,\Theta} \iff (\Gamma,\Theta \vdash t : \tau \wedge \forall \gamma.\ \gamma \in \mathcal{F}_\Theta^\Gamma \implies t\gamma \in \mathcal{F}_\tau^\Theta).$$

Here, γ ranges over substitutions[6] and $\gamma \in \mathcal{F}_\Theta^\Gamma$ holds if the support of γ is Γ and $\gamma(x) \in \mathcal{F}_\tau^\Theta$, for any $(x : \tau) \in \Gamma$.

Notice that Definition 1 ensures first-order real-valued functions to be in $\mathfrak{F}$, and asks for such a property to be hereditary preserved at higher-order types. Lemma 1 states that these conditions are indeed sufficient to guarantee any $\Lambda_\mathfrak{F}^{\times,\to,\mathbb{R}}$ term $\Theta \vdash t : \mathbb{R}$ to denote a function in $\mathfrak{F}$.

Lemma 1 (Fundamental Lemma). *For all environments Γ,Θ as above, and for any expression $\Gamma,\Theta \vdash t : \tau$, we have $t \in \mathcal{F}_\tau^{\Gamma,\Theta}$.*

Proof. By induction on t, observing that $\mathcal{F}_\tau^\Theta$ is closed under denotational semantics: if $s \in \mathcal{F}_\tau^\Theta$ and $[\![\Theta \vdash t : \tau]\!] = [\![\Theta \vdash s : \tau]\!]$, then $t \in \mathcal{F}_\tau^\Theta$. The proof follows the same structure of Lemma 3, and thus we omit details here.   □

Finally, a straightforward application of Lemma 1 gives the desired result, namely Theorem 1.

5   Automatic Differentiation

In this section, we show how we can use open logical relations to prove the correctness of (a fragment of) the automatic differentiation algorithm of [50] (suitably adapted to our calculus).

Automatic differentiation [8,9,35] (AD, for short) is a family of techniques to efficiently compute the *numerical* (as opposed to *symbolical*) derivative of a computer program denoting a real-valued function. Roughly speaking, AD acts on the code of a program by letting variables incorporate values for their derivative, and operators propagate derivatives according to the *chain rule* of differential calculus [52]. Due to its vast applications in machine learning (back-propagation [49] being an example of an AD technique) and, most notably, in deep learning [9], AD is rapidly becoming a topic of interest in the programming language theory community, as witnessed by the new line of research called *differentiable programming* (see, e.g., [28,50,16,1] for some recent results on AD and programming language theory developed in the latter field).

AD comes several modes, the two most important ones being the *forward mode* (also called *tangent mode*) and the *backward mode* (also called *reverse mode*). These can be seen as different ways to compute the chain rule, the former by traversing the chain rule from inside to outside, while the latter from outside to inside.

---

[6] We write $t\gamma$ for the result of applying γ to variables in t.

Here we are concerned with forward mode AD. More specifically, we consider the forward mode AD algorithm recently proposed in [50]. The latter is based on a source-to-source program transformation extracting out of a program t a new program Dt whose evaluation simultaneously gives the result of computing t and its derivative. This is achieved by augmenting the code of t in such a way to handle *dual numbers*[7].

The transformation roughly goes as follows: expressions s of type R are transformed into dual numbers, i.e. expressions s' of type $R \times R$, where the first component of s' gives the original value of s, and the second component of s' gives the derivative of s. Real-valued function symbols are then extended to handle dual numbers by applying the chain rule, while other constructors of the language are extended pointwise.

The algorithm of [50] has been studied by means of benchmarks and, to the best of the authors' knowledge, the only proof of its correctness available in the literature[8] has been given at the time of writing by Huot et al. in [37]. However, the latter proof relies on *denotational* semantics, and no *operational* proof of correctness has been given so far. Differentiability being a first-order concept, open logical relations are thus a perfect candidate for such a job.

An AD Program Transformation In the rest of this section, given a differentiable function $f : \mathbb{R}^n \to \mathbb{R}$, we denote by $\partial_x f : \mathbb{R}^n \to \mathbb{R}$ its partial derivative with respect to the variable x. Let $\mathfrak{D}$ be the collection of (real-valued) differentiable functions, and let us fix a collection $\mathfrak{F}$ of real-valued functions such that, for any $f \in \mathfrak{D}$, both f and $\partial_x f$ belong to $\mathfrak{F}$. We also assume $\mathfrak{F}$ to contain functions for real number arithmetic. Notice that since $\partial_x f$ is not necessarily differentiable, in general $\partial_x f \notin \mathfrak{D}$.

We begin by recalling how the program transformation of [50] works on $\Lambda_{\mathfrak{D}}^{\times, \to, R}$, the extension of $\Lambda^{\times, \to, R}$ with operators for functions in $\mathfrak{D}$. In order to define the derivative of a $\Lambda_{\mathfrak{D}}^{\times, \to, R}$ expression, we first define an intermediate *program transformation* $D : \Lambda_{\mathfrak{D}}^{\times, \to, R} \to \Lambda_{\mathfrak{F}}^{\times, \to, R}$ such that:

$$\Gamma \vdash t : \tau \implies D\Gamma \vdash Dt : D\tau.$$

The action of D on types, environments, and expressions is defined in Figure 2. Notice that t is an expression in $\Lambda_{\mathfrak{D}}^{\times, \to, R}$, whereas Dt is an expression in $\Lambda_{\mathfrak{F}}^{\times, \to, R}$.

Let us comment the definition of D, beginning with its action on types. Following the rationale behind forward-mode AD, the map D associates to the type

---

[7] We represent dual numbers [21] as pairs of the form (x, x'), with $x, x' \in \mathbb{R}$. The first component, namely x, is subject to the usual real number arithmetic, whereas the second component, namely x', obeys to first-order differentiation arithmetic. Dual numbers are usually presented, in analogy with complex numbers, as formal sums of the form $x + x'\varepsilon$, where ε is an abstract number (an infinitesimal) subject to the law $\varepsilon^2 = 0$.

[8] However, we remark that formal approaches to *backward* automatic differentiation for higher-order languages have been recently proposed in [1,16] (see Section 7).

$$DR = R \times R \qquad\qquad D(\cdot) = \cdot$$
$$D(\tau_1 \times \tau_2) = D\tau_1 \times D\tau_2 \qquad\qquad D(x : \tau, \Gamma) = dx : D\tau, D\Gamma$$
$$D(\tau_1 \rightarrow \tau_2) = D\tau_1 \rightarrow D\tau_2$$

$$D\underline{r} = (\underline{r}, \underline{0}) \quad D(\underline{f}(t_1, \ldots, t_n)) = (\underline{f}(Dt_1.1, \ldots, Dt_n.1), \sum_{i=1}^{n} \partial_{x_i} \underline{f}(Dt_1.1, \ldots, Dt_n.1) * Dt_i.2)$$

$$Dx = dx \quad D(\lambda x.t) = \lambda dx.Dt \quad D(st) = (Ds)(Dt) \quad D(t.i) = Dt.i \quad D(t_1, t_2) = (Dt_1, Dt_2)$$

Fig. 2: Intermediate transformation D

R the product type $R \times R$, the first and second components of its inhabitants being the original expression and its derivative, respectively. The action of D on non-basic types is straightforward and it is designed so that the automatic differentiation machinery can handle higher-order expressions in such a way to guarantee correctness at real-valued function types.

The action of D on the usual constructors of the λ-calculus is pointwise, although it is worth noticing that D associates to any variable x of type τ a new variable, which we denote by dx, of type $D\tau$. As we are going to see, if $\tau = R$, then dx acts as a placeholder for a dual number.

More interesting is the action of D on real-valued constructors. To any numeral $\underline{r}$, D associates the pair $D\underline{r} = (\underline{r}, \underline{0})$, the derivative of a number being zero. Let us now inspect the action of D on an operator $\underline{f}$ associated to $f : \mathbb{R}^n \rightarrow \mathbb{R}$ (we treat f as a function in the variables $x_1, \ldots, x_n$). The interesting part is the second component of $D(\underline{f}(t_1, \ldots, t_n))$, namely

$$\sum_{i=1}^{n} \partial_{x_i} f(Dt_1.1, \ldots, Dt_n.1) * Dt_i.2$$

where $\sum_{i=1}^{n}$ and $*$ denote the operators (of $\Lambda_{\mathfrak{F}}^{\times, \rightarrow, R}$) associated to summation and (binary) multiplication (for readability we omit the underline notation), and $\partial_{x_i} f$ is the operator (of $\Lambda_{\mathfrak{F}}^{\times, \rightarrow, R}$) associated to partial derivative $\partial_{x_i} f$ of f in the variable x_i. It is not hard to recognize that the above expression is nothing but an instance of the *chain rule*.

Finally, we notice that if $\Gamma \vdash t : \tau$ is a (derivable) judgment in $\Lambda_{\mathfrak{D}}^{\times, \rightarrow, R}$, then indeed $D\Gamma \vdash Dt : D\tau$ is a (derivable) judgment in $\Lambda_{\mathfrak{F}}^{\times, \rightarrow, R}$.

Example 1. Let us consider the binary function $f(x_1, x_2) = \sin(x_1) + \cos(x_2)$. For readability, we overload the notation writing f in place of $\underline{f}$ (and similarly for $\partial_{x_i} f$). Given expressions t_1, t_2, we compute $D(\sin(t_1) + \cos(t_2))$. Recall that

$\partial_{x_1} f(x_1, x_2) = \cos(x_1)$ and $\partial_{x_2} f(x_1, x_2) = -\sin(x_2)$. We have:

$D(\sin(t_1) + \cos(t_2))$
$= (\sin(Dt_1.1) + \cos(Dt_2.1), \partial_{x_1} f(Dt_1.1, Dt_2.1) * Dt_1.2 + \partial_{x_2} f(Dt_1.1, Dt_2.1) * Dt_2.2)$
$= (\sin(Dt_1.1) + \cos(Dt_2.1), \cos(Dt_1.1) * Dt_1.2 - \sin(Dt_2.1) * Dt_2.2).$

As a consequence, we see that $D(\lambda x. \lambda y. \sin(x) + \cos(y))$ is

$$\lambda dx. \lambda dy. (\sin(dx.1) + \cos(dy.1), \cos(dx.1) * dx.2 - \sin(dy.1) * dy.2).$$

We now aim to define the derivative of an expression $x_1 : R, \ldots, x_n : R \vdash t : R$ with respect to a variable x (of type R). In order to do so we first associate to any variable $y : R$ its dual expression $\text{dual}_x(y) : R \times R$ defined as:

$$\text{dual}_x(y) = \begin{cases} (y, \underline{1}) & \text{if } x = y \\ (y, \underline{0}) & \text{otherwise.} \end{cases}$$

Next, we define for $x_1 : R, \ldots, x_n : R \vdash t : R$ the derivative $\text{deriv}(x, t)$ of t with respect to x as:

$$\text{deriv}(x, t) = Dt[\text{dual}_x(x_1)/dx_1, \ldots, \text{dual}_x(x_n)/dx_n].2$$

Let us clarify this passage with a simple example.

Example 2. Let us compute the derivative of $x : R, y . R \vdash t : R$, where $t = x * y$. We first of all compute Dt, obtaining:

$dx : R \times R, dy : R \times R \vdash ((dx.1) * (dy.1), (dx.1) * (dy.2) + (dx.2) * (dy.1)) : R \times R.$

Observing that $\text{dual}_x(x) = (x, \underline{1})$ and $\text{dual}_x(y) = (y, \underline{0})$, we indeed obtain the desired derivative as $x : R, y : R \vdash Dt[\text{dual}_x(x)/dx, \text{dual}_x(y)/dy].2 : R$. For we have:

$$\llbracket x : R, y : R \vdash Dt[\text{dual}_x(x)/dx, \text{dual}_x(y)/dy].2 : R \rrbracket$$
$$= \llbracket x : R, y : R \vdash (x * y, x * 0 + 1 * y).2 : R \rrbracket$$
$$= \llbracket x : R, y : R \vdash y : R \rrbracket = \partial_x \llbracket x : R, y : R \vdash x * y : R \rrbracket.$$

Remark 1. For $\Theta = x_1 : R, \ldots, x_n : R$ we have $\Theta \vdash \text{dual}_y(x_i) : DR$ and $\Theta \vdash Ds[\text{dual}_y(x_1)/dx_1, \ldots, \text{dual}_y(x_n)/dx_n] : D\tau$, for any variable y and $\Theta \vdash s : \tau$.

Open Logical relations for AD We have claimed that the operation deriv performs automatic differentiation of $\Lambda_{\mathfrak{D}}^{\times, \to, R}$ expressions. By that we mean that once applied to expressions of the form $x_1 : R, \ldots, x_n : R \vdash t : R$, the operation deriv can be used to compute the derivative of $\llbracket x_1 : R, \ldots, x_n : R \vdash t : R \rrbracket$. We now show how we can prove such a statement using open logical relations, this way providing a proof of correctness of our AD program transformation.

We begin by defining a logical relations $\mathcal{R}$ between $\Lambda_{\mathfrak{D}}^{\times, \to, R}$ and $\Lambda_{\mathfrak{Z}}^{\times, \to, R}$ expressions. We design $\mathcal{R}$ in such a way that (i) $t \mathcal{R} Dt$ and (ii) if $t \mathcal{R} s$ and t inhabits a first-order type, then indeed s corresponds to the derivative of t. While (ii) essentially holds by definition, (i) requires some efforts in order to be proved.

Definition 2 (Open Logical Relation). *Let* $\Theta = x_1 : \mathrm{R}, \ldots, x_n : \mathrm{R}$ *be a fixed, arbitrary environment. Define the family of relations* $(\mathcal{R}_\tau^\Theta)_{\Theta,\tau}$ *between* $\Lambda_{\mathfrak{D}}^{\times,\to,\mathrm{R}}$ *and* $\Lambda_{\mathfrak{F}}^{\times,\to,\mathrm{R}}$ *expressions by induction on* τ *as follows:*

$$t \, \mathcal{R}_{\mathrm{R}}^\Theta \, s \iff \begin{cases} \Theta \vdash t : \mathrm{R} \wedge \mathrm{D}\Theta \vdash s : \mathrm{R} \times \mathrm{R} \\ \forall y : \mathrm{R}. \\ [\![\Theta \vdash s[\mathrm{dual}_y(x_1)/\mathrm{d}x_1, \ldots, \mathrm{dual}_y(x_n)/\mathrm{d}x_n].1 : \mathrm{R}]\!] = [\![\Theta \vdash t : \mathrm{R}]\!] \\ [\![\Theta \vdash s[\mathrm{dual}_y(x_1)/\mathrm{d}x_1, \ldots, \mathrm{dual}_y(x_n)/\mathrm{d}x_n].2 : \mathrm{R}]\!] = \partial_y [\![\Theta \vdash t : \mathrm{R}]\!] \end{cases}$$

$$t \, \mathcal{R}_{\tau_1 \to \tau_2}^\Theta \, s \iff \begin{cases} \Theta \vdash t : \tau_1 \to \tau_2 \wedge \mathrm{D}\Theta \vdash s : \mathrm{D}\tau_1 \to \mathrm{D}\tau_2 \\ \forall p, q. \; p \, \mathcal{R}_{\tau_1}^\Theta \, q \implies tp \, \mathcal{R}_{\tau_2}^\Theta \, sq \end{cases}$$

$$t \, \mathcal{R}_{\tau_1 \times \tau_2}^\Theta \, s \iff \begin{cases} \Theta \vdash t : \tau_1 \times \tau_2 \wedge \mathrm{D}\Theta \vdash s : \mathrm{D}\tau_1 \times \mathrm{D}\tau_2 \\ \forall i \in \{1, 2\}. \; t.i \, \mathcal{R}_{\tau_i}^\Theta \, s.i \end{cases}$$

We extend $\mathcal{R}_\tau^\Theta$ *to the family* $(\mathcal{R}_\tau^{\Gamma,\Theta})_{\Gamma,\Theta,\tau}$, *where* Γ *ranges over arbitrary environments (possibly containing variables of type* R*), as follows:*

$$t \, \mathcal{R}_\tau^{\Gamma,\Theta} \, s \iff (\Gamma, \Theta \vdash t : \tau) \wedge (\mathrm{D}\Gamma, \mathrm{D}\Theta \vdash s : \mathrm{D}\tau) \wedge (\forall \gamma, \delta. \; \gamma \, \mathcal{R}_\Theta^\Gamma \, \delta \implies t\gamma \, \mathcal{R}_\tau^\Theta \, s\delta)$$

where γ, δ *range over substitutions, and:*

$$\gamma \, \mathcal{R}_\Theta^\Gamma \, \delta \iff (\mathrm{supp}(\gamma) = \Gamma) \wedge (\mathrm{supp}(\delta) = \mathrm{D}\Gamma) \wedge (\forall (x : \tau) \in \Gamma. \; \gamma(x) \, \mathcal{R}_\tau^\Theta \, \delta(\mathrm{d}x)).$$

Obviously, Definition 2 satisfies condition (ii) above. What remains to be done is to show that it satisfies condition (i) as well. In order to prove such a result, we first need to show that the logical relation respects the denotational semantics of $\Lambda_{\mathfrak{D}}^{\times,\to,\mathrm{R}}$.

Lemma 2. *Let* $\Theta = x_1 : \mathrm{R}, \ldots, x_n : \mathrm{R}$. *Then, the following hold:*

$$t' \, \mathcal{R}_\tau^\Theta \, s \wedge [\![\Theta \vdash t : \tau]\!] = [\![\Theta \vdash t' : \tau]\!] \implies t \, \mathcal{R}_\tau^\Theta \, s$$
$$t \, \mathcal{R}_\tau^\Theta \, s' \wedge [\![\mathrm{D}\Theta \vdash s' : \mathrm{D}\tau]\!] = [\![\mathrm{D}\Theta \vdash s : \mathrm{D}\tau]\!] \implies t \, \mathcal{R}_\tau^\Theta \, s.$$

Proof. A standard induction on τ. □

We are now ready to state and prove the main result of this section.

Lemma 3 (Fundamental Lemma). *For all environments* Γ, Θ *and for any expression* $\Gamma, \Theta \vdash t : \tau$, *we have* $t \, \mathcal{R}_\tau^{\Gamma,\Theta} \, \mathrm{D}t$.

Proof. We prove the following statement, by induction on t:

$$\forall t. \; \forall \tau. \; \forall \Gamma, \Theta. \; (\Gamma, \Theta \vdash t : \tau \implies t \, \mathcal{R}_\tau^{\Gamma,\Theta} \, \mathrm{D}t).$$

We show only the most relevant cases. Suppose t is a variable x. We distinguish whether x belongs to Γ or Θ.

1. Suppose $(x : R) \in \Theta$. We have to show $x \, \mathcal{R}_R^{\Gamma,\Theta} \, dx$, i.e.

$$[\![\Theta \vdash dx[\mathbf{dual}_y(x)/dx].1 : R]\!] = [\![\Theta \vdash x : R]\!]$$
$$[\![\Theta \vdash dx[\mathbf{dual}_y(x)/dx].2 : R]\!] = \partial_y[\![\Theta \vdash x : R]\!]$$

for any variable y (of type R). The first identity obviously holds as

$$[\![\Theta \vdash dx[\mathbf{dual}_y(x)/dx].1 : R]\!] = [\![\Theta \vdash dx[(x,b)/dx].1 : R]\!] = [\![\Theta \vdash x : R]\!],$$

where $b \in \{\underline{0}, \underline{1}\}$. For the second identity we distinguish whether $y = x$ or $y \neq x$. In the former case we have $\mathbf{dual}_y(x) = (x, \underline{1})$, and thus:

$$[\![\Theta \vdash dx[\mathbf{dual}_y(x)/dx].2 : R]\!] = [\![\Theta \vdash \underline{1} : R]\!] = \partial_y[\![\Theta \vdash y : R]\!].$$

In the latter case we have $\mathbf{dual}_y(x) = (x, \underline{0})$, and thus:

$$[\![\Theta \vdash dx[\mathbf{dual}_y(x)/dx].2 : R]\!] = [\![\Theta \vdash \underline{0} : R]\!] = \partial_y[\![\Theta \vdash x : R]\!].$$

2. Suppose $(x : \tau) \in \Gamma$. We have to show $x \, \mathcal{R}^{\Gamma,\Theta} \, dx$, i.e. $\gamma(x) \, \mathcal{R}_\tau^\Theta \, \delta(dx)$, for all substitutions γ, δ such that $\gamma \, \mathcal{R}_\Theta^\Gamma \, \delta$. Since x belongs to Γ, we are trivially done.

Suppose t is $\lambda x.s$, so that we have

$$\frac{\Gamma, \Theta, x : \tau_1 \vdash s : \tau_2}{\Gamma, \Theta \vdash \lambda x.s : \tau_1 \to \tau_2}$$

for some types τ_1, τ_2. As x is bound in $\lambda x.s$, without loss of generality we can assume $(x : \tau_1) \notin \Gamma \cup \Theta$. Let $\Delta = \Gamma, x : \tau_1$, so that we have $\Delta, \Theta \vdash s : \tau_2$, and thus $s \, \mathcal{R}_{\tau_2}^{\Delta,\Theta} \, Ds$, by induction hypothesis. By definition of open logical relation, we have to prove that for arbitrary γ, δ such that $\gamma \, \mathcal{R}_\Theta^\Gamma \, \delta$, we have

$$\lambda x.s\gamma \, \mathcal{R}_{\tau_1 \to \tau_2}^\Theta \, \lambda dx.(Ds)\delta,$$

i.e. $(\lambda x.s\gamma)p \, \mathcal{R}_{\tau_2}^\Theta \, (\lambda dx.(Ds)\delta)q$, for all $p \, \mathcal{R}_{\tau_1}^\Theta \, q$. Let us fix a pair (p, q) as above. By Lemma 2, it is sufficient to show $(s\gamma)[p/x] \, \mathcal{R}_{\tau_2}^\Theta \, ((Ds)\delta)[q/dx]$. Let γ', δ' be the substitutions defined as follows:

$$\gamma'(y) = \begin{cases} p & \text{if } y = x \\ \gamma(y) & \text{otherwise} \end{cases} \qquad \delta'(y) = \begin{cases} q & \text{if } y = dx \\ \delta(y) & \text{otherwise.} \end{cases}$$

It is easy to see that $\gamma' \, \mathcal{R}_\Theta^\Delta \, \delta'$, so that by $s \, \mathcal{R}_{\tau_2}^{\Delta,\Theta} \, Ds$ (recall that the latter follows by induction hypothesis) we infer $s\gamma' \, \mathcal{R}_{\tau_2}^\Theta \, (Ds)\delta'$, by the very definition of open logical relation. As a consequence, the thesis is proved if we show

$$(s\gamma)[p/x] = s\gamma'; \qquad\qquad ((Ds)\delta)[q/dx] = (Ds)\delta'.$$

The above identities hold if $x \notin FV(\gamma(y))$ and $dx \notin FV(\delta(dy))$, for any $(y : \tau) \in \Gamma$. This is indeed the case, since $\gamma(y) \, \mathcal{R}_\tau^\Theta \, \delta(dy)$ implies $\Theta \vdash \gamma(y) : \tau$ and $D\Theta \vdash \delta(dy) : D\tau$, and $x \notin \Theta$ (and thus $dx \notin D\Theta$). $\qquad \square$

A direct application of Lemma 3 allows us to conclude the correctness of the program transformation D. In fact, given a first-order term $\Theta \vdash t : R$, with $\Theta = x_1 : R, \ldots, x_n : R$, by Lemma 3 we have $t\,\mathcal{R}_R^\Theta\,Dt$, and thus

$$\partial_y \llbracket \Theta \vdash t : R \rrbracket = \llbracket \Theta \vdash Dt[\mathrm{dual}_y(x_1)/dx_1, \ldots, \mathrm{dual}_y(x_n)/dx_n].2 : R \rrbracket,$$

for any real-valued variable y, meaning that Dt indeed computes the partial derivative of t.

Theorem 2. *For any term $\Theta \vdash t : R$ as above, the term $D\Theta \vdash Dt : DR$ computes the partial derivative of t, i.e., for any variable y we have*

$$\partial_y \llbracket \Theta \vdash t : R \rrbracket = \llbracket \Theta \vdash Dt[\mathrm{dual}_y(x_1)/dx_1, \ldots, \mathrm{dual}_y(x_n)/dx_n].2 : R \rrbracket.$$

6   On Refinement Types and Local Continuity

In Section 4, we exploited open logical relations to establish a containment theorem for the calculus $\Lambda_{\mathfrak{F}}^{\times,\to,R}$, i.e. the calculus $\Lambda^{\times,\to,R}$ extended with real-valued functions belonging to a set $\mathfrak{F}$ including projections and closed under function composition. Since the collection $\mathfrak{C}$ of (real-valued) *continuous* functions satisfies both constraints, Theorem 1 allows us to conclude that all first order terms of $\Lambda_{\mathfrak{C}}^{\times,\to,R}$ represent continuous functions.

The aim of the present section is the development of a framework to prove continuity properties of programs in a calculus that goes *beyond* $\Lambda_{\mathfrak{C}}^{\times,\to,R}$. More specifically, (i) we do not restrict our analysis to calculi having operators representing continuous real-valued functions only, but consider operators for arbitrary real-valued functions, and (ii) we add to our calculus an if-then-else construct whose static semantics is captured by the following rule:

$$\frac{\Gamma \vdash t : R \quad \Gamma \vdash s : \tau \quad \Gamma \vdash p : \tau}{\Gamma \vdash \text{if } t \text{ then } s \text{ else } p : \tau}$$

The intended dynamic semantics of the term if t then s else p is the same as the one of s whenever t evaluates to any real number $r \neq 0$ and the same as the one of p if it evaluates to 0.

Notice that the crux of the problem we aim to solve is the presence of the if-then-else construct. Indeed, independently of point (i), such a construct breaks the global continuity of programs, as illustrated in Figure 3a. As a consequence we are forced to look at *local* continuity properties, instead: for instance we can say that the program of Figure 3a is continuous both on $\mathbb{R}_{<0}$ and $\mathbb{R}_{\geq 0}$. Observe that guaranteeing local continuity allows us (up to a certain point) to recover the ability of approximating the output of a program by approximating its input. Indeed, if a program $t : R \times \ldots \times R \to R$ is *locally continuous* on a subset X of $\mathbb{R}^n$, then the value of ts (for some input s) can be approximated

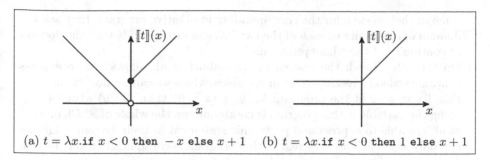

(a) $t = \lambda x.\text{if } x < 0 \text{ then } -x \text{ else } x + 1$ (b) $t = \lambda x.\text{if } x < 0 \text{ then } 1 \text{ else } x + 1$

Fig. 3: Simply typed first-order programs with branches

by passing as argument to t a family $(s_n)_{n \in \mathbb{N}}$ of approximations of s, *as long as* both s and all the $(s_n)_{n \in \mathbb{N}}$ are indeed elements of X. Notice that the continuity domains we are interested in are not necessary open sets: we could for instance be interested in functions that are continuous on the unit circle, i.e. the points $\{(a,b) \mid a^2 + b^2 = 1\} \subseteq \mathbb{R}^2$. For this reason we will work with the notion of *sequential* continuity, instead of the usual topological notion of continuity. It must be observed, however, that these two notions coincide as soon as the continuity domain X is actually an open set.

Definition 3 (Sequential Continuity). *Let $f : \mathbb{R}^n \to \mathbb{R}$, and X be any subset of $\mathbb{R}^n$. We say that f is (sequentially) continuous on X if for every $x \in X$, and for every sequence $(x_n)_{n \in \mathbb{N}}$ of elements of X such that $\lim_{n \to \infty} x_n = x$, it holds that $\lim_{n \to \infty} f(x_n) = f(x)$.*

In [18], Chaudhuri et al. introduced a logical system designed to guarantee local continuity properties on programs in an *imperative* (first-order) programming language with conditional branches and loops. In this section, we develop a similar system in the setting of a *higher-order functional language* with an if-then-else construct, and we use open logical relations to prove the soundness of our system. This witnesses, on yet another situation, the versatility of open logical relations. Compared to [18], we somehow generalize from a result on programs built from only first-order constructs and primitive functions, to a containment result for programs built using also higher-order constructs.

We however mention that, although our system is inspired by the work of Chaudhuri at al., there are significant differences between the two, even at the first-order level. The consequences these differences have on the expressive power of our systems are twofold:

- On the one hand, while inferring continuity on some domain X of a program of the form if t then s else p, we have more flexibility than [18] for the domains of continuity of s and p. To be more concrete, let us consider the program $\lambda x.(\text{if } (x > 0) \text{ then } 0 \text{ else } (\text{if } x = 4 \text{ then } 1 \text{ else } 0))$, which is continuous on $\mathbb{R}$ even though the second branch is continuous on $\mathbb{R}_{\leq 0}$, but not on $\mathbb{R}$. We are able to show in our system that this program is indeed continuous on *the whole* domain $\mathbb{R}$, while Chaudhuri et al. cannot do the same in their system for the corresponding imperative program: they ask the domain of continuity of *each* of the two branches to *coincide* with the domain of continuity of the whole program.

- On the other hand, the system of Chaudhuri at al. allows one to express continuity along a restricted set of variables, which we cannot do. To illustrate this, let us look at the program: $\lambda x, y.\text{if } (x = 0) \text{ then } (3 * y) \text{ else } (4 * y)$: along the variable y, this program is continuous on the whole of $\mathbb{R}$. Chaudhuri et al. are able to express and prove this statement in their system, while we can only say that for every real a, this program is continuous on the domain $\{a\} \times \mathbb{R}$.

For the sake of simplicity, it is useful to slightly simplify our calculus; the ideas we present here, however, would still be valid in a more general setting, but that would make the presentation and proofs more involved. As usual, let $\mathfrak{F}$ be a collection of real-valued functions. We consider the restriction of the calculus $\Lambda_{\mathfrak{F}}^{\times,\to,\mathbb{R}}$ obtained by considering types of the form

$$\tau ::= \mathbb{R} \mid \rho; \qquad \rho ::= \rho_1 \times \cdots \times \rho_n \times \underbrace{\mathbb{R} \times \cdots \times \mathbb{R}}_{m\text{-times}} \to \tau;$$

only. For the sake of readability, we employ the notation $(\rho_1 \ldots, \rho_n, \mathbb{R}, \ldots, \mathbb{R}) \to \tau$ in place of $\rho_1 \times \cdots \times \rho_n \times \mathbb{R} \times \cdots \times \mathbb{R} \to \tau$. We also overload the notation and keep indicating the resulting calculus as $\Lambda_{\mathfrak{F}}^{\times,\to,\mathbb{R}}$. Nonetheless, the reader should keep in mind that from now on, whenever referring to a $\Lambda_{\mathfrak{F}}^{\times,\to,\mathbb{R}}$ term, we are tacitly referring to a term typable according to the restricted type system, but that can indeed contain conditionals.

Since we want to be able to talk about *composition properties* of locally continuous programs, we actually need to talk not only about the points where a program is continuous, but also about the *image* of this continuity domain. In higher-order languages, a well-established framework for the latter kind of specifications is the one of *refinement types*, that have been first introduced by [31] in the context of ML types: the basic idea is to annotate an existing type system with logical formulas, with the aim of being more precise about the underlying program's behaviors than in simple types. Here, we are going to adapt this framework by replacing the image annotations provided by standard refinement types with *continuity annotations*.

6.1   A Refinement Type System Ensuring Local Continuity

Our refinement type system is developed on top of the simple types system of Section 2 (actually, on the simplification of such a system we are considering in this section). We first need to introduce a set of logical formulas which talk about n-uples of real numbers, and which we use as annotations in our refinement types. We consider a set $\mathcal{V}$ of logical variables, and we construct formulas as follows:

$$\psi, \phi \in \mathcal{L} ::= \top \mid (e \leq e) \mid \psi \wedge \phi \mid \neg\psi,$$

$$e \in \mathcal{E} ::= \alpha \mid a \mid f(e, \ldots, e) \qquad \text{with } \alpha \in \mathcal{V}, a \in \mathbb{R}, f : \mathbb{R}^n \to \mathbb{R}.$$

Recall that with the connectives in our logic, we are able to encode logical disjunction and implication, and as customary, we write $\phi \Rightarrow \psi$ for $\neg\phi \vee \psi$. A *real assignment* is a partial map $\sigma : \mathcal{V} \to \mathbb{R}$. When σ has finite support, we sometimes specify σ by writing $(\alpha_1 \mapsto \sigma(\alpha_1), \ldots, \alpha_n \mapsto \sigma(\alpha_n))$. We note $\sigma \models \phi$ when σ is defined on the variables occurring in ϕ, and moreover the real formula obtained when replacing along σ the logical variables of ϕ is true. We write $\models \phi$ when $\sigma \models \phi$ always holds, independently on σ.

We can associate to every formula the subset of $\mathbb{R}^n$ consisting of all points where this formula holds: more precisely, if ϕ is a formula, and $X = \alpha_1, \ldots, \alpha_n$ is a list of logical variables such that $\mathrm{Vars}(\phi) \subseteq X$, we call *truth domain of ϕ w.r.t. X* the set:

$$\mathrm{Dom}(\phi)^X = \{(a_1, \ldots, a_n) \in \mathbb{R}^n \mid (\alpha_1 \mapsto a_1, \ldots, \alpha_n \mapsto a_n) \models \phi\}.$$

We are now ready to define the language of refinement types, which can be seen as simple types annotated by logical formulas. The type R is annotated by logical *variables*: this way we obtain *refinement real types* of the form $\{\alpha \in \mathtt{R}\}$. The crux of our refinement type system consists in the annotations we put *on the arrows*. We introduce two distinct refined arrow constructs, depending on the shape of the target type: more precisely we annotate the arrow of a type $(T_1, \ldots, T_n) \to \mathtt{R}$ with *two* logical formulas, while we annotate $(T_1, \ldots, T_n) \to H$ (where H is an higher-order type) with only *one* logical formula. This way, we obtain refined arrow types of the form $(T_1, \ldots, T_n)^{\psi \leadsto \phi} \to \{\alpha \in \mathtt{R}\}$, and $(T_1, \ldots, T_n) \xrightarrow{\psi} H$: in both cases the formula ψ specifies the continuity domain, while the formula ϕ is an *image annotation* used only when the target type is ground. The intuition is as follows: a program of type $(H_1, \ldots, H_n, \{\alpha_1 \in \mathtt{R}\}, \ldots, \{\alpha_n \in \mathtt{R}\})^{\psi \leadsto \phi} \to \{\alpha \in \mathtt{R}\}$ uses its real arguments continuously on the domain specified by the formula ψ (w.r.t $\alpha_1, \ldots, \alpha_n$), and this domain is sent into the domain specified by the formula ϕ (w.r.t. α). Similarly, a program of the type $(T_1, \ldots, T_n) \xrightarrow{\psi} H$ has its real arguments used in a continuous way on the domain specified by ψ, but it is not possible anymore to specify an image domain, because H is higher-order.

The general form of our refined types is thus as follows:

$$T ::= H \mid F; \qquad F ::= \{\alpha \in \mathtt{R}\};$$

$$H ::= (H_1, \ldots, H_m, F_1, \ldots, F_n) \xrightarrow{\psi} H \mid (H_1, \ldots, H_m, F_1, \ldots, F_n)^{\psi \leadsto \phi} \to F$$

with $n + m > 0$, $\mathrm{Vars}(\phi) \subseteq \{\alpha\}$, $\mathrm{Vars}(\psi) \subseteq \{\alpha_1, \ldots, \alpha_n\}$ when $F = \{\alpha \in \mathtt{R}\}$, $F_i = \{\alpha_i \in \mathtt{R}\}$, and the $(\alpha_i)_{1 \leq i \leq n}$ are distinct. We take refinement types up to renaming of logical variables. If T is a refinement type, we write $\overline{T}$ for the simple type we obtain by forgetting about the annotations in T.

Example 3. We illustrate in this example the intended meaning of our refinement types.

- We first look at how to refine $\mathtt{R} \to \mathtt{R}$: those are types of the form $\{\alpha_1 \in \mathtt{R}\}^{\phi_1 \leadsto \phi_2} \to \{\alpha_2 \in \mathtt{R}\}$. The intended inhabitants of these types are the programs

$t : R \rightarrow R$ such that i) $[\![t]\!]$ is continuous on the truth domain of ϕ_1; and ii) $[\![t]\!]$ sends the truth domain of ϕ_1 into the truth domain of ϕ_2. As an example, ϕ_1 could be $(\alpha_1 < 3)$, and ϕ_2 could be $(\alpha_2 \geq 5)$. An example of a program having this type is $t = \lambda x.(\underline{5} + \underline{f}(x))$, where $f : R \rightarrow R$ is defined as $f(a) = \begin{cases} \frac{1}{3-a} \text{ when } a < 3 \\ 0 \text{ otherwise} \end{cases}$, and moreover we assume that $\{f, +\} \subseteq \mathfrak{F}$.

- We look now at the possible refinements of $R \rightarrow (R \rightarrow R)$: those are of the form $\{\alpha_1 \in R\} \overset{\theta_1}{\rightarrow} (\{\alpha_2 \in R\} \overset{\theta_2 \leadsto \theta_3}{\rightarrow} \{\alpha_3 \in R\})$. The intended inhabitants of these types are the programs $t : R \rightarrow (R \rightarrow R)$ whose interpretation function $(x, y) \in \mathbb{R}^2 \mapsto [\![t]\!](x)(y)$ sends continuously $\text{Dom}(\theta_1)^{\alpha_1} \times \text{Dom}(\theta_2)^{\alpha_2}$ into $\text{Dom}(\theta_3)^{\alpha_3}$. As an example, consider $\theta_1 = (\alpha_1 < 1)$, $\theta_2 = (\alpha_2 \leq 3)$, and $\theta_3 = (\alpha_3 > 0)$. An example of a program having this type is $\lambda x_1.\lambda x_2.\underline{f}(x_1 * x_2)$ where we take f as above.

A refined typing context Γ is a list $x_1 : T_1, \dots, x_n : T_n$, where each T_i is a refinement type. In order to express continuity constraints, we need to *annotate* typing judgments by logical formulas, in a similar way as what we do for arrow types. More precisely, we consider two kinds of refined typing judgments: one for terms of ground type, and one for terms of higher-order type:

$$\Gamma \overset{\psi}{\vdash_r} t : H; \qquad \Gamma \overset{\psi \leadsto \phi}{\vdash_r} t : F.$$

6.2   Basic Typing Rules

We first consider refinement typing rules for the fragment of our language which excludes conditionals: they are given in Figure 4. We illustrate them by way of a series of examples.

Example 4. We first look at the typing rule var-F: if θ implies θ', then the variable x—that, in semantics terms, does the projection of the context Γ to one of its component—sends continuously the truth domain of θ into the truth domain of θ'. Using this rule we can, for instance, derive the following judgment:

$$x : \{\alpha \in R\}, y : \{\beta \in R\} \overset{(\alpha \geq 0 \wedge \beta \geq 0) \leadsto (\alpha \geq 0)}{\vdash_r} x : \{\alpha \in R\}. \tag{1}$$

Example 5. We now look at the Rf rule, that deals with functions from $\mathfrak{F}$. Using this rule, we can show that:

$$x : \{\alpha \in R\}, y : \{\beta \in R\} \overset{(\alpha \geq 0 \wedge \beta \geq 0) \leadsto (\gamma \geq 0)}{\vdash_r} \underline{min}(x, y) : \{\gamma \in R\}. \tag{2}$$

Before giving the refined typing rule for the if-then-else construct, we also illustrate on an example how the rules in Figure 4 allow us to exploit the continuity informations we have on functions in $\mathfrak{F}$, compositionally.

var-H $\dfrac{}{\Gamma, x : H \vdash_r x : H}$ var-F $\dfrac{\models \theta \Rightarrow \theta'}{\Gamma, x : \{\alpha \in \mathsf{R}\} \vdash_r x : \{\alpha \in \mathsf{R}\}}$ $\overset{\psi}{}$ $\overset{\theta \rightsquigarrow \theta'}{}$

Rf $\dfrac{f \in \mathfrak{F} \text{ is continuous on } \mathrm{Dom}(\theta'_1 \wedge \ldots \wedge \theta'_n)^{\alpha_1 \cdots \alpha_n} \qquad \Gamma \vdash_r t_i : \{\alpha_i \in \mathsf{R}\}}{f(\mathrm{Dom}(\theta'_1 \wedge \ldots \wedge \theta'_n)^{\alpha_1 \cdots \alpha_n}) \subseteq \mathrm{Dom}(\theta')^{\beta}}{\Gamma \vdash_r \underline{f}(t_1 \ldots t_n) : \{\beta \in \mathsf{R}\}}$ $\overset{\theta \rightsquigarrow \theta'_i}{}$ $\overset{\theta \rightsquigarrow \theta'}{}$

abs $\dfrac{\Gamma, x_1 : T_1, \ldots, x_n : T_n \vdash_r t : T \qquad \models \psi_1 \wedge \psi_2 \Rightarrow \psi}{\Gamma \vdash_r \lambda(x_1, \ldots, x_n).t : (T_1, \ldots, T_n) \overset{\psi_1(\eta)}{\rightarrow} T}$ $\overset{\psi(\eta)}{}$ $\overset{\psi_2}{}$

app $\dfrac{(\Gamma \vdash_r s_i : H_i)_{1 \leq i \leq m} \quad \Gamma \vdash_r t : (H_1, \ldots, H_m, F_1, \ldots, F_n) \overset{\theta(\eta)}{\rightarrow} T \quad \models \theta_1 \wedge \ldots \wedge \theta_n \Rightarrow \theta \quad (\Gamma \vdash_r p_j : F_j)_{1 \leq j \leq m}}{\Gamma \vdash_r t(s_1, \ldots, s_m, p_1, \ldots, p_m) : T}$ $\overset{\phi}{}$ $\overset{\phi}{}$ $\overset{\phi \rightsquigarrow \theta_j}{}$ $\overset{\phi(\eta)}{}$

The formula $\psi(\eta)$ should be read as ψ when T is a higher-order type, and as $\psi \rightsquigarrow \eta$ when T is a ground type.

Fig. 4: Typing Rules

Example 6. Let $f : \mathbb{R} \to \mathbb{R}$ be the function defined as: $f(x) = \begin{cases} -x \text{ if } x < 0 \\ x + 1 \text{ otherwise} \end{cases}$.
Observe that we can actually regard f as represented by the program in Figure 3a—but we consider it as a primitive function in $\mathfrak{F}$ for the time being, since we have not introduced the typing rule for the if-then-else construct, yet. Consider the program:

$$t = \lambda(x, y).\underline{f}(\underline{min}(x, y)).$$

We see that $[\![t]\!] : \mathbb{R}^2 \to \mathbb{R}$ is continuous on the set $\{(x, y) \mid x \geq 0 \wedge y \geq 0\}$, and that, moreover, the image of f on this set is contained on $[1, +\infty)$. Using the rules in Figure 4, the fact that f is continuous on $\mathbb{R}_{\geq 0}$, and that *min* is continuous on $\mathbb{R}^2$, we see that our refined type system allows us to prove t to be continuous in the considered domain, i.e.:

$$\vdash_r t : (\{\alpha \in \mathsf{R}\}, \{\beta \in \mathsf{R}\}) \overset{(\alpha \geq 0 \wedge \beta \geq 0) \rightsquigarrow (\gamma \geq 1)}{\rightarrow} \{\gamma \in \mathsf{R}\}.$$

6.3   Typing Conditionals

We now look at the rule for the if-then-else construct: as can be seen in the two programs in Figure 3, the use of conditionals *may* or *may not* induce discontinuity points. The crux here is the behaviour of the two branches at the *discontinuity points of the guard function.* In the two programs represented in Figure 3, we see that the only discontinuity point of the guard is in $x = 0$. However, in Figure 3b the two branches return the same value in 0, and the resulting program is thus continuous at $x = 0$, while in Figure 3a the two branches do not coincide in 0, and the resulting program is discontinuous at $x = 0$. We can generalize this observation: for the program if t then s else p to be continuous, we need the branches s and p to be continuous respectively on the domain where t is 1, and on the domain where t is 0, and moreover we need s and p to be continuous *and to coincide* on the points where t is not continuous. Similarly to the logical system designed by Chaudhuri et al [18], the coincidence of the branches in the discontinuity points is expressed as a set of logical rules by way of *observational equivalence.* It should be observed that such an equivalence check is less problematic for first-order programs than it is for higher-order one (the authors of [18] are able to actually check observational equivalence through an SMT solver). On the other hand, various notions of equivalence which are included in contextual equivalence and sometimes coincide with it (e.g., applicative bisimilarity, denotational semantics, or logical relations themselves) have been developed for higher-order languages, and this starts to give rise to actual automatic tools for deciding contextual equivalence [38].

We give in Figure 5 the typing rule for conditionals. The conclusion of the rule guarantees the continuity of the program if t then s else p on a domain specified by a formula θ. The premises of the rule ask for formulas θ_q for $q \in \{t, s, p\}$ that specify continuity domains for the programs t, s, p, and ask also for two additional formulas $\theta_{(t,0)}$ and $\theta_{(t,1)}$ that specify domains where the value of the guard t is 0 and 1, respectively. The target formula θ, and the formulas $(\theta_q)_{q \in \{t,s,p,(t,1),(t,0)\}}$ are related by two side-conditions. Side-condition (1) consists of the following four distinct requirements, that must hold for every point a in the truth domain of θ: i) a is in the truth domain of at least one of the two formulas θ_t, θ_s; ii) if a is not in $\theta_{(t,1)}$ (i.e., we have no guarantee that t will return 1 at point a, meaning that the program p *may* be executed) then a must be in the continuity domain of p; iii) a condition symmetric to the previous one, replacing 1 by 0, and p by s; iv) all points of possible discontinuity (i.e. the points a such that θ^t does not hold) must be in the continuity domain of both s and p, and as a consequence both θ^s and θ^p must hold there. The side-condition (2) uses *typed contextual equivalence* $\equiv^{ctx}$ between terms to express that the two programs s and p must coincide on all inputs such that θ_t does not hold–i.e. that are not in the continuity domain of t. Observe that typed context equivalence here is defined with respect to the system of *simple types.*

Notation 1. *We use the following notations in Figure 5. When Γ is a typing environement, we write $G\Gamma$ and $H\Gamma$ for the ground and higher-order parts of Γ, respectively. Moreover, suppose we have a ground refined typing environment $\Theta = x_1 : \{\alpha_1 \in \mathbb{R}\}, \ldots, x_n : \{\alpha_n \in \mathbb{R}\}$: we say that a logical assignment σ is compatible with Θ when $\{\alpha_i \mid 1 \le i \le n\} \subseteq \mathsf{supp}(\sigma)$. When it is the case, we build in a natural way the substitution associated to σ along Θ by taking $\sigma^\Theta(x_i) = \underline{\sigma(\alpha_i)}$.*

$$\text{If } \frac{\begin{array}{l} \Gamma \overset{\theta_t \rightsquigarrow (\beta=0 \vee \beta=1)}{\vdash_{\mathbf{r}}} t : \{\beta \in \mathbf{R}\} \\[4pt] \Gamma \overset{\theta_{(t,0)} \rightsquigarrow (\beta=0)}{\vdash_{\mathbf{r}}} t : \{\beta \in \mathbf{R}\} \qquad \Gamma \overset{\theta_s(\eta)}{\vdash_{\mathbf{r}}} s : T \qquad \Gamma \overset{\theta_p(\eta)}{\vdash_{\mathbf{r}}} p : T \qquad (1),(2) \\[4pt] \Gamma \overset{\theta_{(t,1)} \rightsquigarrow (\beta=1)}{\vdash_{\mathbf{r}}} t : \{\beta \in \mathbf{R}\} \end{array}}{\Gamma \overset{\theta(\eta)}{\vdash_{\mathbf{r}}} \textbf{if } t \textbf{ then } s \textbf{ else } p : T}$$

Again, the formula $\psi(\eta)$ should be read as ψ when T is a higher-order type, and as $\psi \rightsquigarrow \eta$ when T is a ground type. The side-conditions (1), (2) are given as:

1. $\models \theta \Rightarrow \left((\theta^s \vee \theta^p) \wedge (\theta^{(t,1)} \vee \theta^p) \wedge (\theta^{(t,0)} \vee \theta^s) \wedge (\theta_t \vee (\theta_s \wedge \theta_p)) \right)$.
2. For all logical assignment σ compatible with $G\Gamma$, $\sigma \models \theta \wedge \neg \theta_t$ implies $H\Gamma \vdash s\sigma^{G\Gamma} \equiv^{ctx} p\sigma^{G\Gamma}$.

Fig. 5: Typing Rules for the if-then-else construct

Example 7. Using our if-then-else typing rule, we can indeed type the program in Figure 3b as expected:

$$\vdash \lambda x.\textbf{if } x < 0 \textbf{ then } 1 \textbf{ else } x + 1 : \{\alpha \in \mathbf{R}\} \overset{\top \rightsquigarrow \top}{\rightarrow} \{\beta \in \mathbf{R}\}.$$

6.4   Open-logical Predicates for Refinement Types

Our goal in this section is to show the correctness of our refinement type systems, that we state below.

Theorem 3. *Let t be any program such that:*

$$x_1 : \{\alpha_1 \in \mathbf{R}\}, \ldots, x_n : \{\alpha_n \in \mathbf{R}\} \overset{\theta \rightsquigarrow \theta'}{\vdash_{\mathbf{r}}} t : \{\beta \in \mathbf{R}\}.$$

Then it holds that:

- $[\![t]\!](Dom(\theta)^{\alpha_1, \ldots, \alpha_n}) \subseteq Dom(\theta')^{\beta}$;
- $[\![t]\!]$ *is sequentially continuous on* $Dom(\theta)^{\alpha_1, \ldots, \alpha_n}$.

As a first step, we show that our if-then-else rule is reasonable, i.e. that it behaves well with primitive functions in $\mathfrak{F}$. More precisely, if we suppose that the functions f, g_0, g_1 are such that the premises of the if-then-else rule hold, then the program $\textbf{if } \underline{f}(x_1, \ldots, x_n) \textbf{ then } \underline{g_1}(x_1, \ldots, x_n) \textbf{ else } \underline{g_0}(x_1, \ldots, x_n)$ is indeed continuous in the domain specified by the conclusion of the rule. This is precisely what we prove in the following lemma.

Lemma 4. *Let $f, g_0, g_1 : \mathbf{R}^n \to \mathbf{R}$ be functions in $\mathfrak{F}$, and $\Theta = x_1 : \{\alpha_1 \in \mathbf{R}\}, \ldots, x_n : \{\alpha_n \in \mathbf{R}\}$. We denote $\boldsymbol{\alpha}$ the list of logical variables $\alpha_1, \ldots, \alpha_n$. We consider logical formulas θ and $\theta_f, \theta_{(f,0)}, \theta_{(f,1)}, \phi_{g_0}, \phi_{g_1}$ that have their logical variables in $\boldsymbol{\alpha}$, and such that:*

1. f is continuous on $Dom(\theta)^\alpha$ with $f(Dom(\theta_f)^\alpha) \subseteq \{0,1\}$ and $f(Dom(\theta_{(f,b)})^\alpha) \subseteq \{b\}$ for $b \in \{0,1\}$.

2. g_0 and g_1 are continuous on $Dom(\phi_{g_0})^\alpha$, and $Dom(\phi_{g_1})^\alpha$ respectively, and $(\alpha_1 \mapsto a_1, \ldots, \alpha_n \mapsto a_n) \models \theta \wedge \neg\theta_f$ implies $g_0(a_1, \ldots, a_n) = g_1(a_1, \ldots, a_n)$;

3. $\models \theta \Rightarrow \left((\phi_{g_1} \vee \phi_{g_0}) \wedge (\theta_{(f,0)} \vee \phi_{g_1}) \wedge (\theta_{(f,1)} \vee \phi_{g_0}) \wedge (\theta_f \vee (\phi_{g_0} \wedge \phi_{g_1})) \right)$.

Then it holds that:

$$[\![\overline{\Theta} \vdash \texttt{if } \underline{f}(x_1, \ldots, x_n) \texttt{ then } \underline{g_1}(x_1, \ldots, x_n) \texttt{ else } \underline{g_0}(x_1, \ldots, x_n) : \texttt{R}]\!]$$

is continuous on $Dom(\theta)^\alpha$.

Proof. The proof can be found in the extended version [7]. □

Similarly to what we did in Section 4, we are going to show Theorem 3 by way of a logical predicate. Recall that the logical predicate we defined in Section 4 consists actually of *three* kind of predicates—all defined in Definition 1 of Section 4: $\mathcal{F}_\tau^\Theta$, $\mathcal{F}_\Gamma^\Theta$, $\mathcal{F}_\tau^{\Theta,\Gamma}$, where Θ ranges over ground typing environments, Γ ranges over arbitrary environments, and τ is a type. The first predicate $\mathcal{F}_\tau^\Theta$ contains admissible terms t of type $\Theta \vdash t : \tau$, the second predicate $\mathcal{F}_\Gamma^\Theta$ contains admissible substitutions γ that associate to every $(x : \tau)$ in Γ a term of type τ under the typing context Θ, and the third predicate $\mathcal{F}_\tau^{\Theta,\Gamma}$ contains admissible terms t of type $\Gamma, \Theta \vdash t : \tau$.

Here, we need to adapt the three kinds of logical predicates to a refinement scenario: first, we replace τ and Θ, Γ with refinement types and refined typing contexts respectively. Moreover, for technical reasons, we also need to *generalize* our typing contexts, by allowing them to be annotated with any subset of $\mathbb{R}^n$ instead of restricting ourselves to those subsets generated by logical formulas. Due to this further complexity, we split our definition of logical predicates into two: we first define the counterpart of the ground typing context predicate $\mathcal{F}_\tau^\Theta$ in Definition 4, then the counterpart of the predicate for substitutions $\mathcal{F}_\Gamma^\Theta$ and the counterpart of the predicates $\mathcal{F}_\tau^{\Theta,\Gamma}$ for higher-order typing environment in Definition 5.

Let us first see how we can adapt the predicates $\mathcal{F}_\tau^\Theta$ to our refinement types setting. Recall that in Section 4, we defined the predicate $\mathcal{F}_\texttt{R}^\Theta$ as the collection of terms t such that $\Theta \vdash t : \texttt{R}$, and its semantics $[\![\Theta \vdash t : \texttt{R}]\!]$ belongs to $\mathfrak{F}$. As we are interested in local continuity properties, we need to build a predicate expressing local continuity constraints. Moreover, in order to be consistent with our two arrow constructs and our two kinds of typing judgments, we actually need to consider also *two* kinds of logical predicates, depending on whether the target type we consider is a real type or an higher-order type. We thus introduce the following logical predicates:

$$\mathcal{C}(\Theta, X \rightsquigarrow \phi, F); \qquad \mathcal{C}(\Theta, X, H);$$

where Θ is a ground typing environment, X is a subset of $\mathbb{R}^n$, ϕ is a logical formula, and, as usual, F ranges over the real refinements types, while H ranges over the higher-order refinement types. As expected, X and ϕ are needed to encode continuity constraints inside our logical predicates.

Definition 4. *Let Θ be a* ground *typing context of length n, F and H refined ground type and higher-order type, respectively. We define families of predicates on terms $\mathcal{C}(\Theta, Y \rightsquigarrow \phi, F)$ and $\mathcal{C}(\Theta, Y, H)$, with $Y \subseteq \mathbb{R}^n$ and ϕ a logical formula, as specified in Figure 6.*

- For $F = \{\alpha \in \mathbb{R}\}$ we take:

$$\mathcal{C}(\Theta, Y \rightsquigarrow \psi, F) := \{t \mid x_1 : \mathbb{R}, \ldots, x_n : \mathbb{R} \vdash t : \mathbb{R},$$
$$[\![t]\!](Y) \subseteq \mathrm{Dom}(\psi)^\alpha \wedge [\![t]\!] \text{ continuous over } Y\}.$$

- if H is an arrow type of the form $H = (H_1, \ldots, H_m, \{\alpha_1 \in \mathbb{R}_1\}, \ldots, \{\alpha_p \in \mathbb{R}\}) \overset{\psi(\eta)}{\rightsquigarrow} T$:

$$\mathcal{C}(\Theta, Y, H) := \{t \mid x_1 : \mathbb{R}, \ldots, x_n : \mathbb{R} \vdash t : \overline{H},$$
$$\forall Z, \forall \boldsymbol{s} = (s_1, \ldots, s_m) \text{ with } s_i \in \mathcal{C}(\Theta, Z, H_i),$$
$$\forall \boldsymbol{p} = (p_1, \ldots p_p), \forall \psi^j \text{ with } \models \psi^1 \wedge \ldots \wedge \psi^p \Rightarrow \psi,$$
$$\text{and } p_j \in \mathcal{C}(\Theta, Z \rightsquigarrow \psi^j, \{\alpha_j \in \mathbb{R}\}),$$
$$\text{it holds that } t(\boldsymbol{s}, \boldsymbol{p}) \in \mathcal{C}(\Theta, (Y \cap Z)(\eta), T)\},$$

where as usual we should read $\psi(\eta) = \psi$, $(Y \cap Z)(\eta) = Y \cap Z$ when T is higher-order, and $\psi(\eta) = \psi \rightsquigarrow \eta$, $(Y \cap Z)(\eta) = (Y \cap Z) \rightsquigarrow \eta$ when T is an annotated real type.

Fig. 6: Open Logical Predicates for Refinement Types.

Example 8. We illustrate Definition 4 on some examples. We denote by B° the open unit ball in $\mathbb{R}^2$, i.e. $B^\circ = \{(a, b) \in \mathbb{R}^2 \mid a^2 + b^2 < 1\}$. We consider the ground typing context $\Theta = x_1 : \{\alpha_1 \in \mathbb{R}\}, x_2 : \{\alpha_2 \in \mathbb{R}\}$.

- We look first at the predicate $\mathcal{C}(\Theta, B^\circ \rightsquigarrow (\beta > 0), \{\beta \in \mathbb{R}\})$. It consists of all programs $x_1 : \mathbb{R}, x_2 : \mathbb{R} \vdash t : \mathbb{R}$ such that $[\![x_1 : \mathbb{R}, x_2 : \mathbb{R} \vdash t : \mathbb{R}]\!]$ is continuous on the open unit ball, and takes only strictly positive values there.
- We look now at an example when the target type T is *higher-order*. We take $H = \{\beta_1 \in \mathbb{R}\} \overset{(\beta_1 \geq 0) \rightsquigarrow (\beta_2 \geq 0)}{\rightsquigarrow} \{\beta_2 \in \mathbb{R}\}$, and we look at the logical predicate $\mathcal{C}(\Theta, B^\circ, H)$. We are going to show that the latter contains, for instance, the program:

$$t = \lambda w.\underline{f}(w, x_1^2 + y_1^2) \qquad \text{where } f(w, a) = \frac{w}{1 - a} \text{ if } a < 1; 0 \text{ otherwise.}$$

Looking at Figure 6, we see that it is enough to check that for any $Y \subseteq \mathbb{R}^2$ and any $s \in \mathcal{C}(\Theta, Y \rightsquigarrow (\beta_1 \geq 0), \{\beta_1 \in \mathbb{R}\})$, it holds that:

$$ts \in \mathcal{C}(\Theta, B^\circ \cap Y \rightsquigarrow (\beta_2 \geq 0), \{\beta_2 \in \mathbb{R}\}).$$

Our overall goal—in order to prove Theorem 3—is to show the counterpart of the Fundamental Lemma from Section 4 (i.e. Lemma 1), which states that the logical predicate $\mathcal{F}_R^\Theta$ contains all well-typed terms. This lemma only talks about the logical predicates for *ground typing contexts*, so we can state it as of now, but its proof is based on the fact that we dispose of the *three* predicates. Observe that from there, Theorem 3 follows just from the definition of the logical predicates on base types. Similarly to what we did for Lemma 1 in Section 4, *proving* it requires to define the logical predicates for *substitutions* and *higher-order typing contexts*. We do this in Definition 5 below. As before, they consist in an adaptation to our refinement types framework of the open logical predicates $\mathcal{F}_\Theta^\Gamma$ and $\mathcal{F}_\tau^{\Theta,\Gamma}$ of Section 4: as usual, we need to add continuity annotations, and distinguish whether the target type is a ground type or an higher-order type.

Notation 2. *We need to first introduce the following notation: let Γ, Θ be two ground non-refined typing environments of length m and n respectively–and with disjoint support. Let $\gamma : \mathsf{supp}(\Gamma) \to \{t \mid \overline{\Theta} \vdash t : \mathsf{R}\}$ be a substitution. We write $[\![\gamma]\!]$ for the real-valued function:*

$$[\![\gamma]\!] : \mathbb{R}^n \to \mathbb{R}^{n+m}$$

$$\boldsymbol{a} \mapsto (\boldsymbol{a}, [\![\gamma(x_1)]\!](\boldsymbol{a}), \dots, [\![\gamma(x_m)]\!](\boldsymbol{a}))$$

Definition 5. *Let Θ be a ground typing environment of length n, and Γ an arbitrary typing environment. We note n and m the lengths of respectively Θ and $G\Gamma$.*

- *Let $Z \subseteq \mathbb{R}^n, W \subseteq \mathbb{R}^{n+m}$. We define $\mathcal{C}(\Theta, Z \rightsquigarrow W, \Gamma)$ as the set of those substitutions $\gamma : \mathsf{supp}(\Gamma) \to \{t \mid \overline{\Theta} \vdash t : \mathsf{R}\}$ such that:*
  - *$\forall (x : H) \in H\Gamma,\, \gamma(x) \in \mathcal{C}(\Theta, Z, H)$,*
  - *$[\![\gamma_{|G\Gamma}]\!] : \mathbb{R}^n \to \mathbb{R}^{n+m}$ sends continuously Z into W;*
- *Let $W \subseteq \mathbb{R}^{n+m}$, $F = \{\alpha \in \mathsf{R}\}$ an annotated real type, and ψ a logical formula with $\mathit{Vars}(\psi) \subseteq \{\alpha\}$. We define:*

$$\mathcal{C}((\Gamma; \Theta), W \rightsquigarrow \psi, F) := \{t \mid \overline{\Gamma, \Theta} \vdash t : \mathsf{R}$$
$$\wedge\, \forall X \subseteq \mathbb{R}^n, \forall \gamma \in \mathcal{C}(\Theta, X \rightsquigarrow W, \Gamma),\, t\gamma \in \mathcal{C}(\Theta, X \rightsquigarrow \psi, F)\}.$$

- *Let $W \subseteq \mathbb{R}^{n+m}$, and H an higher-order refined type. We define :*

$$\mathcal{C}((\Gamma; \Theta), W, H) := \{t \mid \overline{\Gamma, \Theta} \vdash t : \overline{H}$$
$$\wedge\, \forall X \subseteq \mathbb{R}^n, \forall \gamma \in \mathcal{C}(\Theta, X \rightsquigarrow W, \Gamma).\, t\gamma \in \mathcal{C}(\Theta, X, H)\}.$$

Example 9. We illustrate Definition 5 on an example. We consider the same context Θ as in Example 8, i.e. $\Theta = x_1 : \{\alpha_1 \in \mathsf{R}\}, x_2 : \{\alpha_2 \in \mathsf{R}\}$, and we take $\Gamma = x_3 : \{\alpha_3 \in \mathsf{R}\}, z : H$, with $H = \{\beta_1 \in \mathsf{R}\}^{(\beta_1 \geq 0) \rightsquigarrow (\beta_2 \geq 0)} \{\beta_2 \in \mathsf{R}\}$. We are interested in the following logical predicate for substitution:

$$\mathcal{C}(\Theta, B^\circ \rightsquigarrow \{(v, |v|) \mid v \in B^\circ)\}, \Gamma)$$

where the norm of the couple (a, b) is taken as: $|(a, b)| = \sqrt{a^2 + b^2}$. We are going to build a substitution $\gamma : \{x_3, z\} \to \Lambda_{\mathfrak{F}}^{\times, \to, \mathsf{R}}$ that belongs to this set. We take:

- $\gamma(z) = \lambda w . f(w, x_1^2 + x_2^2)$ where $f(w, a) = \frac{w}{1-a}$ if $a < 1$; 0 otherwise.
- $\gamma(x_3) = (\sqrt{\cdot})(x_1^2 + x_2^2)$.

We can check that the requirements of Definition 5 indeed hold for γ:

- $\gamma(z) \in \mathcal{C}(\Theta, B^\circ, H)$—see Example 8;
- $[\![\gamma_{|G\Gamma}]\!] : \mathbb{R} \times \mathbb{R} \to \mathbb{R}^3$ is continuous on B°, and moreover sends B° into $\{(v, |v|) \mid v \in B^\circ)\}$. Looking at our definition of the semantics of a substitution, we see that $[\![\gamma_{|G\Gamma}]\!](a, b) = (a, b, |(a, b)|)$, thus the requirements above hold.

Lemma 5 (Fundamental Lemma). *Let Θ be a ground typing context, and Γ an arbitrary typing context–thus Γ can contain both ground type variables and non-ground type variables.*

- *Suppose that $\Gamma, \Theta \vdash_r^{\theta \leadsto \eta} t : F$: then $t \in \mathcal{C}(\Gamma; \Theta, Dom(\theta) \leadsto \eta, F)$.*
- *Suppose that $\Gamma, \Theta \vdash_r^{\theta} t : H$: then $t \in \mathcal{C}(\Gamma; \Theta, Dom(\theta), H)$.*

Proof Sketch. The proof is by induction on the derivation of the refined typing judgment. Along the lines, we need to show that our logical predicates play well with the underlying denotational semantics, but also with logic. The details can be found in the extended version [7]. □

From there, we can finally prove the main result of this section, i.e. Theorem 3, that states the correctness of our refinement type system. Indeed, Lemma 5 has Theorem 3 as a corollary: from there it is enough to look at the definition of the logical predicate for first-order programs to finally show the correctness of our type system.

7 Related Work

Logical relations are certainly one of the most well-studied concepts in higher-order programming language theory. In their unary version, they have been introduced by Tait [54], and further exploited by Girard [33] and Tait [55] himself in giving strong normalization proofs for second-order type systems. The relational counterpart of realizability, namely logical relations proper, have been introduced by Plotkin [48], and further developed along many different axes, and in particular towards calculi with fixpoint constructs or recursive types [3,4,2], probabilistic choice [14], or monadic and algebraic effects [34,11,34]. Without any hope to be comprehensive, we may refer to Mitchell's textbook on programming language theory for a comprehensive account about the earlier, classic definitions [43], or to aforementioned papers for more recent developments.

Extensions of logical relations to open terms have been introduced by several authors [39,47,30,53,15] and were explicitly referred to as *open logical relations* in [59]. However, to the best of the authors' knowledge, all the aforementioned works use open logical relations for specific purposes, and do not investigate their applicability as a general methodology.

Special cases of our Containment Theorem can be found in many papers, typically as auxiliary results. As already mentioned, an example is the one of higher-order polynomials, whose first-order terms are proved to compute proper polynomials in many ways [40,5], none of them in the style of logical relations. The Containment Theorem itself can be derived by a previous result by Lafont [41] (see also Theorem 4.10.7 in [24]). Contrary to such a result, however, our proof of the Containment Theorem is entirely syntactical and consists of a straightforward application of open logical relations.

Algorithms for automatic differentiation have recently been extended to higher-order programming languages [50,46,51,42,45], and have been investigated from a semantical perspective in [16,1] relying on insights from linear logic and denotational semantics. In particular, the work of Huot et al. [37] provides a denotational proof of correctness of the program transformation of [50] that we have studied in Section 5.

Continuity and robustness analysis of imperative first-order programs by way of program logics is the topic of study of a series of papers by Chaudhuri and co-authors [19,18,20]. None of them, however, deal with higher-order programs.

8   Conclusion and Future Work

We have showed how a mild variation on the concept of a logical relation can be fruitfully used for proving both predicative and relational properties of higher-order programming languages, when such properties have a first-order, rather than a ground "flavor". As such, the added value of this contribution is not much in the technique itself, but in showing how it is extremely useful in heterogeneous contexts, this way witnessing the versatility of logical relations.

The three case studies, and in particular the correctness of automatic differentiation and refinement type-based continuity analysis, are given as proof-of-concepts, but this does not mean they do not deserve to be studied more in depth. An example of an interesting direction for future work is the extension of our correctness proof from Section 5 to backward propagation differentiation algorithms. Another one consists in adapting the refinement type system of Section 6.1 to deal with differentiability. That would of course require a substantial change in the typing rule for conditionals, which should take care of checking not only continuity, but also differentiability at the critical points. It would also be interesting to implement the refinement type system using standard SMT-based approaches. Finally, the authors plan to investigate extensions of open logical relations to non-normalizing calculi, as well as to non-simply typed calculi (such as calculi with polymorphic or recursive types).

References

1. Abadi, M., Plotkin, G.D.: A simple differentiable programming language. PACMPL 4(POPL), 38:1–38:28 (2020)

2. Ahmed, A.J.: Step-indexed syntactic logical relations for recursive and quantified types. In: Proc. of ESOP 2006. pp. 69–83 (2006)
3. Appel, A.W., McAllester, D.A.: An indexed model of recursive types for foundational proof-carrying code. ACM Trans. Program. Lang. Syst. 23(5), 657–683 (2001)
4. Appel, A.W., Mellies, P.A., Richards, C.D., Vouillon, J.: A very modal model of a modern, major, general type system. In: ACM SIGPLAN Notices. vol. 42, pp. 109–122. ACM (2007)
5. Baillot, P., Dal Lago, U.: Higher-order interpretations and program complexity. In: Proc. of CSL 2012. Schloss Dagstuhl-Leibniz-Zentrum fuer Informatik (2012)
6. Barendregt, H.P.: The lambda calculus: its syntax and semantics. North-Holland (1984)
7. Barthe, G., Crubillé, R., Dal Lago, U., Gavazzo, F.: On the versatility of open logical relations: Continuity, automatic differentiation, and a containment theorem (long version) (2019), available at https://arxiv.org/abs/2002.08489
8. Bartholomew-Biggs, M., Brown, S., Christianson, B., Dixon, L.: Automatic differentiation of algorithms. Journal of Computational and Applied Mathematics 124(1), 171 – 190 (2000), numerical Analysis 2000. Vol. IV: Optimization and Nonlinear Equations
9. Baydin, A.G., Pearlmutter, B.A., Radul, A.A., Siskind, J.M.: Automatic differentiation in machine learning: a survey. Journal of Machine Learning Research 18, 153:1–153:43 (2017)
10. Benton, N., Hofmann, M., Nigam, V.: Abstract effects and proof-relevant logical relations. In: Proc. of POPL 2014. pp. 619–632 (2014)
11. Biernacki, D., Piróg, M., Polesiuk, P., Sieczkowski, F.: Handle with care: relational interpretation of algebraic effects and handlers. PACMPL 2(POPL), 8:1–8:30 (2018)
12. Birkedal, L., Jaber, G., Sieczkowski, F., Thamsborg, J.: A kripke logical relation for effect-based program transformations. Inf. Comput. 249, 160–189 (2016)
13. Birkedal, L., Sieczkowski, F., Thamsborg, J.: A concurrent logical relation. In: Proc. of CSL 2012. pp. 107–121 (2012)
14. Bizjak, A., Birkedal, L.: Step-indexed logical relations for probability. In: Proc. of FoSSaCS 2015. pp. 279–294 (2015)
15. Bowman, W.J., Ahmed, A.: Noninterference for free. In: Proc. of ICFP 2015. pp. 101–113 (2015)
16. Brunel, A., Mazza, D., Pagani, M.: Backpropagation in the simply typed lambda-calculus with linear negation. PACMPL 4(POPL), 64:1–64:27 (2020)
17. Brunel, A., Terui, K.: Church => scott = ptime: an application of resource sensitive realizability. In: Proc. of DICE 2010. pp. 31–46 (2010)
18. Chaudhuri, S., Gulwani, S., Lublinerman, R.: Continuity analysis of programs. In: Proc. of POPL 2010. pp. 57–70 (2010)
19. Chaudhuri, S., Gulwani, S., Lublinerman, R.: Continuity and robustness of programs. Commun. ACM 55(8), 107–115 (2012)
20. Chaudhuri, S., Gulwani, S., Lublinerman, R., NavidPour, S.: Proving programs robust. In: Proc. of SIGSOFT/FSE 2011. pp. 102–112 (2011)
21. Clifford: Preliminary Sketch of Biquaternions. Proceedings of the London Mathematical Society s1-4(1), 381–395 (11 1871)
22. Cook, S.A., Kapron, B.M.: Characterizations of the basic feasible functionals of finite type (extended abstract). In: 30th Annual Symposium on Foundations of Computer Science, Research Triangle Park, North Carolina, USA, 30 October - 1 November 1989. pp. 154–159 (1989)

23. Crary, K., Harper, R.: Syntactic logical relations for polymorphic and recursive types. Electr. Notes Theor. Comput. Sci. **172**, 259–299 (2007)
24. Crole, R.L.: Categories for Types. Cambridge mathematical textbooks, Cambridge University Press (1993)
25. Dreyer, D., Neis, G., Birkedal, L.: The impact of higher-order state and control effects on local relational reasoning. J. Funct. Program. **22**(4-5), 477–528 (2012)
26. Edalat, A.: The domain of differentiable functions. Electr. Notes Theor. Comput. Sci. **40**, 144 (2000)
27. Edalat, A., Lieutier, A.: Domain theory and differential calculus (functions of one variable). In: Proc. of LICS 2002. pp. 277–286 (2002)
28. Elliott, C.: The simple essence of automatic differentiation. PACMPL **2**(ICFP), 70:1–70:29 (2018)
29. Escardó, M.H., Ho, W.K.: Operational domain theory and topology of sequential programming languages. Inf. Comput. **207**(3), 411–437 (2009)
30. Fiore, M.P.: Semantic analysis of normalisation by evaluation for typed lambda calculus. In: Proc. of PPDP 2002. pp. 26–37 (2002)
31. Freeman, T., Pfenning, F.: Refinement types for ml. In: Proceedings of the ACM SIGPLAN 1991 Conference on Programming Language Design and Implementation. pp. 268–277. PLDI '91 (1991)
32. Gianantonio, P.D., Edalat, A.: A language for differentiable functions. In: Proc. of FOSSACS 2013. pp. 337–352 (2013)
33. Girard, J.Y.: Une extension de l'interpretation de gödel a l'analyse, et son application a l'elimination des coupures dans l'analyse et la theorie des types. In: Studies in Logic and the Foundations of Mathematics, vol. 63, pp. 63–92. Elsevier (1971)
34. Goubault-Larrecq, J., Lasota, S., Nowak, D.: Logical relations for monadic types. In: International Workshop on Computer Science Logic. pp. 553–568. Springer (2002)
35. Griewank, A., Walther, A.: Evaluating Derivatives: Principles and Techniques of Algorithmic Differentiation. Society for Industrial and Applied Mathematics, Philadelphia, PA, USA, second edn. (2008)
36. Hofmann, M.: Logical relations and nondeterminism. In: Software, Services, and Systems - Essays Dedicated to Martin Wirsing on the Occasion of His Retirement from the Chair of Programming and Software Engineering. pp. 62–74 (2015)
37. Huot, M., Staton, S., Vákár, M.: Correctness of automatic differentiation via diffeologies and categorical gluing (2020), to appear in Proc. of ESOP 2020 (long version available at http://arxiv.org/abs/2001.02209
38. Jaber, G.: Syteci: automating contextual equivalence for higher-order programs with references. PACMPL **4**(POPL), 59:1–59:28 (2020)
39. Jung, A., Tiuryn, J.: A new characterization of lambda definability. In: Proc. of TLCA 1993. pp. 245–257 (1993)
40. Kapron, B.M., Cook, S.A.: A new characterization of type-2 feasibility. SIAM J. Comput. **25**(1), 117–132 (1996)
41. Lafont, Y.: Logiques, catégories & machines: implantation de langages de programmation guidée par la logique catégorique. Institut national de recherche en informatique et en automatique (1988)
42. Manzyuk, O., Pearlmutter, B.A., Radul, A.A., Rush, D.R., Siskind, J.M.: Perturbation confusion in forward automatic differentiation of higher-order functions. J. Funct. Program. **29**, e12 (2019)
43. Mitchell, J.C.: Foundations for programming languages. Foundation of computing series, MIT Press (1996)

44. Owens, S., Myreen, M.O., Kumar, R., Tan, Y.K.: Functional big-step semantics. In: Proc. of ESOP 2016. pp. 589–615 (2016)
45. Pearlmutter, B.A., Siskind, J.M.: Lazy multivariate higher-order forward-mode AD. In: Proc. of POPL 2007. pp. 155–160 (2007)
46. Pearlmutter, B.A., Siskind, J.M.: Reverse-mode AD in a functional framework: Lambda the ultimate backpropagator. ACM Trans. Program. Lang. Syst. **30**(2), 7:1–7:36 (2008)
47. Pitts, A.M., Stark, I.D.B.: Observable properties of higher order functions that dynamically create local names, or what's new? In: Proc. of MFCS 1993. pp. 122–141 (1993)
48. Plotkin, G.: Lambda-definability and logical relations. Edinburgh University (1973)
49. Rumelhart, D.E., Hinton, G.E., Williams, R.J.: Neurocomputing: Foundations of research. chap. Learning Representations by Back-propagating Errors, pp. 696–699. MIT Press (1988)
50. Shaikhha, A., Fitzgibbon, A., Vytiniotis, D., Peyton Jones, S.: Efficient differentiable programming in a functional array-processing language. PACMPL **3**(ICFP), 97:1–97:30 (2019)
51. Siskind, J.M., Pearlmutter, B.A.: Nesting forward-mode AD in a functional framework. Higher-Order and Symbolic Computation **21**(4), 361–376 (2008)
52. Spivak, M.: Calculus On Manifolds: A Modern Approach To Classical Theorems Of Advanced Calculus. Avalon Publishing (1971)
53. Staton, S., Yang, H., Wood, F.D., Heunen, C., Kammar, O.: Semantics for probabilistic programming: higher-order functions, continuous distributions, and soft constraints. In: Proc. of LICS 2016. pp. 525–534 (2016)
54. Tait, W.W.: Intensional interpretations of functionals of finite type i. Journal of Symbolic Logic **32**(2), 198–212 (1967)
55. Tait, W.W.: A realizability interpretation of the theory of species. In: Logic Colloquium. pp. 240–251. Springer, Berlin, Heidelberg (1975)
56. Turon, A.J., Thamsborg, J., Ahmed, A., Birkedal, L., Dreyer, D.: Logical relations for fine-grained concurrency. In: Proc. of POPL 2013. pp. 343–356 (2013)
57. Vuillemin, J.: Exact real computer arithmetic with continued fractions. IEEE Trans. Comput. **39**(8), 1087–1105 (1990)
58. Weihrauch, K.: Computable Analysis: An Introduction. Texts in Theoretical Computer Science. An EATCS Series, Springer Berlin Heidelberg (2000)
59. Zhao, J., Zhang, Q., Zdancewic, S.: Relational parametricity for a polymorphic linear lambda calculus. In: Proc. of APLAS 2010. pp. 344–359 (2010)

Constructive Game Logic *

Rose Bohrer[1] and André Platzer[1,2]

[1] Computer Science Department, Carnegie Mellon University, Pittsburgh, USA
aplatzer@cs.cmu.edu
[2] Fakultät für Informatik, Technische Universität München, München, Germany

Abstract. Game Logic is an excellent setting to study proofs-about-programs via the interpretation of those proofs as programs, because constructive proofs for games correspond to effective winning strategies to follow in response to the opponent's actions. We thus develop *Constructive Game Logic*, which extends Parikh's Game Logic (GL) with constructivity and with first-order programs *à la* Pratt's first-order dynamic logic (DL). Our major contributions include: 1. a novel realizability semantics capturing the adversarial dynamics of games, 2. a natural deduction calculus and operational semantics describing the computational meaning of strategies via proof-terms, and 3. theoretical results including soundness of the proof calculus w.r.t. realizability semantics, progress and preservation of the operational semantics of proofs, and Existential Properties enabling the extraction of computational artifacts from game proofs. Together, these results provide the most general account of a Curry-Howard interpretation for any program logic to date, and the first at all for Game Logic.

Keywords: Game Logic, Constructive Logic, Natural Deduction, Proof Terms

1 Introduction

Two of the most essential tools in theory of programming languages are *program logics*, such as Hoare calculi [29] and dynamic logics [45], and the *Curry-Howard correspondence* [17,31], wherein propositions correspond to types, proofs to functional programs, and proof term normalization to program evaluation. Their intersection, the Curry-Howard interpretation of program logics, has received surprisingly little study. We undertake such a study in the setting of Game Logic (GL) [38], because this leads to novel insights, because the Curry-Howard correspondence can be explained particularly intuitively for games, and because our first-order GL is a superset of common logics such as first-order Dynamic Logic (DL).

Constructivity and program verification have met before: Higher-order constructive logics [16] obey the Curry-Howard correspondence and are used to

---

* This research was sponsored by the AFOSR under grant number FA9550-16-1-0288. The authors were also funded by the NDSEG Fellowship and Alexander von Humboldt Foundation, respectively.

P. Müller (Ed.): ESOP 2020, LNCS 12075, pp. 84–111, 2020.
https://doi.org/10.1007/978-3-030-44914-8_4

develop verified functional programs. Program logics are also often embedded in constructive proof assistants such as Coq [48], inheriting constructivity from their metalogic. Both are excellent ways to develop verified software, but we study something else.

We study the computational content of a program logic *itself*. Every fundamental concept of computation is expected to manifest in all three of logic, type systems, and category theory [27]. Because dynamics logics (DL's) such as GL have shown that program execution is a first-class construct in modal logic, the theorist has an imperative to explore the underlying notion of computation by developing a constructive GL with a Curry-Howard interpretation.

The computational content of a proof is especially clear in GL, which generalizes DL to programmatic models of zero-sum, perfect-information games between two players, traditionally named Angel and Demon. Both normal-play and misère-play games can be modeled in GL. In classical GL, the diamond modality $\langle \alpha \rangle \phi$ and box modality $[\alpha]\phi$ say that Angel and Demon respectively have a strategy to ensure ϕ is true at the end of α, which is a model of a game. The difference between classical GL and CGL is that classical GL allows proofs that exclude the middle, which correspond to strategies which branch on undecidable conditions. CGL proofs can branch only on decidable properties, thus they correspond to strategies which are *effective* and can be executed by computer. Effective strategies are crucial because they enable the synthesis of code that implements a strategy. Strategy synthesis is itself crucial because even simple games can have complicated strategies, and synthesis provides assurance that the implementation correctly solves the game. A GL strategy resolves the choices inherent in a game: a diamond strategy specifies every move made by the Angel player, while a box strategy specifies the moves the Demon player will make.

In developing *Constructive Game Logic* (CGL), adding constructivity is a deep change. We provide a natural deduction calculus for CGL equipped with proof terms and an operational semantics on the proofs, demonstrating the meaning of strategies as functional programs and of winning strategies as functional programs that are guaranteed to achieve their objective no matter what counterstrategy the opponent follows. While the proof calculus of a constructive logic is often taken as ground truth, we go a step further and develop a realizability semantics for CGL as programs performing winning strategies for game proofs, then prove the calculus sound against it. We adopt realizability semantics in contrast to the winning-region semantics of classical GL because it enables us to prove that CGL satisfies novel properties (Section 8). The proof of our Strategy Property (Theorem 2) constitutes an (on-paper) algorithm that computes a player's (effective) strategy from a proof that they can win a game. This is the key test of constructivity for CGL, which would not be possible in classical GL. We show that CGL proofs have *two* computational interpretations: the operational semantics interpret an arbitrary proof (strategy) as a functional program which reduces to a normal-form proof (strategy), while realizability semantics interpret Angel strategies as programs which defeat arbitrary Demonic opponents.

While CGL has ample theoretical motivation, the practical motivations from synthesis are also strong. A notable line of work on dGL extends first-order GL to hybrid games to verify safety-critical adversarial cyber-physical systems [42]. We have designed CGL to extend smoothly to hybrid games, where synthesis provides the correctness demanded by safety-critical systems and the synthesis of correct monitors of the external world [36].

2   Related Work

This work is at the intersection of game logic and constructive modal logics. Individually, they have a rich literature, but little work has been done at their intersection. Of these, we are the first for GL and the first with a proofs-as-programs interpretation for a full first-order program logic.

Games in Logic. Parikh's propositional GL [38] was followed by coalitional GL [39]. A first-order version of GL is the basis of differential game logic dGL [42] for hybrid games. GL's are unique in their clear delegation of strategy to the *proof* language rather than the *model* language, crucially allowing succinct game specifications with sophisticated winning strategies. Succinct specifications are important: specifications are *trusted* because proving the *wrong theorem* would not ensure correctness. Relatives without this separation include Strategy Logic [15], Alternating-Time Temporal Logic (ATL) [5], CATL [30], Ghosh's SDGL [24], Ramanujam's structured strategies [46], Dynamic-epistemic logics [6,10,49], evidence logics [9], and Angelic Hoare logic [35].

Constructive Modal Logics. A major contribution of CGL is our constructive semantics for games, not to be confused with game semantics [1], which are used to give programs semantics *in terms of* games. We draw on work in semantics for constructive modal logics, of which two main approaches are intuitionistic Kripke semantics and realizability semantics.

An overview of Intuitionistic Kripke semantics is given by Wijesekera [52]. Intuitionistic Kripke semantics are parameterized over worlds, but in contrast to classical Kripke semantics, possible worlds represent what is currently *known* of the state. Worlds are preordered by $w_1 \geq w_2$ when w_1 contains at least the knowledge in w_2. Kripke semantics were used in Constructive Concurrent DL [53], where both the world and knowledge of it change during execution. A key advantage of realizability semantics [37,33] is their explicit interpretation of constructivity as computability by giving a *realizer*, a program which witnesses a fact. Our semantics combine elements of both: Strategies are represented by realizers, while the game state is a Kripke world. Constructive set theory [2] aids in understanding which set operations are permissible in constructive semantics.

Modal semantics have also exploited mathematical structures such as: i) Neighborhood models [8], topological models for spatial logics [7], and temporal logics of dynamical systems [20]. ii) Categorical [3], sheaf [28], and pre-sheaf [23] models. iii) Coalgebraic semantics for classical Propositional Dynamic Logic

(PDL) [19]. While games are known to exhibit algebraic structure [25], such laws are not essential to this work. Our semantics are also notable for the seamless interaction between a constructive Angel and a classical Demon.

CGL is first-order, so we must address the constructivity of operations that inspect game state. We consider rational numbers so that equality is decidable, but our work should generalize to constructive reals [11,13].

Intuitionistic modalities also appear in dynamic-epistemic logic (DEL) [21], but that work is interested primarily in proof-theoretic semantics while we employ realizability semantics to stay firmly rooted in computation. Intuitionistic Kripke semantics have also been applied to multimodal System K with iteration [14], a weak fragment of PDL.

Constructivity and Dynamic Logic. With CGL, we bring to fruition several past efforts to develop constructive dynamic logics. Prior work on PDL [18] sought an Existential Property for Propositional Dynamic Logic (PDL), but they questioned the practicality of their own implication introduction rule, whose side condition is non-syntactic. One of our results is a first-order Existential Property, which Degen cited as an open problem beyond the methods of their day [18]. To our knowledge, only one approach [32] considers Curry-Howard or functional proof terms for a program logic. While their work is a notable precursor to ours, their logic is a weak fragment of PDL without tests, monotonicity, or unbounded iteration, while we support not only PDL but the much more powerful first-order GL. Lastly, we are preceded by Constructive Concurrent Dynamic Logic, [53] which gives a Kripke semantics for Concurrent Dynamic Logic [41], a proper fragment of GL. Their work focuses on an epistemic interpretation of constructivity, algebraic laws, and tableaux. We differ in our use of realizability semantics and natural deduction, which were essential to developing a Curry-Howard interpretation for CGL. In summary, we are justified in claiming to have the first Curry-Howard interpretation with proof terms and Existential Properties for an *expressive* program logic, the first constructive game logic, and the only with first-order proof terms.

While constructive natural deduction calculi map most directly to functional programs, proof terms can be generated for any proof calculus, including a well-known interpretation of classical logic as continuation-passing style [26]. Proof terms have been developed [22] for a Hilbert calculus for dL, a dynamic logic (DL) for hybrid systems. Their work focuses on a provably correct interchange format for classical dL proofs, not constructive logics.

3   Syntax

We define the language of CGL, consisting of terms, games, and formulas. The simplest terms are *program variables* $x, y \in \mathcal{V}$ where $\mathcal{V}$ is the set of variable identifiers. Globally-scoped mutable program variables contain the state of the game, also called the *position* in game-theoretic terminology. All variables and terms are rational-valued ($\mathbb{Q}$); we also write $\mathbb{B}$ for the set of Boolean values $\{0, 1\}$ for false and true respectively.

Definition 1 (Terms). *A term f, g is a rational-valued computable function over the game state. We give a nonexhaustive grammar of terms, specifically those used in our examples:*

$$f, g ::= \cdots \mid q \mid x \mid f + g \mid f \cdot g \mid f/g \mid f \bmod g$$

where $q \in \mathbb{Q}$ is a rational literal, x a program variable, $f + g$ a sum, $f \cdot g$ a product. Division-with-remainder is intended for use with integers, but we generalize the standard notion to support rational arguments. Quotient f/g is integer even when f and g are non-integer, and thus leaves a rational remainder $f \bmod g$. Divisors g are assumed to be nonzero.

A game in CGL is played between a constructive player named Angel and a classical player named Demon. Our usage of the names Angel and Demon differs subtly from traditional GL usage for technical reasons. Our Angel and Demon are asymmetric: Angel is "our" player, who must play constructively, while the "opponent" Demon is allowed to play classically because our opponent need not be a computer. At any time some player is *active*, meaning their strategy resolves all decisions, and the opposite player is called *dormant*. Classical GL identifies Angel with active and Demon with dormant; the notions are distinct in CGL.

Definition 2 (Games). *The set of* games α, β *is defined recursively as such:*

$$\alpha, \beta ::= ?\phi \mid x := f \mid x := * \mid \alpha \cup \beta \mid \alpha; \beta \mid \alpha^* \mid \alpha^d$$

In the *test game* $?\phi$, the active player wins if they can exhibit a constructive proof that formula ϕ currently holds. If they do not exhibit a proof, the dormant player wins by default and we informally say the active player "broke the rules". In deterministic assignment games $x := f$, neither player makes a choice, but the program variable x takes on the value of a term f. In nondeterministic assignment games $x := *$, the active player picks a value for $x : \mathbb{Q}$. In the choice game $\alpha \cup \beta$, the active player chooses whether to play game α or game β. In the sequential composition game $\alpha; \beta$, game α is played first, then β from the resulting state. In the repetition game α^*, the active player chooses after each repetition of α whether to continue playing, but loses if they repeat α infinitely. Notably, the exact number of repetitions can depend on the dormant player's moves, so the active player need not know, let alone announce, the exact number of iterations in advance. In the dual game α^d, the active player becomes dormant and vice-versa, then α is played. We parenthesize games with braces $\{\alpha\}$ when necessary. Sequential and nondeterministic composition both associate to the right, i.e., $\alpha \cup \beta \cup \gamma \equiv \{\alpha \cup \{\beta \cup \gamma\}\}$. This does not affect their semantics as both operators are associative, but aids in reading proof terms.

Definition 3 (CGL Formulas). *The set of CGL formulas ϕ (also ψ, ρ) is given recursively by the grammar:*

$$\phi ::= \langle \alpha \rangle \phi \mid [\alpha] \phi \mid f \sim g$$

The defining constructs in CGL (and GL) are the modalities $\langle\alpha\rangle\phi$ and $[\alpha]\phi$. These mean that the active or dormant Angel (i.e., constructive) player has a constructive strategy to play α and achieve postcondition ϕ. This paper does not develop the modalities for active and dormant Demon (i.e., classical) players because by definition those cannot be synthesized to executable code. We assume the presence of interpreted comparison predicates $\sim \in \{\leq, <, =, \neq, >, \geq\}$.

The standard connectives of first-order constructive logic can be derived from games and comparisons. Verum ($\mathtt{tt}$) is defined $1 > 0$ and falsum ($\mathtt{ff}$) is $0 > 1$. Conjunction $\phi \wedge \psi$ is defined $\langle ?\phi\rangle\psi$, disjunction $\phi \vee \psi$ is defined $\langle ?\phi\cup?\psi\rangle\mathtt{tt}$, implication $\phi \rightarrow \psi$ is defined $[?\phi]\psi$, universal quantification $\forall x\,\phi$ is defined $[x := *]\phi$, and existential quantification $\exists x\,\phi$ is defined $\langle x := *\rangle\phi$. As usual in logic, equivalence $\phi \leftrightarrow \psi$ can also be defined $(\phi \rightarrow \psi) \wedge (\psi \rightarrow \phi)$. As usual in constructive logics, negation $\neg\phi$ is defined $\phi \rightarrow \mathtt{ff}$, and inequality is defined by $f \neq g \equiv \neg(f = g)$. We will use the derived constructs freely but present semantics and proof rules only for the core constructs to minimize duplication. Indeed, it will aid in understanding of the proof term language to keep the definitions above in mind, because the proof terms for many first-order programs follow those from first-order constructive logic.

For convenience, we also write derived operators where the dormant player is given control of a single choice before returning control to the active player. The *dormant choice* $\alpha \cap \beta$, defined $\{\alpha^d \cup \beta^d\}^d$, says the dormant player chooses which branch to take, but the active player is in control of the subgames. We write ϕ^y_x (likewise for α and f) for the *renaming* of x for y and vice versa in formula ϕ, and write ϕ^f_x for the *substitution* of term f for program variable x in ϕ, if the substitution is admissible (Def. 9 in Section 6).

3.1   Example Games

We demonstrate the meaning and usage of the CGL constructs via examples, culminating in the two classic games of Nim and cake-cutting.

Nondeterministic Programs. Every (possibly nondeterministic) program is also a one-player game. For example, the program $n := 0; \{n := n + 1\}^*$ can nondeterministically sets n to any natural number because Angel has a choice whether to continue after every repetition of the loop, but is not allowed to continue forever. Conversely, games are like programs where the environment (Demon) is adversarial, and the program (Angel) strategically resolves nondeterminism to overcome the environment.

Demonic Counter. Angel's choices often must be *reactive* to Demon's choices. Consider the game $c := 10; \{c := c - 1 \cap c := c - 2\}^*; ?0 \leq c \leq 2$ where Demon repeatedly decreases c by 1 or 2, and Angel chooses when to stop. Angel only wins because she can pass the test $0 \leq c \leq 2$, which she can do by simply repeating the loop until $0 \leq c \leq 2$ holds. If Angel had to decide the loop duration in advance, Demon could force a rules violation by "guessing" the duration and changing his choices of $c := c - 1$ vs. $c := c - 2$.

Coin Toss. Games are perfect-information and do not possess randomness in the probabilistic sense, only (possibilistic) nondeterminism. This standard limitation is shown by attempting to express a coin-guessing game:

$$\{\mathsf{coin} := 0 \cap \mathsf{coin} := 1\}; \{\mathsf{guess} := 0 \cup \mathsf{guess} := 1\}; ?\mathsf{guess} = \mathsf{coin}$$

The Demon player sets the value of a tossed coin, but does so adversarially, not randomly, since strategies in CGL are *pure* strategies. The Angel player has perfect knowledge of coin and can set guess equivalently, thus easily passing the test guess = coin, unlike a real coin toss. Partial information games are interesting future work that could be implemented by limiting the variables visible in a strategy.

Nim. Nim is the standard introductory example of a discrete, 2-player, zero-sum, perfect-information game. We consider misère play (last player loses) for a version of Nim that is also known as the *subtraction game*. The constant NIM defines the game Nim.

$$\text{NIM} = \Big\{ \{\{c := c - 1 \cup c := c - 2 \cup c := c - 3\}; ?c > 0\};$$

$$\{\{c := c - 1 \cup c := c - 2 \cup c := c - 3\}; ?c > 0\}^d \Big\}^*$$

The game state consists of a single counter c containing a natural number, which each player chooses ($\cup$) to reduce by 1, 2, or 3 ($c := c - k$). The counter is non-negative, and the game repeats as long as Angel wishes, until some player empties the counter, at which point that player is declared the loser ($?c > 0$).

Proposition 1 (Dormant winning region). *Suppose $c \equiv 1 \pmod 4$, Then the dormant player has a strategy to ensure $c \equiv 1 \pmod 4$ as an invariant. That is, the following CGL formula is valid (true in every state):*

$$c > 0 \rightarrow c \bmod 4 = 1 \rightarrow [\text{NIM}^*]\, c \bmod 4 = 1$$

This implies the dormant player wins the game because the active player violates the rules once $c = 1$ and no move is valid. We now state the winning region for an active player.

Proposition 2 (Active winning region). *Suppose $c \in \{0, 2, 3\} \pmod 4$ initially, and the active player controls the loop duration. Then the active player can achieve $c \in \{2, 3, 4\}$:*

$$c > 0 \rightarrow c \bmod 4 \in \{0, 2, 3\} \rightarrow \langle \text{NIM}^* \rangle\, c \in \{2, 3, 4\}$$

At that point, the active player will win in one move by setting $c = 1$ which forces the dormant player to set $c = 0$ and fail the test $?c > 0$.

Cake-cutting. Another classic 2-player game, from the study of equitable division, is the cake-cutting problem [40]: The active player cuts the cake in two, then the (initially-)dormant player gets first choice of a piece. This is an optimal protocol for splitting the cake in the sense that the active player is incentivized to split the cake evenly, else the dormant player could take the larger piece. Cake-cutting is also a simple use case for fractional numbers. The constant CC defines the cake-cutting game. Here x is the relative size (from 0 to 1) of the first piece, y is the size of the second piece, a is the size of the active player's piece, and d is the size of dormant player's piece.

$$CC = x := *; ?(0 \leq x \leq 1); y := 1 - x;$$
$$\{a := x; d := y \cap a := y; d := x\}$$

The game is played only once. The active player picks the division of the cake, which must be a fraction $0 \leq x \leq 1$. The dormant player then picks which slice goes to whom.

The active player has a tight strategy to achieve a 0.5 cake share, as stated in Proposition 3.

Proposition 3 (Active winning region). *The following formula is valid:*

$$\langle CC \rangle\, a \geq 0.5$$

The dormant player also has a computable strategy to achieve exactly 0.5 share of the cake (Proposition 4). Division is fair because each player has a strategy to get their fair 0.5 share.

Proposition 4 (Dormant winning region). *The following formula is valid:*

$$[CC]\, d \geq 0.5$$

Computability and Numeric Types. Perfect fair division is only achieved for $a, d \in \mathbb{Q}$ because rational equality is decidable. Trichotomy ($a < 0.5 \lor a = 0.5 \lor a > 0.5$) is a tautology, so the dormant player's strategy can inspect the active player's choice of a. Notably, we intend to support constructive reals in future work, for which exact equality is not decidable and trichotomy is not an axiom. Future work on real-valued CGL will need to employ approximate comparison techniques as is typical for constructive reals [11,13,51]. The examples in this section have been proven [12] using the calculus defined in Section 5.

4   Semantics

We now develop the semantics of CGL. In contrast to classical GL, whose semantics are well-understood [38], the major semantic challenge for CGL is capturing the competition between a *constructive* Angel and *classical* Demon. We base our approach on realizability semantics [37,33], because this approach makes the relationship between constructive proofs and programs particularly clear, and generating programs from CGL proofs is one of our motivations.

Unlike previous applications of realizability, games feature two agents, and one could imagine a semantics with two realizers, one for each of Angel and Demon. However, we choose to use only one realizer, for Angel, which captures the fact that only Angel is restricted to a computable strategy, not Demon. Moreover, a single realizer makes it clear that Angel cannot inspect Demon's strategy, only the game state, and also simplifies notations and proofs. Because Angel is computable but Demon is classical, our semantics has the flavor both of realizability semantics and of a traditional Kripke semantics for programs.

The semantic functions employ *game states* $\omega \in \mathfrak{S}$ where we write $\mathfrak{S}$ for the set of all states. We additionally write $\top, \bot \in \mathfrak{S}$ (not to be confused with formulas $\mathtt{tt}$ and $\mathtt{ff}$) for the pseudo-states $\top$ and $\bot$ indicating that Angel or Demon respectively has won the game early by forcing the other to fail a test. Each $\omega \in \mathfrak{S}$ maps each $x \in \mathcal{V}$ to a value $\omega(x) \in \mathbb{Q}$. We write ω_x^v for the state that agrees with ω except that x is assigned value v where $v \in \mathbb{Q}$.

Definition 4 (Arithmetic term semantics). *A term f is a computable function of the state, so the interpretation $[\![f]\!]\omega$ of term f in state ω is $f(\omega)$.*

4.1   Realizers

To define the semantics of games, we first define realizers, the programs which implement strategies. The language of realizers is a higher-order lambda calculus where variables can range over game states, numbers, or realizers which realize a give proposition ϕ. Gameplay proceeds in continuation-passing style: invoking a realizer returns another realizer which performs any further moves. We describe the typing constraints for realizers informally, and say a is a $\langle\alpha\rangle\phi$-realizer ($a \in \langle\alpha\rangle\phi\,\mathcal{R}z$) if it provides strategic decisions exactly when $\langle\alpha\rangle\phi$ demands them.

Definition 5 (Realizers). *The syntax of realizers $a, b, c \in \mathcal{R}z$ (where $\mathcal{R}z$ is the set of all realizers) is defined coinductively:*

$$a, b, c ::= x \mid () \mid (a, b) \mid \pi_L(a) \mid \pi_R(a) \mid (\lambda\omega : \mathfrak{S}.\ a(\omega)) \mid (\Lambda x : \mathbb{Q}.\ a)$$
$$\mid (\Lambda x : \phi\,\mathcal{R}z.\ a) \mid a\,v \mid a\,b \mid a\,\omega \mid \mathtt{if}\ (f(\omega))\ a\ \mathtt{else}\ b$$

where x is a program (or realizer) variable and f is a term over the state ω. The Roman a, b, c should not be confused with the Greek α, β, γ which range over games. Realizers have access to the game state ω, expressed by lambda realizers $(\lambda\omega : \mathfrak{S}.\ a(\omega))$ which, when applied in a state ν, compute the realizer a with ν substituted for ω. State lambdas λ are distinguished from propositional and first-order lambdas Λ. The unit realizer $()$ makes no choices and is understood as a unit tuple. Units $()$ realize $f \sim g$ because *rational* comparisons, in contrast to real comparisons, are decidable. Conditional strategic decisions are realized by $\mathtt{if}\ (f(\omega))\ a\ \mathtt{else}\ b$ for computable function $f : \mathfrak{S} \to \mathbb{B}$, and execute a if f returns truth, else b. Realizer $(\lambda\omega : \mathfrak{S}.\ f(\omega))$ is a $\langle\alpha \cup \beta\rangle\phi$-realizer if $f(\omega) \in (\{0\} \times \langle\alpha\rangle\phi\,\mathcal{R}z) \cup (\{1\} \times \langle\beta\rangle\phi\,\mathcal{R}z)$ for all ω. The first component determines which branch is taken, while the second component is a continuation which must be able to play the corresponding branch. Realizer $(\lambda\omega : \mathfrak{S}.\ f(\omega))$ can also be a $\langle x := * \rangle\phi$-realizer, which requires $f(\omega) \in \mathbb{Q} \times (\phi\,\mathcal{R}\mathbf{z})$ for all ω. The first component determines the value of x while the second component demonstrates the postcondition ϕ. The pair realizer (a, b) realizes both Angelic tests $\langle ?\phi \rangle\psi$ and dormant choices $[\alpha \cup \beta]\phi$. It is identified with a pair of realizers: $(a, b) \in \mathcal{R}\mathbf{z} \times \mathcal{R}\mathbf{z}$.

A dormant realizer waits and remembers the active Demon's moves, because they typically inform Angel's strategy once Angel resumes action. The first-order realizer $(\Lambda x : \mathbb{Q}.\ b)$ is a $[x := *]\phi$-realizer when b_x^v is a ϕ-realizer for every $v \in \mathbb{Q}$; Demon tells Angel the desired value of x, which informs Angel's continuation b. The higher-order realizer $(\Lambda x : \phi\,\mathcal{R}\mathbf{z}.\ b)$ realizes $[?\phi]\psi$ when b_x^c realizes ψ for every ϕ-realizer c. Demon announces the realizer for ϕ which Angel's continuation b may inspect. Tuples are inspected with projections $\pi_L(a)$ and $\pi_R(a)$. A lambda is inspected by applying arguments $a\,\omega$ for state-lambdas, $a\,v$ for first-order, and $a\,b$ for higher-order. Realizers for sequential compositions $\langle \alpha; \beta \rangle\phi$ (likewise $[\alpha; \beta]\phi$) are $\langle \alpha \rangle\langle \beta \rangle\phi$-realizers: first α is played, and in every case the continuation must play β before showing ϕ. Realizers for repetitions α^* are streams containing α-realizers, possibly infinite by virtue of coinductive syntax. Active loop realizer $\mathsf{ind}(x.\ a)$ is the least fixed point of the equation $b = [b/x]a$, i.e., x is a recursive call which must be invoked only in accordance with some well-order. We realize dormant loops with $\mathsf{gen}(a,\ x.b,\ x.c)$, coinductively generated from initial value a, update b, and post-step c with variable x for current generator value.

Active loops must terminate, so $\langle \alpha^* \rangle\phi$-realizers are constructed inductively using any well-order on states. Dormant loops must be played as long as the opponent wishes, so $[\alpha^*]\phi$-realizers are constructed coinductively, with the invariant that ϕ has a realizer at every iteration.

4.2 Formula and Game Semantics

A state ω paired with a realizer a that continues the game is called a *possibility*. A *region* (written X, Y, Z) is a set of possibilities. We write $[\![\phi]\!] \subseteq \phi\,\mathcal{R}\mathbf{z} \times \mathfrak{S}$ for the region which realizes formula ϕ. A formula ϕ is *valid* iff some a uniformly realizes every state, i.e., $\{a\} \times \mathfrak{S} \subseteq [\![\phi]\!]$. A sequent $\Gamma \vdash \phi$ is *valid* iff the formula $\bigwedge \Gamma \to \phi$ is valid, where $\bigwedge \Gamma$ is the conjunction of all assumptions in Γ.

The game semantics are region-oriented, i.e., they process possibilities in bulk, though Angel commits to a strategy from the start. The region $X\langle\!\langle \alpha \rangle\!\rangle$: $\wp(\mathcal{R}\mathbf{z} \times \mathfrak{S})$ is the union of all end regions of game α which arise when active Angel commits to an element of X, then Demon plays adversarially. In $X[\![\alpha]\!]$: $\wp(\mathcal{R}\mathbf{z} \times \mathfrak{S})$ Angel is the *dormant* player, but it is still Angel who commits to an element of X and Demon who plays adversarially. Recall that pseudo-states $\top$ and $\bot$ represent early wins by each Angel and Demon, respectively. The definitions below implicitly assume $\bot, \top \notin X$, they extend to the case $\bot \in X$ (likewise $\top \in X$) using the equations $(X \cup \{\bot\})[\![\alpha]\!] = X[\![\alpha]\!] \cup \{\bot\}$ and $(X \cup \{\bot\})\langle\!\langle \alpha \rangle\!\rangle = X\langle\!\langle \alpha \rangle\!\rangle \cup \{\bot\}$. That is, if Demon has already won by forcing an Angel violation initially, any remaining game can be skipped with an immediate Demon victory, and vice-versa. The game semantics exploit the *Angelic* projections $Z_{\langle 0 \rangle}, Z_{\langle 1 \rangle}$

and *Demonic* projections $Z_{[0]}, Z_{[1]}$, which represent binary decisions made by a constructive Angel and a classical Demon, respectively. The Angelic projections, which are defined $Z_{\langle 0 \rangle} = \{(\pi_R(a), \omega) \mid \pi_L(a)(\omega) = 0, (a, \omega) \in Z\}$ and $Z_{\langle 1 \rangle} = \{(\pi_R(a), \omega) \mid \pi_L(a)(\omega) = 1, (a, \omega) \in Z\}$, filter by which branch Angel chooses with $\pi_L(a)(\omega) \in \mathbb{B}$, then project the remaining strategy $\pi_R(a)$. The Demonic projections, which are defined $Z_{[0]} \equiv \{(\pi_L(a), \omega) \mid (a, \omega) \in Z\}$ and $Z_{[1]} \equiv \{(\pi_R(a), \omega) \mid (a, \omega) \in Z\}$, contain the same states as Z, but project the realizer to tell Angel which branch Demon took.

Definition 6 (Formula semantics). $[\![\phi]\!] \subseteq \mathcal{R}z \times \mathfrak{S}$ *is defined as:*

$$((), \omega) \in [\![f \sim g]\!] \text{ iff } [\![f]\!]\omega \sim [\![g]\!]\omega$$
$$(a, \omega) \in [\![\langle \alpha \rangle \phi]\!] \text{ iff } \{(a, \omega)\}\langle\!\langle \alpha \rangle\!\rangle \subseteq ([\![\phi]\!] \cup \{\top\})$$
$$(a, \omega) \in [\![[\alpha]\phi]\!] \text{ iff } \{(a, \omega)\}[\![\alpha]\!] \subseteq ([\![\phi]\!] \cup \{\top\})$$

Comparisons $f \sim g$ defer to the term semantics, so the interesting cases are the game modalities. Both $[\alpha]\phi$ and $\langle \alpha \rangle \phi$ ask whether Angel wins α by following the given strategy, and differ only in whether Demon vs. Angel is the active player, thus in both cases *every* Demonic choice must satisfy Angel's goal, and early Demon wins are counted as Angel losses.

Definition 7 (Angel game forward semantics). *We inductively define the region* $X\langle\!\langle \alpha \rangle\!\rangle : \wp(\mathcal{R}z \times \mathfrak{S})$ *in which* α *can end when active Angel plays* X:

$$X\langle\!\langle ?\phi \rangle\!\rangle = \{(\pi_R(a), \omega) \mid (\pi_L(a), \omega) \in [\![\phi]\!] \text{ for some } (a, \omega) \in X \}$$
$$\cup \{\bot \mid (\pi_L(a), \omega) \notin [\![\phi]\!] \text{ for all } (a, \omega) \in X \}$$
$$X\langle\!\langle x := f \rangle\!\rangle = \{(a, \omega_x^{[\![f]\!]\omega}) \mid (a, \omega) \in X\}$$
$$X\langle\!\langle x := * \rangle\!\rangle = \{(\pi_R(a), \omega_x^{\pi_L(a)(\omega)}) \mid (a, \omega) \in X\}$$
$$X\langle\!\langle \alpha; \beta \rangle\!\rangle = (X\langle\!\langle \alpha \rangle\!\rangle)\langle\!\langle \beta \rangle\!\rangle$$
$$X\langle\!\langle \alpha \cup \beta \rangle\!\rangle = X_{\langle 0 \rangle}\langle\!\langle \alpha \rangle\!\rangle \cup X_{\langle 1 \rangle}\langle\!\langle \beta \rangle\!\rangle$$
$$X\langle\!\langle \alpha^* \rangle\!\rangle = \bigcap\{Z_{\langle 0 \rangle} \subseteq \mathcal{R}z \times \mathfrak{S} \mid X \cup (Z_{\langle 1 \rangle}\langle\!\langle \alpha \rangle\!\rangle) \subseteq Z\}$$
$$X\langle\!\langle \alpha^d \rangle\!\rangle = X[\![\alpha]\!]$$

Definition 8 (Demon game forward semantics). *We inductively define the region* $X[\![\alpha]\!] : \wp(\mathcal{R}z \times \mathfrak{S})$ *in which* α *can end when dormant Angel plays* X:

$$X[\![?\phi]\!] = \{(a\,b, \omega) \mid (a, \omega) \in X, (b, \omega) \in [\![\phi]\!], \text{ some } b \in \mathcal{R}z\}$$
$$\cup \{\top \mid (a, \omega) \in X, \text{ but no } (b, \omega) \in [\![\phi]\!]\}$$
$$X[\![x := f]\!] = \{(a, \omega_x^{[\![f]\!]\omega}) \mid (a, \omega) \in X\}$$
$$X[\![x := *]\!] = \{(a\,r, \omega_x^r) \mid r \in \mathbb{Q}\}$$
$$X[\![\alpha; \beta]\!] = (X[\![\alpha]\!])[\![\beta]\!]$$
$$X[\![\alpha \cup \beta]\!] = X_{[0]}[\![\alpha]\!] \cup X_{[1]}[\![\beta]\!]$$
$$X[\![\alpha^*]\!] = \bigcap\{Z_{[0]} \subseteq \mathcal{R}z \times \mathfrak{S} \mid X \cup (Z_{[1]}[\![\alpha]\!]) \subseteq Z\}$$
$$X[\![\alpha^d]\!] = X\langle\!\langle \alpha \rangle\!\rangle$$

Angelic tests $?\phi$ end in the current state ω with remaining realizer $\pi_R(a)$ if Angel can realize ϕ with $\pi_L(a)$, else end in $\bot$. Angelic deterministic assignments consume no realizer and simply update the state, then end. Angelic nondeterministic assignments $x := *$ ask the realizer $\pi_L(a)$ to compute a new value for x from the current state. Angelic compositions $\alpha; \beta$ first play α, then β from the resulting state using the resulting continuation. Angelic choice games $\alpha \cup \beta$ use the Angelic projections to decide which branch is taken according to $\pi_L(a)$. The realizer $\pi_R(a)$ may be reused between α and β, since $\pi_R(a)$ could just invoke $\pi_L(a)$ if it must decide which branch has been taken. This definition of Angelic choice (corresponding to constructive disjunction) captures the reality that realizers in CGL, in contrast with most constructive logics, are entitled to observe a game state, but they must do so in computable fashion.

Repetition Semantics. In any GL, the challenge in defining the semantics of repetition games α^* is that the number of iterations, while finite, can depend on both players' actions and is thus not known in advance, while the DL-like semantics of α^* as the finite reflexive, transitive closure of α gives an advance-notice semantics. Classical GL provides the no-advance-notice semantics as a fixed point [38], and we adopt the fixed point semantics as well. The Angelic choice whether to stop $(Z_{\langle 0 \rangle})$ or iterate the loop $(Z_{\langle 1 \rangle})$ is analogous to the case for $\alpha \cup \beta$.

Duality Semantics. To play the dual game α^d, the active and dormant players switch roles, then play α. In *classical* GL, this characterization of duality is interchangeable with the definition of α^d as the game that Angel wins exactly when it is impossible for Angel to lose. The characterizations are *not* interchangeable in CGL because the Determinacy Axiom (all games have winners) of GL is not valid in CGL:

Remark 1 (Indeterminacy). Classically equivalent determinacy axiom schemata $\neg\langle\alpha\rangle\neg\phi \rightarrow [\alpha]\phi$ and $\langle\alpha\rangle\neg\phi \vee [\alpha]\phi$ of classical GL are not valid in CGL, because they imply double negation elimination.

Remark 2 (Classical duality). In classical GL, Angelic dual games are characterized by the axiom schema $\langle\alpha^d\rangle\phi \leftrightarrow \neg\langle\alpha\rangle\neg\phi$, which is not valid in in CGL. It is classically interdefinable with $\langle\alpha^d\rangle \leftrightarrow [\alpha]\phi$.

The determinacy axiom is not valid in CGL, so we take $\langle\alpha^d\rangle \leftrightarrow [\alpha]\phi$ as primary.

4.3 Demonic Semantics

Demon wins a Demonic test by presenting a realizer b as evidence that the precondition holds. If he cannot present a realizer (i.e., because none exists), then the game ends in $\top$ so Angel wins by default. Else Angel's higher-order realizer a consumes the evidence of the pre-condition, i.e., Angelic strategies are entitled to depend (computably) on *how* Demon demonstrated the precondition. Angel can check that Demon passed the test by executing b. The Demonic repetition game

α^* is defined as a fixed-point [42] with Demonic projections. Computationally, a winning invariant for the repetition is the witness of its winnability.

The remaining cases are innocuous by comparison. Demonic deterministic assignments $x := f$ deterministically store the value of f in x, just as Angelic assignments do. In demonic nondeterministic assignment $x := *$, Demon chooses to set x to *any* value. When Demon plays the choice game $\alpha \cup \beta$, Demon chooses classically between α and β. The dual game α^d is played by Demon becoming dormant and Angel become active in α.

Semantics Examples. The realizability semantics of games are subtle on a first read, so we provide examples of realizers. In these examples, the state argument ω is implicit, and we refer to $\omega(x)$ simply as x for brevity.

Recall that $[?\phi]\psi$ and $\phi \rightarrow \psi$ are equivalent. For any ϕ, the identity function $(\Lambda x : \phi \, \mathcal{R}\mathbf{z}.\ x)$ is a $\phi \rightarrow \phi$-realizer: for every ϕ-realizer x which Demon presents, Angel can present the same x as evidence of ϕ. This confirms expected behavior per propositional constructive logic: the identity function is the proof of self-implication.

In example formula $\langle x := *^d ; \{x := x \cup x := -x\}\rangle x \geq 0$, Demon gets to set x, then Angel decides whether to negate x in order to make it nonnegative. It is realized by $\Lambda x : \mathbb{Q}.\ ((\mathtt{if}\ (x < 0)\ 1\ \mathtt{else}\ 0), ())$: Demon announces the value of x, then Angel's strategy is to check the sign of x, taking the right branch when x is negative. Each branch contains a deterministic assignment which consumes no realizer, then the postcondition $x \geq 0$ has trivial realizer $()$.

Consider the formula $\langle \{x := x + 1\}^* \rangle x > y$, where Angel's winning strategy is to repeat the loop until $x > y$, which will occur as x increases. The realizer is $\mathrm{ind}(w.\ (\mathtt{if}\ (x > y)\ (0, ())\ \mathtt{else}\ (1, w), ()))$, which says that Angel stops the loop if $x > y$ and proves the postcondition with a trivial strategy. Else Angel continues the loop, whose body consumes no realizer, and supplies the inductive call w to continue the strategy inductively.

Consider the formula $[?x > 0; \{x := x + 1\}^*]\exists y\, (y \leq x \wedge y > 0)$ for a subtle example. Our strategy for Angel is to record the initial value of x in y, then maintain a proof that $y \leq x$ as x increases. This strategy is represented by $\Lambda w : (x > 0)\, \mathcal{R}\mathbf{z}.\ \mathrm{gen}((x, ((), w)),\ z.(\pi_L(z), ((), \pi_R(\pi_R(z)))),\ z.z)$. That is, initially Demon announces a proof w of $x > 0$. Angel specifies the initial element of the realizer stream by witnessing $\exists y\, (y \leq x \wedge y > 0)$ with $c_0 = (x, ((), w))$, where the first component instantiates $y = x$, the trivial second component indicates that $y \leq y$ trivially, and the third component reuses w as a proof of $y > 0$. Demon can choose to repeat the loop arbitrarily. When Demon demands the k'th repetition, z is bound to c_{k-1} to compute $c_k = (\pi_L(z), ((), \pi_R(\pi_R(z))))$, which plays the next iteration. That is, at each iteration Angel witnesses $\exists y\, (y \leq x \wedge y > 0)$ by assigning the same value (stored in $\pi_L(z)$) to y, reproving $y \leq x$ with $()$, then reusing the proof (stored in $\pi_R(\pi_R(z))$) that $y > 0$.

5   Proof Calculus

Having settled on the meaning of a game in Section 4, we proceed to develop a calculus for proving CGL formulas syntactically. The goal is twofold: the practical motivation, as always, is that when verifying a concrete example, the realizability semantics provide a notion of ground truth, but are impractical for proving large formulas. The theoretical motivation is that we wish to expose the computational interpretation of the modalities $\langle\alpha\rangle\phi$ and $[\alpha]\phi$ as the types of the players' respective winning strategies for game α that has ϕ as its goal condition. Since CGL is constructive, such a strategy constructs a proof of the postcondition ϕ.

To study the computational nature of proofs, we write proof terms explicitly: the main proof judgement $\Gamma \vdash M : \phi$ says proof term M is a proof of ϕ in context Γ, or equivalently a proof of sequent $(\Gamma \vdash \phi)$. We write M, N, O (sometimes A, B, C) for arbitrary proof terms, and p, q, ℓ, r, s, g for *proof variables*, that is variables that range over proof terms of a given proposition. In contrast to the assignable *program variables*, the proof variables are given their meaning by substitution and are scoped locally, not globally. We adapt propositional proof terms such as pairing, disjoint union, and lambda-abstraction to our context of game logic. To support first-order games, we include first-order proof terms and new terms for features: dual, assignment, and repetition games.

We now develop the calculus by starting with standard constructs and working toward the novel constructs of CGL. The assumptions p in Γ are named, so that they may appear as variable proof-terms p. We write Γ^y_x and M^y_x for the renaming of program variable x to y and vice versa in context Γ or proof term M, respectively. Proof rules for state-modifying constructs explicitly perform renamings, which both ensures they are applicable as often as possible and also ensures that references to proof variables support an intuitive notion of lexical scope. Likewise Γ^f_x and M^f_x are the substitutions of term f for program variable x. We use distinct notation to substitute proof terms for proof variables while avoiding capture: $[N/p]M$ substitutes proof term N for proof variable p in proof term M. Some proof terms such as pairs prove both a diamond formula and a box formula. We write $\langle M, N\rangle$ and $[M, N]$ respectively to distinguish the terms or $\langle\![M, N]\!\rangle$ to treat them uniformly. Likewise we abbreviate $\langle\![\alpha]\!\rangle\phi$ when the same rule works for both diamond and box modalities, using $[\![\alpha]\!]\phi$ to denote its dual modality. The proof terms $\langle x := f^y_x \text{ in } p.\ M\rangle$ and $[x := f^y_x \text{ in } p.\ M]$ introduce an auxiliary ghost variable y for the old value of x, which improves completeness without requiring manual ghost steps.

The propositional proof rules of CGL are in Fig. 1. Formula $[?\phi]\psi$ is constructive implication, so rule $[?]$E with proof term $M\ N$ eliminates M by supplying an N that proves the test condition. Lambda terms $(\lambda p : \phi.\ M)$ are introduced by rule $[?]$I by extending the context Γ. While this rule is standard, it is worth emphasizing that here p is a *proof variable* for which a proof term (like N in $[?]$E) may be substituted, and that the *game state* is untouched by $[?]$I. Constructive disjunction (between the branches $\langle\alpha\rangle\phi$ and $\langle\beta\rangle\phi$) is the choice $\langle\alpha \cup \beta\rangle\phi$. The introduction rules for injections are $\langle\cup\rangle$I1 and $\langle\cup\rangle$I2, and case-analysis is performed with rule $\langle\cup\rangle$E, with two branches that prove a common consequence

$$\langle\cup\rangle E \ \frac{\Gamma \vdash A : \langle\alpha \cup \beta\rangle\phi \quad \Gamma, \ell : \langle\alpha\rangle\phi \vdash B : \psi \quad \Gamma, r : \langle\beta\rangle\phi \vdash C : \psi}{\Gamma \vdash \langle\mathsf{case}\ A\ \mathsf{of}\ \ell \Rightarrow B \mid r \Rightarrow C\rangle : \psi}$$

$$\langle\cup\rangle I1 \ \frac{\Gamma \vdash M : \langle\alpha\rangle\phi}{\Gamma \vdash \langle\ell \cdot M\rangle : \langle\alpha \cup \beta\rangle\phi} \qquad [\cup]E1 \ \frac{\Gamma \vdash M : [\alpha \cup \beta]\phi}{\Gamma \vdash [\pi_1 M] : [\alpha]\phi}$$

$$\langle\cup\rangle I2 \ \frac{\Gamma \vdash M : \langle\beta\rangle\phi}{\Gamma \vdash \langle r \cdot M\rangle : \langle\alpha \cup \beta\rangle\phi} \qquad [\cup]E2 \ \frac{\Gamma \vdash M : [\alpha \cup \beta]\phi}{\Gamma \vdash [\pi_2 M] : [\beta]\phi}$$

$$[\cup]I \ \frac{\Gamma \vdash M : [\alpha]\phi \quad \Gamma \vdash N : [\beta]\phi}{\Gamma \vdash [M, N] : [\alpha \cup \beta]\phi}$$

$$\mathrm{hyp} \ \frac{}{\Gamma, p : \phi \vdash p : \phi}$$

$$\langle?\rangle I \ \frac{\Gamma \vdash M : \phi \quad \Gamma \vdash N : \psi}{\Gamma \vdash \langle M, N\rangle : \langle?\phi\rangle\psi} \qquad \langle?\rangle E1 \ \frac{\Gamma \vdash M : \langle?\phi\rangle\psi}{\Gamma \vdash \langle\pi_1 M\rangle : \phi}$$

$$[?]I \ \frac{\Gamma, p : \phi \vdash M : \psi}{\Gamma \vdash (\lambda p : \phi.\ M) : [?\phi]\psi} \qquad \langle?\rangle E2 \ \frac{\Gamma \vdash M : \langle?\phi\rangle\psi}{\Gamma \vdash \langle\pi_2 M\rangle : \psi}$$

$$[?]E \ \frac{\Gamma \vdash M : [?\phi]\psi \quad \Gamma \vdash N : \phi}{\Gamma \vdash (M\ N) : \psi}$$

Fig. 1. CGL proof calculus: Propositional rules

from each disjunct. The cases $\langle?\phi\rangle\psi$ and $[\alpha \cup \beta]\phi$ are conjunctive. Conjunctions are introduced by $\langle?\rangle I$ and $[\cup]I$ as pairs, and eliminated by $\langle?\rangle E1$, $\langle?\rangle E2$, $[\cup]E1$, and $[\cup]E2$ as projections. Lastly, rule hyp says formulas in the context hold by assumption.

We now begin considering non-propositional rules, starting with the simplest ones. The majority of the rules in Fig. 2, while thoroughly useful in proofs,

$$\langle*\rangle C \ \frac{\Gamma \vdash A : \langle\alpha^*\rangle\phi \quad \Gamma, s : \phi \vdash B : \psi \quad \Gamma, g : \langle\alpha\rangle\langle\alpha^*\rangle\phi \vdash C : \psi}{\Gamma \vdash \langle\mathsf{case}_*\ A\ \mathsf{of}\ s \Rightarrow B \mid g \Rightarrow C\rangle : \psi}$$

$$\mathrm{M} \ \frac{\Gamma \vdash M : \langle\alpha\rangle\phi \quad \Gamma_{\frac{y}{BV(\alpha)}}, p : \phi \vdash N : \psi}{\Gamma \vdash M \circ_p N : \langle\alpha\rangle\psi}$$

$$[*]E \ \frac{\Gamma \vdash M : [\alpha^*]\phi}{\Gamma \vdash [\mathsf{unroll}\ M] : \phi \wedge [\alpha][\alpha^*]\phi} \qquad \langle^d\rangle I \ \frac{\Gamma \vdash M : \langle\!\langle\alpha\rangle\!\rangle\phi}{\Gamma \vdash \langle\mathsf{yield}\ M\rangle : \langle\!\langle\alpha^d\rangle\!\rangle\phi}$$

$$\langle*\rangle S \ \frac{\Gamma \vdash M : \phi}{\Gamma \vdash \langle\mathsf{stop}\ M\rangle : \langle\alpha^*\rangle\phi} \qquad [*]R \ \frac{\Gamma \vdash M : \phi \wedge [\alpha][\alpha^*]\phi}{\Gamma \vdash [\mathsf{roll}\ M] : [\alpha^*]\phi}$$

$$\langle*\rangle G \ \frac{\Gamma \vdash M : \phi \vee \langle\alpha\rangle\langle\alpha^*\rangle\phi}{\Gamma \vdash \langle\mathsf{go}\ M\rangle : \langle\alpha^*\rangle\phi} \qquad \langle;\rangle I \ \frac{\Gamma \vdash M : \langle\!\langle\alpha\rangle\!\rangle\langle\!\langle\beta\rangle\!\rangle\phi}{\Gamma \vdash \langle\!\langle\iota\ M\rangle\!\rangle : \langle\!\langle\alpha; \beta\rangle\!\rangle\phi}$$

Fig. 2. CGL proof calculus: Some non-propositional rules

are computationally trivial. The repetition rules ($[*]E, [*]R$) fold and unfold the notion of repetition as iteration. The rolling and unrolling terms are named in analogy to the *iso-recursive* treatment of recursive types [50], where an explicit operation is used to expand and collapse the recursive definition of a type.

Rules $\langle*\rangle C, \langle*\rangle S, \langle*\rangle G$ are the destructor and injectors for $\langle\alpha^*\rangle\phi$, which are similar to those for $\langle\alpha \cup \beta\rangle\phi$. The duality rules ($\langle^d\rangle I$) say the dual game is proved by proving the game where roles are reversed. The sequencing rules ($\langle;\rangle I$) say a sequential game is played by playing the first game with the goal of reaching a state where the second game is winnable.

Among these rules, monotonicity M is especially computationally rich. The notation $\Gamma \frac{y}{BV(\alpha)}$ says that in the second premiss, the assumptions in Γ have all bound variables of α (written $BV(\alpha)$) renamed to fresh variables y for completeness. In practice, Γ usually contains some assumptions on variables that are not bound, which we wish to access without writing them explicitly in ϕ. Rule M is used to execute programs right-to-left, giving shorter, more efficient proofs. It can also be used to derive the Hoare-logical sequential composition rule, which is frequently used to reduce the number of case splits. Note that like every GL, CGL is subnormal, so the modal modus ponens axiom K and Gödel generalization (or necessitation) rule G are not sound, and M takes over much of the role they usually serve. On the surface, M simply says games are monotonic: a game's goal proposition may freely be replaced with a weaker one. From a computational perspective, Section 7 will show that rule M can be (lazily) eliminated. Moreover, M is an *admissible* rule, one whose instances can all be derived from existing rules. When proofs are written right-to-left with M, the normalization relation translates them to left-to-right normal proofs. Note also that in checking $M \circ_p N$, the context Γ has the bound variables α renamed freshly to some y within N, as required to maintain soundness across execution of α.

Next, we consider *first-order* rules, i.e., those which deal with first-order programs that modify *program* variables. The first-order rules are given in Fig. 3. In $\langle :* \rangle E$, $FV(\psi)$ are the *free variables* of ψ, the variables which can influence its meaning. Nondeterministic assignment provides quantification over rational-

$$
(\lbrack := \rbrack) I \quad \frac{\Gamma^y_x, p : (x = f^y_x) \vdash M : \phi}{\Gamma \vdash \langle\!\langle x := f^y_x \text{ in } p.\ M \rangle\!\rangle : \langle\!\langle x := f \rangle\!\rangle \phi} \qquad (y \text{ fresh})
$$

$$
\langle :* \rangle I \quad \frac{\Gamma^y_x, p : (x = f^y_x) \vdash M : \phi}{\Gamma \vdash \langle f^y_x :* p.\ M \rangle : \langle x := * \rangle \phi} \qquad (y, p \text{ fresh}, f \text{ comp.})
$$

$$
\langle :* \rangle E \quad \frac{\Gamma \vdash M : \langle x := * \rangle \phi \quad \Gamma^y_x, p : \phi \vdash N : \psi}{\Gamma \vdash \text{unpack}(M, py.\ N) : \psi} \qquad (y \text{ fresh}, x \notin FV(\psi))
$$

$$
[:*]I \quad \frac{\Gamma^y_x \vdash M : \phi}{\Gamma \vdash (\lambda x : \mathbb{Q}.\ M) : [x := *] \phi} \qquad (y \text{ fresh})
$$

$$
[:*]E \quad \frac{\Gamma \vdash M : [x := *] \phi}{\Gamma \vdash (M\ f) : \phi^f_x} \qquad (\phi^f_x \text{ admiss.})
$$

Fig. 3. CGL proof calculus: first-order games

valued *program* variables. Rule $[:*]I$ is universal, with proof term $(\lambda x : \mathbb{Q}.\ M)$. While this notation is suggestive, the difference vs. the function proof term $(\lambda p : \phi.\ M)$ is essential: the proof term M is checked (resp. evaluated) in a state where the program variable x has changed from its initial value. For soundness, $[:*]I$ renames x to fresh program variable y throughout context Γ, written Γ^y_x. This means that M can freely refer to all facts of the full context, but they now refer to the state as it was before x received a new value. Elimination $[:*]$E then allows instantiating x to a term f. Existential quantification is introduced by $\langle :*\rangle$I whose proof term $\langle f\frac{y}{x} :* p.\ M\rangle$ is like a dependent pair plus bound renaming of x to y. The witness f is an arbitrary computable term, as always. We write $\langle f_{\tilde{x}} :* M\rangle$ for short when y is not referenced in M. It is eliminated in $\langle :*\rangle$E by unpacking the pair, with side condition $x \notin \mathrm{FV}(\psi)$ for soundness. The assignment rules $\langle\!\!\;:=\;\!\!\rangle$I do not quantify, per se, but always update x to the value of the term f, and in doing so introduce an assumption that x and f (suitably renamed) are now equal. In $\langle :*\rangle$I and $\langle\!\!\;:=\;\!\!\rangle$I, program variable y is fresh.

$$\langle *\rangle\mathrm{I}\ \frac{\Gamma \vdash A:\varphi \quad p:\varphi, q:\mathcal{M}_0 = \mathcal{M} \succ \mathbf{0} \vdash B:\langle\alpha\rangle(\varphi \wedge \mathcal{M}_0 \succ \mathcal{M}) \quad p:\varphi, q:\mathcal{M} = \mathbf{0} \vdash C:\phi}{\Gamma \vdash \mathsf{for}(p:\varphi(\mathcal{M}) = A; q.\,B; C)\{\alpha\}:\langle\alpha^*\rangle\phi}\ (\mathcal{M}_0\ \text{fresh})$$

$$[*]\mathrm{I}\ \frac{\Gamma \vdash M:J \quad p:J \vdash N:[\alpha]J \quad p:J \vdash O:\phi}{\Gamma \vdash (M\ \mathsf{rep}\ p:J.\ N\ \mathsf{in}\ O):[\alpha^*]\phi} \qquad \mathrm{FP}\ \frac{\Gamma \vdash A:\langle\alpha^*\rangle\phi \quad s:\phi \vdash B:\psi \quad g:\langle\alpha\rangle\psi \vdash C:\psi}{\Gamma \vdash FP(A,s.\ B, g.\ C):\psi}$$

$$\text{split}\ \Gamma \vdash (\mathsf{split}\ [f,g]\ ):f \leq g \vee f > g$$

Fig. 4. CGL proof calculus: loops

The looping rules in Fig. 4, especially $\langle *\rangle$I, are arguably the most sophisticated in CGL. Rule $\langle *\rangle$I provides a strategy to repeat a game α until the postcondition ϕ holds. This is done by exhibiting a convergence predicate φ and termination metric $\mathcal{M}$ with terminal value $\mathbf{0}$ and well-ordering $\succ$. Proof term A shows φ holds initially. Proof term B guarantees $\mathcal{M}$ decreases with every iteration where $\mathcal{M}_0$ is a fresh metric variable which is equal to $\mathcal{M}$ at the antecedent of B and is never modified. Proof term C allows any postcondition ϕ which follows from convergence $\varphi \wedge \mathcal{M} = \mathbf{0}$. Proof term $\mathsf{for}(p:\varphi(\mathcal{M}) = A; q.\,B; C)\{\alpha\}$ suggests the computational interpretation as a for-loop: proof A shows the convergence predicate holds in the initial state, B shows that each step reduces the termination metric while maintaining the predicate, and C shows that the postcondition follows from the convergence predicate upon termination. The game α repeats until convergence is reached ($\mathcal{M} = \mathbf{0}$). By the assumption that metrics are well-founded, convergence is guaranteed in finitely (but arbitrarily) many iterations.

A naïve, albeit correct, reading of rule $\langle *\rangle$I says $\mathcal{M}$ is literally some term f. If lexicographic or otherwise non-scalar metrics should be needed, it suffices to interpret φ and $\mathcal{M}_0 \succ \mathcal{M}$ as formulas over several scalar variables.

Rule FP says $\langle\alpha^*\rangle\phi$ is a least pre-fixed-point. That is, if we wish to show a formula ψ holds now, we show that ψ is any pre-fixed-point, then it must hold as it is no lesser than ϕ. Rule $[*]$I is the well-understood induction rule for loops, which applies as well to repeated games. Premiss O ensures $[*]$I supports any provable postcondition, which is crucial for eliminating M in Lemma 7. The elimination form for $[\alpha^*]\phi$ is simply $[*]$E. Like any program logic, reasoning in CGL consists of first applying program-logic rules to decompose a program until the program has been entirely eliminated, then applying first-order logic principles at the leaves of the proof. The *constructive* theory of rationals is undecidable because it can express the undecidable [47] *classical* theory of rationals. Thus facts about rationals require proof in practice. For the sake of space and since our focus is on program reasoning, we defer an axiomatization of rational arithmetic to future work. We provide a (non-effective!) rule FO which says valid first-order formulas are provable.

$$\text{FO} \quad \frac{\Gamma \vdash M : \rho}{\Gamma \vdash \text{FO}[\phi](M) : \phi} \quad (\text{exists } a \text{ s.t. } \{a\} \times \mathfrak{S} \subseteq [\![\rho \to \phi]\!], \ \rho, \phi \text{ F.O.})$$

An effective special case of FO is split (Fig. 4), which says all term comparisons are decidable. Rule split can be generalized to decide termination metrics ($\mathcal{M} = 0 \vee \mathcal{M} \succ 0$). Rule iG says the value of term f can be remembered in fresh ghost variable x:

$$\text{iG} \quad \frac{\Gamma, p : x = f \vdash M : \phi}{\Gamma \vdash \text{Ghost}[x = f](p. \ M) : \phi} \quad (x \text{ fresh except free in } M, p \text{ fresh})$$

Rule iG can be defined using arithmetic and with quantifiers:

$$\text{Ghost}[x = f](p. \ M) \equiv (\lambda x : \mathbb{Q}. \ (\lambda p : (x = f). \ M)) \ f \ (\text{FO}[f = f]())$$

What's Novel in the CGL Calculus? CGL extends first-order reasoning with game reasoning (sequencing [32], assignments, iteration, and duality). The combination of first-order reasoning with game reasoning is synergistic: for example, repetition games are known to be more expressive than repetition systems [42]. We give a new natural-deduction formulation of monotonicity. Monotonicity is admissible and normalization translates monotonicity proofs into monotonicity-free proofs. In doing so, normalization shows that right-to-left proofs can be (lazily) rewritten as left-to-right. Additionally, first-order games are rife with changing state, and soundness requires careful management of the context Γ. The extended version [12] uses our calculus to prove the example formulas.

6 Theory: Soundness

Full versions of proofs outlined in this paper are given in the extended version [12]. We have introduced a proof calculus for CGL which can prove winning strategies for NIM and CC. For any new proof calculus, it is essential to convince ourselves of our soundness, which can be done within several prominent schools of thought. In proof-theoretic semantics, for example, the proof rules are taken as the ground truth, but are validated by showing the rules obey expected properties such as harmony or, for a sequent calculus, cut-elimination. While we will investigate proof terms separately (Section 8), we are already equipped to show soundness by direct appeal to the realizability semantics (Section 4), which we take as an independent notion of ground truth. We show soundness of CGL proof rules against the realizability semantics, i.e., that every provable natural-deduction sequent is valid. An advantage of this approach is that it explicitly connects the notions of provability and computability! We build up to the proof of soundness by proving lemmas on structurality, renaming and substitution.

Lemma 1 (Structurality). *The structural rules W, X, and C are admissible, i.e., the conclusions are provable whenever the premises are provable.*

$$\text{W}\ \frac{\Gamma \vdash M : \phi}{\Gamma, p : \psi \vdash M : \phi} \qquad \text{X}\ \frac{\Gamma, p : \phi, q : \psi \vdash M : \rho}{\Gamma, q : \psi, p : \phi \vdash M : \rho} \qquad \text{C}\ \frac{\Gamma, p : \phi, q : \phi \vdash M : \rho}{\Gamma, p : \phi \vdash [p/q]M : \rho}$$

Proof summary. Each rule is proved admissible by induction on M. Observe that the only premises regarding Γ are of the form $\Gamma(p) = \phi$, which are preserved under weakening. Premises are trivially preserved under exchange because contexts are treated as sets, and preserved modulo renaming by contraction as it suffices to have *any* assumption of a given formula, regardless its name. The context Γ is allowed to vary in applications of the inductive hypothesis, e.g., rules that bind program variables. Some rules discard Γ in checking the subterms inductively, in which case the IH need not be applied at all.   □

Lemma 2 (Uniform renaming). *Let $M\frac{y}{x}$ be the renaming of program variable x to y (and vice-versa) within M, even when neither x nor y is fresh. If $\Gamma \vdash M : \phi$ then $\Gamma\frac{y}{x} \vdash M\frac{y}{x} : \phi\frac{y}{x}$.*

Proof summary. Straightforward induction on the structure of M. Renaming within proof terms (whose definition we omit as it is quite tedious) follows the usual homomorphisms, from which the inductive cases follow. In the case that M is a proof variable z, then $\left(\Gamma\frac{y}{x}\right)(z) = \Gamma(z)\frac{y}{x}$ from which the case follows. The interesting cases are those which modify program variables, e.g., $\langle z := f\frac{w}{z} \text{ in } p. M \rangle$. The bound variable z is renamed to $z\frac{y}{x}$, while the auxiliary variable w is α-varied if necessary to maintain freshness. Renaming then happens recursively in M.   □

Substitution will use proofs of coincidence and bound effect lemmas.

Lemma 3 (Coincidence). *Only the free variables of an expression influence its semantics.*

Lemma 4 (Bound effect). *Only the bound variables of a game are modified by execution.*

Summary. By induction on the expression, in analogy to [43].   □

Definition 9 (Term substitution admissibility). *For simplicity, we say ϕ_x^f (likewise for context Γ, term f, game α, and proof term M) is admissible if ϕ binds neither x nor free variables of f.*

The latter condition can be relaxed in practice [44] to requiring ϕ does not mention x under bindings of free variables.

Lemma 5 (Arithmetic-term substitution). *If $\Gamma \vdash M : \phi$ and the substitutions Γ_x^f, M_x^f, and ϕ_x^f are admissible, then $\Gamma_x^f \vdash M_x^f : \phi_x^f$.*

Summary. By induction on M. Admissibility holds recursively, and so can be assumed at each step of the induction. For non-atomic M that bind no variables, the proof follows from the inductive hypotheses. For M that bind variables, we appeal to Lemma 3 and Lemma 4.   □

Just as arithmetic terms are substituted for program variables, proof terms are substituted for proof variables.

Lemma 6 (Proof term substitution). *Let $[N/p]M$ substitute N for p in M, avoiding capture. If $\Gamma, p : \psi \vdash M : \phi$ and $\Gamma \vdash N : \psi$ then $\Gamma \vdash [N/p]M : \phi$.*

Proof. By induction on M, appealing to renaming, coincidence, and bound effect. When substituting N for p into a term that binds program variables such as $\langle z := f \frac{y}{z}$ in $q.\ M\rangle$, we avoid capture by renaming within occurrences of N in the recursive call, i.e., $[N/p]\langle z := f \frac{y}{z}$ in $q.\ M\rangle = \langle z := f \frac{y}{z}$ in $q.\ [N_y^z/p]M\rangle$, preserving soundness by Lemma 2.   □

Soundness of the proof calculus exploits renaming and substitution.

Theorem 1 (Soundness of proof calculus). *If $\Gamma \vdash M : \phi$ then $(\Gamma \vdash \phi)$ is valid. As a special case for empty context $\cdot$, if $\cdot \vdash M : \phi$, then ϕ is valid.*

Proof summary. By induction on M. Modus ponens case $A\ B$ reduces to Lemma 6. Cases that bind program variables, such as assignment, hold by Lemma 5 and Lemma 2. Rule W is employed when substituting under a binder.   □

We have now shown that the CGL proof calculus is sound, the *sine qua non* condition of any proof system. Because soundness was w.r.t. a realizability semantics, we have shown CGL is constructive in the sense that provable formulas correspond to realizable strategies, i.e., imperative programs executed in an adversarial environment. We will revisit constructivity again in Section 8 from the perspective of proof terms as *functional* programs.

7   Operational Semantics

The Curry-Howard interpretation of games is not complete without exploring the interpretation of proof simplification as normalization of functional programs. To this end, we now introduce a structural operational semantics for CGL proof terms. This semantics provides a view complementary to the realizability semantics: not only do provable formulas correspond to realizers, but proof terms can be directly executed as functional programs, resulting in a *normal* proof term. The chief subtlety of our operational semantics is that in contrast to realizer execution, proof simplification is a static operation, and thus does not inspect game state. Thus the normal form of a proof which branches on the game state is, of necessity, also a proof which branches on the game state. This static-dynamic phase separation need not be mysterious: it is analogous to the monadic phase separation between a functional program which returns an imperative command vs. the execution of the returned command. While the primary motivation for our operational semantics is to complete the Curry-Howard interpretation, proof normalization is also helpful when implementing software tools which process proof artifacts, since code that consumes a normal proof is in general easier to implement than code that consumes an arbitrary proof.

The operational semantics consist of two main judgments: M normal says that M is a normal form, while $M \mapsto M'$ says that M reduces to term M' in one step of evaluation. A normal proof is allowed a case operation at the top-level, either $\langle$case A of $\ell \Rightarrow B \mid r \Rightarrow C\rangle$ or $\langle$case$_*$ A of $s \Rightarrow B \mid g \Rightarrow C\rangle$. Normal proofs M without state-casing are called *simple*, written M simp. The requirement that cases are top-level ensures that proofs which differ only in where the case was applied share a common normal form, and ensures that β-reduction is never blocked by a case interceding between introduction-elimination pairs. Top-level case analyses are analogous to case-tree normal forms in lambda calculi with coproducts [4]. Reduction of proof terms is eager.

Definition 10 (Normal forms). *We say M is* simple, *written M simp, if eliminators occur only under binders. We say M is* normal, *written M normal, if M simp or M has shape $\langle$case A of $\ell \Rightarrow B \mid r \Rightarrow C\rangle$ or $\langle$case$_*$ A of $s \Rightarrow B \mid g \Rightarrow C\rangle$ where A is a term such as (split $[f, g]$ M) that inspects the state. Subterms B and C need not be normal since they occur under the binding of ℓ or r (resp. s or g).*

That is, a normal term has no top-level beta-redexes, and state-dependent cases are top-level. We consider rules $[*]$R, $[:*]$I, $[?]$I, and $\langle:=\rangle$I binding. Rules such as $\langle*\rangle$I have multiple premises but bind only one. While $[*]$R does not introduce a proof variable, it is rather considered binding to prevent divergence, which is in keeping with a coinductive understanding of formula $[\alpha^*]\phi$. If we did not care whether terms diverge, we could have made $[*]$R non-binding.

For the sake of space, this section focuses on the β-rules (Fig. 5). The full calculus, given in the extended version [12], includes structural and commuting-conversion rules, as well as what we call *monotonicity conversion* rules: a proof term $M \circ_p N$ is simplified by structural recursion on M. The capture-avoiding substitution of M for p in N is written $[M/p]N$ (Lemma 6). The propositional cases $\lambda\phi\beta$, $\lambda\beta$, caseβL, caseβR, $\pi_1\beta$, and $\pi_2\beta$ are standard reductions for applications, cases, and projections. Projection terms $\pi_1 M$ and $\pi_2 M$ should not be confused with projection realizers $\pi_L(a)$ and $\pi_R(a)$. Rule unpackβ makes the witness of an existential available in its client as a ghost variable.

Rule FPβ, repβ, and forβ reduce introductions and eliminations of loops. Rule FPβ, which reduces a proof $FP(A, s.\ B, g.\ C)$ says that if α^* has already terminated according to A, then B proves the postcondition. Else the inductive step C applies, but every reference to the IH g is transformed to a recursive application of FP. If A uses only $\langle*\rangle$S and $\langle*\rangle$G, then $FP(A, s.\ B, g.\ C)$ reduces to a simple term, else if A uses $\langle*\rangle$I, then $FP(A, s.\ B, g.\ C)$ reduces to a case. Rule repβ says loop induction (M rep $p : J.\ N$ in O) reduces to a delayed pair

$\lambda\phi\beta$ $(\lambda p:\phi.\ M)\ N \mapsto [N/p]M$ $\quad$ caseβL $\langle$case $\langle\!\langle\ell\cdot A\rangle\!\rangle$ of $\ell \Rightarrow\ B\ |\ r \Rightarrow\ C\rangle \mapsto [A/\ell]B$

$\lambda\beta$ $(\lambda x:Q.\ M)\ f \mapsto M_x^f$ $\quad$ caseβR $\langle$case $\langle\!\langle r\cdot A\rangle\!\rangle$ of $\ell \Rightarrow\ B\ |\ r \Rightarrow\ C\rangle \mapsto [A/r]C$

$\pi_1\beta$ $\langle\!\langle\pi_1\langle\!\langle M,N\rangle\!\rangle\rangle\!\rangle \mapsto M$ $\quad$ unrollβ [unroll [roll M]] $\mapsto M$

$\pi_2\beta$ $\langle\!\langle\pi_2\langle\!\langle M,N\rangle\!\rangle\rangle\!\rangle \mapsto N$

unpackβ unpack$(\langle f\frac{y}{x} :* q.\ M\rangle, py.\ N) \mapsto (\mathsf{Ghost}[x = f\frac{y}{x}](q.\ [M/p]N))\frac{x}{y}$

$\quad$ FPβ $FP(D,s.\ B,g.\ C) \mapsto (\langle\mathsf{case}_* \ D$ of $s \Rightarrow\ B\ |\ g \Rightarrow [(g\circ_z FP(z,s.\ B,g.\ C))/g]C\rangle)$

$\quad$ repβ $(M$ rep $p:J.\ N$ in $O) \mapsto [\mathsf{roll}\ \langle M, ([M/p]N)\circ_q(q$ rep $p:J.\ N$ in $O)\rangle]$

$\quad$ forβ for$(p:\varphi(\mathcal{M}) = A; q.\ B; C)\{\alpha\} \mapsto$

$\langle$case split $[\mathcal{M},0]$ of

$\ell \Rightarrow\ \langle$stop $[(A,\ell)/(p,q)]C\rangle$

$|\ r \Rightarrow\ \mathsf{Ghost}[\mathcal{M}_0 = \mathcal{M}](rr.\ \langle$go $(([A,\langle rr,r\rangle/p,q]B)\circ_t(\mathsf{for}(p:\varphi(\mathcal{M}) = \pi_1 t; q.\ B; C)\{\alpha\}))\rangle)\rangle$

Fig. 5. Operational semantics: β-rules

of the "stop" and "go" cases, where the "go" case first shows $[\alpha]J$, for loop invariant J, then expands $J \to [\alpha^*]\phi$ in the postcondition. Note the laziness of [roll] is essential for normalization: when $(M$ rep $p:J.\ N$ in $O)$ is understood as a coinductive proof, it is clear that normalization would diverge if repβ were applied indefinitely. Rule forβ for for$(p:\varphi(\mathcal{M}) = A; q.\ B; C)\{\alpha\}$ checks whether the termination metric $\mathcal{M}$ has reached terminal value 0. If so, the loop $\langle$stop$\rangle$'s and A proves it has converged. Else, we remember $\mathcal{M}$'s value in a ghost term $\mathcal{M}_0$, and $\langle$go$\rangle$ forward, supplying A and $\langle r, rr\rangle$ to satisfy the preconditions of inductive step B, then execute the loop for$(p:\varphi(\mathcal{M}) = \pi_1 t; q.\ B; C)\{\alpha\}$ in the postcondition. Rule forβ reflects the fact that the exact number of iterations is state dependent.

We discuss the structural, commuting conversion, and monotonicity conversion rules for left injections as an example, with the full calculus in [12]. Structural rule $\ell\cdot$S evaluates term M under an injector. Commuting conversion rule $\langle\!\langle\ell\cdot\rangle\!\rangle$C normalizes an injection of a case to a case with injectors on each branch. Monotonicity conversion rule $\langle\!\langle\ell\cdot\rangle\!\rangle\circ$ simplifies a monotonicity proof of an injection to an injection of a monotonicity proof.

$$\ell\cdot\mathrm{S} \quad \frac{M \mapsto M'}{\langle\!\langle\ell\cdot M\rangle\!\rangle \mapsto \langle\!\langle\ell\cdot M'\rangle\!\rangle}$$

$\langle\!\langle\ell\cdot\rangle\!\rangle$C $\langle\!\langle\ell\cdot\langle$case A of $p \Rightarrow\ B\ |\ q \Rightarrow\ C\rangle\rangle\!\rangle \mapsto \langle$case A of $p \Rightarrow\ \langle\!\langle\ell\cdot B\rangle\!\rangle\ |\ q \Rightarrow\ \langle\!\langle\ell\cdot C\rangle\!\rangle\rangle$

$\langle\!\langle\ell\cdot\rangle\!\rangle\circ$ $\langle\!\langle\ell\cdot M\rangle\!\rangle\circ_p N \mapsto \langle\!\langle\ell\cdot(M\circ_p N)\rangle\!\rangle$

Fig. 6. Operational semantics: structural, commuting conversion, monotonicity rules

8   Theory: Constructivity

We now complete the study of CGL's constructivity. We validate the operational semantics on proof terms by proving that progress and preservation hold, and thus the CGL proof calculus is sound as a type system for the functional programming language of CGL proof terms.

Lemma 7 (Progress). *If* $\cdot \vdash M : \phi$, *then either* M *is normal or* $M \mapsto M'$ *for some* M'.

Summary. By induction on the proof term M. If M is an introduction rule, by the inductive hypotheses the subterms are well-typed. If they are all simple, then M simp. If some subterm (not under a binder) steps, then M steps by a structural rule. Else some subterm is an irreducible case expression not under a binder, it lifts by the commuting conversion rule. If M is an elimination rule, structural and commuting conversion rules are applied as above. Else by Def. 10 the subterm is an introduction rule, and M reduces with a β-rule. Lastly, if M has form $A \circ_x B$ and A simp, then by Def. 10 A is an introduction form, thus reduced by some monotonicity conversion rule.   □

Lemma 8 (Preservation). *Let* $\mapsto^*$ *be the reflexive, transitive closure of the* $\mapsto$ *relation. If* $\cdot \vdash M : \phi$ *and* $M \mapsto^* M'$, *then* $\cdot \vdash M' : \phi$

Summary. Induct on the derivation $M \mapsto^* M'$, then induct on $M \mapsto M'$. The β cases follow by Lemma 6 (for base constructs), and Lemma 6 and Lemma 2 (for assignments). C-rules and $\circ$-rules lift across binders, soundly by W. S-rules are direct by IH.   □

We gave two understandings of proofs in CGL, as imperative strategies and as functional programs. We now give a final perspective: CGL proofs support synthesis in principle, one of our main motivations. Formally, the Existential Property (EP) and Disjunction Property (DP) justify synthesis [18] for existentials and disjunctions: whenever an existential or disjunction has a proof, then we can compute some instance or disjunct that has a proof. We state and prove an EP and DP for CGL, then introduce a Strategy Property, their counterpart for synthesizing strategies from game modalities. It is important to our EP that terms are arbitrary computable functions, because more simplistic term languages are often too weak to witness the existentials they induce.

Example 1 (Rich terms help). Formulas over polynomial terms can have non-polynomial witnesses.

Let $\phi \equiv (x = y \wedge x \geq 0) \vee (x = -y \wedge x < 0)$. Then $f = |x|$ witnesses $\exists y : \mathbb{Q}\ \phi$.

Lemma 9 (Existential Property). *If* $\Gamma \vdash M : (\exists x : \mathbb{Q}\ \phi)$ *then there exists a term* f *and realizer* b *such that for all* $(a, \omega) \in [\![\bigwedge \Gamma]\!]$, *we have* $(b\,a, \omega_x^{f(\omega)}) \in [\![\phi]\!]$.

Proof. By Theorem 1, the sequent $(\Gamma \vdash \exists x : \mathbb{Q}\ \phi)$ is valid. Since $(a, \omega) \in [\![\bigwedge \Gamma]\!]$, then by the definition of sequent validity, there exists a common realizer c such that $(c\,a, \omega) \in [\![\exists x : \mathbb{Q}\ \phi]\!]$. Now let $f = \pi_L(c\,a)$ and $b = \pi_R(c\,a)$ and the result is immediate by the semantics of existentials.   □

Disjunction strategies can depend on the state, so naïve DP does not hold.

Example 2 (Naïve DP). When $\Gamma \vdash M : (\phi \vee \psi)$ there need not be N such that $\Gamma \vdash N : \phi$ or $\Gamma \vdash N : \psi$.

Consider $\phi \equiv x > 0$ and $\psi \equiv x < 1$. Then $\cdot \vdash$ split $[x, 0]$ () $: (\phi \vee \psi)$, but neither $x < 1$ nor $x > 0$ is valid, let alone provable.

Lemma 10 (Disjunction Property). *When $\Gamma \vdash M : \phi \vee \psi$ there exists realizer b and computable f, s.t. for every ω and a such that $(a, \omega) \in [\![\bigwedge \Gamma]\!]$, either $f(\omega) = 0$ and $(\pi_L(b), \omega) \in [\![\phi]\!]$, else $f(\omega) = 1$ and $(\pi_R(b), \omega) \in [\![\psi]\!]$.*

Proof. By Theorem 1, the sequent $\Gamma \vdash \phi \vee \psi$ is valid. Since $(a, \omega) \in [\![\bigwedge \Gamma]\!]$, then by the definition of sequent validity, there exists a common realizer c such that $(c\,a, \omega) \in [\![\phi \vee \psi]\!]$. Now let $f = \pi_L(c\,a)$ and $b = \pi_R(c\,a)$ and the result is immediate by the semantics of disjunction. $\qquad\square$

Following the same approach, we generalize to a Strategy Property. In CGL, strategies are represented by realizers, which implement every computation made throughout the game. Thus, to show provable games have computable winning strategies, it suffices to exhibit realizers.

Theorem 2 (Active Strategy Property). *If $\Gamma \vdash M : \langle \alpha \rangle \phi$, then there exists a realizer b such that for all ω and realizers a such that $(a, \omega) \in [\![\bigwedge \Gamma]\!]$, then $\{(b\,a, \omega)\}\langle\!\langle \alpha \rangle\!\rangle \subseteq [\![\phi]\!] \cup \{\top\}$.*

Theorem 3 (Dormant Strategy Property). *If $\Gamma \vdash M : [\alpha]\phi$, then there exists a realizer b such that for all ω and realizers a such that $(a, \omega) \in [\![\bigwedge \Gamma]\!]$, then $\{(b\,a, \omega)\}[\![\alpha]\!] \subseteq [\![\phi]\!] \cup \{\top\}$.*

Summary. From proof term M and Theorem 1, we have a realizer for formula $\langle \alpha \rangle \phi$ or $[\alpha]\phi$, respectively. We proceed by induction on α: the realizer $b\,a$ contains all realizers applied in the inductive cases composed with their continuations that prove ϕ in each base case. $\qquad\square$

While these proofs, especially EP and DP, are short and direct, we note that this is by design: the challenge in developing CGL is not so much the proofs of this section, rather these proofs become simple because we adopted a realizability semantics. The challenge was in developing the semantics and adapting the proof calculus and theory to that semantics.

9   Conclusion and Future Work

In this paper, we developed a Constructive Game Logic CGL, from syntax and realizability semantics to a proof calculus and operational semantics on the proof terms. We developed two understandings of proofs as programs: semantically, every proof of game winnability corresponds to a realizer which computes the game's winning strategy, while the language of proof terms is also a functional programming language where proofs reduce to their normal forms according to the operational semantics. We completed the Curry-Howard interpretation for games by showing Existential, Disjunction, and Strategy properties: programs can be synthesized that decide which instance, disjunct, or moves are taken in existentials, disjunctions, and games. In summary, we have developed the most comprehensive Curry-Howard interpretation of any program logic to date, for a much more expressive logic than prior work [32]. Because CGL contains constructive Concurrent DL and first-order DL as strict fragments, we have provided a comprehensive Curry-Howard interpretation for them in one fell swoop. The key insights behind CGL should apply to the many dynamic and Hoare logics used in verification today.

Synthesis is the immediate application of CGL. Motivations for synthesis include security games [40], concurrent programs with demonic schedulers (Concurrent Dynamic Logic), and control software for safety-critical cyber-physical systems such as cars and planes. In general, any kind of software program which must operate correctly in an adversarial environment can benefit from game logic verification. The proofs of Theorem 2 and Theorem 3 constitute an (on-paper) algorithm which performs synthesis of guaranteed-correct strategies from game proofs. The first future work is to implement this algorithm in code, providing much-needed assurance for software which is often mission-critical or safety-critical. This paper focused on discrete CGL with one numeric type simply because any further features would distract from the core features. Real applications come from many domains which add features around this shared core.

The second future work is to extend CGL to hybrid games, which provide compelling applications from the domain of adversarial cyber-physical systems. This future work will combine the novel features of CGL with those of the classical logic dGL. The primary task is to define a constructive semantics for differential equations and to give constructive interpretations to the differential equation rules of dGL. Previous work on formalizations of differential equations [34] suggests differential equations can be treated constructively. In principle, existing proofs in dGL might happen to be constructive, but this does not obviate the present work. On the contrary, once a game logic proof is shown to fall in the constructive fragment, our work gives a correct synthesis guarantee for it too!

References

1. Abramsky, S., Jagadeesan, R., Malacaria, P.: Full abstraction for PCF. Inf. Comput. **163**(2), 409–470 (2000), https://doi.org/10.1006/inco.2000.2930
2. Aczel, P., Gambino, N.: The generalised type-theoretic interpretation of constructive set theory. J. Symb. Log. **71**(1), 67–103 (2006), https://doi.org/10.2178/jsl/1140641163
3. Alechina, N., Mendler, M., de Paiva, V., Ritter, E.: Categorical and Kripke semantics for constructive S4 modal logic. In: Fribourg, L. (ed.) CSL. LNCS, vol. 2142, pp. 292–307. Springer (2001), https://doi.org/10.1007/3-ν540-ν44802-ν0_21
4. Altenkirch, T., Dybjer, P., Hofmann, M., Scott, P.J.: Normalization by evaluation for typed lambda calculus with coproducts. In: LICS. pp. 303–310. IEEE Computer Society (2001), https://doi.org/10.1109/LICS.2001.932506

5. Alur, R., Henzinger, T.A., Kupferman, O.: Alternating-time temporal logic. J. ACM **49**(5), 672–713 (2002), https://doi.org/10.1145/585265.585270
6. van Benthem, J.: Logic of strategies: What and how? In: van Benthem, J., Ghosh, S., Verbrugge, R. (eds.) Models of Strategic Reasoning - Logics, Games, and Communities, LNCS, vol. 8972, pp. 321–332. Springer (2015), https://doi.org/10.1007/978-ν3-ν662-ν48540-ν8_10
7. van Benthem, J., Bezhanishvili, G.: Modal logics of space. In: Aiello, M., Pratt-Hartmann, I., van Benthem, J. (eds.) Handbook of Spatial Logics, pp. 217–298. Springer (2007), https://doi.org/10.1007/978-ν1-ν4020-ν5587-ν4_5
8. van Benthem, J., Bezhanishvili, N., Enqvist, S.: A propositional dynamic logic for instantial neighborhood models. In: Baltag, A., Seligman, J., Yamada, T. (eds.) Logic, Rationality, and Interaction - 6th International Workshop, LORI 2017, Sapporo, Japan, September 11-14, 2017, Proceedings. LNCS, vol. 10455, pp. 137–150. Springer (2017), https://doi.org/10.1007/978-ν3-ν662-ν55665-ν8_10
9. van Benthem, J., Pacuit, E.: Dynamic logics of evidence-based beliefs. Studia Logica **99**(1-3), 61–92 (2011), https://doi.org/10.1007/s11225-ν011-ν9347-νx
10. van Benthem, J., Pacuit, E., Roy, O.: Toward a theory of play: A logical perspective on games and interaction. Games (2011), https://doi.org/10.3390/g2010052
11. Bishop, E.: Foundations of constructive analysis (1967)
12. Bohrer, R., Platzer, A.: Constructive hybrid games. CoRR **abs/2002.02536** (2020), https://arxiv.org/abs/2002.02536
13. Bridges, D.S., Vita, L.S.: Techniques of constructive analysis. Springer (2007)
14. Celani, S.A.: A fragment of intuitionistic dynamic logic. Fundam. Inform. **46**(3), 187–197 (2001), http://content.iospress.com/articles/fundamenta-νinformaticae/fi46-ν3-ν01
15. Chatterjee, K., Henzinger, T.A., Piterman, N.: Strategy logic. In: Caires, L., Vasconcelos, V.T. (eds.) CONCUR. LNCS, Springer (2007), https://doi.org/10.1007/978-ν3-ν540-ν74407-ν8_5
16. Coquand, T., Huet, G.P.: The calculus of constructions. Inf. Comput. **76**(2/3), 95–120 (1988), https://doi.org/10.1016/0890-ν5401(88)90005-ν3
17. Curry, H., Feys, R.: Combinatory logic. In: Heyting, A., Robinson, A. (eds.) Studies in logic and the foundations of mathematics. North-Holland (1958)
18. Degen, J., Werner, J.: Towards intuitionistic dynamic logic. Logic and Logical Philosophy **15**(4), 305–324 (2006). https://doi.org/10.12775/LLP.2006.018
19. Doberkat, E.: Towards a coalgebraic interpretation of propositional dynamic logic. CoRR **abs/1109.3685** (2011), http://arxiv.org/abs/1109.3685
20. Fernández-Duque, D.: The intuitionistic temporal logic of dynamical systems. Log. Methods in Computer Science **14**(3) (2018), https://doi.org/10.23638/LMCS-ν14(3:3)2018
21. Frittella, S., Greco, G., Kurz, A., Palmigiano, A., Sikimic, V.: A proof-theoretic semantic analysis of dynamic epistemic logic. J. Log. Comput. **26**(6), 1961–2015 (2016), https://doi.org/10.1093/logcom/exu063
22. Fulton, N., Platzer, A.: A logic of proofs for differential dynamic logic: Toward independently checkable proof certificates for dynamic logics. In: Avigad, J., Chlipala, A. (eds.) CPP. pp. 110–121. ACM (2016). https://doi.org/10.1145/2854065.2854078
23. Ghilardi, S.: Presheaf semantics and independence results for some non-classical first-order logics. Arch. Math. Log. **29**(2), 125–136 (1989), https://doi.org/10.1007/BF01620621
24. Ghosh, S.: Strategies made explicit in dynamic game logic. Workshop on Logic and Intelligent Interaction at ESSLLI pp. 74–81 (2008)

25. Goranko, V.: The basic algebra of game equivalences. Studia Logica **75**(2), 221–238 (2003), https://doi.org/10.1023/A:1027311011342

26. Griffin, T.: A formulae-as-types notion of control. In: Allen, F.E. (ed.) POPL. pp. 47–58. ACM Press (1990), https://doi.org/10.1145/96709.96714

27. Harper, R.: The holy trinity (2011), https://web.archive.org/web/20170921012554/http://existentialtype.wordpress.com/2011/03/27/the-νholy-νtrinity/

28. Hilken, B.P., Rydeheard, D.E.: A first order modal logic and its sheaf models

29. Hoare, C.A.R.: An axiomatic basis for computer programming. Commun. ACM **12**(10), 576–580 (1969). https://doi.org/10.1145/363235.363259

30. van der Hoek, W., Jamroga, W., Wooldridge, M.J.: A logic for strategic reasoning. In: Dignum, F., Dignum, V., Koenig, S., Kraus, S., Singh, M.P., Wooldridge, M.J. (eds.) AAMAS. ACM (2005), https://doi.org/10.1145/1082473.1082497

31. Howard, W.A.: The formulae-as-types notion of construction. To HB Curry: essays on combinatory logic, lambda calculus and formalism **44**, 479–490 (1980)

32. Kamide, N.: Strong normalization of program-indexed lambda calculus. Bull. Sect. Logic Univ. Łódź **39**(1-2), 65–78 (2010)

33. Lipton, J.: Constructive Kripke semantics and realizability. In: Moschovakis, Y. (ed.) Logic from Computer Science. pp. 319–357. Springer (1992). https://doi.org/10.1007/978-1-4612-2822-6_13

34. Makarov, E., Spitters, B.: The Picard algorithm for ordinary differential equations in Coq. In: Blazy, S., Paulin-Mohring, C., Pichardie, D. (eds.) ITP. LNCS, vol. 7998. Springer (2013), https://doi.org/10.1007/978-ν3-ν642-ν39634-ν2_34

35. Mamouras, K.: Synthesis of strategies using the Hoare logic of angelic and demonic nondeterminism. Log. Methods Computer Science **12**(3) (2016), https://doi.org/10.2168/LMCS-ν12(3:6)2016

36. Mitsch, S., Platzer, A.: ModelPlex: Verified runtime validation of verified cyber-physical system models. Form. Methods Syst. Des. **49**(1), 33–74 (2016). https://doi.org/10.1007/s10703-016-0241-z, special issue of selected papers from RV'14

37. van Oosten, J.: Realizability: A historical essay. Mathematical Structures in Computer Science **12**(3), 239–263 (2002), https://doi.org/10.1017/S0960129502003626

38. Parikh, R.: Propositional game logic. In: FOCS. pp. 195–200. IEEE (1983), https://doi.org/10.1109/SFCS.1983.47

39. Pauly, M.: A modal logic for coalitional power in games. J. Log. Comput. **12**(1), 149–166 (2002), https://doi.org/10.1093/logcom/12.1.149

40. Pauly, M., Parikh, R.: Game logic - an overview. Studia Logica **75**(2), 165–182 (2003), https://doi.org/10.1023/A:1027354826364

41. Peleg, D.: Concurrent dynamic logic. J. ACM **34**(2), 450–479 (1987), https://doi.org/10.1145/23005.23008

42. Platzer, A.: Differential game logic. ACM Trans. Comput. Log. **17**(1), 1:1–1:51 (2015). https://doi.org/10.1145/2817824

43. Platzer, A.: A complete uniform substitution calculus for differential dynamic logic. J. Autom. Reas. **59**(2), 219–265 (2017). https://doi.org/10.1007/s10817-016-9385-1

44. Platzer, A.: Uniform substitution for differential game logic. In: Galmiche, D., Schulz, S., Sebastiani, R. (eds.) IJCAR. LNCS, vol. 10900, pp. 211–227. Springer (2018). https://doi.org/10.1007/978-3-319-94205-6_15

45. Pratt, V.R.: Semantical considerations on floyd-hoare logic. In: FOCS. pp. 109–121. IEEE (1976). https://doi.org/10.1109/SFCS.1976.27

46. Ramanujam, R., Simon, S.E.: Dynamic logic on games with structured strategies. In: Brewka, G., Lang, J. (eds.) Knowledge Representation. pp. 49–58. AAAI Press (2008), http://www.aaai.org/Library/KR/2008/kr08-ν006.php
47. Robinson, J.: Definability and decision problems in arithmetic. J. Symb. Log. **14**(2), 98–114 (1949), https://doi.org/10.2307/2266510
48. The Coq development team: The Coq proof assistant reference manual (2019), https://coq.inria.fr/
49. Van Benthem, J.: Games in dynamic-epistemic logic. Bulletin of Economic Research **53**(4), 219–248 (2001)
50. Vanderwaart, J., Dreyer, D., Petersen, L., Crary, K., Harper, R., Cheng, P.: Typed compilation of recursive datatypes. In: Shao, Z., Lee, P. (eds.) Proceedings of TLDI'03: 2003 ACM SIGPLAN International Workshop on Types in Languages Design and Implementation, New Orleans, Louisiana, USA, January 18, 2003. pp. 98–108. ACM (2003), https://doi.org/10.1145/604174.604187
51. Weihrauch, K.: Computable Analysis - An Introduction. Texts in Theoretical Computer Science. An EATCS Series, Springer (2000), https://doi.org/10.1007/978-ν3-ν642-ν56999-ν9
52. Wijesekera, D.: Constructive modal logics I. Ann. Pure Appl. Logic **50**(3), 271–301 (1990), https://doi.org/10.1016/0168-ν0072(90)90059-νB
53. Wijesekera, D., Nerode, A.: Tableaux for constructive concurrent dynamic logic. Ann. Pure Appl. Logic (2005), https://doi.org/10.1016/j.apal.2004.12.001

Optimal and Perfectly Parallel Algorithms for On-demand Data-flow Analysis*

Krishnendu Chatterjee[1], Amir Kafshdar Goharshady[1], Rasmus Ibsen-Jensen[2], and Andreas Pavlogiannis[3]

[1] IST Austria, Klosterneuburg, Austria
[krishnendu.chatterjee, amir.goharshady]@ist.ac.at
[2] University of Liverpool, Liverpool, United Kingdom
r.ibsen-jensen@liverpool.ac.uk
[3] Aarhus University, Aarhus, Denmark
pavlogiannis@cs.au.dk

Abstract. Interprocedural data-flow analyses form an expressive and useful paradigm of numerous static analysis applications, such as live variables analysis, alias analysis and null pointers analysis. The most widely-used framework for interprocedural data-flow analysis is *IFDS*, which encompasses distributive data-flow functions over a finite domain. *On-demand* data-flow analyses restrict the focus of the analysis on specific program locations and data facts. This setting provides a natural split between (i) an *offline (or preprocessing) phase*, where the program is partially analyzed and analysis summaries are created, and (ii) an *online (or query) phase*, where analysis queries arrive on demand and the summaries are used to speed up answering queries.

In this work, we consider on-demand IFDS analyses where the queries concern program locations of the same procedure (aka same-context queries). We exploit the fact that flow graphs of programs have low treewidth to develop faster algorithms that are *space and time optimal* for many common data-flow analyses, in both the preprocessing and the query phase. We also use treewidth to develop query solutions that are *embarrassingly parallelizable*, i.e. the total work for answering each query is split to a number of threads such that each thread performs only a constant amount of work. Finally, we implement a static analyzer based on our algorithms, and perform a series of on-demand analysis experiments on standard benchmarks. Our experimental results show a drastic speed-up of the queries after only a lightweight preprocessing phase, which significantly outperforms existing techniques.

Keywords: Data-flow analysis, IFDS, Treewidth

---

*The research was partly supported by Austrian Science Fund (FWF) Grant No. NFN S11407-N23 (RiSE/SHiNE), FWF Schrödinger Grant No. J-4220, Vienna Science and Technology Fund (WWTF) Project ICT15-003, Facebook PhD Fellowship Program, IBM PhD Fellowship Program, and DOC Fellowship No. 24956 of the Austrian Academy of Sciences (ÖAW). A longer version of this work is available at [17].

P. Müller (Ed.): ESOP 2020, LNCS 12075, pp. 112–140, 2020.
https://doi.org/10.1007/978-3-030-44914-8_5

1   Introduction

Static data-flow analysis. Static program analysis is a fundamental approach
for both analyzing program correctness and performing compiler optimizations
[25,39,44,64,30]. Static data-flow analyses associate with each program location
a set of data-flow facts which are guaranteed to hold under all program executions, and these facts are then used to reason about program correctness,
report erroneous behavior, and optimize program execution. Static data-flow
analyses have numerous applications, such as in pointer analysis (e.g., points-
to analysis and detection of null pointer dereferencing) [46,57,61,62,66,67,69], in
detecting privacy and security issues (e.g., taint analysis, SQL injection analysis)
[3,37,31,33,47,40], as well as in compiler optimizations (e.g., constant propagation, reaching definitions, register allocation) [50,32,55,13,2].

Interprocedural analysis and the IFDS framework. Data-flow analyses fall in two
large classes: *intraprocedural* and *interprocedural*. In the former, each procedure
of the program is analyzed in isolation, ignoring the interaction between procedures which occurs due to parameter passing/return. In the latter, all procedures
of the program are analyzed together, accounting for such interactions, which
leads to results of increased precision, and hence is often preferable to intraprocedural analysis [49,54,59,60]. To filter out false results, interprocedural analyses
typically employ call-context sensitivity, which ensures that the underlying execution paths respect the calling context of procedure invocations. One of the most
widely used frameworks for interprocedural data-flow analysis is the framework
of Interprocedural Finite Distributive Subset (IFDS) problems [50], which offers
a unified formulation of a wide class of interprocedural data-flow analyses as a
reachability problem. This elegant algorithmic formulation of data-flow analysis
has been a topic of active study, allowing various subsequent practical improvements [36,45,8,3,47,56] and implementations in prominent static analysis tools
such as Soot [7] and WALA [1].

On-demand analysis. Exhaustive data-flow analysis is computationally expensive
and often unnecessary. Hence, a topic of great interest in the community is
that of *on-demand* data-flow analysis [4,27,36,51,48,68,45]. On-demand analyses
have several applications, such as (quoting from [36,48]) (i) narrowing down the
focus to specific points of interest, (ii) narrowing down the focus to specific
data-flow facts of interest, (iii) reducing work in preliminary phases, (iv) side-
stepping incremental updating problems, and (v) offering demand analysis as a
user-level operation. On-demand analysis is also extremely useful for speculative
optimizations in just-in-time compilers [24,43,5,29], where dynamic information
can dramatically increase the precision of the analysis. In this setting, it is crucial
that the the on-demand analysis runs fast, to incur as little overhead as possible.

Example 1. As a toy motivating example, consider the partial program shown in
Figure 1, compiled with a just-in-time compiler that uses speculative optimizations. Whether the compiler must compile the expensive function h depends on
whether x is null in line 6. Performing a null-pointer analysis from the entry of

```
1  void f(int b){               9  void g(int *&x, int *y){
2     int *x = NULL, *y = NULL; 10    x=y;
3     if(b > 1)                 11  }
4        y = &b;
5     g(x,y);                   12  void h(){
6     if(x==NULL)               13    //An expensive
7        h();                   14    //function
8  }                            15  }
```

Fig. 1: A partial C++ program.

f reveals that x might be null in line 6. Hence, if the decision to compile h relies only on an offline static analysis, h is always compiled, even when not needed.

Now consider the case where the execution of the program is in line 4, and at this point the compiler decides on whether to compile h. It is clear that given this information, x cannot be null in line 6 and thus h does not have to be compiled. As we have seen above, this decision can not be made based on offline analysis. On the other hand, an *on-demand* analysis starting from the current program location will correctly conclude that x is not null in line 6. Note however, that this decision is made by the compiler during runtime. Hence, such an on-demand analysis is useful only if it can be performed extremely fast. It is also highly desirable that the time for running this analysis is predictable, so that the compiler can decide whether to run the analysis or simply compile h proactively.

The techniques we develop in this paper answer the above challenges rigorously. Our approach exploits a key structural property of flow graphs of programs, called treewidth.

Treewidth of programs. A very well-studied notion in graph theory is the concept of *treewidth* of a graph, which is a measure of how similar a graph is to a tree (a graph has treewidth 1 precisely if it is a tree) [52]. On one hand the treewidth property provides a mathematically elegant way to study graphs, and on the other hand there are many classes of graphs which arise in practice and have constant treewidth. The most important example is that the flow graph for goto-free programs in many classic programming languages have constant treewidth [63]. The low treewidth of flow graphs has also been confirmed experimentally for programs written in Java [34], C [38], Ada [12] and Solidity [15].

Treewidth has important algorithmic implications, as many graph problems that are hard to solve in general admit efficient solutions on graphs of low treewidth. In the context of program analysis, this property has been exploited to develop improvements for register allocation [63,9] (a technique implemented in the Small Device C Compiler [28]), cache management [18], on-demand algebraic path analysis [16], on-demand *intraprocedural* data-flow analysis of concurrent programs [20] and data-dependence analysis [14].

Problem statement. We focus on on-demand data-flow analysis in IFDS [50,36,48]. The input consists of a supergraph G of n vertices, a data-fact domain D and a data-flow transformer function M. Edges of G capture control-flow within each procedure, as well as procedure invocations and returns. The set D defines the domain of the analysis, and contains the data facts to be discovered by the analysis for each program location. The function M associates with every edge (u, v) of G a data-flow transformer $M(u, v) : 2^D \to 2^D$. In words, $M(u, v)$ defines the set of data facts that hold at v in some execution that transitions from u to v, given the set of data facts that hold at u.

On-demand analysis brings a natural separation between (i) an *offline (or preprocessing) phase*, where the program is partially analyzed, and (ii) an *online (or query) phase*, where on-demand queries are handled. The task is to preprocess the input in the offline phase, so that in the online phase, the following types of on-demand queries are answered efficiently:

1. A *pair query* has the form (u, d_1, v, d_2), where u, v are vertices of G in the same procedure, and d_1, d_2 are data facts. The goal is to decide if there exists an execution that starts in u and ends in v, and given that the data fact d_1 held at the beginning of the execution, the data fact d_2 holds at the end. These are known as *same-context* queries and are very common in data-flow analysis [23,50,16].

2. A *single-source* query has the form (u, d_1), where u is a vertex of G and d_1 is a data fact. The goal is to compute for every vertex v that belongs to the same procedure as u, all the data facts that might hold in v as witnessed by executions that start in u and assuming that d_1 holds at the beginning of each such execution.

Previous results. The on-demand analysis problem admits a number of solutions that lie in the preprocessing/query spectrum. On the one end, the preprocessing phase can be disregarded, and every on-demand query be treated anew. Since each query starts a separate instance of IFDS, the time to answer it is $O(n \cdot |D|^3)$, for both pair and single-source queries [50]. On the other end, all possible queries can be pre-computed and cached in the preprocessing phase in time $O(n^2 \cdot |D|^3)$, after which each query costs time proportional to the size of the output (i.e., $O(1)$) for pair queries and $O(n \cdot |D|)$ for single-source queries). Note that this full preprocessing also incurs a cost $O(n^2 \cdot |D|^2)$ in space for storing the cache table, which is often prohibitive. On-demand analysis was more thoroughly studied in [36]. The main idea is that, instead of pre-computing the answer to all possible queries, the analysis results obtained by handling each query are memoized to a cache table, and are used for speeding up the computation of subsequent queries. This is a heuristic-based approach that often works well in practice, however, the only guarantee provided is that of *same-worst-case-complexity*, which states that in the worst case, the algorithm uses $O(n^2 \cdot |D|^3)$ time and $O(n^2 \cdot |D|^2)$ space, similarly to the complete preprocessing case. This guarantee is inadequate for runtime applications such as the example of Figure 1, as it would require either (i) to run a full analysis, or (ii) to run a partial analysis which might wrongly conclude that **h** is reachable, and thus compile it. Both cases incur a large runtime overhead, either because we run a full analysis, or because we compile an expensive function.

Our contributions. We develop algorithms for on-demand IFDS analyses that have strong worst-case time complexity guarantees and thus lead to more predictable performance than mere heuristics. The contributions of this work are as follows:

1. We develop an algorithm that, given a program represented as a supergraph of size n and a data fact domain D, solves the on-demand same-context IFDS problem while spending (i) $O(n \cdot |D|^3)$ time in the preprocessing phase, and (ii) $O(\lceil |D|/\log n \rceil)$ time for a pair query and $O(n \cdot |D|^2/\log n)$ time for a single-source query in the query phase. Observe that when $|D| = O(1)$, the preprocessing and query times are proportional to the size of the input and outputs, respectively, and are thus *optimal*[§]. In addition, our algorithm uses $O(n \cdot |D|^2)$ space at all times, which is proportional to the size of the input, and is thus *space optimal*. Hence, our algorithm not only improves upon previous state-of-the-art solutions, but also ensures optimality in both time and space.

2. We also show that after our one-time preprocessing, each query is *embarrassingly parallelizable*, i.e., every bit of the output can be produced by a single thread in $O(1)$ time. This makes our techniques particularly useful to speculative optimizations, since the analysis is guaranteed to take constant time and thus incur little runtime overhead. Although the parallelization of data-flow analysis has been considered before [41,42,53], this is the first time to obtain solutions that span beyond heuristics and offer theoretical guarantees. Moreover, this is a rather surprising result, given that general IFDS is known to be P-complete.

3. We implement our algorithms on a static analyzer and experimentally evaluate their performance on various static analysis clients over a standard set of benchmarks. Our experimental results show that after only a lightweight preprocessing, we obtain a significant speedup in the query phase compared to standard on-demand techniques in the literature. Also, our parallel implementation achieves a speedup close to the theoretical optimal, which illustrates that the perfect parallelization of the problem is realized by our approach in practice.

Recently, we exploited the low-treewidth property of programs to obtain faster algorithms for algebraic path analysis [16] and intraprocedural reachability [21]. Data-flow analysis can be reduced to these problems. Hence, the algorithms in [16,21] can also be applied to our setting. However, our new approach has two important advantages: (i) we show how to answer queries in a perfectly parallel manner, and (ii) reducing the problem to algebraic path properties and then applying the algorithms in [16,21] yields $O(n \cdot |D|^3)$ preprocessing time and $O(n \cdot \log n \cdot |D|^2)$ space, and has pair and single-source query time $O(|D|)$ and $O(n \cdot |D|^2)$. Hence, our space usage and query times are better by a factor of

---

[§]Note that we count the input itself as part of the space usage.

$\log n$[¶]. Moreover, when considering the complexity wrt n, i.e. considering D to be a constant, these results are optimal wrt both time and space. Hence, no further improvement is possible.

Remark. Note that our approach does not apply to arbitrary CFL reachability in constant treewidth. In addition to the treewidth, our algorithms also exploit specific structural properties of IFDS. In general, small treewidth alone does not improve the complexity of CFL reachability [14].

2   Preliminaries

Model of computation. We consider the standard RAM model with word size $W = \Theta(\log n)$, where n is the size of our input. In this model, one can store W bits in one word (aka "word tricks") and arithmetic and bitwise operations between pairs of words can be performed in $O(1)$ time. In practice, word size is a property of the machine and not the analysis. Modern machines have words of size at least 64. Since the size of real-world input instances never exceeds 2^{64}, the assumption of word size $W = \Theta(\log n)$ is well-realized in practice and no additional effort is required by the implementer to account for W in the context of data flow analysis.

Graphs. We consider directed graphs $G = (V, E)$ where V is a finite set of vertices and $E \subseteq V \times V$ is a set of directed edges. We use the term graph to refer to directed graphs and will explicitly mention if a graph is undirected. For two vertices $u, v \in V$, a path P from u to v is a finite sequence of vertices $P = (w_i)_{i=0}^k$ such that $w_0 = u$, $w_k = v$ and for every $i < k$, there is an edge from w_i to w_{i+1} in E. The length $|P|$ of the path P is equal to k. In particular, for every vertex u, there is a path of length 0 from u to itself. We write $P : u \rightsquigarrow v$ to denote that P is a path from u to v and $u \rightsquigarrow v$ to denote the existence of such a path, i.e. that v is reachable from u. Given a set $V' \subseteq V$ of vertices, the induced subgraph of G on V' is defined as $G[V'] = (V', E \cap (V' \times V'))$. Finally, the graph G is called *bipartite* if the set V can be partitioned into two sets V_1, V_2, so that every edge has one end in V_1 and the other in V_2, i.e. $E \subseteq (V_1 \times V_2) \cup (V_2 \times V_1)$.

2.1   The IFDS Framework

IFDS [50] is a ubiquitous and general framework for interprocedural data-flow analyses that have finite domains and distributive flow functions. It encompasses a wide variety of analyses, including truly-live variables, copy constant propagation, possibly-uninitialized variables, secure information-flow, and gen/kill or bitvector problems such as reaching definitions, available expressions and live variables [50,7]. IFDS obtains *interprocedurally precise* solutions. In contrast to intraprocedural analysis, in which precise denotes "meet-over-all-paths", interprocedurally precise solutions only consider valid paths, i.e. paths in which when

---

[¶]This improvement is due to the differences in the preprocessing phase. Our algorithms for the query phase are almost identical to our previous work.

a function reaches its end, control returns back to the site of the most recent call [58].

Flow graphs and supergraphs. In IFDS, a program with k procedures is specified by a *supergraph*, i.e. a graph $G = (V, E)$ consisting of k flow graphs $G_1, \ldots, G_k$, one for each procedure, and extra edges modeling procedure-calls. Flow graphs represent procedures in the usual way, i.e. they contain one vertex v_i for each statement i and there is an edge from v_i to v_j if the statement j may immediately follow the statement i in an execution of the procedure. The only exception is that a procedure-call statement i is represented by two vertices, a *call* vertex c_i and a *return-site* vertex r_i. The vertex c_i only has incoming edges, and the vertex r_i only has outgoing edges. There is also a *call-to-return-site* edge from c_i to r_i. The call-to-return-site edges are included for passing intraprocedural information, such as information about local variables, from c_i to r_i. Moreover, each flow graph G_l has a unique *start* vertex s_l and a unique *exit* vertex e_l.

The supergraph G also contains the following edges for each procedure-call i with call vertex c_i and return-site vertex r_i that calls a procedure l: (i) an inter-procedural *call-to-start* edge from c_i to the start vertex of the called procedure, i.e. s_l, and (ii) an interprocedural *exit-to-return-site* edge from the exit vertex of the called procedure, i.e. e_l, to r_i.

Example 2. Figure 2 shows a simple C++ program on the left and its supergraph on the right. Each statement i of the program has a corresponding vertex v_i in the supergraph, except for statement 7, which is a procedure-call statement and hence has a corresponding call vertex c_7 and return-site vertex r_7.

```
1   void f(int *&x, int *y){
2       y = new int(1);
3       y = new int(2);
4   }


5   int main(){
6       int *x, *y;
7       f(x,y);
8       *x += *y;
9   }
```

Fig. 2: A C++ program (left) and its supergraph (right).

Interprocedurally valid paths. Not every path in the supergraph G can potentially be realized by an execution of the program. Consider a path P in G and let P' be the sequence of vertices obtained by removing every v_i from P, i.e. P' only consists of c_i's and r_i's. Then, P is called a *same-context valid path* if P' can be generated from S in this grammar:

$$S \to_{c_i} S \ r_i \ S \quad \text{for a procedure-call statement } i$$
$$| \ \varepsilon$$

Moreover, P is called an *interprocedurally valid path* or simply *valid* if P' can be generated from the nonterminal S' in the following grammar:

$$S' \to S' \ c_i \ S \quad \text{for a procedure-call statement } i$$
$$| \ S$$

For any two vertices u, v of the supergraph G, we denote the set of all interprocedurally valid paths from u to v by $\mathsf{IVP}(u, v)$ and the set of all same-context valid paths from u to v by $\mathsf{SCVP}(u, v)$. Informally, a valid path starts from a statement in a procedure p of the program and goes through a number of procedure-calls while respecting the rule that whenever a procedure ends, control should return to the return-site in its parent procedure. A same-context valid path is a valid path in which every procedure-call ends and hence control returns back to the initial procedure p in the same context.

IFDS [50]. An IFDS problem *instance* is a tuple $I = (G, D, F, M, \sqcap)$ where:
- $G = (V, E)$ is a supergraph as above.
- D is a finite set, called the *domain*, and each $d \in D$ is called a *data flow fact*.
- The *meet operator* $\sqcap$ is either intersection or union.
- $F \subseteq 2^D \to 2^D$ is a set of *distributive flow functions* over $\sqcap$, i.e. for each function $f \in F$ and every two sets of facts $D_1, D_2 \subseteq D$, we have $f(D_1 \sqcap D_2) = f(D_1) \sqcap f(D_2)$.
- $M : E \to F$ is a map that assigns a distributive flow function to each edge of the supergraph.

Let $P = (w_i)_{i=0}^k$ be a path in G, $e_i = (w_{i-1}, w_i)$ and $m_i = M(e_i)$. In other words, the e_i's are the edges appearing in P and the m_i's are their corresponding distributive flow functions. The *path function* of P is defined as: $\mathsf{pf}_P := m_k \circ \cdots \circ m_2 \circ m_1$ where $\circ$ denotes function composition. The solution of I is the collection of values $\{\mathsf{MVP}_v\}_{v \in V}$:

$$\mathsf{MVP}_v := \bigsqcap_{P \in \mathsf{IVP}(s_{\mathsf{main}}, v)} \mathsf{pf}_P(D).$$

Intuitively, the solution is defined by taking *meet-over-all-valid-paths*. If the meet operator is union, then MVP_v is the set of data flow facts that *may* hold at v, when v is reached in *some* execution of the program. Conversely, if the meet operator is intersection, then MVP_v consists of data flow facts that *must* hold at v in *every* execution of the program that reaches v. Similarly, we define the same-context solution of I as the collection of values $\{\mathsf{MSCP}_v\}_{v \in V_{\mathsf{main}}}$ defined as follows:

$$\mathsf{MSCP}_v := \bigsqcap_{P \in \mathsf{SCVP}(s_{\mathsf{main}}, v)} \mathsf{pf}_P(D). \tag{1}$$

The intuition behind MSCP is similar to that of MVP, except that in MSCP_v we consider *meet-over-same-context-paths* (corresponding to runs that return to the same stack state).

Remark 1. We note two points about the IFDS framework:
- As in [50], we only consider IFDS instances in which the meet operator is union. Instances with intersection can be reduced to union instances by dualization [50].
- For brevity, we are considering a global domain D, while in many applications the domain is procedure-specific. This does not affect the generality of our approach and our algorithms remain correct for the general case where each procedure has its own dedicated domain. Indeed, our implementation supports the general case.

Succinct representations. A distributive function $f : 2^D \to 2^D$ can be succinctly represented by a relation $R_f \subseteq (D \cup \{\mathbf{0}\}) \times (D \cup \{\mathbf{0}\})$ defined as:

$$R_f := \{(\mathbf{0}, \mathbf{0})\}$$
$$\cup \ \{(\mathbf{0}, b) \mid b \in f(\emptyset)\}$$
$$\cup \ \{(a, b) \mid b \in f(\{a\}) - f(\emptyset)\}.$$

Given that f is distributive over union, we have $f(\{d_1, \ldots, d_k\}) = f(\{d_1\}) \cup \cdots \cup f(\{d_k\})$. Hence, to specify f it is sufficient to specify $f(\emptyset)$ and $f(\{d\})$ for each $d \in D$. This is exactly what R_f does. In short, we have: $f(\emptyset) = \{b \in D \mid (\mathbf{0}, b) \in R_f\}$ and $f(\{d\}) = f(\emptyset) \cup \{b \in D \mid (d, b) \in R_f\}$. Moreover, we can represent the relation R_f as a bipartite graph H_f in which each part consists of the vertices $D \cup \{\mathbf{0}\}$ and R_f is the set of edges. For brevity, we define $D^* := D \cup \{\mathbf{0}\}$.

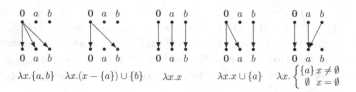

Fig. 3: Succinct representation of several distributive functions.

Example 3. Let $D = \{a, b\}$. Figure 3 provides several examples of bipartite graphs representing distributive functions.

Bounded Bandwidth Assumption. Following [50], we assume that the bandwidth in function calls and returns is bounded by a constant. In other words, there is a small constant b, such that for every edge e that is a call-to-start or exit-to-return-site edge, every vertex in the graph representation $H_{M(e)}$ has degree b or less. This is a classical assumption in IFDS [50,7] and models the fact that every parameter in a called function is only dependent on a few variables in the callee (and conversely, every returned value is only dependent on a few variables in the called function).

Composition of distributive functions. Let f and g be distributive functions and R_f and R_g their succinct representations. It is easy to verify that $g \circ f$ is also distributive, hence it has a succinct representation $R_{g \circ f}$. Moreover, we have $R_{g \circ f} = R_f; R_g = \{(a, b) \mid \exists c \; (a, c) \in R_f \wedge (c, b) \in R_g\}$.

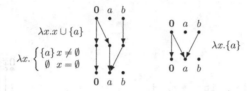

Fig. 4: Obtaining $H_{g \circ f}$ (right) from H_f and H_g (left)

Example 4. In terms of graphs, to compute $H_{g \circ f}$, we first take H_f and H_g, then contract corresponding vertices in the lower part of H_f and the upper part of H_g, and finally compute reachability from the topmost part to the bottommost part of the resulting graph. Consider $f(x) = x \cup \{a\}$, $g(x) = \{a\}$ for $x \neq \emptyset$ and $g(\emptyset) = \emptyset$, then $g \circ f(x) = \{a\}$ for all $x \subseteq D$. Figure 4 shows contracting of corresponding vertices in H_f and H_g (left) and using reachability to obtain $H_{g \circ f}$ (right).

Exploded supergraph. Given an IFDS instance $I = (G, D, F, M, \cup)$ with super-graph $G = (V, E)$, its *exploded supergraph* $\overline{G}$ is obtained by taking $|D^*|$ copies of each vertex in V, one corresponding to each element of D^*, and replacing each edge e with the graph representation $H_{M(e)}$ of the flow function $M(e)$. Formally, $\overline{G} = (\overline{V}, \overline{E})$ where $\overline{V} = V \times D^*$ and

$$\overline{E} = \big\{((u, d_1), (v, d_2)) \mid e = (u, v) \in E \wedge (d_1, d_2) \in R_{M(e)}\big\}.$$

A path $\overline{P}$ in $\overline{G}$ is (same-context) valid, if the path P in G, obtained by ignoring the second component of every vertex in $\overline{P}$, is (same-context) valid. As shown in [50], for a data flow fact $d \in D$ and a vertex $v \in V$, we have $d \in \mathsf{MVP}_v$ iff there is a valid path in $\overline{G}$ from (s_{main}, d') to (v, d) for some $d' \in D \cup \{0\}$. Hence, the IFDS problem is reduced to reachability by valid paths in $\overline{G}$. Similarly, the same-context IFDS problem is reduced to reachability by same-context valid paths in $\overline{G}$.

Example 5. Consider a null pointer analysis on the program in Figure 2. At each program point, we want to know which pointers can potentially be null. We first model this problem as an IFDS instance. Let $D = \{\bar{x}, \bar{y}\}$, where $\bar{x}$ is the data flow fact that x might be null and $\bar{y}$ is defined similarly. Figure 5 shows the same program and its exploded supergraph.

At point 8, the values of both pointers x and y are used. Hence, if either of x or y is null at 8, a null pointer error will be raised. However, as evidenced by the two valid paths shown in red, both x and y might be null at 8. The pointer y might be null because it is passed to the function f by value (instead of by reference) and keeps its local value in the transition from c_7 to r_7, hence the edge $((c_7, \bar{y}), (r_7, \bar{y}))$ is in $\overline{G}$. On the other hand, the function f only initializes y, which is its own local variable, and does not change x (which is shared with main).

```
1   void f(int *&x, int *y) {
2       y = new int(1);
3       y = new int(2);
4   }

5   int main() {
6       int *x, *y;
7       f(x,y);
8       *x += *y;
9   }
```

Fig. 5: A Program (left) and its Exploded Supergraph (right).

2.2 Trees and Tree Decompositions

Trees. A rooted tree $T = (V_T, E_T)$ is an undirected graph with a distinguished "root" vertex $r \in V_T$, in which there is a unique path P_v^u between every pair $\{u, v\}$ of vertices. We refer to the number of vertices in V_T as the *size* of T. For an arbitrary vertex $v \in V_T$, the *depth* of v, denoted by d_v, is defined as the length of the unique path $P_v^r : r \rightsquigarrow v$. The *depth* or *height* of T is the maximum depth among its vertices. A vertex u is called an *ancestor* of v if u appears in P_v^r. In this case, v is called a *descendant* of u. In particular, r is an ancestor of every vertex and each vertex is both an ancestor and a descendant of itself. We denote the set of ancestors of v by $A_v^\uparrow$ and its descendants by $D_v^\downarrow$. It is straightforward to see that for every $0 \le d \le d_v$, the vertex v has a unique ancestor with depth d. We denote this ancestor by a_v^d. The ancestor $p_v = a_v^{d_v - 1}$ of v at depth $d_v - 1$ is called the *parent* of v and v is a *child* of p_v. The subtree $T_v^\downarrow$ corresponding to v is defined as $T[D_v^\downarrow] = (D_v^\downarrow, E_T \cap 2^{D_v^\downarrow})$, i.e. the part of T that consists of v and its descendants. Finally, a vertex $v \in V_T$ is called a *leaf* if it has no children. Given two vertices $u, v \in V_T$, the *lowest common ancestor* $\mathsf{lca}(u, v)$ of u and v is defined as $\operatorname{argmax}_{w \in A_u^\uparrow \cap A_v^\uparrow} d_w$. In other words, $\mathsf{lca}(u, v)$ is the common ancestor of u and v with maximum depth, i.e. which is farthest from the root.

Lemma 1 ([35]). *Given a rooted tree T of size n, there is an algorithm that preprocesses T in $O(n)$ and can then answer lowest common ancestor queries, i.e. queries that provide two vertices u and v and ask for* lca(u,v), *in $O(1)$.*

Tree decompositions [52]. Given a graph $G = (V, E)$, a *tree decomposition* of G is a rooted tree $T = (\mathfrak{B}, E_T)$ such that:

(i) Each vertex $b \in \mathfrak{B}$ of T has an associated subset $V(b) \subseteq V$ of vertices of G and $\bigcup_{b \in \mathfrak{B}} V(b) = V$. For clarity, we call each vertex of T a "bag" and reserve the word vertex for G. Informally, each vertex must appear in some bag.

(ii) For all $(u, v) \in E$, there exists a bag $b \in \mathfrak{B}$ such that $u, v \in V(b)$, i.e. every edge should appear in some bag.

(iii) For any pair of bags $b_i, b_j \in \mathfrak{B}$ and any bag b_k that appears in the path $P : b_i \rightsquigarrow b_j$, we have $V(b_i) \cap V(b_j) \subseteq V(b_k)$, i.e. each vertex should appear in a connected subtree of T.

The *width* of the tree decomposition $T = (\mathfrak{B}, E_T)$ is defined as the size of its largest bag minus 1. The *treewidth* tw(G) of a graph G is the minimal width among its tree decompositions. A vertex $v \in V$ appears in a connected subtree, so there is a unique bag b with the smallest possible depth such that $v \in V(b)$. We call b the *root bag* of v and denote it by rb(v).

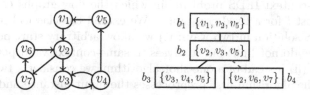

Fig. 6: A Graph G (left) and its Tree Decomposition T (right).

It is well-known that flow graphs of programs have typically small treewidth [63]. For example, programs written in Pascal, C, and Solidity have treewidth at most 3, 6 and 9, respectively. This property has also been confirmed experimentally for programs written in Java [34], C [38] and Ada [12]. The challenge is thus to exploit treewidth for faster interprocedural on-demand analyses. The first step in this approach is to compute tree decompositions of graphs. As the following lemma states, tree decompositions of low-treewidth graphs can be computed efficiently.

Lemma 2 ([11]). *Given a graph G with constant treewidth t, a binary tree decomposition of size $O(n)$ bags, height $O(\log n)$ and width $O(t)$ can be computed in linear time.*

Separators [26]. The key structural property that we exploit in low-treewidth flow graphs is a separation property. Let $A, B \subseteq V$. The pair (A, B) is called a *separation* of G if (i) $A \cup B = V$, and (ii) no edge connects a vertex in $A - B$

to a vertex in $B - A$ or vice versa. If (A, B) is a separation, the set $A \cap B$ is called a *separator*. The following lemma states such a separation property for low-treewidth graphs.

Lemma 3 (Cut Property [26]). *Let $T = (\mathfrak{B}, E_T)$ be a tree decomposition of $G = (V, E)$ and $e = \{b, b'\} \in E_T$. If we remove e, the tree T breaks into two connected components, T^b and $T^{b'}$, respectively containing b and b'. Let $A = \bigcup_{t \in T^b} V(t)$ and $B = \bigcup_{t \in T^{b'}} V(t)$. Then (A, B) is a separation of G and its corresponding separator is $A \cap B = V(b) \cap V(b')$.*

Example 6. Figure 6 shows a graph and one of its tree decompositions with width 2. In this example, we have $\mathsf{rb}(v_5) = b_1, \mathsf{rb}(v_3) = b_2, \mathsf{rb}(v_4) = b_3$, and $\mathsf{rb}(v_7) = b_4$. For the separator property of Lemma 3, consider the edge $\{b_2, b_4\}$. By removing it, T breaks into two parts, one containing the vertices $A = \{v_1, v_2, v_3, v_4, v_5\}$ and the other containing $B = \{v_2, v_6, v_7\}$. We have $A \cap B = \{v_2\} = V(b_2) \cap V(b_4)$. Also, any path from $B - A = \{v_6, v_7\}$ to $A - B = \{v_1, v_3, v_4, v_5\}$ or vice versa must pass through $\{v_2\}$. Hence, (A, B) is a separation of G with separator $V(b_2) \cap V(b_4) = \{v_2\}$.

3   Problem definition

We consider same-context IFDS problems in which the flow graphs G_i have a treewidth of at most t for a fixed constant t. We extend the classical notion of same-context IFDS solution in two ways: (i) we allow arbitrary start points for the analysis, i.e. we do not limit our analyses to same-context valid paths that start at s_{main}; and (ii) instead of a one-shot algorithm, we consider a two-phase process in which the algorithm first preprocesses the input instance and is then provided with a series of queries to answer. We formalize these points below. We fix an IFDS instance $I = (G, D, F, M, \cup)$ with exploded supergraph $\overline{G} = (\overline{V}, \overline{E})$.

Meet over same-context valid paths. We extend the definition of MSCP by specifying a start vertex u and an initial set Δ of data flow facts that hold at u. Formally, for any vertex v that is in the same flow graph as u, we define:

$$\mathsf{MSCP}_{u, \Delta, v} := \bigcap_{P \in \mathsf{SCVP}(u, v)} \mathsf{pf}_P(\Delta). \tag{2}$$

The only difference between (2) and (1) is that in (1), the start vertex u is fixed as s_{main} and the initial data-fact set Δ is fixed as D, while in (2), they are free to be any vertex/set.

Reduction to reachability. As explained in Section 2.1, computing MSCP is reduced to reachability via same-context valid paths in the exploded supergraph $\overline{G}$. This reduction does not depend on the start vertex and initial data flow facts. Hence, for a data flow fact $d \in D$, we have $d \in \mathsf{MSCP}_{u, \Delta, v}$ iff in the exploded supergraph $\overline{G}$ the vertex (v, d) is reachable via same-context valid paths from a vertex (u, δ) for some $\delta \in \Delta \cup \{0\}$. Hence, we define the following types of queries:

Pair query. A pair query provides two vertices (u, d_1) and (v, d_2) of the exploded supergraph $\overline{G}$ and asks whether they are reachable by a same-context valid path. Hence, the answer to a pair query is a single bit. Intuitively, if $d_2 = \mathbf{0}$, then the query is simply asking if v is reachable from u by a same-context valid path in G. Otherwise, d_2 is a data flow fact and the query is asking whether $d_2 \in \mathsf{MSCP}_{u,\{d_1\} \cap D, v}$.

Single-source query. A single-source query provides a vertex (u, d_1) and asks for all vertices (v, d_2) that are reachable from (u, d_1) by a same-context valid path. Assuming that u is in the flow graph $G_i = (V_i, E_i)$, the answer to the single source query is a sequence of $|V_i| \cdot |D^*|$ bits, one for each $(v, d_2) \in V_i \times D^*$, signifying whether it is reachable by same-context valid paths from (u, d_1). Intuitively, a single-source query asks for all pairs (v, d_2) such that (i) v is reachable from u by a same-context valid path and (ii) $d_2 \in \mathsf{MSCP}_{u,\{d_1\} \cap D, v} \cup \{\mathbf{0}\}$.

Intuition. We note the intuition behind such queries. We observe that since the functions in F are distributive over $\cup$, we have $\mathsf{MSCP}_{u,\Delta,v} = \cup_{\delta \in \Delta} \mathsf{MSCP}_{u,\{\delta\},v}$, hence $\mathsf{MSCP}_{u,\Delta,v}$ can be computed by $O(|\Delta|)$ single-source queries.

4 Treewidth-based Data-flow Analysis

4.1 Preprocessing

The original solution to the IFDS problem, as first presented in [50], reduces the problem to reachability over a newly constructed graph. We follow a similar approach, except that we exploit the low-treewidth property of our flow graphs at every step. Our preprocessing is described below. It starts with computing constant-width tree decompositions for each of the flow graphs. We then use standard techniques to make sure that our tree decompositions have a nice form, i.e. that they are balanced and binary. Then comes a reduction to reachability, which is similar to [50]. Finally, we precompute specific useful reachability information between vertices in each bag and its ancestors. As it turns out in the next section, this information is sufficient for computing reachability between any pair of vertices, and hence for answering IFDS queries.

Overview. Our preprocessing consists of the following steps:
(1) **Finding Tree Decompositions.** In this step, we compute a tree decomposition $T_i = (\mathfrak{B}_i, E_{T_i})$ of constant width t for each flow graph G_i. This can either be done by applying the algorithm of [10] directly on G_i, or by using an algorithm due to Thorup [63] and parsing the program.
(2) **Balancing and Binarizing.** In this step, we balance the tree decompositions T_i using the algorithm of Lemma 2 and make them binary using the standard process of [22].
(3) **LCA Preprocessing.** We preprocess the T_i's for answering lowest common ancestor queries using Lemma 1.
(4) **Reduction to Reachability.** In this step, we modify the exploded supergraph $\overline{G} = (\overline{V}, \overline{E})$ to obtain a new graph $\hat{G} = (\overline{V}, \hat{E})$, such that for every pair of vertices (u, d_1) and (v, d_2), there is a path from (u, d_1) to (v, d_2) in

$\hat{G}$ iff there is a *same-context valid path* from (u, d_1) to (v, d_2) in $\overline{G}$. So, this step reduces the problem of reachability via same-context valid paths in $\overline{G}$ to simple reachability in $\hat{G}$.

(5) **Local Preprocessing.** In this step, for each pair of vertices (u, d_1) and (v, d_2) for which there exists a bag b such that both u and v appear in b, we compute and cache whether $(u, d_1) \rightsquigarrow (v, d_2)$ in $\hat{G}$. We write $(u, d_1) \rightsquigarrow_{\text{local}} (v, d_2)$ to denote a reachability established in this step.

(6) **Ancestors Reachability Preprocessing.** In this step, we compute reachability information between each vertex in a bag and vertices appearing in its ancestors in the tree decomposition. Concretely, for each pair of vertices (u, d_1) and (v, d_2) such that u appears in a bag b and v appears in a bag b' that is an ancestor of b, we establish and remember whether $(u, d_1) \rightsquigarrow (v, d_2)$ in $\hat{G}$ and whether $(v, d_2) \rightsquigarrow (u, d_1)$ in $\hat{G}$. As above, we use the notations $(u, d_1) \rightsquigarrow_{\text{anc}} (v, d_2)$ and $(v, d_2) \rightsquigarrow_{\text{anc}} (u, d_1)$.

Steps (1)–(3) above are standard and well-known processes. We now provide details of steps (4)–(6). To skip the details and read about the query phase, see Section 4.3 below.

Step (4): Reduction to Reachability

In this step, our goal is to compute a new graph $\hat{G}$ from the exploded supergraph $\overline{G}$ such that there is a path from (u, d_1) to (v, d_2) in $\hat{G}$ iff there is a same-context valid path from (u, d_1) to (v, d_2) in $\overline{G}$. The idea behind this step is the same as that of the *tabulation algorithm* in [50].

Summary edges. Consider a call vertex c_l in G and its corresponding return-site vertex r_l. For $d_1, d_2 \in D^*$, the edge $((c_l, d_1), (r_l, d_2))$ is called a *summary edge* if there is a same-context valid path from (c_l, d_1) to (r_l, d_2) in the exploded supergraph $\overline{G}$. Intuitively, a summary edge summarizes the effects of procedure calls (same-context interprocedural paths) on the reachability between c_l and r_l. From the definition of *summary edges*, it is straightforward to verify that the graph $\hat{G}$ obtained from $\overline{G}$ by adding every summary edge and removing every interprocedural edge has the desired property, i.e. a pair of vertices are reachable in $\hat{G}$ iff they are reachable by a same-context valid path in $\overline{G}$. Hence, we first find all summary edges and then compute $\hat{G}$. This is shown in Algorithm 1.

We now describe what Algorithm 1 does. Let s_p be the start point of a procedure p. A *shortcut edge* is an edge $((s_p, d_1), (v, d_2))$ such that v is in the same procedure p and there is a same-context valid path from (s_p, d_1) to (v, d_2) in $\overline{G}$. The algorithm creates an empty graph $H = (\overline{V}, E')$. Note that H is implicitly represented by only saving E'. It also creates a queue Q of edges to be added to H (initially $Q = \overline{E}$) and an empty set S which will store the summary edges. The goal is to construct H such that it contains (i) *intraprocedural* edges of $\overline{G}$, (ii) summary edges, and (iii) shortcut edges.

It constructs H one edge at a time. While there is an unprocessed intraprocedural edge $e = ((u, d_1), (v, d_2))$ in Q, it chooses one such e and adds it to H (lines 5–10). Then, if (u, d_1) is reachable from (s_p, d_3) via a same-context valid

---

Algorithm 1: Computing $\hat{G}$ in Step (4)

1    $Q \leftarrow \overline{E}$;
2    $S \leftarrow \emptyset$;
3    $E' \leftarrow \emptyset$;
4   **while** $Q \neq \emptyset$ **do**
5   Choose $e = ((u, d_1), (v, d_2)) \in Q$;
6       $Q \leftarrow Q - \{e\}$;
7   **if** (u, v) *is an interprocedural edge, i.e. a call-to-start or exit-to-return-site edge* **then**
8 | **continue**;
9       $p \leftarrow$ the procedure s.t. $u, v \in V_p$;
10      $E' \leftarrow E' \cup \{e\}$;
11   **foreach** d_3 s.t. $((s_p, d_3), (u, d_1)) \in E'$ **do**
12   **if** $((s_p, d_3), (v, d_2)) \notin E' \cup Q$ **then**
13 | $Q \leftarrow Q \cup \{((s_p, d_3), (v, d_2))\}$;
14   **if** $u = s_p$ and $v = e_p$ **then**
15   **foreach** (c_l, d_3) s.t. $((c_l, d_3), (u, d_1)) \in \overline{E}$ **do**
16   **foreach** d_4 s.t. $((v, d_2), (r_l, d_4)) \in \overline{E}$ **do**
17   **if** $((c_l, d_3), (r_l, d_4)) \notin E' \cup Q$ **then**
18              $S \leftarrow S \cup \{((c_l, d_3), (r_l, d_4))\}$;
19              $Q \leftarrow Q \cup \{((c_l, d_3), (r_l, d_4))\}$;
20   $\hat{G} \leftarrow \overline{G}$;
21 **foreach** $e = ((u, d_1), (v, d_2)) \in \overline{E}$ **do**
22   **if** u and v are not in the same procedure **then**
23 | $\hat{G} = \hat{G} - \{e\}$;
24 $\hat{G} \leftarrow \hat{G} \cup S$;

---

path, then by adding the edge e, the vertex (v, d_2) also becomes accessible from (s_p, d_3). Hence, it adds the shortcut edge $((s_p, d_3), (v, d_2))$ to Q, so that it is later added to the graph H. Moreover, if u is the start s_p of the procedure p and v is its end e_p, then for every call vertex c_l calling the procedure p and its respective return-site r_l, we can add summary edges that summarize the effect of calling p (lines 14–19). Finally, lines 20–24 compute $\hat{G}$ as discussed above.

Correctness. As argued above, every edge that is added to H is either intraprocedural, a summary edge or a shortcut edge. Moreover, all such edges are added to H, because H is constructed one edge at a time and every time an edge e is added to H, all the summary/shortcut edges that might occur as a result of adding e to H are added to the queue Q and hence later to H. Therefore, Algorithm 1 correctly computes summary edges and the graph $\hat{G}$.

Complexity. Note that the graph H has at most $O(|E| \cdot |D^*|^2)$ edges. Addition of each edge corresponds to one iteration of the while loop at line 4 of Algorithm 1. Moreover, each iteration takes $O(|D^*|)$ time, because the loop at line 11 iterates over at most $|D^*|$ possible values for d_3 and the loops at lines 15 and 16 have constantly many iterations due to the bounded bandwidth assumption (Section 2.1). Since $|D^*| = O(|D|)$ and $|E| = O(n)$, the total runtime of Algorithm 1 is $O(|n| \cdot |D|^3)$. For a more detailed analysis, see [50, Appendix].

Step (5): Local Preprocessing

In this step, we compute the set R_{local} of local reachability edges, i.e. edges of the form $((u, d_1), (v, d_2))$ such that u and v appear in the same bag b of a tree decomposition T_i and $(u, d_1) \rightsquigarrow (v, d_2)$ in $\hat{G}$. We write $(u, d_1) \rightsquigarrow_{\text{local}} (v, d_2)$ to denote $((u, d_1), (v, d_2)) \in R_{\text{local}}$. Note that $\hat{G}$ has no interprocedural edges. Hence, we can process each T_i separately. We use a divide-and-conquer technique similar to the kernelization method used in [22] (Algorithm 2).

Algorithm 2 processes each tree decomposition T_i separately. When processing T, it chooses a leaf bag b_l of T and computes all-pairs reachability on the induced subgraph $H_l = \hat{G}[V(b_l) \times D^*]$, consisting of vertices that appear in b_l. Then, for each pair of vertices (u, d_1) and (v, d_2) s.t. u and v appear in b_l and $(u, d_1) \rightsquigarrow (v, d_2)$ in H_l, the algorithm adds the edge $((u, d_1), (v, d_2))$ to both R_{local} and $\hat{G}$ (lines 7–9). Note that this does not change reachability relations in $\hat{G}$, given that the vertices connected by the new edge were reachable by a path before adding it. Then, if b_l is not the only bag in T, the algorithm recursively calls itself over the tree decomposition $T - b_l$, i.e. the tree decomposition obtained by removing b_l (lines 10–11). Finally, it repeats the reachability computation on H_l (lines 12–14). The running time of the algorithm is $O(n \cdot |D^*|^3)$.

Algorithm 2: Local Preprocessing in Step (5)

---

1 $R_{\text{local}} \leftarrow \emptyset$;

2 **foreach** T_i **do**

3 $\quad$ computeLocalReachability(T_i);

4 **Function** computeLocalReachability(T)

5 $\quad$ Choose a leaf bag b_l of T;

6 $\quad$ $b_p \leftarrow$ parent of b_l;

7 $\quad$ **foreach** $u, v \in V(b_l)$, $\ d_1, d_2 \in D^*$ s.t. $(u, d_1) \rightsquigarrow (v, d_2)$ in $\hat{G}[V(b_l) \times D^*]$ **do**

8 $\quad\quad$ $\hat{G} = \hat{G} \cup \{((u, d_1), (v, d_2))\}$;

9 $\quad\quad$ $R_{\text{local}} = R_{\text{local}} \cup \{((u, d_1), (v, d_2))\}$;

10 $\quad$ **if** $b_p \neq$ **null then**

11 $\quad\quad$ computeLocalReachability($T - b_l$);

12 $\quad\quad$ **foreach** $u, v \in V(b_l)$, $\ d_1, d_2 \in D^*$ s.t. $(u, d_1) \rightsquigarrow (v, d_2)$ in $\hat{G}[V(b_l) \times D^*]$ **do**

13 $\quad\quad\quad$ $\hat{G} = \hat{G} \cup \{((u, d_1), (v, d_2))\}$;

14 $\quad\quad\quad$ $R_{\text{local}} = R_{\text{local}} \cup \{((u, d_1), (v, d_2))\}$;

Example 7. Consider the graph G and tree decomposition T given in Figure 6 and let $D^* = \{0\}$, i.e. let $\hat{G}$ and $\bar{G}$ be isomorphic to G. Figure 7 illustrates the steps taken by Algorithm 2. In each step, a bag is chosen and a local all-pairs reachability computation is performed over the bag. Local reachability edges are added to R_{local} and to $\hat{G}$ (if they are not already in $\hat{G}$).

We now prove the correctness and establish the complexity of Algorithm 2.

Correctness. We prove that when computeLocalReachability(T) ends, the set R_{local} contains all the local reachability edges between vertices that appear in the same bag in T. The proof is by induction on the size of T. If T consists of a single bag, then the local reachability computation on H_l (lines 7–9) fills R_{local} correctly. Now assume that T has n bags. Let $H_{-l} = \hat{G}[\cup_{b_i \in T, i \neq l} V(b_i) \times D^*]$. Intuitively, H_{-l} is the part of $\hat{G}$ that corresponds to other bags in T, i.e. every bag except the leaf bag b_l. After the local reachability computation at lines 7–9, (v, d_2) is reachable from (u, d_1) in H_{-l} only if it is reachable in $\hat{G}$. This is because (i) the vertices of H_l and H_{-l} form a separation of $\hat{G}$ with separator $(V(b_l) \cap V(b_p)) \times D^*$ (Lemma 3) and (ii) all reachability information in H_l is now replaced by direct edges (line 8). Hence, by induction hypothesis, line 11 finds all the local reachability edges for $T - b_l$ and adds them to both R_{local} and $\hat{G}$. Therefore, after line 11, for every $u, v \in V(b_l)$, we have $(u, d_1) \leadsto (v, d_2)$ in H_l iff $(u, d_1) \leadsto (v, d_2)$ in $\hat{G}$. Hence, the final all-pairs reachability computation of lines 12–14 adds all the local edges in b_l to R_{local}.

Complexity. Algorithm 2 performs at most two local all-pair reachability computations over the vertices appearing in each bag, i.e. $O(t \cdot |D^*|)$ vertices. Each such computation can be performed in $O(t^3 \cdot |D^*|^3)$ using standard reachability algorithms. Given that the T_i's have $O(n)$ bags overall, the total runtime of Algorithm 2 is $O(n \cdot t^3 \cdot |D^*|^3) = O(n \cdot |D^*|^3)$. Note that the treewidth t is a constant and hence the factor t^3 can be removed.

Step (6): Ancestors Reachability Preprocessing

This step aims to find reachability relations between each vertex of a bag and vertices that appear in the ancestors of that bag. As in the previous case, we compute a set R_{anc} and write $(u, d_1) \leadsto_{\mathsf{anc}} (v, d_2)$ if $((u, d_1), (v, d_2)) \in R_{\mathsf{anc}}$.

This step is performed by Algorithm 3. For each bag b and vertex (u, d) such that $u \in V(b)$ and each $0 \leq j < \mathsf{d}_v$, we maintain two sets: $F(u, d, b, j)$ and $F'(u, d, b, j)$ each containing a set of vertices whose first coordinate is in the ancestor of b at depth j. Intuitively, the vertices in $F(u, d, b, j)$ are reachable from (u, d). Conversely, (u, d) is reachable from the vertices in $F'(u, d, b, j)$. At first all F and F' sets are initialized as $\emptyset$. We process each tree decomposition T_i in a top-down manner and does the following actions at each bag:

– If a vertex u appears in both b and its parent b_p, then the reachability data computed for (u, d) at b_p can also be used in b. So, the algorithm copies this data (lines 4–7).
– If $(u, d_1) \leadsto_{\mathsf{local}} (v, d_2)$, then this reachability relation is saved in F and F' (lines 10–11). Also, any vertex that is reachable from (v, d_2) is reachable from (u, d_1), too. So, the algorithm adds $F(v, d_2, b, j)$ to $F(u, d_1, b, j)$ (line 13). The converse happens to F' (line 14).

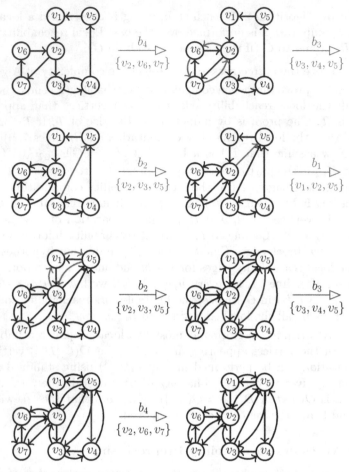

Fig. 7: Local Preprocessing (Step 5) on the graph and decomposition of Figure 6

After the execution of Algorithm 3, we have $(v, d_2) \in F(u, d_1, b, j)$ iff (i) (v, d_2) is reachable from (u, d_1) and (ii) $u \in V(b)$ and $v \in V(a_b^j)$, i.e. v appears in the ancestor of b at depth j. Conversely, $(u, d_1) \in F'(v, d_2, b, j)$ iff (i) (v, d_2) is reachable from (u, d_1) and (ii) $v \in V(b)$ and $u \in V(a_b^j)$. Algorithm 3 has a runtime of $O(n \cdot |D|^3 \cdot \log n)$. See [17] for detailed proofs. In the next section, we show that this runtime can be reduced to $O(n \cdot |D|^3)$ using word tricks.

4.2   Word Tricks

We now show how to reduce the time complexity of Algorithm 3 from $O(n \cdot |D^*|^3 \cdot \log n)$ to $O(n \cdot |D^*|^3)$ using word tricks. The idea is to pack the F and F' sets of Algorithm 3 into words, i.e. represent them by a binary sequence.

Algorithm 3: Ancestors Preprocessing in Step (6)

```
1  foreach Tᵢ = (𝔅ᵢ, E_{Tᵢ}) do
2  │  foreach b ∈ 𝔅ᵢ in top-down order do
3  │  │  bₚ ← parent of b;
4  │  │  foreach u ∈ V(b) ∩ V(bₚ), d ∈ D* do
5  │  │  │  foreach 0 ≤ j < d_b do
6  │  │  │  │  F(u, d, b, j) ← F(u, d, bₚ, j);
7  │  │  │  │  F'(u, d, b, j) ← F'(u, d, bₚ, j);
8  │  │  foreach u, v ∈ V(b), d₁, d₂ ∈ D* do
9  │  │  │  if (u, d₁) ⤳_local (v, d₂) then
10 │  │  │  │  F(u, d₁, b, d_b) ← F(u, d₁, b, d_b) ∪ {(v, d₂)};
11 │  │  │  │  F'(v, d₂, b, d_b) ← F'(v, d₂, b, d_b) ∪ {(u, d₁)};
12 │  │  │  │  foreach 0 ≤ j < d_b do
13 │  │  │  │  │  F(u, d₁, b, j) ← F(u, d₁, b, j) ∪ F(v, d₂, b, j);
14 │  │  │  │  │  F'(v, d₂, b, j) ← F'(v, d₂, b, j) ∪ F'(u, d₁, b, j)
15 R_{anc} ← {((u, d₁), (v, d₂)) | ∃b, j (v, d₂) ∈ F(u, d₁, b, j) ∨ (u, d₁) ∈ F'(v, d₂, b, j)};
```

Given a bag b, we define δ_b as the sum of sizes of all ancestors of b. The tree decompositions are balanced, so b has $O(\log n)$ ancestors. Moreover, the width is t, hence $\delta_b = O(t \cdot \log n) = O(\log n)$ for every bag b. We perform a top-down pass of each tree decomposition T_i and compute δ_b for each b.

For every bag b, $u \in V(b)$ and $d_1 \in D^*$, we store $F(u, d_1, b, -)$ as a binary sequence of length $\delta_b \cdot |D^*|$. The first $|V(b)| \cdot |D^*|$ bits of this sequence correspond to $F(u, d_1, b, d_b)$. The next $|V(b_p)| \cdot |D^*|$ correspond to $F(u, d_1, b, d_b - 1)$, and so on. We use a similar encoding for F'. Using this encoding, Algorithm 3 can be rewritten by word tricks and bitwise operations as follows:

- Lines 5–6 copy $F(u, d, b_p, -)$ into $F(u, d, b, -)$. However, we have to shift and align the bits, so these lines can be replaced by

$$F(u, d, b, -) \leftarrow F(u, d, b_p, -) \ll |V(b)| \cdot |D^*|;$$

- Line 10 sets a single bit to 1.
- Lines 12–13 perform a union, which can be replaced by the bitwise OR operation. Hence, these lines can be replaced by

$$F(u, d_1, b, -) \leftarrow F(u, d_1, b, -) \textbf{ OR } F(v, d_2, b, -);$$

- Computations on F' can be handled similarly.

Note that we do not need to compute R_{anc} explicitly given that our queries can be written in terms of the F and F' sets. It is easy to verify that using these word tricks, every W operations in lines 6, 7, 13 and 14 are replaced by one or two bitwise operations on words. Hence, the overall runtime of Algorithm 3 is reduced to $O\left(\frac{n \cdot |D^*|^3 \cdot \log n}{W}\right) = O(n \cdot |D^*|^3)$.

4.3   Answering Queries

We now describe how to answer pair and single-source queries using the data saved in the preprocessing phase.

Answering a Pair Query. Our algorithm answers a pair query from a vertex (u, d_1) to a vertex (v, d_2) as follows:

(i) If u and v are not in the same flow graph, return 0 (no).

(ii) Otherwise, let G_i be the flow graph containing both u and v. Let $b_u = \mathsf{rb}(u)$ and $b_v = \mathsf{rb}(v)$ be the root bags of u and v in T_i and let $b = \mathsf{lca}(b_u, b_v)$.

(iii) If there exists a vertex $w \in V(b)$ and $d_3 \in D^*$ such that $(u, d_1) \leadsto_{\mathsf{anc}} (w, d_3)$ and $(w, d_3) \leadsto_{\mathsf{anc}} (v, d_2)$, return 1 (yes), otherwise return 0 (no).

Correctness. If there is a path $P : (u, d_1) \leadsto (v, d_2)$, then we claim P must pass through a vertex (w, d_3) with $w \in V(b)$. If $b = b_u$ or $b = b_v$, the claim is obviously true. Otherwise, consider the path $P' : b_u \leadsto b_v$ in the tree decomposition T_i. This path passes through b (by definition of b). Let $e = \{b, b'\}$ be an edge of P'. Applying the cut property (Lemma 3) to e, proves that P must pass through a vertex (w, d_3) with $w \in V(b') \cap V(b)$. Moreover, b is an ancestor of both b_u and b_v, hence we have $(u, d_1) \leadsto_{\mathsf{anc}} (w, d_3)$ and $(w, d_3) \leadsto_{\mathsf{anc}} (v, d_2)$.

Complexity. Computing LCA takes $O(1)$ time. Checking all possible vertices (w, d_3) takes $O(t \cdot |D^*|) = O(|D|)$. This runtime can be decreased to $O\left(\left\lceil \frac{|D|}{\log n} \right\rceil\right)$ by word tricks.

Answering a Single-source Query. Consider a single-source query from a vertex (u, d_1) with $u \in V_i$. We can answer this query by performing $|V_i| \times |D^*|$ pair queries, i.e. by performing one pair query from (u, d_1) to (v, d_2) for each $v \in V_i$ and $d_2 \in D^*$. Since $|D^*| = O(|D|)$, the total complexity is $O\left(|V_i| \cdot |D| \cdot \left\lceil \frac{|D|}{\log n} \right\rceil\right)$ for answering a single-source query. Using a more involved preprocessing method, we can slightly improve this time to $O\left(\frac{|V_i| \cdot |D|^2}{\log n}\right)$. See [17] for more details. Based on the results above, we now present our main theorem:

Theorem 1. *Given an IFDS instance $I = (G, D, F, M, \cup)$, our algorithm preprocesses I in time $O(n \cdot |D|^3)$ and can then answer each pair query and single-source query in time*

$$O\left(\left\lceil \frac{|D|}{\log n} \right\rceil\right) \quad and \quad O\left(\frac{n \cdot |D|^2}{\log n}\right), \quad respectively.$$

4.4   Parallelizability and Optimality

We now turn our attention to parallel versions of our query algorithms, as well as cases where the algorithms are optimal.

Parallelizability. Assume we have k threads in our disposal.

1. Given a pair query of the form (u, d_1, v, d_2), let b_u (resp. b_v) be the root bag u (resp. v), and $b = \mathsf{lca}(b_u, b_v)$ the lowest common ancestor of b_u and b_v. We partition the set $V(b) \times D^*$ into k subsets $\{A_i\}_{1 \le i \le k}$. Then, thread i handles the set A_i, as follows: for every pair $(w, d_3) \in A_i$, the thread sets the output to 1 (yes) iff $(u, d_1) \leadsto_{\mathsf{anc}} (w, d_3)$ and $(w, d_3) \leadsto_{\mathsf{anc}} (v, d_2)$.
2. Recall that a single source query (u, d_1) is answered by breaking it down to $|V_i| \times |D^*|$ pair queries, where G_i is the flow graph containing u. Since all such pair queries are independent, we parallelize them among k threads, and further parallelize each pair query as described above.

With word tricks, parallel pair and single-source queries require $O\left(\left\lceil \frac{|D|}{k \cdot \log n} \right\rceil\right)$ and $O\left(\left\lceil \frac{n \cdot |D|}{k \cdot \log n} \right\rceil\right)$ time, respectively. Hence, for large enough k, each query requires only $O(1)$ time, and we achieve *perfect parallelism*.

Optimality. Observe that when $|D| = O(1)$, i.e. when the domain is small, our algorithm is *optimal*: the preprocessing runs in $O(n)$, which is proportional to the size of the input, and the pair query and single-source query run in times $O(1)$ and $O(n/\log n)$, respectively, each case being proportional to the size of the output. Small domains arise often in practice, e.g. in dead-code elimination or null-pointer analysis.

5   Experimental Results

We report on an experimental evaluation of our techniques and compare their performance to standard alternatives in the literature.

Benchmarks. We used 5 classical data-flow analyses in our experiments, including reachability (for dead-code elimination), possibly-uninitialized variables analysis, simple uninitialized variables analysis, liveness analysis of the variables, and reaching-definitions analysis. We followed the specifications in [36] for modeling the analyses in IFDS. We used real-world Java programs from the DaCapo benchmark suite [6], obtained their flow graphs using Soot [65] and applied the JTDec tool [19] for computing balanced tree decompositions. Given that some of these benchmarks are prohibitively large, we only considered their main Java packages, i.e. packages containing the starting point of the programs. We experimented with a total of 22 benchmarks, which, together with the 5 analyses above, led to a total of 110 instances. Our instance sizes, i.e. number of vertices and edges in the exploded supergraph, range from 22 to 190,591. See [17] for details.

Implementation and comparison. We implemented both variants of our approach, i.e. sequential and parallel, in C++. We also implemented the parts of the classical IFDS algorithm [50] and its on-demand variant [36] responsible for same-context queries. All of our implementations closely follow the pseudocodes of our algorithms and the ones in [50,36], and no additional optimizations are applied. We compared the performance of the following algorithms for randomly-generated queries:

- *SEQ.* The sequential variant of our algorithm.
- *PAR.* A variant of our algorithm in which the queries are answered using perfect parallelization and 12 threads.
- *NOPP.* The classical same-context IFDS algorithm of [50], with *no preprocessing.* NOPP performs a complete run of the classic IFDS algorithm for each query.
- *CPP.* The classical same-context IFDS algorithm of [50], with *complete preprocessing.* In this algorithm, all summary edges and reachability information are precomputed and the queries are simple table lookups.
- *OD.* The on-demand same-context IFDS algorithm of [36]. This algorithm does not preprocess the input. However, it remembers the information obtained in each query and uses it to speed-up the following queries.

For each instance, we randomly generated 10,000 pair queries and 100 single-source queries. In case of single-source queries, source vertices were chosen uniformly at random. For pair queries, we first chose a source vertex uniformly at random, and then chose a target vertex in the same procedure, again uniformly at random.

Experimental setting. The results were obtained on Debian using an Intel Xeon E5-1650 processor (3.2 GHz, 6 cores, 12 threads) with 128GB of RAM. The parallel results used all 12 threads.

Time limit. We enforced a preprocessing time limit of 5 minutes per instance. This is in line with the preprocessing times of state-of-the-art tools on benchmarks of this size, e.g. Soot takes 2-3 minutes to generate all flow graphs for each benchmark.

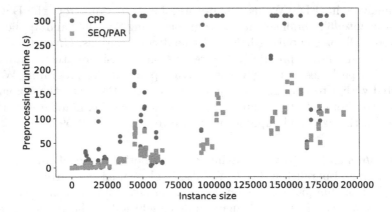

Fig. 8: Preprocessing times of CPP and SEQ/PAR (over all instances). A dot above the 300s line denotes a timeout.

Results. We found that, except for the smallest instances, our algorithm consistently outperforms all previous approaches. Our results were as follows:

Treewidth. The maximum width amongst the obtained tree decompositions was 9, while the minimum was 1. Hence, our experiments confirm the results of [34,19] and show that real-world Java programs have small treewidth. See [17] for more details.

Preprocessing Time. As in Figure 8, our preprocessing is more lightweight and scalable than CPP. Note that CPP preprocessing times out at 25 of the 110 instances, starting with instances of size < 50,000, whereas our approach can comfortably handle instances of size 200,000. Although the theoretical worst-case complexity of CPP preprocessing is $O(n^2 \cdot |D|^3)$, we observed that its runtime over our benchmarks grows more slowly. We believe this is because our benchmark programs generally consist of a large number of small procedures. Hence, the worst-case behavior of CPP preprocessing, which happens on instances with large procedures, is not captured by the DaCapo benchmarks. In contrast, our preprocessing time is $O(n \cdot |D|^3)$ and having small or large procedures does not matter to our algorithms. Hence, we expect that our approach would outperform CPP preprocessing more significantly on instances containing large functions. However, as Figure 8 demonstrates, our approach is faster even on instances with small procedures.

Query Time. As expected, in terms of pair query time, NOPP is the worst performer by a large margin, followed by OD, which is in turn extremely less efficient than CPP, PAR and SEQ (Figure 9, top). This illustrates the underlying trade-off between preprocessing and query-time performance. Note that both CPP and our algorithms (SEQ and PAR), answer each pair query in $O(1)$. They all have pair-query times of less than a millisecond and are indistinguishable in this case. The same trade-off appears in single-source queries as well (Figure 9, bottom). Again, NOPP is the worst performer, followed by OD. SEQ and CPP have very similar runtimes, except that SEQ outperforms CPP in some cases, due to word tricks. However, PAR is extremely faster, which leads to the next point.

Parallelization. In Figure 9 (bottom right), we also observe that single-source queries are handled considerably faster by PAR in comparison with SEQ. Specifically, using 12 threads, the average single-source query time is reduced by a factor of 11.3. Hence, our experimental results achieve near-perfect parallelism and confirm that our algorithm is well-suited for parallel architectures.

Note that Figure 9 combines the results of all five mentioned data-flow analyses. However, the observations above hold independently for every single analysis, as well. See [17] for analysis-specific figures.

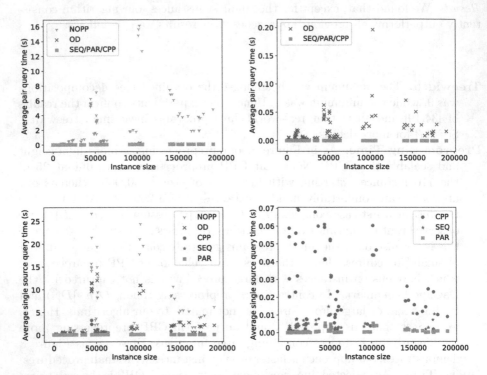

Fig. 9: Comparison of pair query time (top row) and single source query time (bottom row) of the algorithms. Each dot represents one of the 110 instances. Each row starts with a global picture (left) and zooms into smaller time units (right) to differentiate between the algorithms. The plots above contain results over all five analyses. However, our observations hold independently for every single analysis, as well (See [17]).

6   Conclusion

We developed new techniques for on-demand data-flow analyses in IFDS, by exploiting the treewidth of flow graphs. Our complexity analysis shows that our techniques (i) have better worst-case complexity, (ii) offer certain optimality guarantees, and (iii) are embarrassingly paralellizable. Our experiments demonstrate these improvements in practice: after a lightweight one-time preprocessing, queries are answered as fast as the heavyweight complete preprocessing, and the parallel speedup is close to its theoretical optimal. The main limitation of our approach is that it only handles same-context queries. Using treewidth to speedup non-same-context queries is a challenging direction of future work.

References

1. T. J. Watson libraries for analysis (WALA). https://github.com/wala/WALA (2003)
2. Appel, A.W., Palsberg, J.: Modern Compiler Implementation in Java. Cambridge University Press, 2nd edn. (2003)
3. Arzt, S., Rasthofer, S., Fritz, C., Bodden, E., Bartel, A., Klein, J., Le Traon, Y., Octeau, D., McDaniel, P.: FlowDroid: Precise context, flow, field, object-sensitive and lifecycle-aware taint analysis for android apps. In: PLDI. pp. 259–269 (2014)
4. Babich, W.A., Jazayeri, M.: The method of attributes for data flow analysis. Acta Informatica 10(3) (1978)
5. Bebenita, M., Brandner, F., Fahndrich, M., Logozzo, F., Schulte, W., Tillmann, N., Venter, H.: Spur: A trace-based JIT compiler for CIL. In: OOPSLA. pp. 708–725 (2010)
6. Blackburn, S.M., Garner, R., Hoffman, C., Khan, A.M., McKinley, K.S., Bentzur, R., Diwan, A., Feinberg, D., Frampton, D., Guyer, S.Z., Hirzel, M., Hosking, A., Jump, M., Lee, H., Moss, J.E.B., Phansalkar, A., Stefanović, D., VanDrunen, T., von Dincklage, D., Wiedermann, B.: The DaCapo benchmarks: Java benchmarking development and analysis. In: OOPSLA. pp. 169–190 (2006)
7. Bodden, E.: Inter-procedural data-flow analysis with IFDS/IDE and soot. In: SOAP. pp. 3–8 (2012)
8. Bodden, E., Tolêdo, T., Ribeiro, M., Brabrand, C., Borba, P., Mezini, M.: Spllift: Statically analyzing software product lines in minutes instead of years. In: PLDI. pp. 355–364 (2013)
9. Bodlaender, H., Gustedt, J., Telle, J.A.: Linear-time register allocation for a fixed number of registers. In: SODA (1998)
10. Bodlaender, H.L.: A linear-time algorithm for finding tree-decompositions of small treewidth. SIAM Journal on computing 25(6), 1305–1317 (1996)
11. Bodlaender, H.L., Hagerup, T.: Parallel algorithms with optimal speedup for bounded treewidth. SIAM Journal on Computing 27(6), 1725–1746 (1998)
12. Burgstaller, B., Blieberger, J., Scholz, B.: On the tree width of ada programs. In: Ada-Europe. pp. 78–90 (2004)
13. Callahan, D., Cooper, K.D., Kennedy, K., Torczon, L.: Interprocedural constant propagation. In: CC (1986)
14. Chatterjee, K., Choudhary, B., Pavlogiannis, A.: Optimal dyck reachability for data-dependence and alias analysis. In: POPL. pp. 30:1–30:30 (2017)
15. Chatterjee, K., Goharshady, A., Goharshady, E.: The treewidth of smart contracts. In: SAC (2019)
16. Chatterjee, K., Goharshady, A.K., Goyal, P., Ibsen-Jensen, R., Pavlogiannis, A.: Faster algorithms for dynamic algebraic queries in basic RSMs with constant treewidth. ACM Transactions on Programming Languages and Systems 41(4), 1–46 (2019)
17. Chatterjee, K., Goharshady, A.K., Ibsen-Jensen, R., Pavlogiannis, A.: Optimal and perfectly parallel algorithms for on-demand data-flow analysis. arXiv preprint 2001.11070 (2020)
18. Chatterjee, K., Goharshady, A.K., Okati, N., Pavlogiannis, A.: Efficient parameterized algorithms for data packing. In: POPL. pp. 1–28 (2019)
19. Chatterjee, K., Goharshady, A.K., Pavlogiannis, A.: JTDec: A tool for tree decompositions in soot. In: ATVA. pp. 59–66 (2017)

20. Chatterjee, K., Ibsen-Jensen, R., Goharshady, A.K., Pavlogiannis, A.: Algorithms for algebraic path properties in concurrent systems of constant treewidth components. ACM Transactions on Programming Langauges and Systems 40(3), 9 (2018)

21. Chatterjee, K., Ibsen-Jensen, R., Pavlogiannis, A.: Optimal reachability and a space-time tradeoff for distance queries in constant-treewidth graphs. In: ESA (2016)

22. Chaudhuri, S., Zaroliagis, C.D.: Shortest paths in digraphs of small treewidth. part i: Sequential algorithms. Algorithmica 27(3-4), 212–226 (2000)

23. Chaudhuri, S.: Subcubic algorithms for recursive state machines. In: POPL (2008)

24. Chen, T., Lin, J., Dai, X., Hsu, W.C., Yew, P.C.: Data dependence profiling for speculative optimizations. In: CC. pp. 57–72 (2004)

25. Cousot, P., Cousot, R.: Static determination of dynamic properties of recursive procedures. In: IFIP Conference on Formal Description of Programming Concepts (1977)

26. Cygan, M., Fomin, F.V., Kowalik, L., Lokshtanov, D., Marx, D., Pilipczuk, M., Pilipczuk, M., Saurabh, S.: Parameterized algorithms, vol. 4 (2015)

27. Duesterwald, E., Gupta, R., Soffa, M.L.: Demand-driven computation of interprocedural data flow. POPL (1995)

28. Dutta, S.: Anatomy of a compiler. Circuit Cellar 121, 30–35 (2000)

29. Flückiger, O., Scherer, G., Yee, M.H., Goel, A., Ahmed, A., Vitek, J.: Correctness of speculative optimizations with dynamic deoptimization. In: POPL. pp. 49:1–49:28 (2017)

30. Giegerich, R., Möncke, U., Wilhelm, R.: Invariance of approximate semantics with respect to program transformations. In: ECI (1981)

31. Gould, C., Su, Z., Devanbu, P.: Jdbc checker: A static analysis tool for SQL/JDBC applications. In: ICSE. pp. 697–698 (2004)

32. Grove, D., Torczon, L.: Interprocedural constant propagation: A study of jump function implementation. In: PLDI (1993)

33. Guarnieri, S., Pistoia, M., Tripp, O., Dolby, J., Teilhet, S., Berg, R.: Saving the world wide web from vulnerable javascript. In: ISSTA. pp. 177–187 (2011)

34. Gustedt, J., Mæhle, O.A., Telle, J.A.: The treewidth of java programs. In: ALENEX. pp. 86–97 (2002)

35. Harel, D., Tarjan, R.E.: Fast algorithms for finding nearest common ancestors. SIAM Journal on Computing 13(2), 338–355 (1984)

36. Horwitz, S., Reps, T., Sagiv, M.: Demand interprocedural dataflow analysis. ACM SIGSOFT Software Engineering Notes (1995)

37. Hovemeyer, D., Pugh, W.: Finding bugs is easy. ACM SIGPLAN Notices 39(12), 92–106 (Dec 2004)

38. Klaus Krause, P., Larisch, L., Salfelder, F.: The tree-width of C. Discrete Applied Mathematics (03 2019)

39. Knoop, J., Steffen, B.: The interprocedural coincidence theorem. In: CC (1992)

40. Krüger, S., Späth, J., Ali, K., Bodden, E., Mezini, M.: CrySL: An Extensible Approach to Validating the Correct Usage of Cryptographic APIs. In: ECOOP. pp. 10:1–10:27 (2018)

41. Lee, Y.f., Marlowe, T.J., Ryder, B.G.: Performing data flow analysis in parallel. In: ACM/IEEE Supercomputing. pp. 942–951 (1990)

42. Lee, Y.F., Ryder, B.G.: A comprehensive approach to parallel data flow analysis. In: ICS. pp. 236–247 (1992)

43. Lin, J., Chen, T., Hsu, W.C., Yew, P.C., Ju, R.D.C., Ngai, T.F., Chan, S.: A compiler framework for speculative optimizations. ACM Transactions on Architecture and Code Optimization **1**(3), 247–271 (2004)
44. Muchnick, S.S.: Advanced Compiler Design and Implementation. Morgan Kaufmann (1997)
45. Naeem, N.A., Lhoták, O., Rodriguez, J.: Practical extensions to the ifds algorithm. CC (2010)
46. Nanda, M.G., Sinha, S.: Accurate interprocedural null-dereference analysis for java. In: ICSE. pp. 133–143 (2009)
47. Rapoport, M., Lhoták, O., Tip, F.: Precise data flow analysis in the presence of correlated method calls. In: SAS. pp. 54–71 (2015)
48. Reps, T.: Program analysis via graph reachability. ILPS (1997)
49. Reps, T.: Undecidability of context-sensitive data-dependence analysis. ACM Transactions on Programming Languages and Systems **22**(1), 162–186 (2000)
50. Reps, T., Horwitz, S., Sagiv, M.: Precise interprocedural dataflow analysis via graph reachability. In: POPL. pp. 49–61 (1995)
51. Reps, T.: Demand interprocedural program analysis using logic databases. In: Applications of Logic Databases, vol. 296 (1995)
52. Robertson, N., Seymour, P.D.: Graph minors. iii. planar tree-width. Journal of Combinatorial Theory, Series B **36**(1), 49–64 (1984)
53. Rodriguez, J., Lhoták, O.: Actor-based parallel dataflow analysis. In: CC. pp. 179–197 (2011)
54. Rountev, A., Kagan, S., Marlowe, T.: Interprocedural dataflow analysis in the presence of large libraries. In: CC. pp. 2–16 (2006)
55. Sagiv, M., Reps, T., Horwitz, S.: Precise interprocedural dataflow analysis with applications to constant propagation. Theoretical Computer Science (1996)
56. Schubert, P.D., Hermann, B., Bodden, E.: PhASAR: An inter-procedural static analysis framework for C/C++. In: TACAS. pp. 393–410 (2019)
57. Shang, L., Xie, X., Xue, J.: On-demand dynamic summary-based points-to analysis. In: CGO. pp. 264–274 (2012)
58. Sharir, M., Pnueli, A.: Two approaches to interprocedural data flow analysis. In: Program flow analysis: Theory and applications. Prentice-Hall (1981)
59. Smaragdakis, Y., Bravenboer, M., Lhoták, O.: Pick your contexts well: Understanding object-sensitivity. In: POPL. pp. 17–30 (2011)
60. Späth, J., Ali, K., Bodden, E.: Context-, flow-, and field-sensitive data-flow analysis using synchronized pushdown systems. In: POPL. pp. 48:1–48:29 (2019)
61. Sridharan, M., Bodík, R.: Refinement-based context-sensitive points-to analysis for java. ACM SIGPLAN Notices **41**(6), 387–400 (2006)
62. Sridharan, M., Gopan, D., Shan, L., Bodík, R.: Demand-driven points-to analysis for java. In: OOPSLA. pp. 59–76 (2005)
63. Thorup, M.: All structured programs have small tree width and good register allocation. Information and Computation **142**(2), 159–181 (1998)
64. Torczon, L., Cooper, K.: Engineering a Compiler. Morgan Kaufmann, 2nd edn. (2011)
65. Vallée-Rai, R., Co, P., Gagnon, E., Hendren, L.J., Lam, P., Sundaresan, V.: Soot - a Java bytecode optimization framework. In: CASCON. p. 13 (1999)
66. Xu, G., Rountev, A., Sridharan, M.: Scaling cfl-reachability-based points-to analysis using context-sensitive must-not-alias analysis. In: ECOOP (2009)
67. Yan, D., Xu, G., Rountev, A.: Demand-driven context-sensitive alias analysis for java. In: ISSTA. pp. 155–165 (2011)

68. Yuan, X., Gupta, R., Melhem, R.: Demand-driven data flow analysis for communication optimization. Parallel Processing Letters **07**(04), 359–370 (1997)
69. Zheng, X., Rugina, R.: Demand-driven alias analysis for c. In: POPL. pp. 197–208 (2008)

Concise Read-Only Specifications for Better Synthesis of Programs with Pointers

Andreea Costea[1], Amy Zhu[2][*], Nadia Polikarpova[3], and Ilya Sergey[4,1]

[1] School of Computing, National University of Singapore, Singapore
[2] University of British Columbia, Vancouver, Canada
[3] University of California, San Diego, USA
[4] Yale-NUS College, Singapore

Abstract. In program synthesis there is a well-known trade-off between *concise* and *strong* specifications: if a specification is too verbose, it might be harder to write than the program; if it is too weak, the synthesised program might not match the user's intent. In this work we explore the use of annotations for restricting memory access permissions in program synthesis, and show that they can make specifications much stronger while remaining surprisingly concise. Specifically, we enhance Synthetic Separation Logic (SSL), a framework for synthesis of heap-manipulating programs, with the logical mechanism of *read-only borrows*.

We observe that this minimalistic and conservative SSL extension benefits the synthesis in several ways, making it more (a) *expressive* (stronger correctness guarantees are achieved with a modest annotation overhead), (b) *effective* (it produces more concise and easier-to-read programs), (c) *efficient* (faster synthesis), and (d) *robust* (synthesis efficiency is less affected by the choice of the search heuristic). We explain the intuition and provide formal treatment for read-only borrows. We substantiate the claims (a)–(d) by describing our quantitative evaluation of the borrowing-aware synthesis implementation on a series of standard benchmark specifications for various heap-manipulating programs.

1 Introduction

Deductive program synthesis is a prominent approach to the generation of correct-by-construction programs from their declarative specifications [14, 23, 29, 33]. With this methodology, one can represent searching for a program satisfying the user-provided constraints as a proof search in a certain logic. Following this idea, it has been recently observed [34] that the synthesis of correct-by-construction *imperative heap-manipulating* programs (in a language similar to C) can be implemented as a proof search in a version of Separation Logic (SL)—a program logic designed for modular verification of programs with pointers [32, 37].

SL-based deductive program synthesis based on *Synthetic* Separation Logic (SSL) [34] requires the programmer to provide a Hoare-style specification for a program of interest. For instance, given the predicate $\mathsf{ls}(x, S)$, which denotes a symbolic heap corresponding to a linked list starting at a pointer x, ending with `null`, and containing elements from the set S, one can specify the behaviour of the procedure for copying a linked list as follows:

$$\{r \mapsto x * \mathsf{ls}(x, S)\} \; \texttt{listcopy}(r) \; \{r \mapsto y * \mathsf{ls}(x, S) * \mathsf{ls}(y, S)\} \tag{1}$$

---

[*] Work done during an internship at NUS School of Computing in Summer 2019.

P. Müller (Ed.): ESOP 2020, LNCS 12075, pp. 141–168, 2020.
https://doi.org/10.1007/978-3-030-44914-8_6

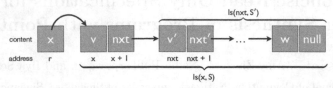

The precondition of specification (1), defining the shape of the initial heap, is illustrated by the figure above. It requires the heap to contain a pointer r, which is taken by the procedure as an argument and whose stored value, x, is the head pointer of the list to be copied. The list itself is described by the symbolic heap predicate instance $ls(x, S)$, whose footprint is assumed to be *disjoint* from the entry $r \mapsto x$, following the standard semantics of the *separating conjunction* operator ($*$) [32]. The postcondition asserts that the final heap, in addition to containing the original list $ls(x, S)$, will contain a new list starting from y whose contents S are the same as of the original list, and also that the pointer r will now point to the head y of the list copy. Our specification is incomplete: it allows, for example, duplicating or rearranging elements. One hopes that such a program is unlikely to be synthesised. In synthesis, it is common to provide incomplete specs: writing complete ones can be as hard as writing the program itself.

1.1   Correct Programs that Do Strange Things

Provided the definition of the heap predicate ls and the specification (1), the SuS-Lik tool, an implementation of the SSL-based synthesis [34], will produce the program depicted in Fig. 1. It is easy to check that this program satisfies the ascribed spec (1). Moreover, it correctly duplicates the original list, faithfully preserving its contents and the ordering. However, an astute reader might notice a certain oddity in the way it treats the initial list provided for copying. According to the postcondition of (1), the value of the pointer r stored in a local immutable variable y1 on line 9 is the head of the copy of the original list's tail. Quite unexpectedly, the pointer y1 becomes the tail of the original list on line 11, while the *original list's* tail pointer nxt, once assigned to $*(y + 1)$ on line 13, becomes the tail of the *copy*!

Indeed, the exercise in tail swapping is totally pointless: not only does it produces less "natural" and readable code, but the

```
1   void listcopy (loc r) {
2     let x = *r;
3     if (x == 0) {
4     } else {
5       let v = *x;
6       let nxt = *(x + 1);
7       *r = nxt;
8       listcopy(r);
9       let y1 = *r;
10      let y = malloc(2);
11      *(x + 1) = y1;
12      *r = y;
13      *(y + 1) = nxt;
14      *y = v;
15  } }
```

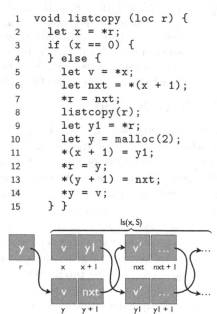

Fig. 1: Result program for spec (1) and the shape of its final heap.

resulting program's locality properties are unsatisfactory; for instance, this program cannot be plugged into a concurrent setting where multiple threads rely on $\mathsf{ls}(x, S)$ to be unchanged.

The issue with the result in Fig. 1 is caused by specification (1) being *too permissive*: it does not prevent the synthesised program from *modifying* the structure of the initial list, while creating its copy. Luckily, the SL community has devised a number of SL extensions that allow one to impose such restrictions, like declaring a part of the provided symbolic heap as *read-only* [5,8,9,11,15,20,21], *i.e.*, forbidden to modify by the specified code.

1.2   Towards Simple Read-Only Specifications for Synthesis

The main challenge of introducing read-only annotations (commonly also referred to as *permissions*)[5] into Separation Logic lies in establishing the discipline for performing sound accounting in the presence of mixed read-only and mutating heap accesses by different components of a program.

As an example, consider a simple symbolic heap $\left\{ x \overset{M}{\mapsto} f * r \overset{M}{\mapsto} h \right\}$ that declares two *mutable* (*i.e.*, allowed to be written to) pointers x and r, that point to unspecified values f and h, correspondingly. With this symbolic heap, is it safe to call the following function that modifies the contents of r but not of x?

$$\left\{ x \overset{RO}{\mapsto} f * r \overset{M}{\mapsto} h \right\} \text{ readX}(x, r) \left\{ x \overset{RO}{\mapsto} f * r \overset{M}{\mapsto} f \right\} \tag{2}$$

The precondition of readX requires a weaker form of access permission for x (read-only, RO), while the considered heap asserts a stronger *write* permission (M). It should be possible to satisfy readX's requirement by providing the necessary read-only permission for x. To do so, we need to agree on a discipline to "adapt" the caller's *write*-permission M to the callee's *read-only* permission RO. While seemingly trivial, if implemented naïvely, accounting of RO permissions in SL might compromise either soundness or completeness of the logical reasoning.

A number of proposals for logically sound interplay between write- and read-only access permissions in the presence of function calls has been described in the literature [7–9,11,13,20,30]. Some of these works manage to maintain the simplicity of having only *mutable/read-only* annotations when confined to the sequential setting [9,11,13]. More general (but harder to implement) approaches rely on *fractional permissions* [8,25], an expressive mechanism for permission accounting, with primary applications in concurrent reasoning [7,28]. We started this project by attempting to adapt some of those logics [9,11,13] as an extension of SSL in order to reap the benefits of read-only annotations for the synthesis of sequential program. The main obstacle we encountered involved definitions of inductive heap predicates with *mixed* permissions. For instance, how can one specify a program that modifies the contents of a linked list, but not its structure? Even though it seemed possible to enable this treatment of predicates via permission multiplication [25], developing support for this machinery on top of existing SuSLik infrastructure was a daunting task. Therefore, we had to look for a technically simpler solution.

---

[5] We will be using the words "annotation" and "permission" interchangeably.

1.3   Our Contributions

Theoretical Contributions. Our main conceptual innovation is the idea of instrumenting SSL with symbolic *read-only borrows* to enable faster and more predictable program synthesis. Borrows are used to annotate symbolic heaps in specifications, similarly to abstract fractional permissions from the deductive verification tools, such as CHALICE and VERIFAST [20,21,27]. They enable simple but principled lightweight threading of heap access permissions from the callers to callees and back, while enforcing *read-only* access whenever it is required. For basic intuition on read-only borrows, consider the specification below:

$$\left\{ x \overset{a}{\mapsto} f * y \overset{b}{\mapsto} g * r \overset{M}{\mapsto} h \right\} \text{ readXY(x, y, r) } \left\{ x \overset{a}{\mapsto} f * y \overset{b}{\mapsto} g * r \overset{M}{\mapsto} (f + g) \right\} \quad (3)$$

The precondition requires a heap with three pointers, x, y, and r, pointing to unspecified f, g, and h, correspondingly. Both x and y are going to be treated as read-only, but now, instead of simply annotating them with RO, we add *symbolic borrowing annotations* a and b. The semantics of these borrowing annotations is the same as that of other ghost variables (such as f). In particular, the *callee* must behave correctly for any valuation of a and b, which leaves it no choice but to treat the corresponding heap fragments as read-only (hence preventing the heap fragments from being written). On the other hand, from the perspective of the *caller*, they serve as formal parameters that are substituted with actuals of caller's choosing: for instance, when invoked with a caller's symbolic heap $\left\{ x \overset{M}{\mapsto} 1 * y \overset{c}{\mapsto} 2 * r \overset{M}{\mapsto} 0 \right\}$ (where c denotes a read-only borrow of the caller), readXY is guaranteed to "restore" the same access permissions in the postcondition, as per the substitution $[M/a, c/b]$. The example above demonstrates that read-only borrows are straightforward to compose when reasoning about code with function calls. They also make it possible to define *borrow-polymorphic* inductive heap predicates, *e.g.*, enhancing ls from spec (1) so it can be used in specifications with mixed access permissions on their components.[6] Finally, read-only borrows make it almost trivial to adapt the existing SSL-based synthesis to work with read-only access permissions; they reduce the complex permission *accounting* to easy-to-implement permission *substitution*.

Practical Contributions. Our first practical contribution is ROBOSUSLIK—an enhancement of the SUSLIK synthesis tool [34] with support for read-only borrows, which required us to modify less than 100 lines of the original code.

   Our second practical contribution is the extensive evaluation of synthesis with read-only permissions, on a standard benchmark suite of specifications for heap-manipulating programs. We compare the behaviour, performance, and the outcomes of the synthesis when run with the standard ("all-mutable") specifications and their analogues instrumented with read-only permissions wherever reasonable. By doing so, we substantiate the following claims regarding the practical impact of using read-only borrows in SSL specifications:

- First, we show that synthesis of read-only specifications is more *efficient*: it does *less backtracking* while searching for a program that satisfies the imposed constraints, entailing better performance.

---

[6] We will present borrow-polymorphic inductive heap predicates in Sec. 2.4.

- Second, we demonstrate that borrowing-aware synthesis is more *effective*: specifications with read-only annotations lead to more concise and human-readable programs, which do not perform redundant operations.
- Third, we observe that read-only borrows increase *expressivity* of the synthesis: in most of the cases enhanced specifications provide stronger correctness guarantees for the results, at almost no additional annotation overhead.
- Finally, we show that read-only borrows make the synthesis more *robust*: its results and performance are less likely to be affected by the unification order or the order of the attempted rule applications during the search.

Paper Outline. We start by showcasing the intricacies and the virtues of SSL-based synthesis with read-only specifications in Sec. 2. We provide the formal account of read-only borrows and present the modified SSL rules, along with the soundness argument in Sec. 3. We report on the implementation and evaluation of the enhanced synthesis in Sec. 4. We conclude with a discussion on the limitations of read-only borrows in Sec. 5 and compare to related work in Sec. 6.

2 Program Synthesis with Read-Only Borrows

We introduce the enhancement of SSL with read-only borrows by walking the reader through a series of small but characteristic examples of deductive synthesis with separation logic. We provide the necessary background on SSL in Sec. 2.1; the readers familiar with the logic may want to skip to Sec. 2.2.

2.1 Basics of SSL-based Deductive Program Synthesis

In a deductive Separation Logic-based synthesis, a client provides a specification of a function of interest as a pair of pre- and post-conditions, such as $\{\mathcal{P}\}$ void foo(loc x, int i) $\{\mathcal{Q}\}$. The precondition $\mathcal{P}$ constrains the symbolic state necessary to run the function safely (*i.e.*, without crashes), while the post-condition $\mathcal{Q}$ constrains the resulting state at the end of the function's execution. A function body c satisfying the provided specification is obtained as a result of deriving the SSL statement, representing the synthesis *goal*:

$$\{x, i\} ; \{\mathcal{P}\} \leadsto \{\mathcal{Q}\} |\, c$$

In the statement above, x and i are *program variables*, and they are explicitly stated in the environment $\Gamma = \{x, i\}$. Variables that appear in $\{\mathcal{P}\}$ and that are not program variables are called (logical) *ghost* variables, while the non-program variables that only appear in $\{\mathcal{Q}\}$ are referred to as (logical) *existential* ones (EV). The meaning of the statement $\Gamma; \{\mathcal{P}\} \leadsto \{\mathcal{Q}\} |\, c$ is the *validity* of the Hoare-style triple $\{\mathcal{P}\}$ c $\{\mathcal{Q}\}$ for all possible values of variables from Γ.[7] Both pre- and postcondition contain a *spatial* part describing the shape of the symbolic state (spatial formulae are ranged over via P, Q, and R), and a *pure* part (ranged over via ϕ, ψ, and ξ), which states the relations between variables (both program and logical). A derivation of an SSL statement is conducted by applying logical

---

[7] We often care only about the *existence* of a program c to be synthesised, not its specific shape. In those cases we will be using a shorter statement: $\Gamma; \{\mathcal{P}\} \leadsto \{\mathcal{Q}\}$.

rules, which reduce the initial goal to a trivial one, so it can be solved by one of the *terminal* rules, such as, *e.g.*, the rule EMP shown below:

$$\text{EMP} \; \frac{\vdash \phi \Rightarrow \psi}{\Gamma; \{\phi; \mathsf{emp}\} \rightsquigarrow \{\psi; \mathsf{emp}\} \,|\, \mathtt{skip}}$$

That is, EMP requires that (i) symbolic heaps in both pre- and post-conditions are empty and (ii) that the pure part ϕ of the precondition implies the pure part ψ of the postcondition. As the result, EMP "emits" a trivial program $\mathtt{skip}$. Some of the SSL rules are aimed at simplifying the goal, bringing it to the shape that can be solved with EMP. For instance, consider the following rules:

$$\text{FRAME} \; \frac{\mathsf{EV}\,(\Gamma, \mathcal{P}, \mathcal{Q}) \cap \mathsf{Vars}\,(\mathsf{R}) = \emptyset \qquad \Gamma; \{\phi; \mathsf{P}\} \rightsquigarrow \{\psi; \mathsf{Q}\} \,|\, \mathsf{c}}{\Gamma; \{\phi; \mathsf{P} * \mathsf{R}\} \rightsquigarrow \{\psi; \mathsf{Q} * \mathsf{R}\} \,|\, \mathsf{c}}$$

$$\text{UNIFYHEAPS} \; \frac{[\sigma]\mathsf{R}' = \mathsf{R} \qquad \emptyset \neq \mathsf{dom}\,(\sigma) \subseteq \mathsf{EV}\,(\Gamma, \mathcal{P}, \mathcal{Q}) \qquad \Gamma; \{\phi; \mathsf{P} * \mathsf{R}\} \rightsquigarrow [\sigma]\{\psi; \mathsf{Q} * \mathsf{R}'\} \,|\, \mathsf{c}}{\Gamma; \{\phi; \mathsf{P} * \mathsf{R}\} \rightsquigarrow \{\psi; \mathsf{Q} * \mathsf{R}'\} \,|\, \mathsf{c}}$$

Neither of the rules FRAME and UNIFYHEAPS "adds" to the program c being synthesised. However, FRAME reduces the goal by removing a matching part R (*a.k.a. frame*) from both the pre- and the post-condition. UNIFYHEAPS non-deterministically picks a substitution σ, which replaces existential variables in a sub-heap R' of the postcondition to match the corresponding symbolic heap R in the precondition. Both of these rules make choices with regard to what frame R to remove or which substitution σ to adopt—a point that will be of importance for the development described in Sec. 2.2.

Finally, the following (simplified) rule for producing a *write* command is *operational*, as it emits a part of the program to be synthesised, while also modifying the goal accordingly. The resulting program will, thus, consist of the emitted store $*\mathtt{x} = \mathtt{e}$ of an expression e to the pointer variable x. The remainder is synthesised by solving the sub-goal produced by applying the WRITE rule.

$$\text{WRITE} \; \frac{\mathsf{Vars}\,(\mathsf{e}) \subseteq \Gamma \qquad \mathsf{e} \neq \mathsf{e}' \qquad \Gamma; \{\phi; \mathsf{x} \mapsto \mathsf{e} * \mathsf{P}\} \rightsquigarrow \{\psi; \mathsf{x} \mapsto \mathsf{e} * \mathsf{Q}\} \,|\, \mathsf{c}}{\Gamma; \{\phi; \mathsf{x} \mapsto \mathsf{e}' * \mathsf{P}\} \rightsquigarrow \{\psi; \mathsf{x} \mapsto \mathsf{e} * \mathsf{Q}\} \,|\, *\mathsf{x} = \mathsf{e}; \mathsf{c}}$$

As it is common with proof search, should no rule apply to an intermediate goal within one of the derivations, the deductive synthesis back-tracks, possibly discarding a partially synthesised program fragment, trying alternative derivation branches. For instance, firing UNIFYHEAPS to unify wrong sub-heaps might lead the search down a path to an unsatisfiable goal, eventually making the synthesis back-track and leading to longer search. Consider also a misguided application of WRITE into a certain location, which can cause the synthesizer to generate a less intuitive program that "makes up" for the earlier spurious writes. This is precisely what we are going to fix by introducing read-only annotations.

2.2 Reducing Non-Determinism with Read-Only Annotations

Consider the following example adapted from the original SSL paper [34]. While the example is intentionally artificial, it captures a frequent synthesis scenario—non-determinism during synthesis. This specification allows a certain degree of freedom in how it can be satisfied:

$$\{x \mapsto 239 * y \mapsto 30\} \text{ void pick(loc x, loc y) } \{z \leq 100; x \mapsto z * y \mapsto z\} \quad (4)$$

It seems logical for the synthesis to start the program derivation by applying the rule UNIFYHEAPS, thus reducing the initial goal to the one of the form

$$\{x, y\}; \{x \mapsto 239 * y \mapsto 30\} \rightsquigarrow \{239 \leq 100; x \mapsto 239 * y \mapsto 239\}$$

This new goal has been obtained by picking one particular substitution $\sigma = [239/z]$ (out of multiple possible ones), which delivers two identical *heaplets* of the form $x \mapsto 239$ in pre- and postcondition. It is time for the WRITE rule to strike to fix the discrepancy between the symbolic heap in the pre- and postcondition by emitting the command $*y = 239$ (at last, some executable code!), and resulting in the following new goal (notice the change of y-related entry in the precondition):

$$\{x, y\}; \{x \mapsto 239 * y \mapsto 239\} \rightsquigarrow \{239 \leq 100; x \mapsto 239 * y \mapsto 239\}$$

What follows are two applications of the FRAME rule to the common symbolic heaps, leading to the goal: $\{x, y\} \{emp\} \rightsquigarrow \{239 \leq 100; emp\}$. At this point, we are clearly in trouble. The pure part of the precondition is simply true, while the postcondition's pure part is $239 \leq 100$, which is unsolvable.

Turns out that our initial pick of the substitution $\sigma = [239/z]$ was an unfortunate one, and we should discard the series of rule applications that followed it, back-track and adopt a different substitution, *e.g.*, $\sigma' = [30/z]$, which will indeed result in solving our initial goal.[8]

Let us now consider the same specification for pick that has been enhanced by explicitly annotating parts of the symbolic heap as mutable and read-only:

$$\left\{x \overset{M}{\mapsto} 239 * y \overset{RO}{\mapsto} 30\right\} \text{ void pick(loc x, loc y) } \left\{z \leq 100; x \overset{M}{\mapsto} z * y \overset{RO}{\mapsto} z\right\} \quad (5)$$

In this version of SSL, the effect of rules such as EMP, FRAME, and UNIFYHEAPS remains the same, while operational rules such as WRITE, become *annotation-aware*. Specifically, the rule WRITE is now replaced by the following one:

$$\text{WRITERO} \quad \frac{\text{Vars}(e) \subseteq \Gamma \quad e \neq e' \quad \Gamma; \left\{\phi; x \overset{M}{\mapsto} e * P\right\} \rightsquigarrow \left\{\psi; x \overset{M}{\mapsto} e * Q\right\} \Big| c}{\Gamma; \left\{\phi; x \overset{M}{\mapsto} e' * P\right\} \rightsquigarrow \left\{\psi; x \overset{M}{\mapsto} e * Q\right\} \Big| *x = e; c}$$

Notice how in the rule above the heaplets of the form $x \overset{M}{\mapsto} e$ are now annotated with the access permission M, which explicitly indicates that the code may modify the corresponding heap location.

Following with the example specification (5), we can imagine a similar scenario when the rule UNIFYHEAPS picks the substitution $\sigma = [239/z]$. Should this be the case, the next application of the rule WRITERO will not be possible, due to the *read-only* annotation on the heaplet $y \overset{RO}{\mapsto} 239$ in the resulting sub-goal:

$$\{x, y\}; \left\{x \overset{M}{\mapsto} 239 * y \overset{RO}{\mapsto} 30\right\} \rightsquigarrow \left\{z \leq 100; x \overset{M}{\mapsto} 239 * y \overset{RO}{\mapsto} 239\right\}$$

As the RO access permission prevents the synthesised code from modifying the greyed heaplets, the synthesis search is forced to back-track, picking an alternative substitution $\sigma' = [30/z]$ and converging on the desirable program $*x = 30$.

---

[8] One might argue that it was possible to detect the unsolvable conjunct $239 \leq 100$ in the postcondition immediately after performing substitution, thus sparing the need to proceed with this derivation further. This is, indeed, a possibility, but in general it is hard to argue which of the heuristics in applying the rules will work better in general. We defer the quantitative argument on this matter until Sec. 4.4.

2.3   Composing Read-Only Borrows

Having synthesised the `pick` function from specification (5), we would like to use it in future programs. For example, imagine that at some point, while synthesising another program, we see the following as an intermediate goal:

$$\{u,v\}\,;\,\left\{u\overset{M}{\mapsto}239*v\overset{M}{\mapsto}30*P\right\}\rightsquigarrow\left\{w\le 200;u\overset{M}{\mapsto}w*v\overset{M}{\mapsto}w*Q\right\}\tag{6}$$

It is clear that, modulo the names of the variables, we can synthesise a part of the desired program by emitting a call $\mathrm{pick}(u,v)$, which we can then reduce to the goal $\{u,v\}\,\{P\}\rightsquigarrow\{w\le 200;Q\}$ via an application of FRAME.

Why is emitting such a call to `pick()` safe? Intuitively, this can be done because the precondition of the spec (5) is *weaker* than the one in the goal (6). Indeed, the precondition of the latter provides the full (mutable) access permission on the heap portion $v\overset{M}{\mapsto}30$, while the pre/postcondition of former requires a weaker form of access, namely read-only: $y\overset{RO}{\mapsto}30$. Therefore, our logical foundations should allow temporary "downgrading" of an access permission, *e.g.*, from M to RO, for the sake of synthesising calls. While allowing this is straightforward and can be done similarly to up-casting a type in languages like Java, what turns out to be less trivial is making sure that the caller's initial stronger access permission (M) is *restored* once $\mathrm{pick}(u,v)$ returns.

Non-solutions. Perhaps, the simplest way to allow the call to a function with a weaker (in terms of access permissions) specification, would be to (a) downgrade the caller's permissions on the corresponding heap fragments to RO, and (b) recover the permissions as per the callee's specification. This approach significantly reduces the expressivity of the logic (and, as a consequence, completeness of the synthesis). For instance, adopting this strategy for using specification (5) in the goal (6) would result in the unsolvable sub-goal of the form $\{u,v\}\,;\,\left\{u\overset{M}{\mapsto}30*v\overset{RO}{\mapsto}30*P\right\}\rightsquigarrow\left\{u\overset{M}{\mapsto}30*v\overset{M}{\mapsto}30*Q\right\}$. This is due to the fact that the postcondition requires the heaplet $v\overset{M}{\mapsto}30$ to have the write-permission M, while the new precondition only provides the RO-access.

Another way to cater for a weaker callee's specification would be to "chip out" a RO-permission from a caller's M-annotation (in the spirit of fractional permissions), offer it to the callee, and then "merge" it back to the caller's full-blown permission upon return. This solution works for simple examples, but not for heap predicates with mixed permissions (discussion in Sec. 6). Yet another approach would be to create a "RO clone" of the caller's M-annotation, introducing an axiom of the form $x\overset{M}{\mapsto}t\dashv\vdash x\overset{M}{\mapsto}t*x\overset{RO}{\mapsto}t$. The created component $x\overset{RO}{\mapsto}t$ could be provided to the callee and discarded upon return since the caller retained the full permission of the original heap. Several works on RO permissions have adopted this approach [9, 11, 13]. While discarding such clones works just fine for sequential program verification, in the case of synthesis guided by pre- and postconditions, *incomplete* postconditions could lead to intractable goals.

Our solution. The key to gaining the necessary expressivity *wrt.* passing/returning access permissions, while maintaining a sound yet simple logic, is *treating access permissions as first-class values*. A natural consequence of this treatment is that immutability annotations can be symbolic (*i.e.*, variables of a special sort "permission"), and the semantics of such variables is well understood; we refer to these symbolic annotations as *read-only borrows*.[9] For instance, using borrows, we can represent the specification (5) as an equivalent one:

$$\left\{x \overset{M}{\mapsto} 239 * y \overset{a}{\mapsto} 30\right\} \text{ void pick(loc x, loc y)} \left\{z \leq 100; x \overset{M}{\mapsto} z * y \overset{a}{\mapsto} z\right\} \quad (7)$$

The only substantial difference with spec (5) is that now the pointer y's access permission is given an *explicit name* a. Such named annotations (*a.k.a.* borrows) are treated as RO by the callee, as long as the pure precondition does not constrain them to be mutable. However, giving these permissions names achieves an important goal: performing accurate accounting while composing specifications with different access permissions. Specifically, we can now emit a call to pick(u, v) as specified by (7) from the goal (6), keeping in mind the substitution $\sigma = [u/x, v/y, M/a]$. This call now accounts for borrows as well, and makes it straightforward to restore v's original permission M upon returning.

Following the same idea, borrows can be naturally composed through capture-avoiding substitutions. For instance, the same specification (7) of pick could be used to advance the following modified version of the goal (6):

$$\{u, v\} ; \left\{u \overset{M}{\mapsto} 239 * v \overset{c}{\mapsto} 30 * P\right\} \leadsto \left\{w \leq 210; u \overset{M}{\mapsto} w * v \overset{c}{\mapsto} w * Q\right\}$$

by means of taking the substitution $\sigma' = [u/x, v/y, c/a]$.

2.4 Borrow-Polymorphic Inductive Predicates

Separation Logic owes its glory to the extensive use of *inductive heap predicates*— a compact way to capture the shape and the properties of finite heap fragments corresponding to recursive linked data structures. Below we provide one of the most widely-used SL predicates, defining the shape of a heap containing a null-terminated singly-linked list with elements from a set S:

$$\begin{aligned} \mathsf{ls}(x, S) \triangleq\ & x = 0 \land \{S = \emptyset; \mathsf{emp}\} \\ |\ & x \neq 0 \land \{S = \{v\} \cup S_1; [x, 2] * x \mapsto v * \langle x, 1 \rangle \mapsto nxt * \mathsf{ls}(nxt, S_1)\} \end{aligned} \quad (8)$$

The predicate contains two clauses describing the corresponding cases of the list's shape depending on the value of the head pointer x. If x is zero, the list's heap representation is empty, and so is the set of elements S. Alternatively, if x is not zero, it stores a record with two items (indicated by the *block assertion* [x, 2]), such that the *payload* pointer x contains the value v (where $S = \{v\} \cup S_1$ for some set S_1), and the pointer, corresponding to x + 1 (denoted as $\langle x, 1 \rangle$) contains the address of the list's tail, *nxt*.

While expressive enough to specify and enable synthesis of various list-traversing and list-generating recursive functions via SSL, the definition (8) does not allow one to restrict the access permissions to different components of the list: all of the involved memory locations can be mutated (which explains the synthesis issue we described in Sec. 1.1). To remedy this weakness of the traditional SL-style predicates, we propose to *parameterise* them with read-only borrows, thus making them aware of different access permissions to their various components. For instance, we propose to redefine the linked list predicate as follows:

---

[9] In this regard, our symbolic borrows are very similar to abstract fractional permissions in CHALICE and VERIFAST [21, 27]. We discuss the relation in detail in Sec. 6.

$$\mathsf{ls}(x, S, a, b, c) \triangleq x = 0 \land \{S = \emptyset; \mathsf{emp}\}$$
$$\mid x \neq 0 \land \left\{ S = \{v\} \cup S_1; [x, 2]^a * x \overset{b}{\mapsto} v * \langle x, 1 \rangle \overset{c}{\mapsto} nxt * \mathsf{ls}(nxt, S_1, a, b, c) \right\} \tag{9}$$

The new definition (9) is similar to the old one (8), but now, in addition to the standard predicate parameters (*i.e.*, the head pointer x and the set S in this case), also features three borrow parameters a, b, and c that stand as place-holders for the access permissions to some particular components of the list. Specifically, the symbolic borrows b and c control the permissions to manipulate the pointers x and x + 1, correspondingly. The borrow a, modifying a block-type heaplet, determines whether the record starting at x can be deallocated with free(x). All the three borrows are passed in the same configuration to the recursive instance of the predicate, thereby imposing the same constraints on the rest of the corresponding list components.

Let us see the borrow-polymorphic inductive predicates in action. Consider the following specification that asks for a function taking a list of arbitrary values and replacing all of them with zeroes:[10]

$$\{\mathsf{ls}(x, S, d, M, e)\} \text{ void } \mathtt{reset(loc\ x)} \ \{\mathsf{ls}(x, \mathbb{O}, d, M, e)\} \tag{10}$$

The spec (10) gives very little freedom to the function that would satisfy it with regard to permissions to manipulate the contents of the heap, constrained by the predicate $\mathsf{ls}(x, S, d, M, e)$. As the first and the third borrow parameters are instantiated with read-only borrows (d and e), the desired function is not going to be able to change the structural pointers or deallocate parts of the list. The only allowed manipulation is, thus, changing the values of the payload pointers.

This concise specification is pleasantly strong. To wit, in plain SSL, a similar spec (without read-only annotations) would also admit an implementation that fully deallocates the list or arbitrarily changes its length. In order to avoid these outcomes, one would, therefore, need to provide an alternative definition of the predicate ls, which would incorporate the length property too.

Imagine now that one would like to use the implementation of reset satisfying specification (10) to generate a function with the following spec, providing stronger access permissions for the list components:

$$\{\mathsf{ls}(y, S, M, M, M)\} \text{ void } \mathtt{call\_reset(loc\ y)} \ \{\mathsf{ls}(y, \mathbb{O}, M, M, M)\}$$

During the synthesis of call_reset, a call to reset is generated. For this purpose the access permissions are borrowed and recovered as per spec (10) via the substitution [y/x, M/d, M/e] in a way described in Sec. 2.3.

2.5   Putting It All Together

We conclude this overview by explaining how synthesis via SSL enhanced with read-only borrows avoids the issue with spurious writes outlined in Sec. 1.1.

To begin, we change the specification to the following one, which makes use of the new list predicate (9) and prevents any modifications in the original list.

$$\left\{ r \overset{M}{\mapsto} x * \mathsf{ls}(x, S, a, b, c) \right\} \text{ listcopy(r) } \left\{ r \overset{M}{\mapsto} y * \mathsf{ls}(x, S, a, b, c) * \mathsf{ls}(y, S, M, M, M) \right\}$$

We should remark that, contrary to the solution sketched at the end of Sec. 1.1, which suggested using the predicate instance of the shape $\mathsf{ls}(x, S)[\mathsf{RO}]$, our concrete proposal does not allow us to constrain the entire predicate with a single

---

[10] We use $\mathbb{O}$ as a notation for a multi-set with an arbitrary finite number of zeroes.

Variable x, y Alpha-numeric identifiers
Size, offset n, ι Non-negative integers
Expression e ::= $0 \mid \mathsf{true} \mid x \mid e = e \mid e \wedge e \mid \neg e$
Command c ::= $\mathsf{let}\ \ x = *(x + \iota) \mid *(x + \iota) = e \mid \mathsf{let}\ \ x = \mathtt{malloc}(n) \mid \mathtt{free}(x)$
$\mid \mathsf{err} \mid f(\overline{e_i}) \mid c; c \mid \mathsf{if}\ (e)\ \{c\}\ \mathsf{else}\ \{c\}$
Fun. dict. Δ ::= $\epsilon \mid \Delta, f\ (\overline{x_i})\ \{\ c\ \}$

Fig. 2: Programming language grammar.

Pure term $\phi, \psi, \chi, \alpha ::= 0 \mid \mathsf{true} \mid \mathsf{M} \mid \mathsf{RO} \mid x \mid \phi = \phi \mid \phi \wedge \phi \mid \neg\phi$
Symbolic heap $\mathsf{P}, \mathsf{Q}, \mathsf{R}$ ::= $\mathsf{emp} \mid \langle e, \iota \rangle \overset{\alpha}{\mapsto} e \mid [e, \iota]^\alpha \mid \mathsf{p}(\overline{\phi_i}) \mid \mathsf{P} * \mathsf{Q}$
Heap predicate $\mathcal{D}$ ::= $\mathsf{p}(\overline{x_i})\ \overline{\langle e_k, \{\chi_k, \mathsf{R}_k\}\rangle}$
Function spec $\mathcal{F}$ ::= $\mathsf{f}(\overline{x_i}) : \{\mathcal{P}\}\{\mathcal{Q}\}$ Assertion $\mathcal{P}, \mathcal{Q}$ ::= $\{\phi; \mathsf{P}\}$
Environment Γ := $\epsilon \mid \Gamma, \mathsf{x}$ Context Σ := $\epsilon \mid \Sigma, \mathcal{D} \mid \Sigma, \mathcal{F}$

Fig. 3: BoSSL assertion syntax.

access permission (*e.g.*, RO). Instead, we allow *fine-grained* access control to its particular elementary components by annotating each one with an individual borrow. The specification above allows the greatest flexibility *wrt.* access permissions to the original list by giving them different names (a, b, c).

In the process of synthesising the non-trivial branch of `listcopy`, the search at some point will come up with the following intermediate goal:

$$\{\mathsf{x, r, nxt, v, y12}\}\ ;$$

$$\left\{ \mathsf{S} = \{\mathsf{v}\} \cup \mathsf{S_1}; \mathsf{r} \overset{\mathsf{M}}{\mapsto} \mathsf{y12} * [\mathsf{x}, 2]^{\mathsf{a}} * \mathsf{x} \overset{\mathsf{b}}{\mapsto} \mathsf{v} * \langle \mathsf{x}, 1 \rangle \overset{\mathsf{c}}{\mapsto} \mathsf{nxt} * \mathsf{ls}(\mathsf{y12}, \mathsf{S_1}, \mathsf{M}, \mathsf{M}, \mathsf{M}) * \ldots \right\}$$

$$\leadsto\ \left\{ [\mathsf{z}, 2]^{\mathsf{M}} * \mathsf{z} \overset{\mathsf{M}}{\mapsto} \mathsf{v} * \langle \mathsf{z}, 1 \rangle \overset{\mathsf{M}}{\mapsto} \mathsf{y12} * \mathsf{ls}(\mathsf{y12}, \mathsf{S_1}, \mathsf{M}, \mathsf{M}, \mathsf{M}) * \ldots \right\}$$

Since the logical variable z in the postcondition is an existential one, the greyed part of the symbolic heap can be satisfied by either (a) re-purposing the greyed part of the precondition (which is what the implementation in Sec. 1.1 does), or (b) allocating a corresponding record of two elements (as should be done). With the read-only borrows in place, the unification of the two greyed fragments in the pre- and postcondition via UNIFYHEAPS fails, because the mutable annotation of $\mathsf{z} \overset{\mathsf{M}}{\mapsto} \mathsf{v}$ in the post cannot be matched by the read-only borrow $\mathsf{x} \overset{\mathsf{b}}{\mapsto} \mathsf{v}$ in the precondition. Therefore, not being able to follow the derivation path (a), the synthesiser is forced to explore an alternative one, eventually deriving the version of `listcopy` without tail-swapping.

3   BoSSL: Borrowing Synthetic Separation Logic

We now give a formal presentation of BoSSL—a version of SSL extended with read-only borrows. Fig. 2 and Fig. 3 present its programming and assertion language, respectively. For simplicity, we formalise a core language without theories (*e.g.*, natural numbers), similar to the one of SMALLFOOT [6]; the only sorts in the core language are locations, booleans, and permissions (where permissions appear only in specifications) and the pure logic only has equality. In contrast, our implementation supports integers and sets (where the latter also only appear in specifications), with linear arithmetic and standard set operations. We do

WRITE

$$\frac{\mathsf{Vars}\,(e) \subseteq \Gamma \quad e \neq e' \quad \Gamma;\,\left\{\phi;\langle x,\iota\rangle \overset{M}{\mapsto} e * P\right\} \leadsto \left\{\psi;\langle x,\iota\rangle \overset{M}{\mapsto} e * Q\right\}\Big|\,c}{\Gamma;\,\left\{\phi;\langle x,\iota\rangle \overset{M}{\mapsto} e' * P\right\} \leadsto \left\{\psi;\langle x,\iota\rangle \overset{M}{\mapsto} e * Q\right\}\Big| * (x+\iota) = e;\,c}$$

ALLOC

$$\frac{R = [z,n]^{\alpha} * \bigstar_{0 \le i < n}\left(\langle z,i\rangle \overset{\alpha_i}{\mapsto} e_i\right) \quad (\{y\} \cup \{\overline{t_i}\}) \cap \mathsf{Vars}\,(\Gamma,\mathcal{P},\mathcal{Q}) = \emptyset \quad z \in \mathsf{EV}\,(\Gamma,\mathcal{P},\mathcal{Q})}{\Sigma;\Gamma;\,\{\phi;P\} \leadsto \{\psi;Q * R\}|\,\mathtt{let}\ y = \mathtt{malloc}(n);c}$$

with $R' \triangleq [y,n]^{M} * \bigstar_{0 \le i < n}\left(\langle y,i\rangle \overset{M}{\mapsto} t_i\right)$, $\Sigma;\Gamma;\,\{\phi;P * R'\} \leadsto \{\psi;Q * R\}|\,c$

FREE

$$\frac{R = [x,n]^{M} * \bigstar_{0 \le i < n}\left(\langle x,i\rangle \overset{M}{\mapsto} e_i\right) \quad \mathsf{Vars}\,(\{x\} \cup \{\overline{e_i}\}) \subseteq \Gamma \quad \Sigma;\Gamma;\,\{\phi;P\} \leadsto \{\mathcal{Q}\}|\,c}{\Sigma;\Gamma;\,\{\phi;P * R\} \leadsto \{\mathcal{Q}\}|\,\mathtt{free}(x);c}$$

Fig. 4: BoSSL derivation rules.

not formalise sort-checking of formulae; however, for readability, we will use the meta-variable α where the intended sort of the pure logic term is "permission", and Perm for the set of all permissions. The permission to allocate or deallocate a memory-block $[x,n]^{\alpha}$ is controlled by α.

3.1 BoSSL rules

New rules of BoSSL are shown in Fig. 4. The figure contains only 3 rules: this minimal adjustment is possible thanks to our approach to unification and permission accounting from first principles. Writing to a memory location requires its corresponding symbolic heap to be annotated as mutable. Note that for a precondition $\left\{a = M;\langle x\rangle \overset{a}{\mapsto} 5\right\}$, a normalisation rule like SUBSTLEFT would first transform it into $\left\{M = M;\langle x\rangle \overset{M}{\mapsto} 5\right\}$, at which point the WRITE rule can be applied. Note also that ALLOC does not require specific permissions on the block in the postcondition; if they turn out to be RO, the resulting goal is unsolvable.

Unsurprisingly, the rule for accessing a memory cell just for reading purposes requires no adjustments since any permission allows reading. Moreover, the CALL rule for method invocation does not need adjustments either. Below, we describe how borrow and return seamlessly operate within a method call:

CALL

$$\frac{\mathcal{F} \triangleq f(\overline{x_i}) : \{\phi_f;P_f\}\{\psi_f;Q_f\} \in \Sigma \quad R = [\sigma]P_f \quad \vdash \phi \Rightarrow [\sigma]\phi_f \quad \overline{e_i} = [\sigma]\overline{x_i}}{\Sigma;\Gamma;\,\{\phi;P * R\} \leadsto \{\mathcal{Q}\}|\,f(\overline{e_i});c}$$

with $\mathsf{Vars}\,(\overline{e_i}) \subseteq \Gamma$, $\phi' \triangleq [\sigma]\psi_f$, $R' \triangleq [\sigma]Q_f$, $\Sigma;\Gamma;\,\{\phi \wedge \phi';P * R'\} \leadsto \{\mathcal{Q}\}|\,c$

The CALL rule fires when a sub-heap R in the precondition of the goal can be unified with the precondition P_f of a function f from context Σ. Some salient points are worth mentioning here: (1) the *annotation borrowing* from R to P_f for those symbolic sub-heaps in P_f which require read-only permissions is handled by the unification of P_f with R, namely $* R = [\sigma]P_f$ (*i.e.*, substitution accounts for borrows: α/a); (2) the *annotation recovery* in the new precondition is implicit via $R' \triangleq [\sigma]Q_f$, where the substitution σ was computed during the unification, that is, while borrowing; (3) finding a substitution σ for $R = [\sigma]P_f$ fails if R does not have sufficient accessibility permissions to call f (*i.e.*, substitutions of the form a/M are disallowed since the domain of σ may only contain existentials). We reiterate that read-only specifications only manipulate symbolic borrows, that is to say, RO constants are not expected in the specification.

3.2 Memory Model

We closely follow the standard SL memory model [32,37] and assume $\text{Loc} \subset \text{Val}$.

(Heap) $h \in \text{Heaps} ::= \text{Loc} \to \text{Val}$ $\qquad$ (Stack) $s \in \text{Stacks} ::= \text{Var} \to \text{Val}$

To enable C-like accounting of dynamically-allocated memory blocks, we assume that the heap h also stores sizes of allocated blocks in dedicated locations. Conceptually, this part of the heap corresponds to the meta-data of the memory allocator. This accounting ensures that only a previously allocated memory block can be disposed (as opposed to any set of allocated locations), enabling the free command to accept a single argument, the address of the block. To model this meta-data, we introduce a function $\text{bl}: \text{Loc} \to \text{Loc}$, where $\text{bl}(x)$ denotes the location in the heap where the block meta-data for the address x is stored, if x is the starting address of a block. In an actual language implementation, $\text{bl}(x)$ might be, *e.g.*, $x - 1$ (*i.e.*, the meta-data is stored right before the block).

Since we have opted for an unsophisticated permission mechanism, where the *heap ownership is not divisible*, but some heap locations are restricted to RO, the definition of the satisfaction relation $\models_{\mathcal{I}}^{\Sigma,R}$ for the annotated assertions in a particular context Σ and given an interpretation $\mathcal{I}$, is parameterised with a fixed set of read-only locations, R:

- $\langle h, s \rangle \models_{\mathcal{I}}^{\Sigma,R} \{\phi; \text{emp}\}$ *iff* $[\![\phi]\!]_s = \text{true}$ and $\text{dom}(h) = \emptyset$.
- $\langle h, s \rangle \models_{\mathcal{I}}^{\Sigma,R} \{\phi; \langle e_1, \iota \rangle \overset{\alpha}{\mapsto} e_2\}$ *iff* $[\![\phi]\!]_s = \text{true}$ and $1 \triangleq [\![e_1]\!]_s + \iota$ and $\text{dom}(h) = \{1\}$ and $h(1) = [\![e_2]\!]_s$ and $1 \in R \Leftrightarrow \alpha = \text{RO}$.
- $\langle h, s \rangle \models_{\mathcal{I}}^{\Sigma,R} \{\phi; [e, n]^\alpha\}$ *iff* $[\![\phi]\!]_s = \text{true}$ and $1 \triangleq \text{bl}([\![e]\!]_s)$ and $\text{dom}(h) = \{1\}$ and $h(1) = n$ and $1 \in R \Leftrightarrow \alpha = \text{RO}$.
- $\langle h, s \rangle \models_{\mathcal{I}}^{\Sigma,R} \{\phi; P_1 * P_2\}$ *iff* $\exists\, h_1, h_2, h = h_1 \uplus h_2$ and $\langle h_1, s \rangle \models_{\mathcal{I}}^{\Sigma,R} \{\phi; P_1\}$ and $\langle h_2, s \rangle \models_{\mathcal{I}}^{\Sigma,R} \{\phi; P_2\}$.
- $\langle h, s \rangle \models_{\mathcal{I}}^{\Sigma,R} \{\phi; p(\overline{\psi_i})\}$ *iff* $[\![\phi]\!]_s = \text{true}$ and $\mathcal{D} \triangleq p(\overline{x_i})\overline{\langle e_k, \{\chi_k, R_k\} \rangle} \in \Sigma$ and $\left\langle h, \overline{[\![\psi_i]\!]_s} \right\rangle \in \mathcal{I}(\mathcal{D})$ and $\bigvee_k (\langle h, s \rangle \models_{\mathcal{I}}^{\Sigma,R} [\psi_i/x_i]\{\phi \wedge e_k \wedge \chi_k; R_k\})$.

There are two non-standard cases: points-to and block, whose permissions must agree with R. Note that in the definition of satisfaction, we only need to consider that case where the permission α is a value (*i.e.*, either RO or M). Although in a specification α can also be a variable, well-formedness guarantees that this variable must be logical, and hence will be substituted away in the definition of validity. We stress the fact that a reference that has RO permissions to a certain symbolic heap still retains the full ownership of that heap, with the restriction that it is not allowed to update or deallocate it. Note that deallocation additionally requires a mutable permission for the enclosing block.

3.3   Soundness

The BoSSL operational semantics is in the spirit of the traditional SL [38], and hence is omitted for the sake of saving space (selected rules are available in the extended version of the paper). The validity definition and the soundness proofs of SSL are ported to BoSSL without any modifications, since our current definition of satisfaction implies the one defined for SSL:

Definition 1 (Validity). *We say that a well-formed Hoare-style specification* $\Sigma; \Gamma; \{\mathcal{P}\} \, c \, \{\mathcal{Q}\}$ *is valid wrt. the function dictionary* Δ *iff whenever* dom $(s) = \Gamma$, $\forall \sigma_{gv} = \overline{[x_i \mapsto d_i]}_{x_i \in GV(\Gamma, \mathcal{P}, \mathcal{Q})}$ *such that* $\langle h, s \rangle \models_{\mathcal{I}}^{\Sigma}[\sigma_{gv}]\mathcal{P}$, *and* $\Delta; \langle h, (c, s) \cdot \epsilon \rangle \rightsquigarrow^*$ $\langle h', (skip, s') \cdot \epsilon \rangle$, *it is also the case that* $\langle h', s' \rangle \models_{\mathcal{I}}^{\Sigma}[\sigma_{ev} \uplus \sigma_{gv}]\mathcal{Q}$ *for some* $\sigma_{ev} = \overline{[y_j \mapsto d_j]}_{y_j \in EV(\Gamma, \mathcal{P}, \mathcal{Q})}$.

The following theorem guarantees that, given a program c generated with BoSSL, a heap model, and a set of read-only locations R that satisfy the program's precondition, executing c does not change those read-only locations:

Theorem 1 (RO Heaps Do Not Change). *Given a Hoare-style specification* $\Sigma; \Gamma; \{\phi; P\}c\{Q\}$, *which is valid wrt. the function dictionary* Δ, *and a set of read-only memory locations* R, *if:*

(i) $\langle h, s \rangle \models_{\mathcal{I}}^{\Sigma, R}[\sigma]\mathcal{P}$, *for some* h, s *and* σ, *and*
(ii) $\Delta; \langle h, (c, s) \cdot \epsilon \rangle \rightsquigarrow^* \langle h', (c', s') \cdot \epsilon \rangle$ *for some* h', s' *and* c'
(iii) $R \subseteq$ dom (h)

then $R \subseteq$ dom (h') *and* $\forall l \in R, \ h(l) = h'(l)$.

Starting from an abstract state where a spatial heap has a read-only permission, under no circumstance can this permission be strengthened to M:

Corollary 1 (No Permission Strengthening). *Given a valid Hoare-style specification* $\Sigma; \Gamma; \{\phi; P\} \, c \, \{\psi; Q\}$ *and a permission* α, *if* $\psi \Rightarrow (\alpha = M)$ *then it is also the case that* $\phi \Rightarrow (\alpha = M)$.

As it turns out, permission weakening is possible, since, though problematic, postcondition weakening is sound in general. However, even though this affects completeness, it does not affect our termination results. For example, given a synthesised auxiliary function $\mathcal{F} \triangleq f(x, r) : \left\{ x \overset{a_1}{\mapsto} t * r \overset{M}{\mapsto} x \right\}\left\{ x \overset{a_2}{\mapsto} t * r \overset{M}{\mapsto} t + 1 \right\}$, and a synthesis goal $\Sigma, \mathcal{F}; \Gamma; \left\{ x \overset{M}{\mapsto} 7 * y \overset{M}{\mapsto} x \right\} \rightsquigarrow \left\{ x \overset{M}{\mapsto} 7 * y \overset{M}{\mapsto} z \right\} \Big| c$, firing the CALL rule for the candidate function $f(x, r)$ would lead to the unsolvable goal $\Sigma, \mathcal{F}; \Gamma;$ $\left\{ x \overset{a_2'}{\mapsto} 7 * y \overset{M}{\mapsto} 8 \right\} \rightsquigarrow \left\{ x \overset{M}{\mapsto} 7 * y \overset{M}{\mapsto} z \right\} \Big| f(x, y); c$. FRAME may never be fired on this new goal since the permission of reference x in the goal's precondition has been permanently weakened. To eliminate such sources of incompleteness we require the user-provided predicates and specifications to be well-formed:

Definition 2 (Well-Formedness of Spatial Predicates). *We say that a spatial predicate* $p(\overline{x_i}) \ \overline{\langle e_k, \{\chi_k, R_k\} \rangle}_{k \in 1..N}$ *is well-formed iff*
$$\left(\bigcup_{k=1}^{N} (\text{Vars}(e_k) \cup \text{Vars}(\chi_k) \cup \text{Vars}(R_k)) \right) \cap \text{Perm} \subseteq (\overline{x_i} \cap \text{Perm}).$$

That is, every accessibility annotation within the predicate's clause is bound by the predicate's parameters.

Definition 3 (Well-Formedness of Specifications). *We say that a Hoare-style specification* $\Sigma; \Gamma; \{\mathcal{P}\}\ c\ \{\mathcal{Q}\}$ *is well-formed iff* $\mathsf{EV}(\Gamma, \mathcal{P}, \mathcal{Q}) \cap \mathtt{Perm} = \emptyset$ *and every predicate instance in* $\mathcal{P}$ *and* $\mathcal{Q}$ *is an instance of a well-formed predicate.*

That is, postconditions are not allowed to have existential accessibility annotations in order to avoid permanent weakening of accessibility.

A callee that requires borrows for a symbolic heap always returns back to the caller its original permission for that respective symbolic heap:

Corollary 2 (Borrows Always Return). *A heaplet with permission* α, *either (a) retains the same permission* α *after a call to a function that is decorated with well-formed specifications and that requires for that heaplet to have read-only permission, or (b) it may be deallocated in case if* $\alpha = \mathsf{M}$.

4   Implementation and Evaluation

We implemented BoSSL in an enhanced version of the SuSLik tool, which we refer to as ROBoSuSLik [12].[11] The changes to the original SuSLik infrastructure affected less than 100 lines of code. The extended synthesis is backwards-compatible with the original benchmarks. To make this possible, we treat the original SSL specifications as annotated/instantiated with M permissions, whenever necessary, which is consistent with treatment of access permissions in BoSSL.

We have conducted an extensive experimental evaluation of ROBoSuSLik, aiming to answer the following research questions:

1. Do borrowing annotations improve the *performance* of SSL-based synthesis when using standard search strategy [34, § 5.2]?
2. Do read-only borrows improve the *quality* of synthesised programs, in terms of size and comprehensibility, *wrt.* to their counterparts obtained from regular, "all-mutable" specifications?
3. Do we obtain *stronger correctness guarantees* for the programs from the standard SSL benchmark suite [34, § 6.1] by simply adding, whenever reasonable, read-only annotations to their specifications?
4. Do borrowing specifications enable more *robust* synthesis? That is, should we expect to obtain better programs/synthesis performance on average *regardless* of the adopted unification and search strategies?

4.1   Experimental Setup

Benchmark Suite. To tackle the above research questions, we have adopted most of the heap-manipulating benchmarks from SuSLik suite [34, § 6.1] (with some variations) into our sets of experiments. In particular we looked at the group of benchmarks which manipulate singly linked list segments, sorted linked list segments and binary trees. We did not include the benchmarks concerning binary search trees (BSTs) for the reasons outlined in the next paragraph.

---

[11] The sources are available at `https://github.com/TyGuS/robosuslik`.

The Tools. For a fair comparison which accounts for the latest advancements to SuSLik, we chose to parameterise the synthesis process with a flag that turns the read-only annotations on and off (off means that they are set to be mutable). Those values which are the result of having this flag set will be marked in the experiments with RO, while those marked with Mut ignore the read-only annotations during the synthesis process. For simplicity, we will refer to the two instances of the tool, namely RO and Mut, as two different tools. Each tool was set to timeout after 2 minutes of attempting to synthesise a program.

Criteria. In an attempt to quantify our results, we have looked at the size of the synthesised program (*AST size*), the absolute time needed to synthesise the code given its specification, averaged over several runs (*Time*), the number of backtrackings in the proof search due to nondeterminism (*#Backtr*), the total number of rule applications that the synthesis fired during the search (*#Rules*), including those that lead to unsolvable goals, and the strength of the guarantees offered by the specifications (*Stronger Guarantees*).

Variables. Some benchmarks have shown improvement over the synthesis process without the read-only annotations. To emphasise the fact that read-only annotations' improvements are not accidental, we have varied the inductive definitions of the corresponding benchmarks to experiment with different properties of the underlying structure: the shape of the structure (in all the definitions), the length of the structure (for those benchmarks tagged with *len*), the values stored within the structure (*val*), a combination of all these properties (*all*) as well as with the sortedness property for the "Sorted list" group of benchmarks.

Experiment Schema. To measure the performance and the quality of the borrowing-aware synthesis we ran the benchmarks against the two different tools and did a one-to-one comparison of the results. We ran each tool three times for each benchmark, and average the resulted synthesis time. All the other evaluation criteria remain constant within all three runs.

To measure the tools' robustness we stressed the synthesis algorithm by altering the default proof search strategy. We prepared 42 such perturbations which we used to run against the different program variants enumerated above. Each pair of program variant and proof strategy perturbation has been then analysed to measure the number of rules that had been fired by RO and Mut.

Hardware Setup. The experiments were conducted on a 64-bit machine running Ubuntu, with an Intel Xeon CPU (6 cores, 2.40GHz) with 32GB RAM.

4.2   Performance and Quality of the Borrowing-Aware Synthesis

Tab. 1 captures the results of running RO and Mut against the considered benchmarks. It provides the empirical proof that the borrowing-aware synthesis improves the performance of the original SSL-based synthesis, or in other words, answering positively the Research Question 1. RO suffers almost no loss in performance (except for a few cases, such as the list segment append where there is a negligible increase in time), while the gain is considerable for those synthesis problems with complex pointer manipulation. For example, if we consider the number of fired rules as the performance measurement criteria, in the worst

Group	Description	AST size RO	AST size Mut	Time (sec) RO	Time (sec) Mut	Time Mut/RO	#Backtr. RO	#Backtr. Mut	#Backtr. Mut/RO	#Rules RO	#Rules Mut	#Rules Mut/RO	Stronger Guarant.
	append	20	20	1.5	1.4	0.9x	8	8	1.0x	77	78	1.0x	YES
	delete	44	44	1.9	2.1	1.1x	67	67	1.0x	180	180	1.0x	same
	dispose	11	11	0.5	0.5	1.0x	0	0	1.0x	8	8	1.0x	same
Linked	init	13	13	0.7	0.7	1.0x	5	5	1.0x	27	27	1.0x	YES
List	lcopy	32	35	1.0	1.0	1.0x	9	14	1.5x	66	82	1.2x	YES
Segment	length	22	22	1.5	1.5	1.0x	2	2	1.0x	38	38	1.0x	YES
	max	28	28	1.4	1.5	1.1x	2	2	1.0x	38	38	1.0x	YES
	min	28	28	1.5	1.5	1.0x	2	2	1.0x	38	38	1.0x	YES
	singleton	11	11	0.5	0.5	1.0x	8	8	1.0x	30	30	1.0x	same
	ins-sort-all	29	29	3.7	3.8	1.0x	5	5	1.0x	60	60	1.0x	YES
Sorted	ins-sort-len	29	29	3.0	3.0	1.0x	7	8	1.1x	59	60	1.0x	YES
List	ins-sort-val	29	29	2.6	2.5	1.0x	5	5	1.0x	57	57	1.0x	YES
	insert	53	53	7.8	8.0	1.0x	35	96	2.7x	214	338	1.6x	YES
	prepend	11	11	0.5	0.6	1.2x	1	1	1.0x	17	17	1.0x	YES
	dispose	16	16	0.4	0.5	1.2x	0	0	1.0x	10	10	1.0x	same
	flatten-acc	35	35	2.1	2.0	1.0x	24	24	1.0x	118	118	1.0x	same
	flatten-app	48	48	1.6	1.7	1.0x	14	14	1.0x	76	76	1.0x	same
	morph	19	19	0.6	0.5	1.0x	1	1	1.0x	24	24	1.0x	YES
	tcopy-all	42	51	1.5	2.2	1.5x	10	88	8.8x	85	296	3.5x	YES
	tcopy-len	36	42	1.3	2.0	1.5x	6	90	15x	72	304	4.2x	YES
Tree	tcopy-val	42	51	1.4	5.3	3.8x	10	1222	122x	82	2673	32x	YES
	tcopy-ptr-all	46	55	1.6	2.4	1.5x	10	88	8.8x	93	303	3.3x	YES
	tcopy-ptr-len	40	46	1.3	2.2	1.7x	6	90	15x	80	311	3.9x	YES
	tcopy-ptr-val	46	55	1.3	5.8	4.5x	10	1222	122x	89	2679	30x	YES
	tsize-all	32	38	1.5	1.4	0.9x	2	4	2.0x	45	51	1.1x	YES
	tsize-len	32	32	1.2	1.1	0.9x	2	2	1.0x	44	46	1.0x	YES
	tsize-ptr-all	36	42	1.6	1.4	0.9x	2	4	2.0x	53	58	1.1x	YES
	tsize-ptr-len	36	36	1.3	1.3	1.0x	2	2	1.0x	52	53	1.0x	YES

Table 1: Benchmarks and comparison between the results for synthesis with read-only annotations (RO) and without them (Mut). For each case study we measure the *AST size* of the synthesised program, the *Time* needed to synthesize the benchmark, the number of times that the synthesiser had to discard a derivation branch (*#Backtr.*), and the total number of fired rules (*#Rules*).

case, RO behaves the same as Mut, while in the best scenario it buys us a 32-fold decrease in the number of applied rules. At the same time, synthesising a few small examples in the RO case is a bit slower, despite the same or smaller number of rule applications. This is due to the increased number of logical variables (because of added borrows) when discharging obligations via SMT solver.

Fig. 5 offers a statistical view of the numbers in the table, where smaller bars mark a better performance. The barplots indicate that as the complexity of the problem increases (approximately from left to right), RO outperforms Mut.

Perhaps the most important take-away from this experiment is that the synthesis with read-only borrows often produces a more concise program (light green cells in the columnt *AST size* of Tab. 1), while retaining the same or better performance *wrt.* all the evaluated criteria. For instance, RO gets rid of the spurious write from the motivating example introduced in Sec. 1, reducing the AST size from 35 nodes down to 32, while in the same time firing fewer rules. That also means that we secure a positive answer for Research Question 2.

4.3   Stronger Correctness Guarantees

To answer Research Question 3, we have manually compared the guarantees offered by the specifications annotated with RO permissions against the default

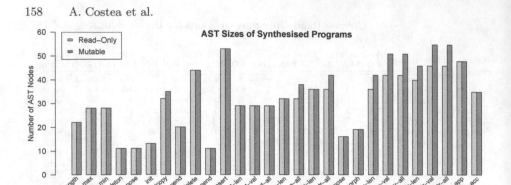

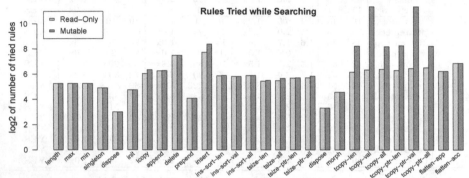

Fig. 5: Statistics for synthesis with and without Read-Only specifications.

ones - the results are summarized in the last column of Tab. 1. For instance, a specification stating that the shape of a linked-list segment is read-only implies that the size of that segment remains constant through the program's execution. In other words, the length property need not be captured separately in the segment's definition. If, in addition to the shape, the payload of the segment is also read-only, then the set of values and their ordering are also invariant.

Consider the goal $\{\mathsf{lseg}(x, y, s, a_1, a_2, a_3)\} \leadsto \{\mathsf{lseg}(x, y, s, a_1, a_2, a_3)\}$, where lseg is an inductive definition of a list segment which ends at y and contains the set of values s. The borrowing-aware synthesiser will produce a program which is guaranteed to treat the segment pointed by x and ending with y as read-only (that is, its shape, length, values and orderings are invariant). At the same time, for a goal $\{\mathsf{lseg}(x, y, s)\} \leadsto \{\mathsf{lseg}(x, y, s)\}$, the guarantees are that the returned segment still ends in y and contains values s. Internal modifications of the segment, such as reordering and duplicating list elements, may still occur.

The few entries marked with same are programs with specifications which have not got stronger when instrumented with RO annotations (*e.g.*, delete). These benchmarks require mutation over the entire data structure, hence the read-only annotations do not influence the offered guarantees. Overall, our observations that read-only annotations offer stronger guarantees are in agreement with the works on SL-based program verification [9, 13], but are promoted here to the more challenging problem of program synthesis.

4.4   Robustness under Synthesis Perturbations

There is no single search heuristics that will work equally well for any given specification: for a particular fixed search strategy, a synthesiser can exhibit suboptimal performance for some goals, while converging quickly on some others. By evaluating robustness *wrt.* to RO and M specification methodologies, we are hoping to show that, provided a large variety of "reasonable" search heuristics, read-only annotations deliver better synthesis performance "on average".

For this set of experiments, we have focused on four characteristic programs from our performance benchmarks based on their pointer manipulation complexity: list segment copy (`lcopy`), insertion into a sorted list segment (`insert`), copying a tree (`tcopy`), and a variation of the tree copy that shares the same pointer for the input tree and its returned copy (`tcopy-ptr`).

Exploring Different Unification Orders. Since spatial unification stays at the core of the synthesis process, we implemented 6 different strategies for choosing a unification candidate based on the following criteria: the size of the heaplet chunk (favor the smallest heap vs. the largest one as the best unification candidate), the name of the predicate (we considered both an ascending as well as a descending priority queue), and a customised ranking function which associates a cost to a symbolic heap based on its kind—a block is cheaper to unify than a points-to which in turn is cheaper than a spatial predicate.

Exploring Different Search Strategies. We next designed 6 strategies for prioritising the rule applications. One of the crux rules in this matter, is the WRITE rule whose different priority schemes might make all the results seem randomly-generated. In the cases where WRITE leads to unsolvable goals, one might rightfully argue that RO has a clear advantage over Mut (*fail fast*). However, for the cases where mutation leads to a solution faster, then Mut might have an advantage over RO (*solve fast*). Because these are just intuitive observations, and for fairness sake, we experimented with both the cases where WRITE has a high and a low priority in the queue of rule phases [34, § 5.2]. Since most of the benchmarks involve recursion, we also chose to shuffle around the priorities of the OPEN and CALL rules. Again, we chose between a stack high and a bottom low priority for these rules to give a fair chance to both tools.

We considered all combinations of the 6 unification permutations and the 6 rule-application permutations (plus the default one) to obtain 42 different proof search perturbations. We will use the following notation in the narrative below:

- S is the set comprising the synthesis problems: `lcopy`, `insert`, `tcopy`, `tcopy-ptr`.
- V is the set of all specification variations: *len, val, all*.
- K is the set of all 42 possible tool perturbations.

The distributions of the number of rules fired for each tool (RO and Mut) with the 42 perturbations over the 4 synthesis problems with 3 variants of specification each, that is 1008 different synthesis runs, are summarised using the boxplots in Fig. 6. There is a boxplot corresponding to each pair of tool and synthesis problem. In the ideal case, each boxplot contains 126 data points corresponding to a unique combination (v, k) of a specification variation $v \in V$ and a tool perturbation $k \in K$. A boxplot is the distribution of such data based on a

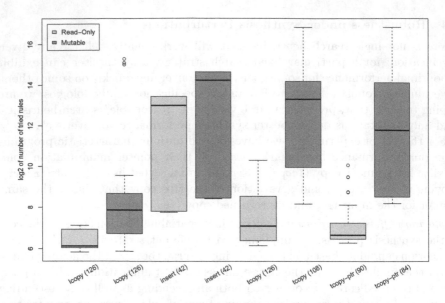

Fig. 6: Boxplots of variations in $\log_2$(numbers of applied rules) for synthesis perturbations. Numbers of data points for each example are given in parentheses.

six number summary: minimum, first quartile, median, third quartile, maximum, outliers. For example, the boxplot for tcopy-ptr corresponding to RO and containing 90 data points, reads as follows: "the synthesis processes fired between 64 and 256 rules, with most of the processes firing between 64 and 128 rules. There are three exception where the synthesiser fired more than 256 rules". Note that the y-axis represents the binary logarithm of the number of fired rules.

Even though we attempted to synthesise each program 126 times for each tool, some attempts hit the timeout and therefore their corresponding data points had to be eliminated from the boxplot. It is of note, though, that whenever RO with configuration (v, k) hit the timeout for the synthesis problem $s \in S$, so did Mut, hence both the $(RO, s, (v, k))$ as well as $(Mut, s, (v, k))$ are omitted from the boxplots. But the inverse did not hold: RO hit the timeout fewer times than Mut, hence RO is measured at disadvantage (i.e., more data points means more opportunities to show worse results). Since insert collected the highest number of timeouts, we equalised it to remove non-matched entries across the two tools.

Despite RO's potential measurement disadvantage, the boxplots depicts it as a clear winner. Not only RO fires fewer rules in all the cases, but with the exception of insert, it is also more stable to the proof search perturbations, it varies a few order of magnitude less than Mut does for the same configurations. Fig. 7 supports this observation by offering a more detailed view on the distributions of the numbers of fired rules per synthesis configuration. Taller bars show that more processes fall in the same range (wrt. the number of fired rules). For lcopy, tcopy, tcopy-ptr it is clear that Mut has a wider distribution of the number of fired rules, that is, Mut is more sensitive to the perturbations than RO. We additionally make some further observations:

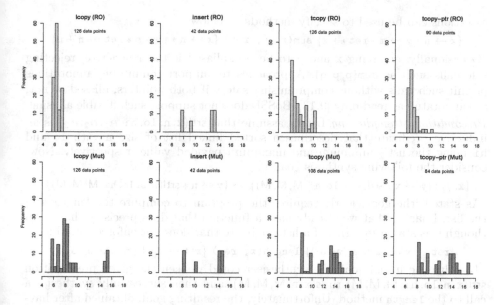

Fig. 7: Distributions of $\log_2$(number of attempted rule applications).

- Despite a similar distribution *wrt.* the numbers of fired rules in the case of `insert`, RO produces compact ASTs of size 53 for all perturbations, while Mut fluctuates between producing ASTs of size 53 and 62.
- For all the synthesis tasks, RO produced the same AST irrespective of the tool's perturbation. In contrast, there were synthesis problems for which Mut produced as many as 3 different ASTs for different perturbations, none of which were as concise as the one produced by RO for the same configuration.
- The outliers of (Mut, `lcopy`) are ridiculously high, firing close to 40k rules.
- The outliers of (RO, `tcopy`) are still below the median values of (Mut, `tcopy`).
- Except for `insert`, the best performance of Mut, in terms of fired rules, barely overlaps with the worst performance of RO.
- Except for `insert`, the medians of RO are closer to the lowest value of the data distribution, as opposed to Mut where the tendancy is to fire more rules.
- In absolute values, RO hit the 2-minutes timeout 102 times compared to Mut, which hit the timeout 132 times.

We believe that the main take-aways from this set of experiments, along with the positive answer to the Research Question 4, are as follows:
- RO is more stable *wrt.* the number of rules fired and the size of the generated AST for many reasonable proof search perturbations.
- RO produces better programs, which avoid spurious statements, irrespective of the perturbation and number of rules fired during the search.

5   Limitations and Discussion

Flexible aliasing. Separating conjunction asserts that the heap can be split into two disjoint parts, or in other words it carries an implicit non-aliasing information. Specifically, $x \mapsto \_ * y \mapsto \_$ states that x and y are non-aliased. Such assertions can be used to specify methods as below:

$$\{x \mapsto n * y \mapsto m * \mathtt{ret} \mapsto x\} \ \mathtt{sum(x, \ y, \ ret)} \ \{x \mapsto n * y \mapsto m * \mathtt{ret} \mapsto n + m\}$$

Occasionally, enforcing x and y to be non-aliased is too restrictive, rejecting safe calls such as $\mathtt{sum}(p, p, q)$. Approaches to support immutable annotations permit such calls without compromising safety if both pointers, aliased or not, are annotated as read-only [9,13]. BoSSL does not support such flexible aliasing.

Precondition strengthening. Let us assume that $\mathsf{srtl}(x, n, lo, hi, \alpha_1, \alpha_2, \alpha_3)$ is an inductive predicate that describes a sorted linked list of size n with lo and hi being the list's minimum and maximum payload value, respectively. Now, consider the following synthesis goal:

$$\{x, y\} ; \{y \mapsto x * \mathsf{srtl}(x, n, lo, hi, M, M, M)\} \rightsquigarrow \{y \mapsto n * \mathsf{srtl}(x, n, lo, hi, M, M, M)\}.$$

As stated, the goal clearly requires the program to compute the length n of the list. Imagine that we already have a function that does precisely that, even though it is stated in terms of a list predicate that does not enforce sortedness:

$$\{\mathtt{ret} \mapsto x * \mathsf{ls}(x, n, a_1, a_2, a_3)\} \ \mathtt{length(x, \ ret)} \ \{\mathtt{ret} \mapsto n * \mathsf{ls}(x, n, a_1, a_2, a_3)\}$$

To solve the initial goal, the synthesiser could weaken the given precondition $\mathsf{srtl}(x, n, lo, hi, M, M, M)$ to $\mathsf{ls}(x, n, M, M, M)$, and then successfully synthesise a call to the length method. Unfortunately, the resulting goal, obtained after having emitted the call to length and applying FRAME, is unsolvable:

$$\{x, y\} \ \{\mathsf{ls}(x, n, M, M, M)\} \rightsquigarrow \{\mathsf{srtl}(x, n, lo, hi, M, M, M)\}.$$

since the logic does not allow to strengthen an arbitrary linked list to a *sorted* linked list without retaining the prior knowledge. Should we have adopted an alternative approach to read-only annotations [9,13] allowing the caller to retain the full permission of the sorted list, then the postcondition of length would *not* contain the list-related part of the heap and would only quantify over the result pointer $\{\mathtt{ret} \mapsto n\}$, thus leading to the solvable goal below:

$$\{x, y\} ; \{\mathsf{srtl}(x, n, lo, hi, M, M, M)\} \rightsquigarrow \{\mathsf{srtl}(x, n, lo, hi, M, M, M)\}.$$

One straightforward way for BoSSL to cope with this limitation is to simply add a version of length annotated with specifications that cater to srtl.

Overcoming the limitations. While the "caller keeps the permission" kind of approach would buy us flexible aliasing and calls with weaker specifications, it would compromise the benefits discussed earlier with respect to the granularity of borrow-polymorphic inductive predicates. One possible solution to gain the best of both worlds would be to design a permission system which allows both borrow-polymorphic inductive predicates as well as read-only modalities to co-exist, where the latter would overwrite the predicate's mixed permissions. In other words, the read-only modality enforces a read-only treatment of the predicate irrespective of its permission arguments, while the permission arguments control the treatment of a mutable predicate. The theoretical implications of such a design choice are left as part of future work.

Extending read-only specifications to concurrency. Thus far we have only investigated the synthesis of sequential programs, for which read-only annotations helped to reduce the synthesis cost. Assuming that the synthesiser has the capability to synthesise concurrent programs as well, the borrows annotation mechanism in its current form may not be able to cope with general resource sharing.

This is because a callee which requires read-only permissions to a particular symbolic heap still consumes the entire required symbolic heap from the caller, despite the read-only requirement; hence, there is no space left for sharing. That said, the recently proposed alternative approaches to introduce read-only annotations [9, 13] have no formal support for heap sharing in the presence of concurrency either. To address these challenges, we could adopt a more sophisticated approach based on fractional permissions mechanism [7,8,20,25,30], but this is left as part of future work since it is orthogonal to the current scope.

6 Related Work

Language design. There is a large body of work on integrating access permissions into practical type systems [5,16,42] (see, *e.g.*, the survey by Clarke *et al.* [10]). One notable such system, which is the closest in its spirit to our proposal, is the borrows type system of the Rust programming language [1] proved safe with RustBelt [22]. Similar to our approach, borrows in Rust are short-lived: in Rust they share the scope with the owner; in our approach they do not escape the scope of a method call. In contrast with our work, Rust's type system carefully manages different references to data by imposing strict sharing constraints, whereas in our approach the treatment of aliasing is taken care of automatically by building on Separation Logic. Moreover, Rust allows read-only borrows to be duplicated, while in the sequential setting of BoSSL this is currently not possible.

Somewhat related to our approach, Naden *et al.* propose a mechanisms for borrowing permissions, albeit integrated as a fundamental part of a type system [31]. Their type system comes equipped with *change permissions* which enforce the borrowing requirements and describe the effects of the borrowing upon return. As a result of treating permissions as first-class values, we do not need to explicitly describe the flow of permissions for each borrow since this is controlled by a mix of the substitution and unification principles.

Program verification with read-only permissions. Boyland introduced fractional permissions to statically reason about interference in the presence of *shared-memory concurrency* [8]. A permission p denotes full resource ownership (i.e. read-write access) when $p = 1$, while $p \in (0, 1)$ denotes a partial ownership (i.e. read-only access). To leverage permissions in practice, a system must support two key operations: permission splitting and permission borrowing. Permission splitting (and merging back) follows the split rule: $x \overset{p}{\mapsto} a = x \overset{p_1}{\mapsto} a * x \overset{p_2}{\mapsto} a$, with $p = p_1 + p_2$ and $p, p_1, p_2 \in (0, 1]$. Permission borrowing refers to the safe manipulation of permissions: a callee may remove some permissions from the caller, use them temporarily, and give them back upon return.

Though it exists, tool support for fractional permissions is still scarce. Leino and Müller introduced a mechanism for storing fractional permissions in data structures via dedicated access predicates in the CHALICE verification tool [27]. To promote generic specifications, Heule *et al.* advanced CHALICE with instatiable abstract permissions, allowing automatic fire of the split rule and symbolic borrowing [20]. VeriFast [21] is guided by contracts written in Separation Logic and assumes the existence of lemmas to cater for permission splitting. Viper [30] is an intermediate language which supports various permission models, including abstract fractional permissions [4, 43]. Similar to CHALICE, the permissions are attached to memory locations using an accessibility predicate. To reason about it, VIPER uses permission-aware assertions and assumptions, which correspond in our approach to the unification and the substitution operations, respectively. Like VIPER, we enhance the basic memory constructors, that is blocks and points-to, to account for permissions, but in contrast, the CALL rule in our approach is standard, *i.e.*, *not* permission-aware.

These tools, along with others [3, 18], offer strong correctness guarantees in the presence of resource sharing. However, there is a class of problems, namely those involving predicates with mixed permissions, whose guarantees are weakened due to the general fractional permissions model behind these tools. We next exemplify this class of problems in a sequential setting. We start by considering a method which resets the values stored in a linked-list while maintaining its shape ($p < 1$ below is to enforce the immutable shape):

$$\{p < 1;\ \mathsf{ls}(x, S)[1, p]\}\ \mathtt{void}\ \mathtt{reset(loc\ x)}\ \{\mathsf{ls}(x, \{0\})[1, p]\}.$$

Assume a call to this method, namely $\mathtt{reset}(y)$. The caller has full permission over the entire list passed as argument, that is $\mathsf{ls}(y, B)[1, 1]$. This attempt leads to two issues. The first has to do with splitting the payload's permission (before the call) such that it matches the callee's postcondition. To be able to modify the list's payload, the callee must get the payload's full ownership, hence the caller should retain 0: $\mathsf{ls}(y, B)[1, 1] = \mathsf{ls}(y, B)[0, 1/2] * \mathsf{ls}(y, B)[1, 1/2]$. But 0 is not a valid fractional permission. The second issue surfaces while attempting to merge the permissions after the call: $\mathsf{ls}(y, B)[0, 1/2] * \mathsf{ls}(y, \{0\})[1, 1/2]$ is invalid since the two instances of ls have incompatible arguments (namely B and $\{0\}$). To avoid such problems, BoSSL abandons the split rule and instead always manipulates full ownership of resources, hence it does not use fractions. This compromise, along with the support for symbolic borrows, allows ROBOSUSLIK to guarantee read-only-ness in a sequential setting while avoiding the aforementioned issues. More investigations are needed in order to lift this result to concurrency reasoning. Another feature which distinguishes the current work from those based on fractional permissions, is the support for permissions as parameters of the predicate, which in turn supports the definition of predicates with mixed permissions.

Immutable specifications on top of Separation Logic have also been studied by David and Chin [13]. Unlike our approach which treats borrows as polymorphic variables that rely on the basic concept of substitution, their annotation mechanism comprises only constants and requires a specially tailored entailment on top of enhanced proof rules. Since callers retain the heap ownership upon calling a method with read-only requirements, their machinery supports flexible aliasing and cut-point preservation—features that we could not find a good use for in the context of program synthesis. An attempt to extend David and Chin's work by adding support for predicates with mixed permissions [11] suffers from significant annotation overhead. Specifically, it employs a mix of mutable, immutable, and *absent* permissions, so that each mutable heaplet in the precondition requires a corresponding matching heaplet annotated with absent in the postcondition.

Charguéraud and Pottier [9] extended Separation Logic with RO assertions that can be freely duplicated or discarded. Their approach creates lexically-scoped copies of the RO-permissions before emitting a call, which, in turn, involves discarding the corresponding heap from the postcondition to guarantee a sound RO-modality. Adapting this modality to program synthesis guided by pre- and postconditions would require a completely new system of deductive synthesis since most of the rules in SSL are not designed to handle the discardable RO-heaps. In contrast, BoSSL supports permission-parametric predicates (*e.g.*, (9)) requiring only minimal adjustments to its host logic, *i.e.*, SSL.

Program synthesis. BoSSL continues a long line of work on program synthesis from formal specifications [26, 36, 40, 41, 44] and in particular, *deductive synthesis* [14, 23, 29, 33, 34], which can be characterised as search in the space of *proofs* of program correctness (rather than in the space of programs). Most directly BoSSL builds upon our prior work on SSL [34] and enhances its specification language with read-only annotations. In that sense, the present work is also related to various approaches that use *non-functional* specifications as input to synthesis. It is common to use *syntactic* non-functional specifications, such as grammars [2], sketches [36, 40], or restrictions on the number of times a component can be used [19]. More recent work has explored *semantic* non-functional specifications, including type annotations for resource consumption [24] and security/privacy [17, 35, 39]. This research direction is promising because (a) annotations often enable the programmer to express a strong specification concisely, and (b) checking annotations is often more compositional (*i.e.*, fails faster) than checking functional specifications, which makes synthesis more efficient. In the present work we have demonstrated that both of these benefits of non-functional specifications also hold for the read-only annotations of BoSSL.

7 Conclusion

In this work, we have advanced the state of the art in program synthesis by highlighting the benefits of guiding the synthesis process with information about memory access permissions. We have designed the logic BoSSL and implemented the tool ROBoSuSLik, showing that a minimalistic discipline for read-only permissions already brings significant improvements *wrt.* the performance and robustness of the synthesiser, as well as *wrt.* the quality of its generated programs.

Acknowledgements. We thank Alexander J. Summers, Cristina David, Olivier Danvy, and Peter O'Hearn for their comments on the preliminary versions of the paper. We are very grateful to the ESOP 2020 reviewers for their detailed feedback, which helped to conduct a more adequate comparison with related approaches and, thus, better frame the conceptual contributions of this work.

Nadia Polikarpova's research was supported by NSF grant 1911149. Amy Zhu's research internship and stay in Singapore during the Summer 2019 was supported by Ilya Sergey's start-up grant at Yale-NUS College, and made possible thanks to UBC Science Co-op Program.

References

1. The Rust Programming Language: References and Borrowing. `https://doc.rust-lang.org/1.8.0/book/references-and-borrowing.html`, 2019.
2. Rajeev Alur, Rastislav Bodík, Garvit Juniwal, Milo M. K. Martin, Mukund Raghothaman, Sanjit A. Seshia, Rishabh Singh, Armando Solar-Lezama, Emina Torlak, and Abhishek Udupa. Syntax-guided synthesis. In *FMCAD*, pages 1–8. IEEE, 2013.
3. Andrew W. Appel. Verified software toolchain - (invited talk). In *ESOP*, volume 6602 of *LNCS*, pages 1–17. Springer, 2011.
4. Vytautas Astrauskas, Peter Müller, Federico Poli, and Alexander J. Summers. Leveraging Rust types for modular specification and verification. *PACMPL*, 3(OOPSLA):147:1–147:30, 2019.
5. Thibaut Balabonski, François Pottier, and Jonathan Protzenko. The Design and Formalization of Mezzo, a Permission-Based Programming Language. *ACM Trans. Program. Lang. Syst.*, 38(4):14:1–14:94, 2016.
6. Josh Berdine, Cristiano Calcagno, and Peter W. O'Hearn. Symbolic execution with separation logic. In *APLAS*, volume 3780 of *LNCS*, pages 52–68. Springer, 2005.
7. Richard Bornat, Cristiano Calcagno, Peter W. O'Hearn, and Matthew J. Parkinson. Permission Accounting in Separation Logic. In *POPL*, pages 259–270. ACM, 2005.
8. John Boyland. Checking Interference with Fractional Permissions. In *SAS*, volume 2694 of *LNCS*, pages 55–72. Springer, 2003.
9. Arthur Charguéraud and François Pottier. Temporary Read-Only Permissions for Separation Logic. In *ESOP*, volume 10201 of *LNCS*, pages 260–286. Springer, 2017.
10. Dave Clarke, Johan Östlund, Ilya Sergey, and Tobias Wrigstad. *Ownership Types: A Survey*, pages 15–58. Springer Berlin Heidelberg, 2013.
11. Andreea Costea, Asankhaya Sharma, and Cristina David. HIPimm: verifying granular immutability guarantees. In *PEPM*, pages 189–194. ACM, 2014.
12. Andreea Costea, Amy Zhu, Nadia Polikarpova, and Ilya Sergey. ROBoSuSLik: ESOP 2020 Artifact. 2020. DOI: `10.5281/zenodo.3630044`.
13. Cristina David and Wei-Ngan Chin. Immutable specifications for more concise and precise verification. In *OOPSLA*, pages 359–374. ACM, 2011.
14. Benjamin Delaware, Clément Pit-Claudel, Jason Gross, and Adam Chlipala. Fiat: Deductive Synthesis of Abstract Data Types in a Proof Assistant. In *POPL*, pages 689–700. ACM, 2015.
15. Robert Dockins, Aquinas Hobor, and Andrew W. Appel. A fresh look at separation algebras and share accounting. In *APLAS*, volume 5904 of *LNCS*, pages 161–177. Springer, 2009.
16. Ronald Garcia, Éric Tanter, Roger Wolff, and Jonathan Aldrich. Foundations of typestate-oriented programming. *ACM Trans. Program. Lang. Syst.*, 36(4):12:1–12:44, 2014.
17. Adrià Gascón, Ashish Tiwari, Brent Carmer, and Umang Mathur. Look for the proof to find the program: Decorated-component-based program synthesis. In *CAV*, volume 10427 of *LNCS*, pages 86–103. Springer, 2017.
18. Colin S. Gordon, Matthew J. Parkinson, Jared Parsons, Aleks Bromfield, and Joe Duffy. Uniqueness and reference immutability for safe parallelism. In *OOPSLA*, pages 21–40. ACM, 2012.
19. Sumit Gulwani, Susmit Jha, Ashish Tiwari, and Ramarathnam Venkatesan. Synthesis of loop-free programs. In *PLDI*, pages 62–73. ACM, 2011.

20. Stefan Heule, K. Rustan M. Leino, Peter Müller, and Alexander J. Summers. Abstract read permissions: Fractional permissions without the fractions. In *VMCAI*, volume 7737 of *LNCS*, pages 315–334. Springer, 2013.
21. Bart Jacobs, Jan Smans, Pieter Philippaerts, Frédéric Vogels, Willem Penninckx, and Frank Piessens. VeriFast: A Powerful, Sound, Predictable, Fast Verifier for C and Java. In *NASA Formal Methods*, volume 6617 of *LNCS*, pages 41–55. Springer, 2011.
22. Ralf Jung, Jacques-Henri Jourdan, Robbert Krebbers, and Derek Dreyer. RustBelt: Securing the foundations of the Rust programming language. *PACMPL*, 2(POPL):66, 2017.
23. Etienne Kneuss, Ivan Kuraj, Viktor Kuncak, and Philippe Suter. Synthesis modulo recursive functions. In *OOPSLA*, pages 407–426. ACM, 2013.
24. Tristan Knoth, Di Wang, Nadia Polikarpova, and Jan Hoffmann. Resource-guided program synthesis. In *PLDI*, pages 253–268. ACM, 2019.
25. Xuan Bach Le and Aquinas Hobor. Logical reasoning for disjoint permissions. In *ESOP*, volume 10801 of *LNCS*, pages 385–414. Springer, 2018.
26. K. Rustan M. Leino and Aleksandar Milicevic. Program Extrapolation with Jennisys. In *OOPSLA*, pages 411–430. ACM, 2012.
27. K. Rustan M. Leino and Peter Müller. A Basis for Verifying Multi-threaded Programs. In *ESOP*, volume 5502 of *LNCS*, pages 378–393. Springer, 2009.
28. K. Rustan M. Leino, Peter Müller, and Jan Smans. Verification of Concurrent Programs with Chalice. In *Foundations of Security Analysis and Design V, FOSAD 2007/2008/2009 Tutorial Lectures*, volume 5705 of *LNCS*, pages 195–222. Springer, 2009.
29. Zohar Manna and Richard J. Waldinger. A deductive approach to program synthesis. *ACM Trans. Program. Lang. Syst.*, 2(1):90–121, 1980.
30. Peter Müller, Malte Schwerhoff, and Alexander J. Summers. Viper: A Verification Infrastructure for Permission-Based Reasoning. In *VMCAI*, volume 9583 of *LNCS*, pages 41–62. Springer, 2016.
31. Karl Naden, Robert Bocchino, Jonathan Aldrich, and Kevin Bierhoff. A type system for borrowing permissions. In *POPL*, pages 557–570. ACM, 2012.
32. Peter W. O'Hearn, John C. Reynolds, and Hongseok Yang. Local reasoning about programs that alter data structures. In *CSL*, volume 2142 of *LNCS*, pages 1–19. Springer, 2001.
33. Nadia Polikarpova, Ivan Kuraj, and Armando Solar-Lezama. Program synthesis from polymorphic refinement types. In *PLDI*, pages 522–538. ACM, 2016.
34. Nadia Polikarpova and Ilya Sergey. Structuring the Synthesis of Heap-Manipulating Programs. *PACMPL*, 3(POPL):72:1–72:30, 2019.
35. Nadia Polikarpova, Jean Yang, Shachar Itzhaky, and Armando Solar-Lezama. Enforcing information flow policies with type-targeted program synthesis. *CoRR*, abs/1607.03445, 2016.
36. Xiaokang Qiu and Armando Solar-Lezama. Natural synthesis of provably-correct data-structure manipulations. *PACMPL*, 1(OOPSLA):65:1–65:28, 2017.
37. John C. Reynolds. Separation logic: A logic for shared mutable data structures. In *LICS*, pages 55–74. IEEE Computer Society, 2002.
38. Reuben N. S. Rowe and James Brotherston. Automatic cyclic termination proofs for recursive procedures in separation logic. In *CPP*, pages 53–65. ACM, 2017.
39. Calvin Smith and Aws Albarghouthi. Synthesizing differentially private programs. *Proc. ACM Program. Lang.*, 3(ICFP):94:1–94:29, July 2019.
40. Armando Solar-Lezama. Program sketching. *STTT*, 15(5-6):475–495, 2013.

41. Saurabh Srivastava, Sumit Gulwani, and Jeffrey S. Foster. From program verification to program synthesis. In *POPL*, pages 313–326. ACM, 2010.
42. Sven Stork, Karl Naden, Joshua Sunshine, Manuel Mohr, Alcides Fonseca, Paulo Marques, and Jonathan Aldrich. Æminium: A Permission-Based Concurrent-by-Default Programming Language Approach. *TOPLAS*, 36(1):2:1–2:42, 2014.
43. Alexander J. Summers and Peter Müller. Automating deductive verification for weak-memory programs. In *TACAS*, volume 10805 of *LNCS*, pages 190–209. Springer, 2018.
44. Emina Torlak and Rastislav Bodík. A lightweight symbolic virtual machine for solver-aided host languages. In *PLDI*, pages 530–541. ACM, 2014.

Soundness conditions for big-step semantics

Francesco Dagnino[1], Viviana Bono[2], Elena Zucca[1], and
Mariangiola Dezani-Ciancaglini[2]

[1] DIBRIS, University of Genova, Italy
[2] Computer Science Department, University of Torino, Italy

Abstract. We propose a general proof technique to show that a predicate is *sound*, that is, prevents stuck computation, *with respect to a big-step semantics*. This result may look surprising, since in big-step semantics there is no difference between non-terminating and stuck computations, hence soundness cannot even be *expressed*. The key idea is to define constructions yielding an extended version of a given arbitrary big-step semantics, where the difference is made explicit. The extended semantics are exploited in the meta-theory, notably they are necessary to show that the proof technique works. However, they remain *transparent* when using the proof technique, since it consists in checking three conditions on the original rules only, as we illustrate by several examples.

1 Introduction

The semantics of programming languages or software systems specifies, for each program/system configuration, its final result, if any. In the case of non-existence of a final result, there are two possibilities:

- either the computation stops with no final result, and there is no means to compute further: *stuck computation*,
- or the computation never stops: *non-termination*.

There are two main styles to define operationally a semantic relation: the *small-step* style [34,35], on top of a reduction relation representing single computation steps, or directly by a set of rules as in the *big-step* style [28]. Within a small-step semantics it is straightforward to make the distinction between stuck and non-terminating computations, while a typical drawback of the big-step style is that they are not distinguished (no judgement is derived in both cases).

For this reason, even though big-step semantics is generally more abstract, and sometimes more intuitive to design and therefore to debug and extend, in the literature much more effort has been devoted to study the meta-theory of small-step semantics, providing properties, and related proof techniques. Notably, the *soundness* of a type system (typing prevents stuck computation) can be proved by *progress* and *subject reduction* (also called *type preservation*) [40].

Our quest is then to provide a general proof technique to prove the soundness of a predicate with respect to an arbitrary big-step semantics. How can we achieve this result, given that in big-step formulation soundness cannot even

P. Müller (Ed.): ESOP 2020, LNCS 12075, pp. 169–196, 2020.
https://doi.org/10.1007/978-3-030-44914-8_7

be *expressed*, since non-termination is modelled as the absence of a final result exactly like stuck computation? The key idea is the following:

1. We define constructions *yielding an extended version of a given arbitrary big-step semantics*, where the difference between stuckness and non-termination is made explicit. In a sense, these constructions show that the distinction was "hidden" in the original semantics.
2. We provide a general proof technique by identifying *three sufficient conditions* on the original big-step rules to prove soundness.

Keypoint (2)'s three sufficient conditions are *local preservation*, $\exists$-*progress*, and $\forall$-*progress*. For *proving* the result that the three conditions actually ensure soundness, the setting up of the extended semantics from the given one is necessary, since otherwise, as said above, we could not even express the property.

However, the three conditions deal only with the original rules of the given big-step semantics. This means that, practically, in order to use the technique there is no need to deal with the extended semantics. This implies, in particular, that our approach does *not* increase the original number of rules. Moreover, the sufficient conditions are checked only on *single rules*, which makes explicit the proof fragments typically needed in a proof of soundness. Even though this is not exploited in this paper, this form of *locality* means *modularity*, in the sense that adding a new rule implies adding the corresponding proof fragment only.

As an important by-product, in order to formally define and prove correct the keypoints (1) and (2), we propose a formalisation of "what is a big-step semantics" which captures its essential features. Moreover, we support our approach by presenting several examples, demonstrating that: on the one hand, their soundness proof can be easily rephrased in terms of our technique, that is, by directly reasoning on big-step rules; on the other hand, our technique is essential when the property to be checked (for instance, the soundness of a type system) is *not preserved* by intermediate computation steps, whereas it holds for the final result. On a side note, our examples concern type systems, but the meta-theory we present in this work holds for any predicate.

We describe now in more detail the constructions of keypoint (1). Starting from an arbitrary big-step judgment $c \Rightarrow r$ that evaluates *configurations* c into *results* r, the *first construction* produces an enriched judgement $c \Rightarrow_{\mathsf{tr}} t$ where t is a *trace*, that is, the (finite or infinite) sequence of all the (sub)configurations encountered during the evaluation. In this way, by interpreting coinductively the rules of the extended semantics, an infinite trace models divergence (whereas no result corresponds to stuck computation). The *second construction* is in a sense dual. It is the *algorithmic* version of the well-known technique presented in Exercise 3.5.16 from the book [33] of adding a special result **wrong** explicitly modelling stuck computations (whereas no result corresponds to divergence).

By trace semantics and **wrong** semantics we can express two flavours of soundness, *soundness-may* and *soundness-must*, respectively, and show the correctness of the corresponding proof technique. This achieves our original aim, and it should be noted that *we define soundness with respect to a big-step semantics* *within a big-step formulation,* without resorting to a small-step style (indeed, the two extended semantics are themselves big-step).

Lastly, we consider the issue of justifying on a formal basis that the two constructions are correct with respect to their expected meaning. For instance, for the wrong semantics we would like to be sure that *all* the cases are covered. To this end, we define a *third construction,* dubbed PEV for "partial evaluation", which makes explicit the *computations* of a big-step semantics, intended as the sequences of execution steps of the naturally associated evaluation algorithm. Formally, we obtain a reduction relation on approximated proof trees, so termination, non-termination and stuckness can be defined as usual. Then, the correctness of traces and wrong constructions is proved by showing they are equivalent to PEV for diverging and stuck computations, respectively.

In Sect. 2 we illustrate the meta-theory on a running example. In Sect. 3 we define the trace and wrong constructions. In Sect. 4 we express soundness in the *must* and *may* flavours, introduce the proof technique, and prove its correctness. In Sect. 5 we show in detail how to apply the technique to the running example, and other significant examples. In Sect. 6 we introduce the third construction and state that the three constructions are equivalent. Finally, in 7 and 8 we discuss related and further work and summarise our contribution. An extended version including an additional example, proofs omitted for lack of space, and technical details on the PEV semantics, can be found at http://arxiv.org/abs/2002.08738.

2   A meta-theory for big-step semantics

We introduce a formalisation of "what is a big-step semantics" that captures its essential features, subsuming a large class of examples (as testified in Sect. 5). This enables a general formal reasoning on an arbitrary big-step semantics.

A *big-step semantics* is a triple $\langle C,\ R,\ \mathcal{R} \rangle$ where:

- C is a set of *configurations* c.
- $R \subseteq C$ is a set of *results* r. We define *judgments* $j \equiv c \Rightarrow r$, meaning that configuration c evaluates to result r. Set $C(j) = c$ and $R(j) = r$.
- $\mathcal{R}$ is a set of *rules* ρ of shape

  $$\frac{j_1 \ \cdots \ j_n \ \ j_{n+1}}{c \Rightarrow R(j_{n+1})} \qquad \text{also written in } \textit{inline format: } \mathsf{rule}(j_1 \ldots j_n, j_{n+1}, c)$$

  with $c \in C \backslash R$, where $j_1 \ldots j_n$ are the *dependencies* and j_{n+1} is the *continuation.* Set $C(\rho){=}c$ and, for $i \in 1..n + 1$, $C(\rho, i){=}C(j_i)$ and $R(\rho, i){=}R(j_i)$.
- For each result $r \in R$, we implicitly assume a single axiom $\dfrac{}{r \Rightarrow r}$. Hence, the only derivable judgment for r is $r \Rightarrow r$, which we will call a *trivial* judgment.

We will use the inline format, more concise and manageable, for the development of the meta-theory, e.g., in constructions.

A rule corresponds to the following evaluation process for a non-result configuration: first, dependencies are evaluated in the given order, then the continuation is evaluated and its result is returned as result of the entire computation.

$e ::= x \mid v \mid e_1 \, e_2 \mid \textbf{succ} \, e \mid e_1 \oplus e_2$ expression
$v ::= n \mid \lambda x.e$ value

$$(\text{VAL}) \; \frac{}{v \Rightarrow v} \qquad (\text{APP}) \; \frac{e_1 \Rightarrow \lambda x.e \quad e_2 \Rightarrow v_2 \quad e[v_2/x] \Rightarrow v}{e_1 \, e_2 \Rightarrow v} \qquad (\text{SUCC}) \; \frac{e \Rightarrow n}{\textbf{succ} \, e \Rightarrow n+1}$$

$$(\text{CHOICE}) \; \frac{e_i \Rightarrow v}{e_1 \oplus e_2 \Rightarrow v} \; i = 1,2$$

(APP) $\mathsf{rule}(e_1 \Rightarrow \lambda x.e \; e_2 \Rightarrow v_2, \, e[v_2/x] \Rightarrow v, \, e_1 \, e_2)$
(SUCC) $\mathsf{rule}(e \Rightarrow n, \, n+1 \Rightarrow n+1, \, \textbf{succ} \, e)$
(CHOICE) $\mathsf{rule}(\epsilon, \, e_i \Rightarrow v, \, e_1 \oplus e_2) \; i = 1,2$

Fig. 1. Example of big-step semantics

Rules as defined above specify an inference system [1,30], whose inductive interpretation is, as usual, the semantic relation. However, they carry slightly more structure with respect to standard inference rules. Notably, premises are a sequence rather than a set, and the last premise plays a special role. Such additional structure does not affect the semantic relation defined by the rules, but allows abstract reasoning about an arbitrary big-step semantics, in particular it is relevant for defining the three constructions. In the following, we will write $\mathcal{R} \vdash c \Rightarrow r$ when the judgment $c \Rightarrow r$ is derivable in $\mathcal{R}$.

As customary, the (infinite) set of rules $\mathcal{R}$ is described by a finite set of meta-rules, each one with a finite number of premises. As a consequence, the number of premises of rules is not only finite but *bounded*. Since we have no notion of meta-rule, we model this feature (relevant in the following) as an explicit assumption:

BP there exists $b \in \mathbb{N}$ such that, for each $\rho \equiv \mathsf{rule}(j_1 \ldots j_n, \, j_{n+1}, \, c)$, $n < b$.

We end this section illustrating the above definitions and conditions by a simple example: a λ-calculus with natural constants, successor and non-deterministic choice shown in Fig. 1. We present this example as an instance of our definition:

- Configurations and results are expressions, and values, respectively.[3]
- To have the set of (meta-)rules in our required shape, abbreviated in inline format in the bottom section of the figure:
  - axiom (VAL) can be omitted (it is implicitly assumed)
  - in (APP) we consider premises as a sequence rather than a set (the third premise is the continuation)
  - in (SUCC), which has no continuation, we add a dummy continuation
  - on the contrary, in (CHOICE) there is only the continuation (dependencies are the empty sequence, denoted ϵ in the inline format).

Note that (APP) corresponds to the standard left-to-right evaluation order. We could have chosen the right-to-left order instead:

(APP-R) $\mathsf{rule}(e_2 \Rightarrow v_2 \; e_1 \Rightarrow \lambda x.e \, , \, e[v_2/x] \Rightarrow v, \, e_1 \, e_2)$

or even opt for a non-deterministic approach by taking both rules (APP) and

---

[3] In general, configurations may include additional components, see Sect. 5.2.

(APP-R). As said above, these different choices do not affect the semantic relation $c \Rightarrow r$ defined by the inference system, which is always the same. However, they will affect the way the extended semantics distinguishing stuck computation and non-termination is constructed. Indeed, if the evaluation of e_1 and e_2 is stuck and non-terminating, respectively, we should obtain stuck computation with rule (APP) and non-termination with rule (APP-R).

In summary, to see a typical big-step semantics as an instance of our definition, it is enough to assume an order (or more than one) on premises, make implicit the axiom for results, and add a dummy continuation when needed. In the examples (Sect. 5), we will assume a left-to-right order on premises, and omit dummy continuations to keep a more familiar style. In the technical part (Sect. 3, Sect. 4 and Sect. 6) we will adopt the inline format.

3   Extended semantics

In the following, we assume a big-step semantics $\langle C, R, \mathcal{R} \rangle$ and describe two constructions which make the distinction between non-termination and stuck computation explicit. In both cases, the approach is based on well-know ideas; the novel contribution is that, thanks to the meta-theory in Sect. 2, we provide a *general* construction working on an arbitrary big-step semantics.

3.1   Traces

We denote by $C^\star$, C^ω, and $C^\infty = C^\star \cup C^\omega$, respectively, the sets of finite, infinite, and possibly infinite *traces*, that is, sequences of configurations. We write $t \cdot t'$ for concatenation of $t \in C^\star$ with $t' \in C^\infty$.

We derive, from the judgement $c \Rightarrow r$, an enriched big-step judgement $c \Rightarrow_{\mathsf{tr}} t$ with $t \in C^\infty$. Intuitively, t keeps trace of all the configurations visited during the evaluation, starting from c itself. To define the trace semantics, we construct, starting from $\mathcal{R}$, a new set of rules $\mathcal{R}_{\mathsf{tr}}$, which are of two kinds:

trace introduction These rules enrich the standard semantics by finite traces: for each $\rho \equiv \mathsf{rule}(j_1 \ldots j_n, j_{n+1}, c)$ in $\mathcal{R}$, and finite traces $t_1, \ldots, t_{n+1} \in C^\star$, we add the rule
$$\frac{C(j_1) \Rightarrow_{\mathsf{tr}} t_1 \cdot R(j_1) \quad \ldots \quad C(j_{n+1}) \Rightarrow_{\mathsf{tr}} t_{n+1} \cdot R(j_{n+1})}{c \Rightarrow_{\mathsf{tr}} c \cdot t_1 \cdot R(j_1) \cdot \ldots \cdot t_{n+1} \cdot R(j_{n+1})}$$
We denote this rule by $\mathsf{trace}(\rho, t_1, \ldots, t_{n+1})$, to highlight the relationship with the original rule ρ. We also add one axiom $\dfrac{}{r \Rightarrow_{\mathsf{tr}} r}$ for each result r.
Such rules derive judgements $c \Rightarrow t$ with $t \in C^\star$, for convergent computations.

divergence propagation These rules propagate divergence, that is, if a (sub)configuration in the premise of a rule diverges, then the subsequent premises are ignored and the configuration in the conclusion diverges as well: for each $\rho \equiv \mathsf{rule}(j_1 \ldots j_n, j_{n+1}, c)$ in $\mathcal{R}$, index $i \in 1..n+1$, finite traces $t_1, \ldots, t_{i-1} \in C^\star$, and infinite trace t, we add the rule:
$$\frac{C(j_1) \Rightarrow_{\mathsf{tr}} t_1 \cdot R(j_1) \quad \ldots \quad C(j_{i-1}) \Rightarrow_{\mathsf{tr}} t_{i-1} \cdot R(j_{i-1}) \quad C(j_i) \Rightarrow t}{c \Rightarrow c \cdot t_1 \cdot R(j_1) \cdot \ldots \cdot t_{i-1} \cdot R(t_{i-1}) \cdot t}$$

$$\text{(APP-TRACE)} \ \frac{e_1 \Rightarrow_{tr} t_1 \cdot \lambda x.e \quad e_2 \Rightarrow_{tr} t_2 \cdot v_2 \quad e[v_2/x] \Rightarrow_{tr} t \cdot v}{e_1 \ e_2 \Rightarrow_{tr} e_1 \ e_2 \cdot t_1 \cdot \lambda x.e \cdot t_2 \cdot v_2 \cdot t \cdot v} \ t_1, t_2, t \in C^\star$$

$$\text{(DIV-APP-1)} \ \frac{e_1 \Rightarrow_{tr} t}{e_1 \ e_2 \Rightarrow_{tr} e_1 \ e_2 \cdot t} \ t \in C^\omega \qquad \text{(DIV-APP-2)} \ \frac{e_1 \Rightarrow_{tr} t_1 \cdot \lambda x.e \quad e_2 \Rightarrow_{tr} t}{e_1 \ e_2 \Rightarrow_{tr} e_1 \ e_2 \cdot t_1 \cdot \lambda x.e \cdot t} \ t_1 \in C^\star, t \in C^\omega$$

$$\text{(DIV-APP-3)} \ \frac{e_1 \Rightarrow_{tr} t_1 \cdot \lambda x.e \quad e_2 \Rightarrow_{tr} t_2 \cdot v_2 \quad e[v_2/x] \Rightarrow_{tr} t}{e_1 \ e_2 \Rightarrow_{tr} e_1 \ e_2 \cdot t_1 \cdot \lambda x.e \cdot t_2 \cdot v_2 \cdot t} \ t_1, t_2 \in C^\star, t \in C^\omega$$

Fig. 2. Trace semantics for application

We denote this rule by $\mathsf{prop}(\rho, i, t_1, \ldots, t_{i-1}, t)$ to highlight the relationship with the original rule ρ. These rules derive judgements $c \Rightarrow_{tr} t$ with $t \in C^\omega$, modelling diverging computations.

The inference system $\mathcal{R}_{tr}$ must be interpreted *coinductively*, to properly model diverging computations. Indeed, since there is no axiom introducing an infinite trace, they can be derived only by an infinite proof tree. We write $\mathcal{R}_{tr} \vdash c \Rightarrow_{tr} t$ when the judgment $c \Rightarrow_{tr} t$ is derivable in $\mathcal{R}_{tr}$.

We show in Fig. 2 the rules obtained starting from meta-rule (APP) of the example (for other meta-rules the outcome is analogous).

For instance, set $\Omega = \omega\omega = (\lambda x.x \ x)(\lambda x.x \ x)$, and t_Ω the infinite trace $\Omega \cdot \omega \cdot \omega \cdot \Omega \cdot \omega \cdot \omega \cdots$, it is easy to see that the judgment $\Omega \Rightarrow_{tr} t_\Omega$ can be derived by the following infinite tree:[4]

$$\text{(DIV-APP3)} \ \frac{\text{(TRACE-VAL)} \ \frac{}{\omega \Rightarrow_{tr} \omega} \quad \text{(TRACE-VAL)} \ \frac{}{\omega \Rightarrow_{tr} \omega} \quad \text{(DIV-APP3)} \ \frac{\vdots}{\omega\omega \equiv (x \ x)[\omega/x] \Rightarrow_{tr} t_\Omega}}{\Omega \Rightarrow \Omega \cdot \omega \cdot \omega \cdot t_\Omega \equiv t_\Omega}$$

Note that *only* the judgment $\Omega \Rightarrow_{tr} t_\Omega$ can be derived, that is, the trace semantics of Ω is uniquely determined to be t_Ω, since the infinite proof tree forces the equation $t_\Omega = \Omega \cdot \omega\omega \cdot t_\Omega$. This example is a cyclic proof, but there are divergent computations with no circular derivation.

The trace construction is *conservative* with respect to the original semantics, that is, converging computations are not affected.

Theorem 1. $\mathcal{R}_{tr} \vdash c \Rightarrow_{tr} t \cdot r$ *for some* $t \in C^\star$ *iff* $\mathcal{R} \vdash c \Rightarrow r$.

3.2 Wrong

A well-known technique [33] (Exercise 3.5.16) to distinguish between stuck and diverging computations, in a sense "dual" to the previous one, is to add a special result wrong, so that $c \Rightarrow$ wrong means that the evaluation of c goes stuck.

In this case, to define an "automatic" version of the construction, starting from $\langle C, R, \mathcal{R} \rangle$, is a non-trivial problem. Our solution is based on defining a relation on rules, modelling *equality up to a certain index* i, also used for other aims

---

[4] To help the reader, we add equivalent expressions with a grey background.

in the following. Consider $\rho \equiv \mathsf{rule}(j_1 \ldots j_n, \, j_{n+1}, \, c)$, $\rho' \equiv \mathsf{rule}(j_1' \ldots j_m', \, j_{m+1}', \, c')$, and an index $i \in 1.. \min(n+1, m+1)$, then $\rho \sim_i \rho'$ if

- $c = c'$
- for all $k < i$, $j_k = j_k'$
- $C(j_i) = C(j_i')$

Intuitively, this means that rules ρ and ρ' model the same computation until the i-th premise. Using this relation, we derive, from the judgment $c \Rightarrow r$, an enriched big-step judgement $c \Rightarrow r_{\mathsf{wr}}$ where $r_{\mathsf{wr}} \in R \cup \{\mathsf{wrong}\}$, defined by a set of rules $\mathcal{R}_{\mathsf{wr}}$ containing all rules in $\mathcal{R}$ and two other kinds of rules:

wrong introduction These rules derive wrong whenever the (sub)configuration in a premise of a rule reduces to a result which is not admitted in such (or any equivalent) rule: for each $\rho \equiv \mathsf{rule}(j_1 \ldots j_n, \, j_{n+1}, \, c)$ in $\mathcal{R}$, index $i \in 1..n+1$, and result $r \in R$, if for all rules ρ' such that $\rho \sim_i \rho'$, $R(\rho', i) \neq r$, then we add the rule $\mathsf{wrong}(\rho, i, r)$ as follows:

$$\frac{j_1 \ldots j_{i-1} \quad C(j_i) \Rightarrow r}{c \Rightarrow \mathsf{wrong}}$$

We also add an axiom $\dfrac{}{c \Rightarrow \mathsf{wrong}}$ for each configuration c which is not the conclusion of any rule.

wrong propagation These rules propagate wrong analogously to those for divergence propagation: for each $\rho \equiv \mathsf{rule}(j_1 \ldots j_n, \, j_{n+1}, \, c)$ in $\mathcal{R}$, and index $i \in 1..n+1$, we add the rule $\mathsf{prop}(\rho, i, \mathsf{wrong})$ as follows:

$$\frac{j_1 \ldots j_{i-1} \quad C(j_i) \Rightarrow \mathsf{wrong}}{c \Rightarrow \mathsf{wrong}}$$

We write $\mathcal{R}_{\mathsf{wr}} \vdash c \Rightarrow r_{\mathsf{wr}}$ when the judgment $c \Rightarrow r_{\mathsf{wr}}$ is derivable in $\mathcal{R}_{\mathsf{wr}}$.

We show in Fig. 3 the meta-rules for wrong introduction and propagation constructed starting from those for application and successor. For instance, rule (WRONG-APP) is introduced since in the original semantics there is rule (APP) with $e_1 \, e_2$ in the consequence and e_1 in the first premise, but there is no equivalent rule (that is, with $e_1 \, e_2$ in the consequence and e_1 in the first premise) such that the result in the first premise is n.

The wrong construction is conservative as well.

Theorem 2. $\mathcal{R}_{\mathsf{wr}} \vdash c \Rightarrow r$ iff $\mathcal{R} \vdash c \Rightarrow r$.

$$(\text{WRONG-APP}) \ \frac{e_1 \Rightarrow n}{e_1 \, e_2 \Rightarrow \mathsf{wrong}} \qquad (\text{WRONG-SUCC}) \ \frac{e \Rightarrow \lambda x.e'}{\mathsf{succ} \ e \Rightarrow \mathsf{wrong}}$$

$$(\text{PROP-APP-1}) \ \frac{e_1 \Rightarrow \mathsf{wrong}}{e_1 \, e_2 \Rightarrow \mathsf{wrong}} \qquad (\text{PROP-APP-2}) \ \frac{e_1 \Rightarrow \lambda x.e \quad e_2 \Rightarrow \mathsf{wrong}}{e_1 \, e_2 \Rightarrow \mathsf{wrong}}$$

$$(\text{PROP-APP-3}) \ \frac{e_1 \Rightarrow \lambda x.e \quad e_2 \Rightarrow v_2 \quad e[v_2/x] \Rightarrow \mathsf{wrong}}{e_1 \, e_2 \Rightarrow \mathsf{wrong}} \qquad (\text{PROP-SUCC}) \ \frac{e \Rightarrow \mathsf{wrong}}{\mathsf{succ} \ e \Rightarrow \mathsf{wrong}}$$

Fig. 3. Semantics with wrong for application and successor

4   Expressing and proving soundness

A predicate (for instance, a typing judgment) is *sound* when, informally, a program satisfying the predicate (e.g., a well-typed program) cannot *go wrong*, following Robin Milner's slogan [31]. In small-step style, as firstly formulated in [40], this is naturally expressed as follows: well-typed programs never reduce to terms which neither are values, nor can be further reduced (called *stuck* terms). The standard technique to ensure soundness is by subject reduction (well-typedness is preserved by reduction) and progress (a well-typed term is not stuck).

We discuss how soundness can be expressed for the two approaches previously presented and we introduce sufficient conditions. In other words, we provide a proof technique to show the soundness of a predicate with respect to a big-step semantics. As mentioned in the Introduction, the extended semantics is only needed to prove the correctness of the technique, whereas to *apply* the technique for a given big-step semantics it is enough to reason on the original rules.

4.1   Expressing soundness

In the following, we assume a big-step semantics $\langle C, R, \mathcal{R} \rangle$, and an *indexed predicate on configurations*, that is, a family $\Pi = (\Pi_\iota)_{\iota \in I}$, for I set of *indexes*, with $\Pi_\iota \subseteq C$. A representative case is that, as in the examples of Sect. 5, the predicate is a typing judgment and the indexes are types; however, the proof technique could be applied to other kinds of predicates. When there is no ambiguity, we also denote by Π the corresponding predicate $\bigcup_{\iota \in I} \Pi_\iota$ on C (e.g., to be well-typed with an arbitrary type).

To discuss how to express soundness of Π, first of all note that, in the nondeterministic case (that is, there is possibly more than one computation for a configuration), we can distinguish two flavours of soundness [21]:

soundness-must (or simply soundness) no computation can be stuck
soundness-may at least one computation is not stuck

Soundness-must is the standard soundness in small-step semantics, and can be expressed in the wrong extension as follows:

soundness-must (wrong) If $c \in \Pi$, then $\mathcal{R}_{\mathsf{wr}} \nvdash c \Rightarrow \mathsf{wrong}$

Instead, soundness-must *cannot* be expressed in the trace extension. Indeed, stuck computations are not explicitly modelled. Conversely, soundness-may can be expressed in the trace extension as follows:

soundness-may (traces) If $c \in \Pi$, then there is t such that $\mathcal{R}_{\mathsf{tr}} \vdash c \Rightarrow_{\mathsf{tr}} t$

whereas cannot be expressed in the wrong semantics, since diverging computations are not modelled.

Of course soundness-must and soundness-may coincide in the deterministic case. Finally, note that indexes (e.g., the specific types of configurations) do not play any role in the above statements. However, they are relevant in the notion of *strong soundness*, introduced by [40]. Strong soundness holds if, for configurations satisfying Π_ι (e.g., having a given type), computation cannot be stuck, and moreover, produces a result satisfying Π_ι (e.g., of the same type) if terminating. Note that soundness alone does not even guarantee to obtain a result satisfying Π (e.g., a well-typed result). The three conditions introduced in the following section actually ensure strong soundness.

In Sect. 4.2 we provide sufficient conditions for soundness-must, showing that they actually ensure soundness in the wrong semantics (Theorem 3). Then, in Sect. 4.3, we provide (weaker) sufficient conditions for soundness-may, and show that they actually ensure soundness-may in the trace semantics (Theorem 4).

4.2   Conditions ensuring soundness-must

The three conditions which ensure the soundness-must property are *local preservation*, $\exists$-*progress*, and $\forall$-progress. The names suggest that the former plays the role of the *type preservation (subject reduction)* property, and the latter two of the *progress* property in small-step semantics. However, as we will see, the correspondence is only rough, since the reasoning here is different.

Considering the first condition more closely, we use the name *preservation* rather than type preservation since, as already mentioned, the proof technique can be applied to arbitrary predicates. More importantly, *local* means that the condition is *on single rules* rather than on the semantic relation as a whole, as standard subject reduction. The same holds for the other two conditions.

Definition 1 (S1: Local Preservation). *For each* $\rho \equiv \mathrm{rule}(j_1 \ldots j_n, j_{n+1}, c)$, *if* $c \in \Pi_\iota$, *then there exist* $\iota_1, \ldots, \iota_{n+1} \in I$, *with* $\iota_{n+1} = \iota$, *such that, for all* $k \in 1..n+1$:

$$\textit{if, for all } h < k, \ R(j_h) \in \Pi_{\iota_h}, \textit{ then } C(j_k) \in \Pi_{\iota_k}.$$

Thinking to the paradigmatic case where the indexes are types, for each rule ρ, if the configuration c in the consequence has type ι, we have to find types $\iota_1, \ldots, \iota_{n+1}$ which can be assigned to (the configurations in) the premises, in particular the same type as c for the continuation. More precisely, we start finding type ι_1, and successively find the type ι_k for (the configuration in) the k-th premise assuming that the results of all the previous premises have the expected types. Indeed, if all such previous premises are derivable, then the expected type should be preserved by their results; if some premise is not derivable, the considered rule is "useless". For instance, considering (an instantiation of) meta-rule (APP) $\mathrm{rule}(e_1 \Rightarrow \lambda x.e \ \ e_2 \Rightarrow v_2, \ e[v_2/x] \Rightarrow v, \ e_1 \ e_2)$ in Sect. 2, we prove that $e[v_2/x]$ has the type T of $e_1 \ e_2$ under the assumption that $\lambda x.e$ has type $T' \to T$, and v_2 has type T' (see the proof example in Sect. 5.1 for more details). A counter-example to condition **S1** is discussed at the beginning of Sect. 5.3.

The following lemma states that local preservation actually implies *preservation* of the semantic relation as a whole.

Lemma 1 (Preservation). *Let* $\mathcal{R}$ *and* Π *satisfy condition* **S1**. *If* $\mathcal{R} \vdash c \Rightarrow r$ *and* $c \in \Pi_\iota$, *then* $r \in \Pi_\iota$.

Proof. The proof is by a double induction. We denote by RH and IH the first and the second induction hypothesis, respectively. The first induction is on big-step rules. Axioms have conclusion $r \Rightarrow r$, hence the thesis holds since $r \in \Pi_\iota$ by hypothesis. Other rules have shape $\mathsf{rule}(j_1 \ldots j_n, j_{n+1}, c)$ with $c \in \Pi_\iota$. We prove by complete induction on $k \in 1..n+1$ that $C(j_k) \in \Pi_{\iota_k}$, for all $k \in 1..n+1$ and for some $\iota_1, \ldots, \iota_{n+1} \in I$. By **S1**, there are $\iota_1, \ldots, \iota_{n+1} \in I$ and $C(j_1) \in \Pi_{\iota_1}$. For $k > 1$, by IH we know that $C(j_h) \in \Pi_{\iota_h}$, for all $h < k$. Then, by RH, we get that $R(j_h) \in \Pi_{\iota_h}$. Moreover by **S1**, $C(j_k) \in \Pi_{\iota_k}$, as needed. In particular, we have just proved that $C(j_{n+1}) \in \Pi_{\iota_{n+1}}$ and, since by **S1** $\iota_{n+1} = \iota$, we get $C(j_{n+1}) \in \Pi_\iota$. Then, by RH, we conclude that $r = R(j_{n+1}) \in \Pi_\iota$, as needed.

The following proposition is a form of local preservation where indexes (e.g., specific types) are not relevant, simpler to use in the proofs of Theorems 3 and 4.

Proposition 1. *Let $\mathcal{R}$ and Π satisfy condition* **S1**. *For each* $\mathsf{rule}(j_1 \ldots j_n, j_{n+1}, c)$ *and $k \in 1..n+1$, if $c \in \Pi$ and, for all $h < k$, $\mathcal{R} \vdash j_h$, then $C(j_k) \in \Pi$.*

The second condition, named ∃-*progress*, ensures that, for configurations satisfying the predicate Π (e.g., well-typed), we can *start constructing* a proof tree.

Definition 2 (S2: ∃-progress). *For each $c \in \Pi \backslash R$, $C(\rho) = c$ for some rule ρ.*

The third condition, named ∀-*progress*, ensures that, for configurations satisfying Π, we can *continue constructing* the proof tree. This condition uses the notion of rules *equivalent up-to an index* introduced at the beginning of Sect. 3.2.

Definition 3 (S3: ∀-progress). *For each $\rho \equiv \mathsf{rule}(j_1 \ldots j_n, j_{n+1}, c)$, if $c \in \Pi$, then, for each $k \in 1..n+1$:*

if, for all $h < k$, $\mathcal{R} \vdash j_h$ and $\mathcal{R} \vdash C(j_k) \Rightarrow r$, for some $r \in R$, then there is a rule $\rho' \sim_k \rho$ such that $R(\rho', k) = r$.

We have to check, for each rule ρ, the following: if the configuration c in the consequence satisfies the predicate (e.g., is well-typed), then, for each k, if the configuration in premise k evaluates to some result r (that is, $\mathcal{R} \vdash C(j_k) \Rightarrow r$), then there is a rule (ρ itself or another rule with the same configuration in the consequence and the first $k-1$ premises) with such judgment as k-th premise. This check can be done under the assumption that all the previous premises are derivable. For instance, consider again (an instantiation of) the meta-rule (APP) $\mathsf{rule}(e_1 \Rightarrow \lambda x.e \; e_2 \Rightarrow v_2, e[v_2/x] \Rightarrow v, e_1 \, e_2)$. Assuming that e_1 evaluates to some v_1, we have to check that there is a rule with first premise $e_1 \Rightarrow v_1$, in pratice, that v_1 is a λ-abstraction; in general, checking **S3** for a (meta-)rule amounts to show that (sub)configurations in the premises evaluate to results with the required shape (see also the proof example in Sect. 5.1).

Soundness-must in **wrong** *semantics* Recall that $\mathcal{R}_{\mathsf{wr}}$ is the extension of $\mathcal{R}$ with **wrong** (Sect. 3.2). We prove the claim of soundness-must with respect to $\mathcal{R}_{\mathsf{wr}}$.

Theorem 3. *Let $\mathcal{R}$ and Π satisfy conditions* **S1**, **S2** *and* **S3**. *If $c \in \Pi$, then* $\mathcal{R}_{wr} \not\vdash c \Rightarrow$ wrong.

Proof. To prove the statement, we assume $\mathcal{R}_{wr} \vdash c \Rightarrow$ wrong and look for a contradiction. The proof is by induction on the derivation of $c \Rightarrow$ wrong.

If the last applied rule is an axiom, then, by construction, there is no rule $\rho \in \mathcal{R}$ such that $C(\rho) = c$, and this violates condition **S2**, since $c \in \Pi$.

If the last applied rule is wrong(ρ, i, r), with $\rho \equiv$ rule($j_1 \ldots j_n, j_{n+1}, c$), then, by hypothesis, for all $k < i$, $\mathcal{R}_{wr} \vdash j_k$, and $\mathcal{R}_{wr} \vdash C(j_i) \Rightarrow r$, and these judgments can also be derived in $\mathcal{R}$ by conservativity (Theorem 2). Furthermore, by construction of this rule, we know that there is no other rule $\rho' \sim_i \rho$ such that $R(\rho', i) = r$, and this violates condition **S3**, since $c \in \Pi$.

If the last applied rule is prop($\rho, i,$ wrong), with $\rho \equiv$ rule($j_1 \ldots j_n, j_{n+1}, c$), then, by hypothesis, for all $k < i$, $\mathcal{R}_{wr} \vdash j_k$, and these judgments can also be derived in $\mathcal{R}$ by conservativity. Then, by Prop. 1 (which requires condition **S1**), since $c \in \Pi$, we have $C(j_i) \in \Pi$, hence we get the thesis by induction hypothesis.

Sect. 5.1 ends with examples not satisfying properties **S2** and **S3**.

4.3 Conditions ensuring soundness-may

As discussed in Sect. 4.1, in the trace semantics we can only express a weaker form of soundness: at least one computation is not stuck (*soundness-may*). As the reader can expect, to ensure this property weaker sufficient conditions are enough: namely, condition **S1**, and another condition named *progress-may* and defined below.

We write $\mathcal{R} \not\vdash c \Rightarrow$ if c *does not converge* (there is no r such that $\mathcal{R} \vdash c \Rightarrow r$).

Definition 4 (S4: progress-may). *For each $c \in \Pi \backslash R$, there is* $\rho \equiv$ rule($j_1 \ldots j_n, j_{n+1}, c$) *such that:*

> *if there is a (first) $k \in 1..n+1$ such that $\mathcal{R} \not\vdash j_k$ and, for all $h < k$,* $\mathcal{R} \vdash j_h$, *then $\mathcal{R} \not\vdash C(j_k) \Rightarrow$.*

This condition can be informally understood as follows: we have to show that there is an either finite or infinite computation for c. If we find a rule where all premises are derivable (no k), then there is a finite computation. Otherwise, c does not converge. In this case, we should find a rule where the configuration in the first non-derivable premise k does not converge as well. Indeed, by coinductive reasoning (use of Lemma 2 below), we obtain that c diverges. The following proposition states that this condition is indeed a weakening of **S2** and **S3**.

Proposition 2. *Conditions* **S2** *and* **S3** *imply condition* **S4**.

Soundness-may in trace semantics Recall that $\mathcal{R}_{tr}$ is the extension of $\mathcal{R}$ with traces, defined in Sect. 3.1, where judgements have shape $c \Rightarrow_{tr} t$, with $t \in C^{\infty}$.

The following lemma provides a proof principle useful to coinductively show that a property ensures the existence of an infinite trace, in particular to show Theorem 4. It is a slight variation of an analogous principle presented in [8].

Lemma 2. *Let $S \subseteq C$ be a set. If, for all $c \in S$, there are $\rho \equiv \mathsf{rule}(j_1 \ldots j_n, j_{n+1}, c)$ and $k \in 1..n+1$ such that*

1. *for all $h < k$, $\mathcal{R} \vdash j_h$, and*
2. *$C(j_k) \in S$*

then, for all $c \in S$, there is $t \in C^\omega$ such that $\mathcal{R}_{\mathsf{tr}} \vdash c \Rightarrow_{\mathsf{tr}} t$.

Theorem 4. *Let $\mathcal{R}$ and Π satisfy conditions **S1** and **S4**. If $c \in \Pi$, then there is t such that $\mathcal{R}_{\mathsf{tr}} \vdash c \Rightarrow_{\mathsf{tr}} t$.*

Proof. First note that, thanks to Theorem 1, the statement is equivalent to the following:

If $c \in \Pi$ and $\mathcal{R} \nvdash c \Rightarrow$, then there is $t \in C^\omega$ such that $\mathcal{R}_{\mathsf{tr}} \vdash c \Rightarrow_{\mathsf{tr}} t$.

Then, the proof follows from Lemma 2. We define $S = \{ c \mid c \in \Pi \text{ and } \mathcal{R} \nvdash c \Rightarrow \}$, and show that, for all $c \in S$, there are $\rho \equiv \mathsf{rule}(j_1 \ldots j_n, j_{n+1}, c)$ and $k \in 1..n+1$ such that, for all $h < k$, $\mathcal{R} \vdash j_h$, and $C(j_k) \in S$.

Consider $c \in S$, then, by **S4**, there is $\rho \equiv \mathsf{rule}(j_1 \ldots j_n, j_{n+1}, c)$. By definition of S, we have $\mathcal{R} \nvdash c \Rightarrow$, hence there exists a (first) $k \in 1..n+1$ such that $\mathcal{R} \nvdash j_k$, since, otherwise, we would have $\mathcal{R} \vdash c \Rightarrow R(j_{n+1})$. Then, since k is the first index with such property, for all $h < k$, we have $\mathcal{R} \vdash j_h$, hence, again by condition **S4**, we have that $\mathcal{R} \nvdash C(j_k) \Rightarrow$. Finally, since for all $h < k$ we have $\mathcal{R} \vdash j_h$, by Prop. 1, we get $C(j_k) \in \Pi$, hence $C(j_k) \in S$, as needed.

5   Examples

Sect. 5.1 explains in detail how a typical soundness proof can be rephrased in terms of our technique, by reasoning directly on big-step rules. Sect. 5.2 shows a case where this is advantageous, since the property to be checked is *not preserved* by intermediate computation steps, whereas it holds for the final result. Sect. 5.3 considers a more sophisticated type system, with intersection and union types. Finally, Sect. 5.4 shows another example where subject reduction is not preserved, whereas soundness can be proved with our technique. This example is intended as a preliminary step towards a more challenging case.

5.1   Simply-typed λ-calculus with recursive types

As a first example, we take the λ-calculus with natural constants, successor, and choice used in Sect. 2 (Fig. 1). We consider a standard simply-typed version with recursive types, obtained by interpreting the production in Fig. 4 coinductively. Introducing recursive types makes the calculus non-normalising and permits to write interesting programs such as Ω (see Sect. 3.1).

The typing rules are recalled in Fig. 4. Type environments, written Γ, are finite maps from variables to types, and $\Gamma\{T/x\}$ denotes the map which returns T on x and coincides with Γ elsewhere. We write $\vdash e : T$ for $\emptyset \vdash e : T$.

Let $\mathcal{R}_1$ be the big-step semantics defined in Fig. 1, and let $\Pi 1_T(e)$ hold if $\vdash e : T$, for T defined in Fig. 4. To prove the three conditions **S1**, **S2** and **S3** of

$$T ::= \mathtt{Nat} \mid T_1 \to T_2 \ \mathtt{type}$$

(T-VAR) $\dfrac{}{\Gamma \vdash x : T}$ $\Gamma(x) = T$ (T-CONST) $\dfrac{}{\Gamma \vdash n : \mathtt{Nat}}$

(T-ABS) $\dfrac{\Gamma\{T'/x\} \vdash e : T}{\Gamma \vdash \lambda x.e : T' \to T}$ (T-APP) $\dfrac{\Gamma \vdash e_1 : T' \to T \quad \Gamma \vdash e_2 : T'}{\Gamma \vdash e_1\, e_2 : T}$

(T-SUCC) $\dfrac{\Gamma \vdash e : \mathtt{Nat}}{\Gamma \vdash \mathtt{succ}\, e : \mathtt{Nat}}$ (T-CHOICE) $\dfrac{\Gamma \vdash e_1 : T \quad \Gamma \vdash e_2 : T}{\Gamma \vdash e_1 \oplus e_2 : T}$

Fig. 4. λ-calculus: type system

Sect. 4.2, we need lemmas of inversion, substitution and canonical forms, as in the standard technique.

Lemma 3 (Inversion).

1. If $\Gamma \vdash x : T$, then $\Gamma(x) = T$.
2. If $\Gamma \vdash n : T$, then $T = \mathtt{Nat}$.
3. If $\Gamma \vdash \lambda x.e : T$, then $T = T_1 \to T_2$ and $\Gamma\{T_1/x\} \vdash e : T_2$.
4. If $\Gamma \vdash e_1\, e_2 : T$, then $\Gamma \vdash e_1 : T' \to T$, and $\Gamma \vdash e_2 : T'$.
5. If $\Gamma \vdash \mathtt{succ}\, e : T$, then $T = \mathtt{Nat}$ and $\Gamma \vdash e : \mathtt{Nat}$.
6. If $\Gamma \vdash e_1 \oplus e_2 : T$, then $\Gamma \vdash e_i : T$ with $i \in 1, 2$.

Lemma 4 (Substitution). If $\Gamma\{T'/x\} \vdash e : T$ and $\Gamma \vdash e' : T'$, then $\Gamma \vdash e[e'/x] : T$.

Lemma 5 (Canonical Forms).

1. If $\vdash v : T' \to T$, then $v = \lambda x.e$.
2. If $\vdash v : \mathtt{Nat}$, then $v = n$.

Theorem 5 (Soundness). *The big-step semantics $\mathcal{R}_1$ and the indexed predicate $\Pi 1$ satisfy the conditions* **S1**, **S2** *and* **S3** *of Sect. 4.2.*

Since the aim of this first example is to illustrate the proof technique, we provide a proof where we explain the reasoning in detail.

Proof of **S1**. We should prove this condition for each (instantiation of meta-)rule. (APP): Assume that $\vdash e_1\, e_2 : T$ holds. We have to find types for the premises, notably T for the last one. We proceed as follows:

1. First premise: by Lemma 3 (4), $\vdash e_1 : T' \to T$.
2. Second premise: again by Lemma 3 (4), $\vdash e_2 : T'$ (without needing the assumption $\vdash \lambda x.e : T' \to T$).
3. Third premise: $\vdash e[v_2/x] : T$ should hold (assuming $\vdash \lambda x.e : T' \to T$, $\vdash v_2 : T'$). Since $\vdash \lambda x.e : T' \to T$, by Lemma 3 (3) we have $x{:}T' \vdash e : T$, so by Lemma 4 and $\vdash v_2 : T'$ we have $\vdash e[v_2/x] : T$.

(succ): This rule has an implicit continuation $n + 1 \Rightarrow n + 1$. Assume that $\vdash$ succ $e : T$ holds. By Lemma 3 (5), $T =$ Nat, and $\vdash e :$ Nat, hence we find Nat as type for the first premise. Moreover, $\vdash n + 1 :$ Nat holds by rule (T-CONST).
(choice): Assume that $\vdash e_1 \oplus e_2 : T$ holds. By Lemma 3 (6), we have $\vdash e_i : T$, with $i \in 1, 2$. Hence we find T as type for the premise.

Proof of S2. We should prove that, for each non-result configuration (here, expression e which is not a value) such that $\vdash e : T$ holds for some T, there is a rule with this configuration in the consequence. The expression e cannot be a variable, since a variable cannot be typed in the empty environment. Application, successor and choice appear as consequence in the reduction rules.

Proof of **S3**. We should prove this condition for each (instantiation of meta-)rule.
(APP): Assuming $\vdash e_1 e_2 : T$, again by Lemma 3 (4) we get $\Gamma \vdash e_1 : T' \to T$.

1. First premise: if $e1 \Rightarrow v$ is derivable, then there should be a rule with $e_1 e_2$ in the consequence and $e1 \Rightarrow v$ as first premise. Since we proved **S1**, by preservation (Lemma 1) $\vdash v : T' \to T$ holds. Then, by Lemma 5 (1), v has shape $\lambda x.e$, hence the required rule exists. As noted at page 10, in practice checking **S3** for a (meta-)rule amounts to show that (sub)configurations in the premises evaluate to results which have the required shape (to be a λ-abstraction in this case).
2. Second premise: if $e_1 \Rightarrow \lambda x.e$, and $e2 \Rightarrow v_2$, then there should be a rule with $e_1 e_2$ in the consequence and $e_1 \Rightarrow \lambda x.e$, $e2 \Rightarrow v$ as first two premises. This is trivial since the meta-variable v_2 can be freely instantiated in the meta-rule.

(succ): Assuming $\vdash$ succ $e : T$, again by Lemma 3 (5) we get $\vdash e :$ Nat. If $e \Rightarrow v$ is derivable, there should be a rule with succ e in the consequence and $e \Rightarrow v$ as first premise. Indeed, by preservation (Lemma 1) and Lemma 5 (2), v has shape n. For the second premise, if $n + 1 \Rightarrow v$ is derivable, then v is necessarily $n + 1$.
(choice): Trivial since the meta-variable v can be freely instantiated.

An interesting remark is that, differently from the standard approach, there is *no induction* in the proof: everything is *by cases*. This is a consequence of the fact that, as discussed in Sect. 4.2, the three conditions are *local*, that is, they are conditions on single rules. Induction is "hidden" in the proof that those three conditions are sufficient to ensure soundness.

If we drop in Fig. 1 rule (succ), then condition **S2** fails, since there is no longer a rule for the well-typed non-result configuration succ n. If we add the (FOOL) rule $\vdash 0\,0 :$ Nat, then condition **S3** fails for rule (APP), since $0 \Rightarrow 0$ is derivable, but there is no rule with $0\,0$ in the conclusion and $0 \Rightarrow 0$ as first premise.

5.2   MiniFJ&λ

In this example, the language is a subset of FJ&λ [12], a calculus extending Featherweight Java (FJ) with λ-abstractions and intersection types, introduced in Java 8. To keep the example small, we do not consider intersections and focus on one key typing feature: λ-abstractions can only be typed when occurring in a context requiring a given type (called the *target type*). In a small-step semantics, this poses a problem: reduction can move λ-abstractions into arbitrary contexts, leading to intermediate terms which would be ill-typed. To maintain subject reduction, in [12] λ-abstractions are decorated with their initial target type. In a big-step semantics, there is no need of intermediate terms and annotations.

The syntax is given in the first part of Fig. 5. We assume sets of *variables* x, *class names* C, *interface names* I, J, *field names* f, and *method names* m. Interfaces which have *exactly* one method (dubbed *functional interfaces*) can be used as target types. Expressions are those of FJ, plus λ-abstractions, and types are class and interface names. In $\lambda xs.e$ we assume that xs is not empty and e is not a λ-abstraction. For simplicity, we only consider *upcasts*, which have no runtime effect, but are important to allow the programmer to use λ-abstractions, as exemplified in discussing typing rules.

To be concise, the class table is abstractly modelled as follows:

- fields(C) gives the sequence of field declarations $T_1 f_1; .. T_n f_n;$ for class C
- mtype(T, m) gives, for each method m in class or interface T, the pair $T_1 \ldots T_n \to T'$ consisting of the parameter types and return type
- mbody(C, m) gives, for each method m in class C, the pair $\langle x_1 \ldots x_n, e \rangle$ consisting of the parameters and body
- <: is the reflexive and transitive closure of the union of the extends and implements relations
- !mtype(I) gives, for each *functional* interface I, mtype(I, m), where m is the only method of I.

The big-step semantics is given in the last part of Fig. 5. MINIFJ&λ shows an example of instantiation of the framework where configurations include an auxiliary structure, rather than being just language terms. In this case, the structure is an *environment* E (a finite map from variables to values) modelling the current stack frame. Results are values, which are either *objects*, of shape $[vs]^C$, or λ-abstractions.

Rules for FJ constructs are straightforward. Note that, since we only consider upcasts, casts have no runtime effect. Indeed, they are guaranteed to succeed on well-typed expressions. Rule (λ-INVK) shows that, when the receiver of a method is a λ-abstraction, the method name is not significant at runtime, and the effect is that the body of the function is evaluated as in the usual application.

The type system is given in Fig. 6. Method bodies are expected to be well-typed with respect to method types. Formally, mbody(C, m) and mtype(C, m) are either both defined or both undefined: in the first case mbody(C, m) = $\langle x_1 \ldots x_n, e \rangle$, mtype(C, m) = $T_1 \ldots T_n \to T$, and $x_1{:}T_1, \ldots, x_n{:}T_n, \text{this}{:}C \vdash e : T$. Moreover, we assume other standard FJ constraints on the class table, such as no field hiding, no method overloading, the same parameter and return types in overriding.

Besides the standard typing features of FJ, the MINIFJ&λ type system ensures the following.

$$e ::= x \mid e.\mathsf{f} \mid \mathbf{new}\ \mathsf{C}(e_1,\dots,e_n) \mid e.\mathsf{m}(e_1,\dots,e_n) \mid \lambda xs.e \mid (T)e \qquad \text{expression}$$
$$xs ::= x_1 \dots x_n \qquad\qquad\qquad\qquad\qquad\qquad\qquad\qquad\qquad\qquad \text{variable list}$$
$$T ::= \mathsf{C} \mid \mathsf{I} \qquad\qquad\qquad\qquad\qquad\qquad\qquad\qquad\qquad\qquad\qquad \text{type}$$

$$c ::= \langle \mathrm{E},\ e \rangle \mid v \qquad\quad \text{configuration}$$
$$v ::= [vs]^{\mathsf{C}} \mid \lambda xs.e \qquad \text{result (value)}$$
$$vs ::= v_1,\dots,v_n \qquad\quad \text{value list}$$

$$(\text{VAR}) \ \frac{}{\langle \mathrm{E},\ x \rangle \Rightarrow v} \quad \mathrm{E}(x) = v$$

$$(\text{FIELD-ACCESS}) \ \frac{\langle \mathrm{E},\ e \rangle \Rightarrow [v_1,\dots,v_n]^{\mathsf{C}} \quad \mathsf{fields}(\mathsf{C}) = T_1\,\mathsf{f}_1\,;\ \dots\ T_n\,\mathsf{f}_n\,;}{\langle \mathrm{E},\ e.\mathsf{f}_i \rangle \Rightarrow v_i \qquad\qquad i \in 1..n}$$

$$(\text{NEW}) \ \frac{\langle \mathrm{E},\ e_i \rangle \Rightarrow v_i\ \ \forall i \in 1..n}{\langle \mathrm{E},\ \mathbf{new}\ \mathsf{C}(e_1,\dots,e_n) \rangle \Rightarrow [v_1,\dots,v_n]^{\mathsf{C}}}$$

$$(\text{INVK}) \ \frac{\begin{array}{l}\langle \mathrm{E},\ e_0 \rangle \Rightarrow [vs]^{\mathsf{C}} \\ \langle \mathrm{E},\ e_i \rangle \Rightarrow v_i\ \ \forall i \in 1..n \\ \langle x_1{:}v_1,\dots,x_n{:}v_n, \mathbf{this}{:}[vs]^{\mathsf{C}},\ e \rangle \Rightarrow v \quad \mathsf{mbody}(\mathsf{C},\mathsf{m}) = \langle x_1 \dots x_n,\ e \rangle\end{array}}{\langle \mathrm{E},\ e_0.\mathsf{m}(e_1,\dots,e_n) \rangle \Rightarrow v}$$

$$(\lambda\text{-INVK}) \ \frac{\begin{array}{l}\langle \mathrm{E},\ e_0 \rangle \Rightarrow \lambda xs.e \\ \langle \mathrm{E},\ e_i \rangle \Rightarrow v_i\ \ \forall i \in 1..n \\ \langle x_1{:}v_1,\dots,x_n{:}v_n,\ e \rangle \Rightarrow v\end{array}}{\langle \mathrm{E},\ e_0.\mathsf{m}(e_1,\dots,e_n) \rangle \Rightarrow v} \qquad (\text{UPCAST}) \ \frac{\langle \mathrm{E},\ e \rangle \Rightarrow v}{\langle \mathrm{E},\ (T)e \rangle \Rightarrow v}$$

Fig. 5. MINIFJ&λ: syntax and big-step semantics

- A functional interface I can be assigned as type to a λ-abstraction which has the functional type of the method, see rule (T-λ).
- A λ-abstraction should have a *target type* determined by the context where the λ-abstraction occurs. More precisely, see [25] page 602, a λ-abstraction in our calculus can only occur as return expression of a method or argument of constructor, method call or cast. Then, in some contexts a λ-abstraction cannot be typed, in our calculus when occurring as receiver in field access or method invocation, hence these cases should be prevented. This is implicit in rule (T-FIELD-ACCESS), since the type of the receiver should be a class name, whereas it is explicitly forbidden in rule (T-INVK). For the same reason, a λ-abstraction cannot be the main expression to be evaluated.
- A λ-abstraction with a given target type J should have type *exactly* J: a subtype I of J is not enough. Consider, for instance, the following program:

```
interface J {}
interface I extends J { A m(A x); }
class C {
  C m(I y) { return new C().n(y); }
  C n(J y) { return new C(); }
}
```

$$(\text{T-CONF}) \quad \frac{\vdash v_i : T_i \ \forall i \in 1..n \quad x_1{:}T_1', \ldots, x_n{:}T_n' \vdash e : T}{\vdash \langle x_1{:}v_1, \ldots, x_n{:}v_n, \ e \rangle : T} \quad T_i <: T_i' \ \forall i \in 1..n$$

$$(\text{T-VAR}) \quad \frac{}{\Gamma \vdash x : T} \quad \Gamma(x) = T \qquad (\text{T-FIELD-ACCESS}) \quad \frac{\Gamma \vdash e : \mathsf{C} \quad \text{fields}(\mathsf{C}) = T_1\,\mathsf{f}_1 ; \ldots T_n\,\mathsf{f}_n ;}{\Gamma \vdash e.\mathsf{f} : T_i \quad i \in 1..n}$$

$$(\text{T-NEW}) \quad \frac{\Gamma \vdash e_i : T_i \ \forall i \in 1..n}{\Gamma \vdash \mathbf{new} \ \mathsf{C}(e_1, \ldots, e_n) : \mathsf{C}} \quad \text{fields}(\mathsf{C}) = T_1\,\mathsf{f}_1 ; \ldots T_n\,\mathsf{f}_n ;$$

$$(\text{T-INVK}) \quad \frac{\Gamma \vdash e_i : T_i \ \forall i \in 0..n}{\Gamma \vdash e_0.\mathsf{m}(e_1, \ldots, e_n) : T} \quad \begin{array}{l} e_0 \ \text{not of shape } \lambda xs.e \\ \text{mtype}(T_0, \mathsf{m}) = T_1 \ldots T_n \to T \end{array}$$

$$(\text{T-}\lambda) \quad \frac{x_1{:}T_1, \ldots, x_n{:}T_n \vdash e : T}{\Gamma \vdash \lambda xs.e : \mathsf{I}} \quad !\text{mtype}(\mathsf{I}) = T_1 \ldots T_n \to T$$

$$(\text{T-UPCAST}) \quad \frac{\Gamma \vdash e : T}{\Gamma \vdash (T)e : T} \qquad (\text{T-OBJECT}) \quad \frac{\Gamma \vdash v_i : T_i' \ \forall i \in 1..n \quad \text{fields}(\mathsf{C}) = T_1\,\mathsf{f}_1 ; \ldots T_n\,\mathsf{f}_n ;}{\Gamma \vdash [v_1, \ldots, v_n]^{\mathsf{C}} : \mathsf{C}} \quad T_i' <: T_i \ \forall i \in 1..n$$

$$(\text{T-SUB}) \quad \frac{\Gamma \vdash e : T \quad e \ \text{not of shape } \lambda xs.e}{\Gamma \vdash e : T' \quad T <: T'}$$

Fig. 6. MINIFJ&λ: type system

and the main expression $\mathbf{new} \ \mathsf{C}().\mathsf{n}(\lambda x.x)$. Here, the λ-abstraction has target type J, which is *not* a functional interface, hence the expression is ill-typed in Java (the compiler has no functional type against which to type-check the λ-abstraction). On the other hand, in the body of method m, the parameter y of type I can be passed, as usual, to method n expecting a supertype. For instance, the main expression $\mathbf{new} \ \mathsf{C}().\mathsf{m}(\lambda x.x)$ is well-typed, since the λ-abstraction has target type I, and can be safely passed to method n, since it is not used as function there. To formalise this behaviour, it is forbidden to apply subsumption to λ-abstractions, see rule (T-SUB).

- However, λ-abstractions occurring as results rather than in source code (that is, in the environment and as fields of objects) are allowed to have a subtype of the required type, see the explicit side condition in rules (T-CONF) and (T-OBJECT). For instance, if C is a class with one field $\mathsf{J}\,\mathsf{f}$, the expression $\mathbf{new} \ \mathsf{C}((\mathsf{I})\lambda x.x)$ is well-typed, whereas $\mathbf{new} \ \mathsf{C}(\lambda x.x)$ is ill typed, since rule (T-SUB) cannot be applied to λ-abstractions. When the expression is evaluated, the result is $[\lambda x.x]^{\mathsf{C}}$, which is well-typed.

As mentioned at the beginning, the obvious small-step semantics would produce not typable expressions. In the above example, we get

$$\mathbf{new} \ \mathsf{C}((\mathsf{I})\lambda x.x) \longrightarrow \mathbf{new} \ \mathsf{C}(\lambda x.x) \longrightarrow [\lambda x.x]^{\mathsf{C}}$$

and $\mathbf{new} \ \mathsf{C}(\lambda x.x)$ has no type, while $\mathbf{new} \ \mathsf{C}((\mathsf{I})\lambda x.x)$ and $[\lambda x.x]^{\mathsf{C}}$ have type C.

We write $\Gamma \vdash e :<: T$ as short for $\Gamma \vdash e : T'$ and $T' <: T$ for some T'. In order to state soundness, set $\mathcal{R}_2$ the big-step semantics defined in Fig. 5, and let

$\Pi2_T(\langle \text{E}, e \rangle)$ hold if $\vdash \langle \text{E}, e \rangle :<: T$, $\Pi2_T(v)$ if $\vdash v :<: T$, for T defined in Fig. 5.

Theorem 6 (Soundness). *The big-step semantics $\mathcal{R}_2$ and the indexed predicate $\Pi2$ satisfy the conditions* **S1**, **S2** *and* **S3** *of Sect. 4.2.*

5.3   Intersection and union types

We enrich the type system of Fig. 4 by adding intersection and union type constructors and the corresponding typing rules, see Fig. 7. As usual we require an infinite number of arrows in each infinite path for the trees representing types. Intersection types for the λ-calculus have been widely studied [11]. Union types naturally model conditionals [26] and non-deterministic choice [22].

$$T ::= \text{Nat} \mid T_1 \to T_2 \mid T_1 \wedge T_2 \mid T_1 \vee T_2 \text{ type}$$

$$(\wedge\,\text{I}) \frac{\Gamma \vdash e : T \quad \Gamma \vdash e : S}{\Gamma \vdash e : T \wedge S} \qquad (\wedge\,\text{E}) \frac{\Gamma \vdash e : T \wedge S}{\Gamma \vdash e : T} \qquad (\wedge\,\text{E}) \frac{\Gamma \vdash e : T \wedge S}{\Gamma \vdash e : S}$$

$$(\vee\,\text{I}) \frac{\Gamma \vdash e : T}{\Gamma \vdash e : T \vee S} \qquad (\vee\,\text{I}) \frac{\Gamma \vdash e : S}{\Gamma \vdash e : T \vee S}$$

Fig. 7. Intersection and union types: syntax and typing rules

The typing rules for the introduction and the elimination of intersection and union are standard, except for the absence of the union elimination rule:

$$(\vee E) \frac{\Gamma\{T/x\} \vdash e : V \quad \Gamma\{S/x\} \vdash e : V \quad \Gamma \vdash e' : T \vee S}{\Gamma \vdash e[e'/x] : V}$$

As a matter of fact rule $(\vee E)$ is unsound for $\oplus$. For example, let split the type Nat into Even and Odd and add the expected typings for natural numbers. The prefix addition $+$ has type

$$(\text{Even} \to \text{Even} \to \text{Even}) \wedge (\text{Odd} \to \text{Odd} \to \text{Even})$$

and we derive

$$\cfrac{x{:}\text{Even} \vdash + x\ x{:}\text{Even} \quad x{:}\text{Odd} \vdash + x\ x{:}\text{Even} \quad \cfrac{\cfrac{\vdash 1 : \text{Odd}}{\vdash 1 : \text{Even} \vee \text{Odd}}\ (\vee\,\text{I}) \quad \cfrac{\vdash 2 : \text{Even}}{\vdash 2 : \text{Even} \vee \text{Odd}}\ (\vee\,\text{I})}{\vdash (1 \oplus 2) : \text{Even} \vee \text{Odd}}\ (\oplus)}{\vdash +(1 \oplus 2)(1 \oplus 2) : \text{Even}}\ (\vee\,\text{E})$$

We cannot assign the type Even to 3, which is a possible result, so strong soundness is lost. In the small-step approach, we cannot assign Even to the intermediate term $+\,1\,2$, so subject reduction fails. In the big-step approach, there is no such intermediate term; however, condition **S1** fails for the reduction rule for $+$. Indeed, considering the following instantiation of the rule:

$$(+) \; \frac{1 \oplus 2 \Rightarrow 1 \quad 1 \oplus 2 \Rightarrow 2 \quad 3 \Rightarrow 3}{+(1 \oplus 2)(1 \oplus 2) \Rightarrow 3}$$

and the type Even for the consequence, we cannot assign this type to the (configuration in) last premise (continuation).

Intersection types allow to derive meaningful types also for expressions containing variables applied to themselves, for example we can derive
$$\vdash \lambda x.x\,x : (T \to S) \wedge T \to S$$
With union types all non-deterministic choices between typable expressions can be typed too, since we can derive $\Gamma \vdash e_1 \oplus e_2 : T_1 \vee T_2$ from $\Gamma \vdash e_1 : T_1$ and $\Gamma \vdash e_2 : T_2$.

In order to state soundness, let $\Pi 3_T(e)$ be $\vdash e : T$, for T defined in Fig. 7.

Theorem 7 (Soundness). *The big-step semantics $\mathcal{R}_1$ and the indexed predicate $\Pi 3$ satisfy the conditions* **S1**, **S2** *and* **S3** *of Sect. 4.2.*

5.4   MiniFJ&O

A well-known example in which proving soundness with respect to small-step semantics is extremely challenging is the standard type system with intersection and union types [10] w.r.t. the pure λ-calculus with full reduction. Indeed, the standard subject reduction technique fails[5], since, for instance, we can derive the type $(T \to T \to V) \wedge (S \to S \to V) \to (U \to T \vee S) \to U \to V$ for both $\lambda x.\lambda y.\lambda z.x((\lambda t.t)(y\,z))((\lambda t.t)(y\,z))$ and $\lambda x.\lambda y.\lambda z.x(y\,z)(y\,z)$, but the intermediate expressions $\lambda x.\lambda y.\lambda z.x((\lambda t.t)(y\,z))(y\,z)$ and $\lambda x.\lambda y.\lambda z.x(y\,z)((\lambda t.t)(y\,z))$ do not have this type.

As the example shows, the key problem is that rule $(\vee E)$ can be applied to expression e where the same subexpression e' occurs more than once. In the non-deterministic case, as shown by the example in the previous section, this is unsound, since e' can reduce to different values. In the deterministic case, instead, this is sound, but cannot be proved by subject reduction. Since using big-step semantics there are no intermediate steps to be typed, our approach seems very promising to investigate an alternative proof of soundness. Whereas we leave this challenging problem to future work, here as first step we describe a (hypothetical) calculus with a much simpler version of the problematic feature.

The calculus is a variant of FJ [27] with intersection and union types. Methods have intersection types with the same return type and different parameter types, modelling a form of *overloading*. Union types enhance typability of conditionals. The more interesting feature is the possibility of replacing an arbitrary number of parameters with the same expression having an union type. We dub this calculus MINIFJ&O.

Fig. 8 gives the syntax, big-step semantics and typing rules of MINIFJ&O. We omit the standard big-step rule for conditional, and typing rules for boolean

---

[5] For this reason, in [10] soundness is proved by an ad-hoc technique, that is, by considering parallel reduction and an equivalent type system à la Gentzen, which enjoys the cut elimination property.

$$e \quad ::= x \mid v \mid e.f \mid e.m(e_1,\ldots,e_n) \mid \text{if } e \text{ then } e_1 \text{ else } e_2 \qquad \text{expression}$$
$$v \quad ::= \text{new } C(v_1,\ldots,v_n) \mid \text{true} \mid \text{false} \qquad \text{value}$$
$$T \quad ::= C \mid \text{Bool} \mid \bigvee_{1\le i \le n} T_i \qquad \text{expression type}$$
$$MT ::= \bigwedge_{1\le i \le m}(C_1^{(i)}\ldots C_n^{(i)} \to D) \qquad \text{method type}$$

$$(\text{FIELD-ACCESS}) \quad \frac{e \Rightarrow \text{new } C(v_1,\ldots,v_n) \quad \text{fields}(C) = T_1\, f_1\,;\,\ldots\, T_n\, f_n\,;}{e.f_i \Rightarrow v_i \qquad i \in 1..n}$$

$$(\text{NEW}) \quad \frac{e_i \Rightarrow v_i \quad \forall i \in 1..n}{\text{new } C(e_1,\ldots,e_n) \Rightarrow \text{new } C(v_1,\ldots,v_n)}$$

$$(\text{INVK}) \quad \frac{\begin{array}{l} e_0 \Rightarrow \text{new } C(vs') \\ e_i \Rightarrow v_i \quad \forall i \in 1..n \\ e[v_1/x_1]\ldots[v_n/x_n][\text{new } C(vs')/\text{this}] \Rightarrow v \end{array}}{e_0.m(e_1,\ldots,e_n) \Rightarrow v} \qquad \text{mbody}(C,m) = \langle x_1 \ldots x_n,\ e \rangle$$

$$(\text{T-VAR}) \quad \frac{}{\Gamma \vdash x : T} \quad \Gamma(x) = T \qquad (\text{T-FIELD-ACCESS}) \quad \frac{\Gamma \vdash e : C \quad \text{fields}(C) = T_1\, f_1\,;\,\ldots\, T_n\, f_n\,;}{\Gamma \vdash e.f_i : C_i \quad i \in 1..n}$$

$$(\text{T-NEW}) \quad \frac{\Gamma \vdash e_i : C_i \quad \forall i \in 1..n}{\Gamma \vdash \text{new } C(e_1,\ldots,e_n) : C} \quad \text{fields}(C) = T_1\, f_1\,;\,\ldots\, T_n\, f_n\,;$$

$$(\text{T-INVK}) \quad \frac{\Gamma \vdash e_i : C_i \quad \forall i \in 0..n \quad \Gamma \vdash e : \bigvee_{1\le i\le m} D_i}{\Gamma \vdash e_0.m(e_1,\ldots,e_n,\underbrace{e,\ldots,e}_{p}) : C} \quad \begin{array}{l} \text{mtype}(C_0,m) <: \\ \bigwedge_{1\le i\le m}(C_1 \ldots C_n \underbrace{D_i \ldots D_i}_{p} \to C) \end{array}$$

$$(\text{T-IF}) \quad \frac{\Gamma \vdash e : \text{Bool} \quad \Gamma \vdash e_1 : T \quad \Gamma \vdash e_2 : T}{\Gamma \vdash \text{if } e \text{ then } e_1 \text{ else } e_2 : T} \qquad (\text{T-SUB}) \quad \frac{\Gamma \vdash e : T}{\Gamma \vdash e : T'} \quad T <: T'$$

Fig. 8. MINIFJ&O: syntax, big-step semantics and type system

constants. The subtyping relation $<:$ is the reflexive and transitive closure of the union of the **extends** relation and the standard rules for union:

$$T_1 <: T_1 \vee T_2 \qquad T_1 <: T_2 \vee T_1$$

On the other hand, *method types* (results of the mtype function) are now *intersection types*, and the subtyping relation on them is the reflexive and transitive closure of the standard rules for intersection:

$$MT_1 \wedge MT_2 <: MT_1 \qquad MT_1 \wedge MT_2 <: MT_2$$

The functions fields and mbody are defined as for MINIFJ&λ.

Instead mtype(C, m) gives, for each method m in class C, an intersection type. We assume mbody(C, m) and mtype(C, m) either both defined or both undefined: in the first case mbody(C, m)=$\langle x_1 \ldots x_n,\ e \rangle$, mtype(C, m)=$\bigwedge_{1\le i\le m}(C_1^{(i)} \ldots C_n^{(i)} \to D)$, and $x_1{:}C_1^{(i)},\ldots,x_n{:}C_n^{(i)},\text{this}{:}C \vdash e : D$ for $i \in 1..m$.

Clearly rule (T-INVK) is inspired by rule ($\vee$E), but the restriction to method calls endows a standard inversion lemma. The subtyping in this rule allows to choose the types for the method best fitting the types of the arguments. Not surprisingly, subject reduction fails for the expected small-step semantics. For

example, let class C have a field point which contains cartesian coordinates and class D have a field point which contains polar coordinates. The method eq takes two objects and compares their point fields returning a boolean value. A type for this method is $(C\,C \to \mathtt{Bool}) \wedge (D\,D \to \mathtt{Bool})$ and we can type $eq(e, e)$, where
$$e = \text{if } \mathtt{false} \text{ then new } C(\dots) \text{ else new } D(\dots)$$
In fact e has type $C \vee D$. Notice that in a standard small-step semantics
$$eq(e, e) \longrightarrow eq(\text{new } D(\dots), \text{if } \mathtt{false} \text{ then new } C(\dots) \text{ else new } D(\dots))$$
and this last expression cannot be typed.

In order to state soundness, let $\mathcal{R}_4$ be the big-step semantics defined in Fig. 8, and let $\Pi 4_T(e)$ hold if $\vdash e : T$, for T defined in Fig. 8.

Theorem 8 (Soundness). *The big-step semantics $\mathcal{R}_4$ and the indexed predicate $\Pi 4$ satisfy the conditions* **S1**, **S2** *and* **S3** *of Sect. 4.2.*

6   The partial evaluation construction

In this section, our aim is to provide a *formal* justification that the constructions in Sect. 3 are correct. For instance, for the wrong semantics we would like to be sure that *all* the cases are covered. To this end, we define a *third construction*, dubbed PEV for "partial evaluation", which makes explicit the *computations* of a big-step semantics, intended as the sequences of execution steps of the naturally associated evaluation algorithm. Formally, we obtain a reduction relation on approximated proof trees, so non-termination and stuck computation are distinguished, and both soundness-must and soundness-may can be expressed.

To this end, first of all we introduce a special result ?, so that a judgment $c \Rightarrow ?$ (called *incomplete*, whereas a judgment in $\mathcal{R}$ is *complete*) means that the evaluation of c is not completed yet. Analogously to the previous constructions, we define an augmented set of rules $\mathcal{R}_?$ for the judgment extended with ?:

? introduction rules These rules derive ? whenever a rule is partially applied: for each rule $\rho \equiv \text{rule}(j_1 \dots j_n, j_{n+1}, c)$ in $\mathcal{R}$, index $i \in 1..n+1$, and result $r \in R$, we define the rule $\text{intro}_?(\rho, i, r)$ as

$$\frac{j_1 \quad \cdots \quad j_{i-1} \quad C(j_i) \Rightarrow r}{c \Rightarrow ?}$$

We also add an axiom $\dfrac{}{c \Rightarrow ?}$ for each configuration $c \in C$.

? propagation rules These rules propagate ? analogously to those for divergence and wrong propagation: for each $\rho \equiv \text{rule}(j_1 \dots j_n, j_{n+1}, c)$ in $\mathcal{R}$, and index $i \in 1..n+1$, we add the rule $\text{prop}(\rho, i, ?)$ as follows:

$$\frac{j_1 \quad \cdots \quad j_{i-1} \quad C(j_i) \Rightarrow ?}{c \Rightarrow ?}$$

Finally, we consider the set $\mathcal{T}$ of the (finite) proof trees τ in $\mathcal{R}_?$. Each τ can be thought as a *partial proof* or *partial evaluation* of the root configuration. In particular, we say it is *complete* if it is a proof tree in $\mathcal{R}$ (that is, it only contains complete judgments), *incomplete* otherwise. We define a reduction relation $\xrightarrow{\mathcal{R}}$

$$(\eta)\ \frac{}{r \Rightarrow ?} \xrightarrow{\mathcal{R}} (r)\ \frac{}{r \Rightarrow r} \qquad (c_?)\ \frac{}{c \Rightarrow ?} \xrightarrow{\mathcal{R}} (\mathsf{prop}(\rho,1,?))\ \frac{c' \Rightarrow ?\quad C(\rho) = c}{c \Rightarrow ?\quad C(\rho,1) = c'}$$

$$(\mathsf{intro}_?(\rho,i,r))\ \frac{\tau_1\ \cdots\ \tau_i}{c \Rightarrow ?} \xrightarrow{\mathcal{R}} (\rho')\ \frac{\tau_1\ \cdots\ \tau_i\quad \begin{array}{c}\rho' \sim_i \rho\\ R(\rho',i) = r\\ \#\rho' = i\end{array}}{c \Rightarrow r}$$

$$(\mathsf{intro}_?(\rho,i,r))\ \frac{\tau_1\ \cdots\ \tau_i}{c \Rightarrow ?} \xrightarrow{\mathcal{R}} (\mathsf{prop}(\rho',i+1,?))\ \frac{\tau_1\ \cdots\ \tau_i\quad c' \Rightarrow ?\quad \begin{array}{c}\rho' \sim_i \rho\\ R(\rho',i) = r\\ C(\rho',i+1) = c'\end{array}}{c \Rightarrow ?}$$

$$(\mathsf{prop}(\rho,i,?))\ \frac{\tau_1\ \cdots\ \tau_i}{c \Rightarrow ?} \xrightarrow{\mathcal{R}} (\mathsf{prop}(\rho,i,?))\ \frac{\tau_1\ \cdots\ \tau_{i-1}\ \tau_i'\quad \tau_i \xrightarrow{\mathcal{R}} \tau_i'}{c \Rightarrow ?\qquad R_?(\mathsf{r}(\tau_i')) = ?}$$

$$(\mathsf{prop}(\rho,i,?))\ \frac{\tau_1\ \cdots\ \tau_i}{c \Rightarrow ?} \xrightarrow{\mathcal{R}} (\mathsf{intro}_?(\rho,i,r))\ \frac{\tau_1\ \cdots\ \tau_{i-1}\ \tau_i'\quad \tau_i \xrightarrow{\mathcal{R}} \tau_i'}{c \Rightarrow ?\qquad R_?(\mathsf{r}(\tau_i')) = r}$$

Fig. 9. Reduction relation on $\mathcal{T}$

on $\mathcal{T}$ such that, starting from the initial proof tree $\dfrac{}{c \Rightarrow ?}$, we derive a sequence where, intuitively, at each step we detail the proof (evaluation). In this way, a sequence ending with a complete tree $\dfrac{\cdots}{c \Rightarrow r}$ models terminating computation, whereas an infinite sequence (tending to an infinite proof tree) models divergence, and a stuck sequence models a stuck computation.

The one-step reduction relation $\xrightarrow{\mathcal{R}}$ on $\mathcal{T}$ is inductively defined by the rules in Fig. 9. In this figure $\#\rho$ denotes the number of premises of ρ, and $\mathsf{r}(\tau)$ the root of τ. We set $R_?(c \Rightarrow u) = u$ where $u \in R \cup \{?\}$. Finally, $\sim_i$ is the *equivalence up-to an index* of rules, introduced at the beginning of Sect. 3.2. As said above, each reduction step makes "less incomplete" the proof tree. Notably, reduction rules apply to nodes with consequence $c \Rightarrow ?$, whereas subtrees with root $c \Rightarrow r$ represent terminated evaluation. In detail:

- If the last applied rule is an axiom, and the configuration is a result r, then we can evaluate r to itself. Otherwise, we have to find a rule ρ with c in the consequence and start evaluating the first premise of such rule.
- If the last applied rule is $\mathsf{intro}_?(\rho, i, r)$, then all subtrees are complete, hence, to continue the evaluation, we have to find another rule ρ', having, for each $k \in 1..i$, as k-th premise the root of τ_k. Then there are two possibilities: if there is an $i + 1$-th premise, we start evaluating it, otherwise, we propagate to the conclusion the result r of τ_i.
- If the last applied rule is a propagation rule $\mathsf{prop}(\rho, i, ?)$, then we simply propagate the step made by τ_i.

In Fig. 10 we report an example of PEV reduction.

We end by stating the three constructions to be equivalent to each other, thus providing a coherency result of the approach. In particular, first we show that PEV is conservative with respect to $\mathcal{R}$, and this ensures the three constructions are equivalent for finite computations. Then, we prove traces and wrong

$$\frac{}{(\lambda x.x)\ n \Rightarrow ?} \xrightarrow{\mathcal{R}} \frac{\lambda x.x \Rightarrow ?}{(\lambda x.x)\ n \Rightarrow ?} \xrightarrow{\mathcal{R}} \frac{\lambda x.x \Rightarrow \lambda x.x}{(\lambda x.x)\ n \Rightarrow ?} \xrightarrow{\mathcal{R}} \frac{\lambda x.x \Rightarrow \lambda x.x \quad n \Rightarrow ?}{(\lambda x.x)\ n \Rightarrow ?}$$

$$\xrightarrow{\mathcal{R}} \frac{\lambda x.x \Rightarrow \lambda x.x \quad n \Rightarrow n}{(\lambda x.x)\ n \Rightarrow ?} \xrightarrow{\mathcal{R}} \frac{\lambda x.x \Rightarrow \lambda x.x \quad n \Rightarrow n \quad n \Rightarrow ?}{(\lambda x.x)\ n \Rightarrow ?}$$

$$\xrightarrow{\mathcal{R}} \frac{\lambda x.x \Rightarrow \lambda x.x \quad n \Rightarrow n \quad n \Rightarrow n}{(\lambda x.x)\ n \Rightarrow ?} \xrightarrow{\mathcal{R}} \frac{\lambda x.x \Rightarrow \lambda x.x \quad n \Rightarrow n \quad n \Rightarrow n}{(\lambda x.x)\ n \Rightarrow n}$$

Fig. 10. The evaluation in PEV of $(\lambda x.x)\ n$.

constructions to be equivalent to PEV for diverging and stuck computations, respectively, and this ensures they cover all possible cases.

Theorem 9. *1.* $\mathcal{R} \vdash c \Rightarrow r$ *iff* $\dfrac{}{c \Rightarrow ?} \xrightarrow{\mathcal{R}}{}^* \tau$, *where* $r(\tau) = c \Rightarrow r$.

2. $\mathcal{R}_{tr} \vdash c \Rightarrow_{tr} t$ *for some* $t \in C^\omega$ *iff* $\dfrac{}{c \Rightarrow ?} \xrightarrow{\mathcal{R}}{}^\omega$.

3. $\mathcal{R}_{wr} \vdash c \Rightarrow \mathsf{wrong}$ *iff* $\dfrac{}{c \Rightarrow ?} \xrightarrow{\mathcal{R}}{}^* \tau$, *where* τ *is stuck.*

7   Related work

Modeling divergence The issue of modelling divergence in big-step semantics dates back to [18], where a stratified approach with a separate coinductive judgment for divergence is proposed, also investigated in [30].

In [5] the authors models divergence by interpreting coinductively standard big-step rules and considering also non-well-founded values. In [17] a similar technique is exploited, by adding a special result modelling divergence. Flag-based big-step semantics [36] captures divergence by interpreting the same semantic rules both inductively and coinductively. In all these approaches, spurious judgements can be derived for diverging computations.

Other proposals [32,3] are inspired by the notion of definitional interpreter [37], where a counter limits the number of steps of a computation. Thus, divergence can be modelled on top of an inductive judgement: a program diverges if the timeout is raised for any value of the counter, hence it is not directly modelled in the definition. Instead, [20] provides a way to directly model divergence using definitional interpreters, relying on the coinductive partiality monad [16].

The trace semantics in Sect. 3.1 has been inspired by [29]. Divergence propagation rules are very similar to those used in [8,9] to define a big-step judgment which directly includes divergence as result. However, this direct definition relies on a non-standard notion of inference system, allowing *corules* [7,19], whereas for the trace semantics presented in this work standard coinduction is enough, since all rules are *productive*, that is, they always add an element to the trace.

Differently from all the previously cited papers which consider specific examples, the work [2] shares with us the aim of providing a *generic construction* to model non-termination, basing on an arbitrary big-step semantics. Ager considers a class of big-step semantics identified by a specific shape of rules, and defines, in a small-step style, a proof-search algorithm which follows the big-step rules; in this way, converging, diverging and stuck computations are distinguished. This approach is somehow similar to our PEV semantics, even tough the transition system we propose is directly defined on proof trees.

There is an extensive body of work on coalgebraic techniques, where the difference between semantics can be simply expressed by a change of functor. In this paper we take a set-theoretic approach, simple and accessible to a large audience. Furthermore, as far as we know [38], coalgebras abstract several kinds of transition systems, thus being more similar to a small-step approach. In our understanding, the coalgebra models a single computation step with possible effects, and from this it is possible to derive a unique morphism into the final coalgebra modelling the "whole" semantics. Our trace semantics, being big-step, seems to roughly correspond to directly get this whole semantics. In other words, we do not have a coalgebra structure on configurations.

Proving soundness As we have discussed, also proving (type) soundness with respect to a big-step semantics is a challenging task, and some approaches have been proposed in the literature. In [24], to show soundness of large steps semantics, they prove a coverage lemma, which ensures that the rules cover all cases, including error situations. In [30] the authors prove a soundness property similar to Theorem 4, but by using a separate judgment to represent divergence, thus avoiding using traces. In [5] there is a proof of soundness of a coinductive type system with respect to a coinductive big-step semantics for a Java-like language, defining a relation between derivations in the type system and in the big-step semantics. In [8] there is a proof principle, used to show type soundness with respect to a big-step semantics defined by an inference system with corules [7]. In [4] the proof of type soundness of a calculus formalising path-dependent types relies on a big-step semantics, while in [3] soundness is shown for the polymorphic type systems $F_{<:}$, and for the DOT calculus, using definitional interpreters to model the semantics. In both cases they extend the original semantics adding error and timeout, and adopt inductive proof strategies, as in [39]. A similar approach is followed by [32] to show type soundness of the Core ML language.

Also [6] proposes an inductive proof of type soundness for the big-step semantics of a Java-like language, but relying on a notion of approximation of infinite derivation in the big-step semantics.

Pretty big-step semantics [17] aims at providing an efficient representation of big-step semantics, so that it can be easily extended without duplication of meta-rules. In order to define and prove soundness, they propose a generic error rule based on a *progress judgment*, whose definition can be easily derived manually from the set of evaluation rules. This is partly similar to our wrong extension, with two main differences. First, by factorising rules, they introduce intermediate steps as in small-step semantics, hence there are similar problems when intermediate steps are ill-typed (as in Sect. 5.2, Sect. 5.4). Second, wrong introduction is handled by the progress judgment, that is, at the level of side-conditions. Moreover, in [13] there is a formalisation of the pretty-big-step rules for performing a generic reasoning on big-step semantics by using abstract interpretation. However, the authors say that they interpret rules inductively, hence non-terminating computations are not modelled.

Finally, some (but not all) infinite trees of our trace semantics can be seen as cyclic proof trees, see end of Sect. 3.1. Proof systems supporting cyclic proofs can be found, e.g., in [14,15] for classical first order logic with inductive definitions.

8 Conclusion and future work

The most important contribution is a general approach for reasoning on soundness with respect to a big-step operational semantics. Conditions can be proven by a case analysis on the semantic (meta-)rules avoiding small-step-style intermediate configurations. This can be crucial since there are calculi where the property to be checked is *not preserved* by such intermediate configurations, whereas it holds for the final result, as illustrated in Sect. 5.

In future work, we plan to use the meta-theory in Sect. 2 as basis to investigate yet other constructions, notably the approach relying on corules [8,9], and that, adding a counter, based on timeout [32,3].

We also plan to compare our proof technique for proving soundness with the standard one for small-step semantics: if a predicate satisfies progress and subject reduction with respect to a small-step semantics, does it satisfy our soundness conditions with respect to an equivalent big-step semantics? To formally prove such a statement, the first step will be to express equivalence between small-step and big-step semantics. On the other hand, the converse does not hold, as shown by the examples in Sect. 5.2 and Sect. 5.4.

For what concerns significant applications, we plan to use the approach to prove soundness for the λ-calculus with full reduction and intersection/union types [10]. The interest of this example lies in the failure of the subject reduction, as discussed in Sect. 5.4. In another direction, we want to enhance MINIFJ&O with λ-abstractions and allowing everywhere intersection and union types [23]. This will extend typability of shared expressions. We plan to apply our approach to the big-step semantics of the statically typed virtual classes calculus developed in [24], discussing also the non terminating computations not considered there.

With regard to proofs, that are mainly omitted here, and can be found in the extended version at http://arxiv.org/abs/2002.08738, we plan to investigate if we can simplify them by means of enhanced conductive techniques.

As a proof-of-concept, we provided a mechanisation[6] in Agda of Lemma 1. The mechanisations of the other proofs is similar. However, as future work, we think it would be more interesting to provide a software for writing big-step definitions and for checking that the soundness conditions hold.

Acknowledgments The authors are grateful to the referees: the paper strongly improved thanks to their useful suggestions and remarks.

---

[6] Available at https://github.com/fdgn/soundness-big-step-semantics.

References

1. Peter Aczel. An introduction to inductive definitions. In *Handbook of Mathematical logic*, pages 739–782, Amsterdam, 1977. North Holland.
2. Mads Sig Ager. From natural semantics to abstract machines. In Sandro Etalle, editor, *LOPSTR 2014 - 14th International Symposium on Logic Based Program Synthesis and Transformation*, volume 3573 of *Lecture Notes in Computer Science*, pages 245–261, Berlin, 2004. Springer. doi:10.1007/11506676_16.
3. Nada Amin and Tiark Rompf. Type soundness proofs with definitional interpreters. In Giuseppe Castagna and Andrew D. Gordon, editors, *POPL'17 - ACM Symp. on Principles of Programming Languages*, pages 666–679, New York, 2017. ACM Press. doi:10.1145/3009837.
4. Nada Amin, Tiark Rompf, and Martin Odersky. Foundations of path-dependent types. In Andrew P. Black and Todd D. Millstein, editors, *OOPSLA'14 - ACM International Conference on Object Oriented Programming Systems Languages and Applications*, pages 233–249, New York, 2014. ACM Press. doi:10.1145/2660193.2660216.
5. Davide Ancona. Soundness of object-oriented languages with coinductive big-step semantics. In James Noble, editor, *ECOOP'12 - Object-Oriented Programming*, volume 7313 of *Lecture Notes in Computer Science*, pages 459–483, Berlin, 2012. Springer. doi:10.1007/978-3-642-31057-7_21.
6. Davide Ancona. How to prove type soundness of Java-like languages without forgoing big-step semantics. In David J. Pearce, editor, *FTfJP'14 - Formal Techniques for Java-like Programs*, pages 1:1–1:6, New York, 2014. ACM Press. doi:10.1145/2635631.2635846.
7. Davide Ancona, Francesco Dagnino, and Elena Zucca. Generalizing inference systems by coaxioms. In Hongseok Yang, editor, *ESOP 2017 - European Symposium on Programming*, volume 10201 of *Lecture Notes in Computer Science*, pages 29–55, Berlin, 2017. Springer. doi:10.1007/978-3-662-54434-1_2.
8. Davide Ancona, Francesco Dagnino, and Elena Zucca. Reasoning on divergent computations with coaxioms. *PACMPL*, 1(OOPSLA):81:1–81:26, 2017. doi:10.1145/3133905.
9. Davide Ancona, Francesco Dagnino, and Elena Zucca. Modeling infinite behaviour by corules. In Todd D. Millstein, editor, *ECOOP'18 - Object-Oriented Programming*, volume 109 of *LIPIcs*, pages 21:1–21:31, Dagstuhl, 2018. Schloss Dagstuhl - Leibniz-Zentrum für Informatik. doi:10.4230/LIPIcs.ECOOP.2018.21.
10. Franco Barbanera, Mariangiola Dezani-Ciancaglini, and Ugo de'Liguoro. Intersection and union types: Syntax and semantics. *Information and Computation*, 119(2):202–230, 1995. doi:10.1006/inco.1995.1086.
11. Hendrik Pieter Barendregt, Wil Dekkers, and Richard Statman. *Lambda Calculus with Types*. Perspectives in logic. Cambridge University Press, Cambridge, 2013.
12. Lorenzo Bettini, Viviana Bono, Mariangiola Dezani-Ciancaglini, Paola Giannini, and Betti Venneri. Java & Lambda: a Featherweight story. *Logical Methods in Computer Science*, 14(3), 2018. doi:10.23638/LMCS-14(3:17)2018.
13. Martin Bodin, Thomas Jensen, and Alan Schmitt. Certified abstract interpretation with pretty-big-step semantics. In Xavier Leroy and Alwen Tiu, editors, *CPP'15 - Proceedings of the 2015 Conference on Certified Programs and Proofs*, pages 29–40, New York, 2015. ACM. doi:10.1145/2676724.2693174.
14. James Brotherston. Cyclic proofs for first-order logic with inductive definitions. In Bernhard Beckert, editor, *Automated Reasoning with Analytic Tableaux and*

Related Methods, International Conference, TABLEAUX 2005, volume 3702 of *Lecture Notes in Computer Science*, pages 78–92. Springer, 2005. doi:10.1007/11554554_8.

15. James Brotherston and Alex Simpson. Sequent calculi for induction and infinite descent. *Journal of Logic and Computation*, 21(6):1177–1216, 2011. doi:10.1093/logcom/exq052.

16. Venanzio Capretta. General recursion via coinductive types. *Logical Methods in Computer Science*, 1(2), 2005. doi:10.2168/LMCS-1(2:1)2005.

17. Arthur Charguéraud. Pretty-big-step semantics. In Matthias Felleisen and Philippa Gardner, editors, *ESOP 2013 - European Symposium on Programming*, volume 7792 of *Lecture Notes in Computer Science*, pages 41–60, Berlin, 2013. Springer. doi:10.1007/978-3-642-37036-6_3.

18. Patrick Cousot and Radhia Cousot. Inductive definitions, semantics and abstract interpretations. In Ravi Sethi, editor, *POPL'92 - ACM Symp. on Principles of Programming Languages*, pages 83–94, New York, 1992. ACM Press. doi:10.1145/143165.143184.

19. Francesco Dagnino. Coaxioms: flexible coinductive definitions by inference systems. *Logical Methods in Computer Science*, 15(1), 2019. doi:10.23638/LMCS-15(1:26)2019.

20. Nils Anders Danielsson. Operational semantics using the partiality monad. In Peter Thiemann and Robby Bruce Findler, editors, *ICFP'12 - International Conference on Functional Programming 2012*, pages 127–138, New York, 2012. ACM Press. doi:10.1145/2364527.2364546.

21. Rocco De Nicola and Matthew Hennessy. Testing equivalences for processes. *Theoretical Computer Science*, 34(1):83 – 133, 1984. doi:https://doi.org/10.1016/0304-3975(84)90113-0.

22. Mariangiola Dezani-Ciancaglini, Ugo de'Liguoro, and Adolfo Piperno. A filter model for concurrent lambda-calculus. *SIAM Journal of Computing*, 27(5):1376–1419, 1998. doi:10.1137/S0097539794275860.

23. Mariangiola Dezani-Ciancaglini, Paola Giannini, and Betti Venneri. Intersection types in Java: Back to the future. In Tiziana Margaria, Susanne Graf, and Kim G. Larsen, editors, *Models, Mindsets, Meta: The What, the How, and the Why Not? - Essays Dedicated to Bernhard Steffen on the Occasion of His 60th Birthday*, volume 11200 of *Lecture Notes in Computer Science*, pages 68–86. Springer, 2018. doi:10.1007/978-3-030-22348-9_6.

24. Erik Ernst, Klaus Ostermann, and William R. Cook. A virtual class calculus. In J. Gregory Morrisett and Simon L. Peyton Jones, editors, *POPL'06 - ACM Symp. on Principles of Programming Languages*, pages 270–282. ACM, 2006. doi:10.1145/1111037.1111062.

25. James Gosling, Bill Joy, Guy L. Steele, Gilad Bracha, and Alex Buckley. *The Java Language Specification, Java SE 8 Edition*. Addison-Wesley Professional, Boston, 1st edition, 2014.

26. Grzegorz Grudzinski. A minimal system of disjunctive properties for strictness analysis. In José D. P. Rolim, Andrei Z. Broder, Andrea Corradini, Roberto Gorrieri, Reiko Heckel, Juraj Hromkovic, Ugo Vaccaro, and J. B. Wells, editors, *ICALP Workshops*, pages 305–322, Waterloo, Ontario, Canada, 2000. Carleton Scientific.

27. Atsushi Igarashi, Benjamin C. Pierce, and Philip Wadler. Featherweight Java: A minimal core calculus for Java and GJ. *ACM Transactions on Programming Languages and Systems*, 23(3):396–450, 2001. doi:10.1145/503502.503505.

28. Gilles Kahn. Natural semantics. In Franz-Josef Brandenburg, Guy Vidal-Naquet, and Martin Wirsing, editors, *STACS'87 - Symposium on Theoretical Aspects of Computer Science*, volume 247 of *Lecture Notes in Computer Science*, pages 22–39, Berlin, 1987. Springer. doi:10.1007/BFb0039592.

29. Jaroslaw D. M. Kusmierek and Viviana Bono. Big-step operational semantics revisited. *Fundamenta Informaticae*, 103(1-4):137–172, 2010. doi:10.3233/FI-2010-323.

30. Xavier Leroy and Hervé Grall. Coinductive big-step operational semantics. *Information and Computation*, 207(2):284–304, 2009. doi:10.1016/j.ic.2007.12.004.

31. Robin Milner. A theory of type polymorphism in programming. *Journal of Computer and System Sciences*, 17(3):348–375, 1978. doi:10.1016/0022-0000(78)90014-4.

32. Scott Owens, Magnus O. Myreen, Ramana Kumar, and Yong Kiam Tan. Functional big-step semantics. In Peter Thiemann, editor, *ESOP 2016 - European Symposium on Programming*, volume 9632 of *Lecture Notes in Computer Science*, pages 589–615, Berlin, 2016. Springer. doi:10.1007/978-3-662-49498-1_23.

33. Benjamin C. Pierce. *Types and programming languages*. MIT Press, Cambridge, Massachusetts, 2002.

34. Gordon D. Plotkin. A structural approach to operational semantics. Technical report, Aarhus University, 1981.

35. Gordon D. Plotkin. A structural approach to operational semantics. *Journal of Logic and Algebraic Programming*, 60-61:17–139, 2004.

36. Casper Bach Poulsen and Peter D. Mosses. Flag-based big-step semantics. *Journal of Logic and Algebraic Methods in Programming*, 88:174–190, 2017. doi:10.1016/j.jlamp.2016.05.001.

37. John C. Reynolds. Definitional interpreters for higher-order programming languages. *Higher-Order and Symbolic Computation*, 11(4):363–397, 1998. doi:10.1023/A:1010027404223.

38. Jan J. M. M. Rutten. Universal coalgebra: a theory of systems. *Theoretical Computer Science*, 249(1):3–80, 2000. doi:10.1016/S0304-3975(00)00056-6.

39. Jeremy Siek. Type safety in three easy lemmas. 2013. URL: http://siek.blogspot.com/2013/05/type-safety-in-three-easy-lemmas.html.

40. A. K. Wright and M. Felleisen. A syntactic approach to type soundness. *Information and Computation*, 115(1):38–94, 1994.

Liberate Abstract Garbage Collection from the Stack by Decomposing the Heap

Kimball Germane[1]([✉]) and Michael D. Adams[2]

[1] Brigham Young University, Provo UT, USA kimball@cs.byu.edu
[2] University of Michigan, Ann Arbor MI, USA adamsmda@umich.edu

Abstract. Abstract garbage collection and the use of pushdown systems each enhance the precision of control-flow analysis (CFA). However, their respective needs conflict: abstract garbage collection requires the stack but pushdown systems obscure it. Though several existing techniques address this conflict, none take full advantage of the underlying interplay. In this paper, we dissolve this conflict with a technique which exploits the precision of pushdown systems to decompose the heap across the continuation. This technique liberates abstract garbage collection from the stack, increasing its effectiveness and the compositionality of its host analysis. We generalize our approach to apply compositional treatment to abstract timestamps which induces the context abstraction of m-CFA, an abstraction more precise than k-CFA's for many common programming patterns.

Keywords: Control-Flow Analysis · Abstract Garbage Collection · Pushdown Systems

1 Introduction

Among the many enhancements available to improve the precision of control-flow analysis (CFA), abstract garbage collection and pushdown models of control flow stand out as particularly effective ones. But their combination is non-trivial.

Abstract garbage collection (GC) [10] is the result of applying standard GC—which calculates the heap data reachable from a root set derived from a given environment and continuation—to an abstract semantics. Though it operates in the same way as *concrete* GC, abstract GC has a different effect on the semantics to which it's applied. Concrete GC is semantically irrelevant in that it has no effect on a program's observable behavior.[3] Abstract GC, on the other hand, is semantically relevant in that, by eliminating some merging in the abstract heap, it prevents a utilizing CFA from conflating some distinct heap data. In the setting of a higher-order language, where data can represent control, this superior approximation of data translates to a superior approximation of control as well, manifest by the CFA exploring fewer infeasible execution paths.

Pushdown models of control flow [16,3] encode the call–return relation of a program's flow of execution as precisely as an unbounded control stack would

---

[3] It is irrelevant only if space consumption is unobservable, as is typical.

© The Author(s) 2020
P. Müller (Ed.): ESOP 2020, LNCS 12075, pp. 197–223, 2020.
https://doi.org/10.1007/978-3-030-44914-8_8

allow. Consequently, and in contrast to the finite-state models which preceded them, pushdown models enable a utilizing CFA—a *stack-precise* CFA—to avoid relating a given return to any but its originating call. Thus, pushdown models also induce CFAs which explore fewer infeasible execution paths.

Not only do abstract GC and pushdown systems each enhance the control precision of CFA, they also appear to do so in complementary ways. Is it possible for a CFA to use both and gain the benefits of each? This question's answer is not immediate, as these techniques have competing requirements: abstract GC must examine the stack to extract the root set of reachability but the use of pushdown models obscures the control stack to the abstract semantics.

This question has been addressed by two techniques: The first *introspective* technique [4] introduces a primitive operation into the analyzing machine which introspects the stack and delivers the set of frames which may be live; this technique has a variety of alternative formulations, some of which alter its complexity–precision profile [8, 7]. The second technique [1], which modifies the first to work with definitional interpreters, dictates that the analyzer implement a set-passing style abstract semantics where each passed set contains the heap addresses present in the continuation at that point. Each of these techniques reconciles the competing requirements of abstract GC and pushdown models of control flow and allows the utilizing CFA to enjoy the precision-enhancing benefits of both at once.

However, each of these techniques—hereafter referred to collectively as *pushdown GC*—yields a setting in which abstract GC and pushdown models of control flow merely coexist. In contrast, this paper prescribes a technique which *exploits* the pushdown model of control flow to enable a new mode of garbage collection—*compositional garbage collection*—which does not require the ability to inspect the continuation.

The key observation is that, in a stack-precise CFA, the heap present at the point of a call is in scope at the point of its return. Thus, the analysis can offload some of the contents of the callee's heap to the caller's—in particular, the data irrelevant to the callee's execution. When this offloading is performed, the final heap of the callee (just as it returns) is incomplete with respect to subsequent execution. But, since the caller's heap is in scope at this point, the analysis can reconstitute the subsequent heap by combining the caller's heap with the callee's final heap.

The data *relevant* to the callee's execution is the data reachable from its local environment and excludes the data reachable from its continuation alone. Offloading heap data, then, consists of GC-ing each callee's heap with respect to its local environment only. When one applies this practice consistently to all calls, one associates with each active call not a heap but a *heap fragment*, effectively decomposing the heap across the continuation. As we will show, careful separation and combination of these heap fragments can perfectly simulate the presence of the full heap.

This liberation of GC from the continuation has several consequences for the host CFA.

1. It simplifies both the formalization and implementation of the host CFA, since it can omit the relatively complex machinery to ensure the continuation-resident addresses are at hand.
2. It reduces the host CFA's workload by not requiring it to traverse full heaps. Earl *et al.* [4] observe that traversal of large heaps observably increases analysis time.
3. It recovers *context irrelevance* in the host CFA's semantics, a property we discuss more in Section 3.4 and Section 6.1.
4. It enables purely-local execution summaries which makes memoization much more effective.

In sum, relative to pushdown GC, compositional GC offers quantitative benefits to the host CFA, being strictly more powerful, as well as qualitative.

1.1   Examples

Let's look at an example where compositional GC makes memoization more effective. Consider the following Scheme program

```
(let* ([id (lambda (x) x)]
       [y (id 42)]
       [z (id y)])
  (+ y z))
```

which calls id twice, each time on 42.

We would hope that a CFA would be able to memoize its analysis of the first call and, upon recognizing that the second call is semantically-identical, reuse its results. However, contemporary CFAs will not because each call is made with a different heap—the second call's heap includes a binding for y that the first's doesn't. Moreover, this distinction persists even with pushdown GC since y's binding is needed to continue execution after the call. Since CFAs have no means but reachability to determine what is relevant to a given execution point, and since what is relevant constitutes a memoization key, pushdown GC is too weak to identify these two calls.

In contrast, a CFA with compositional GC produces a heap fragment for each call which is closed over only data reachable from the local environment—for a call, the procedure and argument values themselves. Accordingly, from its perspective, these two calls are identical and specify a single memoization key.

Now let's look at an example where compositional GC keeps co-live bindings of the same variable distinct. Consider the following Scheme program

```
(letrec ([f (lambda (x)
              (if (prime? x)
                  (let ([y (f (+ x 1))])
                    (+ x y))
                  x))])
  (f 2))
```

which defines and calls a recursive procedure f.

Concrete evaluation of this program proceeds first calls f with 2, and then 3, and then 4, returning 4, and then $3 + 4 = 7$ and then $2 + 7 = 9$. The procedure f is properly recursive—so these calls are nested—and, after f is called with 4 but before it returns, three distinct bindings of x are live. Moreover, since each binding of x is needed until its binding call returns, each is continuation-reachable and therefore not claimed by GC. These facts and limitations translate to the analysis setting: a CFA will discover multiple co-live bindings of x which persist in the face of pushdown GC. Consequently, even with pushdown GC, a CFA will in general join these bindings to some degree, concluding that x can be 2 whenever it can be 3 and can be 3 whenever it can be 4.

In contrast, just before a CFA with compositional GC performs each call to f, it GCs with respect to the operator and argument values which, in each case, consist of the closure of f (which reaches only itself in the heap) and a number (which doesn't reach anything). Thus, each binding to x is the first in its respective heap fragment and doesn't interfere with the live bindings of x in other heap fragments. Using a numeric abstraction in which arithmetic operations propagate but do not introduce approximation [1], a CFA with compositional GC will produce an exact answer (whereas one with pushdown GC will not).

1.2   Generalizing the Approach

The conventional treatment of the heap by CFA is to thread it through execution, allowing it to evolve as it goes. In contrast, compositional GC advocates that the CFA treat the heap with the same discipline that it treats the environment: saved at the evaluation of a subexpression and restored when its evaluation completes and its value is delivered. That is, compositional GC is achieved by, in effect, treating the heap compositionally.

What happens if we impose the same compositional discipline on other threaded components, such as the timestamp? In that case, we move from the last-k-call-sites[4] context abstraction of k-CFA [14] to the top-m-stack-frames[5] context abstraction of m-CFA [11] This appearance of m-CFA's abstraction in a stack-precise CFA is the first such, to our knowledge.

With compositional treatment of both the heap and timestamp, we arrive at a stack-precise CFA which treats each of its components compositionally. This treatment also leads to a CFA closer to being compositional in the sense that the analysis of a compound expression is a function of the analyses of its constituent parts. Accordingly, we refer to such a stack-precise CFA as a *compositional control-flow analysis*.

The remainder of the paper is as follows. We first introduce the syntax of the language we will use throughout the paper in Section 2. We then discuss the enhancements of perfect stack precision, garbage collection, and their combination in Section 3. We then proceed through a series of semantics which transition

---

[4] as in, *most-recent k* call sites
[5] as in, *youngest m* stack frames

from a threaded heap to a compositional, garbage-collected heap in Section 4. We then abstract the compositional semantics to obtain our CFA in Section 5. We discuss the ramifications of the compositional treatment of each of the heap and abstract time in Section 6. We finally discuss related work in Section 7 and conclusions and future work in Section 8.

Note In the remainder of the paper, we use the standard term *store* to refer to the analysis component which models the heap. Thus, we will describe our technique as, e.g., *treating stores compositionally.*

2   A-Normal Form λ-Calculus

For presentation, we keep the language small: we use a unary λ-calculus in $\mathcal{A}$-normal form [5], the grammar of which is given below.

$$Exp \ni e ::= ce \mid \mathsf{let}\, x = ce \,\mathsf{in}\, e$$
$$CExp \ni ce ::= ae \mid (ae_0\, ae_1) \mid \mathsf{set!}\, x\, ae$$
$$AExp \ni ae ::= x \mid \lambda x.e$$
$$Var \ni x \quad [\text{an infinite set of variables}]$$

A proper expression e is a *call expression* ce or a let-expression, which binds a variable to the result of a call expression. (Restricting the bound expression to a call expression prevents let-expressions from nesting there, a hallmark of $\mathcal{A}$-normal form.) A call expression ce is an *atomic expression* ae, an application, or a set!-expression. An atomic expression ae is a variable reference or a λ abstraction.

Atomic expressions are trivial [13]. We include set!-expressions to produce mutative effects that must be threaded through evaluation. (The approach we present in this paper can also handle more-general forms of mutation, such as boxes.) For our purposes, we consider a set!-expression "serious" [13] since it has an effect on the store.

A program is a closed expression; we assume (without loss of generality) that programs are alphatised—that is, that each bound variable has a distinct name.

Expressions of the form $(ae_0\, ae_1)$ for some ae_0 and ae_1 constitute the set *App*; similarly, expressions of the form $\lambda x.e$ for some x and e constitute the set *Lam*.

3   Background

In this section, we review abstract garbage collection and the k-CFA context abstraction. We begin by introducing a small-step concrete semantics which defines the ground truth of evaluation.

3.1   Semantic Domains

First, we introduce some semantic components that we will use heavily through-out the rest of the paper.

$$v \in \mathit{Val} = \mathit{Lam} \times \mathit{Env} \qquad\qquad \rho \in \mathit{Env} = \mathit{Var} \rightharpoonup \mathit{Time}$$

$$t \in \mathit{Time} = \mathit{App}^* \qquad\qquad a \in \mathit{Address} = \mathit{Var} \times \mathit{Time}$$

$$\sigma \in \mathit{Store} = \mathit{Address} \rightharpoonup \mathit{Val} \qquad\qquad \kappa \in \mathit{Cont} ::= \mathsf{mt} \mid \mathsf{lt}(x, \rho, e, \kappa)$$

A value v is closure, a pair of a λ abstraction and an environment which closes it. An environment ρ is a finite map from each variable x to a time t; a time t is a finite sequence of call sites. Let $\rho|_e$ denote the restriction of the domain of the environment ρ to the free variables of e. An address a is a pair of a variable and time and a store σ is a map from addresses to values. A continuation κ is either the empty continuation or the continuation of a let binding.

3.2   Concrete Semantics

We define our concrete semantics as a small-step relation over abstract machine states. The state space of our machine is given formally as follows.

$$\varsigma \in \mathit{State} = \mathit{Eval} + \mathit{Apply}$$

$$\varsigma_{\mathsf{ev}} \in \mathit{Eval} = \mathit{Exp} \times \mathit{Env} \times \mathit{Store} \times \mathit{Cont} \times \mathit{Time}$$

$$\varsigma_{\mathsf{ap}} \in \mathit{Apply} = \mathit{Val} \times \mathit{Store} \times \mathit{Cont} \times \mathit{Time}$$

Machine states come in two variants. An *Eval* machine state represents a point in execution in which an expression will be evaluated; it contains registers for an expression e, its closing environment ρ, the store σ (modelling the heap), the continuation κ (modelling the stack), and the time t. An *Apply* machine state represents a point in execution at which a value is in hand and must be delivered to the continuation; it contains registers for the value v to deliver, the store σ, the continuation κ, and the time t.

Figure 1 contains the definitions of two relations over machine states, the union of which constitutes the small-step relation. The $\rightarrow_{\mathsf{ev}}$ relation transitions an *Eval* state to its successor. The LET rule pushes a continuation frame to save the bound variable, environment, and body expression. The resultant *Eval* state is poised to evaluate the bound expression ce. The CALL rule first uses aeval defined

$$\mathsf{aeval}(\sigma, \rho, x) = \sigma(x, \rho(x)) \qquad\qquad \mathsf{aeval}(\sigma, \rho, \lambda x.e) = (\lambda x.e, \rho|_{\lambda x.e})$$

to obtain values for each of the operator and argument. It then increments the time, extends the store and environment with the incremented time, and arranges evaluation of the operator body at the incremented time. The SET! rule remaps a location in the store designated by a given variable (which is resolved in the environment) to a value obtained by aeval. It returns the identity function.

LET

$$\frac{}{\text{ev}(\text{let } x = ce \text{ in } e, \rho, \sigma, \kappa, t) \rightarrow_{\text{ev}} \text{ev}(ce, \rho, \sigma, \text{lt}(x, \rho, e, \kappa), t)}$$

CALL

$$\frac{(\lambda x.e, \rho') = \text{aeval}(\sigma, \rho, ae_0) \qquad v = \text{aeval}(\sigma, \rho, ae_1) \qquad t' = (ae_0 \ ae_1) :: t}{\sigma' = \sigma[(x, t') \mapsto v] \qquad \rho'' = \rho'[x \mapsto t']}{\text{ev}((ae_0 \ ae_1), \rho, \sigma, \kappa, t) \rightarrow_{\text{ev}} \text{ev}(e, \rho'', \sigma', \kappa, t')}$$

SET!

$$\frac{v = \text{aeval}(\sigma, \rho, ae) \qquad a = (x, \rho(x)) \qquad \sigma' = \sigma[a \mapsto v]}{\text{ev}(\text{set! } x \ ae, \rho, \sigma, \kappa, t) \rightarrow_{\text{ev}} \text{ap}((\lambda x.x, \bot), \sigma', \kappa, t)}$$

ATOMIC

$$\frac{v = \text{aeval}(\sigma, \rho, ae)}{\text{ev}(ae, \rho, \sigma, \kappa, t) \rightarrow_{\text{ev}} \text{ap}(v, \sigma, \kappa, t)}$$

APPLY

$$\frac{\rho' = \rho[x \mapsto t] \qquad \sigma' = \sigma[(x, t) \mapsto v]}{\text{ap}(v, \sigma, \text{lt}(x, \rho, e, \kappa), t) \rightarrow_{\text{ap}} \text{ev}(e, \rho', \sigma', \kappa, t)}$$

Fig. 1. Small-step abstract machine semantics

The ATOMIC rule evaluates an atomic expression. The APPLY rule applies a continuation to a value, extending the environment and store and arranging for the evaluation of the let body.

We *inject* a program pr into the initial evaluation state $\text{ev}(pr, \bot, \bot, \text{mt}, \langle\rangle)$ which arranges evaluation in the empty environment, empty store, halt continuation, and empty time.

Adding Garbage Collection At this point, we have a small-step relation defining execution by abstract machine and are perfectly positioned to apply, e.g., the Abstracting Abstract Machines (AAM) [15] recipe to *abstract* the semantics and thereby obtain a sound, computable CFA. Before doing so, however, we will extend our semantics to garbage-collect the store on each transition. This extension has no semantic effect in the concrete semantics but, as we will discuss, greatly increases the precision of the abstracted (or, simply, *abstract*) semantics.

We extend the semantics by defining two garbage collection transitions, one which collects an *Eval* state and one which collects an *Apply* state. Because our abstract machine explicitly models local environments, heaps (via stores), and stacks (via continuations), we can apply a copying collector to perform garbage collection.

First, we define a family root of metafunctions to extract the reachability root set from values, environments, and continuations.

$$\text{root}_v(\lambda x.e, \rho) = \text{root}_\rho(\rho) \qquad\qquad \text{root}_\kappa(\text{mt}) = \emptyset$$
$$\text{root}_\rho(\rho) = \rho \qquad\qquad \text{root}_\kappa(\text{lt}(x, \rho, e, \kappa)) = \text{root}_\rho(\rho|_e) \cup \text{root}_\kappa(\kappa)$$

The root_v metafunction extracts the root addresses from a closure by using root_ρ to extract the root addresses from its environment. By the root_ρ metafunction, the root addresses of an environment are simply the variable–time pairs that define it—that is, the definition of root_ρ views its argument ρ extensionally as a set of addresses. The root_κ metafunction extracts the root addresses from a continuation. The empty continuation has no root addresses whereas the root addresses of a non-empty continuation are those of its stored environment (restricted to the free variables of the expression it closes) combined with those of the continuation it extends.

Next, we define a reachability relation $\rightarrow_\sigma$ parameterized by a store σ and over addresses by

$$a_0 \rightarrow_\sigma a_1 \Leftrightarrow a_1 \in \mathsf{root}_v(\sigma(a_0))$$

We then define the reachability of a root set with respect to a store

$$\mathcal{R}(\sigma, A) = \{a' : a \in A, a \rightarrow_\sigma^* a'\}$$

where $\rightarrow_\sigma^*$ is the reflexive, transitive closure of $\rightarrow_\sigma$. From here, we obtain the transitions

GC-EVAL
$$\frac{A = \mathsf{root}_\rho(\rho|_e) \cup \mathsf{root}_\kappa(\kappa) \qquad \sigma' = \sigma|_{\mathcal{R}(\sigma, A)}}{\mathsf{ev}(e, \rho, \sigma, \kappa, t) \rightarrow_{\mathsf{GC}} \mathsf{ev}(e, \rho, \sigma', \kappa, t)}$$

GC-APPLY
$$\frac{A = \mathsf{root}_v(v) \cup \mathsf{root}_\kappa(\kappa) \qquad \sigma' = \sigma|_{\mathcal{R}(\sigma, A)}}{\mathsf{ap}(v, \sigma, \kappa, t) \rightarrow_{\mathsf{GC}} \mathsf{ap}(v, \sigma', \kappa, t)}$$

where $\sigma|_{\mathcal{R}(\sigma, A)}$ is σ restricted to the reachable addresses $\mathcal{R}(\sigma, A)$. We compose this garbage-collecting transition with each of $\rightarrow_{\mathsf{ev}}$ and $\rightarrow_{\mathsf{ap}}$. Altogether, the garbage-collecting semantics are given by $\rightarrow_{\mathsf{GC}} \circ [\rightarrow_{\mathsf{ev}} \cup \rightarrow_{\mathsf{ap}}]$.

3.3   Abstracting Abstract Machines with Garbage Collection

Now that we have a small-step abstract machine semantics with GC, we are ready to apply the AAM recipe to obtain a sound, computable CFA with GC.

We apply the AAM recipe in two steps.

First, we refactor the state space so that all inductively-defined components are redirected through the store. Practically, this refactoring has the effect of allocating continuations in the store. For our semantics, this refactoring yields the state space $State_{SA}$ defined

$$State_{SA} = Eval_{SA} + Apply_{SA}$$
$$Eval_{SA} = Exp \times Env \times Store_{SA} \times ContAddr \times Time$$
$$Apply_{SA} = Store_{SA} \times ContAddr \times Val \times Time$$

in which a continuation address $\alpha \in ContAddr$ replaces the continuation drawn from $Cont$. The space of continuations becomes defined by

$$\kappa_{SA} \in Cont_{SA} ::= \mathsf{mt} \mid \mathsf{lt}(x, \rho, e, \alpha)$$

and of stores by

$$Store_{SA} = Address + ContAddr \rightharpoonup Val + Cont_{SA}$$

Not reflected in this structure is the typical constraint that an address a will only ever locate a value and a continuation address α will only ever locate a continuation.

Second, we finitely partition the unbounded address space of the store and treat the constituent sets as abstract addresses (via some finite representative). Practically, this partitioning is achieved by limiting the time t to at most k call sites where k becomes a parameter of the CFA (leading to the designation k-CFA). Any addresses which agree on the k-length prefix of their time component are identified and the finite representative for this set of addresses uses simply that prefix. Accordingly, we define an abstract time domain $\widehat{Time} = Time^{\leq k}$ and let it reverberate through the state space definitions, obtaining

$$\widehat{State} = \widehat{Eval} + \widehat{Apply}$$

$$\widehat{Eval} = Exp \times \widehat{Env} \times \widehat{Store} \times \widehat{ContAddr} \times \widehat{Time}$$

$$\widehat{Apply} = \widehat{Store} \times \widehat{ContAddr} \times \widehat{Val} \times \widehat{Time}$$

(in which we allow the definition of $ContAddr$ to depend, directly or not, on that of $Time$).

Finitization of the address space is key to producing a computable CFA. Practically, however, it means that some values located previously by distinct addresses will after be located by the same abstract address. When this conflation occurs, the CFA must behave as if either access was intended; this behavior is manifested by non-deterministically choosing the value located by a particular address. Because our language is higher-order, this non-determinism also affects the control flows the CFA considers. This effect is evident in the CALL rule defined

CALL
$$\frac{(\lambda x.e, \hat{\rho}') \in \widehat{aeval}(\hat{\sigma}, \hat{\rho}, ae_0) \quad \hat{v} = \widehat{aeval}(\hat{\sigma}, \hat{\rho}, ae_1) \quad \hat{t}' = \lfloor (ae_0\, ae_1) :: \hat{t} \rfloor_k}{\hat{\sigma}' = \hat{\sigma}[(x, \hat{t}') \mapsto \hat{v}] \quad \hat{\rho}'' = \hat{\rho}'[x \mapsto \hat{t}']}{\mathsf{ev}((ae_0\, ae_1), \hat{\rho}, \hat{\sigma}, \hat{\alpha}, \hat{t}) \rightarrow_{\mathsf{ev}} \mathsf{ev}(e, \hat{\rho}'', \hat{\sigma}', \hat{\alpha}, \hat{t}')}$$

which is structurally identical to that of the concrete semantics except in two respects:

1. The abstract evaluation of the operator ae_0 may yield multiple closures and the CFA considers the application of each. Due to the approximation finitization introduces, not every abstractly-applied closure will necessarily appear in a compatible call under the concrete semantics. Such closures, initiating spurious control paths, waste analysis effort and this waste compounds as the exploration of spurious paths leads to the discovery of yet more.
2. The abstract time component is limited to length at most k (obtained by $\lfloor \cdot \rfloor_k$).

In short, a finite address space introduces a value approximation and, in a higher-order language such as ours, a control approximation as well.

While the strategy to store-allocate continuations facilitates the systematic abstraction process of AAM, it also imposes a similar approximation on the continuation space as it does the value space. In consequence, a CFA obtained by AAM approximates not only the value and control flow of the program, but the return flow as well. Return-flow approximation is manifest as a single abstract call returning to caller contexts that did not make that call.[6]

On the other hand, because the AAM abstraction process preserves the overall structure of the state space—in particular, the explicit models of the local environment, heap, and stack—applying GC to an abstract state is straightforward. In addition, GC in the abstract semantics improves precision and reduces the workload of the analyzer [10].

To see how GC improves precision, consider a 0CFA (that is, $[k = 1]$CFA) without GC of the Scheme program

```
(let* ([id (lambda (x) x)]
       [y (id 42)]
       [z (id 35)])
   z)
```

at the call (id 42). As the abstract call is made, the abstract value 42 is stored an address a derived from x. Once the call returns, the abstract value 42 still resides in the heap at a which is now unreachable. However, as the abstract call (id 35) is made, the address a is derived again (a consequence of the finite address space), and the abstract value 35 is merged with the abstract value 42 which persists at a. Since the value at a is returned and becomes the result of the program, the CFA reports that the program results in either 42 or 35.

Now consider a 0CFA with GC of the same program. Once the call (id 42) returns and α becomes unreachable, its heap entry is reaped by GC. The abstract call (id 35) then allocates the abstract value 35 at a which is, from the allocator's perspective, a fresh heap cell. Consequently, the CFA precisely reports that the program results in 35.

The above example also illustrates how GC reduces the workload of the analyzer. Though we didn't call it out, when using a naive continuation allocator without GC, the abstract call (id 35) not only correctly returns to the continuation binding z but also spuriously returns to the continuation binding y. In this example, this spurious control (return) flow does no more damage to the precision of 0CFA's approximation of the final program result, but does cause it to explore infeasible control flows which damage the precision of the 0CFA's approximation of intermediate values. GC prevents the spurious flows in this example from arising at all; however, in general, it does not prevent all spurious return flows.

---

[6] P4F [6] uses a particular continuation allocator which is able to avoid return-flow approximation. However, the P4F technique applies only when the store is globally-widened and, in such a setting, no data ever becomes unreachable which renders GC completely ineffective.

3.4   Stack-Precise CFA with Garbage Collection

In contrast to an AAM-derived analysis, a stack-precise CFA does not approximate the return flow of the program. A stack-precise CFA achieves this feat by modelling control flow with a pushdown system which allows it to precisely match returns with their corresponding calls. However, to do so, it requires full control of the continuation which we abide by factoring it out of the state space, obtaining

$$State_{PD} = Eval_{PD} + Apply_{PD}$$
$$Eval_{PD} = Exp \times Env \times Store \times Time$$
$$Apply_{PD} = Val \times Store \times Time$$

before we abstract it to produce a CFA. (Some CFAs factor the store out of machine states to be managed globally, part of *widening the store*. In a sense, factoring out the continuation is part of *widening the continuation*.) Without a continuation component, an $Eval_{PD}$ state is an *evaluation configuration* and an $Apply_{PD}$ state is an *evaluation result*. Except for the presence of the time component, $State_{PD}$ exhibits precisely the configuration and result shapes one finds in many stack-precise CFAs [17, 8, 1, 18].

However, factoring the continuation out and ceding control of it to the analysis presents an obstacle to abstract GC, which needs to extract the root set of reachable addresses from it. Earl *et al.* [4] developed a technique whereby the analysis could introspect the continuation and extract the root set of reachable addresses from the continuation. Johnson and Van Horn [8] reformulated this *incomplete* technique for an operational setting and offered a *complete*—albeit theoretically more-expensive—technique capable of more precision. Johnson *et al.* [7] unified these techniques within an expanded framework. Darais *et al.* [1] then showed that the *Abstracting Definitional Interpreters*-approach—currently the state of the art—is compatible with the complete technique by including the set of stack root addresses as a component in the evaluation configuration.

Context Irrelevance These techniques indeed reconcile the conflicting needs of GC and stack-precise control yielding an analysis which enjoys the precision-enhancing benefits of each. However, the addition of garbage collection causes the resultant analysis to violate *context irrelevance* [8], the property that the evaluation of a configuration is independent of its continuation. In terms of the concrete semantics of Section 3.2, context irrelevance is the property that $\mathsf{ev}(e, \rho, \sigma, \kappa, t) \to^+ \mathsf{ap}(\sigma', \kappa, v)$ if and only if $\mathsf{ev}(e, \rho, \sigma, \kappa', t) \to^+ \mathsf{ap}(\sigma', \kappa', v)$ for any κ and κ'.

The incomplete and complete techniques to achieve stack-precise abstract GC each violate context irrelevance. Under the incomplete technique, abstract GC prevents spurious paths from being explored and changes the store yielded by those that are explored. Thus, the abstract evaluation of a configuration becomes dependent on (the root set of reachable addresses embedded in) its continuation. The complete technique, achieved by introducing the set of root addresses as a component in the evaluation configuration, vacuously restores context irrelevance by distinguishing otherwise-identical configurations based on the continuation. That is, the states $\mathsf{ev}(e, \rho, \sigma, \kappa, t)$ and $\mathsf{ev}(e, \rho, \sigma, \kappa', t)$ with identical configurations but distinct continuations become the continuation-less evaluation configurations $\mathsf{ev}(e, \rho, \sigma, A, t)$ and $\mathsf{ev}(e, \rho, \sigma, A', t)$ with distinct root address sets A and A'. This address set is a close approximation of the continuation and effectively makes the control context relevant to evaluation.

3.5   The k-CFA Context Abstraction

In the concrete semantics, the time component t serves two purposes. The first purpose is to provide the allocator with a source of freshness, so that when the allocator must furnish a heap cell for a variable bound previously in execution, it is able to furnish a distinct one. Were freshness the only constraint on t, the *Time* domain could simply consist of $\mathbb{N}$. In anticipation of its role in the downstream CFA, the time component assumes a second purpose which is to capture some notion of the context in which execution is occurring. The hope is that the notion of context it captures is semantically meaningful so that, when an unbounded set of times are identified by the process of abstraction, each address, which is qualified by such an abstracted time, locates a semantically-coherent set of values.

To get a better idea of what notion of context our treatment of time captures, let's examine how our concrete semantics treats time, as dictated by k-CFA. Time begins as the empty sequence $\langle\rangle$. It is passed unchanged across all *Eval* transitions, save one, and the *Apply* transition. The exception is the CALL transition, which instead passes the (at-most-)k-length prefix of the application prepended to the incoming time. Hence, the k-CFA context abstraction is the k-most-recent calls made in execution history.

In Section 6.2, we consider the ramifications of threading the time component through evaluation and compare it to an alternative treatment.

4   From Threaded to Compositional Stores

In this section, we present a series of four semantics that gradually transition from a threaded treatment of stores without GC to a compositional treatment of stores with GC. We define each of these semantics in terms of big-step judgments of (or close to) the form $\sigma, \rho, t \vdash e \Downarrow (v, \sigma')$. This judgment expresses that the *evaluation configuration* consisting of the expression e under the store σ, environment ρ, and timestamp t evaluates to the *evaluation result* consisting of the value v and the store σ'. When discussing the evaluation of e, we will refer to σ as the incoming store and σ' as the resultant store. We will also refer to the time component t as the *binding context* since, in the big-step semantics, its connection to the history of execution becomes more distant.

Formulating our semantics in big-step style offers two advantages to our setting: First, we can readily express them by big-step definitional interpreters at which point we can apply systematic abstraction techniques [1, 18] to obtain corresponding CFAs exhibiting perfect stack precision. Second, they emphasize the availability of the configuration store at the delivery point of the evaluation result; this availability is crucial to our ability to shift to a compositional treatment of the store.

4.1 Threaded-Store Semantics

To orient ourselves to the big-step setting, we present the reference semantics for our language in big-step style in Figure 2. This reference semantics is equivalent to the reference semantics given in small-step style in Section 3.2 except that there is no corresponding APPLY rule; its responsibility—to deliver a value to a continuation—is handled implicitly by the big-step formulation. In terms of big-step semantics, this reference semantics is characterized by the threading of the store through each rule; the resultant store of evaluation is the configuration store plus the allocation and mutation incurred during evaluation. Hence, we refer to this semantics as the *threaded-store* semantics. We use natural numbers as store subscripts in each rule to emphasize the store's monotonic increase.

LET
$$\frac{\sigma_0, \rho, t \vdash ce \Downarrow (v_0, \sigma_1) \qquad \rho' = \rho[x \mapsto t] \qquad \sigma_2 = \sigma_1[(x, t) \mapsto v_0] \qquad \sigma_2, \rho', t \vdash e \Downarrow (v, \sigma_3)}{\sigma_0, \rho, t \vdash \mathsf{let}\, x = ce \,\mathsf{in}\, e \Downarrow (v, \sigma_3)}$$

CALL
$$\frac{\begin{array}{c}((\lambda x.e, \rho_0), \sigma_1) = \mathsf{aeval}(\sigma_0, \rho, ae_0) \\ (v_1, \sigma_2) = \mathsf{aeval}(\sigma_1, \rho, ae_1) \qquad t' = (ae_0\, ae_1) :: t \\ \rho_1 = \rho_0[x \mapsto t'] \qquad \sigma_3 = \sigma_2[(x, t') \mapsto v_1] \qquad \sigma_3, \rho_1, t' \vdash e \Downarrow (v, \sigma_4)\end{array}}{\sigma_0, \rho, t \vdash (ae_0\, ae_1) \Downarrow (v, \sigma_4)}$$

SET!
$$\frac{(v, \sigma_1) = \mathsf{aeval}(\sigma_0, \rho, ae) \qquad \sigma_1 = \sigma_0[(x, \rho(x)) \mapsto v]}{\sigma_0, \rho, t \vdash \mathsf{set!}\, x\, ae \Downarrow ((\lambda x.x, \bot), \sigma_1)}$$

ATOMIC
$$\frac{}{\sigma, \rho, t \vdash ae \Downarrow \mathsf{aeval}(\sigma, \rho, ae)}$$

Fig. 2. The threaded-store semantics

A program pr is evaluated in an initial configuration with an empty store $\bot$, an empty environment $\bot$, and an empty binding context $\langle\rangle$. In such a configuration, pr evaluates to a value v if $\bot, \bot, \langle\rangle \vdash pr \Downarrow (v, \sigma)$.

The LET rule evaluates the bound call expression ce under the incoming environment and store. If evaluation results in a value–store pair, this incoming environment is extended with a binding derived from the bound variable and incoming binding context.[7] The resultant store is extended with mapping from that binding to the resultant value. The body expression is evaluated under the extended environment and store and its result becomes that of the overall expression.

Contrasting the treatment of the environment and the store by the LET rule is instructive. On the one hand, the environment is treated compositionally: the incoming environment of evaluation is restored and extended after evaluation of the bound value. On the other hand, the store is treated non-compositionally: the store resulting from the evaluation of the bound expression is extended after it has accumulated the effects of its evaluation.

Under this criteria, we classify the treatment of the binding context as *compositional* rather than *threaded*. This compositional treatment departs from typical practice of CFA and is the first such treatment in a stack-precise CFA to our knowledge. In Section 6.2, we examine the ramifications of this treatment.

The CALL rule evaluates the atomic expressions ae_0 and ae_1 for the operator and argument, respectively. It then derives a new binding context, extends the environment and store with a binding using that context, and evaluates the operator body under the extended environment, store, and derived binding context. The result of evaluation the body is that of the overall expression.

The SET! rule evaluates the atomic body expression ae and updates the binding of the referenced variable in the store. Its result is the identity function paired with the updated store.

The ATOMIC rule evaluates an atomic expression ae using the aeval atomic evaluation metafunction. Foreshadowing the succeeding semantics, we define aeval to return a pair of its calculated value and the given store. In this semantics, the store is passed through unmodified; in forthcoming semantics, it will be altered according to the calculated value. Atomic evaluation is unchanged from the small-step semantics:

$$\mathsf{aeval}(\sigma, \rho, x) = (\sigma(x, \rho(x)), \sigma) \qquad \mathsf{aeval}(\sigma, \rho, \lambda x.e) = ((\lambda x.e, \rho|_{\lambda x.e}), \sigma)$$

4.2 Threaded-Store Semantics with Effect Log

The second semantics enhances the reference semantics with an *effect log* ξ which explicitly records the allocation and mutation that occurs through evaluation. The effect log is considered part of the evaluation result; accordingly the *effect log semantics* are in terms of judgments of the form $\sigma, \rho, t \vdash e \Downarrow_! (v, \sigma'), \xi$. Figure 3 presents the effect log semantics, identical to the reference semantics except for (1) the addition of the effect log and (2) the use of the metavariable a to denote an address (x,t). (This usage persists in all subsequent semantics as well.)

The effect log is represented by a function from store to store. The definition of each log is given by either a literal identity function, a use of the extend$_{log}$

---

[7] Because the program is alphatised, the binding of a let-bound variable in a particular calling context will not interfere with the binding of any other variable.

LET

$$\frac{\rho' = \rho[x \mapsto t] \qquad \sigma_2 = \sigma_1[(x,t) \mapsto v_0] \qquad \begin{array}{c}\sigma_0, \rho, t \vdash ce \Downarrow_! (v_0, \sigma_1), \xi_0 \\ \sigma_2, \rho', t \vdash e \Downarrow_! (v, \sigma_3), \xi_1\end{array}}{\sigma_0, \rho, t \vdash \mathsf{let}\, x = ce \,\mathsf{in}\, e \Downarrow_! (v, \sigma_3), \xi_1 \circ \mathsf{extend}_{log}((x,t), v_0, \sigma_1) \circ \xi_0}$$

CALL

$$\frac{\begin{array}{c}((\lambda x.e, \rho_0), \sigma_1) = \mathsf{aeval}(\sigma_0, \rho, ae_0) \\ (v_1, \sigma_2) = \mathsf{aeval}(\sigma_1, \rho, ae_1) \qquad t' = (ae_0\, ae_1) :: t \\ \rho_1 = \rho_0[x \mapsto t'] \qquad \sigma_3 = \sigma_2[(x,t') \mapsto v_1] \qquad \sigma_3, \rho_1, t' \vdash e \Downarrow_! (v, \sigma_4), \xi\end{array}}{\sigma_0, \rho, t \vdash (ae_0\, ae_1) \Downarrow_! (v, \sigma_4), \xi \circ \mathsf{extend}_{log}((x,t'), v_1, \sigma_2)}$$

SET!

$$\frac{\begin{array}{c}(v, \sigma_1) = \mathsf{aeval}(\sigma_0, \rho, ae) \\ a = (x, \rho(x)) \qquad \sigma_1 = \sigma_0[a \mapsto v]\end{array}}{\sigma_0, \rho, t \vdash \mathsf{set!}\; x\; ae \Downarrow_! ((\lambda \mathrm{x.x}, \bot), \sigma_1), \mathsf{extend}_{log}(a, v, \sigma_1)}$$

ATOMIC

$$\frac{}{\sigma, \rho, t \vdash ae \Downarrow_! \mathsf{aeval}(\sigma, \rho, ae), \lambda\sigma.\sigma}$$

Fig. 3. Threaded-store semantics with an effect log

metafunction, or the composition of effect logs. The extend_{log} metafunction is defined

$$\mathsf{extend}_{log}(a, v, \sigma') = \lambda\sigma.\sigma[a \mapsto v] \cup \sigma'$$

where the union of the extended store $\sigma[a \mapsto v]$ and the value-associated store σ' treats each store extensionally as a set of pairs but the result is always a function—i.e. any given address is paired with at most one value. The effect log of the ATOMIC rule is the identity function, reflecting that no allocation or mutation is performed when evaluating an atomic expression. The effect log of the SET! rule is constructed by the metafunction extend_{log}; the store argument to extend_{log} is the store *after* the mutation has occurred. The use of this store is necessary to propagate the mutative effect and ensures that its union with the store on which this log is replayed agrees on all common bindings. The effect log of the CALL rule is composed of the effect log of evaluation of the body and an entry for the allocation of the bound variable. Finally, the effect log of the LET rule is composed of the effect logs of evaluation of both the body and binding expression interposed by an entry for the allocation of the bound variable.

In this semantics (and the next), the bindings in σ' are redundant: once extend_{log} applies the the mutative or allocative binding to its argument σ, σ already contains all the bindings of σ'. Once we introduce GC to the semantics, however, this will no longer be the case.

The intended role of the effect log is captured by the following lemma, which states that one may obtain the resultant store by applying the resultant log to the initial store of evaluation.

Lemma 1. *If $\sigma, \rho, t \vdash e \Downarrow_! (v, \sigma'), \xi$, then $\sigma' = \xi(\sigma)$.*

The proof proceeds straightforwardly by induction on the judgment's derivation.

4.3   Compositional-Store Semantics

The third semantics (seen in Figure 4) shifts the previous semantics from threading the store to treating it compositionally. Under this treatment, evaluation results still consist of a value, store, and effect log, but the store is associated directly to the value—at least conceptually—and not treated as a global effect repository. This alternative role is particularly apparent in the LET rule: the store resulting from evaluation of the bound expression is not extended to be used as the initial store of evaluation of the body. Instead, the effect log resulting from evaluation of the bound expression is applied to the initial store (of the overall let expression). We emphasize this compositional treatment by no longer using numeric subscripts, which suggest "evolution" of the store, and instead using ticks, which suggest distinct (but related) instances.

LET
$$\frac{\sigma, \rho, t \vdash ce \Downarrow_\circ (v', \sigma_{v'}), \xi' \qquad \sigma' = \xi'(\sigma)}{\sigma, \rho, t \vdash \mathsf{let}\, x = ce\, \mathsf{in}\, e \Downarrow_\circ (v, \sigma_v), \xi \circ \mathsf{extend}_{log}((x, t), v', \sigma_{v'}) \circ \xi'}$$
$$(\rho', \sigma'') = \mathsf{extend}(\rho, \sigma', x, t, v', \sigma_{v'}) \qquad \sigma'', \rho', t \vdash e \Downarrow_\circ (v, \sigma_v), \xi$$

CALL
$$\frac{((\lambda x.e, \rho_0), \sigma_0) = \mathsf{aeval}(\sigma, \rho, ae_0) \qquad (v_1, \sigma_1) = \mathsf{aeval}(\sigma, \rho, ae_1) \qquad t' = (ae_0\ ae_1) :: t}{\sigma, \rho, t \vdash (ae_0\ ae_1) \Downarrow_\circ (v, \sigma_v), \xi \circ \mathsf{extend}_{log}((x, t'), v_1, \sigma_1)}$$
$$(\rho', \sigma') = \mathsf{extend}(\rho_0, \sigma_0, x, t', v_1, \sigma_1) \qquad \sigma', \rho', t' \vdash e \Downarrow_\circ (v, \sigma_v), \xi$$

SET!
$$\frac{(v, \sigma_v) = \mathsf{aeval}(\sigma, \rho, ae)}{\sigma, \rho, t \vdash \mathsf{set!}\, x\, ae \Downarrow_\circ ((\lambda x.x, \bot), \sigma'), \mathsf{extend}_{log}(a, v, \sigma')}$$
$$a = (x, \rho(x)) \qquad \sigma' = \sigma_v[a \mapsto v]$$

ATOMIC
$$\frac{}{\sigma, \rho, t \vdash ae \Downarrow_\circ \mathsf{aeval}(\sigma, \rho, ae), \lambda \sigma. \sigma}$$

Fig. 4. The compositional-store semantics

We use the extend metafunction to bind a value v (with an associated store σ_v) to a variable x in a given binding context t within a given environment ρ and store σ, defined

$$\mathsf{extend}(\rho, \sigma, x, t, v, \sigma_v) = (\rho[x \mapsto t], \sigma[(x, t) \mapsto v] \cup \sigma_v)$$

When we extend σ with a mapping for v, we also copy all of the mappings from σ_v. This copying will yield a well-formed store since $\sigma[(x, t) \mapsto v]$ and σ_v agree on any common bindings.

Although the role of the store has changed, the same lemma holds in this semantics as does in the previous. We repeat it in terms of this semantics.

Lemma 2. *If* $\sigma, \rho, t \vdash e \Downarrow_\circ (v, \sigma_v), \xi$, *then* $\xi(\sigma) = \sigma_v$.

Like the previous lemma, its proof can be obtained by induction on the judgment's derivation.

4.4   Compositional-Store Semantics with Garbage Collection

Our final semantics (seen in Figure 5) continues the compositional treatment of the store but GCs stores to remove irrelevant bindings. Under this compositional treatment, the role of the store is to model the fragment of the heap which is reachable from an associated environment: the store of a configuration closes the associated environment and the store of a result closes the environment of the associated value. Accordingly, the root set of reachability used by GC includes the addresses of the closed environment only and, in particular, does not include addresses from the continuation. We define reachability just as we did for GC in Section 3.2, using the root_v and root_ρ metafunctions to extract a root set from a value and environment, respectively.

In this semantics, we use a modified atomic evaluation function aeval_{gc} which garbage-collects the store associated with a value. It is defined

$$\mathsf{aeval}_{gc}(\sigma, \rho, x) = (v, \mathsf{gc}(v, \sigma)) \text{ where } v = \sigma(x, \rho(x))$$
$$\mathsf{aeval}_{gc}(\sigma, \rho, \lambda x.e) = (v, \mathsf{gc}(v, \sigma)) \text{ where } v = (\lambda x.e, \rho|_{\lambda x.e})$$

where $\mathsf{gc}(v, \sigma)$ prunes the unreachable bindings from σ with respect to v.

This semantics is careful to ensure that each evaluation is performed under a store which contains no values unreachable from the environment via frequent use of the restrict metafunction. For a given expression e, closing environment ρ, and closing store σ, the restrict metafunction first determines the restriction $\rho|_e$ of ρ to the free variables of e and then the bindings of σ reachable from $\rho|_e$; it then garbage-collects the store by pruning unreachable bindings. Formally, restrict is defined

$$\mathsf{restrict}(e, \rho, \sigma) = (\rho|_e, \mathsf{gc}(\rho|_e, \sigma))$$

where $\mathsf{gc}(\rho, \sigma)$ prunes the unreachable bindings from σ with respect to ρ.

The LET rule proceeds by first obtaining the restriction of the environment and store with respect to the bound expression ce, before evaluating ce under that restriction. The evaluation of ce produces a value v', an associated store $\sigma_{v'}$ which closes only that value, and an effect log ξ'. The LET rule then replays the effect log ξ' on the initial store σ thereby accumulating any mutation (and allocation which it depends) which occurred. After replaying the log, it extends the resultant store σ' and initial environment ρ with a binding for v' and copies

LET

$$(\rho_{ce}, \sigma_{ce}) = \text{restrict}(ce, \rho, \sigma)$$

$$\frac{\sigma_{ce}, \rho_{ce}, t \vdash ce \Downarrow_{gc} (v', \sigma_{v'}), \xi' \quad \sigma' = \xi'(\sigma) \quad (\rho', \sigma'') = \text{extend}(\rho, \sigma', x, t, v', \sigma_{v'})}{(\rho_e, \sigma_e) = \text{restrict}(e, \rho', \sigma'') \quad \sigma_e, \rho_e, t \vdash e \Downarrow_{gc} (v, \sigma_v), \xi}{\sigma, \rho, t \vdash \text{let } x = ce \text{ in } e \Downarrow_{gc} (v, \sigma_v), \xi \circ \text{extend}_{log}((x, t), v', \sigma_{v'}) \circ \xi'}$$

CALL

$$\frac{((\lambda x.e, \rho_0), \sigma_0) = \text{aeval}_{gc}(\sigma, \rho, ae_0) \quad (v_1, \sigma_1) = \text{aeval}_{gc}(\sigma, \rho, ae_1)}{t' = (ae_0 \, ae_1) :: t \quad (\rho', \sigma') = \text{extend}(\rho_0, \sigma_0, x, t', v_1, \sigma_1)}{(\rho_e, \sigma_e) = \text{restrict}(e, \rho', \sigma') \quad \sigma_e, \rho_e, t' \vdash e \Downarrow_{gc} (v, \sigma_v), \xi}{\sigma, \rho, t \vdash (ae_0 \, ae_1) \Downarrow_{gc} (v, \sigma_v), \xi \circ \text{extend}_{log}((x, t'), v_1, \sigma_1)}$$

SET!

$$\frac{(v, \sigma_v) = \text{aeval}_{gc}(\sigma, \rho, ae)}{a = (x, \rho(x)) \quad \sigma' = \sigma_v[a \mapsto v]}{\sigma, \rho, t \vdash \text{set! } x \, ae \Downarrow_{gc} ((\lambda \mathbf{x}.\mathbf{x}, \bot), \bot), \text{extend}_{log}(a, v, \sigma')}$$

ATOMIC

$$\frac{}{\sigma, \rho, t \vdash ae \Downarrow_{gc} \text{aeval}_{gc}(\sigma, \rho, ae), \lambda\sigma.\sigma}$$

Fig. 5. The compositional-store semantics with garbage collection

the bindings of its associated store $\sigma_{v'}$. Finally, the extended environment and store are restricted with respect to the body expression e before e's evaluation under them.

The CALL rule proceeds by first evaluating the atomic operator and argument expressions. After calculating the new binding context t', the operator value environment and store are extended with the new binding. Before evaluation of the body e commences, the extended environment and store are restricted with respect to it.

The SET! rule atomically evaluates the expression ae producing the assigned value. It returns the identity function which, with an empty environment, is closed by an empty store.

The ATOMIC rule evaluates an atomic expression with aeval_{gc}.

To connect this semantics to the previous, we show that the addition of GC has no semantic effect by the following lemma.

Lemma 3. If $\sigma, \rho, t \vdash e \Downarrow_\circ (v, \sigma_v), \xi$ and $\sigma' = \text{gc}(\rho|_e, \sigma)$ then $\sigma', \rho, t \vdash e \Downarrow_{gc} (v, \sigma_v'), \xi'$ where $\sigma_v' = \text{gc}(v, \sigma_v)$.

In prose, this lemma states that two evaluation configurations, identical except that one's store is the other's with unreachable bindings pruned, will yield the same evaluation result: their evaluation will produce the same value and, modulo unreachable bindings, the same closing store.

5 Abstract Compositional-Store Semantics with Garbage Collection

We now *abstract* the compositional-store semantics with GC—the final semantics of the preceding section. Abstracting the semantics involves (1) defining a finite counterpart of each component of the evaluation configuration and result and (2) defining a counterpart of each semantic rule in terms of these finite components. With each component of the configuration finite, configurations themselves become finite. Then we show that each abstracted rule *simulates* its counterpart—that it admits the full range of its counterpart's behavior. Doing this for each rule ensures that the abstract semantics includes every behavior included by the exact semantics. Once that's complete, we can directly implement our big-step semantics in an abstract definitional interpreter [1,18] to obtain our stack-precise CFA with GC.

We begin by abstracting each configuration component.

$$\hat{v} \in \widehat{Val} = \mathcal{P}(Lam \times \widehat{Env}) \qquad \hat{\rho} \in \widehat{Env} = Var \rightharpoonup \widehat{Time}$$

$$\hat{t} \in \widehat{Time} = App^{\leq m} \qquad \hat{a} \in \widehat{Address} = Var \times \widehat{Time}$$

$$\hat{\sigma} \in \widehat{Store} = \widehat{Address} \rightarrow \widehat{Val} \qquad \hat{\xi} \in \widehat{Log} = \widehat{Address} \rightarrow \widehat{Val}$$

Like its concrete counterpart, an abstract store $\hat{\sigma}$ maps an abstract address to an abstract value. Abstract addresses remain a pair of a variable and binding context, only the context is abstract. An abstract value $\hat{v}$, however, is a *set* of abstract closures rather than a single closure. An abstract closure is a λ paired with an abstract environment $\hat{\rho}$ which itself is a finite map from variables to binding contexts. An abstract timestamp $\hat{t}$ is a sequence of at most m application sites, where m is a parameter to the analysis.[8] An abstract log $\hat{\xi}$ is an extensional account of the added and modified store mappings relative to the initial store, and takes the same form of an abstract store itself. We define abstract join, composition, and application operators by

$$\hat{\sigma}_0 \sqcup \hat{\sigma}_1 = \lambda\hat{a}.\hat{\sigma}_0(\hat{a}) \cup \hat{\sigma}_1(\hat{a}) \qquad \hat{\xi}_0 \hat{\circ} \hat{\xi}_1 = \hat{\xi}_0 \sqcup \hat{\xi}_1 \qquad \hat{\xi}(\hat{\sigma}) = \hat{\sigma} \sqcup \hat{\xi}$$

To help show that the abstract semantics simulates the concrete, we make a connection between the state space of the abstract and that of the concrete. We make this connection by means of a polymorphic abstraction function $|\cdot|$,[9] defined for all domains except stores by

$$|\rho| = \lambda x.|\rho(x)| \qquad |t| = \lfloor t \rfloor_m \qquad |(\lambda x.e, \rho)| = \{(\lambda x.e, |\rho|)\} \qquad |\xi| = |\xi(\bot)|$$

and for stores by

$$|\sigma| = \lambda\hat{a}. \bigcup_{|a|=\hat{a}} |\sigma(a)|$$

---

[8] The parameter m is used similarly to the parameter k of k-CFA.

[9] The abstraction function is typically accompanied by a complementary *concretization* function to complete a Galois connection. For simplicity here, we leave it incomplete.

Abstracting a store groups entries by their abstracted address in a large set. Abstracting an environment ρ abstracts its range. Abstracting a binding context t takes its at-most-m-length prefix. Abstracting a closure produces a singleton of that closure with an abstracted environment. Finally, abstracting a log ξ produces the abstract store that results from apply the log to the empty store $\perp$ and then abstracting.

Figure 6 defines the abstract compositional-store semantics with garbage collection. Structurally, nearly every rule is identical to the exact counterpart that it abstracts; most of the work of abstraction is defining the abstract domains and metafunctions and connecting them to those of the exact semantics. The CALL rule differs structurally from its exact counterpart in two notable ways: First, because an abstract value is a set of closures, it applies for each such closure in the operator set. Second, it defines the new binding context $\hat{t}'$ to be the prefix of the application site prepended to the previous abstract time $\hat{t}$ and limited to a length of at most m. The abstract $\widehat{\text{aeval}}$ metafunction is defined

$$\widehat{\text{aeval}}(\hat{\sigma}, \hat{\rho}, x) = (\hat{v}, \widehat{\text{gc}}(\hat{v}, \hat{\sigma})) \text{ where } \hat{v} = \hat{\sigma}(\hat{\rho}(x))$$

$$\widehat{\text{aeval}}(\hat{\sigma}, \hat{\rho}, \lambda x.e) = (\hat{v}, \widehat{\text{gc}}(\hat{v}, \hat{\sigma})) \text{ where } \hat{v} = \{(\lambda x.e, \hat{\rho}|_{\lambda x.e})\}$$

We omit the straightforward definitions of the abstract variants of $\widehat{\text{gc}}$, $\widehat{\text{restrict}}$, and $\widehat{\text{extend}}$.

LET
$$(\hat{\rho}_{ce}, \hat{\sigma}_{ce}) = \widehat{\text{restrict}}(ce, \hat{\rho}, \hat{\sigma})$$
$$\hat{\sigma}_{ce}, \hat{\rho}_{ce}, \hat{t} \vdash ce \Downarrow (\hat{v}', \hat{\sigma}_{v'}), \hat{\xi}' \qquad \hat{\sigma}' = \hat{\xi}'(\hat{\sigma}) \qquad (\hat{\rho}', \hat{\sigma}'') = \widehat{\text{extend}}(\hat{\rho}, \hat{\sigma}', x, \hat{t}, \hat{v}', \hat{\sigma}'_v)$$
$$\frac{(\hat{\rho}_e, \hat{\sigma}_e) = \widehat{\text{restrict}}(e, \hat{\rho}', \hat{\sigma}'') \qquad \hat{\sigma}_e, \hat{\rho}_e, \hat{t} \vdash e \Downarrow (\hat{v}, \hat{\sigma}_v), \hat{\xi}}{\hat{\sigma}, \hat{\rho}, \hat{t} \vdash \text{let } x = ce \text{ in } e \Downarrow (\hat{v}, \hat{\sigma}_v), \hat{\xi}\hat{\circ}\hat{\xi}'}$$

CALL
$$(\hat{v}_0, \hat{\sigma}_0) = \widehat{\text{aeval}}(\hat{\sigma}, \hat{\rho}, ae_0) \qquad (\lambda x.e, \hat{\rho}_0) \in \hat{v}_0$$
$$(\hat{v}_1, \hat{\sigma}_1) = \widehat{\text{aeval}}(\hat{\sigma}, \hat{\rho}, ae_1)$$
$$\hat{t}' = \lfloor (ae_0\ ae_1) :: \hat{t} \rfloor_m \qquad (\hat{\rho}', \hat{\sigma}') = \widehat{\text{extend}}(\hat{\rho}_0, \hat{\sigma}_0, x, \hat{t}', \hat{v}_1, \hat{\sigma}_1)$$
$$\frac{(\hat{\rho}_e, \hat{\sigma}_e) = \widehat{\text{restrict}}(e, \hat{\rho}', \hat{\sigma}') \qquad \hat{\sigma}_e, \hat{\rho}_e, \hat{t}' \vdash e \Downarrow (\hat{v}, \hat{\sigma}_v), \hat{\xi}}{\hat{\sigma}, \hat{\rho}, \hat{t} \vdash (ae_0\ ae_1) \Downarrow (\hat{v}, \hat{\sigma}_v), \hat{\xi}}$$

SET!
$$(\hat{v}, \hat{\sigma}_v) = \widehat{\text{aeval}}(\hat{\sigma}, \hat{\rho}, ae)$$
$$\frac{(\_, \hat{\xi}) = \widehat{\text{extend}}(\perp, \perp, x, \hat{\rho}(x), \hat{v}, \hat{\sigma}_v)}{\hat{\sigma}, \hat{\rho}, \hat{t} \vdash \text{set! } x\ ae \Downarrow (\{(\lambda \mathsf{x}.\mathsf{x}, \perp)\}, \perp), \hat{\xi}}$$

ATOMIC
$$\frac{}{\hat{\sigma}, \hat{\rho}, \hat{t} \vdash ae \Downarrow \widehat{\text{aeval}}(\hat{\sigma}, \hat{\rho}, ae), \perp}$$

Fig. 6. The abstract compositional-store semantics with garbage collection

As a final step before we establish the simulation relationship, we define an ordering on stores (and logs, extending it in the natural way):

$$\hat{\sigma}_0 \sqsubseteq \hat{\sigma}_1 \Leftrightarrow \forall \hat{a} \in \widehat{Address}.\hat{\sigma}_0(\hat{a}) \subseteq \hat{\sigma}_1(\hat{a}) \qquad \hat{v}_0 \sqsubseteq \hat{v}_1 \Leftrightarrow \hat{v}_0 \subseteq \hat{v}_1$$

We formally connect this abstract semantics with the concrete compositional-store semantics given in Section 4.4 by the following abstraction theorem.

Theorem 1. *If $|\sigma| \sqsubseteq \hat{\sigma}$ and $|\rho| = \hat{\rho}$ and $|t| = \hat{t}$ and $\sigma, \rho, t \vdash e \Downarrow_{gc} (v, \sigma_v), \xi$, then $\hat{\sigma}, \hat{\rho}, \hat{t} \vdash e \hat{\Downarrow} (\hat{v}, \hat{\sigma}_v), \hat{\xi}$ where $|v| \sqsubseteq \hat{v}$ and $|\sigma_v| \sqsubseteq \hat{\sigma}_v$ and $|\xi| \sqsubseteq \hat{\xi}$.*

This theorem states that if the configuration components are related by abstraction, then, for any given derivation in the exact semantics, there is an derivation in the abstract semantics which yields an abstraction of its results. It can be proved by induction on the derivation.

6   Discussion

Now we examine the ramifications of a compositional treatment of analysis components. We do so in turn, first considering the ramifications of treating the store compositionally and then of treating the time compositionally.

0.1   The Effects of Treating the Store Compositionally

We saw in Section 4.3 that a semantics could treat stores compositionally without employing GC. In this case, the caller's store and callee's final store agreed on common entries and combining them produced the same store as the threaded-store semantics. However, the compositional machinery liberates evaluation from the stack. With evaluation so-liberated, GC need not preserve any heap data reachable solely from the stack. This relaxation

1. simplifies GC and increases its effectiveness;
2. leads to general yet precise summaries; and
3. restores context irrelevance under GC.

We discuss each of these aspects in more detail.

Simplified and More-Effective Garbage Collection Classical abstract GC and its succeeding pushdown GC each preserve heap data reachable from both the local environment and the stack. Once one has determined the root set of reachable addresses from these two components, it determines the transitive closure of reachability. When GC is performed with respect to only the local environment, both the initial root set and its transitive closure are smaller and it requires less work to calculate them. If the CFA employs incomplete garbage collection [8], the garbage collector is also freed from calculating the root set of stack addresses as a fixed point. A smaller transitive closure of reachable addresses is not only less costly to calculate but also leads to more collected garbage.

General Yet Precise Summaries A stack-precise CFA without GC will falsely distinguish abstract evaluations of the same call which are identical modulo GC-able heap data. In such cases, the addition of pushdown GC will allow the CFA to identify them. However, even with pushdown GC, a stack-precise CFA will falsely distinguish abstract evaluations of the same call which are identical modulo continuation-reachable heap data. On the other hand, compositional GC soundly disregards such data and thereby identifies such evaluations.

Compositional GC is able to achieve this feat because its calculates the fragments of the heap reachable from the local environment alone. Since this environment is restricted to the free variables of the expression it closes, the resultant heap fragment includes a tight overapproximation of the actually-relevant heap data. One effect is that evaluation summaries—the association of an evaluation configuration with its results—are general yet precise. They are general since, with a minimum of irrelevant heap data, more contexts are consistent with them. They are precise since, with a minimum of irrelevant heap data, they are less likely to allocate an entry at an existing address. In fact, the precision of compositional GC dominates that of pushdown GC.

Restored Context Irrelevance A semantics determines which parts of a given configuration are *relevant* to its evaluation [8]. When the continuation is irrelevant to evaluation, the semantics exhibits the property of *context irrelevance*. Context irrelevance is an intuitive property: unless our semantics has control effects or some other explicit dependence, we would be surprised if a configuration's continuation was relevant to its evaluation. Even a concrete semantics with GC exhibits context irrelevance since data reachable from the stack alone will not effect the result of evaluation. In an abstract semantics with GC, however, where new allocations can occur at old addresses, the presence of data reachable from the stack alone can affect evaluation. The set of data preserved by GC, which determines how evaluation is affected, is itself determined by the continuation. Thus, an abstract semantics in which GC is defined *with respect to the stack* violates context irrelevance.

Put this way, it is clear why compositional GC restores context irrelevance to the semantics: it removes the dependence on the stack from GC itself and allows all data reachable from the stack alone to be collected. This restoration makes evaluation easier to reason about and increases the effectiveness of memoization.

6.2   The Effect of Treating the Time Compositionally

The k-CFA context abstraction consists of a sequence of k call sites—for each point in execution, the last k call sites encountered. In Section 3.5, we discussed how the last-k-call-sites abstraction arose as a consequence of the semantics threading the abstract time (i.e. the context) through execution.

In contrast, the big-step, concrete semantics of Section 4 and the big-step, abstract semantics of Section 5 didn't thread the abstract time through execution but treated it compositionally, installing a new time at a call but restoring the previous time at the corresponding return. This treatment of time induces a different notion of context than k-CFA; instead of yielding the last-k call sites, it yields the top-m stack frames.

This top-m-stack-frames context abstraction is not novel and originates with m-CFA [11], a family of polynomial-time CFAs. However, to our knowledge, its appearance here is its first in a stack-precise setting: many stack-precise CFAs encode context using other means than a time component (or don't use context in the first place) [16, 3, 1]; still others achieve the last-k-call-sites abstraction, incidentally or intentionally [4, 18].

Using the top-m stack frames to qualify heap allocation has certain advantages to using the last-k call sites; in particular, its power to distinguish bindings is not diluted by static call sequences. To see how k-CFA's and m-CFA's context abstractions compare, let's consider a few examples.

First, consider a $[k = 2]$CFA of the program

```
(define (f x) x)
(define (g y) (f y))
(g 42)
(g 35)
```

the abstract resource 42 is allocated in the heap twice—first when the call to g is made and second when the call to f is made. At the point of the second allocation, the two most-recently-encountered call sites in evaluation are (f y) and (g 42); hence, these call sites are used to qualify the binding of 42 to x in the heap. The treatment of the abstract resource 35 is similar except its second allocation is qualified by (f y) and (g 35). For this program, $[k = 2]$CFA is able to keep the two allocations distinct.

Next, consider a $[k = 2]$CFA of the similar program

```
(define (f x) x)
(define (g y)
  (displayln y)
  (f y))
(g 42)
(g 35)
```

which includes the call (displayln y) in the body of g. As in the previous program, the analysis of this program allocates the abstract resources 42 and 35 twice each. However, in this program, the second of each of their allocations is qualified by (f y) and (displayln y). In fact, every call to f made via g will occur in that same context. In a sense, the static sequence of (displayln y) and (f y) eats up the context budget ensuring that the analysis conflates all bindings made at the call (f y). (Incrementing k would remove the conflation in this example, but it makes the analysis more expensive and such a strategy can always be confounded by a longer "static" trace of calls.)

To constrast, consider an $[m = 2]$CFA of the same program. Because the context consists of the top two stack frames, the allocation of 42 is qualified by (f y) and (g 42) and the allocation of 35 is qualified by (f y) and (g 35). Because the second stack frame of each allocation is distinct, $[m = 2]$CFA is able to keep the bindings distinct in the analysis.

The top-m-stack-frames context abstraction is itself susceptible to deep nests of calls which serve only to pass parameters: if the nesting depth exceeds m, then the analysis will conflate the bindings made by the innermost calls. And, as with k-CFA, an increased m can always be confounded by a deeper nesting. In spite of that, the m-CFA context abstraction has been shown to work well relative to k-CFA in practice in a stack-imprecise setting where variables are aggressively re-bound [11]. Future work is needed to verify that its advantages carry over to a stack-precise setting.

7   Related Work

Broadly, this work is an instance of abstract interpretation and, more specifically, of control-flow analysis (CFA) [9, 14]. It inherits from the *Abstracting Abstract Machines* methodology [15] of systematically deriving CFAs from purely operational specifications. More specifically, this work is an instance of stack-precise CFA which is preceded by many variations [16, 3, 8, 6, 12, 1, 18].

Might and Shivers [10] first introduced GC to CFA. Reconciling GC with stack-precise CFAs has been the focus of significant effort. Earl *et al.* [4] introduced the first technique to do so which approximated the the set of frames that could be on any possible stack at any given control point. Johnson and Van Horn [8] cast this technique into a more operational framework and considered a more-precise variant in which a control point splits for each possible stack with its heap being collected with respect to that stack alone. Johnson *et al.* [7] unified these previous two works in one formal framework. Darais *et al.* [1] show that the *Abstracting Definitional Interpreters* approach easily accommodates abstract GC by introducing a machine component which contains the addresses embedded in stack frames; this realization of GC amounts essentially to the fully-precise technique. Our work sidesteps the need for all of this previous effort by decomposing the heap into continuation-independent fragments.

A significant concept in the work of Johnson and Van Horn [8] is *context irrelevance*, the property that the evaluation of a configuration is independent of its continuation, and they note that the approximate abstract GC technique introduced by Earl *et al.* [4] violates context irrelevance. Once again, the independence of GC from the stack under our technique sidesteps these issues; evaluation under our technique exhibits context irrelevance effortlessly.

As part of the resolution of an apparent paradox regarding the complexities of object-oriented k-CFA and functional k-CFA, Might *et al.* [11] develop m-CFA, a stack-imprecise, polynomial-time family of CFA that employs the top-m stack frames as a context abstraction as opposed to the last-k call sites of k-CFA. They show that this abstraction is more resilient against approximation in the face of the aggressive rebinding that m-CFA effects. Our treatment of the abstract time component induces this same top-m-stack-frames context abstraction but in a stack-precise setting, the first such appearance in the literature, to our knowledge.

Although not inspired by it, our work surprisingly shares much of the perspective and approach of the work of Dillig *et al.* [2] to verify C and C++ programs. In particular, both works employ a compositional approach to analysis by producing evaluation summaries and decompose the heap to support their approach. In addition, both works have some notion of propagation of summary effects: theirs is a *summary transfer function*; ours is an effect log. In contrast, our work does not produce summaries in a bottom-up fashion and is targeted toward explicitly higher-order languages with effects. Interesting future work could explore whether any precision-enhancing techniques of Dillig *et al.* [2] could be ported and applied, whether the bottom-up production of summaries is viable, or whether their general approach can be used for verification in our setting.

8   Conclusion and Future Work

In this paper, we showed that treating the heap compositionally in a stack-precise CFA removes its dependence on the stack, at once simplifying GC and increasing its effectiveness. As a result, the analysis produces more compact and precise evaluation summaries that are more amenable to reuse. We also showed that treating the time component compositionally induces the top-m-stack-frames context abstraction of m-CFA. Unlike k-CFA's last-k-call-sites context abstraction, m-CFA's need not devote any precision to static call sequences.

Interestingly, the notion of context shared by k-CFA and m-CFA—calling context, roughly—seems to be at odds with summary reuse. In a stack-precise 1CFA (which exhibits the same context abstraction whether it is $[k = 1]$CFA or $[m = 1]$CFA), the syntactic call site of the caller is encoded in the summary of the callee, preventing the summary's reuse at any other call site. If this tension is fundamental, it might benefit to look to alternative notions of context—extant and novel.

The complement to abstract GC is abstract counting [10] which keeps track of the number of concrete resources that correspond to an abstract resource and enables certain abstract transitions, such as a strong store update. If an abstact counting can be applied to heap fragments such that the overlap among fragments is accounted for correctly, it might be possible to detect opportunities to perform strong updates to heap bindings which would further increase the precision of our technique.

Finally, Darais *et al.* [1] consider a particular value abstraction in which primitive operations propagate imprecision but do not introduce it. Their abstraction suggests a generalization in which each "basic block" is analyzed at full precision and imprecision occurs only at the join points of control flow. CFA2's stack environments capture an aspect of this generalization and it appears our technique does as well. However, a focused investigation would reveal whether such a generalization can be more-fully realized.

References

1. Darais, D., Labich, N., Nguyen, P.C., Van Horn, D.: Abstracting definitional interpreters (functional pearl). Proceedings of the ACM on Programming Languages **1**(ICFP), 12:1–12:25 (Aug 2017). https://doi.org/10.1145/3110256
2. Dillig, I., Dillig, T., Aiken, A., Sagiv, M.: Precise and compact modular procedure summaries for heap manipulating programs. In: Proceedings of the 32Nd ACM SIGPLAN Conference on Programming Language Design and Implementation. pp. 567–577. PLDI '11, ACM, New York, NY, USA (2011). https://doi.org/10.1145/1993498.1993565
3. Earl, C., Might, M., Van Horn, D.: Pushdown control-flow analysis of higher order programs. Workshop on Scheme and Functional Programming (2010)
4. Earl, C., Sergey, I., Might, M., Van Horn, D.: Introspective pushdown analysis of higher-order programs. In: Proceedings of the 17th ACM SIGPLAN International Conference on Functional Programming. pp. 177–188. ICFP '12, ACM, New York, NY, USA (Sep 2012). https://doi.org/10.1145/2364527.2364576
5. Flanagan, C., Sabry, A., Duba, B.F., Felleisen, M.: The essence of compiling with continuations. In: Proceedings of the ACM SIGPLAN 1993 Conference on Programming Language Design and Implementation. pp. 237–247. PLDI '93, ACM, New York, NY, USA (1993). https://doi.org/10.1145/155090.155113
6. Gilray, T., Lyde, S., Adams, M.D., Might, M., Van Horn, D.: Pushdown control-flow analysis for free. In: Proceedings of the 43rd Annual ACM SIGPLAN-SIGACT Symposium on Principles of Programming Languages. pp. 691–704. POPL '16, ACM, New York, NY, USA (Jan 2016). https://doi.org/10.1145/2837614.2837631
7. Johnson, J.I., Sergey, I., Earl, C., Might, M., Van Horn, D.: Pushdown flow analysis with abstract garbage collection. Journal of Functional Programming **24**, 218–283 (May 2014). https://doi.org/10.1017/s0956796814000100
8. Johnson, J.I., Van Horn, D.: Abstracting abstract control. In: Proceedings of the 10th ACM Symposium on Dynamic Languages. pp. 11–22. DLS '14, ACM, New York, NY, USA (Oct 2014). https://doi.org/10.1145/2661088.2661098
9. Jones, N.D.: Flow analysis of lambda expressions. In: International Colloquium on Automata, Languages, and Programming. pp. 114–128. Springer (1981)
10. Might, M., Shivers, O.: Improving flow analyses via ΓCFA: abstract garbage collection and counting. In: Proceedings of the Eleventh ACM SIGPLAN International Conference on Functional Programming. pp. 13–25. ICFP '06, ACM, New York, NY, USA (Sep 2006). https://doi.org/10.1145/1159803.1159807
11. Might, M., Smaragdakis, Y., Van Horn, D.: Resolving and exploiting the k-CFA paradox: illuminating functional vs. object-oriented program analysis. In: Proceedings of the 31st ACM SIGPLAN Conference on Programming Language Design and Implementation. pp. 305–315. PLDI '10, ACM, New York, NY, USA (Jun 2010). https://doi.org/10.1145/1806596.1806631
12. Peng, F.: h-CFA: A simplified approach for pushdown control flow analysis. Master's thesis, The University of Wisconsin-Milwaukee (2016)
13. Reynolds, J.C.: Definitional interpreters for Higher-Order programming languages. Higher-Order and Symbolic Computation **11**(4), 363–397 (1998)
14. Shivers, O.: Control-Flow Analysis of Higher-Order Languages. Ph.D. thesis, Carnegie Mellon University, Pittsburgh, PA, USA (1991)
15. Van Horn, D., Might, M.: Abstracting abstract machines. In: Proceedings of the 15th ACM SIGPLAN International Conference on Functional Programming. pp. 51–62. ICFP '10, ACM, New York, NY, USA (Sep 2010). https://doi.org/10.1145/1863543.1863553

16. Vardoulakis, D., Shivers, O.: CFA2: A context-free approach to control-flow analysis. In: Gordon, A.D. (ed.) Programming Languages and Systems. pp. 570–589. Springer Berlin Heidelberg, Berlin, Heidelberg (2010)
17. Vardoulakis, D., Shivers, O.: CFA2: a context-free approach to control-flow analysis. Logical Methods in Computer Science **7**(2) (2011). https://doi.org/10.2168/LMCS-7(2:3)2011
18. Wei, G., Decker, J., Rompf, T.: Refunctionalization of abstract abstract machines: bridging the gap between abstract abstract machines and abstract definitional interpreters (functional pearl). Proceedings of the ACM on Programming Languages **2**(ICFP), 105:1–105:28 (Jul 2018). https://doi.org/10.1145/3236800

SMT-Friendly Formalization of the Solidity Memory Model

Ákos Hajdu[1]⋆ and Dejan Jovanović[2]

[1] Budapest University of Technology and Economics, Budapest, Hungary
hajdua@mit.bme.hu
[2] SRI International, New York City, USA
dejan.jovanovic@sri.com

Abstract. Solidity is the dominant programming language for Ethereum smart contracts. This paper presents a high-level formalization of the Solidity language with a focus on the memory model. The presented formalization covers all features of the language related to managing state and memory. In addition, the formalization we provide is effective: all but few features can be encoded in the quantifier-free fragment of standard SMT theories. This enables precise and efficient reasoning about the state of smart contracts written in Solidity. The formalization is implemented in the SOLC-VERIFY verifier and we provide an extensive set of tests that covers the breadth of the required semantics. We also provide an evaluation on the test set that validates the semantics and shows the novelty of the approach compared to other Solidity-level contract analysis tools.

1 Introduction

Ethereum [32] is a public blockchain platform that provides a novel computing paradigm for developing decentralized applications. Ethereum allows the deployment of arbitrary programs (termed smart contracts [31]) that operate over the blockchain state. The public can interact with the contracts via transactions. It is currently the most popular public blockchain with smart contract functionality. While the nodes participating in the Ethereum network operate a low-level, stack-based virtual machine (EVM) that executes the compiled smart contracts, the contracts themselves are mostly written in a high-level, contract-oriented programming language called Solidity [30].

Even though smart contracts are generally short, they are no less prone to errors than software in general. In the Ethereum context, any flaws in the contract code come with potentially devastating financial consequences (such as the infamous DAO exploit [17]). This has inspired a great interest in applying formal verification techniques to Ethereum smart contracts (see e.g., [4] or [14] for surveys). In order to apply formal verification of any kind, be it static analysis or

---

⋆ The author was also affiliated with SRI International as an intern during this project. Supported by the ÚNKP-19-3 New National Excellence Program of the Ministry for Innovation and Technology.

© The Author(s) 2020
P. Müller (Ed.): ESOP 2020, LNCS 12075, pp. 224–250, 2020.
https://doi.org/10.1007/978-3-030-44914-8_9

model checking, the first step is to formalize the semantics of the programming language that the smart contracts are written in. Such semantics should not only remain an exercise in formalization, but should preferably be developed, resulting in precise and automated verification tools.

Early approaches to verification of Ethereum smart contracts focused mostly on formalizing the low-level virtual machine precisely (see, e.g., [11,19,21,22,2]). However, the unnecessary details of the EVM execution model make it difficult to reason about high-level functional properties of contracts (as they were written by developers) in an effective and automated way. For Solidity-level properties of smart contracts, Solidity-level semantics are preferred. While some aspects of Solidity have been studied and formalized [23,10,15,33], the semantics of the Solidity memory model still lacks a detailed and precise formalization that also enables automation.

The memory model of Solidity has various unusual and non-trivial behaviors, providing a fertile ground for potential bugs. Smart contracts have access to two classes of data storage: a permanent storage that is a part of the global blockchain state, and a transient local memory used when executing transactions. While the local memory uses a standard heap of entities with references, the permanent storage has pure value semantics (although pointers to storage can be declared locally). This memory model that combines both value and reference semantics, with all interactions between the two, poses some interesting challenges but also offers great opportunities for automation. For example, the value semantics of storage ensures non-aliasing of storage data. This can, if supported by an appropriate encoding of the semantics, potentially improve both the precision and effectiveness of reasoning about contract storage.

This paper provides a formalization of the Solidity semantics in terms of a simple SMT-based intermediate language that covers all features related to managing contract storage and memory. A major contribution of our formalization is that all but few of its elements can be encoded in the quantifier-free fragment of standard SMT theories. Additionally, our formalization captures the value semantics of storage with implicit non-aliasing information of storage entities. This allows precise and effective verification of Solidity smart contracts using modern SMT solvers. The formalization is implemented in the open-source SOLC-VERIFY tool [20], which is a modular verifier for Solidity based on SMT solvers. We validate the formalization and demonstrate its effectiveness by evaluating it on a comprehensive set of tests that exercise the memory model. We show that our formalization significantly improves the precision and soundness compared to existing Solidity-level verifiers, while remarkably outperforming low-level EVM-based tools in terms of efficiency.

2   Background

2.1   Ethereum

Ethereum [32,3] is a generic blockchain-based distributed computing platform. The Ethereum ledger is a storage layer for a database of accounts (identified by addresses) and the data associated with the accounts. Every account has an associated balance in Ether (the native cryptocurrency of Ethereum). In addition, an account can also be associated with the executable bytecode of a contract and the contract state.

Although Ethereum contracts are deployed to the blockchain in the form of the bytecode of the Ethereum Virtual Machine (EVM) [32], they are generally written in a high-level programming language called Solidity [30] and then compiled to EVM bytecode. After deployment, the contract is publicly accessible and its code cannot be modified. An external user, or another contract, can interact with a contract through its API by invoking its public functions. This can be done by issuing a transaction that encodes the function to be called with its arguments, and contains the contract's address as the recipient. The Ethereum network then executes the transaction by running the contract code in the context of the contract instance.

A contract instance has access to two different kinds of memory during its lifetime: contract storage and memory.[3] *Contract storage* is a dedicated data store for a contract to store its persistent state. At the level of the EVM, it is an array of 256-bit storage *slots* stored on the blockchain. Contract data that fits into a slot, or can be sliced into fixed number of slots, is usually allocated starting from slot 0. More complex data types that do not fit into a fixed number of slots, such as mappings, or dynamic arrays, are not supported directly by the EVM. Instead, they are implemented by the Solidity compiler using storage as a hash table where the structured data is distributed in a deterministic collision-free manner. *Contract memory* is used during the execution of a transaction on the contract, and is deleted after the transaction finishes. This is where function parameters, return values and temporary data can be allocated and stored.

2.2   Solidity

Solidity [30] is the high-level programming language supporting the development of Ethereum smart contracts. It is a full-fledged object-oriented programming language with many features focusing on enabling rapid development of Ethereum smart contracts. The focus of this paper is the semantics of the Solidity memory model: the Solidity view of contract storage and memory, and the operations that can modify it. Thus, we restrict the presentation to a generous fragment of Solidity that is relevant for discussing and formalizing the memory model. An example contract that illustrates relevant features is shown in Figure 1, and the abstract syntax of the targeted fragment is presented in Figure 2. We omit parts of Solidity that are not relevant to the memory model (e.g., inheritance, loops, blockchain-specific members). We also omit low-level, unsafe features that can break the Solidity memory model abstractions (e.g., `assembly` and `delegatecall`).

---

[3] There is an additional data location named *calldata* that behaves the same as memory, but is used to store parameters of external functions. For simplicity, we omit it in this paper.

```
contract DataStorage {
  struct Record {
    bool set;
    int[] data;
  }

  mapping(address=>Record) private records;

  function append(address at, int d) public {
    Record storage r = records[at];
    r.set = true;
    r.data.push(d);
  }
  function isset(Record storage r) internal view returns (bool s) {
    s = r.set;
  }
  function get(address at) public view returns (int[] memory ret) {
    require(isset(records[at]));
    ret = records[at].data;
  }
}
```

Fig. 1: An example contract illustrating commonly used features of the Solidity memory model. The contract keeps an association between addresses and data and allows users to query and append to their data.

Contracts. Solidity contracts are similar to classes in object-oriented programming. A contract can define any additional types needed, followed by the declaration of the *state variables* and contract *functions*, including an optional single *constructor* function. The contract's state variables define the only persistent data that the contract instance stores on the blockchain. The constructor function is only used once, when a new contract instance is deployed to the blockchain. Other public contract functions can be invoked arbitrarily by external users through an Ethereum transaction that encodes the function call data and designates the contract instance as the recipient of the transaction.

Example 1. The contract **DataStorage** in Figure 1 defines a struct type **Record**. Then it defines the contract storage as a single state variable **records**. Finally three contract functions are defined **append()**, **isset()**, and **get()**. Note that a constructor is not defined and, in this case, a default constructor is provided to initialize the contract state to default values.

Solidity supports further concepts from object-oriented programming, such as inheritance, function modifiers, and overloading (also covered by our implementation [20]). However, as these are not relevant for the formalization of the memory model we omit them to simplify our presentation.

Types. Solidity is statically typed and provides two classes of types: *value* types and *reference* types. Value types include elementary types such as addresses, integers, and Booleans that are always passed by value. Reference types, on the other hand, are passed by reference and include structs, arrays and mappings.

TypeName	::= **address** | **int** | **uint** | **bool**	Value types
	| **mapping(** *TypeName* **=>** *TypeName* **)**	Mapping
	| *TypeName* **[]** | *TypeName* **[** *n* **]**	Arrays
	| *StructName*	Struct name
DataLoc	::= **storage** | **memory**	Data location
lval	::= *id*	Identifier
	| *expr* . *id*	Member access
	| *expr* **[** *expr* **]**	Index access
expr	::= *lval*	Lvalue
	| *expr* **?** *expr* **:** *expr*	Conditional
	| **new** *TypeName* **[]** **(** *expr* **)**	New memory array
	| *StructName* **(** *expr** **)**	New memory struct
stmt	::= *TypeName DataLoc*? *id* [**=** *expr*] **;**	Local variable declaration
	| **(** *lval* **)*** **=** **(** *expr* **)*** **;**	Assignment (tuples)
	| *lval* . **push(** *expr* **) ;**	Push
	| *lval* . **pop() ;**	Pop
	| **delete** *lval* **;**	Delete
StructMem	::= *TypeName id* **;**	Struct member
StructDef	::= **struct** *StructName* **{** *StructMem** **}**	Struct definition
StateVar	::= *TypeName id* **;**	State variable definition
FunPar	::= *TypeName DataLoc*? *id*	Function parameter
Fun	::= **function** *id* **(** *FunPar** **)**	Function definition
	[**returns** **(** *FunPar** **)**] **{** *stmt** **}**	
Constr	::= **constructor(** *FunPar** **) {** *stmt** **}**	Constructor definition
Contract	::= **contract** *id*	Contract definition
	{ *StructDef** *StateVar** *Constr*? *Fun** **}**	

Fig. 2: Syntax of the targeted Solidity fragment.

A struct consists of a fixed number of members. An array is either fixed-size or dynamically-sized and besides the elements of the base type, it also includes a **length** field holding the number of elements. A mapping is an associative array mapping keys to values. The important caveat is that the table does not actually store the keys so it is not possible to check if a key is defined in the map.

Example 2. The contract in Figure 1 uses the following types. The **records** variable is a mapping from addresses to **Record** structures which, in turn, consist of a Boolean value and a dynamically-sized integer array. It is a common practice to define a struct with a Boolean member (**set**) to indicate that a mapping value has been set. This is because Solidity mappings do not store keys: any key can be queried, returning a default value if no value was associated previously.

Data locations for reference types. Data of reference types resides in a *data location* that is either *storage* or *memory*. Storage is the persistent store used for state variables of the contract. In contrast, memory is used during execution of a transaction to store function parameters, return values and local variables, and it is deleted after the transaction finishes.

Semantics of reference types differ fundamentally depending on the data location that they are stored in. Layout of data in the memory data location resembles the memory model common in Java-like programming languages: there is a heap where reference types are allocated and any entity in the heap can contain values of value types, and *references* to other memory entities. In contrast, the storage data location treats and stores all entities, including those of reference types, as *values* with no references involved. Mixing storage and memory is not possible: the data location of a reference type is propagated to its elements and members. This means that storage entities cannot have references to memory entities, and memory entities cannot have reference types as values. Storage of a contract can be viewed as a single value with no aliasing possible.

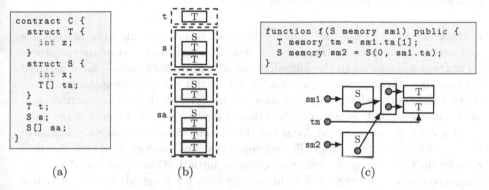

(a)   (b)   (c)

Fig. 3: An example illustrating reference types (structs and arrays) and their layout in storage and memory: (a) a contract defining types and state variables; (b) an abstract representation of the contract storage as values; and, (c) a function using the memory data location and a possible layout of the data in memory.

Example 3. Consider the contract C defined in Figure 3a. The contract defines two reference **struct** types S and T, and declares state variables s, t, and sa. These variables are maintained in storage during the contract lifetime and they are represented as values with no references within. A potential value of these variables is shown in Figure 3b. On the other hand, the top of Figure 3c shows a function with three variables in the memory data location, one as the argument to the function, and two defined within the function. Because they are in memory, these variables are references to heap locations. Any data of reference types, stored within the structures and arrays, is also a reference and can be reallocated or assigned to point to an existing heap location. This means that the layout of the data can contain arbitrary graphs with arbitrary aliasing. A potential layout of these variables is shown at the bottom of Figure 3c.

Functions. Functions are the Solidity equivalent of methods in classes. They receive data as arguments, perform computations, manipulate state variables and interact with other Ethereum accounts. Besides accessing the storage of the contract through its state variables, functions can also define local variables, including function arguments and return values. Variables of value types are stored as values on a stack. Variables of reference types must be explicitly declared with a data location, and are always pointers to an entity in that data location (storage or memory). A pointer to storage is called a *local storage pointer*. As the storage is not memory in the usual sense, but a value instead, one can see storage pointers as encoding a path to one reference type entity in the storage.

Example 4. Consider the example in Figure 1. The local variable r in function `append()` points to the struct at index `at` of the state variable `records` (residing in the contract storage). In contrast, the return value `ret` of function `get()` is a pointer to an integer array in memory.

Statements and expressions. Solidity includes usual programming statements and control structures. To keep the presentation simple, we focus on the statements that are related to the formalization of the memory model: local variable declarations, assignments, array manipulation, and the `delete` statement.[4] Solidity expressions relevant for the memory model are identifiers, member and array accesses, conditionals and allocation of new arrays and structs in memory.

If a value is not provided, local variable declarations automatically initialize the variable to a default value. For reference types in memory, this allocates new entities on the heap and performs recursive initialization of its members. For reference types in storage, the local storage pointers must always be explicitly initialized to point to a storage member. This ensures that no pointer is ever "null". Value types are initialized to their simple default value (0, false). Behavior of assignment in Solidity is complex (see Section 3.5) and depends on the data location of its arguments (e.g., deep copy or pointer assignment). Dynamically-sized storage arrays can be extended by pushing an element to their end, or can be shrunk by popping. The `delete` statement assigns the default value (recursively for reference types) to a given entity based on its type.

Example 5. The assignment r.set = true in the `append()` function of Figure 1 is a simple value assignment. On the other hand, ret = records[at].data in the `get()` function allocates a new array on the heap and performs a deep copy of data from storage to memory.

2.3   SMT-Based Programs

We formalize the semantics of the Solidity fragment by translating it to a simple programming language that uses SMT semantics [9,12] for the types and data. The syntax of this language is shown in Figure 4. The syntax is purposefully

---

[4] Our implementation [20] supports a majority of statements, excluding low-level operations (such as inline assembly). Loops are also supported and can be specified with loop invariants.

TypeName	::= int | bool	Integer, Boolean
	| [TypeName] TypeName	SMT array
	| DataTypeName	SMT datatype
DataTypeDef	::= DataTypeName((id : TypeName)*)	Datatype definition
expr	::= id	Identifier
	| expr[expr]	Array read
	| expr[expr ← expr]	Array write
	| DataTypeName(expr*)	Datatype constructor
	| expr.id	Member selector
	| ite(expr, expr, expr)	Conditional
	| expr + expr | expr − expr	Arithmetic expression
VarDecl	::= id : TypeName	Variable declaration
stmt	::= id := expr	Assignment
	| if expr then stmt* else stmt*	If-then-else
	| assume(expr)	Assumption
Program	::= DataTypeDef* VarDecl* stmt*	Program definition

Fig. 4: Syntax of SMT-based programs.

minimal and generic, so that it can be expressed in any modern SMT-based verification tool (e.g., Boogie [5], Why3 [18] or Dafny [26]).[5]

The types of SMT-based programs are the SMT types: simple value types such as Booleans and mathematical integers, and structured types such as arrays [27,16] and inductive datatypes [8]. The expressions of the language are standard SMT expressions such as identifiers, array reads and writes, datatype constructors, member selectors, conditionals and basic arithmetic [7]. All variables are declared at the beginning of a program. The statements of the language are limited to assignments, the if-then-else statement, and assumption statement.

SMT-based programs are a good fit for modeling of program semantics. For one, they have clear semantics with no ambiguities. Furthermore, any property of the program can be checked with SMT solvers: the program can be translated directly to a SMT formula by a single static assignment (SSA) transformation.

Note that the syntax requires the left hand side of an assignment to be an identifier. However, to make our presentation simpler, we will allow array read, member access and conditional expressions (and their combination) as LHS. Such constructs can be eliminated iteratively in the following way until only identifiers appear as LHS in assignments.

- $a[i] := e$ is equivalent to $a := a[i \leftarrow e]$.
- $d.m_j := e$ is equivalent to $d := D(d.m_1, \ldots, d.m_{j-1}, e, d.m_{j+1}, \ldots, d.m_n)$, where D is the constructor of a datatype with members $m_1, \ldots, m_n$.
- $ite(c, t, f) := e$ is equivalent to $if\ c\ then\ t := e\ else\ f := e$.

---

[5] Our current implementation is based on Boogie, but we have plans to introduce a generic intermediate representation that could incorporate alternate backends such as Why3 or Dafny.

3   Formalization

In this section we present our formalization of the Solidity semantics through a translation that maps Solidity elements to constructs in the SMT-based language. The formalization is described top-down in separate subsections for types, contracts, state variables, functions, statements, and expressions.

3.1   Types

We use $\mathcal{T}(.)$ to denote the function that maps a Solidity type to an SMT type. This function is used in the translation of contract elements and can, as a side effect, introduce datatype definitions and variable declarations. This is denoted with $[decl]$ in the result of the function. To simplify the presentation, we assume that such side effects are automatically added to the preamble of the SMT program. Furthermore, we assume that declarations with the same name are only added once. We use $\mathsf{type}(expr)$ to denote the original (Solidity) type of an expression (to be used later in the formalization). The definition of $\mathcal{T}(.)$ is shown in Figure 5.

$$
\begin{aligned}
&\mathcal{T}(\texttt{bool}) \quad\;\; \doteq bool \\
&\mathcal{T}(\texttt{address}) \doteq \mathcal{T}(\texttt{int}) \doteq \mathcal{T}(\texttt{uint}) \doteq int \\[4pt]
&\mathcal{T}(\texttt{mapping}(K\texttt{=>}V)\ \texttt{storage}) \doteq [\mathcal{T}(K)]\mathcal{T}(V) \\
&\mathcal{T}(\texttt{mapping}(K\texttt{=>}V)\ \texttt{storptr}) \doteq [int]int \\[4pt]
&\mathcal{T}(T\,\texttt{[}n\texttt{]}\ \texttt{storage}) \doteq \mathcal{T}(T\texttt{[]}\ \texttt{storage}) \\
&\mathcal{T}(T\,\texttt{[}n\texttt{]}\ \texttt{storptr}) \doteq \mathcal{T}(T\texttt{[]}\ \texttt{storptr}) \\
&\mathcal{T}(T\,\texttt{[}n\texttt{]}\ \texttt{memory}) \;\doteq \mathcal{T}(T\texttt{[]}\ \texttt{memory}) \\[4pt]
&\mathcal{T}(T\texttt{[]}\ \texttt{storage}) \doteq StorArr_T \text{ with } [StorArr_T(arr:[int]\mathcal{T}(T), length:int)] \\
&\mathcal{T}(T\texttt{[]}\ \texttt{storptr}) \doteq [int]int \\
&\mathcal{T}(T\texttt{[]}\ \texttt{memory}) \;\doteq int \qquad \text{with } [MemArr_T(arr:[int]\mathcal{T}(T), length:int)] \\
&\hspace{16em} [arrheap_T:[int]MemArr_T] \\[4pt]
&\mathcal{T}(\texttt{struct}\ S\ \texttt{storage}) \doteq StorStruct_S \text{ with } [StorStruct_S(\ldots, m_i:\mathcal{T}(S_i),\ldots)] \\
&\mathcal{T}(\texttt{struct}\ S\ \texttt{storptr}) \doteq [int]int \\
&\mathcal{T}(\texttt{struct}\ S\ \texttt{memory}) \;\doteq int \qquad \text{with } [MemStruct_S(\ldots, m_i:\mathcal{T}(S_i),\ldots)] \\
&\hspace{16em} [structheap_S:[int]MemStruct_S]
\end{aligned}
$$

Fig. 5: Formalization of Solidity types. Members of struct S are denoted as m_i with types S_i.

Value types. Booleans are mapped to SMT Booleans while other value types are mapped to SMT integers. Addresses are also mapped to SMT integers so that arithmetic comparison and conversions between integers and addresses is supported. For simplicity, we map all integers (signed or unsigned) to SMT integers.[6] Solidity also allows function types to store, pass around, and call functions, but this is not yet supported by our encoding.

Reference types. The Solidity syntax does not always require the data location for variable and parameter declarations. However, for reference types it is always required (enforced by the compiler), except for state variables that are always implicitly storage. In our formalization, we assume that the data location of reference types is a part of the type. As discussed before, memory entities are always accessed through pointers. However, for storage we distinguish whether it is the storage reference itself (e.g., state variable) or a storage pointer (e.g., local variable, function parameter). We denote the former with `storage` and the latter with `storptr` in the type name. Our modeling of reference types relies on the generalized theory of arrays [16] and the theory of inductive data-types [8], both of which are supported by modern SMT solvers (e.g., CVC4 [6] and Z3 [28]).

Mappings and arrays. For both arrays and mappings, we abstract away the implementation details of Solidity and model them with the SMT theory of arrays and inductive datatypes. We formalize Solidity mappings simply as SMT arrays. Both fixed- and dynamically-sized arrays are translated using the same SMT type and we only treat them differently in the context of statements and expressions. Strings and byte arrays are not discussed here, but we support them as particular instances of the array type. To ensure that array size is properly modeled we keep track of it in the datatype (*length*) along with the actual elements (*arr*).

For *storage array types* with base type T, we introduce an SMT datatype $StorArr_T$ with a constructor that takes two arguments: an inner SMT array (*arr*) associating integer indexes and the recursively translated base type ($\mathcal{T}(T)$), and an integer *length*. The advantage of this encoding is that the value semantics of storage data is provided by construction: each array element is a separate entity (no aliasing) and assigning storage arrays in SMT makes a deep copy. This encoding also generalizes if the base type is a reference type.

For *memory array types* with base type T, we introduce a separate datatype $MemArr_T$ (side effect). However, memory arrays are stored with pointer values. Therefore the memory array type is mapped to integers, and a heap ($arrheap_T$) is introduced to associate integers (pointers) with the actual memory array datatypes. Note that mixing data locations within a reference type is not possible: the element type of the array has the same data location as the array itself. Therefore, it is enough to introduce two datatypes per element type T: one for storage and one for memory. In the former case the element type will have value semantics whereas in the latter case elements will be stored as pointers.

Structs. For each *storage struct type* S the translation introduces an inductive datatype $StorStruct_S$, including a constructor for each struct member with types

---

[6] Note that this does not capture the precise machine integer semantics, but this is not relevant from the perspective of the memory model. Precise computation can be provided by relying on SMT bitvectors or modular arithmetic (see, e.g., [20]).

mapped recursively. Similarly to arrays, this ensures the value semantics of storage such as non-aliasing and deep copy assignments. For each *memory struct S* we also introduce a datatype *MemStruct_S* and a constructor for each member.[7] However, the memory struct type itself is mapped to integers (pointer) and a heap (*structheap_S*) is introduced to associate the pointers with the actual memory struct datatypes. Note that if a memory struct has members with reference types, they are also pointers, which is ensured recursively by our encoding.

3.2   Local Storage Pointers

An interesting aspect of the storage data location is that, although the stored data has value semantics, it is still possible to define pointers to an entity in storage within a local context, e.g., with function parameters or local variables. These pointers are called *local storage pointers*.

Example 6. In the `append()` function of Figure 1 the variable r is defined to be a convenience pointer into the storage map `records[at]`. Similarly, the `isset()` function takes a storage pointer to a `Record` entity in storage as an argument.

Since our formalization uses SMT datatypes to encode the contract data in storage, it is not possible to encode these pointers directly. A partial solution would be to substitute each occurrence of the local pointer with the expression that is assigned to it when it was defined. However, this approach is too simplistic and has limitations. Local storage pointers can be reassigned, or assigned conditionally, or it might not be known at compile time which definition should be used. Furthermore, local storage pointers can also be passed in as function arguments: they can point to different storage entities for different calls.

   We propose an approach to encode local storage pointers while overcoming these limitations. Our encoding relies on the fact that storage data of a contract can be viewed as a finite-depth tree of values. As such, each element of the stored data can be uniquely identified by a finite path leading to it.[8]

Example 7. Consider the contract C in Figure 6a. The contract defines structs T and S, and state variables of these types. If we are interested in all storage entities of type T, we can consider the sub-tree of the contract storage tree that has leaves of type T, as depicted in Figure 6b. The root of the tree is the contract itself, with indexed sub-nodes for state variables, in order. For nodes of struct type there are indexed sub-nodes leading to its members, in order. For each node of array type there is a sub-node for the base type. Every pointer to a storage T entity can be identified by a path in this tree: by fixing the index to each state

---

[7] Mappings in Solidity cannot reside in memory. If a struct defines a mapping member and it is stored in memory, the mapping is simply inaccessible. Such members could be omitted from the constructor.

[8] Solidity does support a limited form of recursive data-types. Such types could make the storage a tree of potentially arbitrary depth. We chose not to support such types as recursion is non-existing in Solidity types used in practice.

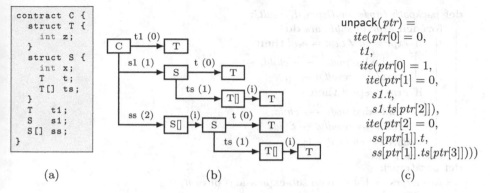

(a)	(b)	(c)

Fig. 6: An example of packing and unpacking: (a) contract with struct definitions and state variables; (b) the storage tree of the contract for type T; and (c) the unpacking expression for storage pointers of type T.

variable, member, and array index, as seen in brackets in Figure 6b, such paths can be encoded as an array of integers. For example, the state variable t1 can be represented as $[0]$, the member s1.t as $[1,0]$, and ss[8].ts[5] as $[2,8,1,5]$.

This idea allows us to encode storage pointer types (pointing to arrays, structs or mappings) simply as SMT arrays ($[int]int$). The novelty of our approach is that storage pointers can be encoded and passed around, while maintaining the value semantics of storage data, without the need for quantifiers to describe non-aliasing. To encode storage pointers, we need to address initialization and dereference of storage pointers, while assignment is simply an assignment of array values. When a storage pointer is initialized to a concrete expression, we *pack* the indexed path to the storage entity (that the expression references) into an array value. When a storage pointer is dereferenced (e.g., by indexing into or accessing a member), the array is *unpacked* into a conditional expression that will evaluate to a storage entity by decoding paths in the tree.

Storage tree. The storage tree for a given type T can be easily obtained by filtering the AST nodes of the contract definition to only include state variable declarations and to, further, only include nodes that lead to a sub-node of type T. We denote the storage tree for type T as tree(T).[9]

Packing. Given an expression (such as ss[8].ts[5]), pack(.) uses the storage tree for the type of the expression and encodes it to an array (e.g., $[2,8,1,5]$) by fitting the expression into the tree. Pseudocode for pack(.) is shown in Figure 7. To start, the expression is decomposed into a list of base sub-expressions. The base expression of an identifier id is id itself. For an array index $e[i]$ or a member

---

[9] In our implementation we do not explicitly compute the storage tree but instead traverse directly the AST provided by the Solidity compiler.

```
def packpath (node, subExprs, d, result):
    foreach expr in subExprs do
        if expr = id ∨ expr = e.id then
                          id (i)
            find edge node ⟶ child;
            result := result[d ← i];
        if expr = e[idx] then
                          (i)
            find edge node ⟶ child;
            result := result[d ← E(idx)];
        node, d := child, d + 1;
    return result
def pack(expr):
    baseExprs := list of base sub-expressions of expr;
    baseExpr := car(baseExprs);
    if baseExpr is a state variable then
        return packpath(tree(type(expr)), baseExprs, 0, constarr[int]int(0))
    if baseExpr is a storage pointer then
        result := constarr[int]int(0);
        prefix := E(baseExpr);
        foreach path to a leaf in tree(type(baseExpr)) do
            pathResult, pathCond := prefix, true;
            foreach kth edge on the path with label id (i) do
                pathCond := pathCond ∧ prefix[k] = i
            pathResult := packpath(leaf, cdr(baseExprs), len(path), pathResult);
            result := ite(pathCond, pathResult, result);
        return result
```

Fig. 7: Packing of an expressions. It returns a symbolic array expression that, when evaluated, can identify the path to the storage entity that the expression references.

access $e.m_i$ it is recursively the base expressions of e. We call the first element of this list (denoted by car) the base expression (the innermost base expression). The base expression is always either a state variable or a storage pointer, and we consider these two cases separately.

If the *base expression is a state variable*, we simply align the expression along the storage tree with the packpath function. The packpath function takes the list of base sub-expressions, and the storage tree to use for alignment, and then processes the expressions in order. If the current expression is an identifier (state variable or member access), the algorithm finds the outgoing edge annotated with the identifier (from the current node) and writes the index into the result array. If the expression is an index access, the algorithm maps and writes the index expression (symbolically) in the array. The expression mapping function $\mathcal{E}(.)$ is introduced later in Section 3.6.

If the *base expression is a storage pointer*, the process is more general since the "start" of the packing must accommodate any point in storage where the base expression can point to. In this case the algorithm finds all paths to leaves in the tree of the base pointer, identifies the condition for taking that path and writes the labels on the path to an array. Then it uses `packpath` to continue writing the array with the rest of the expression (denoted by `cdr`), as before. Finally, a conditional expression is constructed with all the conditions and packed arrays. Note, that the type of this conditional is still an SMT array of integers as it is the case for a single path.

Example 8. For contract in Figure 6a, `pack(ss[8].ts[5])` produces $[2, 8, 1, 5]$ by calling `packpath` on the base sub-expressions $[ss, ss[8], ss[8].ts, ss[8].ts[5]]$. First, 2 is added as `ss` is the state variable with index 2. Then, `ss[8]` is an index access so 8 is mapped to 8 and added to the result. Next, `ss[8].ts` is a member access with `ts` having the index 1. Finally, `ss[8].ts[5]` is an index access so 5 is mapped to 5 and added.

```
def unpack(ptr):
    return unpack(ptr, tree(type(ptr)), empty, 0);
def unpack(ptr, node, expr, d):
    result := empty;
    if node has no outgoing edges then result := expr;
    if node is contract then
        foreach edge node ─id (i)→ child do
            result := ite(ptr[d] = i, unpack(ptr, child, id, d + 1), result);
    if node is struct then
        foreach edge node ─id (i)→ child do
            result := ite(ptr[d] = i, unpack(ptr, child, expr.id, d + 1), result);
    if node is array/mapping with edge node ─(i)→ child then
        result := unpack(ptr, child, expr[ptr[d]], d + 1);
    return result;
```

Fig. 8: Unpacking of a local storage pointer into a conditional expression.

Unpacking. The opposite of `pack()` is `unpack()`, shown in Figure 8. This function takes a storage pointer (of type $[int]int$) and produces a conditional expression that decodes any given path into one of the leaves of the storage tree. The function recursively traverses the tree starting from the contract node and accumulates the expressions leading to the leaves. The function creates conditionals when branching, and when a leaf is reached the accumulated expression is simply returned. For contracts we process edges corresponding to each state variable by setting the subexpression to be the state variable itself. For structs we process edges corresponding to each member by wrapping the subexpression into a member access. For both contracts and structs, the subexpressions are collected into a conditional as separate cases. For arrays and mappings we process the single outgoing edge by wrapping the subexpression into an index access using the current element (at index d) of the pointer.

Example 9. For example, the conditional expression corresponding to the tree in Figure 6b can be seen in Figure 6c. Given a pointer *ptr*, if $ptr[0] = 0$ then the conditional evaluates to *t1*. Otherwise, if $ptr[0] = 1$ then *s1* has to be taken, where two leaves are possible: if $ptr[1] = 0$ then the result is *s1.t* otherwise it is *s1.ts*$[ptr[2]]$, and so on. If *ptr* is $[2, 8, 1, 5]$ then the conditional evaluates exactly to ss[8].ts[5] from which *ptr* was packed.[10]

Note that with inheritance and libraries [30] it is possible that a contract defines a type T but has no nodes in its storage tree. The contract can still define functions with storage pointers to T, which can be called by derived contracts that define state variables of type T. In such cases we declare an array of type $[int]\mathcal{T}(T)$, called the *default context*, and unpack storage pointers to T as if the default context was a state variable. This allows us to reason about abstract contracts and libraries, modeling that their storage pointers can point to arbitrary entities not yet declared.

3.3   Contracts, State Variables, Functions

The focus of our discussion is the Solidity memory model and, for presentation purposes, we assume a minimalist setting where the important aspects of storage and memory can be presented: we assume a single contract and a single function to translate. Interactions between multiple functions are handled differently depending on the verification approach. For example, in modular verification functions are checked individually against specifications (pre- and post-conditions) and function calls are replaced by their specification [20].

State variables. Each state variable s_i of a contract is mapped to a variable declaration $s_i : \mathcal{T}(\text{type}(s_i))$ in the SMT program.[11] The data location of state variables is always storage. As discussed previously, reference types are mapped using SMT datatypes and arrays, which ensures non-aliasing by construction. While Solidity optionally allows inline initializer expressions for state variables, without the loss of generality we can assume that they are initialized in the constructor using regular assignments.

---

[10] Note that due to the "else" branches, unpack is a is a non-injective surjective function. For example, $[a, 8, 1, 5]$ with any $a \geq 2$ would evaluate to the same slot. However this does not affect our encoding as pointers cannot be compared and pack always returns the same (unique) values.

[11] Generalizing this to multiple contracts can be done directly by using a separate one-dimensional heap for each state variable, indexed by a receiver parameter (*this* : *address*) identifying the current contract instance (see, e.g., [20]).

$$\mathsf{defval}(\mathtt{bool}) \;\; \doteq false$$
$$\mathsf{defval}(\mathtt{address}) \doteq \mathsf{defval}(\mathtt{int}) \doteq \mathsf{defval}(\mathtt{uint}) \doteq 0$$

$$\mathsf{defval}(\mathtt{mapping}(K\texttt{=>}V)) \doteq \mathsf{constarr}_{[\mathcal{T}(K)]\mathcal{T}(V)}(\mathsf{defval}(V))$$

$$\mathsf{defval}(T\texttt{[]} \;\; \mathtt{storage}) \doteq \mathsf{defval}(T\texttt{[0]} \;\; \mathtt{storage})$$
$$\mathsf{defval}(T\texttt{[]} \;\; \mathtt{memory}) \;\; \doteq \mathsf{defval}(T\texttt{[0]} \;\; \mathtt{memory})$$

$$\mathsf{defval}(T\texttt{[}n\texttt{]} \;\; \mathtt{storage}) \doteq StorArr_T(\mathsf{constarr}_{[int]\mathcal{T}(T)}(\mathsf{defval}(T)), n)$$
$$\mathsf{defval}(T\texttt{[}n\texttt{]} \;\; \mathtt{memory}) \;\; \doteq [ref : int] \text{ (fresh symbol)}$$
$$ \{ref := refcnt := refcnt + 1\}$$
$$ \{arrheap_T[ref].length := n\}$$
$$ \{arrheap_T[ref].arr[i] := \mathsf{defval}(T)\} \qquad \text{for } 0 \leq i \leq n$$
$$ ref$$

$$\mathsf{defval}(\mathtt{struct} \;\; S \;\; \mathtt{storage}) \doteq StorStruct_S(\ldots, \mathsf{defval}(S_i), \ldots)$$
$$\mathsf{defval}(\mathtt{struct} \;\; S \;\; \mathtt{memory}) \;\; \doteq [ref : int] \text{ (fresh symbol)}$$
$$ \{ref := refcnt := refcnt + 1\}$$
$$ \{structheap_S[ref].m_i = \mathsf{defval}(S_i)\} \text{ for each } m_i$$
$$ ref$$

Fig. 9: Formalization of default values. We denote struct S members as m_i with types S_i.

Functions calls. From the perspective of the memory model, the only important aspect of function calls is the way parameters are passed in and how function return values are treated. Our formalization is general in that it allows us to treat both of the above as plain assignments (explained later in Section 3.5). For each parameter p_i and return value r_i of a function, we add declarations $p_i : \mathcal{T}(\mathsf{type}(p_i))$ and $r_i : \mathcal{T}(\mathsf{type}(r_i))$ in the SMT program. Note that for reference types appearing as parameters or return values of the function, their types are either memory or storage pointers.

Memory allocation. In order to model allocation of new memory entities, while keeping some non-aliasing information, we introduce an allocation counter $refcnt$: int variable in the preamble of the SMT program. This counter is incremented for each allocation of memory entities and used as the address of the new entity. For each parameter p_i with memory data location we include an assumption $assume(p_i \leq refcnt)$ as they can be arbitrary pointers, but should not alias with new allocations within the function. Note that if a parameter of memory pointer type is a reference type containing other references, such non-aliasing constraints need to be assumed recursively [25]. This can be done for structs by enumerating members. But, for dynamic arrays it requires quantification that is nevertheless still decidable (array property fragment [13]).

Initialization and default values. If we are translating the constructor function, each state variable s_i is first initialized to its default value with a statement $s_i := \mathsf{defval}(\mathsf{type}(s_i))$. For regular functions, we set each return value r_i to its default value with a statement $r_i := \mathsf{defval}(\mathsf{type}(r_i))$. We use $\mathsf{defval}(.)$, as defined in Figure 9, to denote the function that maps a Solidity type to its default value as an SMT expression. Note that, as a side effect, this function can do allocations for memory entities, introducing extra declarations and statements, denoted by [*decl*] and {*stmt*}. As expected, the default value is *false* for Booleans and 0 for other primitives that map to integers. For mappings from K to V, the default value is an SMT constant array returning the default value of the value type V for each key $k \in K$ (see, e.g., [16]). The default value of storage arrays is the corresponding datatype value constructed with a constant array of the default value for base type T, and a length of n or 0 for fixed- or dynamically-sized arrays. For storage structs, the default value is the corresponding datatype value constructed with the default values of each member.

The default value of uninitialized memory pointers is unusual. Since Solidity doesn't support "null" pointers, a new entity is automatically allocated in memory and initialized to default values (which might include additional recursive initialization). Note, that for fixed-size arrays Solidity enforces that the array size n must be an integer literal or a compile time constant, so setting each element to its default value is possible without loops or quantifiers. Similarly for structs, each member is recursively initialized, which is again possible by explicitly enumerating each member.

3.4   Statements

We use $\mathcal{S}[\![.]\!]$ to denote the function that translates Solidity statements to a list of statements in the SMT program. It relies on the type mapping function $\mathcal{T}(.)$ (presented previously in Section 3.1) and on the expression mapping function $\mathcal{E}(.)$ (to be introduced in Section 3.6). Furthermore, we define a helper function $\mathcal{A}(.,.)$ dedicated to modeling Solidity assignments (to be discussed in Section 3.5).

The definition of $\mathcal{S}[\![.]\!]$ is shown in Figure 10. As a side effect, extra declarations can be introduced to the preamble of the SMT program (denoted by [*decl*]). The Solidity documentation [30] does not precisely state the order of evaluating subexpressions in statements. It only specifies that subnodes are processed before the parent node. This problem is independent form the discussion of the memory models so we assume that side effects of subexpressions are added in the same order as it is implemented in the compiler. Furthermore, if a subexpression is mapped multiple times, we assume that the side effects are only added once. This makes our presentation simpler by introducing fewer temporary variables.

Local variable declarations introduce a variable declaration with the same identifier in the SMT program by mapping the type.[12] If an initialization expression is given, it is mapped using $\mathcal{E}(.)$ and assigned to the variable. Otherwise, the default value is used as defined by defval(.) in Figure 9. Delete assigns the default value for a type, which is simply mapped to an assignment in our formalization. Solidity supports multiple assignments as one statement with a tuple-like syntax. The documentation [30] does not specify the behavior precisely, but the

---

[12] Without the loss of generality we assume that identifiers in Solidity are unique. The compiler handles scoping and assigns an unique identifier to each declaration.

$$\mathcal{S}[\![T\ id]\!] \quad\quad\ \doteq [id:\mathcal{T}(T)];\ \mathcal{A}(id,\mathsf{defval}(T))$$
$$\mathcal{S}[\![T\ id = expr]\!] \doteq [id:\mathcal{T}(T)];\ \mathcal{A}(id,\mathcal{E}(expr))$$
$$\mathcal{S}[\![\texttt{delete}\ e]\!] \quad\doteq \quad\quad\quad \mathcal{A}(\mathcal{E}(e),\mathsf{defval}(\mathsf{type}(e)))$$

$$\mathcal{S}[\![l_1,\dots,l_n = r_1,\dots,r_n]\!] \doteq [tmp_i:\mathcal{T}(\mathsf{type}(r_i))]\ \text{for}\ 1 \le i \le n\ (\text{fresh symbols})$$
$$\mathcal{A}(tmp_i,\mathcal{E}(r_i)) \quad\quad \text{for}\ 1 \le i \le n$$
$$\mathcal{A}(\mathcal{E}(l_i),tmp_i) \quad\quad \text{for}\ n \ge i \ge 1\ (\text{reversed})$$

$$\mathcal{S}[\![e_1.\texttt{push}(e_2)]\!] \doteq \mathcal{A}(\mathcal{E}(e_1).arr[\mathcal{E}(e_1).length],\mathcal{E}(e_2))$$
$$\mathcal{E}(e_1).length := \mathcal{E}(e_1).length + 1$$
$$\mathcal{S}[\![e.\texttt{pop}()]\!] \quad\doteq \mathcal{E}(e).length := \mathcal{E}(e).length - 1$$
$$\mathcal{A}(\mathcal{E}(e).arr[\mathcal{E}(e).length],\mathsf{defval}(\mathsf{arrtype}(\mathcal{E}(e))))$$

Fig. 10: Formalization of statements.

```
contract C {
  struct S { int x; }

  S s1, s2, s3;

  function primitiveAssign() {
    s1.x = 1; s2.x = 2; s3.x = 3;
    (s1.x, s3.x, s2.x) = (s3.x, s2.x, s1.x);
    // s1.x == 3, s2.x == 1, s3.x == 2
  }
  function storageAssign() {
    s1.x = 1; s2.x = 2; s3.x = 3;
    (s1, s3, s2) = (s3, s2, s1);
    // s1.x, s2.x, s3.x are all equal to 1
  }
}
```

Fig. 11: Example illustrating the right-to-left assignment order and the treatment of reference types in storage in tuple assignment.

```
contract C {
  struct S { int x; }

  S[] a;

  constructor() {
    a.push(S(1));
    S storage s = a[0];
    a.pop();
    assert(s.x == 1); // Ok
    // Following is error
    // assert(a[0].x == 1);
  }
}
```

Fig. 12: Example illustrating a dangling pointer to storage.

compiler first evaluates the RHS and LHS tuples (in this order) from left to right and then assignment is performed component-wise from right to left.

Example 10. Consider the tuple assignment in function `primitiveAssign()` in Figure 11. From right to left, `s2.x` is assigned first with the value of `s1.x` which is 1. Afterwards, when `s3.x` is assigned with `s2.x`, the already evaluated (old) value of 2 is used instead of the new value 1. Finally, `s1.x` gets the old value of `s3.x`, i.e., 3. Note however, that storage expressions on the RHS evaluate to storage pointers. Consider, for example, the function `storageAssign()` in Figure 11. From right to left, `s2` is assigned first, with a pointer to `s1` making `s2.x` become 1. However, as opposed to primitive types, when `s3` is assigned next, `s2` on the RHS is a storage pointer and thus the new value in the storage of `s2` is assigned to `s3` making `s3.x` become 1. Similarly, `s1.x` also becomes 1 as the new value behind `s3` is used.

Array push increases the length and assigns the given expression as the last element. Array pop decreases the length and sets the removed element to its default value. While the removed element can no longer be accessed via indexing into an array (a runtime error occurs), it can still be accessed via local storage pointers (see Figure 12).[13]

3.5   Assignments

Assignments between reference types in Solidity can be either pointer assignments or value assignments, involving deep copying and possible new allocations in the latter case. We use $\mathcal{A}(lhs, rhs)$ to denote the function that assigns a rhs SMT expression to a lhs SMT expression based on their original types and data locations. The definition of $\mathcal{A}(.,.)$ is shown in Figure 13. Value type assignments are simply mapped to an SMT assignment. To make our presentation more clear, we subdivide the other cases into separate functions for array, struct and mapping operands, denoted by $\mathcal{A}_A(.,.)$, $\mathcal{A}_S(.,.)$ and $\mathcal{A}_M(.,.)$ respectively.

Mappings. As discussed previously, Solidity prohibits direct assignment of mappings. However, it is possible to declare a storage pointer to a mapping, in which case the RHS expression is packed. It is also possible to assign two storage pointers, which simply assigns pointers. Other cases are a no-op.[14]

Structs and arrays. For structs and arrays the semantics of assignment is summarized in Figure 14. However, there are some notable details in various cases that we expand on below.

Assigning anything *to storage* LHS always causes a deep copy. If the RHS is storage, this is simply mapped to a datatype assignment in our encoding (with an additional unpacking if the RHS is storage pointer).[15] If the RHS is memory, deep copy for structs can be done member wise by accessing the heap with the RHS pointer and performing the assignment recursively (as members can be reference types themselves). For arrays, we access the datatype corresponding to the array via the heap and do an assignment, which does a deep copy in SMT. Note however, that this only works if the base type of the array is a value type. For reference types, memory array elements are pointers and would require being dereferenced during assignment to storage. As opposed to struct members, the number of array elements is not known at compile time so loops or quantifiers have to be used (as in traditional software analysis). However, this is a

---

[13] The current version (0.5.x) of Solidity supports resizing arrays by assigning to the length member. However, this behavior is dangerous and has been since removed in the next version (0.6.0) (see https://solidity.readthedocs.io/en/v0.6.0/060-breaking-changes.html). Therefore, we do not support this in our encoding.

[14] This is consequence of the fact that keys are not stored in mappings and so the assignment is impossible to perform.

[15] This also causes mappings to be copied, which contradicts the current semantics. However, we chose to keep the deep copy as assignments of mappings is planned to be disallowed in the future (see https://github.com/ethereum/solidity/issues/7739).

$$\mathcal{A}(lhs, rhs) \doteq lhs := rhs \quad \text{for value type operands}$$
$$\mathcal{A}(lhs, rhs) \doteq \mathcal{A}_M(lhs, rhs) \text{ for mapping type operands}$$
$$\mathcal{A}(lhs, rhs) \doteq \mathcal{A}_S(lhs, rhs) \text{ for struct type operands}$$
$$\mathcal{A}(lhs, rhs) \doteq \mathcal{A}_A(lhs, rhs) \text{ for array type operands}$$

$$\mathcal{A}_M(lhs : \mathbf{sp}, rhs : \mathbf{s}) \doteq lhs := \mathsf{pack}(rhs)$$
$$\mathcal{A}_M(lhs : \mathbf{sp}, rhs : \mathbf{sp}) \doteq lhs := rhs$$
$$\mathcal{A}_M(lhs, rhs) \doteq \{\} \qquad \text{(all other cases)}$$

$$\mathcal{A}_S(lhs : \mathbf{s}, rhs : \mathbf{s}) \doteq lhs := rhs$$
$$\mathcal{A}_S(lhs : \mathbf{s}, rhs : \mathbf{m}) \doteq \mathcal{A}(lhs.m_i, structheap_{type(rhs)}[rhs].m_i) \text{ for each } m_i$$
$$\mathcal{A}_S(lhs : \mathbf{s}, rhs : \mathbf{sp}) \doteq \mathcal{A}_S(lhs, \mathsf{unpack}(rhs))$$
$$\mathcal{A}_S(lhs : \mathbf{m}, rhs : \mathbf{m}) \doteq lhs := rhs$$
$$\mathcal{A}_S(lhs : \mathbf{m}, rhs : \mathbf{s}) \doteq lhs := refcnt := refcnt + 1$$
$$\mathcal{A}(structheap_{type(lhs)}[lhs].m_i, rhs.m_i) \text{ for each } m_i$$
$$\mathcal{A}_S(lhs : \mathbf{m}, rhs : \mathbf{sp}) \doteq \mathcal{A}_S(lhs, \mathsf{unpack}(rhs))$$
$$\mathcal{A}_S(lhs : \mathbf{sp}, rhs : \mathbf{s}) \doteq lhs := \mathsf{pack}(rhs)$$
$$\mathcal{A}_S(lhs : \mathbf{sp}, rhs : \mathbf{sp}) \doteq lhs := rhs$$

$$\mathcal{A}_A(lhs : \mathbf{s}, rhs : \mathbf{s}) \doteq lhs := rhs$$
$$\mathcal{A}_A(lhs : \mathbf{s}, rhs : \mathbf{m}) \doteq lhs := arrheap_{type(rhs)}[rhs]$$
$$\mathcal{A}_A(lhs : \mathbf{s}, rhs : \mathbf{sp}) \doteq \mathcal{A}_A(lhs, \mathsf{unpack}(rhs))$$
$$\mathcal{A}_A(lhs : \mathbf{m}, rhs : \mathbf{m}) \doteq lhs := rhs$$
$$\mathcal{A}_A(lhs : \mathbf{m}, rhs : \mathbf{s}) \doteq lhs := refcnt := refcnt + 1$$
$$arrheap_{type(lhs)}[lhs] := rhs$$
$$\mathcal{A}_A(lhs : \mathbf{m}, rhs : \mathbf{sp}) \doteq \mathcal{A}_A(lhs, \mathsf{unpack}(rhs))$$
$$\mathcal{A}_A(lhs : \mathbf{sp}, rhs : \mathbf{s}) \doteq lhs := \mathsf{pack}(rhs)$$
$$\mathcal{A}_A(lhs : \mathbf{sp}, rhs : \mathbf{sp}) \doteq lhs := rhs$$

Fig. 13: Formalization of assignment based on different type categories and data locations for the LHS and RHS. We use $\mathbf{s}$, $\mathbf{sp}$ and $\mathbf{m}$ after the arguments to denote storage, storage pointer and memory types respectively.

special case, which can be encoded in the decidable array property fragment [13]. Assigning storage (or storage pointer) *to memory* is also a deep copy but in the other direction. However, instead overwriting the existing memory entity, a new one is allocated (recursively for reference typed elements or members). We model this by incrementing the reference counter, storing it in the LHS and then accessing the heap for deep copy using the new pointer.

3.6   Expressions

We use $\mathcal{E}(.)$ to denote the function that translates a Solidity expression to an SMT expression. As a side effect, declarations and statements might be introduced (denoted by $[decl]$ and $\{stmt\}$ respectively). The definition of $\mathcal{E}(.)$ is shown in Figure 15. As discussed in Section 3.4 we assume that side effects are added from subexpressions in the proper order and only once.

Member access is mapped to an SMT member access by mapping the base expression and the member name. There is an extra unpacking step for storage

lhs/rhs	Storage	Memory	Stor.ptr.
Storage	Deep copy	Deep copy	Deep copy
Memory	Deep copy	Pointer assign	Deep copy
Stor.ptr.	Pointer assign	Error	Pointer assign

Fig. 14: Semantics of assignment between array and struct operands based on their data location.

$\mathcal{E}(id) \doteq id$

$\mathcal{E}(expr.id) \doteq \mathcal{E}(expr).\mathcal{E}(id)$ if type($expr$) = struct S storage
$\mathcal{E}(expr.id) \doteq$ unpack($\mathcal{E}(expr)$).$\mathcal{E}(id)$ if type($expr$) = struct S storptr
$\mathcal{E}(expr.id) \doteq structheap_S[\mathcal{E}(expr)].\mathcal{E}(id)$ if type($expr$) = struct S memory
$\mathcal{E}(expr.id) \doteq \mathcal{E}(expr).\mathcal{E}(id)$ if type($expr$) = T[] storage
$\mathcal{E}(expr.id) \doteq$ unpack($\mathcal{E}(expr)$).$\mathcal{E}(id)$ if type($expr$) = T[] storptr
$\mathcal{E}(expr.id) \doteq arrheap_T[\mathcal{E}(expr)].\mathcal{E}(id)$ if type($expr$) = T[] memory

$\mathcal{E}(expr[idx]) \doteq \mathcal{E}(expr).arr[\mathcal{E}(idx)]$ if type($expr$) = T[] storage
$\mathcal{E}(expr[idx]) \doteq$ unpack($\mathcal{E}(expr)$).$arr[\mathcal{E}(idx)]$ if type($expr$) = T[] storptr
$\mathcal{E}(expr[idx]) \doteq arrheap_T[\mathcal{E}(expr)].arr[\mathcal{E}(idx)]$ if type($expr$) = T[] memory
$\mathcal{E}(expr[idx]) \doteq \mathcal{E}(expr)[\mathcal{E}(idx)]$ if type($expr$) = mapping(K=>V) storage
$\mathcal{E}(expr[idx]) \doteq$ unpack($\mathcal{E}(expr)$)[$\mathcal{E}(idx)$]   if type($expr$) = mapping(K=>V) storptr

$\mathcal{E}(cond\ ?\ expr_T\ :\ expr_F) \doteq [var_T : \mathcal{T}(\text{type}(cond\ ?\ expr_T\ :\ expr_F))]$ (fresh symbol)
                  $[var_F : \mathcal{T}(\text{type}(cond\ ?\ expr_T\ :\ expr_F))]$ (fresh symbol)
                  $\{\mathcal{A}(var_T, \mathcal{E}(expr_T))\}$
                  $\{\mathcal{A}(var_F, \mathcal{E}(expr_F))\}$
                  $ite(\mathcal{E}(cond), var_T, var_F)$

$\mathcal{E}(\mathbf{new}\ T[](expr)) \doteq [ref : int]$ (fresh symbol)
                $\{ref := refcnt := refcnt + 1\}$
                $\{arrheap_T[ref].length := \mathcal{E}(expr)\}$
                $\{arrheap_T[ref].arr[i] := \text{defval}(T)\}$ for $0 \le i \le \mathcal{E}(expr)$
                ref

$\mathcal{E}(S(\ldots, expr_i, \ldots)) \doteq [ref : int]$ (fresh symbol)
                $\{ref := refcnt := refcnt + 1\}$
                $\{structheap_S[ref].m_i := \mathcal{E}(expr_i)\}$ for each member m_i
                ref

Fig. 15: Formalization of expressions. We denote struct S members as m_i with types S_i.

pointers and a heap access for memory. Note that the only valid member for arrays is length. Index access is mapped to an SMT array read by mapping the base expression and the index, and adding en extra member access for arrays to get the inner array arr of elements from the datatype. Furthermore, similarly to member accesses, an extra unpacking step is needed for storage pointers and a heap access for memory.

Conditionals in Solidity can be mapped to an SMT conditional in general. However, data locations can be different for the true and false branches, causing possible side effects. Therefore, we first introduce fresh variables for the true and false branch with the common type (of the whole conditional), then make assignments using $\mathcal{A}(.,.)$ and finally use the new variables in the conditional. The documentation [30] does not specify the common type, but the compiler returns memory if any of the branches is memory, and storage pointer otherwise.

Allocating a new array in memory increments the reference counter, sets the length and the default values for each element (recursively). Note that in general the length might not be a compile time constant,in which case setting default values could be encoded with the array property fragment (similarly to deep copy in assignments) [13]. Allocating a new memory struct also increments the reference counter and sets each value by translating the provided arguments.

4 Evaluation

The formalization described in this paper serves as the basis of our Solidity verification tool SOLC-VERIFY [20].[16] In this section we provide an evaluation of the presented formalization and our implementation by validating it on a set of relevant test cases. For illustrative purposes we also compare our tool with other available Solidity analysis tools.[17]

"Real world" contracts currently deployed on Ethereum (e.g., contract available on Etherscan) have limited value for evaluating memory model semantics. Many such contracts use old compiler versions with constructs that are not supported anymore, and do not use newer features. There are also many toy and trivial contracts that are deployed but not used, and popular contracts (e.g. tokens) are over-represented with many duplicates. Furthermore, the inconsistent usage of assert and require [20] makes evaluation hard. Evaluating the memory semantics requires contracts that exercise diverse features of the memory model. There are larger dApps that do use more complex features (e.g., Augur or ENS), but these contracts also depend on many other features (e.g. inheritance, modifiers, loops) that would skew the results.

Therefore we have manually developed a set of tests that try to capture the interesting behaviors and corner cases of the Solidity memory semantics. The tests are targeted examples that do not use irrelevant features. The set is structured so that every target test behavior is represented with a test case that sets up the state, exercises a specific feature and checks the correctness of the behavior with assertions. This way a test should only pass if the tool provides a correct verification result by modeling the targeted feature precisely.

---

[16] SOLC-VERIFY is open source, available at https://github.com/SRI-CSL/solidity. Besides certain low-level constructs (such as inline assembly) SOLC-VERIFY supports a majority of Solidity features that we omitted from the presentation, including inheritance, function modifiers, for/while loops and if-then-else.

[17] All tests, with a Truffle test harness, a docker container with all the tools, and all individual results are available at https://github.com/dddejan/solidity-semantics-tests.

The correctness of the tests themselves is determined by running them through the EVM with no assertion failures. Test cases are expanded to use all reference types and combinations of reference types. This includes structures, mappings, dynamic and fixed-size arrays, both single- and multi-dimensional.

The tests are organized into the following classes. Tests in the assignment class check whether the assign statement is properly modeled. This includes assignments in the same data location, but also assignments across data locations that need deep copying, and assignments and re-assignments of memory and storage pointers. The delete class of tests checks whether the delete statement is properly modeled. Tests in the init class check whether variable and data initialization is properly modeled. For variables in storage, we check if they are properly initialized to default values in the contract constructor. Similarly, we check whether memory variables are properly initialized to provided values, or default values when no initializer is provided. The storage class of tests checks whether storage itself is properly modeled for various reference types, including for example non-aliasing. Tests in the storageptr class check whether storage pointers are modeled properly. This includes checking if the model properly treats storage pointers to various reference types, including nested types. In addition, the tests check that the storage pointers can be properly passed to functions and ensure non-aliasing for distinct parts of storage.

For illustrative purposes we include a comparison with the following available Solidity analysis tools: MYTHRIL v0.21.17 [29], VERISOL v0.1.1-alpha [24], and SMT-CHECKER v0.5.12 [1]. MYTHRIL is a Solidity symbolic execution tool that runs analysis at the level of the EVM bytecode. VERISOL is similar to SOLC-VERIFY in that it uses Boogie to model the Solidity contracts, but takes the traditional approach to modeling memory and storage with pointers and quantifiers. SMT-CHECKER is an SMT-based analysis module built into the Solidity compiler itself. There are other tools that can be found in the literature, but they are either basic prototypes that cannot handle realistic features we are considering, or are not available for direct comparison.

We ran the experiments on a machine with Intel Xeon E5-4627 v2 @ 3.30GHz CPU enforcing a 60s timeout and a memory limit of 64GB. Results are shown in Table 1. As expected, MYTHRIL has the most consistent results on our test set. This is because MYTHRIL models contract semantics at the EVM level and does not need to model complex Solidity semantics. Nevertheless, the results also indicate that the performance penalty for this precision is significant (8 timeouts). VERISOL, as the closest to our approach, still doesn't support many features and has a significant amount of false reports for features that it does support. Many false reports are because their model of storage is based on pointers and tries to ensure storage consistency with the use of quantifiers. SMT-CHECKER doesn't yet support the majority of the Solidity features that our tests target.

Based on the results, SOLC-VERIFY performs well on our test set, matching the precision of MYTHRIL at very low computational cost. The few false alarms we have are either due to Solidity features that we chose to not implement (e.g., proper treatment of mapping assignments), or parts of the semantics that we

Table 1: Results of evaluating MYTHRIL, VERISOL, SMT-CHECKER, and SOLC-VERIFY on our test suite.

assignment (102)	correct	incorrect	unsupported	timeout	time (s)
MYTHRIL	94	0	0	8	1655.14
VERISOL	10	61	31	0	175.27
SMT-CHECKER	6	9	87	0	15.25
SOLC-VERIFY	78	8	16	0	62.81
delete (14)	correct	incorrect	unsupported	timeout	time (s)
MYTHRIL	13	1	0	0	47.51
VERISOL	3	8	3	0	24.66
SMT-CHECKER	0	0	14	0	0.30
SOLC-VERIFY	7	1	6	0	9.02
init (18)	correct	incorrect	unsupported	timeout	time (s)
MYTHRIL	15	3	0	0	59.67
VERISOL	7	8	3	0	28.82
SMT-CHECKER	0	0	18	0	0.41
SOLC-VERIFY	13	5	0	0	11.88
storage (27)	correct	incorrect	unsupported	timeout	time (s)
MYTHRIL	27	0	0	0	310.40
VERISOL	12	15	0	0	43.45
SMT-CHECKER	2	0	25	0	1.32
SOLC-VERIFY	27	0	0	0	17.61
storageptr (164)	correct	incorrect	unsupported	timeout	time (s)
MYTHRIL	164	0	0	0	1520.29
VERISOL	128	19	17	0	203.93
SMT-CHECKER	4	18	142	0	21.93
SOLC-VERIFY	164	0	0	0	96.92

only implemented partially (such as deep copy of arrays with reference types and recursively initializing memory objects). There are no technical difficulties in supporting them and they are planned in the future.

5 Related Work

There is a strong push in the Ethereum community to apply formal methods to smart contract verification. This includes many attempts to formalize the semantics of smart contracts, both at the level of EVM and Solidity.

EVM-level semantics. Bhargavan et al. [11] decompile a fragment of EVM to F*, modeling EVM as a stack based machine with word and byte arrays for storage and memory. Grishchenko et al. [19] extend this work by providing a small step semantics for EVM. KEVM [21] provides an executable formal semantics of EVM in the K framework. Hirai [22] formalizes EVM in Lem, a language used by some interactive theorem provers. Amani et al. [2] extends this work by defining a program logic to reason about EVM bytecode.

Solidity-level semantics. Jiao et al. [23] formalize the operational semantics of Solidity in the K framework. Their formalization focuses on the details of bit-precise sizes of types, alignment and padding in storage. They encode storage slots, arrays and mappings with the full encoding of hashing. However, the formalization does not describe assignments (e.g., deep copy) apart from simple cases. Furthermore, user defined structs are also not mentioned. In contrast, our semantics is high-level and abstracts away some details (e.g., hashes, alignments) to enable efficient verification. Additionally, we provide proper modeling of different cases for assignments between storage and memory. Bartotelli et al. [10] propose TINYSOL, a minimal core calculus for a subset of Solidity, required to model basic features such as asset transfer and reentrancy. Contract data is modeled as a key value store, with no differences in storage and memory, or in value and reference types. Crafa et al. [15] introduce Featherweight Solidity, a calculus formalizing core features of the language, with focus on primitive types. Data locations and reference types are not discussed, only mappings are mentioned briefly. The main focus is on the type system and type checking. They propose an improved type system that can statically detect unsafe casts and callbacks. The closest to our work is the work of Zakrzewski [33], a Coq formalization focusing on functions, modifiers, and the memory model. The memory model is treated similarly: storage is a mapping from names to storage objects (values), memory is a mapping from references to memory objects (containing references recursively) and storage pointers define a path in storage. Their formalization is also high-level, without considering alignment, padding or hashing. The formalization is provided as big step functional semantics in Coq. While the paper presents some example rules, the formalization does not cover all cases. For example the details of assignments (e.g., memory to storage), push/pop for arrays, treating memory aliasing and new expressions. Furthermore, our approach focuses on SMT and modular verification, which enables automated reasoning.

6 Conclusion

We presented a high-level SMT-based formalization of the Solidity memory model semantics. Our formalization covers all aspects of the language related to managing both the persistent contract storage and the transient local memory. The novel encoding of storage pointers as arrays allows us to precisely model non-aliasing and deep copy assignments between storage entities without the need for quantifiers. The memory model forms the basis of our Solidity-level modular verification tool SOLC-VERIFY. We developed a suite of test cases exercising all aspects of memory management with different combinations of reference types. Results indicate that our memory model outperforms existing Solidity-level tools in terms of soundness and precision, and is on par with low-level EVM-based implementations, while having a significantly lower computational cost for discharging verification conditions.

References

1. Alt, L., Reitwiessner, C.: SMT-based verification of Solidity smart contracts. In: ISoLA 2018, LNCS, vol. 11247, pp. 376–388. Springer (2018). https://doi.org/10.1007/978-3-030-03427-6_28
2. Amani, S., Bégel, M., Bortin, M., Staples, M.: Towards verifying ethereum smart contract bytecode in Isabelle/HOL. In: Proceedings of the 7th ACM SIGPLAN International Conference on Certified Programs and Proofs. pp. 66–77. ACM (2018)
3. Antonopoulos, A., Wood, G.: Mastering Ethereum: Building Smart Contracts and Dapps. O'Reilly Media, Inc. (2018)
4. Atzei, N., Bartoletti, M., Cimoli, T.: A survey of attacks on Ethereum smart contracts. In: POST 2017, LNCS, vol. 10204, pp. 164–186. Springer (2017). https://doi.org/10.1007/978-3-662-54455-6_8
5. Barnett, M., Chang, B.Y.E., DeLine, R., Jacobs, B., Leino, K.R.M.: Boogie: A modular reusable verifier for object-oriented programs. In: FMCO 2005, LNCS, vol. 4111, pp. 364–387. Springer (2006). https://doi.org/10.1007/11804192_17
6. Barrett, C., Conway, C.L., Deters, M., Hadarean, L., Jovanović, D., King, T., Reynolds, A., Tinelli, C.: CVC4. In: CAV 2011, LNCS, vol. 6806, pp. 171–177. Springer (2011). https://doi.org/10.1007/978-3-642-22110-1_14
7. Barrett, C., Fontaine, P., Tinelli, C.: The Satisfiability Modulo Theories Library (SMT-LIB) (2016), www.SMT-LIB.org
8. Barrett, C., Shikanian, I., Tinelli, C.: An abstract decision procedure for satisfiability in the theory of recursive data types. Journal on Satisfiability, Boolean Modeling and Computation 3, 21–46 (2007)
9. Barrett, C., Tinelli, C.: Satisfiability modulo theories. In: Handbook of Model Checking, pp. 305–343. Springer (2018)
10. Bartoletti, M., Galletta, L., Murgia, M.: A minimal core calculus for Solidity contracts. In: DPM 2019, CBT 2019, LNCS, vol. 11737, pp. 233–243. Springer (2019). https://doi.org/978-3-030-31500-9_15
11. Bhargavan, K., Delignat-Lavaud, A., Fournet, C., Gollamudi, A., Gonthier, G., Kobeissi, N., Kulatova, N., Rastogi, A., Sibut-Pinote, T., Swamy, N., Zanella-Béguelin, S.: Formal verification of smart contracts: Short paper. In: ACM Workshop on Programming Languages and Analysis for Security. pp. 91–96. ACM (2016)
12. Biere, A., Heule, M., van Maaren, H.: Handbook of satisfiability. IOS press (2009)
13. Bradley, A.R., Manna, Z., Sipma, H.B.: What's decidable about arrays? In: VMCAI 2006, LNCS, vol. 3855, pp. 427–442. Springer (2006). https://doi.org/10.1007/11609773_28
14. Chen, H., Pendleton, M., Njilla, L., Xu, S.: A survey on ethereum systems security: Vulnerabilities, attacks and defenses (2019), https://arxiv.org/abs/1908.04507
15. Crafa, S., Pirro, M.D., Zucca, E.: Is solidity solid enough? In: Financial Cryptography Workshops (2019)
16. De Moura, L., Bjørner, N.: Generalized, efficient array decision procedures. In: Formal Methods in Computer-Aided Design. pp. 45–52. IEEE (2009)
17. Dhillon, V., Metcalf, D., Hooper, M.: The DAO hacked. In: Blockchain Enabled Applications, pp. 67–78. Apress (2017)
18. Filliâtre, J.C., Paskevich, A.: Why3 — where programs meet provers. In: ESOP 2013, LNCS, vol. 7792, pp. 125–128. Springer (2013). https://doi.org/10.1007/978-3-642-37036-6_8
19. Grishchenko, I., Maffei, M., Schneidewind, C.: A semantic framework for the security analysis of Ethereum smart contracts. In: POST 2018, LNCS, vol. 10804, pp. 243–269. Springer (2018). https://doi.org/10.1007/978-3-319-89722-6_10

20. Hajdu, Á., Jovanović, D.: SOLC-VERIFY: A modular verifier for Solidity smart contracts. In: VSTTE 2019, LNCS, vol. 12301. Springer (2019), (In press)
21. Hildenbrandt, E., Saxena, M., Zhu, X., Rodrigues, N., Daian, P., Guth, D., Rosu, G.: KEVM: A complete semantics of the Ethereum virtual machine. Tech. rep., IDEALS (2017)
22. Hirai, Y.: Defining the Ethereum virtual machine for interactive theorem provers. In: FC 2017, LNCS, vol. 10323, pp. 520–535. Springer (2017). https://doi.org/10.1007/978-3-319-70278-0_33
23. Jiao, J., Kan, S., Lin, S., Sanán, D., Liu, Y., Sun, J.: Executable operational semantics of Solidity (2018), http://arxiv.org/abs/1804.01295
24. Lahiri, S.K., Chen, S., Wang, Y., Dillig, I.: Formal specification and verification of smart contracts for azure blockchain. In: VSTTE 2019, LNCS, vol. 12301. Springer, (In press)
25. Leino, K.R.M.: Ecstatic: An object-oriented programming language with an axiomatic semantics. In: Proceedings of the Fourth International Workshop on Foundations of Object-Oriented Languages (1997)
26. Leino, K.R.M.: Dafny: An automatic program verifier for functional correctness. In: LPAR 2010, LNCS, vol. 11247, pp. 348–370. Springer (2010). https://doi.org/10.1007/978-3-642-17511-4_20
27. McCarthy, J.: Towards a mathematical science of computation. In: IFIP Congress. pp. 21–28 (1962)
28. de Moura, L., Bjørner, N.: Z3: An efficient SMT solver. In: TACAS 2008, LNCS, vol. 4963, pp. 337–340. Springer (2008). https://doi.org/10.1007/978-3-540-78800-3_24
29. Mueller, B.: Smashing Ethereum smart contracts for fun and real profit. In: Proceedings of the 9th Annual HITB Security Conference (HITBSecConf) (2018)
30. Solidity documentation (2019), https://solidity.readthedocs.io/
31. Szabo, N.: Smart contracts (1994)
32. Wood, G.: Ethereum: A secure decentralised generalised transaction ledger (2017), https://ethereum.github.io/yellowpaper/paper.pdf
33. Zakrzewski, J.: Towards verification of Ethereum smart contracts: A formalization of core of Solidity. In: VSTTE 2018, LNCS, vol. 11294, pp. 229–247. Springer (2018). https://doi.org/10.1007/978-3-030-03592-1_13

Exploring Type-Level Bisimilarity towards More Expressive Multiparty Session Types

Sung-Shik Jongmans[1,2,3] and Nobuko Yoshida[3]

[1] Department of Computer Science, Open University, Heerlen, the Netherlands
[2] CWI, Amsterdam, the Netherlands
[3] Department of Computing, Imperial College, London, UK

Abstract. A key open problem with multiparty session types (MPST) concerns their expressiveness: current MPST have inflexible choice, no existential quantification over participants, and limited parallel composition. This precludes many real protocols to be represented by MPST. To overcome these bottlenecks of MPST, we explore a new technique using weak bisimilarity between global types and endpoint types, which guarantees deadlock-freedom and absence of protocol violations. Based on a process algebraic framework, we present well-formed conditions for global types that guarantee weak bisimilarity between a global type and its endpoint types and prove their check is decidable. Our main practical result, obtained through benchmarks, is that our well-formedness conditions can be checked orders of magnitude faster than directly checking weak bisimilarity using a state-of-the-art model checker.

1 Introduction

Background. To take advantage of modern parallel and distributed computing platforms, message-passing concurrency is becoming increasingly important. Modern programming languages, however, offer insufficiently effective linguistic support to guide programmers towards *safe usage* of message-passing abstractions (e.g., to prevent deadlocks or protocol violations).

Multiparty session types (MPST) [34] constitute a static, correct-by-construction approach to simplify concurrent programming, by offering a type-based framework to specify message-passing protocols and ensure deadlock-freedom and protocol conformance. The idea is to use behavioural types [1,37] to enforce *protocols* (i.e., patterns of admissible communications) between *roles* (e.g., threads, processes, services) to avoid concurrency bugs. The framework is illustrated in Fig. 1: first, a *global type G* (protocol specification; written by the programmer) is *projected* onto every role; then, every resulting *endpoint type (local type) L_i* (role specification) is *type-checked*

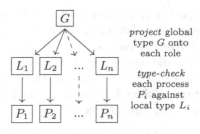

project global type G onto each role

type-check each process P_i against local type L_i

Fig. 1: MPST framework

© The Author(s) 2020
P. Müller (Ed.): ESOP 2020, LNCS 12075, pp. 251–279, 2020.
https://doi.org/10.1007/978-3-030-44914-8_10

with the corresponding *process* P_i (role implementation). If every process is well-typed against its local type, then their parallel composition is guaranteed to be free of deadlocks and protocol violations relative to the global type. Notably, common concurrency bugs as sends without receives, receives without sends, and type mismatches (actual type sent vs. expected type received) are ruled out statically. The MPST framework is *language-agnostic*: in recent years, practical implementations of MPST have been developed for several programming languages, including Erlang, F#, Go, Java, and Scala [18,35,36,45,46,50].

Three open problems. Many practically relevant protocols *cannot* be specified as global types; this limits MPST's applicability to real-world concurrent programs. Specifically, while the original work [33] has been extended with several advanced features (e.g., time [7,44], security [11,12,13,17], and parametrisation [18,25,47]), core features still have significant restrictions: inflexible choice, no existential quantification over participants, and limited parallel composition.

1. Inflexible choice: In the original work [33], if there is a choice between multiple branches, the sender in the first communication of each branch must be the same, the receiver must be the same, and the message type must be different (i.e., no non-determinism). Moreover, each role *not* involved in the first communication of each branch, must have the same behaviour in each continuation. For instance, the following global type specifies a protocol where Client c repeatedly requests an arithmetic Server s to compute the sum or product of two numbers:

$$\mu X. \left[\left[c \rightarrow s : \mathsf{Add} \cdot s \rightarrow c : \mathsf{Sum} \cdot X\right] + \left[c \rightarrow s : \mathsf{Mul} \cdot s \rightarrow c : \mathsf{Prod} \cdot X\right]\right]$$

Here, $c \rightarrow s : \mathsf{Add}$ specifies a communication of an Add-message (with two numbers as payload) from the Client to the Server, while $\cdot$ and $+$ specify sequencing and branching, and square brackets indicate operator precedence. This is a "good" global type that satisfies the conditions. In contrast, the following "bad" global type specifies a protocol where Client c repeatedly requests addition and multiplication Servers s_1 and s_2 via Router r (payload types omitted; $r_1 \rightarrow r_2 \rightarrow r_3 : t$ abbreviates $r_1 \rightarrow r_2 : t \cdot r_2 \rightarrow r_3 : t$):

$$\mu X. \left[\left[c \rightarrow r \rightarrow s_1 : \mathsf{Add} \cdot s_1 \rightarrow c : \mathsf{Sum} \cdot X\right] + \left[c \rightarrow r \rightarrow s_2 : \mathsf{Mul} \cdot s_2 \rightarrow c : \mathsf{Prod} \cdot X\right]\right]$$

Several improvements to the original work have been proposed: Honda et al. managed to allow each role r not involved in a choice to have different behaviour in different branches [15], so long as r is made aware of which branch is chosen in a timely and unambiguous fashion (e.g., the previous global type is still forbidden), while Lange et al., Castagna et al., and Hu & Yoshida managed to allow choices between different receivers [16,23,36,40]. For instance, the following global type (the Client *directly* requests the specialised server) is allowed:

$$\mu X. \left[\left[c \rightarrow s_1 : \mathsf{Add} \cdot s_1 \rightarrow c : \mathsf{Sum} \cdot X\right] + \left[c \rightarrow s_2 : \mathsf{Mul} \cdot s_2 \rightarrow c : \mathsf{Prod} \cdot X\right]\right]$$

But, the following global type (two Clients c_1 and c_2 use Server S) is forbidden:

$$\mu X. \begin{bmatrix} \left[c_1 \rightarrow s : \mathsf{Add} \cdot s \rightarrow c_1 : \mathsf{Sum} \cdot X\right] + \left[c_1 \rightarrow s : \mathsf{Mul} \cdot s \rightarrow c_1 : \mathsf{Prod} \cdot X\right] + \\ \left[c_2 \rightarrow s : \mathsf{Add} \cdot s \rightarrow c_2 : \mathsf{Sum} \cdot X\right] + \left[c_2 \rightarrow s : \mathsf{Mul} \cdot s \rightarrow c_2 : \mathsf{Prod} \cdot X\right] \end{bmatrix}$$

None of the existing works allow the above nondeterministic choices between different senders. We call this the +-**problem**: how to add a choice constructor, denoted by +, to specify choices between disjoint sender-receiver-label triples?

2. No existential quantification: Related to the +-problem is the ∃-**problem**: how to add an existential role quantifier, denoted by ∃, to specify the execution of ∃'s body for <u>some</u> role in ∃'s domain? For instance, instead of writing a separate global type for 2 Clients, 3 Clients, etc., existential role quantification allows us to write *only one* global type for any $n>1$ Clients:

$$\mu X. \exists r \in \{c_i \mid 1 \leq i \leq n\}. \left[\!\left[r \to s : \mathsf{Add} \cdot s \to r : \mathsf{Sum} \cdot X\right] + \left[r \to s : \mathsf{Mul} \cdot s \to r : \mathsf{Prod} \cdot X\right]\!\right]$$

The ∃-problem was first formulated by Deniélou & Yoshida [22] as the dual of the ∀-problem (i.e., specify the execution of ∀'s body for <u>each</u> role in ∀'s domain): the ∀-problem was solved in the same paper, but the ∃-problem "raises many semantic issues" [22] and has remained open for almost a decade.

3. Limited parallel composition: The third open problem related to choice is the ∥-**problem**: how to add a constructor, denoted by ∥, that allows *infinite branching* (i.e., non-finite control) through unbounded parallel interleaving? While extensions of the original work with parallel composition exist (e.g., [16,22,23,43]), none of these works supports unbounded interleaving. For instance, the following global type allows an unbounded number of requests to be served by the Server in parallel (instead of sequentializing them):

$$\mu X. \exists r \in \{c_i \mid 1 \leq i \leq n\}. \left[\!\left[r \to s : \mathsf{Add} \cdot [s \to r : \mathsf{Sum} \parallel X]\right] + \left[r \to s : \mathsf{Mul} \cdot [s \to r : \mathsf{Prod} \parallel X]\right]\!\right]$$

Contributions. We overcome these three bottlenecks of MPST with an approach based on three key novelties: first, we have a new definition of projection that keeps more information in the local types than existing definitions; second, we exploit this extra information to formulate our well-formedness conditions; third, we use an unexplored proof method for MPST, namely to prove the operational equivalence between a global type and its projections modulo weak bisimilarity. This makes the proofs cleaner and ultimately allows for more flexibility (e.g., our approach can be modularly combined with traditional session type checking, but potentially also with other verification methods, such as model checking or conformance testing). To summarise the highlights:

- For the first time, we provide solutions to the +-problem, the ∃-problem, and the ∥-problem, by presenting expressive syntax for global and local types (formulated as process algebraic terms), a refined notion of projection, and novel well-formedness conditions.
- Our main theoretical result is *operational equivalence*: a well-formed global type behaves the same as the parallel composition of its projections, modulo weak bisimulation. This implies freedom of deadlocks and freedom of protocol violations of the projections. Checking this equivalence is decidable.
  To our knowledge, we are the first to use (weak) bisimilarity to prove the correctness of a projection operator from global to local types. By doing so,

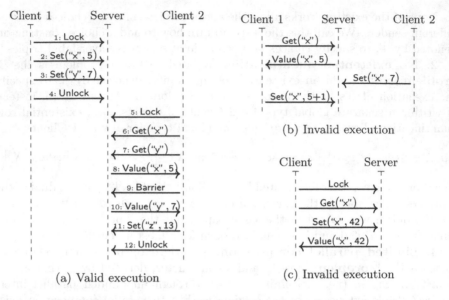

(a) Valid execution

(b) Invalid execution

(c) Invalid execution

Fig. 2: Example executions of the Key-Value Store protocol

we decouple (a) the act of reasoning about projection and (b) the act of establishing compliance between local types and process implementations; until our work, these two concerns have always been conflated.

– Our main practical results are: (1) to provide representative protocols typable in our approach; and (2) the well-formedness conditions of (1) can be checked orders of magnitude faster than directly checking weak bisimilarity using mCRL2 [10,20,29], a state-of-the-art model checker.

In Sect. 2, we present an overview of our contribution through a representative example protocol that is not supported by previous work. In Sect. 3, we present the details of our theoretical contribution. In Sect. 4, we present the details of our practical contribution (implementation and evaluation). In Sect. 5, we discuss related work. We conclude and discuss future work in Sect. 6.

Detailed formal definitions and proofs of all lemmas and theorems can be found in our supplement [38].

2   Overview of our Approach

Scenario. To highlight our solutions to the +-problem, ∃-problem, and ∥-problem, we consider a *Key-Value Store* protocol, similar to those used in modern NoSQL databases [21,27]. Specifically, our Key-Value Store protocol is inspired by the transaction mechanism of the popular Redis database [48,49]. This protocol is not supported by any of the existing MPST works.

The Key-Value Store protocol consists of n *Clients* that require access to the store, represented by role names $c_1, ..., c_n$, and one *Server* that provides access to the store, represented by role name s. The store has keys of type Str (strings) and values of type Nat (numbers). Fig. 2 shows valid and invalid example executions of the protocol ($n{=}2$) as message sequence charts; it works as follows.

First, a Lock-message is communicated from *some* Client c_i ($1{\leq}i{\leq}n$) to Server s (Fig. 2a, arrows 1, 5); this grants c_i exclusive access to the store. Then, a sequence of messages to write and/or read values is communicated:

- To write, a Set-message is communicated from c_i to s (arrows 2, 3, 11).
- To read, a Get-message is communicated from c_i to s (arrows 6, 7). Then, *eventually*, a Value-message is communicated from s to c_i (arrows 8, 10), but in the meantime, additional Get-messages can be communicated from c_i to s. In this way, the Client does not need to await the responses of the Server to perform multiple independent requests. To indicate enough Get-messages have been sent, a Barrier-message is communicated from c_i to s (arrow 9), which serves as a communication fence: the protocol will only proceed once all Value-messages for pending Get-messages have been communicated.

The sequence ends with the communication of an Unlock-message from c_i to s (arrow 12). The protocol is then repeated for *some* Client c_j ($1{\leq}j{\leq}n$); possibly, but not necessarily, $i{=}j$. In this way, the Server *atomically* processes accesses to the store between Lock/Unlock-messages.

Global and local types. The corresponding global type and local types, inferred via projection (for some n), are as follows:

$$G = \mu X.\, \exists r{\in}\{c_i \mid 1{\leq}i{\leq}n\}.\, r{\rightarrow}s{:}\mathsf{Lock}\cdot$$
$$\mu Y.\left[\begin{array}{l}[\mu Z.\,[[r{\rightarrow}s{:}\mathsf{Get}(\mathsf{Str})\cdot[s{\rightarrow}r{:}\mathsf{Value}(\mathsf{Str},\mathsf{Nat})\parallel Z]]{+}r{\rightarrow}s{:}\mathsf{Barrier}]\cdot Y]\\ {+}[r{\rightarrow}s{:}\mathsf{Set}(\mathsf{Str},\mathsf{Nat})\cdot Y]{+}[r{\rightarrow}s{:}\mathsf{Unlock}\cdot X]\end{array}\right]$$

$$L_{C_i} = \mu X.\, c_i s!\mathsf{Lock}\cdot$$
$$\mu Y.\left[\begin{array}{l}[\mu Z.\,[[c_i s!\mathsf{Get}(\mathsf{Str})\cdot[s c_i?\mathsf{Value}(\mathsf{Str},\mathsf{Nat})\parallel Z]]{+}c_i s!\mathsf{Barrier}]\cdot Y]\\ {+}[c_i s!\mathsf{Set}(\mathsf{Str},\mathsf{Nat})\cdot Y]{+}[c_i s!\mathsf{Unlock}\cdot X]\end{array}\right]$$

$$L_S = \mu X.\, \exists r{\in}\{c_i \mid 1 \leq i \leq n\}.\, rs?\mathsf{Lock}\cdot$$
$$\mu Y.\left[\begin{array}{l}[\mu Z.\,[[rs?\mathsf{Get}(\mathsf{Str})\cdot[sr!\mathsf{Value}(\mathsf{Str},\mathsf{Nat})\parallel Z]]{+}rs?\mathsf{Barrier}]\cdot Y]\\ {+}[rs?\mathsf{Set}(\mathsf{Str},\mathsf{Nat})\cdot Y]{+}[rs?\mathsf{Unlock}\cdot X]\end{array}\right]$$

Global type $r_1{\rightarrow}r_2{:}\ell(t)$ specifies the *communication* of a message labelled ℓ with a payload typed t from sender r_1 to receiver r_2; global type $G_1\cdot G_2$ specifies the *sequential composition* of global types G_1 and G_2; global type G_1+G_2 specifies the *alternative composition* (choice) of global types G_1 and G_2; global type $\exists r{\in}\{r_1,...,r_n\}.\,G$ specifies the *existential role quantification* over domain $\{r_1,...,r_n\}$ (i.e., the alternative composition of $G[r_1/r]$ and ... and $G[r_n/r]$, where $G[r_i/r]$ denotes the substitution of r_i for every r in G); global type $G_1 \parallel G_2$ specifies the *interleaving composition* of G_1 and G_2 (free merge [4]); global type $\mu X.\,G$ specifies recursion (i.e., X is bound to $\mu X.\,G$ in G).

Local type $r_1r_2!\ell(t)$ specifies the send of a $\ell(t)$-message through the channel from r_1 to r_2; dually, local type $r_1r_2?\ell(t)$ specifies a receive. Because every Client participates in only one branch of the quantification, their local types do not contain $\exists$ under the recursion. In contrast, because the Server participates in all branches, L_S does contain $\exists$ under the recursion.

By Thm. 3, G and the parallel composition of L_{C_1}, ..., L_{C_n}, L_S are operationally equivalent (weakly bisimilar), which in turn implies deadlock-freedom and absence of protocol violations. Note also that our global type for the Key-Value Store protocol indeed relies on solutions to the $+$-problem (choice between multiple clients that send a Lock-message), the $\exists$-problem (existential quantification over clients), and the $\|$-problem (unbounded interleaving to support asynchronous responses of a statically unknown number of requests).

3   An MPST Theory with $+$, $\exists$, and $\|$

3.1   Types as Process Algebraic Terms

We define our languages of global and local types as *algebras* over sets of (global) communications and (local) sends/receives. This subsection presents preliminaries on the generic algebraic framework we use, based on the existing algebras PA [3] and TCP+REC [2]; the next subsection presents our specific instantiations for global and local types.

Let $\mathbb{A}$ denote a set of *actions*, ranged over by α, and let $\{X_1, X_2, \ldots, Y, \ldots\}$ denote a set of *recursion variables*. Then, let $\mathrm{TERM}(\mathbb{A})$ denote the set of *(algebraic) terms*, ranged over by T, generated by the following grammar:

$$T ::= \mathbb{1} \mid \alpha \mid T_1 + T_2 \mid T_1 \cdot T_2 \mid T_1 \| T_2 \mid X \mid \langle X_k \mid \{X_i \mapsto T_i\}_{i \in I}\rangle \ (k \in I)$$

Term $\mathbb{1}$ specifies a *skip*; the grey background indicates it should not be explicitly written by programmers (but it is used only implicitly in the operational semantics). Term α specifies an atomic *action* from $\mathbb{A}$. Terms $T_1 + T_2$, $T_1 \cdot T_2$, and $T_1 \| T_2$ specify the *alternative composition*, the *sequential composition*, and the *interleaving composition* (free merge [4]; a form of parallel composition without interaction between the operands) of T_1 and T_2. Terms X and $\langle X_k \mid \{X_i \mapsto T_i\}_{i \in I}\rangle$ specify *recursion*, where $\{X_i \mapsto T_i\}_{i \in I}$ is a *recursive specification* that maps recursion variables to terms, X_k is the *initial call* (for T_k), and every X_j that occurs in T_k is a subsequent *recursive call* (for T_j); we write $\mu X.\, T$ instead of $\langle X \mid \{X \mapsto T\}\rangle$.

Let $\mathbb{X} \rightharpoonup \mathrm{TERM}(\mathbb{A})$ denote the set of all *recursive specifications* (i.e., every recursive specification is a partial function), ranged over by E, F, and let $\mathrm{sub}(E, T)$ denote the simultaneous substitution of term $E(X)$ for each recursion variable X in T. Fig. 3 defines the operational semantics of terms. It consists of two components: relation $\rightarrow$ defines reduction of terms, while relation $\downarrow$ defines successful termination of terms. In words, term $T_1 + T_2$ is reduced by reducing either T_1 or T_2; term $T_1 \cdot T_2$ is reduced by reducing first T_1 and then T_2; term

$$\frac{}{\alpha \xrightarrow{\alpha} \boxed{1}} \qquad \frac{T_1 \xrightarrow{\alpha} T_1'}{T_1 \cdot T_2 \xrightarrow{\alpha} T_1' \cdot T_2} \qquad \frac{T_1 \downarrow \quad T_2 \xrightarrow{\alpha} T_2'}{T_1 \cdot T_2 \xrightarrow{\alpha} T_2'} \qquad \frac{T_1 \xrightarrow{\alpha} T_1'}{T_1 + T_2 \xrightarrow{\alpha} T_1'} \qquad \frac{T_2 \xrightarrow{\alpha} T_2'}{T_1 + T_2 \xrightarrow{\alpha} T_2'}$$

$$\frac{T_1 \xrightarrow{\alpha} T_1'}{T_1 \parallel T_2 \xrightarrow{\alpha} T_1' \parallel T_2} \qquad \frac{T_2 \xrightarrow{\alpha} T_2'}{T_1 \parallel T_2 \xrightarrow{\alpha} T_1 \parallel T_2'} \qquad \frac{\mathsf{sub}(E, E(X)) \xrightarrow{\alpha} T'}{\langle X \,|\, E \rangle \xrightarrow{\alpha} T'}$$

(a) Reduction

$$\frac{}{\boxed{1} \downarrow} \qquad \frac{T_1 \downarrow}{T_1 + T_2 \downarrow} \qquad \frac{T_2 \downarrow}{T_1 + T_2 \downarrow} \qquad \frac{T_1 \downarrow \quad T_2 \downarrow}{T_1 \cdot T_2 \downarrow} \qquad \frac{T_1 \downarrow \quad T_2 \downarrow}{T_1 \parallel T_2 \downarrow} \qquad \frac{\mathsf{sub}(E, E(X)) \downarrow}{\langle X \,|\, E \rangle \downarrow}$$

(b) Termination

Fig. 3: Operational semantics of terms

$T_1 \parallel T_2$ is reduced by reducing T_1 and T_2 interleaved; and term $\langle X \,|\, E \rangle$ is reduced by reducing the version of $E(X)$ where recursion variables have been substituted.

A term is $\boxed{1}$-*free* if it has no occurrences of $\boxed{1}$. A term is *closed* if it has no occurrences of free recursion variables. A term T is *deterministic* if (1) for every action α, there exists at most one term T' such that T can reduce to T' by performing α, and (2) every term to which T can reduce is deterministic as well. Henceforth, we consider only $\boxed{1}$-free, closed, and deterministic terms.

We note that $\langle \mathbb{A}, +, \cdot, \parallel \rangle$ is the signature of PA [3], while $\langle \boxed{1}, \mathbb{A}, +, \cdot, \parallel, \mathbb{X}, \langle\text{-}|\text{-}\rangle \rangle$ is a subsignature of TCP+REC [2]. As the operational semantics of terms in $\mathrm{TERM}(\mathbb{A})$ coincides with the operational semantics of terms in (the corresponding subalgebra of) TCP+REC, our languages of global and local types inherit TCP+REC's sound and complete *axiomatisation*, used in our tool (Sect. 4.1).

3.2   Global Types and Local Types

Actions. We instantiate $\mathrm{TERM}(\mathbb{A})$ to obtain languages of global and local types by defining action sets for (global) communications and for (local) sends/receives.

Let $\mathbb{R} = \{\mathsf{a}, \mathsf{b}, ...\}$ denote the set of all *role names*, ranged over by r. Let $\mathrm{LAB} = \{\mathsf{Lock}, \mathsf{Get}, ...\}$ denote the set of all *labels*, ranged over by ℓ. Let $\mathbb{T} = \{\mathsf{Nat}, \mathsf{Bool}, ...\}$ denote the set of all *payload types*, ranged over by t. Let $\mathbb{U} = \mathrm{LAB} \times \mathbb{T}$ denote the set of all *message types*, ranged over by U; we write $\ell(t)$ instead of $\langle \ell, t \rangle$. Finally, let $\mathbb{A}_g$ and $\mathbb{A}_l$ denote the sets of all *(global) communications* and *(local) sends/receives*, ranged over by g and l, generated by:

$$g ::= r_1 \rightarrow r_2 : U \ \ (\textbf{if: } r_1 \neq r_2)$$
$$l ::= r_1 r_2 ! U \mid r_1 r_2 ? U \mid \varepsilon^r_{r_1 r_2} \ \ (\textbf{if: } r_1 \neq r_2 \textbf{ and } r_1 \neq r \neq r_2)$$

Global action $r_1 \rightarrow r_2 : U$ specifies the communication of a U-message from sender r_1 to receiver r_2; we note that communications are synchronous, as actions in the underlying algebra are indivisible [2,3], but asynchrony can be encoded (Exmp. 1, below). Local action $r_1 r_2 ! U$ specifies the send of a U-message through channel $r_1 r_2$ (from r_1 to r_2). Dually, local action $r_1 r_2 ? U$ specifies a receive. Local

$$\mathsf{split}(r, r_1 \twoheadrightarrow r_2 : U) = \begin{cases} (\mathbf{1}, r_1 \twoheadrightarrow r_2 : U) & \textbf{if: } r \in \{r_1, r_2\} \\ (r_1 \twoheadrightarrow r_2 : U, \mathbf{1}) & \textbf{otherwise} \end{cases}$$

$$\mathsf{split}(r, G_1 \cdot G_2) = \begin{cases} (G_1', G_1'' \cdot G_2) & \textbf{if: } \mathsf{split}(r, G_1) = (G_1', G_1'') \text{ and } G_1'' \neq \mathbf{1} \\ (G_1 \cdot G_2', G_2'') & \textbf{if: } \mathsf{split}(r, G_1) = (G_1', G_1'') \text{ and } G_1'' = \mathbf{1} \text{ and} \\ & \quad \mathsf{split}(r, G_2) = (G_2', G_2'') \text{ and } G_2'' \neq \mathbf{1} \\ (G_1 \cdot G_2, \mathbf{1}) & \textbf{otherwise} \end{cases}$$

$$\frac{}{G \rightsquigarrow G} \qquad \frac{M \rightsquigarrow G \quad \mathsf{split}(r_2, G) = (G', G'')}{r_1 \twoheadrightarrow r_2 : U \cdot M \rightsquigarrow r_1 \twoheadrightarrow r_1 r_2 : U \cdot [r_1 r_2 \twoheadrightarrow r_2 : U \,\|\, G'] \cdot G''} \text{ (asynchrony)}$$

$$\frac{}{\Sigma \emptyset \rightsquigarrow \mathbf{1}} \qquad \frac{M_k \rightsquigarrow G_k \quad \Sigma \{M_i\}_{i \in I \setminus \{k\}} \rightsquigarrow G \quad k \in I}{\Sigma \{M_i\}_{i \in I} \rightsquigarrow G_k + G} \text{ (n-ary choice)}$$

$$\frac{}{\overline{\mu}(X, \ell_{\mathbf{c}}, \ell_{\mathbf{e}}, \emptyset) \rightsquigarrow \mathbf{1}} \text{ (finite recursion: base)}$$

$$M_i' = \overline{\mu}(X, \ell_{\mathbf{c}}, \ell_{\mathbf{e}}, \{\langle r_{1j}, r_{2j}, M_j \rangle\}_{j \in I \setminus \{i\}}) \textbf{ for all } i \in I$$
$$\frac{\Sigma \{[r_{1i} \twoheadrightarrow r_{2i} : \ell_{\mathbf{c}} \cdot M_i \cdot X] + [r_{1i} \twoheadrightarrow r_{2i} : \ell_{\mathbf{e}} \cdot M_i']\}_{i \in I} \rightsquigarrow G}{\overline{\mu}(X, \ell_{\mathbf{c}}, \ell_{\mathbf{e}}, \{\langle r_{1i}, r_{2i}, G_i \rangle\}_{i \in I}) \rightsquigarrow \mu X . G} \text{ (finite recursion: step)}$$

$$\frac{\Sigma \{M[r_i/r]\}_{i \in I} \rightsquigarrow G}{\exists r \in \{r_i\}_{i \in I} . M \rightsquigarrow G} \text{ (existential role quantification)}$$

Fig. 4: Macros

action $\varepsilon_{r_1 r_2}^r$ specifies the *idling* of role r during a communication between roles r_1 and r_2. The inclusion of such annotated idling actions in local types is novel; we shortly elaborate on its purpose.

We can now define $\mathbb{GLOB} = \mathrm{TERM}(\mathbb{A}_g)$ and $\mathbb{LOC} = \mathrm{TERM}(\mathbb{A}_l)$ as the sets of all global and local types, ranged over by G and L.

Macros. As a testimony to the unique expressive power of our language of global types, we extend it with a number of *macros* that can be expanded to "normal" global types in $\mathbb{GLOB}$. A macro M is generated by the following grammar:

$$M ::= G \in \mathbb{GLOB} \mid r_1 \twoheadrightarrow r_2 \cdot M \mid \Sigma \{M_i\}_{i \in I} \mid$$
$$\overline{\mu}(X, \ell_{\mathbf{c}}, \ell_{\mathbf{e}}, \{\langle r_{1i}, r_{2i}, M_i \rangle\}_{i \in I}) \mid \exists r \in \{r_i\}_{i \in I} . M$$

Degenerate "macro" G is a normal global type; it is part of the grammar to nest global types inside macros. Macro $r_1 \twoheadrightarrow r_2 \cdot M$ specifies an asynchronous communication from sender r_1 to receiver r_2. Macro $\Sigma \{M_i\}_{i \in I}$ specifies an n-ary choice among $|I|$ alternatives. Macro $\overline{\mu}(X, \ell_{\mathbf{c}}, \ell_{\mathbf{e}}, \{\langle r_{1i}, r_{2i}, M_i \rangle\}_{i \in I})$ specifies finite recursion: at the start of each unfolding of recursion variable X, for some $i \in I$, either an $\ell_{\mathbf{c}}$-message is communicated from sender r_{1i} to receiver r_{2i} (in which case they *continue* their participation in the recursion), or an $\ell_{\mathbf{e}}$-message is communicated (in which case they *exit*). Macro $\exists r \in \{r_i\}_{i \in I} . M$ specifies existential role quantification. Macros can be nested. Slightly abusing notation, we allow macros to occur and be expanded freely in "normal" global types.

Fig. 4 defines the macro expansion rules. We note that the left-hand side of $\rightsquigarrow$ is a macro, while the right-hand side is a normal global type. We demonstrated existential role quantification in Sect. 2; below, we give two more examples to illustrate our encoding of asynchronous communication and finite recursion.

Example 1 (Asynchrony). Although communications are synchronous, we can encode asynchrony by representing *buffered channels* (unordered, as in asynchronous π-calculus [32]) explicitly as roles that participate in a protocol. To this end, assume for all $r_1, r_2 \in \mathbb{R}$, there exists a role $r_1 r_2 \in \mathbb{R}$ as well (to represent the buffer from r_1 to r_2); alternatively $r_1 r_2$ could be any fresh name.

The following global types (message types omitted) specify paradigmatic cases for protocols with asynchronous communications:

$$M_1 = \mathsf{a} \twoheadrightarrow \mathsf{b} \cdot \mathbf{1} \qquad \rightsquigarrow G_1 = \mathsf{a} \rightarrow \mathsf{ab} \cdot \mathsf{ab} \twoheadrightarrow \mathsf{b}$$

$$M_2 = \mathsf{a} \twoheadrightarrow \mathsf{b} \cdot \mathsf{a} \twoheadrightarrow \mathsf{b} \cdot \mathbf{1} \rightsquigarrow G_2 = \mathsf{a} \rightarrow \mathsf{ab} \cdot [\mathsf{ab} \twoheadrightarrow \mathsf{b} \parallel \mathsf{a} \rightarrow \mathsf{ab}] \cdot \mathsf{ab} \twoheadrightarrow \mathsf{b}$$

$$M_3 = \mathsf{a} \twoheadrightarrow \mathsf{b} \cdot \mathsf{b} \twoheadrightarrow \mathsf{a} \cdot \mathbf{1} \rightsquigarrow G_3 = \mathsf{a} \rightarrow \mathsf{ab} \cdot \mathsf{ab} \twoheadrightarrow \mathsf{b} \cdot \mathsf{b} \twoheadrightarrow \mathsf{ba} \cdot \mathsf{ba} \twoheadrightarrow \mathsf{a}$$

$$M_4 = \mathsf{a} \twoheadrightarrow \mathsf{b} \cdot \mathsf{a} \rightarrow \mathsf{b} \qquad \rightsquigarrow G_4 = \mathsf{a} \rightarrow \mathsf{ab} \cdot \mathsf{ab} \twoheadrightarrow \mathsf{b} \cdot \mathsf{a} \twoheadrightarrow \mathsf{b}$$

(For brevity, we omit $\mathbf{1}$ from the resulting global types; this can be incorporated in the macro expansion rules, at the expense of a more complex formulation.)

Global type G_1 specifies an asynchronous communication from Alice to Bob. Global type G_2 specifies two asynchronous communications from Alice to Bob; Alice can do the second send already *before* Bob has done the first receive. Global type G_3 specifies an asynchronous communication from Alice to Bob, followed by one from Bob to Alice; in contrast to G_2, Bob can send only *after* he has received (i.e., this encoding of asynchrony preserves causality of messages sent and received by the same role). Global type G_4 specifies an asynchronous communication from Alice to Bob, followed by a *synchronous* communication from Bob to Alice; it highlights that, unlike existing languages of global types, ours supports mixing synchrony and asynchrony in a single global type. $\square$

Example 2 (Finite recursion). The Key-Value Store protocol in Sect. 2 does not terminate: in its global type, the inner recursions (Y and Z) can be exited, but the outer recursion (X) cannot. A version of this protocol that terminates once each of the Clients has indicated it has finished using the store (e.g., by sending an Exit-message) can also be specified.

We illustrate the key idea in a simplified example:

$$G_1 = \mu X. \big[\big[\mathsf{a} \twoheadrightarrow \mathsf{c} : \mathsf{Con} \cdot X\big] + \mathsf{a} \twoheadrightarrow \mathsf{c} : \mathsf{Exit}\big] \quad G_2 = \mu X. \big[\big[\mathsf{b} \rightarrow \mathsf{c} : \mathsf{Con} \cdot X\big] + \mathsf{b} \rightarrow \mathsf{c} : \mathsf{Exit}\big]$$

$$G = \mu X. \big[\big[\mathsf{a} \twoheadrightarrow \mathsf{c} : \mathsf{Con} \cdot X\big] + \big[\mathsf{a} \twoheadrightarrow \mathsf{c} : \mathsf{Exit} \cdot G_2\big]\big] + \big[\mathsf{b} \rightarrow \mathsf{c} : \mathsf{Con} \cdot X\big] + \big[\mathsf{b} \rightarrow \mathsf{c} : \mathsf{Exit} \cdot G_1\big]$$

Global type G_1 specifies the communication of either a Con-message (to continue the recursion) or an Exit-message (to break it) from Alice to Carol. Global type G_2 is similar. Global type G specifies the communication of a Con-message from

$$\frac{\mathcal{L}(r)\downarrow \quad \text{for all } r \in \operatorname{dom}\mathcal{L}}{\mathcal{L}\downarrow}$$

(a) Termination

$$\frac{\mathcal{L}(r_1) \xrightarrow{r_1 r_2 ! U} L'_{r_1} \quad \mathcal{L}(r_2) \xrightarrow{r_1 r_2 ? U} L'_{r_2}}{\mathcal{L} \xrightarrow{r_1 \twoheadrightarrow r_2 : U} \mathcal{L}[r_1 \mapsto L'_{r_1}, r_2 \mapsto L'_{r_2}]} \qquad \frac{\mathcal{L}(r) \xrightarrow{\varepsilon^r_{r_1 r_2}} L'_r}{\mathcal{L} \xrightarrow{\varepsilon^r_{r_1 r_2}} \mathcal{L}[r \mapsto L'_r]}$$

(b) Reduction

Fig. 5: Operational semantics of groups of local types

$$T\!\upharpoonright\! r = T \quad \text{if: } G \in \{\boxed{1}\} \cup \mathbb{X}$$

$$(G_1 * G_2)\!\upharpoonright\! r = (G_1\!\upharpoonright\! r) * (G_2\!\upharpoonright\! r) \qquad r_1 \twoheadrightarrow r_2 : U\!\upharpoonright\! r = \begin{cases} r_1 r_2 ! U & \text{if: } r_1 = r \neq r_2 \\ r_1 r_2 ? U & \text{if: } r_1 \neq r = r_2 \\ \varepsilon^r_{r_1 r_2} & \text{if: } r_1 \neq r \neq r_2 \end{cases}$$

$$\text{if: } * \in \{+, \cdot, \|\}$$

$$\langle X \,|\, E \rangle \!\upharpoonright\! r = \langle X \,|\, E\!\upharpoonright\! r \rangle \qquad E\!\upharpoonright\! r = \{ X \mapsto E(X)\!\upharpoonright\! r \mid X \in \operatorname{dom} E \}$$

$$G \!\upharpoonright\!\!\upharpoonright R = \{ r \mapsto G\!\upharpoonright\! r \mid r \in R \} \quad \text{if: } \mathsf{r}(G) \subseteq R \neq \emptyset$$

Fig. 6: Projection

either Alice or Bob to Carol, or an Exit-message. In the latter case, Carol stops communicating with a role, while she proceeds communicating with the other role. Thus, the communications between Alice and Carol, and between Bob and Carol, are decoupled (i.e., decisions to continue or break recursions are made per role). Macro $\overline{\mu}$ generalizes this pattern to arbitrary recursion bodies.   □

Groups. Finally, let $\mathbb{R} \rightharpoonup \mathbb{L}\text{OC}$ denote the set of all *groups* of local types (i.e., every group is a partial function from role names to local types), ranged over by $\mathcal{L}$. The idea is that while a global type specifies a protocol among n roles from one global perspective, a group of local types specifies a protocol from the n local perspectives. Fig. 5 defines the operational semantics of groups, built on top of the operational semantics of local types; we use the $f[x \mapsto y]$ notation to update function f with entry $x \mapsto y$. In words, group $\mathcal{L}$ is reduced either by synchronously reducing the local types of a sender r_1 and a receiver r_2 (yielding a communication from r_1 to r_2), or by reducing the local type of an idling role.

3.3   End-Point Projection: from Global Types to Local Types

A key part of MPST (Fig. 1) is a projection operator that consumes a global type G as input and produces a group of local types $\mathcal{L}$ as output; it is *correct* if, under certain well-formedness conditions, G and $\mathcal{L}$ are operationally equivalent.

Let $\mathsf{r}(G)$ denote the set of all role names that occur in G. Fig. 6 defines our projection operator. In words, the projection of a communication $r_1 \twoheadrightarrow r_2 : U$ onto a role r is a send $r_1 r_2 ! U$ if the role is sender in the communication, a receive $r_1 r_2 ? U$ if it is receiver, or an idling action $\varepsilon^r_{r_1 r_2}$ if it is not involved; the projections of all other forms of global types onto r are homomorphic; the projection of a global type onto a set of roles R is the corresponding group of

$$\frac{T\downarrow}{T\Downarrow} \quad \frac{T \xrightarrow{\tau} T'\Downarrow}{T\Downarrow} \qquad \frac{T \xrightarrow{\alpha} T'}{T \xRightarrow{\alpha} T'} \quad \frac{T \xrightarrow{\tau} T' \xRightarrow{\alpha} T''}{T \xRightarrow{\alpha} T''} \quad \frac{T \xRightarrow{\alpha} T' \xrightarrow{\tau} T''}{T \xRightarrow{\alpha} T''} \quad \frac{T \xRightarrow{\sigma} T'}{T \xRightarrow{\tau} T'}$$

(a) Termination   (b) Reduction

Fig. 7: Weak operational semantics; $T, T', T'' \in \text{GLOB} \cup \text{LOC} \cup (\mathbb{R} \rightharpoonup \text{LOC})$

projections, where the side condition implies that the group is nonempty and contains a local type for at least every role name that occurs in G. Thus, a group of projections of G is a *partial* function relative to the set of all roles $\mathbb{R}$, but it is *total* relative to the set of roles $\mathsf{r}(G) \subseteq \mathbb{R}$ that occur in G. (We note that we also continue to assume global types are $\mathbb{1}$-free, closed, and deterministic.)

Our projection operator is similar to existing projection operators in the MPST literature [34], but it also differs on a fundamental account: it produces local types with annotated idling actions. These idling actions will be instrumental in the definition of our well-formedness conditions. We note that no idling actions occur in the local types for the Key-Value Store protocol in Sect. 2. This is because *after* the idling actions have been used to establish well-formedness, they are of no more use and can be eliminated to simplify the local types.

The following lemmas state key properties about termination and reduction behaviour of global types and their projections: Lem. 1 states projection is sound and complete for termination; Lem. 2 states the same for reduction.

Lemma 1. $\big[G\downarrow$ implies $(G \restriction r)\downarrow\big]$ and $\big[(G \restriction r)\downarrow$ implies $G\downarrow\big]$

Proof. By induction on G.   □

Lemma 2. $\big[G \xrightarrow{g} G'$ implies $(G \restriction r) \xrightarrow{g\restriction r} (G' \restriction r)\big]$
     and $\big[(G \restriction r) \xrightarrow{g\restriction r} L'$ implies $\big[G \xrightarrow{g} G'$ and $L = G' \restriction r\big]$ for some $G'\big]\big]$

Proof. Both conjuncts are proven by induction on the structure of G, also using Lem. 1 (needed because termination plays a role in reduction of $\cdot$).   □

3.4   Weak Bisimilarity of Global Types, Local Types, and Groups

The idling actions introduced in local types by our projection operator are *internal*, because they never compose into communications that emerge between local types in groups. Therefore, the operational equivalence relation under which we prove the correctness of projection should be insensitive to idling actions.

First, let $\mathbb{A}_\tau = \{\varepsilon^r_{r_1 r_2} \mid r_1 \neq r_2$ and $r_1 \neq r \neq r_2\}$ denote the set of all *internal actions*, ranged over by τ, σ. Second, Fig. 7 defines an extension of our operational semantics (Fig. 3) with relations that assert *weak termination* and *weak reduction* (i.e., versions of termination and reduction that are insensitive to internal actions). Third, Fig. 8 defines weak bisimilarity ($\approx$), in terms of weak similarity ($\preceq$), in terms of weak termination and weak reduction; it coincides with the definition found in the literature (e.g., [2]), with the administrative

$$T_1 \Downarrow \text{ implies } T_2 \Downarrow \quad \begin{bmatrix} \left[[T_1' \preceq T_2' \text{ and } T_2 \overset{\alpha}{\Rightarrow} T_2'] \text{ for some } T_2'\right] \\ \text{or } [T_1' \preceq T_2 \text{ and } \alpha \in \mathbb{A}_\tau] \\ \text{for all } T_1 \overset{\alpha}{\rightarrow} T_1' \end{bmatrix} \quad \mathcal{R}, \mathcal{R}^{-1} \subseteq \preceq$$
$$\frac{}{T_1 \preceq T_2} \qquad \qquad \frac{T_1 \mathcal{R} T_2}{T_1 \approx T_2}$$

Fig. 8: Weak operational equivalence; $T_1, T_1', T_2, T_2' \in \mathbb{G}\text{LOB} \cup \mathbb{L}\text{OC} \cup (\mathbb{R} \rightharpoonup \text{LOC})$

exception that we need the fourth rule in Fig. 7b to account for the fact we have multiple different internal actions. We use a double horizontal line in the formulation of rules to indicate they should be applied coinductively.

The notion of weak reduction allows us to generalize the soundness and completeness of projection from roles (Lem. 2) to groups of roles: Lem. 3 states (1) if G can g-reduce to G' and the projection of G' is defined, then the group of projections of G can reduce to the group of projections of G', either directly or with a trailing weak τ-reduction; (2) conversely, if the group of projections of G can g-reduce to $\mathcal{L}'$, then G can g-reduce to G' and either $\mathcal{L}'$ equals the group of projections of G', or it can get there with a weak reduction.

Lemma 3. $\begin{bmatrix} \begin{bmatrix} G \overset{g}{\rightarrow} G' \text{ and} \\ G \Uparrow R \text{ is defined} \end{bmatrix} \text{ implies } \begin{bmatrix} \begin{bmatrix} (G \Uparrow R) \overset{g}{\rightarrow} (G' \Uparrow R) \text{ or} \\ (G \Uparrow R) \overset{g}{\rightarrow} \mathcal{L}' \overset{\tau}{\Rightarrow} (G' \Uparrow R) \end{bmatrix} \\ \text{for some } \mathcal{L}', \tau \end{bmatrix} \end{bmatrix}$

and $\begin{bmatrix} (G \Uparrow R) \overset{g}{\rightarrow} \mathcal{L}' \text{ implies } \begin{bmatrix} G \overset{g}{\rightarrow} G' \text{ and } \begin{bmatrix} \mathcal{L}' = G' \Uparrow R \text{ or} \\ \mathcal{L}' \overset{\tau}{\Rightarrow} (G' \Uparrow R) \end{bmatrix} \\ \text{for some } G', \tau \end{bmatrix} \end{bmatrix}$

Proof. Both conjuncts are proven by induction on R, also using Lem. 2.   □

3.5   Well-formedness of Global Types

In general, projection does not preserve weak operational semantics.

Example 3 (Bad protocols). The following global types (message types omitted) specify "bad" protocols that do not permit "good" concurrent implementations:

$$G_1 = \mathsf{a} \rightarrowtail \mathsf{b} + \mathsf{a} \rightarrowtail \mathsf{c} \qquad\qquad G_2 = \mathsf{a} \rightarrowtail \mathsf{b} \cdot \mathsf{c} \rightarrowtail \mathsf{d}$$

$$\underbrace{\mathsf{ab!} + \mathsf{ac!}}_{G_1 \upharpoonright \mathsf{a}} \quad \underbrace{\mathsf{ab?} + \varepsilon^{\mathsf{b}}_{\mathsf{ac}}}_{G_1 \upharpoonright \mathsf{b}} \quad \underbrace{\varepsilon^{\mathsf{c}}_{\mathsf{ab}} + \mathsf{ac?}}_{G_1 \upharpoonright \mathsf{c}} \qquad \underbrace{\mathsf{ab!} \cdot \varepsilon^{\mathsf{a}}_{\mathsf{cd}}}_{G_2 \upharpoonright \mathsf{a}} \quad \underbrace{\mathsf{ab?} \cdot \varepsilon^{\mathsf{a}}_{\mathsf{cd}}}_{G_2 \upharpoonright \mathsf{b}} \quad \underbrace{\varepsilon^{\mathsf{c}}_{\mathsf{ab}} \cdot \mathsf{cd!}}_{G_2 \upharpoonright \mathsf{c}} \quad \underbrace{\varepsilon^{\mathsf{d}}_{\mathsf{ab}} \cdot \mathsf{cd?}}_{G_2 \upharpoonright \mathsf{d}}$$

Global type G_1 specifies a communication from Alice to either Bob or Carol, chosen by Alice. This is a bad protocol, because if Alice chooses Bob, there is no way for Carol to know (and vice versa): Carol cannot locally distinguish between whether Alice has not made her choice yet, or whether Alice has chosen Bob. Formally, this is manifested in the fact that Carol's local type can *at any time* choose to perform idling action ε_{ab}^c (i.e., local type $G_1 \upharpoonright c$ has two reductions, neither one of which has priority), thereby *assuming* that Alice has chosen Bob. However, Bob can symmetrically assume that Alice has chosen Carol. As a result, the group projection can reduce as follows: $G_1 \restriction \{a, b, c\} \xrightarrow{\varepsilon_{ab}^c} \mathcal{L}_1 \xrightarrow{\varepsilon_{ac}^b} \mathcal{L}_2$. Now, $\mathcal{L}_2$ cannot reduce further, but Alice has not terminated yet. This sequence of reductions cannot be (weakly) simulated by G_1.

Global type G_2 specifies a communication from Alice to Bob, followed by a communication from Carol to Dave. This is a bad protocol, because there is no way for Carol and Dave to know when the communication from Alice to Bob has occurred. Formally, this is manifested in the fact that Carol's and Dave's local types can *at any time* choose to perform idling actions, thereby *assuming* that the communication from Alice to Bob has occurred. As a result, the group projection can reduce as follows: $G_2 \restriction \{a, b, c, d\} \xrightarrow{\varepsilon_{ab}^c} \mathcal{L}_1 \xrightarrow{\varepsilon_{ab}^d} \mathcal{L}_2 \xrightarrow{d \to d} \mathcal{L}_3 \xrightarrow{a \to b}$ $\mathcal{L}_4$. This sequence cannot be (weakly) simulated by G_2. □

Next, we define two well-formedness conditions that invalidate the previous examples; in Sect. 3.6, we prove that if these conditions are satisfied by a global type G, it is indeed guaranteed that G and $G \restriction R$ are operationally equivalent (i.e., weakly bisimilar). Instead of defining the conditions in terms of global types, we define them in terms of projections (i.e., local types). Informally:

C For every $r \in R$, for every choice that local type $G \upharpoonright r$ has between a weak reduction $\xRightarrow{l}$ (where l is a send, a receive, or an idling action) and a completely unobservable weak reduction $\xRightarrow{\tau}$, choosing to perform the former does not disable the latter, and vice versa. This can be thought of as a form of *commutativity* between l and τ.

EC For every $r \in R$, one of the following is true:

1. For every every weak reduction $\xRightarrow{l}$ that local type $G \upharpoonright r$ can perform (where l is a send or a receive, but not an idling action), it can perform a reduction $\xrightarrow{l}$. That is, if $G \upharpoonright r$ can perform l in the future after idling actions, it can do l already *eagerly* in the present.

2. Local type $G \upharpoonright r$ is the start of a causal *chain*: a sequence of τ-reductions, followed by a non-τ-reduction, that are "causally related" to each other. An $\varepsilon_{r_1 r_2}^r$-reduction is causally related to a $\varepsilon_{r_3 r_4}^r$-reduction iff $\{r_1, r_2\} \cap \{r_3, r_4\} \neq \emptyset$. Globally speaking, this means communication between r_3 and r_4 must be preceded by communication between r_1 and r_2.

These conditions must hold coinductively for all local types that $G \upharpoonright r$ can reduce to. Essentially, these conditions state that by performing idling actions, a local type can neither *decrease* its possible behaviour (C), nor *increase* it (EC-1), unless it is guaranteed the added behaviour cannot be exercised yet, because it is causally related to other communications that need to happen first (EC-2).

Example 4 (Bad protocols, continued). Global type G_1 (Exmp. 3) is ill-formed: its projections onto b and c violate condition C. Global type G_2 (Exmp. 3) is also ill-formed: its projections onto c and d violate condition EC. □

$$\frac{\left[\begin{array}{l}\left[\varLambda_1'' \approx \varLambda_2'' \text{ and } \varLambda_1' \xrightarrow{\alpha_2} \varLambda_1'' \text{ and } \varLambda_2' \xrightarrow{\alpha_1} \varLambda_2''\right] \text{ or} \\ \left[\varLambda_1'' \approx \varLambda_2' \text{ and } \varLambda_1' \xrightarrow{\alpha_2} \varLambda_1'' \text{ and } \alpha_1 \in \mathbb{A}_\tau\right] \text{ or} \\ \left[\varLambda_1' \approx \varLambda_2'' \text{ and } \varLambda_2' \xrightarrow{\alpha_1} \varLambda_2'' \text{ and } \alpha_2 \in \mathbb{A}_\tau\right] \text{ or} \\ \left[\varLambda_1' \approx \varLambda_2' \text{ and } \alpha_1, \alpha_2 \in \mathbb{A}_\tau\right] \\ \qquad\qquad \textbf{for some } \varLambda_1'', \varLambda_2'' \\ \textbf{for all } \left[\varLambda \xrightarrow{\alpha_1} \varLambda_1' \text{ and } \varLambda \xrightarrow{\alpha_2} \varLambda_2'\right]\end{array}\right]}{\mathsf{C}_{\alpha_2}^{\alpha_1}(\varLambda)} \qquad \frac{\mathsf{C}_\tau^\alpha(\varLambda) \qquad \mathsf{C}(\varLambda')}{\substack{\textbf{for all } \alpha, \tau \quad \textbf{for all } \varLambda \xrightarrow{\alpha} \varLambda' \\ \mathsf{C}(\varLambda)}}$$

$$\frac{\left[\begin{array}{l}\left[\varLambda'' \approx \varLambda^{**} \text{ and } \varLambda \xrightarrow{\alpha_2} \varLambda^* \xrightarrow{\alpha_1} \varLambda^{**}\right] \text{ or} \\ \left[\varLambda'' \approx \varLambda^* \text{ and } \varLambda \xrightarrow{\alpha_2} \varLambda^* \text{ and } \alpha_1 \in \mathbb{A}_\tau\right] \text{ or} \\ \mathsf{Chain}\,\varLambda \\ \qquad\qquad \textbf{for some } \varLambda^*, \varLambda^{**} \\ \textbf{for all } \varLambda \xrightarrow{\alpha_1} \varLambda' \xrightarrow{\alpha_2} \varLambda''\end{array}\right]}{\mathsf{EC}_{\alpha_2}^{\alpha_1}(\varLambda)} \qquad \frac{\mathsf{EC}_\alpha^\tau(\varLambda) \qquad \mathsf{EC}(\varLambda')}{\substack{\textbf{for all } \alpha \notin \mathbb{A}_\tau, \tau \quad \textbf{for all } \varLambda \xrightarrow{\alpha} \varLambda' \\ \mathsf{EC}(\varLambda)}}$$

$$\frac{\left[L_1' = L_2' \text{ and } l_1 = l_2\right] \qquad \left[\mathsf{r}(\tau) \cap \mathsf{r}(l) \neq \emptyset \text{ and } \left[\mathsf{Chain}\,L' \text{ or } l \notin \mathbb{A}_\tau\right]\right]}{\substack{\textbf{for all } \left[L \xrightarrow{l_1} L_1' \text{ and } L \xrightarrow{l_2} L_2'\right] \qquad \textbf{for all } L \xrightarrow{\tau} L' \xrightarrow{l} L'' \\ \mathsf{Chain}\,L}}$$

Fig. 9: Well-formedness conditions; $\varLambda, \varLambda', \varLambda'', \varLambda_1', \varLambda_1'', \varLambda_2', \varLambda_2'' \in \mathbb{L}\textsc{oc} \cup (\mathbb{R} \rightharpoonup \mathbb{L}\textsc{oc})$

Fig. 9 defines C and EC formally. We define C not only for local types, but also for groups of local types, as this simplifies some notation later on. We prove key properties of C: Thm. 1 states commutativity of local sends/receives/idling (l) in local types gets lifted to commutativity of global communications/idling (α) in groups of local types; Lem. 4 states weak bisimilarity preserves commutativity.

Theorem 1. $\left[\left[\left[\begin{array}{l}\mathsf{C}_\tau^l(\mathcal{L}(r)) \\ \textbf{for all } l, \tau\end{array}\right] \textbf{ for all } r \in \operatorname{dom}\mathcal{L}\right] \textbf{ implies } \left[\begin{array}{l}\mathsf{C}_\tau^\alpha(\mathcal{L}) \\ \textbf{for all } \alpha, \tau\end{array}\right]\right]$
$\quad$ **and** $\left[\left[\mathsf{C}(\mathcal{L}(r)) \textbf{ for all } r \in \operatorname{dom}\mathcal{L}\right] \textbf{ implies } \mathsf{C}(\mathcal{L})\right]$

Proof. The first conjunct is proven by induction on the rules of $\Rightarrow$. The second is proven by coinduction on the rule of C, also using the first conjunct. □

Lemma 4. $\left[\left[\mathsf{C}_{\alpha_2}^{\alpha_1}(\mathcal{L}_1) \text{ and } \mathcal{L}_1 \approx \mathcal{L}_2\right] \textbf{ implies } \mathsf{C}_{\alpha_2}^{\alpha_1}(\mathcal{L}_2)\right]$
$\quad$ **and** $\left[\left[\mathsf{C}(\mathcal{L}_1) \text{ and } \mathcal{L}_1 \approx \mathcal{L}_2\right] \textbf{ implies } \mathsf{C}(\mathcal{L}_2)\right]$

Proof. The first conjunct is proven by applying the definitions of C and $\approx$; the second is proven by coinduction on the rule of C, also using the first conjunct. □

We also prove key properties of Chain and EC, both of which work *specifically* for groups of projections: Lem. 5 states if the projections of r_1 and r_2 are both causal chains, they cannot weakly reduce to local types where they can perform reciprocal actions (r_1 the send; r_2 the receive); Thm. 2 states eagerness of local sends/receives (not idling) in projections gets lifted to eagerness of global communications in groups of projections (cf. Thm. 1).

Lemma 5.
$$\begin{bmatrix} \mathsf{Chain}\,(G \upharpoonright R)(r_1) \overset{\tau_1}{\Longrightarrow} \mathcal{L}'(r_1) \xrightarrow{r_1 r_2 ! U} \mathcal{L}''(r_1) \text{ and} \\ \mathsf{Chain}\,(G \upharpoonright R)(r_2) \overset{\tau_2}{\Longrightarrow} \mathcal{L}'(r_2) \xrightarrow{r_1 r_2 ? U} \mathcal{L}''(r_2) \end{bmatrix} \text{ implies false}$$

Proof. By induction on the rules of $\Rightarrow$. □

Theorem 2.
$$\begin{bmatrix} \mathsf{EC}_l^\tau((G \upharpoonright R)(r)) \\ \textbf{for all } l \notin \mathbb{A}_\tau, \tau, r \in R \end{bmatrix} \text{ implies } \begin{bmatrix} \mathsf{EC}_\alpha^\tau(G \upharpoonright R) \\ \textbf{for all } \alpha, \tau \end{bmatrix}$$
$$\textbf{and } [[\mathsf{EC}(\mathcal{L}(r)) \textbf{ for all } r \in \mathrm{dom}\,\mathcal{L}] \textbf{ implies } \mathsf{EC}(\mathcal{L})]$$

Proof. The first conjunct is proven by using Lem. 5; the second is proven by coinduction on the rule of EC, also using the first conjunct. □

We note that, in contrast to Lem. 4 for C, we do not have a lemma that states weak bisimilarity preserves EC. Such a lemma would have been highly useful in our subsequent proofs, but it is unfortunately false, because weak bisimilarity does not preserve Chain. A simple counterexample, for local types, is this: $L_1 = r_1 r_2 ! U$ and $L_2 = \varepsilon_{r_4 r_5}^{r_3} \cdot r_1 r_2 ! U$, where $\{r_1, r_2\} \cap \{r_3, r_4, r_5\} = \emptyset$. While L_1 and L_2 are weakly bisimilar, L_1 is the start of a unary causal chain, but L_2 is not. The problem here is that Chain depends on the role names associated with idling actions, whereas weak bisimilarity abstracts those role names away.

We call a global type *well-formed* if each of its projections satisfies C and EC.

3.6 Correctness of Projection under Well-Formedness

We now to prove our main result: if a global type is well-formed, it is weakly bisimilar to the group of its projections. We start by defining a relation $\bowtie$ to relate global types with groups of local types (denoted by $\mathcal{R}$ in Fig. 8):

$$\frac{\mathsf{C}(G \upharpoonright R) \quad \mathsf{EC}(G \upharpoonright R) \quad (G \upharpoonright R) \overset{*}{\Rightarrow} \mathcal{L}' \overset{*}{\Leftarrow} \mathcal{L} \quad \mathsf{C}(\mathcal{L})}{G \bowtie \mathcal{L}}$$

Here, we write $\mathcal{L}_1 \overset{*}{\Rightarrow} \mathcal{L}_2$ as an abbreviation for:

$$[\mathcal{L}_1 \approx \mathcal{L}_1' \overset{\tau}{\Rightarrow} \mathcal{L}_2' \approx \mathcal{L}_2 \textbf{ for some } \mathcal{L}_1', \mathcal{L}_2'] \textbf{ or } \mathcal{L}_1 \approx \mathcal{L}_2$$

In words, $\mathcal{L}_1 \overset{*}{\Rightarrow} \mathcal{L}_2$ means $\mathcal{L}_1$ has a *silent reduction* (only τ-s) to a term that is weakly bisimilar to $\mathcal{L}_2$, or $\mathcal{L}_1$ is already weakly bisimilar to $\mathcal{L}_2$ (without any reductions). Essentially, if $\mathsf{C}(G \upharpoonright R)$ and $\mathsf{EC}(G \upharpoonright R)$, then $\bowtie$ relates G to a set of groups $S = \{\mathcal{L} \mid G \bowtie \mathcal{L}\}$ that can roughly be characterised as follows:

- (*base*) $G \upharpoonright R$ is in S;
- (*successors*) any group to which $G \upharpoonright R$ can silently reduce, is in S;
- (*predecessors*) any group that can silently reduce to $G \upharpoonright R$, is in S;

- (*pseudo-predecessors*) any group that can silently reduce to a group to which $G \restriction R$ can silently reduce, is in S;
- (*closure*) S is closed under weak bisimilarity.

The following technical lemma states if a well-formed group of projections $G \restriction R$ can weakly g-reduce to some group $\mathcal{L}'$, then the original global type G can g-reduce to some G', and $\mathcal{L}'$ and the group of projections of G' either are weakly bisimilar, or they can weakly reduce to a weakly bisimilar group $\mathcal{L}''$.

Lemma 6. $\left[\!\left[\mathsf{C}(G \restriction R) \text{ and } \mathsf{EC}(G \restriction R) \text{ and } (G \restriction R) \overset{g}{\Rightarrow} \mathcal{L}' \right]\!\right]$

$\qquad$ **implies** $\left[\!\left[G \overset{g}{\to} G' \text{ and } (G' \restriction R) \overset{*}{\Rightarrow} \mathcal{L}'' \overset{*}{\Leftarrow} \mathcal{L}' \right] \text{ for some } \mathcal{L}'' \right]$

Proof. By induction on the rules of $\Rightarrow$, also using Lem. 3. $\qquad\qquad$ □

The following two lemmas state key properties of $\bowtie$: Lem. 7 states $\bowtie$ preserves termination (as weak termination); Lem. 8 states $\bowtie$ coinductively preserves reduction (as weak reduction). Together, these lemmas imply $\bowtie \subseteq \preceq$ and $\bowtie^{-1} \subseteq \preceq$, which in turn imply $\bowtie \subseteq \approx$.

Lemma 7. $\left[\!\left[G \bowtie \mathcal{L} \text{ and } G{\downarrow} \right] \text{ implies } \mathcal{L}{\Downarrow} \right]$

$\qquad$ **and** $\left[\!\left[G \bowtie \mathcal{L} \text{ and } \mathcal{L}{\downarrow} \right] \text{ implies } G{\Downarrow} \right]$

Proof. The first conjunct is proven by induction on the rules of $\Rightarrow$, also using Lem. 1; the second is proven by contradiction (assume **not** $G{\downarrow}$; derive **false**; conclude $G{\downarrow}$; it implies $G{\Downarrow}$). $\qquad\qquad$ □

Lemma 8. $\left[\left[G \bowtie \mathcal{L} \text{ and } G \overset{g}{\to} G' \right] \text{ implies } \left[\begin{array}{c} \left[G' \bowtie \mathcal{L}' \text{ and } \mathcal{L} \overset{g}{\Rightarrow} \mathcal{L}' \right] \\ \text{for some } \mathcal{L}' \end{array} \right] \right]$

$\qquad$ **and** $\left[\left[G \bowtie \mathcal{L} \text{ and } \mathcal{L} \overset{g}{\to} \mathcal{L}' \right] \text{ implies } \left[\begin{array}{c} \left[G' \bowtie \mathcal{L}' \text{ and } G \overset{g}{\to} G' \right] \\ \text{for some } G' \end{array} \right] \right]$

$\qquad$ **and** $\left[\!\left[G \bowtie \mathcal{L} \text{ and } \mathcal{L} \overset{\tau}{\to} \mathcal{L}' \right] \text{ implies } G \bowtie \mathcal{L}' \right]$

Proof. The first and second conjunct are proven by induction on the rules of $\Rightarrow$, also using Lemmas 3–4; the third is proven by induction on the rules of $\Rightarrow$. $\quad$ □

Theorem 3. $\left[\mathsf{C}(G \restriction R) \text{ and } \mathsf{EC}(G \restriction R) \right]$ **implies** $G \approx (G \restriction R)$

Proof. By coinduction on the rule of $\preceq$ (Fig. 8), also using Lemmas 7-8. $\quad$ □

A group of local types $\mathcal{L}$ enjoys *deadlock-freedom* if it either has successfully terminated ($\mathcal{L}{\downarrow}$; Fig. 5a) or can make another reduction. A group of local types $\mathcal{L}$ enjoys *absence of protocol violations* relative to global type G if, coinductively, every non-τ reduction of $\mathcal{L}$ can be simulated by G (i.e., every communication in the group is "permitted" by G). The following corollary relates Thm. 3 of operational equivalence to these classical MPST properties:

Corollary 1. *If global type G is well-formed, then the group of G's projections enjoys deadlock-freedom and absence of protocol violations relative to G.*

The key insight to understand this, is that global types are *by definition* free of deadlocks (they either reduce to $\boxed{1}$, or they never terminate; Fig. 3), while weak bisimilarity preserves deadlock-freedom of global types in their projections (notably, weak bisimilarity is sensitive to termination, and a group of local types terminates only if *all* individual local types terminate; Fig. 5a). Weak bisimilarity also directly implies freedom of protocol violations.

3.7 Decidability of Checking Well-Formedness

We note our proof of Thm. 3 is non-constructive, in the sense that $\bowtie$ is infinitely large (i.e., for each group of local types, there exist infinitely many weakly bisimilar groups). The following proposition states this is not a problem in practice.

Proposition 1. *Checking $\mathsf{C}(\mathcal{L})$ and $\mathsf{EC}(\mathcal{L})$ is decidable.*

The rationale behind this proposition is as follows. First, to check $\mathsf{C}(\mathcal{L})$ and $\mathsf{EC}(\mathcal{L})$, by Thm. 1 and Thm. 2, it suffices to check $\mathsf{C}(\mathcal{L}(r))$ and $\mathsf{EC}(\mathcal{L}(r))$ for each $r \in \operatorname{dom} \mathcal{L}$. For each such local type $\mathcal{L}(r)$, there are two possibilities.

If local type $\mathcal{L}(r)$ has finite control, its state space can be exhaustively explored in finite time, so checking $\mathsf{C}(\mathcal{L}(r))$ and $\mathsf{EC}(\mathcal{L}(r))$ is obviously decidable.

In contrast, if $\mathcal{L}(r)$ has non-finite control, we make two observations. The first observation is that the only possibly source of infinity is the occurrence of recursion variables under parallel composition. The second observation is that C and EC are true for $L_1 \| L_2$ if they are true for L_1 and L_2 separately; this is because C and EC essentially assert a "diamond structure" on the reductions of $L_1 \| L_2$, which is *precisely* the operational semantics of $\|$ (Fig. 3). Thus, we can check $\mathsf{C}(L_1 \| L_2)$ and $\mathsf{EC}(L_1 \| L_2)$ by checking $\mathsf{C}(L_1)$, $\mathsf{C}(L_2)$, $\mathsf{EC}(L_1)$, and $\mathsf{EC}(L_2)$, thereby "avoiding" the possible source of infinity.

We note that splitting the checks for parallel composition in this way not only ensures decidability; it also avoids exponential state explosion (in the number of nested $\|$-operators in a single local type) in local types with finite control.

3.8 Discussion of Challenges

Our use of (weak) bisimilarity, plus the key insight to annotate silent actions with additional information to keep track of choices, made the problem of proving the correctness of projection (Thm. 3) feasible. The major technical challenges to achieve this were defining the right bisimulation relation (Sect. 3.5) and discovering corresponding well-formedness conditions (Sect. 3.6).

A naive weak bisimulation relation, R_{naive}, relates every global type only with its group of projections. R_{naive} is sufficient to prove that every reduction of a global type can be weakly simulated with one non-silent reduction of the group (sender and receiver), followed by a number of silent reductions (idling

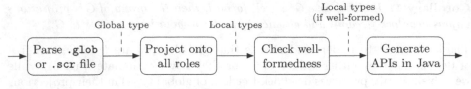

Fig. 10: Overview of mpstpp

processes). In contrast, R_{naive} is insufficient to prove that every reduction of the group can be simulated by its global type, because of silent actions: if global type G is related to group of projections $\mathcal{L}$ by R_{naive}, and a silent action subsequently reduces $\mathcal{L}$ to $\mathcal{L}'$, the simulation fails, as R_{naive} does not relate G to $\mathcal{L}'$.

To alleviate this issue, we defined the bisimulation relation in such a way that it relates every global type G to a group of local types that are not necessarily *equal* to the projections of G, but every local type can be *behind* the corresponding projection (the local type can reach the projection with silent actions) or *ahead* (the projection can reach the local type with silent actions).

4   Practical Experience with the Theory

4.1   Implementation

Tool. We implemented a tool, mpstpp, based on the core theoretical contributions of this paper. Fig. 10 shows a high-level overview of the tool, including the main components (boxes) and data flows (arrows).

First, mpstpp parses an input .glob-file to a data structure for a global type G (programmer-friendly Scribble-style syntax [35] is also supported as input). Then, it projects G onto all roles that occur in G. Then, it checks each of the resulting local types for well-formedness, depending on settings, either sequentially or *in parallel*: a key advantage of the formulation of our well-formedness conditions is that they can be checked modularly for every role in isolation, enabling us to take advantage of modern multicore hardware. Finally, if the local types are well-formed, idling actions are eliminated and *typed communication APIs* are generated from the local types to enable MPST++-based programming in Java.

Optimisations. Parsing, computing projections, and generating APIs is relatively inexpensive; instead, the run times of our tool are dominated by checks for well-formedness. We therefore implemented several optimisations to make these checks more efficient. Before we present these optimisations, we first note that the complexity of checking well-formedness of a local type L is polynomial in the number of *successors* that can be reached from L (Fig. 9).

(1) Our first optimisation targets local types with parallel composition; local type $L_1 \| L_2$ is potentially a serious bottleneck, as its number of successors is *exponential* in the number of nested $\|$-operators. Therefore, even with finite state spaces, we check the well-formedness of $L_1 \parallel L_2$ by checking the well-formedness of L_1 and L_2, without explicitly considering the exponentially many successors of $L_1 \parallel L_2$, exploiting the same observation as with decidability (Sect. 3.7).

(2) Our second optimisation concerns computation of weak reductions. In particular, to check whether C and EC are true for a local type L, according to their definitions (Fig. 9), we need to iterate over each of their weak reductions. Especially if L has many τ-reductions (Fig. 7), computing the set of weak reductions can be expensive. To avoid this, mpstpp computes sound (but incomplete) *approximations* of C and EC. We implemented two kinds of approximations: (a) checking versions of C and EC where every occurrence of $\Rightarrow$ in the definition is replaced with $\rightarrow$, and (b) checking $L \approx L'$ for every τ-reduction from L to L'. Approximation (a) is sound for both C and EC (rationale: if individual reductions can commute, sequences of reductions consisting of those individual reductions can commute as well), but approximation (b) is sound only for C (rationale: auxiliary relation Chain of EC is not preserved by weak bisimilarity). To ensure soundness, thus, mpstpp never uses approximation (b) for EC.

(3) Our third optimisation targets the checks for weak bisimilarity that occur in several places in the definitions of C and EC (Fig. 9). Instead of computing the full reduction relations and run an algorithm to decide their weak bisimilarity (which would be computationally costly), we take advantage of the fact that our language of local types is based on existing algebras (Sect. 3.1) that have sound and complete axiomatisations. Specifically, to check whether two local types are weakly bisimilar, mpstpp applies the axioms as rewrite rules and compares the resulting normal forms for structural equality. To ensure rewriting is fast, we sacrificed completeness (i.e., we use rewriting only to eliminate as many silent actions as possible in a sound way, but for instance, our rewrite procedure cannot prove that $(L_1 \cdot \tau) + L_2$ and $L_2 + L_1$ are weakly bisimilar); however, for the ample examples we tried (including this paper's), this optimisation is highly effective.

Optimisations (2) and (3) are *conservative*: mpstpp may conclude C or EC is false, even though it is actually true. While this affects completeness, soundness is guaranteed: if mpstpp concludes a local type is well-formed, it really is.

4.2   Evaluation of the Approach

Setup. In the previous section, we formulated and proved the theoretical *correctness* of our well-formedness conditions (Thm. 3). In this section, we demonstrate the practical *usefulness* through experimental evaluation in benchmarks. Specifically, we show that checking our well-formedness conditions is faster and more scalable than explicitly checking operational equivalence (which currently seems the only alternative to attain the same level of expressiveness as our work).

In our benchmarks, we compare three approaches to check operational equivalence between a global type and its group of projected local types:

- mpstpp-SEQ (baseline): In this approach, the mpstpp tool is used to check our well-formedness conditions (which imply operational equivalence; Thm. 3), without using any form of parallel processing.

- mpstpp-PAR: Like mpstpp-SEQ, except each projected local type is checked in a separate thread. The fact our well-formedness conditions can be easily parallelised in this way is an important practical advantage.
- EXPLICIT: In this approach, mpstpp is used only for parsing and projecting; after that, we use the state-of-the-art verification tool set mCRL2 [10,20,29] to explicitly check operational equivalence (details below).

We identified six example protocols (details below) that can naturally be scaled in the number of roles N (e.g., the number of Clients in the Key-Value Store protocol). Using each of the three approaches, for each of the protocols, for each value of N between the minimal number of roles N_{min} (e.g, $N_{min}=2$ in the Key-Value Store protocol: the Server and one Client) and 16, we subsequently checked operational equivalence; varying N in this way, yields insights not only in per-case performance, but also scalability. To get statistically reliable results [31], we repeated executions as many times as was necessary until the 95% confidence interval was within 5% of our reported means (i.e., there is a 95% probability that the true mean is within 5% of our reported means).

We ran our benchmarks on a machine with an Intel Xeon 6130 processor (16 cores; no hyper-threading), using Debian 9, Java 13, and mCRL2 201908.0.

Translation to mCRL2. In the EXPLICIT approach, we use mCRL2 [10,20,29] to explicitly check if global type G and its group of projections $\mathcal{L}$ are operationally equivalent. Our choice for mCRL2 is motivated by the fact our languages of global and local types are based on the same process algebra as mCRL2's specification language, so their translation to mCRL2 specifications is direct and straightforward. Moreover, mCRL2 is mature (e.g., used in industry [5]), and it uses optimised, state-of-the-art algorithms to check behavioural equivalences (e.g., [28]), so we are comparing our tool with a serious competitor.

First, we translate global type G to mCRL2 specification $[\![G]\!]$. Then, we use mCRL2 tools mcrl22lps and lps2lts to normalize $[\![G]\!]$ to a *linear process specification* (LPS) and generate a corresponding *labelled transition system* (LTS). Because of the directness of the translation, the transition labels in the resulting LTS are all global communication actions of the form $r_1{\rightarrow}r_2{:}U$.

Second, we translate group of projections $\mathcal{L}$, consisting of roles $r_1,...,r_n$, to mCRL2 specification $[\![\mathcal{L}]\!]$. It looks as follows (in formal mCRL2 notation [29]):

$$\nabla_{\{r_i\rightarrow r_j:U\,|\,1\leq i,j\leq n,i\neq j,U\in\mathbb{U}\}}\big($$
$$\Gamma_{\{(r_ir_j!U\sqcup r_ir_j?U)\rightarrow(r_i\rightarrow r_j:U)\,|\,1\leq i,j\leq n,i\neq j,U\in\mathbb{U}\}}([\![\mathcal{L}(r_1)]\!]\,\|\,...\,\|\,[\![\mathcal{L}(r_n)]\!]))$$

where each $[\![\mathcal{L}(r_i)]\!]$ is a direct translation of local type $\mathcal{L}(r_i)$ to an mCRL2 specification; $\|$ is a form of parallel composition that prescribes both interleaving and synchronisation of operand actions; $\sqcup$ is *synchronous composition* of actions; Γ is the *communication operator* that replaces synchronised local send/receive actions $r_ir_j!U \sqcup r_ir_j?U$ with global communication action $r_i{\rightarrow}r_j{:}U$; and ∇ is the *allow operator* that allows only global communication actions to be executed (i.e., unsynchronized, individual send/receive actions cannot be executed).

When translating a local type $\mathcal{L}(r_i)$ to an mCRL2 specification $[\![\mathcal{L}(r_i)]\!]$, to make mCRL2's subsequent verification easier, we already eliminate as many idling actions $\varepsilon_{r_1 r_2}^r$ as possible (modulo branching bisimulation); those that remain are represented as a general τ action, because mCRL2 does not need the additional information provided by $\varepsilon_{r_1 r_2}^r$. Then, we use mcrl22lps and lps2lts to generate an LPS and LTS for $[\![\mathcal{L}]\!]$.

Third, we use mCRL2 tool ltscompare to check if the LTS for $[\![G]\!]$ is weakly bisimilar to the LTS for $[\![\mathcal{L}]\!]$. We note that normalisation to an LPS using mcrl22lps is a requirement to use ltscompare.

Protocols. We used the following protocols in our benchmarks:

Key-Value Store (KVS): This protocol is the same protocol as the one presented in Sect. 2, except each inner parallel composition ($\|$) is replaced with sequential composition ($\cdot$). This is because mcrl22lps does not support normalisation of mCRL2 specifications where $\|$ occurs under recursion.

Load Balancer (LB): This protocol consists of a *Master* and a number of *Workers*. Iteratively, first, a Request-message is communicated from the Master to one of the Workers; then, a Response-message is communicated from that Worker to the Master.

Work Stealing (WS): This protocol consists of a *Master* and a number of *Workers*. Iteratively, a Job-message is communicated from the Master to one of the Workers. Meanwhile, Workers can try to "steal" jobs from each other: at any point, first, a Steal-message can be communicated from one Worker to another Worker; then, either a Job-message (if the former Worker has a job to spare) or a None-message (otherwise) is communicated from the latter Worker to the former Worker.

Map/Reduce (MR): This protocol consists of a *Master* and a number of *Workers*. First, in no particular order, a Map-message is communicated from the Master to each Worker; then, in no particular order, a Reduce-message is communicated from each Worker to the Master.

Peer-to-Peer (PtP): This protocol consists of a number of *Peers*. Unordered, a Msg-message is communicated from each Peer to each other Peer.

Pub/Sub (PS): This protocol consists of a *Publisher* and a number of *Subscribers*. In no particular order, a Sub-message can be communicated once from each Subscriber to the Publisher to gain a subscription. Concurrently, a Pub-message can be communicated from the Publisher to each Subscriber with a subscription.

The table on the right summarises the features used in each of these protocols.

For each $1 \leq n \leq 15$, we instantiated the Key-Value Store, Load Balancer, Work Stealing, and Map/Reduce protocols with 1 Server/Master + n Clients/Workers.

	KVS	LB	WS	MR	PtP	PS
+	✓		✓			✓
∃	✓	✓	✓			✓
$\|$	✓		✓	✓	✓	

For each $2 \leq n \leq 16$, we instantiated the Peer-to-Peer protocol with n Peers. For

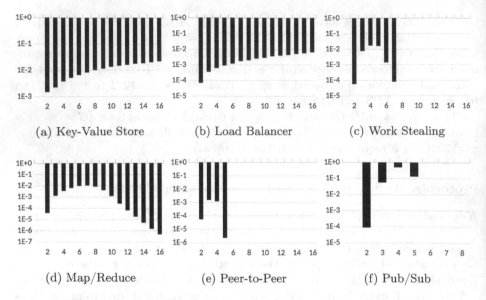

(a) Key-Value Store   (b) Load Balancer   (c) Work Stealing

(d) Map/Reduce   (e) Peer-to-Peer   (f) Pub/Sub

Fig. 11: Speedups (y-axis; y>1E+0 means faster, y<1E+0 means slower) of EX-PLICIT relative to mpstpp-SEQ as the number of roles increases (x-axis)

each $2 \leq n \leq 7$, we instantiated the Pub/Sub protocol with 1 Publisher and n Subscribers; we did not instantiate the Pub/Sub protocol with n>7 Subscribers, as the resulting global types are too large (their size grows exponentially in n).

Benchmark results. Figures 11–12 shows the results of our benchmarks. The x-axis indicates the number of roles; the y-axis indicates relative speed-ups. The baselines are at y=1E+0 and y=1: above it, a competing approach is *faster* than mpstpp-SEQ; below it, it is *slower*. We draw two conclusions.

(1) For each protocol and number of roles, mpstpp-SEQ outperforms EXPLICIT. In the cases of Key-Value Store and Load Balancer, EXPLICIT grows towards mpstpp-SEQ, but the growth levels off as the number of roles increases, while EXPLICIT is still about two order of magnitude slower than mpstpp-SEQ in the best of circumstances. In the cases of Work Stealing, Peer-to-Peer, and Pub/Sub, the LTSs generated from the translated mCRL2 specifications were too large to be compared (i.e., ltscompare produced an error) beyond 7, 5, and 5 roles; this was no issue for mpstpp-SEQ. In the case of Map/Reduce, the LTSs were small enough to compare using mCRL2's ltscompare, but after an initial upwards slope for $2 \leq N \leq 7$ roles, EXPLICIT starts to perform progressively worse.

(2) Especially for larger numbers of roles, parallelisation can yield serious performance improvements. In the cases of Key-Value Store and Load Balancer, mpstpp-PAR outperforms mpstpp-SEQ only with 14–16 roles; for smaller numbers of roles, parallel execution is slower. In the worst case (Load Balancer, 2 roles), the slowdown is roughly $\frac{10.9\mu s}{3.2\mu s} = 3.4$; we hypothesise that be-

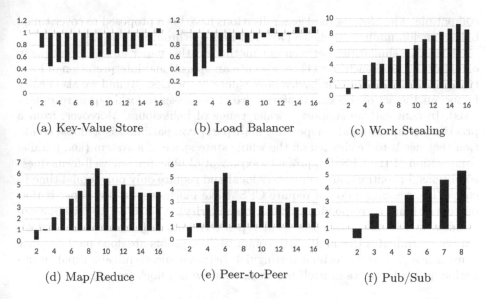

(a) Key-Value Store   (b) Load Balancer   (c) Work Stealing

(d) Map/Reduce   (e) Peer-to-Peer   (f) Pub/Sub

Fig. 12: Speedups (y-axis; $y>1$ means faster, $y<1$ means slower) of mpstpp-PAR relative to mpstpp-SEQ as the number of roles increases (x-axis)

cause of the low absolute execution times, the cost of spawning and synchronising threads outweighs their benefit. However, the ascending gradient indicates that as the number of roles increases, relatively more of the total work can be parallelised, yielding progressive rewards. In the cases of Work Stealing, Map/Reduce, Peer-to-Peer, and Pub/Sub, similar trends can be observed, except $y=1$ is crossed sonner. The absolute execution times for these protocols and for small numbers of roles are higher than for Key-Value Store and Load Balancer.

5   Related Work

Multiparty compatibility. Closest to this paper is existing literature on multiparty compatibility [6,24,40,42]. The key idea, initially developed by Deniélou and Yoshida for the original MPST [23,24], is to represent (groups of) local types operationally as (*systems* of) *communicating finite state machines* (CFSM) [8]. A CFSM M is a state machine where transitions are labelled with sends/receives; a system of CFSMs S is a parallel composition where CFSMs communicate through asynchronous buffers. Multiparty compatibility, then, is a condition on the reachable states and transitions of a system $S = (M_1, ..., M_n)$: if it is satisfied by S, the system is guaranteed to be *safe* (no deadlocks; no unmatched sends/receives) and *live* (S terminates, assuming at least one M_i can terminate). Multiparty compatibility is a sufficient condition to guarantee safety and liveness, but not necessary: there exist safe/live systems that are not multiparty compatible. Therefore, several generalisations have been proposed to cover timed behaviour [6], undirected choice [40], and non-synchronisability [42].

The main similarities between our method in this paper and the multiparty compatibility approach are: (1) we also use an operational interpretation of local types; (2) we guarantee similar liveness/safety properties; (3) and we also neatly factor out the act of checking conformance of processes to local types (resp. CF-SMs). In contrast, we support a wider range of behaviours. Moreover, from a practical/computational perspective, multiparty compatibility is a global condition that needs to be checked on the whole state space of a system (i.e., parallel composition of the CFSMs), prone to exponential blow-up; our well-formedness conditions, in contrast, are completely local and require only polynomial time to check. The reason we do not require CFSM-like machinery in this paper is that our operational correspondence (weak bisimilarity) is sensitive to termination: notably, in Fig. 5a, a group of local types terminates *iff* every individual local type terminates (for multiparty compatibility, proofs are done modulo trace equivalence [24], which cannot distinguish between successful/abnormal termination and is therefore in itself too weak to show deadlock-freedom).

Expressiveness of MPST. In the original MPST theory [33], and many of its descendants (e.g., [14,19,22,24,25,43]), the restrictions on choices are enforced through a combination of syntax and additional well-formedness conditions. Notably, in these works, communications in global types are specified as $r_1 \rightarrow r_2 : \{\ell_i \cdot G_i\}_{i \in I}$, so syntactically, it is impossible to specify choices among senders or receivers. There exist also papers where a seemingly more general binary +-like operator is introduced, particularly those that support choices among receivers [16,23,36,40], but the well-formedness conditions still basically restrict the use of + in these works to $r_1 \rightarrow r_2 : \{\ell_i \cdot G_i\}_{i \in I}$ or $r \rightarrow \{r_i : \ell_i \cdot G_i\}_{i \in I}$.

This is the first paper where well-formedness conditions do not force the use of + into one of those two restricted forms. Moreover, our well-formedness conditions are compatible with unbounded interleaving (recursion under parallel), beyond similar operators in previous work [16,22,23,43]. An alternative approach is to completely omit statically checked well-formedness conditions (and projection), and to only *dynamically* verify communication actions against global types through monitoring, as recently proposed [30]. The language of global types in that paper is more expressive than ours in this paper, but all verification happens at *run-time*, whereas we provide correctness guarantees already at *compile-time*.

Session types and model checking. Recently, there has been growing interest in using model checking to verify properties of (multiparty) session types, similar to our use of mCRL2 as an alternative to checking well-formedness (Sect. 4.2). Lange et al. [39] infer behavioural types from Go programs and use mCRL2 to verify the inferred types, to establish safety properties (combined with another tool, KITTeL [26], to establish liveness). Hu and Yoshida [36] use a custom model checker to verify safety and progress properties of local types (represented as CFSMs) as part of API generation in the Scribble toolchain for MPST [35].

Closest to our use of mCRL2 is the work of Scalas et al. [52,53], where mCRL2 is used to verify properties of local types (e.g., deadlock-freedom), while a form of dependent type-checking is used to verify conformance of processes against those types (i.e., actors in Scala); no global types and projection are used, though (programmers write local types manually). The idea is that properties model-checked on the types carry over to the processes. Similarly, Scalas and Yoshida [51] use mCRL2 to model-check session environments, as a more expressive alternative to the classical consistency condition needed to prove subject reduction. Note that [51, Theorem 5.15] shows that, in the case that a set of processes is typable by a single multiparty session (i.e. a single global type), type-level properties including safety, deadlock-freedom and liveness guarantee the same properties for multiparty session π-processes. Hence our type-level analysis is directly usable to provide decidable procedures to verify session π-calculi with extended expressiveness [51, Theorem 7.2].

6 Conclusion

A key open problems with multiparty session types (MPST) concerns expressiveness: none of the previous languages of global and local types supports arbitrary choice (e.g., choices between different senders), existential quantification over roles, and unbounded interleaving of subprotocols (in the same session). In this paper, we presented the first theory that supports these features. Our main theoretical result is operational equivalence under weak bisimilarity: this guarantees classical MPST properties for groups of local types projected from a global type, namely freedom of deadlocks and absence of protocol violations. Our main practical result is that our well-formedness conditions, which guarantee operational equivalence, can be checked orders of magnitude faster than directly checking weak bisimilarity, which is demonstrated by our benchmark results.

We identify several interesting avenues for future work. First, it is useful to extend our theory with *parametrisation* along the lines of Castro et al. [18] (which currently works only for restrictive choices); their proof technique for correctness seems to offer substantial synergy with our bisimilarity-based approach in this paper. Second, we aim to investigate extensions of our theory with subtyping (e.g., in terms of weak similarity). Notably, while asynchronous communication can be encoded in our current theory, asynchronous subtyping is known to be undecidable [9,41], so the connection between the two is interesting to explore.

Acknowledgments. Funded by the Netherlands Organisation of Scientific Research (NWO): 016.Veni.192.103. This work was carried out on the Dutch national e-infrastructure with the support of SURF Cooperative. Supported by EPSRC projects EP/K034413/1, EP/K011715/1, EP/L00058X/1, EP/N027833/1, EP/N028201/1, EP/T006544/1.

References

1. Ancona, D., Bono, V., Bravetti, M., Campos, J., Castagna, G., Deniélou, P., Gay, S.J., Gesbert, N., Giachino, E., Hu, R., Johnsen, E.B., Martins, F., Mascardi, V., Montesi, F., Neykova, R., Ng, N., Padovani, L., Vasconcelos, V.T., Yoshida, N.: Behavioral types in programming languages. Foundations and Trends in Programming Languages **3**(2-3), 95–230 (2016)
2. Baeten, J.C.M., Bravetti, M.: A ground-complete axiomatisation of finite-state processes in a generic process algebra. Mathematical Structures in Computer Science **18**(6), 1057–1089 (2008)
3. Bergstra, J.A., Fokkink, W., Ponse, A.: Chapter 5 - process algebra with recursive operations. In: Bergstra, J., Ponse, A., Smolka, S. (eds.) Handbook of Process Algebra, pp. 333 – 389. Elsevier Science (2001)
4. Bergstra, J.A., Klop, J.W.: Process algebra for synchronous communication. Information and Control **60**(1-3), 109–137 (1984)
5. van Beusekom, R., Groote, J.F., Hoogendijk, P.F., Howe, R., Wesselink, W., Wieringa, R., Willemse, T.A.C.: Formalising the dezyne modelling language in mcrl2. In: FMICS-AVoCS. Lecture Notes in Computer Science, vol. 10471, pp. 217–233. Springer (2017)
6. Bocchi, L., Lange, J., Yoshida, N.: Meeting deadlines together. In: CONCUR. LIPIcs, vol. 42, pp. 283–296. Schloss Dagstuhl - Leibniz-Zentrum fuer Informatik (2015)
7. Bocchi, L., Yang, W., Yoshida, N.: Timed multiparty session types. In: CONCUR. Lecture Notes in Computer Science, vol. 8704, pp. 419–434. Springer (2014)
8. Brand, D., Zafiropulo, P.: On communicating finite-state machines. J. ACM **30**(2), 323–342 (1983)
9. Bravetti, M., Carbone, M., Zavattaro, G.: Undecidability of asynchronous session subtyping. Inf. Comput. **256**, 300–320 (2017)
10. Bunte, O., Groote, J.F., Keiren, J.J.A., Laveaux, M., Neele, T., de Vink, E.P., Wesselink, W., Wijs, A., Willemse, T.A.C.: The mcrl2 toolset for analysing concurrent systems - improvements in expressivity and usability. In: TACAS (2). Lecture Notes in Computer Science, vol. 11428, pp. 21–39. Springer (2019)
11. Capecchi, S., Castellani, I., Dezani-Ciancaglini, M.: Typing access control and secure information flow in sessions. Inf. Comput. **238**, 68–105 (2014)
12. Capecchi, S., Castellani, I., Dezani-Ciancaglini, M.: Information flow safety in multiparty sessions. Mathematical Structures in Computer Science **26**(8), 1352–1394 (2016)
13. Capecchi, S., Castellani, I., Dezani-Ciancaglini, M., Rezk, T.: Session types for access and information flow control. In: CONCUR. Lecture Notes in Computer Science, vol. 6269, pp. 237–252. Springer (2010)
14. Carbone, M., Montesi, F.: Deadlock-freedom-by-design: multiparty asynchronous global programming. In: POPL. pp. 263–274. ACM (2013)
15. Carbone, M., Yoshida, N., Honda, K.: Asynchronous session types: Exceptions and multiparty interactions. In: SFM. Lecture Notes in Computer Science, vol. 5569, pp. 187–212. Springer (2009)
16. Castagna, G., Dezani-Ciancaglini, M., Padovani, L.: On global types and multiparty session. Logical Methods in Computer Science **8**(1) (2012)
17. Castellani, I., Dezani-Ciancaglini, M., Pérez, J.A.: Self-adaptation and secure information flow in multiparty communications. Formal Asp. Comput. **28**(4), 669–696 (2016)

18. Castro, D., Hu, R., Jongmans, S., Ng, N., Yoshida, N.: Distributed programming using role-parametric session types in go: statically-typed endpoint apis for dynamically-instantiated communication structures. PACMPL 3(POPL), 29:1–29:30 (2019)
19. Coppo, M., Dezani-Ciancaglini, M., Yoshida, N., Padovani, L.: Global progress for dynamically interleaved multiparty sessions. Mathematical Structures in Computer Science 26(2), 238–302 (2016)
20. Cranen, S., Groote, J.F., Keiren, J.J.A., Stappers, F.P.M., de Vink, E.P., Wesselink, W., Willemse, T.A.C.: An overview of the mcrl2 toolset and its recent advances. In: TACAS. Lecture Notes in Computer Science, vol. 7795, pp. 199–213. Springer (2013)
21. Davoudian, A., Chen, L., Liu, M.: A survey on nosql stores. ACM Comput. Surv. 51(2), 40:1–40:43 (2018)
22. Deniélou, P., Yoshida, N.: Dynamic multirole session types. In: POPL. pp. 435–446. ACM (2011)
23. Deniélou, P., Yoshida, N.: Multiparty session types meet communicating automata. In: ESOP. Lecture Notes in Computer Science, vol. 7211, pp. 194–213. Springer (2012)
24. Deniélou, P., Yoshida, N.: Multiparty compatibility in communicating automata: Characterisation and synthesis of global session types. In: ICALP (2). Lecture Notes in Computer Science, vol. 7966, pp. 174–186. Springer (2013)
25. Deniélou, P., Yoshida, N., Bejleri, A., Hu, R.: Parameterised multiparty session types. Logical Methods in Computer Science 8(4) (2012)
26. Falke, S., Kapur, D., Sinz, C.: Termination analysis of imperative programs using bitvector arithmetic. In: VSTTE. Lecture Notes in Computer Science, vol. 7152, pp. 261–277. Springer (2012)
27. Gessert, F., Wingerath, W., Friedrich, S., Ritter, N.: Nosql database systems: a survey and decision guidance. Computer Science - R&D 32(3-4), 353–365 (2017)
28. Groote, J.F., Jansen, D.N., Keiren, J.J.A., Wijs, A.: An $O(m\log n)$ algorithm for computing stuttering equivalence and branching bisimulation. ACM Trans. Comput. Log. 18(2), 13:1–13:34 (2017)
29. Groote, J.F., Mousavi, M.R.: Modeling and Analysis of Communicating Systems. MIT Press (2014)
30. Hamers, R., Jongmans, S.S.: Discourje: Runtime verification of communication protocols in clojure. In: TACAS 2020 (in press)
31. Hoefler, T., Belli, R.: Scientific benchmarking of parallel computing systems: twelve ways to tell the masses when reporting performance results. In: SC. pp. 73:1–73:12. ACM (2015)
32. Honda, K., Tokoro, M.: An object calculus for asynchronous communication. In: ECOOP. Lecture Notes in Computer Science, vol. 512, pp. 133–147. Springer (1991)
33. Honda, K., Yoshida, N., Carbone, M.: Multiparty asynchronous session types. In: POPL. pp. 273–284. ACM (2008)
34. Honda, K., Yoshida, N., Carbone, M.: Multiparty asynchronous session types. J. ACM 63(1), 9:1–9:67 (2016)
35. Hu, R., Yoshida, N.: Hybrid session verification through endpoint API generation. In: FASE. Lecture Notes in Computer Science, vol. 9633, pp. 401–418. Springer (2016)
36. Hu, R., Yoshida, N.: Explicit connection actions in multiparty session types. In: FASE. Lecture Notes in Computer Science, vol. 10202, pp. 116–133. Springer (2017)

37. Hüttel, H., Lanese, I., Vasconcelos, V.T., Caires, L., Carbone, M., Deniélou, P., Mostrous, D., Padovani, L., Ravara, A., Tuosto, E., Vieira, H.T., Zavattaro, G.: Foundations of session types and behavioural contracts. ACM Comput. Surv. **49**(1), 3:1–3:36 (2016)

38. Jongmans, S.S., Yoshida, N.: Exploring Type-Level Bisimilarity towards More Expressive Multiparty Session Types. Tech. Rep. TR-OU-INF-2020-01, Open University of the Netherlands (2020)

39. Lange, J., Ng, N., Toninho, B., Yoshida, N.: A static verification framework for message passing in go using behavioural types. In: ICSE. pp. 1137–1148. ACM (2018)

40. Lange, J., Tuosto, E., Yoshida, N.: From communicating machines to graphical choreographies. In: POPL. pp. 221–232. ACM (2015)

41. Lange, J., Yoshida, N.: On the undecidability of asynchronous session subtyping. In: FoSSaCS. Lecture Notes in Computer Science, vol. 10203, pp. 441–457 (2017)

42. Lange, J., Yoshida, N.: Verifying asynchronous interactions via communicating session automata. In: CAV (1). Lecture Notes in Computer Science, vol. 11561, pp. 97–117. Springer (2019)

43. Mostrous, D., Yoshida, N., Honda, K.: Global principal typing in partially commutative asynchronous sessions. In: ESOP. Lecture Notes in Computer Science, vol. 5502, pp. 316–332. Springer (2009)

44. Neykova, R., Bocchi, L., Yoshida, N.: Timed runtime monitoring for multiparty conversations. Formal Asp. Comput. **29**(5), 877–910 (2017)

45. Neykova, R., Hu, R., Yoshida, N., Abdeljallal, F.: A session type provider: compile-time API generation of distributed protocols with refinements in f#. In: CC. pp. 128–138. ACM (2018)

46. Neykova, R., Yoshida, N.: Let it recover: multiparty protocol-induced recovery. In: CC. pp. 98–108. ACM (2017)

47. Ng, N., Yoshida, N.: Pabble: parameterised scribble. Service Oriented Computing and Applications **9**(3-4), 269–284 (2015)

48. Redis Labs: Redis (nd), accessed 18 October 2019, https://redis.io

49. Redis Labs: Transactions – redis (nd), accessed 18 October 2019, https://redis.io/topics/transactions

50. Scalas, A., Dardha, O., Hu, R., Yoshida, N.: A linear decomposition of multiparty sessions for safe distributed programming. In: ECOOP. LIPIcs, vol. 74, pp. 24:1–24:31. Schloss Dagstuhl - Leibniz-Zentrum fuer Informatik (2017)

51. Scalas, A., Yoshida, N.: Less is more: multiparty session types revisited. PACMPL **3**(POPL), 30:1–30:29 (2019)

52. Scalas, A., Yoshida, N., Benussi, E.: Effpi: verified message-passing programs in dotty. In: SCALA@ECOOP. pp. 27–31. ACM (2019)

53. Scalas, A., Yoshida, N., Benussi, E.: Verifying message-passing programs with dependent behavioural types. In: PLDI. pp. 502–516. ACM (2019)

Verifying Visibility-Based Weak Consistency

Siddharth Krishna[1], Michael Emmi[2], Constantin Enea[3], and Dejan Jovanović[2]

[1] New York University, New York, NY, USA, siddharth@cs.nyu.edu
[2] SRI International, New York, NY, USA, michael.emmi@gmail.com,
dejan.jovanovic@sri.com
[3] Université de Paris, IRIF, CNRS, F-75013 Paris, France, cenea@irif.fr

Abstract. Multithreaded programs generally leverage efficient and thread-safe *concurrent objects* like sets, key-value maps, and queues. While some concurrent-object operations are designed to behave atomically, each witnessing the atomic effects of predecessors in a linearization order, others forego such strong consistency to avoid complex control and synchronization bottlenecks. For example, contains (value) methods of key-value maps may iterate through key-value entries without blocking concurrent updates, to avoid unwanted performance bottlenecks, and consequently overlook the effects of some linearization-order predecessors. While such *weakly-consistent* operations may not be atomic, they still offer guarantees, e.g., only observing values that have been present.

In this work we develop a methodology for proving that concurrent object implementations adhere to weak-consistency specifications. In particular, we consider (forward) simulation-based proofs of implementations against *relaxed-visibility specifications*, which allow designated operations to overlook some of their linearization-order predecessors, i.e., behaving as if they never occurred. Besides annotating implementation code to identify *linearization points*, i.e., points at which operations' logical effects occur, we also annotate code to identify *visible operations*, i.e., operations whose effects are observed; in practice this annotation can be done automatically by tracking the writers to each accessed memory location. We formalize our methodology over a general notion of transition systems, agnostic to any particular programming language or memory model, and demonstrate its application, using automated theorem provers, by verifying models of Java concurrent object implementations.

1   Introduction

Programming efficient multithreaded programs generally involves carefully organizing shared memory accesses to facilitate inter-thread communication while avoiding synchronization bottlenecks. Modern software platforms like Java include reusable abstractions which encapsulate low-level shared memory accesses and synchronization into familiar high-level abstract data types (ADTs). These so-called *concurrent objects* typically include mutual-exclusion primitives like locks, numeric data types like atomic integers, as well as collections like sets, key-value maps, and queues; Java's standard-edition platform contains many implementations of each. Such objects typically provide strong consistency guarantees like *linearizability* [18], ensuring that each operation appears to happen atomically, witnessing the atomic effects of predecessors according to some linearization order among concurrently-executing operations.

P. Müller (Ed.): ESOP 2020, LNCS 12075, pp. 280–307, 2020.
https://doi.org/10.1007/978-3-030-44914-8_11

While such strong consistency guarantees are ideal for logical reasoning about programs which use concurrent objects, these guarantees are too strong for many operations, since they preclude simple and/or efficient implementation — over half of Java's concurrent collection methods forego atomicity for *weak-consistency* [13]. On the one hand, basic operations like the get and put methods of key-value maps typically admit relatively-simple atomic implementations, since their behaviors essentially depend upon individual memory cells, e.g., where the relevant key-value mapping is stored. On the other hand, making aggregate operations like size and contains (value) atomic would impose synchronization bottlenecks, or otherwise-complex control structures, since their atomic behavior depends simultaneously upon the values stored across many memory cells. Interestingly, such implementations are not linearizable even when their underlying memory operations are sequentially consistent, e.g., as is the case with Java 8's concurrent collections, whose memory accesses are data-race free.[4]

For instance, the contains (value) method of Java's concurrent hash map iterates through key-value entries without blocking concurrent updates in order to avoid unreasonable performance bottlenecks. Consequently, in a given execution, a contains-value-v operation o_1 will overlook operation o_2's concurrent insertion of $k_1 \mapsto v$ for a key k_1 it has already traversed. This oversight makes it possible for o_1 to conclude that value v is not present, and can only be explained by o_1 being linearized before o_2. In the case that operation o_3 removes $k_2 \mapsto v$ concurrently before o_1 reaches key k_2, but only after o_2 completes, then atomicity is violated since in every possible linearization, either mapping $k_2 \mapsto v$ or $k_1 \mapsto v$ is always present. Nevertheless, such weakly-consistent operations still offer guarantees, e.g., that values never present are never observed, and initially-present values not removed are observed.

In this work we develop a methodology for proving that concurrent-object implementations adhere to the guarantees prescribed by their weak-consistency specifications. The key salient aspects of our approach are the lifting of existing sequential ADT specifications via *visibility relaxation* [13], and the harnessing of simple and mechanizable reasoning based on *forward simulation* [25] by relaxed-visibility ADTs. Effectively, our methodology extends the predominant forward-simulation based linearizability-proof methodology to concurrent objects with weakly-consistent operations, and enables automation for proving weak-consistency guarantees.

To enable the harnessing of existing sequential ADT specifications, we adopt the recent methodology of *visibility relaxation* [13]. As in linearizability [18], the return value of each operation is dictated by the atomic effects of its predecessors in some (i.e., existentially quantified) linearization order. To allow consistency weakening, operations are allowed, to a certain extent, to overlook some of their linearization-order predecessors, behaving as if they had not occurred. Intuitively, this (also existentially quantified) *visibility* captures the inability or unwillingness to atomically observe the values stored across many memory cells. To provide guarantees, the extent of

---

[4] Java 8 implementations guarantee data-race freedom by accessing individual shared-memory cells with atomic operations via volatile variables and compare-and-swap instructions. Starting with Java 9, the implementations of the concurrent collections use the VarHandle mechanism to specify shared variable access modes. Java's official language and API specifications do not clarify whether these relaxations introduce data races.

visibility relaxation is bounded to varying degrees. Notably, the visibility of an *absolute* operation must include all of its linearization-order predecessors, while the visibility of a *monotonic* operation must include all happens-before predecessors, along with all operations visible to them. The majority of Java's concurrent collection methods are absolute or monotonic [13]. For instance, in the contains-value example described above, by considering that operation o_2 is not visible to o_1, the conclusion that v is not present can be justified by the linearization $o_2; o_3; o_1$, in which o_1 sees o_3's removal of $k_2 \mapsto v$ yet not o_2's insertion of $k_1 \mapsto v$. Ascribing the monotonic visibility to the contains-value method amounts to a guarantee that initially-present values are observed unless removed (i.e., concurrently).

While relaxed-visibility specifications provide a means to describing the guarantees provided by weakly-consistent concurrent-object operations, systematically establishing implementations' adherence requires a strategy for demonstrating *simulation* [25], i.e., that each step of the implementation is simulated by some step of (an operational representation of) the specification. The crux of our contribution is thus threefold: first, to identify the relevant specification-level actions with which to relate implementation-level transitions; second, to identify implementation-level annotations relating transitions to specification-level actions; and third, to develop strategies for devising such annotations systematically. For instance, the existing methodology based on *linearization points* [18] essentially amounts to annotating implementation-level transitions with the points at which its specification-level action, i.e., its atomic effect, occurs. Relaxed-visibility specifications require not only a witness for the existentially-quantified linearization order, but also an existentially-quantified visibility relation, and thus requires a second kind of annotation to resolve operations' visibilities. We propose a notion of *visibility actions* which enable operations to declare their visibility of others, e.g., specifying the writers of memory cells it has read.

The remainder of our approach amounts to devising a systematic means for constructing simulation proofs to enable automated verification. Essentially, we identify a strategy for systematically annotating implementations with visibility actions, given linearization-point annotations and visibility bounds (i.e., absolute or monotonic), and then encode the corresponding simulation check using an off-the-shelf verification tool. For the latter, we leverage CIVL [16], a language and verifier for Owicki-Gries style modular proofs of concurrent programs with arbitrarily-many threads. In principle, since our approach reduces simulation to safety verification, any safety verifier could be used, though CIVL facilitates reasoning for multithreaded programs by capturing interference at arbitrary program points. Using CIVL, we have verified monotonicity of the contains-value and size methods of Java's concurrent hash-map and concurrent linked-queue, respectively — and absolute consistency of add and remove operations. Although our models are written in CIVL and assume sequentially-consistent memory accesses, they capture the difficult aspects of weak-consistency in Java, including heap-based memory access; furthermore, our models are also sound with respect to Java 8's memory model, since their Java 8 implementations guarantee data-race freedom.

In summary, we present the first methodology for verifying weakly-consistent operations using sequential specifications and forward simulation. Contributions include:

- the formalization of our methodology over a general notion of transition systems, agnostic to any particular programming language or memory model (§3);
- the application of our methodology to verifying a weakly-consistent contains-value method of a key-value map (§4); and
- a mechanization of our methodology used for verifying models of weakly-consistent Java methods using automated theorem provers (§5).

Aside from the outline above, this article summarizes an existing weak-consistency specification methodology via visibility relaxation (§2), summarizes related work (§6), and concludes (§7). Proofs of all theorems and lemmas are listed in Appendix A.

2   Weak Consistency

Our methodology for verifying weakly-consistent concurrent objects relies both on the precise characterization of weak consistency specifications, as well as a proof technique for establishing adherence to specifications. In this section we recall and outline a characterization called *visibility relaxation* [13], an extension of sequential abstract data type (ADT) specifications in which the return values of some operations may not reflect the effects of previously-effectuated operations.

Notationally, in the remainder of this article, ε denotes the empty sequence, $\emptyset$ denotes the empty set, _ denotes an unused binding, and $\top$ and $\bot$ denote the Boolean values true and false, respectively. We write $R(x)$ to denote the inclusion $x \in R$ of a tuple x in the relation R; and $R[x \mapsto y]$ to denote the extension $R \cup \{xy\}$ of R to include xy; and $R \mid X$ to denote the projection $R \cap X^*$ of R to set X; and $\overline{R}$ to denote the complement $\{x : x \notin R\}$ of R; and $R(x)$ to denote the image $\{y : xy \in R\}$ of R on x; and $R^{-1}(y)$ to denote the pre-image $\{x : xy \in R\}$ of R on y; whether $R(x)$ refers to inclusion or an image will be clear from its context. Finally, we write x_i to refer to the ith element of tuple $x = x_0 x_1 \ldots$.

2.1   Weak-Visibility Specifications

For a general notion of ADT specifications, we consider fixed sets $\mathbb{M}$ and $\mathbb{X}$ of method names and argument or return values, respectively. An *operation label* $\lambda = \langle m, x, y \rangle$ is a method name $m \in \mathbb{M}$ along with argument and return values $x, y \in \mathbb{X}$. A *read-only predicate* is a unary relation $R(\lambda)$ on operation labels, an *operation sequence* $s = \lambda_0 \lambda_1 \ldots$ is a sequence of operation labels, and a *sequential specification* $S = \{s_0, s_1, \ldots\}$ is a set of operation sequences. We say that R is *compatible* with S when S is closed under deletion of read-only operations, i.e., $\lambda_0 \ldots \lambda_{j-1} \lambda_{j+1} \ldots \lambda_i \in S$ when $\lambda_0 \ldots \lambda_i \in S$ and $R(\lambda_j)$.

Example 1. The *key-value map* ADT sequential specification S_m is the prefix-closed set containing all sequences $\lambda_0 \ldots \lambda_i$ such that λ_i is either:

- $\langle \text{put}, kv, b \rangle$, and $b = \top$ iff some $\langle \text{rem}, k, \_ \rangle$ follows any prior $\langle \text{put}, kv, \_ \rangle$;
- $\langle \text{rem}, k, b \rangle$, and $b = \top$ iff no other $\langle \text{rem}, k, \_ \rangle$ follows some prior $\langle \text{put}, kv, \_ \rangle$;
- $\langle \text{get}, k, v \rangle$, and no $\langle \text{put}, kv', \_ \rangle$ nor $\langle \text{rem}, k, \_ \rangle$ follows some prior $\langle \text{put}, kv, \_ \rangle$, and $v = \bot$ if no such $\langle \text{put}, kv, \_ \rangle$ exists; or

- $\langle has, v, b \rangle$, and $b = \top$ iff no prior $\langle put, kv', \_ \rangle$ nor $\langle rem, k, \_ \rangle$ follows some prior $\langle put, kv, \_ \rangle$.

The read-only predicate R_m holds for the following cases:

$$R_m(\langle put, \_, b \rangle) \text{ if } \neg b \quad R_m(\langle rem, \_, b \rangle) \text{ if } \neg b \quad R_m(\langle get, \_, \_ \rangle) \quad R_m(\langle has, \_, \_ \rangle).$$

This is a simplification of Java's Map ADT, i.e., with fewer methods.[5]

To derive weak specifications from sequential ones, we consider a set $\mathbb{V}$ of exactly two *visibility* labels from prior work [13]: *absolute* and *monotonic*.[6] A *visibility annotation* $V : \mathbb{M} \to \mathbb{V}$ maps each method $m \in \mathbb{M}$ to a visibility $V(m) \in \mathbb{V}$.

Intuitively, absolute visibility requires operations to observe the effects of all of their linearization-order predecessors. The weaker monotonic visibility requires operations to observe the effects of all their happens-before (i.e., program- and synchronization-order) predecessors, along with the effects already observed by those predecessors, i.e., so that sets of visible effects are monotonically increasing over happens-before chains of operations; conversely, operations may ignore effects which have been ignored by their happens-before predecessors, so long as those effects are not transitively related by program and synchronization order.

Definition 1. *A* weak-visibility specification $W = \langle S, R, V \rangle$ *is a sequential specification* S *with a compatible read-only predicate* R *and a visibility annotation* V.

Example 2. The *weakly-consistent contains-value map* $W_m = \langle S_m, R_m, V_m \rangle$ annotates the key-value map ADT methods of S_m from Example 1 with:

$$V_m(put) = V_m(rem) = V_m(get) = absolute, \qquad V_m(has) = monotonic.$$

Java's concurrent hash map appears to be consistent with this specification [13].

We ascribe semantics to specifications by characterizing the values returned by concurrent method invocations, given constraints on invocation order. In practice, the *happens-before* order among invocations is determined by a *program order*, i.e., among invocations of the same thread, and a *synchronization order*, i.e., among invocations of distinct threads accessing the same atomic objects, e.g., locks. A *history* $h = \langle O, inv, ret, hb \rangle$ is a set $O \subseteq \mathbb{N}$ of numeric operation identifiers, along with an invocation function $inv : O \to \mathbb{M} \times \mathbb{X}$ mapping operation identifiers to method names and argument values, a partial return function $ret : O \rightharpoonup \mathbb{X}$ mapping operation identifiers to return values, and a (strict) partial happens-before relation $hb \subseteq O \times O$; the *empty history* $h_\emptyset$ has $O = inv = ret = hb = \emptyset$. An operation $o \in O$ is *complete* when $ret(o)$ is defined, and is otherwise *incomplete*; then h is *complete* when each operation is. The *label* of a complete operation o with $inv(o) = \langle m, x \rangle$ and $ret(o) = y$ is $\langle m, x, y \rangle$.

To relate operations' return values in a given history back to sequential specifications, we consider certain sequencings of those operations. A *linearization* of a history $h = \langle O, \_, \_, hb \rangle$ is a total order $lin \supseteq hb$ over O which includes hb, and a *visibility*

---

[5] For brevity, we abbreviate Java's remove and contains-value methods by rem and has.

[6] Previous work refers to absolute visibility as *complete*, and includes additional visibility labels.

projection vis of *lin* maps each operation $o \in O$ to a subset $vis(o) \subseteq lin^{-1}(o)$ of the operations preceding o in *lin*; note that $\langle o_1, o_2 \rangle \in vis$ means o_1 observes o_2. For a given read-only predicate R, we say o's visibility is *monotonic* when it includes every happens-before predecessor, and operation visible to a happens-before predecessor, which is not read-only,[7] i.e., $vis(o) \supseteq \left(hb^{-1}(o) \cup vis(hb^{-1}(o)) \right) \mid \overline{R}$. We says o's visibility is *absolute* when $vis(o) = lin^{-1}(o)$, and *vis* is itself *absolute* when each $vis(o)$ is. An *abstract execution* $e = \langle h, lin, vis \rangle$ is a history h along with a linearization of h, and a visibility projection *vis* of *lin*. An abstract execution is *sequential* when *hb* is total, *complete* when h is, and *absolute* when *vis* is.

Example 3. An abstract execution can be defined using the linearization[8]

$$\langle \text{put}, \langle 1, 1 \rangle, \top \rangle \; \langle \text{get}, 1, 1 \rangle \; \langle \text{put}, \langle 0, 1 \rangle, \top \rangle \; \langle \text{put}, \langle 1, 0 \rangle, \bot \rangle \; \langle \text{has}, 1, \bot \rangle$$

along with a happens-before order that, compared to the linearization order, keeps $\langle \text{has}, 1, \bot \rangle$ unordered w.r.t. $\langle \text{put}, \langle 0, 1 \rangle, \top \rangle$ and $\langle \text{put}, \langle 1, 0 \rangle, \bot \rangle$, and a visibility projection where the visibility of every put and get includes all the linearization predecessors and the visibility of $\langle \text{has}, 1, \bot \rangle$ consists of $\langle \text{put}, \langle 1, 1 \rangle, \top \rangle$ and $\langle \text{put}, \langle 1, 0 \rangle, \bot \rangle$. Recall that in the argument $\langle k, v \rangle$ to put operations, the key k precedes value v.

To determine the consistency of individual histories against weak-visibility specifications, we consider adherence of their corresponding abstract executions. Let $h = \langle O, inv, ret, hb \rangle$ be a history and $e = \langle h, lin, vis \rangle$ a complete abstract execution. Then e is *consistent* with a visibility annotation V and read-only predicate R if for each operation $o \in \text{dom}(lin)$ with $inv(o) = \langle m, \_ \rangle$, $vis(o)$ is absolute or monotonic, respectively, according to $V(m)$ and R. The *labeling* $\lambda_0 \lambda_1 \ldots$ of a total order $o_0 \prec o_1 \prec \ldots$ of complete operations is the sequence of operation labels, i.e., λ_i is the label of o_i. Then e is *consistent* with a sequential specification S when the labeling[9] of $lin \mid (vis(o) \cup \{o\})$ is included in S, for each operation $o \in \text{dom}(lin)$.[10] Finally, we say e is *consistent* with a weak-visibility specification $\langle S, R, V \rangle$ when it is consistent with S, R, and V.

Example 4. The execution in Example 3 is consistent with the weakly-consistent contains-value map W_m defined in Example 2.

Remark 1. Consistency models suited for modern software platforms like Java are based on *happens-before* relations which abstract away from *real-time* execution order. Since happens-before, unlike real-time, is not necessarily an *interval order*, the composition

---

[7] For convenience we rephrase Emmi and Enea [13]'s notion to ignore read-only predecessors.

[8] For readability, we list linearization sequences with operation labels in place of identifiers.

[9] As is standard, adequate labelings of incomplete executions are obtained by completing each linearized yet pending operation with some arbitrarily-chosen return value [18]. It is sufficient that one of these completions be included in the sequential specification.

[10] We consider a simplification from prior work [13]: rather than allowing the observers of a given operation to pretend they see distinct return values, we suppose that all observers agree on return values. While this is more restrictive in principle, it is equivalent for the simple specifications studied in this article.

of linearizations of two distinct objects in the same execution may be cyclic, i.e., not linearizable. Recovering compositionality in this setting is orthogonal to our work of proving consistency against a given model, and is explored elsewhere [11].

The *abstract executions* $E(W)$ of a weak-visibility specification $W = \langle S, R, V \rangle$ include those complete, sequential, and absolute abstract executions derived from sequences of S, i.e., when $s = \lambda_0 \dots \lambda_n \in S$ then each e_s labels each o_i by λ_i, and orders $hb(o_i, o_j)$ iff $i < j$. In addition, when $E(W)$ includes an abstract execution $\langle h, lin, vis \rangle$ with $h = \langle O, inv, ret, hb \rangle$, then $E(W)$ also includes any:

- execution $\langle h', lin, vis \rangle$ such that $h' = \langle O, inv, ret, hb' \rangle$ and $hb' \subseteq hb$; and
- W-consistent execution $\langle h', lin, vis' \rangle$ with $h' = \langle O, inv, ret', hb \rangle$ and $vis' \subseteq vis$.

Note that while *happens-before weakening* $hb' \subseteq hb$ always yields consistent executions, unguarded *visibility weakening* $vis' \subseteq vis$ generally breaks consistency with visibility annotations and sequential specifications: visibilities can become non-monotonic, and return values can change when operations observe fewer operations' effects.

Lemma 1. *The abstract executions $E(W)$ of a specification W are consistent with W.*

Example 5. The abstract executions of W_m include the complete, sequential, and absolute abstract execution defined by the following happens-before order

$$\langle put, \langle 1, 1 \rangle, \top \rangle \; \langle get, 1, 1 \rangle \; \langle put, \langle 0, 1 \rangle, \top \rangle \; \langle put, \langle 1, 0 \rangle, \bot \rangle \; \langle has, 1, \top \rangle$$

which implies that it also includes one in which just the happens-before order is modified such that $\langle has, 1, \top \rangle$ becomes unordered w.r.t. $\langle put, \langle 0, 1 \rangle, \top \rangle$ and $\langle put, \langle 1, 0 \rangle, \bot \rangle$. Since it includes the latter, it also includes the execution in Example 3 where the visibility of has is weakened which also modifies its return value from $\top$ to $\bot$.

Definition 2. *The* histories *of a weak-visibility specification W are the projections $H(W) = \{h : \langle h, \_, \_ \rangle \in E(W)\}$ of its abstract executions.*

2.2   Consistency against Weak-Visibility Specifications

To define the consistency of implementations against specifications, we leverage a general model of computation to capture the behavior of typical concurrent systems, e.g., including multiprocess and multithreaded systems. A *sequence-labeled transition system* $\langle Q, A, q, \rightarrow \rangle$ is a set Q of states, along with a set A of actions, initial state $q \in Q$ and transition relation $\rightarrow \in Q \times A^* \times Q$. An *execution* is an alternating sequence $\eta = q_0 \vec{a}_0 q_1 \vec{a}_1 \dots q_n$ of states and action sequences starting with $q_0 = q$ such that $q_i \xrightarrow{\vec{a}_i} q_{i+1}$ for each $0 \leq i < n$. The *trace* $\tau \in A^*$ of the execution η is its projection $\vec{a}_0 \vec{a}_1 \dots$ to individual actions.

To capture the histories admitted by a given implementation, we consider sequence-labeled transition systems (SLTSs) which expose actions corresponding to method call, return, and happens-before constraints. We refer to the actions $call(o, m, x)$, $ret(o, y)$, and $hb(o, o')$, for $o, o' \in \mathbb{N}$, $m \in \mathbb{M}$, and $x, y \in \mathbb{X}$, as *the history actions*, and a *history transition system* is an SLTS whose actions include the history actions. We say that an action over operation identifier o is an o-*action*, and assume that executions are *well formed* in the sense that for a given operation identifier o: at most one call o-action occurs, at most one ret o-action occurs, and no ret nor hb o-actions occur prior to a call o-action. Furthermore, we assume call o-actions are enabled, so long as no prior call o-action has occurred. The *history* of a trace τ is defined inductively by $f_h(h_\emptyset, \tau)$, where $h_\emptyset$ is the empty history, and,

$$
\begin{aligned}
f_h(h, \varepsilon) &= h & g_h(h, \text{call}(o, m, x)) &= \langle O \cup \{o\}, inv[o \mapsto \langle m, x \rangle], ret, hb \rangle \\
f_h(h, a\tau) &= f_h(g_h(h, a), \tau) & g_h(h, \text{ret}(o, y)) &= \langle O, inv, ret[o \mapsto y], hb \rangle \\
f_h(h, \tilde{a}\tau) &= f_h(h, \tau) & g_h(h, \text{hb}(o, o')) &= \langle O, inv, ret, hb \cup \langle o, o' \rangle \rangle
\end{aligned}
$$

where $h = \langle O, inv, ret, hb \rangle$, and a is a call, ret, or hb action, and $\tilde{a}$ is not. An *implementation* I is a history transition system, and the *histories* $H(I)$ of I are those of its traces. Finally, we define consistency against specifications via history containment.

Definition 3. *Implementation I is* consistent *with specification W iff $H(I) \subseteq H(W)$.*

3   Establishing Consistency with Forward Simulation

To obtain a consistency proof strategy, we more closely relate implementations to specifications via their admitted abstract executions. To capture the abstract executions admitted by a given implementation, we consider SLTSs which expose not only history-related actions, but also actions witnessing linearization and visibility. We refer to the actions lin(o) and vis(o, o') for $o, o' \in \mathbb{N}$, along with the history actions, as *the abstract-execution actions*, and an *abstract-execution transition system* (AETS) is an SLTS whose actions include the abstract-execution actions. Extending the corresponding notion from history transition systems, we assume that executions are *well formed* in the sense that for a given operation identifier o: at most one lin o-action occurs, and no lin or vis o-actions occur prior to a call o-action. The *abstract execution* of a trace τ is defined inductively by $f_e(e_\emptyset, \tau)$, where $e_\emptyset = \langle h_\emptyset, \emptyset, \emptyset \rangle$ is the empty execution, and,

$$
\begin{aligned}
f_e(e, \varepsilon) &= e & g_e(e, \hat{a}) &= \langle g_h(h), lin, vis \rangle \\
f_e(e, a\tau) &= f_e(g_e(e, a), \tau) & g_e(e, \text{lin}(o)) &= \langle h, lin \cup \{\langle o', o \rangle : o' \in lin\}, vis \rangle \\
f_e(e, \tilde{a}\tau) &= f_e(e, \tau) & g_e(e, \text{vis}(o, o')) &= \langle h, lin, vis \cup \{\langle o, o' \rangle\} \rangle
\end{aligned}
$$

where $e = \langle h, lin, vis \rangle$, and a is a call, ret, hb, lin, or vis action, $\tilde{a}$ is not, and $\hat{a}$ is a call, ret, or hb action. A *witnessing implementation* I is an abstract-execution transition system, and the *abstract executions* $E(I)$ of I are those of its traces.

We adopt forward simulation [25] for proving consistency against weak-visibility specifications. Formally, a *simulation relation* from one system $\Sigma_1 = \langle Q_1, A_1, \chi_1, \rightarrow_1 \rangle$ to another $\Sigma_2 = \langle Q_2, A_2, \chi_2, \rightarrow_2 \rangle$ is a binary relation $R \subseteq Q_1 \times Q_2$ such that initial states are related, $R(\chi_1, \chi_2)$, and: for any pair of related states $R(q_1, q_2)$ and source-system transition $q_1 \xrightarrow{\bar{a}_1}_1 q_1'$, there exists a target-system transition $q_2 \xrightarrow{\bar{a}_2}_2 q_2'$ to related states, i.e., $R(q_1', q_2')$, over common actions, i.e., $(\bar{a}_1 \mid A_2) = (\bar{a}_2 \mid A_1)$. We say Σ_2 *simulates* Σ_1 and write $\Sigma_1 \sqsubseteq \Sigma_2$ when a simulation relation from Σ_1 to Σ_2 exists.

We derive transition systems to model consistency specifications in simulation. The following lemma establishes the soundness and completeness of this substitution, and the subsequent theorem asserts the soundness of the simulation-based proof strategy.

Definition 4. *The* transition system $[\![W]\!]_{\mathrm{s}}$ *of a weak-visibility specification W is the AETS whose actions are the abstract execution actions, whose states are abstract executions, whose initial state is the empty execution, and whose transitions include $e_1 \xrightarrow{\vec{a}} e_2$ iff $f_{\mathrm{e}}(e_1, \vec{a}) = e_2$ and e_2 is consistent with W.*

Lemma 2. *A weak-visibility spec. and its transition system have identical histories.*

Theorem 1. *A witnessing implementation I is consistent with a weak-visibility specification W if the transition system $[\![W]\!]_{\mathrm{s}}$ of W simulates I.*

Our notion of simulation is in some sense *complete* when the sequential specification S of a weak-consistency specification $W = \langle S, R, V \rangle$ is *return-value deterministic*, i.e., there is a single label $\langle m, x, y \rangle$ such that $\vec{\lambda} \cdot \langle m, x, y \rangle \in S$ for any method m, argument-value x, and admitted sequence $\vec{\lambda} \in S$. In particular, $[\![W]\!]_{\mathrm{s}}$ simulates any witnessing implementation I whose abstract executions $E(I)$ are included in $E([\![W]\!]_{\mathrm{s}})$.[11] This completeness, however, extends only to inclusion of abstract executions, and not all the way to consistency, since consistency is defined on histories, and any given operation's return value is not completely determined by the other operation labels and happens-before relation of a given history: return values generally depend on linearization order and visibility as well. Nevertheless, sequential specifications typically are return-value deterministic, and we have used simulation to prove consistency of Java-inspired weakly-consistent objects.

Establishing simulation for an implementation is also helpful when reasoning about clients of a concurrent object. One can use the specification in place of the implementation and encode the client invariants using the abstract execution of the specification in order to prove client properties, following Sergey et al.'s approach [35].

3.1 Reducing Consistency to Safety Verification

Proving simulation between an implementation and its specification can generally be achieved via product construction: complete the transition system of the specification, replacing non-enabled transitions with error-state transitions; then ensure the synchronized product of implementation and completed-specification transition systems is *safe*, i.e., no error state is reachable. Assuming that the individual transition systems are safe, then the product system is safe *iff* the specification simulates the implementation. This reduction to safety verification is also generally applicable to implementation and specification programs, though we limit our formalization to their underlying transition systems for simplicity. By the upcoming Corollary 1, such reductions enable consistency verification with existing safety verification tools.

3.2 Verifying Implementations

While Theorem 1 establishes forward simulation as a strategy for proving the consistency of implementations against weak-visibility specifications, its application to

---

[11] This is a consequence of a generic result stating that the set of traces of an LTS A_1 is included in the set of traces of an LTS A_2 iff A_2 simulates A_1, provided that A_2 is deterministic [25].

real-world implementations requires program-level mechanisms to signal the underlying AETS lin and vis actions. To apply forward simulation, we thus develop a notion of programs whose commands include such mechanisms.

This section illustrates a toy programming language with AETS semantics which provides these mechanisms. The key features are the lin and vis program commands, which emit linearization and visibility actions for the currently-executing operation, along with load, store, and cas (compare-and-swap) commands, which record and return the set of operation identifiers having written to each memory cell. Such augmented memory commands allow programs to obtain handles to the operations whose effects it has observed, in order to signal the corresponding vis actions.

While one can develop similar mechanisms for languages with any underlying memory model, the toy language presented here assumes a sequentially-consistent memory. Note that the assumption of sequentially-consistent memory operations is practically without loss of generality for Java 8's concurrent collections since they are designed to be data-race free — their anomalies arise not from weak-memory semantics, but from non-atomic operations spanning several memory cells.

For generality, we assume abstract notions of commands and memory, using κ, μ, ℓ, and M respectively to denote a *program command*, *memory command*, *local state*, and *global memory*. So that operations can assert their visibilities, we consider memory which stores, and returns upon access, the identifier(s) of operations which previously accessed a given cell. A *program* $P = \langle \text{init}, \text{cmd}, \text{idle}, \text{done} \rangle$ consists of an $\text{init}(m, x) = \ell$ function mapping method name m and argument values x to local state ℓ, along with a $\text{cmd}(\ell) = \kappa$ function mapping local state ℓ to program command κ, and $\text{idle}(\ell)$ and $\text{done}(\ell)$ predicates on local states ℓ. Intuitively, identifying local states with threads, the idle predicate indicates whether a thread is outside of atomic sections, and subject to interference from other threads; meanwhile the done predicate indicates whether whether a thread has terminated.

The *denotation* of a memory command μ is a function $[\![\mu]\!]_m$ from global memory M_1, argument value x, and operation o to a tuple $[\![\mu]\!]_m(M_1, x, o) = \langle M_2, y \rangle$ consisting of a global memory M_2, along with a return value y.

Example 6. A sequentially-consistent memory system which records the set of operations to access each location can be captured by mapping addresses x to value and operation-set pairs $M(x) = \langle y, O \rangle$, along with three memory commands:

$$[\![\text{load}]\!]_m(M, x, \_) = \langle M, M(x) \rangle$$

$$[\![\text{store}]\!]_m(M, xy, o) = \langle M[x \mapsto \langle y, M(x)_1 \cup \{o\} \rangle], \varepsilon \rangle$$

$$[\![\text{cas}]\!]_m(M, xyz, o) = \begin{cases} \langle M[x \mapsto \langle z, M(x)_1 \cup \{o\} \rangle], \langle \text{true}, M(x)_1 \rangle \rangle & \text{if } M(x)_0 = y \\ \langle M, \langle \text{false}, M(x)_1 \rangle \rangle & \text{if } M(x)_0 \neq y \end{cases}$$

where the compare-and-swap (CAS) operation stores value z at address x and returns *true* when y was previously stored, and otherwise returns *false*.

The *denotation* of a program command κ is a function $[\![\kappa]\!]_c$ from local state ℓ_1 to a tuple $[\![\kappa]\!]_c(\ell_1) = \langle \mu, x, f \rangle$ consisting of a memory command μ and argument value x, and a update continuation f mapping the memory command's return value y to a pair $f(y) = \langle \ell_2, \alpha \rangle$, where ℓ_2 is an updated local state, and α maps an operation o to an LTS action $\alpha(o)$. We assume the denotation $[\![\texttt{ret}\ x]\!]_c(\ell_1) = \langle \text{nop}, \varepsilon, \lambda y.\langle \ell_2, \lambda o.\text{ret}(z) \rangle \rangle$ of the $\texttt{ret}$ command yields a local state ℓ_2 with done(ℓ_2) without executing memory commands, and outputs a corresponding LTS ret action.

Example 7. A simple goto language over variables $\texttt{a}, \texttt{b}, \ldots$ for the memory system of Example 6 would include the following commands:

$$[\![\texttt{goto a}]\!]_c(\ell) = \langle \text{nop}, \varepsilon, \lambda y.\langle jump(\ell, \ell(\texttt{a})), \lambda o.\varepsilon \rangle \rangle$$
$$[\![\texttt{assume a}]\!]_c(\ell) = \langle \text{nop}, \varepsilon, \lambda y.\langle next(\ell), \lambda o.\varepsilon \rangle \rangle \text{ if } \ell(\texttt{a}) \neq 0$$
$$[\![\texttt{b, c = load(a)}]\!]_c(\ell) = \langle \text{load}, \ell(\texttt{a}), \lambda y_1, y_2.\langle next(\ell[\texttt{b} \mapsto y_1][\texttt{c} \mapsto y_2]), \lambda o.\varepsilon \rangle \rangle$$
$$[\![\texttt{store(a, b)}]\!]_c(\ell) = \langle \text{store}, \ell(\texttt{a})\ell(\texttt{b}), \lambda y.\langle next(\ell), \lambda o.\varepsilon \rangle \rangle$$
$$[\![\texttt{d, e = cas(a, b, c)}]\!]_c(\ell) = \langle \text{cas}, \ell(\texttt{a})\ell(\texttt{b})\ell(\texttt{c}), \lambda y_1, y_2.\langle next(\ell[\texttt{d} \mapsto y_1][\texttt{e} \mapsto y_2]), \lambda o.\varepsilon \rangle$$

where the *jump* and *next* functions update a program counter, and the load command stores the operation identifier returned from the corresponding memory commands. Linearization and visibility actions are captured as program commands as follows:

$$[\![\texttt{lin}]\!]_c(\ell) = \langle \text{nop}, \varepsilon, \lambda y.\langle next(\ell), \lambda o.\text{lin}(o) \rangle \rangle$$
$$[\![\texttt{vis(a)}]\!]_c(\ell) = \langle \text{nop}, \varepsilon, \lambda y.\langle next(\ell), \lambda o.\text{vis}(o, \ell(\texttt{a})) \rangle \rangle$$

Atomic sections can be captured with a $\texttt{lock}$ variable and a pair of program commands,

$$[\![\texttt{begin}]\!]_c(\ell) = \langle \text{nop}, \varepsilon, \lambda y.\langle next(\ell[\texttt{lock} \mapsto true]), \lambda o.\varepsilon \rangle \rangle$$
$$[\![\texttt{end}]\!]_c(\ell) = \langle \text{nop}, \varepsilon, \lambda y.\langle next(\ell[\texttt{lock} \mapsto false]), \lambda o.\varepsilon \rangle \rangle$$

such that idle states are identified by not holding the lock, i.e., idle(ℓ) $= \neg\ell(\texttt{lock})$, as in the initial state init$(m, x)(\texttt{lock}) = false$.

Figure 1 lists the semantics $[\![P]\!]_p$ of a program P as an abstract-execution transition system. The states $\langle M, L \rangle$ of $[\![P]\!]_p$ include a global memory M, along with a partial function L from operation identifiers o to local states $L(o)$; the initial state is $\langle M_\emptyset, \emptyset \rangle$, where $M_\emptyset$ is an initial memory state. The transitions for call and hb actions are enabled independently of implementation state, since they are dictated by implementations' environments. Although we do not explicitly model client programs and platforms here, in reality, client programs dictate call actions, and platforms, driven by client programs, dictate hb actions; for example, a client which acquires the lock released after operation o_1, before invoking operation o_2, is generally ensured by its platform that o_1 happens before o_2. The transitions for all other actions are dictated by implementation commands. While the ret, lin, and vis commands generate their corresponding LTS actions, all other commands generate ε transitions.

Each atomic $\xrightarrow{a}$ step of the AETS underlying a given program is built from a sequence of $\rightsquigarrow$ steps for the individual program commands in an atomic section. Individual program commands essentially execute one small $\rightsquigarrow$ step from shared memory and local state $\langle M_1, \ell_1 \rangle$ to $\langle M_2, \ell_2 \rangle$, invoking memory command μ with

$$\frac{o \notin \mathrm{dom}(L) \qquad \ell = \mathrm{init}(m, x)}{\langle M, L \rangle \xrightarrow{\mathrm{call}(o,m,x)} \langle M, L[o \mapsto \ell] \rangle} \qquad \frac{\mathrm{done}(L(o_1)) \qquad o_2 \notin \mathrm{dom}(L)}{\langle M, L \rangle \xrightarrow{\mathrm{hb}(o_1,o_2)} \langle M, L \rangle}$$

$$\frac{\langle M_1, \ell_1, o, \varepsilon \rangle \rightsquigarrow^* \langle M_2, \ell_2, o, \vec{a} \rangle \qquad \mathrm{idle}(\ell_2)}{\langle M_1, L[o \mapsto \ell_1] \rangle \xrightarrow{\vec{a}} \langle M_2, L[o \mapsto \ell_2] \rangle}$$

$$\frac{\mathrm{cmd}(\ell_1) = \kappa \qquad [\![\kappa]\!]_{\mathrm{c}}(\ell_1) = \langle \mu, x, f \rangle \\ [\![\mu]\!]_{\mathrm{m}}(M_1, x, o) = \langle M_2, y \rangle \qquad f(y) = \langle \ell_2, \alpha \rangle}{\langle M_1, \ell_1, o, \vec{a} \rangle \rightsquigarrow \langle M_2, \ell_2, o, \vec{a} \cdot \alpha(o) \rangle}$$

Fig. 1. The semantics of program $P = \langle \mathrm{init}, \mathrm{cmd}, \mathrm{idle}, \mathrm{done} \rangle$ as an abstract-execution transition system, where $[\![\cdot]\!]_{\mathrm{c}}$ and $[\![\cdot]\!]_{\mathrm{m}}$ are the denotations of program and memory commands, respectively.

argument x, and emitting action $\alpha(o)$. Besides its effect on shared memory, each step uses the result $\langle M_2, y \rangle$ of memory command μ to update local state and emit an action using the continuation f, i.e., $f(y) = \langle \ell_2, \alpha \rangle$. Commands which do not access memory are modeled by a no-op memory commands. We define the consistency of programs by reduction to their transition systems.

Definition 5. *A program P is* consistent *with a specification iff its semantics $[\![P]\!]_{\mathrm{p}}$ is.*

Thus the consistency of P with W amounts to the inclusion of $[\![P]\!]_{\mathrm{p}}$'s histories in W's. The following corollary of Theorem 1 follows directly by Definition 5, and immediately yields a program verification strategy: validate a simulation relation from the states of $[\![P]\!]_{\mathrm{p}}$ to the states of $[\![W]\!]_{\mathrm{s}}$ such that each command of P is simulated by a step of $[\![W]\!]_{\mathrm{s}}$.

Corollary 1. *A program P is consistent with specification W if $[\![W]\!]_{\mathrm{s}}$ simulates $[\![P]\!]_{\mathrm{p}}$.*

4 Proof Methodology

In this section we develop a systematic means to annotating concurrent objects for relaxed-visibility simulation proofs. Besides leveraging an auxiliary memory system which tags memory accesses with the operation identifiers which wrote read values (see §3.2), annotations signal linearization points with lin commands, and indicate visibility of other operations with vis commands. As in previous works [3, 37, 2, 18] we assume linearization points are given, and focus on visibility-related annotations.

As we focus on data-race free implementations (e.g., Java 8's concurrent collections) for which sequential consistency is sound, it can be assumed without loss of generality that the happens-before order is exactly the *returns-before* order between operations, which orders two operations o_1 and o_2 iff the return action of o_1 occurs in real-time before the call action of o_2. This assumption allows to guarantee that linearizations are consistent with happens-before just by ensuring that the linearization point of each operation occurs in between its call and return action (like in standard linearizability).

```
var table: array of T;

procedure absolute put(k: int, v: T) {
  atomic {
    store(table[k], v);
    vis(getLin());
    lin();
  }
}

procedure absolute get(k: int) {
  atomic{
    v, O = load(table[k]);
    vis(getLin());
    lin();
  }
  return v;
}
```

```
procedure monotonic has(v: T)
  vis(getModLin());
{
  store(k, 0);
  while (k < table.length) {
    atomic{
      tv, O = load(table[k]);
      vis(O ∩ getModLin());
    }
    if (tv = v) then {
      lin();
      return true;
    }
    inc(k);
  }
  lin();
  return false;
}
```

Fig. 2. An implementation I_{chm} modeling Java's concurrent hash map. The command inc(k) increments counter k, and commands within atomic {...} are collectively atomic.

It is without loss of generality because the clients of such implementations can use auxiliary variables to impose synchronization order constraints between every two operations ordered by returns-before, e.g., writing a variable after each operation returns which is read before each other operation is called (under sequential consistency, every write happens-before every other read which reads the written value).

We illustrate our methodology with the key-value map implementation I_{chm} of Figure 2, which models Java's concurrent hash map. The lines marked in blue and red represent linearization/visibility commands added by the instrumentation that will be described below. Key-value pairs are stored in an array table indexed by keys. The implementation of put and get are obvious while the implementation of has returns true iff the input value is associated to some key consists of a while loop traversing the array and searching for the input value. To simplify the exposition, the shared memory reads and writes are already adapted to the memory system described in Section 3.2 (essentially, this consists in adding new variables storing the set of operation identifiers returned by a shared memory read). While put and get are obviously linearizable, has is weakly consistent, with monotonic visibility. For instance, given the two thread program {get(1); has(1)} || {put(1, 1); put(0, 1); put(1, 0)} it is possible that get(1) returns 1 while has(1) returns false. This is possible in an interleaving where has reads table[0] before put(0,1) writes into it (observing the initial value 0), and table[1] after put(1,0) writes into it (observing value 0 as well). The only abstract execution consistent with the weakly-consistent contains-value map W_m (Example 2) which justifies these return values is given in Example 3. We show that this implementation is consistent with a simplification of the contains-value map W_m, without remove key operations, and where put operations return no value.

Given an implementation I, let $\mathcal{L}(I)$ be an instrumentation of I with program commands lin() emitting linearization actions. The execution of lin() in the context of an operation with identifier o emits a linearization action $\text{lin}(o)$. We assume that $\mathcal{L}(I)$ leads to well-formed executions (e.g., at most one linearization action per operation).

Example 8. For the implementation in Figure 2, the linearization commands of put and get are executed atomically with the store to table[k] in put and the load of table[k] in get, respectively. The linearization command of has is executed at any point after observing the input value v or after exiting the loop, but before the return. The two choices correspond to different return values and only one of them will be executed during an invocation.

Given an instrumentation $\mathcal{L}(I)$, a visibility annotation V for I's methods, and a read-only predicate R, we define a witnessing implementation $\mathcal{V}(\mathcal{L}(I))$ according to a generic heuristic that depends only on V and R. This definition uses a program command getLin() which returns the set of operations in the current linearization sequence.[12] The current linearization sequence is stored in a history variable which is updated with every linearization action by appending the corresponding operation identifier. For readability, we leave this history variable implicit and omit the corresponding updates. As syntactic sugar, we use a command getModLin() which returns the set of *modifiers* (non read-only operations) in the current linearization sequence. To represent visibility actions, we use program commands vis(A) where A is a set of operation identifiers. The execution of vis(A) in the context of an operation with identifier o emits the set of visibility actions vis(o, o') for every operation $o' \in A$.

Therefore, $\mathcal{V}(\mathcal{L}(I))$ extends the instrumentation $\mathcal{L}(I)$ with commands generating visibility actions as follows:

- for absolute methods, each linearization command is preceded by vis(getLin()) which ensures that the visibility of an invocation includes all the predecessors in linearization order. This is executed atomically with lin().
- for monotonic methods, the call action is followed by vis(getModLin()) (and executed atomically with this command) which ensures that the visibility of each invocation is monotonic, and every read of a shared variable which has been written by a set of operations O is preceded by vis($O \cap$ getModLin()) (and executed atomically with this command). The latter is needed so that the visibility of such an invocation contains enough operations to explain its return value (the visibility command attached to call actions is enough to ensure monotonic visibilities).

Example 9. The blue lines in Figure 2 demonstrate the visibility commands added by the instrumentation $\mathcal{V}(\cdot)$ to the key-value map in Figure 2 (in this case, the modifiers are put operations). The first visibility command in has precedes the procedure body to emphasize the fact that it is executed *atomically* with the procedure call. Also, note that the read of the array table is the only shared memory read in has.

Theorem 2. *The abstract executions of the witnessing implementation $\mathcal{V}(\mathcal{L}(I))$ are consistent with V and R.*

Proof. Let $\langle h, lin, vis \rangle$ be the abstract execution of a trace τ of $\mathcal{V}(\mathcal{L}(I))$, and let o be an invocation in h of a monotonic method (w.r.t. V). By the definition of $\mathcal{V}$, the call action of o is *immediately* followed in τ by a sequence of visibility actions vis(o, o')

---

[12] We rely on retrieving the identifiers of currently-linearized operations. More complex proofs may also require inspecting, e.g., operation labels and happens-before relationships.

for every modifier o' which has been already linearized. Therefore, any operation which has returned before o (i.e., happens-before o) has already been linearized and it will necessarily have a smaller visibility (w.r.t. set inclusion) because the linearization sequence is modified only by appending new operations. The instrumentation of shared memory reads may add more visibility actions $vis(o, \_)$ but this preserves the monotonicity status of o's visibility. The case of absolute methods is obvious.   □

The consistency of the abstract executions of $\mathcal{V}(\mathcal{L}(I))$ with a given sequential specification S, which completes the proof of consistency with a weak-visibility specification $W = \langle S, R, V \rangle$, can be proved by showing that the transition system $[\![W]\!]_s$ of W simulates $\mathcal{V}(\mathcal{L}(I))$ (Theorem 1). Defining a simulation relation between the two systems is in some part implementation specific, and in the following we demonstrate it for the key-value map implementation $\mathcal{V}(\mathcal{L}(I_{chm}))$.

We show that $[\![W_m]\!]_s$ simulates implementation I_{chm}. A state of I_{chm} in Figure 2 is a valuation of table and the history variable lin storing the current linearization sequence, and a valuation of the local variables for each active operation. Let $ops(q)$ denote the set of operations which are active in an implementation state q. Also, for a has operation $o \in ops(q)$, let $index(o)$ be the maximal index k of the array table such that o has already read table$[k]$ and table$[k] \neq$ v. We assume $index(o) = -1$ if o did not read any array cell.

Definition 6. *Let R_{chm} be a relation which associates every implementation state q with a state of $[\![W_m]\!]_s$, i.e., an $\langle S, R, V \rangle$-consistent abstract execution $e = \langle h, lin, vis \rangle$ with $h = \langle O, inv, ret, hb \rangle$, such that:*

1. *O is the set of identifiers occurring in $ops(q)$ or the history variable lin,*
2. *for each operation $o \in ops(q)$, $inv(o)$ is defined according to its local state, $ret(o)$ is undefined, and o is maximal in the happens-before order hb,*
3. *the value of the history variable lin in q equals the linearization sequence lin,*
4. *every invocation $o \in ops(q)$ of an absolute method (put or get) has absolute visibility if linearized, otherwise, its visibility is empty,*
5. *table is the array obtained by executing the sequence of operations lin,*
6. *for every linearized get(k) operation $o \in ops(q)$, the put(k, _) operation in $vis(o)$ which occurs last in lin writes v to key k, where v is the local variable of o,*
7. *for every has operation $o \in ops(q)$, $vis(o)$ consists of:*
   - *all the put operations o' which returned before o was invoked,*
   - *for each $i \leq index(o)$, all the put$(i, \_)$ operations from a prefix of lin that wrote a value different from v,*
   - *all the put$(index(o) + 1, \_)$ operations from a prefix of lin that ends with a put$(index(o) + 1, v)$ operation, provided that tv = v.*
   Above, the linearization prefix associated to an index $j_1 < j_2$ should be a prefix of the one associated to j_2.

A large part of this definition is applicable to any implementation, only points (5), (6), and (7) being specific to the implementation we consider. The points (6) and (7) ensure that the return values of operations are consistent with S and mimic the effect of the vis commands from Figure 2.

Theorem 3. *R_{chm} is a simulation relation from $\mathcal{V}(\mathcal{L}(I_{chm}))$ to $[\![W_m]\!]_s$.*

5 Implementation and Evaluation

In this section we effectuate our methodology by verifying two weakly-consistent concurrent objects: Java's ConcurrentHashMap and ConcurrentLinkedQueue.[13] We use an off-the-shelf deductive verification tool called CIVL [16], though any concurrent program verifier could suffice. We chose CIVL because comparable verifiers either require a manual encoding of the concurrency reasoning (e.g. Dafny or Viper) which can be error-prone, or require cumbersome reasoning about interleavings of thread-local histories (e.g. VerCors). An additional benefit of CIVL is that it directly proves simulation, thereby tying the mechanized proofs to our theoretical development. Our proofs assume no bound on the number of threads or the size of the memory.

Our use of CIVL imposes two restrictions on the implementations we can verify. First, CIVL uses the Owicki-Gries method [29] to verify concurrent programs. These methods are unsound for weak memory models [22], so CIVL, and hence our proofs, assume a sequentially-consistent memory model. Second, CIVL's strategy for building the simulation relation requires implementations to have statically-known linearization points because it checks that there exists exactly one atomic section in each code path where the global state is modified, and this modification is simulated by the specification.

Given these restrictions, we can simplify our proof strategy of forward refinement by factoring the simulations we construct through an atomic version of the specification transition system. This atomic specification is obtained from the specification AETS $[\![W]\!]_s$ by restricting the interleavings between its transitions.

Definition 7. *The* atomic transition system *of a specification W is the AETS* $[\![W]\!]_a = \langle Q, A, q, \rightarrow_a \rangle$, *where* $[\![W]\!]_s = \langle Q, A, q, \rightarrow \rangle$ *is the AETS of W and* $e_1 \xrightarrow{\vec{a}}_a e_2$ *if and only if* $e_1 \xrightarrow{\vec{a}} e_2$ *and* $\vec{a} \in \{call(o,m,x)\} \cup \{ret(o,y)\} \cup \{hb(o,o')\} \cup \{\vec{a_1} \ lin(o) : \vec{a_1} \in \{vis(o,\_)\}^*\}$.

Note that the language of $[\![W]\!]_a$ is included in the language of $[\![W]\!]_s$ and simulation proofs towards $[\![W]\!]_a$ apply to $[\![W]\!]_s$ as well.

Our CIVL proofs show that there is a simulation from an implementation to its atomic specification, which is encoded as a program whose state consists of the components of an abstract execution, i.e., $\langle O, inv, ret, hb, lin, vis \rangle$. These were encoded as maps from operation identifiers to values, sequences of operation identifiers, and maps from operation identifiers to sets of operation identifiers respectively. Our axiomatization of sequences and sets were adapted from those used by the Dafny verifier [23]. For each method in $\mathbb{M}$, we defined atomic procedures corresponding to call actions, return actions, and combined visibility and linearization actions in order to obtain exactly the atomic transitions of $[\![W]\!]_a$.

It is challenging to encode Java implementations faithfully in CIVL, as the latter's input programming language is a basic imperative language lacking many Java features. Most notable among these is dynamic memory allocation on the heap, used by almost all of the concurrent data structure implementations. As CIVL is a first-order prover, we needed an encoding of the heap that lets us perform reachability reasoning on the

---

[13] Our verified implementations are open source, and available at:
  https://github.com/siddharth-krishna/weak-consistency-proofs.

heap. We adapted the first-order theory of reachability and footprint sets from the GRASShopper verifier [30] for dynamically allocated data structures. This fragment is decidable, but relies on local theory extensions [36], which we implemented by using the trigger mechanism of the underlying SMT solver [27, 15] to ensure that quantified axioms were only instantiated for program expressions. For instance, here is the "cycle" axiom that says that if a node x has a field f[x] that points to itself, then any y that it can reach via that field (encoded using the between predicate Btwn(f, x, y, y)) must be equal to x:

```
axiom (forall f: [Ref]Ref, x: Ref, y:Ref :: {known(x), known(y)}
       f[x] == x && Btwn(f, x, y, y) ==> x == y);
```

We use the trigger known(x), known(y) (known is a dummy function that maps every reference to true) and introduce known(t) terms in our programs for every term t of type Ref (for instance, by adding assert known(t) to the point of the program where t is introduced). This ensures that the cycle axiom is only instantiated for terms that appear in the program, and not for terms that are generated by instantiations of axioms (like f[x] in the cycle axiom). This process was key to keeping the verification time manageable.

Since we consider fine-grained concurrent implementations, we also needed to reason about interference by other threads and show thread safety. CIVL provides Owicki-Gries [29] style thread-modular reasoning, by means of demarcating atomic blocks and providing preconditions for each block that are checked for stability under all possible modifications by other threads. One of the consequences of this is that these annotations can only talk about the local state of a thread and the shared global state, but not other threads. To encode facts such as distinctness of operation identifiers and ownership of unreachable nodes (e.g. newly allocated nodes) in the shared heap, we use CIVL's linear type system [40].

For instance, the proof of the push method needs to make assertions about the value of the newly-allocated node x. These assertions would not be stable under interference of other threads if we didn't have a way of specifying that the address of the new node is known only by the push thread. We encode this knowledge by marking the type of the variable x as linear – this tells CIVL that all values of x across all threads are distinct, which is sufficient for the proof. CIVL ensures soundness by making sure that linear variables are not duplicated (for instance, they cannot be passed to another method and then used afterwards).

We evaluate our proof methodology by considering models of two of Java's weakly-consistent concurrent objects.

Concurrent Hash Map One is the ConcurrentHashMap implementation of the Map ADT, consisting of absolute put and get methods and a monotonic has method that follows the algortihm given in Figure 2. For simplicity, we assume here that keys are integers and the hash function is identity, but note that the proof of monotonicity of has is not affected by these assumptions.[14]

---

[14] Our CIVL implementation assumes the hash function is injective to avoid reasoning about the dynamic bucket-list needed to resolve hash collisions. While such reasoning is possible within

Module	Code	Proof	Total	Time (s)
Sets and Sequences	-	85	85	-
Executions and Consistency	-	30	30	-
Heap and Reachability	-	35	35	-
Map ADT	51	34	85	-
Array-map implementation	138	175	313	6
Queue ADT	50	22	72	-
Linked Queue implementation	280	325	605	13

Fig. 3. Case study detail: for each object we show lines of code, lines of proof, total lines, and verification time in seconds. We also list common definitions and axiomatizations separately.

CIVL can construct a simulation relation equivalent to the one defined in Definition 6 automatically, given an inductive invariant that relates the state of the implementation to the abstract execution. A first attempt at an invariant might be that the value stored at table[k] for every key k is the same as the value returned by adding a get operation on k by the specification AETS. This invariant is sufficient for CIVL to prove that the return value of the absolute methods (put and get) is consistent with the specification.

However, it is not enough to show that the return value of the monotonic has method is consistent with its visibility. This is because our proof technique constructs a visibility set for has by taking the union of the memory tags (the set of operations that wrote to each memory location) of each table entry it reads, but without additional invariants this visibility set could entail a different return value. We thus strengthen the invariant to say that tableTags[k], the memory tags associated with hash table entry k, is exactly the set of linearized put operations with key k. A consequence of this is that the abstract state encoded by tableTags[k] has the same value for key k as the value stored at table[k]. CIVL can then prove, given the following loop invariant, that the value returned by has is consistent with its visibility set.

```
(forall i: int :: 0 <= i && i < k ==> Map.ofVis(my_vis, lin)[i] != v)
```

This loop invariant says that among the entries scanned thus far, the abstract map given by the projection of lin to the current operation's visibility my_vis does not include value v.

Concurrent Linked Queue Our second case study is the ConcurrentLinkedQueue implementation of the Queue ADT, consisting of absolute push and pop methods and a monotonic size method that traverses the queue from head to tail without any locks and returns the number of nodes it sees (see Figure 4 for the full code). We again model the core algorithm (the Michael-Scott queue [26]) and omit some of Java's optimizations, for instance to speed up garbage collection by setting the next field of popped nodes to themselves, or setting the values of nodes to null when popping values.

The invariants needed to verify the absolute methods are a straightforward combination of structural invariants (e.g. that the queue is composed of a linked list from the head to null, with the tail being a member of this list) and a relation between the

---

CIVL, see our queue case study, this issue is orthogonal to the weak-consistency reasoning that we study here.

```
var head, tail: Ref;  struct Node { var data: K; var next: Ref; }
```

```
procedure absolute push(k: K) {          procedure absolute pop() {           procedure monotonic size()
  x = new Node(k, null);                   while (true) {                        vis(getModLin());
  while (true) {                             h, _ = load(head);               {
    t, _ = load(tail);                       t, _ = load(tail);                 store(s, 0);
    tn, _ = load(tail.next);                 hn, _ = load(h.next);              c, _ = load(head);
    if (tn == null) {                        if (h != t) {                      atomic {
      atomic {                                 k, _ = load(hn.data);              cn, 0 = load(c.next);
        b, _ = cas(t.next, tn, x);             atomic {                           vis(0 ∩ getModLin());
        if (b) {                                 b, _ = cas(head, h, hn);       }
          vis(getLin());                         if (b) {                       while (cn != null) {
          lin();                                   vis(getLin());                 inc(s);
        }                                          lin();                         c = cn;
      }                                          }                              atomic {
      if (b) then break;                       }                                  cn, 0 = load(c.next);
    } else {                                   if (b) then return k;               vis(0 ∩ getModLin());
      b, _ = cas(tail, t, tn);               }                                  }
    }                                      }                                    }
  }                                      }                                      lin();
}                                                                              return s;
                                                                             }
```

Fig. 4. The simplified implementation of Java's ConcurrentLinkedQueue that we verify.

abstract and concrete states. Once again, we need to strengthen this invariant in order to verify the monotonic size method, because otherwise we cannot prove that the visibility set we construct (by taking the union of the memory tags of nodes in the list during traversal) justifies the return value.

The key additional invariant is that the memory tags for the next field of each node (denoted x.nextTags for each node x) in the queue contain the operation label of the operation that pushed the next node into the queue (if it exists). Further, the sequence of push operations in lin are exactly the operations in the nextTags field of nodes in the queue, and in the order they are present in the queue.

Figure 5 shows a simplified version of the CIVL encoding of these invariants. In it, we use the following auxiliary variables in order to avoid quantifier alternation: nextInvoc maps nodes to the operation label (type Invoc in CIVL) contained in the nextTags field; nextRef maps operations to the nodes whose nextTags field contains them, i.e. it is the inverse of nextInvoc; and absRefs maps the index of the abstract queue (represented as a mathematical sequence) to the corresponding concrete heap node. We omit the triggers and known predicates for readability; the full invariant can be found in the accompanying proof scripts.

Given these invariants, one can show that the return value s computed by size is consistent with the visibility set it constructs by picking up the memory tags from each node that it traverses. The loop invariant is more involved, as due to concurrent updates size could be traversing nodes that have been popped from the queue; see our CIVL proofs for more details.

Results Figure 3 provides a summary of our case studies. We separate the table into sections, one for each case study, and a common section at the top that contains the common theories of sets and sequences and our encoding of the heap. In each case study section, we separate the definitions of the atomic specification of the ADT (which can

```
// nextTags only contains singleton sets of push operations
(forall y: Ref ::
  (Btwn(next, start, y, null) && y != null && next[y] != null
    ==> nextTags[y] == Set(nextInvoc[y])
      && invoc_m(nextInvoc[y]) == Queue.push))

// nextTags of the last node is the empty set
&& nextTags[absRefs[Queue.stateTail(Queue.ofSeq(lin)) - 1]]
  == Set_empty()

// lin is made up of nextInvoc[y] for y in the queue
&& (forall n: Invoc :: invoc_m(n) == Queue.push
    ==> (Seq_elem(n, lin)
        <==> Btwn(next, start, nextRef[n], null)
          && nextRef[n] != null && next[nextRef[n]] != null))

// lin is ordered by order of nodes in queue
&& (forall n1, n2: Invoc ::
    (invoc_m(n1) == Queue.push && invoc_m(n2) == Queue.push
    && Seq_elem(n1, lin) && Seq_elem(n2, lin)
    ==> (Seq_ord(lin, n1, n2)
        <==> Btwn(next, nextRef[n1], nextRef[n1], nextRef[n2])
          && nextRef[n1] != nextRef[n2])))
```

Fig. 5. A snippet from the CIVL invariant for the queue.

be reused for other implementations) from the code and proof of the implementation we consider. For each resulting module, we list the number of lines of code, lines of proof, total lines, and CIVL's verification time in seconds. Experiments were conducted on an Intel Core i7-4470 3.4 GHz 8-core machine with 16GB RAM.

Our two case studies are representative of the weakly-consistent behaviors exhibited by all the Java concurrent objects studied in [13], both those using fixed-size arrays and those using dynamic memory. As CIVL does not direlcty support dynamic memory and other Java language features, we were forced to make certain simplifications to the algorithms in our verification effort. However, the assumptions we make are orthogonal to the reasoning and proof of weak consistency of the monotonic methods. The underlying algorithm used by, and hence the proof argument for monotonicity of, hash map's has method is the same as that in the other monotonic hash map operations such as elements, entrySet, and toString. Similarly, the argument used for the queue's size can be adapted to other monotonic ConcurrentLinkedQueue and LinkedTransferQueue operations like toArray and toString. Thus, our proofs carry over to the full versions of the implementations as the key invariants linking the memory tags and visibility sets to the specification state are the same.

In addition, CIVL does not currently have any support for inferring the preconditions of each atomic block, which currently accounts for most of the lines of proof in our case studies. However, these problems have been studied and solved in other tools [30, 39], and in theory can be integrated with CIVL in order to simplify these kinds of proofs.

In conclusion, our case studies show that verifying weakly-consistent operations introduces little overhead compared to the proofs of the core absolute operations. The additional invariants needed to prove monotonicity were natural and easy to construct. We also see that our methodology brings weak-consistency proofs within the scope of what is provable by off-the-shelf automated concurrent program verifiers in reasonable time.

6   Related Work

Though *linearizability* [18] has reigned as the de-facto concurrent-object consistency criterion, several recent works proposed weaker criteria, including *quantitative relaxation* [17], *quiescent consistency* [10], and *local linearizability* [14]; these works effectively permit externally-visible interference among threads by altering objects' sequential specifications, each in their own way. Motivated by the diversity of these proposals, Sergey et al. [35] proposed the use of Hoare logic for describing a custom consistency specification for each concurrent object. Raad et al. [31] continued in this direction by proposing declarative consistency models for concurrent objects atop weak-memory platforms. One common feature between our paper and this line of work (see also [21, 9]) is encoding and reasoning directly about the concurrent history. The notion of *visibility relaxation* [13] originates from Burckhardt et al.'s axiomatic specifications [7], and leverages traditional sequential specifications by allowing certain operations to behave as if they are unaware of concurrently-executed linearization-order predecessors. The linearization (and visibility) actions of our simulation-proof methodology are unique to visibility-relaxation based weak-consistency, since they refer to a global linearization order linking executions with sequential specifications.

Typical methodologies for proving linearizability are based on reductions to safety verification [8, 5] and forward simulation [3, 37, 2], the latter generally requiring the annotation of per-operation *linearization points*, each typically associated with a single program statement in the given operation, e.g., a shared memory access. Extensions to this methodology include *cooperation* [38, 12, 41], i.e., allowing operations' linearization points to coincide with other operations' statements, and *prophecy* [33, 24], i.e., allowing operation' linearization points to depend on future events. Such extensions enable linearizability proofs of objects like the Herlihy-Wing Queue (HWQ). While prophecy [25], alternatively backward simulation [25], is generally more powerful than forward simulation alone, Bouajjani et al. [6] described a methodology based on forward simulation capable of proving seemingly future-dependent objects like HWQ by considering fixed linearization points only for value removal, and an additional kind of specification-simulated action, *commit points*, corresponding to operations' final shared-memory accesses. Our consideration of specification-simulated visibility actions follows this line of thinking, enabling the forward-simulation based proof of weakly-consistent concurrent objects.

7   Conclusion and Future Work

This work develops the first verification methodology for weakly-consistent operations using sequential specifications and forward simulation, thus reusing existing sequential ADT specifications and enabling simple reasoning, i.e., without prophecy [1] or backward simulation [25]. This paper demonstrates the application of our methodology to absolute and monotonic methods on sequentially-consistent memory, as these are the consistency levels demonstrated in actual Java implementations of which we are aware. Our formalization is general, and also applicable to the other visibility relaxations, e.g., the *peer* and *weak* visibilities [13], and weaker memory models, e.g., the Java memory model.

Extrapolating, we speculate that handling other visibilities amounts to adding annotations and auxiliary state which mirrors inter-operation communication. For example, while monotonic operations on shared-memory implementations observe mutating linearization-order predecessors – corresponding to a sequence of shared-memory updates – causal operations with message-passing based implementations would observe operations whose messages have (transitively) propagated. The corresponding annotations may require auxiliary state to track message propagation, similar in spirit to the getModLin() auxiliary state that tracks mutating linearization-order predecessors (§4). Since weak memory models essentially alter the mechanics of inter-operation communication, the corresponding visibility annotations and auxiliary state may similarly reflect this communication. Since this communication is partly captured by the denotations of memory commands (§3.2), these denotations would be modified, e.g., to include not one value and tag per memory location, but multiple. While variations are possible depending on the extent to which the proof of a given implementation relies on the details of the memory model, in the worst case the auxiliary state could capture an existing memory model (e.g., operational) semantics exactly.

As with systematic or automated linearizability-proof methodologies, our proof methodology is susceptible to two potential sources of incompleteness. First, as mentioned in Section 3, methodologies like ours based on forward simulation are only complete when specifications are *return-value deterministic*. However, data types are typically designed to be return-value deterministic and this source of incompleteness does not manifest in practice.

Second, methodologies like ours based on annotating program commands, e.g., with linearization points, are generally incomplete since the consistency mechanism employed by any given implementation may not admit characterization according to a given static annotation scheme; the Herlihy-Wing Queue, whose linearization points depend on the results of future actions, is a prototypical example [18]. Likewise, our systematic strategy for annotating implementations with *lin* and *vis* commands (§3) can fail to prove consistency of future-dependent operations. However, we have yet to observe any practical occurrence of such exotic objects; our strategy is sufficient for verifying the weakly-consistent algorithms implemented in the Java development kit. As a theoretical curiosity for future work, investigating the potential for complete annotation strategies would be interesting, e.g., for restricted classes of data types and/or implementations.

Finally, while CIVL's high-degree of automation facilitated rapid prototyping of our simulation proofs, its underlying foundation using Owicki-Gries style proof rules limits the potential for modular reasoning. In particular, while our weak-consistency proofs are thread-modular, our invariants and intermediate assertions necessarily talk about state shared among multiple threads. Since our simulation-based methodology and annotations are completely orthogonal to the underlying program logic, it would be interesting future work to apply our methodology using expressive logics like Rely-Guarantee, e.g. [19, 38], or variations of Concurrent Separation Logic, e.g. [28, 32, 34, 35, 4, 20]. It remains to be seen to what degree increased modularity may sacrifice automation in the application of our weak-consistency proof methodology.

Acknowledgments This material is based upon work supported by the National Science Foundation under Grant No. 1816936, and the European Research Council (ERC) under the European Union's Horizon 2020 research and innovation programme (grant agreement No 678177).

A   Appendix: Proofs to Theorems and Lemmas

Lemma 1. *The abstract executions $E(W)$ of a specification W are consistent with W.*

Proof. Any complete, sequential, and absolute execution is consistent by definition, since the labeling of its linearization is taken from the sequential specification. Then, any happens-before weakening is consistent for exactly the same reason as its source execution, since its linearization and visibility projection are both identical. Finally, any visibility weakening is consistent by the condition of W-consistency in its definition. □

Lemma 2. *A weak-visibility specification and its transition system have identical histories.*

Proof. It follows almost immediately that the abstract executions of $[\![W]\!]_s$ are identical to those of W, since $[\![W]\!]_s$'s state effectively records the abstract execution of a given AETS execution, and only enables those returns that are consistent with W. Since histories are the projections of abstract executions, the corresponding history sets are also identical. □

Theorem 1. *A witnessing implementation I is consistent with a weak-visibility specification W if the transition system $[\![W]\!]_s$ of W simulates I.*

Proof. This follows from standard arguments, given that the corresponding SLTSs include ε transitions to ensure that every move of one system can be matched by stuttering from the other: since both systems synchronize on the call, ret, hb, lin, and vis actions, the simulation guarantees that every abstract execution, and thus history, of I is matched by one of $[\![W]\!]_s$. Then by Lemma 2, the histories of I are included in W. □

Theorem 3. R_{chm} *is a simulation relation from* I_{chm} *to* $[\![W_m]\!]_s$.

Proof Sketch. We show that every step of the implementation, i.e., an atomic section or a program command, is simulated by $[\![W_m]\!]_s$. Given $\langle q, e \rangle \in R_{\text{chm}}$, we consider the different implementation steps which are possible in q.

The case of commands corresponding to procedure calls of put and get is trivial. Executing a procedure call in q leads to a new state q' which differs only by having a new active operation o. We have that $e \xrightarrow{\text{call}(o,\_,\_)} e'$ and $\langle q', e' \rangle \in R_{\text{chm}}$ where e' is obtained from e by adding o with an appropriate value of $inv(o)$ and an empty visibility.

The transition corresponding to the atomic section of put is labeled by a sequence of visibility actions (one for each linearized operation) followed by a linearization action. Let σ denote this sequence of actions. This transition leads to a state q' where the array table may have changed (unless writing the same value), and the history variable lin is extended with the put operation o executing this step. We define an abstract execution e' from e by changing lin to the new value of lin, and defining an absolute visibility for o. We have that $e \xrightarrow{\sigma} e'$ because e' is consistent with W_m. Also, $\langle q', e' \rangle \in R_{\text{chm}}$ because the validity of (3), (4), and (5) follow directly from the definition of e'. The atomic section of get can be handled in a similar way. The simulation of return actions of get operations is a direct consequence of point (6) which ensures consistency with S.

For has, we focus on the atomic sections containing vis commands and the linearization commands (the other internal steps are simulated by ϵ steps of $[\![W_m]\!]_s$, and the simulation of the return step follows directly from (7) which justifies the consistency of the return value). The atomic section around the procedure call corresponds to a transition labeled by a sequence σ of visibility actions (one for each linearized modifier) and leads to a state q' with a new active has operation o (compared to q). We have that $e \xrightarrow{\sigma} e'$ because e' is consistent with W_m. Indeed, the visibility of o in e' is not constrained since o has not been linearized and the W_m-consistency of e' follows from the W_m-consistency of e. Also, $\langle q', e' \rangle \in R_{chm}$ because $index(o) = -1$ and (7) is clearly valid. The atomic section around the read of table[k] is simulated by $[\![W_m]\!]_s$ in a similar way, noticing that (7) models precisely the effect of the visibility commands inside this atomic section. For the simulation of the linearization commands is important to notice that any active has operation in e has a visibility that contains all modifiers which returned before it was called and as explained above, this visibility is monotonic. $\square$

References

[1] Abadi, M., Lamport, L.: The existence of refinement mappings. Theor. Comput. Sci. **82**(2), 253–284 (1991)

[2] Abdulla, P.A., Haziza, F., Holík, L., Jonsson, B., Rezine, A.: An integrated specification and verification technique for highly concurrent data structures for highly concurrent data structures. STTT **19**(5), 549–563 (2017)

[3] Amit, D., Rinetzky, N., Reps, T.W., Sagiv, M., Yahav, E.: Comparison under abstraction for verifying linearizability. In: CAV. Lecture Notes in Computer Science, vol. 4590, pp. 477–490. Springer (2007)

[4] Blom, S., Darabi, S., Huisman, M., Oortwijn, W.: The vercors tool set: Verification of parallel and concurrent software. In: IFM. Lecture Notes in Computer Science, vol. 10510, pp. 102–110. Springer (2017)

[5] Bouajjani, A., Emmi, M., Enea, C., Hamza, J.: On reducing linearizability to state reachability. Inf. Comput. **261**(Part), 383–400 (2018)

[6] Bouajjani, A., Emmi, M., Enea, C., Mutluergil, S.O.: Proving linearizability using forward simulations. In: CAV (2). Lecture Notes in Computer Science, vol. 10427, pp. 542–563. Springer (2017)

[7] Burckhardt, S., Gotsman, A., Yang, H., Zawirski, M.: Replicated data types: specification, verification, optimality. In: POPL. pp. 271–284. ACM (2014)

[8] Chakraborty, S., Henzinger, T.A., Sezgin, A., Vafeiadis, V.: Aspect-oriented linearizability proofs. Logical Methods in Computer Science **11**(1) (2015)

[9] Delbianco, G.A., Sergey, I., Nanevski, A., Banerjee, A.: Concurrent data structures linked in time. In: ECOOP. LIPIcs, vol. 74, pp. 8:1–8:30. Schloss Dagstuhl - Leibniz-Zentrum fuer Informatik (2017)

[10] Derrick, J., Dongol, B., Schellhorn, G., Tofan, B., Travkin, O., Wehrheim, H.: Quiescent consistency: Defining and verifying relaxed linearizability. In: FM. Lecture Notes in Computer Science, vol. 8442, pp. 200–214. Springer (2014)

[11] Dongol, B., Jagadeesan, R., Riely, J., Armstrong, A.: On abstraction and compositionality for weak-memory linearisability. In: VMCAI. Lecture Notes in Computer Science, vol. 10747, pp. 183–204. Springer (2018)

[12] Dragoi, C., Gupta, A., Henzinger, T.A.: Automatic linearizability proofs of concurrent objects with cooperating updates. In: CAV. Lecture Notes in Computer Science, vol. 8044, pp. 174–190. Springer (2013)

[13] Emmi, M., Enea, C.: Weak-consistency specification via visibility relaxation. PACMPL 3(POPL), 60:1–60:28 (2019)

[14] Haas, A., Henzinger, T.A., Holzer, A., Kirsch, C.M., Lippautz, M., Payer, H., Sezgin, A., Sokolova, A., Veith, H.: Local linearizability for concurrent container-type data structures. In: CONCUR. LIPIcs, vol. 59, pp. 6:1–6:15. Schloss Dagstuhl - Leibniz-Zentrum fuer Informatik (2016)

[15] Hawblitzel, C., Petrank, E.: Automated verification of practical garbage collectors. Logical Methods in Computer Science 6(3) (2010)

[16] Hawblitzel, C., Petrank, E., Qadeer, S., Tasiran, S.: Automated and modular refinement reasoning for concurrent programs. In: CAV (2). Lecture Notes in Computer Science, vol. 9207, pp. 449–465. Springer (2015)

[17] Henzinger, T.A., Kirsch, C.M., Payer, H., Sezgin, A., Sokolova, A.: Quantitative relaxation of concurrent data structures. In: POPL. pp. 317–328. ACM (2013)

[18] Herlihy, M., Wing, J.M.: Linearizability: A correctness condition for concurrent objects. ACM Trans. Program. Lang. Syst. 12(3), 463–492 (1990)

[19] Jones, C.B.: Specification and design of (parallel) programs. In: IFIP Congress. pp. 321–332. North-Holland/IFIP (1983)

[20] Jung, R., Krebbers, R., Jourdan, J., Bizjak, A., Birkedal, L., Dreyer, D.: Iris from the ground up: A modular foundation for higher-order concurrent separation logic. J. Funct. Program. 28, e20 (2018)

[21] Khyzha, A., Dodds, M., Gotsman, A., Parkinson, M.J.: Proving linearizability using partial orders. In: ESOP. Lecture Notes in Computer Science, vol. 10201, pp. 639–667. Springer (2017)

[22] Lahav, O., Vafeiadis, V.: Owicki-gries reasoning for weak memory models. In: ICALP (2). Lecture Notes in Computer Science, vol. 9135, pp. 311–323. Springer (2015)

[23] Leino, K.R.M.: Dafny: An automatic program verifier for functional correctness. In: LPAR (Dakar). Lecture Notes in Computer Science, vol. 6355, pp. 348–370. Springer (2010)

[24] Liang, H., Feng, X.: Modular verification of linearizability with non-fixed linearization points. In: PLDI. pp. 459–470. ACM (2013)

[25] Lynch, N.A., Vaandrager, F.W.: Forward and backward simulations: I. untimed systems. Inf. Comput. 121(2), 214–233 (1995)

[26] Michael, M.M., Scott, M.L.: Simple, fast, and practical non-blocking and blocking concurrent queue algorithms. In: PODC. pp. 267–275. ACM (1996)

[27] Moskal, M., Lopuszanski, J., Kiniry, J.R.: E-matching for fun and profit. Electr. Notes Theor. Comput. Sci. **198**(2), 19–35 (2008)

[28] O'Hearn, P.W.: Resources, concurrency and local reasoning. In: CONCUR. Lecture Notes in Computer Science, vol. 3170, pp. 49–67. Springer (2004)

[29] Owicki, S.S., Gries, D.: Verifying properties of parallel programs: An axiomatic approach. Commun. ACM **19**(5), 279–285 (1976)

[30] Piskac, R., Wies, T., Zufferey, D.: Grasshopper - complete heap verification with mixed specifications. In: TACAS. Lecture Notes in Computer Science, vol. 8413, pp. 124–139. Springer (2014)

[31] Raad, A., Doko, M., Rozic, L., Lahav, O., Vafeiadis, V.: On library correctness under weak memory consistency: specifying and verifying concurrent libraries under declarative consistency models. PACMPL **3**(POPL), 68:1–68:31 (2019)

[32] Reynolds, J.C.: Separation logic: A logic for shared mutable data structures. In: LICS. pp. 55–74. IEEE Computer Society (2002)

[33] Schellhorn, G., Wehrheim, H., Derrick, J.: How to prove algorithms linearisable. In: CAV. Lecture Notes in Computer Science, vol. 7358, pp. 243–259. Springer (2012)

[34] Sergey, I., Nanevski, A., Banerjee, A.: Mechanized verification of fine-grained concurrent programs. In: PLDI. pp. 77–87. ACM (2015)

[35] Sergey, I., Nanevski, A., Banerjee, A., Delbianco, G.A.: Hoare-style specifications as correctness conditions for non-linearizable concurrent objects. In: OOPSLA. pp. 92–110. ACM (2016)

[36] Sofronie-Stokkermans, V.: Hierarchic reasoning in local theory extensions. In: CADE. Lecture Notes in Computer Science, vol. 3632, pp. 219–234. Springer (2005)

[37] Vafeiadis, V.: Shape-value abstraction for verifying linearizability. In: VMCAI. Lecture Notes in Computer Science, vol. 5403, pp. 335–348. Springer (2009)

[38] Vafeiadis, V.: Automatically proving linearizability. In: CAV. Lecture Notes in Computer Science, vol. 6174, pp. 450–464. Springer (2010)

[39] Vafeiadis, V.: Rgsep action inference. In: VMCAI. Lecture Notes in Computer Science, vol. 5944, pp. 345–361. Springer (2010)

[40] Wadler, P.: Linear types can change the world! In: Programming Concepts and Methods. p. 561. North-Holland (1990)

[41] Zhu, H., Petri, G., Jagannathan, S.: Poling: SMT aided linearizability proofs. In: CAV (2). Lecture Notes in Computer Science, vol. 9207, pp. 3–19. Springer (2015)

Local Reasoning for Global Graph Properties

Siddharth Krishna[1], Alexander J. Summers[2], and Thomas Wies[1]

[1] New York University, New York, NY, USA, {siddharth, wies}@cs.nyu.edu
[2] ETH Zürich, Zurich, Switzerland, alexander.summers@inf.ethz.ch

Abstract. Separation logics are widely used for verifying programs that manipulate complex heap-based data structures. These logics build on so-called *separation algebras*, which allow expressing properties of heap regions such that modifications to a region do not invalidate properties stated about the remainder of the heap. This concept is key to enabling modular reasoning and also extends to concurrency. While heaps are naturally related to mathematical graphs, many ubiquitous graph properties are non-local in character, such as reachability between nodes, path lengths, acyclicity and other structural invariants, as well as data invariants which combine with these notions. Reasoning modularly about such graph properties remains notoriously difficult, since a local modification can have side-effects on a global property that cannot be easily confined to a small region.

In this paper, we address the question: What separation algebra can be used to avoid proof arguments reverting back to tedious global reasoning in such cases? To this end, we consider a general class of global graph properties expressed as fixpoints of algebraic equations over graphs. We present mathematical foundations for reasoning about this class of properties, imposing minimal requirements on the underlying theory that allow us to define a suitable separation algebra. Building on this theory, we develop a general proof technique for modular reasoning about global graph properties expressed over program heaps, in a way which can be directly integrated with existing separation logics. To demonstrate our approach, we present local proofs for two challenging examples: a priority inheritance protocol and the non-blocking concurrent Harris list.

1 Introduction

Separation logic (SL) [31,37] provides the basis of many successful verification tools that can verify programs manipulating complex data structures [1,4,17,29]. This success is due to the logic's support for reasoning modularly about modifications to heap-based data. For simple inductive data structures such as lists and trees, much of this reasoning can be automated [2,11,20,33]. However, these techniques often fail when data structures are less regular (e.g. multiple overlaid data structures) or provide multiple traversal patterns (e.g. threaded trees). Such idioms are prevalent in real-world implementations such as the fine-grained concurrent data structures found in operating systems and databases. Solutions to these problems have been proposed [14] but remain difficult to automate. For proofs of general graph algorithms, the situation is even more dire. Despite substantial improvements in the verification methodology for such algorithms [35,38], significant parts of the proof argument still typically need to be carried out using non-local reasoning [7,8,13,25]. This paper presents a general technique for local reasoning

P. Müller (Ed.): ESOP 2020, LNCS 12075, pp. 308–335, 2020.
https://doi.org/10.1007/978-3-030-44914-8_12

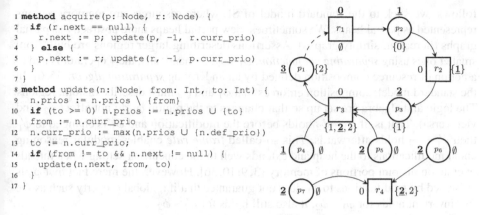

```
1  method acquire(p: Node, r: Node) {
2    if (r.next == null) {
3      r.next := p; update(p, -1, r.curr_prio)
4    } else {
5      p.next := r; update(r, -1, p.curr_prio)
6    }
7  }
8  method update(n: Node, from: Int, to: Int) {
9    n.prios := n.prios \ {from}
10   if (to >= 0) n.prios := n.prios ∪ {to}
11   from := n.curr_prio
12   n.curr_prio := max(n.prios ∪ {n.def_prio})
13   to := n.curr_prio;
14   if (from != to && n.next != null) {
15     update(n.next, from, to)
16   }
17 }
```

Fig. 1: Pseudocode of the PIP and a state of the protocol data structure. Round nodes represent processes and rectangular nodes resources. Nodes are marked with their default priorities def_prio as well as the aggregate priority multiset prios. A node's current priority curr_prio is underlined and marked in bold blue.

about global graph properties that can be used within off-the-shelf separation logics. We demonstrate our technique using two challenging examples for which no fully local proof existed before, respectively, whose proof required a tailor-made logic.

As a motivating example, we consider an idealized priority inheritance protocol (PIP), a technique used in process scheduling [39]. The purpose of the protocol is to avoid *priority inversion*, i.e. a situation where a low-priority process causes a high-priority process to be blocked. The protocol maintains a bipartite graph with nodes representing processes and resources. An example graph is shown in Fig. 1. An edge from a process p to a resource r indicates that p is waiting for r to be available whereas an edge in the other direction means that r is currently held by p. Every node has an associated *default* priority and *current*; these are natural numbers. The current priority is used for scheduling processes. When a process attempts to acquire a resource currently held by another process, the graph is updated to avoid priority inversion. For example, when process p_1 with current priority 3 attempts to acquire the resource r_1 held by process p_2 of priority 1, p_1's higher priority is propagated to p_2 and, transitively, to any other process that p_2 is waiting for (p_3 in this case). As a result, all nodes on the created cycle[3] will get current priority 3. The protocol maintains the following *invariant*: the current priority of each node is the maximum of its default priority and the current priorities of all its predecessors. Priority propagation is implemented by the method update shown in Fig 1. The implementation represents graph edges by next pointers and handles both adding an edge (acquire) and removing one (release - code omitted). To recalculate the current priority of a node (line 12), each node maintains its default priority def_prio and a multiset prios which contains the priorities of all its immediate predecessors.

Verifying that the PIP maintains its invariant using established separation logic (SL) techniques is challenging. In general, SL assertions describe resources and express the fact that the program has permission to access and manipulate these resources. In what

---

[3] The cycle can be used to detect/handle a deadlock; this is not the concern of this data structure.

follows, we stick to the standard model of SL where resources are memory regions represented as partial heaps. We sometimes view partial heaps more abstractly as partial graphs (hereafter, simply graphs). Assertions describing larger regions are built from smaller ones using *separating conjunction*, $\phi_1 * \phi_2$. Semantically, the $*$ operator is tied to a notion of resource composition defined by an underlying *separation algebra* [5,6]. In the standard model, composition enforces that ϕ_1 and ϕ_2 must describe disjoint regions. The logic and algebra are set up so that changes to the region ϕ_1 do not affect ϕ_2 (and vice versa). That is, if $\phi_1 * \phi_2$ holds before the modification and ϕ_1 is changed to ϕ'_1, then $\phi'_1 * \phi_2$ holds afterwards. This so-called *frame rule* enables modular reasoning about modifications to the heap and extends well to the concurrent setting when threads operate on disjoint portions of memory [3,9,10,36]. However, the mere fact that ϕ_2 is preserved by modifications to ϕ_1 does not guarantee that if a global property such as the PIP invariant holds for $\phi_1 * \phi_2$, it also still holds for $\phi'_1 * \phi_2$.

For example, consider the PIP scenario depicted in Fig. 1. If ϕ_1 describes the subgraph containing only node p_1, ϕ_2 the remainder of the graph, and ϕ'_1 the graph obtained from ϕ_1 by adding the edge from p_1 to r_1, then the PIP invariant will no longer hold for the new composed graph described by $\phi'_1 * \phi_2$. On the other hand, if ϕ_1 captures p_1 and the nodes reachable from r_1 (i.e., the set of nodes modified by update), ϕ_2 the remainder of the graph, and we reestablish the PIP invariant locally in ϕ_1 obtaining ϕ'_1 (i.e., run update to completion), then $\phi'_1 * \phi_2$ will also globally satisfy the PIP invariant. The separating conjunction $*$ is not sufficient to differentiate these two cases; both describe valid partitions of a possible program heap. As a consequence, prior techniques have to revert back to non-local reasoning to prove that the invariant is maintained.

A first helpful idea towards a solution to this problem is that of *iterated separating conjunction* [30,44], which describes a graph G consisting of a set of nodes X by a formula $\Psi = \Asterisk_{x \in X} \mathsf{N}(x)$ where $\mathsf{N}(x)$ is some predicate that holds locally for every node $x \in X$. Using such node-local conditions one can naturally express non-inductive properties of graphs (e.g. *"G has no outgoing edges"* or *"G is bipartite"*). The advantages of this style of specification are two-fold. First, one can arbitrarily decompose and recompose Ψ by splitting X into disjoint subsets. For example, if X is partitioned into X_1 and X_2, then Ψ is equivalent to $\Asterisk_{x \in X_1} \mathsf{N}(x) * \Asterisk_{x \in X_2} \mathsf{N}(x)$. Moreover, it is very easy to prove that Ψ is preserved under modifications of subgraphs. For instance, if a program modifies the subgraph induced by X_1 such that $\Asterisk_{x \in X_1} \mathsf{N}(x)$ is preserved locally, then the frame rule guarantees that Ψ will be preserved in the new larger graph. Iterated separating conjunction thus yields a simple proof technique for local reasoning about graph properties that can be described in terms of node-local conditions. However, this idea alone does not actually solve our problem because general global graph properties such as *"G is a direct acyclic graph"*, *"G is an overlay of multiple trees"*, or *"G satisfies the PIP invariant"* cannot be directly described via node-local conditions.

Solution. The key ingredient of our approach is the concept of a *flow* of a graph: a function fl from the nodes of the graph to *flow values*. For the PIP, the flow maps each node to the multiset of its incoming priorities. In general, a flow is a fixpoint of a set of algebraic equations induced by the graph. These equations are defined over a *flow domain*, which determines how flow values are propagated along the edges of the graph and how they are aggregated at each node. In the PIP example, an edge between nodes (n, n') propagates the multiset containing $\max(fl(n), n.\texttt{def\_prio})$ from n to n'. The multisets arriving at n' are aggregated with multiset union to obtain $fl(n')$. Flows enable capturing global graph properties in terms of node-local conditions. For example, the PIP invariant can be expressed by the following node-local condition: $n.\texttt{curr\_prio} = \max(fl(n), n.\texttt{def\_prio})$. To enable compositional reasoning about such properties we need an appropriate separation algebra allowing us to prove locally that modifications to a subgraph do not affect the flow of the remainder of the graph.

To this end, we make the useful observation that a separation algebra induces a notion of an *interface of a resource*: we say that two resources a and a' are equivalent if they compose with the same resources. The interface of a resource a could then be defined as a's equivalence class, but more-succinct and simpler representations may be possible. In the standard model of SL where resources are graphs and composition is disjoint graph union, the interface of a graph G is the set of all graphs G' that have the same domain as G; in this model, a graph's domain could be defined to be its interface.

The interfaces of resources described by assertions capture the information that is implicitly communicated when these assertions are conjoined by separating conjunction. As we discussed earlier, in the standard model of SL, this information is too weak to enable local reasoning about global properties of the composed graphs because some additional information about the subgraphs' structure other than which nodes they contain must be communicated. For instance, if the goal is to verify the PIP invariant, the interfaces must capture information about the multisets of priorities propagated between the subgraphs. We define a separation algebra achieving exactly this: the induced *flow interface* of a graph G in this separation algebra captures how values of the flow domain must enter and leave G such that, when composed with a compatible graph G', the imposed local conditions on the flow of each node are satisfied in the composite graph.

This is the key to enabling SL-style framing for global graph properties. Using iterated separating conjunctions over the new separation algebra, we obtain a compositional proof technique that yields succinct proofs of programs such as the PIP, whose proofs with existing techniques would involve non-trivial global reasoning steps.

Contributions. In §2, we present mathematical foundations for flow domains, imposing the minimal requirements on the underlying algebra that allow us to capture a broad range of data structure invariants and graph properties and reason locally about them in a suitable separation algebra. Building on this theory we develop a general proof technique for modular reasoning about global graph properties that can be integrated with existing separation logics (§3). We further identify general mathematical conditions that can be used when desired to guarantee unique flows, and provide local proof arguments to check the preservation of these conditions (§4). We demonstrate the versatility of our approach by presenting local proofs for two challenging examples: the PIP and the concurrent non-blocking list due to Harris [12].

Flows Redesigned. Our work is inspired by the recent flow framework explored by some of the authors [22], but was redesigned from the ground up. We revisit the core algebra behind flow reasoning, and derive a different algebraic foundation by analysing the minimal requirements for general local reasoning; we call our newly-designed reasoning framework the *foundational flow framework*. Our new framework makes several significant improvements over [22] and eliminates its most stark limitations. We provide a detailed technical comparison with [22] and discuss other related work in §5.

2   The Foundational Flow Framework

In this section, we introduce the foundational flow framework, explaining the motivation for its design with respect to local reasoning principles. We aim for a general technique for modularly proving the preservation of recursively-defined invariants over (partial) graphs, with well-defined decomposition and composition operations.

2.1   Preliminaries and Notation

The term $(b \; ? \; t_1 : t_2)$ denotes t_1 if condition b holds and t_2 otherwise. We write $f \colon A \to B$ for a function from A to B, and $f \colon A \rightharpoonup B$ for a partial function from A to B. For a partial function f, we write $f(x) = \bot$ if f is undefined at x. We use lambda notation $(\lambda x. \; E)$ to denote a function that maps x to the expression E (typically containing x). If f is a function from A to B, we write $f[x \mapsto y]$ to denote the function from $A \cup \{x\}$ defined by $f[x \mapsto y](z) := (z = x \; ? \; y : f(z))$. We use $\{x_1 \mapsto y_1, \ldots, x_n \mapsto y_n\}$ for pairwise different x_i to denote the function $\epsilon[x_1 \mapsto y_1] \cdots [x_n \mapsto y_n]$, where ϵ is the function on an empty domain. Given functions $f_1 \colon A_1 \to B$ and $f_2 \colon A_2 \to B$ we write $f_1 \uplus f_2$ for the function $f \colon A_1 \uplus A_2 \to B$ that maps $x \in A_1$ to $f_1(x)$ and $x \in A_2$ to $f_2(x)$ (if A_1 and A_2 are not disjoint sets, $f_1 \uplus f_2$ is undefined).

We write $\delta_{n=n'} \colon M \to M$ for the function defined by $\delta_{n=n'}(m) := m$ if $n = n'$ else 0. We also write $\lambda_0 := (\lambda m. \; 0)$ for the identically zero function, $\lambda_{\text{id}} := (\lambda m. \; m)$ for the identity function, and use $e \equiv e'$ to denote function equality. For $e \colon M \to M$ and $m \in M$ we write $m \triangleright e$ to denote the function application $e(m)$. We write $e \circ e'$ to denote function composition, i.e. $(e \circ e')(m) = e(e'(m))$ for $m \in M$, and use superscript notation e^p to denote the function composition of e with itself p times.

For multisets S, we use standard set notation when clear from the context. We write $S(x)$ to denote the number of occurrences of x in S. We write $\{x_1 \mapsto i_1, \ldots, x_n \mapsto i_n\}$ for the multiset containing i_1 occurrences of x_1, i_2 occurrences of x_2, etc.

A *partial monoid* is a set M, along with a partial binary operation $+ \colon M \times M \rightharpoonup M$, and a special zero element $0 \in M$, such that (1) $+$ is associative, i.e., $(m_1 + m_2) + m_3 = m_1 + (m_2 + m_3)$; and (2) 0 is an identity, i.e., $m + 0 = 0 + m = m$. Here, $=$ means either both sides are defined and equal, or both are undefined. We identify a partial monoid with its support set M. If $+$ is a total function, then we call M a monoid. Let $m_1, m_2, m_3 \in M$ be arbitrary elements of the (partial) monoid in the following. We call a (partial) monoid M *commutative* if $+$ is commutative, i.e., $m_1 + m_2 = m_2 + m_1$. Similarly, a commutative monoid M is *cancellative* if $+$ is cancellative, i.e., if $m_1 + m_2 = m_1 + m_3$ is defined, then $m_2 = m_3$.

A *separation algebra* [5] is a cancellative, partial, commutative monoid.

2.2   Flows

Recursive properties of graphs naturally depend on non-local information; e.g. we cannot express that a graph is acyclic directly as a conjunction of per-node invariants. Our foundational flow framework defines *flow values* at each node that capture non-local graph properties, and enables local specification and reasoning about such properties. Flow values are drawn from a *flow domain*, an algebraic structure which also specifies the operations used to define a flow via recursive computations over the graph. Our entire theory is parametric with the choice of a flow domain, whose components will be explained and motivated in the rest of this section.

Definition 1 (Flow Domain). *A* flow domain $(M, +, 0, E)$ *consists of a commutative cancellative (total) monoid* $(M, +, 0)$ *and a set of* edge functions $E \subseteq M \to M$.

Example 1. The *path-counting* flow domain is $(\mathbb{N}, +, 0, \{\lambda_{\mathrm{id}}, \lambda_0\})$, consisting of the monoid of natural numbers under addition and the set of edge functions containing only the identity function and the zero function. This can be used to define a flow where the values at each node represent the number of paths to this node from a distinguished node n. Path-counting provides enough information to express locally per node that e.g. (a) all nodes are reachable from n (all path counts are non-zero), or (b) that the graph forms a tree rooted at n (all path counts are exactly 1).

Example 2. We use $(\mathbb{N}^{\mathbb{N}}, \cup, \emptyset, \{\lambda_0\} \cup \{(\lambda m. \{\max(m \cup \{p\})\}) \mid p \in \mathbb{N}\})$ as flow domain for the PIP example (Figure 1). This consists of the monoid of multisets of natural numbers under multiset union and two kinds of edge functions: λ_0 and functions mapping a multiset m to the singleton multiset containing the maximum value between m and a fixed value p (used to represent a node's default priority). This can define a flow which locally captures the appropriate current node priorities as the graph is modified.

Further definitions in this section assume a fixed flow domain $(M, +, 0, E)$ and a (potentially infinite) set of nodes $\mathfrak{N}$. For this section, we abstract heaps using directed partial graphs; integration of our graph reasoning with direct proofs over program heaps is explained in §3.

Definition 2 (Graph). *A* (partial) graph $G = (N, e)$ *consists of a finite set of nodes* $N \subseteq \mathfrak{N}$ *and a mapping from pairs of nodes to edge functions* $e \colon N \times \mathfrak{N} \to E$.

Flow Values and Flows. Flow values (taken from M; the first element of a flow domain) are used to capture sufficient information to express desired non-local properties of a graph. In Example 1, flow values are non-negative integers; for the PIP (Example 2) we instead use *multisets* of integers, representing relevant *non-local* information: the priorities of nodes currently referencing a given node in the graph. Given such flow values, a node's correct priority can be defined locally per node in the graph. This definition requires only the *maximum* value of these multisets, but as we will see shortly these multisets enable local *recomputation* of a correct priority when the graph is changed.

For a graph $G = (N, e)$ we express properties of G in terms of node-local conditions that may depend on the nodes' *flow*. A flow is a function $fl \colon N \to M$ assigning every node a flow value and must be some fixpoint of the following *flow equation*:

$$\forall n \in N.\ fl(n) = in(n) + \sum_{n' \in N} fl(n') \triangleright e(n', n) \qquad \text{(FlowEqn)}$$

Intuitively, one can think of the flow as being obtained by a fold computation over the graph:[4] the *inflow* $in\colon N \to M$ defines an initial flow at each node. This initial flow is then updated recursively for each node n: the current flow value at its predecessor nodes n' is transferred to n via *edge functions* $e(n', n)\colon M \to M$. These flow values are aggregated using the *summation operation* $+$ of the flow domain to obtain an updated flow of n; a flow for the graph is some fixpoint satisfying this equation at all nodes. [5]

Definition 3 (Flow Graph). *A flow graph* $H = (N, e, \mathit{fl})$ *is a graph* (N, e) *and function* $\mathit{fl}\colon N \to M$ *such that there exists an* inflow $in\colon N \to M$ *satisfying* FlowEqn(in, e, fl).

We let $\mathrm{dom}(H) = N$, and sometimes identify H and $\mathrm{dom}(H)$ to ease notational burden. For $n \in H$ we write H_n for the singleton flow subgraph of H induced by n.

Edge Functions. In any flow graph, the flow value assigned to a node n by a flow is propagated to its neighbours n' (and transitively) according to the edge function $e(n, n')$ labelling the edge (n, n'). The edge function maps the flow value at the *source node* n to one propagated on *this edge* to the *target node* n'. Note that we require such a labelling for *all* pairs consisting of a source node n inside the graph and a target node $n' \in \mathfrak{N}$ (i.e., possibly outside the graph). The 0 flow value (the third element of our flow domains) is used to represent no flow; the corresponding (constant) zero *function* $\lambda_0 = (\lambda m.\ 0)$ is used as edge function to model the *absence* of an edge in the graph. A set of edge functions E from which this labelling is chosen can, other than the requirement $\lambda_0 \in E$, be chosen as desired. As we will see in §4.4, restrictions to particular sets of edge functions E can be exploited to further strengthen our overall technique. Edge functions can depend on the local state of the source node (as in the following example); dependencies from elsewhere in the graph must be represented by the node's flow.

Example 3. Consider the graph in Figure 1 and the flow domain as in Example 2. We choose the edge functions to be λ_0 where no edge exists in the PIP structure, and otherwise $(\lambda m.\ \{\max(m \cup \{d\})\})$ where d is the default priority of the source of the edge. For example, in Figure 1, $e(r_3, p_2) = \lambda_0$ and $e(r_3, p_1) = (\lambda m.\ \{\max(m \cup \{0\})\})$. Since the flow value at r_3 is $\{1, 2, 2\}$, the edge (r_3, p_1) propagates the value $\{2\}$ to p_1, correctly representing the current priority of r_3.

Flow Aggregation and Inflows. The flow value at a node is defined by those propagated to it from each node in a graph via edge functions, along with an additional *inflow* value explained here. Since multiple non-zero flow values can be propagated to a node, we require an aggregation of these values via a binary $+$ operator on flow values : the second element of our flow domains. The edges from which the aggregated values originate are unordered. Thus, we require $+$ to be commutative and associative, making this aggregation order-independent. The 0 flow value must act as a unit for $+$. For example, in the path-counting flow domain $+$ means addition on natural numbers, while for the multisets employed for the PIP it means multiset union.

---

[4] We note that flows are not generally defined in this manner as we consider any fixpoint of the flow equation to be a flow. Nonetheless, the analogy helps to build an initial intuition.

[5] We discuss questions regarding the existence and uniqueness of such fixpoints in §4.

Each node in a flow graph has an *inflow*, modelling contributions to its flow value which do *not* come from inside the graph. Inflows play two important roles: first, since our graphs are partial, they model contributions from nodes *outside of the graph*. Second, inflow can be artificially added as a means of specialising the computation of flow values to characterise specific graph properties. For example, in the path-counting domain, we give an inflow of 1 to the node from which we are counting paths, and 0 to all others.

Example 4. Let the edges in the graph in Figure 1 be labelled as described in Example 3. If the inflow function in assigns the empty multiset to every node n and we let $fl(n)$ be the multiset labelling every node in the figure, then $\mathsf{FlowEqn}(in, e, fl)$ holds.

The flow equation ($\mathsf{FlowEqn}$) defines the flow of a node n to be the aggregation of flow values coming from other nodes n' inside the graph (as given by the respective edge function $e(n', n)$) as well as the inflow $in(n)$. Preserving solutions to this equation across updates to the graph structure is a fundamental goal of our technique. The following lemma (which relies on the fact that $+$ is required to be cancellative) states that any correct flow values uniquely determine appropriate inflow values:

Lemma 1. *Given a flow graph* (N, e, fl)*, there exists a unique inflow* in *such that* $\mathsf{FlowEqn}(in, e, fl)$*.*

We now turn to how solutions of the flow equation can be preserved or appropriately updated under *changes* to the underlying graph.

Graph Updates and Cancellativity. Given a flow graph with known flow and inflow values, suppose we *remove* an edge from n_1 to n_2 (replacing the edge function with λ_0). For the same inflow, such an update will potentially affect the flow at n_2 and nodes to which n_2 (transitively) propagates flow. Starting from the simple case that n_2 has no outgoing edges, we need to recompute a suitable flow at n_2. Knowing the old flow value (say, m) and the contribution $m' = fl(n_1) \triangleright e(n_1, n_2)$ *previously* provided along the removed edge, we know that the correct new flow value is some m'' such that $m' + m'' = m$. This constraint has a unique solution (and thus, we can unambiguously recompute a new flow value) exactly when the aggregation $+$ is *cancellative*; we therefore make cancellativity a *requirement* on the $+$ of any flow domain.

Cancellativity intuitively enforces that the flow domain carries enough information to enable adaptation to local updates (in particular, removal of edges[6]). Returning to the PIP example, cancellativity requires us to carry multisets as flow values rather than only the maximum priority value: $+$ cannot be the maximum operation, as this would not be cancellative. The resulting multisets (like the `prio` fields in the actual code) provide the information necessary to recompute corrected priority values locally.

For example, in the PIP graph shown in Figure 1, removing the edge from p_6 to r_4 would not affect the current priority of r_4 whereas if p_7 had current priority 1 instead of 2, then the current priority of r_4 would have to decrease. In either case, recomputing the flow value for r_4 is simply a matter of subtraction (removing $\{2\}$ from the multiset at r_4); cancellativity guarantees that our flow domains will always provide the information

---

[6] As we will show in §2.3, an analogous problem for composition of flow graphs is also directly solved by this choice to force aggregation to be cancellative.

needed for this recomputation. Without this property, the recomputation of a flow value for the target node n_2 would, in general, entail recomputing the incoming flow values from all remaining edges from scratch. Cancellativity is also crucial for Lemma 1 above, forcing uniqueness of inflows, given known flow values in a flow graph. This allows us to define natural but powerful notions of flow graph decomposition and recomposition.

2.3 Flow Graph Composition and Abstraction

Building towards the core of our reasoning technique, we now turn to the question of decomposition and recomposition of flow graphs. Two flow graphs with disjoint domains always compose to a graph, but this will be a *flow graph* only if their flows are chosen consistently to admit a solution to the resulting flow equation (i.e. the flow graph composition operator $\odot$ defined below is *partial*).

Definition 4 (Flow Graph Algebra). *The* flow graph algebra $(\mathsf{FG}, \odot, H_\emptyset)$ *for the flow domain* $(M, +, 0, E)$ *is defined by*

$$\mathsf{FG} := \{(N, e, f\!l) \mid (N, e, f\!l) \text{ is a flow graph}\}, \qquad H_\emptyset := (\emptyset, e_\emptyset, f\!l_\emptyset),$$

$$(N_1, e_1, f\!l_1) \odot (N_2, e_2, f\!l_2) := \begin{cases} (N_1 \uplus N_2, e_1 \uplus e_2, f\!l_1 \uplus f\!l_2) & \text{if in } \mathsf{FG} \\ \bot & \text{otherwise,} \end{cases}$$

where $e_\emptyset$ and $f\!l_\emptyset$ are the edge functions and flow on the empty set of nodes $N = \emptyset$.

Intuitively, two flow graphs compose to a flow graph if their contributions to each others' flow (along edges from one to the other) are reflected in the corresponding inflow of the other graph. For example, consider the subgraph from Figure 1 consisting of the single node p_7 (with 0 inflow). This will compose with the remainder of the graph depicted only if this remainder subgraph has an inflow which, at node r_4, includes at least the multiset $\{2\}$, reflecting the propagated value from p_7.

We use this intuition to extract an *abstraction* of flow graphs which we call *flow interfaces*. Given a flow (sub)graph, its flow interface consists of the node-wise inflow and *outflow* (the flow contributions its nodes make to all nodes outside of the graph, defined below). It is thus an abstraction that hides the flow values and edges that are wholly *inside* the flow graph. Flow graphs that have the same flow interface "look the same" to the external graph, as the same values are propagated inwards and outwards.

Definition 5 (Flow Interface). *For a given flow domain M, a* flow interface *is a pair $I = (in, out)$ where $in \colon N \to M$ and $out \colon \mathfrak{N} \setminus N \to M$ for some $N \subseteq \mathfrak{N}$.*

We write $I.in, I.out$ for the two components of the interface $I = (in, out)$. We will again sometimes identify I and $\mathrm{dom}(I.in)$ to ease notational burden.

Given a flow graph $H \in \mathsf{FG}$, we can compute its interface as follows. Recall that Lemma 1 implies that any flow graph has a unique inflow. Thus, we can define an inflow function that maps each flow graph $H = (N, e, f\!l)$ to the unique inflow $\inf(H) \colon H \to M$ such that $\mathsf{FlowEqn}(\inf(H), e, f\!l)$. Dually, we define the *outflow* of H as the function $\mathrm{outf}(H) \colon \mathfrak{N} \setminus N \to M$ defined by $\mathrm{outf}(H)(n) := \sum_{n' \in N} f\!l(n') \triangleright e(n', n)$. The *flow interface of H*, written $\mathrm{int}(H)$, is the pair $(\inf(H), \mathrm{outf}(H))$ consisting of its inflow and its outflow. Returning to the previous example, if H is the singleton subgraph consisting of node p_7 from Figure 1 with flow and edges as depicted, then $\text{int}(H) = (\lambda n. \emptyset, \lambda n. (n{=}r_4 ? \{2\} : \emptyset))$.

This abstraction, while simple, turns out to be powerful enough to build a separation algebra over our flow graphs, allowing them to be decomposed, locally modified and recomposed in ways yielding all the local reasoning benefits of separation logics. In particular, for graph operations within a subgraph with a certain interface, we need to prove: (a) that the modified subgraph is still a flow graph (by checking that the flow equation still has a solution locally in the subgraph) and (b) that it satisfies the same interface (in other words, the effect of the modification on the flow is contained within the subgraph); the meta-level results for our technique then justify that we can recompose the modified subgraph with any graph that the original could be composed with.

We define the corresponding *flow interface algebra* as follows:

Definition 6 (Flow Interface Algebra). *For a given flow domain M, the* flow interface algebra *over M is defined to be* $(\mathsf{FI}, \oplus, I_\emptyset)$, *where:*

$$\mathsf{FI} := \{I \mid I \text{ is a flow interface}\}, \qquad I_\emptyset := \text{int}(H_\emptyset),$$

$$I_1 \oplus I_2 := \begin{cases} I & I_1 \cap I_2 = \emptyset \\ & \wedge \forall i \neq j \in \{1,2\}, n \in I_i.\ I_i.in(n) = I.in(n) + I_j.out(n) \\ & \wedge \forall n \notin I.\ I.out(n) = I_1.out(n) + I_2.out(n) \\ \bot & otherwise. \end{cases}$$

Flow interface composition is well-defined because of cancellativity of the underlying flow domain (it is also, exactly as flow graph composition, partial). We next show the key result for this abstraction: the ability for two flow graphs to compose depends only on their interfaces; flow interfaces implicitly define a congruence relation on flow graphs.

Lemma 2. $\text{int}(H_1) = I_1 \wedge \text{int}(H_2) = I_2 \Rightarrow \text{int}(H_1 \odot H_2) = I_1 \oplus I_2.$

Crucially, the following result shows that we can use our flow interfaces as an abstraction directly compatible with existing separation logics.

Theorem 1. *The flow interface algebra* $(\mathsf{FI}, \oplus, I_\emptyset)$ *is a separation algebra.*

This result forms the core of our reasoning technique; it enables us to make modifications within a chosen subgraph and, by proving preservation of its interface, know that the result composes with any context exactly as the original did. Flow interfaces capture precisely the information relevant about a flow graph, with respect to composition with other flow graphs. In Appendix B of the accompanying technical report (hereafter, TR) [23] we provide additional examples of flow domains that demonstrate the range of data structures and graph properties that can be expressed using flows, including a notion of *universal flow* that in a sense provides a completeness result for the expressivity of the framework. We now turn to constructing proofs atop these new reasoning principles.

3   Proof Technique

This section shows how to integrate flow reasoning into a standard separation logic, using the priority inheritance protocol (PIP) algorithm to illustrate our proof techniques.

Since flow graphs and flow interfaces form separation algebras, it is possible in principle to define a separation logic (SL) using these notions as a custom *semantic model* (indeed, this is the proof approach taken in [22]). By contrast, we integrate flow interfaces with a *standard* separation logic without modifying its semantics. This has the important technical advantage that our proof technique can be naturally integrated with existing separation logics and verification tools supporting SL-style reasoning. We consider a standard *sequential* SL in this section, but our technique can also be directly integrated with a concurrent SL such as RGSep (as we show in §4.5) or frameworks such as Iris [18] supporting (ghost) resources ranging over user-defined separation algebras.

3.1   Encoding Flow-based Proofs in SL

Proofs using our flow framework can employ a combination of specifications enforced at the node level and in terms of the flow graphs and interfaces corresponding to larger heap regions such as entire data structures (henceforth, *composite graphs* and *composite interfaces*). At the node level, we write invariants that every node is intended to satisfy, typically relating the node's flow value to its local state (fields). For example, in the PIP, we use node-local invariants to express that a node's current priority is the maximum of the node's default priority and those in its current flow value. We typically express such specifications in terms of *singleton (flow) graphs*, and their *singleton interfaces*.

Specification in terms of *composite* interfaces has several important purposes. One is to define custom inflows: e.g. in the path-counting flow domain, specifying that the inflow of a composite interface is 1 at some designated node r and 0 elsewhere enforces in any underlying flow graph that each node n's flow value will be the number of paths from r to n.[7] Composite interfaces can also be used to express that, in two states of execution, a portion of the heap "looks the same" with respect to composition (it has the same interface, and so can be composed with the same flow graphs), or to capture by *how much* there is an observable difference in inflow or outflow; we employ this idea in the PIP proof below.

We now define an assertion syntax convenient for capturing both node-level and composite-level constraints, defined within an SL-style proof system. We assume an *intuitionistic, garbage-collected* SL [6] with standard syntax and semantics:[8] see Appendix A of the TR [23] for more details.

Node Predicates. The basic building block of our flow-based specifications is a node predicate $N(x, H)$, representing ownership of the fields of a single node x, as well as

---

[7] Note that the analogous property cannot be captured at the node level; when considering singleton interfaces per node in a tree rooted at r, *every* singleton interface has an inflow of 1.

[8] As $P * \phi \equiv P \wedge \phi$ for pure formulas P in garbage-collected SLs, we use $*$ instead of $\wedge$ throughout this paper.

capturing its corresponding singleton flow graph H:

$$N(x, H) := \exists fs, fl.\ x \mapsto fs * H = (\{x\},\ (\lambda y.\ \mathsf{edge}(x, fs, y)),\ fl) * \gamma(x, fs, fl(x))$$

N is implicitly parameterised by fs, edge and γ; these are explained next and are typically fixed across any given flow-based proof. The N predicate expresses that we have a heap cell at location x containing fields fs (a list of field-name/value mappings).[9] It also says that H is a singleton flow graph with domain $\{x\}$ with some flow fl, whose edge functions are defined by a user-defined abstraction function $\mathsf{edge}(x, fs, y)$; this function allows us to define edges in terms of x's field values. Finally, the node, its fields, and its flow in this flow graph satisfy the custom predicate γ, used to encode node-local properties such as constraints in terms of the flow values of nodes.

Graph Predicates. The analogous predicate for composite graphs is Gr. It carries ownership to the nodes making up a potentially unbounded graph, using iterated separating conjunction over a *set* of nodes X as mentioned in §1:

$$Gr(X, H) := \exists \mathcal{H}.\ \underset{x \in X}{\bigstar}\ N(x, \mathcal{H}(x)) * H = \underset{x \in X}{\bigodot} \mathcal{H}(x)$$

Gr is also implicitly parameterised by fs, edge and γ. The existentially-quantified $\mathcal{H}$ is a logical variable representing a *function* from nodes in X to corresponding singleton flow graphs. $Gr(X, H)$ describes a set of nodes X, such that each $x \in X$ is an N (in particular, it satisfies γ), whose singleton flow graphs compose back to H. As well as carrying ownership of the underlying heap locations, Gr's definition allows us to connect a node-level view of the region X (each $\mathcal{H}(x)$) with a composite-level view defined by H, on which we can impose appropriate graph-level properties such as constraints on the region's inflow.

Lifting to Interfaces. Flow based proofs can often be expressed more elegantly and abstractly using predicates in terms of node and composite-level interfaces rather than flow graphs. To this end, we overload both our node and graph predicates with analogues whose second parameter is a flow interface, defined as follows:

$$N(x, I) := \exists H.\ N(x, H) * I = \mathsf{int}(H)$$
$$Gr(X, I) := \exists H.\ Gr(x, H) * I = \mathsf{int}(H)$$

We will use these versions in the PIP proof below; interfaces capture all relevant properties for decomposition and composition of these flow graphs.

Flow Lemmas. We first illustrate our N and Gr predicates (which capture SL ownership of heap regions and abstract these with flow interfaces) by identifying a number of lemmas which are generically useful in flow-based proofs. Reasoning at the level of flow interfaces is entirely in the *pure* world (mathematics independent of heap-ownership and

---

[9] For simplicity, we assume that all fields of a flow graph node are to be handled by our flow-based technique, and that their ownership (via $\mapsto$ points-to predicates) is always carried around together; lifting these restrictions would be straightforward.

$$\begin{aligned}
\mathsf{Gr}(X_1 \uplus X_2, H) &\models \exists H_1, H_2.\, \mathsf{Gr}(X_1, H_1) * \mathsf{Gr}(X_2, H_2) \\
&\quad * H_1 \odot H_2 = H &\text{(DECOMP)} \\
\mathsf{Gr}(X_1, H_1) * \mathsf{Gr}(X_2, H_2) * H_1 \odot H_2 \neq \perp &\models \mathsf{Gr}(X_1 \uplus X_2, H_1 \odot H_2) &\text{(COMP)} \\
\mathsf{N}(x, H) &\equiv \mathsf{Gr}(\{x\}, H) &\text{(SING)} \\
emp &\models \mathsf{Gr}(\emptyset, H_\emptyset) &\text{(GREMP)} \\
\mathsf{Gr}(X_1, H_1') * \mathsf{Gr}(X_2, H_2) * H = H_1 \odot H_2 &\models \mathsf{Gr}(X_1 \uplus X_2, H_1' \odot H_2) &\text{(REPL)} \\
* \operatorname{int}(H_1) = \operatorname{int}(H_1') &\quad * \operatorname{int}(H) = \operatorname{int}(H_1' \odot H_2)
\end{aligned}$$

Fig. 2: Some useful lemmas for proving entailments between flow-based specifications.

resources) with respect to the underlying SL reasoning; these lemmas are consequences of our predicate definitions and the foundational flow framework definitions themselves.

Examples of these lemmas are shown in Figure 2. (DECOMP) shows that we can always decompose a valid flow graph into subgraphs which are themselves flow graphs. Recomposition (COMP) is possible only if the subgraphs compose. These rules, as well as (SING), and (GREMP) follow directly from the definition of Gr and standard SL properties of iterated separating conjunction. The final rule (REPL) is a direct consequence of rules (COMP), (DECOMP) and the congruence relation on flow graphs induced by their interfaces (cf. Lemma 2). Conceptually, it expresses that after decomposing any flow graph into two parts H_1 and H_2, we can *replace* H_1 with a new flow graph H_1' with the same interface; when recomposing, the overall graph will be a flow graph with the same overall interface.

Note the connection between rules (COMP)/(DECOMP) and the algebraic laws of standard inductive predicates such as ls describing a segment of a linked list [2]. For instance by combining the definition of Gr with these rules and (SING) we can prove the following graph analogue of the rule to separate a list into the head node and the tail:

$$\mathsf{Gr}(X \uplus \{y\}, H) \equiv \exists H_y, H'.\mathsf{N}(y, H_y) * \mathsf{Gr}(X, H') * H = H_y \odot H' \quad \text{((UN)FOLD)}$$

However, crucially (and unlike when using general inductive predicates [32]), this rule is symmetrical for any node x in X; it works analogously for any desired order of decomposition of the graph, and for any data structure specified using flows.

When working with our overloaded N and Gr predicates, similar steps to those described by the above lemmas are useful. Given these overloaded predicates, we simply apply the lemmas above to the *existentially quantified* flow-graphs in their definitions and then lift the consequence of the lemma back to the interface level using the congruence between our flow graph and interface composition notions (Lemma 2).

3.2   Proof of the PIP

We now have all the tools necessary to verify the priority inheritance protocol (PIP). Figure 3 gives the full algorithm with flow-based specifications; we also include some intermediate assertions to illustrate the reasoning steps for the `acquire` method, which

```
1 // Let  δ(m, q₁, q₂) := m \ (q₁ ≥ 0 ? {q₁} : ∅) ∪ (q₂ ≥ 0 ? {q₂} : ∅)
2
3 method update(n: Ref, from: Int, to: Int)
4   requires N(n, Iₙ) * Gr(X \ {n}, I') * I = I'ₙ ⊕ I' * φ(I) * n ∈ X
5   requires I'ₙ = ({n ↦ δ(Iₙ.in(n), from, to)}, Iₙ.out) * from ≠ to
6   ensures Gr(X, I)
7 {
8   n.prios := n.prios \ {from}
9   if (to >= 0) {
10    n.prios := n.prios ∪ {to}
11  }
12  from := n.curr_prio
13  n.curr_prio := max(n.prios ∪ {n.def_prio})
14  to := n.curr_prio
15
16  if (from != to && n.next != null) {
17    update(n.next, from, to)
18  }
19 }
20
21 method acquire(p: Ref, r: Ref)
22   requires Gr(X, I) * φ(I) * p ∈ X * r ∈ X * p ≠ r
23   ensures Gr(X, I)
24 {
25   {∃Iᵣ, Iₚ, I₁. N(r, Iᵣ) * N(p, Iₚ) * Gr(X \ {r, p}, I₁) * I = Iᵣ ⊕ Iₚ ⊕ I₁ * φ(I)}
26   if (r.next == null) {
27     r.next := p;
28     // Let  qᵣ = r.curr_prio
29   {∃Iᵣ, I'ᵣ, Iₚ, I₁. N(r, I'ᵣ) * N(p, Iₚ) * Gr(X \ {r, p}, I₁) * I = Iᵣ ⊕ Iₚ ⊕ I₁ }
       { * I'ᵣ = (Iᵣ.in, {p ↦ {qᵣ}}) * Iᵣ.out = λ₀ * ···                          }
30   ⊨ {∃Iₚ, I'ₚ, I₂. N(p, Iₚ) * Gr(X \ {p}, I₂) * I = I'ₚ ⊕ I₂                      }
       { * I'ₚ = ({p ↦ δ(Iₚ.in(p), -1, qᵣ)}, Iₚ.out) * ···                         }
31     update(p, -1, r.curr_prio)
32   {Gr(X, I)}
33   } else {
34     p.next := r; update(r, -1, p.curr_prio)
35   }
36 }
37
38 method release(p: Ref, r: Ref)
39   requires Gr(X, I) * φ(I) * p ∈ X * r ∈ X * p ≠ r
40   ensures Gr(X, I)
41 { r.next := null; update(p, r.curr_prio, -1) }
```

Fig. 3: Full PIP code and specifications, with proof sketch for `acquire`. The comments and coloured annotations (lines 29 to 32) are used to highlight steps in the proof, and are explained in detail in the text.

we explain in more detail below. [10] We instantiate our framework in order to capture the PIP invariants as follows:

$$fs := \{\text{next}: y, \text{curr\_prio}: q, \text{def\_prio}: q^0, \text{prios}: Q\}$$

$$\text{edge}(x, fs, z) := \begin{cases} (\lambda m. \ \max(m \cup \{q^0\})) & \text{if } z = y \neq null \\ \lambda_0 & \text{otherwise} \end{cases}$$

$$\gamma(x, fs, m) := q^0 \geq 0 \ * \ (\forall q' \in Q. \ q' \geq 0) \ * \ m = Q \ * \ q = \{\max(Q \cup \{q^0\})\}$$

$$\varphi(I) := I = (\lambda_0, \lambda_0)$$

Each node has the four fields listed in fs. fs also defines variables such as y to denote field values that are used in the definitions of edge and γ; these variables are bound to the heap by N. edge abstracts the heap into a flow graph by letting each node have an edge to its next successor labelled by a function that passes to it the maximum incoming priority or the node's default priority: whichever is larger. With this definition, one can see that the flow of every node will be the multiset containing exactly the priorities of its predecessors. The node-local invariant γ says that all priorities are non-negative, the flow m of each node is stored in the prios field, and its current priority is the maximum of its default and incoming priorities. Finally, the constraint φ on the global interface expresses that the graph is closed – it has no inflow or outflow.

Flows Specifications for the PIP. Our specifications of acquire and release guarantee that if we start with a valid flow graph (closed, according to φ), we are guaranteed to return a valid flow graph with the same interface (i.e. the graph remains closed). For clarity of the exposition, we focus here on how we prove that being a flow graph that satisfies the PIP invariant is preserved (as is the composite flow graph's interface). Extending this specification to one which proves, e.g., that acquire adds the expected edge is straightforward (see Appendix C of the TR [23]). [11]

The specification for update is somewhat subtle, and exploits the full flexibility of flow interfaces as a specification medium. The preconditions of update describe an update to the graph which is not yet completed. There are three complementary aspects to this specification. Firstly, (as for acquire and release), node-local invariants (γ) hold for all nodes in the graph (enforced via N and Gr predicates). Secondly, we employ flow interfaces to express a decomposition of the original top-level interface I into compatible (primed) sub-interfaces. The key to understanding this specification is that I'_n is in some sense a *fake* interface; it does not abstract the current state of the heap node n. Instead, I'_n expresses the way in which the node n's current inflow *hasn't yet* been accounted for in the heap: that *if* n could adjust its inflow according to the propagated priority change *without* changing its outflow, then it would compose back with the rest of the graph, and restore the graph's overall interface. The shorthand δ defines the required change to n's inflow.

In general (except when n's next field is null, or n's flow value is unchanged), it is not even possible for n's fields to be updated to satisfy I'_n; by updating n's inflow,

---

[10] In specifications, we implicitly quantify at the top level over free variables such as I. λ_0 denotes an identically zero function on an unconstrained domain.

[11] We also omit acquire's precondition that p.next == null for brevity.

we will necessarily update its outflow. However, we can then construct a corresponding "fake" interface for the next node in the graph, reflecting the update yet to be accounted for, and establishing the precondition for the recursive call to `update`.

The third specification aspect is the *connection* between heap-level nodes and interfaces. The $N(n, I_n)$ predicate connects n with a *different* interface; I_n is the actual current abstraction of n's state. Conceptually, the key property which is broken at this point is this connection between the interface-level specification and the heap at node n, reflected by the decomposition in the specification between $X \setminus \{n\}$ and $\{n\}$.

We note that the same specification ideas and proof style can be easily adapted to other data structure implementations with an update-notify style, including well-known designs such as Subject-Observer patterns, or the Composite pattern [27].

Proof Outline. To illustrate the application of flows reasoning to our PIP specification ideas more clearly, we examine in detail the first `if`-branch in the proof of `acquire`. Our intermediate proof steps are shown as purple annotations surrounded by braces. The first step, as shown in the first line inside the method body, is to apply ((UN)FOLD) twice (on the flow graphs represented by these predicates) and peel off N predicates for each of r and p. The update to r's `next` field (line 27) causes the correct singleton interface of r to change to I'_r: its outflow (previously none, since the `next` field was null) now propagates flow to p. We summarise this state in the assertion on line 29 (we omit e.g. repetition of properties from the function's precondition, focusing on the flow-related steps of the argument). We now rewrite this state: using the definition of interface composition (Definition 6) we deduce that although I'_r and I_p do not compose (since the former has outflow that the latter does not account for as inflow), the alternative "fake" interface I'_p for p (which artificially accounts for the missing inflow) *would* do so (cf. line 30). Essentially, we show $I_r \oplus I_p = I'_r \oplus I'_p$, that the interface of $\{r, p\}$ would be unchanged if p could somehow have interface I'_p. Now by setting $I_2 = I'_r \oplus I_1$ and using algebraic properties of interfaces, we assemble the precondition expected by `update`. After the call, `update`'s postcondition gives us the desired postcondition.

We focused here on the details of `acquire`'s proof, but very similar manipulations are required for reasoning about the recursive call in `update`'s implementation.[12] The main difference there is that if the if-condition wrapping the recursive call is false then either the last-modified node has no successor (and so there is no outstanding inflow change needed), or we have `from = to` which implies that the "fake" interface is actually the same as the currently correct one.

Despite the property proved for the PIP example being a rather delicate recursive invariant over the (potentially cyclic) graph, the power of our framework enables extremely succinct specifications for the example, and proofs which require the application of relatively few generic lemmas. The integration with standard separation logic reasoning, and the complementary separation algebras provided by flow interfaces allow decomposition and recomposition to be simple proof steps. For this proof, we integrated with standard sequential separation logic, but in the next section we will show that compatibility with concurrent SL techniques is similarly straightforward.

---

[12] We provide further proof outlines in Appendix C of the TR [23].

324   S. Krishna et al.

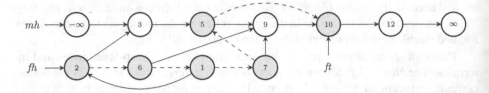

Fig. 4: A potential state of the Harris list with explicit memory management. fnext pointers are shown with dashed edges, marked nodes are shaded gray, and null pointers are omitted for clarity.

4 Advanced Flow Reasoning and the Harris List

This section introduces some advanced foundational flow framework theory and demonstrates its use in the proof of the Harris list. We note that [22] presented a proof of this data structure in the original flow framework. The proof given here shows that the new framework eliminates the need for the customized concurrent separation logic defined in [22]. We start with a recap of Harris' algorithm adapted from [22].

4.1 The Harris List Algorithm

The power of flow-based reasoning is exhibited in the proof of overlaid data structures such as the Harris list, a concurrent non-blocking linked list algorithm [12]. This algorithm implements a set data structure as a sorted list, and uses atomic compare-and-swap (CAS) operations to allow a high degree of parallelism. As with the sequential linked list, Harris' algorithm inserts a new key k into the list by finding nodes k_1, k_2 such that $k_1 < k < k_2$, setting k to point to k_2, and using a CAS to change k_1 to point to k only if it was still pointing to k_2. However, a similar approach fails for the delete operation. If we had consecutive nodes k_1, k_2, k_3 and we wanted to delete k_2 from the list (say by setting k_1 to point to k_3), there is no way to ensure with one CAS that k_2 and k_3 are also still adjacent (another thread could have inserted/deleted in between them).

Harris' solution is a two step deletion: first atomically mark k_2 as deleted (by setting a mark bit on its successor field) and then later remove it from the list using a single CAS. After a node is marked, no thread can insert or delete to its right, hence a thread that wanted to insert k' to the right of k_2 would first remove k_2 from the list and then insert k' as the successor of k_1.

In a non-garbage-collected environment, unlinked nodes cannot be immediately freed as suspended threads might continue to hold a reference to them. A common solution is to maintain a second "free list" to which marked nodes are added before they are unlinked from the main list (this is the so-called drain technique). These nodes are then labelled with a timestamp, which is used by a maintenance thread to free them when it is safe to do so. This leads to the kind of data structure shown in Figure 4, where each node has two pointer fields: a next field for the main list and an fnext field for the free list (the list from fh to ft via dashed edges). Threads that have been suspended while holding

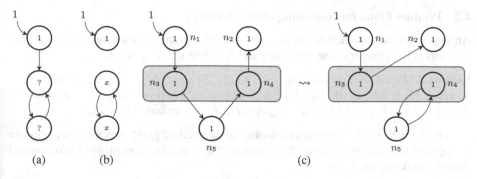

Fig. 5: Examples of graphs that motivate effective acyclicity. All graphs use the path-counting flow domain, the flow is displayed inside each node, and the inflow is displayed as curved arrows to the top-left of nodes. (a) shows a graph and inflow that has no solution to (FlowEqn); (b) has many solutions. (c) shows a modification that preserves the interface of the modified nodes, yet goes from a graph that has a unique flow to one that has many solutions to (FlowEqn).

a reference to a node that was added to the free list can simply continue traversing the next pointers to find their way back to the unmarked nodes of the main list.

Even for seemingly simple properties such as that the Harris list is memory safe and not leaking memory, the proof will rely on the following non-trivial invariants:

(a) The data structure consists of two (potentially overlapping) lists: a list on next edges beginning at mh and one on fnext edges beginning at fh.
(b) The two lists are null terminated and next edges from nodes in the free list point to nodes in the free list or main list.
(c) All nodes in the free list are marked.
(d) ft is an element in the free list (due to concurrency, it's not always the tail).

Challenges. To prove that Harris' algorithm maintains the invariants listed above we must tackle a number of challenges. First, we must construct flow domains that allow us to describe overlaid data structures, such as the overlapping main and free lists (§4.2). Second, the flow-based proofs we have seen so far work by showing that the interface of some modified region is unchanged. However, if we consider a program that allocates and inserts a new node into a data structure (like the insert method of Harris), then the interface cannot be the same since the domain has changed (it has increased by the newly allocated node). We must thus have a means to reason about preservation of flows by modifications that allocate new nodes (§4.3). The third issue is that in some flow domains, there exist graphs G and inflows in for which no solutions to the flow equation (FlowEqn) exist. For instance, consider the path-counting flow domain and the graph in Figure 5(a). Since we would need to use the path-counting flow in the proof of the Harris list to encode its structural invariants, this presents a challenge (§4.4).

We will next see how to overcome these three challenges in turn, and then apply those solution to the proof of the Harris list in §4.5.

4.2 Product Flows for Reasoning about Overlays

An important fact about flows is that any flow of a graph over a product of two flow domains is the product of the flows on each flow domain component.

Lemma 3. *Given two flow domains* $(M_1, +_1, 0_1, E_1)$ *and* $(M_2, +_2, 0_2, E_2)$, *the product domain* $(M_1 \times M_2, +, (0_1, 0_2), E)$ *is a flow domain, where* $+$ *and* E *are the pointwise liftings of* $(+_1, +_2)$ *and* (E_1, E_2), *respectively, to the domain* $M_1 \times M_2$.

This lemma greatly simplifies reasoning about overlaid graph structures; we will use the product of two path-counting flows to describe a structure consisting of two overlaid lists that make up the Harris list.

4.3 Contextual Extensions and the Replacement Theorem

In general, when modifying a flow graph H to another flow graph H', requiring that H' satisfies *precisely* the same interface $\text{int}(H)$ can be too strong a condition as it does not permit allocating new nodes. Instead, we want to allow $\text{int}(H')$ to differ from $\text{int}(H)$ in that the new interface could have a larger domain, as long as the edges from the new nodes do not change the outflow of the modified region.

Definition 7. *An interface* $I = (in, out)$ *is* contextually extended *by* $I' = (in', out')$, *written* $I \precsim I'$, *if and only if the following conditions all hold:*

(1) $\text{dom}(in) \subseteq \text{dom}(in')$,
(2) $\forall n \in \text{dom}(in).\ in(n) = in'(n)$, *and*
(3) $\forall n' \notin \text{dom}(in').\ out(n') = out'(n')$.

The following theorem states that contextual extension preserves composability and is itself preserved under interface composition.

Theorem 2 (Replacement Theorem). *If* $I = I_1 \oplus I_2$, *and* $I_1 \precsim I_1'$ *are all valid interfaces such that* $I_1' \cap I_2 = \emptyset$ *and* $\forall n \in I_1' \setminus I_1.\ I_2.out(n) = 0$, *then there exists a valid* $I' = I_1' \oplus I_2$ *such that* $I \precsim I'$.

In terms of our flow predicates, this theorem gives rise to the following adaptation of the (REPL) rule:

$$\mathsf{Gr}(X_1', H_1') * \mathsf{Gr}(X_2, H_2) * H = H_1 \odot H_2 * \text{int}(H_1) \precsim \text{int}(H_1')$$
$$\models \exists H'.\ \mathsf{Gr}(X_1' \uplus X_2, H') * H = H_1' \odot H_2 * \text{int}(H) \precsim \text{int}(H') \qquad \text{(REPL+)}$$

The rule (REPL+) is derived from the Replacement Theorem by instantiating with $I = \text{int}(H), I_1 = \text{int}(H_1), I_2 = \text{int}(H_2)$ and $I_1' = \text{int}(H_1')$. We know $I_1 \precsim I_1'$; $H = H_1 \odot H_2$ tells us (by Lemma 2) that $I = I_1 \oplus I_2$, and $\mathsf{Gr}(X_1', H_1') * \mathsf{Gr}(X_2, H_2)$ gives us $I_1' \cap I_2 = \emptyset$. The final condition of the Replacement Theorem is to prove that there is no outflow from X_2 to any newly allocated node in X_1'. While we can use additional ghost state to prove such constraints in our proofs, if we assume that the memory allocator only allocates fresh addresses and restrict the abstraction function edge to only propagate flow along an edge (n, n') if n has a (non-ghost) field with a reference to n' then this condition is always true. For simplicity, and to keep the focus of this paper on the flow reasoning, we make this assumption in the Harris list proof.

4.4 Existence and Uniqueness of Flows

We typically express global properties of a graph $G = (N, e)$ by fixing a global inflow $in\colon N \to M$ and then constraining the flow of each node in N using node-local conditions. However, as we discussed at the beginning of this section, there is no general guarantee that a flow exists or is unique for a given in and G. The remainder of this section presents two complementary conditions under which we can prove that our flow fixpoint equation always has a unique solution. To this end, we say that a flow domain $(M, +, 0, E)$ has *unique flows* if for every graph (N, e) over this flow domain and inflow $in\colon N \to M$, there exists a unique fl that satisfies the flow equation $\mathsf{FlowEqn}(in, e, fl)$. But first, we briefly recall some more monoid theory.

We say M is *positive* if $m_1 + m_2 = 0$ implies that $m_1 = m_2 = 0$. For a positive monoid M, we can define a partial order $\leq$ on its elements as $m_1 \leq m_2$ if and only if $\exists m_3.\ m_1 + m_3 = m_2$. This definition implies that every $m \in M$ satisfies $0 \leq m$.

For $e, e'\colon M \to M$, we write $e + e'$ for the function that maps $m \in M$ to $e(m) + e'(m)$. We lift this construction to a set of functions E and write it as $\sum_{e \in E} e$.

Definition 8. *A function* $e\colon M \to M$ *is called an* endomorphism *on* M *if for every* $m_1, m_2 \in M$, $e(m_1 + m_2) = e(m_1) + e(m_2)$. *We denote the set of all endomorphisms on* M *by* $\mathsf{End}(M)$.

Note that for cancellative M, $e(0) = 0$ for every endomorphism $e \in \mathsf{End}(M)$. Note further that $e + e' \in \mathsf{End}(M)$ for any $e, e' \in \mathsf{End}(M)$. Similarly, for finite sets $E \subseteq \mathsf{End}(M)$, $\sum_{e \in E} e \in \mathsf{End}(M)$. We say that a set of endomorphisms $E \subseteq \mathsf{End}(M)$ is *closed* if for every $e, e' \in E$, $e \circ e' \in E$ and $e + e' \in E$.

Nilpotent Cycles. Let $(M, +, 0, E)$ be a flow domain where every edge function $e \in E$ is an endomorphism on M. In this case, we can show that the flow of a node n is the sum of the flow as computed along *each path* in the graph that ends at n. Suppose we additionally know that the edge functions are defined such that their composition along any *cycle* in the graph eventually becomes the identically zero function. We then need only consider finitely many paths to compute the flow of a node, which means the flow equation has a unique solution.

Definition 9. *A closed set of endomorphisms* $E \subseteq \mathsf{End}(M)$ *is called* nilpotent *if there exists* $p > 1$ *such that* $e^p \equiv 0$ *for every* $e \in E$.

Example 5. The flow domain $(\mathbb{N}^2, +, (0, 0), \{(\lambda(x, y).\ (0, c \cdot x)) \mid c \in \mathbb{N}\})$ contains nilpotent edge functions that shift the first component of the flow to the second (with a scaling factor). This domain can be used to express the property that every node in a graph is reachable from the root via a single edge (by requiring the flow of every node to be $(0, 1)$ under the inflow $(\lambda n.\ (n = r\ ?\ (1, 0) : (0, 0)))$).

Before we prove that nilpotent endomorphisms lead to unique flows, we present a useful notion when dealing with endomorphic flow domains.

Definition 10. *The* capacity *of a flow graph* $G = (N, e)$ *is* $\mathsf{cap}(G)\colon N \times \mathfrak{N} \to (M \to M)$, *defined inductively as* $\mathsf{cap}(G) := \mathsf{cap}^{|G|}(G)$, *where* $\mathsf{cap}^0(G)(n, n') := \delta_{n=n'}$ *and*

$$\mathsf{cap}^{i+1}(G)(n, n') := \delta_{n=n'} + \sum_{n'' \in G} \mathsf{cap}^i(G)(n, n'') \circ e(n'', n').$$

For a flow graph $H = (N, e, \mathit{fl})$, we write $\mathsf{cap}(H)(n, n') = \mathsf{cap}((N, e))(n, n')$ for the capacity of the underlying graph. Intuitively, $\mathsf{cap}(G)(n, n')$ is the function that summarizes how flow is routed from any source node n in G to any other node n', including those outside of G.

We can now show that if all edges of a flow graph are labelled with edges from a nilpotent set of endomorphisms, then the flow equation has a unique solution:

Lemma 4. *If $(M, +, 0, E)$ is a flow domain such that M is a positive monoid and E is a nilpotent set of endomorphisms, then this flow domain has unique flows.*

Effectively Acyclic Flow Graphs. There are some flow domains that compute flows useful in practice, but which do not guarantee either existence or uniqueness of fixpoints *a priori* for all graphs. For example, the path-counting flow from Example 1 is one where for certain graphs, there exist no solutions to the flow equation (see Figure 5(a)), and for others, there can exist more than one (in Figure 5(b), the nodes marked with x can have any path count, as long as they both have the same value).

In such cases, we explore how to restrict the class of *graphs* we use in our flow-based proofs such that each graph has a unique fixpoint; the difficulty is that this restriction must be respected for composition of our graphs. Here, we study the class of flow domains $(M, +, 0, E)$ such that M is a positive monoid and E is a set of *reduced* endomorphisms (defined below). In such domains we can decompose the flow computations into the various paths in the graph, and achieve unique fixpoints by restricting the kinds of cycles graphs can have.

Definition 11. *A flow graph $H = (N, e, \mathit{fl})$ is effectively acyclic (EA) if for every $1 \le k$ and $n_1, \ldots, n_k \in N$,*

$$\mathit{fl}(n_1) \rhd e(n_1, n_2) \cdots e(n_{k-1}, n_k) \rhd e(n_k, n_1) = 0.$$

The simplest example of an effectively acyclic graph is one where the edges with non-zero edge functions form an acyclic graph. However, our semantic condition is weaker: for example, when reasoning about two overlaid acyclic lists whose union happens to form a cycle, a product of two path-counting domains will satisfy effective acyclicity because the composition of different types of edges results in the zero function.

Lemma 5. *Let $(M, +, 0, E)$ be a flow domain such that M is a positive monoid and E is a closed set of endomorphisms. Given a graph (N, e) over this flow domain and inflow $\mathsf{in} \colon N \to M$, if there exists a flow graph $H = (N, e, \mathit{fl})$ that is effectively acyclic, then fl is unique.*

While the restriction to effectively acyclic flow graphs guarantees us that the flow is the unique fixpoint of the flow equation, it is not easy to show that modifications to the graph preserve EA while reasoning locally. Even modifying a subgraph to another with the same flow interface (which we know guarantees that it will compose with any context) can inadvertently create a cycle in the larger composite graph. For instance, consider Figure 5(c), that shows a modification to nodes $\{n_3, n_4\}$ (the boxed blue region). The interface of this region is $(\{n_3 \rightarrowtail 1, n_4 \rightarrowtail 1\}, \{n_5 \rightarrowtail 1, n_2 \rightarrowtail 1\})$, and so swapping the edges of n_3 and n_4 preserves this interface. However, the resulting graph, despite composing with the context to form a valid flow graph, is not EA (in this case, it has multiple solutions to the flow equation). This shows that flow interfaces are not powerful enough to preserve effective acyclicity. For a special class of endomorphisms, we show that a local property of the modified subgraph can be checked, which implies that the modified composite graph continues to be EA.

Definition 12. *A closed set of endomorphisms* $E \subseteq \mathsf{End}(M)$ *is called* reduced *if* $e \circ e \equiv \lambda_0$ *implies* $e \equiv \lambda_0$ *for every* $e \in E$.

Note that if E is reduced, then no $e \in E$ can be nilpotent. In that sense, this class of instantiations is complementary to the nilpotent class.

Example 6. Examples of flow domains that fall into this class include positive semirings of reduced rings (with the additive monoid of the semiring being the aggregation monoid of the flow domain and E being any set of functions that multiply their argument with a constant flow value). Note that any direct product of integral rings is a reduced ring. Hence, products of the path counting flow domain are a special case.

For reduced endomorphisms, it suffices to check that a modification preserves the flow routed between every pair of source and sink node in order to ensure that it does not create any new cycles in any composite graph.

Definition 13. *A flow graph* H' *is a* subflow-preserving extension *of* H, *for which we write* $H \precsim_s H'$, *if the following conditions all hold:*

(1) $\mathsf{int}(H) \precsim \mathsf{int}(H')$
(2) $\forall n \in H, n' \notin H', m.\ m \leq \mathsf{inf}(H)(n) \Rightarrow m \triangleright \mathsf{cap}(H)(n, n') = m \triangleright \mathsf{cap}(H')(n, n')$
(3) $\forall n \in H' \setminus H, n' \notin H', m.\ m \leq \mathsf{inf}(H')(n) \Rightarrow m \triangleright \mathsf{cap}(H')(n, n') = 0$

This pairwise check, apart from requiring the interface of the modified region to be unchanged, also permits allocating new nodes as long as no flow is routed via the new nodes (condition (3)). We now show that it is sufficient to check that a modification is a subflow-preserving extension to guarantee composition back to an effectively-acyclic composite graph:

Theorem 3. *Let* $(M, +, 0, E)$ *be a flow domain such that* M *is a positive monoid and* E *is a reduced set of endomorphisms. If* $H = H_1 \odot H_2$ *and* $H_1 \precsim_s H_1'$ *are all effectively acyclic flow graphs such that* $H_1' \cap H_2 = \emptyset$ *and* $\forall n \in H_1' \setminus H_1.\ \mathsf{outf}(H_2)(n) = 0$, *then there exists an effectively acyclic flow graph* $H' = H_1' \odot H_2$ *such that* $H \precsim_s H'$.

We define effectively acyclic versions of our flow graph predicates, $\mathsf{N_a}(x, H)$ and $\mathsf{Gr_a}(X, H)$, that additionally constrain H to be effectively acyclic. The above theorem yields the following variant of the (REPL) rule for EA graphs:

$$\mathsf{Gr_a}(X_1', H_1') * \mathsf{Gr_a}(X_2, H_2) * H = H_1 \odot H_2 * H_1 \precsim_s H_1'$$
$$\models \exists H'.\ \mathsf{Gr_a}(X_1' \uplus X_2, H') * H' = H_1' \odot H_2 * H \precsim_s H' \qquad \text{(REPLEA)}$$

4.5 Proof of the Harris List

We use the techniques seen in this section in the proof of the Harris list. As the data structure consists of two potentially overlapping lists, we use Lemma 3 to construct a product flow domain of two path-counting flows: one tracks the path count from the head of the main list, and one from the head of the free list. We also work under the effectively acyclic restriction (i.e. we use the N_a and Gr_a predicates), both in order to obtain the desired interpretation of the flow as well as to ensure existence of flows in this flow domain.

We instantiate the framework using the following definitions of parameters:

$$fs := \{\text{key}: k, \text{next}: y, \text{fnext}: z\}$$
$$\text{edge}(x, fs, v) := (v = null \; ? \; \lambda_0 : (v = y \land y \neq z \; ? \; \lambda_{(1,0)}$$
$$: (v \neq y \land y = z \; ? \; \lambda_{(0,1)} : (v = y \land y = z \; ? \; \lambda_{\text{id}} : \lambda_0))))$$
$$\gamma(x, fs, I) := (I.in(x) \in \{(1,0), (0,1), (1,1)\}) * (I.in(x) \neq (1,0) \Rightarrow M(y))$$
$$* (x = ft \Rightarrow I.in(x) = (\_, 1)) * (\neg M(y) \Rightarrow z = null)$$
$$\varphi(I) := I = (\lambda_0[mh \rightarrowtail (1,0)][fh \rightarrowtail (0,1)], \lambda_0)$$

Here, edge encodes the edge functions needed to compute the product of two path counting flows, the first component tracks path-counts from mh on next edges and the second tracks path-counts from fh on fnext edges [13]. The node-local invariant γ says: the flow is one of $\{(1,0), (0,1), (1,1)\}$ (meaning that the node is on one of the two lists, invariant (a)); if the flow is not $(1,0)$ (the node is not only on the main list, i.e. it is on the free list) then the node is marked (indicated by $M(y)$, invariant (c)); and if the node is ft then it must be on the free list (invariant (d)). The constraint on the global interface, φ, says that the inflow picks out mh and fh as the roots of the lists, and there is no outgoing flow (thus, all non-null edges must stay within the graph, invariant (b)).

Since the Harris list is a concurrent algorithm, we perform the proof in rely-guarantee separation logic (RGSep) [41]. Like in §3, we do not need to modify the semantics of RGSep in any way; our flow-based predicates can be defined and reasoning using our lemmas can be performed in the logic out-of-the-box. For space reasons, the full proof can be found in Appendix D of the TR [23].

5 Related Work

As mentioned in §1, the most closely related work is the flow framework developed by some of the authors in [22]. We here present a simplified and generalized meta theory of flows that makes the approach much more broadly applicable. There were a number of limitations of the prior framework that prevented its application to more general classes of examples.

First, [22] required flow domains to form a semiring; the analogue of edge functions are restricted to multiplication with a constant which must come from the same flow

---

[13] We use the shorthands $\lambda_{(1,0)} := (\lambda(m_1, m_2). (m_1, 0))$ and $\lambda_{(0,1)} := (\lambda(m_1, m_2). (0, m_2))$, and denote an anonymous existentially-quantified variable by $\_$.

value set. This restriction made it complex to encode many graph properties of interest. For example, one could not easily encode the PIP flow, or a simple flow that counts the number of incoming edges to each node. Our foundational flow framework decouples the algebraic structure defining how flow is *aggregated* from the algebraic structure of the edge functions. In this way, we obtain a more general framework that applies to many more examples, and with simpler flow domains.

Second, in [22], a flow graph did not uniquely determine its inflow (cf. Lemma 1). Correspondingly, [22]'s notion of interface included an *equivalence class* of inflows (all those that induce the same flow values). Since, in [22], the interface also determines which modifications are permitted by the framework, [22] could only handle modifications that preserve the inflow equivalence class. For example, this prevents one from reasoning locally about the removal of a single edge from a graph in certain cases (in particular, like `release` does in the PIP). Our foundational flow framework solves this problem by requiring that the aggregation operation on flow values is cancellative, guaranteeing unique inflows.

Cancellativity is fundamentally incompatible with [22], which requires the flow domain to form an ω-CPO in order to guarantee the existence of unique flows. For example, in a graph with two nodes n and n' with identity edges between them and all other edges zero (in [22], edges labelled with 1 and 0), if we have $in(n) = 0$ and $in(n) = m$ for some non-zero m, a solution to the flow equation must satisfy $fl(n) = m + fl(n)$. [22] forces such solutions to exist, ruling out cancellativity. To solve this problem, we present a new theory which can optionally guarantee unique flows when desired and show that requiring cancellativity does not limit expressivity.

Next, the proofs of programs shown in [22] depend on a bespoke program logic. This logic requires new reasoning primitives that are not supported by the logics implemented in existing SL-based verification tools. Our general proof technique eliminates the need for a dedicated program logic and can be implemented on top of standard separation logics and existing SL-based tools. Finally, the underlying separation algebra of the original framework makes it hard to use equational reasoning, which is a critical prerequisite for enabling proof automation.

An abundance of SL variants provide complementary mechanisms for modular reasoning about programs (e.g. [18, 36, 38]). Most are parameterized by the underlying separation algebra; our flow-based reasoning technique easily integrates with these existing logics.

The most common approach to reason about irregular graph structures in SL is to use iterated separating conjunction [30, 44] and describe the graph as a set of nodes each of which satisfies some local invariant. This approach has the advantage of being able to naturally describe general graphs. However, it is hard to express non-local properties that involve some form of fixpoint computation over the graph structure. One approach is to abstract the program state as a mathematical graph using iterated separating conjunction and then express non-local invariants in terms of the abstract graph rather than the underlying program state [14, 35, 38]. However, a proof that a modification to the state maintains a global invariant of the abstract graph must then often revert back to non-local and manual reasoning, involving complex inductive arguments about paths, transitive closure, and so on. Our technique also exploits iterated separating conjunction for the underlying heap ownership, with the key benefit that flow interfaces exactly capture the necessary conditions on a modified subgraph in order to compose with *any* context and preserve desired non-local invariants.

In recent work, Wang et al. present a Coq-mechanised proof of graph algorithms in C, based on a substantial library of graph-related lemmas, both for mathematical and heap-based graphs [42]. They prove rich functional properties, integrated with the VST tool. In contrast to our work, a substantial suite of lemmas and background properties are necessary, since these specialise to particular properties such as reachability. We believe that our foundational flow framework could be used to simplify framing lemmas in a way which remains parameteric with the property in question.

Proofs of a number of graph algorithms have been mechanized in various verification tools and proof assistants, including Tarjan's SCC algorithm [8], union-find [7], Kruskal's minimum spanning tree algorithm [13], and network flow algorithms [25]. These proofs generally involve non-local reasoning arguments about mathematical graphs.

An alternative approach to using SL-style reasoning is to commit to global reasoning but remain within decidable logics to enable automation [16, 21, 24, 28, 43]. However, such logics are restricted to certain classes of graphs and certain types of properties. For instance, reasoning about reachability in unbounded graphs with two successors per node is undecidable [15]. Recent work by Ter-Gabrielyan et al. [40] shows how to deal with modular framing of *pairwise reachability* specifications in an imperative setting. Their framing notion has parallels to our notion of interface composition, but allows subgraphs to *change* the paths visible to their context. The work is specific to a reachability relation, and cannot express the rich variety of custom graph properties available in our technique.

Dynamic frames [19] (e.g. implemented in Dafny [26]), can be used to explicitly reason about framing of heap information in a first-order logic. However, by itself, this theory does not enable modular reasoning about global graph properties. We believe that the flow framework could in principle be adapted to the dynamic frames setting.

6   Conclusions and Future Work

We have presented the foundational flow framework, enabling local modular reasoning about recursively-defined properties over general graphs. The core reasoning technique has been designed to make minimal mathematical requirements, providing great flexibility in terms of potential instantiations and applications. We identified key classes of these instantiations for which we can provide existence and uniqueness guarantees for the fixpoint properties our technique addresses and demonstrate our proof technique on several challenging examples. As future work, we plan to automate flow-based proofs in our new framework using existing tools that support SL-style reasoning such as Viper [29] and GRASShopper [34].

Acknowledgments. This work is funded in parts by the National Science Foundation under grants CCF-1618059 and CCF-1815633.

References

1. Appel, A.W.: Verified software toolchain. In: NASA Formal Methods. Lecture Notes in Computer Science, vol. 7226, p. 2. Springer (2012)
2. Berdine, J., Calcagno, C., O'Hearn, P.W.: A decidable fragment of separation logic. In: FSTTCS. Lecture Notes in Computer Science, vol. 3328, pp. 97–109. Springer (2004)
3. Brookes, S., O'Hearn, P.W.: Concurrent separation logic. SIGLOG News 3(3), 47–65 (2016)
4. Calcagno, C., Distefano, D., Dubreil, J., Gabi, D., Hooimeijer, P., Luca, M., O'Hearn, P.W., Papakonstantinou, I., Purbrick, J., Rodriguez, D.: Moving fast with software verification. In: NFM. Lecture Notes in Computer Science, vol. 9058, pp. 3–11. Springer (2015)
5. Calcagno, C., O'Hearn, P.W., Yang, H.: Local action and abstract separation logic. In: LICS. pp. 366–378. IEEE Computer Society (2007)
6. Cao, Q., Cuellar, S., Appel, A.W.: Bringing order to the separation logic jungle. In: APLAS. Lecture Notes in Computer Science, vol. 10695, pp. 190–211. Springer (2017)
7. Charguéraud, A., Pottier, F.: Verifying the correctness and amortized complexity of a union-find implementation in separation logic with time credits. J. Autom. Reasoning 62(3), 331–365 (2019)
8. Chen, R., Cohen, C., Lévy, J., Merz, S., Théry, L.: Formal proofs of tarjan's strongly connected components algorithm in why3, coq and isabelle. In: ITP. LIPIcs, vol. 141, pp. 13:1–13:19. Schloss Dagstuhl - Leibniz-Zentrum für Informatik (2019)
9. Dockins, R., Hobor, A., Appel, A.W.: A fresh look at separation algebras and share accounting. In: APLAS. Lecture Notes in Computer Science, vol. 5904, pp. 161–177. Springer (2009)
10. Dodds, M., Jagannathan, S., Parkinson, M.J., Svendsen, K., Birkedal, L.: Verifying custom synchronization constructs using higher-order separation logic. ACM Trans. Program. Lang. Syst. 38(2), 4.1–4:72 (2016)
11. Enea, C., Lengál, O., Sighireanu, M., Vojnar, T.: SPEN: A solver for separation logic. In: NFM. Lecture Notes in Computer Science, vol. 10227, pp. 302–309 (2017)
12. Harris, T.L.: A pragmatic implementation of non-blocking linked-lists. In: DISC. Lecture Notes in Computer Science, vol. 2180, pp. 300–314. Springer (2001)
13. Haslbeck, M.P.L., Lammich, P., Biendarra, J.: Kruskal's algorithm for minimum spanning forest. Archive of Formal Proofs 2019 (2019)
14. Hobor, A., Villard, J.: The ramifications of sharing in data structures. In: POPL. pp. 523–536. ACM (2013)
15. Immerman, N., Rabinovich, A.M., Reps, T.W., Sagiv, S., Yorsh, G.: The boundary between decidability and undecidability for transitive-closure logics. In: CSL. Lecture Notes in Computer Science, vol. 3210, pp. 160–174. Springer (2004)
16. Itzhaky, S., Banerjee, A., Immerman, N., Nanevski, A., Sagiv, M.: Effectively-propositional reasoning about reachability in linked data structures. In: CAV. Lecture Notes in Computer Science, vol. 8044, pp. 756–772. Springer (2013)
17. Jacobs, B., Smans, J., Philippaerts, P., Vogels, F., Penninckx, W., Piessens, F.: Verifast: A powerful, sound, predictable, fast verifier for C and java. In: NASA Formal Methods. Lecture Notes in Computer Science, vol. 6617, pp. 41–55. Springer (2011)
18. Jung, R., Krebbers, R., Jourdan, J., Bizjak, A., Birkedal, L., Dreyer, D.: Iris from the ground up: A modular foundation for higher-order concurrent separation logic. J. Funct. Program. 28, e20 (2018)
19. Kassios, I.T.: Dynamic frames: Support for framing, dependencies and sharing without restrictions. In: FM. Lecture Notes in Computer Science, vol. 4085, pp. 268–283. Springer (2006)
20. Katelaan, J., Matheja, C., Zuleger, F.: Effective entailment checking for separation logic with inductive definitions. In: TACAS (2). Lecture Notes in Computer Science, vol. 11428, pp. 319–336. Springer (2019)

21. Klarlund, N., Schwartzbach, M.I.: Graph types. In: POPL. pp. 196–205. ACM Press (1993)
22. Krishna, S., Shasha, D.E., Wies, T.: Go with the flow: compositional abstractions for concurrent data structures. PACMPL **2**(POPL), 37:1–37:31 (2018)
23. Krishna, S., Summers, A.J., Wies, T.: Local reasoning for global graph properties. CoRR **abs/1911.08632** (2019)
24. Lahiri, S.K., Qadeer, S.: Back to the future: revisiting precise program verification using SMT solvers. In: POPL. pp. 171–182. ACM (2008)
25. Lammich, P., Sefidgar, S.R.: Formalizing network flow algorithms: A refinement approach in isabelle/hol. J. Autom. Reasoning **62**(2), 261–280 (2019)
26. Leino, K.R.M.: Dafny: An automatic program verifier for functional correctness. In: LPAR (Dakar). Lecture Notes in Computer Science, vol. 6355, pp. 348–370. Springer (2010)
27. Leino, K.R.M., Moskal, M.: Vacid-0: Verification of ample correctness of invariants of data-structures, edition 0. Microsoft Research Technical Report (2010)
28. Madhusudan, P., Qiu, X., Stefanescu, A.: Recursive proofs for inductive tree data-structures. In: POPL. pp. 123–136. ACM (2012)
29. Müller, P., Schwerhoff, M., Summers, A.J.: Viper: A verification infrastructure for permission-based reasoning. In: Jobstmann, B., Leino, K.R.M. (eds.) Verification, Model Checking, and Abstract Interpretation (VMCAI). LNCS, vol. 9583, pp. 41–62. Springer-Verlag (2016)
30. Müller, P., Schwerhoff, M., Summers, A.J.: Automatic verification of iterated separating conjunctions using symbolic execution. In: CAV (1). Lecture Notes in Computer Science, vol. 9779, pp. 405–425. Springer (2016)
31. O'Hearn, P.W., Reynolds, J.C., Yang, H.: Local reasoning about programs that alter data structures. In: CSL. Lecture Notes in Computer Science, vol. 2142, pp. 1–19. Springer (2001)
32. Parkinson, M.J., Bierman, G.M.: Separation logic and abstraction. In: Palsberg, J., Abadi, M. (eds.) Principles of Programming Languages (POPL). pp. 247–258. ACM (2005)
33. Piskac, R., Wies, T., Zufferey, D.: Automating separation logic using SMT. In: CAV. Lecture Notes in Computer Science, vol. 8044, pp. 773–789. Springer (2013)
34. Piskac, R., Wies, T., Zufferey, D.: Grasshopper - complete heap verification with mixed specifications. In: TACAS. Lecture Notes in Computer Science, vol. 8413, pp. 124–139. Springer (2014)
35. Raad, A., Hobor, A., Villard, J., Gardner, P.: Verifying concurrent graph algorithms. In: APLAS. Lecture Notes in Computer Science, vol. 10017, pp. 314–334 (2016)
36. Raad, A., Villard, J., Gardner, P.: Colosl: Concurrent local subjective logic. In: ESOP. Lecture Notes in Computer Science, vol. 9032, pp. 710–735. Springer (2015)
37. Reynolds, J.C.: Separation logic: A logic for shared mutable data structures. In: LICS. pp. 55–74. IEEE Computer Society (2002)
38. Sergey, I., Nanevski, A., Banerjee, A.: Mechanized verification of fine-grained concurrent programs. In: PLDI. pp. 77–87. ACM (2015)
39. Sha, L., Rajkumar, R., Lehoczky, J.P.: Priority inheritance protocols: An approach to real-time synchronization. IEEE Trans. Computers **39**(9), 1175–1185 (1990)
40. Ter-Gabrielyan, A., Summers, A.J., Müller, P.: Modular verification of heap reachability properties in separation logic. PACMPL **3**(OOPSLA), 121:1–121:28 (2019)
41. Vafeiadis, V.: Modular fine-grained concurrency verification. Ph.D. thesis, University of Cambridge, UK (2008)
42. Wang, S., Cao, Q., Mohan, A., Hobor, A.: Certifying graph-manipulating C programs via localizations within data structures. PACMPL **3**(OOPSLA), 171:1–171:30 (2019)
43. Wies, T., Muñiz, M., Kuncak, V.: An efficient decision procedure for imperative tree data structures. In: CADE. Lecture Notes in Computer Science, vol. 6803, pp. 476–491. Springer (2011)
44. Yang, H.: An example of local reasoning in BI pointer logic: the Schorr-Waite graph marking algorithm. In: Proceedings of the SPACE Workshop (2001)

Aneris: A Mechanised Logic for Modular Reasoning about Distributed Systems

Morten Krogh-Jespersen, Amin Timany ⓘ*, Marit Edna Ohlenbusch,
Simon Oddershede Gregersen ⓘ, and Lars Birkedal ⓘ

Aarhus University, Aarhus, Denmark

Abstract. Building network-connected programs and distributed systems is a powerful way to provide scalability and availability in a digital, always-connected era. However, with great power comes great complexity. Reasoning about distributed systems is well-known to be difficult.

In this paper we present Aneris, a novel framework based on separation logic supporting modular, node-local reasoning about concurrent and distributed systems. The logic is higher-order, concurrent, with higher-order store and network sockets, and is fully mechanized in the Coq proof assistant. We use our framework to verify an implementation of a load balancer that uses multi-threading to distribute load amongst multiple servers and an implementation of the *two-phase-commit* protocol with a replicated logging service as a client. The two examples certify that Aneris is well-suited for both horizontal and vertical modular reasoning.

Keywords: Distributed systems · Separation logic · Higher-order logic · Concurrency · Formal verification

1 Introduction

Reasoning about distributed systems is notoriously difficult due to their sheer complexity. This is largely the reason why previous work has traditionally focused on verification of protocols of core network components. In particular, in the context of model checking, where safety and liveness assertions [29] are considered, tools such as SPIN [9], TLA+ [23], and Mace [17] have been developed. More recently, significant contributions have been made in the field of formal proofs of *implementations* of challenging protocols, such as two-phase-commit, lease-based key-value stores, Paxos, and Raft [7, 25, 30, 35, 40]. All of these developments define domain specific languages (DSLs) specialized for distributed systems verification. Protocols and modules proven correct can be compiled to an executable, often relying on some trusted code-base.

Formal reasoning about distributed systems has often been carried out by giving an abstract model in the form of a *state transition system* or *flow-chart* in the tradition of Floyd [5], Lamport [21, 22]. A state is normally taken to be a

---

* This research was carried out while Amin Timany was at KU Leuven, working as a postdoctoral fellow of the Flemish research fund (FWO).

P. Müller (Ed.): ESOP 2020, LNCS 12075, pp. 336–365, 2020.
https://doi.org/10.1007/978-3-030-44914-8_13

view of the global state and events are observable changes to this state. State transition systems are quite versatile and have been used in other verification applications. However, reasoning based on state transition systems often suffer from a lack of modularity due to their very global. As a consequence, separate nodes or components cannot be verified in isolation and the system has to be verified as a whole.

IronFleet [7] is the first system that supports node-local reasoning for verifying the implementation of programs that run on different nodes. In IronFleet, a distributed system is modeled by a transition system. This transition system is shown to be refined by the composition of a number of transition systems, each pertaining to one of the nodes in the system. Each node in the distributed system is shown to be correct and a refinement of its corresponding transition system. Nevertheless, IronFleet does not allow you to reason compositionally; a correctness proof for a distributed system cannot be used to show the correctness of a larger system.

Higher-order concurrent separation logics (CSLs) [3, 4, 13, 15, 18, 26, 27, 28, 33, 34, 36, 39] simplify reasoning about higher-order imperative concurrent programs by offering facilities for specifying and proving correctness of programs in a modular way. Indeed, their support for modular reasoning (a.k.a. compositional reasoning) is the key reason for their success. Disel [35] is a separation logic that does support compositional reasoning about distributed systems, allowing correctness proofs of distributed systems to be used for verifying larger systems. However, Disel struggles with node-local reasoning in that it cannot hide node-local usage of mutable state. That is, the use of internal state in nodes must be exposed in the high-level protocol of the system and changes to the internal state are only possible upon sending and receiving messages over the network.

Finally, both Disel and IronFleet restrict nodes to run only sequential programs and no node-level concurrency is supported.

In this paper we present Aneris, a framework for implementing and reasoning about functional correctness of distributed systems. Aneris is based on concurrent separation logic and supports modular reasoning with respect to both nodes (node-local reasoning) and threads within nodes (thread-local reasoning). The Aneris framework consists of a programming language, AnerisLang, for writing realistic, real-world distributed systems and a higher-order concurrent separation logic for reasoning about these systems. AnerisLang is a concurrent ML-like programming language with higher-order functions, local state, threads, and network primitives. The operational semantics of the language, naturally, involves multiple hosts (each with their own heap and multiple threads) running in a network. The Aneris logic is build on top of the Iris framework [13, 15, 18] and supports machine-verified formal proofs in the Coq proof assistant about distributed systems written in AnerisLang.

Networking. There are several ways of adding network primitives to a programming language. One approach is *message-passing* using first-class communication channels á la the π-calculus or using an implementation of the actor model as done in high-level languages like Erlang, Elixir, Go, and Scala. However, any such implementation is an abstraction built on top of network sockets where all data has to be serialized, data packets may be dropped, and packet reception may not follow the transmission order. Network sockets are a quintessential part of building efficient, real-world distributed systems and all major operating systems provide an application programming interface (API) to them. Likewise, AnerisLang provides support for datagram-like sockets by directly exposing a simple API with the core methods necessary for socket-based communication using the User Datagram Protocol (UDP) with duplicate protection. This allows for a wide range of real-world systems and protocols to be implemented (and verified) using the Aneris framework.

Modular Reasoning in Aneris. In general, there are two different ways to support modular reasoning about distributed systems corresponding to how components can be composed. Aneris enables simultaneously both:

- *Vertical composition*: when reasoning about programs within each node, one is able to compose proofs of different components to prove correctness of the whole program. For instance, the specification of a verified data structure, e.g. a concurrent queue, should suffice for verifying programs written against that data structure, independently of its implementation.
- *Horizontal composition*: at each node, a verified thread is composable with other verified threads. Similarly, a verified node is composable with other verified nodes which potentially engage in different protocols. This naturally aids implementing and verifying large-scale distributed systems.

Node-local variants of the standard rules of CSLs like, for example, the bind rule and the frame rule (as explained in Sect. 2) enable vertical reasoning. Sect. 6 showcases vertical reasoning in Aneris using a replicated distributed logging service that is implemented and verified using a separate implementation and specification of the two-phase commit protocol.

Horizontal reasoning in Aneris is achieved through the THREAD-PAR-rule and the NODE-PAR-rule (further explained in Sect. 2) which intuitively says that to verify a distributed system, it suffices to verify each thread and each node in isolation. This is analogous to how CSLs allow us to reason about multi-threaded programs by considering individual threads in isolation; in Aneris we extend this methodology to include both threads and nodes. Where most variants of concurrent separation logic use some form of an invariant mechanism to reason about shared-memory concurrency, we abstract the communication between nodes over the network through *socket protocols* that restrict what can be sent and received on a socket and allow us to share ownership of logical resources among nodes. Sect. 5 showcases horizontal reasoning in Aneris using an implementation and a correctness proof for a simple addition service that uses a load balancer to distribute the workload among several addition servers. Each node is verified in isolation and composed to form the final distributed system.

Contributions. In summary, we make the following contributions:

- We present AnerisLang, a formalized higher-order functional programming language for writing distributed systems. The language features higher-order store, node-local concurrency, and network sockets, allowing for dynamic creation and binding of sockets to addresses with serialization and deserialization primitives for encoding and parsing messages.
- We define the Aneris logic, the first higher-order concurrent separation logic with support for network sockets and with support for both node-local and thread-local reasoning.
- We introduce a simple and novel approach to specifying network protocols; a mechanism that supports separation-logic-style modular specifications of distributed systems.
- We conduct two case studies that showcase how our framework aids the implementation and verification of real-world distributed systems using compositional reasoning:
  - A replicated logging service that is implemented and verified using a separate implementation and specification of the two-phase commit protocol, demonstrating vertical compositional reasoning.
  - A load balancer that distributes work on multiple servers by means of node-local multi-threading. We use this to verify a simple addition service that uses the load balancer to distribute its requests over multiple servers, demonstrating horizontal compositional reasoning.
- We have formalized all of the theory and examples on top of Iris in the Coq proof assistant using the MoSeL framework [19]. The Coq formalization can be found online at https://iris-project.org/artifacts/2020-esop-aneris.tar.gz.

Outline. We start by describing the core concepts of the Aneris framework in Sec. 2. We then describe the AnerisLang programming language (Sec. 3) before presenting the Aneris logic proof rules and stating our adequacy theorem, *i.e.*, soundness of Aneris, in Sec. 4. Subsequently, we use the logic to verify a load balancer (Sec. 5) and a two-phase-commit implementation with a replicated logging client (Sec. 6). We discuss related work in Sec. 7 and conclude in Sec. 8.

2   The Core Concepts of Aneris

In this section we present our methodology to modular verification of distributed systems. We begin by recalling the ideas of thread-local reasoning and protocols from concurrent separation logic and explain how we lift those ideas to *node-local* reasoning. Finally, we illustrate the Aneris methodology for specifying, implementing, and verifying distributed systems by developing a simple addition service and a lock server. The distributed systems are composed of individually verified concurrently running nodes communicating asynchronously by exchanging messages that can be reordered or dropped.

2.1   Local and Thread-Local Reasoning

The most important feature of (concurrent) separation logic is, arguably, how it enables scalable modular reasoning about pointer-manipulating programs.

Separation logic is a resource logic, in the sense that propositions denote not only facts about the state, but *ownership* of resources. Originally, separation logic [32] was introduced for modular reasoning about the heap—i.e. the notion of resource was fixed to be logical pieces of the heap. The essential idea is that we can give a local specification $\{P\} e \{v.Q\}$ to a program e involving only the *footprint* of e. Hence, while verifying e, we need not consider the possibility that another piece of code in the program might interfere with e; the program e can be verified without concern for the environment in which e may occur. Local specifications can then be lifted to more global specifications by framing and binding:

$$\frac{\{P\} e \{v.Q\}}{\{P * R\} e \{v.Q * R\}} \qquad \frac{\{P\} e \{v.Q\} \qquad \forall v.\{Q\} K[v] \{w.R\}}{\{P\} K[e] \{w.R\}}$$

where K denotes an evaluation context. The symbol $*$ denotes separating conjunction. Intuitively, $P * Q$ holds for a given resource (in this case a heap) if it can be divided into two disjoint resources such that P holds for one and Q holds for the other. Thus, the frame rule essentially says that executing e for which we know $\{P\} e \{x.Q\}$ cannot possibly affect parts of the heap that are *separate* from its footprint. Another related separation logic connective is $-\!*$, the separating implication. Proposition $P -\!* Q$ describes a resource that, combined with a disjoint resource satisfying P, results in a resource satisfying Q.

Since its introduction, separation logic has been extended to resources beyond heaps and with more sophisticated mechanisms for modular control of interference. Concurrent separation logics (CSLs) [28] allow reasoning about concurrent programs and a preeminent feature of these program logics is again the support for modular reasoning, in this case with respect to concurrency through *thread-local* reasoning. When reasoning about a concurrent program we consider threads one at a time and need not reason about interleavings of threads explicitly. In a way, our frame here includes, in addition to the shared fragments of the heap and other resources, the execution of other threads which can be interleaved throughout the execution of the thread being verified. This can be seen from the following disjoint concurrency rule:

THREAD-PAR
$$\frac{\{P_1\} \langle n; e_1 \rangle \{v.Q_1\} \qquad \{P_2\} \langle n; e_2 \rangle \{v.Q_2\}}{\{P_1 * P_2\} \langle n; e_1 \parallel e_2 \rangle \{v.\exists v_1, v_2.v = (v_1, v_2) * Q_1[v_1/v] * Q_2[v_2/v]\}}$$

where $e_1 \parallel e_2$ denotes parallel composition of expressions e_1 and e_2 and we use the notation $\langle n; e \rangle$ to denote an expression e running on a node with identifier n.[1]

Inevitably, at some point threads typically have to communicate with one another through some kind of shared state, an unavoidable form of interference. The original CSL used a simple form of resource invariant in which ownership of a shared resource can be transferred between threads.

---

[1] In a language with fork-based concurrency, the parallel composition operator is an easily defined construct and the rule is derivable from a more general fork-rule.

A notable program logic in the family of concurrent separation logics is Iris that is specifically designed for reasoning about programs written in concurrent higher-order imperative programming languages. Iris has already proven to be versatile for reasoning about a number of sophisticated properties of programming languages [12, 16, 37]. In order to support modular reasoning about concurrent programs Iris features (1) *impredicative invariants* for expressing protocols on shared state among multiple threads and (2) allows for encoding of *higher-order ghost state* using a form of partial commutative monoids for reasoning about resources. We will give examples of these features and explain them in more detail as needed.

2.2 Node-Local Reasoning

Programs written in AnerisLang are higher-order imperative concurrent programs that run on multiple nodes in a distributed system. When reasoning about distributed systems in Aneris, alongside heap-local and thread-local reasoning, we also reason *node-locally*. When proving correctness of AnerisLang programs we reason about each node of the system in isolation, akin to how we in CSLs reason about each thread in isolation.

By virtue of building on Iris, reasoning in Aneris is naturally modular with respect to separation logic frames and with respect to threads. What Aneris adds on top of this is support for *node-local* reasoning about programs. This is expressed by the following rule:

NODE-PAR
$$\frac{\{P_1 * \mathsf{IsNode}(n_1) * \mathsf{FreePorts}(ip_1, \mathfrak{P})\} \langle n_1; e_1 \rangle \{\mathsf{True}\}}{\{P_2 * \mathsf{IsNode}(n_2) * \mathsf{FreePorts}(ip_2, \mathfrak{P})\} \langle n_2; e_2 \rangle \{\mathsf{True}\}}{\{P_1 * P_2 * \mathsf{FreeIp}(ip_1) * \mathsf{FreeIp}(ip_2)\} \langle \mathfrak{S}; (n_1; ip_1; e_1) \mid\mid\mid (n_2; ip_2; e_2) \rangle \{\mathsf{True}\}}$$

where $\mid\mid\mid$ denotes parallel composition of two nodes with identifier n_1 and n_2 running expressions e_1 and e_2 with IP addresses ip_1 and ip_2.[2] The set $\mathfrak{P} = \{p \mid 0 \leq p \leq 65535\}$ denotes a finite set of ports.

Note that only a distinguished system node $\mathfrak{S}$ can start new nodes (as elaborated on in Sect. 3). In Aneris, the execution of the distributed system starts with the execution of $\mathfrak{S}$ as the only node in the system. In order to start a new node associated with ip address ip one provides the resource $\mathsf{FreeIp}(ip)$ which indicates that ip is not used by other nodes. The node can then rely on the fact that when it starts, all ports on ip are available. The resource $\mathsf{IsNode}(n)$ indicates that the node n is a node in the system and keeps track of abstract state related to our modeling of node n's heap and allocated sockets. To facilitate modular reasoning, free ports can be split: if $A \cap B = \emptyset$ then $\mathsf{FreePorts}(ip, A) * \mathsf{FreePorts}(ip, B) \dashv\vdash \mathsf{FreePorts}(ip, A \cup B)$ where $\dashv\vdash$ denotes

---

[2] In the same way as the parallel composition rule is derived from a more general fork-based rule, this composition rule is also an instance of a more general rule for spawning nodes shown in Sect. 3.

logical equivalence of Aneris propositions (of type *iProp*). We will use FreePort(a) as shorthand for FreePorts($ip, \{p\}$) where $a = (ip, p)$.

Finally, observe that the node-local postconditions are simply True, in contrast to the arbitrary thread-local postconditions in the THREAD-PAR-rule that carry over to the main thread. In the concurrent setting, shared memory provides reliable communication and synchronization between the child threads and the main thread; in the rule for parallel composition, the main thread will wait for the two child processes to finish. In the distributed setting, there are no such guarantees and nodes are separate entities that cannot synchronize with the distinguished system node.

Socket Protocols. Similar to how classical CSLs introduce the concept of resource invariants for expressing protocols on shared state among multiple threads, we introduce the simple and novel concept of *socket protocols* for expressing protocols among multiple nodes. With each socket address—a pair of an IP address and a port—a protocol is associated, which restricts what can be communicated on that socket.

A socket protocol is a predicate $\Phi : Message \to iProp$ on incoming messages received on a particular socket. One can think of this as a form of rely-guarantee reasoning since the socket protocol will be used to restrict the distributed environment's interference with a node on a particular socket. In Aneris we write $a \mapsto \Phi$ to mean that socket address a is governed by the protocol Φ. In particular, if $a \mapsto \Phi$ and $a \mapsto \Psi$ then Φ and Ψ are equivalent.[3] Moreover, the proposition is duplicable: $a \mapsto \Phi \dashv\vdash a \mapsto \Phi * a \mapsto \Phi$.

Conceptually, a socket is an abstract representation of a handle for a local endpoint of some channel. We further restrict channels to use the User Datagram Protocol (UDP) which is *asynchronous*, *connectionless*, and *stateless*. In accordance with UDP, Aneris provides no guarantee of delivery or ordering although we assume duplicate protection. We assume duplicate protection to simplify our examples, as otherwise the code of all of our examples would have to be adapted to cope with duplication of messages. One can think of sockets in Aneris as open-ended multi-party communication channels without synchronization.

It is noteworthy that inter-process communication can happen in two ways. Thread-concurrent programs can communicate both through the shared heap and by sending messages through sockets. For memory-separated programs running on different nodes all communication is by message-passing.

In the logic, we consider both *static* and *dynamic* socket addresses. This distinction is entirely abstract and at the level of the logic. Static addresses come with primordial protocols, agreed upon before starting the distributed system, whereas dynamic addresses do not. Protocols on static addresses are primarily intended for addresses pointing to nodes that offer a service.

To distinguish between static and dynamic addresses, we use a resource Fixed(A) which denotes that the addresses in A are static and should have a fixed

---

[3] The predicate equivalence is under a later modality in order to avoid self-referential paradoxes. We omit it for the sake of presentation as this is an orthogonal issue.

interpretation. This proposition expresses knowledge without asserting ownership of resources and is duplicable: $\mathsf{Fixed}(A) \dashv\vdash \mathsf{Fixed}(A) * \mathsf{Fixed}(A)$.

Corresponding to the two kinds of addresses we have two different rules, SOCKETBIND-STATIC and SOCKETBIND-DYNAMIC, for binding an address to a socket as seen below. Both rules consume an instance of $\mathsf{Fixed}(A)$ and $\mathsf{FreePort}(a)$ as well as a resource $z \hookrightarrow_n \mathsf{None}$. The latter keeps track of the address associated with the socket handle z on node n and ensures that the socket is bound only once as further explained in Sect. 4. Notice that the protocol Φ in SOCKETBIND-DYNAMIC can be freely chosen.

SOCKETBIND-STATIC
$$\{\mathsf{Fixed}(A) * a \in A * \mathsf{FreePort}(a) * z \hookrightarrow_n \mathsf{None}\}$$

$$\langle n; \mathsf{socketbind}\ z\ a \rangle$$

$$\{x.\ x = 0 * z \hookrightarrow_n \mathsf{Some}\ a\}$$

SOCKETBIND-DYNAMIC
$$\{\mathsf{Fixed}(A) * a \notin A * \mathsf{FreePort}(a) * z \hookrightarrow_n \mathsf{None}\}$$

$$\langle n; \mathsf{socketbind}\ z\ a \rangle$$

$$\{x.\ x = 0 * z \hookrightarrow_n \mathsf{Some}\ a * a \Mapsto \Phi\}$$

In the remainder of the paper we will use the following shorthands in order to simplify the presentation of our specifications.

$$\mathsf{Static}(a, A, \Phi) \triangleq \mathsf{Fixed}(A) * a \in A * \mathsf{FreePort}(a) * a \Mapsto \Phi$$
$$\mathsf{Dynamic}(a, A) \triangleq \mathsf{Fixed}(A) * a \notin A * \mathsf{FreePort}(a)$$

2.3   Example: An Addition Service

To illustrate node-local reasoning, socket protocols, and the Aneris methodology for specifying, implementing, and verifying distributed systems we develop a simple addition service that offers to add numbers for clients.

Fig. 1 depicts an implementation of a server and a client written in AnerisLang. Notice that the programs look as if they were written in a realistic functional language with sockets like OCaml. Messages are strings to make programming with sockets easier (similar to send_substring in the Unix module in OCaml).

The server is parameterized over an address on which it will listen for requests. The server allocates a new socket and binds the address to the socket. Then the server starts listening for an incoming message on the socket, calling a handler function on the message, if any. The handler function will deserialize the message, perform the addition, serialize the result, and return it to the sender before recursively listening for new messages.

The client is parameterized over two numbers to compute on, a server address, and a client address. The client allocates a new socket, binds the address to the socket, and serializes the two numbers. In the end, it sends the serialized message

```
rec server a =                        rec client x y srv a =
  let skt = socket () in                let skt = socket () in
  socketbind skt a;                     socketbind skt a;
  listen skt (rec handler msg from =    let m = serialize (x, y) in
    let m = deserialize msg in          sendto skt m srv;
    let res = serialize (π₁ m + π₂ m) in let res = listenwait skt in
    sendto skt res from;                deserialize (π₁ res)
    listen skt handler)
```

Fig. 1. An implementation of an addition service and a client written in AnerisLang. listen and listenwait are convenient helper functions to be found in the appendix [20].

to the server address using the socket and waits for a response, projecting out the result of the addition on arrival and deserializing it.

In order to give the server code a specification we will fix a primordial socket protocol that will govern the address given to the server. The protocol will spell out how the server relies on the socket. We will use $\mathsf{from}(m)$ and $\mathsf{body}(m)$ for projections of the sender and the message body, respectively, from the message m. We define Φ_{add} as follows:

$$\Phi_{add}(m) \triangleq \exists \Psi, x, y. \, \mathsf{from}(m) \mapsto \Psi * \mathsf{body}(m) = serialize(x, y) *$$
$$\forall m', \mathsf{body}(m') = serialize(x + y) \mathbin{-\!*} \Psi(m')$$

Intuitively, the protocol demands that the sender of a message m is governed by some protocol Ψ and that the message body $\mathsf{body}(m)$ must be the serialization of two numbers x and y. Moreover, the sender's protocol must be satisfied if the serialization of $x + y$ is sent as a response.

Using Φ_{add} as the socket protocol, we can give server the specification

$$\{\mathsf{Static}(a, A, \Phi_{add}) * \mathsf{IsNode}(n)\} \, \langle n; \mathsf{server} \ a \rangle \, \{\mathsf{False}\}.$$

The postcondition is allowed to be False as the program does not terminate. The triple guarantees safety which, among others, means that *if* the server responds to communication on address a it does so according to Φ_{add}.

Similarly, using Φ_{add} as a primordial protocol for the server address, we can also give client a specification

$$\{srv \mapsto \Phi_{add} * srv \in A * \mathsf{Dynamic}(a, A) * \mathsf{IsNode}(m)\}$$
$$\langle m; \mathsf{client} \ x \ y \ srv \ a \rangle$$
$$\{v.v = x + y\}$$

that showcases how the client is able to conclude that the response from the server is the sum of the numbers it sent to it. In the proof, when binding a to the socket using SOCKETBIND-DYNAMIC, we introduce the proposition $a \mapsto \Phi_{client}$ where

$$\Phi_{client}(m) \triangleq \mathsf{body}(m) = serialize(x + y)$$

and use it to instantiate Ψ when satisfying Φ_{add}. Using the two specifications and the NODE-PAR-rule it is straightforward to specify and verify a distributed system composed of, e.g., a server and multiple clients.

2.4   Example: A Lock Server

Mutual exclusion in distributed systems is often a necessity and there are many different approaches for providing it. The simplest solution is a centralized algorithm with a single node acting as the coordinator. We will develop this example to showcase a more interesting protocol that relies on ownership transfer of spatial resources between nodes to ensure correctness.

The code for a centralized lock server implementation is shown in Fig. 2.

```
rec lockserver a =
  let lock = ref NONE in
  let skt = socket () in
  socketbind skt a;
  listen skt (rec handler msg from =
    if (msg = "LOCK") then
      match !lock with
        NONE ⇒ lock ← SOME (); sendto skt "YES" from
      | SOME _ ⇒ sendto skt "NO" from
      end
    else lock ← NONE; sendto skt "RELEASED" from
    listen skt handler)
```

Fig. 2. A lock server in AnerisLang.

The lock server declares a node-local variable lock to keep track of whether the lock is taken or not. It allocates a socket, binds the input address to the socket and continuously listens for incoming messages. When a "LOCK" message arrives and the lock is available, the lock gets taken and the server responds "YES". If the lock was already taken, the server will respond "NO". Finally, if the message was not "LOCK", the lock is released and the server responds with "RELEASED".

Our specification of the lock server will be inspired by how a lock can be specified in concurrent separation logic. Thus we first recall how such a specification usually looks like.

Conceptually, a lock can either be unlocked or locked, as described by a two-state labeled transition system.

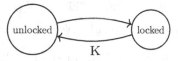

In concurrent separation logic, the lock specification does not describe this transition system directly, but instead focuses on the resources needed for the transitions to take place. In the case of the lock, the resources are simply a non-duplicable resource K, which is needed in order to call the lock's release method. Intuitively, this resource corresponds to the key of the lock.

A typical concurrent separation logic specification for a spin lock module looks roughly like the following:

$$\exists\,\mathsf{isLock}\,.$$
$$\wedge \quad \forall v, K.\ \mathsf{isLock}(v, K) \dashv\vdash \mathsf{isLock}(v, K) * \mathsf{isLock}(v, K)$$
$$\wedge \quad \forall v, K.\ \mathsf{isLock}(v, K) \vdash K * K \Rightarrow \mathsf{False}$$
$$\wedge \quad \{\mathsf{True}\}\ \mathsf{newLock}\ ()\ \{v.\ \exists K.\ \mathsf{isLock}(v, K)\}$$
$$\wedge \quad \forall v.\ \{\mathsf{isLock}(v, K)\}\ \mathsf{acquire}\ v\ \{v.K\}$$
$$\wedge \quad \forall v.\ \{\mathsf{isLock}(v, K) * K\}\ \mathsf{release}\ v\ \{\mathsf{True}\}$$

The intuitive reading of such a specification is:

- Calling newLock will lead to the duplicable knowledge of the return value v being a lock.
- Knowing that a value is a lock, a thread can try to acquire the lock and when it eventually succeeds it will get the key K.
- Only a thread holding this key is allowed to call release.

Sharing of the lock among several threads is achieved by the isLock predicate being duplicable. Mutual exclusion is ensured by the last bullet point together with the requirement of K being non-duplicable whenever we have $\mathsf{isLock}(v, K)$. For a leisurely introduction to such specifications, the reader may consult Birkedal and Bizjak [1].

Let us now return to the distributed lock synchronization. To give clients the possibility of interacting with the lock server as they would with such a concurrent lock module, the specification for the lock server will look like follows.

$$\{K * \mathsf{Static}(a, A, \Phi_{lock})\}\ \langle n;\ \mathtt{lockserver}\ a\rangle\ \{\mathsf{False}\}.$$

This specification simply states that a lock server should have a primordial protocol Φ_{lock} and that it needs the key resource to begin with. To allow for the desired interaction with the server, we define the socket protocol Φ_{lock} as follows:

$$acq(m, \Psi) \triangleq (\mathsf{body}(m) = \text{"LOCK"}) *$$
$$\forall m'.\ (\mathsf{body}(m') = \text{"NO"}) \vee (\mathsf{body}(m') = \text{"YES"} * K) \rightarrow\!\!* \Psi(m')$$
$$rel(m, \Psi) \triangleq (\mathsf{body}(m) = \text{"RELEASE"}) * K *$$
$$\forall m'.\ (\mathsf{body}(m') = \text{"RELEASED"}) \rightarrow\!\!* \Psi(m')$$
$$\Phi_{lock}(m) \triangleq \exists \Psi.\ \mathsf{from}(m) \mapsto \Psi * (acq(m, \Psi) \vee rel(m, \Psi))$$

The protocol Φ_{lock} demands that a client of the lock has to be bound to some protocol Ψ and that the server can receive two types of messages fulfilling either $acq(m, \Psi)$ or $rel(m, \Psi)$. These correspond to the module's two methods acquire and release respectively. In the case of a "LOCK" message, the server will answer either "NO" or "YES" along with the key resource. In either case, the answer should suffice for fulfilling the client protocol Ψ.

Receiving a "RELEASE" request is similar, but the important part is that we require a client to send the key resource K along with the message, which ensures that only the current holder can release the lock.

One difference between the distributed and the concurrent specification is that we allow for the distributed lock to directly deny access. The client can use a simple loop, asking for the lock until it is acquired, if it wishes to wait until the lock can be acquired.

There are several interesting observations one can make about the lock server example: (1) The lock server can allocate, read, and write node-local references but these are hidden in the specification. (2) There are no channel descriptors or assertions on the socket in the code. (3) The lock server provides mutual exclusion by requiring clients to satisfy a sufficient protocol.

3   AnerisLang

AnerisLang is an untyped functional language with higher-order functions, fork-based concurrency, higher-order mutable references, and primitives for communicating over network sockets. The syntax is as follows:

$$v \in Val ::= () \mid b \mid i \mid s \mid \ell \mid z \mid \mathsf{rec}\, f\, x = e \mid \ldots$$
$$e \in Expr ::= v \mid x \mid \mathsf{rec}\, f\, x = e \mid e_1\, e_2 \mid \mathsf{ref}\, e \mid\, !e \mid e_1 \leftarrow e_2 \mid \mathsf{cas}\, e_1\, e_2\, e_3$$
$$\mid \mathsf{find}\, e_1\, e_2\, e_3 \mid \mathsf{substring}\, e_1\, e_2\, e_3 \mid \mathsf{i2s}\, e \mid \mathsf{s2i}\, e$$
$$\mid \mathsf{fork}\, \{e\} \mid \mathsf{start}\, \{n; ip; e\} \mid \mathsf{makeaddress}\, e_1\, e_2$$
$$\mid \mathsf{socket}\, e \mid \mathsf{socketbind}\, e_1\, e_2 \mid \mathsf{sendto}\, e_1\, e_2\, e_3 \mid \mathsf{receivefrom}\, e \mid \ldots$$

We omit the usual operations on pairs, sums, booleans $b \in \mathbb{B}$, and integers $i \in \mathbb{Z}$ which are all standard. We introduce the following syntactic sugar: lambda abstractions $\lambda x.\, e$ defined as $\mathsf{rec}\, \_\, x = e$, let-bindings $\mathsf{let}\, x = e_1\, \mathsf{in}\, e_2$ defined as $(\lambda x.\, e_2)(e_1)$, and sequencing $e_1; e_2$ defined as $\mathsf{let}\, \_ = e_1\, \mathsf{in}\, e_2$.

We have the usual operations on locations $\ell \in Loc$ in the heap: $\mathsf{ref}\, v$ for allocating a new reference, $!\ell$ for dereferencing, and $\ell \leftarrow v$ for assignment. $\mathsf{cas}\, \ell\, v_1\, v_2$ is an atomic compare-and-set operation used to achieve synchronization between threads on a specific memory location ℓ. Operationally, it tests whether ℓ has value v_1 and if so, updates the location to v_2, returning a boolean indicating whether the swap succeeded or not.

The operation find finds the index of a particular substring in a string $s \in String$ and $\mathsf{substring}$ splits a string at given indices, producing the corresponding substring. $\mathsf{i2s}$ and $\mathsf{s2i}$ convert between integers and strings. These operations are mainly used for serialization and deserialization purposes.

The expression $\mathsf{fork}\, \{e\}$ forks off a new (node-local) thread and $\mathsf{start}\, \{n; ip; e\}$ will spawn a new node $n \in Node$ with ip address $ip \in Ip$ running the program e. Note that it is only at the bootstrapping phase of a distributed system that a special system-node $\mathfrak{S}$ will be able to spawn nodes.

We use $z \in Handle$ to range over socket handles created by the socket operation. $\mathsf{makeaddress}$ constructs an address given an ip address and a port, and the network primitives socketbind, sendto, and receivefrom correspond to the similar BSD-socket API methods.

Operational Semantics. We define the operational semantics of AnerisLang in three stages.

We first define a node-local, thread-local, head step reduction $(e, h) \rightsquigarrow (e', h')$ for $e, e' \in Expr$ and $h, h' \in Loc \xrightarrow{\text{fin}} Val$ that handles all pure and heap-related node-local reductions. All rules of the relation are standard.

Next, the node-local head step reduction induces a network-aware head step reduction $(\langle n; e \rangle, \Sigma) \rightarrow (\langle n; e' \rangle, \Sigma')$.

$$\frac{(e, h) \rightsquigarrow (e', h')}{\langle n; e \rangle, (\mathcal{H}[n \mapsto h], \mathcal{S}, \mathcal{P}, \mathcal{M}) \rightarrow \langle n; e' \rangle, (\mathcal{H}[n \mapsto h'], \mathcal{S}, \mathcal{P}, \mathcal{M})}.$$

Here $n \in Node$ denotes a node identifier and $\Sigma, \Sigma' \in NetworkState$ the global network state. Elements of *NetworkState* are tuples $(\mathcal{H}, \mathcal{S}, \mathcal{P}, \mathcal{M})$ tracking heaps $\mathcal{H} \in Node \xrightarrow{\text{fin}} Heap$ and sockets $\mathcal{S} \in Node \xrightarrow{\text{fin}} Handle \xrightarrow{\text{fin}} Option\ Address$ for all nodes, ports in use $\mathcal{P} \in Ip \xrightarrow{\text{fin}} \wp^{\text{fin}}(Port)$, and messages sent $\mathcal{M} \in Id \xrightarrow{\text{fin}} Message$. The induced network-aware reduction is furthermore extended with rules for the network primitives as seen in Fig. 3. The socket operation allocates a new

$$\frac{z \notin \text{dom}(\mathcal{S}(n)) \qquad \mathcal{S}' = \mathcal{S}[n \mapsto \mathcal{S}(n)[z \mapsto \text{None}]]}{\langle n; \text{socket ()} \rangle, (\mathcal{H}, \mathcal{S}, \mathcal{P}, \mathcal{M}) \rightarrow \langle n; z \rangle, (\mathcal{H}, \mathcal{S}', \mathcal{P}, \mathcal{M})}$$

$$\frac{p \notin \mathcal{P}(ip) \qquad \mathcal{S}' = \mathcal{S}[n \mapsto \mathcal{S}(n)[z \mapsto \text{Some } (ip, p)]] \qquad \mathcal{P}' = \mathcal{P}[ip \mapsto \mathcal{P}(ip) \cup \{p\}]}{\langle n; \text{socketbind } z\ (ip, p) \rangle, (\mathcal{H}, \mathcal{S}, \mathcal{P}, \mathcal{M}) \rightarrow \langle n; 0 \rangle, (\mathcal{H}, \mathcal{S}', \mathcal{P}', \mathcal{M})}$$

$$\frac{\mathcal{S}(n)(z) = \text{Some } from \qquad i \notin dom(\mathcal{M}) \qquad \mathcal{M}' = \mathcal{M}[i \mapsto (from, to, msg, \text{SENT})]}{\langle n; \text{sendto } z\ msg\ to \rangle, (\mathcal{H}, \mathcal{S}, \mathcal{P}, \mathcal{M}) \rightarrow \langle n; |msg| \rangle, (\mathcal{H}, \mathcal{S}, \mathcal{P}, \mathcal{M}')}$$

$$\frac{\mathcal{S}(n)(z) = \text{Some } to \qquad \mathcal{M}' = \mathcal{M}[i \mapsto (from, to, msg, \text{RECEIVED})]}{\langle n; \text{receivefrom } z \rangle, (\mathcal{H}, \mathcal{S}, \mathcal{P}, \mathcal{M}) \rightarrow \langle n; \text{Some } (msg, from) \rangle, (\mathcal{H}, \mathcal{S}, \mathcal{P}, \mathcal{M}')}$$

$$\frac{\mathcal{S}(n)(z) = \text{Some } to}{\langle n; \text{receivefrom } z \rangle, (\mathcal{H}, \mathcal{S}, \mathcal{P}, \mathcal{M}) \rightarrow \langle n; \text{None} \rangle, (\mathcal{H}, \mathcal{S}, \mathcal{P}, \mathcal{M})}$$

Fig. 3. An excerpt of the rules for network-aware head reduction.

unbound socket using a fresh handle z for a node n and socketbind binds a socket address a to an unbound socket z if the address and port p is not already in use. Hereafter, the port is no longer available in $\mathcal{P}'(ip)$. For bound sockets, sendto sends a message msg to a destination address to from the sender's address *from* found in the bound socket. The message is assigned a unique identifier and tagged with a status flag SENT indicating that the message has been sent and not received. The operation returns the number of characters sent.

To model possibly dropped or delayed messages we introduce two rules for receiving messages using the receivefrom operation that on a bound socket either returns a previously unreceived message or nothing. If a message is received the status flag of the message is updated to RECEIVED

Third and finally, using standard *call-by-value right-to-left evaluation contexts* $K \in Ectx$ we lift the node-local head reduction to a *distributed systems* reduction $\twoheadrightarrow$ shown below. We write $\twoheadrightarrow^*$ for its reflexive-transitive closure. The distributed systems relation reduces by picking a thread on any node or forking off a new thread on a node.

$$\frac{(\langle n; e \rangle, \Sigma) \to (\langle n; e' \rangle, \Sigma')}{(\boldsymbol{T_1} + [\langle n; K[e] \rangle] + \boldsymbol{T_2}, \Sigma) \twoheadrightarrow (\boldsymbol{T_1} + [\langle n; K[e'] \rangle] + \boldsymbol{T_2}; \Sigma')}$$

$$(\boldsymbol{T_1} + [\langle n; K[\textsf{fork } \{e\}] \rangle] + \boldsymbol{T_2}, \Sigma) \twoheadrightarrow (\boldsymbol{T_1} + [\langle n; K[()] \rangle] + \boldsymbol{T_2} + [\langle n; e \rangle], \Sigma)$$

4   The Aneris Logic

As a consequence of building on the Iris framework, the Aneris logic features all the usual connectives and rules of higher-order separation logic, some of which are shown in the grammar below.[4] The full expressiveness of the logic can be exploited when giving specifications to programs or stating protocols.

$$P, Q \in iProp ::= \textsf{True} \mid \textsf{False} \mid P \wedge Q \mid P \vee Q \mid P \Rightarrow Q \mid$$
$$\forall x. P \mid \exists x. P \mid P * Q \mid P \twoheadrightarrow Q \mid t = u \mid$$
$$\ell \mapsto_n v \mid \boxed{P} \mid \lceil \boxed{a} \rceil^\gamma \mid \{P\} \langle n; e \rangle \{x. Q\} \mid \dots$$

Note that in Aneris the usual points-to connective about the heap, $\ell \mapsto_n v$, is indexed by a node identifier $n \in Node$, asserting ownership of the singleton heap mapping ℓ to v on node n.

The logic features (impredicative) invariants $\boxed{P}$ and user-definable ghost state via the proposition $\lceil \boxed{a} \rceil^\gamma$, which asserts ownership of a piece of ghost state a at ghost location γ. The logical support for user-defined invariants and ghost state allows one to relate (ghost and physical) resources to each other; this is vital for our specifications as will become evident in Sect. 5 and Sect. 6. We refer to Jung et al. [14] for a more thorough treatment of user-defined ghost state.

To reason about AnerisLang programs, the logic features Hoare triples.[5] The intuitive reading of the Hoare triple $\{P\} \langle n; e \rangle \{x. Q\}$ is that if the program e on

---

[4] To avoid the issue of reentrancy, invariants are annotated with a *namespace* and Hoare triples with a *mask*. We omit both for the sake of presentation as they are orthogonal issues.

[5] In both Iris and Aneris the notion of a Hoare triple is defined in terms of a *weakest precondition* but this will not be important for the remainder of this paper.

node n is run in a distributed system s satisfying P, then the computation does not get stuck and, moreover, if it terminates with a value v and in a system s', then s' satisfies $Q[v/x]$. In other words, a Hoare triple implies safety and states that all spatial resources that are used by e are contained in the precondition P.

In contrast to spatial propositions that express *ownership*, e.g., $\ell \mapsto_n v$, propositions like $\boxed{P}$ and $\{P\} \langle n; e\rangle \{x.\, Q\}$ express *knowledge* of properties that, once true, hold true forever. We call this class of propositions *persistent*. Persistent propositions P can be freely duplicated: $P \dashv\vdash P * P$.

4.1   The Program Logic

The Aneris proof rules include the usual rules of concurrent separation logic for Hoare triples, allowing formal reasoning about node-local pure computations, manipulations of the the heap, and forking of threads. Expressions e are annotated with a node identifier n, but the rules are otherwise standard.

To reason about individual nodes in a distributed system in isolation, Aneris introduces the following rule:

$$\text{START} \atop \dfrac{\{P * \mathsf{IsNode}(n) * \mathsf{FreePorts}(ip, \mathfrak{P})\} \langle n; e\rangle \{\mathsf{True}\}}{\{P * \mathsf{Freelp}(ip)\} \langle \mathfrak{S}; \mathsf{start}\ \{n; ip; e\}\rangle \{x.\, x = ()\}}$$

where $\mathfrak{P} = \{p \mid 0 \le p \le 65535\}$. This rule is the key rule allowing node-local reasoning; the rule expresses exactly that to reason about a distributed system it suffices to reason about each node in isolation.

As described in Sect. 3, only the distinguished system node $\mathfrak{S}$ can start new nodes—this is also reflected in the START-rule. In order to start a new node associated with IP address ip, the resource $\mathsf{Freelp}(ip)$ is provided. This indicates that ip is not used by other nodes. When reasoning about the node n, the proof can rely on all ports on ip being available. The resource $\mathsf{IsNode}(n)$ indicates that the node n is a valid node in the system and keeps track of abstract state related to the modeling of node n's heap and sockets. $\mathsf{IsNode}(n)$ is persistent and hence duplicable.

Network Communication. To reason about network communication in a distributed system, the logic includes a series of rules for reasoning about socket manipulation: allocation of sockets, binding of addresses to sockets, sending via sockets, and receiving from sockets.

To allocate a socket it suffices to prove that the node n is valid by providing the $\mathsf{IsNode}(n)$ resource. In return, an unbound socket resource $z \hookrightarrow_n \mathsf{None}$ is given.

$$\text{SOCKET} \atop \{\mathsf{IsNode}(n)\} \langle n; \mathsf{socket}\ ()\rangle \{z.\, z \hookrightarrow_n \mathsf{None}\}$$

The socket resource $z \hookrightarrow_n o$ keeps track of the address associated with the socket handle z on node n and takes part in ensuring that the socket is bound only once. It behaves similarly to the points-to connective for the heap, e.g., $z \hookrightarrow_n o * z \hookrightarrow_n o' \Rightarrow$ False.

As briefly touched upon in Sect. 2, the logic offers two different rules for binding an address to a socket depending on whether or not the address has a (at the level of the logic) primordial, agreed upon protocol. To distinguish between such static and dynamic addresses, we use a persistent resource $\mathsf{Fixed}(A)$ to keep track of the set of addresses that have a fixed socket protocol.

To reason about a static address binding to a socket z it suffices to show that the address a being bound has a fixed interpretation (by being in the "fixed" set), that the port of the address is free, and that the socket is not bound.

> SOCKETBIND-STATIC
> $\{\mathsf{Fixed}(A) * a \in A * \mathsf{FreePort}(a) * z \hookrightarrow_n \mathsf{None}\}$
>
> $\langle n; \mathsf{socketbind}\ z\ a\rangle$
>
> $\{x.\, x = 0 * z \hookrightarrow_n \mathsf{Some}\ a\}$

In accordance with the BSD-socket API, the bind operation returns the integer 0 and the socket resource gets updated, reflecting the fact that the binding took place.

The rule for dynamic address binding is similar but the address a should not have a fixed interpretation. Moreover, the user of the logic is free to pick the socket protocol Φ to govern address a.

> SOCKETBIND-DYNAMIC
> $\{\mathsf{Fixed}(A) * a \notin A * \mathsf{FreePort}(a) * z \hookrightarrow_n \mathsf{None}\}$
>
> $\langle n; \mathsf{socketbind}\ z\ a\rangle$
>
> $\{x.\, x = 0 * z \hookrightarrow_n \mathsf{Some}\ a * a \mapsto \Phi\}$

To reason about sending a message on a socket z it suffices to show that z is bound, that the destination of the message is governed by a protocol Φ, and that the message satisfies the protocol.

> SENDTO
> $\{z \hookrightarrow_n \mathsf{Some}\ from * to \mapsto \Phi * \Phi((from, to, msg, \mathrm{SENT}))\}$
>
> $\langle n; \mathsf{sendto}\ z\ msg\ to\rangle$
>
> $\{x.\, x = |msg| * z \hookrightarrow_n \mathsf{Some}\ from\}$

Finally, to reason about receiving a message on a socket z the socket must be bound to an address governed by a protocol Φ.

> RECEIVEFROM
> $\{z \hookrightarrow_n \mathsf{Some}\ to * to \mapsto \Phi\}$
>
> $\langle n; \mathsf{receivefrom}\ z\rangle$
>
> $\left\{ \begin{array}{l} x.\, z \hookrightarrow_n \mathsf{Some}\ to * \\ \quad \left(x = \mathsf{None} \vee \left(\exists m.\, x = \mathsf{Some}\,(\mathsf{body}(m), \mathsf{from}(m)) * \Phi(m) * \mathsf{R}(m)\right)\right) \end{array} \right\}$

When trying to receive a message on a socket, either a message will be received or no message is available. This is reflected directly in the logic: if no message was received, no resources are obtained. If a message m is received, the resources prescribed by $\Phi(m)$ are transferred together with an unmodifiable certificate $\mathsf{R}(m)$ accounting logically for the fact that message m was received. This certificate can in the logic be used to talk about messages that has actually been received in contrast to arbitrary messages. In our specification of the two-phase commit protocol presented in Sect. 6, the notion of a vote denotes not just a message with the right content but only one that has been sent by a participant and received by the coordinator.

4.2 Adequacy for Aneris

We now state a formal adequacy theorem, which expresses that Aneris guarantees both safety, and, that all protocols are adhered to.

To state our theorem we introduce a notion of *initial state coherence*: A set of addresses $A \subseteq Address = Ip \times Port$ and a map $\mathcal{P} : Ip \xrightarrow{\text{fin}} \wp^{\text{fin}}(Port)$ are said to satisfy initial state coherence if the following hold: (1) if $(i, p) \in A$ then $i \in \text{dom}(\mathcal{P})$, and (2) if $i \in \text{dom}(\mathcal{P})$ then $\mathcal{P}(i) = \emptyset$.

Theorem 1 (Adequacy). *Let φ be a first-order predicate over values, i.e., a meta logic predicate (as opposed to Iris predicates), let $\mathcal{P}$ be a map $Ip \xrightarrow{\text{fin}} \wp^{\text{fin}}(Port)$, and $A \subseteq Address$ such that A and $\mathcal{P}$ satisfy initial state coherence. Given a primordial socket protocol Φ_a for each $a \in A$, suppose that the Hoare triple*

$$\left\{ \mathsf{Fixed}(A) * \underset{a \in A}{\text{\Large\bigstar}} a \mapsto \Phi_a * \underset{i \in \text{dom}(\mathcal{P})}{\text{\Large\bigstar}} \mathsf{Freelp}(i) \right\} \langle n_1; e \rangle \{ v.\varphi(v) \}$$

is derivable in Aneris.
If we have

$$(\langle n_1; e \rangle, (\emptyset, \emptyset, \mathcal{P}, \emptyset)) \rightarrow^* ([\langle n_1; e_1 \rangle, \langle n_2; e_2 \rangle, \ldots \langle n_m; e_m \rangle], \Sigma)$$

then the following properties hold:

1. *If e_1 is a value, then $\varphi(e_1)$ holds at the meta-level.*
2. *Each e_i that is not a value can make a node-local, thread-local reduction step.*

Given predefined socket protocols for all primordial protocols and the necessary free IP addresses, this theorem provides the normal adequacy guarantees of Iris-like logics, namely *safety*, i.e., that nodes and threads on nodes cannot get stuck and that the postcondition holds for the resulting value. Notice, however, that this theorem also implies that all nodes adhere to the agreed upon protocols; otherwise, a node not adhering to a protocol would be able to cause another node to get stuck, which the adequacy theorem explicitly guarantees against.

5   Case Study 1: A Load Balancer

AnerisLang supports concurrent execution of threads on nodes through the
fork $\{e\}$ primitive. We will illustrate the benefits of node-local concurrency
by presenting an example of server-side load balancing.

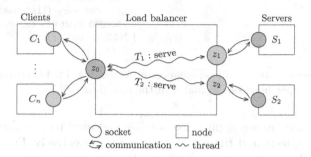

Fig. 4. The architecture of a distributed system with a load balancer and two servers.

Implementation. In the case of server-side load balancing, the work distribution
is implemented by a program listening on a socket that clients send their requests
to. The program forwards the requests to an available server, waits for the
response from the server, and sends the answer back to the client. In order to
handle requests from several clients simultaneously, the load balancer can employ
concurrency by forking off a new thread for every available server in the system
that is capable of handling such requests. Each of these threads will then listen
for and forward requests. The architecture of such a system with two servers and
n clients is illustrated in Fig. 4.

An implementation of a load balancer is shown in Fig. 5. The load balancer is
parameterized over an IP address, a port, and a list of servers. It creates a socket
(corresponding to z_0 in Fig. 4), binds the address, and folds a function over the
list of servers. This function forks off a new thread (corresponding to T_1 and T_2
in Fig. 4) for each server that runs the serve function with the newly-created
socket, the given IP address, a fresh port number, and a server as arguments.

The serve function creates a new socket (corresponding to z_1 and z_2 in Fig. 4),
binds the given address to the socket, and continuously tries to receive a client
request on the main socket (z_0) given as input. If a request is received, it forwards
the request to its server and waits for an answer. The answer is passed on to
the client via the main socket. In this way, the entire load balancing process is
transparent to the client, whose view will be the same as if it was communicating
with just a single server handling all requests itself as the load balancer is simply
relaying requests and responses.

Specification and Protocols. To provide a general, reusable specification of the
load balancer, we will parameterize its socket protocol by two predicates P_{in}
and P_{out} that are both predicates on a message m and a meta-language value

```
rec load_balancer ip port servers =          rec serve main ip port srv =
  let skt = socket () in                       let skt = socket () in
  let a = makeaddress ip port in               let a = makeaddress ip port in
  socketbind skt a;                            socketbind skt a;
  listfold (λ server, acc.                     (rec loop () =
    fork { serve skt ip acc server };            match receivefrom main with
    acc + 1) 1100 servers                          SOME m =>
                                                     sendto skt (π₁ m) srv;
                                                     let res = π₁ (listenwait skt) in
                                                     sendto main res (π₂ m); loop ()
                                                 | NONE => loop ()
                                               end) ()
```

Fig. 5. An implementation of a load balancer in AnerisLang. listfold and listenwait
are convenient helper functions available in the appendix [20].

v. The two predicates are application specific and used to give logical accounts
of the client requests and the server responses, respectively. Furthermore, we
parameterize the protocol by a predicate P_{val} on a meta-language value that
will allows us to maintain ghost state between the request and response as will
become evident in following.

In our specification, the sockets where the load balancer and the servers
receive requests (the blue sockets in Fig. 4) will all be governed by the same
socket protocol Φ_{rel} such that the load balancer may seamlessly relay requests
and responses between the main socket and the servers, without invalidating any
socket protocols. We define the generic relay socket protocol Φ_{rel} as follows:

$$\Phi_{rel}(P_{val}, P_{in}, P_{out})(m) \triangleq \exists \Psi, v.\, \mathsf{from}(m) \Rightarrow \Psi * P_{in}(m,v) * P_{val}(v) *$$
$$(\forall m'.\, P_{val}(v) * P_{out}(m',v) \ast\!\!-\!\!* \Psi(m'))$$

When verifying a request, this protocol demands that the sender (corresponding
to the red sockets in Fig. 4) is governed by some protocol Ψ, that the request
fulfills the P_{in} and P_{val} predicates, and that Ψ is satisfied given a response that
maintains P_{val} and satisfies P_{out}.

When verifying the load balancer receiving a request m from a client, we
obtain the resources $P_{in}(m,v)$ and $P_{val}(v)$ for some v according to Φ_{rel}. This
suffices for passing the request along to a server. However, to forward the server's
response to the client we must know that the server behaves faithfully and
gave us the response to the right request value v. Φ_{rel} does not give us this
immediately as the v is existentially quantified. Hence we define a ghost resource
$\mathsf{LB}(\pi, s, v)$ that provides fractional ownership for $\pi \in (0,1]$, which satisfies
$\mathsf{LB}(1,s,v) \dashv\vdash \mathsf{LB}(\frac{1}{2},s,v) * \mathsf{LB}(\frac{1}{2},s,v)$, and for which v can only get updated if
$\pi = 1$ and in particular $\mathsf{LB}(\pi,s,v) * \mathsf{LB}(\pi,s,v') \implies v = v'$ for any π. Using
this resource, the server with address s will have $P_{LB}(s)$ as its instantiation of
P_{val} where

$$P_{LB}(s)(v) \triangleq \mathsf{LB}(\tfrac{1}{2}, s, v).$$

When verifying the load balancer, we will update this resource to the request
value v when receiving a request (as we have the full fraction) and transfer

$LB(\frac{1}{2}, s, v)$ to the server with address s handling the request and, according to Φ_{rel}, it will be required to send it back along with the result. Since the server logically only gets half ownership, the value cannot be changed. Together with the fact that v is also an argument to P_{in} and P_{out}, this ensures that the server fulfills P_{out} for the same value as it received P_{in} for. The socket protocol for the serve function's socket (z_1 and z_2 in Fig. 4) that communicates with a server with address s can now be stated as follows.

$$\Phi_{serve}(s, P_{out})(m) \triangleq \exists v.\, LB(\tfrac{1}{2}, s, v) * P_{out}(m, v)$$

Since all calls to the serve function need access to the main socket in order to receive requests, we will keep the socket resource required in an invariant I_{LB} which is shared among all the threads:

$$I_{LB}(n, z, a) \triangleq \boxed{z \hookrightarrow_n \mathsf{Some}\ a}$$

The specification for the serve function becomes:

$$\left\{ \begin{array}{l} I_{LB}(n, main, a_{main}) * \mathsf{Dynamic}((ip, p), A) * \mathsf{IsNode}(n) * LB(1, s, v) * \\ a_{main} \mapsto \Phi_{rel}(\lambda\_.\mathsf{True}, P_{in}, P_{out}) * s \mapsto \Phi_{rel}(P_{LB}(s), P_{in}, P_{out}) \end{array} \right\}$$

$$\langle n;\, \mathtt{serve}\ main\ ip\ p\ s \rangle$$

$$\{\mathsf{False}\}$$

The specification requires the address a_{main} of the socket $main$ to be governed by Φ_{rel} with a trivial instantiation of P_{val} and the address s of the server to be governed by Φ_{rel} with P_{val} instantiated by P_{LB}. The specification moreover expects resources for a dynamic setup, the invariant that owns the resource needed to verify use of the $main$ socket, and a full instance of the $LB(1, s, v)$ resource for some arbitrary v.

With this specification in place the complete specification of our load balancer is immediate (note that it is parameterized by P_{in} and P_{out}):

$$\left\{ \begin{array}{l} \mathsf{Static}((ip, p), A, \phi_{rel}(\lambda\_.\mathsf{True}, P_{in}, P_{out})) * \mathsf{IsNode}(n) * \\[6pt] \left(\displaystyle\mathop{\Asterisk}_{p' \in ports} \mathsf{Dynamic}((ip, p'), A) \right) * \\[12pt] \left(\displaystyle\mathop{\Asterisk}_{s \in srvs} \exists v.\, LB(1, s, v) * s \mapsto \phi_{rel}(P_{LB}(s), P_{in}, P_{out}) \right) \end{array} \right\}$$

$$\langle n;\, \mathtt{load\_balancer}\ ip\ p\ srvs \rangle$$

$$\{\mathsf{True}\}$$

where $ports = [1100, \cdots, 1100 + |srvs|]$. In addition to the protocol setup for each server as just described, for each port $p' \in ports$ which will become the endpoint for a corresponding server, we need the resources for a dynamic setup, and we need the resource for a static setup on the main input address (ip, p).

In the accompanying Coq development we provide an implementation of the addition service from Sect. 2.3, both in the single server case and in a load balanced case. For this particular proof we let the meta-language value v be a pair of integers corresponding to the expected arguments. In order to instantiate the load balancer specification we choose

$$P_{in}^{add}(m, (v_1, v_2)) \triangleq \mathsf{body}(m) = serialize(v_1, v_2)$$

$$P_{out}^{add}(m, (v_1, v_2)) \triangleq \mathsf{body}(m) = serialize(v_1 + v_2)$$

with $serialize$ being the same serialization function from Sect. 2.3. We build and verify two distributed systems, (1) one consisting of two clients and an addition server and (2) one including two clients, a load balancer and three addition servers. We prove both of these systems safe and the proofs utilize the specifications we have given for the individual components. Notice that $\Phi_{rel}(\lambda\_.\mathsf{True}, P_{in}^{add}, P_{out}^{add})$ and Φ_{add} from Sect. 2.3 are the same. This is why we can use the same client specification in both system proofs. Hence, we have demonstrated Aneris' ability and support for horizontal composition of the same modules in different systems.

While the load balancer demonstrates the use of node-local concurrency, its implementation does not involve shared memory concurrency, i.e., synchronization among the node-local threads. The appendix [20] includes an example of a distributed system, where clients interact with a server that implements a bag. The server uses multiple threads to handle client requests concurrently and the threads use a *shared* bag data structure governed by a lock. This example demonstrates Aneris' ability to support both shared-memory concurrency and distributed networking.

6   Case Study 2: Two-Phase Commit

A typical problem in distributed systems is that of consensus and distributed commit; an operation should be performed by all participants in a system or none at all. The *two-phase commit* protocol (TPC) by Gray [6] is a classic solution to this problem. We study this protocol in Aneris as (1) it is widely used in the real-world, (2) it is a complex network protocol and thus serves as a decent benchmark for reasoning in Aneris, and (3) to show how an implementation can be given a specification that is usable for a client that abstractly relies on some consensus protocol.

The two-phase commit protocol consists of the following two phases, each involving two steps:

1. (a) The coordinator sends out a vote request to each participant.
   (b) A participant that receives a vote request replies with a vote for either commit or abort.
2. (a) The coordinator collects all votes and determines a result. If all participants voted commit, the coordinator sends a global commit to all. Otherwise, the coordinator sends a global abort to all.

(b) All participants that voted for a commit wait for the final verdict from the coordinator. If the participant receives a global commit it locally commits the transaction, otherwise the transaction is locally aborted. All participants must acknowledge.

Our implementation and specification details can be found in the appendix [20] and in the accompanying Coq development, but we will emphasize a few key points.

To provide general, reusable implementations and specifications of the coordinator and participants implementing TPC, we do not define how requests, votes, nor decisions look like. We leave it to a user of the module to provide decidable predicates matching the application specific needs and to define the logical, local pre- and postconditions, P and Q, of participants for the operation in question.

Our specifications use fractional ghost resources to keep track of coordinator and participant state w.r.t. the coordinator and participant transition systems indicated in the protocol description above. Similar to our previous case study, we exploit partial ownership to limit when transitions can be made. When verifying a participant, we keep track of their state and the coordinator's state and require all participants' view of the coordinator state to be in agreement through an invariant.

In short, our specification of TPC

- ensures the participants and coordinator act according to the protocol, *i.e.*,
  - the coordinator decides based on all the participant votes,
  - participants act according to the global decision,
  - if the decision was to commit, we obtain the resources described by Q for all participants,
  - if the decision was to abort, we still have the resources described by P for all participants,
- does not require the coordinator to be primordial, so the coordinator could change from round to round.

6.1   A Replicated Log

In a distributed replicated logging system, a log is stored on several databases distributed across several nodes where the system ensures consistency among the logs through a consensus protocol. We have verified such a system implemented on top of the TPC coordinator and participant modules to showcase vertical composition of complex protocols in Aneris as illustrated in Fig. 6. The blue parts of the diagram constitute node-local instantiations of the TPC modules invoked by the nodes to handle the consensus process. As noted by Sergey et al. [35], clients of core consensus protocols have not received much focus from other major verification efforts [7, 30, 40].

Our specification of a replicated logging system draws on the generality of the TPC specification. In this case, we use fractional ghost state to keep track of two related pieces of information. The first keeps a logical account of the log l already

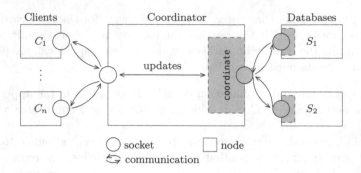

Fig. 6. The architecture of a replicated logging system implemented using the TPC modules (the blue parts of the diagram) with a coordinator and two databases (S_1 and S_2) each storing a copy of the log.

stored in the database at a node at address a, $\mathsf{LOG}(\pi, a, l)$. The second one keeps track of what the log should be updated to, if the pending round of consensus succeeds. This is a pair of the existing log l and the (pending) change s proposed in this round, $\mathsf{PEND}(\pi, a, (l, s))$. We exploit fractional resource ownership by letting the coordinator, logically, keep half of the pending log resources at all times. Together with suitable local pre- and postconditions for the databases, this prevents the databases from doing arbitrary changes to the log. Concretely, we instantiate P and Q of the TPC module as follows:

$$P_{rep}(p)(m) \triangleq \exists l, s. (m = \text{"REQUEST\_"} @ s) * \mathsf{LOG}(\tfrac{1}{2}, p, l) * \mathsf{PEND}(\tfrac{1}{2}, p, (l, s))$$

$$Q_{rep}(p)(n) \triangleq \exists l, s. \mathsf{LOG}(\tfrac{1}{2}, p, l@s) * \mathsf{PEND}(\tfrac{1}{2}, p, (l, s))$$

where @ denotes string concatenation. Note how the request message specifies the proposed change (since the string that we would like to add to the log is appended to the requests message) and how we ensure consistency by making sure the two ghost assertions hold for the same log. Even though l and s are existentially quantified, we know the logs cannot be inconsistent since the coordinator retains partial knowledge of the log. Due to the guarantees given by TPC specification, this implies that if the global decision was to commit a change this change will have happened locally on all databases, cf. $\mathsf{LOG}(\tfrac{1}{2}, p, l@s)$ in Q_{rep}, and if the decision was to abort, then the log remains unchanged on all databases, cf. $\mathsf{LOG}(\tfrac{1}{2}, p, l)$ in P_{rep}. We refer to the appendix [20] or the Coq development for further details.

7   Related Work

Verification of distributed systems has received a fair amount of attention. In order to give a better overview, we have divided related work into four categories.

Model-Checking of Distributed Protocols. Previous work on verification of distributed systems has mainly focused on verification of protocols or core network components through model-checking. Frameworks for showing safety and liveness properties, such as SPIN [9], and TLA+ [23], have had great success. A benefit of using model-checking frameworks is that they allow to state both safety and liveness assertions as LTL assertions [29]. Mace [17] provides a suite for building and model-checking distributed systems with asynchronous protocols, including liveness conditions. Chapar [25] allows for model-checking of programs that use causally consistent distributed key-value stores. Neither of these languages provide higher-order functions or thread-based concurrency.

Session Types for Giving Types to Protocols. Session types have been studied for a wide range of process calculi, in particular, typed π-calculus. The idea is to describe two-party communication protocols as a type to ensure communication safety and progress [10]. This has been extended to multi-party asynchronous channels [11], multi-role types [2] which informally model topics of actor-based message-passing and dependent session types allowing quantification over messages [38]. Our socket protocol definitions are quite similar to the multi-party asynchronous session types with progress encoded by having suitable ghost-assertions and using the magic wand. Actris [8] is a logic for session-type based reasoning about message-passing in actor-based languages.

Hoare Style Reasoning About Distributed Systems. Disel [35] is a Hoare Type Theory for distributed program verification in Coq with ideas from separation logic. It provides the novel protocol-tailored rules WithInv and Frame which allow for modularity of proofs under the condition of an inductive invariant and distributed systems composition. In Disel, programs can be extracted into runnable OCaml programs, which is on our agenda for future work.

IronFleet [7] allows for building provably correct distributed systems by combining TLA-style state-machine refinement with Hoare-logic verification in a layered approach, all embedded in Dafny [24]. IronFleet also allows for liveness assertions. For a comparison of Disel and IronFleet to Aneris from a modularity point of view we refer to the Introduction section.

Other Distributed Verification Efforts. Verdi [40] is a framework for writing and verifying implementations of distributed algorithms in Coq, providing a novel approach to network semantics and fault models. To achieve compositionality, the authors introduced *verified system transformers*, that is, a function that transforms one implementation to another implementation with different assumptions about its environment. This makes vertical composition difficult for clients of proven protocols and in comparison AnerisLang seems more expressive.

EventML [30, 31] is a functional language in the ML family that can be used for coding distributed protocols using high-level combinators from the Logic of Events, and verify them in the Nuprl interactive theorem prover. It is not quite clear how modular reasoning works, since one works within the model, however, the notion of a central main observer is akin to our distinguished system node.

8 Conclusion

Distributed systems are ubiquitous and hence it is essential to be able to verify them. In this paper we presented Aneris, a framework for writing and verifying distributed systems in Coq built on top of the Iris framework. From a programming point of view, the important aspect of AnerisLang is that it is feature-rich: it is a concurrent ML-like programming language with network primitives. This allows individual nodes to internally use higher-order heap and concurrency to write efficient programs.

The Aneris logic provides node-local reasoning through socket protocols. That is, we can reason about individual nodes in isolation as we reason about individual threads. We demonstrate the versatility of Aneris by studying interesting distributed systems both implemented and verified within Aneris. The adequacy theorem of Aneris implies that these programs are safe to run.

Table 1. Sizes of implementations, specifications, and proofs in lines of code. When proving adequacy, the system must be closed.

Module	Implementation	Specification	Proofs
Load Balancer (Sect. 5)			
Load balancer	18	78	95
Addition Service			
Server	11	15	38
Client	9	14	26
Adequacy (1 server, 2 clients)	5	12	62
Adequacy w. Load Balancing (3 servers, 2 clients)	16	28	175
Two-phase commit (Sect. 6)			
Coordinator	18	181	265
Participant	11		280
Replicated logging (Sect. 6 + appendix [20])			
Instantiation of TPC	-	85	-
Logger	22	19	95
Database	24	20	190
Adequacy (2 dbs, 1 coordinator, 2 clients)	13	-	137

Relating the verification sizes of the modules from Table 1 to other formal verification efforts in Coq indicates that it is easier to specify and verify systems in Aneris. The total work required to prove two-phase commit with replicated logging is 1,272 lines which is just half of the lines needed for proving the inductive invariant for TPC in other works [35]. However, extensive work has gone into Iris Proof Mode thus it is hard to conclude that Aneris requires less verification effort and does not just have richer tactics.

Acknowledgments

This work was supported in part by the ModuRes Sapere Aude Advanced Grant from The Danish Council for Independent Research for the Natural Sciences (FNU); a Villum Investigator grant (no. 25804), Center for Basic Research in Program Verification (CPV), from the VILLUM Foundation; and the Flemish research fund (FWO).

Bibliography

[1] Birkedal, L., Bizjak, A.: Lecture notes on Iris: Higher-order concurrent separation logic (2017), URL http://iris-project.org/tutorial-pdfs/iris-lecture-notes.pdf

[2] Deniélou, P., Yoshida, N.: Dynamic multirole session types. In: Ball, T., Sagiv, M. (eds.) Proceedings of the 38th ACM SIGPLAN-SIGACT Symposium on Principles of Programming Languages, POPL 2011, Austin, TX, USA, January 26-28, 2011, pp. 435–446, ACM (2011), https://doi.org/10.1145/1926385.1926435

[3] Dinsdale-Young, T., Birkedal, L., Gardner, P., Parkinson, M.J., Yang, H.: Views: compositional reasoning for concurrent programs. In: Giacobbazzi, R., Cousot, R. (eds.) The 40th Annual ACM SIGPLAN-SIGACT Symposium on Principles of Programming Languages, POPL '13, Rome, Italy - January 23 - 25, 2013, pp. 287–300, ACM (2013), https://doi.org/10.1145/2429069.2429104

[4] Dinsdale-Young, T., Dodds, M., Gardner, P., Parkinson, M.J., Vafeiadis, V.: Concurrent abstract predicates. In: D'Hondt, T. (ed.) ECOOP 2010 - Object-Oriented Programming, 24th European Conference, Maribor, Slovenia, June 21-25, 2010. Proceedings, Lecture Notes in Computer Science, vol. 6183, pp. 504–528, Springer (2010), https://doi.org/10.1007/978-3-642-14107-2_24

[5] Floyd, R.W.: Assigning meanings to programs. Mathematical aspects of computer science **19**(19-32), 1 (1967)

[6] Gray, J.: Notes on data base operating systems. In: Flynn, M.J., Gray, J., Jones, A.K., Lagally, K., Opderbeck, H., Popek, G.J., Randell, B., Saltzer, J.H., Wiehle, H. (eds.) Operating Systems, An Advanced Course, Lecture Notes in Computer Science, vol. 60, pp. 393–481, Springer (1978), https://doi.org/10.1007/3-540-08755-9_9

[7] Hawblitzel, C., Howell, J., Kapritsos, M., Lorch, J.R., Parno, B., Roberts, M.L., Setty, S.T.V., Zill, B.: Ironfleet: proving practical distributed systems correct. In: Miller, E.L., Hand, S. (eds.) Proceedings of the 25th Symposium on Operating Systems Principles, SOSP 2015, Monterey, CA, USA, October 4-7, 2015, pp. 1–17, ACM (2015), https://doi.org/10.1145/2815400.2815428

[8] Hinrichsen, J.K., Bengtson, J., Krebbers, R.: Actris: session-type based reasoning in separation logic. PACMPL **4**, 6:1–6:30 (2020), https://doi.org/10.1145/3371074

[9] Holzmann, G.J.: The model checker SPIN. IEEE Trans. Software Eng. **23**(5), 279–295 (1997), https://doi.org/10.1109/32.588521

[10] Honda, K., Vasconcelos, V.T., Kubo, M.: Language primitives and type discipline for structured communication-based programming. In: Hankin, C. (ed.) Programming Languages and Systems - ESOP'98, 7th European Symposium on Programming, Held as Part of the European Joint Conferences on the Theory and Practice of Software, ETAPS'98, Lisbon, Portugal, March

28 - April 4, 1998, Proceedings, Lecture Notes in Computer Science, vol. 1381, pp. 122–138, Springer (1998), https://doi.org/10.1007/BFb0053567

[11] Honda, K., Yoshida, N., Carbone, M.: Multiparty asynchronous session types. In: Necula, G.C., Wadler, P. (eds.) Proceedings of the 35th ACM SIGPLAN-SIGACT Symposium on Principles of Programming Languages, POPL 2008, San Francisco, California, USA, January 7-12, 2008, pp. 273–284, ACM (2008), https://doi.org/10.1145/1328438.1328472

[12] Jung, R., Jourdan, J., Krebbers, R., Dreyer, D.: Rustbelt: securing the foundations of the rust programming language. PACMPL 2(POPL), 66:1–66:34 (2018), https://doi.org/10.1145/3158154

[13] Jung, R., Krebbers, R., Birkedal, L., Dreyer, D.: Higher-order ghost state. In: Proceedings of the 21st ACM SIGPLAN International Conference on Functional Programming, p. 256–269, ICFP 2016, Association for Computing Machinery, New York, NY, USA (2016), ISBN 9781450342193, https://doi.org/10.1145/2951913.2951943

[14] Jung, R., Krebbers, R., Jourdan, J., Bizjak, A., Birkedal, L., Dreyer, D.: Iris from the ground up: A modular foundation for higher-order concurrent separation logic. J. Funct. Program. 28, e20 (2018), https://doi.org/10.1017/S0956796818000151

[15] Jung, R., Swasey, D., Sieczkowski, F., Svendsen, K., Turon, A., Birkedal, L., Dreyer, D.: Iris: Monoids and invariants as an orthogonal basis for concurrent reasoning. In: Rajamani, S.K., Walker, D. (eds.) Proceedings of the 42nd Annual ACM SIGPLAN-SIGACT Symposium on Principles of Programming Languages, POPL 2015, Mumbai, India, January 15-17, 2015, pp. 637–650, ACM (2015), https://doi.org/10.1145/2676726.2676980

[16] Kaiser, J., Dang, H., Dreyer, D., Lahav, O., Vafeiadis, V.: Strong logic for weak memory: Reasoning about release-acquire consistency in Iris. In: Müller, P. (ed.) 31st European Conference on Object-Oriented Programming, ECOOP 2017, June 19-23, 2017, Barcelona, Spain, LIPIcs, vol. 74, pp. 17:1–17:29, Schloss Dagstuhl - Leibniz-Zentrum fuer Informatik (2017), https://doi.org/10.4230/LIPIcs.ECOOP.2017.17

[17] Killian, C.E., Anderson, J.W., Braud, R., Jhala, R., Vahdat, A.: Mace: language support for building distributed systems. In: Ferrante, J., McKinley, K.S. (eds.) Proceedings of the ACM SIGPLAN 2007 Conference on Programming Language Design and Implementation, San Diego, California, USA, June 10-13, 2007, pp. 179–188, ACM (2007), https://doi.org/10.1145/1250734.1250755

[18] Krebbers, R., Jung, R., Bizjak, A., Jourdan, J., Dreyer, D., Birkedal, L.: The essence of higher-order concurrent separation logic. In: Yang, H. (ed.) Programming Languages and Systems - 26th European Symposium on Programming, ESOP 2017, Held as Part of the European Joint Conferences on Theory and Practice of Software, ETAPS 2017, Uppsala, Sweden, April 22-29, 2017, Proceedings, Lecture Notes in Computer Science, vol. 10201, pp. 696–723, Springer (2017), https://doi.org/10.1007/978-3-662-54434-1_26

[19] Krebbers, R., Timany, A., Birkedal, L.: Interactive proofs in higher-order concurrent separation logic. In: Castagna, G., Gordon, A.D. (eds.) Proceed-

ings of the 44th ACM SIGPLAN Symposium on Principles of Programming Languages, POPL 2017, Paris, France, January 18-20, 2017, pp. 205–217, ACM (2017)

[20] Krogh-Jespersen, M., Timany, A., Ohlenbusch, M.E., Gregersen, S.O., Birkedal, L.: Aneris: A mechanised logic for modular reasoning about distributed systems - technical appendix (2020), URL https://iris-project.org/pdfs/2020-esop-aneris-final-appendix.pdf

[21] Lamport, L.: Proving the correctness of multiprocess programs. IEEE Trans. Software Eng. **3**(2), 125–143 (1977), https://doi.org/10.1109/TSE.1977.229904

[22] Lamport, L.: The implementation of reliable distributed multiprocess systems. Computer Networks **2**, 95–114 (1978), https://doi.org/10.1016/0376-5075(78)90045-4

[23] Lamport, L.: Hybrid systems in TLA$^+$. In: Grossman, R.L., Nerode, A., Ravn, A.P., Rischel, H. (eds.) Hybrid Systems, Lecture Notes in Computer Science, vol. 736, pp. 77–102, Springer (1992), https://doi.org/10.1007/3-540-57318-6_25

[24] Leino, K.R.M.: Dafny: An automatic program verifier for functional correctness. In: Clarke, E.M., Voronkov, A. (eds.) Logic for Programming, Artificial Intelligence, and Reasoning - 16th International Conference, LPAR-16, Dakar, Senegal, April 25-May 1, 2010, Revised Selected Papers, Lecture Notes in Computer Science, vol. 6355, pp. 348–370, Springer (2010), https://doi.org/10.1007/978-3-642-17511-4_20

[25] Lesani, M., Bell, C.J., Chlipala, A.: Chapar: certified causally consistent distributed key-value stores. In: Bodík, R., Majumdar, R. (eds.) Proceedings of the 43rd Annual ACM SIGPLAN-SIGACT Symposium on Principles of Programming Languages, POPL 2016, St. Petersburg, FL, USA, January 20 - 22, 2016, pp. 357–370, ACM (2016), https://doi.org/10.1145/2837614.2837622

[26] Ley-Wild, R., Nanevski, A.: Subjective auxiliary state for coarse-grained concurrency. In: Giacobazzi, R., Cousot, R. (eds.) The 40th Annual ACM SIGPLAN-SIGACT Symposium on Principles of Programming Languages, POPL '13, Rome, Italy - January 23 - 25, 2013, pp. 561–574, ACM (2013), https://doi.org/10.1145/2429069.2429134

[27] Nanevski, A., Ley-Wild, R., Sergey, I., Delbianco, G.A.: Communicating state transition systems for fine-grained concurrent resources. In: Shao, Z. (ed.) Programming Languages and Systems - 23rd European Symposium on Programming, ESOP 2014, Held as Part of the European Joint Conferences on Theory and Practice of Software, ETAPS 2014, Grenoble, France, April 5-13, 2014, Proceedings, Lecture Notes in Computer Science, vol. 8410, pp. 290–310, Springer (2014), https://doi.org/10.1007/978-3-642-54833-8_16

[28] O'Hearn, P.W.: Resources, concurrency, and local reasoning. Theor. Comput. Sci. **375**(1-3), 271–307 (2007), https://doi.org/10.1016/j.tcs.2006.12.035

[29] Pnueli, A.: The temporal logic of programs. In: 18th Annual Symposium on Foundations of Computer Science, Providence, Rhode Island, USA, 31 October - 1 November 1977, pp. 46–57, IEEE Computer Society (1977), https://doi.org/10.1109/SFCS.1977.32

M. Krogh-Jespersen et al.

[30] Rahli, V., Guaspari, D., Bickford, M., Constable, R.L.: Formal specification, verification, and implementation of fault-tolerant systems using EventML. ECEASST **72** (2015), https://doi.org/10.14279/tuj.eceasst.72.1013

[31] Rahli, V., Guaspari, D., Bickford, M., Constable, R.L.: EventML: Specification, verification, and implementation of crash-tolerant state machine replication systems. Sci. Comput. Program. **148**, 26–48 (2017), https://doi.org/10.1016/j.scico.2017.05.009

[32] Reynolds, J.C.: Separation logic: A logic for shared mutable data structures. In: 17th IEEE Symposium on Logic in Computer Science (LICS 2002), 22-25 July 2002, Copenhagen, Denmark, Proceedings, pp. 55–74, IEEE Computer Society (2002), https://doi.org/10.1109/LICS.2002.1029817

[33] da Rocha Pinto, P., Dinsdale-Young, T., Gardner, P.: Tada: A logic for time and data abstraction. In: Jones, R.E. (ed.) ECOOP 2014 - Object-Oriented Programming - 28th European Conference, Uppsala, Sweden, July 28 - August 1, 2014. Proceedings, Lecture Notes in Computer Science, vol. 8586, pp. 207–231, Springer (2014), https://doi.org/10.1007/978-3-662-44202-9_9

[34] Sergey, I., Nanevski, A., Banerjee, A.: Mechanized verification of fine-grained concurrent programs. In: Grove, D., Blackburn, S. (eds.) Proceedings of the 36th ACM SIGPLAN Conference on Programming Language Design and Implementation, Portland, OR, USA, June 15-17, 2015, pp. 77–87, ACM (2015), https://doi.org/10.1145/2737924.2737964

[35] Sergey, I., Wilcox, J.R., Tatlock, Z.: Programming and proving with distributed protocols. PACMPL **2**(POPL), 28:1–28:30 (2018), https://doi.org/10.1145/3158116

[36] Svendsen, K., Birkedal, L.: Impredicative concurrent abstract predicates. In: Shao, Z. (ed.) Programming Languages and Systems - 23rd European Symposium on Programming, ESOP 2014, Held as Part of the European Joint Conferences on Theory and Practice of Software, ETAPS 2014, Grenoble, France, April 5-13, 2014, Proceedings, Lecture Notes in Computer Science, vol. 8410, pp. 149–168, Springer (2014), https://doi.org/10.1007/978-3-642-54833-8_9

[37] Timany, A., Stefanesco, L., Krogh-Jespersen, M., Birkedal, L.: A logical relation for monadic encapsulation of state: proving contextual equivalences in the presence of runST. PACMPL **2**(POPL), 64:1–64:28 (2018), https://doi.org/10.1145/3158152

[38] Toninho, B., Caires, L., Pfenning, F.: Dependent session types via intuitionistic linear type theory. In: Schneider-Kamp, P., Hanus, M. (eds.) Proceedings of the 13th International ACM SIGPLAN Conference on Principles and Practice of Declarative Programming, July 20-22, 2011, Odense, Denmark, pp. 161–172, ACM (2011), https://doi.org/10.1145/2003476.2003499

[39] Turon, A., Dreyer, D., Birkedal, L.: Unifying refinement and hoare-style reasoning in a logic for higher-order concurrency. In: Morrisett, G., Uustalu, T. (eds.) ACM SIGPLAN International Conference on Functional Programming, ICFP'13, Boston, MA, USA - September 25 - 27, 2013, pp. 377–390, ACM (2013), https://doi.org/10.1145/2500365.2500600

[40] Wilcox, J.R., Woos, D., Panchekha, P., Tatlock, Z., Wang, X., Ernst, M.D., Anderson, T.E.: Verdi: a framework for implementing and formally verifying distributed systems. In: Grove, D., Blackburn, S. (eds.) Proceedings of the 36th ACM SIGPLAN Conference on Programming Language Design and Implementation, Portland, OR, USA, June 15-17, 2015, pp. 357–368, ACM (2015), https://doi.org/10.1145/2737924.2737958

Continualization of Probabilistic Programs With Correction

Jacob Laurel[✉] and Sasa Misailovic

University of Illinois Urbana-Champaign, Department of Computer Science
Urbana, Illinois 61820, USA
{jlaurel2,misailo}@illinois.edu

Abstract. Probabilistic Programming offers a concise way to represent stochastic models and perform automated statistical inference. However, many real-world models have discrete or hybrid discrete-continuous distributions, for which existing tools may suffer non-trivial limitations. Inference and parameter estimation can be exceedingly slow for these models because many inference algorithms compute results faster (or exclusively) when the distributions being inferred are continuous. To address this discrepancy, this paper presents Leios. Leios is the first approach for systematically approximating arbitrary probabilistic programs that have discrete, or hybrid discrete-continuous random variables. The approximate programs have all their variables fully continualized. We show that once we have the fully continuous approximate program, we can perform inference and parameter estimation faster by exploiting the existing support that many languages offer for continuous distributions. Furthermore, we show that the estimates obtained when performing inference and parameter estimation on the continuous approximation are still comparably close to both the true parameter values and the estimates obtained when performing inference on the original model.

Keywords: Probabilistic Programming · Program Transformation · Continuity · Parameter Synthesis · Program Approximation

1   Introduction

Probabilistic programming languages (PPLs) offer an intuitive way to model uncertainty by representing complex probability models as simple programs [28]. A probabilistic programming system then performs fully automated statistical inference on this program by conditioning on observed data, to obtain a posterior distribution, all while hiding the intricate details of this inference process.

Probabilistic inference is a computationally hard task, even for programs containing only Bernoulli distributions (#P-complete [18]), but prior work has shown that for many inference algorithms, continuous and smooth distributions (such as Gaussians) can be *significantly* easier to handle than the distributions having discrete components or discontinuities in their densities [15, 53, 52, 9, 56].

© The Author(s) 2020
P. Müller (Ed.): ESOP 2020, LNCS 12075, pp. 366–393, 2020.
https://doi.org/10.1007/978-3-030-44914-8_14

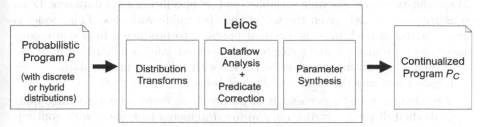

Fig. 1: Overview of Leios

However, many popular Bayesian models can have distributions which are discrete or hybrid discrete-continuous mixtures (denoted simply as "hybrid") leading to computationally inefficient inference for much the same reason. Particularly when the observed variable is a discrete-continuous mixture, inference may fail altogether [65]. Likewise even if the observed variable and likelihood are continuous, the prior or important latent variables, may be discrete (e.g., Binomial) leading to an equally difficult discrete inference problem [61, 50].

In fact, a number of popular inference algorithms such as Hamiltonian Monte Carlo [48], NUTS [31, 50], or versions of Variational Inference (VI) [9] only work for restricted classes of programs (e.g. by requiring each latent be continuous) to avoid these problems. Furthermore, we cannot always marginalize away the program's discrete component since it is often precisely the one we are interested in. Even if the parameter was one which could be safely marginalized out, doing so may require the programmer to use advanced domain knowledge to analytically solve and obtain a new model and re-write the program completely, which can be well beyond the abilities of the average PPL user.

Problem statement: We address the question of how to accurately approximate the semantics of a probabilistic program P whose prior or likelihood is either discrete or hybrid, with a new program P_C, where all variables follow continuous distributions, so that we can exploit the aforementioned inference algorithms to improve inference in an easy, off-the-shelf fashion.

While a programmer could manually rewrite the probabilistic program or model and apply approximations in an ad hoc manner, such as simply adding Gaussian noise to each variable, this would be neither sufficient nor wise. For instance, it has been shown that when a model contains Gaussians, *how* they are programatically written and parametrized can impact the inference time and quality [29, 5]. Also, by not correcting for continuity in the program's branch conditions, one could significantly alter the probability of executing a particular program branch, and hence alter the overall distribution represented by the probabilistic program.

Leios: We introduce a fully automated program analysis framework to continualize probabilistic programs for significantly improved inference performance, especially in cases where inference was originally intractable or prohibitively slow.

An input to Leios is a probabilistic program, which consists of (1) *model* that specifies the prior distributions and how the latent variables are related,

(2) specifications of observable variables, and (3) specifications of data sets. Leios transforms the model, given the set of the observable variables. This model is then substituted back into the original program to produce a fully continuous probabilistic program leading to greatly improved inference. Furthermore the approximated program can easily be reused with different, unseen data.

Figure 1 presents the main workflow of Leios :

- *Distribution transformer and Boolean predicate correction:* Leios first finds individual discrete distribution sample statements to replace with continuous approximations based on known convergence theorems that specifically match the distributions' first moments [23]. Leios then performs a dataflow analysis to identify and then correct Boolean predicates in branches to best preserve the original program's probabilistic control flow. To correct Boolean predicates, we convert the program to a *sketch* and fill in the predicates with holes that will then be synthesized with the optimal values. We ensure that the distribution of the model's observed variables is fully continuous with a differentiable density function, by transforming it using an approach that adapts Smooth Interpretation [14] to probabilistic programs. We describe the transformations in Section 4.

- *Parameter Synthesizer:* Leios determines the optimal parameters which minimize a numerical approximation of the Wasserstein Distance to fill in the holes in the program sketch. This step of the algorithm can be thought of as a "training phase" much like in machine learning, and we need only perform it once for a given program, regardless of the number of times we will later perform inference on different data sets. These parameters correspond to *continuity correction factors* in classical probability theory [23]. We describe the synthesizer in Section 5.

Contributions: This paper makes the following main contributions:

- **Concept**: To the best of our knowledge, Leios is the first technique to automate program transformations that approximate discrete or hybrid discrete-continuous *probabilistic programs* with fully continuous ones to improve inference. It combines insights from probability theory, program analysis, compiler autotuning, and machine learning.

- **Program Transformation**: Leios implements a set of transformations on distributions and the conditional statements that can produce provably continuous probabilistic programs that approximate the original ones.

- **Parameter Synthesis**: We present a synthesis algorithm that corrects the probabilities of taking specific branches in the probabilistic program and improves the overall inference accuracy.

- **Evaluation**: We evaluated Leios on a set of ten benchmarks from existing literature and two systems, WebPPL (using MCMC sampling) and Pyro (using stochastic variational inference). The results demonstrate that Leios can achieve a substantial decrease in inference time compared to the original model, while still achieving high inference accuracy. We also show how a continualized program allows for easy off-the-shelf inference that is not always readily available to discrete or hybrid models.

```
 1  Data := [12,8, ... ];
 2
 3  Model {
 4    prior = Uniform(20,50);
 5    Recruiters = Poisson(prior);
 6
 7    perfGPA = 4;
 8    regGPA = 4*Beta(7,3);
 9    GPA = Mix(perfGPA,.05,regGPA,.95)
10
11    if (GPA == 4) {
12      Interviews = Bin(Recruiters,.9);
13    } else if (GPA > 3.5) {
14      Interviews = Bin(Recruiters,.6);
15    } else {
16      Interviews = Bin(Recruiters,.5);
17    }
18
19    Offers = Bin(Interviews,0.4);
20  }
21
22  for d in Data {
23    factor(Offers,d);
24  }
25
26  return prior;
```

```
 1  Model {
 2    prior = Uniform(20,50);
 3    mu_p = prior;
 4    sigma_p = sqrt(prior);
 5    Recruiters = Gaussian(mu_p,sigma_p);
 6
 7    perfGPA = Gaussian(4,β);
 8    regGPA = 4*Beta(7,3);
 9    GPA = Mix(perfGPA,.05,regGPA,.95)
10
11    if (4 - θ₁ < GPA < 4+ θ₂){
12      mu = Recruiters * 0.9;
13      sigma = sqrt(Recruiters*0.9*0.1);
14      Interviews = Gaussian(mu,sigma);
15    } else if (GPA > 3.5 + θ₃){
16      mu = Recruiters * 0.6;
17      sigma= sqrt(Recruiters*0.6*0.4);
18    Interviews = Gaussian(mu,sigma);
19    } else {
20      mu = Recruiters * 0.5;
21      sigma = sqrt(Recruiters*0.5*0.5);
22      Interviews = Gaussian(mu,sigma);
23    }
24    mu2 = Interviews * 0.4;
25    sigma2 = sqrt(Interviews*0.4*0.6);
26    Offers = Gaussian(mu2,sigma2);
27  }
```

(a)   (b)

Fig. 2: (a) Program P and (b) the Continualized Model Sketch

2   Example

Figure 2 (a) presents a program that infers the parameters of the distribution modeling the number of recruiters coming to a recruiting fair given both the number of offers multiple students receive (line 1). As the number of recruiters may vary year to year, we model this count as a Poisson distribution (line 5). However, to accurately quantify how *much* this count varies year to year, we want to estimate the unknown parameter of this Poisson variable. We thus place a uniform prior over this parameter (line 4).

The example represents the student GPAs in lines 7-9: it is either a perfect 4.0 score or any number between 0 and 4. We model the perfect GPA with a discrete distribution that has all the probability mass at 4.0 (line 7). To model the imperfect GPA, we use a Beta distribution (line 8), scaled by 4 to lie in the range $[0.0, 4.0]$. Finally, the distribution of the GPAs is a *mixture* of these two components (line 9). Our mixture assumes that 5% of students obtain perfect GPAs.

Because the GPA impacts the number of interviews a student receives, our model incorporates control flow where each branch captures the distribution of interviews received, conditioned on the GPA being in a certain range (lines 11-17). Each student's resume is available to all recruiters and each recruiter can request an interview or not, hence all three of the `Interviews` distributions follow a Binomial distribution (here denoted as `bin`) with the same n (number of recruiters) but with different probabilities (higher probabilities for higher GPAs). From the factor statement (line 23) we see that the `Offers` variable governs the distribution of the observed data, hence it is the *observed* variable. Furthermore, given the values of all latent variables, `Offers` follows a Binomial distribution (line 19), hence the *likelihood function* of this program is discrete.

This program poses several challenges for inference. First, it contains discrete latent variables (such as the Binomials), which are expensive to sample from or rule out certain inference methods [26]. Second, it contains a hybrid discrete-continuous distribution governing the student GPA, and such hybrid distributions are challenging for inference algorithms [65]. Third, the model has complex control flow introduced by the `if` statements, making the observable data follow a (potentially multimodal) mixture distribution, which is yet another obstacle to efficient inference [43, 17]. Lastly, the discrete distribution of the observed data and likelihood also hinder the inference efficiency [61, 50, 59].

2.1   Continualization

Our approach starts from the observation that inference with continuous distributions is often more efficient for several inference algorithms [53, 52, 56]. Leios first continualizes discrete and hybrid distributions in the original model. Starting in line 5 in Figure 2 (b), we approximate the Poisson variable with a Gaussian using a classical result [16], hence relaxing the constraint that the number of recruiters be an integer. (For ease of presentation we created new variables `mu_p` and `sigma_p` corresponding to the parameters of the approximation; Leios simply inlines these.) We next approximate the discrete component of the GPA hybrid mixture distribution by a Gaussian centered at 4 and small tunable standard deviation β (line 7). The GPA is now a mixture of two *continuous* distributions. We then transform all of the Binomials to Gaussians (lines 14, 18, 22, and 26) using another classic approximation [23].

Finally, Leios smooths the observed variables by a Gaussian to ensure the likelihood function is both fully continuous *and* differentiable. In this example we see that the approximation of the Binomial already makes the distribution of `Offers` (given all latent values) a Gaussian, hence this final step is not needed.

After continualization, the GPA cannot be *exactly* 4.0, thus we need to repair the first conditional branch of the continualized program. In line 11, we replace the exact equality predicate with the interval predicate $4-\theta_1 <$ `GPA` $< 4+\theta_2$ where each θ is a hole whose value Leios will *synthesize*. Leios finds all such branching predicates by tracking transitive data dependencies of all continualized variables.

2.2   Parameter Synthesis

Our continuous approximation should be close enough to the original model such that upon performing inference on the approximation, the estimations obtained will also be close to the ground-truth values. Hence Leios needs to ensure that the values synthesized for each θ are such that for every conditional statement, the probability of executing the true branch in the continualized program roughly matches the original (ensuring similar likelihoods). In probability theory, this value has a natural interpretation as a *continuity correction factor* as

```
1   Model {
2       prior = Uniform(20,50);
3       mu_p = prior;
4       sigma_p = sqrt(prior);
5       Recruiters = Gaussian(mu_p,sigma_p);
6
7       perfGPA = Gaussian(4, 0.1);
8       regGPA = 4*Beta(7,3);
9       GPA = Mix(perfGPA,.05,regGPA,.95);
10
11      if (3.99999 < GPA < 4.95208){
12          mu = Recruiters * 0.9;
13          sigma = sqrt(Recruiters*0.9*0.1);
14          Interviews = Gaussian(mu,sigma);
15      } else if (GPA > 3.500122){
16          mu = Recruiters * 0.6;
17          sigma = sqrt(Recruiters*0.6*0.4);
18          Interviews = Gaussian(mu,sigma);}
19      } else {
20          mu = Recruiters * 0.5;
21          sigma = sqrt(Recruiters*0.5*0.5);
22          Interviews = Gaussian(mu,sigma);
23      }
24
25      mu2 = Interviews * 0.4;
26      sigma2 = sqrt(Interviews*0.4*0.6);
27      Offers = Gaussian(mu2,sigma2);
28  }
```

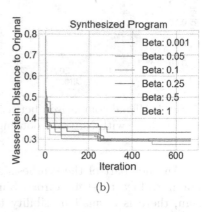

(b)

(a)

Fig. 3: (a) the fully continualized model and (b) Convergence of the Synthesis Step for multiple β.

it "corrects' the probability of a predicate being true after applying continuous approximations. For the (GPA == 4) condition, we might think about using a typical continuity correction factor of 0.5 [23], and transform it to 4-0.5 < GPA < 4+0.5. However, in that case, the second else if (GPA > 3.5) branch would never execute, thus significantly changing the program's semantics (and thus the likelihood function). Experimentally, such an error can lead to highly inaccurate inference results.

Hence we must *synthesize* a better continuity correction factor that makes the approximated model "closest" to the original program's with respect to a well-defined distance metric between probability distributions. In this paper, we will use the common Wasserstein distance, which we describe later in Section 5. The objective function aims to find the continuity correction factors that minimize the Wasserstein distance between the original and continualized models.

Figure 3 (a) shows the continualized model. Leios calculated that the optimal values for the first branch are $\theta_1 = 0.00001$ (hence the lower bound is 3.99999) and $\theta_2 = 0.95208$ (hence the upper bound is 4.95208) in line 11, and $\theta_3 = 0.00012$ (hence the lower bound is 3.500122) for the branch in line 15. Intuitively the synthesizer found the upper bound 4.95208 so that any sample larger than 4 (which must have come from the right tail of the continualized perfect GPA) is consumed by the first branch, instead of accidentally being consumed by the second branch.

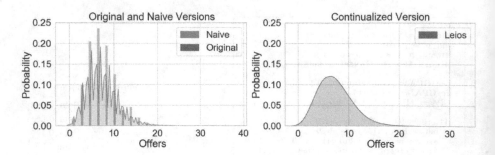

Fig. 4: Visual comparison between Model Distribution of Original Program with Naive Smoothing and Leios (both with $\beta = 0.1$)

Another part of the synthesis step is to make sure that approximations do not introduce run-time errors. Since `Interviews` is now sampled from Gaussian, there is a small possibility that it could become negative, thus causing a runtime error (since we later take its square root). By dynamically sampling the continualized model during the parameter synthesis, as part of a light-weight *auto-tuning* step, Leios checks if such an error exists. If it does, Leios can instead use a Gamma approximation (which is always non-negative).

While continualization incurs additional computational cost, this cost is typically amortized. In particular, continualization needs to be performed only once. The continualized model can be then be used multiple times for inference on different data-sets. Further, we experimentally observed that our synthesis step is fast. In this example, for all the values of β we evaluated, this step required only a few hundred iterations to converge to the optimal continuity correction factors, as shown in Figure 3 (b).

2.3 Improving Inference

Upon constructing the continuous approximation of the model, we now wish to perform inference by conditioning upon the outcomes of 25 sampled students. To make a fair comparison, we compile both the original and continuous versions down to Webppl [26] and run MCMC inference (with 3500 samples and a burn-in of 700). We also seek to understand how smoothing latent variables improves inference, thus we also compare against a naively continualized version *where only the observed variable* was smoothed using the same β, number of MCMC samples and burn-in.

Figure 4 presents the distribution of the `Offers` variable in the original model, naively smoothed model, and the Leios-optimized model. The continuous approximation achieved by Leios is smooth and unimodal, unlike the naively smoothed approximation, which is highly multimodal. However all models have similar means

Using these three models for inference, Figure 5 (a) presents the posterior distribution of the variable `param` for each approach. We finally take the *mean* as

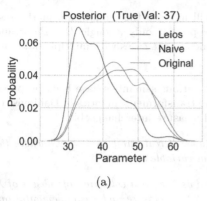

Posterior (True Val: 37)

(a)

Metric	Leios	Naive	Original
Accuracy	0.058	0.069	0.090
Runtime (s)	0.604	0.631	0.805

(b)

Fig. 5: (a) *Posteriors* of each method – the true value is equal to 37. (b) Avg. Accuracy and Inference time; the bars represent accuracy (left Y-axis), the lines represent time (right Y-axis).

the point-estimate, τ_{est}, of the parameter's true value τ. Figure 5 (b) presents the run time and the error ratio, $|\frac{\tau - \tau_{est}}{\tau}|$, for each approach (for the given true value of 37). It shows that our continualized version leads to the fastest inference.

3   Syntax and Semantics of Programs

We present the syntax and semantics of the probabilistic programming language on which our analyses is defined

3.1   Source Language Syntax

Program	::=	*DataBlock?* ; *Model* { *Stmt*$^+$ } ; *ObserveBlock?*; *return Var*;
Stmt	::=	*skip* | *abort* | *Var := Expr* | *Var := Dist* | CONST *Var := Expr*
	|	*Stmt* ; *Stmt* | { *Stmt* } | *condition* (*BExpr*)
	|	*if* (*BExpr*) *Stmt else Stmt* | *for i = Int to Int Stmt*
	|	*while* (*BExpr*) *Stmt*
Expr	::=	*Expr ArithOp Expr* | *f(Expr)* | *Real* | *Int* | *Var*
BExpr	::=	*BExpr or BExpr* | *BExpr and BExpr* | *not BExpr*
	|	*Expr RelOp Expr* | (*BExpr*)
DataBlock	::=	*Data:=* [(*Int* | *Real*)*]
ObserveBlock	::=	*for D in Data* { *factor(Var,D);* }
Dist	::=	*ContDist* | *DiscDist*

$ContDist \in \{Gaussian, Uniform, etc.\}, DiscDist \in \{Binomial, Bernoulli, etc.\}$
$ArithOp \in \{+, -, *, /, **\}, f \in \{log, abs, sqrt, exp\}, RelOp \in \{<, \leq, ==\}$

The syntax is similar to the ones used in [24, 51]. Unlike [51], our syntax *does* include exact equality predicates, which introduce difficulties during the approximation. To give the developer the flexibility in selecting which parts of the program to continualize, we add the CONST annotation. It indicates that the variable's distribution should not be continualized. Until explicitly noted, we will not use this annotation in the rest of the paper. For simplicity of exposition, we present only a single *DataBlock* and *ObserveBlock*, but our approach naturally extends to the cases with multiple data and observed variables.

Measure Theory Preliminaries Though various semantics have been proposed [44, 36, 7], we adapt the sub-probability measure transformer semantics of Dahlqvist et al. [19]. We will use the terms distribution and measure interchangeably.

Definition 1. *A program state* $\sigma \in \mathbb{S}$ *is a n-tuple of real numbers:* $\mathbb{S} = \mathbb{R}^n$ *where the* i^{th} *tuple element corresponds to the* i^{th} *program variable's value.*

Definition 2. *A* Σ*-algebra on a set* X *(denoted as* Σ_X*) is a collection of subsets of* X *such that (1)* $X \in \Sigma_X$ *and (2)* $X_i \in \Sigma_X \Rightarrow X_i^c \in \Sigma_X$ *(closure under complementation) and (3)* $X_1, X_2 \in \Sigma_X \Rightarrow X_1 \vee X_2 \in \Sigma_X$ *(closure under countable union). The tuple of* (X, Σ_X) *is called a measurable space. Our semantics is defined on the Borel measurable space* $(\mathbb{R}^n, \mathcal{B}\{\mathbb{R}^n\})$ *where* $\mathcal{B}\{\mathbb{R}^n\}$ *is the standard Borel* Σ*-algebra over* $\mathbb{R}^n$*.*

Definition 3. *A measure* μ *over* $\mathbb{R}^n$ *is a mapping from* $\mathcal{B}\{\mathbb{R}^n\}$ *to* $[0, +\infty)$ *such that* $\mu(\emptyset) = 0$ *and* $\mu(\bigcup_{i \in \mathbb{N}} X_i) = \sum_{i \in \mathbb{N}} \mu(X_i)$ *when all* X_i *are mutually disjoint. A probability measure is a measure that satisfies* $\mu(\mathbb{R}^n) = 1$ *and a sub-probability measure is one satisfying* $\mu(\mathbb{R}^n) \leq 1$*. The simplest measure is the Dirac measure denoted as* $\delta_{a_i}(S) = 1$ *if* a_i *in* S *else 0. We denote the set of all sub-probability measures as* $\mathrm{M}(\mathbb{R}^n)$*.*

Definition 4. *Given measures* $\mu_1, \mu_2 \in \mathrm{M}(\mathbb{R})$*, the product measure* $\mu_1 \otimes \mu_2 \in \mathrm{M}(\mathbb{R}^2)$ *is defined as* $\mu_1 \otimes \mu_2(B_1 \times B_2) = \mu_1(B_1)\mu_2(B_2)$ *for* $B_1, B_2 \in \mathcal{B}\{\mathbb{R}\}$

Definition 5. *Given a measure* $\mu \in \mathrm{M}(\mathbb{R}^n)$ *the marginal measure of a variable* x_i *is defined as* $\mu_{x_i}(B_i) = \mu(\mathbb{R} \times ... \mathbb{R} \times B_i \times \mathbb{R}...)$ *for* $B_i \in \mathcal{B}\{\mathbb{R}\}$

Definition 6. *A kernel is a function* $\kappa : \mathbb{S} \to \mathrm{M}(\mathbb{R}^n)$ *mapping states to measures.*

Definition 7. *The Lebesgue measure on* $\mathbb{R}$ *(denoted Leb) is the measure that maps any interval to its length, e.g.,* $Leb([a, b]) = b - a$*. The Lebesgue measure in* $\mathbb{R}^n$ *is simply the n-fold product measure of n copies of the Lebesgue measure on* $\mathbb{R}$*.*

Definition 8. *A measure* μ *is absolutely continuous with respect to the Lebesgue measure Leb (denoted as* $\mu \ll Leb$ *or simply* μ *is A.C.) iff for any measurable set* S $Leb(S) = 0 \Rightarrow \mu(S) = 0$*.*

3.2   Semantics

Expression Level Semantics Arithmetic Expression semantics are standard, they map states $\sigma \in \mathbb{R}^n$ to values, equivalently $[\![Expr]\!] : \mathbb{R}^n \to \mathbb{R}$. Boolean Expression Semantics, denoted $[\![BExpr]\!]$, simply return the set of states $B_i \in \mathcal{B}\{\mathbb{R}^n\}$ satisfying the Boolean conditional.

$$[\![c]\!](\sigma) = c \quad [\![x_i]\!](\sigma) = \sigma[x_i] \quad [\![t_1 \ op \ t_2]\!](\sigma) = [\![t_1]\!](\sigma) \ op \ [\![t_2]\!](\sigma) \quad [\![f(t_1)]\!](\sigma) = f([\![t_1]\!](\sigma))$$

$$[\![B_1 \ \textbf{and} \ B_2]\!] = [\![B_1]\!] \cap [\![B_2]\!] \quad [\![B_1 \ \textbf{or} \ B_2]\!] = [\![B_1]\!] \cup [\![B_2]\!] \quad [\![\textbf{not} \ B_1]\!] = \mathbb{R}^n \setminus [\![B_1]\!]$$

$$[\![e_1 \ relop \ e_2]\!] = \{\sigma \in \mathbb{R}^n \mid [\![e_1]\!](\sigma) \ relop \ [\![e_2]\!](\sigma)\}$$

Distribution Semantics The interpretation of a distribution is a kernel, κ, mapping a state to the measure associated with the specific parametrization of the distribution in that state. Since measures are set functions we will represent them as λ abstractions. The signature is $[\![Dist]\!] : \mathbb{R}^n \to (\mathcal{B}\{\mathbb{R}\} \to [0,1])$

$$\kappa_{Cont}(\sigma) = [\![ContDist(e_1, e_2, ...)]\!](\sigma) = \lambda S. \int_{v \in \mathbb{R}} 1_S(v) \cdot f_{Cont}(v; [\![e_1]\!](\sigma), [\![e_2]\!](\sigma), ...)$$

$$\kappa_{Disc}(\sigma) = [\![DiscDist(e_1, e_2, ...)]\!](\sigma) = \lambda S. \sum_{v \in Supp \cap S} f_{Disc}(v; [\![e_1]\!](\sigma), [\![e_2]\!](\sigma), ...)$$

Where f_{Cont} and f_{Disc} are the density and mass functions, respectively, of the primitive distribution being sampled from (e.g., $f_{Gauss}(x; \mu, \sigma) = \frac{1}{\sigma\sqrt{2\pi}} e^{\frac{-(x-\mu)^2}{2\sigma^2}} \cdot 1_{\{\sigma > 0\}}$) and $Supp$ is the distribution's support.

Statement Level Semantics The statement-level semantics are shown in Figure 6. We interpret each statement as a (sub) measure transformer, hence the semantic signature is $[\![Statement]\!] : M(\mathbb{R}^n) \to M(\mathbb{R}^n)$. The skip statement returns the original measure and the abort statement transforms any measure to the **0** sub-measure. The condition statement removes measure from regions not satisfying the Boolean guard B. The factor statement can be seen as a "smoothed" version of condition that uses g, a function of the observed data and its distribution, to re-weight the measure associated with a set by some real value in $[0,1]$ (as opposed to strictly 0 or 1). Deterministic assignment transforms the measure into one which assigns to any set of states S the same value that the original measure μ would have assigned to all states that end up in S after executing the assignment statement. Probabilistic Assignment updates the measure so that x_i's marginal is the measure associated with Dist, but with the parameters governed by μ.

An if else statement can be decomposed into the sum of the true branch's measure and the false branch's measure. The while loop semantics are the solution to the standard least fixed point equation [19], but can also be viewed as a mixture distribution where each mixture component corresponds to going through the loop k times. A for loop is just syntactic sugar for a sequencing of a fixed number of statements. We note that the Data block does not affect the measure (it is also syntactic sugar, and could simply be inlined in the Observe block). The program can be thought of as starting in some initial input measure μ_0 where each variable is undefined (which could simply mean initialized to some special value or even just zero), and as each variable gets defined, that variable's marginal (and hence the joint measure μ) gets updated.

4   Continualizing Probabilistic Programs

Our goal is to synthesize a new continuous approximation of the original program P. We formally define this via a transformation operator $\mathcal{T}_P^\beta[\bullet]: Program \to Program$. Our approach operates in two main steps:

(1) We first *locally* approximate the program's prior and latent variables using a series of program transformations to best preserve the local structural properties of the program and then apply smoothing *globally* to ensure that the likelihood function is both fully continuous and differentiable.

$$[\![\texttt{skip}]\!](\mu) = \mu \qquad [\![\texttt{abort}]\!](\mu) = \lambda S.0 \qquad [\![P_1; P_2]\!](\mu) = [\![P_2]\!]([\![P_1]\!](\mu))$$

$$[\![\texttt{condition(B)}]\!](\mu) = \lambda S.\mu(S \cap [\![B]\!]) \qquad [\![\texttt{factor(x}_i\texttt{,t)}]\!](\mu) = \lambda S. \int_{\mathbb{R}^n} \mathbf{1}_S \cdot g(t, \sigma) \cdot \mu(d\sigma)$$

$$[\![\texttt{x}_i \texttt{ := e}]\!](\mu) = \lambda S.\mu(\{(x_1, ..., x_n) \in \mathbb{R}^n \mid (x_1, ..., x_{i-1}, [\![e]\!](x_1, ..x_n), x_{i+1}..., x_n) \in S\})$$

$$[\![\texttt{x}_i \texttt{ := Dist(e}_1,\ldots\texttt{e}_k\texttt{)}]\!](\mu) = \lambda S. \int_{\mathbb{R}^n} \mu(d\sigma) \cdot \delta_{x_1} \otimes ... \delta_{x_{i-1}} \otimes [\![\texttt{Dist(e}_1,\ldots\texttt{e}_k\texttt{)}]\!](\sigma) \otimes \delta_{x_{i+1}} ... (S)$$

$$[\![\texttt{if (B) } \{P_1\} \texttt{ else } \{P_2\}]\!](\mu) = [\![P_1]\!]([\![\texttt{condition(B)}]\!](\mu)) + [\![P_2]\!]([\![\texttt{condition(not B)}]\!](\mu))$$

$$[\![\texttt{while (B) } \{\ P_1\ \}]\!](\mu) = \sum_{k=0}^{\infty} [\![(\texttt{condition(B)}; \ P_1)^k; \texttt{condition(not B)}]\!](\mu)$$

Fig. 6: Denotational Semantics of Probabilistic Programs

(2) We next synthesize a set of parameters that (approximately) minimize the distance metric between the distributions of the original and continualized models and we use light-weight *auto-tuning* to ensure the approximations do not introduce runtime errors.

4.1   Overview of the Algorithm

Algorithm 1 presents the technique for continualizing programs. It takes as input a program P containing a prior or observed variable that is discrete (or hybrid) and returns $\mathcal{T}_{\mathcal{P}}^{\beta}[P]$, a probabilistic program representing a fully continuous random variable with a differentiable likelihood function. The algorithm uses a tunable hyper-parameter $\beta \in (0, \infty)$ to control the amount of smoothing (like in [14]). A smaller β leads to less smoothing, while a larger β leads to more smoothing, however the smallest β does not always lead to the best inference, and vice-versa, as can be seen in section 7.

In line 3 of Algorithm 1 Leios constructs a standard control flow graph (CFG) to represent the program, using a method called GetCFG(). This data structure will form the basis of Leios's future analyses. Each CFG node corresponds to a single statement and contains all relevant attributes of that statement. Leios then uses this CFG to build a data dependency graph (line 4) which will be used for checking which variables are tainted by the approximations. In line 5 Leios then applies $\mathcal{T}_{\mathcal{P}}^{\beta}[\bullet]$ to obtain a continualized sketch, P_C. Lastly, Leios synthesizes the optimal continuity correction parameters (line 7), and in doing so, samples the program to detect if a runtime error occurred, also returning a Boolean flag *success* to convey this information. If a runtime error *did* occur we find the expression causing it (line 9) and then in lines 10-12 reapply the safer transformations (e.g., Gamma instead of Gaussian) to all possible dependencies which could have contributed to the runtime error.

4.2   Distribution and Expression Transformations

To continualize each variable, Leios mutates the individual distributions and expressions assigned to latent variables within the program. We use a transform operator for expressions and distributions $\mathcal{T}_{\mathcal{E}}^{\beta}[\bullet] \colon Expr \cup Dist \to Expr \cup Dist$, which we define next.

Algorithm 1: Procedure for Continualizing a Probabilistic Program

---

1 <u>function Continualize</u> (P, β);

   Input : A probabilistic program P containing discrete/hybrid observable
              variables and/or priors and a smoothing factor $\beta > 0$

   Output: A fully continuous probabilistic program P_C

2 $Acceptable \leftarrow False$;

3 $CFG \leftarrow \texttt{GetCFG}(P)$;

4 $DataDepGraph \leftarrow \texttt{ComputeDataFlow}(CFG)$;

5 $P_C \leftarrow \mathcal{T}_P^\beta[P]$;   /* apply all continuous transformations */

6 **while** *not Acceptable* **do**

7     $P_C, success \leftarrow \texttt{Synthesize}(P_C, P)$;

8   **if** *not success*:

9        $D \leftarrow \texttt{getInvalidExpression}()$;

10       $Deps \leftarrow \texttt{getDependencies}(\texttt{DataDepGraph},\texttt{D})$;

11   **forall** *Expression* **in** *Deps* **do**

12          $P_C \leftarrow \texttt{reapplySafeTransformation}(P_C, Expression)$;

13   **else**:

14       $Acceptable \leftarrow True$;

15 **end**

16 **return** P_C

Transform Operator For Distributions and Expressions We now detail
the full list of continuous probability distribution transformations that $\mathcal{T}_\mathcal{E}^\beta[\bullet]$ uses.

$$\mathcal{T}_\mathcal{E}^\beta[E] = \begin{cases} Gaussian(\lambda, \sqrt{\lambda}) & E = Poisson(\lambda) \\ Gamma(\lambda, 1) & E = Poisson(\lambda) \text{ \& } Gaussian \text{ fails} \\ Gaussian(np, \sqrt{np(1-p)}) & E = Binomial(n, p) \\ Gamma(n, p) & E = Binomial(n, p) \text{ \& } Gaussian \text{ fails} \\ Uniform(a, b) & E = DiscUniform(a, b) \\ Exponential(p) & E = Geometric(p) \\ MixOfGauss_\beta([(1, p), (0, 1-p)]) & E = Bernoulli(p) \\ Beta(\beta, \beta\frac{1-p}{p}) & E = Bernoulli(p) \text{ \& } MixOfGauss \text{ fails} \\ Mixture([(\mathcal{T}_\mathcal{E}^\beta[D_1], p_1), ...(\mathcal{T}_\mathcal{E}^\beta[D_2], p_2)]) & E = Mixture([(D_1, p_1), ...(D_2, p_2)]) \\ Gaussian(c, \beta) & E = c \ (constant) \\ E & E = a \cdot x_i + b \ (a \neq 0) \\ KDE(\beta) & E \in DiscDist \text{ \& not covered} \\ Gaussian(E, \beta) & otherwise \end{cases}$$

The rationale for this definition is that these approximations all preserve key structural properties of the distributions' shape (e.g., the number of modes) which have been
shown to strongly affect the quality of inference [25, 45, 17]. Second, these continuous
approximations all match the first moment of their corresponding discrete distributions,
which is another important feature that affects the quality of approximation [53]. We
refer the reader to [54] to see that for each distribution on the left, the corresponding

continuous distribution on the right has the same mean. These approximations are best when certain limit conditions are satisfied, e.g. $\lambda \geq 10$ for approximating a Poisson distribution with Gaussian, hence the values in the program itself do affect the overall approximation accuracy.

However, if we are not careful, a statement level transformation could introduce runtime errors. For example, a Binomial is always non-negative, but its Gaussian approximation could be negative. This is why $\mathcal{T}_{\mathcal{E}}^{\beta}[\bullet]$ has *multiple* transformations for the same distribution. For example, in addition to using a Gaussian to approximate both a Binomial and a Poisson, we also have a Gamma approximation since a Gamma distribution is *always non-negative*. Likewise we have a Beta approximation to a Bernoulli if we require that the approximation also have support in the range $[0, 1]$. Leios uses auto-tuning to safeguard against such errors during the synthesis phase, whereby when sampling the transformed program, if we encounter a run-time error of this nature, we simply go back and try a safer (but possibly slower) alternative (Algorithm 1 line 12). Since there are only finitely many variables and (safer) transformations to apply, this process will eventually terminate. For discrete distributions *not* supported by the specific approximations, but with fixed parameters, we empirically sample them to get a set of samples and then use a Kernel Density Estimate (KDE) [62] with a Gaussian kernel (the KDE bandwidth is precisely β) as the approximation.

Lastly, by default *all* discrete random variables become approximated with continuous versions, however we leave the option to the user to manually specify CONST in front of a variable if they *do not* wish for it to be approximated (in which case we no longer make any theoretical guarantees about continuity).

4.3   Influence Analysis and Control-Flow Correction of Predicates

Simply changing all instances of discrete distributions in the program to continuous ones is not enough to closely approximate the semantics of the original program. We additionally need to ensure that such changes do not introduce *control flow errors* into the program, in the sense that quantitative properties such as the probability of taking a particular branch need to be reasonably preserved.

Avoiding Zero Probability Events   A major concern of the approximation is to ensure that no zero-probability events are introduced, such as when we have an exact equality "==" predicate in an if, observe or while statement and the variable being checked was transformed from a discrete to a continuous type. For example, discrete programs commonly have a statement like x := Poisson(1) followed by a conditional such as if (x==4), because the probability that a discrete random variable is *exactly* equal to a value can be non-zero. However upon applying our distribution transformations and transforming the distribution of x from a discrete Poisson to a continuous Gaussian, the conditional statement "if (x==4)" now corresponds to a **zero probability** (or measure zero) event, as the probability that an absolutely continuous probability measure assigns to the singleton set $\{4\}$ is by definition zero. Thus, if not corrected for, we could significantly change the probabilities of taking certain branches and hence the overall distribution of the program.

The converse can also be true: applying approximations can make a zero probability event in the original program now have non-zero probability. For example, in x := DiscUniform(1,5); if (x<3 and x>2) the true branch has probability zero of executing but this becomes non-zero after approximations are applied. However, the branch paths like these in the original model could be identified by symbolic analysis (e.g., [24]) and removed via dead code elimination during pre-processing.

Correcting Control Flow Probabilities via Static Analysis To prevent zero-probability events and ensure that the branch execution probabilities of the continualized program closely matches the original's, we use data dependence analysis to track which `if`, `while` or `condition` statements have logical comparisons with variables "tainted" by the approximations. A variable v is "tainted" if it has a transitive data dependence on an approximated variable, and we use *reaching definitions analysis* [35] on the program's CFG to identify these.

As shown in Algorithm 1 line 4, to compute the reaching definitions analysis we use a method called `ComputeDataFlow()` as part of a pre-transformation pass whereby for each program point in the CFG, each variable is marked with all the other variables on which it has a data-dependence. These annotations are stored in a data structure called *DataDepGraph* which maps *nodes* (program points) to *sets of tuples* where each tuple contains a variable, the other variables it depends on (and where they are assigned), and lastly, whether it will become tainted. Note that in the algorithm this step is done *before* the previously discussed expression-level transformations, hence why `ComputeDataFlow()` marks which variables will *become* continualized and which ones will not (i.e if a variable already defines a continuous random variable or was annotated with `CONST`). Furthermore, though we are computing the data dependencies before the approximations, because the approximations do not re-order or remove statements, all data dependencies will be the same before and after applying the approximations.

Transform Operator For Boolean Expressions We take all such control predicates that contain an exact equality "==" comparison with a tainted variable and transform these predicates from exact equality predicates to interval-style predicates. Thus if we originally had a predicate of the form `if(x==4)` we will mutate this into a predicate of the form `if(x>4-`θ_1` && x<4+`θ_2`)` where θ are now placeholder values that will need to be filled with a concrete value during the synthesis phase (Section 5). Hence checking for exact equality gets relaxed to checking for containment within the interval $(4 - \theta_1, 4 + \theta_2)$. We also need to correct `<` and `<=` predicates if one of the variables was approximated or transitively affected by an approximation.

Hence we also define our transform operator $\mathcal{T}_B^\beta [\bullet] : BExpr \to BExpr$ at the level of Boolean expressions:

$$\mathcal{T}_B^\beta[(x == y)] = \begin{cases} (y - \theta_1 < x) \ and \ (x < y + \theta_2) & default \\ (x == y) & CONST \ x \ and \ CONST \ y \ specified \end{cases}$$

$$\mathcal{T}_B^\beta[(x < y)] = \begin{cases} (x < y + \theta) & if \ x \ or \ y \ tainted \\ (x < y) & otherwise \end{cases}$$

$$\mathcal{T}_B^\beta[(x \leq y)] = \begin{cases} (x \leq y + \theta) & if \ x \ or \ y \ tainted \\ (x \leq y) & otherwise \end{cases}$$

Because we have already pre-computed *DataDepGraph* one can check if a variable in a given statement or expression is tainted (or marked as `CONST`) in constant time.

This correction has a natural interpretation in classical probability theory. It is well known that to approximate a discrete distribution X with a continuous one $\hat{X}$, we need a continuity correction factor, θ, such that $P(X < x) \approx P(\hat{X} < x + \theta)$ (hence why $\mathcal{T}_B^\beta[\bullet]$ also corrects `<` and `<=` predicates). For simple approximations (i.e Binomial to Gaussian), the canonical correction factor is known ($\theta = 0.5$) [23], however for the general case, it is not. Furthermore, it has been shown that in many cases, 0.5 is *not* the best correction factor [3].

4.4   Bringing it all together: Full Program Transformations

Having defined the transformation for distributions, arithmetic and Boolean expressions, we now define the *program* transformation operator $\mathcal{T}_{\mathcal{P}}^{\beta}[\bullet]: Program \to Program$ inductively:

$$\mathcal{T}_{\mathcal{P}}^{\beta}[P_1; P_2] = \mathcal{T}_{\mathcal{P}}^{\beta}[P_1]; \mathcal{T}_{\mathcal{P}}^{\beta}[P_2]$$

$$\mathcal{T}_{\mathcal{P}}^{\beta}[\texttt{if (B) } \{P_1\} \texttt{ else } \{P_2\}] = \texttt{if } (\mathcal{T}_{\mathcal{B}}^{\beta}[B]) \ \mathcal{T}_{\mathcal{P}}^{\beta}[P_1] \texttt{ else } \mathcal{T}_{\mathcal{P}}^{\beta}[P_2]$$

$$\mathcal{T}_{\mathcal{P}}^{\beta}[\texttt{while(B) } P_1] = \texttt{while}(\mathcal{T}_{\mathcal{B}}^{\beta}[B]) \ \mathcal{T}_{\mathcal{P}}^{\beta}[P_1]$$

$$\mathcal{T}_{\mathcal{P}}^{\beta}[\texttt{condition(B)}] = \texttt{condition}(\mathcal{T}_{\mathcal{B}}^{\beta}[B])$$

$$\mathcal{T}_{\mathcal{P}}^{\beta}[\texttt{x := E}] = \texttt{x := } \mathcal{T}_{\mathcal{E}}^{\beta}[E]$$

$$\mathcal{T}_{\mathcal{P}}^{\beta}[\texttt{CONST x := E}] = \texttt{x := E}$$

The **abort**, **factor** and **skip** statements and the *DataBlock* remain the same after applying the transformation operator $\mathcal{T}_{\mathcal{P}}^{\beta}[\bullet]$.

Ensuring Smoothness Upon applying the statement-level transformations and performing both dataflow analysis and predicate mutations, Leios ensures each latent variable comes from a continuous distribution. However a continuous distribution may still have jump discontinuities or non-differentiable regions in its density function (such as a uniform distribution), which can make inference difficult [66]. Furthermore it is known that performing parameter estimation on data that is distributed according to a discontinuous or non-smooth density function, or on distributions with a non-smooth likelihoods can be just as challenging [50, 1, 59]. Thus to make the Program's likelihood function and density function of the observed data fully *smooth*, we need to apply additional Gaussian smoothing.

Since it would be redundant to apply smoothing if we already knew this variable came from a smooth distribution (as in the example) hence we make this simple check first. The following transformation performs this on the observed variables (which appear in the factor statement).

$$\mathcal{T}_{\mathcal{P}}^{\beta}[\texttt{x}_o \texttt{ := E}] = \begin{cases} \texttt{x}_o \texttt{ := E} & \textit{if x already smooth} \\ \texttt{x}_o \texttt{ := Gaussian(E,} \beta \texttt{);} & \textit{otherwise} \end{cases}$$

We could perform additional smoothing for *every* variable to ensure each has a differentiable density, however we empirically observed that the variance added up enough to where inference quality deteriorated, hence we only apply the additional smoothing to observed variables.

Having defined the statement-level transformations we now state a theorem about $\mathcal{T}_{\mathcal{P}}^{\beta}[\bullet]$ preserving continuity. As many applications may invoke inference at any point in the program [46, 60], it is important that absolute continuity of each marginal hold at *every* point.

Theorem 1. *In the transformed program, $\mathcal{T}_{\mathcal{P}}^{\beta}[P]$, the marginal sub-probability measure of each variable, denoted μ_{x_i}, is absolutely continuous with respect to the Lebesgue measure (denoted μ_{x_i} is A.C.) at each program point for which that variable is defined.*

Proof. (sketch) To prove the theorem we will show that when any variable x_i is initially defined, it comes from an absolutely continuous distribution and furthermore that the semantics of each statement in $\mathcal{T}_{\mathcal{P}}^{\beta}[P]$ preserves the absolute continuity of each marginal measure (where $\mu_{x_i} \equiv \mu(\mathbb{R} \times ... \times B_i \times \mathbb{R}... \times \mathbb{R}))$, equivalently for any statement, any (already defined) variable x_i and any Borel set $B_i \in \mathcal{B}\{\mathbb{R}\}$:

$$\mu(\mathbb{R} \times ... \times B_i \times \mathbb{R}... \times \mathbb{R}) \ is \ A.C. \Rightarrow [\![statement]\!](\mu)(\mathbb{R} \times ... \times B_i \times \mathbb{R}... \times \mathbb{R}) \ is \ A.C.$$

Case 1. skip and abort: Since skip is the identity measure transformer of each defined marginal measure μ_{x_i} was A.C. before, then they will trivially be so afterward since they are unchanged. abort sends each marginal to the $\mathbf{0}$ sub-measure (which is trivially A.C.).

Case 2. condition and factor: Since factor and condition only lose measure we have $[\![condition(B)]\!](\mu)(S) \leq \mu(S)$ and $[\![factor(x_k,t)]\!](\mu)(S) \leq \mu(S)$ for any Borel set S. Thus $\mu(S) = 0 \Rightarrow [\![condition(B)]\!](\mu)(S) = 0$ and $\mu(S) = 0 \Rightarrow [\![factor(x_k,t)]\!](\mu)(S) = 0$ since all measures are non-negative. Hence by transitivity, since $\mu(\mathbb{R} \times ...B_i \times \mathbb{R}...) \ is \ A.C.$, $[\![factor(x_k,t)]\!](\mu)(S)(\mathbb{R} \times ...B_i \times \mathbb{R}... \times \mathbb{R}) \ is \ A.C.$ and likewise for similar reasons, we have that $[\![condition(B)]\!](\mu)(\mathbb{R} \times ...B_i \times \mathbb{R}... \times \mathbb{R}) \ is \ A.C.$

Case 3. Assignment: Probabilistic assignment is straightforward. Since the continualized program only samples from absolutely continuous distributions, the marginal of the sampled variable x_i will be A.C. and all other marginals μ_{x_j} were A.C. by assumption. Deterministic assignment has to be handled carefully. In the continualized program the only deterministic assignments will be $x_i := a*x_j+b$; for $a \neq 0$ (all other assignments are smoothed). The marginal $\mu_{x_i}(S)$ is just $\mu_{x_j}(aS + b)$ where the set $aS + b \equiv \{s \in \mathbb{R} \mid a \cdot s + b \in S\}$. However by assumption of the A.C. of x_j, $Leb(aS + b) = 0 \Rightarrow \mu_{x_j}(aS + b) = 0$, but $Leb(S) = 0 \Leftrightarrow Leb(aS + b) = 0$ [55], hence: $Leb(S) = 0 \Rightarrow Leb(aS + b) = 0 \Rightarrow \mu_{x_j}(aS + b) = 0$. Lastly by the semantic definition of x_i, we have that $\mu_{x_j}(aS + b) = 0 \Rightarrow \mu_{x_i}(S) = 0$, hence $Leb(S) = 0 \Rightarrow \mu_{x_i}(S) = 0$ by transitivity. All other marginals are unchanged, hence A.C. of each is preserved.

Case 4. Sequencing, if and while: Intuitively since the above statements each preserve A.C of each marginal, any sequencing of them should too. Since the sum of two measures that are both A.C. in each marginal is also A.C. in each marginal, if statements preserve A.C. of each marginal. For this same reason while loops also preserve A.C.

5   Synthesis of Continuity Correction Parameters

We now present our procedure for synthesizing optimal continuity correction parameters which covers lines 6 to 15 in Algorithm 1. This can be thought of as a "training" step which fits the continualized model to the original one. It is important to note that this step is agnostic to the observed data (it only fits to the *Model*), hence it need only be done *once* off-line, regardless of how many times we perform inference on new data sets. Furthermore, even if we do not have parameters to synthesize, this step is still useful for catching runtime errors caused by the approximations, so that we can go back and apply safer approximations if necessary.

5.1   Optimization Framework

Ideally the posteriors of our approximated program $\mathcal{T}_{\mathcal{P}}^{\beta}[P]$ and the original P, should be reasonably close. However a specific posterior is induced by the corresponding dataset, if our optimization objective tries to minimize the statistical distance from $\mathcal{T}_{\mathcal{P}}^{\beta}[P]$

to P, we would simply be over-fitting to the data and we would not be able to re-use $\mathcal{T}_{\mathcal{P}}^{\beta}[P]$ for new data sets with different true parameters. Instead our objective is to minimize the distance between the original *model* M, which is simply the fragment of P that does not contain the data or observe block (and hence only defines the prior, likelihood and latent variables), and the corresponding continualized approximation, $\mathcal{T}_{\mathcal{P}}^{\beta}[M]$. To do so, we need to choose the best possible continuity correction factors, θ, for $\mathcal{T}_{\mathcal{P}}^{\beta}[M]$. Thus we define the "optimal" parameters as those which minimize a distance metric d between probability measures $d : \mathrm{M}(\mathbb{R}^n) \times \mathrm{M}(\mathbb{R}^n) \to [0, \infty)$. We also need to ensure that the metric can (a) compute the distance between discrete and continuous distributions and (b) is such that if models or likelihoods are close with respect to d, the posteriors should be as well.

Wasserstein Distance We choose to use the Wasserstein distance primarily because (1) it can measure the distance between a continuous and discrete distribution (unlike KL-Divergence or Total Variation Distance) and (2) prior work has shown that when performing inference, if using the Wasserstein distance as the chosen metric to approximate a likelihood, the (approximate) posteriors induced are comparable to the true posteriors (obtainable if one used the true likelihood) [49]. Additionally, unlike other metrics, the Wasserstein metric incorporates the underlying difference in geometry of the distributions (which strongly affects inference accuracy [37, 59]).

Let $[\![M]\!](\mu_0)$ represent the *renormalized* measure associated to the observed variables of the original model and let $[\![\mathcal{T}_{\mathcal{P}}^{\beta}[M_\theta]]\!](\mu_0)$ represent the observed variables of the continualized model, but where a given continuity correction factor θ has been substituted in (both measures start in initial distribution μ_0). Furthermore, let $\mathbf{J} \subseteq \mathrm{M}(\mathbb{R}^2)$ represent the set of all joint measures with marginal measures $[\![M]\!](\mu_0)$ and $[\![\mathcal{T}_{\mathcal{P}}^{\beta}[M_\theta]]\!](\mu_0)$. Hence we now define the 1-Wasserstein Distance:

$$W([\![M]\!](\mu_0), [\![\mathcal{T}_{\mathcal{P}}^{\beta}[M_\theta]]\!](\mu_0)) = \inf_{J \in \mathbf{J}} \int ||x - y|| dJ(x, y) \tag{1}$$

We also provide further justification why the Wasserstein Distance is a sensible metric to use. It is well known that a mixture of Gaussians can converge in distribution to any continuous random variable, however existing work has shown that a mixture of Gaussians can approximate any *discrete* distribution *in the Wasserstein Distance* arbitrarily well [20].

Objective Function We now formulate our optimization approach as follows, where $\hat{\theta}$ is the parameter vector minimizing the Wasserstein Distance with respect to the original model M, and d is the number of parameters to synthesize.

$$\hat{\theta} = \operatorname*{argmin}_{\theta \in (0,1)^d} W([\![M]\!](\mu_0), [\![\mathcal{T}_{\mathcal{P}}^{\beta}[M_\theta]]\!](\mu_0)) \tag{2}$$

To restrict the search space we follow common practice [23, 3] by requiring each $\theta_i \in (0, 1)$. Such optimization problem lacks a closed form solution. Symbolically computing the Wasserstein Distance is intractable, hence we numerically approximate it via the empirical Wasserstein Distance (EWD) between observed samples of M and $\mathcal{T}_{\mathcal{P}}^{\beta}[M_\theta]$. Because this step is fully dynamic (we run and sample the model), the samples are conditioned upon successfully terminating, and hence the model's sub-measure has been implicitly *renormalized* to a full probability measure, thus justifying the use of a fully renormalized measure in equations (1) and (2).

Algorithm 2: Synthesizing Optimal Continuity Correction Parameters

---

1 Function Synthesize $P, \mathcal{T}_P^\beta[P]$;

    Input   : A program P and a continualized sketch $\mathcal{T}_P^\beta[P]$ with d parameters to be synthesized

    Output: A fully continuous probabilistic program P_C and a binary flag denoting the existence of a runtime error

2 **if** $d==0$ **then**

3     $s \leftarrow$ sample$(\mathcal{T}_P^\beta[P], n)$;

4   **if** $s==Error$ **then**

5 | **return** $\mathcal{T}_P^\beta[P]$, *false*

6   **end**

7 **end**

8 **else**

9     $M, \mathcal{T}_P^\beta[M] \leftarrow$ getModel$(P, \mathcal{T}_P^\beta[P])$;

10   **for** $\theta_i \in Grid([0,1]^d)$ **do**

11       $p, s \leftarrow$ Nelder-Mead$(W, \theta_i, M, \mathcal{T}_P^\beta[M], \eta, \epsilon, n)$;

12   **if** $s==Error$ **then**

13 | **return** $\mathcal{T}_P^\beta[P]$, *false*

14   **end**

15   **if** $W(p) < W(\hat{\theta})$ **then**

16 | $\hat{\theta} \leftarrow p$

17   **end**

18   **end**

19 **end**

20 **return** substitute$(\mathcal{T}_P^\beta[P], \hat{\theta})$, *true*

Though intuitively we would expect that as we apply less smoothing (i.e. $\beta < 1$), the optimal θ_i should also be smaller (less need for correction) and the continualized program should become closer to the original, a simple negative result illustrates this is not always the case and that the dependence between the smoothing and continuity correction *must be* non-linear.

Remark 1. $\hat{\theta}$ **cannot be linearly proportional** to β.

Proof. Let X be the constant random variable that is 0 with probability 1 and let $X' \sim Gaussian(0, \beta)$. Furthermore, let $I := (X == 0)$ and $I_c := (c\beta \leq X' \leq c\beta)$ be two indicator random variables. Intuitively we want I_c to have the same probability of being true as I for *any* β. However if c is constant (such as 1) then $Pr(c\beta \leq X' \leq c\beta)$ will **always** be the same regardless of β (when $c = 1$, the probability is always 0.68).

5.2 Optimization Algorithm

Algorithm 2 presents our approximate synthesis algorithm, which is called as a subroutine in the main algorithm. As seen in line 2, if there are no parameters to be synthesized ($d == 0$) we still sample the continualized program in hopes of uncovering a possible runtime error (or gaining statistical confidence that one does not occur). We check for such an error in line 4 and if one exists, we return immediately, with the flag variable set to *false* (line 5).

To evaluate the EWD objective function (when there are parameters to synthesize), Algorithm 2 follows a technique from [14] and uses a Nelder-Mead search (line 11), due to Nelder-Mead's well known success in solving non-convex program synthesis problems. We first extract the fragment of the programs corresponding to the models, M and $\mathcal{T}_{\mathcal{P}}^{\beta}[M]$, respectively in line 9. In each step of the Nelder-Mead search we take n samples ($n \approx 500$) of $\mathcal{T}_{\mathcal{P}}^{\beta}[M]$, but with a fixed value of θ_i substituted into $\mathcal{T}_{\mathcal{P}}^{\beta}[M]$, to compute the EWD with respect to samples of the original model M (which have been cached to avoid redundant resampling). The Nelder-Mead search steps through the parameter space (with step size $\eta > 0$), substituting different values of θ into $\mathcal{T}_{\mathcal{P}}^{\beta}[M]$. This process continues until the search converges to a minimizing parameter, p, that is within the stopping threshold $\epsilon > 0$ or encounters a runtime error during the sampling (which is checked in line 12). As before, if we encounter such an error we immediately return with the flag set to false (line 13). Following [14], we successively restart the Nelder-Mead search from k evenly spaced grid points in $[0, 1]^d$ (hence the loop in line 10), to find the globally optimal parameter (hence our approach is robust to local minima), which we successively update in lines 15-16. If no runtime error was ever encountered, we substitute in the parameters with the minimum EWD over all runs, $\hat{\theta}$, to the fully continuous program $\mathcal{T}_{\mathcal{P}}^{\beta}[P]$ and return (line 20). Though it can be argued this sampling is potentially as difficult as the original inference, we reiterate that we need only do this once offline, hence the cost is easily *amortized*.

6   Methodology

6.1   Benchmarks

Table 1 presents the benchmarks. For each benchmark, Columns 2 and 3 present the original prior and likelihood type, respectively. Column 4 presents whether the continuity correction was applied. Column 5 presents the time to continualize the program, $T_{Cont.}$. As can be seen in Columns 4 and 5 the *total* continualization time, $T_{Cont.}$, depends on whether parameters had to be synthesized. GPAExample had the longest $T_{Cont.}$ at $3.6s$, due to the complexity of the multiple predicates, however these times are *amortized* as our synthesis step is done only once.

As our problem has received little attention, no standard benchmark suites exist. In fact, to make inference tractable, for many models, developers would construct continuous approximations by hand, in an ad hoc fashion. However we wanted a benchmark suite that showcased all 3 inference scenarios that our approach works for: (1) discrete/hybrid prior and discrete/hybrid likelihood (2) continuous prior but discrete/hybrid likelihood and (3) discrete/hybrid prior but a continuous likelihood. Therefore, we obtained the benchmarks in two ways. First, we looked at variations of the mixed distributions benchmarks previously published in the machine learning community, e.g., [65, 58], which served as the inspiration for our GPAExample. Second, we took existing benchmarks [27, 30] for which designers modeled certain distributions with continuous approximations, and we retro-fitted these models with the corresponding discrete distributions. This step was done for Election, Fairness, SVMfairness, SVE, and TrueSkill. These discretizations were only applied where they made sense, e.g., the Gauss(np,np(1-p)) in the original Election program became discretized as Binomial(n,p). We also took popular Bayesian models from Cognitive Science literature which use multiple discrete latent variables [39] and these models

Table 1: Description of Benchmarks

Program	Prior	Likelihood	Correction?	$T_{Cont.}$ (s)
GPAExample	Uniform	Discrete	✓	3.643
Election [27]	DiscUniform	Bernoulli	✓	1.139
Fairness [2]	DiscUniform	Bernoulli	✓	1.809
SVMfairness [2]	Binomial	Continuous	✓	1.578
TrueSkill [30]	Poisson	Bernoulli	✓	1.149
DiscreteDisease	DiscUniform	Discrete	✗	0.006
SVE [58]	Uniform	Hybrid	✗	0.009
BetaBinomial [39]	Beta	Discrete	✗	0.006
Exam [39]	Uniform	Discrete	✗	0.008
Plankton [10]	DiscUniform	Discrete	✗	0.006

are `BetaBinomial` and `Exam`. Lastly we took population models from the mathematical biology literature [10, 4] to build benchmarks since populations are by nature discrete. This was done for `Plankton` and `DiscreteDisease`. We present the original programs in the appendix [38].

Implementation We implemented Leios in Python (~4.5K LoC). All experiments were run on an Intel Xeon, multi-core desktop running Ubuntu 16.04 with a 3.7 GHz CPU and with 32GB RAM. All results are obtained from single-core executions.

6.2 Experimental Setup

Continualized Versions As there are no other general tools that automatically continualize probabilistic programs in mainstream languages, we compare Leios with:

- *Original Program*: inference done in standard fashion on the original model, and
- *Naive Smoothing*: inference done on a KDE style model in which Gaussian smoothing is applied *only* to the observed variable, but no approximations are applied to the inner latent variables.

We will refer to these as simply "Original" and "Naive" respectively.

Inference Accuracy Comparison using Ground Truth Our experimental design compares the respective inference estimates with the *ground truth*. We set the experiments as follows: For each of the original discrete or hybrid programs P, we replace the program variable corresponding to the prior distribution with a fixed value τ (the ground-truth) to obtain $P(\tau)$. We then sample $P(\tau)$ to obtain 25 observed data points, which will be used to test inference performance on P, P_{NS}, and P_{Leios} respectively. To test inference performance we then score P (original program), P_{NS} (naively smoothed program), and P_{Leios} against the observed data points to infer the posterior over the ground truth parameter τ. Note the programs only have access to the data samples, but not τ.

For each of the 3 versions: P, P_{NS}, and P_{Leios}, we take the inferred posterior means as the estimates of the value, and then compare it with the ground-truth value τ to measure the error ratio $E = \left| \frac{\tau - \tau_{est}}{\tau} \right|$. This entire procedure is repeated for 10 different values of τ to get a representative average of inference performance over a wide range of true parameter values.

Table 2: Inference Times (s) and Error Ratios for each model, $\beta = 0.1$

Program	Original Time	Original Error	Naive Time	Naive Error	Leios Time	Leios Error
GPAExample	0.806	0.090	0.631	0.070	0.605	0.058
Election	-	-	3.232	0.051	0.616	0.036
Fairness	4.396	0.057	0.563	0.056	0.603	0.093
SVMfairness	-	-	0.626	0.454	0.980	0.261
TrueSkill	3.668	0.009	0.494	0.059	0.586	0.053
DiscreteDisease	4.944	0.009	1.350	0.013	0.490	0.008
SVE	-	-	0.522	0.045	0.516	0.091
BetaBinomial	1.224	0.028	0.564	0.024	0.459	0.013
Exam	3.973	0.087	0.504	0.126	0.527	0.133
Plankton	0.570	0.017	0.457	0.080	0.453	0.042
Average	2.797	0.043	0.894	0.098	0.584	0.079

Analyzed Probabilistic Programming Systems. We used two languages in our development: WebPPL [26] (with MCMC inference) and Pyro [8] (with Variational inference). Our implementation automatically generates WebPPL code for all the programs. We used 3500 MCMC samples (with burn-in of 700 samples) in the simulation. For Pyro, we only wanted to test *fully-automatic* black-box Variational Inference, hence we did not manually marginalize out discrete variables (which is often not even applicable, as the discrete variables are the one we wish to estimate).

Inference Time Measurement We measure the time taken for inference for each version using built-in timers (which exclude file reading and warm-up). A timeout of 10 minutes was used for the inference step. We used this same procedure for both MCMC-based sampling in WebPPL and Variational Inference in Pyro.

7   Evaluation

We study the following three research questions:

RQ1 Can program continualization make inference faster, while still maintaining a high degree of accuracy, compared to the original program and naive smoothing?

RQ2 How do performance and accuracy vary for different smoothing factors β?

RQ3 Can program continualization enable running transformed programs with off-the-shelf inference algorithms that cannot execute the original programs?

7.1   RQ1: Benefits of Continualization

Table 2 presents detailed timing and accuracy errors for a single smoothing factor β on WebPPL programs. Columns 2 and 3 present the time and error (compared to the ground truth) for the original program. Columns 4 and 5 present time/error for the naive smoothing and Columns 6 and 7 present time/error for Leios.

From Table 2 we can see that on average, Leios leads to faster inference than both the Original (no approximations) and Naive (0.584s vs 2.797s and 0.894s, respectively). The Naive version was also faster than the original, giving more evidence that continuous models (even when just the observed variable is continualized) yield faster inference.

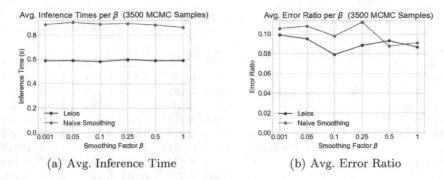

(a) Avg. Inference Time   (b) Avg. Error Ratio

Fig. 7: Inference Times and Error ratios for Leios and Naive for different β

For accuracy, inference performed via Leios was on average more accurate than Naive ($E = 0.079$ vs. 0.098, respectively). Both were slightly less accurate than inference performed on Original ($E = 0.043$). This is not unreasonable as Original has *no* approximations applied (which are the main source of inference error). However the Original failed on `Election`, `SVE`, and `SVMfairness`. For `Election`, a large Binomial latent led to a timeout, and it also slowed the Naive version relative to Leios (3.23s vs 0.61s). The Original failed on `SVE` since it is a hybrid discrete-continuous model (which can make inference intractable [65, 6]). `SVMfairness` is a non-linear model where many latent variables have high variances, leading to inference on the Original failing to converge; Leios and Naive had higher error on this benchmark, for much the same reason (though Leios was still significantly better than Naive, $E = 0.261$ vs 0.454).

Although Leios was faster than Original in all cases, for `TrueSkill` and `SVMfairness`, Leios was somewhat slower than Naive. This is likely because the discrete latent variables in these benchmarks had small enough parameters (Binomial with small n). Similarly, for `Fairness`, Leios was slightly less accurate than Naive because the Gaussian approximation can be less accurate for smaller n.

7.2   RQ2: Impact of Smoothing Factors

Figure 7 presents the average inference times and ERs for different smoothing factors β. In both cases, X-axes represent smoothing factors. The Y-Axis of the left subfigure presents time, and Y-Axis of the right presents error ratio compared to the ground truth (less is better).

Figure 7 (a) shows that Inference on the programs constructed by Leios is non-trivially faster than inference done on the naively smoothed version, regardless of the β used (which has negligible affect on the inference time for the β we examined).

Figure 7 (b) presents how accuracy directly depends on β. The Error Ratio for Leios reaches a local minimum when $\beta = 0.1$. Because Leios achieves "global" smoothing by approximating each latent, a larger value for β is not needed (unlike Naive). We also noticed for many benchmarks, smaller β led to better continuity correction parameters which also leads to better inference. Naive's performance suffers for smaller β, which we attribute to small β creating a highly multimodal observed variable distribution (also presented in Section 2) which hampers inference [37, 59]. Consequently, Naive performs best when $\beta = 0.5$, however this β introduces non-trivially higher variance, which may often negatively affect the precision of inference.

Table 3: Variational Inference Times (s) and Error Ratios for selected β

Program	T_{org}	E_{org}	T_{NS}	E_{NS}	$\beta : 0.25$		$\beta : 0.5$		$\beta : 0.75$	
					T_{Leios}	E_{Leios}	T_{Leios}	E_{Leios}	T_{Leios}	E_{Leios}
GPAExample	-	-	-	-	3.111	0.207	3.341	0.241	3.435	0.321
Election	-	-	-	-	1.762	0.070	1.755	0.110	1.764	0.064
Fairness	-	-	-	-	1.813	0.722	1.827	0.769	1.830	0.753
SVMfairness	-	-	-	-	1.800	0.201	1.806	0.293	1.804	0.301
TrueSkill	-	-	-	-	1.809	0.119	1.802	0.062	1.790	0.090
DiscreteDisease	-	-	-	-	1.734	0.248	1.731	0.471	1.747	0.553
SVE	0.677	0.684	1.478	3.095	1.471	0.587	1.460	0.566	1.448	0.348
BetaBinomial	-	-	-	-	1.605	0.834	1.596	0.708	1.587	0.497
Exam	-	-	-	-	0.603	0.222	0.602	0.213	0.603	0.285
Plankton	-	-	-	-	3.432	0.297	3.427	0.763	3.434	0.530

7.3   RQ3: Extending Results to Other Systems

Table 3 presents the results for running translated programs in Pyro. Columns 2-5 present the inference times and result errors for the original and naively smoothed program. These columns are "-" when Pyro cannot successfully perform inference (i.e. the model contains a discrete variable that is unsupported by the auto guide). Columns 6-11 present Leios' time and error for each model, for three different smoothing parameters.

Fully-automated Variational Inference failed on all but one of the examples for both the Original and Naive. This is because in both cases the program still contains latent or observed discrete random variables. For most of the benchmarks (**Election**, **GPA**, **TrueSkill**) the program optimized with Leios had errors comparable to those computed previously with MCMC in WebPPL. For some the error was over 0.5 for all β (**BetaBinomial**, **Fairness**), which is in part a consequence of limitations of automatic VI, and hence for certain models manual fine-tuning may be unavoidable. These results illustrate that Leios can be used to create an efficient program in situations when the original language does not easily support non-continuous distributions.

8   Related Work

Probabilistic Program Synthesis To the best of our knowledge, we are the first to study program transformations that approximate discrete or hybrid discrete-continuous *probabilistic programs* with fully continuous ones to improve inference. Probabilistic program synthesis takes a more ambitious task of generating probabilistic programs with certain properties directly from data. For instance, Nori et al. [51] aim to synthesize a probabilistic program given a program sketch and a data-set to fit the program to. However, it merely fits the distribution parameters to the sketch. Furthermore their language lacks '==' comparisons. Chasins et al. [11] takes a similar approach but only apply continuous approximations to *already* continuous variables.

Probabilistic Inference with Discrete and Hybrid Distributions Recent work [65, 66] has explored developing languages and semantics to encode discrete-continuous mixtures, however these all restrict the types of programs that can be expressed and require specialized inference algorithms. In contrast, Leios can work with a variety of off-the-shelf inference algorithms that operate on arbitrary models and does not need to define its own inference algorithm. In [66] the authors explored a restricted programming language that can statically detect which parameters the program's density is discontinuous in. However they did not address the question of continuous approximation, rather their approach was to develop a custom inference scheme and restrict the language so that pathological models cannot be written (they also disallow '==' predicates). In [65], Wu et al. develop a custom inference method for discrete-continuous mixtures but only for models encodeable as a Bayesian network, furthermore as pointed out by [47], the specialized inference method of Wu et al. is restrictive since it cannot be composed with other program transformations.

Additionally, Machine Learning researchers have developed other continuous relaxation techniques to address the inherent problems of non-differentiable models. One other popular method is to reparametrize the gradient estimator during Variational Inference (VI) computation, commonly called the "reparameterization trick" [42, 61]. However, this approach suffers from the fact that not all distributions support such gradient reparameterizations, and also this method is only limited to Variational Inference. Conversely our approach allows one to still use *any* inference scheme. Further, even though these techniques have been attempted in the probabilistic programming setting, [40], such work still inherits the aforementioned weaknesses.

We also draw upon Kernel Density Estimation (KDE) [62], a common approximation scheme in statistics. KDE fits a Kernel density to each observed data point, hence constructing a smooth approximation. Naive Smoothing is essentially a KDE (with a Gaussian Kernel) of the original while Leios employs additional continualizations. Furthermore, our smoothing factor β is analogous to the *bandwidth* of a KDE.

Program Analysis for Probabilistic Programs Multiple Program Analysis frameworks and systems have been developed for Probabilistic Programming [57, 33, 63, 32, 22]. Additionally these analyses make use of a rich set of semantics [44, 36, 7, 64, 19], however of particular note is recent work by Lew et al. [41], which provides a type system for reasoning about variational approximations; however they focus on continuous approximations of already continuous variables.

Benefits of Continuity in Conventional Programs The idea of smoothing and working with continuous functions in non-probabilistic programs has found success in a variety of applications [21, 12, 34, 13]. Our work derives inspiration mainly from Smooth interpretation [14], which provides a semantics for smoothing *deterministic* programs encoding a discontinuous or discrete function.

9   Conclusion

We presented Leios as a method for approximating probabilistic programs with fully continuous versions. Our approach shows that by continualizing probabilistic programs, it is possible to achieve substantial speed-ups in inference performance whilst still preserving a high degree of accuracy. To this effect we combined two key techniques: statement level program transformations to continualize latent variables and a novel continuity correction synthesis procedure to correct branch conditions.

Acknowledgements

We would like to thank the anonymous reviewers for their constructive feedback. We thank Darko Marinov for his helpful feedback during early stages of the work. We thank Adithya Murali for valuable feedback about the semantics. We thank Zixin Huang and Saikat Dutta for helpful discussions about the evaluation and Vimuth Fernando and Keyur Joshi for helpful proofreads. JL is grateful for support from the Alfred P. Sloan foundation for a Sloan Scholar award used to support much of this work. The research presented in this paper has been supported in part by NSF, Grant no. CCF-1846354.

References

1. Aigner, D.J., Amemiya, T., Poirier, D.J.: On the estimation of production frontiers: maximum likelihood estimation of the parameters of a discontinuous density function. International Economic Review pp. 377–396 (1976)
2. Albarghouthi, A., D'Antoni, L., Drews, S., Nori, A.V.: Fairsquare: Probabilistic verification of program fairness. Proc. ACM Program. Lang. (OOPSLA) (2017)
3. Bar-Lev, S.K., Fuchs, C.: Continuity corrections for discrete distributions under the edgeworth expansion. Methodology And Computing In Applied Probability 3(4), 347–364 (2001)
4. Becker, N.: A general chain binomial model for infectious diseases. Biometrics 37(2), 251–258 (1981)
5. Betancourt, M., Girolami, M.: Hamiltonian monte carlo for hierarchical models. Current trends in Bayesian methodology with applications 79, 30 (2015)
6. Bhat, S., Borgström, J., Gordon, A.D., Russo, C.: Deriving probability density functions from probabilistic functional programs. In: International Conference on Tools and Algorithms for the Construction and Analysis of Systems. pp. 508–522. TACAS'13 (2013)
7. Bichsel, B., Gehr, T., Vechev, M.T.: Fine-grained semantics for probabilistic programs. In: Programming Languages and Systems - 27th European Symposium on Programming, ESOPh. pp. 145–185 (2018)
8. Bingham, E., Chen, J.P., Jankowiak, M., Obermeyer, F., Pradhan, N., Karaletsos, T., Singh, R., Szerlip, P., Horsfall, P., Goodman, N.D.: Pyro: Deep Universal Probabilistic Programming. arXiv preprint arXiv:1810.09538 (2018)
9. Blei, D.M., Kucukelbir, A., McAuliffe, J.D.: Variational inference: A review for statisticians. Journal of the American Statistical Association 112(518) (2017)
10. Blumenthal, S., Dahiya, R.C.: Estimating the binomial parameter n. Journal of the American Statistical Association 76(376), 903–909 (1981)
11. Chasins, S., Phothilimthana, P.M.: Data-driven synthesis of full probabilistic programs. In: CAV (2017)
12. Chaudhuri, S., Clochard, M., Solar-Lezama, A.: Bridging boolean and quantitative synthesis using smoothed proof search. In: ACM SIGPLAN-SIGACT Symposium on Principles of Programming Languages. POPL '14 (2014)
13. Chaudhuri, S., Gulwani, S., Lublinerman, R.: Continuity and robustness of programs. In: Communications of the ACM, Research Highlights. vol. 55 (2012)
14. Chaudhuri, S., Solar-Lezama, A.: Smooth interpretation. In: Proceedings of the 31st ACM SIGPLAN Conference on Programming Language Design and Implementation. pp. 279–291. PLDI '10 (2010)

15. Chen, Y., Ghahramani, Z.: Scalable discrete sampling as a multi-armed bandit problem. In: Proceedings of the 33rd International Conference on International Conference on Machine Learning - Volume 48. pp. 2492–2501. ICML'16 (2016)
16. Cheng, T.T.: The normal approximation to the poisson distribution and a proof of a conjecture of ramanujan. Bull. Amer. Math. Soc. **55**(4), 396–401 (04 1949)
17. Chung, H., Loken, E., Schafer, J.L.: Difficulties in drawing inferences with finite-mixture models. The American Statistician **58**(2), 152–158 (2004)
18. Cooper, G.F.: The computational complexity of probabilistic inference using bayesian belief networks. Artificial Intelligence **42**(2), 393 – 405 (1990)
19. Dahlqvist, F., Kozen, D., Silva, A.: Semantics of probabilistic programming: A gentle introduction. In: Foundations of Probabilistic Programming (2020)
20. Delon, J., Desolneux, A.: A wasserstein-type distance in the space of gaussian mixture models. arXiv preprint arXiv:1907.05254 (2019)
21. DeMillo, R.A., Lipton, R.J.: Defining software by continuous, smooth functions. IEEE Trans. Softw. Eng. **17**(4) (Apr 1991)
22. Dutta, S., Zhang, W., Huang, Z., Misailovic, S.: Storm: program reduction for testing and debugging probabilistic programming systems. In: Proceedings of the 2019 27th ACM Joint Meeting on European Software Engineering Conference and Symposium on the Foundations of Software Engineering. pp. 729–739 (2019)
23. Feller, W.: On the normal approximation to the binomial distribution. Ann. Math. Statist. **16**(4), 319–329 (12 1945)
24. Gehr, T., Misailovic, S., Vechev, M.T.: PSI: exact symbolic inference for probabilistic programs. In: Computer Aided Verification, CAV. pp. 62–83 (2016)
25. Gelman, A.: Parameterization and bayesian modeling. Journal of the American Statistical Association **99**(466), 537–545 (2004)
26. Goodman, N.D., Stuhlmüller, A.: The Design and Implementation of Probabilistic Programming Languages (2014)
27. Goodman, N.D., Tenenbaum, J.B., Contributors, T.P.: Probabilistic Models of Cognition (2016)
28. Gordon, A.D., Henzinger, T.A., Nori, A.V., Rajamani, S.K.: Probabilistic programming. In: Proceedings of the on Future of Software Engineering (2014)
29. Gorinova, M.I., Moore, D., Hoffman, M.D.: Automatic reparameterisation in probabilistic programming (2019)
30. Herbrich, R., Minka, T., Graepel, T.: Trueskill^{TM}: A bayesian skill rating system. In: Proceedings of the 19th International Conference on Neural Information Processing Systems. pp. 569–576. NIPS'06 (2006)
31. Hoffman, M.D., Gelman, A.: The no-u-turn sampler: Adaptively setting path lengths in hamiltonian monte carlo (2011)
32. Huang, Z., Wang, Z., Misailovic, S.: Psense: Automatic sensitivity analysis for probabilistic programs. In: Automated Technology for Verification and Analysis - 15th International Symposium, ATVA 2018, Los Angeles, California, October 7-10, 2018, Proceedings (2018)
33. Hur, C.K., Nori, A.V., Rajamani, S.K., Samuel, S.: Slicing probabilistic programs. In: Proceedings of the 35th ACM SIGPLAN Conference on Programming Language Design and Implementation. pp. 133–144 (2014)
34. Inala, J.P., Gao, S., Kong, S., Solar-Lezama, A.: REAS: combining numerical optimization with SAT solving (2018)
35. Kildall, G.A.: A unified approach to global program optimization. In: Proceedings of the 1st Annual ACM SIGACT-SIGPLAN Symposium on Principles of Programming Languages. pp. 194–206. POPL '73 (1973)

36. Kozen, D.: Semantics of probabilistic programs. Journal of Computer and System Sciences **22**(3), 328 – 350 (1981)
37. Lan, S., Streets, J., Shahbaba, B.: Wormhole hamiltonian monte carlo. In: Proceedings of the Twenty-Eighth AAAI Conference on Artificial Intelligence. pp. 1953–1959. AAAI'14 (2014)
38. Laurel, J., Misailovic, S.: Continualization of probabilistic programs with correction (appendix) (2020), https://jsl1994.github.io/papers/ESOP2020_appendix.pdf
39. Lee, M.D., Wagenmakers, E.J.: Bayesian cognitive modeling: A practical course. Cambridge University Press (2014)
40. Lee, W., Yu, H., Yang, H.: Reparameterization gradient for non-differentiable models. In: Advances in Neural Information Processing Systems. pp. 5553–5563 (2018)
41. Lew, A.K., Cusumano-Towner, M.F., Sherman, B., Carbin, M., Mansinghka, V.K.: Trace types and denotational semantics for sound programmable inference in probabilistic languages. Proc. ACM Program. Lang. **4**(POPL) (2019)
42. Maddison, C.J., Mnih, A., Teh, Y.W.: The Concrete Distribution: A Continuous Relaxation of Discrete Random Variables. In: International Conference on Learning Representations (2017)
43. Marin, J.M., Mengersen, K., Robert, C.P.: Bayesian modelling and inference on mixtures of distributions. Handbook of statistics **25**, 459–507 (2005)
44. Morgan, C., McIver, A., Seidel, K.: Probabilistic predicate transformers. ACM Trans. Program. Lang. Syst. **18**(3), 325–353 (May 1996)
45. Murray, I., Salakhutdinov, R.: Evaluating probabilities under high-dimensional latent variable models. In: Proceedings of the 21st International Conference on Neural Information Processing Systems. pp. 1137–1144. NIPS'08 (2008)
46. Nandi, C., Grossman, D., Sampson, A., Mytkowicz, T., McKinley, K.S.: Debugging probabilistic programs. In: Proceedings of the 1st ACM SIGPLAN International Workshop on Machine Learning and Programming Languages. MAPL 2017 (2017)
47. Narayanan, P., Shan, C.c.: Symbolic disintegration with a variety of base measures (2019), http://homes.sice.indiana.edu/ccshan/rational/disint2arg.pdf
48. Neal, R.M.: Mcmc using hamiltonian dynamics. In: Handbook of Markov Chain Monte Carlo, chap. 5 (2012)
49. Nguyen, V.A., Abadeh, S.S., Yue, M.C., Kuhn, D., Wiesemann, W.: Optimistic distributionally robust optimization for nonparametric likelihood approximation. In: Advances in Neural Information Processing Systems. pp. 15846–15856 (2019)
50. Nishimura, A., Dunson, D., Lu, J.: Discontinuous hamiltonian monte carlo for discrete parameters and discontinuous likelihoods (2017), https://arxiv.org/abs/1705.08510
51. Nori, A.V., Ozair, S., Rajamani, S.K., Vijaykeerthy, D.: Efficient synthesis of probabilistic programs. In: Proceedings of the 36th ACM SIGPLAN Conference on Programming Language Design and Implementation. pp. 208 217. PLDI '15 (2015)
52. Opper, M., Archambeau, C.: The variational gaussian approximation revisited. Neural Computation **21**(3), 786–792 (2009)
53. Opper, M., Winther, O.: Expectation consistent approximate inference. J. Mach. Learn. Res. **6**, 2177–2204 (Dec 2005)
54. Ross, S.: A First Course in Probability. Pearson (2010)
55. Rudin, W.: Real and complex analysis. McGraw-Hill Education (2006)
56. Salimans, T., Kingma, D.P., Welling, M.: Markov chain monte carlo and variational inference: Bridging the gap. In: Proceedings of the 32nd International Conference on International Conference on Machine Learning. pp. 1218–1226. ICML (2015)

57. Sankaranarayanan, S., Chakarov, A., Gulwani, S.: Static analysis for probabilistic programs: inferring whole program properties from finitely many paths. In: Proceedings of the 34th ACM SIGPLAN conference on Programming language design and implementation. pp. 447–458 (2013)
58. Sanner, S., Abbasnejad, E.: Symbolic variable elimination for discrete and continuous graphical models. In: Proceedings of the Twenty-Sixth AAAI Conference on Artificial Intelligence. pp. 1954–1960. AAAI'12 (2012)
59. Smith, J., Croft, J.: Bayesian networks for discrete multivariate data: an algebraic approach to inference. Journal of Multivariate Analysis **84**(2), 387 – 402 (2003)
60. Tolpin, D., van de Meent, J.W., Yang, H., Wood, F.: Design and implementation of probabilistic programming language anglican. In: Proceedings of the 28th Symposium on the Implementation and Application of Functional Programming Languages. IFL 2016 (2016)
61. Tucker, G., Mnih, A., Maddison, C.J., Sohl-Dickstein, J.: REBAR : Low-variance, unbiased gradient estimates for discrete latent variable models. In: Neural Information Processing Systems (2017)
62. Wand, M., Jones, M.: Kernel Smoothing (Chapman & Hall/CRC Monographs on Statistics and Applied Probability) (1995)
63. Wang, D., Hoffmann, J., Reps, T.: Pmaf: An algebraic framework for static analysis of probabilistic programs. In: Proceedings of the 39th ACM SIGPLAN Conference on Programming Language Design and Implementation. PLDI 2018 (2018)
64. Wang, D., Hoffmann, J., Reps, T.: A denotational semantics for low-level probabilistic programs with nondeterminism. Electronic Notes in Theoretical Computer Science **347** (2019), proceedings of the Thirty-Fifth Conference on the Mathematical Foundations of Programming Semantics
65. Wu, Y., Srivastava, S., Hay, N., Du, S., Russell, S.: Discrete-continuous mixtures in probabilistic programming: Generalized semantics and inference algorithms. In: Proceedings of the 35th International Conference on Machine Learning. Proceedings of Machine Learning Research, vol. 80, pp. 5343–5352 (2018)
66. Zhou, Y., Gram-Hansen, B.J., Kohn, T., Rainforth, T., Yang, H., Wood, F.: LF-PPL: A low-level first order probabilistic programming language for non-differentiable models. In: The 22nd International Conference on Artificial Intelligence and Statistics, AISTATS. Proceedings of Machine Learning Research, vol. 89, pp. 148–157 (2019)

Semantic Foundations for Deterministic Dataflow and Stream Processing

Konstantinos Mamouras

Rice University, Houston TX 77005, USA
mamouras@rice.edu

Abstract. We propose a denotational semantic framework for deterministic dataflow and stream processing that encompasses a variety of existing streaming models. Our proposal is based on the idea that data streams, stream transformations, and stream-processing programs should be classified using types. The type of a data stream is captured formally by a monoid, an algebraic structure with a distinguished binary operation and a unit. The elements of a monoid model the finite fragments of a stream, the binary operation represents the concatenation of stream fragments, and the unit is the empty fragment. Stream transformations are modeled using monotone functions on streams, which we call stream transductions. These functions can be implemented using abstract machines with a potentially infinite state space, which we call stream transducers. This abstract typed framework of stream transductions and transducers can be used to (1) verify the correctness of streaming computations, that is, that an implementation adheres to the desired behavior, (2) prove the soundness of optimizing transformations, e.g. for parallelization and distribution, and (3) inform the design of programming models and query languages for stream processing. In particular, we show that several useful combinators can be supported by the full class of stream transductions and transducers: serial composition, parallel composition, and feedback composition.

Keywords: Data streams · Denotational semantics · Type system

1   Introduction

Stream processing is the computational paradigm where the input is not presented in its entirety at the beginning of the computation, but instead it is given in an incremental fashion as a potentially unbounded sequence of elements or data items. This paradigm is appropriate in settings where data is created continually in real-time and has to be processed immediately in order to extract actionable insights and enable timely decision-making. Examples of such datasets are streams of business events in an enterprise setting [26], streams of packets that flow through computer networks [37], time-series data that is captured by sensors in healthcare applications [33], etc.

Due to the great variety of streaming applications, there are various proposals for specialized languages, compilers, and runtime systems that deal with the

P. Müller (Ed.): ESOP 2020, LNCS 12075, pp. 394–427, 2020.
https://doi.org/10.1007/978-3-030-44914-8_15

processing of streaming data. Relational database systems and SQL-based languages have been adapted to the streaming setting [1,2,15,16,18,19,32,37,57,91]. Recently, several systems have been developed for the distributed processing of data streams that are based on the distributed dataflow model of computation [6, 7, 70, 86, 92, 94, 108, 112, 113]. Languages for detecting complex events in distributed systems, which draw on the theory of regular expressions and finite-state automata, have also been proposed [29,40,41,50,53,88,99,111]. The synchronous dataflow formalisms [20, 24, 28, 51, 73, 107] are based on Kahn's seminal work [59], and they have been used for exposing and exploiting task-level and pipeline parallelism within streaming computations in the context of embedded systems. Several formalisms for the runtime verification of reactive systems have been proposed, many of which are based on variants of Temporal Logic and its timed/quantitative extensions [39, 43, 52, 74, 105]. Finally, there is a large collection of languages and systems for reactive programming [34,36,38,46,47,55,68,69,77,89,93,103], which focus on the development of event-driven and interactive applications such as GUIs and web programming.

The aforementioned languages and systems have been successfully used in the application domains for which they were developed. However, each one of them typically introduces a unique variant of the streaming model in terms of: (1) the form of the input and output data, (2) the class of expressible stream-processing computations, and (3) the syntax employed to describe these computations. This has resulted in an enormous proliferation of semantic models for stream processing that are difficult to compare. For this reason, we are interested in identifying a semantic unification of several existing streaming models.

This paper introduces a *typed semantic framework* for reasoning about languages and systems for stream processing. Three key questions are tackled:

1. How do we model *streams* and what is the form of the data that they carry?
2. How do we capture mathematically the notion of a *stream transformation*?
3. What is a general *programming model* for specifying streaming computations?

The first two questions concern the discovery of an appropriate **denotational model** for streaming computation. The third question concerns the design of programming and query languages, where a key requirement is that the behavior of a streaming program/query admits a precise mathematical description. Existing works have addressed these questions in the context of specific classes of applications. Here are examples of various perspectives:

– *Transductions of strings* [8, 100, 104, 110]: A stream is viewed as an unbounded sequence of letters, and a stream transformation is a translation from input sequences to output sequences, which is typically called string/word transduction. These translations are commonly described using finite-state transducers, a class of automata that extend acceptors with output.

– *The streaming dataflow model of Gilles Kahn* [59, 60]: The input and output consist of multiple independent channels that carry unbounded sequences of elements. A transformation is a function from a tuple of input sequences to a tuple of output sequences. Such transformations are specified with dataflow graphs whose nodes describe single-process computations.

- **Relational transformations** [71]: A stream is an unbounded multiset (bag) of tuples, and a stream transformation is a monotone operator (w.r.t. multiset containment) on multisets. This can be generalized to consider more than one input stream. An interesting subclass of these operators can be described syntactically using monotone relational algebra.

- **Processing of time-varying relations** [16, 17]: A stream is a time-varying finite multiset of tuples, i.e. an unbounded sequence of finite multisets of tuples. In this setting, a stream transformation processes the input in a way that preserves the notion of time: after processing t input multisets (i.e., t time units) the output consists of t output multisets. The query language CQL [16] defines a class of such computations that involve relational and windowing operators.

- **Transformations of continuous-time signals** [27]: An input stream is a continuous-time signal, that is, a function from the real numbers $\mathbb{R}$ to an n-dimensional space $\mathbb{R}^n$. A stream transformation is a mapping from input signals to output signals that is *causal*, which means that the value of the output at time t depends on the values of input signal up to (and including) time t. Systems of differential equations can be used to describe classes of such transformations.

We are interested here in a unifying framework that encompasses all the aforementioned concrete instances of streaming models and enables formal reasoning about the composition of streaming computations from different models. In order to achieve this we take an **abstract algebraic approach** that retains only the essential aspects of stream processing without any unnecessary specialization. The rest of the section outlines our proposal.

At the most fundamental level, stream processing is computation over input that is not given at the beginning in full, but rather is presented incrementally as the computation evolves. Since the input is presented piece by piece, the basic concepts that need to be captured mathematically are: (1) what is a *piece* or *fragment of the input*, and (2) how do we *extend the input*. The most general class of algebraic structures that model these notions is the class of **monoids**, the collection of algebras that have a distinguished binary associative multiplication operation · and an identity element 1 for this operation. A monoid $(A, \cdot, 1)$ then constitutes a **type of data streams**, where the elements of the monoid are all the possible *finite stream fragments*, the identity $1 \in A$ is the *empty stream* fragment, and the multiplication operation $\cdot : A \times A \to A$ models the *concatenation* of stream fragments. Using monoids, we can organize several notions of data streams using types that describe the form of the data, as well any invariants or assumptions about them. Monoids encompass the kinds of data streams that we mentioned earlier and many more: strings of letters, linear sequences of data items, tuples of sequences, multisets (bags) of data items, sets of data items, time-varying relations/multisets, (potentially disordered) timestamped sequences of data items, continuous-time signals, and so on.

Stream transformations can be classified according to the type of their input and output streams, which we call a **transduction type**. They are modeled using *monotone functions* that map an input stream history (i.e., the fragment of the input stream that has been received from the beginning of the computation until now) to an output stream history (i.e., the fragment of the output stream produced so far). The monotonicity requirement captures the idea that a stream transformation cannot retract the output that has already been emitted. We call such functions **stream transductions**, and we propose them as a denotational semantic model for stream processing. This model encompasses string transductions, non-diverging Kahn-computable [59] functions on streams, monotone relational transformations [71], the CQL-definable [16] transformations on time-varying relations, and transformations of continuous-time signals [27].

We also introduce an abstract model of computation for stream processing. The considered programs or abstract machines are called **stream transducers**, and they are organized using **transducer types** that specify the input and output stream types. A stream transducer processes the input stream in an incremental fashion, by consuming it fragment by fragment. The consumption of an input fragment results in the emission of an output fragment. Our algebraic setting brings in an unavoidable complication compared to the classical theory of word transducers: not all stream transducers describe a stream transduction. This phenomenon has to do with the generalization of the input and output data streams from sequences of atomic data items to elements of arbitrary monoids. A stream transducer has to respect its input/output type, which means that the way in which the input stream is fragmented into pieces and fed to the transducer does not affect the cumulative output. More concisely, this says that the cumulative output is independent from the fragmentation of the input. In order to formalize this notion, we say that a *factorization* of an input history u is a sequence of stream fragments $u_1, u_2, \ldots, u_n$ whose concatenation is equal to the input history, i.e. $u_1 \cdot u_2 \cdots u_n = u$. Now, the desired restriction can be described as follows: for every input history w and any two factorizations $u_1, \ldots, u_m$ and $v_1, \ldots, v_m$ of w, the cumulative output that the transducer emits when consuming the fragments $u_1, \ldots, u_m$ in sequence is equal to the cumulative output when consuming the fragments $v_1, \ldots, v_n$. Fortunately, this complex property can be distilled into an equivalent property on the structure of the stream transducer that we call **coherence property**. Every stream transducer that is coherent has a well-defined semantics or *denotation* in terms of a stream transduction.

We have already outlined the basics of our general framework for streaming computation, which includes: (1) a classification of streams using monoids as types, (2) a denotational semantic model that employs monotone functions from input histories to output histories, and (3) a programming model that generalizes transducers to compute meaninfully on elements of arbitrary monoids. This already allows us to address important questions about specific computations:

– Does a streaming program (transducer) behave as intended? This amounts to checking whether the denotation of the transducer is the desired function.
– Are two streaming programs (transducers) equivalent? This means that their denotations in terms of stream transductions are the same.

The first question is a *correctness* property. The second question is relevant for *semantics-preserving program optimization*. We will turn now to the issue of how to modularly specify complex stream transductions and transducers.

One of the most common ways to conceptually organize complex streaming computations is to view the overall computation as the composition of several processes that run independently and are connected with directed communication channels on which streams of data flow. This way of structuring computations is called the *dataflow programming model*. The simple deterministic parallel model of Karp and Miller [61] is one of the first variants of dataflow, and other notable early works on dataflow models include Dennis's parallel language of actors and links [42] and Kahn's networks [59] of computing stations and communication lines. We investigate three key *dataflow combinators* for composing stream transductions (i.e., semantic-level) and stream transducers (i.e., program-level): *serial* composition, *parallel* composition, and *feedback* composition. Serial composition is useful for describing pipelines of processing stages, where the output of one stage is streamed as input into the next stage. Parallel composition describes the independent and concurrent computation of two or more components. Feedback composition supports computations whose current output depends on previously produced outputs. We show that our framework supports all these combinators, which facilitate the modular description of complex computations and expose pipeline and task-based parallelism.

Outline of paper. In Sect. 2 we introduce the idea that data streams can be classified using monoids as their types, and in Sect. 3 we propose the semantic model of stream transductions. Sect. 4 is devoted to the description of an abstract model of streaming computation, called stream transducer, and the main properties that it satisfies. In Sect. 5 we show that our abstract model is closed under a fundamental set of dataflow combinators: serial, parallel, and feedback composition. In Sect. 6 we prove the soundness of a streaming optimizing transformation using denotational arguments and algebraic rewriting. Sect. 7 contains related work, and Sect. 8 concludes with a brief summary of our proposal.

2 Monoids as Types for Streams

Data streams are typically viewed as unbounded linear sequences of data items, where a data item can be thought of as a small indivisible piece of data. This viewpoint is sufficient for describing many useful semantic and programming models, but it is too concrete and unnecessarily restricts the notion of a data stream. In order to see this, consider a computation where the specific order in which the data items arrive is not relevant. Counting is a trivial example of such a computation, and it can be described operationally as follows: every time a new data item arrives, the counting stream algorithm emits the total number of items that have been seen so far. This can be described mathematically by the function β, given by $\beta(\langle x_1, x_2, \ldots, x_n \rangle) = \langle 1, 2, \ldots, n \rangle$, where $\langle x_1, x_2, \ldots, x_n \rangle$ is the input and $\langle 1, 2, \ldots, n \rangle$ is the cumulative output of the computation. For this computation, the input can be meaningfully viewed as a *multiset* (or bag) instead of a sequence, since the ordering of the data items is irrelevant. This means that multisets can also be viewed as data streams, and in some cases this viewpoint is preferable to the traditional one of "streams = sequences".

The example of the previous paragraph raises an obvious question: What class of mathematical objects can meaningfully serve as data streams? Linear sequences and multisets should certainly be included, but it would be desirable to generalize the notion of streams as much as possible. Recent works explore the idea of generalizing streams to encompass a large class of *partial orders* [13, 85], but we will see later that this approach excludes many useful instances. Stream processing is the computational paradigm where the input is not presented in full at the beginning of the computation, but instead it is given in an incremental fashion or *piece by piece*. For this reason, there are just three notions that need to be modeled mathematically: (1) a *fragment* or piece of a data stream, (2) the *extension* of data with an additional fragment of data, and (3) the *empty* data stream, i.e. the data seen at the very beginning of the computation. This leads us to consider a *kind* or *type of a data stream* as an algebraic structure that satisfies the following: (1) its elements model data stream fragments, (2) it has a distinguished associative operation $\cdot$ for the concatenation of stream fragments, and (3) it has a distinguished element 1 that represents the empty fragment so that 1 is a unit for concatenation. The class of monoids is the largest class of algebraic structures that fulfill these requirements.

More formally, a *monoid* is an algebraic structure $(A, \cdot, 1)$, where $\cdot : A \times A \to A$ is a binary operation called *multiplication* and $1 \in A$ is a constant called *unit*, that satisfies the following two axioms: (I) $(x \cdot y) \cdot z = x \cdot (y \cdot z)$ for all $x, y, z \in A$, and (II) $1 \cdot x = x \cdot 1 = x$ for all $x \in A$. The first axiom says that $\cdot$ is associative, and the second axiom says that 1 is a left and right identity for the $\cdot$ operation. For brevity, we will sometimes write xy to denote $x \cdot y$.

Suppose that A is a monoid. We write A^* for the set of all finite sequences of elements of A and ε for the empty sequence. The *finite multiplication* function $\pi : A^* \to A$ is given by $\pi(\varepsilon) = 1$ and $\pi(\bar{x} \cdot \langle y \rangle) = \pi(\bar{x}) \cdot y$ for $\bar{x} \in A^*$ and $y \in A$. For sequences $\bar{x}, \bar{y} \in A^*$, it holds that $\pi(\bar{x} \cdot \bar{y}) = \pi(\bar{x}) \cdot \pi(\bar{y})$. So, π generalizes the binary multiplication $\cdot$ to a finite but arbitrary number of arguments.

Let $(A, \cdot_A, 1_A)$ and $(B, \cdot_B, 1_B)$ be monoids. Their *product* is the monoid $(A \times B, \cdot, 1)$, where the multiplication operation is given by $(x, y) \cdot (x', y') = (x \cdot_A x', y \cdot_B y')$ for $x, x' \in A$ and $y, y' \in B$, and the identity is $1 = (1_A, 1_B)$.

A *monoid homomorphism* from a monoid $(A, \cdot, 1)$ to a monoid $(B, \cdot, 1)$ is a function $h : A \to B$ that commutes with the monoid operations, that is, $h(1) = 1$ and $h(x \cdot y) = h(x) \cdot h(y)$ for all $x, y \in A$.

As we discussed earlier, we can think of a monoid as a *type of data streams*. The elements of the monoid represent *finite stream fragments*. The multiplication operation $\cdot$ models the *concatenation* of stream fragments, and the unit of the monoid is the *empty stream fragment*.

For a monoid $(A, \cdot, 1)$ we define the binary relation $\preccurlyeq$ as follows: for all $x, y \in A$, we put $x \preccurlyeq y$ if and only if $xz = y$ for some $z \in A$. Since the relation $\preccurlyeq$ is reflexive and transitive, we call it the *prefix preorder* for the monoid A. The unit 1 is a minimal element w.r.t. the $\preccurlyeq$ relation: $1 \cdot x = x$ and hence $1 \preccurlyeq x$ for every $x \in A$. Define the function prefix $: A \times A \to \mathcal{P}(A)$ as follows: prefix$(x, y) = \{z \in A \mid xz = y\}$ for all $x, y \in A$. This implies that $x \preccurlyeq y$ iff

$\mathsf{prefix}(x,y) \neq \emptyset$. In other words, $\mathsf{prefix}(x,y)$ is the set of all witnesses for $x \preccurlyeq y$. A partial function $\partial : A \times A \rightharpoonup A$ is said to be a *prefix witness function* (or simply a *witness function*) for the monoid A if its domain is equal to $\preccurlyeq$ and it satisfies: $\partial(x,y) \in \mathsf{prefix}(x,y)$ for every $x,y \in A$ with $x \preccurlyeq y$. We can express this equivalently by requiring that the type of the function ∂ is $\prod_{(x,y) \in \preccurlyeq} \mathsf{prefix}(x,y)$.

We say that a monoid A satisfies the *left cancellation* property if $xy = xz$ implies $y = z$ for all $x,y,z \in A$. In this case we say that A is *left-cancellative*. If A is left-cancellative, then it has a unique prefix witness function, because $x \preccurlyeq y$ implies that there is a unique z with $xz = y$.

Example 1 (Finite Sequences). Consider the algebra $(\mathsf{FSeq}(A), \cdot, \varepsilon)$, where $\mathsf{FSeq}(A)$ is the set A^* of all finite words (strings) over a set A, $\cdot$ is word concatenation, and ε is the empty word. This algebra is a monoid. In fact, it is the *free monoid* with generators A. For $u,v \in A^*$, $u \preccurlyeq v$ iff the word u is a prefix of the word v. There is a unique prefix witness function, because for every $x,y \in A^*$ with $x \preccurlyeq y$ there is a unique $z \in A^*$ such that $xz = y$.

Let us consider now a variant of Example 1 in order to clear any misunderstandings regarding the $\preccurlyeq$ order. The set A^*, together with the empty sequence ε, and the operation $\circ$ given by $x \circ y = yx$ is a monoid. For the monoid $(A^*, \varepsilon, \circ)$, we have that $x \preccurlyeq y$ iff $x \circ z = zx = y$ for some $z \in A^*$. So, $x \preccurlyeq y$ iff the word x is a *suffix* of the word y.

Example 2 (Finite Multisets). Consider the algebra $(\mathsf{FBag}(A), \cup, \emptyset)$, where $\mathsf{FBag}(A)$ is the set of all finite multisets (bags) over a set A, $\cup$ is multiset union, and $\emptyset$ is the empty multiset. This algebra is a monoid. In fact, it is the *free commutative monoid* with generators A. It is also left cancellative. For $x,y \in \mathsf{FBag}(A)$, $x \preccurlyeq y$ iff x is contained in y. So, we also use the notation $\subseteq$ instead of $\preccurlyeq$. There is a unique prefix witness function, because for every $x,y \in \mathsf{FBag}(A)$ with $x \subseteq y$ there is a unique $z \in \mathsf{FBag}(A)$ such that $xz = y$.

Example 3 (Finite Sets). Let A be a set. Consider the algebra $(\mathsf{FSet}(A), \cup, \emptyset)$, where $\mathsf{FSet}(A)$ is the set of all finite subsets of A, $\cup$ is set union, and $\emptyset$ is the empty set. This algebra is a monoid. In fact, it is the *free commutative idempotent monoid* with generators A. For $x,y \in \mathsf{FBag}(A)$, $x \preccurlyeq y$ iff x is contained in y. So, we also use the notation $\subseteq$ instead of $\preccurlyeq$.

For $x \subseteq y$, define $\partial(x,y) = y \setminus x$, where $\setminus$ is the set difference operation. Since $x \cup (y \setminus x) = y$ for $x \subseteq y$, ∂ is a prefix witness function. We also define $\tau(x,y) = y$ for $x \subseteq y$. Since $x \cup y = y$ for $x \subseteq y$, τ is a prefix witness function. So, $\mathsf{FSet}(A)$ has several distinct prefix witness functions.

Example 4 (Finite Maps). Let K be a set of keys, and V be a set of values. Consider the algebra $(\mathsf{FMap}(K,V), \cdot, \emptyset)$, where $\mathsf{FMap}(K,V)$ is the set of all partial maps $K \rightharpoonup V$ with a finite domain, $\emptyset$ is the partial map with empty domain, and $\cdot$ is defined as follows:

$$(f \cdot g)(k) = \begin{cases} g(k), & \text{if } g(k) \text{ is defined} \\ f(k), & \text{if } g(k) \text{ is undefined and } f(k) \text{ is defined} \\ \text{undefined}, & \text{otherwise} \end{cases}$$

for every $f, g \in \mathsf{FMap}(K, V)$ and $k \in K$. We leave it to the reader to check that $\emptyset \cdot f = f \cdot \emptyset = f$ and $(f \cdot g) \cdot h = f \cdot (g \cdot h)$ for all $f, g, h \in \mathsf{FMap}(K, V)$. So, the algebra $\mathsf{FMap}(K, V)$ is a monoid.

Let $f, g \in \mathsf{FMap}(A)$. We write $\mathrm{dom}(f) = \{k \in K \mid f(k) \text{ is defined}\}$ for the domain of f. It holds that $\mathrm{dom}(f \cdot g) = \mathrm{dom}(f) \cup \mathrm{dom}(g)$. Using this property, we see that $f \preccurlyeq g$ iff $\mathrm{dom}(f) \subseteq \mathrm{dom}(g)$.

Let $f, g \in \mathsf{FMap}(K, V)$ with $f \preccurlyeq g$. Define $\partial(f, g) = g$. Since $\mathrm{dom}(f) \subseteq \mathrm{dom}(g)$, we have that $f \cdot \partial(f, g) = g$. It follows that ∂ is a prefix witness function. Define $g \setminus f \in \mathsf{FMap}(K, V)$ as follows:

$$(g \setminus f)(k) = \begin{cases} g(k), & \text{if } g(k) \text{ is defined and } f(k) \text{ is undefined} \\ g(k), & \text{if } g(k), f(k) \text{ are defined and } g(k) \neq f(k) \\ \text{undefined}, & \text{otherwise} \end{cases}$$

for every $k \in K$. From $f \preccurlyeq g$ we get $f \cdot (g \setminus f) = g$. So, $\setminus$ is a prefix witness function. This means that $\mathsf{FMap}(K, V)$ has several distinct prefix witness functions.

Example 5 (Bounded-Domain Continuous-Time Signals). Let A be an arbitrary set, and $\mathbb{R}$ be the set of real numbers. A bounded-domain continuous-time signal with values in A is a function $f : [0, u) \to A$ where $u \geq 0$ is a real number and $[u, v) = \{t \in \mathbb{R} \mid u \leq t < v\}$. We define the *concatenation* operation $\cdot$ for such signals as follows:

$$\frac{f : [0, u) \to A \qquad g : [0, v) \to A}{f \cdot g : [0, u + v) \to A} \qquad (f \cdot g)(t) = \begin{cases} f(t), & \text{if } t \in [0, u) \\ g(t - u), & \text{if } t \in [u, u + v) \end{cases}$$

We write $\mathsf{BSig}(A)$ for the set of all these bounded-domain continuous-time signals. The *unit* signal is the unique function of type $[0, 0) \to A$, whose domain of definition is empty. Observe that $\mathsf{BSig}(A)$ is a monoid. For signals $f : [0, u) \to A$ and $g : [0, v) \to A$, it holds that $f \preccurlyeq g$ iff $u \leq v$ and $f(t) = g(t)$ for every $t \in [0, u)$. There is a unique prefix witness function, because for every $f, g \in \mathsf{BSig}(A)$ with $f \preccurlyeq g$ there is a unique $h \in \mathsf{BSig}(A)$ such that $f \cdot h = g$.

Example 6 (Timed Finite Sequences). We write $\mathbb{N}$ to denote the set of natural numbers (non-negative integers). A *timed sequence* over A is an alternating sequence $s_0 a_1 s_1 a_2 \ldots a_n s_n$, where $s_i \in \mathbb{N}$ and $a_i \in A$ for every i. The occurrences $s_0, s_1, \ldots$ are called *time punctuations* and indicate the passage of time. So, the set of all timed sequences over A is equal to $\mathsf{TFSeq}(A) = \mathbb{N} \cdot (A \cdot \mathbb{N})^*$. We define the *fusion product* $\diamond$ of timed sequences as follows: $s_0 a_1 s_1 \ldots a_m s_m \diamond t_0 b_1 t_1 \ldots b_n t_n = s_0 a_1 s_1 \ldots a_m (s_m + t_0) b_1 t_1 \ldots b_n t_n$. The *unit* timed sequence is the singleton sequence 0. The algebra $(\mathsf{TFSeq}(A), \diamond, 0)$ is easily shown to be a monoid. There is a unique prefix witness function, because for all $x, y \in \mathsf{TFSeq}(A)$ with $x \preccurlyeq y$ there is a unique $z \in \mathsf{TFSeq}(A)$ s.t. $x \diamond z = y$.

Example 7 (Finite Time-Varying Multisets). A *finite time-varying multiset* over A is a partial function $f : \mathbb{N} \rightharpoonup \mathsf{FBag}(A)$ whose domain is equal to

$[0..n] = \{0, \ldots, n\}$ for some integer $n \geq 0$. We also use the notation $f : [0..n] \to$ FBag(A) to convey this information regarding the domain of f. We define the *concatenation* operation $\cdot$ for finite time-varying multisets as follows:

$$\frac{f : [0..m] \to \mathsf{FBag}(A) \qquad g : [0..n] \to \mathsf{FBag}(A)}{f \cdot g : [0..m+n] \to \mathsf{FBag}(A)} \qquad (f \cdot g)(t) = \begin{cases} f(t), & \text{if } t \in [0..m-1] \\ f(t) \cup g(0), & \text{if } t = m \\ g(t-m), & \text{if } t \in [m+1..n] \end{cases}$$

We write TFBag(A) to denote the set of all finite time-varying multisets over A. The *unit* time-varying multiset $\mathsf{Id} : [0..0] \to \mathsf{FBag}(A)$ is given by $\mathsf{Id}(0) = \emptyset$. It is easy to see that $f \cdot \mathsf{Id} = f$ and that $\mathsf{Id} \cdot f = f$ for every $f : [0..n] \to \mathsf{FBag}(A)$. We leave it to the reader to also verify that $(f \cdot g) \cdot h = f \cdot (g \cdot h)$ for finite time-varying multisets f, g and h. So, the set TFBag(A) together with $\cdot$ and Id is a monoid. It is not difficult to show that it is left-cancellative.

Let us consider now the prefix preorder $\preccurlyeq$ on finite time-varying multisets. For $f : [0..m] \to \mathsf{FBag}(A)$ and $g : [0..n] \to \mathsf{FBag}(A)$, it holds that $f \preccurlyeq g$ iff $m \leq n$ and $f(t) = g(t)$ for every $t \in [0..m]$.

The examples above highlight the variety of mathematical objects that can be meaningfully viewed as streams. These streams can be organized elegantly using the structure of monoids. The sequences of Example 1, the multisets of Example 2, and the finite time-varying multisets of Example 7 can be described equivalently in terms of the partial orders of [13, 85], which have also been suggested as an approach to unify notions of streams. Using partial orders it is also possible to model the timed finite sequences of Example 6, but only with a non-succinct encoding: every time punctuation $t \in \mathbb{N}$ is encoded with a sequence $11 \ldots 1$ of t punctuations, one for each time unit. Partial orders cannot encode the sets of Example 3, the maps of Example 4, or the signals of Example 5. Informally, the reason for this is that partial orders can only encode *commutation equations*, which are insufficient for objects such as sets and maps.

3 Stream Transductions

In this section we will introduce *stream transductions* as semantic denotational models of stream transformations. At any given point in a streaming computation, we have seen an *input history* (the part of the stream from the beginning of the computation until now) and we have produced an *output history* (the cumulative output that has been emitted from the beginning until now). As a first approximation, a streaming computation can be described mathematically by a function $\beta : A \to B$, where A and B are monoids that describe the input and output type respectively, which maps an input history $x \in A$ to an output history $\beta(x) \in B$. The function β has to be *monotone* because the output is cumulative, which means that it can only be extended with more output items as the computation proceeds. An equivalent way to understand the monotonicity property is that it captures the idea that any output that has already been emitted cannot be retracted. Since β takes an entire input history as its argument, it can describe stateful computations, where the output that is emitted at every step potentially depends on the entire input history.

Definition 8 (Stream Transduction & Incremental Form). Let A and B be monoids. A function $\beta : A \to B$ is said to be *monotone* (with respect to the prefix preorder) if $x \preccurlyeq y$ implies $\beta(x) \preccurlyeq \beta(y)$ for all $x, y \in A$. For a monotone $\beta : A \to B$, we say that the partial function μ is a *monotonicity witness function* if it maps elements $x, y \in A$ and $z \in \mathsf{prefix}(x, y)$ witnessing that $x \preccurlyeq y$ to a witness $\mu(x, y, z) \in \mathsf{prefix}(\beta(x), \beta(y))$ for $\beta(x) \preccurlyeq \beta(y)$. That is, we require that the type of μ is $\prod_{x,y \in A} \mathsf{prefix}(x, y) \to \mathsf{prefix}(\beta(x), \beta(y))$. So, the defining property of μ is that for all $x, y, z \in A$ with $xz = y$ it holds that $\beta(x) \cdot \mu(x, y, z) = \beta(y)$. For brevity, we will sometimes write $\mu(x, z)$ to denote $\mu(x, xz, z)$. The defining property of μ is then written as $\beta(x) \cdot \mu(x, z) = \beta(xz)$ for all $x, z \in A$.

A *stream transduction* from A to B is a function $\beta : A \to B$ that is monotone with respect to the prefix preorder, together with a monotonicity witness function $\mu : \prod_{x,y \in A} \mathsf{prefix}(x, y) \to \mathsf{prefix}(\beta(x), \beta(y))$. We write $\mathsf{STrans}(A, B)$ to denote the set of all stream transductions from A to B.

The *incremental form* of a stream transduction $\langle \beta, \mu \rangle \in \mathsf{STrans}(A, B)$ is a function $\mathsf{F}(\beta, \mu) : A^* \to B^*$, which is defined inductively by $\mathsf{F}(\beta, \mu)(\varepsilon) = \langle \beta(1) \rangle$ and $\mathsf{F}(\beta, \mu)(\langle x_1, \ldots, x_n, x_{n+1} \rangle) = \mathsf{F}(\beta, \mu)(\langle x_1, \ldots, x_n \rangle) \cdot \langle \mu(x_1 \cdots x_n, x_{n+1}) \rangle$ for every sequence $\langle x_1, \ldots, x_{n+1} \rangle \in A^*$.

Consider the stream transduction $\langle \beta, \mu \rangle : \mathsf{STrans}(A, B)$ and the input fragments $x, y \in A$. Notice that $\mu(x, y)$ gives the *output increment* that the streaming computation generates when the input history x is extended into xy. For an arbitrary output monoid B, the output increment $\mu(x, y)$ is generally not uniquely determined by $\beta(x)$ and $\beta(xy)$. This means that the monotonicity witness function μ generally provides some additional information about the streaming computation that cannot be obtained purely from β. However, if the output monoid B is left-cancellative then there is a unique function μ that witnesses the monotonicity of β.

Suppose that $\langle \beta, \mu \rangle : \mathsf{STrans}(A, B)$ is a stream transduction. The incremental form $\mathsf{F}(\beta, \mu)$ of the transduction $\langle \beta, \mu \rangle$ describes the stream transformation in explicit input/output increments. For example, $\mathsf{F}(\beta, \mu)(\langle x_1 \rangle) = \langle \beta(1), \mu(1, x_1) \rangle$ and $\mathsf{F}(\beta, \mu)(\langle x_1, x_2 \rangle) = \langle \beta(1), \mu(1, x_1), \mu(x_1, x_2) \rangle$. The key property of the incremental form is that $\pi(\mathsf{F}(\beta, \mu)(\bar{x})) = \beta(\pi(\bar{x}))$ for every $\bar{x} \in A^*$. For example, $\pi(\mathsf{F}(\beta, \mu)(\langle x_1, x_2, x_3 \rangle)) = \beta(1) \cdot \mu(1, x_1) \cdot \mu(x_1, x_2) \cdot \mu(x_1 x_2, x_3) = \beta(x_1) \cdot \mu(x_1, x_2) \cdot \mu(x_1 x_2, x_3) = \beta(x_1 x_2) \cdot \mu(x_1 x_2, x_3) = \beta(x_1 x_2 x_3)$.

Example 9 (Counting). Let A be an arbitrary set. We will describe a streaming computation whose input type is the monoid $\mathsf{FBag}(A)$ and whose output type is the monoid $\mathsf{FSeq}(\mathbb{N})$. The informal operational description is as follows: there is no initial output, and every time a new data item arrives the computation emits the total number of items seen so far. The formal description is given by the stream transduction $\beta : \mathsf{FBag}(A) \to \mathsf{FSeq}(\mathbb{N})$, defined by $\beta(\emptyset) = \varepsilon$ and $\beta(x) = \langle 1, 2, \ldots, |x| \rangle$ for every non-empty $x \in \mathsf{FBag}(A)$, where $|x|$ denotes the size of the multiset x. It is easy to see that β is monotone. Since $\mathsf{FSeq}(\mathbb{N})$

is left-cancellative, the monotonicity witness function is uniquely determined: $\mu(x, \emptyset) = \varepsilon$ and $\mu(x, y) = \langle |x| + 1, \ldots, |x| + |y| \rangle$ when $y \neq \emptyset$.

Example 10 (Per-Key Aggregation). Let K be a set of keys, and V be a set of values. The elements of $K \times V$ are typically called key-value pairs. Suppose that $\mathsf{op} : V \times V \to V$ is an associative and commutative operation. So, op can be generalized to an aggregation operation that takes non-empty finite multisets over V as input. We will describe a streaming computation whose input type is the monoid $\mathsf{FBag}(K \times V)$ and whose output type is the monoid $\mathsf{FMap}(K, V)$. Informally, every time an item (k, v) is processed, the output map is updated so that the k-indexed entry contains the aggregate (using op) of all values seen so far for the key k. The formal description of this computation is given by the stream transduction $\beta : \mathsf{FBag}(K \times V) \to \mathsf{FMap}(K, V)$, defined by $\beta(x) = \{k \mapsto \mathsf{op}(x|_k) \mid k \text{ appears in } x\}$ for every multiset x, where $x|_k$ denotes the multiset that results from x by keeping only the pairs whose key is equal to k. That is, the domain of $\beta(x)$ is equal to $\mathrm{dom}(\beta(x)) = \{k \in K \mid k \text{ appears in } x\}$ and $\beta(x)(k) = \mathsf{op}(x|_k)$ for every k that appears in x. The monotonicity witness function μ is defined as follows: $\mu(x, y)$ is equal to the restriction of the map $\beta(x \cup y)$ to the set of all keys that appear in y.

We saw in Sect. 2 that we can form products of monoids: if A and B are monoids, then so is $A \times B$. Intuitively, we can think of $A \times B$ as the data stream type that involves two parallel and independent *channels*: one channel for streams of type A and another channel for streams of type B.

Example 11 (Merging of Multiple Input Channels). Given a set A, we want to describe a transformation with two input channels of type $\mathsf{FBag}(A)$ and one output channel of type $\mathsf{FBag}(A)$. The monotone function $\beta : \mathsf{FBag}(A) \times \mathsf{FBag}(A) \to \mathsf{FBag}(A)$, given by $\beta(x, y) = x \cup y$ for multisets x and y, describes the merging of the two input substreams. Operationally, whenever a new data item arrives (regardless of channel) it is propagated to the output channel. Since $\mathsf{FBag}(A)$ is left-cancellative, the monotonicity witness function is uniquely determined: $\mu(\langle x_1, y_1 \rangle, \langle x_2, y_2 \rangle) = (x_2 \cup y_2) \setminus (x_1 \cup y_1)$ for all $x_1, y_1, x_2, y_2 \in \mathsf{FBag}(A)$.

Example 12 (Flatten). Let A be a monoid. The function $\beta : \mathsf{FSeq}(A) \to A$, given by $\beta(\bar{x}) = \pi(\bar{x})$ for every $\bar{x} \in \mathsf{FSeq}(A)$, describes the *flattening* of a sequence of monoid elements. The function β is monotone, and its monotonicity witness function μ is given by $\mu(\bar{x}, \bar{y}) = \pi(\bar{y})$ for all $\bar{x}$ and $\bar{y}$. The stream transduction $flatten(A) = \langle \beta, \mu \rangle$ has type $\mathsf{STrans}(\mathsf{FSeq}(A), A)$.

Example 13 (Split in Batches). Let $\Sigma = \{a, b\}$ be an alphabet of symbols. Suppose that we want to describe the decomposition of an element of Σ^* into batches of size exactly 3. We describe this using two functions $r_1 : \Sigma^* \to \mathsf{FSeq}(\Sigma^*)$ and $r_2 : \Sigma^* \to \Sigma^*$. Informally, r_1 gives the sequence of full batches of size 3, and r_2 gives the remaining incomplete batch. For example, $r_1(abbaabba) = \langle abb, aab \rangle$ and $r_2(abbaabba) = ba$.

This idea of splitting in batches can be generalized from the monoid Σ^* to an arbitrary monoid A. We say that a *splitter* for A is a pair $r = (r_1, r_2)$ of functions $r_1 : A \to \mathsf{FSeq}(A)$ and $r_2 : A \to A$ satisfying the following properties: (1) the equality $x = \pi(r_1(x)) \cdot r_2(x)$ says that r_1 and r_2 decompose $x \in A$, (2) $r_1(1_A) = \varepsilon$ says that the unit cannot be decomposed, (3) $r_1(x \cdot y) = r_1(x) \cdot r_1(r_2(x) \cdot y)$ and (4) $r_2(x \cdot y) = r_2(r_2(x) \cdot y)$ describe how to decompose the concatenation of two monoid elements. The first two properties imply that $r_2(1_A) = 1_A$. The third property implies that r_1 is monotone. Define $\mu(x, y) = r_1(r_2(x) \cdot y)$ for $x, y \in A$ and observe that $r_1(x) \cdot \mu(x, y) = r_1(xy)$. It follows that $split(r) = \langle r_1, \mu \rangle$ is a stream transduction of type $\mathsf{STrans}(A, \mathsf{FSeq}(A))$.

Our denotational model of a stream transformation uses a monotone function whose domain is the monoid of (finite) input histories. We emphasize that such a denotation can also describe the transformation of an **infinite stream**. To illustrate this point in simple terms, consider a monotone function $\beta : A^* \to B^*$, where A (resp., B) is the type of input (resp., output) items. This function extends uniquely to the ω-continuous function $\beta^\infty : A^\infty \to B^\infty$, where $A^\infty = A^* \cup A^\omega$ is the set of finite and infinite sequences over A, as follows: $\beta^\infty(a_0 a_1 a_2 \ldots)$ is equal to the supremum of the chain $\beta(\varepsilon) \le \beta(a_0) \le \beta(a_0 a_1) \le \ldots$

4   Model of Computation

We will present an abstract model of computation for stream processing, where the input and output data streams are elements of monoids A and B respectively. A streaming algorithm is described by a transducer, a kind of automaton that produces output values. We consider transducers that can have a potentially infinite state space, which we denote by St. The computation starts at a distinguished initial state $\mathsf{init} \in \mathsf{St}$, and the initialization triggers some initial output $\mathsf{o} \in B$. The computation then proceeds by consuming the input stream incrementally, i.e. fragment by fragment. One step of the computation from a state $s \in \mathsf{St}$ involves consuming an input fragment $x \in A$, producing an output increment $\mathsf{out}(s, x) \in B$ and transitioning to the next state $\mathsf{next}(s, x) \in \mathsf{St}$.

Definition 14 (Stream Transducer). Let A, B be monoids. A *stream transducer* with inputs from A and outputs from B is a tuple $\mathcal{G} = (\mathsf{St}, \mathsf{init}, \mathsf{o}, \mathsf{next}, \mathsf{out})$, where St is a nonempty set of *states*, $\mathsf{init} \in \mathsf{St}$ is the *initial state*, $\mathsf{o} \in B$ is the *initial output*, $\mathsf{next} : \mathsf{St} \times A \to \mathsf{St}$ is the *transition function*, and $\mathsf{out} : \mathsf{St} \times A \to B$ is the *output function*. We write $\mathsf{G}(A, B)$ to denote the set of all stream transducers with inputs from A and outputs from B.

We define the *generalized transition function* $\mathsf{gnext} : \mathsf{St} \times A^* \to \mathsf{St}$ by induction: $\mathsf{gnext}(s, \varepsilon) = s$ and $\mathsf{gnext}(s, \langle x \rangle \cdot \bar{y}) = \mathsf{gnext}(\mathsf{next}(s, x), \bar{y})$ for all $s \in \mathsf{St}$, $x \in A$ and $\bar{y} \in A^*$. A state $s \in \mathsf{St}$ is said to be *reachable* in $\mathcal{G}$ if there exists a sequence $\bar{x} \in A^*$ such that $\mathsf{gnext}(\mathsf{init}, \bar{x}) = s$.

We define the *generalized output function* $\mathsf{gout} : \mathsf{St} \times A^* \to B$ by induction on the second argument: $\mathsf{gout}(s, \varepsilon) = 1$ and $\mathsf{gout}(s, \langle x \rangle \cdot \bar{y}) = \mathsf{out}(s, x) \cdot \mathsf{gout}(\mathsf{next}(s, x), \bar{y})$ for all $s \in \mathsf{St}$, $x \in A$ and $\bar{y} \in A^*$. The *extended output function* $\mathsf{eout} : \mathsf{St} \times A^* \to B^*$ is defined similarly: $\mathsf{eout}(s, \varepsilon) = \varepsilon$ and $\mathsf{eout}(x, \langle x \rangle \cdot \bar{y}) = \langle \mathsf{out}(s, x) \rangle \cdot \mathsf{eout}(\mathsf{next}(s, x), \bar{y})$ for all $s \in \mathsf{St}$, $x \in A$ and $\bar{y} \in A^*$.

Example 15 (Transducer for Counting). Recall the counting streaming computation that was described in Example 9. We will describe a stream transducer that implements the counting computation. The input monoid is $\mathsf{FBag}(A)$ and the output monoid is $\mathsf{FSeq}(\mathbb{N})$. The state space is $\mathsf{St} = \mathbb{N}$, because the transducer has to maintain a counter that remembers the number of data items seen so far. The initial state is $\mathsf{init} = 0$ and the initial output is $\mathsf{o} = \varepsilon$. The transition function increments the counter, i.e. $\mathsf{next}(s, x) = s + |x|$ for every $s \in \mathsf{St}$ and $x \in \mathsf{FBag}(A)$. The output function is defined by $\mathsf{out}(s, \emptyset) = \varepsilon$ and $\mathsf{out}(s, x) = \langle s + 1, \ldots, s + |x| \rangle$ for a nonempty multiset x. The type of this transducer is $\mathsf{G}(\mathsf{FBag}(A), \mathsf{FSeq}(\mathbb{N}))$.

Example 16 (Transducer for Merging). We will implement the merging computation of Example 11, where there are two input channels of type $\mathsf{FBag}(A)$ and one output channel of type $\mathsf{FBag}(A)$. The transducer does not need memory, so $\mathsf{St} = \mathsf{Unit}$, where $\mathsf{Unit} = \{\star\}$ is a singleton set. The initial state is $\mathsf{init} = \star$ and the initial output is $\mathsf{o} = \emptyset$. There is only one possibility for the transition function: $\mathsf{next}(s, \langle x, y \rangle) = \star$. The output function describes the propagation of the input increments of both input channels to the output channel: $\mathsf{out}(s, \langle x, y \rangle) = x \cup y$ for all multisets x, y. The type of this transducer is $\mathsf{G}(\mathsf{FBag}(A) \times \mathsf{FBag}(A), \mathsf{FBag}(A))$.

Example 17 (Flatten). For a monoid A, we define a transducer $\mathtt{Flatten}(A) = (\mathsf{St}, \mathsf{init}, \mathsf{o}, \mathsf{next}, \mathsf{out}) : \mathsf{G}(\mathsf{FSeq}(A), A)$ that implements the flattening transduction of Example 12. This computation does not require memory, so we define $\mathsf{St} = \mathsf{Unit}$ and $\mathsf{init} = \star$. The initial output is $\mathsf{o} = 1_A$, the transition function is uniquely determined by $\mathsf{next}(s, x) = \star$, and the output function is given by $\mathsf{out}(s, \langle a_1, \ldots, a_n \rangle) = a_1 \cdots a_n$.

Example 18 (Split in Batches). For a monoid A and a splitter $r = (r_1, r_2)$ for A (Example 13), we describe a transducer $\mathtt{Split}(r) = (\mathsf{St}, \mathsf{init}, \mathsf{o}, \mathsf{next}, \mathsf{out})$ that implements the transduction $split(r) : \mathsf{STrans}(A, \mathsf{FSeq}(A))$. We define $\mathsf{St} = A$, because the transducer needs to remember the remainder of the cumulative input that does not yet form a complete batch, and $\mathsf{init} = 1_A$. The initial output $\mathsf{o} = \varepsilon$ is the empty sequence. The transition and output functions are defined by $\mathsf{next}(s, x) = r_2(s \cdot x)$ and $\mathsf{out}(s, x) = r_1(s \cdot x)$.

Definition 14 does not capture a key requirement for streaming computations over monoids, namely that the cumulative output of a transducer $\mathcal{G}$ should be independent of the particular way in which the input history is split into the fragments that are fed to it. More precisely, suppose that w is an input history that can be fragmented (factorized) in two different ways: $w = u_1 \cdot u_2 \cdots u_m$ and $w = v_1 \cdot v_2 \cdots v_n$. Then, the cumulative output of the transducer $\mathcal{G}$ when consuming the sequence of fragments (factorization) $u_1, u_2, \ldots, u_m$ should be equal to the cumulative output when consuming $v_1, v_2, \ldots, v_n$. In Definition 20 below, we formulate a set of *coherence conditions* that a transducer must adhere to in order to satisfy this "factorization independence" requirement.

Definition 19 (Bisimulation & Bisimilarity). Let $\mathcal{G} = (\mathsf{St}, \mathsf{init}, \mathsf{o}, \mathsf{next}, \mathsf{out})$ be a transducer with inputs from A and outputs from B. A relation $R \subseteq \mathsf{St} \times \mathsf{St}$ is a *bisimulation* for $\mathcal{G}$ if for every $s, t \in \mathsf{St}$ and $x \in A$ we have that $(s, t) \in R$ implies $\mathsf{out}(s, x) = \mathsf{out}(t, x)$ and $(\mathsf{next}(s, x), \mathsf{next}(t, x)) \in R$. We will also use the notation sRt to mean $(s, t) \in R$. We say that the states $s, t \in R$ are *bisimilar*, denoted $s \sim t$, if there exists a bisimulation R for $\mathcal{G}$ such that sRt. The relation $\sim$ is called the *bisimilarity relation* for $\mathcal{G}$.

It is well-known that the bisimilarity relation for $\mathcal{G}$ is an equivalence relation (reflexive, symmetric, and transitive), and for all $s, t \in \mathsf{St}$ and $x \in A$ it satisfies the following **extension property**: $s \sim t$ implies that $\mathsf{next}(s, x) \sim \mathsf{next}(t, x)$. It can then be easily seen that the bisimilarity relation is a bisimulation. In fact, it is the largest bisimulation for the transducer $\mathcal{G}$.

Definition 20 (Coherence). Suppose $\mathcal{G} = (\mathsf{St}, \mathsf{init}, \mathsf{o}, \mathsf{next}, \mathsf{out}) : \mathsf{G}(A, B)$ is a stream transducer. We say that $\mathcal{G}$ is *coherent* if it satisfies the following:
(N1) $\mathsf{next}(\mathsf{init}, 1) \sim \mathsf{init}$.
(N2) $\mathsf{next}(\mathsf{init}, xy) \sim \mathsf{next}(\mathsf{next}(\mathsf{init}, x), y)$ for every $x, y \in A$.
(O1) $\mathsf{o} \cdot \mathsf{out}(\mathsf{init}, 1) = \mathsf{o}$.
(O2) $\mathsf{o} \cdot \mathsf{out}(\mathsf{init}, xy) = \mathsf{o} \cdot \mathsf{out}(\mathsf{init}, x) \cdot \mathsf{out}(\mathsf{next}(\mathsf{init}, x), y)$ for every $x, y \in A$.

The coherence conditions of Definition 20 capture the idea that the transducer behaves in "essentially the same way" regardless of how the input is split into fragments. For example, the condition (N2) says that the two-step transition $\mathsf{init} \to^x s_1 \to^y s_2$ and the single-step transition $\mathsf{init} \to^{xy} t_1$ end up in states (s_2 and t_1) that will have exactly the same behavior in the subsequent computation. In other words, it does not matter whether the input xy was fed to the transducer as a single fragment xy or as a sequence of two fragments $\langle x, y \rangle$.

Let $(A, \cdot, 1)$ be a monoid. A *factorization* of an element $x \in A$ is a sequence $x_1, \ldots, x_n$ of elements of A such that $x = x_1 \cdots x_n$. In particular, the empty sequence $\varepsilon \in A^*$ is a factorization of 1. In other words, $\bar{x} \in A^*$ is a factorization of $x \in A$ if $\pi(\bar{x}) = x$.

Theorem 21 (Factorization Independence). Let $\mathcal{G} = (\mathsf{St}, \mathsf{init}, \mathsf{o}, \mathsf{next}, \mathsf{out})$ be a stream transducer of type $\mathsf{G}(A, B)$. If $\mathcal{G}$ is coherent, then for every $x \in A$ and every factorization $\bar{x} \in A^*$ of x we have that $\mathsf{o} \cdot \mathsf{gout}(\mathsf{init}, \bar{x}) = \mathsf{o} \cdot \mathsf{out}(\mathsf{init}, x)$.

Proof. For clarity, we write $\langle x_1, x_2, \ldots, x_n \rangle \in A^*$ to denote a finite sequence of elements of A. The following properties hold for all $s \in \mathsf{St}$, $\bar{x} \in A^*$ and $y \in A$:

$$\mathsf{gnext}(s, \bar{x} \cdot \langle y \rangle) = \mathsf{next}(\mathsf{gnext}(s, \bar{x}), y) \tag{1}$$

$$\mathsf{gout}(s, \bar{x} \cdot \langle y \rangle) = \mathsf{gout}(s, \bar{x}) \cdot \mathsf{out}(\mathsf{gnext}(s, \bar{x}), y) \tag{2}$$

$$\mathsf{eout}(s, \bar{x} \cdot \langle y \rangle) = \mathsf{eout}(s, \bar{x}) \cdot \langle \mathsf{out}(\mathsf{gnext}(s, \bar{x}), y) \rangle \tag{3}$$

Each property shown above can be proved by induction on the sequence $\bar{x}$.

Consider an arbitrary *coherent* stream transducer $\mathcal{G} = (\mathsf{St}, \mathsf{init}, \mathsf{o}, \mathsf{next}, \mathsf{out})$. We claim that $\mathcal{G}$ satisfies the following coherence property:

$$\mathsf{gnext}(\mathsf{init}, \langle x_1, \ldots, x_n \rangle) \sim \mathsf{next}(\mathsf{init}, x_1 \cdots x_n) \text{ for all } \langle x_1, \ldots, x_n \rangle \in A^*. \tag{N*}$$

The proof is by induction on the length of the sequence. For the base case, we have that $\mathsf{gnext}(\mathsf{init}, \varepsilon) = \mathsf{init}$ and $\mathsf{next}(\mathsf{init}, 1)$ are bisimilar because $\mathcal{G}$ is coherent (recall Property (N1) of Definition 20). For the induction step we have:

$$\mathsf{gnext}(\mathsf{init}, \bar{x} \cdot \langle y \rangle) = \mathsf{next}(\mathsf{gnext}(\mathsf{init}, \bar{x}), y) \qquad \text{[Equation (1)]}$$
$$\sim \mathsf{next}(\mathsf{next}(\mathsf{init}, \pi(\bar{x})), y), \qquad \text{[I.H., extension]}$$
$$\sim \mathsf{next}(\mathsf{init}, \pi(\bar{x}) \cdot y), \qquad \text{[coherence (N2)]}$$

which is equal to $\mathsf{next}(\mathsf{init}, \pi(\bar{x} \cdot \langle y \rangle))$. This concludes the proof of the claim (N*).

The proof of the theorem proceeds by induction on $\bar{x} \in A^*$. For the base case, observe that $\mathsf{o} \cdot \mathsf{gout}(\mathsf{init}, \varepsilon) = \mathsf{o} \cdot 1 = \mathsf{o}$ is equal to $\mathsf{o} \cdot \mathsf{out}(\mathsf{init}, 1) = \mathsf{o}$ (property (O1) for $\mathcal{G}$). For the induction step, we have:

$$\mathsf{o} \cdot \mathsf{gout}(\mathsf{init}, \bar{x} \cdot \langle y \rangle) = \mathsf{o} \cdot \mathsf{gout}(\mathsf{init}, \bar{x}) \cdot \mathsf{out}(\mathsf{gnext}(\mathsf{init}, \bar{x}), y) \qquad \text{[Eq. (2)]}$$
$$= \mathsf{o} \cdot \mathsf{out}(\mathsf{init}, \pi(\bar{x})) \cdot \mathsf{out}(\mathsf{gnext}(\mathsf{init}, \bar{x}), y) \qquad \text{[I.H.]}$$
$$= \mathsf{o} \cdot \mathsf{out}(\mathsf{init}, \pi(\bar{x})) \cdot \mathsf{out}(\mathsf{next}(\mathsf{init}, \pi(\bar{x})), y) \qquad \text{[Prop. (N*)]}$$
$$= \mathsf{o} \cdot \mathsf{out}(\mathsf{init}, \pi(\bar{x}) \cdot y) \qquad \text{[Prop. (O2)]}$$

which is equal to $\mathsf{o} \cdot \mathsf{out}(\mathsf{init}, \pi(\bar{x} \cdot \langle y \rangle))$. $\qquad \square$

Theorem 21 says that the condition of coherence guarantees a basic correctness property for stream transducers: the output that they produce does not depend on the specific way in which the input was partitioned into fragments.

For a transducer $\mathcal{G} = (\mathsf{St}, \mathsf{init}, \mathsf{o}, \mathsf{next}, \mathsf{out})$ we define the function $[\![G]\!] : A^* \to B^*$ as follows: $[\![G]\!](\bar{x}) = \langle \mathsf{o} \rangle \cdot \mathsf{eout}(\mathsf{init}, \bar{x})$ for every $\bar{x} \in A^*$. We call $[\![\mathcal{G}]\!]$ the *interpretation* or *denotation* of $\mathcal{G}$. The definition of $[\![\mathcal{G}]\!]$ implies that $[\![\mathcal{G}]\!](\varepsilon) = \langle \mathsf{o} \rangle$ and the following holds for every $\bar{x} \in A^*$ and $y \in A$:

$$[\![\mathcal{G}]\!](\bar{x} \cdot \langle y \rangle) = [\![\mathcal{G}]\!](\bar{x}) \cdot \langle \mathsf{out}(\mathsf{gnext}(\mathsf{init}, \bar{x}), y) \rangle \qquad (4)$$

When $\mathcal{G}$ is coherent, Theorem 21 says that the denotation gives the same cumulative output for any two factorizations of the input. We say that the transducers $\mathcal{G}_1$ and $\mathcal{G}_2$ are *equivalent* if their denotations are equal, i.e. $[\![\mathcal{G}_1]\!] = [\![\mathcal{G}_2]\!]$.

Definition 22 (The Implementation Relation). Let A, B be monoids, $\mathcal{G} : \mathsf{G}(A, B)$ be a stream transducer, and $\langle \beta, \mu \rangle : \mathsf{STrans}(A, B)$ be a stream transduction. We say that $\mathcal{G}$ *implements* $\langle \beta, \mu \rangle$ if $[\![\mathcal{G}]\!](\bar{x}) = \mathsf{F}(\beta, \mu)(\bar{x})$ for every $\bar{x} \in A^*$.

Theorem 23 (Implementation & Coherence). A stream transducer $\mathcal{G} : \mathsf{G}(A, B)$ is coherent if and only if it implements some stream transduction.

Proof. Suppose that $\mathcal{G} = (\mathsf{St}, \mathsf{init}, \mathsf{o}, \mathsf{next}, \mathsf{out}) : \mathsf{G}(A, B)$ is a coherent transducer. Define the function $\beta : A \to B$ by $\beta(x) = \mathsf{o} \cdot \mathsf{out}(\mathsf{init}, x)$ for every $x \in A$, and the function $\mu : A \times A \to B$ by $\mu(x, y) = \mathsf{out}(\mathsf{next}(\mathsf{init}, x), y)$ for all $x, y \in A$. For any $x, y \in A$, we have to establish that $\beta(x) \cdot \mu(x, y) = \beta(xy)$. This follows immediately from Part (O2) of the coherence property for $\mathcal{G}$. So, $\langle \beta, \mu \rangle$ is a stream transduction. It remains to prove that $\mathcal{G}$ implements $\langle \beta, \mu \rangle$, that is,

$[\![\mathcal{G}]\!](\bar{x}) = F(\beta, \mu)(\bar{x})$ for every $\bar{x} \in A^*$. For the base case, we have $[\![\mathcal{G}]\!](\varepsilon) = \langle \mathsf{o} \rangle$ and $F(\beta, \mu)(\varepsilon) = \langle \beta(1) \rangle$, which are equal because $\beta(1) = \mathsf{o} \cdot \mathsf{out}(\mathsf{init}, 1) = \mathsf{o}$ by (O1). For the step case, we observe that:

$$[\![\mathcal{G}]\!](\bar{x} \cdot \langle y \rangle) = [\![\mathcal{G}]\!](\bar{x}) \cdot \langle \mathsf{out}(\mathsf{gnext}(\mathsf{init}, \bar{x}), y) \rangle \qquad [\text{Equation (4)}]$$

$$F(\beta, \mu)(\bar{x} \cdot \langle y \rangle) = F(\beta, \mu)(\bar{x}) \cdot \langle \mu(\pi(\bar{x}), y) \rangle \qquad [\text{def. of } F(\beta, \mu)]$$

By the induction hypothesis, it suffices to show that $\mathsf{out}(\mathsf{gnext}(\mathsf{init}, \bar{x}), y)$ is equal to $\mu(\pi(\bar{x}), y) = \mathsf{out}(\mathsf{next}(\mathsf{init}, \pi(\bar{x})), y)$. This follows from the fact that $\mathsf{gnext}(\mathsf{init}, \bar{x})$ and $\mathsf{next}(\mathsf{init}, \pi(\bar{x}))$ are bisimilar, see Property (N*).

For the converse, suppose that $\mathcal{G} = (\mathsf{St}, \mathsf{init}, \mathsf{o}, \mathsf{next}, \mathsf{out}) : \mathsf{G}(A, B)$ is a transducer that implements $\langle \beta, \mu \rangle : \mathsf{STrans}(A, B)$. Define the relation R as:

$$R = \{(s, t) \in \mathsf{St} \times \mathsf{St} \mid \text{there are } \bar{x}, \bar{y} \in A^* \text{ with } \pi(\bar{x}) = \pi(\bar{y}) \text{ s.t.}$$
$$s = \mathsf{gnext}(\mathsf{init}, \bar{x}) \text{ and } t = \mathsf{gnext}(\mathsf{init}, \bar{y})\}.$$

We claim that R is a bisimulation. Consider arbitrary states $s, t \in \mathsf{St}$ with sRt and $z \in A$. It follows that there are $\bar{x}, \bar{y} \in A^*$ with $\pi(\bar{x}) = \pi(\bar{y})$ such that $s = \mathsf{gnext}(\mathsf{init}, \bar{x})$ and $t = \mathsf{gnext}(\mathsf{init}, \bar{y})$. We have to show that $\mathsf{out}(s, z) = \mathsf{out}(t, z)$ and $\mathsf{next}(s, z) \, R \, \mathsf{next}(t, z)$. First, notice that:

$$[\![\mathcal{G}]\!](\bar{x} \cdot \langle z \rangle) = [\![\mathcal{G}]\!](\bar{x}) \cdot \langle \mathsf{out}(s, z) \rangle \qquad [\text{Equation (4), def. of } s]$$

$$F(\beta, \mu)(\bar{x} \cdot \langle z \rangle) = F(\beta, \mu)(\bar{x}) \cdot \langle \mu(\pi(\bar{x}), z) \rangle \qquad [\text{def. of } F(\beta, \mu)]$$

Since $\mathcal{G}$ implements $\langle \beta, \mu \rangle$, we have that $[\![\mathcal{G}]\!](\bar{x} \cdot \langle z \rangle) = F(\beta, \mu)(\bar{x} \cdot \langle z \rangle)$ and therefore $\mathsf{out}(s, z) = \mu(\pi(\bar{x}), z)$. Similarly, we can obtain that $\mathsf{out}(t, z) = \mu(\pi(\bar{y}), z)$. From $\pi(\bar{x}) = \pi(\bar{y})$ we get that $\mu(\pi(\bar{x}), z) = \mu(\pi(\bar{y}), z)$, and therefore $\mathsf{out}(s, z) = \mathsf{out}(t, z)$. Now, observe that $s' = \mathsf{next}(s, z) = \mathsf{next}(\mathsf{gnext}(\mathsf{init}, \bar{x}), z) = \mathsf{gnext}(\bar{x} \cdot \langle z \rangle)$ using Property 1. Similarly, we have that $t' = \mathsf{next}(t, z) = \mathsf{gnext}(\bar{y} \cdot \langle z \rangle)$. From $\pi(\bar{x} \cdot \langle z \rangle) = \pi(\bar{x})z = \pi(\bar{y})z = \pi(\bar{y} \cdot \langle z \rangle)$ we conclude that $s'Rt'$. We have thus established that R is a bisimulation.

Now, we are ready to prove that $\mathcal{G}$ is coherent. We will only present the cases of Part (N2) and Part (O2), since they are the most interesting ones. Let $x, y \in A$. For Part (N2), we have to show that the states $s = \mathsf{next}(\mathsf{next}(\mathsf{init}, x), y)$ and $t = \mathsf{next}(\mathsf{init}, xy)$ are bisimilar. Since R (previous paragraph) is a bisimulation, it suffices to show that $(s, t) \in R$. Indeed, this is true because $s = \mathsf{gnext}(\mathsf{init}, \langle x, y \rangle)$, $t = \mathsf{gnext}(\mathsf{init}, \langle xy \rangle)$ and $\pi(\langle x, y \rangle) = xy = \pi(\langle xy \rangle)$. For Part (O2), we have that $[\![G]\!](\langle xy \rangle) = \langle \mathsf{o}, \mathsf{out}(\mathsf{init}, xy) \rangle$ and $F(\beta, \mu)(\langle xy \rangle) = \langle \beta(1), \mu(1, xy) \rangle$, as well as

$$[\![\mathcal{G}]\!](\langle x, y \rangle) = \langle \mathsf{o}, \mathsf{out}(\mathsf{init}, x), \mathsf{out}(\mathsf{next}(\mathsf{init}, x), y) \rangle \text{ and}$$

$$F(\beta, \mu)(\langle x, y \rangle) = \langle \beta(1), \mu(1, x), \mu(x, y) \rangle,$$

using the definitions of $[\![G]\!]$ and F. Since $\mathcal{G}$ implements $\langle \beta, \mu \rangle$, we know that $[\![\mathcal{G}]\!](\langle x, y \rangle) = F(\beta, \mu)(\langle x, y \rangle)$ and $[\![G]\!](\langle xy \rangle) = F(\beta, \mu)(\langle xy \rangle)$. Using all the above, we get that $\mathsf{o} \cdot \mathsf{out}(\mathsf{init}, x) \cdot \mathsf{out}(\mathsf{next}(\mathsf{init}, x), y) = \beta(1) \cdot \mu(1, x) \cdot \mu(x, y) = \beta(x) \cdot \mu(x, y) = \beta(xy)$ and $\mathsf{o} \cdot \mathsf{out}(\mathsf{init}, xy) = \beta(1) \cdot \mu(1, xy) = \beta(xy)$. So, Part (O2) of the coherence property holds. $\qquad \square$

Theorem 23 provides justification for our definition of the coherence property for stream transducers (recall Definition 20). It says that the definition is exactly appropriate, because it is a necessary and sufficient condition for a stream transducer to have a stream transduction as its denotation. In other words, the coherence property characterizes the transducers have a well-defined denotational semantics in terms of transductions. It offers this guarantee of correctness without limiting their expressive power as implementations of transductions.

Theorem 24 (Expressive Completeness). Let A and B be monoids, and $\langle \beta, \mu \rangle$ be a stream transduction in $\mathsf{STrans}(A, B)$. There exists a coherent stream transducer that implements $\langle \beta, \mu \rangle$.

Proof. Recall from Definition 8 that the monotonicity witness function μ satisfies the following property: $\beta(x) \cdot \mu(x, y) = \beta(xy)$ for every $x, y \in A$. Now, we define the transducer $\mathcal{G} = (\mathsf{St}, \mathsf{init}, \mathsf{o}, \mathsf{next}, \mathsf{out})$ as follows: $\mathsf{St} = A$, $\mathsf{init} = 1$, $\mathsf{o} = \beta(1)$, $\mathsf{next}(s, x) = s \cdot x$ and $\mathsf{out}(s, x) = \mu(s, x)$ for every state $s \in \mathsf{St}$ and input $x \in A$. The following properties hold for every $s \in \mathsf{St}$ and $\langle x_1, \dots, x_n \rangle \in A^*$:

$$\mathsf{gnext}(s, \langle x_1, \dots, x_n \rangle) = s \cdot x_1 \cdots x_n \quad \text{and} \tag{5}$$

$$\langle \mathsf{o} \rangle \cdot \mathsf{eout}(\mathsf{init}, \langle x_1, \dots, x_n \rangle) = \mathsf{F}(\beta, \mu)(\langle x_1, \dots, x_n \rangle) \tag{6}$$

Both these properties are shown by induction on the sequence $\langle x_1, \dots, x_n \rangle$. It follows that $[\![\mathcal{G}]\!](\bar{x}) = \langle \mathsf{o} \rangle \cdot \mathsf{eout}(\mathsf{init}, \bar{x}) = \mathsf{F}(\beta, \mu)(\bar{x})$ for every $\bar{x} \in A^*$. So, $\mathcal{G}$ implements the transduction $\langle \beta, \mu \rangle$. Finally, $\mathcal{G}$ is coherent by Theorem 23.   □

Theorem 24 assures us that the abstract computational model of coherent stream transducers is expressive enough to implement any stream transduction. For this reason, we will be using stream transducers as the basic programming model for describing streaming computations.

Example 25 (Correctness of Flatten). Using induction, we will show that the transducer $\mathcal{G} = \mathtt{Flatten}(A) = (\mathsf{Unit}, \star, 1_A, \mathsf{next}, \mathsf{out})$ implements the transduction $\langle \pi, \mu \rangle = \mathit{flatten}(A)$ for a monoid A (recall Examples 12 and 17). We show by induction that $[\![\mathcal{G}]\!](\bar{x}) = \mathsf{F}(\pi, \mu)(\bar{x})$ for every $\bar{x} \in \mathsf{FSeq}(A)^*$. For the base case, we have that $[\![\mathcal{G}]\!](\varepsilon) = \langle 1_A \rangle$ and $\mathsf{F}(\pi, \mu)(\varepsilon) = \langle \pi(\varepsilon) \rangle = \langle 1_A \rangle$. Now,

$$
\begin{aligned}
[\![\mathcal{G}]\!](\bar{x} \cdot \langle y \rangle) &= [\![\mathcal{G}]\!](\bar{x}) \cdot \langle \mathsf{out}(\mathsf{gnext}(\mathsf{init}, \bar{x}), y) \rangle && [\text{def. of } [\![\mathcal{G}]\!]] \\
&= \mathsf{F}(\pi, \mu)(\bar{x}) \cdot \langle \pi(y) \rangle && [\text{I.H. and def. of out}] \\
&= \mathsf{F}(\pi, \mu)(\bar{x}) \cdot \langle \mu(\pi(\bar{x}), y) \rangle && [\text{def. of } \mu] \\
&= \mathsf{F}(\pi, \mu)(\bar{x} \cdot \langle y \rangle) && [\text{def. of F}]
\end{aligned}
$$

for all $\bar{x} \in \mathsf{FSeq}(A)^*$ and $y \in \mathsf{FSeq}(A)$. We have thus proved that $\mathtt{Flatten}(A)$ is correct: its denotation is equal to the intended semantics.

Example 26 (Correctness of Split). We will establish that the transducer for splitting in batches is correct, namely that $\mathcal{G} = \mathtt{Split}(r) = (A, 1_A, \varepsilon, \mathsf{next}, \mathsf{out})$ implements $\langle r_1, \mu \rangle = \mathit{split}(r)$ for a splitter $r = (r_1, r_2)$ for the monoid A (recall

Examples 13 and 18). Using the properties of splitters and an argument by induction, we obtain that $\mathsf{gnext}(\mathsf{init}, \bar{x}) = r_2(\pi(\bar{x}))$ for every $\bar{x} \in A^*$. We show by induction that $[\![\mathcal{G}]\!](\bar{x}) = \mathsf{F}(r_1, \mu)(\bar{x})$ for every $\bar{x} \in A^*$. For the base case, we have that $[\![\mathcal{G}]\!](\varepsilon) = \langle \varepsilon \rangle$ and $\mathsf{F}(r_1, \mu)(\varepsilon) = \langle r_1(1_A) \rangle = \langle \varepsilon \rangle$. Now,

$$
\begin{aligned}
[\![\mathcal{G}]\!](\bar{x} \cdot \langle y \rangle) &= [\![\mathcal{G}]\!](\bar{x}) \cdot \langle \mathsf{out}(\mathsf{gnext}(\mathsf{init}, \bar{x}), y) \rangle && \text{[Equation (4)]} \\
&= \mathsf{F}(r_1, \mu)(\bar{x}) \cdot \langle \mathsf{out}(r_2(\pi(\bar{x})), y) \rangle && \text{[I.H. and previous claim]} \\
&= \mathsf{F}(r_1, \mu)(\bar{x}) \cdot \langle r_1(r_2(\pi(\bar{x})) \cdot y) \rangle && \text{[def. of out]} \\
&= \mathsf{F}(r_1, \mu)(\bar{x}) \cdot \langle \mu(\pi(\bar{x}), y) \rangle && \text{[def. of } \mu] \\
&= \mathsf{F}(r_1, \mu)(\bar{x} \cdot \langle y \rangle) && \text{[def. of F]}
\end{aligned}
$$

for all $\bar{x} \in A^*$ and $y \in A$. We have thus established that $\mathtt{Split}(r)$ is correct: its denotation is equal to the intended semantics.

5   Combinators for Deterministic Dataflow

We consider four dataflow combinators: (1) the *lifting* of pure morphisms to streaming computations, (2) *serial composition* for exposing pipeline parallelism, (3) *parallel composition* for exposing task-based parallelism, and (4) *feedback composition* for describing computations whose current output depends on previously produced output. The combinators are defined both for stream transductions (semantic objects) and for stream transducers (programs). Table 1 shows the definitions. The lifting of pure morphisms is implemented with a stateless transducer (i.e., the state space is a singleton set). Both parallel and serial composition are implemented using a product construction on transducers. In the case of parallel composition, each component computes independently. In the case of serial composition, the output of the first component is passed as input to the second component. In the case of feedback composition, the computation proceeds in well-defined rounds in order to prevent divergence.

We prove a precise correspondence between the semantics-level and program-level combinators for all cases: lifting (Proposition 27), parallel composition (Propsition 28), serial composition (Proposition 29), and feedback composition (Proposition 30). These are essentially **correctness properties** for the implementations of the combinators $\mathtt{Lift}$, $\mathtt{Par}$, $\mathtt{Serial}$, $\mathtt{Loop}$. They establish that our typed framework is appropriate for the modular specification of complex streaming computations, as it can support composition constructs that are essential for parallelization and distribution.

Proposition 27 (Lifting). Let $h : A \to B$ be a monoid homomorphism. Then, $\mathtt{Lift}(h)$ is a coherent transducer and it implements the transduction $\mathrm{lift}(h)$.

Proposition 28 (Parallel Composition). Let A_1, A_2, B_1, B_2 be monoids, $\langle \beta_1, \mu_1 \rangle : \mathsf{STrans}(A_1, B_1)$ and $\langle \beta_2, \mu_2 \rangle : \mathsf{STrans}(A_2, B_2)$ be transductions, and $\mathcal{G}_1 : \mathsf{G}(A_1, B_1)$ and $\mathcal{G}_2 : \mathsf{G}(A_2, B_2)$ be transducers.
(1) IMPLEMENTATION: If $\mathcal{G}_1$ implements $\langle \beta_1, \mu_1 \rangle$ and $\mathcal{G}_2$ implements $\langle \beta_2, \mu_2 \rangle$, then $\mathtt{Par}(\mathcal{G}_1, \mathcal{G}_2)$ implements $\langle \beta_1, \mu_1 \rangle \parallel \langle \beta_2, \mu_2 \rangle$.

Table 1. Combinators for deterministic dataflow.

Lifting of monoid homomorphisms

$$\frac{\text{monoid homomorphism } h : A \to B}{\text{lift}(h) = \langle \beta, \mu \rangle : \text{STrans}(A, B)} \qquad \begin{array}{l} \beta(x) = h(x) \\ \mu(x, y) = h(y) \end{array}$$

$$\texttt{Lift}(h) = (\text{St}, \text{init}, \text{o}, \text{next}, \text{out}) \qquad \text{init} = \star \qquad \text{next}(s, x) = s$$
$$\text{St} = \text{Unit} \qquad\qquad\qquad \text{o} = h(1) \qquad\qquad \text{out}(s, x) = h(x)$$

Parallel composition

$$\frac{\langle \beta_1, \mu_1 \rangle : \text{STrans}(A_1, B_1) \qquad \langle \beta_2, \mu_2 \rangle : \text{STrans}(A_2, B_2)}{\langle \beta_1, \mu_1 \rangle \parallel \langle \beta_2, \mu_2 \rangle = \langle \beta, \mu \rangle : \text{STrans}(A_1 \times A_2, B_1 \times B_2)}$$

$$\beta(\langle x_1, x_2 \rangle) = \langle \beta_1(x_1), \beta_2(x_2) \rangle \qquad \mu(\langle x_1, x_2 \rangle, \langle y_1, y_2 \rangle) = \langle \mu_1(x_1, y_1), \mu_2(x_2, y_2) \rangle$$

$$\mathcal{G}_1 = (\text{St}_1, \text{init}_1, \text{o}_1, \text{next}_1, \text{out}_1) \qquad\qquad\qquad \text{init} = \langle \text{init}_1, \text{init}_2 \rangle$$
$$\mathcal{G}_2 = (\text{St}_2, \text{init}_2, \text{o}_2, \text{next}_2, \text{out}_2) \qquad\qquad\qquad \text{o} = \langle \text{o}_1, \text{o}_2 \rangle$$
$$\texttt{Par}(\mathcal{G}_1, \mathcal{G}_2) = (\text{St}, \text{init}, \text{o}, \text{next}, \text{out}) \qquad \text{next}(\langle s_1, s_2 \rangle, \langle a, c \rangle) = \langle \text{next}_1(s_1, a), \text{next}_2(s_2, c) \rangle$$
$$\text{St} = \text{St}_1 \times \text{St}_2 \qquad\qquad\qquad \text{out}(\langle s_1, s_2 \rangle, \langle a, c \rangle) = \langle \text{out}_1(s_1, a), \text{out}_2(s_2, c) \rangle$$

Serial composition

$$\frac{\langle \beta_1, \mu_1 \rangle : \text{STrans}(A, B) \qquad \langle \beta_2, \mu_2 \rangle : \text{STrans}(B, C)}{\langle \beta_1, \mu_1 \rangle \gg \langle \beta_2, \mu_2 \rangle = \langle \beta, \mu \rangle : \text{STrans}(A, C)} \qquad \begin{array}{l} \beta(x) = \beta_2(\beta_1(x)) \\ \mu(x, y) = \mu_2(\beta_1(x), \mu_1(x, y)) \end{array}$$

$$\mathcal{G}_1 = (\text{St}_1, \text{init}_1, \text{o}_1, \text{next}_1, \text{out}_1) \qquad\qquad \text{o} = \text{o}_2 \cdot \text{out}_2(\text{init}_2, \text{o}_1)$$
$$\mathcal{G}_2 = (\text{St}_2, \text{init}_2, \text{o}_2, \text{next}_2, \text{out}_2) \quad \text{next}(\langle s_1, s_2 \rangle, a) = \langle \text{next}_1(s_1, a),$$
$$\texttt{Serial}(\mathcal{G}_1, \mathcal{G}_2) = (\text{St}_1 \times \text{St}_2, \text{init}, \text{o}, \text{next}, \text{out}) \qquad\qquad \text{next}_2(s_2, \text{out}_1(s_1, a)) \rangle$$
$$\text{init} = \langle \text{init}_1, \text{next}_2(\text{init}_2, \text{o}_1) \rangle \qquad \text{out}(\langle s_1, s_2 \rangle, a) = \text{out}_2(s_2, \text{out}_1(s_1, a))$$

Feedback composition

$$\frac{\langle \beta, \mu \rangle : \text{STrans}(A \times B, B)}{loopB(\beta, \mu) = \langle \gamma, \nu \rangle : \text{STrans}(\text{FSeq}(A), \text{FSeq}(B))}$$

$$\gamma(\langle a_1, \ldots, a_n \rangle) = \langle b_0, b_1, \ldots, b_n \rangle$$
$$\gamma(\varepsilon) = \langle b_0 \rangle, \text{ where } b_0 = \beta(1_A, 1_B)$$
$$\gamma(\langle a_1, \ldots, a_n, a_{n+1} \rangle) = \gamma(\langle a_1, \ldots, a_n \rangle) \cdot \langle b_{n+1} \rangle, \text{ where}$$
$$b_{n+1} = \mu(\langle a_1 \cdots a_n, b_0 b_1 \cdots b_{n-1} \rangle, \langle a_{n+1}, b_n \rangle)$$

$$\mathcal{G} = (\text{St}, \text{init}, \text{o}, \text{next}, \text{out}) : \text{G}(A \times B, B)$$
$$\texttt{LoopB}(\mathcal{G}) = (\text{St}', \text{init}', \text{o}', \text{next}', \text{out}') : \text{G}(\text{FSeq}(A), \text{FSeq}(B))$$
$$\text{St}' = \text{St} \times B \quad \text{(second component: last output batch)}$$
$$\text{init}' = \langle \text{init}, \text{o} \rangle \text{ and } \text{o}' = \langle \text{o} \rangle$$
$$\text{next}'(\langle s, b \rangle, a) = \langle \text{next}(s, \langle a, b \rangle), \text{out}(s, \langle a, b \rangle) \rangle$$
$$\text{out}'(\langle s, b \rangle, a) = \langle \text{out}(s, \langle a, b \rangle) \rangle$$

$$\frac{\langle \beta, \mu \rangle : \text{STrans}(A \times B, B) \qquad \text{splitter } r \text{ for } A}{loop(\beta, \mu, r) = split(r) \gg loopB(\beta, \mu) \gg flatten(B) : \text{STrans}(A, B)}$$

$$\frac{\mathcal{G} : \text{G}(A \times B, B) \qquad \text{splitter } r \text{ for } A}{\texttt{Loop}(\mathcal{G}, r) = \texttt{Serial}(\texttt{Split}(r), \texttt{LoopB}(\mathcal{G}), \texttt{Flatten}(B)) : \text{G}(A, B)}$$

(2) COHERENCE: If $\mathcal{G}_1$ and $\mathcal{G}_2$ are coherent, then so is $\text{Par}(\mathcal{G}_1, \mathcal{G}_2)$.

Proof. Notice that Part (2) follows immediately from Part (1) and Theorem 23. Define $f = [\![\text{Par}(\mathcal{G}_1, \mathcal{G}_2)]\!]$ and $\langle \beta, \mu \rangle = \langle \beta_1, \mu_1 \rangle \parallel \langle \beta_2, \mu_2 \rangle$. We will show that $f(\bar{w}) = F(\beta, \mu)(\bar{w})$ for every $\bar{w} \in (A_1 \times A_2)^*$. Suppose that fst is the (elementwise) left projection function. We claim that $\text{fst}(\text{gnext}(s, \bar{w})) = \text{gnext}_1(\text{fst}(s), \text{fst}(\bar{w}))$ and $\text{fst}(\text{eout}(s, \bar{w})) = \text{eout}_1(\text{fst}(s), \text{fst}(\bar{w}))$ for all $s \in \text{St}$ and $\bar{w} \in (A_1 \times A_2)^*$. Both claims are shown by induction on the length of $\bar{w}$. With similar arguments we can obtain that $\text{snd}(f(\bar{w})) = [\![\mathcal{G}_2]\!](\text{snd}(\bar{w}))$ for every $\bar{w} \in (A_1 \times A_2)^*$. It can be shown by induction that $\text{fst}(F(\beta, \mu)(\bar{w})) = F(\beta_1, \mu_1)(\text{fst}(\bar{w}))$ and $\text{snd}(F(\beta, \mu)(\bar{w})) = F(\beta_1, \mu_1)(\text{snd}(\bar{w}))$ for all $\bar{w} \in (A_1 \times A_2)^*$. In order to establish that $f(\bar{w}) = F(\beta, \mu)(\bar{w})$, it suffices to show that $\text{fst}(f(\bar{w})) = \text{fst}(F(\beta, \mu)(\bar{w}))$ and $\text{snd}(f(\bar{w})) = \text{snd}(F(\beta, \mu)(\bar{w}))$. Given the claims shown previously, these equalities are equivalent to $[\![\mathcal{G}_1]\!](\text{fst}(\bar{w})) = F(\beta_1, \mu_1)(\text{fst}(\bar{w}))$ and $[\![\mathcal{G}_2]\!](\text{snd}(\bar{w})) = F(\beta_2, \mu_2)(\text{snd}(\bar{w}))$ respectively. These equalities follow from the assumptions that $\mathcal{G}_1$ implements $\langle \beta_1, \mu_1 \rangle$ and $\mathcal{G}_2$ implements $\langle \beta_2, \mu_2 \rangle$. $\square$

Proposition 29 (Serial Composition). Let A, B, C be monoids, $\langle \beta_1, \mu_1 \rangle :$ $\text{STrans}(A, B)$ and $\langle \beta_2, \mu_2 \rangle : \text{STrans}(B, C)$ be transductions, and $\mathcal{G}_1 : G(A, B)$ and $\mathcal{G}_2 : G(B, C)$ be transducers.
(1) IMPLEMENTATION: If $\mathcal{G}_1$ implements $\langle \beta_1, \mu_1 \rangle$ and $\mathcal{G}_2$ implements $\langle \beta_2, \mu_2 \rangle$, then $\text{Serial}(\mathcal{G}_1, \mathcal{G}_2)$ implements $\langle \beta_1, \mu_1 \rangle \gg \langle \beta_2, \mu_2 \rangle$.
(2) COHERENCE: If $\mathcal{G}_1$ and $\mathcal{G}_2$ are coherent, then so is $\text{Serial}(\mathcal{G}_1, \mathcal{G}_2)$.

Proof. Part (2) follows easily from Part (1) and Theorem 23. In order to prove Part (1) we have to first establish a number of preliminary facts. We define the function $M_2 : A^* \to A$ as follows: $M_2(\varepsilon) = 1$, $M_2(\langle x \rangle) = x$ for $x \in A$, and $M_2(\langle x, y \rangle \cdot \bar{z}) = \langle xy \rangle \cdot \bar{z}$ for $x, y \in A$ and $\bar{z} \in A^*$. We write $\mathcal{G}$ to denote $\mathcal{G}_1 \gg \mathcal{G}_2$.

$$\text{fst}(\text{gnext}(s, \bar{x})) = \text{gnext}_1(\text{fst}(s), \bar{x}) \text{ for all } s \in \text{St and } \bar{x} \in A^* \quad (7)$$

$$\text{snd}(\text{gnext}(s, \bar{x})) = \text{gnext}_2(\text{snd}(s), \text{eout}_1(\text{fst}(s), \bar{x})) \text{ for all } s \in \text{St and } \bar{x} \in A^* \quad (8)$$

$$[\![\mathcal{G}]\!](\bar{x}) = M_2([\![\mathcal{G}_2]\!]([\![\mathcal{G}_1]\!](\bar{x}))) \text{ for all } \bar{x} \in A^* \quad (9)$$

$$F(\beta, \mu)(\bar{x}) = M_2(F(\beta_2, \mu_2)(F(\beta_1, \mu_1)(\bar{x}))) \text{ for all } \bar{x} \in A^* \quad (10)$$

where $\langle \beta, \mu \rangle = \langle \beta_1, \mu_1 \rangle \gg \langle \beta_2, \mu_2 \rangle$. All four claims above are proved by induction on the sequence $\bar{x}$. Equations (7) and (8) are needed to prove Equation (9). Now, we will establish that $\mathcal{G}$ implements $\langle \beta, \mu \rangle$. Indeed, we have that

$$
\begin{aligned}
[\![\mathcal{G}]\!](\bar{x}) &= M_2([\![\mathcal{G}_2]\!]([\![\mathcal{G}_1]\!](\bar{x}))) && \text{[Equation (9)]} \\
&= M_2([\![\mathcal{G}_2]\!](F(\beta_1, \mu_1)(\bar{x}))) && [\mathcal{G}_1 \text{ implements } \langle \beta_1, \mu_1 \rangle] \\
&= M_2(F(\beta_2, \mu_2)(F(\beta_1, \mu_1)(\bar{x}))) && [\mathcal{G}_2 \text{ implements } \langle \beta_2, \mu_2 \rangle] \\
&= F(\beta, \mu)(\bar{x}) && \text{[Equation (10)]}
\end{aligned}
$$

for every $\bar{x} \in A^*$. So, we conclude that $\mathcal{G}$ implements $\langle \beta, \mu \rangle$. $\square$

Let us give an example of how to construct complex computations from simpler ones using the dataflow combinators. Let A, B be sets and $\text{op} : A \to B$

be a function. We want to describe a streaming computation with two input channels, both of type $\mathsf{FBag}(A)$, and one output channel of type $\mathsf{FBag}(B)$. The computation transforms both input channels in the same way, namely by applying the function op to each element. This gives two output substreams, both of type $\mathsf{FBag}(B)$, that are merged into the output stream. The function $\mathsf{op} : A \to B$ lifts to a monoid homomorphism $\mathsf{op} : \mathsf{FBag}(A) \to \mathsf{FBag}(B)$, given by $\mathsf{op}(x) = \{\mathsf{op}(a) \mid a \in x\}$ for every multiset x. The streaming computation described previously can be visualized using the dataflow graph shown below.

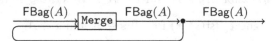

Each edge of the graph represents a communication channel along which a stream flows, and it is annotated with the type of the stream. The dataflow graph above represents the transducer $\mathcal{G} = \mathsf{Serial}(\mathsf{Par}(\mathsf{Lift}(\mathsf{op}), \mathsf{Lift}(\mathsf{op})), \mathsf{Merge})$, where $\mathsf{Merge} : \mathsf{G}(\mathsf{FBag}(A) \times \mathsf{FBag}(A), \mathsf{FBag}(A))$ is the transducer of Example 16. From Propositions 27, 29 and 28 we obtain that $\mathcal{G}$ implements the transduction $(\mathsf{lift}(\mathsf{op}) \parallel \mathsf{lift}(\mathsf{op})) \gg \mathsf{merge}$, where merge is described in Example 11.

We will now consider the feedback combinator, which introduces cycles in the dataflow graph. One consequence of cyclic graphs in the style of Kahn-MacQueen [60] is that divergence can be introduced, that is, a finite amount of input can cause an operator to enter an infinite loop. For example, consider the transducer $\mathsf{Merge} : \mathsf{G}(\mathsf{FBag}(A) \times \mathsf{FBag}(A), \mathsf{FBag}(A))$ of Example 16. The figure below visualizes the dataflow graph, where the output channel of Merge is connected to one of its input channels, thus forming a feedback loop.

$$\mathsf{FBag}(A) \xrightarrow{} \boxed{\mathsf{Merge}} \xrightarrow{\mathsf{FBag}(A)} \bullet \xrightarrow{\mathsf{FBag}(A)}$$

Suppose that the singleton input $\{a\}$ is fed to the input of the dataflow graph above, which corresponds to the first input channel of Merge. This will cause Merge to emit $\{a\}$, which will be sent again to the second input channel of Merge. Intuitively, this will cause the computation to enter an infinite loop (divergence) of consuming and emitting $\{a\}$. This behavior is undesirable in systems that process data streams, because divergence can make the system unresponsive. For this reason, we will consider here a form of feedback that eliminates this problem by ensuring that the computation of a feedback loop proceeds in a *sequence of rounds*. This avoid divergence, because the computation always makes progress by moving from one round to the next, as dictated by the input data. We describe this organization in rounds by requiring that the programmer specifies a *splitter* (recall Example 18). The splitter decomposes the input stream into *batches*, and one round of computation for the feedback loop corresponds to consuming one batch of data, generating the corresponding output batch, and sending the output batch along the feedback loop to be available for the next round of processing. This form of feedback allows flexibility in specifying what constitutes a single *batch* (and thus a single *round*), and therefore generalizes the feedback combinator of Synchronous Languages such as Lustre [31].

Proposition 30 (Feedback Composition). Let A and B be monoids, $\langle \beta, \mu \rangle$: $\mathrm{STrans}(A, B)$ be a transduction, $\mathcal{G}$: $\mathrm{G}(A, B)$ be a transducer, and $r = (r_1, r_2)$ be a splitter for A (see Example 13).
(1) IMPLEM.: If $\mathcal{G}$ implements $\langle \beta, \mu \rangle$, then $\mathrm{Loop}(\mathcal{G}, r)$ implements $loop(\beta, \mu, r)$.
(2) COHERENCE: If $\mathcal{G}$ is coherent, then so is $\mathrm{Loop}(\mathcal{G}, r)$.

Proof. We leave to the reader the proofs that Split (Example 18) implements *split* and that $\mathrm{Flatten}$ (Example 17) implements *flatten*. Given Proposition 29, it suffices to show that $\mathcal{G}' = \mathrm{LoopB}(\mathcal{G})$ implements $\langle \gamma, \nu \rangle = loopB(\beta, \mu)$. Since $\mathcal{G}'$ is of type $\mathrm{G}(\mathrm{FSeq}(A), \mathrm{FSeq}(B))$ it suffices to define the transition and output functions on singleton sequences (as done in Table 1), because there is a unique way to extend them so that $\mathcal{G}'$ is coherent. It remains to show that $[\![\mathcal{G}']\!](\bar{x}) = \mathrm{F}(\gamma, \nu)(\bar{x})$ for every $\bar{x} \in \mathrm{FSeq}(A)^*$. The base case is easy, and for the step case it suffices to show that $\mathrm{out}'(\mathrm{gnext}'(\mathrm{init}', \bar{x}), y) = \nu(\pi(\bar{x}), y)$ for every $\bar{x} \in \mathrm{FSeq}(A)^*$ and $y \in \mathrm{FSeq}(A)$. As we discussed before, gnext' and out' can be viewed as being defined on elements of A rather than sequences of $\mathrm{FSeq}(A)$, so we can equivalently prove that $\mathrm{out}'(\mathrm{gnext}'(\mathrm{init}', \langle a_1, \ldots, a_n \rangle), a_{n+1}) = \nu(\langle a_1, \ldots, a_n \rangle, a_{n+1})$ with each a_i an element of A. Given that $\mathcal{G}$ implements $\langle \beta, \mu \rangle$, the key observation to finish the proof is $\mathrm{gnext}'(\mathrm{init}', \langle a_1, \ldots, a_n \rangle) = \langle \mathrm{gnext}(\mathrm{init}, \langle \langle a_1, b_0 \rangle, \ldots, \langle a_n, b_{n-1} \rangle \rangle), b_n \rangle$, where $\gamma(\langle a_1, \ldots, a_n \rangle) = \langle b_0, b_1, \ldots, b_n \rangle$. $\square$

Example 31. For an example of using the feedback combinator, consider the transduction $\langle \beta, \mu \rangle$ which adds two input streams of numbers pointwise. That is, $\beta : \mathrm{FSeq}(\mathbb{N}) \times \mathrm{FSeq}(\mathbb{N}) \to \mathrm{FSeq}(\mathbb{N})$ is defined by $\beta(x_1 x_2 \ldots x_m, y_1 y_2 \ldots y_n) = 0(x_1 + y_1)(x_2 + y_2) \ldots (x_k + y_k)$ where $k = \min(m, n)$. Additionally, consider the trivial splitter $r = (r_1, r_2)$ for sequences where each batch is a singleton: $r_1(x_1 \ldots x_n) = \langle x_1, \ldots, x_n \rangle$ and $r_2(x_1 \ldots x_n) = \varepsilon$. We use this splitter to enforce that each batch is a single element and that each round of the computation involves consuming one element. Finally, the transduction $loop(\beta, \mu, r) = \langle \gamma, \nu \rangle$ describes the *running sum*, that is, $\gamma(x_1 \ldots x_n) = 0 x_1 (x_1 + x_2) \ldots (x_1 + \cdots + x_n)$.

The dataflow combinators of this section could form the basis of query language design. The StreamQRE language [10,84] and related formalisms [9,11,12, 14] are based on a set of combinators for efficiently processing linearly-ordered streams (e.g., time series [3,4]). Extending a language like StreamQRE to the typed setting of stream transductions is an interesting research direction.

6   Algebraic Reasoning for Optimizing Transformations

Our typed denotational framework can be used to validate optimizing transformations using algebraic reasoning. This amounts to establishing that the original transducer is equivalent to the optimized one. A fundamental approach for showing equivalence of composite transducers is to establish algebraic laws between basic building blocks, and then use algebraic rewriting.

As a concrete example, consider the per-key streaming aggregation of Example 10, which is described by the transduction reduce(K, op) : STrans(FBag($K \times V$), FMap(K, V)), where K is the set of keys, V is the set of values, and op : $V \times V \to V$ is an associative and commutative aggregation operation. Let $h : K \to \{1, \ldots, n\}$ be a hash function for the keys, and define $K_i^h = h^{-1}(i) = \{k \in K \mid h(k) = i\}$ for every i. Consider two variants of the merging operation of Example 11: (1) kmerge(h) merges n input streams of types FBag($K_1^h \times V$), …, FBag($K_n^h \times V$) respectively into an output stream of type FBag($K \times V$), and (2) mmerge(h) merges n input streams of types FMap(K_1^h, V), …, FMap(K_n^h, V) respectively into an output stream of type FMap(K, V). We also consider the transduction ksplit(h) that partitions an input stream of type FBag($K \times V$) into n output substreams of types FBag($K_1^h \times V$), …, FBag($K_n^h \times V$) respectively. Using elementary set-theoretic arguments, the following equalities can be established: ksplit(h) $\gg$ kmerge(h) = id and

$$\text{kmerge}(h) \gg \text{rd}(K, \text{op}) = (\text{rd}(K_1^h, \text{op}) \parallel \cdots \parallel \text{rd}(K_n^h, \text{op})) \gg \text{mmerge}(h),$$

where rd abbreviates reduce. Next, we consider the corresponding transducers KSplit(h), KMerge(h), Id, Reduce(K, op) (abbreviation Rd) and MMerge(h) and establish that they implement the respective transductions. This can be shown with induction proofs as shown earlier in Example 25 and Example 26. Using these facts and the propositions of Sect. 5, the equalities between transductions shown earlier give the following equations (equivalences) between transducers: KSplit(h) $\gg$ KMerge(h) $\equiv$ Id and

$$\text{KMerge}(h) \gg \text{Rd}(K, \text{op}) \equiv (\text{Rd}(K_1^h, \text{op}) \parallel \cdots \parallel \text{Rd}(K_n^h, \text{op})) \gg \text{MMerge}(h).$$

Using these equations, we can establish the following optimizing transformation for *data parallelization*, which is useful when processing high-rate data streams.

$$\begin{aligned} \text{Reduce}(K, \text{op}) &\equiv \text{Id} \gg \text{Reduce}(K, \text{op}) \\ &\equiv \text{KSplit}(h) \gg \text{KMerge}(h) \gg \text{Reduce}(K, \text{op}) \\ &\equiv \text{KSplit}(h) \gg (\text{Rd}(K_1^h, \text{op}) \parallel \cdots \parallel \text{Rd}(K_n^h, \text{op})) \gg \text{MMerge}(h). \end{aligned}$$

The above equation illustrates our proposed style of reasoning for establishing the soundness of optimizing streaming transformations: (1) prove equalities between transductions using elementary set-theoretic arguments, (2) prove that the transducers (programs) implement the transductions (denotations) using induction, (3) translate the equalities between transductions into equivalences between transducers using the results of Sect. 5, and finally (4) use algebraic reasoning to establish more complex equivalences.

The example of this section is simple but illustrates two key points: (1) our data types for streams (monoids) capture important invariants about the streams that enable transformations, and (2) useful program transformations can be established with denotational arguments that require an appropriate notion of transduction. This approach opens up the possibility of formally verifying the wealth of optimizing transformations that are used in stream processing systems.

The papers [54, 101] describe several of them, but use informal arguments that rely on the operational intuition about streaming computations. Our approach here, on the other hand, relies on rigorous denotational arguments.

The equational axiomatizations of arrows [56] and traced monoidal categories [58] are relevant to our setting, but would require adaptation. An interesting question is whether a *complete axiomatization* can be provided for the basic dataflow combinators of Sect. 5, similarly to how Kleene Algebra (KA) [62,63] and its extensions [49,64,79,83] (as well as other program logics [65,66,78,80–82]) capture properties of imperative programs at the propositional level. We also leave for future work the development of the coalgebraic approach [96–98] for reasoning about the equivalence of stream transducers. We have already defined a notion of bisimulation in Sect. 4, which could give an alternative approach for proving equivalence using coinduction on the transducers.

7 Related Work

Sect. 1 contains several pointers to related literature for stream processing. In this section, we will focus on prior work that specifically addresses aspects of formal semantics for streaming computation.

The seminal work of Gilles Kahn [59] is exemplary in its rigorous treatment of denotational semantics for a language of *deterministic dataflow* graphs of independent processes, which access their input channels using blocking read statements and the output channels using nonblocking write statements. The language Lustre [31] is a synchronous restriction of Kahn's model, which introduces the semantic idea of a clock for specifying the rate of a stream. Other notable synchronous formalisms are the language Signal [21,72] and Esterel [22,28], and the synchronous dataflow graphs of [73] and [24]. These formalisms are all deterministic, in the sense the the output is determined purely by the input data. Nondeterminism creates unavoidable semantic complications [30].

The CQL language [16] is a streaming extension of a *relational* database language with additional constructs for time-based windowing. The denotational semantics of CQL [17] can be reconstructed and greatly simplified within our framework using the notion of stream described in Example 7 (finite time-varying multisets). There are several works that deal with the semantics of specific language constructs (e.g., windows), notions of time, punctuations and disordered streams, but do not give a mathematical description of the overall streaming computation [5, 7, 25, 44, 67, 75, 76, 109].

The literature on Functional Reactive Programming (*FRP*) [34, 46, 47, 55, 68, 69, 93, 103] is closely related to the deterministic dataflow formalisms mentioned earlier. The main abstractions in FRP are signals and event sequences, which are linearly ordered data. Processing unordered data (e.g., multisets and maps) and extracting data parallelism (e.g., the per-key aggregation of Sect. 6) require a data model that goes beyond linear orders. In particular, the axioms of *arrows* [56] (often used in FRP) cannot prove the soundness of the optimizing transformation of Sect. 6, which requires reasoning about multisets.

The idea of using *types* to classify streams has been recently explored in [85] (see also [13]), but only for a restricted class of types that correspond to partial orders. No general abstract model of computation is presented in [85], and many of the examples in this paper cannot be adequately accomodated.

The mathematical framework of *coalgebras* [97] has been used to describe streams [98]. One advantage of this approach is that proofs of equivalence can be given using the proof principle of coinduction [96], which in many cases offers a useful alternative to proofs by induction. This line of work mostly focuses on infinite sequences of elements, whereas here we focus on the transformation of streams of data that can be of various different forms (not just sequences).

The idea to model the input/output of automata using monoids has appeared in the *algebraic theory* of automata and transducers. Monoids (non-free, e.g. $A^* \times B^*$) have been used to generalize automata from recognizers of languages to recognizers of relations [45], which are sometimes called *rational transducers* [100]. Our focus here is on (deterministic) functions, as models that recognize relations can give rise to the Brock-Ackerman anomaly [30]. The automata models (with inputs from a free monoid A^*) most closely related to our stream transducers are deterministic: Mealy machines [87], Moore machines [90], sequential transducers [48,95], and sub-sequential transducers [102]. The concept of coherence that we introduce here (Definition 20) does not arise in these models, because they do not operate on input batches. An algebraic generalization of a deterministic acceptor is provided by a *right monoid action* $\delta : \mathsf{St} \times A \to \mathsf{St}$ (see page 231 of [100]), which satisfies the following properties for all $s \in \mathsf{St}$ and $x, y \in A$: (1) $\delta(s, 1) = s$, and (2) $\delta(\delta(s, x), y) = \delta(s, xy)$. These properties look similar to (N1) and (N2) of Definition 20. They are, however, too restrictive for our stream transducers, as they would falsify Theorem 23.

8   Conclusion

We have presented a typed semantic framework for stream processing, based on the idea of abstracting data streams as elements of algebraic structures called *monoids*. Data streams are thus classified using monoids as *types*. Stream transformations are modeled as monotone functions, which are organized by input/output type. We have adapted the classical model of string transducers to our setting, and we have developed a general theory of streaming computation with a formal denotational semantics. The entire technical development in this paper is constructive, and therefore lends itself well to formalization in a proof assistant such as Coq [23,35,106]. Our framework can be used for the formalization of streaming models, and the validation of subtle optimizations of streaming programs (e.g., Sect. 6), such as the ones described in [54,101]. We have restricted our attention in this paper to *deterministic* streaming computation, in the sense that the behaviors that we model have predictable and reproducible results. Nondeterminism causes fundamental semantic difficulties [30], and it is undesirable in applications where repeatability is important.

References

1. Abadi, D.J., Ahmad, Y., Balazinska, M., Cetintemel, U., Cherniack, M., Hwang, J.H., Lindner, W., Maskey, A., Rasin, A., Ryvkina, E., Tatbul, N., Xing, Y., Zdonik, S.: The design of the Borealis stream processing engine. In: Proceedings of the 2nd Biennial Conference on Innovative Data Systems Research (CIDR '05). pp. 277–289 (2005), http://cidrdb.org/cidr2005/papers/P23.pdf
2. Abadi, D.J., Carney, D., Cetintemel, U., Cherniack, M., Convey, C., Lee, S., Stonebraker, M., Tatbul, N., Zdonik, S.: Aurora: A new model and architecture for data stream management. The VLDB Journal **12**(2), 120–139 (2003). https://doi.org/10.1007/s00778-003-0095-z
3. Abbas, H., Alur, R., Mamouras, K., Mangharam, R., Rodionova, A.: Real-time decision policies with predictable performance. Proceedings of the IEEE, Special Issue on Design Automation for Cyber-Physical Systems **106**(9), 1593–1615 (2018). https://doi.org/10.1109/JPROC.2018.2853608
4. Abbas, H., Rodionova, A., Mamouras, K., Bartocci, E., Smolka, S.A., Grosu, R.: Quantitative regular expressions for arrhythmia detection. IEEE/ACM Transactions on Computational Biology and Bioinformatics **16**(5), 1586–1597 (2019). https://doi.org/10.1109/TCBB.2018.2885274
5. Affetti, L., Tommasini, R., Margara, A., Cugola, G., Della Valle, E.: Defining the execution semantics of stream processing engines. Journal of Big Data **4**(1) (2017). https://doi.org/10.1186/s40537-017-0072-9
6. Akidau, T., Balikov, A., Bekiroğlu, K., Chernyak, S., Haberman, J., Lax, R., McVeety, S., Mills, D., Nordstrom, P., Whittle, S.: MillWheel: Fault-tolerant stream processing at Internet scale. Proceedings of the VLDB Endowment **6**(11), 1033–1044 (2013). https://doi.org/10.14778/2536222.2536229
7. Akidau, T., Bradshaw, R., Chambers, C., Chernyak, S., Fernández-Moctezuma, R.J., Lax, R., McVeety, S., Mills, D., Perry, F., Schmidt, E., Whittle, S.: The dataflow model: A practical approach to balancing correctness, latency, and cost in massive-scale, unbounded, out-of-order data processing. Proceedings of the VLDB Endowment **8**(12), 1792–1803 (2015). https://doi.org/10.14778/2824032.2824076
8. Alur, R., Černý, P.: Streaming transducers for algorithmic verification of single-pass list-processing programs. In: Proceedings of the 38th Annual ACM SIGPLAN-SIGACT Symposium on Principles of Programming Languages. pp. 599–610. POPL '11, ACM, New York, NY, USA (2011). https://doi.org/10.1145/1926385.1926454
9. Alur, R., Fisman, D., Mamouras, K., Raghothaman, M., Stanford, C.: Streamable regular transductions. Theoretical Computer Science **807**, 15–41 (2020). https://doi.org/10.1016/j.tcs.2019.11.018
10. Alur, R., Mamouras, K.: An introduction to the StreamQRE language. Dependable Software Systems Engineering **50**, 1–24 (2017). https://doi.org/10.3233/978-1-61499-810-5-1
11. Alur, R., Mamouras, K., Stanford, C.: Automata-based stream processing. In: Chatzigiannakis, I., Indyk, P., Kuhn, F., Muscholl, A. (eds.) Proceedings of the 44th International Colloquium on Automata, Languages, and Programming (ICALP '17). Leibniz International Proceedings in Informatics (LIPIcs), vol. 80, pp. 112:1–112:15. Schloss Dagstuhl–Leibniz-Zentrum fuer Informatik, Dagstuhl, Germany (2017). https://doi.org/10.4230/LIPIcs.ICALP.2017.112
12. Alur, R., Mamouras, K., Stanford, C.: Modular quantitative monitoring. Proceedings of the ACM on Programming Languages **3**(POPL), 50:1–50:31 (2019). https://doi.org/10.1145/3290363

13. Alur, R., Mamouras, K., Stanford, C., Tannen, V.: Interfaces for stream process-
    ing systems. In: Lohstroh, M., Derler, P., Sirjani, M. (eds.) Principles of Modeling:
    Essays Dedicated to Edward A. Lee on the Occasion of His 60th Birthday, Lec-
    ture Notes in Computer Science, vol. 10760, pp. 38–60. Springer, Cham (2018).
    https://doi.org/10.1007/978-3-319-95246-8_3
14. Alur, R., Mamouras, K., Ulus, D.: Derivatives of quantitative regular expressions.
    In: Aceto, L., Bacci, G., Bacci, G., Ingólfsdóttir, A., Legay, A., Mardare, R.
    (eds.) Models, Algorithms, Logics and Tools: Essays Dedicated to Kim Guldstrand
    Larsen on the Occasion of His 60th Birthday, Lecture Notes in Computer Science,
    vol. 10460, pp. 75–95. Springer, Cham (2017). https://doi.org/10.1007/978-3-319-
    63121-9_4
15. Arasu, A., Babcock, B., Babu, S., Cieslewicz, J., Datar, M., Ito, K., Motwani,
    R., Srivastava, U., Widom, J.: STREAM: The Stanford data stream management
    system. Tech. Rep. 2004-20, Stanford InfoLab (2004), http://ilpubs.stanford.edu:
    8090/641/
16. Arasu, A., Babu, S., Widom, J.: The CQL continuous query language: Seman-
    tic foundations and query execution. The VLDB Journal 15(2), 121–142 (2006).
    https://doi.org/10.1007/s00778-004-0147-z
17. Arasu, A., Widom, J.: A denotational semantics for continuous queries
    over streams and relations. SIGMOD Record 33(3), 6–11 (2004).
    https://doi.org/10.1145/1031570.1031572
18. Babcock, B., Babu, S., Datar, M., Motwani, R., Widom, J.: Models
    and issues in data stream systems. In: Proceedings of the Twenty-first
    ACM SIGMOD-SIGACT-SIGART Symposium on Principles of Database
    Systems. pp. 1–16. PODS '02, ACM, New York, NY, USA (2002).
    https://doi.org/10.1145/543613.543615
19. Bai, Y., Thakkar, H., Wang, H., Luo, C., Zaniolo, C.: A data stream
    language and system designed for power and extensibility. In: Proceedings
    of the 15th ACM International Conference on Information and Knowledge
    Management. pp. 337–346. CIKM '06, ACM, New York, NY, USA (2006).
    https://doi.org/10.1145/1183614.1183664
20. Benveniste, A., Caspi, P., Edwards, S.A., Halbwachs, N., Guernic, P.L., de Si-
    mone, R.: The synchronous languages 12 years later. Proceedings of the IEEE
    91(1), 64–83 (2003). https://doi.org/10.1109/JPROC.2002.805826
21. Benveniste, A., Guernic, P.L., Jacquemot, C.: Synchronous programming with
    events and relations: The SIGNAL language and its semantics. Science of
    Computer Programming 16(2), 103–149 (1991). https://doi.org/10.1016/0167-
    6423(91)90001-E
22. Berry, G., Gonthier, G.: The Esterel synchronous programming language: De-
    sign, semantics, implementation. Science of Computer Programming 19(2), 87–
    152 (1992). https://doi.org/10.1016/0167-6423(92)90005-V
23. Bertot, Y., Castéran, P.: Interactive Theorem Proving and Program Development.
    Springer (2013). https://doi.org/10.1007/978-3-662-07964-5
24. Bilsen, G., Engels, M., Lauwereins, R., Peperstraete, J.: Cyclo-static
    dataflow. IEEE Transactions on Signal Processing 44(2), 397–408 (1996).
    https://doi.org/10.1109/78.485935
25. Botan, I., Derakhshan, R., Dindar, N., Haas, L., Miller, R.J., Tatbul, N.: SE-
    CRET: A model for analysis of the execution semantics of stream process-
    ing systems. Proceedings of the VLDB Endowment 3(1-2), 232–243 (2010).
    https://doi.org/10.14778/1920841.1920874

26. Bouillet, E., Kothari, R., Kumar, V., Mignet, L., Nathan, S., Ranganathan, A., Turaga, D.S., Udrea, O., Verscheure, O.: Processing 6 billion CDRs/day: From research to production (experience report). In: Proceedings of the 6th ACM International Conference on Distributed Event-Based Systems. pp. 264–267. DEBS '12, ACM, New York, NY, USA (2012). https://doi.org/10.1145/2335484.2335513

27. Bourke, T., Pouzet, M.: Zélus: A synchronous language with ODEs. In: Proceedings of the 16th International Conference on Hybrid Systems: Computation and Control. pp. 113–118. HSCC '13, ACM, New York, NY, USA (2013). https://doi.org/10.1145/2461328.2461348

28. Boussinot, F., de Simone, R.: The ESTEREL language. Proceedings of the IEEE **79**(9), 1293–1304 (1991). https://doi.org/10.1109/5.97299

29. Brenna, L., Demers, A., Gehrke, J., Hong, M., Ossher, J., Panda, B., Riedewald, M., Thatte, M., White, W.: Cayuga: A high-performance event processing engine. In: Proceedings of the 2007 ACM SIGMOD International Conference on Management of Data. pp. 1100–1102. SIGMOD '07, ACM, New York, NY, USA (2007). https://doi.org/10.1145/1247480.1247620

30. Brock, J.D., Ackerman, W.B.: Scenarios: A model of non-determinate computation. In: Díaz, J., Ramos, I. (eds.) Proceedings of the International Colloquium on the Formalization of Programming Concepts (ICFPC '81). Lecture Notes in Computer Science, vol. 107, pp. 252–259. Springer, Berlin, Heidelberg (1981). https://doi.org/10.1007/3-540-10699-5_102

31. Caspi, P., Pilaud, D., Halbwachs, N., Plaice, J.A.: LUSTRE: A declarative language for real-time programming. In: Proceedings of the 14th ACM SIGACT-SIGPLAN Symposium on Principles of Programming Languages. pp. 178–188. POPL '87, ACM, New York, NY, USA (1987). https://doi.org/10.1145/41625.41641

32. Chandrasekaran, S., Cooper, O., Deshpande, A., Franklin, M.J., Hellerstein, J.M., Hong, W., Krishnamurthy, S., Madden, S., Raman, V., Reiss, F., Shah, M.: TelegraphCQ: Continuous dataflow processing for an uncertain world. In: Proceedings of the First Biennial Conference on Innovative Data Systems Research (CIDR '03) (2003), http://cidrdb.org/cidr2003/program/p24.pdf

33. Chen, C.M., Agrawal, H., Cochinwala, M., Rosenbluth, D.: Stream query processing for healthcare bio-sensor applications. In: Proceedings of the 20th International Conference on Data Engineering. pp. 791–794. ICDE '04, IEEE (2004). https://doi.org/10.1109/ICDE.2004.1320048

34. Cooper, G.H., Krishnamurthi, S.: Embedding dynamic dataflow in a call-by-value language. In: Sestoft, P. (ed.) Proceedings of the 15th European Symposium on Programming (ESOP '06). Lecture Notes in Computer Science, vol. 3924, pp. 294–308. Springer, Berlin, Heidelberg (2006). https://doi.org/10.1007/11693024_20

35. Coquand, T., Huet, G.: The calculus of constructions. Information and Computation **76**(2), 95–120 (1988). https://doi.org/10.1016/0890-5401(88)90005-3

36. Courtney, A.: Frappé: Functional reactive programming in Java. In: Ramakrishnan, I.V. (ed.) Proceedings of the 3rd International Symposium on Practical Aspects of Declarative Languages (PADL '01). Lecture Notes in Computer Science, vol. 1990, pp. 29–44. Springer, Berlin, Heidelberg (2001). https://doi.org/10.1007/3-540-45241-9_3

37. Cranor, C., Johnson, T., Spataschek, O., Shkapenyuk, V.: Gigascope: A stream database for network applications. In: Proceedings of the 2003 ACM SIGMOD International Conference on Management of Data. pp. 647–651. SIGMOD '03, ACM, New York, NY, USA (2003). https://doi.org/10.1145/872757.872838

38. Czaplicki, E., Chong, S.: Asynchronous functional reactive programming for GUIs. In: Proceedings of the 34th ACM SIGPLAN Conference on Programming Language Design and Implementation. pp. 411–422. PLDI '13, ACM, New York, NY, USA (2013). https://doi.org/10.1145/2491956.2462161

39. D'Angelo, B., Sankaranarayanan, S., Sanchez, C., Robinson, W., Finkbeiner, B., Sipma, H.B., Mehrotra, S., Manna, Z.: LOLA: Runtime monitoring of synchronous systems. In: Proceedings of the 12th International Symposium on Temporal Representation and Reasoning (TIME '05). pp. 166–174. IEEE (2005). https://doi.org/10.1109/TIME.2005.26

40. Demers, A., Gehrke, J., Hong, M., Riedewald, M., White, W.: Towards expressive publish/subscribe systems. In: Ioannidis, Y., Scholl, M.H., Schmidt, J.W., Matthes, F., Hatzopoulos, M., Boehm, K., Kemper, A., Grust, T., Boehm, C. (eds.) Proceedings of the 10th International Conference on Extending Database Technology (EDBT '06). Lecture Notes in Computer Science, vol. 3896, pp. 627–644. Springer, Berlin, Heidelberg (2006). https://doi.org/10.1007/11687238_38

41. Demers, A., Gehrke, J., Panda, B., Riedewald, M., Sharma, V., White, W.: Cayuga: A general purpose event monitoring system. In: Proceedings of the 3rd Biennial Conference on Innovative Data Systems Research (CIDR '07). pp. 412–422 (2007), http://cidrdb.org/cidr2007/papers/cidr07p47.pdf

42. Dennis, J.B.: First version of a data flow procedure language. In: Robinet, B. (ed.) Programming Symposium. Lecture Notes in Computer Science, vol. 19, pp. 362–376. Springer, Berlin, Heidelberg (1974). https://doi.org/10.1007/3-540-06859-7_145

43. Deshmukh, J.V., Donzé, A., Ghosh, S., Jin, X., Juniwal, G., Seshia, S.A.: Robust online monitoring of signal temporal logic. Formal Methods in System Design 51(1), 5–30 (2017). https://doi.org/10.1007/s10703-017-0286-7

44. Dindar, N., Tatbul, N., Miller, R.J., Haas, L.M., Botan, I.: Modeling the execution semantics of stream processing engines with SECRET. The VLDB Journal 22(4), 421–446 (2013). https://doi.org/10.1007/s00778-012-0297-3

45. Elgot, C.C., Mezei, J.E.: On relations defined by generalized finite automata. IBM Journal of Research and Development 9(1), 47–68 (1965). https://doi.org/10.1147/rd.91.0047

46. Elliott, C., Hudak, P.: Functional reactive animation. In: Proceedings of the Second ACM SIGPLAN International Conference on Functional Programming. pp. 263–273. ICFP '97, ACM, New York, NY, USA (1997). https://doi.org/10.1145/258948.258973

47. Elliott, C.M.: Push-pull functional reactive programming. In: Proceedings of the 2nd ACM SIGPLAN Symposium on Haskell. pp. 25–36. Haskell '09, ACM, New York, NY, USA (2009). https://doi.org/10.1145/1596638.1596643

48. Ginsburg, S., Rose, G.F.: A characterization of machine mappings. Canadian Journal of Mathematics 18, 381—-388 (1966). https://doi.org/10.4153/CJM-1966-040-3

49. Grathwohl, N.B.B., Kozen, D., Mamouras, K.: KAT + B! In: Proceedings of the Joint Meeting of the Twenty-Third EACSL Annual Conference on Computer Science Logic (CSL) and the Twenty-Ninth Annual ACM/IEEE Symposium on Logic in Computer Science (LICS). pp. 44:1–44:10. CSL-LICS '14, ACM, New York, NY, USA (2014). https://doi.org/10.1145/2603088.2603095

50. Gyllstrom, D., Wu, E., Chae, H.J., Diao, Y., Stahlberg, P., Anderson, G.: SASE: Complex event processing over streams. In: Proceedings of the 3rd Biennial Conference on Innovative Data Systems Research (CIDR '07). pp. 407–411 (2007), http://cidrdb.org/cidr2007/papers/cidr07p46.pdf

51. Halbwachs, N., Caspi, P., Raymond, P., Pilaud, D.: The synchronous data flow programming language LUSTRE. Proceedings of the IEEE **79**(9), 1305–1320 (1991). https://doi.org/10.1109/5.97300

52. Havelund, K., Roşu, G.: Efficient monitoring of safety properties. International Journal on Software Tools for Technology Transfer **6**(2), 158–173 (2004). https://doi.org/10.1007/s10009-003-0117-6

53. Hirzel, M.: Partition and compose: Parallel complex event processing. In: Proceedings of the 6th ACM International Conference on Distributed Event-Based Systems. pp. 191–200. DEBS '12, ACM, New York, NY, USA (2012). https://doi.org/10.1145/2335484.2335506

54. Hirzel, M., Soulé, R., Schneider, S., Gedik, B., Grimm, R.: A catalog of stream processing optimizations. ACM Computing Surveys (CSUR) **46**(4), 46:1–46:34 (2014). https://doi.org/10.1145/2528412

55. Hudak, P., Courtney, A., Nilsson, H., Peterson, J.: Arrows, robots, and functional reactive programming. In: Jeuring, J., Jones, S.L.P. (eds.) Revised Lectures of the 4th International School on Advanced Functional Programming: AFP 2002, Oxford, UK, August 19-24, 2002., Lecture Notes in Computer Science, vol. 2638, pp. 159–187. Springer, Berlin, Heidelberg (2003). https://doi.org/10.1007/978-3-540-44833-4_6

56. Hughes, J.: Generalising monads to arrows. Science of Computer Programming **37**(1), 67–111 (2000). https://doi.org/10.1016/S0167-6423(99)00023-4

57. Jain, N., Mishra, S., Srinivasan, A., Gehrke, J., Widom, J., Balakrishnan, H., Çetintemel, U., Cherniack, M., Tibbetts, R., Zdonik, S.: Towards a streaming SQL standard. Proceedings of the VLDB Endowment **1**(2), 1379–1390 (2008). https://doi.org/10.14778/1454159.1454179

58. Joyal, A., Street, R., Verity, D.: Traced monoidal categories. Mathematical Proceedings of the Cambridge Philosophical Society **119**(3), 447—-468 (1996). https://doi.org/10.1017/S0305004100074338

59. Kahn, G.: The semantics of a simple language for parallel programming. Information Processing **74**, 471–475 (1974)

60. Kahn, G., MacQueen, D.B.: Coroutines and networks of parallel processes. Information Processing **77**, 993–998 (1977)

61. Karp, R.M., Miller, R.E.: Properties of a model for parallel computations: Determinacy, termination, queueing. SIAM Journal on Applied Mathematics **14**(6), 1390–1411 (1966). https://doi.org/10.1137/0114108

62. Kozen, D.: A completeness theorem for Kleene algebras and the algebra of regular events. Information and Computation **110**(2), 366–390 (1994). https://doi.org/10.1006/inco.1994.1037

63. Kozen, D.: Kleene algebra with tests. ACM Transactions on Programming Languages and Systems (TOPLAS) **19**(3), 427–443 (1997). https://doi.org/10.1145/256167.256195

64. Kozen, D., Mamouras, K.: Kleene algebra with equations. In: Esparza, J., Fraigniaud, P., Husfeldt, T., Koutsoupias, E. (eds.) Proceedings of the 41st International Colloquium on Automata, Languages and Programming (ICALP '14). Lecture Notes in Computer Science, vol. 8573, pp. 280–292. Springer, Berlin, Heidelberg (2014). https://doi.org/10.1007/978-3-662-43951-7_24

65. Kozen, D., Parikh, R.: An elementary proof of the completeness of PDL. Theoretical Computer Science **14**(1), 113–118 (1981). https://doi.org/10.1016/0304-3975(81)90019-0

66. Kozen, D., Tiuryn, J.: On the completeness of propositional Hoare logic. Information Sciences **139**(3—4), 187–195 (2001). https://doi.org/10.1016/S0020-0255(01)00164-5

67. Krämer, J., Seeger, B.: Semantics and implementation of continuous sliding window queries over data streams. ACM Transactions on Database Systems (TODS) **34**(1), 4:1–4:49 (2009). https://doi.org/10.1145/1508857.1508861

68. Krishnaswami, N.R.: Higher-order functional reactive programming without spacetime leaks. In: Proceedings of the 18th ACM SIGPLAN International Conference on Functional Programming. pp. 221–232. ICFP '13, ACM, New York, NY, USA (2013). https://doi.org/10.1145/2500365.2500588

69. Krishnaswami, N.R., Benton, N.: Ultrametric semantics of reactive programs. In: Proceedings of the 26th Annual IEEE Symposium on Logic in Computer Science (LICS '11). pp. 257–266. IEEE (2011). https://doi.org/10.1109/LICS.2011.38

70. Kulkarni, S., Bhagat, N., Fu, M., Kedigehalli, V., Kellogg, C., Mittal, S., Patel, J.M., Ramasamy, K., Taneja, S.: Twitter Heron: Stream processing at scale. In: Proceedings of the 2015 ACM SIGMOD International Conference on Management of Data. pp. 239–250. SIGMOD '15, ACM, New York, NY, USA (2015). https://doi.org/10.1145/2723372.2742788

71. Law, Y.N., Wang, H., Zaniolo, C.: Relational languages and data models for continuous queries on sequences and data streams. ACM Transactions on Database Systems (TODS) **36**(2), 8:1–8:32 (2011). https://doi.org/10.1145/1966385.1966386

72. Le Guernic, P., Benveniste, A., Bournai, P., Gautier, T.: SIGNAL–a data flow-oriented language for signal processing. IEEE Transactions on Acoustics, Speech, and Signal Processing **34**(2), 362–374 (1986). https://doi.org/10.1109/TASSP.1986.1164809

73. Lee, E.A., Messerschmitt, D.G.: Synchronous data flow. Proceedings of the IEEE **75**(9), 1235–1245 (1987). https://doi.org/10.1109/PROC.1987.13876

74. Leucker, M., Schallhart, C.: A brief account of runtime verification. The Journal of Logic and Algebraic Programming **78**(5), 293–303 (2009). https://doi.org/10.1016/j.jlap.2008.08.004

75. Li, J., Maier, D., Tufte, K., Papadimos, V., Tucker, P.A.: Semantics and evaluation techniques for window aggregates in data streams. In: Proceedings of the 2005 ACM SIGMOD International Conference on Management of Data. pp. 311–322. SIGMOD '05, ACM, New York, NY, USA (2005). https://doi.org/10.1145/1066157.1066193

76. Maier, D., Li, J., Tucker, P., Tufte, K., Papadimos, V.: Semantics of data streams and operators. In: Eiter, T., Libkin, L. (eds.) Proceedings of the 10th International Conference on Database Theory (ICDT '05). Lecture Notes in Computer Science, vol. 3363, pp. 37–52. Springer, Berlin, Heidelberg (2005). https://doi.org/10.1007/978-3-540-30570-5_3

77. Maier, I., Odersky, M.: Higher-order reactive programming with incremental lists. In: Castagna, G. (ed.) Proceedings of the 27th European Conference on Object-Oriented Programming (ECOOP '13). Lecture Notes in Computer Science, vol. 7920, pp. 707–731. Springer, Berlin, Heidelberg (2013). https://doi.org/10.1007/978-3-642-39038-8_29

78. Mamouras, K.: On the Hoare theory of monadic recursion schemes. In: Proceedings of the Joint Meeting of the 23rd EACSL Annual Conference on Computer Science Logic (CSL) and the 29th Annual ACM/IEEE Symposium on Logic in Computer Science (LICS). pp. 69:1–69:10. CSL-LICS '14, ACM, New York, NY, USA (2014). https://doi.org/10.1145/2603088.2603157

79. Mamouras, K.: Extensions of Kleene Algebra for Program Verification. Ph.D. thesis, Cornell University, Ithaca, NY (August 2015), http://hdl.handle.net/1813/40960
80. Mamouras, K.: Synthesis of strategies and the Hoare logic of angelic nondeterminism. In: Pitts, A. (ed.) Proceedings of the 18th International Conference on Foundations of Software Science and Computation Structures (FoSSaCS '15). Lecture Notes in Computer Science, vol. 9034, pp. 25–40. Springer, Berlin, Heidelberg (2015). https://doi.org/10.1007/978-3-662-46678-0_2
81. Mamouras, K.: The Hoare logic of deterministic and nondeterministic monadic recursion schemes. ACM Transactions on Computational Logic (TOCL) 17(2), 13:1–13:30 (2016). https://doi.org/10.1145/2835491
82. Mamouras, K.: Synthesis of strategies using the Hoare logic of angelic and demonic nondeterminism. Logical Methods in Computer Science 12(3) (2016). https://doi.org/10.2168/LMCS-12(3:6)2016
83. Mamouras, K.: Equational theories of abnormal termination based on Kleene algebra. In: Esparza, J., Murawski, A.S. (eds.) Proceedings of the 20th International Conference on Foundations of Software Science and Computation Structures (FoSSaCS '17). Lecture Notes in Computer Science, vol. 10203, pp. 88–105. Springer, Berlin, Heidelberg (2017). https://doi.org/10.1007/978-3-662-54458-7_6
84. Mamouras, K., Raghothaman, M., Alur, R., Ives, Z.G., Khanna, S.: StreamQRE: Modular specification and efficient evaluation of quantitative queries over streaming data. In: Proceedings of the 38th ACM SIGPLAN Conference on Programming Language Design and Implementation. pp. 693–708. PLDI '17, ACM, New York, NY, USA (2017). https://doi.org/10.1145/3062341.3062369
85. Mamouras, K., Stanford, C., Alur, R., Ives, Z.G., Tannen, V.: Data-trace types for distributed stream processing systems. In: Proceedings of the 40th ACM SIGPLAN Conference on Programming Language Design and Implementation. pp. 670–685. PLDI '19, ACM, New York, NY, USA (2019). https://doi.org/10.1145/3314221.3314580
86. McSherry, F., Murray, D.G., Isaacs, R., Isard, M.: Differential dataflow. In: Proceedings of the 6th Biennial Conference on Innovative Data Systems Research (CIDR '13) (2013), http://cidrdb.org/cidr2013/Papers/CIDR13_Paper111.pdf
87. Mealy, G.H.: A method for synthesizing sequential circuits. The Bell System Technical Journal 34(5), 1045–1079 (1955). https://doi.org/10.1002/j.1538-7305.1955.tb03788.x
88. Mei, Y., Madden, S.: ZStream: A cost-based query processor for adaptively detecting composite events. In: Proceedings of the 2009 ACM SIGMOD International Conference on Management of Data. pp. 193–206. SIGMOD '09, ACM, New York, NY, USA (2009). https://doi.org/10.1145/1559845.1559867
89. Meyerovich, L.A., Guha, A., Baskin, J., Cooper, G.H., Greenberg, M., Bromfield, A., Krishnamurthi, S.: Flapjax: A programming language for Ajax applications. In: Proceedings of the 24th ACM SIGPLAN Conference on Object Oriented Programming Systems Languages and Applications. pp. 1–20. OOPSLA '09, ACM, New York, NY, USA (2009). https://doi.org/10.1145/1640089.1640091
90. Moore, E.F.: Gedanken-Experiments on Sequential Machines, Annals of Mathematics Studies, vol. 34, pp. 129–153. Princeton University Press (1956)
91. Motwani, R., Widom, J., Arasu, A., Babcock, B., Babu, S., Datar, M., Manku, G.S., Olston, C., Rosenstein, J., Varma, R.: Query processing, approximation, and resource management in a data stream management system. In: Proceedings of the First Biennial Conference on Innovative Data Systems Research (CIDR '03) (2003), http://cidrdb.org/cidr2003/program/p22.pdf

92. Murray, D.G., McSherry, F., Isaacs, R., Isard, M., Barham, P., Abadi, M.: Naiad: A timely dataflow system. In: Proceedings of the Twenty-Fourth ACM Symposium on Operating Systems Principles. pp. 439–455. SOSP '13, ACM, New York, NY, USA (2013). https://doi.org/10.1145/2517349.2522738

93. Nilsson, H., Courtney, A., Peterson, J.: Functional reactive programming, continued. In: Proceedings of the 2002 ACM SIGPLAN Workshop on Haskell. pp. 51––64. Haskell '02, ACM, New York, NY, USA (2002). https://doi.org/10.1145/581690.581695

94. Noghabi, S.A., Paramasivam, K., Pan, Y., Ramesh, N., Bringhurst, J., Gupta, I., Campbell, R.H.: Samza: Stateful scalable stream processing at LinkedIn. Proceedings of the VLDB Endowment **10**(12), 1634–1645 (2017). https://doi.org/10.14778/3137765.3137770

95. Raney, G.N.: Sequential functions. Journal of the ACM **5**(2), 177––180 (1958). https://doi.org/10.1145/320924.320930

96. Rutten, J.J.M.M.: Automata and coinduction (an exercise in coalgebra). In: Sangiorgi, D., de Simone, R. (eds.) Proceedings of the 9th International Conference on Concurrency Theory (CONCUR '98). Lecture Notes in Computer Science, vol. 1466, pp. 194–218. Springer, Berlin, Heidelberg (1998). https://doi.org/10.1007/BFb0055624

97. Rutten, J.J.M.M.: Universal coalgebra: A theory of systems. Theoretical Computer Science **249**(1), 3–80 (2000). https://doi.org/10.1016/S0304-3975(00)00056-6

98. Rutten, J.J.M.M.: A coinductive calculus of streams. Mathematical Structures in Computer Science **15**(1), 93–147 (2005). https://doi.org/10.1017/S0960129504004517

99. Sadri, R., Zaniolo, C., Zarkesh, A., Adibi, J.: Expressing and optimizing sequence queries in database systems. ACM Transactions on Database Systems **29**(2), 282–318 (2004). https://doi.org/10.1145/1005566.1005568

100. Sakarovitch, J.: Elements of Automata Theory. Cambridge University Press (2009)

101. Schneider, S., Hirzel, M., Gedik, B., Wu, K.L.: Safe data parallelism for general streaming. IEEE Transactions on Computers **64**(2), 504–517 (2015). https://doi.org/10.1109/TC.2013.221

102. Schützenberger, M.P.: Sur une variante des fonctions séquentielles. Theoretical Computer Science **4**(1), 47–57 (1977). https://doi.org/10.1016/0304-3975(77)90055-X

103. Sculthorpe, N., Nilsson, H.: Safe functional reactive programming through dependent types. In: Proceedings of the 14th ACM SIGPLAN International Conference on Functional Programming. pp. 23––34. ICFP '09, ACM, New York, NY, USA (2009). https://doi.org/10.1145/1596550.1596558

104. Shivers, O., Might, M.: Continuations and transducer composition. In: Proceedings of the 27th ACM SIGPLAN Conference on Programming Language Design and Implementation. pp. 295––307. PLDI '06, ACM, New York, NY, USA (2006). https://doi.org/10.1145/1133981.1134016

105. Thati, P., Roşu, G.: Monitoring algorithms for metric temporal logic specifications. Electronic Notes in Theoretical Computer Science **113**, 145–162 (2005). https://doi.org/10.1016/j.entcs.2004.01.029

106. The Coq development team: The Coq proof assistant. https://coq.inria.fr (2020), [Online; accessed February 22, 2020]

107. Thies, W., Karczmarek, M., Amarasinghe, S.: StreamIt: A language for streaming applications. In: Horspool, R.N. (ed.) Proceedings of the 11th International Conference on Compiler Construction (CC '02). Lecture Notes in Computer Science, vol. 2304, pp. 179–196. Springer, Berlin, Heidelberg (2002). https://doi.org/10.1007/3-540-45937-5_14

108. Toshniwal, A., Taneja, S., Shukla, A., Ramasamy, K., Patel, J.M., Kulkarni, S., Jackson, J., Gade, K., Fu, M., Donham, J., Bhagat, N., Mittal, S., Ryaboy, D.: Storm @ Twitter. In: Proceedings of the 2014 ACM SIGMOD International Conference on Management of Data. pp. 147–156. SIGMOD '14, ACM, New York, NY, USA (2014). https://doi.org/10.1145/2588555.2595641

109. Tucker, P.A., Maier, D., Sheard, T., Fegaras, L.: Exploiting punctuation semantics in continuous data streams. IEEE Transactions on Knowledge and Data Engineering 15(3), 555–568 (2003). https://doi.org/10.1109/TKDE.2003.1198390

110. Veanes, M., Hooimeijer, P., Livshits, B., Molnar, D., Bjorner, N.: Symbolic finite state transducers: Algorithms and applications. In: Proceedings of the 39th Annual ACM SIGPLAN-SIGACT Symposium on Principles of Programming Languages. pp. 137–150. POPL '12, ACM, New York, NY, USA (2012). https://doi.org/10.1145/2103656.2103674

111. Wu, E., Diao, Y., Rizvi, S.: High-performance complex event processing over streams. In: Proceedings of the 2006 ACM SIGMOD International Conference on Management of Data. pp. 407–418. SIGMOD '06, ACM, New York, NY, USA (2006). https://doi.org/10.1145/1142473.1142520

112. Zaharia, M., Das, T., Li, H., Hunter, T., Shenker, S., Stoica, I.: Discretized streams: Fault-tolerant streaming computation at scale. In: Proceedings of the Twenty-Fourth ACM Symposium on Operating Systems Principles. pp. 423–438. SOSP '13, ACM, New York, NY, USA (2013). https://doi.org/10.1145/2517349.2522737

113. Zaharia, M., Xin, R.S., Wendell, P., Das, T., Armbrust, M., Dave, A., Meng, X., Rosen, J., Venkataraman, S., Franklin, M.J., Ghodsi, A., Gonzalez, J., Shenker, S., Stoica, I.: Apache Spark: A unified engine for big data processing. Communications of the ACM 59(11), 56–65 (2016). https://doi.org/10.1145/2934664

Connecting Higher-Order Separation Logic to a First-Order Outside World

William Mansky[1], Wolf Honoré[2], and Andrew W. Appel[3]

[1] University of Illinois at Chicago, Chicago, IL, USA
[2] Yale University, New Haven, CT, USA
[3] Princeton University, Princeton, NJ, USA

Abstract. Separation logic is a useful tool for proving the correctness of programs that manipulate memory, especially when the model of memory includes higher-order state: Step-indexing, predicates in the heap, and higher-order ghost state have been used to reason about function pointers, data structure invariants, and complex concurrency patterns. On the other hand, the behavior of system features (e.g., operating systems) and the external world (e.g., communication between components) is usually specified using first-order formalisms. In principle, the soundness theorem of a separation logic is its interface with first-order theorems, but the soundness theorem may implicitly make assumptions about how other components are specified, limiting its use. In this paper, we show how to extend the higher-order separation logic of the Verified Software Toolchain to interface with a first-order verified operating system, in this case CertiKOS, that mediates its interaction with the outside world. The resulting system allows us to prove the correctness of C programs in separation logic based on the semantics of system calls implemented in CertiKOS. It also demonstrates that the combination of interaction trees + CompCert memories serves well as a *lingua franca* to interface and compose two quite different styles of program verification.

Keywords: formal verification · verifying communication · modular verification · interaction trees · VST · CertiKOS

1 Introduction

Separation logic allows us to verify programs by stating pre- and postconditions that describe the memory usage of a program. Modern variants include reasoning principles for shared-memory concurrency, invariants of locks and shared data structures, function pointers, rely-guarantee-style reasoning, and various other interesting features of programming languages. To support these features, the "memory" that is the subject of their assertions is not just a map from addresses to values, but something more complex: it may contain "predicates in the heap" to allow reasoning about invariants attached to dynamically allocated objects such as semaphores, it may be step-indexed to allow higher-order assertions, and it may contain various forms of ghost state describing resources that exist only

P. Müller (Ed.): ESOP 2020, LNCS 12075, pp. 428–455, 2020.
https://doi.org/10.1007/978-3-030-44914-8_16

for the purposes of verification. The soundness proof of the logic then relates these decorated heaps to the simple address-map view of memory used in the semantics of the target language.

This works well as long as every piece of the system is verified with respect to decorated heaps, but what if we have multiple verification tools, some of which provide correctness results in terms of undecorated memory (or, still worse, memory with a different set of decorations)? To take advantage of the correctness theorem of a function verified with one of these tools, we will need to translate our decorated memory into an undecorated one, demonstrate that it meets the function's undecorated precondition, and then take the memory output by the function and use it to reconstruct a decorated memory. In this paper, we demonstrate a technique to do exactly that, allowing higher-order separation logics (in this instance, the Verified Software Toolchain) to take advantage of correctness proofs generated by other tools (in this case, the CertiKOS verified operating system). This allows us to remove the separation-logic-level specifications of system calls from our trusted computing base, instead relying on the operating system's proofs of its own calls. In particular, we are interested in functions that do more than just manipulate memory (which is separation logic's specialty)—they communicate with the outside world, which may not know anything about program memory or higher-order state.

```
int main(void) {
    unsigned int n, d; char c;
    n=0;
    c=getchar();
    while (n<1000) {
        d = ((unsigned)c)-(unsigned)'0';
        if (d>=10) break;
        n+=d;
        print_int(n);
        putchar('\n');
        c=getchar();
    }
    return 0;
}
```

Fig. 1: A simple communicating program

Consider the program in Figure 1. It repeatedly reads a digit from the console, adds it to the sum of the digits seen so far, and prints the current sum to the console. Although this is a very simple program, it is not a natural fit for separation-logic-based verification tools, which model the behavior of C programs in terms of computation and memory rather than I/O. Several approaches have been suggested for reasoning about I/O in separation logic, for instance by Penninckx et al. [18] and Koh et al. [13]. Using the latter approach, we might specify the behavior of getchar with the Hoare triple $\{\mathsf{ITree}(r \leftarrow \mathsf{read};; \ k\ r)\}\ \mathsf{x} = \mathsf{getchar}()\ \{\mathsf{ITree}(k\ \mathsf{x})\}$, relating the function call to an external read event: the program before the call to getchar must have permission to perform a sequence of operations beginning with a read, and after the call it has permission to perform the remaining operations (with values that may depend upon the received value). By adding these specifications as axioms to VST's separation logic, we can use standard separation logic techniques to prove the correctness of programs such as the one above. But when we compile and run this C program, putchar and getchar are not axiomatized functions; they are system calls provided by the operating system, which may have an effect on kernel memory, user memory, and of course the console itself. If we prove a specification of this C program using the separation logic rules for putchar and getchar, what does that tell us about the behavior of the program when it runs? For programs without external calls, we can answer this question with the soundness proof of the logic. To extend this soundness proof to programs with external calls, we must relate the pre- and postconditions of the external calls to both the semantics of C and their implementations in the operating system.

In this paper, we describe a modular approach to proving soundness of a verification system for communicating programs, including the following elements:

- An extension of VST with support for generic ghost state.
- A generic mechanism for reasoning about external communication in a higher-order separation logic, built on top of ghost state.
- A technique for relating pre- and postconditions for external functions in higher-order separation logic to first-order specifications of the same functions in the verified operating system CertiKOS, with a general approach to "de-step-indexing" a certain class of step-indexed specifications.
- A new notion of correctness of the implementation of external communication, by relating user-level traces of external behavior to I/O operations inside the operating system.

The result is the first soundness proof of a separation logic that can be extended with first-order specifications of system calls. All proofs are formalized in the Coq proof assistant.

To understand the scope of our results, it is important to clarify exactly how much of CertiKOS we have brought into our proofs of correctness for C programs, and how much of a gap remains. The semantics on which we prove the soundness of our separation logic is the standard CompCert semantics of C, extended with the specifications of system calls provided by CertiKOS. Our model does not include the process by which CertiKOS switches from user mode to kernel mode when executing a system call, but rather assumes that CertiKOS implements this process so that the user cannot distinguish it from a normal function call. To prove this assertion rather than assuming it, we would need to transfer our soundness proof to the whole-system assembly-language semantics used by CertiKOS, and interface with not just CertiKOS's system call specifications but also its top-level correctness theorem. We discuss this last gap further in Section 7, but in summary, we prove that our client-side programs and OS-side system calls are correct, while *assuming* that CertiKOS correctly implements its transition between user mode and kernel mode.

The rest of the paper proceeds as follows. In Section 2, we describe generic ghost state in separation logic. In Section 3, we show how to encode the state of the outside world as ghost state that can only be changed through calls to external functions, allowing us to describe external communication in separation logic specifications. In Section 4, we use this approach to specify console I/O operations, and demonstrate the verification of a simple communicating program. In Sections 5 and 6, we describe the process of verifying the implementation of an external call, by first connecting its VST specification to a first-order specification on memory and then relating that "dry" specification to the functional specification of the same call in CertiKOS. This allows us to state our central theorem, which guarantees that programs verified in VST run correctly given the CertiKOS system call specifications. In Section 7, we address the relationship between user-level events and the actual communication performed by the OS. In Sections 8 and 9, we review related work and summarize our results.

2 Background: Ghost State in Separation Logic

2.1 Ghost Algebras

The fundamental insight behind ghost state is that if a mathematical object has the same basic properties as a separation logic heap, it can be injected into separation logic as a resource, even if it is not actually present in program memory. This insight was discovered independently by many people [4,3,19], and the "basic properties" required have been characterized in many ways: partial commutative monoids (PCMs), resource algebras, separation algebras, etc. They all include the idea that the ghost state must support an *operator*, often written as ·, for combining it in the same way heaps are combined by disjoint union, and they require that operator to have some of the properties of heap union (associativity, commutativity) but not all (for instance, it may be possible to combine two identical pieces of ghost state). Crucially, the operator · may be *partial*, so that the very existence of one piece of state means that another piece cannot possibly exist in the same program (just as ownership of one piece of the heap means that no other thread can hold the same piece). We follow Iris [11] in also including a *validity* predicate valid that marks out the elements of an algebra that represent well-formed ghost state.

Ghost state appears in the logic in a new kind of assertion, which we write as own, asserting that the current thread owns a certain ghost resource. In the assertion own g a pp, g is an identifier (analogous to a location in the heap), a is an element of the underlying algebra, and pp is a predicate, allowing for a limited form of higher-order ghost state—for instance, we can store separation logic assertions in ghost state to implement global invariants. The key property of the own assertion is that separating conjunction on it corresponds to the · operator of the underlying algebra (see rule own_op in Figure 2). By defining different algebras with different operators, we can define different sharing protocols for the ghost state. For instance, if we only want to count the number of times some shared resource is used, the state may be a number and the operator

$$\text{own\_op} \; \frac{a1 \cdot a2 = a3}{\text{own } g \; a3 \; pp \Leftrightarrow \text{own } g \; a1 \; pp * \text{own } g \; a2 \; pp}$$

$$\text{own\_update} \; \frac{\text{fp\_update } a \; b}{\text{own } g \; a \; pp \Rrightarrow \text{own } g \; b \; pp}$$

$$\text{consequence} \; \frac{P \Rrightarrow P' \qquad \{P'\} \; C \; \{Q'\} \qquad Q' \Rrightarrow Q}{\{P\} \; C \; \{Q\}}$$

Fig. 2: Key separation logic rules for ghost state

may be addition; if we want to describe the pattern of sharing more precisely, as with ghost variables, the state may be a pair of the variable's value and a fraction of ownership, with a guarantee that two fractions are only compatible if they agree on the value. More complex sharing patterns correspond to more complicated join operations; for instance, Jung et al. [11] showed that any acyclic state machine can be encoded as ghost state, with the join operation computing the closest common successor of two states. The ghost state is not explicitly referenced by program instructions, but it can be modified at any time via a *frame-preserving update*: ghost state a can be replaced with b as long as any third party's ghost state c that is consistent with a is also consistent with b, formally expressed as $\text{fp\_update } a \; b \triangleq \forall c, a \cdot c \Rightarrow b \cdot c$, where we write $a \cdot b$ to mean $\exists d. \; a \cdot b = d$, i.e., a and b are compatible pieces of ghost state. This frame-preserving update is embedded into the logic using a *view-shift* operator $\Rrightarrow$, as shown in rule own_update of Figure 2.

```
            x = 0;
    acquire(1); acquire(1);
    x++;        x++;
    release(1); release(1);
```

Fig. 3: The increment example

Figure 3 shows the canonical example of a program where ghost state increases the verification power of separation logic. Using concurrent separation logic as originally presented by O'Hearn [17], we can prove that the value of x at the end of the program is at least 0, but we cannot prove that it is exactly 2. This limitation comes from the fact that we can associate an *invariant* with the lock 1, but that invariant cannot express *progress* properties such as a change in the value of x. We can get around this limitation by adding ghost state that captures the contribution of each thread to x, and then use the invariant to ensure that the value of x is the sum of all contributions. (This approach is due to Ley-Wild and Nanevski [16].) We begin with ghost state that models the central operation of the program:

Definition 1. *The* sum *ghost algebra is the algebra* $(\mathbb{N}, +, \lambda n.\text{True})$ *of natural numbers with addition, in which every number is a valid element.*

Intuitively, the lock invariant should remember every addition to x, while each individual thread only knows its own contribution. This is actually an instance of a very general pattern: the *reference* pattern, in which one party holds a complete and correct "reference" copy of some ghost state, and one or more other parties hold possibly incomplete "partial" copies. Because the reference copy must always be completely up to date, the partial copies cannot be modified without access to the reference copy. When all the partial copies are gathered together, they are guaranteed to accurately represent the state of the data structure. The reference ghost algebra is built as follows:

Definition 2. *Given a ghost algebra G, we define the* positive *ghost algebra on G, written $\mathsf{pos}(G)$, as an algebra whose carrier set is $(\Pi \times G) \cup \{\bot\}$, where Π is a set of shares.[4] An element of $\mathsf{pos}(G)$ is* valid *if it has a nonempty share, and the operator $\cdot$ is defined such that $(\pi_1, a_1) \cdot (\pi_2, a_2) = (\pi_1 + \pi_2, a_1 \cdot a_2)$ and $x \cdot \bot = x$ for all x.*

The *positive* ghost algebra contains pairs of a nonempty share and an element of G, with join defined pointwise, representing partial ownership of an element of G. Total ownership of the element can be recovered by combining all of the pieces, obtaining a full share, and combining all of the G elements accordingly.

Definition 3. *Given a ghost algebra G, let the* reference *ghost algebra on G, written $\mathsf{ref}(G)$, be the algebra $(\mathsf{pos}(G) \times (G \cup \bot), \cdot, \{(p, r) \mid r = \bot \vee p \sqsubseteq r\})$, where $(p_1, r) \cdot (p_2, \bot) = (p_1 \cdot p_2, r)$, and $p \sqsubseteq r \triangleq \exists q.\ p \cdot q = (\top, r)$.*

An element of the *reference* ghost algebra is a pair of a positive share of G (partial element) and an optional reference element of G, where the reference element is unique and indivisible, and the partial element must be completable to the reference element if one exists. This ensures that when all the shares are gathered, i.e., when the partial element is $(\top, a)$, then it exactly matches the reference element, but no changes can be made to the partial element without the reference element present. To more clearly relate elements of this algebra to their intended meanings, we write ref r for the reference element $(\bot, r)$ and part s v for the partial element $((s, v), \bot)$.

Now we can formalize our intuition about what each party knows about the sum. We let the lock invariant for 1 be $\exists v.\ x \mapsto v * \mathsf{own}\ g\ (\mathsf{ref}\ v)$, and start each thread with a partial element part $\frac{1}{2}$ 0. When each thread acquires its lock and increments x, it also uses the own_update rule to increment its partial ghost state. At the end of the program, we can combine the two partial elements to obtain part $\top$ 2, which in combination with the lock invariant is sufficient to guarantee that the value of x is 2. This pattern can be used for a wide range of applications

---

[4] We use tree shares [1, Chapter 41] in the Coq proofs, but for simplicity of presentation in this paper we will use fractional shares: $\bot$ is the empty share, $\frac{1}{2}$ is a half share, and $\top$ is the full share.

by replacing the sum algebra with one appropriate to the application or data structure in question. We will also make use of it later to model the state of the external world as a separation logic resource.

2.2   Semantics of Ghost State

To support the use of ghost state in a separation logic, we need to make two main changes in the construction of the logic. First, we need to extend the underlying model of the logic with ghost state: rather than being predicates on the heap, our assertions are now predicates on the combination of heap and ghost state. Once ghost state exists in the model, we can give semantics to the own assertion.

Second, we need to change our definition of Hoare triples to allow for the possibility of frame-preserving updates to ghost state at any point in a program's execution. In a ghost-free separation logic, we might define Hoare triples with respect to an operational semantics for the language as follows:

$$[\![\{P\}\ c\ \{Q\}]\!] \triangleq \forall h, P(h) \Rightarrow (c, h) \rightarrow^* (\mathsf{done}, h') \Rightarrow Q(h')$$

where $(c, h) \rightarrow (c', h')$ means that the program c executed with starting heap h may take a step to a new program c' with heap h'. For a step-indexed logic, it is more convenient to write this definition inductively:

Definition 4 (Safety). *A configuration (c, h) is safe for n steps with postcondition Q if:*

 - *n is 0, or*
 - *c has terminated and $Q(h)$ holds to approximation (step-index) n, or*
 - *$(c, h) \rightarrow (c', h')$ and (c', h') is safe for $n - 1$ steps with Q.*

We can then define $\{P\}\ c\ \{Q\}$ (at step-index n) to mean that $\forall h.\ P(h) \Rightarrow (c, h)$ is safe for n steps with Q.

Once we have added ghost state, our heap h is now a pair (h, g) of physical and ghost state, and between any two steps the ghost state may change. This leads us to a ghost-augmented version of safety.

Definition 5 (Safety with Ghost State). *A configuration (c, h, g) is safe for n steps with postcondition Q if:*

 - *n is 0, or*
 - *c has terminated and $Q(h, g)$ holds to approximation n, or*
 - *$(c, h) \rightarrow (c', h')$ and $\forall g_{\mathsf{frame}}.\ g \cdot g_{\mathsf{frame}} \Rightarrow \exists g'.\ (g' \cdot g_{\mathsf{frame}} \wedge (c', h', g')$ is safe for $n - 1$ steps with Q).*

The program must be able to continue executing under any g_{frame} consistent with its current ghost state, but its choice of new ghost state g' may depend on the frame. This quantifier alternation captures the essence of ghost state: the ghost state held by the program constrains any other ghost state held by the notional "rest of the system", and may be changed arbitrarily in any way that does not invalidate that other ghost state.

3   External State as Ghost State

An I/O-performing program modifies the state of the outside world. We would like to treat this external state as a kind of ghost state, since it is not in the program's memory and yet can be described by separation logic assertions. At the same time, we would emphatically *not* like to allow users to make arbitrary frame-preserving updates to external state: the external environment should have complete control of the external state, and the program should never be able to change it except by calling external functions. Furthermore, VST's semantic model (used to prove soundness) already includes an external state element[5], a black box of arbitrary type that is carried around by the program and passed to the environment at each external call, allowing the effects of external calls to be stateful without explicitly representing their state in program memory. While this external state is present in the operational semantics of VST, prior to the changes we describe it could not be referred to by separation logic assertions and was never instantiated with anything other than the singleton type unit. In this section, we describe how we combine ghost state with the built-in external state to make the external state visible in the separation logic.

Intuitively, external state is just another kind of shared resource, and we should be able to model it with a form of ghost state. However, one of the key features of ghost state is that programs can make arbitrary frame-preserving updates to it, while programs should never be able to modify external state. We can accomplish this using the reference ghost algebra of Section 2: the reference element ref a will be held by the external environment, while the program holds a partial element part $\top$ a. This ensures that the program cannot make any frame-preserving updates without the reference element, which is only available when the program passes control to the external environment via an external call. It then remains to choose the underlying algebra G of the external state. Different applications may call for external state with different carrier sets and operations, but in the simplest case, the VST user will not want to split or combine the local copy of the external state[6]. In this case, they can pick a type Z and make G the *exclusive* ghost algebra for Z, which holds only an empty unit element and an indivisible ownership element, preventing the local copy from being divided. Then the user program holds an element part $\top$ a that cannot be divided or modified, but only passed to the external environment, where $a : Z$ is the current value of the external state. We encapsulate the ghost state construction in an assertion has_ext $a \triangleq$ own 0 (part $\top$ a), where 0 is the identifier reserved for the external ghost state. Now, when verifying a program with external state, the user simply provides the starting state a, and receives in the precondition of the **main** function the assertion has_ext a, with no need to use or understand the ghost state mechanism.

---

[5] Appel et al. [1] call this the *external oracle*, but we refer to it as simply "external state" to avoid confusion with the environment oracles of CertiKOS.

[6] One example of a use case that benefits from nontrivial external state structure is a multithreaded web server in which different threads serve different clients simultaneously; in this case, each thread might have its own piece of the external state.

On the back end, we must still modify VST's semantics to connect the ghost state a to the actual external state, and to prevent the "ghost steps" of the semantics from changing the external state. Recall from Section 2 that in order for a non-terminated configuration (c, h, g) to be safe for a nonzero number of steps, it must be the case that $(c, h) \rightarrow (c', h')$ and $\forall g_{\text{frame}}.\ g \cdot g_{\text{frame}} \Rightarrow \exists g'.\ g' \cdot g_{\text{frame}} \wedge (c', h', g')$ is safe. To connect the external ghost state to a real external state z, we simply extend this definition to require that g_{frame} include an element $(\bot, z)$ at identifier 0. This enforces the requirement that the value of the external ghost state always be the same as the value of the external state, and ensures that frame-preserving updates cannot change the value of the external state. Re-proving the separation logic rules of Verifiable C with this new definition of Hoare triple required only minor changes, since internal program steps never change the external ghost state.

When the semantics reaches an external call, the call is allowed to make arbitrary changes to the state consistent with its pre- and postcondition, including changing the value of the external ghost state (as well as the actual external state). We can use has_ext assertions in the pre- and postcondition of an external function to describe how that function affects the external state. For instance, we might give a console write function the "consuming-style" specification $\{\text{has\_ext}(\text{write}(v);;\ k)\}$ write(v) $\{\text{has\_ext}(k)\}$, stating that if before calling write(v) the program has permission to write the value v and then do the operations in k, then after the call it is left with permission to do k. (We could reverse the pre- and postcondition for a "trace-style" specification, in which the external state records the history of operations performed by the program instead of the future operations allowed.) In this paper, we use *interaction trees* [13] as a means of describing a collection of allowed traces of external events. Interaction trees can be thought of as "abstract traces with binding"; for instance, we can write $x \leftarrow \text{read};; \text{write}\ (x + 1);; k\ x$ to mean "read a value, call it x, write the value $x + 1$, and then continue to do the actions in k using the same value of x."

In the end, we have a new assertion has_ext on external state that works in exactly the way we expect: it can hold external state of any type, it cannot be modified by user code, it can be freely modified by external calls, it always has exactly the same value as the external state already present in VST's semantics, and it exposes no ghost-state functionality to the user. If the user wants more fine-grained control over external state (for instance, to split it into pieces so multiple threads can make concurrent calls to external functions), they can define their own ghost algebra for the state and pass around part elements explicitly, but for the common case, has_ext provides seamless separation-logic reasoning about C programs that interact with an external environment.

4 Verifying C Programs with I/O in VST

Once we have separation logic specifications for external function calls, verifying a communicating program is no different from verifying any other program. We demonstrate this with the example program excerpted in Figure 1, shown in

$\{\mathsf{ITree}(\mathsf{write\_list}(\mathsf{decimal\_rep}'(i));;\ k)\}$

```
void print_intr(unsigned int i) {
  unsigned int q,r;
  if (i!=0) {
    q=i/10u;
    r=i%10u;
    print_intr(q);
    putchar(r+'0');
  }
}
```

$\{\mathsf{ITree}(k)\}$

$\{\mathsf{ITree}(\mathsf{write\_list}(\mathsf{decimal\_rep}(i));;\ k)\}$

```
void print_int(unsigned int i) {
  if (i==0)
    putchar('0');
  else print_intr(i);
}
```

$\{\mathsf{ITree}(k)\}$

$\{\mathsf{ITree}(c \leftarrow \mathsf{read};;\ \mathsf{main\_loop}(0, c))\}$

```
int main(void) {
  unsigned int n, d; char c;
  n=0;
  c=getchar();
  while (n<1000) {
    d = ((unsigned)c)-
(unsigned)'0';
    if (d>=10) break;
    n+=d;
    print_int(n);
    putchar('\n');
    c=getchar();
  }
  return 0;
}
```

$\{\mathsf{ITree}(\mathsf{done})\}$

Fig. 4: A simple communicating program, with specifications for each function

full in Figure 4. The print_intr function uses external calls to putchar to print the decimal representation of its argument, as long as that argument is nonzero; print_int handles the zero case as well. The main function repeatedly reads in digits using getchar and then prints the running total of the digits read so far. The ITree predicate is simply a wrapper around the has_ext predicate of the previous section (i.e., an assertion on the external ghost state), specialized to interaction trees on I/O operations. We can then write simple specifications for getchar and putchar, using interaction trees to represent external state:

$$\{\mathsf{ITree}(r \leftarrow \mathsf{read};;\ k\ r)\}\ x = \mathsf{getchar}()\ \{\mathsf{ITree}(k\ x)\}$$
$$\{\mathsf{ITree}(\mathsf{write}(x);;\ k)\}\ \mathsf{putchar}(x)\ \{\mathsf{ITree}(k)\}$$

Next, we annotate each function with separation logic pre- and postconditions; the program does not manipulate memory, so the specifications only describe the I/O behavior of each function. The effect of print_intr is to make a series of calls to putchar, printing the digits of the argument i as computed by the meta-level function decimal_rep' (where write_list($[i_0; i_1; ...; i_n]$) is an abbreviation for the series of outputs write(i_0);; write(i_1);; ...;; write(i_n)). When the value of i is 0, print_intr assumes that the number has been completely printed, so print_int adds a special case for 0 as the initial input. The specification for the main loop is a recursive sequence of read and write operations, taking the running total (which starts at 0) and the most recent input as arguments:

$\mathsf{main\_loop}(n, d) \triangleq \mathbf{if}\ n < 1000$

$\quad \mathbf{then}\ \mathsf{write\_list}(\mathsf{decimal\_rep}(n + d));; c \leftarrow \mathsf{read};;\ \mathsf{main\_loop}(n + d, c)\ \mathbf{else}\ \mathsf{done}$

Using the specifications for putchar and getchar as axioms, we can easily prove the specifications of print_intr, print_int, and main. (The following sections show how we substantiate these axioms.)

$\{\mathsf{ITree}(\ell \leftarrow \mathsf{read\_list}(n);;\ k\ \ell) * buf \mapsto \_\}$
$x = \mathsf{getchars}(buf, n)$
$\{\exists vs.\ \mathsf{length}(vs) = n \wedge x = n \wedge \mathsf{ITree}(k\ vs) * buf \mapsto vs\}$

$\{\mathsf{length}(vs) = n \wedge \mathsf{ITree}(\mathsf{write\_list}(vs);;\ k) * buf \mapsto vs\}$
$\mathsf{putchars}(buf, n)$
$\{\mathsf{ITree}(k) * buf \mapsto vs\}$

Fig. 5: Separation logic specifications for I/O calls with memory

More complicated programs may manipulate memory as well as communicating, and we can easily combine the two. For instance, if we want to read or write several characters in a single call, the standard C idiom is to pass a buffer in memory as an argument. Figure 5 shows the specifications for functions putchars and getchars in this style, where each function takes as arguments a buffer to hold the input/output and a number indicating the size of the buffer[7]. The pre- and postconditions of these functions now involve both the external state and a standard points-to assertion for the buffer. (Note that $\ell \leftarrow \mathsf{read\_list}(n)$ is an abbreviation for the series of inputs $\ell_0 \leftarrow \mathsf{read};;\ \ell_1 \leftarrow \mathsf{read};;\ ...;;\ \ell_{n-1} \leftarrow \mathsf{read}$.)

Figures 6 and 7 show a variant of the previous program that uses these external functions with memory. The print_intr function now populates a buffer with the characters to be written and returns the length of the decimal representation of its argument (retval in the postcondition refers to the return value of the function), while print_int makes a single call to putchars with the populated buffer. The main function now reads four characters at a time and then processes them one by one, ultimately producing the same output as the previous program. The specifications for putchars and getchars describe changes to both external state and memory, as shown in Figure 5. Proving the specifications for the functions in this program is not any more difficult than in the memoryless case: we define an interaction tree main_loop capturing the slightly different pattern of interaction in this program, and then apply the appropriate separation logic rule to each command. The external calls affect both memory and the ITree predicate, while all other commands affect only memory and local variables, as usual.

---

[7] While these are not standard POSIX I/O functions, they are close to the behavior of POSIX read/write, socket operations, and other common forms of I/O.

$\{\mathsf{length}(\mathsf{decimal\_rep}'(i)) \leq \mathsf{length}(contents) \wedge$
   $buf \mapsto contents\}$

```
int print_intr(unsigned int i,
        unsigned char *buf) {
  unsigned int q;
  unsigned char r;
  int k = 1;
  if (i!=0) {
    q=i/10u;
    r=i%10u;
    k = print_intr(q, buf);
    buf[k] = r+'0';
  }
  return k + 1;
}
```

$\{buf \mapsto contents[0...(\text{retval} - 1) :=$
   $\mathsf{decimal\_rep}'(i)]\}$

$\{\mathsf{ITree}(\mathsf{write\_list}(\mathsf{decimal\_rep}(i));; \ k)\}$

```
void print_int(unsigned int i) {
  unsigned char *buf = malloc(5);
  if (!buf) exit(1);
  int k;
  if (i==0){
    buf[0] = '0';
    buf[1] = '\n';
    k = 2;
  }
  else{
    k = print_intr(i, buf);
    buf[k] = '\n';
    k++;
  }
  putchars(buf, k);
  free(buf);
}
```

$\{\mathsf{ITree}(k)\}$

Fig. 6: A communicating program with memory (part 1)

5   Soundness of External-State Reasoning

The soundness proof of VST [1] describes the guarantees that the Hoare-logic proof of correctness for a C program provides about the actual execution of that program. A C program P is represented as a list $P_1, ..., P_n$ of function definitions in CompCert Clight, a Coq representation of the abstract syntax of C. The program is annotated with a collection of function specifications (i.e., separation logic pre- and postconditions) $\Gamma = \Gamma_1, ..., \Gamma_n$, one for each function. We then prove that each P_i satisfies its specification Γ_i, which we write as $\Gamma \vdash P_i : \Gamma_i$ (note that each function may call on the specification of any function, including itself). The soundness theorem of VST without external function calls is then:

Theorem 1 (VST Soundness). *Let P be a program with specification Γ. Suppose for every function P_i there is a proof $\Gamma \vdash P_i : \Gamma_i$ that P_i satisfies its specification. Then the* main *function of P can run according to the Comp-Cert Clight semantics for any number of steps without getting stuck, and if it terminates then it does so in a state that satisfies its postcondition.*

Proof. First, make a nonstandard, ownership-annotated, resource-annotated, step-indexed small-step semantics for Clight. Define Verifiable C's Hoare triple as a shallowly embedded statement about safe executions in this "juicy" semantics. Then show that executions in the juicy semantics *erase* to corresponding safe executions in Clight's standard "dry" small-step semantics.

$\{\mathsf{ITree}(cs \leftarrow \mathsf{read\_list}(4);; \ \mathsf{main\_loop}'(0, cs))\}$

```
int main(void) {
  unsigned int n, d; unsigned char c;
  unsigned char *buf;
  int i, j;

  n=0;
  buf = malloc(4);
  if (!buf) exit(1);
  i = getchars(buf, 4);
  while (n<1000) {
    for(j = 0; j < i; j++){
      c = buf[j];
      d = ((unsigned)c)-(unsigned)'0';
      if (d>=10) { free(buf); return 0; }
      n+=d;
      print_int(n);
    }
    i = getchars(buf, 4);
  }
  free(buf);
  return 0;
}
```

$\{\mathsf{ITree}(\mathsf{done})\}$

Fig. 7: A communicating program with memory (part 2)

Corollary 1. *Since null pointer dereferences, integer overflows, etc. are all stuck in CompCert's small-step semantics, this means that a verified program will be free of all of these kinds of errors.*

This soundness theorem expresses the relationship between the juicy semantics described by VST's separation logic and the dry semantics under which C programs actually execute[8]. The proof of correctness of a program gives us enough information to construct a corresponding dry execution for each juicy execution[9]. However, we may not have access to the code of external functions, and in some cases (e.g., system calls) they may not even be implemented in C. In this section, we generalize the soundness theorem to include external functions.

---

[8] Of course, a C program *actually* executes by running machine code, but the relationship between the dry C semantics and the semantics of assembly language is already proved in CompCert, as is assembly-to-machine language [20].

[9] Theorem 1 blurs the line between juicy and dry by saying that a dry execution "terminates in a state that satisfies its postcondition", where the postcondition is stated in separation logic. In the original proof of soundness [1], this is resolved by assuming that the postcondition of main is always true. The techniques we use in this section can also be applied to more refined specifications of main.

In order to prove correctness of a C program with external calls in our separation logic, we must have a pre- and postcondition Γ_i for each external function. At this level these specifications are taken as axioms, since we do not have access to the code of the external functions. To be able to describe the dry executions of programs that call these functions, we also need simpler specifications on dry states. Each *dry external specification* contains a pre- and postcondition for the function, which may refer to the memory state, arguments/return values, the external state, and a *witness* used to provide logical parameters to the pre- and postcondition. The core of our approach is to prove the correspondence between the juicy specification and the dry specification of each external function.

If we can relate every juicy specification to a dry specification, then why bother with the juicy specifications at all? The answer is, not every function can be specified "dry." Higher-order functions in object-oriented patterns, dynamically created locks with self-referential resource invariants, and many other C programming patterns cannot be given simple first-order specifications. But the *external functions* that correspond to ordinary input/output *can* be given first-order specifications. Therefore, users can write higher-order object-oriented programs, in which the *internal* functions have (only) juicy specifications, so long as the external functions have (also) dry specifications. For instance, consider the specification of the putchars function from the previous section:

$$\{\text{length}(vs) = n \wedge \text{ITree}(\text{write\_list}(vs); ; \ k) * buf \mapsto vs\} \ \text{putchars}(buf, n)$$
$$\{\text{ITree}(k) * buf \mapsto vs\}$$

The pre- and postcondition each make one assertion about memory (that the buffer buf points to the string of bytes vs) and one assertion about the external state[10] (that the interaction tree allows write_list(vs) followed by k before the call, and k afterward). The corresponding first-order specification on dry memory and external state is:

$$\text{Pre}((vs, k), (buf, n), m, z) \triangleq \text{length}(vs) = n \wedge z = (\text{write\_list}(vs); ; \ k) \wedge$$
$$\forall i < n. \ m(buf + i) = vs[i]$$
$$\text{Post}((vs, k), (buf, n), m_0, m, z) \triangleq m_0 = m \wedge z = k$$

where (vs, k) is the witness (i.e., the parameters to the specification), buf and n are the arguments passed to the function, m is the current memory, z is the external state, and m_0 in the postcondition is the memory before the call (allowing us to state that memory is unchanged). Of the roughly 210 Linux system calls that are not Linux- or platform-specific, about 140 fall into this pattern, including socket, console, and file I/O, memory allocation, or are simpler informational calls like gethostname that do not involve memory.

Once we have a juicy and a dry specification for a given external function, what is the relationship between them? Intuitively, if the juicy specification for a function f is $\{P_j\} \ f(args); \ \{Q_j\}$, the Hoare logic proof for a program that calls

---

[10] ITree is actually an assertion on the *external ghost state*, which is connected to the true external state as described in Section 3, and is erased at the dry level.

f guarantees that P_j is satisfied before every call to f, and relies on Q_j holding after each such call returns. To know that the program will run without getting stuck, on the other hand, we must know that the dry precondition P_d is satisfied before each call, and we can assume that the dry postcondition Q_d is satisfied after each return. So informally, we need to know that P_j implies P_d and that Q_d implies Q_j. This cannot be a simple logical implication, however, because P_j and Q_j are predicates on juicy memories, while P_d and Q_d are predicates on dry memories. A juicy memory jm is a dependent triple (m, ϕ, pf), where m is a dry memory, ϕ is a higher-order, step-indexed memory with ghost state, and pf is a proof of the relationship between m and ϕ. We can easily extract the dry memory m from a juicy memory (we write this as $\mathsf{dry}(jm)$), but there are many possible ϕ's that may correspond to a single m: we need to make decisions about ownership information and ghost state that is not present at the CompCert level.

In order to relate the juicy and dry specifications, we must erase the juice from the precondition, $P_j \Rightarrow P_d$, and then reconstruct the juice in the postcondition, $Q_d \Rightarrow Q_j$. The key to this erasure is that, as explained above, the P_j and Q_j for external functions generally make only first-order assertions on memory (memory buffers passed to system calls don't contain higher-order objects such as function pointers and locks). The rest of the memory is implicitly the *frame*, and will not be changed by the external call. For first-order predicates, erasure is injective, and the associated juicy memory can be uniquely reconstructed once the buffer has been modified. The frame *can* contain noninjective juice, but we can reuse the same juice in going from $Q_d \Rightarrow Q_j$ that we erased in going from $P_j \Rightarrow P_d$, since the external function does not modify the frame. In practice, the story is not quite so simple: the external function might allocate or free memory, the dry witness (used in P_d and Q_d) must be derived from the juicy witness (used in P_j and Q_j), and so on. We now formalize the details, culminating in Definition 6, the formal correspondence between juicy and dry specifications.

First, we address the problem of reconstructing a juicy memory from a dry memory. While there are many juicy memories that correspond to a given Comp-Cert memory, it is easy to start with a (precondition) juicy memory and change it to reflect (postcondition) modifications to the associated dry memory, as long as those changes fall within certain limits. In particular, a memory location may be newly allocated or deallocated, or its value may be changed while staying at the same permission level, but its permissions should not otherwise be changed[11]. If a dry specification ensures that memory is changed in only (at most) these ways, we say that it *safely evolves* memory. When a user adds a new set of external functions to VST, this safe evolution property will be one of their proof obligations. As long as an external function satisfies a specification that safely evolves memory, we can always reconstruct the juicy memory after the call by modifying the original juicy memory to reflect the changes to the dry memory. This

---

[11] Any function that interacts with memory through the standard interface of load, store, alloc, and free will fall within these limits; concurrency operations, such as acquiring or releasing a lock, may not, and proving that lock operations are correctly implemented is outside the scope of this work.

reconstruction captures the effects of the external call on the program's memory; to reflect the changes to the external state, we must also set the external ghost state of the reconstructed juicy memory to match the external state returned by the call. We define a reconstruct operation such that $\mathsf{reconstruct}(jm, m, z)$ is a version of the juicy memory jm that has been modified to take into account the changes in the dry memory m and the external state z.

Second, we need a way to transform a juicy witness into the corresponding dry witness. When a user adds a new external call to VST, they must provide a dessicate function that performs this transformation. Fortunately, the dessicate operation usually follows a simple pattern. Components of the witness that are not memory objects are generally identical in their juicy and dry versions. The frame is usually the only memory object in the juicy witness; while it is possible in VST to write a Hoare triple that quantifies over other memory objects explicitly, it is very unusual and runs counter to the spirit of separation logic. Similarly, the postcondition of the dry specification may refer to the memory state before the call (to express properties such as "this call stored value v at location ℓ"), but there is rarely a reason to refer to any other memory object. Thus, the dessicate operation for each function can simply discard the frame (juicy) memory and replace it with the dry memory from before the call. This standard dessicate operation works for all external functions shown in this paper.

This leads to the following definition and theorem:

Definition 6 (Juicy-Dry Correspondence). *A juicy specification* (P_j, Q_j) *and a dry specification* (P_d, Q_d) *for an external function correspond if, for a suitable* dessicate *operation:*

- *for all witnesses* w, *arguments* a, *external states* z, *and juicy memories* jm, *if* $P_j(w, a, z, jm)$, *then* $P_d(\mathsf{dessicate}(jm, w), a, z, \mathsf{dry}(jm))$; *and*
- *for all witnesses* w, *arguments* a, *return values* r, *external states* z, *initial juicy memories* jm_0, *initial external states* z_0, *and dry memories* m, *if* $P_d(\mathsf{dessicate}(jm_0, w), a, z_0, \mathsf{dry}(jm_0))$ *and* $Q_d(\mathsf{dessicate}(jm_0, w), r, z, m)$, *then* $Q_j(w, r, z, \mathsf{reconstruct}(jm_0, m, z))$.

Theorem 2 (VST Soundness with External Functions). *Let P be a program with n functions, calling also upon m external functions. The internal functions have (juicy) specifications $\Gamma_1 \ldots \Gamma_n$ and the external functions have (juicy) specifications $\Gamma_{n+1} \ldots \Gamma_{n+m}$. Suppose P is proved correct in Verifiable C—there is a derivation $\Gamma \vdash P_1 : \Gamma_1, \ldots, P_n : \Gamma_n$. Let $D_{n+1}, \ldots, D_{n+m}$ be dry specifications that safely evolve memory, and that correspond to $\Gamma_{n+1} \ldots \Gamma_{n+m}$. Then the* main *function of P can run according to the CompCert C semantics, using D as the semantics of external function calls, for any number of steps without getting stuck, and if it terminates then it satisfies its postcondition.*

Proof. We extend the juicy semantics of Theorem 1 with a rule for external calls that uses their juicy pre- and postconditions, and then prove that executions in this semantics erase to safe executions in the dry semantics, using the correspondence to relate juicy and dry behaviors of external calls.

Although this theorem does not explicitly mention external communication, it implies that any I/O operations performed by P conform to the description of allowed communication in the specification of `main`. This follows from the fact that only external calls can change the external state, and only external calls can communicate with the outside world. Thus, if P performs a sequence of external function calls $f_1, ..., f_n$, the external communication performed by P must be consistent with the specifications $D_{f_1}, ..., D_{f_n}$. In the case of the examples above, this means that at any point in a program's execution, its communication so far will be a prefix of the operations allowed by the initial ITree predicate, as desired.

Proving the correspondence between the juicy and dry specifications is the primary proof burden for a VST user who wants to use a new external function in their program. Fortunately, this proof only needs to be done once per external function rather than once per program (as long as the original specification is general enough to be usable in many different programs), and soundness (Theorem 2) has been proved once and for all. As a result, a VST user can prove that their program with external calls runs correctly as follows:

1. For each external function used in the program (that has not already been specified in VST), write a separation logic specification for that function.
2. Prove correctness of the program in VST as usual using the separation-logic-level external specifications.
3. For each external function used in the program (again, that has not already been specified), write a dry specification describing its effects on CompCert memories, and prove that the dry specification corresponds to the juicy specification and safely evolves memory.
4. Show immediately that the program runs correctly for any number of steps by applying Theorem 2.

For instance, we have already seen the VST-level specifications for putchars and getchars, and used them to prove correctness of a simple program; we can complete the process with the following lemma.

Lemma 1. *The juicy specifications of putchars and getchars correspond to their dry specifications.*

As a result, we now know that the sample program in Figure 7 runs correctly for any implementation of putchars and getchars that satisfy their dry specifications.

6   Connecting VST to CertiKOS

In the previous section, we showed how to connect a step-indexed separation logic specification of an external function to a "dry" specification on non-step-indexed CompCert memories and external state. This gives us a correctness property for C programs with external functions, but it still treats the dry specifications of the external functions as axioms. In this section, we show how to discharge these axioms by connecting dry specifications to implementations of the corresponding functions in the verified operating system CertiKOS [7].

```
Definition serial_in (port : Z) (st : OSState) : OSState * Z :=
 ... (* read buffers, compare bits, etc *)
 let new := st.(serial_oracle) st.(serial_trace) in
 match new with
 | SerialRecv data ⇒
   let (st', byte) := ... in (* manipulate data *)
   (st'/[serial_trace := st.(serial_trace) ++ [new]], byte)
 | ... (* handle other events *) end.
```

Fig. 8: A specification of a serial driver

6.1 CertiKOS Specifications

In order to explain how to connect VST and CertiKOS specifications, we first summarize how their specification styles differ. In VST, a specification is a pre- and postcondition on the (step-indexed, ghost-state-augmented) memory state of a program. In CertiKOS, a specification is a function representing a state transition from the current OS state to a new one with an (optional) return value. The OS state is a record with fields for each piece of concrete or logical state that CertiKOS maintains, such as page table maps and console buffers. Specifications are organized into "Certified Abstraction Layers" [6], which can be independently proven to refine higher-level abstractions, and then composed with other layers to build more complex systems. The concrete CertiKOS kernel implementation, in C and assembly, is verified with respect to high-level specifications using this layer framework and the CompCert compiler.

Because the specifications are pure, deterministic functions, something more is needed to model functions with externally visible effects such as I/O. To handle such functions, CertiKOS parameterizes specifications by "environment contexts" [8], which act as oracles that take a log of the events up to that point and return the next steps taken by the environment. Each oracle has a fixed set of events it can produce, along with a trace well-formedness invariant that it must preserve. For example, the oracle for modeling the behavior of the serial device can return events indicating the successful completion of a send or the arrival of some data, and it is assumed to only receive values that fit in a byte ([0, 255]). Although any particular choice of oracle is a deterministic function, its implementation is completely opaque to the specification, so that proofs about the specification's behavior hold given any oracle and environment state.

As a concrete example, consider the abridged specification of part of the serial driver in CertiKOS (Figure 8). After some initial work, the specification needs to know what bits came in from the physical device, so it consults the oracle and branches based on the next serial event. If the next event is a receive, it manipulates the received data to extract a byte and returns it along with a new state in which the trace is updated to include the processed event.

6.2   Relating OS and User State

```
Definition serial_putc (c : Z) (st : OSState) : option (OSState * Z) :=
  let c' := c mod 256 in
  if st.(ikern) && st.(init) && st.(ihost) then
    if st.(drv_serial).(serial_exists) then
      match st.(com1) with
      | mkDevData (mkSerialState _ true _ _ txbuf nil false) _ ltx _ ⇒
        let cs := if c' =? CHAR_LF then [CHAR_LF;CHAR_CR] else [c'] in
        Some (st/[com1/s/TxBuf := cs,
                  serial_log := st.(serial_log) ++ [IOEvPutc c]], c')
      | _ ⇒ None end
    else Some (st, -1)
  else None.
```

$$\text{Pre}(k, c, m, z) \triangleq (\text{write}(c); ; \ k) \sqsubseteq z$$
$$\text{Post}(k, c, m_0, m, z) \triangleq m_0 = m \wedge z \sqsubseteq k$$

Fig. 9: The core of the putchar system call vs. its dry specification

User-level programs cannot directly interact with the outside environment, and must instead communicate through the OS using the system call interface it provides. System calls in CertiKOS are specified just like any other operation, i.e., as a state transition function. For each system call, we would like to relate its dry pre- and postcondition (as described in Section 5) to its functional specification in CertiKOS. The property we would like to prove is something like: *for any initial state s, if the dry precondition holds for s, then the value v and state s' returned by the functional specification satisfy the dry postcondition.* Combined with the correspondence between juicy and dry specifications, this implies that the system call specification correctly implements the behavior expected by the user program (as expressed by its separation logic specification in VST). However, this property cannot be proven in its current form because the dry pre- and postconditions are predicates on CompCert memories and external state, which differ from CertiKOS's state, much of which is invisible and irrelevant to the user program, as can be seen in Figure 9. Instead, we must restate the correctness property in terms of relations between the common elements of the two state representations. The key components to relate are the return value of the system call, the representation of the user program's memory, and the model of external behaviors. The return value is a CompCert value in both systems, but the other two require additional work to translate between them.

Although, like VST, the CertiKOS kernel uses the CompCert C semantics and memory model, user-process memory is represented as a flat physical address space rather than a set of disjoint blocks. The OS state also includes page tables to map virtual to physical addresses and a record of which addresses are allocated. Fortunately, aside from these differences, the flat memory model is quite similar to CompCert's (see Figure 10). We assume the existence of a relation R_{mem} that maps blocks to virtual addresses. Other than the restriction

```
Inductive flatmem_val :=        Inductive memval :=
| HUndef                        | Undef: memval
| HByte: byte → flatmem_val.    | Byte: byte → memval
                                | Pointer: block → int → nat → memval.
(* Map from address to value *)  (* Map from block and offset to value *)
Definition flatmem :=           Record mem := mkmem {
  ZMap.t flatmem_val.             mem_contents: PMap.t (ZMap.t memval);
                                  ... }.
```

Fig. 10: A comparison of CertiKOS flat memory and CompCert memory

that blocks fit in the virtual address space and map to nonoverlapping regions, the exact mapping has no effect on the system call correctness, so it can be completely arbitrary. To relate a CompCert memory to a CertiKOS one, we define a relation $\mathsf{inj}(m, \mathsf{flat}(s), \mathsf{ptbl}(s))$, which states that if a block and offset in the CompCert memory m is valid, then it contains the same data as the corresponding location (according to R_{mem} and the page table) in the flat memory of the OS state s. Note that inj is parameterized by the page table to allow a system call to alter the address mapping, for example by allocating new memory.

At the user level, the precondition contains an interaction tree (or similar external specification) that specifies the allowed external behaviors, and the postcondition contains a smaller tree that continues using the return value of the "consumed" actions. On the other hand, in CertiKOS, specifications begin with a trace of the events that have already happened and extend it with new events by querying the external environment. To reconcile these two views, we can first relate an interaction tree to a (possibly infinite) set of (possibly infinitely long) traces, each of which intuitively is the result of following one path in the tree. Then any trace allowed by the output interaction tree should be a suffix of a trace allowed by the input tree, and the difference between the two should be exactly the trace of events generated during the system call:

Definition 7. *We write* $\mathsf{consume}(\mathcal{T}, \mathcal{T}', tr)$ *to mean that, if* tr' *is a trace of* $\mathcal{T}'$, *then* $tr \mathbin{+\!\!+} tr'$ *(concatenation of* tr *and* tr'*) is a trace of* $\mathcal{T}$.

Equipped with the relations defined above, we can define more precisely what it means for a system call to satisfy its dry specification.

Definition 8 (Dry-Syscall Correspondence). *A system call f with functional specification O_f correctly implements a dry specification (P_d, Q_d) if for any arguments v, CompCert memory m, interaction tree $\mathcal{T}$, and OS state s, if $P_d(v, m, \mathcal{T})$, $\mathsf{inj}(m, \mathsf{flat}(s), \mathsf{ptbl}(s))$, and $O_f(v, s) = (s', v', t_{\mathrm{new}})$, then for all m' such that $\mathsf{inj}(m', \mathsf{flat}(s'), \mathsf{ptbl}(s'))$, there exists $\mathcal{T}'$ such that $\mathsf{consume}(\mathcal{T}, \mathcal{T}', t_{\mathrm{new}})$, and $Q_d(v, v', m', \mathcal{T}')$.*

That is, if f correctly implements a dry specification then for any state that satisfies the dry precondition P_d, we can inject the relevant piece of memory into an OS state s, apply the functional specification O_f, and then extract a resulting state that satisfies the dry postcondition Q_d. The inj relation may relate multiple CompCert memories to a given OS state (hence the universal quantification over the resulting memory m'), but all such memories must agree on the contents of all valid addresses, so the postcondition will usually hold for all m' if it holds for any m'.

Theorem 3. *Putchar and getchar in CertiKOS correctly implement their dry specifications.*

While this correspondence is specific to CertiKOS, we can adapt it to other verified operating systems by replacing the CertiKOS system call specification, user memory model, and external event representation with those of the other OS. For example, in the case of the seL4 microkernel [12], inj could be redefined to relate a CompCert memory to certain capability slots that represent the virtual memory, and the system call might send a message to a device driver running in another process. Despite these changes, most of the theorems in this paper aside from Theorem 3 would continue to hold with minor or no alterations.

6.3   Soundness of VST + CertiKOS

In Section 5, we described a correspondence between "juicy" separation logic specifications for external functions and "dry" CompCert-level specifications that is sufficient to guarantee that verified C programs behave correctly when run, as long as the external functions actually satisfy their dry specifications. Now we have seen how to prove that an external function satisfies its dry specification, by relating it to its CertiKOS specification. We combine these two proofs to get a stronger correctness property for programs that use CertiKOS system calls. This will also allow us to formalize the idea that at each point in a program's execution, it has performed some prefix of the communication operations specified in its precondition.

First, we define the semantics of programs with respect to the implementation of external functions:

Definition 9 (OS Safety). *Suppose that we have a set of external calls F such that each $f \in F$ has a functional specification O_f. Then a configuration $(c, m, t, \mathcal{T})$, where c is a C program state, m is a memory, t is a trace of events performed so far, and $\mathcal{T}$ is an interaction tree specifying the allowed future events, is safe for n steps with respect to a set of traces T if:*

- *n is 0 and T is $\{\epsilon\}$, or*
- *$(c, m) \to (c', m')$ and $(c', m', t, \mathcal{T})$ is safe for $n - 1$ steps with respect to T, or*
- *c is at a call to an external function f with arguments $\boldsymbol{v}$, and for all s consistent with t such that $\mathsf{inj}(m, \mathsf{flat}(s), \mathsf{ptbl}(s))$, if $O_f(\boldsymbol{v}, s) = (s', v', t_{\mathrm{new}})$, then there is some new interaction tree $\mathcal{T}'$ such that $(c', m', t ++ t_{\mathrm{new}}, \mathcal{T}')$ is safe for $n - 1$ steps with respect to T', where c' is the program state after the call (using the return value v'), $\mathsf{inj}(m', \mathsf{flat}(s'), \mathsf{ptbl}(s'))$, and $\mathsf{consume}(\mathcal{T}, \mathcal{T}', t_{\mathrm{new}})$, and T is the union of $\{t_{\mathrm{new}} ++ t' \mid t' \in T'\}$ for all such $\mathcal{T}'$.*

The C program has states (c, m), where c holds the values of local variables and the control stack, and m is the memory. Our small-step relation $(c, m) \rightarrow (c', m')$ characterizes *internal* C execution, and therefore if c is at a call to an external function then $(c, m) \not\rightarrow (c', m')$. The operating system has states s that contain the physical memory flat(s) and many other components used internally by the OS (and its proof of correctness), including a trace of past events; we say that s is consistent with t when the trace in s is exactly t.

Definition 9 has several important differences from our original definition of safety in Section 2. First, configurations include the trace t of events performed so far, as well as $\mathcal{T}$, the high-level specification of the allowed communication events (here it is taken to be an interaction tree, but it could easily be defined in another formalism just by changing the definition of consume). Second, our external functions are not simply axiomatized with pre- and postconditions, but implemented by the executable specifications O_f provided by the operating system. We use the ideas of the previous section to relate the execution of C programs to the behavior of system calls: we inject the user memory into the OS state, extract the resulting memory from the resulting state, and require that the new interaction tree $\mathcal{T}'$ reflect the communication events t_{new} performed by the call. Note the quantification over the current OS state s: the details of the OS state, such as the buffer of values received, are unknown to the C program (and may change arbitrarily between steps, for instance, if an interrupt occurs), and so it must be safe under all possible OS states consistent with the events t. The set T contains all possible communication traces from the program's execution, so by proving that every trace in T is allowed by the initial interaction tree $\mathcal{T}$, we show that the program's communication is always constrained by $\mathcal{T}$.

Lemma 2 (Trace Correctness). *If $(c, m, \mathcal{T})$ is safe for n steps with respect to T, then for all traces $t \in T$, there exists some interaction tree $\mathcal{T}'$ such that* consume$(\mathcal{T}, \mathcal{T}', t)$.

Proof. By induction on n. Since the consume relation holds for the trace segment produced by each external call, it suffices to show that it is transitive, i.e., that consume(a, b, t_1) and consume(b, c, t_2) imply consume$(a, c, t_1 ++ t_2)$.

Theorem 4 (Soundness of VST + CertiKOS). *Let P be a program with n functions, calling also upon m external functions. The internal functions have (juicy) specifications $\Gamma_1 \ldots \Gamma_n$ and the external functions have (juicy) specifications $\Gamma_{n+1} \ldots \Gamma_{n+m}$. Suppose P is proved correct in Verifiable C with initial interaction tree $\mathcal{T}$. Let $D_{n+1}, \ldots, D_{n+m}$ be dry specifications that safely evolve memory, and that correspond to $\Gamma_{n+1} \ldots \Gamma_{n+m}$. Further, let each D_i be correctly implemented by an OS function f_i with executable specification O_{f_i}. Then for all n, the* main *function of P is safe for n steps with respect to some set of traces T, and for every trace $t \in T$, there exists some interaction tree $\mathcal{T}'$ such that* consume$(\mathcal{T}, \mathcal{T}', t)$.

Proof. By the combination of the soundness of VST with external functions (Theorem 2), Lemma 2, and a proof relating our previous definition of safety to the new definition.

This is our main result: by combining the results of the previous sections, we obtain a soundness theorem down to the operating system's implementation of system calls, one that guarantees that the actual communication operations performed by the program are always a prefix of the initial specification of allowed operations. By instantiating the theorem with a set of verified system calls, we obtain a strong correctness result for our VST-verified programs, such as:

Theorem 5. *Let P be a program that uses the putchar and getchar system calls provided by CertiKOS, such as the one in Figure 4. Suppose P is proved correct with initial interaction tree $\mathcal{T}$. Then for all n, the main function of P is safe for n steps with respect to some set of traces T, and for every trace $t \in T$, there exists some interaction tree $\mathcal{T}'$ such that* consume($\mathcal{T}, \mathcal{T}', t$).

7   From syscall-level to hardware-level interactions

Thus far, we have assumed that the events in a program's trace are exactly the events described in the user-level interaction tree $\mathcal{T}$. In practice, however, the communication performed by the OS may differ from that observed by the user. For example, like all operating systems, CertiKOS uses a kernel buffer of finite size to store characters received from the serial device; if the buffer is full, incoming characters are discarded without being read. To represent this distinction, we distinguish between the user-visible events produced by system calls, and *external events*, which are generated by the environment oracle and recorded in the trace at the time that they occur. For the system call events to be meaningful, they must correspond in some way to the external events, but this correspondence may not be one-to-one. In the case of console I/O, each character received by the serial device should be returned by getchar at most once, and in the order they arrived, but characters may be dropped. This leads us to the condition that the user events should be a subsequence of the environment events, which is proved in CertiKOS.

Lemma 3. *The getchar system call maintains the invariant that there exists an injective map from a system call event with value v in the OS trace to an external event with value v earlier in the trace.*

Corollary 2. *Let P be a verified program as described in Theorem 4, in which getchar is the only system call performed. Then for all n, the main function of P is safe for n steps with respect to some set of traces T, and for every trace $t \in T$, there exists some interaction tree $\mathcal{T}'$ such that* consume($\mathcal{T}, \mathcal{T}', t$), *and the events in t correspond to external events performed as described in Lemma 3.*

Unlike Theorem 4, this corollary is specific to a particular system call, but it gives a stronger correctness property: the events in the user-level interaction tree are now interpreted in terms of actual bytes received by the OS, in the form of external events. Note that Lemma 3 does not require that every external event has a corresponding system call event; if the buffer fills up and characters are dropped before a getchar call, then there will be external events that do not correspond to anything in the interaction tree, and this is the intended semantics of buffered communication without flow control. A similar corollary can be proved for any set of system calls, but the precise correspondence between user events and external events will depend on the particular system calls involved.

There is one more soundness theorem we might want to prove, asserting that the combined system of program and operating system executes correctly according to the assembly-level semantics of the OS. We should be able to obtain this theorem by connecting Theorem 4 with the soundness theorem of CertiKOS, which guarantees that the behavior of the operating system running a program P refines the behavior of a system $K \bowtie P$ consisting of the program along with an abstract model of the operating system. However, this connection is far from trivial: it involves lowering our soundness result from C to assembly (using the correctness theorem of CompCert), modeling the switch from user to kernel mode (including the semantics of the trap instruction), and considering the effects of other OS features on program behavior (e.g., context switching). We estimate that we have covered more than half of the distance between VST and CertiKOS with our current result, but there is still work to be done to complete the connection. We can now remove the OS's implementation of each system call from the trusted computing base; it remains to remove the OS entirely.

8   Related Work

The most comprehensive prior work connecting verified programs to the implementation of I/O operations is that of Férée et al. [5] in CakeML, a functional language with I/O connected to a verified compiler and verified hardware. As in our approach, the language is parameterized by functional specifications for external functions, backed by proofs at a lower level. However, while CakeML does support a separation logic [9], it is not higher-order, so all of the components are specified in the same basic style. Our approach could enable higher-order separation logic reasoning about CakeML programs. Ironclad Apps [10] also includes verified communicating code, for user-level networking applications running on the Verve operating system [21]. However, their network stack is implemented outside of the operating system, so proofs about I/O operations are carried out within the same framework as the programs that use the operations.

One major category of system calls is file I/O operations. The FSCQ file system [2] is verified using Crash Hoare Logic, a separation logic which accounts for possible crashes at any point in a program. File system assertions are similar to the ordinary points-to assertions of separation logic, but may persist through crashes while memory is reset. In Crash Hoare Logic, the implementation-level model of the file state is the same as the user's model, and the approach does not obviously generalize to other forms of external communication.

Another related area is the extension of separation logic to distributed systems, which necessarily involves reasoning about communication with external entities. The most closely related such logic is Aneris [14], which is built on

Iris, the inspiration for VST's approach to ghost state. The adequacy theorem of Aneris proves the connection between higher-order separation logic specifications of socket operations and a language that includes first-order operational semantics for those functions. In our approach, this would correspond to directly adding the "dry" specifications for each operation to the language semantics, and building the correspondence proof for those particular operations into the soundness theorem of the logic; our more generic style of soundness theorem would make it easier to plug in new external calls. The bottom half of our approach—showing that the language-level semantics of the operations are implemented by an OS such as CertiKOS—could be applied to Aneris more or less as is. Another interesting feature of Aneris is that the communication allowed on each socket is specified by a user-provided protocol, an arbitrary separation logic predicate on messages and resources. In our examples thus far, we have assumed that the external world does not share any notion of resource with the program, and so our external state only mentions the messages to be sent and received; however, the construction of Section 3 does allow the external state to have arbitrary ghost-state structure, which we could use to define similarly expressive protocols.

9   Conclusion and Future Work

We have now seen how to connect programs verified using higher-order separation logic to external functions provided by a first-order verified system, effectively importing the results of outside verification (e.g. OS verification) into our separation logic. The approach consists of two halves: we first relate separation logic specifications for the external functions to "dry" first-order specifications on CompCert memories [15] and interaction trees [13], and then relate these dry specifications to the system that implements the functions (CertiKOS in our example). In the process, we interpret the C-level communication constraints in terms of OS-level events that more accurately represent the communication that occurs in the real world. Our approach works for any type of external communication, and allows users to extend the system with new external functions as needed. Each new correspondence proof for an external function modularly extends the soundness theorem of VST, removing the separation-logic specification of the function from the trusted computing base.

The combination of CompCert memories with interaction trees has served as a robust specification interface between two quite different approaches to verification: VST's higher-order impredicative concurrent separation logic, and CertiKOS's certified concurrent abstraction layers. This strongly suggests that the combination of CompCert memories and interaction trees can serve as a *lingua franca* to interface with other verification systems for client programs and for operating systems.

References

1. Appel, A.W., Dockins, R., Hobor, A., Beringer, L., Dodds, J., Stewart, G., Blazy, S., Leroy, X.: Program Logics for Certified Compilers. Cambridge University Press

(2014), http://www.cambridge.org/de/academic/subjects/computer-science/programming-languages-and-applied-logic/program-logics-certified-compilers?format=HB

2. Chen, H., Ziegler, D., Chajed, T., Chlipala, A., Kaashoek, M.F., Zeldovich, N.: Using Crash Hoare Logic for certifying the FSCQ file system. In: Proceedings of the 25th Symposium on Operating Systems Principles. pp. 18–37. SOSP '15, ACM, New York, NY, USA (2015). https://doi.org/10.1145/2815400.2815402

3. Dinsdale-Young, T., Birkedal, L., Gardner, P., Parkinson, M.J., Yang, H.: Views: compositional reasoning for concurrent programs. In: Giacobazzi, R., Cousot, R. (eds.) The 40th Annual ACM SIGPLAN-SIGACT Symposium on Principles of Programming Languages, POPL '13, Rome, Italy - January 23 - 25, 2013. pp. 287–300. ACM (2013). https://doi.org/10.1145/2429069.2429104

4. Dinsdale-Young, T., Dodds, M., Gardner, P., Parkinson, M.J., Vafeiadis, V.: Concurrent abstract predicates. In: D'Hondt, T. (ed.) ECOOP 2010 - Object-Oriented Programming, 24th European Conference, Maribor, Slovenia, June 21-25, 2010. Proceedings. Lecture Notes in Computer Science, vol. 6183, pp. 504–528. Springer (2010). https://doi.org/10.1007/978-3-642-14107-2_24

5. Férée, H., Pohjola, J.Å., Kumar, R., Owens, S., Myreen, M.O., Ho, S.: Program verification in the presence of I/O - semantics, verified library routines, and verified applications. In: Piskac, R., Rümmer, P. (eds.) Verified Software. Theories, Tools, and Experiments - 10th International Conference, VSTTE 2018, Oxford, UK, July 18-19, 2018, Revised Selected Papers. Lecture Notes in Computer Science, vol. 11294, pp. 88–111. Springer (2018). https://doi.org/10.1007/978-3-030-03592-1_6

6. Gu, R., Koenig, J., Ramananandro, T., Shao, Z., Wu, X.N., Weng, S.C., Zhang, H., Guo, Y.: Deep specifications and certified abstraction layers. In: Proceedings of the 42nd Annual ACM SIGPLAN-SIGACT Symposium on Principles of Programming Languages. pp. 595–608. POPL '15, ACM, New York, NY, USA (2015). https://doi.org/10.1145/2676726.2676975

7. Gu, R., Shao, Z., Chen, H., Wu, X.N., Kim, J., Sjöberg, V., Costanzo, D.: Certikos: An extensible architecture for building certified concurrent OS kernels. In: 12th USENIX Symposium on Operating Systems Design and Implementation, OSDI 2016, Savannah, GA, USA, November 2-4, 2016. pp. 653–669 (2016), https://www.usenix.org/conference/osdi16/technical-sessions/presentation/gu

8. Gu, R., Shao, Z., Kim, J., Wu, X.N., Koenig, J., Sjöberg, V., Chen, H., Costanzo, D., Ramananandro, T.: Certified concurrent abstraction layers. In: Proceedings of the 39th ACM SIGPLAN Conference on Programming Language Design and Implementation, PLDI 2018, Philadelphia, PA, USA, June 18-22, 2018. pp. 646–661 (2018). https://doi.org/10.1145/3192366.3192381

9. Guéneau, A., Myreen, M.O., Kumar, R., Norrish, M.: Verified characteristic formulae for CakeML. In: Yang, H. (ed.) Programming Languages and Systems. pp. 584–610. Springer Berlin Heidelberg, Berlin, Heidelberg (2017)

10. Hawblitzel, C., Howell, J., Lorch, J.R., Narayan, A., Parno, B., Zhang, D., Zill, B.: Ironclad apps: End-to-end security via automated full-system verification. In: 11th USENIX Symposium on Operating Systems Design and Implementation, OSDI '14, Broomfield, CO, USA, October 6-8, 2014. pp. 165–181 (2014), https://www.usenix.org/conference/osdi14/technical-sessions/presentation/hawblitzel

11. Jung, R., Krebbers, R., Birkedal, L., Dreyer, D.: Higher-order ghost state. In: Proceedings of the 21st ACM SIGPLAN International Conference on Functional Programming. pp. 256–269. ICFP 2016, ACM, New York, NY, USA (2016). https://doi.org/10.1145/2951913.2951943

12. Klein, G., Elphinstone, K., Heiser, G., Andronick, J., Cock, D., Derrin, P., Elka-duwe, D., Engelhardt, K., Kolanski, R., Norrish, M., Sewell, T., Tuch, H., Win-wood, S.: seL4: Formal verification of an OS kernel. In: Proceedings of the ACM SIGOPS 22nd Symposium on Operating Systems Principles. pp. 207–220. SOSP '09, ACM, New York, NY, USA (2009). https://doi.org/10.1145/1629575.1629596
13. Koh, N., Li, Y., Li, Y., Xia, L.y., Beringer, L., Honoré, W., Mansky, W., Pierce, B.C., Zdancewic, S.: From C to interaction trees: Specifying, verifying, and test-ing a networked server. In: Proceedings of the 8th ACM SIGPLAN International Conference on Certified Programs and Proofs. pp. 234–248. CPP 2019, ACM, New York, NY, USA (2019). https://doi.org/10.1145/3293880.3294106
14. Krogh-Jespersen, M., Timany, A., Ohlenbusch, M.E., Birkedal, L.: Aneris: A logic for node-local, modular reasoning of distributed systems (2019), https://iris-project.org/pdfs/2019-aneris-submission.pdf, unpublished draft
15. Leroy, X., Appel, A.W., Blazy, S., Stewart, G.: The CompCert memory model. In: Appel, A.W. (ed.) Program Logics for Certified Compilers, chap. 32. Cambridge University Press (2014)
16. Ley-Wild, R., Nanevski, A.: Subjective auxiliary state for coarse-grained concur-rency. In: Proceedings of the 40th Annual ACM SIGPLAN-SIGACT Symposium on Principles of Programming Languages. pp. 561–574. POPL '13, ACM, New York, NY, USA (2013). https://doi.org/10.1145/2429069.2429134
17. O'Hearn, P.W.: Resources, concurrency, and local reasoning. Theor. Comput. Sci. 375(1-3), 271–307 (Apr 2007). https://doi.org/10.1016/j.tcs.2006.12.035
18. Penninckx, W., Jacobs, B., Piessens, F.: Sound, modular and compositional ver-ification of the input/output behavior of programs. In: Programming Languages and Systems - 24th European Symposium on Programming, ESOP 2015, Held as Part of the European Joint Conferences on Theory and Practice of Software, ETAPS 2015, London, UK, April 11-18, 2015. Proceedings. pp. 158–182 (2015). https://doi.org/10.1007/978-3-662-46669-8_7
19. Sergey, I., Nanevski, A., Banerjee, A.: Specifying and verifying concurrent algo-rithms with histories and subjectivity. In: Vitek, J. (ed.) Proceedings of the 24th European Symposium on Programming (ESOP 2015). Lecture Notes in Computer Science, vol. 9032, pp. 333–358. Springer (2015). https://doi.org/10.1007/978-3-662-46669-8_14
20. Wang, Y., Wilke, P., Shao, Z.: An abstract stack based approach to verified com-positional compilation to machine code. Proceedings of the ACM on Programming Languages 3(POPL), 62 (2019)
21. Yang, J., Hawblitzel, C.: Safe to the last instruction: automated verifica-tion of a type-safe operating system. In: Proceedings of the 2010 ACM SIG-PLAN Conference on Programming Language Design and Implementation, PLDI 2010, Toronto, Ontario, Canada, June 5-10, 2010. pp. 99–110 (2010). https://doi.org/10.1145/1806596.1806610

Modular Inference of Linear Types for Multiplicity-Annotated Arrows

Kazutaka Matsuda[1]

Graduate School of Information Sciences, Tohoku University, Sendai 980-8579, Japan
kztk@ecei.tohoku.ac.jp

Abstract. Bernardy et al. [2018] proposed a linear type system $\lambda^q_\to$ as a core type system of Linear Haskell. In the system, linearity is represented by annotated arrow types $A \to_m B$, where m denotes the multiplicity of the argument. Thanks to this representation, existing non-linear code typechecks as it is, and newly written linear code can be used with existing non-linear code in many cases. However, little is known about the type inference of $\lambda^q_\to$. Although the Linear Haskell implementation is equipped with type inference, its algorithm has not been formalized, and the implementation often fails to infer principal types, especially for higher-order functions. In this paper, based on OUTSIDEIN(X) [Vytiniotis et al., 2011], we propose an inference system for a rank 1 qualified-typed variant of $\lambda^q_\to$, which infers principal types. A technical challenge in this new setting is to deal with ambiguous types inferred by naive qualified typing. We address this ambiguity issue through quantifier elimination and demonstrate the effectiveness of the approach with examples.

Keywords: Linear Types · Type Inference · Qualified Typing.

1 Introduction

Linearity is a fundamental concept in computation and has many applications. For example, if a variable is known to be used only once, it can be freely inlined without any performance regression [29]. In a similar manner, destructive updates are safe for such values without the risk of breaking referential transparency [32]. Moreover, linearity is useful for writing transformation on data that cannot be copied or discarded for various reasons, including reversible computation [19, 35] and quantum computation [2, 25]. Another interesting application of linearity is that it helps to bound the complexity of programs [1, 5, 13]

Linear type systems use types to enforce linearity. One way to design a linear type system is based on Curry-Howard isomorphism to linear logic. For example, in Wadler [33]'s type system, functions are linear in the sense that their arguments are used exactly once, and any exception to this must be marked by the type operator (!). Such an approach is theoretically elegant but cumbersome in programming; a program usually contains both linear and unrestricted code, and many manipulations concerning (!) are required in the latter and around the

© The Author(s) 2020
P. Müller (Ed.): ESOP 2020, LNCS 12075, pp. 456–483, 2020.
https://doi.org/10.1007/978-3-030-44914-8_17

interface between the two. Thus, there have been several proposed approaches for more practical linear type systems [7, 21, 24, 28].

Among these approaches, a system called $\lambda_{\rightarrow}^q$, the core type system of Linear Haskell, stands out for its ability to have linear code in large unrestricted code bases [7]. With it, existing unrestricted code in Haskell typechecks in Linear Haskell without modification, and if one desires, some of the unrestricted code can be replaced with linear code, again without any special programming effort. For example, one can use the function *append* in an unrestricted context as $\lambda x.tail$ (*append* x x), regardless of whether *append* is a linear or unrestricted function. This is made possible by their representation of linearity. Specifically, they annotate function type with its argument's multiplicity ("linearity via arrows" [7]) as $A \rightarrow_m B$, where $m = 1$ means that the function of the type uses its argument linearly, and $m = \omega$ means that there is no restriction in the use of the argument, which includes all non-linear standard Haskell code. In this system, linear functions can be used in an unrestricted context if their arguments are unrestricted. Thus, there is no problem in using *append* : List $A \rightarrow_1$ List $A \rightarrow_1$ List A as above, provided that x is unrestricted. This promotion of linear expressions to unrestricted ones is difficult in other approaches [21, 24, 28] (at least in the absence of bounded kind-polymorphism), where linearity is a property of a type (called "linearity via kinds" in [7]).

However, as far as we are aware, little is known about *type inference* for $\lambda_{\rightarrow}^q$. It is true that Linear Haskell is implemented as a fork[1] of the Glasgow Haskell Compiler (GHC), which of course comes with type inference. However, the algorithm has not been formalized and has limitations due to a lack of proper handling of multiplicity constraints. Indeed, Linear Haskell gives up handling complex constraints on multiplicities such as those with multiplications $p \cdot q$; as a result, Linear Haskell sometimes fails to infer principal types, especially for higher-order functions.[2] This limits the reusability of code. For example, Linear Haskell cannot infer an appropriate type for function composition to allow it to compose both linear and unrestricted functions.

A classical approach to have both separated constraint solving that works well with the usual unification-based typing and principal typing (for a rank 1 fragment) is qualified typing [15]. In qualified typing, constraints on multiplicities are collected, and then a type is qualified with it to obtain a principal type. Complex multiplicities are not a problem in unification as they are handled by a constraint solver. For example, consider $app = \lambda f.\lambda x.f\ x$. Suppose that f has type $a \rightarrow_p b$, and x has type a (here we focus only on multiplicities). Let us write the multiplicities of f and x as p_f and p_x, respectively. Since x is passed to f, there is a constraint that the multiplicity p_x of x must be ω if the multiplicity p of the f's argument also is. In other words, p_x must be no less than p, which is represented by inequality $p \leq p_x$ under the ordering $1 \leq \omega$. (We could represent the constraint as an equality $p_x = p \cdot p_x$, but using inequality is simpler here.)

---

[1] https://github.com/tweag/ghc/tree/linear-types
[2] Confirmed for commit `1c80dcb424e1401f32bf7436290dd698c739d906` at May 14, 2019.

For the multiplicity p_f of f, there is no restriction because f is used exactly once; linear use is always legitimate even when $p_f = \omega$. As a result, we obtain the inferred type $\forall p\, p_f\, p_x\, a\, b.\, p \leq p_x \Rightarrow (a \rightarrow_p b) \rightarrow_{p_f} a \rightarrow_{p_x} b$ for app. This type is a principal one; it is intuitively because only the constraints that are needed for typing $\lambda f.\lambda x.f\ x$ are gathered. Having separate constraint solving phases itself is rather common in the context of linear typing [3, 4, 11, 12, 14, 23, 24, 29, 34]. Qualified typing makes the constraint solving phase local and gives the principal typing property that makes typing modular. In particular, in the context of linearity via kinds, qualified typing is proven to be effective [11, 24].

As qualified typing is useful in the context of linearity via kinds, one may expect that it also works well for linearity via arrows such as $\lambda^q_\rightarrow$. However, naive qualified typing turns out to be impractical for $\lambda^q_\rightarrow$ because it tends to infer ambiguous types [15, 27]. As a demonstration, consider a slightly different version of app defined as $app' = \lambda f.\lambda x.app\ f\ x$. Standard qualified typing [15, 31] infers the type

$$\forall q\, q_f\, q_x\, p_f\, p_x\, a\, b.\, (q \leq q_x \wedge q_f \leq p_f \wedge q_x \leq p_x) \Rightarrow (a \rightarrow_q b) \rightarrow_{p_f} a \rightarrow_{p_x} b$$

by the following steps:

- The polymorphic type of app is instantiated to $(a \rightarrow_q b) \rightarrow_{q_f} a \rightarrow_{q_x} b$ and yields a constraint $q \leq q_x$ (again we focus only on multiplicity constraints).
- Since f is used as the first argument of app, f must have type $a \rightarrow_q b$. Also, since the multiplicity of app's first argument is q_f, there is a restriction on the multiplicity of f, say p_f, that $q_f \leq p_f$.
- Similarly, since x is used as the second argument of app, x must have type a, and there is a constraint on the multiplicity of x, say p_x, that $q_x \leq p_x$.

This inference is unsatisfactory, as the inferred type leaks internal details and is ambiguous [15, 27] in the sense that one cannot determine q_f and q_x from an instantiation of $(a \rightarrow_q b) \rightarrow_{p_f} a \rightarrow_{p_x} b$. Due to this ambiguity, the types of app and app' are not judged as equivalent; in fact, the standard qualified typing algorithms [15, 31] reject $app' : \forall p\, p_f\, p_x\, a\, b.\, p \leq p_x \Rightarrow (a \rightarrow_p b) \rightarrow_{p_f} a \rightarrow_{p_x} b$. We conjecture that the issue of inferring ambiguous types is intrinsic to linearity via arrows because of the separation of multiplicities and types, unlike the case of linearity via kinds, where multiplicities are always associated with types. Simple solutions such as rejecting ambiguous types are not desirable as this case appears very often. Defaulting ambiguous variables (such as q_f and q_x) to 1 or ω is not a solution either because it loses principality in general.

In this paper, we propose a type inference method for a rank 1 qualified-typed variant of $\lambda^q_\rightarrow$, in which the ambiguity issue is addressed without compromising principality. Our type inference system is built on top of OUTSIDEIN(X) [31], an inference system for qualified types used in GHC, which can handle local assumptions to support **let**, existential types, and GADTs. An advantage of using OUTSIDEIN(X) is that it is parameterized over theory X of constraints. Thus, applying it to linear typing boils down to choosing an appropriate X. We choose X carefully so that the representation of constraints is closed under quantifier elimination, which is the key to addressing the ambiguity issue. Specifically, in this paper:

- We present a qualified typing variant of a rank-1 fragment of $\lambda^q_\to$ without local definitions, in which manipulation of multiplicities is separated from the standard unification-based typing (Sect. 2).
- We give an inference method for the system based on gathering constraints and solving them afterward (Sect. 3). This step is mostly standard, except that we solve multiplicity constraints in time polynomial in their sizes.
- We address the ambiguity issue by quantifier elimination under the assumption that multiplicities do not affect runtime behavior (Sect. 4).
- We extend our technique to local assumptions (Sect. 5), which enables **let** and GADTs, by showing that the disambiguation in Sect. 4 is compatible with OUTSIDEIN(X).
- We report experimental results using our proof-of-concept implementation (Sect. 6). The experiments show that the system can infer unambiguous principal types for selected functions from Haskell's `Prelude`, and performs well with acceptable overhead.

Finally, we discuss related work (Sect. 7) and then conclude the paper (Sect. 8). The prototype implementation is available as a part of a reversible programming system SPARCL, available from https://bitbucket.org/kztk/partially-reversible-lang-impl/. Due to space limitation, we omit some proofs from this paper, which can be found in the full version [20].

2   Qualified-Typed Variant of $\lambda^q_\to$

In this section, we introduce a qualified-typed [15] variant of $\lambda^q_\to$ [7] for its rank 1 fragment, on which we base our type inference. Notable differences to the original $\lambda^q_\to$ include: (1) multiplicity abstractions and multiplicity applications are implicit (as type abstractions and type applications), (2) this variant uses qualified typing [15], (3) conditions on multiplicities are inequality based [6], which gives better handling of multiplicity variables, and (4) local definitions are excluded as we postpone the discussions to Sect. 5 due to their issues in the handling of local assumptions in qualified typing [31].

2.1   Syntax of Programs

Programs and expressions, which will be typechecked, are given below.

$$
\begin{aligned}
prog &::= bind_1; \ldots; bind_n \\
bind &::= f = e \mid f : A = e \\
e\ \ \ &::= x \mid \lambda x.e \mid e_1\ e_2 \mid \mathsf{C}\ \bar{e} \mid \textbf{case}\ e_0\ \textbf{of}\ \{\mathsf{C}_i\ \bar{x_i} \to e_i\}_i
\end{aligned}
$$

A program is a sequence of bindings with or without type annotations, where bound variables can appear in following bindings. As mentioned at the beginning

$$
\begin{array}{llll}
A, B & ::= \forall \overline{pa}.Q \Rightarrow \tau & \text{(polytypes)} & Q & ::= \bigwedge_i \phi_i & \text{(constraints)} \\
\sigma, \tau & ::= a \mid \mathsf{D}\,\overline{\mu}\,\overline{\tau} \mid \sigma \to_\mu \tau & \text{(monotypes)} & \phi & ::= M \le M' & \text{(predicates)} \\
\mu & ::= p \mid 1 \mid \omega & \text{(multiplicities)} & M, N & ::= \prod_i \mu_i & \text{(multiplications)}
\end{array}
$$

Fig. 1. Types and related notions: a and p are type and multiplicity variables, respectively, and D represents a type constructor.

of this section, we shall postpone the discussions of local bindings (i.e., **let**) to Sect. 5. Expressions consist of variables x, applications $e_1\,e_2$, λ-abstractions $\lambda x.e$, constructor applications $\mathsf{C}\,\overline{e}$, and (shallow) pattern matching **case** e_0 **of** $\{\mathsf{C}_i\,\overline{x_i} \to e_i\}_i$. For simplicity, we assume that constructors are fully-applied and patterns are shallow. As usual, patterns $\mathsf{C}_i\,\overline{x_i}$ must be linear in the sense that each variable in $\overline{x_i}$ is different. Programs are assumed to be appropriately α-renamed so that newly introduced variables by λ and patterns are always fresh. We do not require the patterns of a **case** expression to be exhaustive or no overlapping, following the original $\lambda^q_\to$ [7]; the linearity in $\lambda^q_\to$ cares only for successful computations. Unlike the original $\lambda^q_\to$, we do not annotate λ and **case** with the multiplicity of the argument and the scrutinee, respectively.

Constructors play an important role in $\lambda^q_\to$. As we will see later, they can be used to witness unrestrictedness, similarly to ! of !e in a linear type system [33].

2.2 Types

Types and related notations are defined in Fig. 1. Types are separated into monotypes and polytypes (or, type schemes). Monotypes consist of (rigid) type variables a, datatypes $\mathsf{D}\,\overline{\mu}\,\overline{\tau}$, and multiplicity-annotated function types $\tau_1 \to_\mu \tau_2$. Here, a multiplicity μ is either 1 (linear), ω (unrestricted), or a (rigid) multiplicity variable p. Polytypes have the form $\forall \overline{pa}.Q \Rightarrow \tau$, where Q is a constraint that is a conjunction of predicates. A predicate ϕ has the form of $M \le M'$, where M' and M are multiplications of multiplicities. We shall sometimes treat Q as a set of predicates, which means that we shall rewrite Q according to contexts by the idempotent commutative monoid laws of $\wedge$. We call both multiplicity (p) and type (a) variables *type-level variables*, and write $\mathsf{ftv}(\overline{t})$ for the set of free type-level variables in syntactic objects (such as types and constraints) $\overline{t}$.

The relation ($\le$) and operator ($\cdot$) in predicates denote the corresponding relation and operator on $\{1, \omega\}$, respectively. On $\{1, \omega\}$, ($\le$) is defined as the reflexive closure of $1 \le \omega$; note that $(\{1, \omega\}, \le)$ forms a total order. Multiplication ($\cdot$) on $\{1, \omega\}$ is defined by

$$
1 \cdot m = m \cdot 1 = m \qquad \omega \cdot m = m \cdot \omega = \omega.
$$

For simplicity, we shall sometimes omit ($\cdot$) and write $m_1 m_2$ for $m_1 \cdot m_2$. Note that, for $m_1, m_2 \in \{1, \omega\}$, $m_1 \cdot m_2$ is the least upper bound of m_1 and m_2 with respect to $\le$. As a result, $m_1 \cdot m_2 \le m$ holds if and only if $(m_1 \le m) \wedge (m_2 \le m)$ holds; we will use this property for efficient handling of constraints (Sect. 3.2).

We assume a fixed set of constructors given beforehand. Each constructor is assigned a type of the form $\forall \overline{pa}.\ \tau_1 \to_{\mu_1} \cdots \to_{\mu_{n_1}} \tau_n \to_{\mu_n} D\ \overline{p}\ \overline{a}$ where each τ_i and μ_i do not contain free type-level variables other than $\{\overline{pa}\}$, i.e., $\bigcup_i \mathsf{ftv}(\tau_i, \mu_i) \subseteq \{\overline{pa}\}$. For simplicity, we write the above type as $\forall \overline{pa}.\ \overline{\tau} \to_{\overline{\mu}} D\ \overline{p}\ \overline{a}$. We assume that types are well-kinded, which effectively means that D is applied to the same numbers of multiplicity arguments and type arguments among the constructor types. Usually, it suffices to use constructors of linear function types as below because they can be used in both linear and unrestricted code.

$$(-,-) : \forall a\,b.\ a \to_1 b \to_1 a \otimes b$$
$$\mathsf{Nil} : \forall a.\ \mathsf{List}\ a \qquad \mathsf{Cons} : \forall a.\ a \to_1 \mathsf{List}\ a \to_1 \mathsf{List}\ a$$

In general, constructors can encapsulate arguments' multiplicities as below, which is useful when a function returns both linear and unrestricted results.

$$\mathsf{MkUn} : \forall a.\ a \to_\omega \mathsf{Un}\ a \qquad \mathsf{MkMany} : \forall p\,a.\ a \to_p \mathsf{Many}\ p\ a$$

For example, a function that reads a value from a mutable array at a given index can be given as a primitive of type $readMArray : \forall a.\ \mathsf{MArray}\ a \to_1 \mathsf{Int} \to_\omega$ ($\mathsf{MArray}\ a \otimes \mathsf{Un}\ a$) [7]. Multiplicity-parameterized constructors become useful when the multiplicity of contents can vary. For example, the type $\mathsf{IO}_\mathsf{L}\ p\ a$ with the constructor $\mathsf{MkIO}_\mathsf{L} : (\mathsf{World} \to_1 (\mathsf{World} \otimes \mathsf{Many}\ p\ a)) \to_1 \mathsf{IO}_\mathsf{L}\ p\ a$ can represent the IO monad [7] with methods $return : \forall p\,a.\ a \to_p \mathsf{IO}_\mathsf{L}\ p\ a$ and ($\succ\!\!=$) : $\forall p\,q\,a\,b.\ \mathsf{IO}_\mathsf{L}\ p\ a \to_1 (a \to_p \mathsf{IO}_\mathsf{L}\ q\ b) \to_1 \mathsf{IO}_\mathsf{L}\ q\ b$.

2.3 Typing Rules

Our type system uses two sorts of environments A *typing environment* maps variables into polytypes (as usual in non-linear calculi), and a *multiplicity environment* maps variables into multiplications of multiplicities. This separation of the two will be convenient when we discuss type inference. As usual, we write $x_1 : A_1, \ldots, x_n : A_n$ instead of $\{x_1 \mapsto A_1, \ldots, x_n \mapsto A_n\}$ for typing environments. For multiplicity environments, we use multiset-like notation as $x_1{}^{M_1}, \ldots, x_n{}^{M_n}$.

We use the following operations on multiplicity environments:[3]

$$(\Delta_1 + \Delta_2)(x) = \begin{cases} \omega & \text{if } x \in \mathsf{dom}(\Delta_1) \cap \mathsf{dom}(\Delta_2) \\ \Delta_i(x) & \text{if } x \in \mathsf{dom}(\Delta_i) \setminus \mathsf{dom}(\Delta_j)\ (i \neq j \in \{1,2\}) \end{cases}$$

$$(\mu\Delta)(x) = \mu \cdot \Delta(x)$$

$$(\Delta_1 \sqcup \Delta_2)(x) = \begin{cases} \Delta_1(x) \cdot \Delta_2(x) & \text{if } x \in \mathsf{dom}(\Delta_1) \cap \mathsf{dom}(\Delta_2) \\ \omega & \text{if } x \in \mathsf{dom}(\Delta_i) \setminus \mathsf{dom}(\Delta_j)\ (i \neq j \in \{1,2\}) \end{cases}$$

---

[3] In these definitions, we implicitly consider multiplicity 0 and regard $\Delta(x) = 0$ if $x \notin \mathsf{dom}(\Delta)$. It is natural that $0 + m = m + 0$. With 0, multiplication $\cdot$, which is extended as $0 \cdot m = m \cdot 0 = 0$, no longer computes the least upper bound. Therefore, we use $\sqcup$ for the last definition; in fact, the definition corresponds to the pointwise computation of $\Delta_1(x) \sqcup \Delta_2(x)$, where $\leq$ is extended as $0 \leq \omega$ but not $0 \leq 1$. This treatment of 0 coincides with that in the Linear Haskell proposal [26].

$$\frac{Q;\Gamma;\Delta' \vdash e : \tau'}{Q;\Gamma;\Delta \vdash e : \tau} \quad Q \models \Delta = \Delta' \quad Q \models \tau \sim \tau'}{Q;\Gamma;\Delta \vdash e : \tau} \text{ EQ} \qquad \frac{\Gamma(x) = \forall \overline{pa}.Q' \Rightarrow \tau}{Q \models Q'[\overline{p \mapsto \mu}] \quad Q \models x^1 \leq \Delta}{Q;\Gamma;\Delta \vdash x : \tau[\overline{p \mapsto \mu}, \overline{a \mapsto \tau}]} \text{ VAR}$$

$$\frac{Q;\Gamma,x : \sigma; \Delta, x^\mu \vdash e : \tau}{Q;\Gamma;\Delta \vdash \lambda x.e : \sigma \rightarrow_\mu \tau} \text{ ABS} \qquad \frac{Q;\Gamma;\Delta_1 \vdash e_1 : \sigma \rightarrow_\mu \tau \quad Q;\Gamma;\Delta_2 \vdash e_2 : \sigma}{Q;\Gamma;\Delta_1 + \mu\Delta_2 \vdash e_1\, e_2 : \tau} \text{ APP}$$

$$\frac{\mathsf{C} : \forall \overline{pa}.\ \overline{\tau} \rightarrow_{\overline{v}} \mathsf{D}\ \overline{p}\ \overline{a} \quad \{Q;\Gamma;\Delta_i \vdash e_i : \tau_i[\overline{p \mapsto \mu}, \overline{a \mapsto \sigma}]\}_i}{Q;\Gamma;\omega\Delta_0 + \sum_i \nu_i[\overline{p \mapsto \mu}]\Delta_i \vdash \mathsf{C}\ \overline{e} : \mathsf{D}\ \overline{\mu}\ \overline{\sigma}} \text{ CON}$$

$$\frac{Q;\Gamma;\Delta_0 \vdash e_0 : \mathsf{D}\ \overline{\mu}\ \overline{\sigma} \quad \left\{ \begin{matrix} \mathsf{C}_i : \forall \overline{pa}.\ \overline{\tau_i} \rightarrow_{\overline{v_i}} \mathsf{D}\ \overline{p}\ \overline{a} \\ Q;\Gamma, \overline{x_i : \tau_i[\overline{p \mapsto \mu}, \overline{a \mapsto \sigma}]}; \Delta_i, \overline{x_i}^{\mu_0 \nu_i[\overline{p \mapsto \mu}]} \vdash e_i : \tau' \end{matrix} \right\}_i}{Q;\Gamma;\mu_0\Delta_0 + \bigsqcup_i \Delta_i \vdash \mathbf{case}\ e_0\ \mathbf{of}\ \{\mathsf{C}_i\ \overline{x_i} \rightarrow e_i\}_i : \tau'} \text{ CASE}$$

Fig. 2. Typing relation for expressions

Intuitively, $\Delta(x)$ represents the number of uses of x. So, in the definition of $\Delta_1 + \Delta_2$, we have $(\Delta_1 + \Delta_2)(x) = \omega$ if $x \in \mathsf{dom}(\Delta_1) \cap \mathsf{dom}(\Delta_2)$ because this condition means that x is used in two places. Operation $\Delta_1 \sqcup \Delta_2$ is used for **case** branches. Suppose that a branch e_1 uses variables as Δ_1 and another branch e_2 uses variables as Δ_2. Then, putting the branches together, variables are used as $\Delta_1 \sqcup \Delta_2$. The definition says that x is considered to be used linearly in the two branches put together if and only if both branches use x linearly, where non-linear use includes unrestricted use ($\Delta_i(x) = \omega$) and non-use ($x \notin \mathsf{dom}(\Delta)$).

We write $Q \models Q'$ if Q logically entails Q'. That is, for any valuation of multiplicity variables $\theta(p) \in \{1, \omega\}$, $Q'\theta$ holds if $Q\theta$ does. For example, we have $p \leq r \wedge r \leq q \models p \leq q$. We extend the notation to multiplicity environments and write $Q \models \Delta_1 \leq \Delta_2$ if $\mathsf{dom}(\Delta_1) \subseteq \mathsf{dom}(\Delta_2)$ and $Q \models \bigwedge_{x \in \mathsf{dom}(\Delta)} \Delta_1(x) \leq \Delta_2(x) \wedge \bigwedge_{x \in \mathsf{dom}(\Delta_2) \setminus \mathsf{dom}(\Delta_1)} \omega \leq \Delta_2(x)$ hold. We also write $Q \models \Delta_1 = \Delta_2$ if both $Q \models \Delta_1 \leq \Delta_2$ and $Q \models \Delta_2 \leq \Delta_1$ hold. We then have the following properties.

Lemma 1. Suppose $Q \models \Delta \leq \Delta'$ and $Q \models \Delta = \Delta_1 + \Delta_2$. Then, there are some Δ_1' and Δ_2' such that $Q \models \Delta' = \Delta_1' + \Delta_2'$, $Q \models \Delta_1 \leq \Delta_1'$ and $Q \models \Delta_2 \leq \Delta_2'$. $\square$

Lemma 2. $Q \models \mu\Delta \leq \Delta'$ implies $Q \models \Delta \leq \Delta'$. $\square$

Lemma 3. $Q \models \Delta_1 \sqcup \Delta_2 \leq \Delta'$ implies $Q \models \Delta_1 \leq \Delta'$ and $Q \models \Delta_2 \leq \Delta'$. $\square$

Constraints Q affect type equality; for example, under $Q = p \leq q \wedge q \leq p$, $\sigma \rightarrow_p \tau$ and $\sigma \rightarrow_q \tau$ become equivalent. Formally, we write $Q \models \tau \sim \tau'$ if $\tau\theta = \tau'\theta$ for any valuation θ of multiplicity variables that makes $Q\theta$ true.

Now, we are ready to define the *typing judgment for expressions*, $Q;\Gamma;\Delta \vdash e : \tau$, which reads that under assumption Q, typing environment Γ, and multiplicity environment Δ, expression e has monotype τ, by the typing rules in Fig. 2. Here, we assume $\mathsf{dom}(\Delta) \subseteq \mathsf{dom}(\Gamma)$. Having $x \in \mathsf{dom}(\Gamma) \setminus \mathsf{dom}(\Delta)$ means that the multiplicity of x is essentially 0 in e.

Rule EQ says that we can replace τ and Δ with equivalent ones in typing.

$$\frac{}{\Gamma \vdash \varepsilon} \text{ Empty} \qquad \frac{Q; \Gamma; \Delta \vdash e : \tau \quad \overline{pa} = \mathsf{ftv}(Q, \tau) \quad \Gamma, f : \forall \overline{pa}.Q \Rightarrow \tau \vdash prog}{\Gamma \vdash f = e; prog} \text{ Bind}$$

$$\frac{Q; \Gamma; \Delta \vdash e : \tau \quad \overline{pa} = \mathsf{ftv}(Q, \tau) \quad \Gamma, f : \forall \overline{pa}.Q \Rightarrow \tau \vdash prog}{\Gamma \vdash f : (\forall \overline{pa}.Q \Rightarrow \tau) = e; prog} \text{ BindA}$$

Fig. 3. Typing rules for programs

Rule VAR says that x is used once in a variable expression x, but it is safe to regard that the expression uses x more than once and uses other variables ω times. At the same time, the type $\forall \overline{pa}.Q' \Rightarrow \tau$ of x instantiated to $\tau[\overline{p \mapsto \mu}, \overline{a \mapsto \sigma}]$ with yielding constraints $Q'[\overline{p \mapsto \mu}]$, which must be entailed from Q.

Rule ABS says that $\lambda x.e$ has type $\sigma \to_\mu \tau$ if e has type τ, assuming that the use of x in e is μ. Unlike the original $\lambda^q_\to$ [7], in our system, multiplicity annotations on arrows must be μ, i.e., 1, ω, or a multiplicity variable, instead of M. This does not limit the expressiveness because such general arrow types can be represented by type $\sigma \to_p \tau$ with constraints $p \le M \wedge M \le p$.

Rule APP sketches an important principle in $\lambda^q_\to$; when an expression with variable use Δ is used μ-many times, the variable use in the expression becomes $\mu\Delta$. Thus, since we pass e_2 (with variable use Δ_2) to e_1, where e_1 uses the argument μ-many times as described in its type $\sigma \to_\mu \tau$, the use of variables in e_2 of $e_1 \, e_2$ becomes $\mu\Delta_2$. For example, for $(\lambda y.42) \, x$, x is considered to be used ω times because $(\lambda y.42)$ has type $\sigma \to_\omega \mathsf{Int}$ for any σ.

Rule CON is nothing but a combination of VAR and APP. The $\omega\Delta_0$ part is only useful when C is nullary; otherwise, we can weaken Δ at leaves.

Rule CASE is the most complicated rule in this type system. In this rule, μ_0 represents how many times the scrutinee e_0 is used in the **case**. If $\mu_0 = \omega$, the pattern bound variables can be used unrestrictedly, and if $\mu_0 = 1$, the pattern bound variables can be used according to the multiplicities of the arguments of the constructor.[4] Thus, in the ith branch, variables in $\overline{x_i}$ can be used as $\overline{\mu_0 \nu_i [p \mapsto \mu]}$, where $\mu_i[\overline{p \mapsto \mu}]$ represents the multiplicities of the arguments of the constructor C_i. Other than $\overline{x_i}$, each branch body e_i can contain free variables used as Δ_i. Thus, the uses of free variables in the whole branch bodies are summarized as $\bigsqcup_i \Delta_i$. Recall that the **case** uses the scrutinee μ_0 times; thus, the whole uses of variables are estimated as $\mu_0 \Delta_0 + \bigsqcup_i \Delta_i$.

Then, we define the *typing judgment for programs*, $\Gamma \vdash prog$, which reads that program $prog$ is well-typed under Γ, by the typing rules in Fig. 3. At this place, the rules BIND and BINDA have no significant differences; their difference will be clear when we discuss type inference. In the rules BIND and BINDA, we assumed that Γ contains no free type-level variables. Therefore, we can safely generalize all free type-level variables in Q and τ. We do not check the use Δ in both rules

---

[4] This behavior, inherited from $\lambda^q_\to$ [7], implies the isomorphism $!(A \otimes B) \equiv !A \otimes !B$, which is not a theorem in the standard linear logic. The isomorphism intuitively means that unrestricted products can (only) be constructed from unrestricted components, as commonly adopted in linearity-via-kind approaches [11, 21, 24, 28, 29].

as bound variables are assumed to be used arbitrarily many times in the rest of the program; that is, the multiplicity of a bound variable is ω and its body uses variable as $\omega\Delta$, which maps $x \in \mathsf{dom}(\Delta)$ to ω and has no free type-level variables.

2.4   Metatheories

Lemma 4 is the standard weakening property. Lemma 5 says that we can replace Q with a stronger one, Lemma 6 says that we can replace Δ with a greater one, and Lemma 7 says that we can substitute type-level variables in a term-in-context without violating typeability. These lemmas state some sort of weakening, and the last three lemmas clarify the goal of our inference system discussed in Sect. 3.

Lemma 4. $Q; \Gamma; \Delta \vdash e : \tau$ implies $Q; \Gamma, x : A; \Delta \vdash e : \tau$.   □

Lemma 5. $Q; \Gamma; \Delta \vdash e : \tau$ and $Q' \models Q$ implies $Q'; \Gamma; \Delta \vdash e : \tau$.   □

Lemma 6. $Q; \Gamma; \Delta \vdash e : \tau$ and $Q \models \Delta \leq \Delta'$ implies $Q; \Gamma; \Delta' \vdash e : \tau$.   □

Lemma 7. $Q; \Gamma; \Delta \vdash e : \tau$ implies $Q\theta; \Gamma\theta; \Delta\theta \vdash e : \tau\theta$.   □

We have the following form of the substitution lemma:

Lemma 8 (Substitution). Suppose $Q_0; \Gamma, \overline{x : \sigma}; \Delta_0, \overline{x^\mu} \vdash e : \tau$, and $Q_i; \Gamma; \Delta_i \vdash e'_i : \sigma_i$ for each i. Then, $Q_1 \wedge \bigwedge_i Q_i; \Gamma; \Delta_0 + \sum_i \mu_i \Delta_i \vdash e[\overline{x \mapsto e'}] : \tau$.   □

Subject Reduction We show the subject reduction property for a simple call-by-name semantics. Consider the standard small-step call-by-name relation $e \longrightarrow e'$ with the following β-reduction rules (we omit the congruence rules):

$$(\lambda x.e_1)\, e_2 \longrightarrow e_1[x \mapsto e_2] \qquad \mathbf{case}\ \mathsf{C}_j\ \overline{e}_j\ \mathbf{of}\ \{\mathsf{C}_i\ \overline{x}_i \to e'_i\}_i \longrightarrow e'_j[\overline{x_j \mapsto e_j}]$$

Then, by Lemma 8, we have the following subjection reduction property:

Lemma 9 (Subject Reduction). $Q; \Gamma; \Delta \vdash e : \tau$ and $e \longrightarrow e'$ implies $Q; \Gamma; \Delta \vdash e' : \tau$.   □

Lemma 9 holds even for the call-by-value reduction, though with a caveat. For a program $f_1 = e_1; \ldots; f_n = e_n$, it can happen that some e_i is typed only under unsatisfiable (i.e., conflicting) Q_i. As conflicting Q_i means that e_i is essentially ill-typed, evaluating e_i may not be safe. However, the standard call-by-value strategy evaluates e_i, even when f_i is not used at all and thus the type system does not reject this unsatisfiability. This issue can be addressed by the standard witness-passing transformation [15] that converts programs so that $Q \Rightarrow \tau$ becomes $W_Q \to \tau$, where W_Q represents a set of witnesses of Q. Nevertheless, it would be reasonable to reject conflicting constraints locally.

We then state the correspondence with the original system [7] (assuming the modification [6] for the variable case[5]) to show that the qualified-typed version

---

[5] In the premise of VAR, the original [7] uses $\exists \Delta'. \Delta = x^1 + \omega\Delta'$, which is modified to $x^1 \leq \Delta$ in [6]. The difference between the two becomes clear when $\Delta(x) = p$, for which the former one does not hold as we are not able to choose Δ' depending on p.

captures the linearity as the original. While the original system assumes the call-by-need evaluation, Lemma 9 could be lifted to that case.

Theorem 1. If $\top; \Gamma; \Delta \vdash e : \tau$ where Γ contains only monotypes, e is also well-typed in the original $\lambda^q_\rightarrow$ under some environment. $\qquad\square$

The main reason for the monotype restriction is that our polytypes are strictly more expressive than their (rank-1) polytypes. This extra expressiveness comes from predicates of the form $\cdots \leq M \cdot M'$. Indeed, $f = \lambda x.\mathbf{case}\ x\ \mathbf{of}\ \{\mathsf{MkMany}\ y \rightarrow (y, y)\}$ has type $\forall p\, q\, a.\, \omega \leq p \cdot q \Rightarrow \mathsf{MkMany}\ p\ a \rightarrow_q a \otimes a$ in our system, while it has three incomparable types in the original $\lambda^q_\rightarrow$.

3 Type Inference

In this section, we give a type inference method for the type system in the previous section. Following [31, Section 3], we adopt the standard two-phase approach; we first gather constraints on types and then solve them. As mentioned in Sect. 1, the inference system described here has the issue of ambiguity, which will be addressed in Sect. 4.

3.1 Inference Algorithm

We first extend types τ and multiplicities μ to include *unification variables*.

$$\tau ::= \cdots \mid \alpha \qquad \mu ::= \cdots \mid \pi$$

We call α/π a unification type/multiplicity variable, which will be substituted by a concrete type/multiplicity (including rigid variables) during the inference. Similarly to $\mathsf{ftv}(\bar{t})$, we write $\mathsf{fuv}(\bar{t})$ for the unification variables (of both sorts) in $\bar{t}$, where each t_i ranges over any syntactic element (such as τ, Q, Γ, and Δ).

Besides Q, the algorithm will generate equality constraints $\tau \sim \tau'$. Formally, the sets of *generated constraints* C and *generated predicates* ψ are given by

$$C ::= \bigwedge_i \psi_i \qquad \psi ::= \phi \mid \tau \sim \tau'$$

Then, we define *type inference judgment for expressions*, $\Gamma \Vdash e : \tau \rightsquigarrow \Delta; C$, which reads that, given Γ and e, type τ is inferred together with variable use Δ and constraints C, by the rules in Fig. 4. Note that Δ is also synthesized as well as τ and C in this step. This difference in the treatment of Γ and Δ is why we separate multiplicity environments Δ from typing environments Γ.

Gathered constraints are solved when we process top-level bindings. Figure 5 defines *type inference judgment for programs*, $\Gamma \Vdash prog$, which reads that the inference finds $prog$ well-typed under Γ. In the rules, manipulation of constraints is done by the *simplification judgment* $Q \Vdash_{\mathrm{simp}} C \rightsquigarrow Q'; \theta$, which simplifies C under the assumption Q into the pair (Q', θ) of residual constraints Q' and substitution θ for unification variables, where (Q', θ) is expected to be equivalent

$$\frac{\Gamma(x) = \forall \overline{pa}.Q \Rightarrow \tau \quad \overline{\alpha}, \overline{\pi} : \text{fresh}}{\Gamma \Vdash x : \tau[\overline{p \mapsto \pi}, \overline{a \mapsto \alpha}] \leadsto x^1; Q[\overline{p \mapsto \pi}]} \qquad \frac{\Gamma, x : \alpha \Vdash e : \tau \leadsto \Delta, x^M; C \quad \alpha, \pi : \text{fresh}}{\Gamma \Vdash \lambda x.e : \alpha \to_\pi \tau \leadsto \Delta; C \wedge M \leq \pi}$$

$$\frac{\Gamma \Vdash e_1 : \tau_1 \leadsto \Delta_1; C_2 \quad \Gamma \Vdash e_2 : \tau_2 \leadsto \Delta_2; C_1 \quad \beta, \pi : \text{fresh}}{\Gamma \Vdash e_1\, e_2 : \beta \leadsto \Delta_1 + \pi\Delta_2; C_1 \wedge C_2 \wedge \tau_1 \sim (\tau_2 \to_\pi \beta)}$$

$$\frac{\mathsf{C} : \forall \overline{pa}.\, \overline{\sigma} \to_{\overline{v}} \mathsf{D}\, \overline{p}\, \overline{a} \quad \{\Gamma \Vdash e_i : \tau_i \leadsto \Delta_i; C_i\}_i \quad \overline{\alpha}, \overline{\pi} : \text{fresh}}{\Gamma \Vdash \mathsf{C}\, \overline{e} : \mathsf{D}\, \overline{\pi}\, \overline{\alpha} \leadsto \sum_i \nu_i[\overline{p \mapsto \pi}]\Delta_i; \bigwedge_i C_i \wedge \tau_i \sim \sigma_i[\overline{p \mapsto \pi}, \overline{a \mapsto \alpha}]}$$

$$\frac{\begin{array}{c} \Gamma \Vdash e_0 : \tau_0 \leadsto \Delta_0; C_0 \quad \pi_0, \overline{\pi_i}, \overline{\alpha_i}, \beta : \text{fresh} \\[4pt] \left\{ \begin{array}{l} \mathsf{C}_i : \forall \overline{pa}.\, \overline{\tau_i} \to_{\overline{v_i}} \mathsf{D}\, \overline{p}\, \overline{a} \\ \Gamma, \overline{x_i : \tau_i}[p \mapsto \pi_i, a \mapsto \alpha_i] \Vdash e_i : \tau'_i \leadsto \Delta_i, \overline{x_i{}^{M_i}}; C_i \end{array} \right\}_i \\[10pt] C' = C_0 \wedge \bigwedge_i \left(C_i \wedge \beta \sim \tau'_i \wedge (\tau_0 \sim \mathsf{D}\, \overline{\pi_i}\, \overline{\alpha_i}) \wedge \bigwedge_j M_{ij} \leq \pi_0 \nu_{ij}[p \mapsto \pi_i] \right) \end{array}}{\Gamma \Vdash \mathbf{case}\ e_0\ \mathbf{of}\ \{\mathsf{C}_i\, \overline{x_i} \to e_i\}_i : \beta \leadsto \pi_0 \Delta_0 + \bigsqcup_i \Delta_i; C'}$$

Fig. 4. Type inference rules for expressions

$$\frac{}{\Gamma \Vdash \varepsilon} \qquad \frac{\begin{array}{c} \Gamma \Vdash e : \tau \leadsto \Delta; C \quad \top \Vdash_{\text{simp}} C \leadsto Q; \theta \quad \{\overline{\pi\alpha}\} = \mathsf{fuv}(Q, \tau\theta) \\ \overline{p}, \overline{a} : \text{fresh} \quad \Gamma, f : \forall \overline{pa}.(Q \Rightarrow \tau\theta)[\overline{\alpha \mapsto a}, \overline{\pi \mapsto p}] \Vdash prog \end{array}}{\Gamma \Vdash f = e; prog}$$

$$\frac{\Gamma \Vdash e : \sigma \leadsto \Delta; C \quad Q \Vdash_{\text{simp}} C \wedge \tau \sim \sigma \leadsto \top; \theta \quad \Gamma, f : \forall \overline{pa}.Q \Rightarrow \tau \Vdash prog}{\Gamma \Vdash f : (\forall \overline{pa}.Q \Rightarrow \tau) = e; prog}$$

Fig. 5. Type inference rules for programs

in some sense to C under the assumption Q. The idea underlying our simplification is to solve type equality constraints in C as much as possible and then remove predicates that are implied by Q. Rules S-Fun, s-Data, s-Uni, and S-Triv are responsible for the former, which decompose type equality constraints and yield substitutions once either of the sides becomes a unification variable. Rules S-Entail and S-Rem are responsible for the latter, which remove predicates implied by Q and then return the residual constraints. Rule S-Entail checks $Q \models \phi$; a concrete method for this check will be discussed in Sect. 3.2.

Example 1 (app). Let us illustrate how the system infers a type for *app* = $\lambda f.\lambda x.f\ x$. We have the following derivation for its body $\lambda f.\lambda x.f\ x$:

$$\frac{\dfrac{f : \alpha_f \Vdash f : \alpha_f \leadsto f^1; \top \quad x : \alpha_x \Vdash x : \alpha_x \leadsto x^1; \top}{f : \alpha_f, x : \alpha_x \Vdash f\ x : \beta \leadsto f^1, x^\pi; \alpha_f \sim (\alpha_x \to_\pi \beta)}}{\dfrac{f : \alpha_f \Vdash \lambda x.f\ x : \alpha_x \to_{\pi_x} \beta \leadsto f^1; \alpha_f \sim (\alpha_x \to_\pi \beta) \wedge \pi_x \leq \pi}{\Vdash \lambda f.\lambda x.f\ x : \alpha_f \to_{\pi_f} \alpha_x \to_{\pi_x} \beta \leadsto \emptyset; \alpha_f \sim (\alpha_x \to_\pi \beta) \wedge \pi_x \leq \pi \wedge 1 \leq \pi_f}}$$

The highlights in the above derivation are:

- In the last two steps, f is assigned to type α_f and multiplicity π_f, and x is assigned to type α_x and multiplicity π_x.

$$\frac{Q \Vdash_{\mathsf{simp}} \sigma \sim \sigma' \wedge \mu \leq \mu' \wedge \mu' \leq \mu \wedge \tau \sim \tau' \leadsto Q'; \theta}{Q \Vdash_{\mathsf{simp}} (\sigma \rightarrow_\mu \tau) \sim (\sigma' \rightarrow_{\mu'} \tau') \wedge C \leadsto Q'; \theta} \text{S-Fun}$$

$$\frac{Q \Vdash_{\mathsf{simp}} \overline{\mu \leq \mu'} \wedge \overline{\mu' \leq \mu} \wedge \overline{\sigma \sim \sigma'} \wedge C \leadsto Q'; \theta}{Q \Vdash_{\mathsf{simp}} (\mathsf{D}\ \overline{\mu}\ \overline{\sigma}) \sim (\mathsf{D}\ \overline{\mu'}\ \overline{\sigma'}) \wedge C \leadsto Q'; \theta} \text{S-Data}$$

$$\frac{\alpha \notin \mathsf{fuv}(\tau) \quad Q \Vdash_{\mathsf{simp}} C[\alpha \mapsto \tau] \leadsto Q'; \theta}{Q \Vdash_{\mathsf{simp}} \alpha \sim \tau \wedge C \leadsto Q'; \theta \circ [\alpha \mapsto \tau]} \text{S-Uni} \qquad \frac{Q \Vdash_{\mathsf{simp}} C \leadsto Q'; \theta}{Q \Vdash_{\mathsf{simp}} \tau \sim \tau \wedge C \leadsto Q'; \theta} \text{S-Triv}$$

$$\frac{Q \wedge Q_{\mathsf{w}} \models \phi \quad Q \Vdash_{\mathsf{simp}} Q_{\mathsf{w}} \wedge C \leadsto Q'; \theta}{Q \Vdash_{\mathsf{simp}} \phi \wedge Q_{\mathsf{w}} \wedge C \leadsto Q'; \theta} \text{S-Entail} \qquad \frac{\text{no other rules can apply}}{Q \Vdash_{\mathsf{simp}} Q' \leadsto Q'; \emptyset} \text{S-Rem}$$

Fig. 6. Simplification rules (modulo commutativity and associativity of $\wedge$ and commutativity of $\sim$)

- Then, in the third last step, for $f\ x$, the system infers type β with constraint $\alpha_f \sim (\alpha_x \rightarrow_\pi \beta)$. At the same time, the variable use in $f\ x$ is also inferred as f^1, x^π. Note that the use of x is π because it is passed to $f : \alpha_x \rightarrow_\pi \beta$.
- After that, in the last two steps again, the system yields constraints $\pi_x \leq \pi$ and $1 \leq \pi_f$.

As a result, the type $\tau = \alpha_f \rightarrow_{\pi_f} \alpha_x \rightarrow_{\pi_x} \beta$ is inferred with the constraint $C = \alpha_f \sim (\alpha_x \rightarrow_\pi \beta) \wedge \pi_x \leq \pi \wedge 1 \leq \pi_f$.

Then, we try to assign a polytype to *app* by the rules in Fig. 4. By simplification, we have $\top \Vdash_{\mathsf{simp}} C \leadsto \pi_x \leq \pi; [\alpha_f \mapsto (\alpha_x \rightarrow_\pi \beta)]$. Thus, by generalizing $\tau[\alpha_f \mapsto (\alpha_x \rightarrow_\pi \beta)] = (\alpha_x \rightarrow_\pi \beta) \rightarrow_{\pi_f} \alpha_x \rightarrow_{\pi_x} \beta$ with $\pi_x \leq \pi$, we obtain the following type for *app*:

$$app : \forall p\, p_f\, p_x\, a\, b.\ p \leq p_x \Rightarrow (a \rightarrow_p b) \rightarrow_{p_f} a \rightarrow_{p_x} b \qquad \square$$

Correctness We first prepare some definitions for the correctness discussions. First, we allow substitutions θ to replace unification multiplicity variables as well as unification type variables. Then, we extend the notion of $\models$ and write $C \models C'$ if $C'\theta$ holds when $C\theta$ holds. From now on, we require that substitutions are idempotent, i.e., $\tau\theta\theta = \tau\theta$ for any τ, which excludes substitutions $[\alpha \mapsto \mathsf{List}\ \alpha]$ and $[\alpha \mapsto \beta, \beta \mapsto \mathsf{Int}]$ for example. Let us write $Q \models \theta = \theta'$ if $Q \models \tau\theta \sim \tau\theta'$ for any τ. The restriction of a substitution θ to a domain X is written by $\theta|_X$.

Consider a pair $(Q_{\mathsf{g}}, C_{\mathsf{w}})$, where we call Q_{g} and C_{w} given and wanted constraints, respectively. Then, a pair (Q, θ) is called a (sound) *solution* [31] for the pair $(Q_{\mathsf{g}}, C_{\mathsf{w}})$ if $Q_{\mathsf{g}} \wedge Q \models C_{\mathsf{w}}\theta$, $\mathsf{dom}(\theta) \cap \mathsf{fuv}(Q_{\mathsf{g}}) = \emptyset$, and $\mathsf{dom}(\theta) \cap \mathsf{fuv}(Q) = \emptyset$. A solution is called *guess-free* [31] if it satisfies $Q_{\mathsf{g}} \wedge C_{\mathsf{w}} \models Q \wedge \bigwedge_{\pi \in \mathsf{dom}(\theta)}(\pi = \theta(\pi)) \wedge \bigwedge_{\alpha \in \mathsf{dom}(\theta)}(\alpha \sim \theta(\alpha))$ in addition. Intuitively, a guess-free solution consists of necessary conditions required for a wanted constraint C_{w} to hold, assuming a given constraint Q_{g}. For example, for $(\top, \alpha \sim (\beta \rightarrow_1 \beta))$, $(\top, [\alpha \mapsto (\mathsf{Int} \rightarrow_1 \mathsf{Int}), \beta \mapsto \mathsf{Int}])$ is a solution but not guess-free. Very roughly speaking, being for (Q, θ) a guess-free solution of $(Q_{\mathsf{g}}, C_{\mathsf{w}})$ means that (Q, θ) is equivalent to C_{w} under the assumption Q_{g}. There can be multiple guess-free solutions; for example, for $(\top, \pi \leq 1)$, both $(\pi \leq 1, \emptyset)$ and $(\top, [\pi \mapsto 1])$ are guess-free solutions.

Lemma 10 (Soundness and Principality of Simplification). *If $Q \Vdash_{simp}$ $C \leadsto Q'; \theta$, (Q', θ) is a guess-free solution for (Q, C).* □

Lemma 11 (Completeness of Simplification). *If (Q', θ) is a solution for (Q, C) where Q is satisfiable, then $Q \Vdash_{simp} C \leadsto Q''; \theta'$ for some Q'' and θ'.* □

Theorem 2 (Soundness of Inference). *Suppose $\Gamma \Vdash e : \tau \leadsto \Delta; C$ and there is a solution (Q, θ) for $(\top, C)$. Then, we have $Q; \Gamma\theta; \Delta\theta \vdash e : \tau\theta$.* □

Theorem 3 (Completeness and Principality of Inference). *Suppose $\Gamma \Vdash e : \tau \leadsto \Delta; C$. Suppose also that $Q'; \Gamma\theta'; \Delta' \vdash e : \tau'$ for some substitution θ' on unification variables such that $\mathsf{dom}(\theta') \subseteq \mathsf{fuv}(\Gamma)$ and $\mathsf{dom}(\theta') \cap \mathsf{fuv}(Q') = \emptyset$. Then, there exists θ such that $\mathsf{dom}(\theta) \setminus \mathsf{dom}(\theta') \subseteq X$, (Q', θ) is a solution for $(\top, C)$, $Q' \models \theta|_{\mathsf{dom}(\theta')} = \theta'$, $Q' \models \tau\theta \sim \tau'$, and $Q' \models \Delta\theta \leq \Delta'$, where X is the set of unification variables introduced in the derivation.* □

Note that the constraint generation $\Gamma \Vdash e : \tau \leadsto \Delta; C$ always succeeds, whereas the generated constraints may possibly be conflicting. Theorem 3 states that such a case cannot happen when e is well-typed under the rules in Fig. 2.

Incompleteness in Typing Programs. It may sound contradictory to Theorem 3, but the type inference is indeed incomplete for checking type-annotated bindings. Recall that the typing rule for type-annotated bindings requires that the resulting constraint after simplification must be $\top$. However, even when there exists a solution of the form $(\top, \theta)$ for (Q, C), there can be no guess-free solution of this form. For example, $(\top, \pi \leq \pi')$ has a solution $(\top, [\pi \mapsto \pi'])$, but there are no guess-free solutions of the required form. Also, even though there exists a guess-free solution of the form $(\top, \theta)$, the simplification may not return the solution, as guess-free solutions are not always unique. For example, for $(\top, \pi \leq \pi' \wedge \pi' \leq \pi)$, $(\top, [\pi \mapsto \pi'])$ is a guess-free solution, whereas we have $\top \Vdash_{simp} \pi \leq \pi' \wedge \pi' \leq \pi \leadsto \pi \leq \pi' \wedge \pi' \leq \pi; \emptyset$. The source of the issue is that constraints on multiplicities can (also) be solved by substitutions.

Fortunately, this issue disappears when we consider disambiguation in Sect. 4. By disambiguation, we can eliminate constraints for internally-introduced multiplicity unification variables that are invisible from the outside. As a result, after processing equality constraints, we essentially need only consider rigid multiplicity variables when checking entailment for annotated top-level bindings.

Promoting Equalities to Substituions. The inference can infer polytypes $\forall p. \, p \leq 1 \Rightarrow \mathsf{Int} \to_p \mathsf{Int}$ and $\forall p_1 p_2. \, (p_1 \leq p_2 \wedge p_2 \leq p_1) \Rightarrow \mathsf{Int} \to_{p_1} \mathsf{Int} \to_{p_2} \mathsf{Int}$, while programmers would prefer more simpler types $\mathsf{Int} \to_1 \mathsf{Int}$ and $\forall p. \, \mathsf{Int} \to_p \mathsf{Int} \to_p \mathsf{Int}$; the simplification so far does not yield substitutions on multiplicity unification variables. Adding the following rule remedies the situation:

$$\frac{\pi \notin \mathsf{fuv}(Q) \quad \pi \neq \mu \qquad Q \wedge Q_{\mathrm{w}} \models \pi \leq \mu \wedge \mu \leq \pi \quad Q \Vdash_{simp} (Q_{\mathrm{w}} \wedge C)[\pi \mapsto \mu] \leadsto Q'; \theta}{Q \Vdash_{simp} Q_{\mathrm{w}} \wedge C \leadsto Q'; \theta \circ [\pi \mapsto \mu]} \text{S-Eq}$$

This rule says that if $\pi = \mu$ must hold for $Q_w \wedge C$ to hold, the simplification yields the substitution $[\pi \mapsto \mu]$. The condition $\pi \notin \mathsf{fuv}(Q)$ is required for Lemma 10; a solution cannot substitute variables in Q. Note that this rule essentially finds an improving substitution [16].

Using the rule is optional. Our prototype implementation actually uses S-EQ only for Q_w for which we can find μ easily: $M \leq 1$, $\omega \leq \mu$, and looping chains $\mu_1 \leq \mu_2 \wedge \cdots \wedge \mu_{n-1} \leq \mu_n \wedge \mu_n \leq \mu_1$.

3.2 Entailment Checking by Horn SAT Solving

The simplification rules rely on the check of entailment $Q \models \phi$. For the constraints in this system, we can perform this check in quadratic time at worst but in linear time for most cases. Specifically, we reduce the checking $Q \models \phi$ to satisfiability of propositional Horn formulas (Horn SAT), which is known to be solved in linear time in the number of occurrences of literals [10], where the reduction (precisely, the preprocessing of the reduction) may increase the problem size quadratically. The idea of using Horn SAT for constraint solving in linear typing can be found in Mogensen [23].

First, as a preprocess, we normalize both given and wanted constraints by the following rules:

- Replace $M_1 \cdot M_2 \leq M$ with $M_1 \leq M \wedge M_2 \leq M$.
- Replace $M \cdot 1$ and $1 \cdot M$ with M, and $M \cdot \omega$ and $\omega \cdot M$ with ω.
- Remove trivial predicates $1 \leq M$ and $M \leq \omega$.

After this, each predicate ϕ has the form $\mu \leq \prod_i \nu_i$.

After the normalization above, we can reduce the entailment checking to satisfiability. Specifically, we use the following property:

$$Q \models \mu \leq \prod_i \nu_i \quad \text{iff} \quad Q \wedge \bigwedge_i (\nu_i \leq 1) \wedge (\omega \leq \mu) \text{ is unsatisfiable}$$

Here, the constraint $Q \wedge \bigwedge_i (\nu_i \leq 1) \wedge (\omega \leq \mu)$ intuitively asserts that there exists a counterexample of $Q \models \mu \leq \prod_i \nu_i$.

Then, it is straightforward to reduce the satisfiability of Q to Horn SAT; we just map 1 to true and ω to false and accordingly map $\leq$ and $\cdot$ to $\Leftarrow$ and $\wedge$, respectively. Since Horn SAT can be solved in linear time in the number of occurrences of literals [10], the reduction also shows that the satisfiability of Q is checked in linear time in the size of Q if Q is normalized.

Corollary 1. Checking $Q \models \phi$ is in linear time if Q and ϕ are normalized. □

The normalization of constraints can duplicate M of $\cdots \leq M$, and thus increases the size quadratically in the worst case. Fortunately, the quadratic increase is not common because the size of M is bounded in practice, in many cases by one. Among the rules in Fig. 2, only the rule that introduces non-singleton M in the right-hand side of $\leq$ is CASE for a constructor whose arguments' multiplicities are non-constants, such as MkMany : $\forall p\, a.\, a \rightarrow_p$ Many $p\, a$. However, it often suffices to use non-multiplicity-parameterized constructors, such as Cons : $\forall a.\, a \rightarrow_1$ List $a \rightarrow_1$ List a, because such constructors can be used to construct or deconstruct both linear and unrestricted data.

3.3   Issue: Inference of Ambiguous Types

The inference system so far looks nice; the system is sound and complete, and infers principal types. However, there still exists an issue to overcome for the system to be useful: it often infers ambiguous types [15, 27] in which internal multiplicity variables leak out to reveal internal implementation details.

Consider $app' = \lambda f.\lambda x.app\, f\, x$ for $app = \lambda f.\lambda x.f\, x$ from Example 1. We would expect that equivalent types are inferred for app' and app. However, this is not the case for the inference system. In fact, the system infers the following type for app' (here we reproduce the inferred type of app for comparison):

$$app\ :\qquad \forall p\, p_f\, p_x\, a\, b.\ (p \le p_x) \qquad\qquad\qquad \Rightarrow (a \rightarrow_p b) \rightarrow_{p_f} a \rightarrow_{p_x} b$$
$$app'\ :\ \forall q\, q_f\, q_x\, p_f\, p_x\, a\, b.\ (q \le q_x \wedge q_f \le p_f \wedge q_x \le p_x) \Rightarrow (a \rightarrow_q b) \rightarrow_{p_f} a \rightarrow_{p_x} b$$

We highlight why this type is inferred as follows.

- By abstractions, f is assigned to type α_f and multiplicity π_f, and x is assigned to type α_x and multiplicity π_x.
- By its use, app is instantiated to type $(\alpha' \rightarrow_{\pi'} \beta') \rightarrow_{\pi'_f} \alpha' \rightarrow_{\pi'_x} \beta'$ with constraint $\pi' \le \pi'_x$.
- For $app\, f$, the system infers type β with constraint $((\alpha' \rightarrow_{\pi'} \beta') \rightarrow_{\pi'_f} \alpha' \rightarrow_{\pi'_x} \beta') \sim (\alpha_f \rightarrow_{\pi_1} \beta)$. At the same time, the variable use in the expression is inferred as app^1, f^{π_1}.
- For $(app\, f\, x)$, the system infers type γ with constraint $\beta \sim (\alpha' \rightarrow_{\pi_2} \gamma)$. At the same time, the variable use in the expression is inferred as $app^1, f^{\pi_1}, x^{\pi_2}$.
- As a result, $\lambda f.\lambda x.app\, f\, x$ has type $\alpha_f \rightarrow_{\pi_f} \alpha_x \rightarrow_{\pi_x} \gamma$, yielding constraints $\pi_1 \le \pi_f \wedge \pi_2 \le \pi_x$.

Then, for the gathered constraints, by simplification (including S-EQ), we obtain a (guess-free) solution (Q, θ) such that $Q = (\pi'_f \le \pi_f \wedge \pi' \le \pi'_x \wedge \pi'_x \le \pi_x)$ and $\theta = [\alpha_f \mapsto (\alpha' \rightarrow_{\pi'} \beta'), \pi'_1 \mapsto \pi'_f, \beta \mapsto (\alpha_f \rightarrow_{\pi'_x} \beta'), \pi_2 \mapsto \pi'_x, \gamma \mapsto \beta'])$. Then, after generalizing $(\alpha_f \rightarrow_{\pi_f} \alpha_x \rightarrow_{\pi_x} \gamma)\theta = (\alpha' \rightarrow_{\pi'} \beta') \rightarrow_{\pi_f} \alpha' \rightarrow_{\pi_x} \beta$, we obtain the inferred type above.

There are two problems with this inference result:

- The type of app' is *ambiguous* in the sense that the type-level variables in the constraint cannot be determined only by those that appear in the type [15, 27]. Usually, ambiguous types are undesirable, especially when their instantiation affects runtime behavior [15, 27, 31].
- Due to this ambiguity, the types of app and app' are not judged equivalent by the inference system. For example, the inference rejects the binding $app'' : \forall p\, p_f\, p_x\, a\, b.\ (p \le p_x) \Rightarrow (a \rightarrow_p b) \rightarrow_{p_f} a \rightarrow_{p_x} b = app'$ because the system does not know how to instantiate the ambiguous type-level variables q_f and q_x, while the binding is valid in the type system in Sect. 2.

Inference of ambiguous types is common in the system; it is easily caused by using defined variables. Rejecting ambiguous types is not a solution for our case because it rejects many programs. Defaulting such ambiguous type-level variables to 1 or ω is not a solution either because it loses principality in general. However, we have no other choices than to reject ambiguous types, *as long as multiplicities are relevant in runtime behavior.*

In the next section, we will show how we address the ambiguity issue under the assumption that multiplicities are irrelevant at runtime. Under this assumption, it is no problem to have multiplicity-monomorphic primitives such as array processing primitives (e.g., *readMArray* : $\forall a.$ MArray $a \to_1$ Int $\to_\omega$ (MArray $a \otimes$ Un a)) [31]. Note that this assumption does not rule out all multiplicity-polymorphic primitives; it just prohibits the primitives from inspecting multiplicities at runtime.

4   Disambiguation by Quantifier Elimination

In this section, we address the issue of ambiguous and leaky types by using quantifier elimination. The basic idea is simple; we just view the type of *app'* as

$$app' : \forall q\, p_f\, p_x\, a\, b.\, (\exists q_x\, q_f.\, q \le q_x \wedge q_f \le p_f \wedge q_x \le p_x) \Rightarrow (a \to_q b) \to_{p_f} a \to_{p_x} b$$

In this case, the constraint $(\exists q_x\, q_f.\, q \le q_x \wedge q_f \le p_f \wedge q_x \le p_x)$ is logically equivalent to $q \le p_x$, and thus we can infer the equivalent types for both *app* and *app'*. Fortunately, such quantifier elimination is always possible for our representation of constraints; that is, for $\exists p.Q$, there always exists Q' that is logically equivalent to $\exists p.Q$. A technical subtlety is that, although we perform quantifier elimination after generalization in the above explanation, we actually perform quantifier elimination just before generalization, or more precisely, as a final step of simplification, for compatibility with the simplification in OUTSIDEIN(X) [31], especially in the treatment of local assumptions.

4.1   Elimination of Existential Quantifiers

The elimination of existential quantifiers is rather easy; we simply use the well-known fact that a disjunction of a Horn clause and a definite clause can also be represented as a Horn clause. Regarding our encoding of normalized predicates (Sect. 3.2) that maps $\mu \le M$ to a Horn clause, the fact can be rephrased as:

Lemma 12. $(\mu \le M \vee \omega \le M') \equiv \mu \le M \cdot M'.$ $\square$

Here, we extend constraints to include $\vee$ and write $\equiv$ for the logical equivalence; that is, $Q \equiv Q'$ if and only if $Q \models Q'$ and $Q' \models Q$.

As a corollary, we obtain the following result:

Corollary 2. There effectively exists a quantifier-free constraint Q', denoted by $\mathsf{elim}(\exists \pi.Q)$, such that Q' is logically equivalent to $\exists \pi.Q$.

Proof. Note that $\exists \pi.Q$ means $Q[\pi \mapsto 1] \vee Q[\pi \mapsto \omega]$ because π ranges over $\{1, \omega\}$. We safely assume that Q is normalized (Sect. 3.2) and that Q does not contain a predicate $\pi \leq M$ where π appears also in M, because such a predicate trivially holds.

We define Φ_1, Φ_ω, and Q_{rest} as $\Phi_1 = \{\mu \leq M \mid (\mu \leq \pi \cdot M) \in Q, \mu \neq \pi\}$, $\Phi_\omega = \{\omega \leq M \mid (\pi \leq M) \in Q, \pi \notin \text{fuv}(M)\}$, and $Q_{\text{rest}} = \bigwedge \{\phi \mid \phi \in Q, \pi \notin \text{fuv}(\phi)\}$. Here we abused the notation to write $\phi \in Q$ to mean that $Q = \bigwedge_i \phi_i$ and $\phi = \phi_i$ for some i. In the construction of Φ_1, we assumed the monoid laws of $(\cdot)$; the definition says that we remove π from the right-hand sides and M becomes 1 if the right-hand side is π. By construction, $Q[p \mapsto 1]$ and $Q[p \mapsto \omega]$ are equivalent to $(\bigwedge \Phi_1) \wedge Q_{\text{rest}}$ and $(\bigwedge \Phi_\omega) \wedge Q_{\text{rest}}$, respectively. Thus, by Lemma 12 and by the distributivity of $\vee$ over $\wedge$ it suffices to define Q' as $Q' = (\bigwedge \{\mu \leq M \cdot M' \mid \mu \leq M \in \Phi_1, \omega \leq M' \in \Phi_\omega\}) \wedge Q_{\text{rest}}$. □

Example 2. Consider $Q = (\pi_f' \leq \pi_f \wedge \pi' \leq \pi_x' \wedge \pi_x' \leq \pi_x)$; this is the constraint obtained from $\lambda f.\lambda x.app\ f\ x$ (Sect. 3.3). Since π_f' and π_x' do not appear in the inferred type $(\alpha' \to_{\pi'} \beta') \to_{\pi_f} \alpha' \to_{\pi_x} \beta$, we want to eliminate them by the above step. There is a freedom to choose which variable is eliminated first. Here, we shall choose π_f' first.

First, we have $\text{elim}(\exists \pi_f'.Q) = \pi' \leq \pi_x' \wedge \pi_x' \leq \pi_x$ because for this case we have $\Phi_1 = \emptyset$, $\Phi_\omega = \{\omega \leq \pi_f\}$, and $Q_{\text{rest}} = \pi' \leq \pi_x' \wedge \pi_x' \leq \pi_x$. We then have $\text{elim}(\exists \pi_x'.\pi' \leq \pi_x' \wedge \pi_x' \leq \pi_x) = \pi' \leq \pi_x$ because for this case we have $\Phi_1 = \{\pi' \leq 1\}$, $\Phi_2 = \{\omega \leq \pi_x\}$, and $Q_{\text{rest}} = \top$. □

In the worst case, the size of $\text{elim}(\exists \pi.Q)$ can be quadratic to that of Q. Thus, repeating elimination can make the constraints exponentially bigger. We believe that such blow-up rarely happens because it is usual that π occurs only in a few predicates in Q. Also, recall that non-singleton right-hand sides are caused only by multiplicity-parameterized constructors. When each right-hand side of $\leq$ is a singleton in Q, the same holds in $\text{elim}(\exists \pi.Q)$. For such a case, the exponential blow-up cannot happen because the size of constraints in the form is at most quadratic in the number of multiplicity variables.

4.2   Modified Typing Rules

As mentioned at the begging of this section, we perform quantifier elimination as the last step of simplification. To do so, we define $Q \Vdash^\tau_{\text{simp}} C \rightsquigarrow Q''; \theta$ as follows:

$$\frac{Q \Vdash_{\text{simp}} C \rightsquigarrow Q'; \theta \quad \{\overline{\pi}\} = \text{fuv}(Q') \setminus \text{fuv}(\tau\theta) \quad Q'' = \text{elim}(\exists \overline{\pi}.Q')}{Q \Vdash^\tau_{\text{simp}} C \rightsquigarrow Q''; \theta}$$

Here, τ is used to determine which unification variables will be ambiguous after generalization. We simply identify variables ($\overline{\pi}$ above) that are not in τ as ambiguous [15] for simplicity. This check is indeed conservative in a more general definition of ambiguity [27], in which $\forall p\,r\,a.\ (p \leq r, r \leq p) \Rightarrow a \rightarrow_p a$ for example is not judged as ambiguous because r is determined by p.

Then, we replace the original simplification with the above-defined version.

$$\frac{\Gamma \Vdash e : \tau \rightsquigarrow \Delta; C \quad \top \Vdash^{\tau}_{\text{simp}} C \rightsquigarrow Q; \theta \quad \{\overline{\pi\alpha}\} = \mathsf{fuv}(Q, \tau\theta) \quad \overline{p}, \overline{a} : \text{fresh} \quad \Gamma, f : \forall \overline{pa}.(Q \Rightarrow \tau\theta)[\overline{\alpha \mapsto a, \pi \mapsto p}] \Vdash prog}{\Gamma \Vdash f = e; prog}$$

$$\frac{\Gamma \Vdash e : \sigma \rightsquigarrow \Delta; C \quad Q \Vdash^{\sigma}_{\text{simp}} C \wedge \tau \sim \sigma \rightsquigarrow \top; \theta \quad \Gamma, f : \forall \overline{pa}.Q \Rightarrow \tau \Vdash prog}{\Gamma \Vdash f : (\forall \overline{pa}.Q \Rightarrow \tau) = e; prog}$$

Here, the changed parts are highlighted for readability.

Example 3. Consider (Q, θ) in Sect. 3.3 such that $Q = (\pi'_f \leq \pi_f \wedge \pi' \leq \pi'_x \wedge \pi'_x \leq \pi_x)$ and $\theta = [\alpha_f \mapsto (\alpha' \rightarrow_{\pi'} \beta'), \pi'_1 \mapsto \pi'_f, \beta \mapsto (\alpha_f \rightarrow_{\pi'_x} \beta'), \pi_2 \mapsto \pi'_x, \gamma \mapsto \beta'])$, which is obtained after simplification of the gathered constraint. Following Example 2, eliminating variables that are not in $\tau\theta = (\alpha' \rightarrow_{\pi'} \beta') \rightarrow_{\pi_f} \alpha' \rightarrow_{\pi_x} \beta$ yields the constraint $\pi' \leq \pi_x$. As a result, by generalization, we obtain the polytype

$$\forall q\, p_f\, p_x\, a\, b. \, (q \leq p_x) \Rightarrow (a \rightarrow_q b) \rightarrow_{p_f} a \rightarrow_{p_x} b$$

for *app'*, which is equivalent to the inferred type of *app*.   □

Note that (Q', θ) of $Q \Vdash^{\tau}_{\text{simp}} C \rightsquigarrow Q'; \theta$ is no longer a solution of (Q, C) because C can have eliminated variables. However, it is safe to use this version when generalization takes place, because, for variables $\overline{q}$ that do not occur in τ, $\forall \overline{pqa}.\, Q \Rightarrow \tau$ and $\forall \overline{pa}.\, Q' \Rightarrow \tau$ have the same set of monomorphic instances, if $\exists \overline{q}.Q$ is logically equivalent to Q'. Note that in this type system simplification happens only before (implicit) generalization takes place.

5   Extension to Local Assumptions

In this section, following OUTSIDEIN(X) [31], we extend our system with local assumptions, which enable us to have **let**s and GADTs. We focus on the treatment of **let**s in this section because type inference for **let**s involves a linearity-specific concern: the multiplicity of a **let**-bound variable.

5.1   "Let Should Not Be Generalized" for Our Case

We first discuss that even for our case "**let** should not be generalized" [31]. That is, generalization of **let** sometimes results in counter-intuitive typing and conflicts with the discussions so far.

Consider the following program:

$$h = \lambda f. \lambda k. \mathbf{let} \; y = f \; (\lambda x. k \; x) \; \mathbf{in} \; 0$$

Suppose for simplicity that f and x have types $(a \rightarrow_{\pi_1} b) \rightarrow_{\pi_2} c$ and $a \rightarrow_{\pi_3} b$, respectively (here we only focus on the treatment of multiplicity). Then, $f \; (\lambda x. k \; x)$

has type c with the constraint $\pi_3 \leq \pi_1$. Thus, after generalization, y has type $\pi_3 \leq \pi_1 \Rightarrow c$, where π_3 and π_1 are neither generalized nor eliminated because they escape from the definition of y. As a result, h has type $\forall p_1 \, p_2 \, p_3 \, a \, b \, c. \, ((a \rightarrow_{p_1} b) \rightarrow_{p_2} c) \rightarrow_\omega (a \rightarrow_{p_3} b) \rightarrow_\omega$ Int; there is no constraint $p_3 \leq p_1$ because the definition of y does not yield a constraint. This nonexistence of the constraint would be counter-intuitive because users wrote $f \, (\lambda x.k \, x)$ while the constraint for the expression is not imposed. In particular, it does not cause an error even when $f : (a \rightarrow_1 b) \rightarrow_1 c$ and $k : a \rightarrow_\omega b$, while $f \, (\lambda x.k \, x)$ becomes illegal for this case. Also, if we change 0 to y, the error happens at the use site instead of the definition site. Moreover, the type is fragile as it depends on whether y occurs or not; for example, if we change 0 to $const \, 0 \, y$ where $const = \lambda a.\lambda b.a$, the type of h changes to $\forall p_1 \, p_2 \, p_3 \, a \, b \, c. \, p_1 \leq p_3 \Rightarrow ((a \rightarrow_{p_1} b) \rightarrow_{p_2} c) \rightarrow_\omega (a \rightarrow_{p_3} b) \rightarrow_\omega$ Int. In this discussion, we do not consider type-equality constraints, but there are no legitimate reasons why type-equality constraints are solved on the fly in typing y.

As demonstrated in the above example, "**let** should not be generalized" [30,31] in our case. Thus, we adopt the same principle in OUTSIDEIN(X) that **let** will be generalized only if users write a type annotation for it [31]. This principle is also adopted in GHC (as of 6.12.1 when the language option `MonoLocalBinds` is turned on) with a slight relaxation to generalize closed bindings.

5.2   Multiplicity of Let-Bound Variables

Another issue with **let**-generalization, which is specific to linear typing, is that a generalization result depends on the multiplicity of the **let**-bound variable. Let us consider the following program, where we want to generalize the type of y (even without a type annotation):

$$g = \lambda x.\mathbf{let} \, y = \lambda f.f \, x \, \mathbf{in} \, y \, not$$

Suppose for simplicity that not has type Bool $\rightarrow_1$ Bool and x has type Bool already in typing **let**. Then, y's body $\lambda f.f \, x$ has a monotype $(\text{Bool} \rightarrow_\pi r) \rightarrow_{\pi'} r$ with no constraints (on multiplicity). There are two generalization results depending on the multiplicity π_y of y because the use of x also escapes in the type system.

- If $\pi_y = 1$, the type is generalized into $\forall q \, r. \, (\text{Bool} \rightarrow_\pi r) \rightarrow_q r$, where π is not generalized because the use of x in y's body is π.
- If $\pi_y = \omega$, the type is generalized into $\forall p \, q \, r. \, (\text{Bool} \rightarrow_p r) \rightarrow_q r$, where π is generalized (to p) because the use of x in y's body is ω.

A difficulty here is that π_y needs to be determined at the definition of y, while the constraint on π_y is only obtained from the use of y.

Our design choice is the latter; the multiplicity of a generalizable **let**-bound variable is ω in the system. One justification for this choice is that a motivation of polymorphic typing is to enhance reusability, while reuse is not possible for variables with multiplicity 1. Another justification is compatibility with recursive definitions, where recursively-defined variables must have multiplicity ω; it might be confusing, for example, if the multiplicity of a list-manipulation function changes after we change its definition from an explicit recursion to *foldr*.

5.3 Inference Rule for Lets

In summary, the following are our criteria about **let** generalization:

- Only **let**s with polymorphic type annotations are generalized.
- Variables introduced by **let** to be generalized have multiplicity ω.

This idea can be represented by the following typing rule:

$$\frac{\begin{array}{c}\Gamma \Vdash e_1 : \tau_1 \rightsquigarrow \Delta_1; C_1 \quad \{\overline{\pi\alpha}\} = \mathsf{fuv}(\tau_1, C_1) \setminus \mathsf{fuv}(\Gamma) \\ C_1' = \exists \overline{\pi\alpha}.(Q \models^{\tau_1} C_1 \wedge \tau \sim \tau_1) \\ \Gamma\theta_1, x : (\forall \overline{pa}.Q \Rightarrow \tau) \Vdash e_2 : \tau_2 \rightsquigarrow \Delta_2, x^M; C_2\end{array}}{\Gamma \Vdash \mathbf{let}\ x : (\forall \overline{pa}.Q \Rightarrow \tau) = e_1\ \mathbf{in}\ e_2 : \tau_2 \rightsquigarrow \omega\Delta_1 + \Delta_2; C_1' \wedge C_2} \textsc{LetA}$$

(We do not discuss non-generalizable **let** because they are typed as $(\lambda x.e_2)\,e_1$.)
Constraints like $\exists \overline{\pi\alpha}.(Q \models^{\tau_1} C_1 \wedge \tau \sim \tau_1)$ above are called *implication con-straints* [31], which states that the entailment must hold only by instantiating unification variables in $\overline{\pi\alpha}$. There are two roles of implication constraints. One is to delay the checking because τ_1 and C_1 contain some unification variables that will be made concrete at this point by solving C_2. The other is to guard constraints; in the above example, since the constraints $C_1 \wedge \tau \sim \tau_1$ hold by assuming Q, it is not safe to substitute variables outside $\overline{\pi\alpha}$ in solving the constraints because the equivalence might be a consequence of Q; recall that Q affects type equality. We note that there is a slight deviation from the original approach [31]; an implication constraint in our system is annotated by τ_1 to identify for which subset of $\{\overline{\pi\alpha}\}$ the existence of a unique solution is not required and thus quantifier elimination is possible, similarly to Sect. 4.

5.4 Solving Constraints

Now, the set of constraints is extended to include implication constraints.

$$C ::= \bigwedge_i \psi_i \qquad \psi_i ::= \cdots \mid \exists \overline{\pi\alpha}.(Q \models^\tau C)$$

As we mentioned above, an implication constraint $\exists \overline{\pi\alpha}.(Q \models^\tau C)$ means that $Q \models C$ must hold by substituting $\overline{\pi}$ and $\overline{\alpha}$ with appropriate values, where we do not require uniqueness of solutions for unification variables that do not appear in τ. That is, $Q \Vdash^\tau_{\mathsf{simp}} C \rightsquigarrow \top; \theta$ must hold with $\mathsf{dom}(\theta) \subseteq \{\overline{\pi\alpha}\}$.
    Then, following OUTSIDEIN(X) [31], we define the *solving judgment* $\overline{\pi\alpha}.Q \Vdash^\tau_{\mathsf{solv}}$ $C \rightsquigarrow Q'; \theta$, which states that we solve (Q, C) as (Q', θ) where θ only touches variables in $\overline{\pi\alpha}$, where τ is used for disambiguation (Sect. 4). Let us write $\mathsf{impl}(C)$ for all the implication constraints in C, and $\mathsf{simpl}(C)$ for the rest. Then, we can define the inference rules for the judgment simply by recursive simplification, similarly to the original [31].

$$\frac{\overline{\pi\alpha}.\,Q \Vdash^\tau_{\mathsf{simpl}} \mathsf{simpl}(C) \rightsquigarrow Q_{\mathrm{r}}; \theta \qquad \{\overline{\pi_i\alpha_i}.\,Q \wedge Q_i \wedge Q_{\mathrm{r}} \Vdash^{\tau_i}_{\mathsf{solv}} C_i \rightsquigarrow \top; \theta_i\}_{(\exists \overline{\pi_i\alpha_i}.(Q_i \models^{\tau_i} C_i)) \in \mathsf{impl}(C\theta)}}{\overline{\pi\alpha}.\,Q \Vdash^\tau_{\mathsf{solv}} C \rightsquigarrow Q_{\mathrm{r}}; \theta}$$

Here, $\overline{\pi\alpha}.\ Q \Vdash^\tau_{\text{simpl}} C \rightsquigarrow Q_r; \theta$ is a simplification relation defined similarly to $Q \Vdash^\tau_{\text{simp}} C \rightsquigarrow Q_r; \theta$ except that we are allowed to touch only variables in $\overline{\pi\alpha}$. We omit the concrete rules for this version of simplification relation because they are straightforward except that unification caused by S-Uni and S-Eq and quantifier elimination (Sect. 4) are allowed only for variables in $\{\overline{\pi\alpha}\}$.

Accordingly, we also change the typing rules for bindings to use the solving relation instead of the simplification relation.

$$\frac{\Gamma \Vdash e : \tau \rightsquigarrow \Delta; C \quad \boxed{\mathsf{fuv}(C, \tau).\ \top \Vdash^\tau_{\text{solv}} C \rightsquigarrow Q; \theta} \quad \{\overline{\pi\alpha}\} = \mathsf{fuv}(Q, \tau\theta)}{\overline{p}, \overline{a} : \text{fresh} \quad \Gamma, f : \forall \overline{pa}.(Q \Rightarrow \tau\theta)[\overline{\alpha} \mapsto a, \overline{\pi} \mapsto p] \Vdash prog}{\Gamma \Vdash f = e; prog}$$

$$\frac{\Gamma \Vdash e : \sigma \rightsquigarrow \Delta; C \quad \boxed{\mathsf{fuv}(C, \sigma).\ Q \Vdash^\sigma_{\text{solv}} C \wedge \tau \sim \sigma \rightsquigarrow \top; \theta} \quad \Gamma, f : \forall \overline{pa}.Q \Rightarrow \tau \Vdash prog}{\Gamma \Vdash f : (\forall \overline{pa}.Q \Rightarrow \tau) = e; prog}$$

Above, there are no unification variables other than $\mathsf{fuv}(C, \tau)$ or $\mathsf{fuv}(C, \sigma)$.

The definition of the solving judgment and the updated inference rules for programs are the same as those in the original OUTSIDEIN(X) [31] except τ for disambiguation. This is one of the advantages of being based on OUTSIDEIN(X).

6 Implementation and Evaluation

In this section, we evaluate the proposed inference method using our prototype implementation. We first report what types are inferred for functions from Prelude to see whether or not inferred types are reasonably simple. We then report the performance evaluation that measures efficiency of type inference and the overhead due to entailment checking and quantifier elimination.

6.1 Implementation

The implementation follows the present paper except for a few points. Following the implementation of OUTSIDEIN(X) in GHC, our type checker keeps a natural number, which we call an implication level, corresponding to the depth of implication constraints, and a unification variable also accordingly keeps the implication level at which the variable is introduced. As usual, we represent unification variables by mutable references. We perform unification on the fly by destructive assignment, while unification of variables that have smaller implication levels than the current level is recorded for later checking of implication constraints; such a variable cannot be in $\overline{\pi\alpha}$ of $\exists \overline{\pi\alpha}.Q \models^\tau C$. The implementation supports GADTs because they can be implemented rather easily by extending constraints Q to include type equalities, but does not support type classes because the handling of them requires another X of OUTSIDEIN(X).

Although we can use a linear-time Horn SAT solving algorithm [10] for checking $Q \models \phi$, the implementation uses a general SAT solver based on DPLL [8, 9] because the unit propagation in DPLL works efficiently for Horn formulas. We do not use external solvers, such as Z3, as we conjecture that the sizes of formulas are usually small, and overhead to use external solvers would be high.

$$(\circ) : (q \le s \land q \le t \land p \le t) \Rightarrow (b \to_q c) \to_r (a \to_p b) \to_s a \to_t c$$
$$curry : (p \le r \land p \le s) \Rightarrow ((a \otimes b) \to_p c) \to_q a \to_r b \to_s c$$
$$uncurry : (p \le s \land q \le s) \Rightarrow (a \to_p b \to_q c) \to_r (a \otimes b) \to_s c$$
$$either : (p \le r \land q \le r) \Rightarrow (a \to_p c) \to_\omega (b \to_q c) \to_\omega \mathsf{Either}\ a\ b \to_r c$$
$$foldr : (q \le r \land p \le s \land q \le s) \Rightarrow (a \to_p b \to_q b) \to_\omega b \to_r \mathsf{List}\ a \to_s b$$
$$foldl : (p \le r \land r \le s \land q \le s) \Rightarrow (b \to_p a \to_q b) \to_\omega b \to_r \mathsf{List}\ a \to_s b$$
$$map : (p \le q) \Rightarrow (a \to_p b) \to_\omega \mathsf{List}\ a \to_q \mathsf{List}\ b$$
$$filter : (a \to_p \mathsf{Bool}) \to_\omega \mathsf{List}\ a \to_\omega \mathsf{List}\ a$$
$$append : \mathsf{List}\ a \to_p \mathsf{List}\ a \to_q \mathsf{List}\ a$$
$$reverse : \mathsf{List}\ a \to_p \mathsf{List}\ a$$
$$concat : \mathsf{List}\ (\mathsf{List}\ a) \to_p \mathsf{List}\ a$$
$$concatMap : (p \le q) \Rightarrow (a \to_p \mathsf{List}\ b) \to_\omega \mathsf{List}\ a \to_q \mathsf{List}\ b$$

Fig. 7. Inferred types for selected functions from `Prelude` (quantifications are omitted)

6.2 Functions from Prelude

We show how our type inference system works for some polymorphic functions from Haskell's `Prelude`. Since we have not implemented type classes and I/O in our prototype implementation and since we can define copying or discarding functions for concrete first-order datatypes, we focus on the unqualified polymorphic functions. Also, we do not consider the functions that are obviously unrestricted, such as *head* and *scanl*, in this examination. In the implementation of the examined functions, we use natural definitions as possible. For example, a linear-time accumulative definition is used for *reverse*. Some functions can be defined by both explicit recursions and *foldr*/*foldl*; among the examined functions, *map*, *filter*, *concat*, and *concatMap* can be defined by *foldr*, and *reverse* can be defined by *foldl*. For such cases, both versions are tested.

Fig. 7 shows the inferred types for the examined functions. Since the inferred types coincide for the two variations (by explicit recursions or by folds) of *map*, *filter*, *append*, *reverse*, *concat*, and *concatMap*, the results do not refer to these variations. Most of the inferred types look unsurprising, considering the fact that the constraint $p \le q$ is yielded usually when an input that corresponds to q is used in an argument that corresponds to p. For example, consider *foldr f e xs*. The constraint $q \le r$ comes from the fact that e (corresponding to r) is passed as the second argument of f (corresponding to q) via a recursive call. The constraint $p \le s$ comes from the fact that the head of *xs* (corresponding to s) is used as the first argument of f (corresponding to p). The constraint $q \le s$ comes from the fact that the tail of *xs* is used in the second argument of f. A little explanation is needed for the constraint $r \le s$ in the type of *foldl*, where both r and s are associated with types with the same polarity. Such constraints usually come from recursive definitions. Consider the definition of *foldl*:

$$foldl = \lambda f.\lambda e.\lambda x.\mathbf{case}\ x\ \mathbf{of}\ \{\mathsf{Nil} \to e; \mathsf{Cons}\ a\ y \to foldl\ f\ (f\ e\ a)\ y\}$$

Here, we find that a, a component of x (corresponding to s), appears in the second argument of *fold* (corresponding to r), which yields the constraint $r \le s$.

Note that the inference results do not contain $\to_1$; recall that there is no problem in using unrestricted inputs linearly, and thus the multiplicity of a linear input can be arbitrary. The results also show that the inference algorithm successfully detected that *append*, *reverse*, and *concat* are linear functions.

It is true that these inferred types indeed leak some internal details into their constraints, but those constraints can be understood only from their extensional behaviors, at least for the examined functions. Thus, we believe that the inferred types are reasonably simple.

6.3 Performance Evaluation

We measured the elapsed time for type checking and the overhead of implication checking and quantifier elimination. The following programs were examined in the experiments: funcs: the functions in Fig. 7, gv: an implementation of a simple

Table 1. Experimental results

Program	LOC	Total Elapsed	SAT Elapsed (#)	QE Elapsed (#)
funcs	40	4.3	0.70 (42)	0.086 (15)
gv	53	3.9	0.091 (9)	0.14 (17)
app1	4	0.34	0.047 (4)	0.012 (2)
app10	4	0.84	0.049 (4)	0.038 (21)

(times are measured in ms)

communication in a session-type system GV [17] taken from [18, Section 4] with some modifications,[6] app1: a pair of the definitions of *app* and *app'*, and app10: a pair of the definitions of *app* and $app10 = \lambda f.\lambda x. \underbrace{app \ldots app}_{10} f \, x$. The former two programs are intended to be miniatures of typical programs. The latter two programs are intended to measure the overhead of quantifier elimination. Although the examined programs are very small, they all involve the ambiguity issues. For example, consider the following fragment of the program gv:

```
answer : Int = fork prf calculator $ \c -> left c & \c ->
               send (MkUn 3) c & \c -> send (MkUn 4) c & \c ->
               recv c & \(MkUn z, c) -> wait c & \() -> MkUn z
```

(Here, we used our paper's syntax instead of that of the actual examined code.) Here, both $ and & are operator versions of *app*, where the arguments are flipped in &. As well as treatment of multiplicities, the disambiguation is crucial for this expression to have type Int.

The experiments were conducted on a MacBook Pro (13-inch, 2017) with Mac OS 10.14.6, 3.5 GHz Intel Core i7 CPU, and 16 GB memory. GHC 8.6.5 with -O2 was used for compiling our prototype system.

Table 1 lists the experimental results. Each elapsed time is the average of 1,000 executions for the first two programs, and 10,000 executions for the last two. All columns are self-explanatory except for the # column, which counts the number of

---

[6] We changed the type of *fork* : Dual $s \, s' \to_\omega$ (Ch $s \to_1$ Ch End) $\to_1$ (Ch $s' \to_1$ Un r) $\to_1 r$, as their type Dual $s \, s' \Rightarrow$ (Ch $s \to_1$ Ch End) $\to_1$ Ch s' is incorrect for the multiplicity erasing semantics. A minor difference is that we used a GADT to witness duality because our prototype implementation does not support type classes.

executions of corresponding procedures. We note that the current implementation restricts Q_w in S-ENTAIL to be $\top$ and removes redundant constraints afterward. This is why the number of SAT solving in app1 is four instead of two. For the artificial programs (app1 and app10), the overhead is not significant; typing cost grows faster than SAT/QE costs. In contrast, the results for the latter two show that SAT becomes heavy for higher-order programs (funcs), and quantifier elimination becomes heavy for combinator-heavy programs (gv), although we believe that the overhead would still be acceptable. We believe that, since we are currently using naive algorithms for both procedures, there is much room to reduce the overhead. For example, if users annotate most general types, the simplification invokes trivial checks $\bigwedge_i \phi_i \models \phi_i$ often. Special treatment for such cases would reduce the overhead.

7   Related Work

Borrowing the terminology from Bernardy et al. [7], there are two approaches to linear typing: linearity via arrows and linearity via kinds. The former approaches manage how many times an assumption (i.e., a variable) can be used; for example, in Wadler [33]'s linear λ calculus, there are two sort of variables: linear and unrestricted, where the latter variables can only be obtained by decomposing let $!x = e_1$ in e_2. Since primitive sources of assumptions are arrow types, it is natural to annotate them with arguments' multiplicities [7,12,22]. For multiplicities, we focused on 1 and ω following Linear Haskell [6,7,26]. Although $\{1,\omega\}$ would already be useful for some domains including reversible computation [19,35] and quantum computation [2,25], handling more general multiplicities, such as $\{0,1,\omega\}$ and arbitrary semirings [12], is an interesting future direction. Our discussions in Sect. 2 and 3, similarly to Linear Haskell [7], could be extended to more general domains with small modifications. In contrast, we rely on the particular domains $\{1,\omega\}$ of multiplicities for the crucial points of our inference, i.e., entailment checking and quantifier elimination. Igarashi and Kobayashi [14]'s linearity analysis for π calculus, which assigns input/output usage (multiplicities) to channels, has similarity to linearity via arrows. Multiplicity 0 is important in their analysis to identify input/output only channels. They solve constraints on multiplicities separately in polynomial time, leveraging monotonicity of multiplicity operators with respect to ordering $0 \le 1 \le \omega$. Here, $0 \le 1$ comes from the fact that 1 in their system means "at-most once" instead of "exactly once".

The "linearity via kinds" approaches distinguish types of which values are treated linearly and types of which values are not [21,24,28], where the distinction usually is represented by kinds [21,28]. Interestingly, they also have two function types—function types that belong to the linear kind and those that belong to the unrestricted kind—because the kind of a function type cannot be determined solely by the argument and return types. Mazurak et al. [21] use subkinding to avoid explicit conversions from unrestricted values to linear ones. However, due to the variations of the function types, a function can have multiple incompatible types; e.g., the function *const* can have four incompatible types [24] in the system.

Universal types accompanied by kind abstraction [28] address the issue to some extent; it works well for *const*, but still gives two incomparable types to the function composition (∘) [24]. Morris [24] addresses this issue of principality with qualified typing [15]. Two forms of predicates are considered in the system: Un τ states that τ belongs to the unrestricted kind, and $\sigma \leq \tau$ states that Un σ implies Un τ. This system is considerably simple compared with the previous systems. Turner et al. [29]'s type-based usage analysis has a similarity to the linearity via kinds; in the system, each type is annotated by usage (a multiplicity) as $(\mathsf{List}\ \mathsf{Int}^\omega)^\omega$. Wansbrough and Peyton Jones [34] extends the system to include polymorphic types and subtyping with respect to multiplicities, and have discussions on multiplicity polymorphism. Mogensen [23] is a similar line of work, which reduces constraint solving on multiplicities to Horn SAT. His system concerns multiplicities $\{0, 1, \omega\}$ with ordering $0 \leq 1 \leq \omega$, and his constraints can involve more operations including additions and multiplications but only in the left-hand side of $\leq$.

Morris [24] uses improving substitutions [16] in generalization, which sometimes are effective for removing ambiguity, though without showing concrete algorithms to find them. In our system, as well as S-EQ, $\mathsf{elim}(\exists \pi.Q)$ can be viewed as a systematic way to find improving substitutions. That is, $\mathsf{elim}(\exists \pi.Q)$ improves Q by substituting π with $\min\{M_i \mid \omega \leq M_i \in \Phi_\omega\}$, i.e., the largest possible candidate of π. Though the largest solution is usually undesirable, especially when the right-hand sides of $\leq$ are all singletons, we can also view that $\mathsf{elim}(\exists \pi.Q)$ substitutes π by $\prod_{\mu_i \leq 1 \in \Phi_1} \mu_i$, i.e., the smallest possible candidate.

8   Conclusion

We designed a type inference system for a rank 1 fragment of $\lambda_\rightarrow^q$ [7] that can infer principal types based on the qualified typing system OUTSIDEIN(X) [31]. We observed that naive qualified typing infers ambiguous types often and addressed the issue based on quantifier elimination. The experiments suggested that the proposed inference system infers principal types effectively, and the overhead compared with unrestricted typing is acceptable, though not negligible.

Since we based our work on the inference algorithm used in GHC, the natural expectation is to implement the system into GHC. A technical challenge to achieve this is combining the disambiguation techniques with other sorts of constraints, especially type classes, and arbitrarily ranked polymorphism.

Acknowledgments

We thank Meng Wang, Atsushi Igarashi, and the anonymous reviewers of ESOP 2020 for their helpful comments on the preliminary versions of this paper. This work was partially supported by JSPS KAKENHI Grant Numbers 15H02681 and 19K11892, JSPS Bilateral Program, Grant Number JPJSBP120199913, the Kayamori Foundation of Informational Science Advancement, and EPSRC Grant *EXHIBIT: Expressive High-Level Languages for Bidirectional Transformations* (EP/T008911/1).

References

1. Aehlig, K., Berger, U., Hofmann, M., Schwichtenberg, H.: An arithmetic for non-size-increasing polynomial-time computation. Theor. Comput. Sci. **318**(1-2), 3–27 (2004). https://doi.org/10.1016/j.tcs.2003.10.023

2. Altenkirch, T., Grattage, J.: A functional quantum programming language. In: 20th IEEE Symposium on Logic in Computer Science (LICS 2005), 26-29 June 2005, Chicago, IL, USA, Proceedings. pp. 249–258. IEEE Computer Society (2005). https://doi.org/10.1109/LICS.2005.1

3. Baillot, P., Hofmann, M.: Type inference in intuitionistic linear logic. In: Kutsia, T., Schreiner, W., Fernández, M. (eds.) Proceedings of the 12th International ACM SIGPLAN Conference on Principles and Practice of Declarative Programming, July 26-28, 2010, Hagenberg, Austria. pp. 219–230. ACM (2010). https://doi.org/10.1145/1836089.1836118

4. Baillot, P., Terui, K.: A feasible algorithm for typing in elementary affine logic. In: Urzyczyn, P. (ed.) Typed Lambda Calculi and Applications, 7th International Conference, TLCA 2005, Nara, Japan, April 21-23, 2005, Proceedings. Lecture Notes in Computer Science, vol. 3461, pp. 55–70. Springer (2005). https://doi.org/10.1007/11417170_6

5. Baillot, P., Terui, K.: Light types for polynomial time computation in lambda calculus. Inf. Comput. **207**(1), 41–62 (2009). https://doi.org/10.1016/j.ic.2008.08.005

6. Bernardy, J.P., Boespflug, M., Newton, R., Jones, S.P., Spiwack, A.: Linear minicore. GHC Developpers Wiki, https://gitlab.haskell.org/ghc/ghc/wikis/uploads/ceaedb9ec409555c80ae5a97cc47470e/minicore.pdf, visited Oct. 14, 2019.

7. Bernardy, J., Boespflug, M., Newton, R.R., Peyton Jones, S., Spiwack, A.: Linear haskell: practical linearity in a higher-order polymorphic language. PACMPL **2**(POPL), 5:1–5:29 (2018). https://doi.org/10.1145/3158093

8. Davis, M., Logemann, G., Loveland, D.W.: A machine program for theorem-proving. Commun. ACM **5**(7), 394–397 (1962). https://doi.org/10.1145/368273.368557

9. Davis, M., Putnam, H.: A computing procedure for quantification theory. J. ACM **7**(3), 201–215 (1960). https://doi.org/10.1145/321033.321034

10. Dowling, W.F., Gallier, J.H.: Linear-time algorithms for testing the satisfiability of propositional horn formulae. J. Log. Program. **1**(3), 267–284 (1984). https://doi.org/10.1016/0743-1066(84)90014-1

11. Gan, E., Tov, J.A., Morrisett, G.: Type classes for lightweight substructural types. In: Alves, S., Cervesato, I. (eds.) Proceedings Third International Workshop on Linearity, LINEARITY 2014, Vienna, Austria, 13th July, 2014. EPTCS, vol. 176, pp. 34–48 (2014). https://doi.org/10.4204/EPTCS.176.4

12. Ghica, D.R., Smith, A.I.: Bounded linear types in a resource semiring. In: Shao, Z. (ed.) Programming Languages and Systems - 23rd European Symposium on Programming, ESOP 2014, Held as Part of the European Joint Conferences on Theory and Practice of Software, ETAPS 2014, Grenoble, France, April 5-13, 2014, Proceedings. Lecture Notes in Computer Science, vol. 8410, pp. 331–350. Springer (2014). https://doi.org/10.1007/978-3-642-54833-8_18

13. Girard, J., Scedrov, A., Scott, P.J.: Bounded linear logic: A modular approach to polynomial-time computability. Theor. Comput. Sci. **97**(1), 1–66 (1992). https://doi.org/10.1016/0304-3975(92)90386-T

14. Igarashi, A., Kobayashi, N.: Type reconstruction for linear -calculus with I/O subtyping. Inf. Comput. **161**(1), 1–44 (2000). https://doi.org/10.1006/inco.2000.2872

15. Jones, M.P.: Qualified Types: Theory and Practice. Cambridge University Press, New York, NY, USA (1995)

16. Jones, M.P.: Simplifying and improving qualified types. In: Williams, J. (ed.) Proceedings of the seventh international conference on Functional programming languages and computer architecture, FPCA 1995, La Jolla, California, USA, June 25-28, 1995. pp. 160–169. ACM (1995). https://doi.org/10.1145/224164.224198

17. Lindley, S., Morris, J.G.: A semantics for propositions as sessions. In: Vitek, J. (ed.) Programming Languages and Systems - 24th European Symposium on Programming, ESOP 2015, Held as Part of the European Joint Conferences on Theory and Practice of Software, ETAPS 2015, London, UK, April 11-18, 2015. Proceedings. Lecture Notes in Computer Science, vol. 9032, pp. 560–584. Springer (2015). https://doi.org/10.1007/978-3-662-46669-8_23

18. Lindley, S., Morris, J.G.: Embedding session types in haskell. In: Mainland, G. (ed.) Proceedings of the 9th International Symposium on Haskell, Haskell 2016, Nara, Japan, September 22-23, 2016. pp. 133–145. ACM (2016). https://doi.org/10.1145/2976002.2976018

19. Lutz, C.: Janus: a time-reversible language. *Letter to R. Landauer.* (1986), available on: http://tetsuo.jp/ref/janus.pdf

20. Matsuda, K.: Modular inference of linear types for multiplicity-annotated arrows (2020), http://arxiv.org/abs/1911.00268v2

21. Mazurak, K., Zhao, J., Zdancewic, S.: Lightweight linear types in system fdegree. In: TLDI. pp. 77–88. ACM (2010)

22. McBride, C.: I got plenty o' nuttin'. In: Lindley, S., McBride, C., Trinder, P.W., Sannella, D. (eds.) A List of Successes That Can Change the World - Essays Dedicated to Philip Wadler on the Occasion of His 60th Birthday. Lecture Notes in Computer Science, vol. 9600, pp. 207–233. Springer (2016). https://doi.org/10.1007/978-3-319-30936-1_12

23. Mogensen, T.Æ.: Types for 0, 1 or many uses. In: Clack, C., Hammond, K., Davie, A.J.T. (eds.) Implementation of Functional Languages, 9th International Workshop, IFL'97, St. Andrews, Scotland, UK, September 10-12, 1997, Selected Papers. Lecture Notes in Computer Science, vol. 1467, pp. 112–122. Springer (1997). https://doi.org/10.1007/BFb0055427

24. Morris, J.G.: The best of both worlds: linear functional programming without compromise. In: Garrigue, J., Keller, G., Sumii, E. (eds.) Proceedings of the 21st ACM SIGPLAN International Conference on Functional Programming, ICFP 2016, Nara, Japan, September 18-22, 2016. pp. 448–461. ACM (2016). https://doi.org/10.1145/2951913.2951925

25. Selinger, P., Valiron, B.: A lambda calculus for quantum computation with classical control. Mathematical Structures in Computer Science **16**(3), 527–552 (2006). https://doi.org/10.1017/S0960129506005238

26. Spiwack, A., Domínguez, F., Boespflug, M., Bernardy, J.P.: Linear types. GHC Proposals, https://github.com/tweag/ghc-proposals/blob/linear-types2/proposals/0000-linear-types.rst, visited Sep. 11, 2019.

27. Stuckey, P.J., Sulzmann, M.: A theory of overloading. ACM Trans. Program. Lang. Syst. **27**(6), 1216–1269 (2005). https://doi.org/10.1145/1108970.1108974

28. Tov, J.A., Pucella, R.: Practical affine types. In: Ball, T., Sagiv, M. (eds.) Proceedings of the 38th ACM SIGPLAN-SIGACT Symposium on Principles of Programming Languages, POPL 2011, Austin, TX, USA, January 26-28, 2011. pp. 447–458. ACM (2011). https://doi.org/10.1145/1926385.1926436

29. Turner, D.N., Wadler, P., Mossin, C.: Once upon a type. In: Williams, J. (ed.) Proceedings of the seventh international conference on Functional programming languages and computer architecture, FPCA 1995, La Jolla, California, USA, June 25-28, 1995. pp. 1–11. ACM (1995). https://doi.org/10.1145/224164.224168
30. Vytiniotis, D., Peyton Jones, S.L., Schrijvers, T.: Let should not be generalized. In: Kennedy, A., Benton, N. (eds.) Proceedings of TLDI 2010: 2010 ACM SIGPLAN International Workshop on Types in Languages Design and Implementation, Madrid, Spain, January 23, 2010. pp. 39–50. ACM (2010). https://doi.org/10.1145/1708016.1708023
31. Vytiniotis, D., Peyton Jones, S.L., Schrijvers, T., Sulzmann, M.: Outsidein(x) modular type inference with local assumptions. J. Funct. Program. **21**(4-5), 333–412 (2011). https://doi.org/10.1017/S0956796811000098
32. Wadler, P.: Linear types can change the world! In: Broy, M. (ed.) Programming concepts and methods: Proceedings of the IFIP Working Group 2.2, 2.3 Working Conference on Programming Concepts and Methods, Sea of Galilee, Israel, 2-5 April, 1990. p. 561. North-Holland (1990)
33. Wadler, P.: A taste of linear logic. In: Borzyszkowski, A.M., Sokolowski, S. (eds.) Mathematical Foundations of Computer Science 1993, 18th International Symposium, MFCS'93, Gdansk, Poland, August 30 - September 3, 1993, Proceedings. Lecture Notes in Computer Science, vol. 711, pp. 185–210. Springer (1993). https://doi.org/10.1007/3-540-57182-5_12
34. Wansbrough, K., Peyton Jones, S.L.: Once upon a polymorphic type. In: Appel, A.W., Aiken, A. (eds.) POPL '99, Proceedings of the 26th ACM SIGPLAN-SIGACT Symposium on Principles of Programming Languages, San Antonio, TX, USA, January 20-22, 1999. pp. 15–28. ACM (1999). https://doi.org/10.1145/292540.292545
35. Yokoyama, T., Axelsen, H.B., Glück, R.: Towards a reversible functional language. In: Vos, A.D., Wille, R. (eds.) RC. Lecture Notes in Computer Science, vol. 7165, pp. 14–29. Springer (2011). https://doi.org/10.1007/978-3-642-29517-1_2

RustHorn: CHC-based Verification for Rust Programs*

Yusuke Matsushita[1], Takeshi Tsukada[1], and Naoki Kobayashi[1]

The University of Tokyo, Tokyo, Japan
{yskm24t,tsukada,koba}@is.s.u-tokyo.ac.jp

Abstract. Reduction to the satisfiablility problem for constrained Horn clauses (CHCs) is a widely studied approach to automated program verification. The current CHC-based methods for pointer-manipulating programs, however, are not very scalable. This paper proposes a novel translation of pointer-manipulating Rust programs into CHCs, which clears away pointers and heaps by leveraging ownership. We formalize the translation for a simplified core of Rust and prove its correctness. We have implemented a prototype verifier for a subset of Rust and confirmed the effectiveness of our method.

1 Introduction

Reduction to *constrained Horn clauses (CHCs)* is a widely studied approach to automated program verification [22,6]. A CHC is a Horn clause [30] equipped with constraints, namely a formula of the form $\varphi \Longleftarrow \psi_0 \wedge \cdots \wedge \psi_{k-1}$, where φ and $\psi_0, \ldots, \psi_{k-1}$ are either an atomic formula of the form $f(t_0, \ldots, t_{n-1})$ (f is a *predicate variable* and $t_0, \ldots, t_{n-1}$ are terms), or a constraint (e.g. $a < b+1$).[1] We call a finite set of CHCs a *CHC system* or sometimes just CHC. *CHC solving* is an act of deciding whether a given CHC system S has a *model*, i.e. a valuation for predicate variables that makes all the CHCs in S valid. A variety of program verification problems can be naturally reduced to CHC solving.

For example, let us consider the following C code that defines McCarthy's 91 function.

```
int mc91(int n) {
    if (n > 100) return n - 10; else return mc91(mc91(n + 11));
}
```

Suppose that we wish to prove $\mathtt{mc91}(n)$ returns 91 whenever $n \leq 101$ (if it terminates). The wished property is equivalent to the satisfiability of the following CHCs, where $Mc91(n,r)$ means that $\mathtt{mc91}(n)$ returns r if it terminates.

$$Mc91(n,r) \Longleftarrow n > 100 \wedge r = n - 10$$

---

* The full version of this paper is available as [47].
[1] Free variables are universally quantified. Terms and variables are governed under sorts (e.g. int, bool), which are made explicit in the formalization of §3.

© The Author(s) 2020
P. Müller (Ed.): ESOP 2020, LNCS 12075, pp. 484–514, 2020.
https://doi.org/10.1007/978-3-030-44914-8_18

$$Mc91(n, r) \Longleftarrow n \le 100 \land Mc91(n + 11, res') \land Mc91(res', r)$$
$$r = 91 \Longleftarrow n \le 101 \land Mc91(n, r)$$

The property can be verified because this CHC system has a model:

$$Mc91(n, r) :\Longleftrightarrow r = 91 \lor (n > 100 \land r = n - 10).$$

A CHC solver provides a common infrastructure for a variety of programming languages and properties to be verified. There have been effective CHC solvers [40,18,29,12] that can solve instances obtained from actual programs[2] and many program verification tools [23,37,25,28,38,60] use a CHC solver as a backend.

However, the current CHC-based methods do not scale very well for programs using *pointers*, as we see in § 1.1. We propose a novel method to tackle this problem for pointer-manipulating programs under *Rust-style ownership*, as we explain in § 1.2.

1.1   Challenges in Verifying Pointer-Manipulating Programs

The standard CHC-based approach [23] for pointer-manipulating programs represents the memory state as an *array*, which is passed around as an argument of each predicate (cf. the *store-passing style*), and a pointer as an index.

For example, a pointer-manipulating variation of the previous program

```
void mc91p(int n, int* r) {
    if (n > 100) *r = n - 10;
    else { int s; mc91p(n + 11, &s); mc91p(s, r); }
}
```

is translated into the following CHCs by the array-based approach:[3]

$$Mc91p(n, r, h, h') \Longleftarrow n > 100 \land h' = h\{r \leftarrow n - 10\}$$
$$Mc91p(n, r, h, h') \Longleftarrow n \le 100 \land Mc91p(n + 11, s, h, h'')$$
$$\land Mc91p(h''[s], r, h'', h')$$
$$h'[r] = 91 \Longleftarrow n \le 101 \land Mc91p(n, r, h, h').$$

Mc91p additionally takes two arrays h, h' representing the (heap) memory states before/after the call of mc91p. The second argument r of *Mc91p*, which corresponds to the pointer argument r in the original program, is an index for the arrays. Hence, the assignment *r = n - 10 is modeled in the first CHC as an update of the r-th element of the array. This CHC system has a model

$$Mc91p(n, r, h, h') :\Longleftrightarrow h'[r] = 91 \lor (n > 100 \land h'[r] = n - 10),$$

which can be found by some array-supporting CHC solvers including Spacer [40], thanks to evolving SMT-solving techniques for arrays [62,10].

However, the array-based approach has some shortcomings. Let us consider, for example, the following innocent-looking code.[4]

---

[2] For example, the above CHC system on *Mc91* can be solved instantly by many CHC solvers including Spacer [40] and HoIce [12].

[3] $h\{r \leftarrow v\}$ is the array made from h by replacing the value at index r with v. $h[r]$ is the value of array h at index r.

[4] rand() is a non-deterministic function that can return any integer value.

```
bool just_rec(int* ma) {
    if (rand() >= 0) return true;
    int old_a = *ma; int b = rand(); just_rec(&b);
    return (old_a == *ma);
}
```

It can immediately return `true`; or it recursively calls itself and checks if the target of `ma` remains unchanged through the recursive call. In effect this function *does nothing* on the allocated memory blocks, although it can possibly modify some of the unused parts of the memory.

Suppose we wish to verify that `just_rec` never returns `false`. The standard CHC-based verifier for C, SeaHorn [23], generates a CHC system like below:[5][6]

$$JustRec(ma, h, h', r) \Longleftarrow h' = h \land r = \mathsf{true}$$
$$JustRec(ma, h, h', r) \Longleftarrow mb \neq ma \land h'' = h\{mb \leftarrow b\}$$
$$\land \; JustRec(mb, h'', h', r') \land r = (h[ma] == h'[ma])$$
$$r = \mathsf{true} \Longleftarrow JustRec(ma, h, h', r)$$

Unfortunately the CHC system above is *not* satisfiable and thus SeaHorn issues a false alarm. This is because, in this formulation, mb may not necessarily be completely fresh; it is assumed to be different from the argument ma of the current call, but may coincide with ma of some deep ancestor calls.[7]

The simplest remedy would be to explicitly specify the way of memory allocation. For example, one can represent the memory state as a pair of an array h and an index sp indicating the maximum index that has been allocated so far.

$$JustRec_+(ma, h, sp, h', sp', r) \Longleftarrow h' = h \land sp' = sp \land r = \mathsf{true}$$
$$JustRec_+(ma, h, sp, h', sp', r) \Longleftarrow mb = sp'' = sp + 1 \land h'' = h\{mb \leftarrow b\}$$
$$JustRec_+(mb, h'', sp'', h', sp', r') \land r = (h[ma] == h'[ma])$$
$$r = \mathsf{true} \Longleftarrow JustRec_+(ma, h, sp, h', sp', r) \land ma \leq sp$$

The resulting CHC system now has a model, but it involves quantifiers:

$$JustRec_+(ma, h, sp, h', sp', r) :\Longleftrightarrow r = \mathsf{true} \land \forall i \leq sp. \, h[i] = h'[i]$$

Finding quantified invariants is known to be difficult in general despite active studies on it [41,2,36,26,19] and most current array-supporting CHC solvers give up finding quantified invariants. In general, much more complex operations on pointers can naturally take place, which makes the universally quantified invariants highly involved and hard to automatically find. To avoid complexity of models, CHC-based verification tools [23,24,37] tackle pointers by pointer analysis [61,43]. Although it does have some effects, the current applicable scope of pointer analysis is quite limited.

---

[5] $==, !=, >=, \&\&$ denote binary operations that return boolean values.

[6] We omitted the allocation for `old_a` for simplicity.

[7] Precisely speaking, SeaHorn tends to even omit shallow address-freshness checks like $mb \neq ma$.

1.2   Our Approach: Leverage Rust's Ownership System

This paper proposes a novel approach to CHC-based verification of pointer-manipulating programs, which makes use of *ownership* information to avoid an explicit representation of the memory.

Rust-style Ownership. Various styles of *ownership/permission/capability* have been introduced to control and reason about usage of pointers on programming language design, program analysis and verification [13,31,8,31,9,7,64,63]. In what follows, we focus on the ownership in the style of the Rust programming language [46,55].

Roughly speaking, the ownership system guarantees that, for each memory cell and at each point of program execution, either (i) only one alias has the *update* (write & read) permission to the cell, with any other alias having *no* permission to it, or (ii) some (or no) aliases have the *read* permission to the cell, with no alias having the update permission to it. In summary, *when an alias can read some data* (with an update/read permission), *any other alias cannot modify the data.*

As a running example, let us consider the program below, which follows Rust's ownership discipline (it is written in the C style; the Rust version is presented at Example 1):

```
int* take_max(int* ma, int* mb) {
    if (*ma >= *mb) return ma; else return mb;
}
bool inc_max(int a, int b) {
    {
        int* mc = take_max(&a, &b);    // borrow a and b
        *mc += 1;
    }                                  // end of borrow
    return (a != b);
}
```

Figure 1 illustrates which alias has the update permission to the contents of a and b during the execution of `take_max(5,3)`.

A notable feature is *borrow*. In the running example, when the pointers &a and &b are taken for `take_max`, the *update permissions* of a and b are *temporarily transferred* to the pointers. The original variables, a and b, *lose the ability to access their contents* until the end of borrow. The function `take_max` returns a pointer having the update permission until the end of borrow, which justifies the *update operation* `*mc += 1`. In this example, the end of borrow is at the end of the inner block of `inc_max`. At this point, *the permissions are given back* to the original variables a and b, allowing to compute a `!=` b. Note that mc can point to a and also to b and that this choice is determined *dynamically*. The values of a and b after the borrow *depend on the behavior of the pointer* mc.

The end of each borrow is statically managed by a *lifetime*. See §2 for a more precise explanation of ownership, borrow and lifetimes.

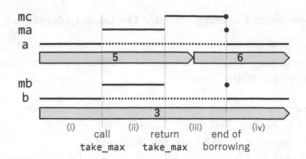

Fig. 1. Values and aliases of a and b in evaluating `inc_max(5,3)`. Each line shows each variable's permission timeline: a solid line expresses the update permission and a bullet shows a point when the borrowed permission is given back. For example, `b` has the update permission to its content during (i) and (iv), but not during (ii) and (iii) because the pointer `mb`, created at the call of `take_max`, *borrows* `b` until the end of (iii).

Key Idea. The key idea of our method is to *represent a pointer* `ma` *as a pair* $\langle a, a_\circ \rangle$ *of the current target value* a *and the target value* $a_\circ$ *at the end of borrow.*[8][9] This representation employs *access to the future information* (it is related to *prophecy variables*; see § 5). This simple idea turns out to be very powerful.

In our approach, the verification problem "Does `inc_max` always return `true`?" is reduced to the satisfiability of the following CHCs:

$$TakeMax(\langle a, a_\circ \rangle, \langle b, b_\circ \rangle, r) \impliedby a \geq b \wedge b_\circ = b \wedge r = \langle a, a_\circ \rangle$$
$$TakeMax(\langle a, a_\circ \rangle, \langle b, b_\circ \rangle, r) \impliedby a < b \wedge a_\circ = a \wedge r = \langle b, b_\circ \rangle$$
$$IncMax(a, b, r) \impliedby TakeMax(\langle a, a_\circ \rangle, \langle b, b_\circ \rangle, \langle c, c_\circ \rangle) \wedge c' = c + 1$$
$$\wedge \; c_\circ = c' \wedge r = (a_\circ \mathrel{!=} b_\circ)$$
$$r = \mathsf{true} \impliedby IncMax(a, b, r).$$

The mutable reference `ma` is now represented as $\langle a, a_\circ \rangle$, and similarly for `mb` and `mc`. The first CHC models the then-clause of `take_max`: the return value is `ma`, which is expressed as $r = \langle a, a_\circ \rangle$; in contrast, `mb` is released, which *constrains* $b_\circ$, the value of `b` at the end of borrow, to the current value b. In the clause on `IncMax`, `mc` is represented as a pair $\langle c, c_\circ \rangle$. The constraint $c' = c + 1 \wedge c_\circ = c'$ models the increment of `mc` (in the phase (iii) in Fig. 1). Importantly, the final check `a != b` is simply expressed as $a_\circ \mathrel{!=} b_\circ$; the updated values of `a`/`b` are available as $a_\circ/b_\circ$. Clearly, the CHC system above has a simple model.

Also, the `just_rec` example in § 1.1 can be encoded as a CHC system

$$JustRec(\langle a, a_\circ \rangle, r) \impliedby a_\circ = a \wedge r = \mathsf{true}$$
$$JustRec(\langle a, a_\circ \rangle, r) \impliedby mb = \langle b, b_\circ \rangle \wedge JustRec(mb, r')$$
$$\wedge \; a_\circ = a \wedge r = (a == a_0)$$

---

[8] Precisely, this is the representation of a pointer with a borrowed update permission (i.e. *mutable reference*). Other cases are discussed in § 3.

[9] For example, in the case of Fig. 1, when `take_max` is called, the pointer `ma` is $\langle 5, 6 \rangle$ and `mb` is $\langle 3, 3 \rangle$.

$$r = \mathsf{true} \impliedby \mathit{JustRec}(\langle a, a_\circ\rangle, r).$$

Now it has a simple model: $\mathit{JustRec}(\langle a, a_\circ\rangle, r) :\iff r = \mathsf{true} \wedge a_\circ = a$. Remarkably, arrays and quantified formulas are not required to express the model, which allows the CHC system to be easily solved by many CHC solvers. More advanced examples are presented in §3.4, including one with destructive update on a singly-linked list.

Contributions. Based on the above idea, we formalize the translation from programs to CHC systems for a core language of Rust, prove correctness (both soundness and completeness) of the translation, and confirm the effectiveness of our approach through preliminary experiments. The core language supports, among others, recursive types. Remarkably, our approach enables us to automatically verify some properties of a program with destructive updates on recursive data types such as lists and trees.

The rest of the paper is structured as follows. In §2, we provide a formalized core language of Rust supporting recursions, lifetime-based ownership and recursive types. In §3, we formalize our translation from programs to CHCs and prove its correctness. In §4, we report on the implementation and the experimental results. In §5 we discuss related work and in §6 we conclude the paper.

2   Core Language: Calculus of Ownership and Reference

We formalize a core of Rust as *Calculus of Ownership and Reference (COR)*, whose design has been affected by the safe layer of λ_{Rust} in the RustBelt paper [32]. It is a typed procedural language with a Rust-like ownership system.

2.1   Syntax

The following is the syntax of COR.

$$
\begin{aligned}
\text{(program)} \ \Pi &::= F_0 \cdots F_{n-1} \\
\text{(function definition)} \ F &::= \mathsf{fn}\ f\ \Sigma\ \{L_0\colon S_0\ \cdots\ L_{n-1}\colon S_{n-1}\} \\
\text{(function signature)} \ \Sigma &::= \langle \alpha_0, \ldots, \alpha_{m-1} \mid \alpha_{a_0} \leq \alpha_{b_0}, \ldots, \alpha_{a_{l-1}} \leq \alpha_{b_{l-1}}\rangle \\
& \quad\ (x_0\colon T_0, \ldots, x_{n-1}\colon T_{n-1}) \to U \\
\text{(statement)} \ S &::= I;\ \mathsf{goto}\ L \mid \mathsf{return}\ x \\
& \quad\ \mid\ \mathsf{match}\ {*}x\ \{\mathsf{inj}_0{*}y_0 \to \mathsf{goto}\ L_0,\ \mathsf{inj}_1{*}y_1 \to \mathsf{goto}\ L_1\} \\
\text{(instruction)} \ I &::= \mathsf{let}\ y = \mathsf{mutbor}_\alpha\ x \mid \mathsf{drop}\ x \mid \mathsf{immut}\ x \mid \mathsf{swap}({*}x, {*}y) \\
& \quad\ \mid\ \mathsf{let}\ {*}y = x \mid \mathsf{let}\ y = {*}x \mid \mathsf{let}\ {*}y = \mathsf{copy}\ {*}x \mid x\ \mathsf{as}\ T \\
& \quad\ \mid\ \mathsf{let}\ y = f\langle \alpha_0, \ldots, \alpha_{m-1}\rangle(x_0, \ldots, x_{n-1}) \\
& \quad\ \mid\ \mathsf{intro}\ \alpha \mid \mathsf{now}\ \alpha \mid \alpha \leq \beta \\
& \quad\ \mid\ \mathsf{let}\ {*}y = \mathit{const} \mid \mathsf{let}\ {*}y = {*}x\ op\ {*}x' \mid \mathsf{let}\ {*}y = \mathsf{rand}() \\
& \quad\ \mid\ \mathsf{let}\ {*}y = \mathsf{inj}_i^{T_0+T_1}\ {*}x \mid \mathsf{let}\ {*}y = ({*}x_0, {*}x_1) \mid \mathsf{let}\ ({*}y_0, {*}y_1) = {*}x \\
\text{(type)} \ T, U &::= X \mid \mu X.T \mid P\,T \mid T_0{+}T_1 \mid T_0{\times}T_1 \mid \mathsf{int} \mid \mathsf{unit} \\
\text{(pointer kind)} \ P &::= \mathsf{own} \mid R_\alpha \quad \text{(reference kind)} \ R ::= \mathsf{mut} \mid \mathsf{immut}
\end{aligned}
$$

$$\alpha, \beta, \gamma ::= \text{(lifetime variable)} \quad X, Y ::= \text{(type variable)}$$
$$x, y ::= \text{(variable)} \quad f, g ::= \text{(function name)} \quad L ::= \text{(label)}$$
$$const ::= n \mid () \quad \text{bool} := \text{unit} + \text{unit} \quad op ::= op_{\text{int}} \mid op_{\text{bool}}$$
$$op_{\text{int}} ::= + \mid - \mid \cdots \quad op_{\text{bool}} ::= \mathord{>=} \mid \mathord{==} \mid \mathord{!=} \mid \cdots$$

Program, Function and Label. A program (denoted by Π) is a set of function definitions. A function definition (F) consists of a function name, a function signature and a set of labeled statements ($L\colon S$). In COR, for simplicity, the input/output types of a function are restricted to *pointer types*. A function is parametrized over lifetime parameters under constraints; polymorphism on types is not supported for simplicity, just as λ_{Rust}. For the lifetime parameter receiver, often $\langle \alpha_0, \cdots \mid \rangle$ is abbreviated to $\langle \alpha_0, \ldots \rangle$ and $\langle \mid \rangle$ is omitted.

A label (L) is an abstract program point to be jumped to by goto.[10] Each label is assigned a *whole context* by the type system, as we see later. This style, with unstructured control flows, helps the formal description of CHCs in §3.2. A function should have the label entry (entry point), and every label in a function should be syntactically reachable from entry by goto jumps.[11]

Statement and Instruction. A statement (S) performs an instruction with a jump (I; goto L), returns from a function (return x), or branches (match $*x \{\cdots\}$).

An instruction (I) performs an elementary operation: mutable (re)borrow (let $y = \text{mutbor}_\alpha\, x$), releasing a variable (drop x), weakening ownership (immut x),[12] swap (swap($*x, *y$)), creating/dereferencing a pointer (let $*y = x$, let $y = *x$), copy (let $*y = \text{copy}\, *x$),[13] type weakening (x as T), function call (let $y = f\langle \cdots \rangle(\cdots)$), lifetime-related ghost operations (intro α, now α, $\alpha \leq \beta$; explained later), getting a constant / operation result / random integer (let $*y = const$ / $*x\, op\, *x'$ / rand()), creating a variant (let $*y = \text{inj}_i^{T_0 + T_1}\, *x$), and creating/destructing a pair (let $*y = (*x_0, *x_1)$, let $(*y_0, *y_1) = *x$). An instruction of form let $*y = \cdots$ implicitly allocates new memory cells as y; also, some instructions deallocate memory cells implicitly. For simplicity, every variable is designed to be a *pointer* and every *release of a variable* should be explicitly annotated by 'drop x'. In addition, we provide swap instead of assignment; the usual assignment (of copyable data from $*x$ to $*y$) can be expressed by let $*x' = \text{copy}\, *x$; swap($*y, *x'$); drop x'.

Type. As a type (T), we support recursive types ($\mu X.T$), pointer types (PT), variant types ($T_0 + T_1$), pair types ($T_0 \times T_1$) and basic types (int, unit).

A pointer type PT can be an *owning pointer* own T (Box<T> in Rust), *mutable reference* mut$_\alpha T$ (&'a mut T) or *immutable reference* immut$_\alpha T$ (&'a T). An

---

[10] It is related to a *continuation* introduced by letcont in λ_{Rust}.

[11] Here 'syntactically' means that detailed information such that a branch condition on match or non-termination is ignored.

[12] This instruction turns a mutable reference to an immutable reference. Using this, an immutable borrow from x to y can be expressed by let $y = \text{mutbor}_\alpha\, x$; immut y.

[13] Copying a pointer (an immutable reference) x to y can be expressed by let $*ox = x$; let $*oy = \text{copy}\, *ox$; let $y = *oy$.

owning pointer has data in the heap memory, can freely update the data (unless it is borrowed), and has the obligation to clean up the data from the heap memory. In contrast, a *mutable/immutable reference* (or *unique/shared reference*) borrows an update/read permission from an owning pointer or another reference with the deadline of a *lifetime* α (introduced later). A mutable reference cannot be copied, while an immutable reference can be freely copied. A reference loses the permission at the time when it is released.[14]

A type T that appears in a program (not just as a substructure of some type) should satisfy the following condition (if it holds we say the type is *complete*): every type variable X in T is bound by some μ and guarded by a pointer constructor (i.e. given a binding of form $\mu X.U$, every occurrence of X in U is a part of a pointer type, of form $P U'$).

Lifetime. A *lifetime* is an *abstract time point in the process of computation*,[15] which is statically managed by *lifetime variables* α. A lifetime variable can be a *lifetime parameter* that a function takes or a *local lifetime variable* introduced within a function. We have three lifetime-related ghost instructions: intro α introduces a new local lifetime variable, now α sets a local lifetime variable to the current moment and eliminates it, and $\alpha \leq \beta$ asserts the ordering on local lifetime variables.

Expressivity and Limitations. COR can express most borrow patterns in the core of Rust. The set of moments when a borrow is active forms a continuous time range, even under *non-lexical lifetimes* [54].[16]

A major limitation of COR is that it does not support *unsafe code blocks* and also lacks *type traits and closures*. Still, our idea can be combined with unsafe code and closures, as discussed in §3.5. Another limitation of COR is that, unlike Rust and λ_{Rust}, we *cannot directly modify/borrow a fragment of a variable* (e.g. an element of a pair). Still, we can eventually modify/borrow a fragment by borrowing the whole variable and *splitting pointers* (e.g. 'let $(*y_0, *y_1) = *x$'). This borrow-and-split strategy, nevertheless, yields a subtle obstacle when we extend the calculus for advanced data types (e.g. `get_default` in 'Problem Case #3' from [54]). For future work, we pursue a more expressive calculus modeling Rust and extend our verification method to it.

Example 1 (COR Program). The following program expresses the functions `take_max` and `inc_max` presented in §1.2. We shorthand sequential executions

---

[14] In Rust, even after a reference loses the permission and the lifetime ends, its address data can linger in the memory, although dereferencing on the reference is no longer allowed. We simplify the behavior of lifetimes in COR.

[15] In the terminology of Rust, a lifetime often means a time range where a borrow is active. To simplify the discussions, however, we in this paper use the term lifetime to refer to a *time point when a borrow ends*.

[16] Strictly speaking, this property is broken by recently adopted implicit two-phase borrows [59,53]. However, by shallow syntactical reordering, a program with implicit two-phase borrows can be fit into usual borrow patterns.

by '$;^L$' (e.g. $L_0\colon I_0;^{L_1} I_1;$ goto L_2 stands for $L_0\colon I_0;$ goto L_1 $L_1\colon I_1;$ goto L_2).[17]

```
fn take-max ⟨α⟩ (ma: mutα int, mb: mutα int) → mutα int {
    entry: let *ord = *ma >= *mb;^L1 match *ord {inj1 *ou → goto L2,  inj0 *ou → goto L5}
    L2: drop ou;^L3 drop mb;^L4 return ma    L5: drop ou;^L6 drop ma;^L7 return mb
}
fn inc-max(oa: own int, ob: own int) → own bool {
    entry: intro α;^L1 let ma = mutborα oa;^L2 let mb = mutborα ob;^L3
    let mc = take-max⟨α⟩(ma, mb);^L4 let *o1 = 1;^L5 let *oc' = *mc + *o1;^L6 drop o1;^L7
    swap(mc, oc');^L8 drop oc';^L9 drop mc;^L10 now α;^L11 let *or = *oa != *ob;^L12
    drop oa;^L13 drop ob;^L14 return or
}
```

In take-max, conditional branching is performed by match and its goto directions (at L1). In inc-max, increment on the mutable reference mc is performed by calculating the new value (at L4, L5) and updating the data by swap (at L7).

The following is the corresponding Rust program, with ghost annotations (marked italic and dark green, e.g. *drop ma*) on lifetimes and releases of mutable references.

```
fn take_max<'a>(ma: &'a mut i32, mb: &'a mut i32) -> &'a mut i32 {
    if *ma >= *mb { drop mb; ma } else { drop ma; mb }
}
fn inc_max(mut a: i32, mut b: i32) -> bool {
    { intro 'a;
        let mc = take_max<'a>(&'a mut a, &'a mut b); *mc += 1;
    drop mc; now 'a; }
    a != b
}
```

2.2   Type System

The type system of COR assigns to each label a *whole context* $(\Gamma, \mathbf{A})$. We define below the whole context and the typing judgments.

Context. A *variable context* Γ is a finite set of items of form $x\colon^{\mathbf{a}} T$, where T should be a complete *pointer* type and $\mathbf{a}$ (which we call *activeness*) is of form 'active' or '$\dagger\alpha$' (*frozen until lifetime* α). We abbreviate $x\colon^{\text{active}} T$ as $x\colon T$. A variable context should not contain two items on the same variable. A *lifetime context* $\mathbf{A} = (A, R)$ is a finite preordered set of lifetime variables, where A is the underlying set and R is the preorder. We write $|\mathbf{A}|$ and $\leq_{\mathbf{A}}$ to refer to A and R. Finally, a *whole context* $(\Gamma, \mathbf{A})$ is a pair of a variable context Γ and a lifetime context $\mathbf{A}$ such that every lifetime variable in Γ is contained in $\mathbf{A}$.

---

[17] The first character of each variable indicates the pointer kind (o/m corresponds to own/mut$_\alpha$). We swap the branches of the match statement in take-max, to fit the order to C/Rust's if.

Notations. The set operation $A + B$ (or more generally $\sum_\lambda A_\lambda$) denotes the disjoint union, i.e. the union defined only if the arguments are disjoint. The set operation $A - B$ denotes the set difference defined only if $A \supseteq B$. For a natural number n, $[n]$ denotes the set $\{0, \dots, n-1\}$.

Generally, an auxiliary definition for a rule can be presented just below, possibly in a dotted box.

Program and Function. The rules for typing programs and functions are presented below. They assign to each label a whole context $(\mathbf{\Gamma}, \mathbf{A})$. '$S{:}_{\Pi,f} (\mathbf{\Gamma}, \mathbf{A}) \mid (\mathbf{\Gamma}_L, \mathbf{A}_L)_L \mid U$' is explained later.

$$\frac{\text{for any } F \text{ in } \Pi,\ F{:}_\Pi (\mathbf{\Gamma}_{\text{name}(F),L}, \mathbf{A}_{\text{name}(F),L})_{L \in \text{Label}_F}}{\Pi{:} (\mathbf{\Gamma}_{f,L}, \mathbf{A}_{f,L})_{(f,L)\,\in\,\text{FnLabel}_\Pi}}$$

name(F): the function name of F Label$_F$: the set of labels in F

FnLabel$_\Pi$: the set of pairs (f, L) such that a function f in Π has a label L

$$F = \mathsf{fn}\ f\langle\alpha_0, \dots, \alpha_{m-1} \mid \alpha_{a_0} \leq \alpha_{b_0}, \dots, \alpha_{a_{l-1}} \leq \alpha_{b_{l-1}}\rangle(x_0{:}T_0, \dots, x_{n-1}{:}T_{n-1}) \to U\,\{\cdots\}$$

$$\mathbf{\Gamma}_{\text{entry}} = \{x_i{:}T_i \mid i \in [n]\} \quad A = \{\alpha_j \mid j \in [m]\} \quad \mathbf{A}_{\text{entry}} = \left(A, (\text{Id}_A \cup \{(\alpha_{a_k}, \alpha_{b_k}) \mid k \in [l]\})^+\right)$$

$$\frac{\text{for any } L'{:}S \in \text{LabelStmt}_F,\ S{:}_{\Pi,f} (\mathbf{\Gamma}_{L'}, \mathbf{A}_{L'}) \mid (\mathbf{\Gamma}_L, \mathbf{A}_L)_{L \in \text{Label}_F} \mid U}{F{:}_\Pi (\mathbf{\Gamma}_L, \mathbf{A}_L)_{L \in \text{Label}_F}}$$

LabelStmt$_F$: the set of labeled statements in F

Id$_A$: the identity relation on A R^+: the transitive closure of R

On the rule for the function, the initial whole context at entry is specified (the second and third preconditions) and also the contexts for other labels are checked (the fourth precondition). The context for each label (in each function) can actually be determined in the order by the distance in the number of goto jumps from entry, but that order is not very obvious because of *unstructured control flows*.

Statement. '$S{:}_{\Pi,f} (\mathbf{\Gamma}, \mathbf{A}) \mid (\mathbf{\Gamma}_L, \mathbf{A}_L)_L \mid U$' means that running the statement S (under Π, f) with the whole context $(\mathbf{\Gamma}, \mathbf{A})$ results in a jump to a label with the whole contexts specified by $(\mathbf{\Gamma}_L, \mathbf{A}_L)_L$ or a return of data of type U. Its rules are presented below. '$I{:}_{\Pi,f} (\mathbf{\Gamma}, \mathbf{A}) \to (\mathbf{\Gamma}', \mathbf{A}')$' is explained later.

$$\frac{I{:}_{\Pi,f} (\mathbf{\Gamma}, \mathbf{A}) \to (\mathbf{\Gamma}_{L_0}, \mathbf{A}_{L_0})}{I;\ \mathsf{goto}\ L_0{:}_{\Pi,f} (\mathbf{\Gamma}, \mathbf{A}) \mid (\mathbf{\Gamma}_L, \mathbf{A}_L)_L \mid U} \qquad \frac{\mathbf{\Gamma} = \{x{:}U\} \quad |\mathbf{A}| = A_{\text{ex}\,\Pi,f}}{\mathsf{return}\ x{:}_{\Pi,f} (\mathbf{\Gamma}, \mathbf{A}) \mid (\mathbf{\Gamma}_L, \mathbf{A}_L)_L \mid U}$$

$A_{\text{ex}\,\Pi,f}$: the set of lifetime parameters of f in Π

$$\frac{x{:}P(T_0{+}T_1) \in \mathbf{\Gamma}}{\text{for } i = 0, 1,\ (\mathbf{\Gamma}_{L_i}, \mathbf{A}_{L_i}) = (\mathbf{\Gamma} - \{x{:}P(T_0{+}T_1)\} + \{y_i{:}P\,T_i\}, \mathbf{A})}$$

$$\mathsf{match}\ {*}x\ \{\mathsf{inj}_0\ {*}y_0 \to \mathsf{goto}\ L_0,\ \mathsf{inj}_1\ {*}y_1 \to \mathsf{goto}\ L_1\}{:}_{\Pi,f} (\mathbf{\Gamma}, \mathbf{A}) \mid (\mathbf{\Gamma}_L, \mathbf{A}_L)_L \mid U$$

The rule for the return statement ensures that there remain no extra variables and local lifetime variables.

Instruction. '$I{:}_{\Pi,f} (\mathbf{\Gamma}, \mathbf{A}) \to (\mathbf{\Gamma}', \mathbf{A}')$' means that running the instruction I (under Π, f) updates the whole context $(\mathbf{\Gamma}, \mathbf{A})$ into $(\mathbf{\Gamma}', \mathbf{A}')$. The rules are designed so that, for any $I, \Pi, f, (\mathbf{\Gamma}, \mathbf{A})$, there exists at most one $(\mathbf{\Gamma}', \mathbf{A}')$ such that

$I:_{\Pi,f} (\mathbf{\Gamma}, \mathbf{A}) \to (\mathbf{\Gamma}', \mathbf{A}')$ holds. Below we present some of the rules; the complete rules are presented in the full paper. The following is the typing rule for mutable (re)borrow.

$$\frac{\alpha \notin A_{\mathrm{ex}\,\Pi,f} \quad P = \mathsf{own}, \mathsf{mut}_\alpha \quad \text{for any } \beta \in \mathrm{Lifetime}_{P\,T},\ \alpha \leq_\mathbf{A} \beta}{\mathsf{let}\, y = \mathsf{mutbor}_\alpha\, x :_{\Pi,f} (\mathbf{\Gamma}+\{x\!:\!P\,T\}, \mathbf{A}) \to (\mathbf{\Gamma}+\{y\!:\!\mathsf{mut}_\alpha\, T,\ x\!:\!^{\dagger\alpha} P\,T\}, \mathbf{A})}$$
$$\text{Lifetime}_T\text{: the set of lifetime variables occurring in } T$$

After you mutably (re)borrow an owning pointer / mutable reference x until α, x is *frozen* until α. Here, α should be a local lifetime variable[18] (the first precondition) that does not live longer than the data of x (the third precondition). Below are the typing rules for local lifetime variable introduction and elimination.

$$\mathsf{intro}\,\alpha :_{\Pi,f} (\mathbf{\Gamma}, (A, R)) \to (\mathbf{\Gamma}, (\{\alpha\}+A, \{\alpha\}\times(\{\alpha\}+A_{\mathrm{ex}\,\Pi,f})+R))$$

$$\frac{\alpha \notin A_{\mathrm{ex}\,\Pi,f}}{\mathsf{now}\,\alpha :_{\Pi,f} (\mathbf{\Gamma}, (\{\alpha\}+A, R)) \to (\{\mathsf{thaw}_\alpha(x\!:\!^\mathbf{a} T) \mid x\!:\!^\mathbf{a} T \in \mathbf{\Gamma}\}, (A, \{(\beta,\gamma)\in R \mid \beta\neq\alpha\}))}$$
$$\mathsf{thaw}_\alpha(x\!:\!^\mathbf{a} T) := \begin{cases} x\!:\!T & (\mathbf{a} = \dagger\alpha) \\ x\!:\!^\mathbf{a} T & (\text{otherwise}) \end{cases}$$

On $\mathsf{intro}\,\alpha$, it just ensures the new local lifetime variable to be earlier than any lifetime parameters (which are given by exterior functions). On $\mathsf{now}\,\alpha$, the variables frozen with α get active again. Below is the typing rule for dereference of a pointer to a pointer, which may be a bit interesting.

$$\mathsf{let}\, y = *x :_{\Pi,f} (\mathbf{\Gamma}+\{x\!:\!P\,P'\,T\}, \mathbf{A}) \to (\mathbf{\Gamma}+\{y\!:\!(P\circ P')\,T\}, \mathbf{A})$$

$$P \circ \mathsf{own} = \mathsf{own} \circ P := P \quad R_\alpha \circ R'_\beta := R''_\alpha \text{ where } R'' = \begin{cases} \mathsf{mut} & (R = R' = \mathsf{mut}) \\ \mathsf{immut} & (\text{otherwise}) \end{cases}$$

The third precondition of the typing rule for mutbor justifies taking just α in the rule '$R_\alpha \circ R'_\beta := R''_\alpha$'.

Let us interpret $\Pi\colon(\mathbf{\Gamma}_{f,L}, \mathbf{A}_{f,L})_{(f,L)\,\in\,\mathrm{FnLabel}_\Pi}$ as "the program Π has the type $(\mathbf{\Gamma}_{f,L}, \mathbf{A}_{f,L})_{(f,L)\,\in\,\mathrm{FnLabel}_\Pi}$". The type system ensures that any program has at most one type (which may be a bit unclear because of unstructured control flows). Hereinafter, we implicitly assume that a program has a type.

2.3   Concrete Operational Semantics

We introduce for COR *concrete operational semantics*, which handles a concrete model of the heap memory.

The basic item, *concrete configuration* $\mathbf{C}$, is defined as follows.

$$\mathbf{S} ::= \mathsf{end} \mid [f, L]\, x, \mathbf{F}; \mathbf{S} \quad \text{(concrete configuration)} \quad \mathbf{C} ::= [f, L]\, \mathbf{F}; \mathbf{S} \mid \mathbf{H}$$

Here, $\mathbf{H}$ is a *heap*, which maps addresses (represented by integers) to integers (data). $\mathbf{F}$ is a *concrete stack frame*, which maps variables to addresses. The stack

[18] In COR, a reference that lives after the return from the function should be created by splitting a reference (e.g. 'let $(*y_0, *y_1) = *x$') given in the inputs; see also Expressivity and Limitations.

part of $\mathbf{C}$ is of form '$[f, L]\,\mathbf{F}$; $[f', L']\,x, \mathbf{F}'$; $\cdots$; end' (we may omit the terminator '; end'). $[f, L]$ on each stack frame indicates the program point. 'x,' on each non-top stack frame is the receiver of the value returned by the function call.

Concrete operational semantics is characterized by the one-step transition relation $\mathbf{C} \rightarrow_\Pi \mathbf{C}'$ and the termination relation $\mathrm{final}_\Pi(\mathbf{C})$, which can be defined straightforwardly. Below we show the rules for mutable (re)borrow, swap, function call and return from a function; the complete rules and an example execution are presented in the full paper. $S_{\Pi, f, L}$ is the statement for the label L of the function f in Π. $\mathrm{Ty}_{\Pi, f, L}(x)$ is the type of variable x at the label.

$$\frac{S_{\Pi, f, L} = \mathsf{let}\,y = \mathsf{mutbor}_\alpha\,x;\,\mathsf{goto}\,L' \quad \mathbf{F}(x) = a}{[f, L]\,\mathbf{F};\,\mathbf{S}\mid\mathbf{H} \rightarrow_\Pi [f, L']\,\mathbf{F}+\{(y, a)\};\,\mathbf{S}\mid\mathbf{H}}$$

$$\frac{S_{\Pi, f, L} = \mathsf{swap}(*x, *y);\,\mathsf{goto}\,L' \quad \mathrm{Ty}_{\Pi, f, L}(x) = P\,T \quad \mathbf{F}(x) = a \quad \mathbf{F}(y) = b}{\begin{array}{c}[f, L]\,\mathbf{F};\,\mathbf{S}\mid\mathbf{H}+\{(a+k, m_k)\mid k\in[\#T]\}+\{(b+k, n_k)\mid k\in[\#T]\} \\ \rightarrow_\Pi [f, L']\,\mathbf{F};\,\mathbf{S}\mid\mathbf{H}+\{(a+k, n_k)\mid k\in[\#T]\}+\{(b+k, m_k)\mid k\in[\#T]\}\end{array}}$$

$$\frac{\begin{array}{c}S_{\Pi, f, L} = \mathsf{let}\,y = g\langle\cdots\rangle(x_0, \ldots, x_{n-1});\,\mathsf{goto}\,L' \\ \Sigma_{\Pi, g} = \langle\cdots\rangle(x_0' : T_0, \ldots, x_{n-1}' : T_{n-1}) \rightarrow U\end{array}}{[f, L]\,\mathbf{F}+\{(x_i, a_i)\mid i\in[n]\};\,\mathbf{S}\mid\mathbf{H} \rightarrow_\Pi [g, \mathsf{entry}]\,\{(x_i', a_i)\mid i\in[n]\};\,[f, L]\,y, \mathbf{F};\,\mathbf{S}\mid\mathbf{H}}$$

$$\frac{S_{\Pi, f, L} = \mathsf{return}\,x}{[f, L]\,\{(x, a)\};\,[g, L']\,x', \mathbf{F}';\,\mathbf{S}\mid\mathbf{H} \rightarrow_\Pi [g, L']\,\mathbf{F}'+\{(x', a)\};\,\mathbf{S}\mid\mathbf{H}}$$

$$\frac{S_{\Pi, f, L} = \mathsf{return}\,x}{\mathrm{final}_\Pi([f, L]\,\{(x, a)\}\mid\mathbf{H})}$$

Here we introduce '$\#T$', which represents how many memory cells the type T takes (at the outermost level). $\#T$ is defined for every *complete* type T, because every occurrence of type variables in a complete type is guarded by a pointer constructor.

$$\#(T_0 + T_1) := 1 + \max\{\#T_0, \#T_1\} \quad \#(T_0 \times T_1) := \#T_0 + \#T_1$$
$$\#\mu X.T := \#T[\mu X.T/X] \quad \#\,\mathsf{int} = \#\,P\,T := 1 \quad \#\,\mathsf{unit} = 0$$

3 CHC Representation of COR Programs

To formalize the idea discussed in §1, we give a translation from COR programs to CHC systems, which precisely characterize the input-output relations of the COR programs. We first define the logic for CHCs (§3.1). We then formally describe our translation (§3.2) and prove its correctness (§3.3). Also, we examine effectiveness of our approach with advanced examples (§3.4) and discuss how our idea can be extended and enhanced (§3.5).

3.1 Multi-sorted Logic for Describing CHCs

To begin with, we introduce a first-order multi-sorted logic for describing the CHC representation of COR programs.

Syntax. The syntax is defined as follows.

$$(\text{CHC}) \ \varPhi ::= \forall x_0 {:} \sigma_0, \ldots, x_{m-1} {:} \sigma_{m-1}. \ \check{\varphi} \Longleftarrow \psi_0 \wedge \cdots \wedge \psi_{n-1}$$

$$\top := \text{the nullary conjunction of formulas}$$

$$(\text{formula}) \ \varphi, \psi ::= f(t_0, \ldots, t_{n-1}) \quad (\text{elementary formula}) \ \check{\varphi} ::= f(p_0, \ldots, p_{n-1})$$

$$(\text{term}) \ t ::= x \mid \langle t \rangle \mid \langle t_*, t_\circ \rangle \mid \text{inj}_i t \mid (t_0, t_1) \mid {*}t \mid \circ t \mid t.i \mid const \mid t \ op \ t'$$

$$(\text{value}) \ v, w ::= \langle v \rangle \mid \langle v_*, v_\circ \rangle \mid \text{inj}_i v \mid (v_0, v_1) \mid const$$

$$(\text{pattern}) \ p, q ::= x \mid \langle p \rangle \mid \langle p_*, p_\circ \rangle \mid \text{inj}_i p \mid (p_0, p_1) \mid const$$

$$(\text{sort}) \ \sigma, \tau ::= X \mid \mu X.\sigma \mid C\,\sigma \mid \sigma_0 + \sigma_1 \mid \sigma_0 \times \sigma_1 \mid \text{int} \mid \text{unit}$$

$$(\text{container kind}) \ C ::= \text{box} \mid \text{mut} \quad const ::= \text{same as COR} \quad op ::= \text{same as COR}$$

$$\text{bool} := \text{unit} + \text{unit} \quad \text{true} := \text{inj}_1 () \quad \text{false} := \text{inj}_0 ()$$

$$X ::= (\text{sort variable}) \quad x, y ::= (\text{variable}) \quad f ::= (\text{predicate variable})$$

We introduce $\text{box}\,\sigma$ and $\text{mut}\,\sigma$, which correspond to $\text{own}\,T/\text{immut}_\alpha T$ and $\text{mut}_\alpha T$ respectively. $\langle t \rangle / \langle t_*, t_\circ \rangle$ is the constructor for $\text{box}\,\sigma/\text{mut}\,\sigma$. $*t$ takes the body/first value of $\langle - \rangle / \langle -, - \rangle$ and $\circ t$ takes the second value of $\langle -, - \rangle$. We restrict the form of CHCs here to simplify the proofs later. Although the logic does not have a primitive for equality, we can define the equality in a CHC system (e.g. by adding $\forall x {:} \sigma. \ Eq(x, x) \Longleftarrow \top$).

A *CHC system* $(\boldsymbol{\Phi}, \boldsymbol{\Xi})$ is a pair of a finite set of CHCs $\boldsymbol{\Phi} = \{\varPhi_0, \ldots, \varPhi_{n-1}\}$ and $\boldsymbol{\Xi}$, where $\boldsymbol{\Xi}$ is a finite map from predicate variables to tuples of sorts (denoted by $\varXi$), specifying the sorts of the input values. Unlike the informal description in § 1, we add $\boldsymbol{\Xi}$ to a CHC system.

Sort System. '$t {:}_{\boldsymbol{\Delta}} \sigma$' (the term t has the sort σ under $\boldsymbol{\Delta}$) is defined as follows. Here, $\boldsymbol{\Delta}$ is a finite map from variables to sorts. $\sigma \sim \tau$ is the congruence on sorts induced by $\mu X.\sigma \sim \sigma[\mu X.\sigma/X]$.

$$\frac{\boldsymbol{\Delta}(x) = \sigma}{x {:}_{\boldsymbol{\Delta}} \sigma} \quad \frac{t {:}_{\boldsymbol{\Delta}} \sigma}{\langle t \rangle {:}_{\boldsymbol{\Delta}} \text{box}\,\sigma} \quad \frac{t_*, t_\circ {:}_{\boldsymbol{\Delta}} \sigma}{\langle t_*, t_\circ \rangle {:}_{\boldsymbol{\Delta}} \text{mut}\,\sigma} \quad \frac{t {:}_{\boldsymbol{\Delta}} \sigma_i}{\text{inj}_i t {:}_{\boldsymbol{\Delta}} \sigma_0 + \sigma_1} \quad \frac{t_0 {:}_{\boldsymbol{\Delta}} \sigma_0 \quad t_1 {:}_{\boldsymbol{\Delta}} \sigma_1}{(t_0, t_1) {:}_{\boldsymbol{\Delta}} \sigma_0 \times \sigma_1}$$

$$\frac{t {:}_{\boldsymbol{\Delta}} C\sigma}{{*}t {:}_{\boldsymbol{\Delta}} \sigma} \quad \frac{t {:}_{\boldsymbol{\Delta}} \text{mut}\,\sigma}{\circ t {:}_{\boldsymbol{\Delta}} \sigma} \quad \frac{t {:}_{\boldsymbol{\Delta}} \sigma_0 + \sigma_1}{t.i {:}_{\boldsymbol{\Delta}} \sigma_i} \quad \frac{}{const {:}_{\boldsymbol{\Delta}} \sigma_{const}} \quad \frac{t, t' {:}_{\boldsymbol{\Delta}} \text{int}}{t \ op \ t' {:}_{\boldsymbol{\Delta}} \sigma_{op}} \quad \frac{t {:}_{\boldsymbol{\Delta}} \sigma \quad \sigma \sim \tau}{t {:}_{\boldsymbol{\Delta}} \tau}$$

$$\sigma_{const}: \text{the sort of } const \qquad \sigma_{op}: \text{the output sort of } op$$

'wellSorted$_{\boldsymbol{\Delta},\boldsymbol{\Xi}}(\varphi)$' and 'wellSorted$_{\boldsymbol{\Xi}}(\boldsymbol{\Phi})$', the judgments on well-sortedness of formulas and CHCs, are defined as follows.

$$\frac{\boldsymbol{\Xi}(f) = (\sigma_0, \ldots, \sigma_{n-1}) \quad \text{for any } i \in [n], \ t_i {:}_{\boldsymbol{\Delta}} \sigma_i}{\text{wellSorted}_{\boldsymbol{\Delta},\boldsymbol{\Xi}}(f(t_0, \ldots, t_{n-1}))}$$

$$\frac{\boldsymbol{\Delta} = \{(x_i, \sigma_i) \mid i \in [m]\} \quad \text{wellSorted}_{\boldsymbol{\Delta},\boldsymbol{\Xi}}(\check{\varphi}) \quad \text{for any } j \in [n], \ \text{wellSorted}_{\boldsymbol{\Delta},\boldsymbol{\Xi}}(\psi_j)}{\text{wellSorted}_{\boldsymbol{\Xi}}(\forall x_0 {:} \sigma_0, \ldots, x_{m-1} {:} \sigma_{m-1}. \ \check{\varphi} \Longleftarrow \psi_0 \wedge \cdots \wedge \psi_{n-1})}$$

The CHC system $(\boldsymbol{\Phi}, \boldsymbol{\Xi})$ is said to be well-sorted if wellSorted$_{\boldsymbol{\Xi}}(\varPhi)$ holds for any $\varPhi \in \boldsymbol{\Phi}$.

Semantics. '$[\![t]\!]_{\mathbf{I}}$', the interpretation of the term t as a value under $\mathbf{I}$, is defined as follows. Here, $\mathbf{I}$ is a finite map from variables to values. Although the definition is partial, the interpretation is defined for all well-sorted terms.

$$[\![x]\!]_{\mathbf{I}} := \mathbf{I}(x) \quad [\![\langle t\rangle]\!]_{\mathbf{I}} := \langle [\![t]\!]_{\mathbf{I}} \rangle \quad [\![\langle t_*, t_\circ\rangle]\!]_{\mathbf{I}} := \langle [\![t_*]\!]_{\mathbf{I}}, [\![t_\circ]\!]_{\mathbf{I}} \rangle \quad [\![\mathsf{inj}_i\, t]\!]_{\mathbf{I}} := \mathsf{inj}_i [\![t]\!]_{\mathbf{I}}$$

$$[\![(t_0, t_1)]\!]_{\mathbf{I}} := ([\![t_0]\!]_{\mathbf{I}}, [\![t_1]\!]_{\mathbf{I}}) \quad [\![*t]\!]_{\mathbf{I}} := \begin{cases} v & ([\![t]\!]_{\mathbf{I}} = \langle v\rangle) \\ v_* & ([\![t]\!]_{\mathbf{I}} = \langle v_*, v_\circ\rangle) \end{cases} \quad [\![\circ t]\!]_{\mathbf{I}} := v_\circ \text{ if } [\![t]\!]_{\mathbf{I}} = \langle v_*, v_\circ\rangle$$

$$[\![t.i]\!]_{\mathbf{I}} := v_i \text{ if } [\![t]\!]_{\mathbf{I}} = (v_0, v_1) \quad [\![const]\!]_{\mathbf{I}} := const \quad [\![t\ op\ t']\!]_{\mathbf{I}} := [\![t]\!]_{\mathbf{I}} [\![op]\!] [\![t']\!]_{\mathbf{I}}$$

$$[\![op]\!]\colon \text{the binary operation on values corresponding to } op$$

A *predicate structure* $\mathbf{M}$ is a finite map from predicate variables to (concrete) predicates on values. $\mathbf{M}, \mathbf{I} \models f(t_0, \ldots, t_{n-1})$ means that $\mathbf{M}(f)([\![t_0]\!]_{\mathbf{I}}, \ldots, [\![t_{m-1}]\!]_{\mathbf{I}})$ holds. $\mathbf{M} \models \Phi$ is defined as follows.

$$\frac{\text{for any } \mathbf{I} \text{ s.t. } \forall i \in [m].\, \mathbf{I}(x_i){:}_\varnothing\, \sigma_i,\ \mathbf{M}, \mathbf{I} \models \psi_0, \ldots, \psi_{n-1} \text{ implies } \mathbf{M}, \mathbf{I} \models \check{\varphi}}{\mathbf{M} \models \forall x_0{:}\sigma_0, \ldots, x_{m-1}{:}\sigma_{m-1}.\ \check{\varphi} \Longleftarrow \psi_0 \wedge \cdots \wedge \psi_{n-1}}$$

Finally, $\mathbf{M} \models (\Phi, \Xi)$ is defined as follows.

$$\frac{\text{for any } (f, (\sigma_0, \ldots, \sigma_{n-1})) \in \Xi,\ \mathbf{M}(f) \text{ is a predicate on values of sort } \sigma_0, \ldots, \sigma_{n-1}}{\mathrm{dom}\, \mathbf{M} = \mathrm{dom}\, \Xi \quad \text{for any } \Phi \in \Phi,\ \mathbf{M} \models \Phi}{\mathbf{M} \models (\Phi, \Xi)}$$

When $\mathbf{M} \models (\Phi, \Xi)$ holds, we say that $\mathbf{M}$ is a *model* of (Φ, Ξ). Every well-sorted CHC system (Φ, Ξ) has the *least model* on the point-wise ordering (which can be proved based on the discussions in [16]), which we write as $\mathbf{M}^{\text{least}}_{(\Phi, \Xi)}$.

3.2 Translation from COR Programs to CHCs

Now we formalize our translation of Rust programs into CHCs. We define $(\!|\Pi|\!)$, which is a CHC system that represents the input-output relations of the functions in the COR program Π.

Roughly speaking, the least model $\mathbf{M}^{\text{least}}_{(\!|\Pi|\!)}$ for this CHC system should satisfy: for any values $v_0, \ldots, v_{n-1}, w$, $\mathbf{M}^{\text{least}}_{(\!|\Pi|\!)} \models f_{\text{entry}}(v_0, \ldots, v_{n-1}, w)$ holds exactly if, in COR, a function call $f(v_0, \ldots, v_{n-1})$ can return w. Actually, in concrete operational semantics, such values should be read out from the heap memory. The formal description and proof of this expected property is presented in § 3.3.

Auxiliary Definitions. The sort corresponding to the type T, $(\!|T|\!)$, is defined as follows. $\check{P}$ is a meta-variable for a non-mutable-reference pointer kind, i.e. own or immut$_\alpha$. Note that the information on lifetimes is all stripped off.

$$(\!|X|\!) := X \quad (\!|\mu X.T|\!) = \mu X.(\!|T|\!) \quad (\!|\check{P}\,T|\!) := \mathsf{box}\,(\!|T|\!) \quad (\!|\mathsf{mut}_\alpha\,T|\!) := \mathsf{mut}\,(\!|T|\!)$$

$$(\!|\mathsf{int}|\!) := \mathsf{int} \quad (\!|\mathsf{unit}|\!) := \mathsf{unit} \quad (\!|T_0{+}T_1|\!) := (\!|T_0|\!) + (\!|T_1|\!) \quad (\!|T_0{\times}T_1|\!) := (\!|T_0|\!) \times (\!|T_1|\!)$$

We introduce a special variable res to represent the result of a function.[19] For a label L in a function f in a program Π, we define $\check{\varphi}_{\Pi,f,L}$, $\Xi_{\Pi,f,L}$ and $\Delta_{\Pi,f,L}$

---

[19] For simplicity, we assume that the parameters of each function are sorted respecting *some fixed order* on variables (with res coming at the last), and we enumerate various items in this fixed order.

as follows, if the items in the variable context for the label are enumerated as $x_0\!:^{a_0} T_0, \ldots, x_{n-1}\!:^{a_{n-1}} T_{n-1}$ and the return type of the function is U.

$$\check{\varphi}_{\Pi,f,L} := f_L(x_0, \ldots, x_{n-1}, \mathsf{res}) \quad \varXi_{\Pi,f,L} := (\langle\!| T_0 |\!\rangle, \ldots, \langle\!| T_{n-1} |\!\rangle, \langle\!| U |\!\rangle)$$

$$\boldsymbol{\Delta}_{\Pi,f,L} := \{(x_i, \langle\!| T_i |\!\rangle) \mid i \in [n]\} + \{(\mathsf{res}, \langle\!| U |\!\rangle)\}$$

$\forall(\boldsymbol{\Delta})$ stands for $\forall\, x_0\!:\sigma_0, \ldots, x_{n-1}\!:\sigma_{n-1}$, where the items in $\boldsymbol{\Delta}$ are enumerated as $(x_0, \sigma_0), \ldots, (x_{n-1}, \sigma_{n-1})$.

CHC Representation. Now we introduce '$\langle\!| L\!:S |\!\rangle_{\Pi,f}$', the set (in most cases, singleton) of CHCs modeling the computation performed by the labeled statement $L\!:S$ in f from Π. Unlike informal descriptions in §1, we turn to *pattern matching* instead of equations, to simplify the proofs. Below we show some of the rules; the complete rules are presented in the full paper. The variables marked green (e.g. $x_\circ$) should be fresh. The following is the rule for mutable (re)borrow.

$$\langle\!| L\!:\mathsf{let}\, y = \mathsf{mutbor}_\alpha\, x;\ \mathsf{goto}\, L' |\!\rangle_{\Pi,f}$$
$$:= \begin{cases} \left\{ \begin{array}{l} \forall(\boldsymbol{\Delta}_{\Pi,f,L}\!+\!\{(x_\circ, \langle\!| T |\!\rangle)\}). \\ \check{\varphi}_{\Pi,f,L} \Longleftarrow \check{\varphi}_{\Pi,f,L'}[\langle *x, x_\circ\rangle/y, \langle x_\circ\rangle/x] \end{array} \right\} & (\mathrm{Ty}_{\Pi,f,L}(x) = \mathsf{own}\, T) \\[2ex] \left\{ \begin{array}{l} \forall(\boldsymbol{\Delta}_{\Pi,f,L}\!+\!\{(x_\circ, \langle\!| T |\!\rangle)\}). \\ \check{\varphi}_{\Pi,f,L} \Longleftarrow \check{\varphi}_{\Pi,f,L'}[\langle *x, x_\circ\rangle/y, \langle x_\circ, \circ x\rangle/x] \end{array} \right\} & (\mathrm{Ty}_{\Pi,f,L}(x) = \mathsf{mut}_\alpha\, T) \end{cases}$$

The value at the end of borrow is represented as a newly introduced variable $x_\circ$. Below is the rule for release of a variable.

$$\langle\!| L\!:\mathsf{drop}\, x;\ \mathsf{goto}\, L' |\!\rangle_{\Pi,f}$$
$$:= \begin{cases} \left\{ \forall(\boldsymbol{\Delta}_{\Pi,f,L}).\ \check{\varphi}_{\Pi,f,L} \Longleftarrow \check{\varphi}_{\Pi,f,L'} \right\} & (\mathrm{Ty}_{\Pi,f,L}(x) = \check{P}\, T) \\[2ex] \left\{ \begin{array}{l} \forall(\boldsymbol{\Delta}_{\Pi,f,L}\!-\!\{(x, \mathsf{mut}\, \langle\!| T |\!\rangle)\}\!+\!\{(x_*, \langle\!| T |\!\rangle)\}). \\ \check{\varphi}_{\Pi,f,L}[\langle x_*, x_*\rangle/x] \Longleftarrow \check{\varphi}_{\Pi,f,L'} \end{array} \right\} & (\mathrm{Ty}_{\Pi,f,L}(x) = \mathsf{mut}_\alpha\, T) \end{cases}$$

When a variable x of type $\mathsf{mut}_\alpha\, T$ is dropped/released, we check the prophesied value at the end of borrow. Below is the rule for a function call.

$$\langle\!| L\!:\mathsf{let}\, y = g\langle\cdots\rangle(x_0, \ldots, x_{n-1});\ \mathsf{goto}\, L' |\!\rangle_{\Pi,f}$$
$$:= \{\forall(\boldsymbol{\Delta}_{\Pi,f,L}\!+\!\{(y, \langle\!| \mathrm{Ty}_{\Pi,f,L'}(y) |\!\rangle)\}).\ \check{\varphi}_{\Pi,f,L} \Longleftarrow g_{\mathsf{entry}}(x_0, \ldots, x_{n-1}, y) \wedge \check{\varphi}_{\Pi,f,L'}\}$$

The body (the right-hand side of $\Longleftarrow$) of the CHC contains two formulas, which yields a kind of call stack at the level of CHCs. Below is the rule for a return from a function.

$$\langle\!| L\!:\mathsf{return}\, x |\!\rangle_{\Pi,f} := \{\forall(\boldsymbol{\Delta}_{\Pi,f,L}).\ \check{\varphi}_{\Pi,f,L}[x/\mathsf{res}] \Longleftarrow \top\}$$

The variable res is forced to be equal to the returned variable x.

Finally, $\langle\!| \Pi |\!\rangle$, the CHC system that represents the COR program Π (or the *CHC representation of Π*), is defined as follows.

$$\langle\!| \Pi |\!\rangle := \left(\textstyle\sum_{F \text{ in } \Pi,\, L:S\, \in\, \mathrm{LabelStmt}_F} \langle\!| L\!:S |\!\rangle_{\Pi,\mathsf{name}_F},\ (\varXi_{\Pi,f,L})_{f_L \text{ s.t. } (f,L)\, \in\, \mathrm{FnLabel}_\Pi} \right)$$

Example 2 (CHC Representation). We present below the CHC representation of take-max described in §2.1. We omit CHCs on inc-max here. We have also excluded the variable binders '$\forall \cdots$'.[20]

$$\mathsf{take\text{-}max}_{\mathsf{entry}}(ma, mb, \mathsf{res}) \Longleftarrow \mathsf{take\text{-}max}_{\mathsf{L1}}(ma, mb, \langle *ma \ge *mb\rangle, \mathsf{res})$$

---

[20] The sorts of the variables are as follows: ma, mb, res: mut int; ma_*, mb_*: int; ou: box unit.

$$\text{take-max}_{\text{L1}}(ma, mb, \langle\text{inj}_1 * ou\rangle, \text{res}) \iff \text{take-max}_{\text{L2}}(ma, mb, ou, \text{res})$$
$$\text{take-max}_{\text{L1}}(ma, mb, \langle\text{inj}_0 * ou\rangle, \text{res}) \iff \text{take-max}_{\text{L5}}(ma, mb, ou, \text{res})$$
$$\text{take-max}_{\text{L2}}(ma, mb, ou, \text{res}) \iff \text{take-max}_{\text{L3}}(ma, mb, \text{res})$$
$$\text{take-max}_{\text{L3}}(ma, \langle mb_*, mb_*\rangle, \text{res}) \iff \text{take-max}_{\text{L4}}(ma, \text{res})$$
$$\text{take-max}_{\text{L4}}(ma, ma) \iff \top$$
$$\text{take-max}_{\text{L5}}(ma, mb, ou, \text{res}) \iff \text{take-max}_{\text{L6}}(ma, mb, \text{res})$$
$$\text{take-max}_{\text{L6}}(\langle ma_*, ma_*\rangle, mb, \text{res}) \iff \text{take-max}_{\text{L7}}(mb, \text{res})$$
$$\text{take-max}_{\text{L7}}(mb, mb) \iff \top$$

The fifth and eighth CHC represent release of mb/ma. The sixth and ninth CHC represent the determination of the return value res.

3.3 Correctness of the CHC Representation

Now we formally state and prove the correctness of the CHC representation.

Notations. We use $\{\!|\cdots|\!\}$ (instead of $\{\cdots\}$) for the intensional description of a multiset. $A \oplus B$ (or more generally $\bigoplus_\lambda A_\lambda$) denotes the multiset sum (e.g. $\{\!|0, 1|\!\} \oplus \{\!|1|\!\} = \{\!|0, 1, 1|\!\} \neq \{\!|0, 1|\!\}$).

Readout and Safe Readout. We introduce a few judgments to formally describe how read out data from the heap.

First, the judgment 'readout$_\mathbf{H}(*a :: T \mid v; \mathcal{M})$' (the data at the address a of type T can be read out from the heap $\mathbf{H}$ as the value v, yielding the memory footprint $\mathcal{M}$) is defined as follows.[21] Here, a *memory footprint* $\mathcal{M}$ is a finite multiset of addresses, which is employed for monitoring the memory usage.

$$\frac{\mathbf{H}(a) = a' \quad \text{readout}_\mathbf{H}(*a' :: T \mid v; \mathcal{M})}{\text{readout}_\mathbf{H}(*a : \text{own } T \mid \langle v\rangle; \mathcal{M} \oplus \{\!|a|\!\})} \quad \frac{\text{readout}_\mathbf{H}(*a :: T[\mu X.T/X] \mid v; \mathcal{M})}{\text{readout}_\mathbf{H}(*a :: \mu X.T/X \mid v; \mathcal{M})}$$

$$\frac{\mathbf{H}(a) = n}{\text{readout}_\mathbf{H}(*a :: \text{int} \mid n; \{\!|a|\!\})} \quad \text{readout}_\mathbf{H}(*a :: \text{unit} \mid (); \varnothing)$$

$$\frac{\mathbf{H}(a) = i \in [2] \quad \text{for any } k \in [(\#T_{1-i} - \#T_i)_{\geq 0}], \ \mathbf{H}(a+1+\#T_i+k) = 0}{\text{readout}_\mathbf{H}(*(a+1) :: T_i \mid v; \mathcal{M})}$$
$$\text{readout}_\mathbf{H}\big(*a :: T_0 + T_1 \mid \text{inj}_i v; \mathcal{M} \oplus \{\!|a|\!\} \oplus \{\!|a+1+\#T_i+k \mid k \in [(\#T_{1-i} - \#T_i)_{\geq 0}]|\!\}\big)$$
$$(n)_{\geq 0} := \max\{n, 0\}$$

$$\frac{\text{readout}_\mathbf{H}\big(*a :: T_0 \mid v_0; \mathcal{M}_0\big) \quad \text{readout}_\mathbf{H}\big(*(a+\#T_0) :: T_1 \mid v_1; \mathcal{M}_1\big)}{\text{readout}_\mathbf{H}\big(*a :: T_0 \times T_1 \mid (v_0, v_1); \mathcal{M}_0 \oplus \mathcal{M}_1\big)}$$

For example, 'readout$_{\{(100,7),(101,5)\}}(*100 :: \text{int} \times \text{int} \mid (7, 5); \{\!|100, 101|\!\})$' holds.

Next, 'readout$_\mathbf{H}(\mathbf{F} :: \Gamma \mid \mathcal{F}; \mathcal{M})$' (the data of the stack frame $\mathbf{F}$ respecting the variable context Γ can be read out from $\mathbf{H}$ as $\mathcal{F}$, yielding $\mathcal{M}$) is defined as follows. dom Γ stands for $\{x \mid x:^{\text{a}} T \in \Gamma\}$.

$$\frac{\text{dom } \mathbf{F} = \text{dom } \Gamma \quad \text{for any } x: \text{own } T \in \Gamma, \ \text{readout}_\mathbf{H}(*\mathbf{F}(x) :: T \mid v_x; \mathcal{M}_x)}{\text{readout}_\mathbf{H}(\mathbf{F} :: \Gamma \mid \{(x, \langle v_x\rangle) \mid x \in \text{dom } \mathbf{F}\}; \bigoplus_{x \in \text{dom } \mathbf{F}} \mathcal{M}_x)}$$

---

[21] Here we can ignore mutable/immutable references, because we focus on what we call *simple* functions, as explained later.

Finally, 'safe$_\mathbf{H}$($\mathbf{F} :: \mathbf{\Gamma} \mid \mathcal{F}$)' (the data of $\mathbf{F}$ respecting $\mathbf{\Gamma}$ can be *safely* read out from $\mathbf{H}$ as $\mathcal{F}$) is defined as follows.

$$\frac{\text{readout}_\mathbf{H}(\mathbf{F} :: \mathbf{\Gamma} \mid \mathcal{F}; \mathcal{M}) \quad \mathcal{M} \text{ has no duplicate items}}{\text{safe}_\mathbf{H}(\mathbf{F} :: \mathbf{\Gamma} \mid \mathcal{F})}$$

Here, the 'no duplicate items' precondition checks the safety on the ownership.

COS-based Model. Now we introduce the *COS-based model* (COS stands for concrete operational semantics) f_Π^{COS} to formally describe the expected input-output relation. Here, for simplicity, f is restricted to one that does not take lifetime parameters (we call such a function *simple*; the input/output types of a simple function cannot contain references). We define f_Π^{COS} as the predicate (on values of sorts $(\!|T_0|\!), \ldots, (\!|T_{n-1}|\!), (\!|U|\!)$ if f's input/output types are $T_0, \ldots, T_{n-1}, U$) given by the following rule.

$$\frac{\mathbf{C}_0 \to_\Pi \cdots \to_\Pi \mathbf{C}_N \quad \text{final}_\Pi(\mathbf{C}_N) \quad \mathbf{C}_0 = [f, \text{entry}]\,\mathbf{F} \mid \mathbf{H} \quad \mathbf{C}_N = [f, L]\,\mathbf{F}' \mid \mathbf{H}' \quad \text{safe}_\mathbf{H}\big(\mathbf{F} :: \mathbf{\Gamma}_{\Pi,f,\text{entry}} \mid \{(x_i, v_i) \mid i \in [n]\}\big) \quad \text{safe}_{\mathbf{H}'}\big(\mathbf{F}' :: \mathbf{\Gamma}_{\Pi,f,L} \mid \{(y, w)\}\big)}{f_\Pi^{\text{COS}}(v_0, \ldots, v_{n-1}, w)}$$

$\mathbf{\Gamma}_{\Pi,f,L}$: the variable context for the label L of f in the program Π

Correctness Theorem. Finally, the correctness (both soundness and completeness) of the CHC representation is simply stated as follows.

Theorem 1 (Correctness of the CHC Representation). *For any program Π and simple function f in Π, f_Π^{COS} is equivalent to $\mathbf{M}_{(\!|\Pi|\!)}^{\text{least}}(f_{\text{entry}})$.*

Proof. The details are presented in the full paper. We outline the proof below.

First, we introduce *abstract operational semantics*, where we get rid of heaps and directly represent each variable in the program simply as a value with *abstract variables*, which is strongly related to *prophecy variables* (see § 5). An abstract variable represents the undetermined value of a mutable reference at the end of borrow.

Next, we introduce *SLDC resolution* for CHC systems and find a *bisimulation* between abstract operational semantics and SLDC resolution, whereby we show that the *AOS-based model*, defined analogously to the COS-based model, is *equivalent* to the least model of the CHC representation. Moreover, we find a *bisimulation* between concrete and abstract operational semantics and prove that the COS-based model is *equivalent* to the AOS-based model.

Finally, combining the equivalences, we achieve the proof for the correctness of the CHC representation.   □

Interestingly, as by-products of the proof, we have also shown the *soundness of the type system* in terms of preservation and progression, in both concrete and abstract operational semantics. Simplification and generalization of the proofs is left for future work.

3.4   Advanced Examples

We give advanced examples of pointer-manipulating Rust programs and their CHC representations. For readability, we write programs in Rust (with ghost annotations) instead of COR. In addition, CHCs are written in an informal style like § 1, preferring equalities to pattern matching.

Example 3. Consider the following program, a variant of `just_rec` in § 1.1.

```
fn choose<'a>(ma: &'a mut i32, mb: &'a mut i32) -> &'a mut i32 {
   if rand() { drop ma; mb } else { drop mb; ma }
}
fn linger_dec<'a>(ma: &'a mut i32) -> bool {
   *ma -= 1; if rand() >= 0 { drop ma; return true; }
   let mut b = rand(); let old_b = b; intro 'b; let mb = &'b mut b;
   let r2 = linger_dec<'b>(choose<'b>(ma, mb)); now 'b;
   r2 && old_b >= b
}
```

Unlike `just_rec`, the function `linger_dec` can modify the local variable of an arbitrarily deep ancestor. Interestingly, each recursive call to `linger_dec` can introduce a new lifetime `'b`, which yields arbitrarily many layers of lifetimes.

Suppose we wish to verify that `linger_dec` never returns `false`. If we use, like $JustRec_+$ in § 1.1, a predicate taking the memory states h, h' and the stack pointer sp, we have to discover the quantified invariant: $\forall i \leq sp. h[i] \geq h'[i]$. In contrast, our approach reduces this verification problem to the following CHCs:

$$Choose(\langle a, a_o \rangle, \langle b, b_o \rangle, r) \Longleftarrow b_o = b \land r = \langle a, a_o \rangle$$
$$Choose(\langle a, a_o \rangle, \langle b, b_o \rangle, r) \Longleftarrow a_o = a \land r = \langle b, b_o \rangle$$
$$LingerDec(\langle a, a_o \rangle, r) \Longleftarrow a' = a - 1 \land a_o = a' \land r = \mathsf{true}$$
$$LingerDec(\langle a, a_o \rangle, r) \Longleftarrow a' = a - 1 \land oldb = b \land Choose(\langle a', a_o \rangle, \langle b, b_o \rangle, mc)$$
$$\land LingerDec(mc, r') \land r = (r' \text{ \&\& } oldb >= b_o)$$
$$r = \mathsf{true} \Longleftarrow LingerDec(\langle a, a_o \rangle, r).$$

This can be solved by many solvers since it has a very simple model:

$$Choose(\langle a, a_o \rangle, \langle b, b_o \rangle, r) :\Longleftrightarrow (b_o = b \land r = \langle a, a_o \rangle) \lor (a_o = a \land r = \langle b, b_o \rangle)$$
$$LingerDec(\langle a, a_o \rangle, r) :\Longleftrightarrow r = \mathsf{true} \land a \geq a_o.$$

Example 4. Combined with *recursive data structures*, our method turns out to be more interesting. Let us consider the following Rust code:[22]

```
enum List { Cons(i32, Box<List>), Nil } use List::*;
fn take_some<'a>(mxs: &'a mut List) -> &'a mut i32 {
   match mxs {
      Cons(mx, mxs2) => if rand() { drop mxs2; mx }
                        else { drop mx; take_some<'a>(mxs2) }
      Nil => { take_some(mxs) }
```

---

[22] In COR, `List` can be expressed as $\mu X.\mathsf{int} \times \mathsf{own}\, X + \mathsf{unit}$.

```
    }
}
fn sum(xs: &List) -> i32 {
    match xs { Cons(x, xs2) => x + sum(xs2), Nil => 0 }
}
fn inc_some(mut xs: List) -> bool {
    let n = sum(&xs); intro 'a; let my = take_some<'a>(&'a mut xs);
    *my += 1; drop my; now 'a; let m = sum(&xs); m == n + 1
}
```

This is a program that manipulates singly linked integer lists, defined as a recursive data type. `take_some` takes a mutable reference to a list and returns a mutable reference to some element of the list. `sum` calculates the sum of the elements of a list. `inc_some` increments some element of a list via a mutable reference and checks that the sum of the elements of the list has increased by 1.

Suppose we wish to verify that `inc_some` never returns `false`. Our method translates this verification problem into the following CHCs.[23]

$$TakeSome(\langle[x|xs'], xs_o\rangle, r) \iff xs_o = [x_o|xs'_o] \land xs'_o = xs' \land r = \langle x, x_o\rangle$$
$$TakeSome(\langle[x|xs'], xs_o\rangle, r) \iff xs_o = [x_o|xs'_o] \land x_o = x \land TakeSome(\langle xs', xs'_o\rangle, r)$$
$$TakeSome(\langle[], xs_o\rangle, r) \iff TakeSome(\langle[], xs_o\rangle, r)$$
$$Sum(\langle[x|xs']\rangle, r) \iff Sum(\langle xs'\rangle, r') \land r = x + r'$$
$$Sum(\langle[]\rangle, r) \iff r = 0$$
$$IncSome(xs, r) \iff Sum(\langle xs\rangle, n) \land TakeSome(\langle xs, xs_o\rangle, \langle y, y_o\rangle) \land y_o = y + 1$$
$$\land \ Sum(\langle xs_o\rangle, m) \land r = (m == n+1).$$

A crucial technique used here is *subdivision of a mutable reference*, which is achieved with the constraint $xs_o = [x_o|xs'_o]$.

We can give this CHC system a very simple model, using an auxiliary function sum (satisfying $\mathsf{sum}([x|xs']) := x + \mathsf{sum}(xs')$, $\mathsf{sum}([]) := 0$):

$$TakeSome(\langle xs, xs_o\rangle, \langle y, y_o\rangle) \iff y_o - y = \mathsf{sum}(xs_o) - \mathsf{sum}(xs)$$
$$Sum(\langle xs\rangle, r) \iff r = \mathsf{sum}(xs)$$
$$IncSome(xs, r) \iff r = \mathsf{true}.$$

Although the model relies on the function sum, the validity of the model can be checked without induction on sum (i.e. we can check the validity of each CHC just by properly unfolding the definition of sum a few times).

The example can be *fully automatically and promptly* verified by our approach using HoIce [12,11] as the back-end CHC solver; see § 4.

3.5   Discussions

We discuss here how our idea can be extended and enhanced.

---

[23] $[x|xs]$ is the cons made of the head x and the tail xs. $[]$ is the nil. In our formal logic, they are expressed as $\mathsf{inj}_0(x, \langle xs\rangle)$ and $\mathsf{inj}_1()$.

Applying Various Verification Techniques. Our idea can also be expressed as a translation of a pointer-manipulating Rust program into a program of a *stateless functional programming language*, which allows us to use *various verification techniques* not limited to CHCs. Access to future information can be modeled using *non-determinism*. To express the value $a_\circ$ coming at the end of mutable borrow in CHCs, we just *randomly guess* the value with non-determinism. At the time we actually release a mutable reference, we just *check* a' = a and cut off execution branches that do not pass the check.

For example, `take_max`/`inc_max` in § 1.2/Example 1 can be translated into the following OCaml program.

```
let rec assume b = if b then () else assume b
let take_max (a, a') (b, b') =
  if a >= b then (assume (b' = b); (a, a'))
            else (assume (a' = a); (b, b'))
let inc_max a b =
  let a' = Random.int(0) in let b' = Random.int(0) in
  let (c, c') = take_max (a, a') (b, b') in
  assume (c' = c + 1); not (a' = b')
let main a b = assert (inc_max a b)
```

'let a' = Random.int(0)' expresses a *random guess* and 'assume (a' = a)' expresses a *check*. The original problem "Does `inc_max` never return false?" is reduced to the problem "Does `main` never fail at assertion?" on the OCaml program.[24]

This representation allows us to use various verification techniques, including model checking (higher-order, temporal, bounded, etc.), semi-automated verification (e.g. on Boogie [48]) and verification on proof assistants (e.g. Coq [15]). The property to be verified can be not only partial correctness, but also total correctness and liveness. Further investigation is left for future work.

Verifying Higher-order Programs. We have to care about the following points in modeling closures: **(i)** A closure that encloses mutable references can be encoded as a pair of the main function and the 'drop function' called when the closure is released; **(ii)** A closure that updates enclosed data can be encoded as a function that returns, with the main return value, the updated version of the closure; **(iii)** A closure that updates external data through enclosed mutable references can also be modeled by combination of (i) and (ii). Further investigation on verification of higher-order Rust programs is left for future work.

Libraries with Unsafe Code. Our translation does not use lifetime information; the correctness of our method is guaranteed by the nature of borrow. Whereas

---

[24] MoCHi [39], a higher-order model checker for OCaml, successfully verified the safety property for the OCaml representation above. It also successfully and instantly verified a similar representation of `choose`/`linger_dec` at Example 3.

lifetimes are used for *static check* of the borrow discipline, many libraries in Rust (e.g. RefCell) provide a mechanism for *dynamic ownership check*.

We believe that such libraries with *unsafe code* can be verified for our method by a separation logic such as Iris [35,33], as RustBelt [32] does. A good news is that Iris has recently incorporated *prophecy variables* [34], which seems to fit well with our approach. This is an interesting topic for future work.

After the libraries are verified, we can turn to our method. For an easy example, Vec [58] can be represented simply as a functional array; a mutable/immutable slice &mut[T]/&[T] can be represented as an array of mutable/immutable references. For another example, to deal with RefCell [56], we pass around an *array* that maps a RefCell<T> address to data of type T equipped with an ownership counter; RefCell itself is modeled simply as an address.[25][26] Importantly, *at the very time we take a mutable reference $\langle a, a_\circ \rangle$ from a ref-cell, the data at the array should be updated into $a_\circ$*. Using methods such as pointer analysis [61], we can possibly shrink the array.

Still, our method does not go quite well with *memory leaks* [52] caused for example by combination of RefCell and Rc [57], because they obfuscate the ownership release of mutable references. We think that use of Rc etc. should rather be restricted for smooth verification. Further investigation is needed.

4   Implementation and Evaluation

We report on the implementation of our verification tool and the preliminary experiments conducted with small benchmarks to confirm the effectiveness of our approach.

4.1   Implementation of RustHorn

We implemented a prototype verification tool *RustHorn* (available at https://github.com/hopv/rust-horn) based on the ideas described above. The tool supports basic features of Rust supported in COR, including recursions and recursive types especially.

The implementation translates the MIR (Mid-level Intermediate Representation) [45,51] of a Rust program into CHCs quite straightforwardly.[27] Thanks to the nature of the translation, RustHorn can just rely on Rust's borrow check and forget about lifetimes. For efficiency, the predicate variables are constructed by the granularity of the vertices in the control-flow graph in MIR, unlike the per-label construction of § 3.2. Also, assertions in functions are taken into account unlike the formalization in § 3.2.

---

[25] To borrow a mutable/immutable reference from RefCell, we check and update the counter and take out the data from the array.

[26] In Rust, we can use RefCell to naturally encode data types with circular references (e.g. doubly-linked lists).

[27] In order to use the MIR, RustHorn's implementation depends on the unstable nightly version of the Rust compiler, which causes a slight portability issue.

4.2   Benchmarks and Experiments

To measure the performance of RustHorn and the existing CHC-based verifier SeaHorn [23], we conducted preliminary experiments with benchmarks listed in Table 1. Each benchmark program is designed so that the Rust and C versions match. Each benchmark instance consists of either one program or a pair of safe and unsafe programs that are very similar to each other. The benchmarks and experimental results are accessible at https://github.com/hopv/rust-horn.

The benchmarks in the groups simple and bmc were taken from SeaHorn (https://github.com/seahorn/seahorn/tree/master/test), with the Rust versions written by us. They have been chosen based on the following criteria: they (i) consist of only features supported by core Rust, (ii) follow Rust's ownership discipline, and (iii) are small enough to be amenable for manual translation from C to Rust.

The remaining six benchmark groups are built by us and consist of programs featuring mutable references. The groups inc-max, just-rec and linger-dec are based on the examples that have appeared in § 1 and § 3.4. The group swap-dec consists of programs that perform repeated involved updates via mutable references to mutable references. The groups lists and trees feature destructive updates on recursive data structures (lists and trees) via mutable references, with one interesting program of it explained in § 3.4.

We conducted experiments on a commodity laptop (2.6GHz Intel Core i7 MacBook Pro with 16GB RAM). First we translated each benchmark program by RustHorn and SeaHorn (version 0.1.0-rc3) [23] translate into CHCs in the SMT-LIB 2 format. Both RustHorn and SeaHorn generated CHCs sufficiently fast (about 0.1 second for each program). After that, we measured the time of CHC solving by Spacer [40] in Z3 (version 4.8.7) [69] and HoIce (version 1.8.1) [12,11] for the generated CHCs. SeaHorn's outputs were not accepted by HoIce, especially because SeaHorn generates CHCs with arrays. We also made modified versions for some of SeaHorn's CHC outputs, adding constraints on address freshness, to improve accuracy of representations and reduce false alarms.[28]

4.3   Experimental Results

Table 1 shows the results of the experiments.

Interestingly, the combination of RustHorn and HoIce succeeded in verifying many programs with recursive data types (lists and trees), although it failed at difficult programs.[29] HoIce, unlike Spacer, can find models defined with primitive recursive functions for recursive data types.[30]

---

[28] For base/3 and repeat/3 of inc-max, the address-taking parts were already removed, probably by inaccurate pointer analysis.

[29] For example, inc-some/2 takes two mutable references in a list and increments on them; inc-all-t destructively increments all elements in a tree.

[30] We used the latest version of HoIce, whose algorithm for recursive types is presented in the full paper of [11].

Group	Instance	Property	RustHorn w/Spacer	w/HoIce	SeaHorn w/Spacer as is	modified
simple	01	safe	<0.1	<0.1	<0.1	
	04-recursive	safe	0.5	timeout	0.8	
	05-recursive	unsafe	<0.1	<0.1	<0.1	
	06-loop	safe	timeout	0.1	timeout	
	hhk2008	safe	timeout	40.5	<0.1	
	unique-scalar	unsafe	<0.1	<0.1	<0.1	
bmc	1	safe	0.2	<0.1	<0.1	
		unsafe	0.2	<0.1	<0.1	
	2	safe	timeout	0.1	<0.1	
		unsafe	<0.1	<0.1	<0.1	
	3	safe	<0.1	<0.1	<0.1	
		unsafe	<0.1	<0.1	<0.1	
	diamond-1	safe	0.1	<0.1	<0.1	
		unsafe	<0.1	<0.1	<0.1	
	diamond-2	safe	0.2	<0.1	<0.1	
		unsafe	<0.1	<0.1	<0.1	
inc-max	base	safe	<0.1	<0.1	false alarm	<0.1
		unsafe	<0.1	<0.1	<0.1	<0.1
	base/3	safe	<0.1	<0.1	false alarm	
		unsafe	0.1	<0.1	<0.1	
	repeat	safe	0.1	timeout	false alarm	0.1
		unsafe	<0.1	0.4	<0.1	<0.1
	repeat/3	safe	0.2	timeout	<0.1	
		unsafe	<0.1	1.3	<0.1	
swap-dec	base	safe	<0.1	<0.1	false alarm	<0.1
		unsafe	0.1	timeout	<0.1	<0.1
	base/3	safe	0.2	timeout	false alarm	<0.1
		unsafe	0.4	0.9	<0.1	0.1
	exact	safe	0.1	0.5	false alarm	timeout
		unsafe	<0.1	26.0	<0.1	<0.1
	exact/3	safe	timeout	timeout	false alarm	false alarm
		unsafe	<0.1	0.4	<0.1	<0.1
just-rec	base	safe	<0.1	<0.1	<0.1	
		unsafe	<0.1	0.1	<0.1	
linger-dec	base	safe	<0.1	<0.1	false alarm	
		unsafe	<0.1	0.1	<0.1	
	base/3	safe	<0.1	<0.1	false alarm	
		unsafe	<0.1	7.0	<0.1	
	exact	safe	<0.1	<0.1	false alarm	
		unsafe	<0.1	0.2	<0.1	
	exact/3	safe	<0.1	<0.1	false alarm	
		unsafe	<0.1	0.6	<0.1	
lists	append	safe	tool error	<0.1	false alarm	
		unsafe	tool error	0.2	0.1	
	inc-all	safe	tool error	<0.1	false alarm	
		unsafe	tool error	0.3	<0.1	
	inc-some	safe	tool error	<0.1	false alarm	
		unsafe	tool error	0.3	0.1	
	inc-some/2	safe	tool error	timeout	false alarm	
		unsafe	tool error	0.3	0.4	
trees	append-t	safe	tool error	<0.1	timeout	
		unsafe	tool error	0.3	0.1	
	inc-all-t	safe	tool error	timeout	timeout	
		unsafe	tool error	0.1	<0.1	
	inc-some-t	safe	tool error	timeout	timeout	
		unsafe	tool error	0.3	0.1	
	inc-some/2-t	safe	tool error	timeout	false alarm	
		unsafe	tool error	0.4	0.1	

Table 1. Benchmarks and experimental results on RustHorn and SeaHorn, with Spacer/Z3 and HoIce. "timeout" denotes timeout of 180 seconds; "false alarm" means reporting 'unsafe' for a safe program; "tool error" is a tool error of Spacer, which currently does not deal with recursive types well.

False alarms of SeaHorn for the last six groups are mainly due to problematic approximation of SeaHorn for pointers and heap memories, as discussed in § 1.1. On the modified CHC outputs of SeaHorn, five false alarms were erased and four of them became successful. For the last four groups, unboundedly many memory cells can be allocated, which imposes a fundamental challenge for SeaHorn's array-based approach as discussed in § 1.1.[31] The combination of RustHorn and HoIce took a relatively long time or reported timeout for some programs, including unsafe ones, because HoIce is still an unstable tool compared to Spacer; in general, automated CHC solving can be rather unstable.

5   Related Work

CHC-based Verification of Pointer-Manipulating Programs. SeaHorn [23] is a representative existing tool for CHC-based verification of pointer-manipulating programs. It basically represents the heap memory as an array. Although some pointer analyses [24] are used to optimize the array representation of the heap, their approach suffers from the scalability problem discussed in § 1.1, as confirmed by the experiments in § 4. Still, their approach is quite effective as automated verification, given that many real-world pointer-manipulating programs do not follow Rust-style ownership.

Another approach is taken by JayHorn [37,36], which translates Java programs (possibly using object pointers) to CHCs. They represent store invariants using special predicates *pull* and *push*. Although this allows faster reasoning about the heap than the array-based approach, it can suffer from more false alarms. We conducted a small experiment for JayHorn (0.6-alpha) on some of the benchmarks of § 4.2; unexpectedly, JayHorn reported 'UNKNOWN' (instead of 'SAFE' or 'UNSAFE') for even simple programs such as the programs of the instance unique-scalar in simple and the instance basic in inc-max.

Verification for Rust. Whereas we have presented the first CHC-based (fully automated) verification method specially designed for Rust-style ownership, there have been a number of studies on other types of verification for Rust.

RustBelt [32] aims to formally prove high-level safety properties for Rust libraries with unsafe internal implementation, using manual reasoning on the higher-order concurrent separation logic Iris [35,33] on the Coq Proof Assistant [15]. Although their framework is flexible, the automation of the reasoning on the framework is little discussed. The language design of our COR is affected by their formal calculus λ_{Rust}.

Electrolysis [67] translates some subset of Rust into a purely functional programming language to manually verify functional correctness on Lean Theorem Prover [49]. Although it clears out pointers to get simple models like our approach, Electrolysis' applicable scope is quite limited, because it deals with mutable references by *simple static tracking of addresses based on lenses* [20], not

---

[31] We also tried on Spacer *JustRec+*, the stack-pointer-based accurate representation of just_rec presented in § 1.1, but we got timeout of 180 seconds.

supporting even basic use cases such as dynamic selection of mutable references (e.g. take_max in §1.2) [66], which our method can easily handle. Our approach covers *all* usages of pointers of the safe core of Rust as discussed in §3.

Some serial studies [27,3,17] conduct (semi-)automated verification on Rust programs using Viper [50], a verification platform based on separation logic with fractional ownership. This approach can to some extent deal with unsafe code [27] and type traits [17]. Astrauskas et al. [3] conduct semi-automated verification (manually providing pre/post-conditions and loop invariants) on many realistic examples. Because Viper is based on *fractional ownership*, however, their platforms have to use *concrete indexing on the memory* for programs like take_max/inc_max. In contrast, our idea leverages *borrow-based ownership*, and it can be applied also to semi-automated verification as suggested in §3.5.

Some researches [65,4,44] employ bounded model checking on Rust programs, especially with unsafe code. Our method can be applied to bounded model checking as discussed in §3.5.

Verification using Ownership. Ownership has been applied to a wide range of verification. It has been used for detecting race conditions on concurrent programs [8,64] and analyzing the safety of memory allocation [63]. Separation logic based on ownership is also studied well [7,50,35]. Some verification platforms [14,5,21] support simple ownership. However, most prior studies on ownership-based verification are based on fractional or counting ownership. Verification under *borrow-based ownership* like Rust was little studied before our work.

Prophecy Variables. Our idea of taking a future value to represent a mutable reference is linked to the notion of *prophecy variables* [1,68,34]. Jung et al. [34] propose a new Hoare-style logic with prophecy variables. In their logic, prophecy variables are not copyable, which is analogous to uncopyability of mutable references in Rust. This logic can probably be used for generalizing our idea as suggested in §3.5.

6   Conclusion

We have proposed a novel method for CHC-based program verification, which represents a mutable reference as a pair of values, the current value and the future value at the time of release. We have formalized the method for a core language of Rust and proved its correctness. We have implemented a prototype verification tool for a subset of Rust and confirmed the effectiveness of our approach. We believe that this study establishes the foundation of verification leveraging borrow-based ownership.

Acknowledgments. This work was supported by JSPS KAKENHI Grant Number JP15H05706 and JP16K16004. We are grateful to the anonymous reviewers for insightful comments.

References

1. Abadi, M., Lamport, L.: The existence of refinement mappings. Theor. Comput. Sci. **82**(2), 253–284 (1991). https://doi.org/10.1016/0304-3975(91)90224-P
2. Alberti, F., Bruttomesso, R., Ghilardi, S., Ranise, S., Sharygina, N.: Lazy abstraction with interpolants for arrays. In: Bjørner, N., Voronkov, A. (eds.) Logic for Programming, Artificial Intelligence, and Reasoning - 18th International Conference, LPAR-18, Mérida, Venezuela, March 11-15, 2012. Proceedings. Lecture Notes in Computer Science, vol. 7180, pp. 46–61. Springer (2012). https://doi.org/10.1007/978-3-642-28717-6_7
3. Astrauskas, V., Müller, P., Poli, F., Summers, A.J.: Leveraging Rust types for modular specification and verification (2018). https://doi.org/10.3929/ethz-b-000311092
4. Baranowski, M.S., He, S., Rakamaric, Z.: Verifying Rust programs with SMACK. In: Lahiri and Wang [42], pp. 528–535. https://doi.org/10.1007/978-3-030-01090-4_32
5. Barnett, M., Fähndrich, M., Leino, K.R.M., Müller, P., Schulte, W., Venter, H.: Specification and verification: The Spec# experience. Commun. ACM **54**(6), 81–91 (2011). https://doi.org/10.1145/1953122.1953145
6. Bjørner, N., Gurfinkel, A., McMillan, K.L., Rybalchenko, A.: Horn clause solvers for program verification. In: Beklemishev, L.D., Blass, A., Dershowitz, N., Finkbeiner, B., Schulte, W. (eds.) Fields of Logic and Computation II - Essays Dedicated to Yuri Gurevich on the Occasion of His 75th Birthday. Lecture Notes in Computer Science, vol. 9300, pp. 24–51. Springer (2015). https://doi.org/10.1007/978-3-319-23534-9_2
7. Bornat, R., Calcagno, C., O'Hearn, P.W., Parkinson, M.J.: Permission accounting in separation logic. In: Palsberg, J., Abadi, M. (eds.) Proceedings of the 32nd ACM SIGPLAN-SIGACT Symposium on Principles of Programming Languages, POPL 2005, Long Beach, California, USA, January 12-14, 2005. pp. 259–270. ACM (2005). https://doi.org/10.1145/1040305.1040327
8. Boyapati, C., Lee, R., Rinard, M.C.: Ownership types for safe programming: Preventing data races and deadlocks. In: Ibrahim, M., Matsuoka, S. (eds.) Proceedings of the 2002 ACM SIGPLAN Conference on Object-Oriented Programming Systems, Languages and Applications, OOPSLA 2002, Seattle, Washington, USA, November 4-8, 2002. pp. 211–230. ACM (2002). https://doi.org/10.1145/582419.582440
9. Boyland, J.: Checking interference with fractional permissions. In: Cousot, R. (ed.) Static Analysis, 10th International Symposium, SAS 2003, San Diego, CA, USA, June 11-13, 2003, Proceedings. Lecture Notes in Computer Science, vol. 2694, pp. 55–72. Springer (2003). https://doi.org/10.1007/3-540-44898-5_4
10. Bradley, A.R., Manna, Z., Sipma, H.B.: What's decidable about arrays? In: Emerson, E.A., Namjoshi, K.S. (eds.) Verification, Model Checking, and Abstract Interpretation, 7th International Conference, VMCAI 2006, Charleston, SC, USA, January 8-10, 2006, Proceedings. Lecture Notes in Computer Science, vol. 3855, pp. 427–442. Springer (2006). https://doi.org/10.1007/11609773_28
11. Champion, A., Chiba, T., Kobayashi, N., Sato, R.: ICE-based refinement type discovery for higher-order functional programs. In: Beyer, D., Huisman, M. (eds.) Tools and Algorithms for the Construction and Analysis of Systems - 24th International Conference, TACAS 2018, Held as Part of the European Joint Conferences

on Theory and Practice of Software, ETAPS 2018, Thessaloniki, Greece, April 14-20, 2018, Proceedings, Part I. Lecture Notes in Computer Science, vol. 10805, pp. 365–384. Springer (2018). https://doi.org/10.1007/978-3-319-89960-2_20

12. Champion, A., Kobayashi, N., Sato, R.: HoIce: An ICE-based non-linear Horn clause solver. In: Ryu, S. (ed.) Programming Languages and Systems - 16th Asian Symposium, APLAS 2018, Wellington, New Zealand, December 2-6, 2018, Proceedings. Lecture Notes in Computer Science, vol. 11275, pp. 146–156. Springer (2018). https://doi.org/10.1007/978-3-030-02768-1_8

13. Clarke, D.G., Potter, J., Noble, J.: Ownership types for flexible alias protection. In: Freeman-Benson, B.N., Chambers, C. (eds.) Proceedings of the 1998 ACM SIGPLAN Conference on Object-Oriented Programming Systems, Languages & Applications (OOPSLA '98), Vancouver, British Columbia, Canada, October 18-22, 1998. pp. 48–64. ACM (1998). https://doi.org/10.1145/286936.286947

14. Cohen, E., Dahlweid, M., Hillebrand, M.A., Leinenbach, D., Moskal, M., Santen, T., Schulte, W., Tobies, S.: VCC: A practical system for verifying concurrent C. In: Berghofer, S., Nipkow, T., Urban, C., Wenzel, M. (eds.) Theorem Proving in Higher Order Logics, 22nd International Conference, TPHOLs 2009, Munich, Germany, August 17-20, 2009. Proceedings. Lecture Notes in Computer Science, vol. 5674, pp. 23–42. Springer (2009). https://doi.org/10.1007/978-3-642-03359-9_2

15. Coq Team: The Coq proof assistant (2020), https://coq.inria.fr/

16. van Emden, M.H., Kowalski, R.A.: The semantics of predicate logic as a programming language. Journal of the ACM 23(4), 733–742 (1976). https://doi.org/10.1145/321978.321991

17. Erdin, M.: Verification of Rust Generics, Typestates, and Traits. Master's thesis, ETH Zürich (2019)

18. Fedyukovich, G., Kaufman, S.J., Bodík, R.: Sampling invariants from frequency distributions. In: Stewart, D., Weissenbacher, G. (eds.) 2017 Formal Methods in Computer Aided Design, FMCAD 2017, Vienna, Austria, October 2-6, 2017. pp. 100–107. IEEE (2017). https://doi.org/10.23919/FMCAD.2017.8102247

19. Fedyukovich, G., Prabhu, S., Madhukar, K., Gupta, A.: Quantified invariants via syntax-guided synthesis. In: Dillig, I., Tasiran, S. (eds.) Computer Aided Verification - 31st International Conference, CAV 2019, New York City, NY, USA, July 15-18, 2019, Proceedings, Part I. Lecture Notes in Computer Science, vol. 11561, pp. 259–277. Springer (2019). https://doi.org/10.1007/978-3-030-25540-4_14

20. Foster, J.N., Greenwald, M.B., Moore, J.T., Pierce, B.C., Schmitt, A.: Combinators for bidirectional tree transformations: A linguistic approach to the view-update problem. ACM Trans. Program. Lang. Syst. 29(3), 17 (2007). https://doi.org/10.1145/1232420.1232424

21. Gondelman, L.: Un système de types pragmatique pour la vérification déductive des programmes. (A Pragmatic Type System for Deductive Verification). Ph.D. thesis, University of Paris-Saclay, France (2016), https://tel.archives-ouvertes.fr/tel-01533090

22. Grebenshchikov, S., Lopes, N.P., Popeea, C., Rybalchenko, A.: Synthesizing software verifiers from proof rules. In: Vitek, J., Lin, H., Tip, F. (eds.) ACM SIGPLAN Conference on Programming Language Design and Implementation, PLDI '12, Beijing, China - June 11 - 16, 2012. pp. 405–416. ACM (2012). https://doi.org/10.1145/2254064.2254112

23. Gurfinkel, A., Kahsai, T., Komuravelli, A., Navas, J.A.: The SeaHorn verification framework. In: Kroening, D., Pasareanu, C.S. (eds.) Computer Aided Verification

- 27th International Conference, CAV 2015, San Francisco, CA, USA, July 18-24, 2015, Proceedings, Part I. Lecture Notes in Computer Science, vol. 9206, pp. 343–361. Springer (2015). https://doi.org/10.1007/978-3-319-21690-4_20

24. Gurfinkel, A., Navas, J.A.: A context-sensitive memory model for verification of C/C++ programs. In: Ranzato, F. (ed.) Static Analysis - 24th International Symposium, SAS 2017, New York, NY, USA, August 30 - September 1, 2017, Proceedings. Lecture Notes in Computer Science, vol. 10422, pp. 148–168. Springer (2017). https://doi.org/10.1007/978-3-319-66706-5_8

25. Gurfinkel, A., Shoham, S., Meshman, Y.: SMT-based verification of parameterized systems. In: Zimmermann, T., Cleland-Huang, J., Su, Z. (eds.) Proceedings of the 24th ACM SIGSOFT International Symposium on Foundations of Software Engineering, FSE 2016, Seattle, WA, USA, November 13-18, 2016. pp. 338–348. ACM (2016). https://doi.org/10.1145/2950290.2950330

26. Gurfinkel, A., Shoham, S., Vizel, Y.: Quantifiers on demand. In: Lahiri and Wang [42], pp. 248–266. https://doi.org/10.1007/978-3-030-01090-4_15

27. Hahn, F.: Rust2Viper: Building a Static Verifier for Rust. Master's thesis, ETH Zürich (2016). https://doi.org/10.3929/ethz-a-010669150

28. Hoenicke, J., Majumdar, R., Podelski, A.: Thread modularity at many levels: A pearl in compositional verification. In: Castagna, G., Gordon, A.D. (eds.) Proceedings of the 44th ACM SIGPLAN Symposium on Principles of Programming Languages, POPL 2017, Paris, France, January 18-20, 2017. pp. 473–485. ACM (2017). https://doi.org/10.1145/3009837

29. Hojjat, H., Rümmer, P.: The ELDARICA Horn solver. In: Bjørner, N., Gurfinkel, A. (eds.) 2018 Formal Methods in Computer Aided Design, FMCAD 2018, Austin, TX, USA, October 30 - November 2, 2018. pp. 1–7. IEEE (2018). https://doi.org/10.23919/FMCAD.2018.8603013

30. Horn, A.: On sentences which are true of direct unions of algebras. The Journal of Symbolic Logic 16(1), 14–21 (1951), http://www.jstor.org/stable/2268661

31. Jim, T., Morrisett, J.G., Grossman, D., Hicks, M.W., Cheney, J., Wang, Y.: Cyclone: A safe dialect of C. In: Ellis, C.S. (ed.) Proceedings of the General Track: 2002 USENIX Annual Technical Conference, June 10-15, 2002, Monterey, California, USA. pp. 275–288. USENIX (2002), http://www.usenix.org/publications/library/proceedings/usenix02/jim.html

32. Jung, R., Jourdan, J., Krebbers, R., Dreyer, D.: RustBelt: Securing the foundations of the Rust programming language. PACMPL 2(POPL), 66:1–66:34 (2018). https://doi.org/10.1145/3158154

33. Jung, R., Krebbers, R., Jourdan, J., Bizjak, A., Birkedal, L., Dreyer, D.: Iris from the ground up: A modular foundation for higher-order concurrent separation logic. J. Funct. Program. 28, e20 (2018). https://doi.org/10.1017/S0956796818000151

34. Jung, R., Lepigre, R., Parthasarathy, G., Rapoport, M., Timany, A., Dreyer, D., Jacobs, B.: The future is ours: Prophecy variables in separation logic. PACMPL 4(POPL), 45:1–45:32 (2020). https://doi.org/10.1145/3371113

35. Jung, R., Swasey, D., Sieczkowski, F., Svendsen, K., Turon, A., Birkedal, L., Dreyer, D.: Iris: Monoids and invariants as an orthogonal basis for concurrent reasoning. In: Rajamani, S.K., Walker, D. (eds.) Proceedings of the 42nd Annual ACM SIGPLAN-SIGACT Symposium on Principles of Programming Languages, POPL 2015, Mumbai, India, January 15-17, 2015. pp. 637–650. ACM (2015). https://doi.org/10.1145/2676726.2676980

36. Kahsai, T., Kersten, R., Rümmer, P., Schäf, M.: Quantified heap invariants for object-oriented programs. In: Eiter, T., Sands, D. (eds.) LPAR-21, 21st International Conference on Logic for Programming, Artificial Intelligence and Reasoning,

Maun, Botswana, May 7-12, 2017. EPiC Series in Computing, vol. 46, pp. 368–384. EasyChair (2017)

37. Kahsai, T., Rümmer, P., Sanchez, H., Schäf, M.: JayHorn: A framework for verifying Java programs. In: Chaudhuri, S., Farzan, A. (eds.) Computer Aided Verification - 28th International Conference, CAV 2016, Toronto, ON, Canada, July 17-23, 2016, Proceedings, Part I. Lecture Notes in Computer Science, vol. 9779, pp. 352–358. Springer (2016). https://doi.org/10.1007/978-3-319-41528-4_19

38. Kalra, S., Goel, S., Dhawan, M., Sharma, S.: ZEUS: Analyzing safety of smart contracts. In: 25th Annual Network and Distributed System Security Symposium, NDSS 2018, San Diego, California, USA, February 18-21, 2018. The Internet Society (2018)

39. Kobayashi, N., Sato, R., Unno, H.: Predicate abstraction and CEGAR for higher-order model checking. In: Hall, M.W., Padua, D.A. (eds.) Proceedings of the 32nd ACM SIGPLAN Conference on Programming Language Design and Implementation, PLDI 2011, San Jose, CA, USA, June 4-8, 2011. pp. 222–233. ACM (2011). https://doi.org/10.1145/1993498.1993525

40. Komuravelli, A., Gurfinkel, A., Chaki, S.: SMT-based model checking for recursive programs. In: Biere, A., Bloem, R. (eds.) Computer Aided Verification - 26th International Conference, CAV 2014, Held as Part of the Vienna Summer of Logic, VSL 2014, Vienna, Austria, July 18-22, 2014. Proceedings. Lecture Notes in Computer Science, vol. 8559, pp. 17–34. Springer (2014). https://doi.org/10.1007/978-3-319-08867-9_2

41. Lahiri, S.K., Bryant, R.E.: Constructing quantified invariants via predicate abstraction. In: Steffen, B., Levi, G. (eds.) Verification, Model Checking, and Abstract Interpretation, 5th International Conference, VMCAI 2004, Venice, Italy, January 11-13, 2004, Proceedings. Lecture Notes in Computer Science, vol. 2937, pp. 267–281. Springer (2004). https://doi.org/10.1007/978-3-540-24622-0_22

42. Lahiri, S.K., Wang, C. (eds.): Automated Technology for Verification and Analysis - 16th International Symposium, ATVA 2018, Los Angeles, CA, USA, October 7-10, 2018, Proceedings, Lecture Notes in Computer Science, vol. 11138. Springer (2018). https://doi.org/10.1007/978-3-030-01090-4

43. Lattner, C., Adve, V.S.: Automatic pool allocation: Improving performance by controlling data structure layout in the heap. In: Sarkar, V., Hall, M.W. (eds.) Proceedings of the ACM SIGPLAN 2005 Conference on Programming Language Design and Implementation, Chicago, IL, USA, June 12-15, 2005. pp. 129–142. ACM (2005). https://doi.org/10.1145/1065010.1065027

44. Lindner, M., Aparicius, J., Lindgren, P.: No panic! Verification of Rust programs by symbolic execution. In: 16th IEEE International Conference on Industrial Informatics, INDIN 2018, Porto, Portugal, July 18-20, 2018. pp. 108–114. IEEE (2018). https://doi.org/10.1109/INDIN.2018.8471992

45. Matsakis, N.D.: Introducing MIR (2016), https://blog.rust-lang.org/2016/04/19/MIR.html

46. Matsakis, N.D., Klock II, F.S.: The Rust language. In: Feldman, M., Taft, S.T. (eds.) Proceedings of the 2014 ACM SIGAda annual conference on High integrity language technology, HILT 2014, Portland, Oregon, USA, October 18-21, 2014. pp. 103–104. ACM (2014). https://doi.org/10.1145/2663171.2663188

47. Matsushita, Y., Tsukada, T., Kobayashi, N.: RustHorn: CHC-based verification for Rust programs (full version). CoRR (2020), https://arxiv.org/abs/2002.09002

48. Microsoft: Boogie: An intermediate verification language (2020), https://www.microsoft.com/en-us/research/project/boogie-an-intermediate-verification-language/

49. de Moura, L.M., Kong, S., Avigad, J., van Doorn, F., von Raumer, J.: The Lean theorem prover (system description). In: Felty, A.P., Middeldorp, A. (eds.) Automated Deduction - CADE-25 - 25th International Conference on Automated Deduction, Berlin, Germany, August 1-7, 2015, Proceedings. Lecture Notes in Computer Science, vol. 9195, pp. 378–388. Springer (2015). https://doi.org/10.1007/978-3-319-21401-6_26

50. Müller, P., Schwerhoff, M., Summers, A.J.: Viper: A verification infrastructure for permission-based reasoning. In: Jobstmann, B., Leino, K.R.M. (eds.) Verification, Model Checking, and Abstract Interpretation - 17th International Conference, VMCAI 2016, St. Petersburg, FL, USA, January 17-19, 2016. Proceedings. Lecture Notes in Computer Science, vol. 9583, pp. 41–62. Springer (2016). https://doi.org/10.1007/978-3-662-49122-5_2

51. Rust Community: The MIR (Mid-level IR) (2020), https://rust-lang.github.io/rustc-guide/mir/index.html

52. Rust Community: Reference cycles can leak memory - the Rust programming language (2020), https://doc.rust-lang.org/book/ch15-06-reference-cycles.html

53. Rust Community: RFC 2025: Nested method calls (2020), https://rust-lang.github.io/rfcs/2025-nested-method-calls.html

54. Rust Community: RFC 2094: Non-lexical lifetimes (2020), https://rust-lang.github.io/rfcs/2094-nll.html

55. Rust Community: Rust programming language (2020), https://www.rust-lang.org/

56. Rust Community: std::cell::RefCell - Rust (2020), https://doc.rust-lang.org/std/cell/struct.RefCell.html

57. Rust Community: std::rc::Rc - Rust (2020), https://doc.rust-lang.org/std/rc/struct.Rc.html

58. Rust Community: std::vec::Vec - Rust (2020), https://doc.rust-lang.org/std/vec/struct.Vec.html

59. Rust Community: Two-phase borrows (2020), https://rust-lang.github.io/rustc-guide/borrow_check/two_phase_borrows.html

60. Sato, R., Iwayama, N., Kobayashi, N.: Combining higher-order model checking with refinement type inference. In: Hermenegildo, M.V., Igarashi, A. (eds.) Proceedings of the 2019 ACM SIGPLAN Workshop on Partial Evaluation and Program Manipulation, PEPM@POPL 2019, Cascais, Portugal, January 14-15, 2019. pp. 47–53. ACM (2019). https://doi.org/10.1145/3294032.3294081

61. Steensgaard, B.: Points-to analysis in almost linear time. In: Boehm, H., Jr., G.L.S. (eds.) Conference Record of POPL'96: The 23rd ACM SIGPLAN-SIGACT Symposium on Principles of Programming Languages, Papers Presented at the Symposium, St. Petersburg Beach, Florida, USA, January 21-24, 1996. pp. 32–41. ACM Press (1996). https://doi.org/10.1145/237721.237727

62. Stump, A., Barrett, C.W., Dill, D.L., Levitt, J.R.: A decision procedure for an extensional theory of arrays. In: 16th Annual IEEE Symposium on Logic in Computer Science, Boston, Massachusetts, USA, June 16-19, 2001, Proceedings. pp. 29–37. IEEE Computer Society (2001). https://doi.org/10.1109/LICS.2001.932480

63. Suenaga, K., Kobayashi, N.: Fractional ownerships for safe memory deallocation. In: Hu, Z. (ed.) Programming Languages and Systems, 7th Asian Symposium, APLAS 2009, Seoul, Korea, December 14-16, 2009. Proceedings. Lecture Notes in Computer Science, vol. 5904, pp. 128–143. Springer (2009). https://doi.org/10.1007/978-3-642-10672-9_11

64. Terauchi, T.: Checking race freedom via linear programming. In: Gupta, R., Amarasinghe, S.P. (eds.) Proceedings of the ACM SIGPLAN 2008 Conference on Programming Language Design and Implementation, Tucson, AZ, USA, June 7-13, 2008. pp. 1–10. ACM (2008). https://doi.org/10.1145/1375581.1375583
65. Toman, J., Pernsteiner, S., Torlak, E.: CRUST: A bounded verifier for Rust. In: Cohen, M.B., Grunske, L., Whalen, M. (eds.) 30th IEEE/ACM International Conference on Automated Software Engineering, ASE 2015, Lincoln, NE, USA, November 9-13, 2015. pp. 75–80. IEEE Computer Society (2015). https://doi.org/10.1109/ASE.2015.77
66. Ullrich, S.: Electrolysis reference (2016), http://kha.github.io/electrolysis/
67. Ullrich, S.: Simple Verification of Rust Programs via Functional Purification. Master's thesis, Karlsruhe Institute of Technology (2016)
68. Vafeiadis, V.: Modular fine-grained concurrency verification. Ph.D. thesis, University of Cambridge, UK (2008), http://ethos.bl.uk/OrderDetails.do?uin=uk.bl.ethos.612221
69. Z3 Team: The Z3 theorem prover (2020), https://github.com/Z3Prover/z3

A First-Order Logic with Frames

Adithya Murali[*][†] ⓘ, Lucas Peña[*][†]✉, Christof Löding[‡], and P. Madhusudan[†] ⓘ

[†] University of Illinois at Urbana-Champaign, Department of Computer Science,
Urbana, IL, USA {adithya5,lpena7, madhu}@illinois.edu
[‡] RWTH Aachen University, Department of Computer Science, Aachen, Germany
loeding@automata.rwth-aachen.de

Abstract. We propose a novel logic, called *Frame Logic* (FL), that extends first-order logic (with recursive definitions) using a construct $Sp(\cdot)$ that captures the *implicit supports* of formulas— the precise subset of the universe upon which their meaning depends. Using such supports, we formulate proof rules that facilitate frame reasoning elegantly when the underlying model undergoes change. We show that the logic is expressive by capturing several data-structures and also exhibit a translation from a *precise* fragment of separation logic to frame logic. Finally, we design a program logic based on frame logic for reasoning with programs that dynamically update heaps that facilitates local specifications and frame reasoning. This program logic consists of both localized proof rules as well as rules that derive the weakest tightest preconditions in FL.

Keywords: Program Verification, Program Logics, Heap Verification, First-Order Logic, First-Order Logic with Recursive Definitions

1 Introduction

Program logics for expressing and reasoning with programs that dynamically manipulate heaps is an active area of research. The research on separation logic has argued convincingly that it is highly desirable to have *localized logics* that talk about small states (heaplets rather than the global heap), and the ability to do *frame reasoning*. Separation logic achieves this objective by having a tight heaplet semantics and using special operators, primarily a separating conjunction operator ∗ and a separating implication operator (the magic wand −∗).

In this paper, we ask a fundamental question: can classical logics (such as FOL and FOL with recursive definitions) be extended to support localized specifications and frame reasoning? Can we utilize classical logics for reasoning effectively with programs that dynamically manipulate heaps, with the aid of local specifications and frame reasoning?

The primary contribution of this paper is to endow a classical logic, namely first-order logic with recursive definitions (with least fixpoint semantics) with frames and frame reasoning.

---

[*] Equal contribution ✉ Corresponding Author

© The Author(s) 2020
P. Müller (Ed.): ESOP 2020, LNCS 12075, pp. 515–543, 2020.
https://doi.org/10.1007/978-3-030-44914-8_19

A formula in first-order logic with recursive definitions (FO-RD) can be naturally associated with a *support*— the subset of the universe that determines its truth. By using a more careful syntax such as guarded quantification (which continue to have a classical interpretation), we can in fact write specifications in FO-RD that have very precise supports. For example, we can write the property that x points to a linked list using a formula $list(x)$ written purely in FO-RD so that its support is precisely the locations constituting the linked list.

In this paper, we define an extension of FO-RD, called Frame Logic (FL) where we allow a new operator $Sp(\alpha)$ which, for an FO-RD formula α, evaluates to the support of α. Logical formulas thus have access to supports and can use it to *separate* supports and do frame reasoning. For instance, the logic can now express that two lists are disjoint by asserting that $Sp(list(x)) \cap Sp(list(y)) = \emptyset$. It can then reason that in such a program heap configuration, if the program manipulates only the locations in $Sp(list(y))$, then $list(x)$ would continue to be true, using simple frame reasoning.

The addition of the support operator to FO-RD yields a very natural logic for expressing specifications. First, formulas in FO-RD have the same meaning when viewed as FL formulae. For example, $f(x) = y$ (written in FO-RD as well as in FL) is true in any model that has x mapped by f to y, instead of a specialized "tight heaplet semantics" that demands that f be a partial function with the domain only consisting of the location x. The fact that the support of this formula contains only the location x is important, of course, but is made accessible using the support operator, i.e., $Sp(f(x) = y)$ gives the set containing the sole element interpreted for x. Second, properties of supports can be naturally expressed using set operations. To state that the lists pointed to by x and y are disjoint, we don't need special operators (such as the $*$ operator in separation logic) but can express this as $Sp(list(x)) \cap Sp(list(y)) = \emptyset$. Third, when used to annotate programs, pre/post specifications for programs written in FL can be made *implicitly* local by interpreting their supports to be the localized heaplets accessed and modified by programs, yielding frame reasoning akin to program logics that use separation logic. Finally, as we show in this paper, the weakest precondition of specifications across basic loop-free paths can be expressed in FL, making it an expressive logic for reasoning with programs. Separation logic, on the other hand, introduces the magic wand operator $-*$ (which is inherently higher-order) in order to add enough expressiveness to be closed under weakest preconditions [38].

We define frame logic (FL) as an extension of FO with recursive definitions (FO-RD) that operates over a multi-sorted universe, with a particular foreground sort (used to model locations on the heap on which pointers can mutate) and several background sorts that are defined using separate theories. Supports for formulas are defined with respect to the foreground sort only. A special background sort of *sets* of elements of the foreground sort is assumed and is used to model the supports for formulas. For any formula φ in the logic, we have a special construct $Sp(\varphi)$ that captures its support, a set of locations in the foreground sort, that intuitively corresponds to the precise subdomain of functions the value of φ depends on. We then prove a *frame theorem* (Theorem 1) that says that changing a model M by changing the interpretation of functions that are not in the support of φ will not affect the truth of the formula φ. This theorem then directly supports frame reasoning; if a model satisfies φ and the model is changed so that the changes made are disjoint from the support of φ, then φ will continue to hold. We also show that FL formulae can be translated to vanilla FO-RD logic (without support operators); in other words, the semantics for the support of a formula can be captured in FO-RD itself. Consequently, we can use any FO-RD reasoning mechanism (proof systems [19, 20] or heuristic algorithms such as the natural proof techniques [24, 32, 37, 41]) to reason with FL formulas.

We illustrate our logic using several examples drawn from program verification; we show how to express various data-structure definitions and the elements they contain and various measures for them using FL formulas (e.g., linked lists, sorted lists, list segments, binary search trees, AVL trees, lengths of lists, heights of trees, set of keys stored in the data-structure, etc.)

While the sensibilities of our logic are definitely inspired by separation logic, there are some fundamental differences beyond the fact that our logic extends the syntax and semantics of classical logics with a special support operator and avoids operators such as $*$ and $-*$. In separation logic, there can be many supports of a formula (also called heaplets)— a heaplet for a formula is one that *supports its truth*. For example, a formula of the form $\alpha \vee \beta$ can have a heaplet that supports the truth of α or one that supports the truth of β. However, the philosophy that we follow in our design is to have a *single* support that supports the truth value of a formula, whether it be *true or false*. Consequently, the support of the formula $\alpha \vee \beta$ is the *union* of the supports of the formulas α and β.

The above design choice of the support being *determined* by the formula has several consequences that lead to a deviation from separation logic. For instance, the support of the negation of a formula φ is the same as the support of φ. And the support of the formula $f(x) = y$ and its negation are the same, namely the singleton location interpreted for x. In separation logic, the corresponding formula will have the same heaplet but its negation will include *all* other heaplets. The choice of having determined supports or heaplets is not new, and there have been several variants and sublogics of separation logics that have been explored. For example, the logic DRYAD [32, 37] is a separation logic that insists on determined heaplets to support automated reasoning, and the *precise* fragment of separation logic studied in the literature [29] defines a sublogic that has (essentially) determined heaplets. The second main contribution in this paper is to show that this fragment of separation logic (with slight changes for technical reasons) can be translated to frame logic, such that the unique heaplet that satisfies a precise separation logic formula is its support of the corresponding formula in frame logic.

The third main contribution of this paper is a program logic based on frame logic for a simple while-programming language destructively updating heaps. We present two kinds of proof rules for reasoning with such programs annotated with pre- and post-conditions written in frame logic. The first set of rules are local rules that axiomatically define the semantics of the program, using the smallest supports for each command. We also give a frame rule that allows arguing preservation of properties whose supports are disjoint from the heaplet modified by a program. These rules are similar to analogous rules in separation logic. The second class of rules work to give a *weakest tightest precondition* for any postcondition with respect to non-recursive programs. In separation logic, the corresponding rules for weakest preconditions are often expressed using separating implication (the magic-wand operator). Given a small change made to the heap and a postcondition β, the formula $\alpha -\!* \beta$ captures all heaplets H where if a heaplet that satisfies α is joined with H, then β holds. When α describes the change effected by the program, $\alpha -\!* \beta$ captures, essentially, the weakest precondition. However, the magic wand is a very powerful operator that calls for quantifications over heaplets and submodels, and hence involves second order quantification. In our logic, we show that we can capture the weakest precondition with only first-order quantification, and hence first-order frame logic is closed under weakest preconditions across non-recursive programs blocks. This means that when inductive loop invariants are given also in FL, reasoning with programs reduces to reasoning with FL. By translating FL to pure FO-RD formulas, we can use FO-RD reasoning techniques to reason with FL, and hence programs.

In summary, the contributions of this paper are:

- A logic, called *frame logic* (FL) that extends FO-RD with a support operator and supports frame reasoning. We illustrate FL with specifications of various data-structures. We show a translation to equivalent formulas in FO-RD.

- A program logic and proof system based on FL including local rules and rules for computing the weakest tightest precondition. FL reasoning required for proving programs is hence reducible to reasoning with FO-RD.

- A separation logic fragment that can generate only precise formulas, and a translation from this logic to equivalent FL formulas.

The paper is organized as follows. Section 2 sets up first-order logics with recursive definitions (FO-RD), with a special uninterpreted foreground sort of locations and several background sorts/theories. Section 3 introduces Frame Logic (FL), its syntax, its semantics which includes a discussion of design choices for supports, proves the frame theorem for FL, shows a reduction of FL to FO-RD, and illustrates the logic by defining several data-structures and their properties using FL. Section 4 develops a program logic based on FL, illustrating them with proofs of verification of programs. Section 5 introduces a precise fragment of separation logic and shows its translation to FL. Section 6 discusses comparisons of FL to separation logic, and some existing first-order techniques that can be used to reason with FL. Section 7 compares our work with the research literature and Section 8 has concluding remarks.

2   Background: First-Order Logic with Recursive Definitions and Uninterpreted Combinations of Theories

The base logic upon which we build frame logic is a first order logic with recursive definitions (FO-RD), where we allow a foreground sort and several background sorts, each with their individual theories (like arithmetic, sets, arrays, etc.). The foreground sort and functions involving the foreground sort are *uninterpreted* (not constrained by theories). This hence can be seen as an uninterpreted combination of theories over disjoint domains. This logic has been defined and used to model heap verification before [23].

We will build frame logic over such a framework where supports are modeled as subsets of elements of the foreground sort. When modeling heaps in program verification using logic, the foreground sort will be used to model *locations of the heap*, uninterpreted functions from the foreground sort to foreground sort will be used to model *pointers*, and uninterpreted functions from the foreground sort to the background sort will model *data fields*. Consequently, supports will be subsets of locations of the heap, which is appropriate as these are the domains of pointers that change when a program updates a heap.

We define a signature as $\Sigma = (S; C; F; \mathcal{R}; \mathcal{I})$, where S is a finite non-empty set of sorts. C is a set of constant symbols, where each $c \in C$ has some sort $\tau \in S$. F is a set of function symbols, where each function $f \in F$ has a type of the form $\tau_1 \times \ldots \times \tau_m \to \tau$ for some m, with $\tau_i, \tau \in S$. The sets $\mathcal{R}$ and $\mathcal{I}$ are (disjoint) sets of relation symbols, where each relation $R \in \mathcal{R} \cup \mathcal{I}$ has a type of the form $\tau_1 \times \ldots \times \tau_m$. The set $\mathcal{I}$ contains those relation symbols for which the corresponding relations are inductively defined using formulas (details are given below), while those in $\mathcal{R}$ are given by the model.

We assume that the set of sorts contains a designated "foreground sort" denoted by σ_f. All the other sorts in S are called background sorts, and for each such background sort σ we allow the constant symbols of type σ, function symbols that have type $\sigma^n \to \sigma$ for some n, and relation symbols have type σ^m for some m, to be constrained using an arbitrary theory T_σ.

A formula in first-order logic with recursive definitions (FO-RD) over such a signature is of the form $(\mathcal{D}, \alpha)$, where $\mathcal{D}$ is a set of recursive definitions of the form $R(\overline{x}) := \rho_R(\overline{x})$, where $R \in \mathcal{I}$ and $\rho_R(\overline{x})$ is a first-order logic formula, in which the relation symbols from $\mathcal{I}$ occur only positively. α is also a first-order logic formula over the signature. We assume $\mathcal{D}$ has at most one definition for any inductively defined relation, and that the formulas ρ_R and α use only inductive relations defined in $\mathcal{D}$.

The semantics of a formula is standard; the semantics of inductively defined relations are defined to be the least fixpoint that satisfies the relational equations, and the semantics of α is the standard one defined using these semantics for relations. We do not formally define the semantics, but we will formally define the semantics of frame logic (discussed in the next section and whose semantics is defined in the Technical Report [25]) which is an extension of FO-RD.

3   Frame Logic

We now define Frame Logic (FL), the central contribution of this paper.

FL formulas: $\varphi ::= t_\tau = t_\tau \mid R(t_{\tau_1}, \ldots, t_{\tau_m}) \mid \varphi \wedge \varphi \mid \neg\varphi \mid ite(\gamma : \varphi, \varphi) \mid \exists y : \gamma. \ \varphi$
$\qquad\qquad\quad \tau \in S, \ R \in \mathcal{R} \cup \mathcal{I}$ of type $\tau_1 \times \cdots \times \tau_m$

Guards: $\gamma ::= t_\tau = t_\tau \mid R(t_{\tau_1}, \ldots, t_{\tau_m}) \mid \gamma \wedge \gamma \mid \neg\gamma \mid ite(\gamma : \gamma, \gamma) \mid \exists y : \gamma. \ \gamma$
$\qquad\qquad\quad \tau \in S \setminus \{\sigma_{\mathsf{S(f)}}\}, \ R \in \mathcal{R}$ of type $\tau_1 \times \cdots \times \tau_m$

Terms: $t_\tau ::= c \mid x \mid f(t_{\tau_1}, \ldots, t_{\tau_m}) \mid ite(\gamma : t_\tau, t_\tau) \mid$
$\qquad\qquad Sp(\varphi) \ \ (\text{if } \tau = \sigma_{\mathsf{S(f)}}) \mid Sp(t_{\tau'}) \ \ (\text{if } \tau = \sigma_{\mathsf{S(f)}})$
$\qquad\qquad \tau, \tau' \in S$ with constants c, variables x of type τ,
$\qquad\qquad$ and functions f of type $\tau_1 \times \cdots \times t_m \to \tau$

Recursive definitions: $R(\overline{x}) := \rho_R(\overline{x})$ with $R \in \mathcal{I}$ of type $\tau_1 \times \cdots \times \tau_m$ with
$\qquad\qquad \tau_i \in S \setminus \{\sigma_{\mathsf{S(f)}}\}$, FL formula $\rho_R(\overline{x})$ where all relation symbols
$\qquad\qquad R' \in \mathcal{I}$ occur only positively or inside a support expression.

Fig. 1. Syntax of frame logic: γ for guards, t_τ for terms of sort τ, and general formulas φ. Guards cannot use inductively defined relations or support expressions.

We consider a universe with a foreground sort and several background sorts, each restricted by individual theories, as described in Section 2. We consider the elements of the foreground sort to be *locations* and consider supports as *sets of locations*, i.e., sets of elements of the foreground sort. We hence introduce a background sort $\sigma_{\mathsf{S(f)}}$; the elements of sort $\sigma_{\mathsf{S(f)}}$ model sets of elements of sort σ_{f}. Among the relation symbols in $\mathcal{R}$ there is the relation $\in$ of type $\sigma_{\mathsf{f}} \times \sigma_{\mathsf{S(f)}}$ that is interpreted as the usual element relation. The signature includes the standard operations on sets $\cup, \cap$ with the usual meaning, the unary function $\tilde{}$ that is interpreted as the complement on sets (with respect to the set of foreground elements), and the constant $\emptyset$. For these functions and relations we assume a background theory $B_{\sigma_{\mathsf{S(f)}}}$ that is an axiomatization of the theory of sets. We further assume that the signature does not contain any other function or relation symbols involving the sort $\sigma_{\mathsf{S(f)}}$.

For reasoning about changes of the structure over the locations, we assume that there is a subset $F_m \subseteq F$ of function symbols that are declared mutable. These functions can be used to model mutable pointer fields in the heap that can be manipulated by a program and thus change. Formally, we require that each $f \in F_m$ has at least one argument of sort σ_{f}.

For variables, let Var_τ denote the set of variables of sort τ, where $\tau \in S$. We let $\overline{x}$ abbreviate tuples $x_1, \ldots, x_n$ of variables.

Our frame logic over uninterpreted combinations of theories is a variant of first-order logic with recursive definitions that has an additional operator $Sp(\varphi)$ that assigns to each formula φ a set of elements (its support or "heaplet" in the context of heaps) in the foreground universe. So $Sp(\varphi)$ is a term of sort $\sigma_{\mathsf{S(f)}}$.

The intended semantics of $Sp(\varphi)$ (and of the inductive relations) is defined formally as a least fixpoint of a set of equations. This semantics is presented in Section 3.3. In the following, we first define the syntax of the logic, then discuss informally the various design decisions for the semantics of supports, before proceeding to a formal definition of the semantics

3.1 Syntax of Frame Logic (FL)

The syntax of our logic is given in the grammar in Figure 1. This extends FO-RD with the rule for building *support expressions*, which are terms of sort $\sigma_{S(f)}$ of the form $Sp(\alpha)$ for a formula α, or $Sp(t)$ for a term t.

The formulas defined by γ are used as *guards* in existential quantification and in the if-then-else-operator, which is denoted by *ite*. The restriction compared to general formulas is that guards cannot use inductively defined relations (R ranges only over $\mathcal{R}$ in the rule for γ, and over $\mathcal{R} \cup \mathcal{I}$ in the rule for φ), nor terms of sort $\sigma_{S(f)}$ and thus no support expressions (τ ranges over $S \setminus \{\sigma_{S(f)}\}$ in the rules for γ and over S in the rule for φ). The requirement that the guard does not use the inductive relations and support expressions is used later to ensure the existence of least fixpoints for defining semantics of inductive definitions. The semantics of an *ite*-formula $ite(\gamma, \alpha, \beta)$ is the same as the one of $(\gamma \wedge \alpha) \vee (\neg \gamma \wedge \beta)$; however, the *supports* of the two formulas will turn out to be different (i.e., $Sp(ite(\gamma : \alpha, \beta))$ and $Sp((\gamma \wedge \alpha) \vee (\neg \gamma \wedge \beta))$ are different), as explained in Section 3.2. The same is true for existential formulas, i.e., $\exists y : \gamma.\varphi$ has the same semantics as $\exists y.\gamma \wedge \varphi$ but, in general, has a different support.

For recursive definitions (throughout the paper, we use the terms recursive definitions and inductive definitions with the same meaning), we require that the relation R that is defined does not have arguments of sort $\sigma_{S(f)}$. This is another restriction in order to ensure the existence of a least fixpoint model in the definition of the semantics.[1]

3.2 Semantics of Support Expressions: Design Decisions

We discuss the design decisions that go behind the semantics of the support operator Sp in our logic, and then give an example for the support of an inductive definition. The formal conditions that the supports should satisfy are stated in the equations in Figure 2, and are explained in Section 3.3. Here, we start by an informal discussion.

The first decision is to have every formula uniquely define a support, which roughly captures the subdomain of mutable functions that a formula φ's truth-hood depends on, and have $Sp(\varphi)$ evaluate to it.

The choice for supports of atomic formulae are relatively clear. An atomic formula of the kind $f(x)=y$, where x is of the foreground sort and f is a mutable function, has as its support the singleton set containing the location interpreted

---

[1] It would be sufficient to restrict formulas of the form $R(t_1, \ldots, t_n)$ for inductive relations R to not contain support expressions as subterms.

for x. And atomic formulas that do not involve mutable functions over the foreground have an empty support. Supports for terms can also be similarly defined. The support of a conjunction $\alpha \wedge \beta$ should clearly be the union of the supports of the two formulas.

Remark 1. In traditional separation logic, each pointer field is stored in a separate location, using integer offsets. However, in our work, we view pointers as references and disallow pointer arithmetic. A more accurate heaplet for such references can be obtained by taking heaplet to be the pair (x, f) (see [30]), capturing the fact that the formula depends only on the field f of x. Such accurate heaplets can be captured in FL as well— we can introduce a *non-mutable field lookup pointer* L_f and use $x.L_f.f$ in programs instead of $x.f$.

What should the support of a formula $\alpha \vee \beta$ be? The choice we make here is that its support is the *union* of the supports of α and β. Note that in a model where α is true and β is false, we still include the heaplet of β in $Sp(\alpha \vee \beta)$. In a sense, this is an overapproximation of the support as far as frame reasoning goes, as surely preserving the model's definitions on the support of α will preserve the truth of α, and hence of $\alpha \vee \beta$.

However, we prefer the support to be the union of the supports of α and β. We think of the support as the subdomain of the universe that determines the meaning of the formula, whether it be *true* or *false*. Consequently, we would like the support of a formula and its negation to be the same. Given that the support of the negation of a disjunction, being a conjunction, is the union of the frames of α and β, we would like this to be the support.

Separation logic makes a different design decision. Logical formulas are not associated with tight supports, but rather, the semantics of the formula is defined for models with given supports/heaplets, where the idea of a heaplet is whether it supports the *truthhood* of a formula (and not its falsehood). For example, for a model, the various heaplets that satisfy $\neg(f(x) = y)$ in separation logic would include all heaplets where the location of x is not present, which does not coincide with the notion we have chosen for supports. However, for positive formulas, separation logic handles supports more accurately, as it can associate several supports for a formula, yielding two heaplets for formulas of the form $\alpha \vee \beta$ when they are both true in a model. The decision to have a single support for a formula compels us to take the union of the supports to be the support of a disjunction.

There are situations, however, where there are disjunctions $\alpha \vee \beta$, where only *one* of the disjuncts can possibly be true, and hence we would like the support of the formula to be the support of the disjunct that happens to be true. We therefore introduce a new syntactical form $ite(\gamma : \alpha, \beta)$ in frame logic, whose heaplet is the union of the supports of γ and α, if γ is true, and the supports of γ and β if γ is false. While the truthhood of $ite(\gamma : \alpha, \beta)$ is the same as that of $(\gamma \wedge \alpha) \vee (\neg\gamma \wedge \beta)$, its supports are potentially smaller, allowing us to write formulas with tighter supports to support better frame reasoning. Note that the support of $ite(\gamma : \alpha, \beta)$ and its negation $ite(\gamma : \neg\alpha, \neg\beta)$ are the same, as we desired.

Turning to quantification, the support for a formula of the form $\exists x.\alpha$ is hard to define, as its truthhood could depend on the entire universe. We hence provide a mechanism for *guarded* quantification, in the form $\exists x : \gamma.\ \alpha$. The semantics of this formula is that there exists some location that satisfies the guard γ, for which α holds. The support for such a formula includes the support of the guard, and the supports of α when x is interpreted to be a location that satisfies γ. For example, $\exists x : (x = f(y)).\ g(x) = z$ has as its support the locations interpreted for y and $f(y)$ only.

For a formula $R(\bar{t})$ with an inductive relation R defined by $R(\bar{x}) := \rho_R(\bar{x})$, the support descends into the definition, changing the variable assignment of the variables in $\bar{x}$ from the inductive definition to the terms in $\bar{t}$. Furthermore, it contains the elements to which mutable functions are applied in the terms in $\bar{t}$.

Recursive definitions are designed such that the evaluation of the equations for the support expressions is independent of the interpretation of the inductive relations. The equations mainly depend on the syntactic structure of formulas and terms. Only the semantics of guards, and the semantics of subterms under a mutable function symbol play a role. For this reason, we disallow guards to contain recursively defined relations or support expressions. We also require that the only functions involving the sort $\sigma_{S(f)}$ are the standard functions involving sets. Thus, subterms of mutable functions cannot contain support expressions (which are of sort $\sigma_{S(f)}$) as subterms.

These restrictions ensure that there indeed exists a unique simultaneous least solution of the equations for the inductive relations and the support expressions.

We end this section with an example.

Example 1. Consider the definition of a predicate $tree(x)$ w.r.t. two unary mutable functions *left* and *right*:

$$tree(x) := ite(x = nil : true, \alpha) \text{ where}$$
$$\alpha = \exists \ell, r : (\ell = left(x) \wedge r = right(x)).tree(\ell) \wedge tree(r) \wedge$$
$$Sp(tree(\ell)) \cap Sp(tree(r)) = \emptyset \wedge \neg(x \in Sp(tree(\ell)) \cup Sp(tree(r)))$$

This inductive definition defines binary trees with pointer fields *left* and *right* for left- and right-pointers, by stating that x points to a tree if either x is equal to *nil* (in this case its support is empty), or $left(x)$ and $right(x)$ are trees with disjoint supports. The last conjunct says that x does not belong to the support of the left and right subtrees; this condition is, strictly speaking, not required to define trees (under least fixpoint semantics). Note that the access to the support of formulas eases defining disjointness of heaplets, like in separation logic. The support of $tree(x)$ turns out to be precisely the nodes that are reachable from x using *left* and *right* pointers, as one would desire. Consequently, if a pointer outside this support changes, we would be able to conclude using frame reasoning that the truth value of $tree(x)$ does not change.   □

3.3   Formal Semantics of Frame Logic

Before we explain the semantics of the support expressions and inductive definitions, we introduce a semantics that treats support expressions and the symbols

$$\llbracket Sp(c) \rrbracket_M(\nu) = \llbracket Sp(x) \rrbracket_M(\nu) = \emptyset \text{ for a constant } c \text{ or variable } x$$

$$\llbracket Sp(f(t_1,\ldots,t_n)) \rrbracket_M(\nu) = \begin{cases} \displaystyle\bigcup_{i \text{ with } t_i \text{ of sort } \sigma_f} \{\llbracket t_i \rrbracket_{M,\nu}\} \cup \bigcup_{i=1}^{n} \llbracket Sp(t_i) \rrbracket_M(\nu) & \text{if } f \in F_m \\ \displaystyle\bigcup_{i=1}^{n} \llbracket Sp(t_i) \rrbracket_M(\nu) & \text{if } f \notin F_m \end{cases}$$

$$\llbracket Sp(Sp(\varphi)) \rrbracket_M(\nu) = \llbracket Sp(\varphi) \rrbracket_M(\nu)$$

$$\llbracket Sp(Sp(t)) \rrbracket_M(\nu) = \llbracket Sp(t) \rrbracket_M(\nu)$$

$$\llbracket Sp(t_1 = t_2) \rrbracket_M(\nu) = \llbracket Sp(t_1) \rrbracket_M(\nu) \cup \llbracket Sp(t_2) \rrbracket_M(\nu)$$

$$\llbracket Sp(R(t_1,\ldots,t_n)) \rrbracket_M(\nu) = \bigcup_{i=1}^{n} \llbracket Sp(t_i) \rrbracket_M(\nu) \text{ for } R \in \mathcal{R}$$

$$\llbracket Sp(R(\bar{t})) \rrbracket_M(\nu) = \llbracket Sp(\rho_R(\overline{x})) \rrbracket_M(\nu[\overline{x} \leftarrow \llbracket \overline{t} \rrbracket_{M,\nu}]) \cup \bigcup_{i=1}^{n} \llbracket Sp(t_i) \rrbracket_M(\nu)$$
$$\text{for } R \in \mathcal{I} \text{ with definition } R(\overline{x}) := \rho_R(\overline{x}),$$
$$\bar{t} = (t_1,\ldots,t_n), \overline{x} = (x_1,\ldots,x_n)$$

$$\llbracket Sp(\alpha \wedge \beta) \rrbracket_M(\nu) = \llbracket Sp(\alpha) \rrbracket_M(\nu) \cup \llbracket Sp(\beta) \rrbracket_M(\nu)$$

$$\llbracket Sp(\neg\varphi) \rrbracket_M(\nu) = \llbracket Sp(\varphi) \rrbracket_M(\nu)$$

$$\llbracket Sp(ite(\gamma : \alpha, \beta)) \rrbracket_M(\nu) = \llbracket Sp(\gamma) \rrbracket_M(\nu) \cup \begin{cases} \llbracket Sp(\alpha) \rrbracket_M(\nu) \text{ if } M, \nu \models \gamma \\ \llbracket Sp(\beta) \rrbracket_M(\nu) \text{ if } M, \nu \not\models \gamma \end{cases}$$

$$\llbracket Sp(ite(\gamma : t_1, t_2)) \rrbracket_M(\nu) = \llbracket Sp(\gamma) \rrbracket_M(\nu) \cup \begin{cases} \llbracket Sp(t_1) \rrbracket_M(\nu) \text{ if } M, \nu \models \gamma \\ \llbracket Sp(t_2) \rrbracket_M(\nu) \text{ if } M, \nu \not\models \gamma \end{cases}$$

$$\llbracket Sp(\exists y : \gamma.\varphi) \rrbracket_M(\nu) = \bigcup_{u \in D_y} \llbracket Sp(\gamma) \rrbracket_M(\nu[y \leftarrow u]) \cup \bigcup_{u \in D_y ; M,\nu[y \leftarrow u] \models \gamma} \llbracket Sp(\varphi) \rrbracket_M(\nu[y \leftarrow u])$$

Fig. 2. Equations for support expressions

from $\mathcal{I}$ as uninterpreted symbols. We refer to this semantics as *uninterpreted semantics*. For the formal definition we need to introduce some terminology first.

An occurrence of a variable x in a formula is free if it does not occur under the scope of a quantifier for x. By renaming variables we can assume that each variable only occurs freely in a formula or is quantified by exactly one quantifier in the formula. We write $\varphi(x_1,\ldots,x_k)$ to indicate that the free variables of φ are among $x_1,\ldots,x_k$. Substitution of a term t for all free occurrences of variable x in a formula φ is denoted $\varphi[t/x]$. Multiple variables are substituted simultaneously as $\varphi[t_1/x_1,\ldots,t_n/x_n]$. We abbreviate this by $\varphi[\bar{t}/\overline{x}]$.

A model is of the form $M = (U; \llbracket \cdot \rrbracket_M)$ where $U = (U_\sigma)_{\sigma \in S}$ contains a universe for each sort, and an interpretation function $\llbracket \cdot \rrbracket_M$. The universe for the sort $\sigma_{S(f)}$ is the powerset of the universe for σ_f.

A variable assignment is a function ν that assigns to each variable a concrete element from the universe for the sort of the variable. For a variable x, we write D_x for the universe of the sort of x (the domain of x). For a variable x and an element $u \in D_x$ we write $\nu[x \leftarrow u]$ for the variable assignment that is obtained from ν by changing the value assigned for x to u.

The interpretation function $\llbracket \cdot \rrbracket_M$ maps each constant c of sort σ to an element $\llbracket c \rrbracket_M \in U_\sigma$, each function symbol $f : \tau_1 \times \ldots \times \tau_m \to \tau$ to a concrete function $\llbracket f \rrbracket_M : U_{\tau_1} \times \ldots \times U_{\tau_m} \to U_\tau$, and each relation symbol $R \in \mathcal{R} \cup \mathcal{I}$ of type $\tau_1 \times \ldots \times \tau_m$ to a concrete relation $\llbracket R \rrbracket_M \subseteq U_{\tau_1} \times \ldots \times U_{\tau_m}$. These interpretations are assumed to satisfy the background theories (see Section 2). Furthermore, the interpretation function maps each expression of the form $Sp(\varphi)$ to a function $[\![Sp(\varphi)]\!]_M$ that assigns to each variable assignment ν a set $[\![Sp(\varphi)]\!]_M(\nu)$ of foreground elements. The set $[\![Sp(\varphi)]\!]_M(\nu)$ corresponds to the support of the formula when the free variables are interpreted by ν. Similarly, $[\![Sp(t)]\!]_M$ is a function from variable assignments to sets of foreground elements.

Based on such models, we can define the semantics of terms and formulas in the standard way. The only construct that is non-standard in our logic are terms of the form $Sp(\varphi)$, for which the semantics is directly given by the interpretation function. We write $[\![t]\!]_{M,\nu}$ for the interpretation of a term t in M with variable assignment ν. With this convention, $[\![Sp(\varphi)]\!]_M(\nu)$ denotes the same thing as $[\![Sp(\varphi)]\!]_{M,\nu}$. As usual, we write $M, \nu \models \varphi$ to indicate that the formula φ is true in M with the free variables interpreted by ν, and $[\![\varphi]\!]_M$ denotes the relation defined by the formula φ with free variables $\overline{x}$.

We refer to the above semantics as the *uninterpreted semantics* of φ because we do not give a specific meaning to inductive definitions and support expressions.

Now let us define the true semantics for FL. The relation symbols $R \in \mathcal{I}$ represent inductively defined relations, which are defined by equations of the form $R(\overline{x}) := \rho_R(\overline{x})$ (see Figure 1). In the intended meaning, R is interpreted as the least relation that satisfies the equation

$$[\![R(\overline{x})]\!]_M = [\![\rho_R(\overline{x})]\!]_M.$$

The usual requirement for the existence of a unique least fixpoint of the equation is that the definition of R does not negatively depend on R. For this reason, we require that in $\rho_R(\overline{x})$ each occurrence of an inductive predicate $R' \in \mathcal{I}$ is either inside a support expression, or it occurs under an even number of negations.[2]

Every support expression is evaluated on a model to a set of foreground elements (under a given variable assignment ν). Formally, we are interested in models in which the support expressions are interpreted to be the sets that correspond to the *smallest solution of the equations given in Figure 2*. The intuition behind these definitions was explained in Section 3.2

Example 2. Consider the inductive definition $tree(x)$ defined in Example 1. To check whether the equations from Figure 2 indeed yield the desired support, note that the supports of $Sp(x = nil) = Sp(x) = Sp(true) = \emptyset$. Below, we write $[u]$ for a variable assignment that assigns u to the free variable of the formula that we are considering. Then we obtain that $Sp(tree(x))[u] = \emptyset$ if $u = nil$, and $Sp(tree(x))[u] = Sp(\alpha)[u]$ if $x \neq nil$. The formula α is existentially quantified with guard $\ell = left(x) \wedge r = right(x)$. The support of this guard is $\{u\}$ because mutable functions are applied to x. The support of the remaining part of α is the union of the supports of $tree(\ell)[left(u)]$ and $tree(r)[right(u)]$ (the assignments for ℓ and r that make the guard true). So we obtain for the case that $u \neq nil$ that the element u enters the support, and the recursion further descends into the subtrees of u, as desired.   □

---

[2] As usual, it would be sufficient to forbid negative occurrences of inductive predicates in mutual recursion.

A *frame model* is a model in which the interpretation of the inductive relations and of the support expressions corresponds to the least solution of the
respective equations (see the Technical Report [25] for a rigorous formalisation).

Proposition 1. *For each model M, there is a unique frame model over the
same universe and the same interpretation of the constants, functions, and non-
inductive relations.*

3.4   A Frame Theorem

The support of a formula can be used for frame reasoning in the following sense:
if we modify a model M by changing the interpretation of the mutable functions
(e.g., a program modifying pointers), then truth values of formulas do not change
if the change happens outside the support of the formula. This is formalized
below and proven in the Technical Report [25].

Given two models M, M' over the same universe, we say that M' is a *mutation
of M* if $[\![R]\!]_M = [\![R]\!]_{M'}$, $[\![c]\!]_M = [\![c]\!]_{M'}$, and $[\![f]\!]_M = [\![f]\!]_{M'}$, for all constants c,
relations $R \in \mathcal{R}$, and functions $f \in F \setminus F_{\mathsf{m}}$. In other words, M can only be
different from M' on the interpretations of the mutable functions, the inductive
relations, and the support expressions.

Given a subset $X \subseteq U_{\sigma_{\mathsf{f}}}$ of the elements from the foreground universe, we say
that the *mutation is stable on X* if the values of the mutable functions did not
change on arguments from X, that is, $[\![f]\!]_M(u_1, \ldots, u_n) = [\![f]\!]_{M'}(u_1, \ldots, u_n)$ for
all mutable functions $f \in F_{\mathsf{m}}$ and all appropriate tuples $u_1, \ldots, u_n$ of arguments
with $\{u_1, \ldots, u_n\} \cap X \neq \emptyset$.

Theorem 1 (Frame Theorem). *Let M, M' be frame models such that M' is
a mutation of M that is stable on $X \subseteq U_{\sigma_{\mathsf{f}}}$, and let ν be a variable assignment.
Then $M, \nu \models \alpha$ iff $M', \nu \models \alpha$ for all formulas α with $[\![Sp(\alpha)]\!]_M(\nu) \subseteq X$, and
$[\![t]\!]_{M,\nu} = [\![t]\!]_{M',\nu}$ for all terms t with $[\![Sp(t)]\!]_M(\nu) \subseteq X$.*

3.5   Reduction from Frame Logic to FO-RD

The only extension of frame logic compared to FO-RD is the operator Sp, which
defines a function from interpretations of free variables to sets of foreground
elements. The semantics of this operator can be captured within FO-RD itself,
so reasoning within frame logic can be reduced to reasoning within FO-RD.

A formula $\alpha(\overline{y})$ with $\overline{y} = y_1, \ldots, y_m$ has one support for each interpretation of the free variables. We capture these supports by an inductively defined
relation $Sp_\alpha(\overline{y}, z)$ of arity $m + 1$ such that for each frame model M, we have
$(u_1, \ldots, u_m, u) \in [\![Sp_\alpha]\!]_M$ if $u \in [\![Sp(\alpha)]\!]_M(\nu)$ for the interpretation ν that interprets y_i as u_i.

Since the semantics of $Sp(\alpha)$ is defined over the structure of α, we introduce
corresponding inductively defined relations Sp_β and Sp_t for all subformulas β
and subterms t of either α or of a formula ρ_R for $R \in \mathcal{I}$.

$$list(x) := ite(x = nil, true, \exists z : z = next(x).\ list(z) \land x \notin Sp(list(z)))$$
$$\text{(linked list)}$$

$$dll(x) := ite(x = nil : \top, ite(next(x) = nil : \top, \exists z : z = next(x).$$
$$prev(z) = x \land dll(z) \land x \notin Sp(dll(z))))) \qquad \text{(doubly linked list)}$$

$$lseg(x, y) := ite(x = y : \top, \exists z : z = next(x).\ lseg(z, y) \land x \notin Sp(lseg(z, y)))$$
$$\text{(linked list segment)}$$

$$length(x, n) := ite(x = nil : n = 0, \exists z : z = next(x).\ length(z, n - 1))$$
$$\text{(length of list)}$$

$$slist(x) := ite(x = nil : \top, ite(next(x) = nil, \top, \exists z : z = next(x).$$
$$key(x) \leq key(z) \land slist(z) \land x \notin Sp(slist(z))))) \qquad \text{(sorted list)}$$

$$mkeys(x, M) := ite(x = nil : M = \emptyset, \exists z, M_1 : z = next(x).$$
$$M = M_1 \cup_m \{key(x)\} \land mkeys(z, M_1)) \land x \notin Sp(mkeys(z, M_1))$$
$$\text{(multiset of keys in linked list)}$$

$$btree(x) := ite(x = nil : \top, \exists \ell, r : \ell = left(x) \land r = right(x).$$
$$btree(\ell) \land btree(r) \land x \notin Sp(btree(\ell)) \land x \notin Sp(btree(r)) \land$$
$$Sp(btree(\ell)) \cap Sp(btree(r)) = \emptyset) \qquad \text{(binary tree)}$$

$$bst(x) := ite(x = nil : \top, ite(left(x) = nil \land right(x) = nil : \top, ite(left(x) = nil :$$
$$\exists r : r = right(x).\ key(x) \leq key(r) \land bst(r) \land x \notin Sp(bst(r)),$$
$$ite(right(x) = nil : \exists \ell : \ell = left(x).\ key(\ell) \leq key(x) \land bst(\ell) \land x \notin Sp(bst(\ell)),$$
$$\exists \ell, r : \ell = left(x) \land r = right(x).\ key(x) \leq key(r) \land key(\ell) \leq key(x) \land$$
$$bst(\ell) \land bst(r) \land x \notin Sp(bst(\ell)) \land x \notin Sp(bst(r)) \land$$
$$Sp(bst(\ell)) \cap Sp(bst(r)) = \emptyset)))) \qquad \text{(binary search tree)}$$

$$height(x, n) := ite(x = nil : n = 0, \exists \ell, r, n_1, n_2 : \ell = left(x) \land r = right(x).$$
$$height(\ell, n_1) \land height(r, n_2) \land ite(n_1 > n_2 : n = n_1 + 1, n = n_2 + 1))$$
$$\text{(height of binary tree)}$$

$$bfac(x, b) := ite(x = nil : 0, \exists \ell, r, n_1, n_2 : \ell = left(x) \land r = right(x).$$
$$height(\ell, n_1) \land height(r, n_2) \land b = n_2 - n_1)$$
$$\text{(balance factor (for AVL tree))}$$

$$avl(x) := ite(x = nil : \top, \exists \ell, r : \ell = left(x) \land r = right(x).$$
$$avl(\ell) \land avl(r) \land bfac(x) \in \{-1, 0, 1\} \land$$
$$x \notin Sp(avl(\ell)) \cup Sp(avl(r)) \land Sp(avl(\ell)) \cap Sp(avl(r)) = \emptyset) \quad \text{(avl tree)}$$

$$ttree(x) := pttree(x, nil) \qquad \text{(threaded tree)}$$

$$pttree(x, p) := ite(x = nil : \top, \exists \ell, r : \ell = left(x) \land r = right(x).$$
$$((r = nil \land tnext(x) = p) \lor (r \neq nil \land tnext(x) = r)) \land$$
$$pttree(\ell, x) \land pttree(r, p) \land x \notin Sp(pttree(\ell, x)) \cup Sp(pttree(r, p)) \land$$
$$Sp(pttree(\ell, x)) \cap Sp(pttree(r, p)) = \emptyset)$$
$$\text{(threaded tree auxiliary definition)}$$

Fig. 3. Example definitions of data-structures and other predicates in Frame Logic

The equations for supports from Figure 2 can be expressed by inductive definitions for the relations Sp_β. The translations are shown in the Technical Report [25]. It is not hard to see that general frame logic formulas can be translated to FO-RD formulas that make use of these new inductively defined relations.

Proposition 2. *For every frame logic formula there is an equisatisfiable FO-RD formula with the signature extended by auxiliary predicates for recursive definitions of supports.*

3.6   Expressing Data-Structures Properties in FL

We now present the formulation of several data-structures and properties about them in FL. Figure 3 depicts formulations of singly- and doubly-linked lists, list segments, lengths of lists, sorted lists, the multiset of keys stored in a list (assuming a background sort of multisets), binary trees, their heights, and AVL trees. In all these definitions, the support operator plays a crucial role. We also present a formulation of *single threaded binary trees* (adapted from [7]), which are binary trees where, apart from tree-edges, there is a pointer *tnext* that connects every tree node to the inorder successor in the tree; these pointers go from leaves to ancestors arbitrarily far away in the tree, making it a nontrivial definition.

We believe that FL formulas naturally and succinctly express these data-structures and their properties, making it an attractive logic for annotating programs.

4   Programs and Proofs

In this section, we develop a program logic for a while-programming language that can destructively update heaps. We assume that location variables are denoted by variables of the form x and y, whereas variables that denote other data (which would correspond to the *background* sorts in our logic) are denoted by v. We omit the grammar to construct background terms and formulas, and simply denote such 'background expressions' with *be* and clarify the sort when it is needed. Finally, we assume that our programs are written in Single Static Assignment (SSA) form, which means that every variable is assigned to at most once in the program text. The grammar for our programming language is in Figure 4.

$$S ::= x := c \mid x := y \mid x := y.f \mid v := be \mid x.f := y$$
$$\mid \mathsf{alloc}(x) \mid \mathsf{free}(x) \mid \text{if } be \text{ then } S \text{ else } S \mid \text{while } be \text{ do } S \mid S\,;\,S$$

Fig. 4. Grammar of while programs. c is a constant location, f is a field pointer, and *be* is a background expression. In our logic, we model every field f as a function $f()$ from locations to the appropriate sort.

4.1   Operational Semantics

A configuration $\mathcal{C}$ is of the form (M, H, U) where M contains interpretations for the store and the heap. The store is a partial map that interprets variables, constants, and non-mutable functions (a function from location variables to locations) and the heap is a total map on the domain of locations that interprets mutable functions (a function from pointers and locations to locations). H is a subset of locations denoting the set of allocated locations, and U is a subset of locations denoting a *subset* of unallocated locations that can be allocated in the future. We introduce a special configuration $\bot$ that the program transitions to when it dereferences a variable not in H.

A configuration (M, H, U) is *valid* if all variables of the location sort map only to locations not in U, locations in H do not point to any location in U, and U is a subset of the complement of H that does not contain *nil* or the locations mapped to by the variables. We denote this by $valid(M, H, U)$. Initial configurations and reachable configurations of any program will be valid.

The transition of configurations on various commands that manipulate the store and heap are defined in the natural way. Allocation adds a new location from U into H with pointer-fields defaulting to *nil* and default data fields. See the Technical Report [25] for more details.

4.2   Triples and Validity

We express specifications of programs using triples of the form $\{\alpha\}S\{\beta\}$ where α and β are FL formulae and S is a program. The formulae are, however, restricted— for simplicity, we disallow atomic relations on locations, and functions with arity greater than one. We also disallow functions from a background sort to the foreground sort (see Section 3). Lastly, quantified formulae can have supports as large as the entire heap. However, our program logic covers a more practical fragment without compromising expressivity. Thus, we require guards in quantification to be of the form $f(z') = z$ or $z \in U$ (z is the quantified variable).

We define a triple to be *valid* if every valid configuration with heaplet being precisely the support of α, when acted on by the program, yields a configuration with heaplet being the support of β. More formally, a triple is valid if for every valid configuration (M, H, U) such that $M \models \alpha$, $H = [\![Sp(\alpha)]\!]_M$:

- it is never the case that the abort state $\bot$ is encountered in the execution on S.
- if (M, H, U) transitions to (M', H', U') on S, then $M' \models \beta$ and $H' = [\![Sp(\beta)]\!]_{M'}$

4.3   Program Logic

First, we define a set of *local rules* and rules for conditionals, while, sequence, consequence, and framing:

Assignment: $\{true\}\ x := y\ \{x = y\}$ $\{true\}\ x := c\ \{x = c\}$

Lookup: $\{f(y) = f(y)\}\ x := y.f\ \{x = f(y)\}$

Mutation: $\{f(x) = f(x)\}\ x.f := y\ \{f(x) = y\}$

Allocation: $\{true\}\ \mathsf{alloc}(x)\ \{\ \bigwedge_{f \in F} f(x) = def_f\}$

Deallocation: $\{f(x) = f(x)\}\ \mathsf{free}(x)\ \{true\}$

Conditional: $\dfrac{\{be \wedge \alpha\}\ S\ \{\beta\} \quad \{\neg be \wedge \alpha\}\ T\ \{\beta\}}{\{\alpha\}\ \mathsf{if}\ be\ \mathsf{then}\ S\ \mathsf{else}\ T\ \{\beta\}}$

While: $\dfrac{\{\alpha \wedge be\}\ S\ \{\alpha\}}{\{\alpha\}\ \mathsf{while}\ be\ \mathsf{do}\ S\ \{\neg be \wedge \alpha\}}$

Sequence: $\dfrac{\{\alpha\}\ S\ \{\beta\} \quad \{\beta\}\ T\ \{\mu\}}{\{\alpha\}\ S\ ;\ T\ \{\mu\}}$

Consequence: $\dfrac{\alpha' \implies \alpha \quad \{\alpha\}\ S\ \{\beta\} \quad Sp(\alpha) = Sp(\alpha') \quad \beta \implies \beta' \quad Sp(\beta) = Sp(\beta')}{\{\alpha'\}\ S\ \{\beta'\}}$

Frame: $\dfrac{Sp(\alpha) \cap Sp(\mu) = \emptyset \quad \{\alpha\}\ S\ \{\beta\}}{\{\alpha \wedge \mu\}\ S\ \{\beta \wedge \mu\}}\ vars(S) \cap fv(\mu) = \emptyset$

The above rules are intuitively clear and are similar to the local rules in separation logic [38]. The rules for statements capture their semantics using minimal/tight heaplets, and the frame rule allows proving triples with larger heaplets. In the rule for alloc, the postcondition says that the newly allocated location has default values for all pointer fields and datafields (denoted as def_f). The soundness of the frame rule relies crucially on the frame theorem for FL (Theorem 1). The full soundness proof can be found in the Technical Report [25].

Theorem 2. *The above rules are sound with respect to the operational semantics.*

4.4   Weakest-Precondition Proof Rules

We now turn to the much more complex problem of designing rules that give weakest preconditions for arbitrary postconditions, for loop-free programs. In separation logic, such rules resort to using the magic-wand operator $-*$ [12, 27, 28, 38], The magic-wand operator, a complex operator whose semantics calls for *second-order quantification* over arbitrarily large submodels. In our setting, our main goal is to show that FL is itself capable of expressing weakest preconditions of postconditions written in FL.

First, we define a notion of *Weakest Tightest Precondition* (WTP) of a formula β with respect to each command in our operational semantics. To define this notion, we first define a preconfiguration, and use that definition to define weakest tightest preconditions:

Definition 1. *The preconfigurations corresponding to a valid configuration (M, H, U) with respect to a program S are a set of valid configurations of the form (M_p, H_p, U_p) (with M_p being a model, H_p and U_p a subuniverse of the locations in M_p, and U_p being unallocated locations) such that when S is executed on M_p with unallocated set U_p it dereferences only locations in H_p and results (using the operational semantics rules) in (M, H, U) or gets stuck (no transition is available). That is:*

$$preconfigurations((M, H, U), S) =$$

$$\{(M_p, H_p, U_p) \mid valid(M_p, H_p, U_p) \text{ and } (M_p, H_p, U_p) \overset{S}{\Rightarrow} (M, H, U) \text{ or}$$
$$(M_p, H_p, U_p) \text{ gets stuck on } S\}$$

Definition 2. *α is a WTP of a formula β with respect to a program S if*

$$\{(M_p, H_p, U_p) \mid M_p \models \alpha, H_p = [\![Sp(\alpha)]\!]_{M_p}, valid(M_p, H_p, U_p)\}$$
$$= \{preconfigurations((M, H, U), S) \mid M \models \beta, H = [\![Sp(\beta)]\!]_M, valid(M, H, U)\}$$

With the notion of weakest tightest preconditions, we define global program logic rules for each command of our language. In contrast to local rules, global specifications contain heaplets that may be larger than the smallest heap on which one can execute the command.

Intuitively, a WTP of β for lookup states that β must hold in the precondition when x is interpreted as x', where $x' = f(y)$, and further that the location y must belong to the support of β. The rules for mutation and allocation are more complex. For mutation, we define a transformation $MW^{x.f:=y}(\beta)$ that evaluates a formula β in the pre-state as though it were evaluated in the post-state. We similarly define such a transformation $MW_v^{\text{alloc}(x)}$ for allocation. We will define these in detail later. Finally, the deallocation rule ensures x is not in the support of the postcondition. The conjunct $f(x) = f(x)$ is provided to satisfy the tightness condition, ensuring the support of the precondition is the support of the postcondition with x added. The rules can be seen below, and the proof of soundness for these global rules can be found in the Technical Report [25].

Assignment-G: $\{\beta[y/x]\}\ x := y\ \{\beta\}$ $\{\beta[c/x]\}\ x := c\ \{\beta\}$

Lookup-G: $\{\exists x' : x' = f(y).\ (\beta \wedge y \in Sp(\beta))[x'/x]\}\ x := y.f\ \{\beta\}$
(where x' does not occur in β)

Mutation-G: $\{MW^{x.f:=y}(\beta \wedge x \in Sp(\beta))\}\ x.f := y\ \{\beta\}$

Allocation-G: $\{\forall v : (v \in U).(v \neq nil \Rightarrow MW_v^{\text{alloc}(x)}(\beta))\}\ \text{alloc}(x)\ \{\beta\}$
(for some fresh variable v)

Deallocation-G: $\{\beta \wedge x \notin Sp(\beta) \wedge f(x) = f(x)\}\ \text{free}(x)\ \{\beta\}$
(where $f \in F_m$ is an arbitrary (unary) mutable function)

4.5 Definitions of MW Primitives

Recall that the MW^3 primitives $MW^{x.f:=y}$ and $MW_v^{\mathsf{alloc}(x)}$ need to evaluate a formula β in the pre-state as it would evaluate in the post-state after mutation and allocation statements. The definition of $MW^{x.f:=y}$ is as follows:

$$MW^{x.f:=y}(\beta) = \beta[\lambda z.\ ite(z = x : ite(f(x) = f(x) : y, y), f(z))/f]$$

The $\beta[\lambda z.\rho(z)/f]$ notation is shorthand for saying that each occurrence of a term of the form $f(t)$, where t is a term, is substituted (recursively, from inside out) by the term $\rho(t)$. The precondition essentially evaluates β taking into account f's transformation, but we use the *ite* expression with a tautological guard $f(x) = f(x)$ (which has the support containing the singleton x) in order to preserve the support. The definition of $MW_v^{\mathsf{alloc}(x)}$ is similar. Refer to the Technical Report [25] for details.

Theorem 3. *The rules above suffixed with -G are sound w.r.t the operational semantics. And, each precondition corresponds to the weakest tightest precondition of β.*

4.6 Example

In this section, we will see an example of using our program logic rules that we described earlier. This will demonstrate the utility of Frame Logic as a logic for annotating and reasoning with heap manipulating programs, as well as offer some intuition about how our program logic can be deployed in a practical setting. The following program performs in-place list reversal: `j := nil ; while (i != nil) do k := i.next ; i.next := j ; j := i ; i := k` For the sake of simplicity, instead of proving that this program reverses a list, we will instead prove the simpler claim that after executing this program j is a *list*. The recursive definition of *list* we use for this proof is the one from Figure 3:

$$list(x) := ite(x = nil, true, \exists z : z = next(x).\ list(z) \wedge x \notin Sp(list(z)))$$

We need to also give an invariant for the while loop, simply stating that i and j point to disjoint lists: $list(i) \wedge list(j) \wedge Sp(list(i)) \cap Sp(list(j)) = \emptyset$.

We prove that this is indeed an invariant of the while loop below. Our proof uses a mix of both local and global rules from Sections 4.3 and 4.4 above to demonstrate how either type of rule can be used. We also use the consequence rule along with the program rule to be applied in several places in order to simplify presentation. As a result, some detailed analysis is omitted, such as proving supports are disjoint in order to use the frame rule.

$$\{\,list(i) \wedge list(j) \wedge Sp(list(i)) \cap Sp(list(j)) = \emptyset \wedge i \neq nil\}\qquad \text{(consequence rule)}$$

---

[3] The acronym MW is a shout-out to the Magic-Wand operator, as these serve a similar function, except that they are definable in FL itself.

$\{ list(i) \wedge list(j) \wedge Sp(list(i)) \cap Sp(list(j)) = \emptyset \wedge i \neq nil \wedge i \notin Sp(list(j)) \}$
$\qquad\qquad\qquad\qquad$ (consequence rule: unfolding list definition)

$\{ \exists k' : k' = next(i). \; list(k') \wedge i \notin Sp(list(k')) \wedge list(j)$
$\qquad\qquad \wedge \, i \notin Sp(list(j)) \wedge Sp(list(k')) \cap Sp(list(j)) = \emptyset \}$ (consequence rule)

$\{ \exists k' : k' = next(i). \; next(i) = next(i) \wedge list(k') \wedge i \notin Sp(list(k')) \wedge list(j)$
$\qquad\qquad \wedge \, i \notin Sp(list(j)) \wedge Sp(list(k')) \cap Sp(list(j)) = \emptyset \}$

$\qquad$ **k := i.next ;** $\qquad\qquad\qquad\qquad$ (consequence rule, lookup-G rule)

$\{ next(i) = next(i) \wedge list(k) \wedge i \notin Sp(list(k)) \wedge list(j)$
$\qquad\qquad \wedge \, i \notin Sp(list(j)) \wedge Sp(list(k)) \cap Sp(list(j)) = \emptyset \}$

$\qquad$ **i.next := j ;** $\qquad\qquad\qquad\qquad$ (mutation rule, frame rule)

$\{ next(i) = j \wedge list(k) \wedge i \notin Sp(list(k)) \wedge list(j)$
$\qquad\qquad \wedge \, i \notin Sp(list(j)) \wedge Sp(list(k)) \cap Sp(list(j)) = \emptyset \}$ (consequence rule)

$\{ list(k) \wedge next(i) = j \wedge i \notin Sp(list(j)) \wedge list(j) \wedge Sp(list(k)) \cap Sp(list(j)) = \emptyset \}$
$\qquad\qquad\qquad\qquad$ (consequence rule: folding list definition)

$\{ list(k) \wedge list(i) \wedge Sp(list(k)) \cap Sp(list(i)) = \emptyset \}$

$\qquad$ **j := i ; i := k** $\qquad\qquad\qquad\qquad$ (assignment-G rule)

$\{ list(i) \wedge list(j) \wedge Sp(list(i)) \cap Sp(list(j)) = \emptyset \}$

Armed with this, proving j is a list after executing the full program above is a trivial application of the assignment, while, and consequence rules, which we omit for brevity.

Observe that in the above proof we were apply the frame rule because of the fact that i belongs neither to $Sp(list(k))$ nor $Sp(list(j))$. This can be dispensed with easily using reasoning about first-order formulae with least-fixpoint definitions, techniques for which are discussed in Section 6.

Also note the invariant of the loop is precisely the intended meaning of $list(i) *$ $list(j)$ in separation logic. In fact, as we will see in Section 6, we can define a *first-order* macro *Star* as $Star(\varphi, \psi) = \varphi \wedge \psi \wedge Sp(\varphi) \cap Sp(\psi) = \emptyset$. We can use this macro to represent disjoint supports in similar proofs.

These proofs demonstrate what proofs of actual programs look like in our program logic. They also show that frame logic and our program logic can prove many results similarly to traditional separation logic. And, by using the derived operator *Star*, very little even in terms of verbosity is sacrificed in gaining the flexibility of Frame Logic(please see Section 6 for a broader discussion of the ways in which Frame Logic differs from Separation Logic and in certain situations offers many advantages in stating and reasoning with specifications/invariants).

5   Expressing a Precise Separation Logic

In this section, we show that FL is expressive by capturing a fragment of separation logic in frame logic; the fragment is a syntactic fragment of separation logic that defines only *precise formulas*— formulas that can be satisfied in at most one heaplet for any store. The translation also shows that frame logic can naturally and compactly capture such separation logic formulas.

5.1 A Precise Separation Logic

As discussed in Section 1, a crucial difference between separation logic and frame logic is that formulas in separation logic have uniquely determined supports/heaplets, while this is not true in separation logic. However, it is well known that in verification, determined heaplets are very natural (most uses of separation logic in fact are precise) and sometimes desirable. For instance, see [8] where precision is used crucially to give sound semantics to concurrent separation logic and [29] where precise formulas are proposed in verifying modular programs as imprecision causes ambiguity in function contracts.

We define a fragment of separation logic that defines precise formulas (more accurately, we handle a slightly larger class inductively: formulas that when satisfiable have unique minimal heaplets for any given store). The fragment we capture is similar to the notion of precise predicates seen in [29]:

Definition 3. *PSL Fragment:*

- *sf: formulas over the stack only (nothing dereferenced). Includes isatom?(), $m(x) = y$ for immutable m, true, background formulas, etc.*
- $x \xrightarrow{f} y$
- *$ite(sf, \varphi_1, \varphi_2)$ where sf is from the first bullet*
- *$\varphi_1 \wedge \varphi_2$ and $\varphi_1 * \varphi_2$*
- *I where $\mathcal{I}$ contains all unary inductive definitions I that have unique heaplets inductively (list, tree, etc.). In particular, the body ρ_I of I is a formula in the PSL fragment ($\rho_I[I \leftarrowtail \varphi]$ is in the PSL fragment provided φ is in the PSL fragment). Additionally, for all x, if $s, h \models I(x)$ and $s, h' \models I(x)$, then $h = h'$.[4]*
- *$\exists y. (x \xrightarrow{f} y) * \varphi_1$*

Note that in the fragment negation and disjunction are disallowed, but mutually exclusive disjunction using *ite* is allowed. Existential quantification is only present when the topmost operator is a $*$ and where one of the formulas guards the quantified variable uniquely.

The semantics of this fragment follows the standard semantics of separation logic [12, 27, 28, 38], with the heaplet of $x \xrightarrow{f} y$ taken to be $\{x\}$. See Remark 1 in Section 3.2 for a discussion of a more accurate heaplet for $x \xrightarrow{f} y$ being the set containing the pair (x, f), and how this can be modeled in the above semantics by using field-lookups using non-mutable pointers.

Theorem 4 (Minimum Heap). *For any formula φ in the PSL fragment, if there is an s and h such that $s, h \models \varphi$ then there is a h_φ such that $s, h_\varphi \models \varphi$ and for all h' such that $s, h' \models \varphi$, $h_\varphi \subseteq h'$.*

---

[4] While we only assume unary inductive definitions here, we can easily generalize this to inductive definitions with multiple parameters.

5.2   Translation to Frame Logic

For a separation logic store and heap s, h (respectively), we define the corresponding interpretation $\mathcal{M}_{s,h}$ such that variables are interpreted according to s and values of pointer functions on $dom(h)$ are interpreted according to h. For φ in the PSL fragment, we first define a formula $P(\varphi)$, inductively, that captures whether φ is precise. φ is a precise formula iff, when it is satisfiable with a store s, there is exactly one h such that $s, h \models \varphi$. The formula $P(\varphi)$ is in separation logic and will be used in the translation. To see why this formula is needed, consider the formula $\varphi_1 \wedge ite(sf, \varphi_2, \varphi_3)$. Assume that φ_1 is imprecise, φ_2 is precise, and φ_3 is imprecise. Under conditions where sf is true, the heaplets for φ_1 and φ_2 must align. However, when sf is false, the heaplets for φ_1 and φ_3 can be anything. Because we cannot initially know when sf will be true or false, we need this separation logic formula $P(\varphi)$ that is true exactly when φ is precise.

Definition 4. *Precision predicate P:*

- $P(sf) = \bot$ and $P(x \xrightarrow{f} y) = \top$
- $P(ite(sf, \varphi_1, \varphi_2)) = (sf \wedge P(\varphi_1)) \vee (\neg sf \wedge P(\varphi_2))$
- $P(\varphi_1 \wedge \varphi_2) = P(\varphi_1) \vee P(\varphi_2)$
- $P(\varphi_1 * \varphi_2) = P(\varphi_1) \wedge P(\varphi_2)$
- $P(I) = \top$ *where* $I \in \mathcal{I}$ *is an inductive predicate*
- $P(\exists y.\ (x \xrightarrow{f} y) * \varphi_1) = P(\varphi_1)$

Note that this definition captures precision within our fragment since stack formulae are imprecise and pointer formulae are precise. The argument for the rest of the cases follow by simple structural induction.

Now we define the translation T inductively:

Definition 5. *Translation from PSL to Frame Logic:*

- $T(sf) = sf$ and $T(x \xrightarrow{f} y) = (f(x) = y)$
- $ite(sf, \varphi_1, \varphi_2) = ite(T(sf), T(\varphi_1), T(\varphi_2))$
- $T(\varphi_1 \wedge \varphi_2) = T(\varphi_1) \wedge T(\varphi_2) \wedge T(P(\varphi_1)) \implies Sp(T(\varphi_2)) \subseteq Sp(T(\varphi_1))$
  $\wedge\ T(P(\varphi_2)) \implies Sp(T(\varphi_1)) \subseteq Sp(T(\varphi_2))$
- $T(\varphi_1 * \varphi_2) = T(\varphi_1) \wedge T(\varphi_2) \wedge Sp(T(\varphi_1)) \cap Sp(T(\varphi_2)) = \emptyset$
- $T(I) = T(\rho_I)$ *where* ρ_I *is the definition of the inductive predicate I as in Section 3.*
- $T(\exists y.\ (x \xrightarrow{f} y) * \varphi_1) = \exists y : [f(x) = y].\ [T(\varphi_1) \wedge x \notin Sp(T(\varphi_1))]$

Finally, recall that any formula φ in the PSL fragment has a unique minimal heap (Theorem 4). With this (and a few auxiliary lemmas that can be found in the Technical Report [25]), we have the following theorem, which captures the correctness of the translation:

Theorem 5. *For any formula φ in the PSL fragment, we have the following implications:* $s, h \models \varphi \implies \mathcal{M}_{s,h} \models T(\varphi)$
$$\mathcal{M}_{s,h} \models T(\varphi) \implies s, h' \models \varphi \text{ where } h' \equiv \mathcal{M}_{s,h}(Sp(T(\varphi)))$$
Here, $\mathcal{M}_{s,h}(Sp(T(\varphi)))$ *is the interpretation of $Sp(T(\varphi))$ in the model $\mathcal{M}_{s,h}$. Note h' is minimal and is equal to h_φ as in Theorem 4.*

6 Discussion

Comparison with Separation Logic. The design of frame logic is, in many ways, inspired by the design choices of separation logic. Separation logic formulas implicitly hold on *tight* heaplets— models are defined on pairs (s, h), where s is a store (an interpretation of variables) and h is a heaplet that defines a subset of the heap as the domain for functions/pointers. In Frame Logic, we choose to not define satisfiability with respect to heaplets but define it with respect to the entire heap. However, we give access to the implicitly defined heaplet using the operator Sp, and give a logic over *sets* to talk about supports. The separating conjunction operation $*$ can then be expressed using normal conjunction and a constraint that says that the support of formulae are disjoint.

We do not allow formulas to have *multiple* supports, which is crucial as Sp is a function, and this roughly corresponds to *precise* fragments of separation logic. Precise fragments of separation logic have already been proposed and accepted in the separation logic literature for giving robust handling of modular functions, concurrency, etc. [8, 29]. Section 5 details a translation of a precise fragment of separation logic (with $*$ but not magic wand) to frame logic that shows the natural connection between precise formulas in separation logic and frame logic.

Frame logic, through the support operator, facilitates local reasoning much in the same way as separation logic does, and the frame rule in frame logic supports frame reasoning in a similar way as separation logic. The key difference between frame logic and separation logic is the adherence to a first-order logic (with recursive definitions), both in terms of syntax and expressiveness.

First and foremost, in separation logic, the magic wand is needed to express the weakest precondition [38]. Consider for example computing the weakest precondition of the formula $list(x)$ with respect to the code $y.n := z$. The weakest precondition should essentially describe the (tight) heaplets such that changing the n pointer from y to z results in x pointing to a list. In separation logic, this is expressed typically (see [38]) using magic wand as $(y \xrightarrow{n} z) \mathbin{-\!*} (list(x))$. However, the magic wand operator is inherently a *second-order* property. The formula $\alpha \mathbin{-\!*} \beta$ holds on a heaplet h if for any *disjoint* heaplet that satisfies α, β will hold on the conjoined heaplet. Expressing this property (for arbitrary α, whose heaplet can be *unbounded*) requires quantifying over unbounded heaplets satisfying α, which is not first order expressible.

In frame logic, we instead rewrite the recursive definition $list(\cdot)$ to a new one $list'(\cdot)$ that captures whether x points to a list, assuming that $n(y) = z$ (see Section 4.4). This property continues to be expressible in frame logic and can be converted to first-order logic with recursive definitions (see Section 3.5). Note that we are exploiting the fact that there is only a bounded amount of change to the heap in straight-line programs in order to express this in FL.

Let us turn to expressiveness and compactness. In separation logic, separation of structures is expressed using $*$, and in frame logic, such a separation is expressed using conjunction and an additional constraint that says that the supports of the two formulas are disjoint. A precise separation logic formula of the form $\alpha_1 * \alpha_2 * \ldots \alpha_n$ is compact and would get translated to a much larger formula in frame logic as it would have to state that the supports of each pair of formulas is disjoint. We believe this can be tamed using macros $(Star(\alpha, \beta) = \alpha \wedge \beta \wedge Sp(\alpha) \cap Sp(\beta) = \emptyset)$.

There are, however, several situations where frame logic leads to more compact and natural formulations. For instance, consider expressing the property that x and y point to lists, which may or may not overlap. In Frame Logic, we simply write $list(x) \wedge list(y)$. The support of this formula is the union of the supports of the two lists. In separation logic, we cannot use $*$ to write this compactly (while capturing the tightest heaplet). Note that the formula $(list(x) * true) \wedge (list(y) * true)$ is *not* equivalent, as it is true in heaplets that are larger than the set of locations of the two lists. The simplest formulation we know is to write a recursive definition $lseg(u, v)$ for list segments from u to v and use quantification: $(\exists z. \ lseg(x, z) * lseg(y, z) * list(z)) \vee (list(x) * list(y))$ where the definition of $lseg$ is the following: $lseg(u, v) \equiv (u = v \wedge emp) \vee (\exists w. \ u \to w * lseg(w, v))$.

If we wanted to say $x_1, \ldots, x_n$ all point to lists, that may or may not overlap, then in FL we can say $list(x_1) \wedge list(x_2) \wedge \ldots \wedge list(x_n)$. However, in separation logic, the simplest way seems to be to write using $lseg$ and a linear number of quantified variables and an exponentially-sized formula. Now consider the property saying $x_1, \ldots, x_n$ all point to binary trees, with pointers *left* and *right*, and that can overlap arbitrarily. We can write it in FL as $tree(x_1) \wedge \ldots \wedge tree(x_n)$, while a formula in (first-order) separation logic that expresses this property seems very complex.

In summary, we believe that frame logic is a logic that supports frame reasoning built on the same principles as separation logic, but is still translatable to first-order logic (avoiding the magic wand), and makes different choices for syntax/semantics that lead to expressing certain properties more naturally and compactly, and others more verbosely.

Reasoning with Frame Logic using First-Order Reasoning Mechanisms. An advantage of the adherence of frame logic to being translatable to a first-order logic with recursive definitions is the power to reason with it using first-order theorem proving techniques. While we do not present tools for reasoning in this paper, we note that there are several reasoning schemes that can readily handle first-order logic with recursive definitions.

The theory of dynamic frames [18] has been proposed for frame reasoning for heap manipulating programs and has been adopted in verification engines like Dafny [21] that provide automated reasoning. A key aspect of dynamic frames is the notion of regions, which are subsets of locations that can be used to define subsets of the heap that change or do not change when a piece of code is executed. Program logics such as region logic have been proposed for object-oriented programs using such regions [1–3]. The supports of formulas in frame logic are also used to express such regions, but the key difference is that the definition of regions is given *implicitly* using supports of formulas, as opposed to explicitly defining them. Separation logic also defines regions implicitly, and in fact, the work on implicit dynamic frames [31, 39] provides translations from separation logic to regions for reasoning using dynamic frames.

Reasoning with regions using set theory in a first-order logic with recursive definitions has been explored by many works to support automated reasoning. Tools like VAMPIRE [20] for first-order logic have been extended in recent work to handle algebraic datatypes [19]; many data-structures in practice can be modeled as algebraic datatypes and the schemes proposed in [19] are powerful tools to reason with them using first-order theorem provers.

A second class of tools are those proposed in the work on natural proofs [23, 32, 37]. Natural proofs explicitly work with first order logic with recursive definitions (FO-RD), implementing validity through a process of unfolding recursive definitions, uninterpreted abstractions, and proving inductive lemmas using induction schemes. Natural proofs are currently used primarily to reason with separation logic by first translating verification conditions arising from Hoare triples with separation logic specifications (without magic wand) to first-order logic with recursive definitions. Frame logic reasoning can also be done in a very similar way by translating it first to FO-RD.

The work in [23] considers natural proofs and quantifier instantiation heuristics for FO-RD (using a similar setup of foreground sort for locations and background sorts), and the work identifies a fragment of FO-RD (called safe fragment) for which this reasoning is *complete* (in the sense that a formula is detected as unsatisfiable by quantifier instantiation iff it is unsatisfiable with the inductive definitions interpreted as fixpoints and not least fixpoints). Since FL can be translated to FO-RD, it is possible to deal with FL using the techniques of [23]. The conditions for the safe fragment of FO-RD are that the quantifiers over the foreground elements are the outermost ones, and that terms of foreground type do not contain variables of any background type. As argued in [23], these restrictions are typically satisfied in heap logic reasoning applications.

7   Related Work

The frame problem [13] is an important problem in many different domains of research. In the broadest form, it concerns representing and reasoning about the effects of a local action without requiring explicit reasoning regarding static changes to the global scope. For example, in artificial intelligence one wants a logic that can seamlessly state that if a door is opened in a lit room, the lights continue to stay switched on. This issue is present in the domain of verification as well, specifically with heap-manipulating programs.

There are many solutions that have been proposed to this problem. The most prominent proposal in the verification context is separation logic [12, 27, 28, 38], which we discussed in detail in the previous section.

In contrast to separation logic, the work on Dynamic Frames [17, 18] and similarly inspired approaches such as Region Logic [1–3] allow methods to explicitly specify the portion of the support that may be modified. This allows fine-grained control over the modifiable section, and avoids special symbols like

* and $-*$. However, explicitly writing out frame annotations can become verbose and tedious.

The work on Implicit Dynamic Frames [22, 39, 40] bridges the worlds of separation logic (without magic wand) and dynamic frames— it uses separation logic and fractional permissions to implicitly define frames (reducing annotation burden), allows annotations to access these frames, and translates them into set regions for first-order reasoning. Our work is similar in that frame logic also implicitly defines regions and gives annotations access to these regions, and can be easily translated to pure FO-RD for first-order reasoning.

One distinction with separation logic involves the non-unique heaplets in separation logic and the unique heaplets in frame logic. Determined heaplets have been used [29, 32, 37] as they are more amenable to automated reasoning. In particular a separation logic fragment with determined heaplets known as precise predicates is defined in [29], which we capture using frame logic in Section 5.

There is also a rich literature on reasoning with these heap logics for program verification. Decidability is an important dimension and there is a lot of work on decidable logics for heaps with separation logic specifications [4–6, 11, 26, 33]. The work based on EPR (Effectively Propositional Reasoning) for specifying heap properties [14–16] provides decidability, as does some of the work that translates separation logic specifications into classical logic [34].

Finally, translating separation logic into classical logics and reasoning with them is another solution pursued in a lot of recent efforts [10, 23, 24, 32, 32, 34–37, 41]. Other techniques including recent work on cyclic proofs [9, 42] use heuristics for reasoning about recursive definitions.

8 Conclusions

Our main contribution is to propose *Frame Logic*, a classical first-order logic endowed with an explicit operator that recovers the implicit supports of formulas and supports frame reasoning. we have argued its expressive by capturing several properties of data-structures naturally and succinctly, and by showing that it can express a precise fragment of separation logic. The program logic built using frame logic supports local heap reasoning, frame reasoning, and weakest tightest preconditions across loop-free programs.

We believe that frame logic is an attractive alternative to separation logic, built using similar principles as separation logic while staying within the first-order logic world. The first-order nature of the logic makes it potentially amenable to easier automated reasoning.

A practical realization of a tool for verifying programs in a standard programming language with frame logic annotations by marrying it with existing automated techniques and tools for first-order logic (in particular [19, 24, 32, 37, 41]), is the most compelling future work.

Acknowledgements: We thank ESOP'20 reviewers for their comments that helped improve this paper. This work is based upon research supported by the National Science Foundation under Grant NSF CCF 1527395.

Bibliography

[1] Banerjee, A., Naumann, D.: Local reasoning for global invariants, Part II: Dynamic boundaries. Journal of the ACM (JACM) **60** (06 2013)

[2] Banerjee, A., Naumann, D.A., Rosenberg, S.: Regional logic for local reasoning about global invariants. In: Vitek, J. (ed.) ECOOP 2008 – Object-Oriented Programming. pp. 387–411. Springer Berlin Heidelberg, Berlin, Heidelberg (2008)

[3] Banerjee, A., Naumann, D.A., Rosenberg, S.: Local reasoning for global invariants, Part I: Region logic. J. ACM **60**(3), 18:1–18:56 (Jun 2013), http://doi.acm.org/10.1145/2485982

[4] Berdine, J., Calcagno, C., O'Hearn, P.W.: A decidable fragment of separation logic. In: Proceedings of the 24th International Conference on Foundations of Software Technology and Theoretical Computer Science. pp. 97–109. FSTTCS'04 (2004)

[5] Berdine, J., Calcagno, C., O'Hearn, P.W.: Symbolic execution with separation logic. In: Proceedings of the Third Asian Conference on Programming Languages and Systems. pp. 52–68. APLAS'05 (2005)

[6] Berdine, J., Calcagno, C., O'Hearn, P.W.: Smallfoot: Modular automatic assertion checking with separation logic. In: Proceedings of the 4th International Conference on Formal Methods for Components and Objects. pp. 115–137. FMCO'05, Springer-Verlag, Berlin, Heidelberg (2006). https://doi.org/10.1007/11804192_6

[7] Brinck, K., Foo, N.Y.: Analysis of algorithms on threaded trees. The Computer Journal **24**(2), 148–155 (01 1981). https://doi.org/10.1093/comjnl/24.2.148

[8] Brookes, S.: A semantics for concurrent separation logic. Theor. Comput. Sci. **375**(1-3), 227–270 (Apr 2007). https://doi.org/10.1016/j.tcs.2006.12.034

[9] Brotherston, J., Distefano, D., Petersen, R.L.: Automated cyclic entailment proofs in separation logic. In: Proceedings of the 23rd International Conference on Automated Deduction. pp. 131–146. CADE'11, Springer-Verlag, Berlin, Heidelberg (2011), http://dl.acm.org/citation.cfm?id=2032266.2032278

[10] Chin, W.N., David, C., Nguyen, H.H., Qin, S.: Automated verification of shape, size and bag properties. In: 12th IEEE International Conference on Engineering Complex Computer Systems (ICECCS 2007). pp. 307–320 (2007)

[11] Cook, B., Haase, C., Ouaknine, J., Parkinson, M., Worrell, J.: Tractable reasoning in a fragment of separation logic. In: Proceedings of the 22nd International Conference on Concurrency Theory. pp. 235–249. CONCUR'11 (2011)

[12] Demri, S., Deters, M.: Separation logics and modalities: a survey. Journal of Applied Non-Classical Logics **25**, 50–99 (2015)

[13] Hayes, P.J.: The frame problem and related problems in artificial intelligence. In: Webber, B.L., Nilsson, N.J. (eds.) Readings in Artificial Intelligence, pp. 223 – 230. Morgan Kaufmann (1981). https://doi.org/10.1016/B978-0-934613-03-3.50020-9

[14] Itzhaky, S., Banerjee, A., Immerman, N., Lahav, O., Nanevski, A., Sagiv, M.: Modular reasoning about heap paths via effectively propositional formulas. In: Proceedings of the 41st ACM SIGPLAN-SIGACT Symposium on Principles of Programming Languages. pp. 385–396. POPL '14, ACM, New York, NY, USA (2014). https://doi.org/10.1145/2535838.2535854

[15] Itzhaky, S., Banerjee, A., Immerman, N., Nanevski, A., Sagiv, M.: Effectively-propositional reasoning about reachability in linked data structures. In: Proceedings of the 25th International Conference on Computer Aided Verification. pp. 756–772. CAV'13, Springer-Verlag, Berlin, Heidelberg (2013). https://doi.org/10.1007/978-3-642-39799-8_53

[16] Itzhaky, S., Bjørner, N., Reps, T., Sagiv, M., Thakur, A.: Property-directed shape analysis. In: Proceedings of the 16th International Conference on Computer Aided Verification. pp. 35–51. CAV'14, Springer-Verlag, Berlin, Heidelberg (2014). https://doi.org/10.1007/978-3-319-08867-9_3

[17] Kassios, I.T.: The dynamic frames theory. Form. Asp. Comput. 23(3), 267–288 (May 2011). https://doi.org/10.1007/s00165-010-0152-5

[18] Kassios, I.T.: Dynamic frames: Support for framing, dependencies and sharing without restrictions. In: Misra, J., Nipkow, T., Sekerinski, E. (eds.) FM 2006: Formal Methods. pp. 268–283. Springer-Verlag, Berlin, Heidelberg (2006)

[19] Kovács, L., Robillard, S., Voronkov, A.: Coming to terms with quantified reasoning. In: Proceedings of the 44th ACM SIGPLAN Symposium on Principles of Programming Languages. pp. 260–270. POPL '17, ACM, New York, NY, USA (2017). https://doi.org/10.1145/3009837.3009887

[20] Kovács, L., Voronkov, A.: First-order theorem proving and Vampire. In: CAV '13. pp. 1–35 (2013). https://doi.org/10.1007/978-3-642-39799-8_1

[21] Leino, K.R.M.: Dafny: An automatic program verifier for functional correctness. In: Proceedings of the 16th International Conference on Logic for Programming, Artificial Intelligence, and Reasoning. p. 348–370. LPAR'10, Springer-Verlag, Berlin, Heidelberg (2010). https://doi.org/10.5555/1939141.1939161

[22] Leino, K.R.M., Müller, P.: A basis for verifying multi-threaded programs. In: Castagna, G. (ed.) Programming Languages and Systems. pp. 378–393. Springer Berlin Heidelberg, Berlin, Heidelberg (2009). https://doi.org/10.1007/978-3-642-00590-9_27

[23] Löding, C., Madhusudan, P., Peña, L.: Foundations for natural proofs and quantifier instantiation. PACMPL 2(POPL), 10:1–10:30 (2018). https://doi.org/10.1145/3158098

[24] Madhusudan, P., Qiu, X., Ştefănescu, A.: Recursive proofs for inductive tree data-structures. In: Proceedings of the 39th Annual ACM SIGPLAN-SIGACT Symposium on Principles of Programming Lan-

guages. pp. 123–136. POPL '12, ACM, New York, NY, USA (2012). https://doi.org/10.1145/2103656.2103673

[25] Murali, A., Peña, L., Löding, C., Madhusudan, P.: A first order logic with frames. CoRR (2019), http://arxiv.org/abs/1901.09089

[26] Navarro Pérez, J.A., Rybalchenko, A.: Separation logic + superposition calculus = heap theorem prover. In: Proceedings of the 32nd ACM SIG-PLAN Conference on Programming Language Design and Implementation. pp. 556–566. PLDI '11, ACM, New York, NY, USA (2011)

[27] O'Hearn, P.W.: A primer on separation logic (and automatic program verification and analysis). In: Software Safety and Security (2012)

[28] O'Hearn, P.W., Reynolds, J.C., Yang, H.: Local reasoning about programs that alter data structures. In: Proceedings of the 15th International Workshop on Computer Science Logic. pp. 1–19. CSL '01, Springer-Verlag, London, UK, UK (2001), http://dl.acm.org/citation.cfm?id=647851.737404

[29] O'Hearn, P.W., Yang, H., Reynolds, J.C.: Separation and information hiding. In: Proceedings of the 31st ACM SIGPLAN-SIGACT Symposium on Principles of Programming Languages. pp. 268–280. POPL '04, ACM, New York, NY, USA (2004). https://doi.org/10.1145/964001.964024

[30] Parkinson, M., Bierman, G.: Separation logic and abstraction. In: Proceedings of the 32nd ACM SIGPLAN-SIGACT Symposium on Principles of Programming Languages. pp. 247–258. POPL '05, ACM, New York, NY, USA (2005). https://doi.org/10.1145/1040305.1040326

[31] Parkinson, M.J., Summers, A.J.: The relationship between separation logic and implicit dynamic frames. In: Barthe, G. (ed.) Programming Languages and Systems. pp. 439–458. Springer Berlin Heidelberg, Berlin, Heidelberg (2011). https://doi.org/10.1007/978-3-642-19718-5_23

[32] Pek, E., Qiu, X., Madhusudan, P.: Natural proofs for data structure manipulation in C using separation logic. In: Proceedings of the 35th ACM SIGPLAN Conference on Programming Language Design and Implementation. pp. 440–451. PLDI '14, ACM, New York, NY, USA (2014). https://doi.org/10.1145/2594291.2594325

[33] Pérez, J.A.N., Rybalchenko, A.: Separation logic modulo theories. In: Programming Languages and Systems (APLAS). pp. 90–106. Springer International Publishing, Cham (2013)

[34] Piskac, R., Wies, T., Zufferey, D.: Automating separation logic using SMT. In: Proceedings of the 25th International Conference on Computer Aided Verification. pp. 773–789. CAV'13, Springer-Verlag, Berlin, Heidelberg (2013). https://doi.org/10.1007/978-3-642-39799-8_54

[35] Piskac, R., Wies, T., Zufferey, D.: Automating separation logic with trees and data. In: Proceedings of the 16th International Conference on Computer Aided Verification. pp. 711–728. CAV'14, Springer-Verlag, Berlin, Heidelberg (2014)

[36] Piskac, R., Wies, T., Zufferey, D.: Grasshopper. In: Ábrahám, E., Havelund, K. (eds.) Tools and Algorithms for the Construction and Analysis of Systems. pp. 124–139. Springer Berlin Heidelberg, Berlin, Heidelberg (2014)

[37] Qiu, X., Garg, P., Ştefănescu, A., Madhusudan, P.: Natural proofs for structure, data, and separation. In: Proceedings of the 34th ACM SIG-PLAN Conference on Programming Language Design and Implementation. pp. 231–242. PLDI '13, ACM, New York, NY, USA (2013). https://doi.org/10.1145/2491956.2462169

[38] Reynolds, J.C.: Separation logic: A logic for shared mutable data structures. In: Proceedings of the 17th Annual IEEE Symposium on Logic in Computer Science. pp. 55–74. LICS '02 (2002)

[39] Smans, J., Jacobs, B., Piessens, F.: Implicit dynamic frames: Combining dynamic frames and separation logic. In: Drossopoulou, S. (ed.) ECOOP 2009 – Object-Oriented Programming. pp. 148–172. Springer Berlin Heidelberg, Berlin, Heidelberg (2009). https://doi.org/10.1007/978-3-642-03013-0_8

[40] Smans, J., Jacobs, B., Piessens, F.: Implicit dynamic frames. ACM Trans. Program. Lang. Syst. 34(1), 2:1–2:58 (May 2012). https://doi.org/10.1145/2160910.2160911

[41] Suter, P., Dotta, M., Kunčak, V.: Decision procedures for algebraic data types with abstractions. In: Proceedings of the 37th Annual ACM SIGPLAN-SIGACT Symposium on Principles of Programming Languages. pp. 199–210. POPL '10, ACM, New York, NY, USA (2010). https://doi.org/10.1145/1706299.1706325

[42] Ta, Q.T., Le, T.C., Khoo, S.C., Chin, W.N.: Automated mutual explicit induction proof in separation logic. In: Fitzgerald, J., Heitmeyer, C., Gnesi, S., Philippou, A. (eds.) FM 2016: Formal Methods. pp. 659–676. Springer International Publishing, Cham (2016). https://doi.org/10.1007/978-3-319-48989-6_40

Proving the safety of highly-available distributed objects

Sreeja S Nair[1], Gustavo Petri[2], and Marc Shapiro[1]

[1] Sorbonne Université—LIP6 & Inria, Paris, France
[2] ARM Research, Cambridge, UK

Abstract. To provide high availability in distributed systems, object replicas allow concurrent updates. Although replicas eventually converge, they may diverge temporarily, for instance when the network fails. This makes it difficult for the developer to reason about the object's properties, and in particular, to prove invariants over its state. For the subclass of state-based distributed systems, we propose a proof methodology for establishing that a given object maintains a given invariant, taking into account any concurrency control. Our approach allows reasoning about individual operations separately. We demonstrate that our rules are sound, and we illustrate their use with some representative examples. We automate the rule using Boogie, an SMT-based tool.

Keywords: Replicated objects · Consistency · Automatic verification · Distributed application design · Tool support

1 Introduction

Many modern applications serve users accessing shared data in different geographical regions. Examples include social networks, multi-user games, cooperative engineering, collaborative editors, source-control repositories, or distributed file systems. One approach would be to store the application's data (which we call object) in a single central location, accessed remotely. However, users far from the central location would suffer long delays and outages.

Instead, the object is *replicated* to several locations. A user accesses the closest available replica. To ensure *availability*, an update must not synchronise across replicas; otherwise, when a network partition occurs, the system would block. Thus, a replica executes both queries and updates locally, and propagates its updates to other replicas asynchronously.

Updates at different locations are concurrent; this may cause replicas to diverge, at least temporarily. Replicas may diverge, but if the system ensures Strong Eventual Consistency (SEC), this ensures that replicas that have received the same set of updates have the same state [25], simplifying the reasoning.

The replicated object may also require to maintain some (application-specific) *invariant*, an assertion about the object. We say a state is safe if the invariant is true in that state; the system is safe if every reachable state is safe. In a sequential system, this is straightforward (in principle): if the initial state is safe,

P. Müller (Ed.): ESOP 2020, LNCS 12075, pp. 544–571, 2020.
https://doi.org/10.1007/978-3-030-44914-8_20

and the final state of every update individually is safe, then the system is safe. However, these conditions are not sufficient in the replicated case, because concurrent updates at different replicas may interfere with one another. This can be fixed by synchronising between some or all types of updates. To maximise availability and latency, such synchronisation should be minimised. In this paper, we propose a proof methodology to ensure that a given object is system-safe, for a given invariant and a given amount of concurrency control. In contrast to previous works, we consider state-based objects.[1] Indeed, the specific properties of state-based propagation enable simple modular reasoning despite concurrency, thanks to the concept of *concurrency invariant*. Our proof methodology derives the concurrency invariant automatically from the sequential specification. Now, if the initial state is safe, and every update maintains both the application invariant and the concurrency invariant, then every reachable state is safe, even in concurrent executions, regardless of network partitions. We have developed a tool named Soteria, to automate our proof methodology. Soteria analyses the specification to detect concurrency bugs and provides counterexamples.

The contributions of this paper are as follows:

- We propose a novel proof system specialised to proving the safety of available objects that converge by propagating state. This specialisation supports modular reasoning, and thus it enables automation.
- We demonstrate that this proof system is sound. Moreover, we provide a simple semantics for state-propagating systems that allows us to ignore network messages altogether.
- We present Soteria, to the best of our knowledge the first tool supporting the verification of program invariants for state-based replicated objects. When Soteria succeeds it ensures that every execution, whether replicas are partitioned or concurrent, is safe.
- We present a number of representative case studies, which we run through Soteria.

2   Background

As a running example, consider a simple auction system (for simplicity, we consider a single auction). An auction object is composed of the following parts:

- Its Status, that can move from initial state INVALID (under preparation) to ACTIVE (can receive bids) and then to CLOSED (no more bids accepted).
- The Winner of the auction, that is initially ⊥ and can become the bid taking the highest amount. In case of ties, the bid with the lowest id wins.
- The set of Bids placed, that is initially empty. A bid is a tuple composed of
  - BidId: A unique identifier
  - Placed: A boolean flag to indicate whether the bid has been placed or not. Initially, it is FALSE. Once placed, a bid cannot be withdrawn.
  - The monetary Amount of the bid; this cannot be modified once the bid is created.

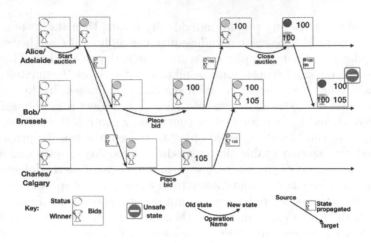

Fig. 1: Evolution of state of an auction object

Figure 1 illustrates how the auction state evolves over time. The state of the object is geo-replicated at data centers in Adelaide, Brussels, and Calgary. Users at different locations can start an auction, place bids, close the auction, declare a winner, inspect the local replica, and observe if a winner is declared and who it is. The updates are propagated asynchronously to other replicas. All replicas will eventually agree on the same auction status, the same set of bids and the same winner.

There are two basic approaches to propagating updates. The operation-based approach applies an update to some origin replica, then transmits the operation itself to be replayed at other replicas. If messages are delivered in causal order, exactly once, and concurrent operations are commutative, then two replicas that received the same updates reach the same state (this is the Strong Eventual Consistency guarantee, or SEC) [25].

The state-based approach applies an update to some origin replica. Occasionally, a replica sends its full state to some other replica, which *merges* the received state into its own. If the state space forms a monotonic semi-lattice, an update is an inflation (its output state is not lesser than the input state), and *merge* computes the least-upper-bound of the local and received states, then SEC is guaranteed [25]. As long as every update eventually reaches every replica, messages may be dropped, re-ordered or duplicated, and the set of replicas may be unknown. Due to these relaxed requirements, state-based propagation is widely used in industry. Figure 1 shows the state-based approach with local operations and merges. Alternatives exist where only a delta of the state —that is, the portion of the state not known to be part of the other replicas— is sent as a message [1]; since this is an optimisation, it is of no consequence to the results of this paper.

---

[1]   As opposed to operation-based. These terms are defined in Section 2.

Looking back to Figure 1, we can see that replicas diverge temporarily. This temporary divergence can lead to an unsafe state, in this case declaring a wrong winner. This correctness problem has been addressed before; however, previous works mostly consider the operation-based propagation approach [11, 13, 19, 24].

3   System Model

In this section, we first introduce the object components, explain the underlying system model informally, and then formalise the operational semantics.

3.1   General Principles

An object consists of a state, a set of operations, a merge function and an invariant. Figure 1 illustrates three replicas of an auction object, at three different locations, represented by the horizontal lines. The object evolves through a set of states. Each line depicts the evolution of the state of the corresponding replica; time flows from left to right.

State. A distributed system consists of a number of servers, with disjoint memory and processing capabilities. The servers might be distributed over geographical regions. A set of servers at a single location stores the state of the object. This is called a single *replica*. The object is replicated at different geographical locations, each location having a full copy of the state. In the simplest case (for instance at initialisation) the state at all replicas will be identical. The state of each replica is called a *local state*. The global view, comprising all local states is called the *global state*.

Operations. Each replica may perform the operations defined for the object. To support availability, an operation modifies the local state at some arbitrary replica, the *origin replica* for that operation, without synchronising with other replicas (the cost of synchronisation being significant at scale). An operation might consist of several changes; these are applied to the replica as a single atomic unit.

Executing an operation on its origin replica has an immediate effect. However, the state of the other replicas, called *remote replicas*, remains unaltered at this point. The remote replicas get updated when the state is eventually propagated. An immediate consequence of this execution model is that in the presence of concurrent operations, replicas can reach different states, i.e. they diverge.

Let us illustrate this with our example in Figure 1. Initially, the auction is yet to start, the winner is not declared and no bids are placed. By default, a replica can execute any operation - start_auction, place_bid, and close_auction - locally without synchronising with other replicas. We see that the local states of replicas occasionally diverge. For example at the point where operation close_auction completes at the Adelaide replica, the Adelaide replica is aware of only a $100 bid, the Brussels replica has two bids, and the Calgary replica observes only one bid for $105.

State Propagation. A replica occasionally propagates its state to other replicas in the system and a replica receiving a remote state *merges* it into its own.

In Figure 1, the arrows crossing between replicas represent the delivery of a message containing the state of the source replica, to be merged into the target replica. A message is labelled with the state propagated. For instance, the first message delivery at the Brussels replica represents the result of updating the local state (setting auction status to `ACTIVE`), with the state originating in the replica at Adelaide (auction started).

Similar to the operations, a merge is atomic. In Figure 1, Alice closes the auction at the Adelaide replica. This atomically sets the status of the auction to `CLOSED` and declares a winner from the set of bids it is aware of. The updated auction state and winner are transmitted together. Merging is performed atomically by the Brussels replica.[2]

We now specify the `merge` operation for an auction. The receiving replica's local state is denoted $\sigma = $ (status, winner, Bids), the received state is denoted $\sigma' = $ (status', winner', Bids') and the result of merge is denoted as $\sigma_{new} = $ (status$_{new}$, winner$_{new}$, Bids$_{new}$).

```
merge((status,winner,Bids),(status',winner',Bids')) :
  status_new := max(status,status')
  winner_new := winner' ≠ ⊥ ? winner' : winner
  for (b in Bids ∪ Bids')
    Bids_new.b.placed := Bids.b.placed ∨ Bids'.b.placed
    Bids_new.b.amount := max(Bids.b.amount, Bids'.b.amount)
```

Furthermore, we require the operations and merge to be defined in a way that ensures convergence. We discuss the relevant properties later in Section 6.1.

Invariants. An invariant is an assertion that must evaluate to true in every local state of every replica. Although evaluated locally at each replica, the invariant is in effect global, since it must be true at all replicas, and replicas eventually converge. For our running example, the invariant can be stated as follows:

- Only an active auction can receive bids, and
- the highest unique bid wins when the auction closes (breaking ties using bid identifiers).

This condition must hold true in all possible executions of the object.

3.2   Notations and Assumptions

First, we introduce some notations and assumptions:

- We assume a fixed set of replicas, ranged over with the meta-variable $r \in R$ sampled from the domain of unique replica names R.
- We denote a local state with the meta-variable $\sigma \in \Sigma$ ranged over the domain of states of the object Σ.

---

[2] We see that this leads to an unsafe state, we discuss this in detail in Section 4.2

- The *local semantic* function $[\![\,]\!]$ takes an operation and a state, and returns the state after applying the operation. We write $[\![\mathrm{op}]\!](\sigma) = \sigma_{new}$ for executing operation op on state σ resulting in a new state σ_{new}.
- Ω denotes a partial function returning the current state of a replica. For instance $\Omega(\mathbf{r}) = \sigma$ means that in global state Ω, replica $\mathbf{r}$ is in local state σ. We will use the notation $\Omega[\mathbf{r} \leftarrow \sigma]$ to denote the global state resulting from replacing the local state of replica $\mathbf{r}$ with σ. The local state of all other replicas remains unchanged in the resulting global state.[3]
- A message propagating states between replicas is denoted $\langle\, \mathbf{r} \xrightarrow{\sigma} \mathbf{r}' \,\rangle$. This represents the fact that replica $\mathbf{r}$ has sent a message (possibly not yet received) to replica $\mathbf{r}'$, with the state σ as its payload. The meta-variable M denotes the messages in transit in the network.
- In the following sub-section, we will utilise a set of states to record the history of the execution. The set of past states will be ranged over with the variable $\mathbf{S} \in \mathbb{P}(\Sigma)$.
- All replicas are assumed to start in the same initial state σ_i. Formally, for each replica $\mathbf{r} \in \mathsf{dom}(\Omega_i)$ we have $\Omega_i(\mathbf{r}) = \sigma_i$.

3.3   Operational Semantics

In this and the following subsections we will present two semantics for systems propagating states. Importantly, while the first semantics takes into account the effects of the network on the propagation of the states, and is hence an accurate representation of the execution of systems with state propagation, we will show in the next subsection that reasoning about the network is unnecessary in this kind of system. We will demonstrate this claim by presenting a much simpler semantics in which the network is abstracted away. The importance of this reduction is that the number of events to be considered, both when conducting proofs and when reasoning about applications, is greatly reduced. As informal evidence of this claim, we point at the difference in complexity between the semantic rules presented in Figure 2 and Figure 3. We postpone the equivalence argument to Theorem 1.

Figure 2 presents the semantic rules describing what we shall call the *precise semantics* (we will later present a more abstract version) defining the transition relations describing how the state of the object evolves.

The figure defines a semantic judgement of the form $(\Omega, \mathtt{M}) \to (\Omega_{new}, \mathtt{M}_{new})$ where $(\Omega, \mathtt{M})$ is a configuration where the replica states are given by Ω as shown above, and M is a set of messages that have been transmitted by different replicas and are pending to be received by their target replicas.

Rule OPERATION presents the state transition resulting from a replica $\mathbf{r}$ executing an operation op. The operation queries the state of replica $\mathbf{r}$, evaluates the semantic function for operation op and updates its state with the result. The

---

[3] This notation of a global state is used only to explain and prove our proof rule. In fact, the rule is based only on the local state of each replica.

OPERATION

$$\frac{\Omega(r) = \sigma \qquad [\![op]\!](\sigma) = \sigma_{new} \qquad \Omega_{new} = \Omega[r \leftarrow \sigma_{new}]}{(\Omega, M) \rightarrow (\Omega_{new}, M)}$$

SEND

$$\frac{\Omega(r) = \sigma \qquad r' \in dom(\Omega) \setminus \{r\} \qquad M_{new} = M \cup \{\langle\, r \xrightarrow{\sigma} r'\,\rangle\}}{(\Omega, M) \rightarrow (\Omega, M_{new})}$$

MERGE

$$\frac{\Omega(r) = \sigma}{M_{new} = M \setminus \{\langle\, r' \xrightarrow{\sigma'} r\,\rangle\} \qquad [\![merge]\!](\sigma, \sigma') = \sigma_{new} \qquad \Omega_{new} = \Omega[r \leftarrow \sigma_{new}]}{(\Omega, M) \rightarrow (\Omega_{new}, M_{new})}$$

OP & BROADCAST

$$\frac{\Omega(r) = \sigma \qquad [\![op]\!](\sigma) = \sigma_{new} \qquad \Omega_{new} = \Omega[r \leftarrow \sigma_{new}]}{M_{new} = M \cup \{\, \langle\, r \xrightarrow{\sigma_{new}} r'\,\rangle \mid r' \in dom(\Omega) \setminus \{r\}\,\}}{(\Omega, M) \rightarrow (\Omega_{new}, M_{new})}$$

MERGE & BROADCAST

$$\frac{\Omega(r) = \sigma}{M_{new} = M \setminus \{\langle\, r' \xrightarrow{\sigma'} r\,\rangle\} \qquad [\![merge]\!](\sigma, \sigma') = \sigma_{new} \qquad \Omega_{new} = \Omega[r \leftarrow \sigma_{new}]}{M_{new'} = M_{new} \cup \{\, \langle\, r \xrightarrow{\sigma_{new}} r''\,\rangle \mid r'' \in dom(\Omega) \setminus \{r\}\,\}}{(\Omega, M) \rightarrow (\Omega_{new}, M_{new'})}$$

Fig. 2: Precise Operational Semantics: Messages

set of messages M does not change. The second rule, SEND, represents the non-deterministic sending of the state of replica r to replica r'. The rule has no other effect than to add a message to the set of pending messages M. The MERGE rule picks any message, $\langle\, r' \xrightarrow{\sigma'} r\,\rangle$, in the set of pending messages M, and applies the merge function to the destination replica with the state in the payload of the message, removing $\langle\, r' \xrightarrow{\sigma'} r\,\rangle$ from M.

The final two rules, OP & BROADCAST and MERGE & BROADCAST represent the specific case when the states are immediately sent to all replicas. These rules are not strictly necessary since they are subsumed by the application of either OPERATION or MERGE followed by one SEND per replica. We will, however, use them to simplify a simulation argument in what follows.

We remark at this point that no assumptions are made about the duplication of messages or the order in which messages are delivered. This is in contrast to other works on the verification of properties of replicated objects [11, 13]. The reason why this assumption is not a problem in our case is that the least-upper-bound assumption of the merge function, as well as the inflation assumptions on the states considered in Item 2 (Section 6.1) mean that delayed messages have no effect when they are merged.

OPERATION

$$\frac{\Omega(\mathbf{r}) = \sigma \qquad [\![\mathtt{op}]\!](\sigma) = \sigma_{new} \qquad \Omega_{new} = \Omega[\mathbf{r} \leftarrow \sigma_{new}]}{(\Omega, \mathsf{S}) \to (\Omega_{new}, \mathsf{S} \cup \{\sigma_{new}\})}$$

MERGE

$$\frac{\Omega(\mathbf{r}) = \sigma \qquad \sigma' \in \mathsf{S} \qquad [\![\mathtt{merge}]\!](\sigma, \sigma') = \sigma_{new} \qquad \Omega_{new} = \Omega[\mathbf{r} \leftarrow \sigma_{new}]}{(\Omega, \sigma) \to (\Omega_{new}, \mathsf{S} \cup \{\sigma_{new}\})}$$

Fig. 3: Semantic Rules with a History of States

As customary we will denote with $(\Omega, \mathsf{M}) \xrightarrow{*} (\Omega_{new}, \mathsf{M}_{new})$ the repeated application of the semantic rules zero or more times, from the state (Ω, M) resulting in the state $(\Omega_{new}, \mathsf{M}_{new})$.

It is easy to see how the example in Figure 1 proceeds according to these rules for the auction.

The following lemma,[4] to be used later, establishes that whenever we use only the broadcast rules, for any intermediate state in the execution, and for any replica, when considering the final state of the trace, either the replica has already observed a fresher version of the state in the execution, or there is a message pending for it with that state. This is an obvious consequence of broadcasting.

Lemma 1. *If we consider a restriction to the semantics of Figure 2 where instead of applying the* OPERATION *rule of Figure 2 we apply the* OP & BROADCAST *rule always, and instead of applying the* MERGE *rule we apply* MERGE & BROADCAST *always, we can conclude that given an execution starting from an initial global state Ω_i with*

$$(\Omega_i, \emptyset) \xrightarrow{*} (\Omega, \mathsf{M}) \xrightarrow{*} (\Omega_{new}, \mathsf{M}_{new})$$

for any two replicas $\mathbf{r}$ and $\mathbf{r}'$ and a state σ such that $\Omega(\mathbf{r}) = \sigma$, then either:

- $\Omega_{new}(\mathbf{r}') \geq \sigma$, or
- $\langle\, \mathbf{r} \xrightarrow{\sigma} \mathbf{r}' \,\rangle \in \mathsf{M}_{new}$.

3.4   Operational Semantics with State History

We now turn our attention to a simpler semantics where we omit messages from configurations, but instead, we record in a separate set all the states occurring in any replica throughout the execution.

The semantics in Figure 3 presents a judgement of the form $(\Omega, \mathsf{S}) \to (\Omega_{new}, \mathsf{S}_{new})$ between configurations of the form (Ω, S) as before, but where the set of messages is replaced by a set of states denoted with the meta-variable $\mathsf{S} \in \mathbb{P}(\Sigma)$.

---

[4] The proofs for the lemmas are included in the extended version[23].

The rules are simple. OPERATION executes an operation as before, and it adds the resulting new state to the set of observed states. The rule MERGE non-deterministically selects a state in the set of states and it merges a non-deterministically chosen replica with it. The resulting state is also added to the set of observed states.

Lemma 2. *Consider a state* (Ω, S) *reachable from an initial global state* Ω_i *with the semantics of Figure 3. Formally:* $(\Omega_i, \{\sigma_i\}) \xrightarrow{*} (\Omega, \mathsf{S})$. *We can conclude that the set of recorded states in the final configuration* S *includes all of the states present in any of the replicas*

$$\left(\bigcup_{\mathrm{r} \in \mathsf{dom}(\Omega)} \{\Omega(\mathrm{r})\} \right) \subseteq \mathsf{S}$$

3.5   Correspondence between the semantics

In this section, we show that removing the messages from the semantics, and choosing to record states instead renders the same executions. To that end, we will define the following relation between configurations of the two semantics which will be later shown to be a bisimulation.

Definition 1 (Bisimulation Relation). *We define the relation* $\mathcal{R}_{\Omega_i}$ *between a configuration* (Ω, M) *of the semantics of Figure 2 and a configuration* (Ω, S) *of the semantics of Figure 3 parameterized by an initial global state* Ω_i *and denoted by*

$$(\Omega, \mathsf{M}) \; \mathcal{R}_{\Omega_i} \; (\Omega, \mathsf{S})$$

when the following conditions are met:

1. $(\Omega_i, \emptyset) \xrightarrow{*} (\Omega, \mathsf{M})$, *and*
2. $(\Omega_i, \{\sigma_i\}) \xrightarrow{*} (\Omega, \mathsf{S})$, *and*
3. $\{ \sigma \mid \langle \mathrm{r} \xrightarrow{\sigma} \mathrm{r}' \rangle \in \mathsf{M} \} \subseteq \mathsf{S}$

In other words, two states represented in the two configurations are related if both are reachable from an initial global state and all the states transmitted by the messages (M) is present in the history (S).

We can now show that this relation is indeed a bisimulation. We first show that the semantics of Figure 3 simulates that of Figure 2. That is, all behaviours produced by the precise semantics with messages can also be produced by the semantics with history states. This is illustrated in the commutative diagram of Figure 4a and Figure 4b, where the dashed arrows represent existentially quantified components that are proven to exist in the theorem.

Lemma 3 (State-semantics simulates Messages-semantics). *Consider a reachable state* (Ω, M) *from the initial state* Ω_i *in the semantics of Figure 2. Consider moreover that according to that semantics there exists a transition of the form*

$$(\Omega, \mathsf{M}) \to (\Omega_{new}, \mathsf{M}_{new})$$

$$(\Omega_i, \emptyset) \xrightarrow{\;*\;} (\Omega, \mathsf{M}) \longrightarrow (\Omega_{new}, \mathsf{M}_{new}) \qquad (\Omega_i, \{\sigma_i\}) \xrightarrow{\;*\;} (\Omega, \mathsf{S}) \longrightarrow (\Omega_{new}, \mathsf{S}_{new})$$

$$\left\downarrow \mathcal{R}_{\Omega_i} \qquad\qquad \vdots \mathcal{R}_{\Omega_i} \qquad\qquad\qquad\qquad \left\downarrow \mathcal{R}_{\Omega_i} \qquad\qquad \vdots \mathcal{R}_{\Omega_i} \right.\right.$$

$$(\Omega_i, \{\sigma_i\}) \xrightarrow{\quad} (\Omega, \mathsf{S}) \dashrightarrow (\Omega_{new}, \mathsf{S}_{new}) \qquad (\Omega_i, \emptyset) \xrightarrow{\;*\;} (\Omega, \mathsf{M}) \dashrightarrow (\Omega_{new}, \mathsf{M}_{new})$$

(a) Precise to History-preserving Simulation

(b) History-preserving to Precise Simulation

Fig. 4: Simulation Schema

and consider that there exists a state (Ω, S) of the history preserving semantics of Figure 3 such that they are related by the simulation relation

$$(\Omega, \mathsf{M}) \; \mathcal{R}_{\Omega_i} \; (\Omega, \mathsf{S})$$

We can conclude that, as illustrated in Figure 4a, there exists a state $(\Omega_{new}, \mathsf{S}_{new})$ such that

$$(\Omega, \mathsf{S}) \to (\Omega_{new}, \mathsf{S}_{new}) \qquad and \qquad (\Omega_{new}, \mathsf{M}_{new}) \; \mathcal{R}_{\Omega_i} \; (\Omega_{new}, \mathsf{S}_{new})$$

We will now consider the lemma showing the inverse relation. To that end we will consider a special case of the semantics of Figure 2 where instead of applying the OPERATION rule, we will always apply the OP & BROADCAST rule, and instead of the MERGE rule, we will apply MERGE & BROADCAST. As we mentioned before, this is equivalent to the application of the OPERATION/MERGE rule, followed by a sequence of applications of SEND. The reason we will do this is that we are interested in showing that for any execution of the semantics in Figure 3 there is an equivalent (simulated) execution of the semantics of Figure 2. Since all states can be merged in the semantics of Figure 3 we have to assume that in the semantics of Figure 2 the states have been sent with messages. Fortunately, we can choose how to instantiate the existential send messages to apply the rules as necessary, and that justifies this choice.

Lemma 4 (Messages-semantics simulates State-semantics). *Consider a reachable state (Ω, S) from the initial state Ω_i in the semantics of Figure 3. Consider moreover that according to that semantics there exists a transition of the form*

$$(\Omega, \mathsf{S}) \to (\Omega_{new}, \mathsf{S}_{new})$$

and consider that there exists a state (Ω, M) of the state-preserving semantics of Figure 3 such that they are related by the simulates relation

$$(\Omega, \mathsf{M}) \; \mathcal{R}_{\Omega_i} \; (\Omega, \mathsf{S})$$

We can conclude that there exists a state $(\Omega_{new}, \mathsf{M}_{new})$ such that

$$(\Omega, \mathsf{M}) \to (\Omega_{new}, \mathsf{M}_{new}) \qquad and \qquad (\Omega_{new}, \mathsf{M}_{new}) \; \mathcal{R}_{\Omega_i} \; (\Omega_{new}, \mathsf{S}_{new})$$

As before, an illustration of this lemma is presented in Figure 4b.

We can now conclude that the two semantics are bisimilar:

Theorem 1 (Bisimulation). *The semantics of Figure 2 and Figure 3 are bisimilar as established by the relation defined in Definition 1.*

The theorem above justifies carrying out our proofs with respect to the semantics of Figure 3, which has fewer rules and it better aligns with our proof methodology. This is also justifies that when reasoning semantically about state-propagating object systems we can generally ignore the effects of network delays and messages.

From the standpoint of concurrency, the system model allows the execution of asynchronous concurrent operations, where each operation is executed atomically in each replica, and the aggregation of results of different operations is performed lazily as replicas exchange their state. At this point, we assume the set of states, along with the operations and merge, forms a monotonic semi-lattice. This is a sufficient condition for Strong Eventual Consistency [3, 4, 25].

We have seen that even though we achieve convergence later, there can be instances or even long periods of time during which replicas might diverge. We need to ensure that the concurrent executions are still safe. In the next section, we discuss how to ensure safety of distributed objects built on top of the system model we described.

4   Proving Invariants

In this section, we report our invariant verification strategy. Specifically, we consider the problem of verifying *invariants* of highly-available distributed objects.

To support the verification of invariants we will consider a syntactic-driven approach based on program logic. Bailis et al.[2] identifies necessary and sufficient run-time conditions to establish the security of application invariants for highly-available distributed databases in a criterion dubbed I-confluence. Moreover, they consider the validity of a number of typical invariants and applications. Our work improves on the I-confluence criterion defined in [2] by providing a static, syntax-driven, and mostly-automatic mechanism to verify the correctness of an invariant for an application. We will address the specific differences in Section 7, the related work.

An important consequence of our verification strategy is that while we are proving invariants about a concurrent highly-distributed system, our verification conditions are modular (on the number of API operations), and can be carried out using standard sequential Hoare-style reasoning. These verification conditions in turn entail stability of the assertions as one would have in a logic like Rely/Guarantee.

Let us start by assuming that a given initial state for the object is denoted σ_i. Initially, all replicas have σ_i as their local state. As explained earlier, each replica executes a sequence of state transitions, due either to a local update or to a merge incorporating remote updates.

Let us call *safe state* a replica state that satisfies the invariant. Assuming the current state is safe, any update (local or merge) must result in a safe state. To ensure this, every update is equipped with a precondition that disallows any unsafe execution.[5] Thus, a local update executes only when, at the origin replica, the current state is safe and its precondition currently holds.

Formally, an update u (an operation or a merge), mutates the local state σ, to a new state $\sigma_{new} = u(\sigma)$. To preserve the invariant, Inv, we require that the local state respects the precondition of the update, Pre_u: $\sigma \in \mathsf{Pre}_u \implies u(\sigma) \in Inv$

To illustrate local preconditions, consider an operation `close_auction(w: BidId)`, which sets auction status to `CLOSED` and the winner to `w` (of type BidId). The developer may have written a precondition such as `status = ACTIVE` because closing an auction doesn't make sense otherwise. In order to ensure the invariant that the winner has the highest amount, one needs to strengthen it with the clause `is_highest(Bids, w)`, defined as

```
∀ b ∈ Bids, b.placed ⟹ b.Amount ≤ w.Amount
```

Similarly, merge also needs to be safe. To illustrate merge precondition, let us use our running example. We wish to maintain the invariant that the highest bid is the winner. Assume a scenario where the local replica declared a winner and closed the auction. An incoming state from a remote replica contains a bid with a higher amount. When the two states are merged, we see that the resulting state is unsafe. So we must strengthen the merge operation with a precondition. The strengthened precondition looks like this:

```
status = CLOSED  ⟹ ∀ Bids ∈ ℙ(Bids), is_highest(Bids, w)
∧ status' = CLOSED  ⟹ ∀ Bids ∈ ℙ(Bids), is_highest(Bids, w')
```

This means that if the status is `CLOSED` in either of the two states, the winner should be the highest bid in any state. This condition ensures that when a winner is declared, it is the highest bid among the set of bids in any state at any replica.

Since merge can happen at any time, it must be the case that its precondition is always true, i.e., it constitutes an additional invariant. We call this as the *concurrency invariant*. Now our global invariant consists of two parts: first, the invariant (Inv), and second, the concurrency invariant(Inv_{conc}).

4.1   Invariance Conditions

The verification conditions in Figure 5 ensure that for any reachable local state of a replica, the global invariant $\mathsf{Inv} \wedge \mathsf{Inv}_{conc}$, is a valid assertion. We assume the invariant to be a Hoare-logic style assertion over the state of the object. In a nutshell, all of these conditions check (i) the precondition of each of the operations, and that of the merge operation uphold the global invariant, and (ii) the global invariant of the object consists of the invariant and the concurrency invariant (precondition of `merge`).

We will develop this intuition in what follows. Let us now consider each of the rules:

---

[5] Technically, this is at least the weakest-precondition of the update for safety. It strengthens any *a priori* precondition that the developer may have set.

$$\sigma_i \vDash \mathsf{Inv} \qquad (1)$$

$$\forall\, op, \sigma, \sigma_{new}, \left(\begin{array}{c} \sigma \vDash \mathsf{Pre_{op}} \wedge \\ \sigma \vDash \mathsf{Inv} \wedge \\ [\![op]\!](\sigma) = \sigma_{new} \end{array} \right) \Rightarrow \qquad \sigma_{new} \vDash \mathsf{Inv} \qquad (2)$$

$$\forall\, \sigma, \sigma', \sigma_{new}, \left(\begin{array}{c} (\sigma, \sigma') \vDash \mathsf{Pre_{merge}} \wedge \\ \sigma \vDash \mathsf{Inv} \wedge \\ \sigma' \vDash \mathsf{Inv} \wedge \\ [\![merge]\!](\sigma, \sigma') = \sigma_{new} \end{array} \right) \Rightarrow \qquad \sigma_{new} \vDash \mathsf{Inv} \qquad (3)$$

$$(\sigma_i, \sigma_i) \vDash \mathsf{Inv}_{conc} \qquad (4)$$

$$\forall\, op, \sigma, \sigma', \sigma_{new}, \left(\begin{array}{c} \sigma \vDash \mathsf{Pre_{op}} \wedge \\ (\sigma, \sigma') \vDash \mathsf{Inv}_{conc} \wedge \\ [\![op]\!](\sigma) = \sigma_{new} \end{array} \right) \Rightarrow \qquad (\sigma_{new}, \sigma') \vDash \mathsf{Inv}_{conc} \qquad (5)$$

$$\forall\, \sigma, \sigma', \sigma_{new}, \left(\begin{array}{c} (\sigma, \sigma') \vDash \mathsf{Pre_{merge}} \wedge \\ (\sigma, \sigma') \vDash \mathsf{Inv}_{conc} \wedge \\ [\![merge]\!](\sigma, \sigma') = \sigma_{new} \end{array} \right) \Rightarrow \qquad (\sigma_{new}, \sigma') \vDash \mathsf{Inv}_{conc} \qquad (6)$$

Fig. 5: Invariant Conditions

- Clearly, the initial state of the object must satisfy the global invariant, this is checked by conditions (1) and (4).

The rest of the rules perform a kind of inductive reasoning. Assuming that we start in a state that satisfies the global invariant, we need to check that any state update preserves the validity of said invariant. Importantly, this reasoning is not circular, since the initial state is known by the rule above to be safe.[6]

- Condition (2) checks that each of the operations, when executed starting in a state satisfying its precondition and the invariant, is safe. Notice that we require that the precondition of the operation be satisfied in the starting state. This is the core of the inductive argument alluded to above, all operations – which as we mentioned in Section 3 execute atomically w.r.t. concurrency – preserve the invariant Inv.

Other than the execution of operations, the other source of local state changes is the execution of the merge function in a replica. It is not true in general that for any two given states of an object, the merge should compute a safe state. In particular, it could be the case that the merge function needs a precondition that is stronger than the conjunction of the invariants in the two states to be merged. The following rules deal with these cases.

- We require the merge function to be annotated with a precondition strong enough to guarantee that merge will result in a safe state. Generally, this

---

[6] Indeed, the proof of soundness of program logics such as Rely/Guarantee are typically inductive arguments of this nature.

precondition can be obtained by calculating the weakest precondition [9] of merge w.r.t. the desired invariant. Since merge is the only operation that requires two states as input, the precondition of merge has two states. We can then verify that merging two states is safe. This is the purpose of rule (3).

As per the program model of Section 3, any two replicas can exchange their states at any given point of time and trigger the execution of a merge operation. Thus, it must be the case that the precondition of the merge function is enabled at all times between any two replica local states. Since merge is the only point where a local replica can observe the result of concurrent operations in other replicas, we call this a *concurrency invariant* (Inv_{conc}). In other words: the *concurrency invariant is part of the global invariant* of the object. This is the main insight that allows us to reduce the proof of the distributed object to checking that both the invariant Inv and the concurrency invariant Inv_{conv} are global invariants. In particular, the latter implies the former, but for exposition purposes we shall preserve the invariant Inv in the rules.

- Just as we did with the operations above, we now need to check that whenever we have a pair of states that satisfy the concurrency invariant, if one of these states changes, the resulting pair still satisfies the concurrency invariant. This is exactly the purpose of rule (5) in the case where the state change originates from an operation execution in one of the replicas of the pair. This rule is similar to rule (2) above, where the invariant Inv has been replaced by Inv_{conc}, and consequently we have a pair of states.
- Finally, as we did with rule (3), we need to check the case where one of the states of a pair of states satisfying Inv_{conc} is updated because of yet another merge happening (w.r.t. yet another replica) in one of these states. This is the purpose of rule (6) which is similar to rule (3), with Inv replaced for Inv_{conc}.

As anticipated at the beginning of this section, the reasoning about the concurrency is performed in a completely local manner, by carefully choosing the verification conditions, and it avoids the stability blow-up commonly found in concurrent program logics. The program model, and the verification conditions allow us to effectively reduce the problem of verifying safety of an asynchronous concurrent distributed system, to the modular verification of the global invariant ($\mathsf{Inv} \wedge \mathsf{Inv}_{conc}$) as pre and post conditions of all operations and merge.

Proposition 1 (Soundness). *The proof rules in equations (1)-(6) guarantee that the implementation is safe.*

To conduct an inductive proof of this lemma we need to strengthen the argument to include the set of observed states as given by the semantics of Figure 3.

Lemma 5 (Strengthening of Soundness). *Assuming that the equations (1)-(6) hold for an implementation of a replicated object with initial state Ω_i. For any state (Ω, S) reachable from $(\Omega_i, \{\sigma_i\})$, that is $(\Omega_i, \{\sigma_i\}) \xrightarrow{*} (\Omega, \mathsf{S})$, we have that:*

1. *for all states* $\sigma, \sigma' \in S$, $(\sigma, \sigma') \vDash \mathsf{Inv}_{conc}$, *and*
2. *for any state* $\sigma \in S$, $\sigma \vDash \mathsf{Inv}$.

Corollary 1. *The soundness proposition (1) is a direct consequence of Lemma 5.*

We remark at this point that there are numerous program logic approaches to proving invariants of shared-memory concurrent programs, with Rely/Guarantee [15] and concurrent separation logic [6] underlying many of them. While these approaches could be adapted to our use case (propagating-state distributed systems), this adaptation is not evident. As an indication of this complexity: one would have to predicate about the different states of the different replicas, restate the invariant to talk about these different versions of the state, encode the non-deterministic behaviour of merge, etc. Instead, we argue that our specialised rules are much simpler, allowing for a purely sequential and modular verification that we can mechanise and automate. This reduction in complexity is the main theoretical contribution of this paper.

4.2   Applying the proof rule

Let us apply the proof methodology to the auction object. Its invariant is the following conjunction:

1. Only an `ACTIVE` auction can receive bids, and
2. the highest bid, also unique, wins when the auction is `CLOSED`.

Computing the weakest precondition of each update operation, for this invariant is obvious. For instance, as discussed earlier, `close_auction(w)` gets precondition `is_highest(Bids, w)`, because of Invariant Item 2 above.

Despite local updates to each replica respecting the invariant Inv, Figure 1 showed that it is susceptible of being violated by merging. This is the case if Bob's $100 bid in Brussels wins, even though Charles concurrently placed a $105 bid in Calgary; this occurred because `status` became `CLOSED` in Brussels while still `ACTIVE` in Calgary. The weakest precondition of merge for safety expresses that, if `status` in either state is `CLOSED`, the winner should be the bid with the highest amount in both the states. This merge precondition, now called the concurrency invariant, strengthens the global invariant to be safe in concurrent executions.

Let us now consider how this strengthening impacts the local update operations. Since starting the auction doesn't modify any bids, the operation trivially preserves it. Placing a bid might violate Inv_{conc} if the auction is concurrently closed in some other replica; conversely, closing the auction could also violate Inv_{conc}, if a higher bid is concurrently placed in a remote replica. Thus, the auction object is safe when executed sequentially, but it is unsafe when updates are concurrent. This indicates the specification has a bug, which we now proceed to fix.

4.3   Concurrency Control for Invariant Preservation

As we discussed earlier, the preconditions of operations and merge are strengthened in order to be sequentially safe. An object must also preserve the concurrency invariant in order to ensure concurrent safety. Violating this indicates the presence of a concurrency bug in the specification. In that case, the operations that fail to preserve the concurrency invariant might need to synchronise. The developer adds the required concurrency control mechanisms as part of the state in our model. The modified state is now composed of the state and the concurrency control mechanism.

Recall that in the auction example, placing bids and closing the auction did not preserve the precondition of merge. This requires strengthening the specification by adding a concurrency control mechanism to restrict these operations. We can enforce them to be strictly sequential, thereby avoiding any concurrency at all. But this will affect the availability of the object.

A concurrency control can be better designed with the workload characteristics in mind. For this particular use case, we know that placing bids are much more frequent operations than closing an auction. Hence we try to formulate a concurrency control like a readers-writer lock. In order to realise this we distribute tokens to each replica. As long as a replica has the token, it can allow placing bids. Closing the auction requires recalling the tokens from all replicas. This ensures that there are no concurrent bids placed and thus a winner can be declared, respecting the invariant. The addition of this concurrency control also updates the Inv_{conc}. Clearly, all operations must respect this modification for the specification to be considered safe.

Note that the token model described here restricts availability in order to ensure safety. Adding efficient synchronization is not a problem to be solved only with application specification in hand, it rather requires the knowledge of the application dynamics such as the workload characteristics and is part of our future work.

Figure 6 shows the evolution of the modified auction object with concurrency control. The keys shown are the tokens distributed to each replica. When a replica wants to close the auction, it can request tokens from other replicas. When a replica releases its token, it is indicated by a cross mark on the key. This concurrency control mechanism makes sure that the object is safe during concurrent executions as well. The specification including the concurrency control is given in the extended version[23].

To summarize, all updates (operations and merge) have to respect the global invariant $(Inv \land Inv_{conc})$. If an update violates Inv, the developer must strengthen its precondition. If an update violates Inv_{conc}, the developer must add concurrency control mechanisms.

5   Case Studies

This section presents three representative examples of different consistency requirements of several distributed applications. The consensus object is an ex-

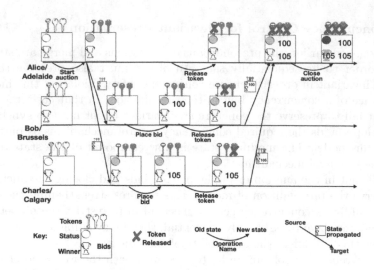

Fig. 6: Evolution of state in an auction object with concurrency control

ample of a coordination-free design, illustrating a safe object with just eventual consistency. The next example of a distributed lock shows a design that maintains a total order, illustrating strong consistency. And the final example of courseware shows a mix of concurrent operations and operations with restrained concurrency. This example, similar to our auction example, illustrates applications that might require coordination for some operations to ensure safety.

For each case study, we give an overview of the operational semantics informally. We then discuss how the design preserves the safety conditions discussed in Section 4. We also provide pseudocode for better comprehension.

5.1 Consensus application

Consensus is required in distributed systems when all replicas have to agree upon a single value. We consider the specification of a consensus object with a fixed number of replicas. We assume that replica failures are solved locally by redundancy or other means, and all replicas participate.

The state consists of a boolean flag indicating the result of consensus, and a boolean array indicating the votes from replicas. Each replica agrees on a proposal by setting its dedicated entry in the boolean array. A replica cannot withdraw its agreement. A replica sets the consensus flag when it sees all entries of the boolean array set.

The consistency between the values of agree flag and the boolean array is ensured by the invariant. The merge function is the disjunction of the individual components. In this case study, we can see that the merge ensures safety without any additional precondition. This means that the object is trivially safe under concurrent executions.

```
Initial state:                  Comparison function:
  ¬B ∧ ¬flag                      flag ∨ (¬flag₀ ∧ (B ∨ ¬B₀))

Invariant:                      {Pre_mark: True}
  flag ⟹ B                       # no precondition
                                mark():
{Pre_merge: True}                 B.me := true
# no precondition
merge(B, flag, B₀, flag₀):      {Pre_agree: B}
    B := B ∨ B₀                  agree():
    flag := flag ∨ flag₀           flag := true
```

Fig. 7: Pseudocode for consensus

```
                                Comparison function:
  Initial state:                  t > t₀
    ∃ r, V.r ∧ t = 0              ∨ (t = t₀ ∧ V = V₀)

  {Pre_transfer: V.me}          {Pre_merge:
  transfer(r_o):                  (t = t₀ ⟹ V = V₀)
      t = t+1                     ∧ (V.me ⟹ t ≥ t₀)}
      V.me := false             merge((t,V),(t₀,V₀)):
      V.r₀ := true                 t = max(t,t₀)
                                   v = (t₀<t)?V:V₀

Invariant:
  ∃ r, V.r ∧ ∀ r, r₀, (V.r ∧ V.r₀) ⟹ r = r₀
```

Fig. 8: Specification of a distributed lock

The pseudo code of the consensus example is shown in Figure 7. The design for consensus can be relaxed, requiring only the majority of replicas to mark their boxes. The extension for that is trivial.

5.2   A replicated concurrency control

We now discuss an object, a distributed lock, that ensures mutual exclusion. We use an array of boolean values, one entry per replica, to model a lock. If a replica owns the lock, the corresponding array entry is set to true. The lock is transferred to any other replica by using the transfer function. The full specification is shown in Figure 8.

We need to ensure that the lock is owned by exactly one replica at any given point in time, which is the invariant here. For simplicity, we are not considering failures. In order to preserve safety, we need to enforce a precondition on the transfer operation such that the operation can only transfer the ownership of its origin replica. For state inflation, a timestamp associated with the lock is incremented during each transfer.

A merge of two states of this distributed lock will preserve the state with the highest timestamp. In order for the merge function to be the least upper bound, we must specify that if the timestamps of the two states are equal, their corresponding boolean arrays are also equal. Also if the origin replica owns the lock, it has the highest timestamp. The conjunction of these two restrictions which form the precondition of merge, Pre_{merge}, is the concurrency invariant, Inv_{conc}.

Consider the case of three replicas r_1, r_2 and r_3 sharing a distributed lock. Assume that initially replica r_1 owns the lock. Replicas r_2 and r_3 concurrently place a request for the lock. The current owner r_1, has to make a decision on the priority of the requests based on the business logic. r_1 calculates a higher priority for r_3 and transfers the lock to r_3. Since r_1 no longer has the lock, it cannot issue any further transfer operations. We see here clearly that the transfer operation is safe. In the new state, r_3 is the only replica that can perform a transfer operation. We can also note that this prevents any concurrent transfer operations. This can guarantee mutual exclusion and hence ensures safety in a concurrent execution environment.

An interesting property we can observe from this example is total order. Due to the preconditions imposed in order to be safe, we see that the states progress through a total order, ordered by the timestamp. The transfer function increases the timestamp and merge function preserves the highest timestamp.

5.3   Courseware

We now look at an application that allows students to register and enroll in a course. For space reasons, we elide the pseudocode which can be found in the extended version[23]. The state consists of a set of students, a set of courses and enrollments of students for different courses. Students can register and deregister, courses can be created and deleted, and a student can enroll for a course. The invariant requires enrolled students and courses to be registered and created respectively.

The set of students and courses consists of two sets - one to track registrations or creations and another to track deregistrations or deletions. Registration or creation monotonically adds the student or course to the registered sets respectively and deregistration or deletion monotonically adds them to the unregistered sets. The semantics currently doesn't support re-registration, but that can be fixed by using a slightly modified data structure that counts the number of times the student has been registered/unregistered and decides on the status of registration. Enrollment adds the student-course pair to the set. Currently, we do not consider canceling an enrollment, but it is a trivial extension. Merging two states takes the union of the sets.

Let us consider the safety of each operation. The operations to register a student and create a course are safe without any restrictions. Therefore they do not need any precondition. The remaining three operations might violate the invariant in some cases. This leads to strengthening their preconditions. The precondition of the operation for deregistering a student and deleting a course requires no existing enrollments for them. For enrollment, both the student and the course should be registered/created and not unregistered/deleted.

Merge also requires strengthening of its precondition. It requires the set of enrolled students and courses to be registered and not unregistered in all the remote states as well. This is the concurrent invariant (Inv_{conc}) for this object.

Running this specification through our tool which we describe in Section 6 reveals concurrency issues for deregistering a student, deleting a course and enrollment. This means that we need to add concurrency control to the state.

For this use case, we know that enrolling will be more frequent than deregistering a student or deleting a course. So, we model a concurrency control mechanism as in the case of the auction object discussed earlier. We assign a token to each replica for each student and course, called a student token and course token respectively. A replica will have a set of student tokens indicating the registered students and course tokens indicating the created courses. In order to deregister a student or delete a course, all replicas must have released their tokens for that particular student/course. Enroll operations can progress as long as the student token and course token are available at the local replica for the student and course for that particular enrollment.

This concurrency control mechanism now forms part of the state. The preconditions of operations and merge are recomputed and the concurrency invariant is updated. The edited specification passes all checks and is deemed safe.

6   Automation

In this section, we present a tool to automate the verification of invariants as discussed in the previous sections. Our tool, called *Soteria* is based on the Boogie [5] verification framework. The input to Soteria is a specification of the object written as Boogie procedures, augmented with a number of domain-specific annotations needed to check the properties described in Section 4.

Let us now consider how a distributed object is specified in Soteria.:

- **State:** We require the programmer to provide a declaration of the state using the global variables in Boogie. The data types can be either built-in or user defined.
- **Comparison function:** Next we require the programmer to provide a comparison function. This function determines the partial order on states. Again, we shall use this comparison function as a basis to check the lattice conditions, and whether each operation is an inflation on the lattice. We use the keyword @gteq to annotate the comparison function in the tool. This comparison function returns true when all the components of the first state are greater than or equal to the corresponding components in the other state. It is encoded as a function in Boogie.
- **Operations:** We require the programmer to provide the implementation of the operations of the object. Moreover, for each operation op we require the

programmer to provide the precondition Pre_{op}. In general, operations are encoded as Boogie procedures. Alternatively, we could just require only a post-condition describing how the state transitions from the precondition to the post-condition. Notice that since in our program model operations are atomic, this is an unambiguous encoding of the operations.

A few things are important in this code. The specification declares operations that can modify the contents of the global variables as declared in the `modifies` clause. Preconditions are annotated with the `requires` clauses, and the postcondition is specified by the `ensures` clauses. The semantics of multiple `requires` and `ensures` clauses is conjunction.

- **Merge function:** We require the special `merge` operation to be distinguished from other operations. To that end, we use the annotation `@merge`. While, as mentioned before, the precondition of `merge` can be obtained by calculating the weakest precondition to ensure safety. The current version of Soteria does not perform this step automatically, it relies on the developer to provide the preconditions. Notice that, as we argued in Section 4.1, Soteria will consider this as the concurrency invariant (Inv_{conc}).

  While in Section 3 we mentioned that the `merge` procedure takes two states as arguments, in the specification input to Soteria, the procedure merge takes only one state as the argument. This is because this procedure assumes that the merge is being applied in a replica, and therefore, the local state of the replica is captured by the global variables.

- **Invariant:** Clearly, we require the programmer to provide the invariant to be verified by the tool. This invariant is simply provided as a Boogie assertion over the state of the object. Once more, we require the invariant to be annotated with the special keyword `@invariant`.

While these are the components required by Soteria to check the safety, often Boogie requires additional information to verify the procedures. Some of these components are:

- User-defined data types,
- Constants to declare special objects such as the origin replica me, or to bound the quantifiers,
- We sometimes make recourse to inductively-defined functions over aggregate data structures, for instance, to obtain the maximum in a set of values. Since we would like to use these functions in the specifications, we axiomatise their semantics to enable the SMT solver used by Boogie to discharge our proof obligations. This is particularly important for list comprehensions, and array operations. We follow the approach of Leino et al.[18].
- When we iterate over lists, arrays or matrices, we need to provide Boogie with loop invariants. Loops are part of the programs, and thus, verified by Boogie.

6.1   Verification passes

The verification of a specification is performed in multiple stages. Let us consider these in order:

1. **Syntax checks**
   The first simple checks validate that the specification provided respects Boogie syntax when ignoring Soteria annotations. It also calls Boogie to validate that the types are correct and that the pre/post conditions provided are sound.
   Then it checks that the specification provides all the elements necessary for a complete specification. Specifically, it checks the function signatures marked by @gteq and @invariant and the procedure marked by @merge.

2. **Convergence check**
   This stage checks the convergence of the specification. Specifically, it checks whether the specification respects Strong Eventual Consistency. The *Strong Eventual Consistency* (SEC) property states that any two replicas that received the same set of updates are in the same state. To guarantee this, objects are designed to have certain sufficient properties in the encoding of the state [3, 4, 25], which can be summarised as follows:
   - The state space is equipped with an ordering operator, comparing two states.
   - The ordering forms a join-semilattice.
   - Each individual operation is an inflation in the semilattice.
   - The merge operation, composing states from two replicas, computes the least-upper-bound of the given states in the semilattice.
   We present the conditions formally in the extended version[23].
   An alternative is to make use of the CALM theorem [12]. This allows non-monotonic operations, but requires them to coordinate. However, our aim is to provide maximum possible availability with SEC. [7]
   To ensure these conditions of Strong Eventual Consistency, the tool performs the following checks:
   - That each operation is an inflation. In a nutshell, we prove using Boogie the following Hoare-logic triple:

     ```
     assume σ ∈ Pre_op
     call σ_new := op(σ)
     assert σ_new ≥ σ
     ```

   - Merge computes the least upper bound. The verification condition discharged is shown below:

     ```
     assume (σ, σ') ∈ Pre_merge
     call σ_new := merge(σ, σ')
     assert σ_new ≥ σ ∧ σ_new ≥ σ'
     assert ∀σ*, σ* ≥ σ ∧ σ* ≥ σ' ⟹ σ* ≥ σ_new
     ```

3. **Safety check** This stage verifies the safety of the specification as discussed in Section 4. This stage is divided further into two sub-stages:
   - *Sequential safety:* Soteria checks whether each individual operation is safe. This corresponds to the conditions (2) and (3) in Figure 5. The verification condition discharged by the tool to ensure sequential safety of operations is:

---

[7] Convergence of our running example is discussed in the extended version[23].

```
assume  σ ∈ Pre_op ∧ Inv
call  σ_new := op(σ)
assert  σ_new ∈ Inv
```

The special case of the **merge** function is verified with the following verification condition:

```
assume  (σ, σ') ∈ Pre_merge ∧ σ ∈ Inv ∧ σ' ∈ Inv
call  σ_new := merge(σ, σ')
assert  σ_new ∈ Inv
```

Notice that in this condition we assume that there are two copies of the state, the state of the replica applying the merge, and the state with superscript representing a state arriving from another replica. In case of failure of the sequential safety check, the designer needs to strengthen the precondition of the operation (or merge) which was unsafe.

– *Concurrent safety:* Here we check whether each operation upholds the precondition of merge. This corresponds to the conditions (5) and (6) in Figure 5. Notice that while this check relates to the concurrent behaviour of the distributed object, the check itself is completely sequential; it does not require reasoning about operations performed by other processes. As shown in Section 4, this ensures safety during concurrent operation. The verification conditions are:

```
assume  σ ∈ Pre_op ∧ Inv ∧ (σ, σ') ∈ Inv_conc
call  σ_new := op(σ)
assert  (σ_new, σ') ∈ Inv_conc
```

to validate each operation **op**, and

```
assume  (σ, σ') ∈ Inv_conc ∧ σ ∈ Inv ∧ σ' ∈ Inv
call  σ_new := merge(σ, σ')
assert  (σ_new, σ) ∈ Inv_conc
```

to validate a call to **merge**. If the concurrent safety check fails, the design of the distributed object needs a replicated concurrency control mechanism embedded as part of the state.

When all checks are validated, the tool reports that the specification is safe. Whenever a check fails, Soteria provides a counterexample [8] along with the failure message tailored to the type of check. This can help the developer identify issues with the specification and fix it.

Once the invariants and specification of an application is given, Soteria is fully automatic, thanks to Z3, an SMT solver that is fully automated. The specification of the application includes the state, all the operations including the pre and post conditions (including merge). In case the invariant cannot be proven, Soteria provides counter-examples. The programmer can leverage these to update the specification with appropriate concurrency control, rerun Soteria, and so on until the application is correct. As far as the proof system is concerned, no programmer involvement is required. Currently, the effort of adding the required synchronization conditions is manual, but as the next step, we are working on

---

[8] Soteria uses the counter model provided by Boogie.

automating the efficient generation of synchronization control considering the workload characteristics. The tool and the full specifications in the form of the tool input are available at Soteria [22]. [9]

7   Related Work

Several works have concentrated on the formalisation and specification of eventually consistent systems [7, 8, 27] to mention but a few.

A number of works concentrate on the specification and correct implementation of replicated data types [10, 14]. Unlike these works, we are not concerned with the correctness of the data type implementation with respect to a specification, but rather on proving properties that hold of a distributed object.

Gotsman et al.[11] present a proof methodology for proving invariants of distributed objects. In fact, that work has been extended with a tool called CISE [24] which, similar to Soteria, performs the check using an SMT solver as a backend. Another more user-friendly tool was developed by Marcelino et al.[19] based on the principle of CISE. It is named Correct Eventual Consistency(CEC) Tool. The tool is based on Boogie verification framework and also proposes sets of tokens that the developer might use. An improved token generation by using the counterexamples generated by Boogie is discussed by Nair and Shapiro[20].

Unlike our work, CISE and CEC (and more generally the work of Gotsman et al.[11]) consider the implementation of operation-based objects. As a consequence, they assume that the underlying network model ensures causal consistency, and the proof methodology therein presented requires reasoning about concurrent behaviours (reflected as stability verification conditions on assertions). We position Soteria as a *complementary* tool to CISE, since CISE is not well-adapted to reason about systems that propagate state, and Soteria is not well-adapted to reason about objects that propagate operations. We consider, as part of our future work, the use of both CISE and Soteria in tandem to prove properties depending on the implementation of the objects at hand.

Houshmand et al.[13] extends CISE by lowering the causal consistency requirements and generating concurrency control protocols. It still requires reasoning about concurrent behaviours.

As anticipated in Section 4, Bailis et al. [2] introduced the concept of *I*-confluence based on a similar system model. *I*-confluence states that for an invariant to hold in a lattice-based state-propagating distributed application, the set of *reachable* valid (i.e. invariant preserving) states must be closed under operations and merge. This condition is similar to the ones presented in Figure 5. However, there is a fundamental difference: while Bailis et al. [2] recognises that one needs to consider only *reachable* states when checking that the merge operation satisfies the invariant, they do not provide means to identify these reachable states. This is indeed a hard problem. In Soteria, we instead *over-approximate the set of reachable states* by ignoring whether the states are indeed reachable,

---

[9] Experimental results with verification time is provided in the extended version[23].

but requiring that their merge satisfies the invariant. This is captured in the concurrency invariant, Inv_{conc}, which is synthesised from the user provided invariant. How to obtain this invariant is understandably not addressed in Bailis et al.[2] since no proof technique is provided. Notice that this is a sound approximation since it guarantees the invariant is satisfied, and we also verify that every operation preserves this condition as shown in Corollary 1. In this sense we say that the pre-condition of merge for a given invariant I, is also an invariant of the system. It is this abstraction step that makes the analysis performed by Soteria to be syntax-driven, automated, and machine-checked. The fact that Soteria is an analysis of a program is in contrast with I-confluence [2] where no means to link a given program text to the semantical model, let alone rules to show that the syntax implies invariant preservation, are provided. In other words, I-confluence [2] does not provide a program logic, but rather a meta-theoretical proof about lattice-based state-propagating systems.

Our previous work [21], provides an informal proof methodology for ensuring safety of Convergent Replicated Data Types(CvRDTs), which are a group of specialised data structures used to ensure convergence in distributed programming. This work builds upon it, and formalises the proof rules and prove them sound. We relax the requirement of CvRDTs by allowing the usage of any data types, that together respect the lattice conditions mentioned in Section 3. We also show several case studies which demonstrate the use of the rule.

A final interesting remark is that we can show how our methodology can aid in the verification of distributed objects mediated by concurrency control. Some works [16, 17, 26, 27] have considered this problem from the standpoint of synthesis, or from the point of view of which mechanisms can be used to check a certain property of the system.

8   Conclusion

We have presented a sound proof rule to verify invariants of state-based distributed objects, i.e., the objects that propagate state. We present the proof obligations guaranteeing that the implementation is safe in concurrent execution by reducing the problem to checking that each operation of the object satisfies a precondition of the `merge` function of the state.

We presented Soteria, a tool sitting on top of the Boogie verification framework. This tool can be used to identify the concurrency bugs in the design of a distributed object. Soteria also checks convergence by checking the lattice conditions on the state, described by [3]. We have shown multiple compelling case-studies showing how Soteria can be leveraged to ensure the correctness of distributed objects that propagate state. It would be an interesting next step to look into automatic concurrency control synthesis. The synthesised concurrency control can be analysed and adapted dynamically to minimise the cost of synchronisation.

Acknowledgements. This research is supported in part by the RainbowFS project (*Agence Nationale de la Recherche*, France, number ANR-16-CE25-0013-01) and by European H2020 project 732 505 LightKone (2017–2020).

Bibliography

[1] Almeida, P.S., Shoker, A., Baquero, C.: Delta state replicated data types. J. Parallel Distrib. Comput. **111**, 162–173 (2018), https://doi.org/10.1016/j.jpdc.2017.08.003

[2] Bailis, P., Fekete, A., Franklin, M.J., Ghodsi, A., Hellerstein, J.M., Stoica, I.: Coordination avoidance in database systems. Proc. VLDB Endow. **8**(3), 185–196 (Nov 2014), http://dx.doi.org/10.14778/2735508.2735509, int. Conf. on Very Large Data Bases (VLDB) 2015, Waikoloa, Hawai'i, USA

[3] Baquero, C., Almeida, P.S., Cunha, A., Ferreira, C.: Composition in state-based replicated data types. Bulletin of the EATCS **123** (2017), http://eatcs.org/beatcs/index.php/beatcs/article/view/507

[4] Baquero, C., Moura, F.: Using structural characteristics for autonomous operation. Operating Systems Review **33**(4), 90–96 (1999), https://doi.org/10.1145/334598.334614

[5] Barnett, M., Chang, B.Y.E., DeLine, R., Jacobs, B., Leino, K.R.M.: Boogie: A modular reusable verifier for object-oriented programs. In: Proceedings of the 4th International Conference on Formal Methods for Components and Objects. pp. 364–387. FMCO'05, Springer-Verlag, Berlin, Heidelberg (2006), http://dx.doi.org/10.1007/11804192_17

[6] Brookes, S., O'Hearn, P.W.: Concurrent separation logic. SIGLOG News **3**(3), 47–65 (2016), https://dl.acm.org/citation.cfm?id=2984457

[7] Burckhardt, S.: Principles of eventual consistency. Foundations and Trends in Programming Languages **1**(1-2), 1–150 (2014), https://doi.org/10.1561/2500000011

[8] Burckhardt, S., Gotsman, A., Yang, H., Zawirski, M.: Replicated data types: Specification, verification, optimality. In: Symp. on Principles of Prog. Lang. (POPL). pp. 271–284. San Diego, CA, USA (Jan 2014), http://doi.acm.org/10.1145/2535838.2535848

[9] Dijkstra, E.: A discipline of programming. Prentice-Hall series in automatic computation, Prentice-Hall (1976)

[10] Gomes, V.B.F., Kleppmann, M., Mulligan, D.P., Beresford, A.R.: A framework for establishing strong eventual consistency for conflict-free replicated datatypes. Archive of Formal Proofs **2017** (2017), https://www.isa-afp.org/entries/CRDT.shtml

[11] Gotsman, A., Yang, H., Ferreira, C., Najafzadeh, M., Shapiro, M.: 'Cause I'm Strong Enough: Reasoning about consistency choices in distributed systems. In: Symp. on Principles of Prog. Lang. (POPL). pp. 371–384. St. Petersburg, FL, USA (2016), http://dx.doi.org/10.1145/2837614.2837625

[12] Hellerstein, J.M., Alvaro, P.: Keeping CALM: when distributed consistency is easy. CoRR **abs/1901.01930** (2019), http://arxiv.org/abs/1901.01930

[13] Houshmand, F., Lesani, M.: Hamsaz: Replication coordination analysis and synthesis. Proc. ACM Program. Lang. **3**(POPL), 74:1–74:32 (Jan 2019), http://doi.acm.org/10.1145/3290387

[14] Jagadeesan, R., Riely, J.: Eventual consistency for crdts. In: Ahmed, A. (ed.) Programming Languages and Systems - 27th European Symposium on Programming, ESOP 2018, Held as Part of the European Joint Conferences on Theory and Practice of Software, ETAPS 2018, Thessaloniki, Greece, April 14-20, 2018, Proceedings. Lecture Notes in Computer Science, vol. 10801, pp. 968–995. Springer (2018), https://doi.org/10.1007/978-3-319-89884-1_34

[15] Jones, C.B.: Specification and design of (parallel) programs. In: Mason, R. (ed.) Information Processing 83. IFIP Congress Series, vol. 9, pp. 321–332. IFIP, North-Holland/IFIP, Paris, France (Sep 1983)

[16] Kaki, G., Earanky, K., Sivaramakrishnan, K., Jagannathan, S.: Safe replication through bounded concurrency verification. Proc. ACM Program. Lang. 2(OOPSLA), 164:1–164:27 (Oct 2018), http://doi.acm.org/10.1145/3276534

[17] Kaki, G., Nagar, K., Najafzadeh, M., Jagannathan, S.: Alone together: Compositional reasoning and inference for weak isolation. In: Symp. on Principles of Prog. Lang. (POPL). Proc. ACM Program. Lang., vol. 2, pp. 27:1–27:34. Assoc. for Computing Machinery, Assoc. for Computing Machinery, Los Angeles, CA, USA (Dec 2017), http://doi.acm.org/10.1145/3158115

[18] Leino, K.R.M., Monahan, R.: Reasoning about comprehensions with first-order smt solvers. In: Proceedings of the 2009 ACM Symposium on Applied Computing. pp. 615–622. SAC '09, ACM, New York, NY, USA (2009), http://doi.acm.org/10.1145/1529282.1529411

[19] Marcelino, G., Balegas, V., Ferreira, C.: Bringing hybrid consistency closer to programmers. In: W. on Principles and Practice of Consistency for Distr. Data (PaPoC). pp. 6:1–6:4. PaPoC '17, Euro. Conf. on Comp. Sys. (EuroSys), ACM, Belgrade, Serbia (2017), http://doi.acm.org/10.1145/3064889.3064896

[20] Nair, S., Shapiro, M.: Improving the "Correct Eventual Consistency" tool. Rapport de recherche RR-9191, Institut National de la Recherche en Informatique et Automatique (Inria), Paris, France (Jul 2018), https://hal.inria.fr/hal-01832888

[21] Nair, S.S., Petri, G., Shapiro, M.: Invariant safety for distributed applications. In: W. on Principles and Practice of Consistency for Distr. Data (PaPoC). pp. 4:1–4:7. Assoc. for Computing Machinery, Assoc. for Computing Machinery, Dresden, Germany (Mar 2019), https://doi.org/10.1145/3301419.3323970

[22] Nair, S.S., Petri, G., Shapiro, M.: Soteria. https://github.com/sreeja/soteria_tool (2019)

[23] Nair, S.S., Petri, G., Shapiro, M.: Proving the safety of highly-available distributed objects (Extended version). Tech. rep. (Feb 2020), https://hal.archives-ouvertes.fr/hal-02492599

[24] Najafzadeh, M., Gotsman, A., Yang, H., Ferreira, C., Shapiro, M.: The CISE tool: Proving weakly-consistent applications correct. In: W. on Principles and Practice of Consistency for Distr. Data (PaPoC). EuroSys 2016

workshops, Assoc. for Computing MachinerySpecial Interest Group on Op. Sys. (SIGOPS), Assoc. for Computing Machinery, London, UK (Apr 2016), http://dx.doi.org/10.1145/2911151.2911160

[25] Shapiro, M., Preguiça, N., Baquero, C., Zawirski, M.: Conflict-free replicated data types. In: Défago, X., Petit, F., Villain, V. (eds.) Int. Symp. on Stabilization, Safety, and Security of Dist. Sys. (SSS). Lecture Notes in Comp. Sc., vol. 6976, pp. 386–400. Springer-Verlag, Grenoble, France (Oct 2011)

[26] Shapiro, M., Saeida Ardekani, M., Petri, G.: Consistency in 3D. In: Desharnais, J., Jagadeesan, R. (eds.) Int. Conf. on Concurrency Theory (CONCUR). Leibniz Int. Proc. in Informatics (LIPICS), vol. 59, pp. 3:1–3:14. Schloss Dagstuhl – Leibniz-Zentrum für Informatik, Dagstuhl Publishing, Germany, Québec, Québec, Canada (Aug 2016), http://dx.doi.org/10.4230/LIPIcs.CONCUR.2016.3

[27] Sivaramakrishnan, K., Kaki, G., Jagannathan, S.: Declarative programming over eventually consistent data stores. In: Assoc. for Computing MachinerySpecial Interest Group on Pg. Lang. (SIGPLAN). pp. 413–424. PLDI '15, Assoc. for Computing Machinery, Assoc. for Computing Machinery, Portland, OR, USA (2015), http://doi.acm.org/10.1145/2737924.2737981

Solving Program Sketches with Large Integer Values

Rong Pan[1], Qinheping Hu[2], Rishabh Singh[3], and Loris D'Antoni[2]

[1] The University of Texas at Austin, Austin, USA
[2] University of Wisconsin-Madison, Madison, USA
[3] Google, Mountain View, USA

Abstract. Program sketching is a program synthesis paradigm in which the programmer provides a partial program with holes and assertions. The goal of the synthesizer is to automatically find integer values for the holes so that the resulting program satisfies the assertions. The most popular sketching tool, SKETCH, can efficiently solve complex program sketches, but uses an integer encoding that often performs poorly if the sketched program manipulates large integer values. In this paper, we propose a new solving technique that allows SKETCH to handle large integer values while retaining its integer encoding. Our technique uses a result from number theory, the Chinese Remainder Theorem, to rewrite program sketches to only track the remainders of certain variable values with respect to several prime numbers. We prove that our transformation is sound and the encoding of the resulting programs are exponentially more succinct than existing SKETCH encodings. We evaluate our technique on a variety of benchmarks manipulating large integer values. Our technique provides speedups against both existing SKETCH solvers and can solve benchmarks that existing SKETCH solvers cannot handle.

1 Introduction

Program synthesis, the art of automatically generating programs that meet a user's intent, promises to increase the productivity of programmers by automating tedious, error-prone, and time-consuming tasks. Syntax-guided Synthesis (SyGuS) [2], where the search space of possible programs is defined using a grammar or a domain-specific language, has emerged as a common program synthesis paradigm for many synthesis domains. One of the earliest and successful syntax-guided program synthesis frameworks is program sketching [19], where (*i*) the search space of the synthesis problem is described using a partial program in which certain integer constants are left unspecified (represented as holes), and (*ii*) the specification is provided as a set of assertions describing the intended behavior of the program. The goal of the synthesizer is to automatically replace the holes in the program with integer values so that the resulting complete program satisfies all the assertions. Thanks to its simplicity, program sketching has found wide adoption in applications such as data-structure design [20], personalized education [18], program repair [7], and many others.

P. Müller (Ed.): ESOP 2020, LNCS 12075, pp. 572–598, 2020.
https://doi.org/10.1007/978-3-030-44914-8_21

The most popular sketching tool, SKETCH [21], can efficiently solve complex program sketches with hundreds of lines of code. However, SKETCH often performs poorly if the sketched program manipulates large integer values. SKETCH's synthesis is based on an algorithm called *counterexample-guided inductive synthesis* (CEGIS) [21]. The CEGIS algorithm iteratively considers a finite set I of inputs for the program and performs SAT queries to identify values for the holes so that the resulting program satisfies all the assertions for the inputs in I. Further SAT queries are then used to verify whether the generated solution is correct on all the possible inputs of the program. SKETCH represents integers using a unary encoding (a variable for each integer value) so that arithmetic computations such as addition, multiplication etc. can be represented efficiently in the SAT formulas as lookup operations. This unary encoding, however, results in huge formulas for solving sketches with larger integer values as we also observe in our evaluation. Recently, an SMT-like technique that extends the SAT solver with native integer variables and integer constraints was proposed to alleviate this issue in SKETCH. It guesses values for the integer variables and propagates them through the integer constraints, and learns from conflict clauses. However, this technique does not scale well when the sketches contain complex arithmetic operations—e.g., non-linear integer arithmetic.

In this paper, we propose a program transformation technique that allows SKETCH to solve program sketches involving large integer values while retaining the unary encoding used by the traditional SKETCH solver. Our technique rewrites a SKETCH program into an equivalent one that performs computations over smaller values. The technique is based on the well-known Chinese Remainder Theorem, which states that, given distinct prime numbers $p_1, \ldots, p_n$ such that $N = p_1 \cdot \ldots \cdot p_n$, for every two distinct numbers $0 \le k_1, k_2 < N$, there exists a p_i such that $k_1 \bmod p_i \ne k_2 \bmod p_i$. Intuitively, this theorem states that tracking the modular values of a number smaller than N for each p_i is enough to uniquely recover the actual value of the number itself. We use this idea to replace a variable x in the program with n variables $x_{p_1}, \ldots, x_{p_n}$, so that for every i, $x_{p_i} = x \bmod p_i$. Using closure properties of modular arithmetic we show that, as long as the program uses the operators $+, -, *, ==$, tracking the modular values of variables and performing the corresponding operations on such values is enough to ensure correctness. For example, to reflect the variable assignment $x = y + z$, we perform the assignment $x_{p_i} = (y_{p_i} + z_{p_i}) \bmod p_i$, for every p_i. Similarly, the Boolean operation $x == y$ will only hold if $x_{p_i} = y_{p_i}$, for every p_i. To identify what variables and values in the program can be rewritten, we develop a data-flow analysis that computes what variables *may* flow into operations that are not sound in modular arithmetic—e.g., $<, >, \le$, and $/$.

We provide a comprehensive theoretical analysis of the complexity of the proposed transformation. First, we derive how many prime numbers are needed to track values in a certain integer range. Second, we analyze the number of bits required to encode values in the original and rewritten program and show that, for the unary encoding used by SKETCH, our technique offers an exponential saving in the number of required bits.

We evaluate our technique on 181 benchmarks from various applications of program sketching. Our results show that our technique results in significant speedups over existing SKETCH solvers and is able to solve 48 benchmarks on which SKETCH times out.

Contributions. In summary, our contributions are:

- A language IMP-MOD together with a *modular semantics* that represents integer values using their remainders for a given set of primes and a proof that this semantics is equivalent to the standard *integer semantics* (§ 4).
- A data-flow analysis for detecting variables that can be soundly executed in the modular semantics and an algorithm for translating IMP programs into IMP-MOD ones (§ 5).
- A synthesis algorithm for IMP-MOD programs and incremental synthesis algorithm that lazily increases the number of primes used in the modular semantics (§ 6).
- A complexity analysis that shows that synthesis for IMP-MOD programs requires exponentially smaller SAT queries than synthesis in IMP (§ 7).
- An evaluation of our technique on 181 benchmarks that manipulate large integer values. Our solver outperforms the default SKETCH unary solver, it can solve 48 new benchmarks that no SKETCH solver can solve, and is 15.9X faster than the SKETCH SMT-like integer solver on the hard benchmarks that take more than 10 seconds to solve (§ 8).

An extended version containing all proofs and further details has been uploaded to arXiv as supplementary material.

2 Motivating Example

In this section, we use a simple example to illustrate our technique and its effectiveness. Consider the SKETCH program polyArray presented in Figure 1b. The goal of this synthesis problem is to synthesize a two-variable quadratic polynomial (lines 7–8) whose evaluation p on given inputs x and y is equal to a given expected-output array z (line 9). Solving the problem amounts to finding non-negative integer values for the holes (??) and sign values, i.e., -1 or 1, for the holes (??^{s}) such that the assertion becomes true.[1] In this case, a possible solution is the polynomial:

```
p[i] = -17*y[i]^2-8*x[i]*y[i]-17*x[i]^2-3*x[i];
```

When attempting to solve this problem, the SKETCH synthesizer times out at 300 seconds. To solve this problem, SKETCH creates SAT queries where the variables are the holes. Due to the large numbers involved in the computation of this program, the unary encoding of SKETCH ends up with SAT formulas with approximately 45 *million* clauses.

---

[1] In SKETCH, holes can only assume positive values. This is why we need the sign holes, which are implemented using regular holes as follows: if(??) then 1 else -1.

```
1  // n=4, x=[24,-1,0,-19], y=[-7,11,-3,13]
2  // z=[-9353,-1983,-153,-6977]
3  polyArray(int n, int[n] x, int[n] y, int[n] z){
4    int[n] p;
5    int i=0;
6    while (i<n){
7      p[i]=??s1*??1*y[i]^2+??s2*??2*x[i]^2+??s3*??3*x[i]*y[i]
8          +??s4*??4*y[i]+??s5*??5*x[i]+??s6*??6;
9      assert p[i] == z[i];
10     i++; }
11 }
```

(a) Original sketch program.

```
1  // n=4, x=[24,-1,0,-19], y=[-7,11,-3,13]
2  // z=[-9353,-1983,-153,-6977]
3  pAPrime(int n, int[n] x, int[n] y, int[n] z){
4    int[n] x2,x3,x5,x7,x11,x13,x17;
5    while (i<n){    // Initialize modular variables
6      x2[i]=x[i]%2;
7      x3[i]=x[i]%3;
8      ... i++; }
9    int i=0;
10   int[n] p2,p3,p5,p7,p11,p13,p17;
11   while (i<n){
12     p2[i]=(??s1*(??1%2)*(y2[i]^2%2)%2
13          +??s2*(??2%2)*(x2[i]^2%2)%2
14          +??s3*(??3%2)*(x2[i]%2)*(y2[i]%2)%2
15          +??s4*(??4%2)*(y2[i]%2)%2
16          +??s5*(??5%2)*(x2[i]%2)%2
17          +??s6*(??6%2)%2)%2;
18     ...
19     assert p2[i] = z2[i];
20     assert p3[i] = z3[i];
21     ...
22     i++; }
23 }
```

(b) Rewritten sketch program.

Fig. 1: SKETCH program (a) and rewritten version with values tracked for different moduli (b).

Sketch Program with Modular Arithmetic The technique we propose in this paper has the goal of reducing the complexity of the synthesis problem by transforming the program into an equivalent one that manipulates smaller integer values and that yields easier SAT queries. Given the SKETCH program in Figure 1b, our technique produces the modified SKETCH program pAPrime in Figure 1a. The new SKETCH program has the same control flow graph as the original one, but instead of computing the actual values of the expressions x[·] and y[·], it tracks their remainders for the set of prime numbers $\{2, 3, 5, 7, 11, 13, 17\}$ using new variables—e.g., x2[i] tracks the remainder of x[i] modulo 2.

The program pAPrime initializes the modular variables with the corresponding modular values (lines 5–8). When rewriting a computation over modular variables, the same computation is performed modularly (lines 12–17). For example, the term $??_1^s * ??_1 * y[i]^2$ when tracked modulo 2 is rewritten as

$$(??_1^s * (??_1 \% 2) * ((y2[i] \% 2)^2 \% 2)) \% 2$$

In the rewritten program, the variables i and n are not tracked modularly, since such a transformation would incorrectly access array indices. Finally, the assertions for different moduli share the same holes as the solution to the SKETCH has to be correct for all modular values. In the rest of the paper, we develop a data flow analysis that detects when variables can be tracked modularly.

SKETCH can solve the rewritten program in less than 2 seconds and produce hole values that are correct solutions for the original program. This speedup is due to the small integer values manipulated by the modular computations. In fact, the intermediate SAT formulas generated by SKETCH for the program pAPrime have approximately 120 *thousand* clauses instead of the 45 *million* clauses for polyArray. Due to the complex arithmetic in the formulas, even if SKETCH uses the SMT-like native integer encoding, it still requires more than 300 seconds to solve this problem.

While this technique is quite powerful, it does have some limitations. In particular, the solution to the rewritten SKETCH is guaranteed to be a correct solution only for inputs that cause intermediate values of the program to be in a range $[d_1, d_2]$ such that $d_2 - d_1 \leq 2 \times 3 \times 5 \times 7 \times 11 \times 13 \times 17 = 510,510$. We will prove this result in Section 4.

3   Preliminaries

In this section, we describe the IMP language that we will consider throughout the paper and briefly recall the counter-example guided inductive synthesis algorithm employed by the SKETCH solver.

For simplicity, we consider a simple imperative language IMP with integer holes for defining the hypothesis space of programs. The syntax and semantics of IMP are shown in Appendix ??. Without loss of generality, we assume the programs consists of a single program $f(v_1, \cdots, v_n, ??_1, \ldots ??_m)$ with n integer variables and m integer holes. The body of the program f consists of a sequence of statements, where a statement s can either be a variable assignment, a while loop statement, an if conditional statement, or an assert statement. The holes ?? denote integer constant values that are unknown and the goal of the synthesis process is to compute these values such that a set of desired program assertions are satisfied for every possible input values to f.[2]

---

[2] Our implementation also supports for-loops, recursion, arrays, and complex types.

Example 1. An example IMP sketch denoting a partial program is shown below.

```
triple(n,h,??){ h=??; assert h*n==n+n+n; }
```

The goal of the synthesizer is to compute the value of the hole ?? such that the assertion is true for all possible input values of n and h. For this example, ?? = 3 is a valid solution.

The SKETCH solver uses the counter-example guided inductive synthesis algorithm (CEGIS) to find hole values such that the desired assertions hold for all input values. Formally, the SKETCH synthesizer solves the following constraint:

$$\exists?? \equiv (??_1, \cdots, ??_m) \in \mathbb{Z}^m. \ \forall in \in \mathcal{I}. \ [\![f(in, ??)]\!]^{\mathrm{IMP}} \neq \bot$$

where $\mathbb{Z}$ denotes the domain of all integer values, ?? denotes the list of unknown hole values $(??_1, \cdots, ??_m) \in \mathbb{Z}^m$, $\mathcal{I}$ denotes the domain of all input argument values to the function f, and $[\![f(in, ??)]\!]^{\mathrm{IMP}} \neq \bot$ denotes that the program satisfies all assertions. The synthesis problem is in general undecidable for a language with complex operations such as the IMP language because of the infinite size of possible hole and input values. To make the synthesis process more tractable, SKETCH imposes a bound on the sizes of both the input domain $(\mathcal{I}_b)$ and the domain of hole values $(\mathbb{Z}_b)$ to obtain the following constraint:

$$\exists?? \equiv (??_1, \cdots, ??_m) \in \mathbb{Z}_b^m. \ \forall in \in \mathcal{I}_h. \ [\![f(in, ??)]\!]^{\mathrm{IMP}} \neq \bot$$

The bounded domains make the synthesis problem decidable, but the second-order quantified formula results in a search space of hole values that is still huge for any reasonable bounds. To solve such bounded equations efficiently, SKETCH uses the CEGIS algorithm to incrementally add inputs from the domain until obtaining hole values ?? that satisfy the assertion predicates for all the input values in the bounded domain. The algorithm solves the second-order formula by iteratively solving a series of first-order queries. It first encodes the existential query (synthesis query) over a randomly selected input value in_0 to find the hole values H that satisfy the predicate for in_0 using a SAT solver in the backend.

$$\exists?? \equiv (??_1, \cdots, ??_m) \in \mathbb{Z}_b^m. \ [\![f(in_0, ??)]\!]^{\mathrm{IMP}} \neq \bot$$

It then encodes another existential query (verification) to now find a counter-example in_1 for which the predicate is not satisfied for the previously found hole values.

$$\exists in \in \mathcal{I}_b. \ \neg [\![f(in, H)]\!]^{\mathrm{IMP}} \neq \bot$$

If no counter-example input can be found, the hole values are returned as the desired solution. Otherwise, the algorithm computes a new hole value that satisfies the assertion for all the counter-example inputs found so far. This process continues iteratively until either a desired hole value is found (i.e. no counter-example input exists), no satisfiable hole value is found (i.e. the synthesis problem is infeasible), or the SAT solver times out.

Integer Encoding The SKETCH solver can efficiently solve the synthesis constraint in many domains, but it does not scale well for sketches manipulating large numbers. SKETCH uses a unary encoding to represent integers, where the encoded formula consists of a variable for each integer value. The unary encoding allows for simplifying the representation of complex non-linear arithmetic operations. For example, a multiplication operation can be represented as simply a lookup table using this encoding. In practice, the unary encoding results in magnitudes of faster solving times compared to the logarithmic encoding for many synthesis problems. However, this also results in huge SAT formulas in presence of large integers. Recently, a new SMT-like technique based on extending the SAT solver with native integer variables and constraints was proposed to alleviate this issue in SKETCH. Similar to the Boolean variables, this extended solver guesses for integer values and propagates them in the constraints while also learning from conflict clauses. Note that SKETCH uses these SAT extensions and encodings instead of an SMT solver as SMT doesn't scale well for the non-linear constraints typically found in the synthesis problems. Our new technique for handling computations over large numbers still maintains the efficient unary encoding of integers and computations over them.

4   Modular Arithmetic Semantics

In this section, we present the language IMP-MOD in which variables can be tracked using modular arithmetic. We start by recalling the Chinese Remainder Theorem, then define both a modular and integer semantics for the IMP-MOD language, and show that the two semantics are equivalent.

4.1   The Chinese Remainder Theorem

The Chinese Remainder Theorem is a powerful number theory result that shows the following: given a set of distinct primes $\mathbb{P} = \{p_1, \ldots, p_k\}$, any number n in an interval of size $p_1 \cdot \ldots \cdot p_k$ can be uniquely identified from the remainders $[n \bmod p_1, \cdots, n \bmod p_k]$. In Section 4.2, we will use this idea to define the semantics of the IMP-MOD language. The main benefit of this idea is that the remainders could be much smaller than actual program values.

Example 2. For $\mathbb{P} = [3, 5, 7]$ and an integer 101, its remainders $[2, 1, 3]$ are much smaller than 101. However, any number of the form $101 + 105 \times n$ also has remainders $[2, 1, 3]$ with respect to the same prime set.

In general, one cannot uniquely determine an arbitrary integer value from its remainders for some set $\mathbb{P}$—i.e., the mapping from a number to its remainders is an abstraction in the sense of abstract interpretation [6]. However, if we are interested in a limited range of integer values $[L, U)$, one can choose a set of primes $\mathbb{P} = \{p_1, \ldots, p_k\}$ such that, for values $L \leq x < U$, the map $[r_1, \cdots, r_k] \mapsto x$, where $x \equiv r_i \bmod p_i$, is an injection.

Modular Expr $a^\mathbb{P} := c^\mathbb{P} \mid v^\mathbb{P} \mid a_1^\mathbb{P} \ op_a^\mathbb{P} \ a_2^\mathbb{P} \mid \textsc{toPrime}(a)$
Modular Op $op_a^\mathbb{P} := + \mid - \mid *$

Arith Expr $a := \ ?? \mid c \mid v \mid a_1 \ op_a \ a_2$
Arith Op $op_a := + \mid - \mid * \mid /$
Bool Expr $b := \text{not } b \mid a_1 \ op_c \ a_2 \mid b_1 \text{ and } b_2 \mid b_1 \text{ or } b_2 \mid a_1^\mathbb{P}{==}a_2^\mathbb{P}$
Comp Op $op_c := \ < \mid > \mid \leq \mid \geq$

Stmt $s := v = a \mid v^\mathbb{P} = a^\mathbb{P} \mid s_1; s_2$
$\mid \text{while}(b) \ \{s\} \mid \text{if}(b) \ s_1 \text{ else } s_2 \mid \text{assert } b$
Program $P := f(v_1, \cdots, v_n, v_1^\mathbb{P}, \cdots, v_m^\mathbb{P}, ??_1, \ldots, ??_l) \ \{s\}$

Fig. 2: Syntax of the IMP-MOD language.

Theorem 1 (Chinese Remainder Theorem [4]). *Let $p_1, ..., p_k$ be positive integers that are pairwise co-prime—i.e., no two numbers share a divisor larger than 1. Denote $N = \prod_{i=1}^{k} p_i$, and let $d, r_1, r_2, \ldots, r_k$ be any integers. Then there is one and only one integer $d \leq x < d + N$ such that $x \equiv r_i \bmod p_i$ for every $1 \leq i \leq k$.*

We define the translation function $m_\mathbb{P}(x) := [x \bmod p_l, \cdots, x \bmod p_k]$ that maps an integer to its set of remainders with respect to $\mathbb{P}$. When $m_\mathbb{P}(x)$ is bijective on some set R, we denote with $m_\mathbb{P}^{-1,R} : [0, p_1) \times \cdots \times [0, p_k) \to R$ its inverse function.

Example 3. Let x be a integer in the range $[0, 105)$ (note that $105 = 3 \times 5 \times 7$). If we know that the value of x is congruent to $[2, 1, 3]$ modulo $\{3, 5, 7\}$, we can uniquely identify the value of x to be 101 by observing that $101 \equiv 2 \bmod 3$, $101 \equiv 1 \bmod 5$, and $101 \equiv 3 \bmod 7$.

The following lemma shows that the function $m_\mathbb{P}$ is closed under addition, subtraction and multiplication of integers.

Lemma 1. *For every set of primes $\mathbb{P}$, integers x and y, and $op \in \{+, -, *\}$, the following holds: $m_\mathbb{P}(x \ op \ y) = m_\mathbb{P}(x) \ op \ m_\mathbb{P}(y)$.*

4.2 The IMP-MOD Language

In this section, we define the IMP-MOD language (syntax in Figure 2), a variant of the IMP language for which the semantics can be defined using modular arithmetic.[3] An IMP-MOD program is parametric on a set $\mathbb{P} = \{p_1, \ldots, p_k\}$ of distinct

---

[3] We consider the simple subset for a clear presentation of the semantics, but our framework works for the full IMP language (and for more complex language constructs) as we will see in the later sections.

$$[\![\text{TOPRIME}(a)]\!]^{\mathbb{P}}_{\sigma,\sigma^{\mathbb{P}}} := [\ [\![a]\!]^{\mathbb{P}}_{\sigma,\sigma^{\mathbb{P}}} \bmod p_1, \cdots\ ]$$

$$[\![v^{\mathbb{P}}]\!]^{\mathbb{P}}_{\sigma,\sigma^{\mathbb{P}}} := \sigma^{\mathbb{P}}(v) \qquad [\![c^{\mathbb{P}}]\!]^{\mathbb{P}}_{\sigma,\sigma^{\mathbb{P}}} := [\ c \bmod p_1, \cdots, c \bmod p_k\ ]$$

$$[\![a^{\mathbb{P}}_1\ op^{\mathbb{P}}_a\ a^{\mathbb{P}}_2]\!]^{\mathbb{P}}_{\sigma,\sigma^{\mathbb{P}}} := [\ (x^1_1\ op^{\mathbb{P}}_a\ x^2_1) \bmod p_1, \cdots\ ] \text{ where } [\![a^{\mathbb{P}}_i]\!]^{\mathbb{P}} = [\ x^i_1, \cdots, x^i_k\ ]$$

$$[\![a^{\mathbb{P}}_1 == a^{\mathbb{P}}_2]\!]^{\mathbb{P}}_{\sigma,\sigma^{\mathbb{P}}} := x^1_1 == x^2_1 \wedge \cdots \wedge x^1_k == x^2_k \text{ where } [\![a^{\mathbb{P}}_i]\!]^{\mathbb{P}} = [\ x^i_1, \cdots, x^i_k\ ]$$

$$[\![c]\!]^{\mathbb{P}}_{\sigma,\sigma^{\mathbb{P}}} := c \qquad [\![v]\!]^{\mathbb{P}}_{\sigma,\sigma^{\mathbb{P}}} := \sigma(v) \qquad [\![a_1\ op_a\ a_2]\!]^{\mathbb{P}}_{\sigma,\sigma^{\mathbb{P}}} := [\![a_1]\!]^{\mathbb{P}}_{\sigma,\sigma^{\mathbb{P}}}\ op_a\ [\![a_2]\!]^{\mathbb{P}}_{\sigma,\sigma^{\mathbb{P}}}$$

$$[\![v = a]\!]^{\mathbb{P}}_{\sigma,\sigma^{\mathbb{P}}} := (\sigma[v \hookleftarrow [\![a]\!]^{\mathbb{P}}_{\sigma,\sigma^{\mathbb{P}}}], \sigma^{\mathbb{P}}) \qquad [\![v^{\mathbb{P}} = a^{\mathbb{P}}]\!]^{\mathbb{P}}_{\sigma,\sigma^{\mathbb{P}}} := (\sigma, \sigma^{\mathbb{P}}[v^{\mathbb{P}} \hookleftarrow [\![a^{\mathbb{P}}]\!]^{\mathbb{P}}_{\sigma,\sigma^{\mathbb{P}}}])$$

Fig. 3: Modular semantics.

prime numbers. The structure of an `IMP-MOD` program is similar to an `IMP` program, but `IMP-MOD` supports two types of variables and arithmetic expressions: the regular `IMP` ones (i.e., v, a, and b), which operate over an integer semantics, and the modular ones (i.e., $v^{\mathbb{P}}$, $a^{\mathbb{P}}$, and $b^{\mathbb{P}}$), which take as an additional parameter the set of primes $\mathbb{P}$ and operate over a modular semantics. The semantics of some of the key constructs of `IMP-MOD` is shown in Figure 3.

The key idea of the modular semantics is that the value of each program variable in $v^{\mathbb{P}}$ and arithmetic expressions in $a^{\mathbb{P}}$ is denoted by a tuple of values, one for each prime number $p_i \in \mathbb{P}$. For example, the value of the constant $c^{\mathbb{P}}$ is represented by the tuple $[c \bmod p_1, \cdots, c \bmod p_k]$, where each individual value denotes the remainder of c when divided by the prime number $p_i \in \mathbb{P}$. Formally, the program f has two sets of variables $V^{\mathbb{Z}} = \{v_1, \cdots, v_n\}$ and $V^{\mathbb{P}} = \{v^{\mathbb{P}}_1, \cdots, v^{\mathbb{P}}_m\}$, which contain all the integer and prime variables respectively, and a set of holes $H = \{??_1, \ldots, ??_k\}$. The denotation function, uses two valuation functions: (i) $\sigma : V^{\mathbb{Z}} \cup H \to \mathbb{Z}$, which maps variables and holes to integer values, (ii) $\sigma^{\mathbb{P}} : V^{\mathbb{P}} \to [0, p_1) \times \cdots \times [0, p_k)$, which maps primed variables to modular values. The expression $\text{TOPRIME}(a)$ converts the integer value of an integer expression a to a modular tuple. Arithmetic expressions in $a^{\mathbb{P}}$ are computed using modular values with the result being obtained using modular arithmetic with respect to the corresponding primes in $\mathbb{P}$. Note that the only comparison operator allowed over modular expressions is $==$ and that the division operator *cannot* be applied to modular expressions. While the syntax does not directly allow for holes to be represented modularly—i.e., we do not have expressions of the form $??^{\mathbb{P}}$—an expression of the form $\text{TOPRIME}(??)$ effectively achieves the objective of representing a hole $??$ modularly.

4.3 Equivalence between the two Semantics

Next, we provide an alternative integer semantics, which applies the `IMP` integer semantics to modular expressions and show that, under some assumptions on the values manipulated by the program, the modular and integer semantics are equivalent. We will use this result to build our modified synthesis algorithm.

$$[\![\text{TOPRIME}(a)]\!]_{\sigma_1,\sigma_2} := [\![a]\!]_{\sigma_1,\sigma_2} \qquad [\![v^{\mathbb{P}}]\!]_{\sigma_1,\sigma_2} := \sigma_2(v^{\mathbb{P}}) \qquad [\![c^{\mathbb{P}}]\!]_{\sigma_1,\sigma_2} := c$$

$$[\![a_1^{\mathbb{P}} \ op_a \ a_2^{\mathbb{P}}]\!]_{\sigma_1,\sigma_2} := [\![a_1^{\mathbb{P}}]\!]_{\sigma_1,\sigma_2} \ op_a \ [\![a_2^{\mathbb{P}}]\!]_{\sigma_1,\sigma_2} \qquad [\![a_1^{\mathbb{P}}==a_2^{\mathbb{P}}]\!]_{\sigma_1,\sigma_2} := [\![a_1^{\mathbb{P}}]\!]_{\sigma_1,\sigma_2}==[\![a_2^{\mathbb{P}}]\!]_{\sigma_1,\sigma_2}$$

$$[\![c]\!]_{\sigma_1,\sigma_2} := c \qquad [\![v]\!]_{\sigma_1,\sigma_2} := \sigma_1(v) \qquad [\![a_1 \ op_a \ a_2]\!]_{\sigma_1,\sigma_2} := [\![a_1]\!]_{\sigma_1,\sigma_2} \ op_a \ [\![a_2]\!]_{\sigma_1,\sigma_2}$$

$$[\![v = a]\!]_{\sigma_1,\sigma_2} := (\sigma_1[v \hookleftarrow [\![a]\!]_{\sigma_1,\sigma_2}], \sigma_2) \qquad [\![v^{\mathbb{P}} = a^{\mathbb{P}}]\!]_{\sigma_1,\sigma_2} := (\sigma_1, \sigma_2[v^{\mathbb{P}} \hookleftarrow [\![a^{\mathbb{P}}]\!]_{\sigma_1,\sigma_2}])$$

Fig. 4: Integer semantics.

Integer Semantics The *integer semantics* of IMP-MOD is shown in Figure 4 (denoted $[\![\cdot]\!]_{\sigma_1,\sigma_2}$). In this semantics, modular expressions are evaluated as integer expressions using the same semantics as for IMP—i.e., the values of modular variables and modular arithmetic expressions are denoted by integer values. Therefore, in the integer semantics, we use two valuation functions $\sigma_1 : V^{\mathbb{Z}} \cup H \mapsto \mathbb{Z}$ mapping variables and holes to integers and $\sigma_2 : V^{\mathbb{P}} \mapsto \mathbb{Z}$ mapping modular variables to integers.

Relation between the Two Semantics We now show that the modular semantics is, in some sense, equivalent to the integer semantics. For the rest of this section, we fix a set of distinct primes $\mathbb{P} = \{p_1, \cdots, p_k\}$.

To prove the equivalence of the two program semantics, we will require the values of modular expressions to lie in some range that is covered by the prime numbers in $\mathbb{P}$. The following definition captures this restriction.

Definition 1. *Given a modular arithmetic expression $a^{\mathbb{P}}$ (resp. Boolean expression b) and some integers $L < U$, we say $a^{\mathbb{P}}$ with context (σ_1, σ_2) is* uniformly in the range $R := [L, U)$ —$a^{\mathbb{P}} \in_{\sigma_1,\sigma_2} R$ *for short—if under the integer semantics, all evaluation of modular subexpressions of $a^{\mathbb{P}}$ (resp. b) are in the range R:*

- $a^{\mathbb{P}} \in_{\sigma_1,\sigma_2} R$, *iff* $[\![a^{\mathbb{P}}]\!]_{\sigma_1,\sigma_2} \in R$;
- $a_1^{\mathbb{P}} == a_2^{\mathbb{P}} \in_{\sigma_1,\sigma_2} R$, *iff* $a_1^{\mathbb{P}} \in_{\sigma_1,\sigma_2} R$, $a_2^{\mathbb{P}} \in_{\sigma_1,\sigma_2} R$;
- b_1 *and* $b_2 \in_{\sigma_1,\sigma_2} R$, *iff* $b_1 \in_{\sigma_1,\sigma_2} R$, $b_2 \in_{\sigma_1,\sigma_2} R$;
- b_1 *or* $b_2 \in_{\sigma_1,\sigma_2} R$, *iff* $b_1 \in_{\sigma_1,\sigma_2} R$, $b_2 \in_{\sigma_1,\sigma_2} R$;
- *not* $b \in_{\sigma_1,\sigma_2} R$, *iff* $b \in_{\sigma_1,\sigma_2} R$;
- $a_1 \ op_c \ a_2 \in_{\sigma_1,\sigma_2} R$ *for any arithmetic expressions a_1, a_2 and operator op_c.*

Given a valuation function $\sigma : V^{\mathbb{P}} \mapsto \mathbb{Z}$, we write $m_{\mathbb{P}} \circ \sigma$ to denote the modular valuation obtained by applying the $m_{\mathbb{P}}$ function to σ—i.e., for every $v^{\mathbb{P}} \in V^{\mathbb{P}}$, $(m_{\mathbb{P}} \circ \sigma)(v^{\mathbb{P}}) = m_{\mathbb{P}}(\sigma(v^{\mathbb{P}}))$. Similarly, for a modular valuation function $\sigma^{\mathbb{P}} : V^{\mathbb{P}} \to [0, p_1) \times \cdots [0, p_k)$, we denote $m_{\mathbb{P}}^{-1,R} \circ \sigma^{\mathbb{P}}$ the integer valuation from $V^{\mathbb{P}}$ to R such that, for every $v^{\mathbb{P}} \in V^{\mathbb{P}}$, $(m_{\mathbb{P}}^{-1,R} \circ \sigma^{\mathbb{P}})(v^{\mathbb{P}}) = m_{\mathbb{P}}^{-1,R}(\sigma^{\mathbb{P}}(v^{\mathbb{P}}))$. The following lemma shows that, when the values of modular arithmetic expressions lay in an interval of size $N = p_1 \cdot \ldots \cdot p_k$ the modular and integer semantics of modular arithmetic expressions are equivalent.

Lemma 2. *Given a set of primes* $\mathbb{P} = \{p_1, \cdots, p_k\}$*, an arithmetic expression* $a^{\mathbb{P}}$*, and two valuation functions* $\sigma_1 : V^{\mathbb{Z}} \cup H \mapsto \mathbb{Z}$ *and* $\sigma_2 : V^{\mathbb{P}} \mapsto \mathbb{Z}$*, we have*

$$m_{\mathbb{P}}(\llbracket a^{\mathbb{P}} \rrbracket_{\sigma_1,\sigma_2}) = \llbracket a^{\mathbb{P}} \rrbracket^{\mathbb{P}}_{\sigma_1, m_{\mathbb{P}} \circ \sigma_2}$$

Moreover, if there exists an interval R *of size* $N = p_1 \cdot \ldots \cdot p_k$ *such that* $a^{\mathbb{P}} \in_{\sigma_1,\sigma_2} R$*, then*

$$m_{\mathbb{P}}^{-1,R}(\llbracket a^{\mathbb{P}} \rrbracket^{\mathbb{P}}_{\sigma_1, m_{\mathbb{P}} \circ \sigma_2}) = \llbracket a^{\mathbb{P}} \rrbracket_{\sigma_1,\sigma_2}.$$

Similarly, we show that the two semantics are also equivalent for Boolean expressions.

Lemma 3. *Given a set of primes* $\mathbb{P} = \{p_1, \cdots, p_k\}$*, an interval* R *of size* $N = p_1 \cdot \ldots \cdot p_k$*, a Boolean expression* b*, and two valuation functions* $\sigma_1 : V^{\mathbb{Z}} \cup H \mapsto \mathbb{Z}$ *and* $\sigma_2 : V^{\mathbb{P}} \mapsto \mathbb{Z}$*, if* $b \in_{\sigma_1,\sigma_2} R$*, then* $\llbracket b \rrbracket_{\sigma_1,\sigma_2} = \llbracket b \rrbracket^{\mathbb{P}}_{\sigma_1, m_{\mathbb{P}} \circ \sigma_2}.$

We are now ready to show the equivalence between the modular semantics and the integer semantics for programs $P \in \text{IMP-MOD}$. The semantics of a program $P = f(V^{\mathbb{Z}}, V^{\mathbb{P}}, H) \{s\}$ is a map from valuations to valuations, i.e., given a valuation $\sigma_1 : V^{\mathbb{Z}} \to \mathbb{Z}$ for integer variables, a valuation $\sigma_2 : V^{\mathbb{P}} \to \mathbb{Z}$ for modular variables and a valuation $\sigma^H : H \to \mathbb{Z}$ for holes, we have $\llbracket P \rrbracket(\sigma_1, \sigma_2, \sigma^H) = \llbracket s \rrbracket_{\sigma_1 \cup \sigma^H, \sigma_2}$ and $\llbracket P \rrbracket^{\mathbb{P}}(\sigma_1, \sigma_2, \sigma^H) = \llbracket s \rrbracket^{\mathbb{P}}_{\sigma_1 \cup \sigma^H, m_{\mathbb{P}} \circ \sigma_2}$. Therefore, it is sufficient to show that the two semantics are equivalent for any statement s.

The two semantics are equivalent for a statement s if, under the same input valuations, the resulting valuations of the semantics can be translated to each other. Formally, given valuations σ_1, σ_2 and an interval R of size N, we say $\llbracket s \rrbracket_{\sigma_1,\sigma_2} \equiv_{\mathbb{P}} \llbracket s \rrbracket^{\mathbb{P}}_{\sigma_1, m_{\mathbb{P}} \circ \sigma_2}$ iff $\sigma_1' = \sigma_1''$, $m_{\mathbb{P}} \circ \sigma_2' = \sigma_2^{\mathbb{P}}$ and $\sigma_2' = m_{\mathbb{P}}^{-1,R} \circ \sigma_2^{\mathbb{P}}$ where $\llbracket s \rrbracket_{\sigma_1,\sigma_2} = (\sigma_1', \sigma_2')$ and $\llbracket s \rrbracket^{\mathbb{P}}_{\sigma_1, m_{\mathbb{P}} \circ \sigma_2} = (\sigma_1'', \sigma_2^{\mathbb{P}})$.

We define uniform inclusion for statements.

Definition 2. *Given a set of primes* $\mathbb{P}$*, two integers* $L < U$ *and a statement* s*, we say* s *with context* (σ_1, σ_2) *is uniformly in the range* $R := [L, U)$—$s \in_{\sigma_1,\sigma_2} R$ *for short—if under the integer semantics, all evaluation of modular subexpressions of* s *are in the range* R*:*

- $(v^{\mathbb{P}} = a^{\mathbb{P}}) \in_{\sigma_1,\sigma_2} R$ *iff* $a^{\mathbb{P}} \in_{\sigma_1,\sigma_2} R$*.*
- $while(b)\{s\} \in_{\sigma_1,\sigma_2} R$ *iff* $s \in_{\sigma_1,\sigma_2} R$ *and* $b \in_{\sigma_1,\sigma_2} R$*.*
- $s_1; s_2 \in_{\sigma_1,\sigma_2} R$ *iff* $s_1 \in_{\sigma_1,\sigma_2} R$ *and* $s_2 \in_{\sigma_1,\sigma_2} R$*.*
- $if(b) \ s_1 \ else \ s_2 \in_{\sigma_1,\sigma_2} R$ *iff* $s_1 \in_{\sigma_1,\sigma_2} R$*,* $s_2 \in_{\sigma_1,\sigma_2} R$ *and* $b \in_{\sigma_1,\sigma_2} R$*.*
- $assert \ b \in_{\sigma_1,\sigma_2} R$ *iff* $b \in_{\sigma_1,\sigma_2} R$*.*

At last, the two semantics are equivalent for statements.

Theorem 2. *Given a set of primes* $\mathbb{P} = [p_1, \cdots, p_k]$*, a statement* s *and two valuation functions* $\sigma_1 : V^{\mathbb{Z}} \cup H \to \mathbb{Z}$ *and* $\sigma_2 : V^{\mathbb{P}} \to \mathbb{Z}$*, if there exists an interval* R *of size* N *such that* $s \in_{\sigma_1,\sigma_2} R$*, then* $\llbracket s \rrbracket_{\sigma_1,\sigma_2} \equiv_{\mathbb{P}} \llbracket s \rrbracket^{\mathbb{P}}_{\sigma_1, m_{\mathbb{P}} \circ \sigma_2}.$

Algorithm 1: returns variables that should be tracked using modular/integer semantics.

```
/* f: sketched function, V^P variables to be tracked modularly, V^Z
   variables to be tracked with integer values                    */
1 function DataFlowAnalysis(f)
2 │   S ← {/, <, >, ≤, ≥}; V^Z ← ∅
3 │   for op ∈ S do
  │   │   /* Compute all variables v that may flow into op         */
4 │   └   V^Z ← V^Z ∪ Dataflow(op, f)
5 │   V^P ← V \ V^Z
6 └   return (V^Z, V^P)
```

5   From IMP to IMP-MOD Programs

In this section, we develop a data flow analysis for detecting variables in IMP programs for which it is sound to track values modularly. We then use this data flow analysis to rewrite an IMP program to an equivalent IMP-MOD program.

5.1   Data Flow Analysis

The formalization of IMP-MOD in Section 4.2 made it clear that the modular semantics is only appropriate when integer values are manipulated using addition, multiplication, subtraction, and equality. Other operations like division and less-than comparison cannot be computed soundly in modular arithmetic.

Example 4. Consider an integer variable x with modular value x_2 under modulus 2 and x_3 under modulus 3, and an integer variable y with modular value y_2, y_3 under corresponding moduli. Then the assignment of $x = y + y$; implies $x_2 = (y_2 + y_2) \mod 2$; and $x_3 = (y_3 + y_3) \mod 3$. However, $x = x/y$; does not imply $x_2 = (x_2/y_2) \mod 2$; and $x_3 = (x_3/y_3) \mod 3$.

We now define a data flow analysis (shown in Algorithm 1) for computing which variables in a program must be tracked with the integer semantics (i.e., the set V^Z) and which variables can be soundly tracked using the modular semantics (i.e., the set V^P). For each operator op in $\{/, <, >, ≤, ≥\}$, the analysis computes the set of variables that *may* flow into the operands of an expression of the form $e_1 \ op \ e_2$. In practice, this is done via *backward may analysis*, noted as Dataflow procedure in Algorithm 1. The obtained set of variables must be tracked using the integer semantics. The remaining variables will never flow into a problematic operator and can therefore be tracked using the modular semantics.

Implementation Remark Since our implementation also supports arrays and recursion, the data flow analysis in Algorithm 1 is inter-procedural and the set S also contains the array indexing operator [ ]—i.e., given an expression $arr[a]$, if a variable v may flow into a, then a must be tracked using the integer semantics.

$$R_a(a) = \begin{cases} v^{\mathbb{P}} & \text{if } a \equiv v \text{ and } v \in V^{\mathbb{P}} \\ c^{\mathbb{P}} & \text{if } a \equiv c \\ R_a(a_1) \ op_a^{\mathbb{P}} \ R_a(a_2) & \text{if } a \equiv a_1 \ op_a^{\mathbb{P}} \ a_2 \\ \text{TOPRIME}(a) & \text{otherwise} \end{cases}$$

$$R_b(b) = \begin{cases} R_a(a_1) \ \texttt{==} \ R_a(a_2) & \text{if } b \equiv a_1 \ \texttt{==} \ a_2 \\ R_b(b_1) \ \textbf{and} \ R_b(b_2) & \text{if } b \equiv b_1 \ \textbf{and} \ b_2 \\ \textbf{not} \ R_b(b_1) & \text{if } b \equiv \textbf{not} \ b_2 \\ b & \text{otherwise} \end{cases}$$

$$R_s(s) = \begin{cases} R_s(s_1); R_s(s_2) & \text{if } s \equiv s_1; s_2 \\ v \ = \ a & \text{if } s \equiv v = a \text{ and } v \in V^{\mathbb{Z}} \\ v^{\mathbb{P}} \ = \ R_a(a) & \text{if } s \equiv v = a \text{ and } v \in V^{\mathbb{P}} \\ \texttt{if}(R_b(b)) \ R_s(s_0) \ \texttt{else} \ R_s(s_1) & \text{if } s \equiv \texttt{if}(b) \ s_0 \ \texttt{else} \ s_1 \\ \texttt{while}(R_b(b)) \ \{R_s(s)\} & \text{if } s \equiv \texttt{while} \ b \ \{s\} \\ \texttt{assert} \ R_b(b) & \text{if } s \equiv \texttt{assert} \ b \end{cases}$$

Fig. 5: Subset of rules for the translation from IMP to IMP-MOD programs. Rules are parametric in $V^{\mathbb{Z}}$, $V^{\mathbb{P}}$ with $\mathbb{P}$: $R_f(f(V, \texttt{??})\{s\}) = f(V^{\mathbb{Z}}, V^{\mathbb{P}}, \texttt{??})\{R_s(s)\}$.

Furthermore, while in our formalization we allow variables to be tracked using only one of the two semantics, in our implementation, we allow variables to be tracked differently (using actual values or modular values) at different program points by tracking, for each variable v, the program points for which the actual value of v is needed, which is done by using the same data-flow analysis. In this case, a variable might initially need to be tracked using actual values but can later be tracked using modular values.

Example 5. Consider the sketch program `polyArray` in Figure 1b. For this program, Algorithm 1 will return that the variables x and y can be tracked modularly. However, the variables i and n must be tracked using the integer semantics since they are used in a < operation and as array indices.

5.2   From IMP to IMP-MOD

Now that we have computed what sets of variables can be tracked modularly, we can transform the IMP program into an IMP-MOD program. The transformation R_f that rewrites f into an IMP-MOD program is shown in Figure 5. The key idea of the program transformation is to use the sets $V^{\mathbb{Z}}$ and $V^{\mathbb{P}}$ to only rewrite variables and sub-expressions of f for which the modular arithmetic can be performed soundly.

Once we get a solution for the IMP-MOD program as hole values, we can get a solution for the IMP program by mapping the hole to integer values given by the integer semantics.

Example 6. Consider a program where the dataflow analysis computes $V^{\mathbb{Z}} = \{i, n\}$ and $V^{\mathbb{P}} = \{x\}$. The statement $x = x + i + 1$ is rewritten to $x^{\mathbb{P}} = x^{\mathbb{P}} +$ TOPRIME$(i) + 1^{\mathbb{P}}$.

The transformation R_f is sound.

Theorem 3. *Given an IMP program f, and sets $V^{\mathbb{Z}}$ and $V^{\mathbb{P}}$ resulting from the data flow analysis on f, the program $R_f(f)$ is in the IMP-MOD language. Moreover, $[\![f]\!]^{IMP} = [\![R_f(f)]\!]$.*

6   Solving IMP-MOD Sketches

In this section, we discuss how synthesis in the modular semantics relates to synthesis in the integer semantics and provide an incremental algorithm for solving IMP-MOD sketches.

6.1   Synthesis in IMP-MOD

Given a set of integers R we say that a variable valuation σ is in R (denoted $\sigma \in R$) if for every v, we have $\sigma(v) \in R$. Similarly to what we saw in Section 3, we assume that the sketch has to be solved for finite ranges of possible values for the hole (R_H) and input values (R_{in}). Solving an IMP-MOD problem $P - f(V, V^{\mathbb{P}}, H)\{s\}$ for the integer semantics amounts to solving the following constraint:

$$\exists \sigma^H \in R_H . \forall \sigma_1, \sigma_2 \in R_{in} . [\![s]\!]_{\sigma_1 \cup \sigma^H, \sigma_2} \neq \bot .$$

According to Theorem. 2, given a set of distinct primes $\mathbb{P} = \{p_1, \cdots, p_k\}$ and variable valuations σ^H, σ_1, and σ_2, if there exists a range R of size $N = p_1 \cdots \cdots \cdots p_k$ such that $s \in_{\sigma_1 \cup \sigma^H, \sigma_2} R$, the modular semantics and the integer semantics are equivalent to each other. Using this observation, we can define the set of variable valuations for which the two semantics are guaranteed to be equivalent:

$$\mathcal{I}_R^{\mathbb{P}} := \left\{ (\sigma_1, \sigma_2) \mid \forall \sigma^H \in R_H . \exists R. \ |R| = N \wedge s \in_{\sigma_1 \cup \sigma^H, \sigma_2} R \right\} .$$

Since for every $\sigma^H \in R_H$ and $\sigma_1, \sigma_2 \in \mathcal{I}_R^{\mathbb{P}}$ we have that $[\![s]\!]_{\sigma_1 \cup \sigma^H, m_{\mathbb{P}} \circ \sigma_2}^{\mathbb{P}} = [\![s]\!]_{\sigma_1 \cup \sigma^H, \sigma_2}$, any solution to an IMP-MOD program in the modular semantics is also a solution to the following formula in the integer semantics:

$$\exists \sigma^H \in R_H . \forall \sigma_1, \sigma_2 \in \mathcal{I}_R^{\mathbb{P}} . [\![s]\!]_{\sigma_1 \cup \sigma^H, \sigma_2} \neq \bot .$$

When all valuations in $\sigma_1, \sigma_2 \in R_{in}$ are also elements of $\mathcal{I}_R^{\mathbb{P}}$, any solution to an IMP-MOD program in the modular semantics is guaranteed to be a correct solution under the integer semantics.

To summarize, if the synthesizer returns UNSAT for the IMP-MOD program, the problem is unrealizable and does not admit a solution. When it returns a solution, the solution is correct if it only produces valuations in the range allowed by

---

Algorithm 2: Incremental synthesis for IMP-MOD.

```
/* f: function, P: set of primes                                        */
1 function IncrementalSynthesis(f, P)
2 |   P' ← [p₁]
3 |   f_syn ← Synthesis(f, P')
4 |   while ∃p_cex ∈ P : ¬Verify(f_syn, p_cex) do
5 |   |   P' ← P' ∪ p_cex
6 |   |   f_syn ← Synthesis(f, P')
7 |   |   if f_syn == UNSAT then return ∅ ;
8 |   return f_syn
```

---

the choice of prime numbers. In practice, one can use a verifier to check the correctness of the synthesized solution and add more prime numbers to the modular synthesizer if needed. In fact, this is the main idea behind the counterexample-guided inductive synthesis algorithm used by SKETCH (Section 3).

6.2 Incremental Synthesis Algorithm

In this section, we propose an incremental synthesis algorithm that builds on the following observation. The set of variable valuations for which modular and integer semantics are equivalent increases monotonically in the size of $\mathbb{P}$:

$$\mathbb{P}_1 \subseteq \mathbb{P}_2 \implies \mathcal{I}_R^{\mathbb{P}_1} \subseteq \mathcal{I}_R^{\mathbb{P}_2}. \tag{1}$$

Algorithm 2 uses Equation 1 to add prime numbers lazily during the synthesis process. The algorithm first constructs a set $\mathbb{P}' = \{p_1\}$ with the first prime number $p_1 \in \mathbb{P}$ and synthesizes a solution that is correct for computations modulo the set $\mathbb{P}'$. It then checks if the synthesized solution f_{syn} satisfies the assertions with respect to all prime numbers in $\mathbb{P}$. If yes, f_{syn} is returned as the solution. Otherwise, the algorithm finds a prime $p_{\mathsf{cex}} \in \mathbb{P}$ where $\mathsf{Verify}(f_{\mathsf{syn}}, p_{\mathsf{cex}})$ does not hold and it adds it to the set $\mathbb{P}'$ continuing the iterative algorithm. Due to Equation 1, Algorithm 2 is sound and complete with respect to the synthesis algorithm that considers the full prime set $\mathbb{P}$ all at once.

In practice, the user could use domain knowledge to estimate a suitable set of primes or alternatively use our incremental algorithm to discover appropriate prime sets. The set of prime numbers $\{2, 3, 5, 7, 11, 13, 17\}$ could usually instantiate a range R that is large enough for most synthesis tasks based on SKETCH.

7 Complexity of Rewritten Programs

In this section, we analyze how many bits are necessary to encode numbers for both semantics using unary and binary bit-vector encodings of integers (Sec. 7.1 and 7.2), and show how many prime numbers are necessary in the modular semantics to cover values up to a certain bound (Sec. 7.3). The following results build upon several number theory results that the reader can consult at [9, 15].

7.1   Bit-complexity of Binary Encoding

In this section, we analyze how many bits are necessary when representing an interval of size N in binary in our modular semantics. In the rest of the section, we consider the set of primes $\mathbb{P}_n = \{p \mid p < n\} = \{p_1, \ldots, p_k\}$ containing the prime numbers that have value smaller than n. We will show in Section 8 that this choice of prime number also yields good performance in practice. Concretely, we are interested in knowing what is the magnitude of the number $N = p_1 \cdot \ldots \cdot p_k$ and how many bits are used to represent the numbers in $\mathbb{P}_n$.

We start by introducing the notion of primorial.

Definition 3 (Primorial). *Given a number n, the* primorial $n\#$ *is defined as the product of all primes smaller than n—i.e., $n\# = \prod\limits_{p \in \mathbb{P}_n} p$.*

The primorial captures the size N of the interval covered by the Chinese Remainder Theorem when using prime numbers up to n. The following number theory result gives us a close form for the primorial and shows that the number N has approximately n bits.

$$n\# = e^{(1+o(1))n} = 2^{(1+o(1))n} \tag{2}$$

We use another number theory notion to quantify the number of bits in $\mathbb{P}_n$.

Definition 4 (Chebyshev function). *Given a number n, the* Chebyshev function $\vartheta(n)$ *is the sum of the logarithms of all the prime numbers smaller than n—i.e., $\vartheta(n) = \sum\limits_{p \in \mathbb{P}_n} \log p$.*

The following number theory result relates the primorial to the Chebyshev function.

$$\vartheta(n) = \log(n\#) = \log 2^{(1+o(1))n} = (1 + o(1))n \tag{3}$$

Aside from rounding errors, the Chebyshev function captures the number of bits required to represent the numbers in $\mathbb{P}_n$. To obtain a more precise bound on this number, we need a bound for the formula $\sum\limits_{p \in \mathbb{P}_n} \lceil \log p \rceil$.

We start by recalling the following fundamental number theory result.

Theorem 4 (Prime number theorem). *The set $\mathbb{P}_n$ has size approximately $n / \log n$.*

Using Theorem 4, we get the following result.

$$\sum_{p \in \mathbb{P}_n} \lceil \log p \rceil \leq n / \log n + \sum_{p \in \mathbb{P}_n} \log p \approx (1 + o(1))n \tag{4}$$

Representing a number e^n in a classic binary encoding requires $\log_2(e^n) = (1 + o(1))n$ bits and, combining Equations 2 and 4, we get the following result.

Theorem 5. *Representing a number 2^n in binary requires $(1+o(1))n$ bits under both modular and integer semantics.*

Hence, representing a number in binary requires the same number of bits in the both semantics.

Example 7. Consider the set $\mathbb{P}_{18} = \{2, 3, 5, 7, 11, 13, 17\}$, which can model an interval of $N = 510, 510$ integers (i.e., $n = 18$ in Theorem 5). Representing N in binary requires 19 bits while the binary representations of all the primes in $\mathbb{P}_{18}$ use 22 bits. Both numbers are close to 18 as predicted by the theorem.

7.2   Bit-complexity of Unary Encoding

As discussed in Sec. 3, the default SKETCH solver encodes numbers using a unary encoding—i.e., SKETCH requires 2^n bits to encode the number 2^n. Representing the same number in unary under the modular semantics requires only prime numbers smaller than n and therefore $\sum_{p \in \mathbb{P}_n} p$ bits. We can then use the following closed form to approximate this quantity.

$$\sum_{p \in \mathbb{P}_n} p \sim \frac{n^2}{2 \log n} \tag{5}$$

Equation 5 yields the following theorem.

Theorem 6. *Representing a number 2^n in unary requires 2^n bits in the integer semantics and approximately $\frac{n^2}{2 \log n}$ bits in the modular semantics.*

These results show that, under a unary encoding, the modular semantics is exponentially more succinct than the integer semantics.

Example 8. Consider again the prime set $\mathbb{P}_{18} = \{2, 3, 5, 7, 11, 13, 17\}$, which can model an interval of $N = 510, 510$ integers. Representing N in unary requires 510,510 bits. On the other hand, the sum of the bits in the unary encoding of the primes in $\mathbb{P}_{18}$ is 58.

7.3   Number of Required Primes

We analyze how many primes are needed to represent a certain number in the modular semantics. We start by introducing the following alternative version of the primorial.

Definition 5 (Prime Primorial). *For the n-th prime number p_n, the* prime primorial $p_n\#$ *is defined as the product of the first n primes—i.e., $p_n\# = \prod_{k=1}^{n} p_i$.*

The following known number theory result gives us an approximation for the prime primorial.

$$p_n\# = e^{(1+o(1))n \log n} \tag{6}$$

Notice how the approximation of the primorial differs from that of the prime primorial. This is due to the fact that prime numbers are sparse—i.e., the n-th prime number is approximately $n \log n$.

Using Equation 6 we obtain the following result.

Theorem 7. *Representing numbers in an interval of size $N = e^{n \log n}$ in the modular semantics requires the first n prime numbers.*

Since the relation $k = n \log n$ does not admit a closed form for n, we cannot derive exactly how many primes are needed to represent a number 2^k with k bits. It is however clear from the theorem that the number of required primes grows slower than k.

8 Evaluation

We implemented a prototype of our technique as a simple compiler in Java. Our implementation provides a simplified SKETCH frontend, which only allows the limited syntax we support. Given a SKETCH file, our tool rewrites it into a different SKETCH file that operates according to the modular semantics. We will use UNARY to denote the result obtained by running the default version of SKETCH with unary integer encoding on the original SKETCH file, BINARY to denote the result obtained by running the version of SKETCH using an SMT-like native integer solver based on binary integer encoding, UNARY-P to denote the result of running the default SKETCH version on our modified SKETCH file, and UNARY-P-INC to denote the result of running the default version of SKETCH on the file generated by the incremental version of our algorithm described in Section 6. As expected from our theory, the prime technique is not beneficial for the SMT-like native integer solver and always results in worse runtime. Therefore, we do not present data for this solver. All experiments were performed on a machine with 4.0GHz Intel Core i7 CPU with 16GB RAM with SKETCH-1.7.5 and we use a timeout value of 300 seconds (we also report out-of-memory errors as timeouts).

Our evaluation answers the following research questions:

Q1 How does the performance of UNARY-P compare to UNARY and BINARY?
Q2 How does the incremental algorithm compare to the non-incremental one?
Q3 Is UNARY-P's performance sensitive to the set of selected prime numbers?
Q4 How many primes are needed by UNARY-P to produce correct solutions?
Q5 Does UNARY generate larger SAT queries than UNARY-P?

8.1 Benchmarks

We perform our evaluation on three families of programs.

Polynomials The first set of benchmarks contains 81 variants of the polynomial synthesis problem presented in Figure 1. The original version of this benchmark appears in the SKETCH benchmark suite under the name `polynomial.sk`. For each benchmark, we generate a random polynomial f, random inputs $\{\vec{x}\}$, and take the set $\{(\vec{x}, f(x))\}$ as specification. Each benchmark in this set has the following parameters: #Ex$\in \{2, 4, 6\}$ is the number of input-output examples as specification, cbits$\in \{5, 6, 7\}$ denote the number of bits hole values can use, exIn$\in \{[-10, 10], [-30, 30], [-50, 50]\}$ denotes the range of randomly generated input examples and coeff$\in \{[-10, 10], [-30, 30], [-50, 50]\}$ denotes the range of randomly generated coefficients in the polynomial f.

Invariants The second set of benchmarks contain 46 variants of two invariant generation problems obtained from a public set of programs that require polynomial invariants to be verified [8]. We selected the two programs in which at least one variable could be tracked modularly by our tool (the other programs involved complex array operations or inequality operators) and turned the verification problems into synthesis problems by asking SKETCH to find a polynomial equality (using the program variables) that is an invariant for the loop in the program. To control the size of the magnitudes of the inputs, we only require the invariants to hold for a fixed set of input examples.

The first problem, mannadiv, iteratively computes the remainder and the quotient of two numbers given as input. The invariant required to verify mannadiv is a polynomial equality of degree 2 involving 5 variables. The SKETCH template required to describe the space of all polynomial equalities has 32 holes and cannot be handled by any of the SKETCH solvers we consider. We therefore simplify the invariant synthesis problems in two ways. In the first variant, we reduce the ranges of the hole values in the templates by considering cbits $\in \{2, 3\}$. In the second variant, we set cbits $= \{5, 6, 7\}$, but reduce the number of missing hole values to 4 (i.e., we provide part of the invariant). Each benchmark takes two random inputs and we consider the following input ranges $\{[1, 50], [1, 100]\}$. In total, we have 10 benchmarks for mannadiv.

The second problem, petter, iteratively computes the sum $\sum_{1 \leq i \leq n} i^5$ for a given input n. The invariant required to verify petter is a polynomial equality of degree 6 involving 3 variables. The SKETCH template required to describe all such polynomial equalities has 56 holes and cannot be handled by any of the SKETCH solvers we consider. We consider the following simplified variants of the problem: (*i*) petter_0 computes $\sum_{1 \leq i \leq n} 1$ and requires a polynomial invariant of degree one, (*ii*) petter_x computes $\sum_{1 \leq i \leq n} x$ for a given input variable x and requires a polynomial invariant of degree two, (*iii*) petter_1 computes $\sum_{1 \leq i \leq n} i$ and requires a polynomial invariant of degree two, and (*iv*) petter_10 computes $\sum_{1 \leq i \leq n} i + 1$ and requires a polynomial invariant of degree two. Each benchmark takes two random inputs and we consider the following input ranges $\{[1, 10], [1, 100], [1, 1000]\}$. In total, we have 12 variants of petter, each run for values of cbits $\in \{5, 6, 7\}$—i.e., a total of 36 benchmarks.

Program Repair The third set of benchmarks contains 54 variants of SKETCH problems from the domain of automatic feedback generation for introductory programming assignments [7]. Each benchmark corresponds to an incorrect program submitted by a student and the goal of the synthesizer is to find a small variation of the program that behaves correctly on a set of test cases. We select the 6/11 benchmarks from the tool Qlose [7] for which (*i*) our implementation can support all the features in the program, and (*ii*) our data flow analysis identifies at least one variable that can be tracked modularly. Of the remaining benchmarks, 3/11 do not contain variables that can be tracked modularly, and 2/11 call auxiliary functions that cannot be translated into SKETCH. For each

Table 1: Effectiveness of different solvers. SAT (resp. UNSAT) denotes the number of benchmarks for which solver could find a solution to the benchmarks (resp. prove no solution existed) while TO denotes the number of timeouts.

Solver	Solved	Polynomials			Invariants			Program repair		
		SAT	UNSAT	TO	SAT	UNSAT	TO	SAT	UNSAT	TO
UNARY	69/181	12	4	65	5	0	41	48	0	6
BINARY	127/181	70	6	5	17	0	29	34	0	20
UNARY-P	169/181	73	5	3	41	2	3	48	0	6
UNARY-P-INC	172/181	73	6	2	41	2	3	50	0	4

program, we consider the original problem and two variants where the integer inputs are multiplied by 10 and 100, respectively. Further, for each program variants, we impose an assertion specifying that the distance between the original program and the repaired program is within a certain bound. We select three different bounds for each program: the minimum cost c, $c + 100$, and $c + 200$.

8.2 Performance of UNARY-P

Table 1 summarizes our comparison. First, we compare the performance of UNARY-P and UNARY. We use $\mathbb{P} = \{2, 3, 5, 7, 11, 13, 17\}$, which is enough for UNARY-P to always find correct solutions (we verify the correctness of a solution by instantiating the hole values in the original sketch programs). UNARY can only solve 69/181 benchmarks while UNARY-P can solve 169/181. Figure 7a shows a scatter plot (log scale) of the solving times for the two techniques: each point below the diagonal line denotes a benchmark on which UNARY-P was faster than UNARY. Points on the extreme right-hand side of the plot denote timeout for UNARY. When both solvers terminate, UNARY-P (avg. 1.7s) is 6.1X (geometric mean) faster than UNARY (avg. 25.0s).

Next, we compare the performance of UNARY-P and BINARY (Figure 7b). On the 64 easier benchmarks that BINARY can solve in less than 1 second, BINARY (avg. 0.55s) outperforms UNARY-P (avg. 2.32s), but UNARY-P still has reasonable performance. On the 49 benchmarks that BINARY can solve between 1 and 10 seconds, UNARY-P (avg. 3.5s) is on average 1.9X faster than BINARY (avg. 6.9s). Most interestingly, for the 14 harder benchmarks for which BINARY takes more than 10 seconds, UNARY-P (avg. 5.7s) is on average 15.9X faster than BINARY (avg. 90.9s). Remarkably, UNARY-P *solved 43 of the benchmarks (in less than 8s each) for which* BINARY *timed out*[4], and UNARY-P only timed out for two benchmarks that BINARY could solve in less than a second and one benchmark that BINARY could solve in 260s. Finally, we would like to highlight that for 41/208 benchmarks, even UNARY outperforms BINARY. As expected from

---

[4] During our experiment, we observed that BINARY *incorrectly* reported UNSAT for 10 satisfiable benchmarks. We reported these benchmarks as timeouts and have contacted the authors of SKETCH to address the issue.

the discussion throughout the paper, these are benchmarks typically involving complex operations but not involving overly large numbers.

We can now answer **Q1**. First, UNARY-P consistently outperforms UNARY across all benchmarks. Second, **UNARY-P outperforms BINARY on hard-to-solve problems and can solve problems that BINARY cannot solve—** e.g., UNARY-P solved 28/46 invariant problems that SKETCH could not solve. UNARY-P and BINARY have similar performance on easy problems.

Comparison to full SMT encoding For completeness, we also compare our approach to a tool that uses SMT solvers to model the entire synthesis problem. We choose the state-of-the-art SMT-based synthesizer ROSETTE [23] for our comparison. ROSETTE is a programming language that encodes verification and synthesis constraints written in a domain-specific language into SMT formulas that can be solved using SMT solvers.

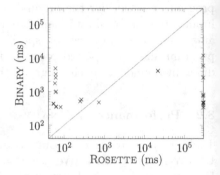

Fig. 6: ROSETTE vs BINARY

We only run ROSETTE on the set of Polynomials because ROSETTE does support the theories of integers, but does not have native support for loops, so there is no direct way to encode Invariants and Program Repair benchmarks. To our knowledge, ROSETTE provides a way to specify the number k it uses to model integers and reals as k-bit words, but the user has no control over how many bits it uses for unknown holes specifically. So we evaluate 27 instead of 81 variants of the polynomial synthesis problem on ROSETTE, i.e., we consider different numbers of cbits.

Figure 6 shows the running times (log scale) for ROSETTE and BINARY with cbits=6. ROSETTE successfully solved 16/27 benchmarks and it terminates quickly (avg. 2.9s) when it can find a solution. However, ROSETTE times out on 11 benchmarks for which BINARY terminates. The timeouts are due to the fact that ROSETTE employs full SMT encodings that combine multiple theories while BINARY uses a SAT solver that is only modified to accommodate SMT-like integer constraints. Since we now know full SMT encodings are not as general and efficient as the encodings used in SKETCH, we will only evaluate the effectiveness of our technique based on comparison with BINARY.

Finally, we tried applying our prime-based technique to ROSETTE and, as expected, the technique is not beneficial due to the binary encoding of numbers in SMT, and causes all benchmarks to timeout. To summarize, (*i*) SMT solvers cannot efficiently handle the synthesis problems considered in this paper, and (*ii*) our technique is better suited for SAT solvers than SMT solvers.

8.3   Performance of Incremental Solving

Our implementation of the incremental solver UNARY-P-INC first attempts to find a solution with the prime set $\mathbb{P} = \{2, 3, 5, 7\}$. If the solver returns a correct

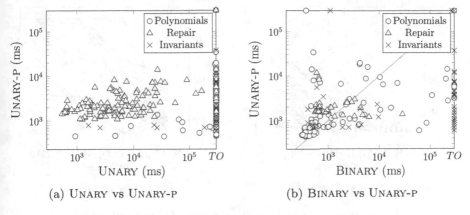

(a) UNARY vs UNARY-P   (b) BINARY vs UNARY-P

Fig. 7: Performance of UNARY, BINARY, and UNARY-P.

solution, UNARY-P-INC terminates. Otherwise, UNARY-P-INC incrementally adds the next prime to $\mathbb{P}$ until it finds a correct solution, it proves there is no solution, or it times out. UNARY-P-INC is 25.2% (geometric mean) slower than UNARY-P (Figure 8 (log scale)). UNARY-P-INC can solve three benchmarks for which both UNARY-P and BINARY timed out. To answer **Q3**, **UNARY-P-INC and UNARY-P have similar performance.**

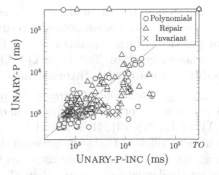

Fig. 8: UNARY-P-INC vs UNARY-P

8.4 Varying the Prime Number Set $\mathbb{P}$

In this experiment, we evaluate how different prime number sets affect UNARY-P.

We consider the 5 increasing sets of primes: $\mathbb{P}_5 = \{2, 3, 5\}$, $\mathbb{P}_7 = \{2, 3, 5, 7\}$, $\mathbb{P}_{11} = \{2, 3, 5, 7, 11\}$, $\mathbb{P}_{13} = \{2, 3, 5, 7, 11, 13\}$, and $\mathbb{P}_{17} = \{2, 3, 5, 7, 11, 13, 17\}$. Figure 9a (log scale) shows the running times for all the polynomial benchmarks with `cbits=7` (showing all benchmarks would clutter the plot). The points where the lines change from dashed to solid denote the number of primes for which the algorithm starts yielding correct solutions. As expected, a smaller set of primes leads to faster solving times as the resulting constraints are smaller and fewer bits are needed for encoding intermediate values. The runtime on average grows with the increasing size of the primes. For example, across all benchmarks, using $\mathbb{P}_{17}$ takes 23% longer on average than using $\mathbb{P}_{11}$. To answer **Q3**, UNARY-P is **slower when using increasingly large sets of prime**.

In terms of correctness, we find that smaller prime sets often yield incorrect solutions ($\mathbb{P}_5$ (37% correct), $\mathbb{P}_7$ (70%), $\mathbb{P}_{11}$ (86%), $\mathbb{P}_{13}$ (97 %), and $\mathbb{P}_{17}$ (100%)) because there is not enough discriminative power with fewer primes and the

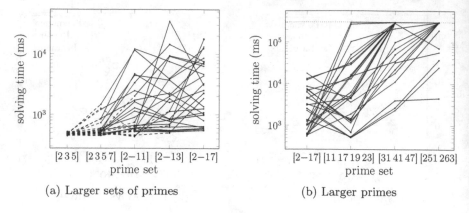

(a) Larger sets of primes   (b) Larger primes

Fig. 9: Performance for different sets of prime numbers.

solutions may overfit to the smaller set of intermediate values. It is interesting to note that even prime sets of intermediate size often lead to correct solutions in practice, which explains some of the speedups observed in the incremental synthesis algorithm. To answer **Q4, UNARY-P is able to synthesize correct solutions even with intermediate sized sets of primes.**

Changing Magnitude of Primes We also evaluate the performance of UNARY-P when using primes of different magnitudes. We consider the sets of primes $\{11, 17, 19, 23\}$, $\{31, 41, 47\}$, and $\{251, 263\}$, which define similar integer ranges, but pose different trade-offs between the number of used primes and their sizes— e.g., the set $\{251, 263\}$ only uses two very large primes. Since the different sets cover similar integer ranges, they all produce correct solutions. Figure 9b (log scale) shows the running time of UNARY-P for the same benchmarks as Figure 9a. Larger prime sets of smaller prime values require less time to solve than smaller prime sets of larger prime values. This result is expected since, in the unary encoding of numbers, representing larger numbers requires more bits.

8.5   Size of SAT Formulas

In this experiment, we compare the sizes of the intermediate SAT formulas generated by UNARY-P and UNARY. Figure 10a shows a scatter plot (log scale) of the number of clauses of the largest intermediate SAT query generated by the CEGIS algorithm for the two techniques. We only plot the instances in which UNARY was able to produce at least a SAT formula. UNARY produces SAT formulas that are on average 19.3X larger than those produced by UNARY-P. To answer **Q5**, as predicted by our theory, **UNARY-P produces significantly smaller SAT queries than UNARY.**

Performance vs Size of SAT Queries We also evaluate the correlation between synthesis time and size of SAT queries. Figure 10b plots the synthesis times of both solvers against the sizes of the SAT queries. It is clear that the synthesis

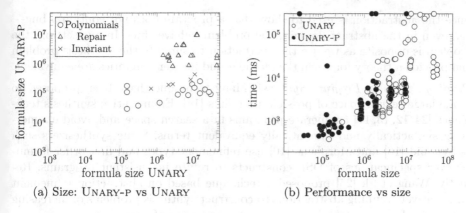

(a) Size: UNARY-P vs UNARY   (b) Performance vs size

Fig. 10: SAT formulas sizes and performance.

time increases with larger SAT queries. The plot illustrates how the solving time strongly depends on the size of the generated formulas.

9 Related Work

Program Sketching Program sketching was designed to automatically synthesize efficient bit-vector manipulations from inefficient iterative implementations [21]. The SKETCH tool has since been engineered to support complex language features and operations [19]. Thanks to its simplicity, sketching has found wide adoption in applications such as optimizing database queries [3], automated feedback generation [18], program repair [7], and many others. Our work further extends the capabilities of SKETCH in a new direction by leveraging number theory results. In particular, our technique allows SKETCH to handle sketches manipulating large integer numbers. To the best of our knowledge, our technique is the first one that can solve many of the benchmarks presented in this paper.

Uses of Chinese Remainder Theorem The Chinese Remainder Theorem and its derivative corollaries have found wide application in several branches of Computer Science and, in particular, in Cryptography [11, 26].

The idea of using modular arithmetic to abstract integer values has been used in program analysis. Since modular fields are finite, they can be used as an abstract domain for verifying programs manipulating integers [5]—e.g., the abstract domain can track whether a number is even or odd. Our work extends this idea to the domain of program synthesis and requires us to solve several challenges. First, when used for verifying programs, the modular abstraction is used to overapproximate the set of possible values of the program and does not need to be precise. In particular, Clark et al. [5] allow program operations that are in the IMP language but not in the IMP-MOD language and lose precision when modeling such operations—e.g., when performing the assignment $x = x/2$ the value of x mod 2 can be either 0 or 1. Such imprecision is fine in program analysis since the abstraction is used to show that a program does not contain a bug—i.e., even in the abstract domain, the problem behaves fine. In our setting, the problem is opposite as we use the abstraction to simplify the synthesis problem and provide a theory for when the modular and integer semantics are equivalent.

Pruning Spaces in Program Synthesis Many techniques have been proposed to prune large search space of possible programs [14]. Enumerative synthesis techniques [24, 12, 13, 17] enumerate programs in a search space and avoid enumerating syntactically and semantically equivalent terms. Some synthesizers such as Synquid [16] and Morpheus [10] use refinement types and first-order formulas over specifications of DSL constructs to refute inconsistent programs. Recently, Wang et al. [25] proposed a technique based on abstraction refinement for iteratively refining abstractions to construct synthesis problems of increasing complexity for incremental search over a large space of programs.

Instead of pruning programs in the syntactic space, our technique uses modular arithmetic to prune the semantic space—i.e., the complexity of verifying the correctness of the synthesized solution—while maintaining the syntactic space of programs. Our approach is related to that of Tiwari et al. [22], who present a technique for component-based synthesis using dual semantics—where syntactic symbols in a language are provided two different semantics to capture different requirements. Our technique is similar in the sense that we also provide an additional semantics based on modular arithmetic. However, we formalize our analysis based on number theory results and develop it in the context of general-purpose SKETCH programs that manipulate integer values, unlike Tiwari et al.'s work that is developed for straight-line programs composed of components.

Synthesis for Large Integer Values Abate et al. propose a modification of the CEGIS algorithm for solving *syntax-guided synthesis* (SyGuS) problems with large constants [1]. SyGuS differs from program sketching in how the synthesis problem is posed and in the type of programs that can be modeled. In particular, in SyGuS one can only describe programs representing *SMT formulas* and the logical specification for the problem can only relate the input and output of the program—i.e., there cannot be intermediate assertions within the program. The problem setup and the solving algorithms proposed in this paper are orthogonal to those of Abate et al. First, we focus on program sketching, which is orthogonal to SyGuS as sketching allows for richer and more generic program spaces as well as richer specifications. While it is true that certain synthesis problems can be expressed both as sketches and as SyGuS problems, this is not the case for our benchmarks programs, which use loops, arrays and non-linear integer arithmetic, all of which are not supported by SyGuS. Second, our technique is motivated by how SKETCH encodes and solves program sketches through SAT solving. While the traditional SKETCH encoding can explode for large constants, the same encoding allows SKETCH to solve program sketches involving complex arithmetic and complex programming constructs. The algorithm proposed by Abate et al. iteratively builds SMT (not SAT) formulas that are required to be in a decidable logical theory. Such an encoding only works for the restricted programming models used in SyGuS problems.

References

1. A. Abate, C. David, P. Kesseli, D. Kroening, and E. Polgreen. Counterexample guided inductive synthesis modulo theories. In *CAV*, Lecture Notes in Computer Science. Springer, 2018.
2. R. Alur, R. Bodík, G. Juniwal, M. M. K. Martin, M. Raghothaman, S. A. Seshia, R. Singh, A. Solar-Lezama, E. Torlak, and A. Udupa. Syntax-guided synthesis. In *Formal Methods in Computer-Aided Design, FMCAD 2013, Portland, OR, USA, October 20-23, 2013*, pages 1–8, 2013.
3. A. Cheung, A. Solar-Lezama, and S. Madden. Optimizing database-backed applications with query synthesis. In *Proceedings of the 34th ACM SIGPLAN Conference on Programming Language Design and Implementation*, PLDI '13, pages 3–14, 2013.
4. L. N. Childs, editor. *The Chinese Remainder Theorem*, pages 253–281. Springer New York, New York, NY, 2009.
5. E. M. Clarke, O. Grumberg, and D. E. Long. Model checking and abstraction. *ACM Trans. Program. Lang. Syst.*, 16(5):1512–1542, Sept. 1994.
6. P. Cousot and R. Cousot. Abstract interpretation: A unified lattice model for static analysis of programs by construction or approximation of fixpoints. In *Proceedings of the 4th ACM SIGACT-SIGPLAN Symposium on Principles of Programming Languages*, POPL '77, pages 238–252, New York, NY, USA, 1977. ACM.
7. L. D'Antoni, R. Samanta, and R. Singh. Qlose: Program repair with quantitative objectives. In *CAV (2)*, volume 9780 of *Lecture Notes in Computer Science*, pages 383–401. Springer, 2016.
8. S. de Oliveira, S. Bensalem, and V. Prevosto. Polynomial invariants by linear algebra. In C. Artho, A. Legay, and D. Peled, editors, *Automated Technology for Verification and Analysis*, pages 479–494, Cham, 2016. Springer International Publishing.
9. P. Dusart. Estimates of ψ, ϑ for large values of x without the riemann hypothesis. *Math. Comput.*, 85(298):875–888, 2016.
10. Y. Feng, R. Martins, J. Van Geffen, I. Dillig, and S. Chaudhuri. Component-based synthesis of table consolidation and transformation tasks from examples. In *Proceedings of the 38th ACM SIGPLAN Conference on Programming Language Design and Implementation*, PLDI 2017, pages 422–436, New York, NY, USA, 2017. ACM.
11. J. Grobchadl. The chinese remainder theorem and its application in a high-speed rsa crypto chip. In *Proceedings of the 16th Annual Computer Security Applications Conference*, ACSAC '00, pages 384–, Washington, DC, USA, 2000. IEEE Computer Society.
12. S. Gulwani. Automating string processing in spreadsheets using input-output examples. In *Proceedings of the 38th ACM SIGPLAN-SIGACT Symposium on Principles of Programming Languages*, POPL 2011, Austin, TX, USA, January 26-28, 2011, pages 317–330, 2011.
13. S. Gulwani, W. R. Harris, and R. Singh. Spreadsheet data manipulation using examples. *Commun. ACM*, 55(8):97–105, 2012.
14. S. Gulwani, O. Polozov, and R. Singh. Program synthesis. *Foundations and Trends in Programming Languages*, 4(1-2):1–119, 2017.
15. G. J. O. Jameson. *The Prime Number Theorem*. London Mathematical Society Student Texts. Cambridge University Press, 2003.

16. N. Polikarpova, I. Kuraj, and A. Solar-Lezama. Program synthesis from polymorphic refinement types. In *Proceedings of the 37th ACM SIGPLAN Conference on Programming Language Design and Implementation, PLDI 2016, Santa Barbara, CA, USA, June 13-17, 2016*, pages 522–538, 2016.
17. R. Singh and S. Gulwani. Transforming spreadsheet data types using examples. In *Proceedings of the 43rd Annual ACM SIGPLAN-SIGACT Symposium on Principles of Programming Languages, POPL 2016, St. Petersburg, FL, USA, January 20 - 22, 2016*, pages 343–356, 2016.
18. R. Singh, S. Gulwani, and A. Solar-Lezama. Automated feedback generation for introductory programming assignments. In *ACM SIGPLAN Conference on Programming Language Design and Implementation, PLDI '13, Seattle, WA, USA, June 16-19, 2013*, pages 15–26, 2013.
19. A. Solar-Lezama. Program sketching. *STTT*, 15(5-6):475–495, 2013.
20. A. Solar-Lezama, C. G. Jones, and R. Bodík. Sketching concurrent data structures. In *Proceedings of the ACM SIGPLAN 2008 Conference on Programming Language Design and Implementation, Tucson, AZ, USA, June 7-13, 2008*, pages 136–148, 2008.
21. A. Solar-Lezama, L. Tancau, R. Bodik, S. Seshia, and V. Saraswat. Combinatorial sketching for finite programs. *SIGOPS Oper. Syst. Rev.*, 40(5):404–415, Oct. 2006.
22. A. Tiwari, A. Gascón, and B. Dutertre. Program synthesis using dual interpretation. In *Automated Deduction - CADE-25 - 25th International Conference on Automated Deduction, Berlin, Germany, August 1-7, 2015, Proceedings*, pages 482–497, 2015.
23. E. Torlak and R. Bodik. A lightweight symbolic virtual machine for solver-aided host languages. In *Proceedings of the 35th ACM SIGPLAN Conference on Programming Language Design and Implementation, PLDI '14*, pages 530–541, New York, NY, USA, 2014. ACM.
24. A. Udupa, A. Raghavan, J. V. Deshmukh, S. Mador-Haim, M. M. Martin, and R. Alur. Transit: Specifying protocols with concolic snippets. In *Proceedings of the 34th ACM SIGPLAN Conference on Programming Language Design and Implementation, PLDI '13*, pages 287–296, 2013.
25. X. Wang, I. Dillig, and R. Singh. Program synthesis using abstraction refinement. *PACMPL*, 2(POPL):63:1–63:30, 2018.
26. S.-M. Yen, S. Kim, S. Lim, and S.-J. Moon. Rsa speedup with chinese remainder theorem immune against hardware fault cryptanalysis. *IEEE Trans. Comput.*, 52(4):461–472, Apr. 2003.

Modular Relaxed Dependencies in Weak Memory Concurrency*

Marco Paviotti[12], Simon Cooksey[2], Anouk Paradis[3], Daniel Wright[2], Scott Owens[2], and Mark Batty[2]

[1] Imperial College London, United Kingdom
m.paviotti@ic.ac.uk
[2] University of Kent, Canterbury, United Kingdom
{m.paviotti, sjc205, daw29, S.A.Owens, M.J.Batty}@kent.ac.uk
[3] ETH Zurich, Switzerland
anouk.paradis@polytechnique.org

Abstract. We present a denotational semantics for weak memory concurrency that avoids *thin-air reads*, provides data-race free programs with sequentially consistent semantics (DRF-SC), and supports a compositional refinement relation for validating optimisations. Our semantics identifies false program dependencies that might be removed by compiler optimisation, and leaves in place just the dependencies necessary to rule out thin-air reads. We show that our dependency calculation can be used to rule out thin-air reads in any axiomatic concurrency model, in particular C++. We present a tool that automatically evaluates litmus tests, show that we can augment C++ to fix the thin-air problem, and we prove that our augmentation is compatible with the previously used compilation mappings over key processor architectures. We argue that our dependency calculation offers a practical route to fixing the longstanding problem of thin-air reads in the C++ specification.

Keywords: Thin-air problem · Weak memory concurrency · Compiler Optimisations · Denotational Semantics · Compositionality

1 Introduction

It has been a longstanding problem to define the semantics of programming languages with shared memory concurrency in a way that does not allow unwanted behaviours – especially observing *thin-air* values [8,7] – and that does not forbid compiler optimisations that are important in practice, as is the case with Java and Hotspot [30,29]. Recent attempts [16,11,25,15] have abandoned the style of *axiomatic models*, which is the de facto paradigm of industrial specification [8,2,6]. Axiomatic models comprise rules that allow or forbid individual program executions. While it is impossible to solve all of the problems in an

* This work was funded by EPSRC Grants EP/M017176/1, EP/R020566/1 and EP/S028129/1, the Lloyds Register Foundation, and the Royal Academy of Engineering.

© The Author(s) 2020
P. Müller (Ed.): ESOP 2020, LNCS 12075, pp. 599–625, 2020.
https://doi.org/10.1007/978-3-030-44914-8_22

axiomatic setting [7], abandoning it completely casts aside mature tools for automatic evaluation [3], automatic test generation [32], and model checking [23], as well as the hard-won refinements embodied in existing specifications like C++, where problems have been discovered and fixed [8,7,18]. Furthermore, the industrial appetite for fundamental change is limited. In this paper we offer a solution to the thin-air problem that integrates with existing axiomatic models.

The thin-air problem in C++ stems from a failure to account for dependencies [22]: *false dependencies* are those that optimisation might remove, and *real dependencies* must be left in place to forbid unwanted behaviour [7]. A single execution is not sufficient to discern real and false dependencies. A key insight from previous work [14,15] is that event structures [33,34] give us a simultaneous overview of all traces at once, allowing us to check whether a write is sure to happen in every branch of execution. Unfortunately, previous work does not integrate well with axiomatic models, nor lend itself to automatic evaluation.

To address this, we construct a denotational semantics in which the meaning of an entire program is constructed by combining the meanings of its subcomponents via a compositional function over the program text. This approach can be particularly amenable to automatic evaluation, reasoning and compiler certification [19,24], and fits with the prevailing axiomatic approach.

This paper uses this denotational approach to capturing program dependencies to explore the thin-air problem, resulting in a concrete proposal for fixing the thin-air problem in the ISO standard for C++.

Contributions. There are two parts to the paper. In the first, we develop a denotational model called "Modular Relaxed Dependencies model" (MRD) and build metatheory around it. The model uses a relatively simple account of synchronisation, but it demonstrates separation between the calculation of dependency and the enforcement of synchronisation. In the second, we evaluate the dependency calculation by combining it with the fully-featured axiomatic models RC11 [18] and IMM [26].

The denotational semantics has the following advantages:

1. It is the first thin-air solution to support fork/join (§2.2).
2. It satisfies the DRF-SC property for a compositional model (§5): programs without data races behave according to sequential consistency.
3. It comes with a refinement relation that validates program transformations, including the optimisation that makes Hotspot unsound for Java [30,29], and a list of others from the Java Causality Tests [27] (§7).
4. It is shown to be equivalent to a global semantics that first performs a dependency calculation and then applies an axiomatic model.
5. An example in Section 10 illustrates a case in which thin-air values are observable in the current state-of-the-art models but forbidden in ours.

We adopt the dependency calculation from the global semantics of point 4 as the basis of our C++ model, which we call MRD-C11. We establish the C++ DRF-SC property described in the standard [13] (§9.1) and we provide several desirable properties for a solution to the thin-air problem in C++:

5. We show that our dependency calculation is the first that can be applied to any axiomatic model, and in particular the RC11 and IMM models that cover C++ concurrency (§8).
6. Our augmented IMM model, which we call MRD+IMM, is provably implementable over x86, Power, ARMv8, ARMv7 and RISC-V, with the compiler mappings provided by the IMM [26] (§8.1).
7. These augmented models of C++ are the first that solve the thin-air problem to have a tool that can automatically evaluate litmus tests (§11).

1.1 Modular Relaxed Dependency by example

To simplify things for now, we will attach an Init program to the beginning of each example to initialise all global variables to zero. Doing this makes the semantics non-compositional, but it is a natural starting place and aligns well with previous work in the area. Later, after we have made all of our formal definitions, we will see why the Init program is not necessary.

For now, consider a simple programming language where all values are booleans, registers (ranging over r) are thread-local, and variables (ranging over x, y) are global. Informally, an event structure for a program consists of a directed graph of events. Events represent the global variable reads and writes that occur on all possible paths that the program can take. This can be built up over the program as follows: each write generates a single event, while each read generates two – one for each possible value that could be read. These read events are put in *conflict* with each other to indicate that they cannot both happen in a single execution, this is indicated with a zig-zag red arrow between the two events. Additionally, the event structure tracks true dependencies via an additional relation which we call *semantic dependencies* (DP). These are yellow arrows from read events to write events.

For example, consider the program

$$(r_1 := x; \; y := r_1) \tag{LB_1}$$

that reads from a variable x and then writes the result to y. The interpretation of this program is an event structure depicted as follows:

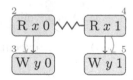

Each event has a unique identifier (the number attached to the box). The straight black arrows represent program order, the curved yellow arrows indicate a causal dependency between the reads and writes, and the red zigzag represents a conflict between two events. If two events are in conflict, then their respective continuations are in conflict too.

If we interpret the program Init; LB_1, as below, we get a program where the Init event sets the variables to zero.

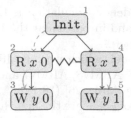

In the above event structure, we highlight events $\{1, 2, 3\}$ to identify an execution. The green dotted arrow indicates that event 2 reads its value from event 1, we call this relation *reads-from* (RF). This execution is *complete* as all of its reads read from a write and it is closed w.r.t conflict-free program order.

We interpret the following program similarly,

$$(r_2 := y; \; x := r_2) \tag{LB_2}$$

leading to a symmetrical event structure where the write to x is dependent on the read from y.

The interpretation of Init; $(LB_1 \parallel LB_2)$ gives the event structure where (LB_1) and (LB_2) are simply placed alongside one another.

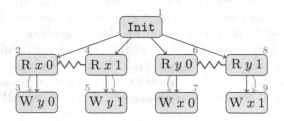

The interpretation of parallel composition is the union of the event structures from LB_1 and LB_2 without any additional conflict edges. When parallel composing the semantics of two programs, we add all RF-edges that satisfy a coherence axiom. Here we present an axiom that provides desirable behaviour in this example (Section 4 provides our model's complete axioms).

$$(\text{DP} \cup \text{RF}) \text{ is acyclic}$$

The program Init; $(LB_1 \parallel LB_2)$ allows executions of the following three shapes.

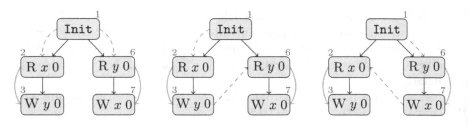

Note that in this example, we are not allowed to read the value 1 – reading a value that does not appear in the program is one sort of thin-air behaviour, as described by Batty et al. [7]. For example, the execution $\{1, 4, 5, 8, 9\}$ does not satisfy the coherence axiom as $4 \xrightarrow{\text{DP}} 5 \xrightarrow{\text{RF}} 8 \xrightarrow{\text{DP}} 9 \xrightarrow{\text{RF}} 4$ forms a cycle.

We now substitute (LB_2) with the following code snippet

$$r_1 := y;\ x := 1 \qquad\qquad (LB_3)$$

where the value written to the variable x is a constant. Its generated event structure is depicted as follows

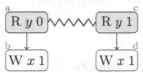

In this program, for each branch, we can reach a write of value 1 to location x. Hence, this will happen no matter which branch is chosen: we say b and d are *independent writes* and we draw no dependency edges from their preceding reads.

Consider now the program (LB_3) in parallel with LB_1 introduced earlier in this section. As usual, we interpret the Init program in sequence with $(LB_1 \parallel LB_3)$ as follows:

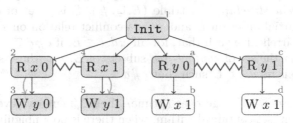

The resulting event structure is very similar to that of $(LB_1 \parallel LB_2)$, but the executions permitted in this event structure are different. The dependency edges calculated when adding the read are preserved, and now executions $\{1, 2, 3, a, b\}$ and $\{1, a, b, 4, 5\}$ are allowed. However, this event structure also contains the execution in which d is independent.

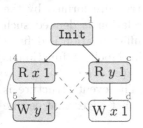

In the execution $\{d \xrightarrow{\text{RF}} 4 \xrightarrow{\text{DP}} 5 \xrightarrow{\text{RF}} c\}$ there is no RF or DP edge between d and c that can create a cycle, hence this is a valid complete execution in which we can observe $x = 1, y = 1$. Note that the Init is irrelevant in the consistency of this execution.

Modularity. It is worthwhile underlining the role that modularity plays here. In order to compute the behaviour of $(LB_1 \parallel LB_2)$ and $(LB_1 \parallel LB_3)$ we did not have to compute the behaviour of LB_1 again. In fact, we computed the semantics of LB_1, LB_2 and LB_3 in isolation and then we observed the behaviour in parallel composition.

Thin-air values. The program $(LB_1 \parallel LB_3)$ is a standard example in the weak memory literature called *load buffering*. In the program $(LB_1 \parallel LB_2)$, if event 5 or 9 were allowed in a complete execution, that would be an undesirable thin-air behaviour: there is no value 1 in the program text, nor does any operation in the program compute the value 1. The program $(LB_1 \parallel LB_3)$ is similar, but now contains a write of value 1 in the program text, so this is no longer a thin-air value. Note that the execution given for it is not sequentially consistent, but nonetheless a weak memory model needs to allow it so that a compiler can, for example, swap the order of the two commands in LB_3, which are completely independent of each other from its perspective.

2   Event Structures

Event structures will form the semantic domain of our denotational semantics in Section 5. Our presentation follows the essential ideas of Winskel [33] and is further influenced by the treatment of shared memory by Jeffrey and Riely [15].

2.1   Background

A partial order $(E, \sqsubseteq)$ is a set E equipped with a reflexive, transitive and antisymmetric relation $\sqsubseteq$. A well-founded partial order is a partial order that has no infinite decreasing chains of the form $\cdots \sqsubseteq e_{i-1} \sqsubseteq e_i \sqsubseteq e_{i+1} \cdots$.

A *prime event structure* is a triple $(E, \sqsubseteq, \#)$. E is a set of events, $\sqsubseteq$ is a well-founded partial order on E and $\#$ is a conflict relation on E. $\#$ is binary, symmetric and irreflexive such that, for all $c, d, e \in E$, if $c\#d \sqsubseteq e$ then $c\#e$. We write $\mathrm{Con}(E)$ for the set of *conflict-free* subsets of E, *i.e.* those subsets $C \subseteq E$ for which there is no $c, d \in C$ such that $c\#d$.

Notation. We use E to range over (prime/labelled/memory) event structures, and also the event set contained within, when there is no ambiguity. We also use $\mathcal{E}$ for event structures.

A *labelled event structure* $(E, \sqsubseteq, \#, \lambda)$, over a set of labels Σ, is a prime event structure together with a function $\lambda : E \to \Sigma$ which assigns a label to an event. We make events explicit using the notation $\{e : \sigma\}$ for $\lambda(e) = \sigma$. We sometimes avoid using names and just write the label σ when there is no risk of confusion.

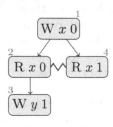

Consider the labelled event structure formed by the set $\{1, 2, 3, 4\}$, where the order relation is defined such that $1 \sqsubseteq 2 \sqsubseteq 3$ and $1 \sqsubseteq 4$, the conflict relation is defined such that $2\#4$ and $3\#4$, and the labelling function is defined such that $\lambda(1) = (\mathrm{W}\ x\ 0)$, $\lambda(2) = (\mathrm{R}\ x\ 0)$, $\lambda(3) = (\mathrm{W}\ y\ 1)$ and $\lambda(4) = (\mathrm{R}\ x\ 1)$. The event structure is visualised on the left (we elide conflict edges that can be inferred from order).

Given labelled event structures $\mathcal{E}_1$ and $\mathcal{E}_2$ define the *product* labelled event structure $\mathcal{E}_1 \times \mathcal{E}_2 \triangleq (E, \sqsubseteq, \#, \lambda)$. E is $E_1 \cup E_2$, assuming E_1 and E_2 to be disjoint, $\sqsubseteq$ is $\sqsubseteq_1 \cup \sqsubseteq_2$, $\#$ is $\#_1 \cup \#_2$ and λ is $\lambda_1 \cup \lambda_2$.

The *coproduct* labelled event structure $\mathcal{E}_1 + \mathcal{E}_2$ is the same as the product, except that the conflict relation $\#$ is $\#_1 \cup \#_2 \cup \{E_1 \times E_2\} \cup \{E_2 \times E_1\}$. We can use a similar construction for the co-product of an infinite set of pairwise-disjoint labelled event structures, indexed by I: we take infinite unions on the underlying sets and relations, along with extra conflicts for every pair of indices. Where the $\mathcal{E}_i$ are not disjoint, we can make them so by renaming with fresh event identifiers. In particular, we will need the infinite coproduct $\sum_{i \in I} \mathcal{E}$ with as many copies of $\mathcal{E}$ as the cardinality of the set I, and all the events between each copy in conflict. Each of these copies will by referred to as $\mathcal{E}^i$.

For a labelled event structure $\mathcal{E}_0$ and an event e, where $e \notin E_0$, define the *prefix* labelled event structure, $e \bullet \mathcal{E}_0$, as a labelled event structure $(E, \sqsubseteq, \#, \lambda)$ where E equals $E_0 \cup \{e\}$, $\sqsubseteq$ equals $\sqsubseteq_0 \cup (\{e\} \times E)$, and $\#$ equals $\#_0$.

2.2 The fork-join event structure

Our language supports parallel composition nested under sequential composition, so we will need to model spawning threads and a subsequent wait for their termination. To support this, we define the *fork-join* composition of two labelled event structures, $\mathcal{E}_1 \star \mathcal{E}_2$. First we define the leaves, $\downarrow (\mathcal{E})$, as the $\sqsubseteq$-maximal elements of $\mathcal{E}$. Let I be the set of maximal conflict-free subsets of $\downarrow (\mathcal{E}_1)$. Intuitively, each event set in I corresponds to the last events[4] of one way of executing the concurrent threads in $\mathcal{E}_1$. We then generate a fresh copy of $\mathcal{E}_2$ for each of the executions: $\mathcal{E}_3 = \sum_{i \in I} \mathcal{E}_2$.

Now $\mathcal{E}_1 \star \mathcal{E}_2 \triangleq (E, \sqsubseteq, \#, \lambda)$ such that E is $E_1 \cup E_3$, $\#$ is $\#_1 \cup \#_3$, λ is $\lambda_1 \cup \lambda_3$, $\sqsubseteq$ is the transitive closure of

$$\sqsubseteq_1 \cup \sqsubseteq_3 \cup \bigcup_{i \in I} \{(e, e') \mid e \in i \wedge e' \in \mathcal{E}_2^E\}$$

The set of events, E, is the set E_1 plus all the elements from the copies of E_3. The order, $\sqsubseteq$, is constructed by linking every event in the copy $\mathcal{E}_2^i$, with all the events in the set i, plus the obvious order from E_1 and the order in the local copy $\mathcal{E}_2^i$. Finally, the conflict relation is the union of the conflict in $\mathcal{E}_1$ and $\mathcal{E}_3$.

3 Coherent event structure

The signature of labels, Σ, is defined as follows:

$$\Sigma = (\{R, W\} \times \mathcal{X} \times \mathcal{V}) + \{L\} + \{U\}$$

where $(W\ x\ v) \in \Sigma$ and $(R\ x\ v) \in \Sigma$ are the usual write and read operations and L, U are the lock and unlock operations respectively.

A *coherent event structure* is a tuple $(E, S, \vdash, \leq)$ where E is a labeled event structure. S is a set of *partial executions*, where each execution is a tuple comprising a maximal conflict-free set of events, together with an intra-thread reads-from

---

[4] We assume that there are no infinite increasing $\sqsubseteq$-chains in $\mathcal{E}_1$.

relation RF_i, an extra-thread reads-from RF_e, a dependency relation DP, and a *partial order* on lock/unlock events LK. The justification relation, $\vdash$, is a relation between conflict-free sets and events. Finally, the *preserved program order*, $\leq^{\mathcal{X}}$, is a restriction of the program order, $\sqsubseteq$, for events on the same variable. $\leq^L$ is the restriction of program order on events related in program order with locks or unlocks. Finally, we define RF to be $RF_e \cup RF_i$ and $\leq$ to be $\leq^{\mathcal{X}} \cup \leq^L$. For a partial execution, $X \in S$, we denote its components as LK_X, RF_X and DP_X.

Justification, $\vdash$, collects dependency information in the program and is used to calculate DP_X. For a conflict-free set C and an event e, we say C *justifies* e or e *depends* on C whenever $C \vdash e$. We collect dependencies between events modularly in order to identify the so-called independent writes which will be introduced shortly.

For a given partial execution, X, we define the order HB_X as the reflexive transitive closure of $(\sqsubseteq \cup LK_X)$. A coherent event structure contains a *data race* if there exists an execution X, with two events on the same variable x, at least one of which is a write, that are not ordered by HB_X. A coherent event structure is *data-race-free* if it does not contain any data race. A *racy* RF_X-*edge* is when two events w and r are racy and $w \xrightarrow{RF_e}_X r$. Note that RF_i edges cannot ever be racy. We now define a coherent partial execution.

Definition 1 (Coherent Partial Execution). *A partial execution X is coherent if and only if:*

1. $(\leq^L \cup LK_X \cup DP_X \cup RF_e X)$ *is acyclic, and*
2. *if $(w : W\ x\ v) \xrightarrow{RF}_X (r : R\ x\ v)$ there are no $(e : R\ x\ v')$ or $(e : W\ x\ \_)$ such that $w \xrightarrow{HB_X} e \xrightarrow{HB_X} r$ with $v \neq v'$.*

A *complete execution X* is an execution where all read events r have a write w that they read from, i.e. $w \xrightarrow{RF}_X r$.

4   Weak memory model

Central to the model is the way it records program dependencies in $\vdash$ and DP. Justification, $\vdash$, records the structure of those dependencies in the program that may be influenced by further composition. As we shall see, composing programs may add or remove dependencies from justification: for example, composing a read may make later writes dependent, or the coproduct mechanism, introduced shortly, may remove them. In some parts of the program, e.g. inside locked regions, dependencies do not interact with the context. In this case, we *freeze* the justifications, using them to calculate DP. Following a freeze, the justification relation is redundant and can be forgotten – DP can be used to judge which executions are coherent.

Freezing. Here we define a function *freeze* which takes a justification $C \vdash (w : W\ x\ v)$ and gives the corresponding dependency relation $(r : R\ x\ v) \xrightarrow{DP} (w : W\ x\ v)$ iff $r \in C$. We lift *freeze* to a function on an event structure as follows:

$$freeze(E_1, S_1, \vdash_1, \leq_1) \triangleq (E_1, S, \emptyset, \leq_1) \qquad (1)$$

where S contains all the executions

$$(X_1, \text{LK}_{X_1}, (\text{DP}_{X_1} \cup \text{DP}), \text{RF}_{X_1})$$

where for each write, $w_i \in X_1$, we choose a justification so that $C_1 \vdash_1 w_1, ..., C_n \vdash_1 w_n$ covers all writes in X_1. Furthermore, with DP defined as follows:

$$\text{DP} = \Big(\bigcup_{i \in \{1, \cdots n\}} freeze(C_i \vdash w_i) \Big)$$

X_1 must be a *coherent execution*. We prove that for a coherent execution there always exists a choice of write justifications that freeze into dependencies to form a coherent execution.

We will illustrate freezing of the program,

$$r_1 := x;\ r_2 := t;\ \text{if}\,(r_1 == 1 \lor r_2 == 1)\{y := 1\}$$

whose event structure is as follows:

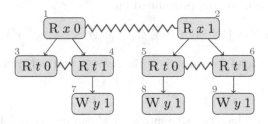

The rules later on in this section will provide us with justifications $\{(6 : R\ t\ 1)\} \vdash (9 : W\ y\ 1)$ and $\{(2 : R\ x\ 1)\} \vdash (9 : W\ y\ 1)$ (but not the *independent justification* $\vdash (9 : W\ y\ 1)$). So in this program there are two *minimal* justifications of $(9 : W\ y\ 1)$. The result of freezing is to duplicate all partial executions for each choice of write justifications. In this case, we get an execution containing $2 \xrightarrow{\text{DP}} 9$ and another one containing $6 \xrightarrow{\text{DP}} 9$.

4.1 Prepending single events

When prepending loads and stores, we model forwarding optimisations by updating the justification relation: e.g. when prepending a write, $(w : W\ x\ 0)$, to an event structure where $\{(r : R\ x\ 0)\} \vdash w'$, write forwarding satisfies the read of the justification, leaving an independently justified write, $\vdash w'$.

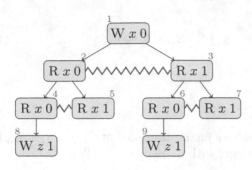

Forwarding is forbidden if there exists e in E such that $w \leq e \leq r$, as in the example on the left. In this example we do not forward 1 to 6. The rules of this section give us that $\{1, 3, 6\} \vdash 9$: we have preserved program order over the accesses of x, $1 \leq 3 \leq 6$, and we do not forward across the intervening read 3.

Read Semantics We now define the semantics of read prepending as follows:

$$(r : \text{R } x \, v) \bullet (E_1, S_1, \vdash_1, \leq_1) \triangleq ((r : \text{R } x \, v) \bullet E_1, S, \vdash, \leq) \tag{2}$$

where preserved program order $\leq$ is built straightforwardly out of $\leq_1$, ordering locks, unlocks and same-location accesses, and S is defined as the set of all $(X \cup \{r\}, \text{LK}_X, \text{RF}_X, \text{DP}_X)$, where X is a partial execution of S_1 and $\vdash$ is the smallest relation such that for all $C \vdash_1 e$ we have

$$C_1 \cup \{r\} \setminus \text{LF} \vdash e$$

with LF being the *"Load Forwarded"* set of reads, *i.e.* the set of reads consecutively following the matching prepended one:

$$\text{LF} = \{(r' : \text{R } x \, v) \in C_1 \mid \nexists e', r \leq^{x} e' \leq^{x} r'\}$$

This allows for load forwarding optimisations and coherence is satisfied by construction.

Write Semantics The write semantics are then defined as follows:

$$(w : \text{W } x \, v) \bullet (E_1, S_1, \vdash_1, \leq_1) \triangleq ((w : \text{W } x \, v) \bullet E_1, S, \vdash, \leq) \tag{3}$$

where $\leq$ is built as in the read rule and S contains all *coherent* executions of the form,

$$(X \cup \{w\}, \text{LK}_X, (\text{RF}_X \cup \text{RF}_i), \text{DP}_X)$$

where $X \in S_1$, and $w \xrightarrow{\text{RF}_i} r$ for any set of matching reads r in E_1 such that condition (1.2) of coherence is satisfied. Adding RF_i edges leaves condition (1.1) satisfied.

The justification relation $\vdash$ is the smallest upward-closed relation such that for all $C \vdash_1 e$:

1. $\vdash w$
2. $C \setminus \text{SF} \cup \{w\} \vdash e$ if there exists $e' \in C$ s.t. $w \leq^{x} e'$
3. $C \setminus \text{SF} \vdash e$ otherwise

with SF being the *Store Forwarding* set of reads, *i.e.* the set of reads that we are going to remove from the justification set for later events that are matching the write we are prepending. This is defined as follows:

$$\text{SF} = \{(r' : \text{R } x \ v) \mid \nexists e, w \leq^{\mathcal{X}} e \leq^{\mathcal{X}} r'\}$$

When prepending a write to an event structure, we add it to justifications that contain a read to the same variable. Failing to do so would invalidate the DRF-SC property. We provide an example in Section 6.3, but we need to complete the definition of the semantics first, in particular, we need to explain first how the writes are lifted. This is coming in the next section (Section 4.2).

4.2 Coproduct semantics

The coproduct mechanism is responsible for making writes independent of prior reads if they are sure to happen, regardless of the value read. It produces the independent writes that enabled relaxed behaviour in the example in Section 1.

In the definition of coproduct we use an upward-closure of justification to enable the lifting of more dependencies. Whenever $C \vdash e$ we define $\uparrow (C)$ as the upward-closed justification set, i.e. $D \vdash e$ if $C \vdash e$, D is a conflict-free lock-free set with $C \subseteq D$, such that for all $e' \in D$ if e'' is an event such that $e'' \leq e'$ then $e'' \subseteq D$.

Now we define the coproduct operation. If E_1 is a labelled event structure of the form $(r_1 : \text{R } x \ v_1) \bullet E_1'$ and, similarly, E_2 is of the form $(r_2 : \text{R } x \ v_2) \bullet E_2'$, the coproduct of event structures is defined as,

$$(E_1, S_1, \vdash_1, \leq_1) + (E_2, S_2, \vdash_2, \leq_2) \triangleq (E_1 + E_2, S_1 \cup S_2, (\vdash_1 \cup \vdash_2 \cup \vdash), \leq)$$

where whenever $\{r_1\} \cup C_1 \vdash_1 (w : \text{W } y \ v)$ and $\{r_2\} \cup C_2 \vdash_2 (w' : \text{W } y \ v)$ then if the following conditions hold, we have $D' \vdash w$ and $D'' \vdash w'$:

1. there exists a $D' \in \uparrow (C_1)$ that is isomorphic to a $D'' \in \uparrow (C_2)$, that is, there exists $f : D' \rightarrow D''$ that is a λ-preserving and $\leq^{\mathcal{X}}$-preserving bijection,
2. there is no event e in D' such that $r_1 \leq^{\mathcal{X}} e$

The example of Section 1 illustrates the application of condition (1) of coproduct. Recall the event structures of (LB_1) and (LB_3) respectively.

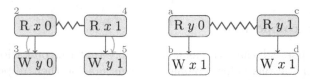

In each case, the event structure is built as the coproduct of the conflicting events. In (LB_3), prior to applying coproduct we have $\{a\} \vdash b$ and $\{c\} \vdash d$. The writes have the same label for both read values so, taking C_1 and C_2 to be empty, coproduct makes them independent, adding the independent writes $\vdash b$ and $\vdash d$.

In contrast, the values of writes 3 and 5 differ in (LB_1), so the coproduct has $\{2\} \vdash 3$ and $\{4\} \vdash 5$. When ultimately frozen, the justifications of (LB_1) will produce the dependency edges $(2,3)$ and $(4,5)$ as described in Section 1.

As for condition (2), if there is an event in the justification set that is ordered in $\leq^{\mathcal{X}}$ with the respective top read, then the top read cannot be erased from the justification. Doing so would break the $\leq^{\mathcal{X}}$ link.

When having value sets that contain more than two values, we use $\sum_{v \in V}$ to denote a *simultaneous coproduct* (rather than the infinite sum). More precisely, if we coproduct the event structures $E_0, E_1, \cdots, E_n$ in a pairwise fashion as follows,

$$(\cdots (E_0 + E_1) + \cdots) + E_v$$

we would get liftings that are undesirable. To see this, it suffices to consider the program,

$$\texttt{if}\,(\texttt{r==3})\,\{\texttt{x := 2}\}\{\texttt{x := 1}\}$$

where the write to x of 1 is independent for a coproduct over values 1 and 2, but not when considering the event structure following (R x 3).

4.3   Lock semantics

When prepending a lock, we order the lock before following events in $\leq$ and we freeze the justifications into dependencies. By freezing, we prevent justifications from events after the lock from interacting with newly appended events. This disables optimisations across the lock, e.g. store and load forwarding.

We define the semantics of locks as follows,

$$(l : L) \bullet (E_1, \vdash_1, S_1, \leq_1) \triangleq ((l : L) \bullet E_1, \emptyset, S, \leq) \tag{4}$$

where $\leq^{\mathcal{X}}$ remains unchanged and $(E_1', \emptyset, S_1', \leq_1') = \textit{freeze}(E_1, \vdash_1, S_1, \leq_1)$, where S contains all partial executions of the form,

$$(X \cup \{l\}, (\textsc{lk}_X \cup \textsc{lk}), \textsc{dp}_X, \textsc{rf}_X)$$

where $X \in S_1'$ and the lock order $\textsc{lk}$ is such that for all lock or unlock event $l' \in X$, $l \xrightarrow{\textsc{lk}} l'$. Finally, $\leq^L$ is $\leq^L{}_1'$ extended with the lock ordered before all events in E_1'.

The semantics for the unlock is similar.

4.4   Parallel composition

We define the parallel semantics as follows. Note that this operation freezes the constituent denotations before combining them, erasing their respective justification relations. This choice prevents the optimisation of dependencies across forks and it makes thread inlining optimisations unsound, as they are in the Promising Semantics [16] and the Java memory model [21].

$$(E_1, S_1, \vdash_1, \leq_1) \times (E_2, S_2, \vdash_2, \leq_2) \triangleq (E_1 \times E_2, S, \emptyset, \leq_1 \cup \leq_2)$$

where, S are all *coherent* partial executions of the form,

$$(X_1 \cup X_2, (\text{LK}_{X_1} \cup \text{LK}_{X_2} \cup \text{LK}), (\text{DP}_{X_1} \cup \text{DP}_{X_2}), (\text{RF}_{X_1} \cup \text{RF}_{X_2} \cup \text{RF}_e))$$

where $X_1 \in S_1^F$, $X_2 \in S_2^F$ and

- $\textit{freeze}(E_1, S_1, \vdash_1, \leq_1) = (E_1, S_1^F, \emptyset, \leq_1)$
- $\textit{freeze}(E_2, S_2, \vdash_2, \leq_2) = (E_2, S_2^F, \emptyset, \leq_2)$

Furthermore, LK is constrained so that $(\text{LK}_{X_1} \cup \text{LK}_{X_2} \cup \text{LK})$ is a *total* order over the lock/unlock operations such that no lock/unlock operation is introduced between a lock and the next unlock on the same thread. Finally, we add all $(w : \text{W } x\ v) \xrightarrow{\text{RF}_e} (r : \text{R } x\ v)$ edges such that the execution satisfies condition (1.1) of coherence[1] and such that w belongs to S_1^F and r belongs to S_2^F or vice versa.

4.5 Join Semantics

We define the join composition as follows:

$$(E_1, S_1, \vdash_1, \leq_1) \star (E_2, S_2, \vdash_2, \leq_2) \triangleq (E_1 \star E_2, S, \vdash_1, \leq) \tag{5}$$

where $\leq$ is built as in the read rule and S are all executions of the form

$$(X_1 \cup X_2, (\text{LK}_{X_1} \cup \text{LK}_{X_2} \cup \text{LK}), (\text{DP}_{X_1} \cup \text{DP}_{X_2}), (\text{RF}_{X_1} \cup \text{RF}_{X_2} \cup \text{RF}_i))$$

where $X_1 \in S_1$ and $X_2 \in S_2$ with X_1 and X_2 conflict-free. Lock order LK orders all lock/unlock of X_1 before all lock/unlock of X_2 and $w \xrightarrow{\text{RF}_i} r$ whenever $w \in X_1$ and $r \in X_2$ such that the execution is still coherent.

5 Language and Semantics

We consider an imperative language that has sequential and parallel composition, and mutable shared memory.

Definition 2 (Language).

$$B := M = M \mid B \wedge B \mid B \vee B \mid \neg B \qquad\qquad M := n \mid \text{r}$$
$$P ::= \textbf{skip} \mid \text{r} := \text{x} \mid \text{x} := M \mid P_1;\ P_2 \mid P_1 \parallel P_2 \mid \textbf{if}(B)\{P_1\}\{P_2\}$$
$$\mid \textbf{while}(B)\{P\} \mid \text{L} \mid \text{U}$$

We have standard boolean expressions, B, and expressions, M, represented by natural numbers, n, or registers, r. Finally we have the set of command statements, P, where **skip** is the command that performs no action, $\text{r} := \text{x}$ reads from a global variable and stores the value in r, $\text{x} := M$ computes the expression M and stores its value to the global variable x, $P_1;\ P_2$ is sequential composition,

---

[1] Note that condition (1.2) does not need to be checked.

and $P_1 \parallel P_2$ is parallel composition. We have standard conditional statements, while loops, locks and unlocks. Moreover, a program P is *lock-well-formed*[5] if on every thread, every lock is paired with a following unlock instruction and vice versa, and there is no lock or unlock operation between pairs.

A *register environment*, $\mathcal{R} \to \mathcal{V}$, is a function from the set of local registers, $\mathcal{R}$, to the set of values, $\mathcal{V}$. A *continuation* is a function taking a register environment, $\mathcal{R} \to \mathcal{V}$, to an event structure, $\mathcal{E}$. We write $\underline{\emptyset}$ as a short-hand for $\lambda\rho.\emptyset$, the continuation returning the empty event structure.

We interpret the syntax defined above into the semantic domain defined in Section 4. In Figure 1, we define $[\![\cdot]\!]$ as a function which takes a *step-index* n, a register environment ρ, and a continuation κ, and returns a coherent event structure.

The interpretation function $[\![\cdot]\!]$ is defined first by induction on the step-index and then by induction on the syntax of the program. When $n = 1$ the interpretation gives the empty event structure (undefined). Otherwise we proceed by induction on the structure of the program. skip is just the continuation applied to the environment. A read is interpreted as a set of conflicting read events for each value v attached with a continuation applied to the environment where the register is updated with v.

A write is interpreted as a write with a following continuation. We interpret sequencing by interpreting the second program and passing it on to the interpretation of the first as a continuation. Parallel composition is the interpretation of the two programs with empty continuations passed to the $\times$ operator. The conditional statement is interpreted as usual. For interpreting the while-loops we use the induction hypothesis on the step-index [9].

When parallel composing two threads, we want to forbid any reordering with events sequenced before or after the composition (as thread inlining would do). To forbid this local reordering we surround this composition with two lock-unlock pairs.

5.1   Compositionality

We define the language of contexts inductively in the standard way.

Definition 3 (Context).

$$\mathcal{C} ::= [-] \mid P; \mathcal{C} \mid \mathcal{C}; P \mid (\mathcal{C} \parallel P) \mid (P \parallel \mathcal{C})$$
$$\mid \mathbf{if}(B)\{\mathcal{C}\}\{P\} \mid \mathbf{if}(B)\{P\}\{\mathcal{C}\} \mid \mathbf{while}(B)\{\mathcal{C}\}$$

In the base case, the context is a hole, denoted by $[-]$. The inductive cases follow the structure of the program syntax. In particular, a context can be a program P in sequence with a context, a context in sequence with a program P and so on. For a context $\mathcal{C}$ we denote $\mathcal{C}[P]$ by the inductively defined function on the context $\mathcal{C}$ that substitutes the program P in every hole.

---

[5] Jeffrey and Riely [15] adopt the same restriction. We conjecture that modelling blocking locks [4] would not affect the DRF-SC property.

$$[\![P]\!]_{1\,\rho\,\kappa} = \underline{\emptyset}$$

$$[\![\mathbf{skip}]\!]_{n\,\rho\,\kappa} = \kappa(\rho)$$

$$[\![\mathbf{r} := \mathbf{x}]\!]_{n\,\rho\,\kappa} = \Sigma_{v\in V}(\mathrm{R}\;x\;v \bullet \kappa(\rho[r \mapsto v]))$$

$$[\![\mathbf{x} := M]\!]_{n\,\rho\,\kappa} = (\mathrm{W}\;x\;[\![M]\!]_\rho) \bullet \kappa(\rho)$$

$$[\![P_1;\,P_2]\!]_{n\,\rho\,\kappa} = [\![P_1]\!]_{n\,\rho\,(\lambda\rho.[\![P_2]\!]_{n\,\rho\,\kappa})}$$

$$[\![\mathrm{L}]\!]_{n\,\rho\,\kappa} = (\mathrm{L} \bullet E_1, \vdash_1)$$

$$\text{where } (E_1, \vdash_1) = \kappa(\rho)$$

$$[\![\mathrm{U}]\!]_{n\,\rho\,\kappa} = (\mathrm{U} \bullet E_1, \vdash_1)$$

$$\text{where } (E_1, \vdash_1) = \kappa(\rho)$$

$$[\![P_1 \parallel P_2]\!]_{n\,\rho\,\kappa} = [\![\mathrm{L};\mathrm{U}]\!]_{n\,\rho\,\kappa'}$$

$$\text{where } \kappa' = (\lambda\rho.([\![P_1]\!]_{n\,\rho\,\underline{\emptyset}}) \times ([\![P_2]\!]_{n\,\rho\,\underline{\emptyset}}) \star ([\![\mathrm{L};\,\mathrm{U}]\!]_{n\,\rho\,\kappa}))$$

$$[\![\mathbf{if}\,(B)\{P_1\}\{P_2\}]\!]_{n\,\rho\,\kappa} = \begin{cases} [\![P_1]\!]_{n\,\rho\,\kappa} & [\![B]\!]_\rho = \mathrm{T} \\ [\![P_2]\!]_{n\,\rho\,\kappa} & [\![B]\!]_\rho = \mathrm{F} \end{cases}$$

$$[\![\mathbf{while}\,(B)\{P\}]\!]_{n\,\rho\,\kappa} = \begin{cases} [\![P;\mathbf{while}\,(B)\{P\}]\!]_{(n-1)\,\rho\,\kappa} & [\![B]\!]_\rho = \mathrm{T} \\ [\![\mathbf{skip}]\!]_{n\,\rho\,\kappa} & [\![B]\!]_\rho = \mathrm{F} \end{cases}$$

Fig. 1: Semantic interpretation

The following lemma shows that the semantics preserve context application. This falls out from the fact that the semantic interpretation is compositional, that is, we define every constructor in terms of its subcomponents.

Lemma 1 (Compositionality). *For all programs P_1, P_2, if $[\![P_1]\!] = [\![P_2]\!]$ then for all contexts C, $[\![C[P_1]]\!] = [\![C[P_2]]\!]$.*

The proof is a straightforward induction on the context C and it follows from the fact that semantics is inductively defined on the program syntax. The attentive reader may note that to prove $[\![P_1]\!] = [\![P_2]\!]$ in the first place we have to assume n, ρ and κ and prove $[\![P_1]\!]_{n\,\rho\,\kappa} = [\![P_2]\!]_{n\,\rho\,\kappa}$. It is customary however in denotational semantics to have programs denoted by functions that are equal if they are equal at all inputs [31].

5.2   Data Race Freedom

Data race freedom ensures that we forbid optimisations which could lead to unexpected behaviour even in the absence of data races. We first define the *closed semantics* for a program P. For all n, the semantics of P, namely $[\![P]\!]$ is $[\![\mathtt{Init}(P)]\!]_{n\,\lambda x.0\,\underline{\emptyset}}$, where $\mathtt{Init}(P)$ is the program that takes the global variables in P and initialises them to 0. We now establish that race-free programs interpreted in the closed semantics have sequentially consistent behaviour.

DRF semantics. Rather than proving DRF-SC directly, we prove that race-free programs behave according to an intermediate semantics $(\!|\cdot|\!)$. This semantics differs from $[\![\cdot]\!]$ in only two ways: program order is used in the calculation of coherence instead of preserved program order, and no dependency edges are recorded (as these are subsumed by program order). More precisely, the semantics is calculated as in Figure 1 but we check that $(\mathrm{RF}_e \cup \mathrm{LK} \cup \sqsubseteq)$ is acyclic.

Note that race-free executions of the intermediate semantics $(\!|\cdot|\!)$ satisfy the constraints of the model of Boehm and Adve [10], and the definition of race is the same between the two models. Boehm and Adve prove that in the absence of races, their model provides sequential consistency.

The DRF-SC theorem is stated as follows.

Theorem 1. *For any program P, if $(\!|P|\!)$ is data race free then every execution D in $[\![P]\!]$ is a sequentially consistent execution, i.e. D is in $(\!|P|\!)$.*

6   Tests and Examples

In this section, four examples demonstrate aspects of the semantics: the first recognises a false dependency, the second forbids unintended behaviour allowed by Jeffrey and Riely [15], the third motivates the choice to add forwarded writes to justification, and the last shows how we support an optimisation forbidden by Java but performed by the Hotspot compiler.

6.1   LB+ctrl-double

In the first example, from Batty et al. [7], the compiler collapses conditionals to transform P_1 to P_2.

Coproduct ensures that the denotations of P_1 and P_2 are identical, with the event structure above, together with justification $\vdash b$ and $\vdash d$. From compositionality (Lemma 1) and equality of the denotations, we have equal behaviour of P_1 and P_2 in any context, and the optimisation is allowed.

6.2   Jeffrey and Riely's TC7

The next test is Java TC7. The outcome where r_1, r_2 and r_3 all have value 1 is forbidden by Jeffrey and Riely [15, Section 7], but allowed in the Java Causality Test Cases [27].

$$
\begin{array}{c|c}
T_1 & T_2 \\
\hline
\texttt{r}_1 := \texttt{z}; & \texttt{r}_3 := \texttt{y}; \\
\texttt{r}_2 := \texttt{x}; & \texttt{z} := \texttt{r}_3; \\
\texttt{y} := \texttt{r}_2; & \texttt{x} := \texttt{1}
\end{array}
\qquad \text{(TC7)}
$$

As noted by Jeffrey and Riely [15], the failure of this test "indicates a failure to validate the reordering of independent reads".

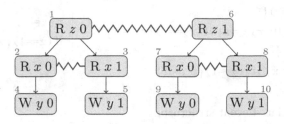

In the event structure of T_1 above, the justification relation is constructed according to Section 5. In particular, the rule for prepending reads (equation (4.1)) gives us $\{1,2\} \vdash_{T_1} 4$ and $\{1,3\} \vdash_{T_1} 5$ on the left-hand side, and $\{6,7\} \vdash_{T_1} 9$ and $\{6,8\} \vdash_{T_1} 10$ on the right. When composing the left and right sides, the coproduct rule (Section 4.2) makes four independent links, namely, $\{2\} \vdash_{T_1} 4$, $\{3\} \vdash_{T_1} 5$, $\{7\} \vdash_{T_1} 9$, and $\{8\} \vdash_{T_1} 10$. This is because, at the top level, for both branches, we can choose a write with the same label that is dependent on the same reads (plus the top ones on z). More precisely, on the left-hand side $C_1 = \{1,2\}$ is such that $C_1 \vdash_{T_1} 4$, and on the right-hand side $C_2 = \{6,7\}$ is such that $C_2 \vdash_{T_1} 9$. When the top events, 1 and 6 respectively, are removed, these contexts become isomorphic ($C_1[1] \cong C_2[6]$). Hence, $\{2\} \vdash_{T_1} 4$ and $\{7\} \vdash_{T_1} 9$, and $\{3\} \vdash_{T_1} 5$ and $\{8\} \vdash_{T_1} 10$.

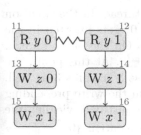

Now consider the event structure for the thread T_2. Here we have two independent writes, namely $\vdash_{T_2} (15 : W\ x\ 1)$ and $\vdash_{T_2} (16 : W\ x\ 1)$, arising in the coproduct from justifications $\{11\} \vdash_{T_2} (15 : W\ x\ 1)$ and $\{12\} \vdash_{T_2} (16 : W\ x\ 1)$. Notice that by definition (3), we do not add the writes 13 and 14 to the justification sets of any $W\ x\ 1$, and because they write different values to z depending on the value of y, we have the dependencies $\{11\} \vdash_{T_2} 13$ and $\{12\} \vdash_{T_2} 14$.

When parallel composing, we connect the RF-edges that respect coherence. Thus we obtain the execution $\{16 \xrightarrow{\text{RF}} 8 \xrightarrow{\text{DP}} 10 \xrightarrow{\text{RF}} 12 \xrightarrow{\text{DP}} 14 \xrightarrow{\text{RF}} 6\}$, which is coherent, allowing the outcome with r_1, r_2 and r_3 all 1 as desired.

6.3   Adding writes to justifications

In the definition of prepending writes (equation (3), condition (2)) we state that for any given justification, if there is an event in the justification set that is related via $\leq^{\mathcal{X}}$ with the write we are prepending, then that write must be in the justification set as well.

To see why we made this choice consider the following program,

```
x := 1;
r₁ := y;
if(r₁==0){                                      r₃ := z;
    x := 0; r₂ := x; if(r₂==1){z := 1}          if(z==1){y := 1}
} else {
    r₃ := x; if(r₃==1){z := 1}
}
```

and its associated event structure,

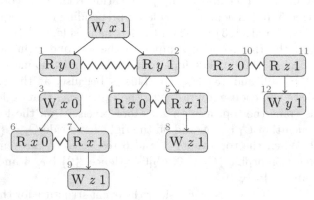

We focus on the interpretation of the left-hand side thread. In the equation (3), because $\{7\} \vdash 9$ and $3 \leq^x 7$, the event $(3 : W\ x\ 0)$ gets inserted in the justification set, leading to the justification $\{3, 7\} \vdash 9$. On the other branch, up until the coproduct of the read on y, we have $\{5\} \vdash 8$. At this point, the justifications $\{7\} \vdash 9$ and $\{5\} \vdash 8$ are not lifted because 9 requires 3 as well. Event 3 may not be removed because of the condition in the write prepending rule. Without this condition 3 would not be necessary to justify 9, yielding the lifting of the link $\{5\} \vdash 8$. This would also cause the execution $\{0 \xrightarrow{\text{RF}} 5 \xrightarrow{\text{DP}} 8 \xrightarrow{\text{RF}} 11 \xrightarrow{\text{DP}} 12 \xrightarrow{\text{RF}} 2\}$ to be coherent due to the lack of a dependency between 2 and 5.

This execution is not sequentially consistent, but under SC, the program is race free. Without writes in justifications, the model would violate the DRF-SC property described in Section 5.2.

6.4   Java memory model, Hotspot.

Finally, we discuss redundant read after read elimination, an optimisation performed by the Hotspot compiler but forbidden by the Java memory model. It is the first optimisation in the following sequence from Ševčík and Aspinall [30, Figure 5], used to demonstrate that the Java memory model is too strict, and unsound with respect to the observable behaviour of Sun's Hotspot compiler.

T_3	T_2	T_1
r₂ := y;		

```
         T₃                    T₂              T₁
   ──────────────────────────────────────────────────
   r₂ := y;
   if(r₂== 1)
                          r₂ := y;        x := 1;
      {r₃ := y; x := r₃} ⟶                ⟶
                          x := 1;         r₂ := y;
   else
      {x := 1}
```

Consider the event structures of the unoptimised T_3 and optimised T_1.

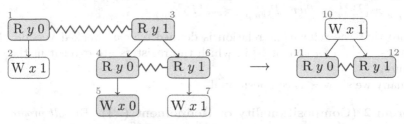

The optimisation removes the apparently redundant pair of reads $(4, 6)$, then reorders the now-independent write. This redundancy is represented in justification: when prepending the top read of y to the right-hand side of the event structure, the existing justification $6 \vdash 7$ is replaced by $3 \vdash 7$. When coproduct is applied, this matches with justification $1 \vdash 2$, leading to the independent writes $\vdash 2$ and $\vdash 7$. In a weak memory context however, a parallel thread could write a value to y between the two reads, thereby changing the value written to x. For this reason, we keep event 4 in the denotation and create the dependency edge $4 \xrightarrow{\text{DP}} 5$.

Despite exhibiting the same behaviour here, the denotations of T_3 and T_2 do not match. We establish that the optimisation is sound in any context in the next section.

7   Refinement

We have shown in Section 5.1 that our semantics enjoys a compositionality property: if we can prove that two programs have the same semantics (w.r.t set-theoretical equality) then they cannot be distinguished by any context. We also explained how equality is too strict, as it does not allow us to relate all programs that ought to be deemed semantically equivalent. Our Java Hotspot compiler example in Section 6 shows that the program T_3 is in practice optimised to T_2 and then to T_1. However, it is clearly not true that $\llbracket T_1 \rrbracket_{n\, \rho\, \kappa}$ is a subset of $\llbracket T_2 \rrbracket_{n\, \rho\, \kappa}$.

In this section we present a coarser-grained relation, which we call *refinement* ($\preccurlyeq$). This relation permits the optimisations we want, but remains sound w.r.t. the intuitive notion of observational equivalence, and that it is closed under context application in the same way as equality.

To show soundness we define *observational refinement* ($\preccurlyeq_{OBS}$) which captures the intuitive notion of program equivalence: one program is a permissible optimisation of another if it does not increase the set of observable behaviours, defined here as changes to values of observed variables. The definition identifies related executions and compares the ordering of observable events, recognising that adding happens-before edges restricts behaviour. We then define a *refinement* relation and show this relation is a subset of observational refinement. This is formally stated in the following lemma:

Lemma 2 (Soundness of Refinement ($\preccurlyeq \subseteq \preccurlyeq_{Obs}$)). *For all P_1 and P_2, if* $[\![P_1]\!]^T_{n \, \rho \, \emptyset} \preccurlyeq [\![P_2]\!]^T_{n \, \rho \, \emptyset}$ *then* $[\![P_1]\!]^T_{n \, \rho \, \emptyset} \preccurlyeq_{obs} [\![P_2]\!]^T_{n \, \rho \, \emptyset}$

Note that the refinement relation is defined over a tweaked version of the semantics, $[\![\cdot]\!]^T$, a variant of $[\![\cdot]\!]$ in which the registers are explicit in the event structure.

Finally we show $\preccurlyeq$ is compositional:

Theorem 2 (Compositionality of Refinement ($\preccurlyeq$)). *For all programs P_1 and P_2, and indexes n, if for all ρ, $[\![P_1]\!]^T_{n \, \rho \, \emptyset} \preccurlyeq [\![P_2]\!]^T_{n \, \rho \, \emptyset}$ then for all contexts C, ρ, κ and κ' such that $\kappa \preccurlyeq \kappa'$ we have that $[\![C[P_1]]\!]^T_{n \, \rho \, \kappa} \preccurlyeq [\![C[P_2]]\!]^T_{n \, \rho \, \kappa'}$*

8   Showing implementability via IMM

In this section we show that our calculation of relaxed dependencies can easily be reused to solve the thin-air problem in other state-of-the-art axiomatic models, drawing the advantages of these models over to ours. In particular, we augment the IMM and RC11 models of Podkopaev et al. [26]. We adopt their language, given below. It covers C++ atomics, fences, fetch-and-add and compare-and-swap operations but excludes locks. Note that locks are implementable using compare and swap operations.

$$M := n \mid r$$
$$B := M = M \mid B \wedge B \mid B \vee B \mid \neg B$$
$$T ::= \mathbf{skip} \mid r :=^{o_R} x \mid x :=^{o_W} M \mid T_1 ; T_2$$
$$\mid \mathbf{if}\,(B)\{P_1\}\{P_2\} \mid \mathbf{while}\,(B)\{P\}$$
$$\mid \mathbf{fence}^{o_F} \mid r := \mathbf{FADD}^{o_R, o_W}_{o_{RMW}}(x, M)$$
$$\mid \mathbf{CAS}^{o_R, o_W}_{o_{RMW}}(x, M, M)$$

$$P ::= T_1 \parallel \cdots \parallel T_n$$
$$o_R ::= rlx \mid acq$$
$$o_W ::= rlx \mid rel$$
$$o_F ::= acq \mid rel \mid acqrel \mid sc$$
$$o_{RMW} ::= normal \mid strong$$

First we provide a model, written (for a program P) as $[\![P]\!]_{MRD+IMM}$, that combines our relaxed dependencies to the axiomatic model of IMM , here written as $[\![P]\!]_{IMM}$. We will make these definitions precise shortly. We then show that $[\![P]\!]_{MRD+IMM}$ is weaker than $[\![P]\!]_{IMM}$, making $[\![P]\!]_{MRD+IMM}$ implementable over hardware architectures like x86-TSO, ARMv7, ARMv8 and Power. Secondly, we relax the RC11 axiomatic model by using our relaxed dependencies model MRD to create a new model $[\![P]\!]_{MRD-C11}$, and show this model weaker than the RC11 model. We argue that the mathematical description of $[\![P]\!]_{\text{MRD-C11}}$ is lightweight and close to the C++ standard, it would therefore require minimal work to augment the standard with the ideas presented in this paper.

To prove implementability over hardware architectures we define a *pre-execution* semantics, where the relaxed dependency relation DP is calculated along with the data and control dependencies from IMM . To combine our model with IMM , we redefine the AR relation (we refer the reader to the IMM paper [26] for the details on AR) such that it is parametrised by an arbitrary relation which we put in place of the relations (data ∪ ctrl). AR(data ∪ ctrl) equals the original axiom AR and AR(DP) is the same axiom where DP is put in place of data ∪ ctrl.

We define the executions in $[\![P]\!]_{\text{MRD+IMM}}$ as the maximal conflict-free sets such that AR(DP) is acyclic, and executions in $[\![P]\!]_{\text{IMM}}$ as the maximal conflict-free sets such that AR(data ∪ ctrl) is acyclic.

8.1   Implementability

We can now state and prove that the MRD model is implementable over IMM, which gives us that MRD is implementable over x86-TSO, ARMv7, ARMv8, Power and RISC-V by combining our result with the implementability result of IMM .

Theorem 3 (MRD ⊦IMM **is weaker than** IMM). *For all programs P by the* IMM *model,*

$$[\![P]\!]_{\text{MRD+IMM}} \supseteq [\![P]\!]_{\text{IMM}}$$

9   Modular Relaxed Dependencies in RC11: MRD-C11

We refer to the RC11 [18] model, as specified in Podkopaev et al. [26]. We call this model $[\![P]\!]_{\text{RC11}}$. While $[\![P]\!]_{\text{RC11}}$ forbids thin-air executions, it is not weak enough: it forbids common compiler optimisations by imposing that (⊑ ∪ RF) is acyclic. We relax this condition by similarly replacing ⊑ with our relaxed dependency relation DP, this time calculated on our preserved program order relation (≤). We call this model $[\![P]\!]_{\text{MRD-C11}}$. Mathematically, this is done by imposing that (DP ∪ RF) is acyclic.

At this point, we prove the following lemma:

Lemma 3 (Implementability of MRD-C11). *For all programs P,*

$$[\![P]\!]_{\text{MRD-C11}} \supseteq [\![P]\!]_{\text{RC11}}$$

To show this it suffices to show that there always exists DP ⊆ ⊑. This is straightforward by induction on the structure of P, observing that the only place where dependencies go against ⊑ is when hoisting a write in the coproduct case. However, in the same construction we always preserve the dependencies coming from the different branches of the structure which are, by inductive hypothesis, always agreeing with program order.

9.1   MRD-C11 is **DRF-SC**

We show that MRD-C11 validates the DRF-SC theorem of the C++ standard [13, §6.8.2.1 paragraph 20].

Theorem 4 (MRD-C11 is **DRF-SC**). *For a program whose atomic accesses are all SC-ordered, if there are no SC-consistent executions with a race over non-atomics, then the outcomes of P under* MRD-C11 *coincide with those under SC.*

Sketch proof. In the absence of races and relaxed atomics, the no-thin-air guarantee of RC11 is made redundant by the guarantee of happens-before acyclicity shared by RC11 and MRD-C11. The result follows from this observation, lemma 3 and Theorem 4 from Lahav et al. [18].

10   On the Promising Semantics and WEAKESTMO

In this section we present examples that differentiate the Promising Semantics and WEAKESTMO from our MRD and MRD-C11 models.

First, we show that MRD correctly forbids the out-of-thin-air behaviour in the litmus test Coh-CYC from Chakraborty and Vafeiadis [11]. The test, given below, differentiates Promising and WEAKESTMO: only the latter avoids the outcome $r_1 = 3$, $r_2 = 2$ and $r_3 = 1$.

$$
\begin{array}{c|c}
\begin{array}{l}
\texttt{x := 2;} \\
\texttt{r}_1 \texttt{ := x; \textbackslash\textbackslash 3} \\
\texttt{if}(\texttt{r}_1\texttt{!= 2})\{\texttt{y := 1}\}
\end{array}
&
\begin{array}{l}
\texttt{x := 1;} \\
\texttt{r}_2 \texttt{ := x; \textbackslash\textbackslash 2} \\
\texttt{r}_3 \texttt{ := y; \textbackslash\textbackslash 1} \\
\texttt{if}(\texttt{r}_3\texttt{!= 0})\{\texttt{x := 3}\}
\end{array}
\end{array}
$$

MRD correctly forbids this outcome: it identifies a dependency on the left-hand thread from the read of 3 from x to the write y := 1, and on the right-hand thread from the read of 1 from y to the write x := 3. The desired outcome then has a cycle in dependency and reads-from, and it is forbidden.

Chakraborty and Vafeiadis ascribe the behaviour to "a violation of coherence or a circular dependency", and include specific machinery to WEAKESTMO that checks for global coherence violations at each step of program execution. These global checks forbid the unwanted outcome.

The Promising Semantics, on the other hand, can make promises that are not sensitive to coherence order, and therefore allows the above outcome erroneously.

In Coh-CYC, enforcing coherence ordering at each step in WEAKESTMO was enough to forbid the thin-air behaviour, but it is not adequate in all cases. The example below features an outcome that Promising and WEAKESTMO allow, and that MRD-C11 and MRD forbid. It demonstrates that cycles in dependency can arise without violating coherence in WEAKESTMO.

$$
\texttt{z := 1} \quad \| \quad \texttt{y := x} \quad \| \quad \texttt{if}(\texttt{z!= 0})\{\texttt{x := 1}\}\{\texttt{r}_0 \texttt{ := y; x := r}_0\texttt{; a := r}_0\}
$$

The program is an adaptation[6] of a Java test, where the the unwanted outcome represents a violation of type safety [20]. Observing the thin-air behaviour where a = 1 in the adaptation above is the analogue of the unwanted outcome in the original test. If in the end a = 1, then the second branch of the conditional in the rightmost thread must execute. It contains a read of 1 from y, and a dependent write of x := 1. On the middle thread there is a read of 1 from x, and a dependent write of y := 1. These dependencies form the archetypal thin-air shape in the execution where a = 1. MRD correctly identifies these dependencies and the outcome is prohibited due to its cycle in reads-from and dependency.

The a = 1 outcome is allowed in the Promising Semantics: a promise can be validated against the write of x := 1 in the true branch of the righthand thread, and later switched to a validation with x := r_0 from the false branch, ignoring the dependency on the read of y.

In the previous example, Coh-CYC, a stepwise global coherence check caused WEAKESTMO to forbid the unwanted behaviour allowed by Promising, but that machinery does not apply here. WEAKESTMO allows the unwanted outcome, and we conjecture that this deficiency stems from the structure of the model. Dependencies are not represented as a relation at the level of the global axiomatic constraint, so one cannot check that they are consistent with the dynamic execution of memory, as represented by the other relations. Adopting a coherence check in the stepwise generation of the event structure mitigates this concern for Coh-CYC, but not for the test above.

In contrast, MRD does represent dependencies as a relation, allowing us to check consistency with the RF relation here. The axiom that requires acyclicity of (DP ∪ RF) forbids the unwanted outcome, as desired.

11   Evaluating MRD-C11 with the MRD-er tool

MRD-C11 is the first weak memory model to solve the thin-air problem for C++ atomics that has a tool for automatically evaluating litmus tests. Our tool, MRD-er, evaluates litmus tests under the base model, RC11 augmented with MRD, and IMM augmented with MRD. It has been used to check the result of every litmus test in this paper, together with many tests from the literature, including the Java Causality Test cases [7,11,15,16,18,25,26,27].

When evaluating whether a particular execution is allowed for a given test, a model that solves the thin-air problem must take other executions of the program into account. For example, the semantics of Pichon-Pharabod et al., having explored one execution path, may ultimately backtrack [25]. Jeffrey and Riely phrase their semantics as a two player game where at each turn, the player explores all forward executions of the program [15]. At each operational step, the Promising Semantics [16] has to run forwards in a limited local way to validate

---

[6] James Riely, Alan Jeffrey and Radha Jagadeesan provided the precise example presented here [28]. It is based on Fig. 8 of Lochbihler [20], and its problematic execution under Promising was confirmed with the authors of Promising.

that promised writes will be reached. The invisible events of Chakraborty et al. [11] are used to similar effect.

In MRD-C11, it is the calculation of justification that draws in information from other executions. This mechanism is localised, it avoids making choices about the execution that prune behaviours, and it does not require backtracking. MRD-C11 acts in a "bottom-up" fashion, and modularity ensures that justifications drawn from the continuation need not be recalculated. These properties have supported the development of MRD-er: automation of the model requires only a single pass across the program text to construct the denotation.

12   Discussion

Four recent papers have presented models that forbid thin-air values and permit previously challenging compiler optimisations. The key insight from these papers is that it is necessary to consider multiple program executions simultaneously. To do this, three of the four [15,25,11] use event structures, while the Promising Semantics [16] is a small-step operational semantics that explores future traces in order to take a step.

Although the Promising Semantics [16] is quite different from MRD, its mechanism for promising focuses on future writes, and MRD has parallels in its calculation of independent writes. Note also that both Promising's certification mechanism and MRD's lifting are thread-local.

The previous event-structure-based models are superficially similar to MRD, but all have a fundamentally different approach from ours: Pichon-Pharabod and Sewell [25] use event structures as the state of a rewriting system; Jeffrey and Riely [14,15] build whole-program event structures and then use a global mechanism to determine which executions are allowed; and Chakraborty et al. [11] transform an event structure using an operational semantics. In contrast, we follow a more traditional approach [33] where our event structures are used as the co-domain of a denotational semantics. Further, Jeffrey and Riely [14,15] and Pichon-Pharabod and Sewell [25] do not cover a significant subset set of C++ relaxed concurrency primitives.

MRD does not suffer from known problems with existing models. As noted by Kang et al. [16], the Pichon-Pharabod and Sewell model produces behaviour incompatible with the ARM architecture. The Jeffrey and Riely model forbids the reordering of independent reads, as demonstrated by Java Causality Test 7 (see Section 6.2). The Promising semantics allows the cyclic coherence ordering of the problematic Coh-CYC example [11]. WEAKESTMO allows the thin-air outcome in the Java-inspired test of Section 10. In all four cases MRD provides the correct behaviour.

MRD is also highly compatible with the existing C++ standard text. The DP relation generated by MRD can be used directly in the axiomatic model to forbid thin-air behaviour. We are working on standards text with the ISO C++ committee based on this work, and have a current working paper with them [5].

The notion in C++ that data-race free programs should not exhibit observable weak behaviours goes back to Adve and Hill [1], and formed the basis of the original proposal for C++ [10]. This was formalised by Batty et al. [8] and adopted into the ISO standard. Despite the pervasiveness of DRF-SC theorems for weak memory models, these have remained whole-program theorems that do not support breaking a program into separate DRF and racy components. Our DRF theorem for our denotational model demonstrates a limited form of modularity that merits further exploration.

Other denotational approaches to relaxed concurrency have not tackled the thin-air problem. Dodds et al. [12] build a denotational model based on an axiomatic model similar to C++. It forms the basis of a sound refinement relation and is used to validate data-structures and optimisations. Their context language is too restrictive to support a compositional semantics, and their compromise to disallow thin-air executions forbids important optimisations. Kavanagh and Brookes [17] provide a denotational account of TSO concurrency, but their model is based on pomsets and suffers from the same limitation as axiomatic models [7]: it cannot be made to recognise false dependencies.

Future Work. We envisage a generalised theorem that would, on augmentation with MRD, extend an axiomatic DRF-SC proof to a proof that applies to the augmented model.

The ISO have struggled to define memory_order::consume [13]. It is intended to provide ordering through dependencies that the compiler will not optimise away. The semantic dependency relation calculated by MRD identifies just these dependencies, and may support a better definition.

Finally, where we have used a global semantics to provide a full C++ model, it would be interesting to extend the denotational semantics to also cover all of C++, thereby allowing reasoning about C++ code in isolation from its context.

13   Conclusions

We have used the relatively recent insight that to avoid thin-air problems, a semantics should consider some information about what might happen in other program executions. We codify that into a modular notation of justification, leading to a semantic notion of independent writes, and finally of dependency (DP). We demonstrate the effectiveness of these concepts in three ways. One, we define a denotational semantics for a weak memory model, show it supports DRF-SC, and build a compositional refinement relation strong enough to verify difficult optimisations. Two, we show how to use DP with other axiomatic models, supporting the first optimal implementability proof for a thin-air solution via IMM , and showing how to repair the ISO C++ model. Three, we build a tool for executing litmus tests allowing us to check a large number of examples.

References

1. Adve, S.V., Hill, M.D.: Weak ordering — a new definition. In: ISCA (1990)
2. Alglave, J., Maranget, L., McKenney, P.E., Parri, A., Stern, A.: Frightening small children and disconcerting grown-ups: Concurrency in the linux kernel. In: ASPLOS (2018)
3. Alglave, J., Maranget, L., Tautschnig, M.: Herding cats: modelling, simulation, testing, and data-mining for weak memory. In: PLDI (2014)
4. Batty, M.: The C11 and C++11 Concurrency Model. Ph.D. thesis, University of Cambridge, UK (2015)
5. Batty, M., Cooksey, S., Owens, S., Paradis, A., Paviotti, M., Wright, D.: Modular Relaxed Dependencies: A new approach to the Out-Of-Thin-Air Problem (2019), http://www.open-std.org/jtc1/sc22/wg21/docs/papers/2019/p1780r0.html
6. Batty, M., Donaldson, A.F., Wickerson, J.: Overhauling SC atomics in C11 and OpenCL. In: POPL (2016)
7. Batty, M., Memarian, K., Nienhuis, K., Pichon-Pharabod, J., Sewell, P.: The problem of programming language concurrency semantics. In: ESOP (2015)
8. Batty, M., Owens, S., Sarkar, S., Sewell, P., Weber, T.: Mathematizing C++ concurrency. In: POPL (2011)
9. Benton, N., Hur, C.: Step-indexing: The good, the bad and the ugly. In: Modelling, Controlling and Reasoning About State, 29.08. - 03.09.2010 (2010)
10. Boehm, H.J., Adve, S.V.: Foundations of the C++ concurrency model. In: PLDI (2008)
11. Chakraborty, S., Vafeiadis, V.: Grounding thin-air reads with event structures. In: POPL (2019)
12. Dodds, M., Batty, M., Gotsman, A.: Compositional verification of compiler optimisations on relaxed memory. In: ESOP (2018)
13. ISO/IEC JTC 1/SC 22 Programming languages, their environments and system software interfaces: ISO/IEC 14882:2017 Programming languages — C++ (2017)
14. Jeffrey, A., Riely, J.: On thin air reads towards an event structures model of relaxed memory. In: LICS (2016)
15. Jeffrey, A., Riely, J.: On thin air reads: Towards an event structures model of relaxed memory. Logical Methods in Computer Science 15(1) (2019)
16. Kang, J., Hur, C.K., Lahav, O., Vafeiadis, V., Dreyer, D.: A promising semantics for relaxed-memory concurrency. In: POPL (2017)
17. Kavanagh, R., Brookes, S.: A denotational semantics for SPARC TSO. MFPS (2018)
18. Lahav, O., Vafeiadis, V., Kang, J., Hur, C., Dreyer, D.: Repairing sequential consistency in C/C++11. In: PLDI (2017)
19. Leroy, X., Grall, H.: Coinductive big-step operational semantics. Inf. Comput. (2009)
20. Lochbihler, A.: Making the Java memory model safe. ACM Trans. Program. Lang. Syst. (2013)
21. Manson, J., Pugh, W., Adve, S.V.: The Java Memory Model. In: POPL (2005)
22. McKenney, P.E., Jeffrey, A., Sezgin, A., Tye, T.: Out-of-Thin-Air Execution is Vacuous (2016), http://www.open-std.org/jtc1/sc22/wg21/docs/papers/2016/p0422r0.html
23. Michalis Kokologiannakis, Azalea Raad, V.V.: Model checking for weakly consistent libraries. In: PLDI (2019)

24. Owens, S., Myreen, M.O., Kumar, R., Tan, Y.K.: Functional big-step semantics. In: Programming Languages and Systems - 25th European Symposium on Programming, ESOP 2016, Held as Part of the European Joint Conferences on Theory and Practice of Software, ETAPS 2016, Eindhoven, The Netherlands, April 2-8, 2016, Proceedings (2016)
25. Pichon-Pharabod, J., Sewell, P.: A concurrency semantics for relaxed atomics that permits optimisation and avoids thin-air executions. In: POPL (2016)
26. Podkopaev, A., Lahav, O., Vafeiadis, V.: Bridging the gap between programming languages and hardware weak memory models. PACMPL (POPL) (2019)
27. Pugh, W.: Java causality tests. http://www.cs.umd.edu/~pugh/java/memoryModel/CausalityTestCases.html (2004), accessed: 2018-11-17
28. Riely, J., Jagadeesan, R., Jeffrey, A.: private correspondence (2020)
29. Ševčík, J.: Program transformations in weak memory models. Ph.D. thesis, University of Edinburgh, UK (2009)
30. Ševčík, J., Aspinall, D.: On validity of program transformations in the Java memory model. In: ECOOP (2008)
31. Streicher, T.: Domain-theoretic foundations of functional programming (01 2006)
32. Wickerson, J., Batty, M., Sorensen, T., Constantinides, G.A.: Automatically comparing memory consistency models. In: POPL (2017)
33. Winskel, G.: Event structures. In: Petri Nets: Central Models and Their Properties, Advances in Petri Nets 1986, Part II, Proceedings of an Advanced Course, Bad Honnef, 8.-19. September 1986 (1986)
34. Winskel, G.: An introduction to event structures (1989)

ARMv8-A system semantics: instruction fetch in relaxed architectures

Ben Simner[1], Shaked Flur[1]*, Christopher Pulte[1]*, Alasdair Armstrong[1], Jean Pichon-Pharabod[1], Luc Maranget[2], and Peter Sewell[1]

[1] University of Cambridge, UK
[2] INRIA Paris, France
* These authors contributed equally

Abstract. Computing relies on *architecture specifications* to decouple hardware and software development. Historically these have been prose documents, with all the problems that entails, but research over the last ten years has developed rigorous and executable-as-test-oracle specifications of mainstream architecture instruction sets and "user-mode" concurrency, clarifying architectures and bringing them into the scope of programming-language semantics and verification. However, the *system semantics*, of instruction-fetch and cache maintenance, exceptions and interrupts, and address translation, remains obscure, leaving us without a solid foundation for verification of security-critical systems software.

In this paper we establish a robust model for one aspect of system semantics: instruction fetch and cache maintenance for ARMv8-A. Systems code relies on executing instructions that were written by data writes, e.g. in program loading, dynamic linking, JIT compilation, debugging, and OS configuration, but hardware implementations are often highly optimised, e.g. with instruction caches, linefill buffers, out-of-order fetching, branch prediction, and instruction prefetching, which can affect programmer-observable behaviour. It is essential, both for programming and verification, to abstract from such microarchitectural details as much as possible, but no more. We explore the key architecture design questions with a series of examples, discussed in detail with senior Arm staff; capture the architectural intent in operational and axiomatic semantic models, extending previous work on "user-mode" concurrency; make these models executable as test oracles for small examples; and experimentally validate them against hardware behaviour (finding a bug in one hardware device). We thereby bring these subtle issues into the mathematical domain, clarifying the architecture and enabling future work on system software verification.

1   Introduction

Computing relies on the *architectural abstraction*: the specification of an envelope of allowed hardware behaviour that hardware implementations should lie within, and that software should assume. These interfaces, defined by hardware vendors and relatively stable over time, notionally decouple hardware and

© The Author(s) 2020
P. Müller (Ed.): ESOP 2020, LNCS 12075, pp. 626–655, 2020.
https://doi.org/10.1007/978-3-030-44914-8_23

software development; they are also, in principle, the foundation for software verification. In practice, however, industrial architectures have accumulated great complexity and subtlety: the ARMv8-A and Intel architecture reference manuals are now 7476 and 4922 pages [9,26], and hardware optimisations, including outof-order and speculative execution, result in surprising and poorly-understood programmer-observable behaviour. Architecture specifications have historically also been entirely informal, describing these complex envelopes of allowed behaviour solely in prose and pseudocode. This is problematic in many ways: do not serve as clear documentation, with the inevitable ambiguity and incompleteness of informal prose leaving major questions unanswered; without a specification that is executable as a test oracle (that can decide whether some observed behaviour is allowed or not), hardware validation relies on test suites that must be manually curated; without an architecturally-complete emulator (that can exhibit all allowed behaviour), it is very hard for software developers to "program to the specification" – they rely on test-and-debug development, and can only test above the hardware implementation(s) they have; and without a mathematically rigorous semantics, formal verification of hardware or software is impossible.

Over the last 10 years, much has been done to put architecture specifications on a more rigorous footing, so that a single specification can serve all those purposes. There are three main problems, two of which are now largely solved.

The first is the instruction-set architecture (ISA): the specification of the sequential behaviour of individual instructions. This is chiefly a problem of scale: modern industrial architectures such as Arm or x86 have large instruction sets, and each instruction involves many details, including its behaviour at different privilege levels, virtual-to-physical address translation, and so on – a single Arm instruction might involve hundreds of auxiliary functions. Recent work by Reid et al. within Arm [40,41,42] transitioned their internal ISA description into a mechanised form, used both for documentation and testing, and with him we automatically translated this into publicly available Sail definitions and thence into theorem-prover definitions [11,10]. Other related work is in §7.

The second is the relaxed-memory concurrent behaviour of "user-mode" operations: memory writes and reads, and the mechanisms that architectures provide to enforce ordering and atomicity (dependencies, memory barriers, load-linked/store-conditional operations, etc.). In 2008, for ARMv7, IBM POWER, and x86, this was poorly understood, and the architects regarded even their own prose specifications as inscrutable. Now, following extensive work by many people [36,37,19,18,22,8,31,45,7,46,48,35,6,2,47,13,1], ARMv8-A has a well-defined and simplified model as part of its specification [9, B2.3], including a prose transcription of a mathematical model [15], and an equivalence proof between operational and axiomatic presentations [36,37]; RISC-V has adopted a similar model [52]; and IBM POWER and x86 have well-established de-facto-standard models. All of these are experimentally validated against hardware, and supported by tools for exhaustively running tests [17,4]. The combination of these models and the ISA semantics above is enough to let one reason about or model-check concurrent algorithms.

That leaves the third part of the problem: the "system" semantics, of instruction-fetch and cache maintenance, exceptions and interrupts, and address translation and TLB (translation lookaside buffer) maintenance. Just as for "user-mode" relaxed memory, these are all areas where microarchitectural optimisations can have surprising programmer-visible effects, especially in the concurrent context. The mechanisms are relied on by all code, but they are explicitly managed only by systems code, in just-in-time (JIT) compilers, dynamic loaders, operating-system (OS) kernels, and hypervisors. This is, of course, exactly the security-critical computing base, currently trusted but not trustworthy, that is especially in need of verification – which requires a precise and well-validated definition of the architectural abstraction. Previous work has scarcely touched on this: none of seL4 [27], CertiKOS [24,23], Komodo [16], or [25,12], address realistic architecture concurrency, and they use (at best) idealised models of the sequential systems architecture. The CakeML [51,28] and CompCert [29] verified compilers target only sequential user-mode ISA fragments.

In this paper we focus on one aspect of system semantics: instruction fetch and cache maintenance, for ARMv8-A. The ability to execute code that has previously been written to data memory is fundamental to computing: fine-grained self-modifying code is now rare, and (rightly) deprecated, but program loading, dynamic linking, JIT compilation, debugging, and OS configuration all rely on executing code from data writes. However, because these are relatively infrequent operations, hardware designers have been able to optimise by partially separating the instruction and data paths, e.g. with distinct instruction caching, which by default may not be coherent with data accesses. This can introduce programmer-visible behaviour analogous to that of user-mode relaxed-memory concurrency, and require specific additional synchronisation to correctly pick up code modifications. Exactly what these are is not entirely clear in the current ARMv8-A architecture text, just as pre-2018 user-mode concurrency was not.

Our main contribution is to clarify this situation, developing precise abstractions that bring the instruction-fetch part of ARMv8-A system behaviour into the domain of rigorous semantics. Arm have stated [private communication] that they intend to incorporate a version of this into their architecture. We aim thereby to enable future work on system software verification using the techniques of programming languages research: program analysis, model-checking, program logics, etc. We begin (§2) by recalling the informal architectural guarantees that Arm provide, and the ways in which real-world software systems such as Linux, JavaScript, and WebAssembly change instruction memory. Then:

(1) **We explore the fundamental phenomena and architecture design questions with a series of examples** (§3). We explore the interactions between instruction fetching, cache maintenance and the 'usual' relaxed memory stores and loads, showing that instruction fetches are more relaxed, and how even fundamental coherence guarantees for data memory do not apply to instruction fetches. Most of these questions arose during the development of our models, in detailed ongoing discussion with the Arm Chief Architect and other Arm staff. They include questions of several different kinds. Six are clear from

the Arm prose specification. Of the others: two are not implied by the prose but are natural choices; five involved substantive new choices by Arm that had not previously been considered and/or documented; for two, either choice could be reasonable, and Arm chose the simpler (and weaker) option; and for one, Arm were independently already strengthening the architecture to accommodate existing software.

(2) **We give an operational semantics for Arm instruction fetch and icache maintenance** (§4). This is in an abstract-microarchitectural style that supports an operational intuition for how hardware actually works, while abstracting from the mass of detail and the microarchitectural variation of actual hardware implementations. We do so by extending the Flat model [37] with simple abstractions of instruction caches and the coherent data cache network, in a way that captures the architectural intent, defining the entire envelope of behaviours that implementations should be allowed to exhibit.

(3) **We give a more concise presentation of the model in an axiomatic style** (§5), extending the "user-mode" axiomatic model from previous work [37,36,15,9], and intended to be functionally equivalent. We discuss how this too matches the architectural intent.

(4) **We validate all this** in two ways: by the extensive discussion with Arm staff mentioned above, and by experimental testing of hardware behaviour, on a selection of ARMv8-A cores designed by multiple vendors (§6). We run tests on hardware with a mild extension of the Litmus tool [5,7]. We make the operational model executable as a test oracle by integrating it into the RMEM tool and its web interface [17], introducing optimisations that make it possible to exhaustively execute the examples. We make the axiomatic model executable as a test oracle with a new tool that takes litmus tests and uses a Sail [11] definition of a fragment of the ARMv8-A ISA to generate SMT problems for the model. We then compare hardware and the two models for the handwritten tests (modulo two tests not supported by the axiomatic checker), compare hardware and the operational model on a suite of 1456 tests, automatically generated with an extension of the diy tool [3], and check the operational and axiomatic models against sets of previous non-ifetch tests. In all this data our models are equivalent to each other and consistent with hardware observations, except for one case where our testing uncovered a hardware bug on a Qualcomm device.

Finally, we discuss other related work (§7) and conclude (§8). We do all this for ARMv8-A, but other relaxed architectures, e.g. IBM POWER and RISC-V, face similar issues; our tests and tooling should enable corresponding work there.

The models are too large to include or explain in full here, so we focus on explaining the motivating examples, the main intuition and style of the operational model, in a prose rendering of its executable mathematics, and the definition of the axiomatic model. Appendices provide additional examples, a complete prose description of the operational model, and additional explanation of the axiomatic model. The complete executable mathematics version, the web-interface tool for running it, and our test results are at https: //www.cl.cam.ac.uk/~pes20/iflat/.

Caveats and Limitations Our executable models are integrated with a substantial fragment of the Sail ARMv8-A ISA (similar to that used for CakeML), but not yet with the full ISA model [11,40,41,42]; this is just a matter of additional engineering. We only handle the 64-bit AArch64 part of ARMv8-A, not AArch32. We do not handle the interaction between instruction fetch and mixed-size accesses, or other variants of the cache maintenance instructions, e.g. those used for interaction with DMA engines, and variants by set or way instead of by virtual address. Finally, the equivalence between our operational and axiomatic models is validated experimentally. A proof of this equivalence is essential in the long term, but would be a major work in itself: the complexity makes mechanisation essential, but the operational model (in all its scale and complexity) has not yet been subject to mechanised proof. Without instruction fetch, a non-mechanised proof was the main result of an entire PhD thesis [36], and we expect the addition of instruction fetch to require global changes to the argument.

2 Industry Practice and the Existing ARMv8-A Prose

Computer architecture relies on a host of sophisticated techniques, including buffering, caching, prediction, and pipelining, for performance. For the normal memory reads and writes of "user-mode" concurrency, the programmer-visible relaxed-memory effects largely arise from store buffering and from out-of-order and speculative pipeline behaviour, not from the cache hierarchy (though some IBM POWER phenomena do arise from the interconnect, and from late processing of cache invalidates). All major architectures provide a strong per-location guarantee of *coherence*: for each memory location, different threads cannot observe the writes to that location in different orders. This is implemented in hardware by coherent cache protocols, ensuring (roughly) that each cache line is writable by at most one hardware thread at a time, and by additional machinery restricting store buffer and pipeline behaviour. Then each architecture provides additional synchronisation mechanisms to let the programmer enforce ordering properties involving multiple locations.

At first sight, one might expect instruction fetches to act like other memory reads but, because writes to instruction memory are relatively rare, hardware designers have adopted different caching mechanisms. The Arm architecture carefully does not mandate exactly what these must be, to allow a wide range of possible hardware implementations, but, for example, a high-performance Arm processor might have per-core separate L1 instruction and data caches, above a unified per-core L2 cache and an L3 cache shared between cores. There may also be additional structures, e.g. per-core fetch queues, and caching of decoded micro-operations. This instruction caching is not necessarily coherent with data memory accesses: *"the architecture does not require the hardware to ensure coherency between instruction caches and memory"* [9, B2.4.4 (B2-114)]; instead, programmers must use explicit cache maintenance instructions. The documentation gives a particular sequence of these: *"If software requires coherency between instruction execution and memory, it must manage this coherency using Context*

synchronization events and cache maintenance instructions. The following code
sequence can be used to allow a processing element (PE) to execute code that the
same PE has written."

```
; Coherency example for data and instruction accesses [...]
; Enter this code with <Wt> containing a new 32-bit instruction,
; to be held in Cacheable space at a location pointed to by Xn.
STR Wt, [Xn]; Store new instruction
DC CVAU, Xn ; Clean data cache by virtual address (VA) to PoU
DSB ISH     ; Ensure visibility of the data cleaned from cache
IC IVAU, Xn ; Invalidate instruction cache by VA to PoU
DSB ISH     ; Ensure completion of the invalidations
ISB         ; Synchronize the fetched instruction stream
```

At first sight, this may be entirely mysterious. The remainder of the paper establishes precise semantics for each instruction, explaining why each is required, but as a rough intuition:

1. The DC CVAU,Xn cleans this core's data cache for address Xn, pushing the new write far enough down the hierarchy for an instruction fetch that misses in the instruction cache to be guaranteed to see the new value. This point is the *Point of Unification* (PoU) and is usually the point where the instruction and data caches become unified (L2 for most modern devices).

2. The DSB ISH waits for the clean to have happened before letting the later instructions execute (without this, the sequence itself can execute out-of-order, and the clean might not have pushed the write down far enough before the instruction cache is updated). The ISH makes this specific to the *Inner Shareable Domain*: the processor itself, not the system-on-chip. We do not model shareability domains in this paper, so this is equivalent to a DSB SY.

3. The IC IVAU,Xn invalidates any entry for that address in the instruction caches for all cores, forcing any future fetch to miss in the instruction cache, and instead read the new value from the data memory hierarchy; it also touches some fetch queue machinery.

4. The second DSB ISH ensures the invalidation completes.

5. The final ISB flushes this core's pipeline, forcing a re-fetch of all program-order-later instructions.

Some hardware implementations provide extra guarantees, rendering the DC or IC instructions unnecessary. Arm allow software to discover this in an architectural way, by reading the CTR_EL0 register's DIC and IDC bits. Our modelling handles this, but for brevity we only discuss the weakest case, with CTR_EL0.DIC=CTR_EL0.IDC=0, that requires full cache maintenance.

Arm make clear that instructions can be prefetched (perhaps speculatively): *"How far ahead of the current point of execution instructions are fetched from is IMPLEMENTATION DEFINED. Such prefetching can be either a fixed or a dynamically varying number of instructions, and can follow any or all possible future execution paths. For all types of memory, the PE might have fetched the instructions from memory at any time since the last Context synchronization event on that PE."*

Concurrent modification and instruction fetch require the same sequence, with an ISB on each thread that executes the new instructions, and the rest of the sequence on the modifying thread [9, B2.2.5 (B2-94)]. Concurrent modification without synchronisation is restricted to particular instructions (B (branch), BL (branch-and-link), BRK (break), SMC, HVC, SVC (secure monitor, hypervisor, and supervisor calls), ISB, and NOP), otherwise there could be *constrained unpredictable behaviour*: *"any behavior that can be achieved by executing any sequence of instructions that can be executed from the same Exception level"*. Concurrent modification of conditional branches is allowed but can result in the old condition with the new target address or vice versa.

All this gives some guidance for programmers, but it leaves the exact semantics of instruction fetch and those cache maintenance instructions unclear, and in practice software typically does not use the above sequence verbatim. For example, it may synchronise a range of addresses at once, looping the DC and IC parts, or the final ISB may be subsumed by instruction synchronisation from exception entry or return. Linux has many places where it modifies code at runtime: in boot-time patching of *alternatives*, modifying kernel code to specialise it to the particular hardware being run on; when the kernel loads code (e.g. when the user calls dl_open); and in the ptrace system call, used e.g. by the GDB debugger to patch arbitrary instructions with breakpoints at runtime. In Google's *Chrome* web browser, its WebAssembly and JavaScript just-in-time (JIT) compilers are required to both write new code during execution and modify existing code at runtime. In JavaScript, this modification happens inside a single thread and so is quite straightforward. The WebAssembly case is more complex, as one thread is modifying the code of another. A software thread can also be moved (by the OS or hypervisor) from one hardware thread to another, perhaps while it is in the middle of some instruction cache maintenance. Moreover, for security reasoning, we have to be able to bound the possible behaviour of arbitrary code.

All this means that we cannot treat the above sequence as a whole, as an opaque black box. Instead, we need a precise semantics for each individual instruction, but the existing prose documentation does not provide that.

The problem we face is to give such a semantics, that correctly defines behaviour in arbitrary concurrent contexts, that captures the Arm architectural intent, that is strong enough for software, and that abstracts from the variety of hardware implementations (e.g. with differing cache structures) that the architecture intends to allow – but which programmers should not have to think about.

3 Instruction Fetch Phenomena and Examples

We now describe the main instruction-fetch phenomena and architecture design questions for ARMv8-A, illustrated by handwritten litmus tests, to guide the following model design.

3.1   Instruction-Fetch Atomicity

The first point, as mentioned in §2, is that concurrent modification and fetch is only permitted if the original and modified instructions are in a particular set: various branches, supervisor/hypervisor/secure-monitor calls, the ISB instruction synchronisation barrier, and NOP. Otherwise, the architecture permits *constrained unpredictable* behaviour, meaning that the resulting machine state could be anything that would be reachable by arbitrary instructions at the same exception level. The following W+F test illustrates this.

W+F	AArch64
Initial state: 0:W0="SUB X0,X0,#1", 0:X1=l	
Thread 0	**Thread 1**
STR W0,[X1] // modify Thread 1 at l	l: ADD X0,X0,#1 // initial code
Allowed: constrained-unpredictable final state	

In this test Thread 0 performs a memory store (with the STR instruction) to the code that Thread 1 is executing; overwriting the ADD X0,X0,#1 instruction with the 32-bit encoding of the SUB X0,X0,#1 instruction. If the fetch were atomic, the outcome of this test would be the result of executing either the ADD or the SUB instruction, but, since at least one of those is not in the set of the 8 atomically-fetchable instructions given previously, Thread 1 has constrained-unpredictable behaviour and the final state is very loosely constrained. Note, however, that this is nonetheless much stronger than the C/C++ whole-program undefined behaviour in the presence of a data race: unlike C/C++, a hardware architecture has to define a useful envelope of behaviour for arbitrary code, to provide guarantees for the rest of the system when one user thread has a race.

Conditional Branches For conditional branches, the Arm architecture provides a specific non-single-copy-atomic fetch guarantee: the execution will be consistent with either the old or new target, and either the old or new condition.

For example, this W+F+branches test can overwrite a B.EQ g with a B.NE h, and end up executing B.NE g or B.EQ h instead of one of those. Our future examples will only modify NOPs and unconditional branch instructions.

W+F+branches	AArch64
Initial state: 0:W0="B.NE h", 0:X1=l	
Thread 0	**Thread 1**
STR W0,[X1]	l: B.EQ g
Allowed: execute "B.NE g"	

3.2   Coherence

Data writes and reads are coherent, in Arm and in other major architectures: in any execution, for each address, the reads of each hardware thread must see a subsequence of the total *coherence order* of all writes to that address. The plain-data CoRR test [46] illustrates one case of this: it is forbidden for a thread to read a new write of x and then the initial state for x. However, instruction fetches are not necessarily coherent: one instruction fetch may be inconsistent with a program-order-previous fetch, and the data and instruction streams can become out-of-sync with each other. We explore three kinds of coherence:

- Instruction-to-Instruction Coherence: whether fetches of the same location must observe writes to the same location coherently.
- Data-to-Instruction Coherence: whether fetches and then reads to the same location must observe writes to the same location coherently.
- Instruction-to-Data Coherence: whether reads and then fetches of the same location must observe writes to the same location coherently.

Instruction-to-Instruction Coherence Arm explicitly do not guarantee any consistency between fetches of the same location: fetching an instruction does not mean that a later fetch of that location will not see an older instruction [9, B2.4.4]. This is illustrated by CoFF, like CoRR but with fetches instead of reads.

CoFF			AArch64
Initial state: 0:W0="B l1", 0:X1=f			
Thread 0	**Thread 1**	**Common**	
STR W0,[X1] //a	BL f	f: B l0	
	MOV X0,X10	l1: MOV X10,#2	
	BL f	RET	
	MOV X1,X10	l0: MOV X10,#1	
		RET	
Allowed: 1:X0=2, 1:X1=1			

Thread 0 → Thread 1 diagram:
a:write f=B l1 ──irf──▶ b:fetch f=B l1
                                │ fpo
                                ▼
             ──irf──▶ c:fetch f=B l0

Here Thread 1 makes two calls to address f (BL is branch-and-link), while Thread 0 overwrites the instruction at that address. The interesting potential execution is that in which the first call to f fetches and executes the newly-written B l1, but the second call fetches and executes the original B l0. We can view such executions as graphs, similar to previous axiomatic-model candidate executions but with new fetch events, one per instruction, and new edges. As usual, we use po and rf edges for the program-order and reads-from relations, together with:

- fe (fetch-to-execute), which relates the fetch event of an instruction to all the execution events (memory writes, reads or barriers) of the instruction;
- irf (instruction-read-from), relating a write to all fetches that read from it (analogous to reads-from, rf); and
- fpo (fetch-program-order), relating fetches of instructions that are in program order (analogous to program order, po).

Edges from the initial state are drawn from a small circle. Since we do not modify the code of most locations, we usually omit the fetch events for those instructions, showing only a subgraph of the interesting events, e.g. as on the right above. For Arm, this execution is both architecturally allowed and experimentally observed.

Here, and in future tests, we assume some common code consisting of a function at address f which always has the same shape: a branch that might be overwritten, which selects a block that writes a value to register X10 before returning. This is sometimes duplicated at different addresses (f1, f2, ...) or extended to g, with three cases. We sometimes elide the common code.

Data-to-Instruction Coherence Fetching from a particular write does imply that program-order-later reads from the same address will see that write (or a coherence successor thereof). This is a *data-to-instruction* coherence property, illustrated by CoFR below. Here Thread 1 fetches the newly-written B l1 at f and then, when reading from f with its LDR load instruction, cannot read the original B l0 instruction (it can only read the new B l1).

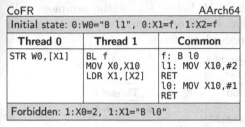

CoFR   AArch64

Initial state: 0:W0="B l1", 0:X1=f, 1:X2=f		
Thread 0	**Thread 1**	**Common**
STR W0,[X1]	BL f	f: B l0
	MOV X0,X10	l1: MOV X10,#2
	LDR X1,[X2]	RET
		l0: MOV X10,#1
		RET
Forbidden: 1:X0=2, 1:X1="B l0"		

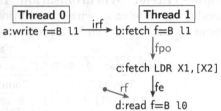

This is not clear in the existing prose specification, but the architectural intent that emerged during discussion with Arm is that the given execution should be forbidden, reflecting microarchitectural choices that (1) instructions decode in order, so the fetch b must occur before the read d, and (2) fetches that miss in the instruction cache must read from data storage, so the instruction cache cannot be ahead of the available data. This ensures that fetching from a write means that all threads are now guaranteed to read from that write (or another coherence-after it).

Instruction-to-Data Coherence In the other direction, reading from a particular write to some location does *not* imply that later fetches of that location will see that write (or a coherence successor), as in the following CoRF+ctrl-isb.

CoRF+ctrl-isb   AArch64

Initial state: 0:W0="B l1", 0:X1=f, 1:X2=f		
Thread 0	**Thread 1**	**Common**
STR W0,[X1]	LDR X0,[X2]	f: B l0
	CBNZ X0,l	l1: MOV X10,#2
	l: ISB	RET
	BL f	l0: MOV X10,#1
	MOV X1,X10	RET
Allowed: 1:X0="B l1", 1:X1=1		

Here Thread 1 has a control dependency and an instruction synchronisation barrier (the CBNZ conditional branch, dependent on the value read by its LDR load, and ISB), abbreviated to ctrl+isb, between its load and the fetch from f. If the latter were a data load, this would ensure the two loads are satisfied in order. This is not explicit in the existing prose, but it is what one would expect, and it is observed in practice. Microarchitecturally, it is easily explained by an out-of-date entry for f in the instruction cache of Thread 1: if Thread 1 had previously fetched f (perhaps speculatively), and that instruction cache entry has not been evicted or explicitly invalidated since, then this fetch of f will simply read the old value from the instruction cache without going out to data memory. The ISB ensures that f is freshly fetched, but does not ensure that Thread 1's instruction cache is up-to-date with respect to data memory.

3.3 Instruction Synchronisation

Instruction fetches satisfy few guarantees, so explicit synchronisation must be performed when modifying the instruction stream.

Same-Thread Synchronisation Test SM below shows the simplest self-modifying code case: without additional synchronisation, a write to program memory can be ignored by a program-order-later fetch.

SM		AArch64
Initial state: 0:W0="B l1", 0:X1=f		
Thread 0	**Common**	

STR W0,[X1] // a
BL f
MOV X0,X10
	f: B l0
	l1: MOV X10,#2
	    RET
	l0: MOV X10,#1
	    RET	

Allowed: 1:X0=1		

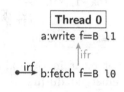

In this execution, the fetch b, fetching the instruction at f, fetches a value from a write coherence-before a, even though b is the fetch of an instruction program-order after a. We illustrate this with an *instruction from-reads* (ifr) edge. This is a derived relation, analogous to the usual *from-reads* (fr) relation, that relates each fetch to all writes that are coherence-after the write it read from; it is defined as ifr = irf^{-1};co. If the fetch were a data read, this would be a forbidden coherence shape (COWR). As it is, it is architecturally allowed, as described explicitly by Arm [9, B2.4.4], and it is experimentally observed on all devices we have tested. Microarchitecturally, this too is simply due to fetches from old instruction cache entries.

Cache Maintenance As we saw in §2, the Arm architecture provides cache maintenance instructions to synchronise the instruction and data streams: the DC data-cache clean and IC instruction-cache invalidate instructions. To forbid the relaxed outcome of SM, by forcing a fetch of the modified code, the specified sequence of cache maintenance instructions must be inserted, with an ISB.

SM+cachesync-isb	AArch64
Initial state: 0:W0="B l1", 0:X1=f	
Thread 0	
STR W0,[X1] //overwrite f with branch **DC** CVAU,X1 //clean data cache DSB ISH **IC** IVAU,X1 //invalidate instruction cache DSB ISH **ISB** //flush pipeline BL f MOV X0,X10	
Forbidden: 1:X0=1	

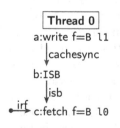

Now the outcome is forbidden. The cache synchronisation sequence DC CVAU; DSB ISH; IC IVAU; DSB ISH (which we abbreviate to a single cachesync edge) ensures that by the time the ISB executes, the instruction and data memory have been made coherent with each other for f. The ISB then ensures the final fetch of f is ordered after this sequence. The microarchitectural intuition for this was in §2; our §4 operational model will describe the semantics of each instruction.

Cross-Thread Synchronisation We now consider modifying code that can be fetched by other threads, using variants of the standard message-passing shape MP. That checks whether two writes (to different locations) on one thread can be seen out-of-order by two reads on another thread; here we replace one or both of those reads by fetches, and ask what synchronisation is required to ensure that the relaxed outcome is forbidden. Consider first an MP variant where the first write is of a new instruction, and the second is just a simple data memory flag:

MP.RF+dmb+ctrl-isb	AArch64
Initial state: 0:W0="B l1", 0:X1=f, 0:X2=1, 0:X3=x, 1:X2=x, [x]=0	

Thread 0	Thread 1
STR W0,[X1]	LDR X0,[X2]
DMB ISH	CBNZ X0,l
STR X2,[X3]	l: ISB
	BL f
	MOV X1,X10

Allowed: 1:X0=1, 1:X1=1

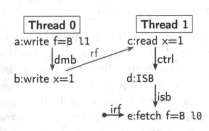

This test includes sufficient synchronisation on each thread to enforce thread-local ordering of data accesses: the DMB in Thread 0 ensures the writes a and b propagate to memory in program order, and the control-dependency into an ISB on Thread 1 ensures the read c and the fetch e happen in program order. However, as we saw in §2, this is not enough to synchronise concurrent modification and execution of code in ARMv8-A. Thread 0 needs the entire cache synchronization sequence (giving test MP.RF+cachesync+ctrl-isb, not shown), not just a DMB, to forbid this outcome.

Another variant of this MP-shape test where the message passing itself is done using modification of code gives a much stronger guarantee, as can be seen from the following MP.FR+dmb+fpo-fe test. This is not clear from the

MP.FR+dmb+fpo-fe	AArch64
Initial state: 0:X0=1, 0:X1=x, 1:X2=x, [x]=0, 0:W2="B l1", 0:X3=f	

Thread 0	Thread 1
STR X0,[X1]	BL f
DMB ISH	MOV X0,X10
STR W2,[X3]	LDR X1,[X2]

Forbidden: 1:X0=2, 1:X1=0

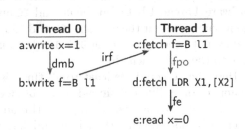

architecture manual, but this outcome is already forbidden with only the DMB.

This is for similar reasons to the above CoFR test: since Thread 1 fetched the updated value for f, we know that value must have reached at least the data caches (since that is where the instruction cache reads from) and therefore multi-copy atomicity guarantees that a normal load instruction will observe it.

The final variant of these MP-shaped tests has both Thread 0 writes be of new instructions. This idiom is very common in practice; it is currently how Chrome's WebAssembly JIT synchronises the modified thread with the new code.

MP.FF+dmb+fpo	AArch64
Initial state: 0:W0="B l1", 0:X1=f1, 0:W2="B l1", 0:X3=f2	

Thread 0	Thread 1
STR W0,[X1]	BL f2
DMB ISH	MOV X0,X10
STR W2,[X3]	BL f1
	MOV X1,X10

| Allowed: 1:X0=2, 1:X1=1 | |

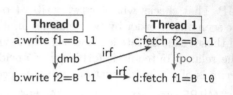

Without the full cachesync sequence on Thread 0, this is an allowed outcome. Interestingly, adding the cachesync sequence to Thread 0 (Test MP.FF+cachesync+fpo, not shown) is sufficient to make the outcome forbidden, without an ISB in Thread 1, as the cachesync sequence is intended to make it appear that fetches occur in program order. Microarchitecturally, that could be ensured in two ways: either by actually fetching in-order, or by making the IC instruction not only invalidate all the instruction caches (for this address) but also clean any core's pre-fetch buffer stale entries (for this address). Architecturally, this is not clear in the current prose, but, concurrent with this work, Arm were independently strengthening their definition to make it so.

Incremental Synchronisation The cache synchronisation sequence need not be contiguous, or even all in the same thread. So long as the sequence in its entirety has been performed by the time the fetch happens, then the instruction stream will have been made consistent with the data stream for that address.

This is demonstrated by the following test, where Thread 0 performs a write to f and then only a DC before synchronizing with Thread 1, which performs the IC, while Thread 2 observes the modified code. This can happen in practice when a software thread is migrated between hardware threads at runtime, by a hypervisor or OS. Thread 0 and Thread 1 may just represent the runtime scheduling of a single process, beginning execution on hardware Thread 0 but migrated to hardware Thread 1 between the DC and IC instructions. In the graph, the dcsync and icsync represent the DC;DSB ISH and DSB ISH;IC;DSB ISH combinations. The DC does not need a preceding DSB ISH because it is ordered w.r.t. the preceding store to the same cache line.

Here the IC gets broadcast to all threads [9, B2.2.5p3], and so the fact that it happens on a different thread to the DC does not affect the outcome. Similarly, if the DC were to happen on another thread first (to get the test MP.RF+[dc]-ic+ctrl-isb, not shown), then it would have the effect of ensuring consistency globally, for all threads.

SA2.F+dc+ic+ctrl-isb		AArch64
Initial state: 0:W0="B l1", 0:X1=f, 0:X2=1, 0:X3=x, [x]=0, 1:X4=f, 1:X1=x, 1:X2=1, 1:X3=y, [y]=0, 2:X2=y		
Thread 0	Thread 1	Thread 2
STR W0,[X1]	LDR X0,[X1]	LDR X0,[X2]
DC CVAU, X1	DSB ISH	CBZ X0,l
DSB ISH	IC IVAU, X4	l:ISB
STR X2,[X3]	DSB ISH	BL f
	STR X2,[X3]	MOV X1,X10
Forbidden: 1:X0=1, 1:X1=1		

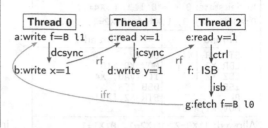

3.4 Multi-Copy Atomicity

For data accesses, the question of whether they are *multi-copy atomic* is a crucial one for relaxed architectures. IBM POWER, ARMv7, and pre-2018 ARMv8-A are/were non-multi-copy atomic: two writes to different addresses could become visible to distinct other threads in different orders. Post-2018 ARMv8-A and RISC-V are multi-copy atomic (or "other multi-copy-atomic" in Arm terminology) [37,36,9]: the programmer can assume there is a single shared memory, with all relaxed-memory effects due to thread-local out-of-order execution.

However, for fetches, due to the lack of any fetch atomicity guarantee for most instructions (§3.1), and the lack of coherent fetches for the others (§3.2), the question of multi-copy atomicity is not particularly interesting. Tests are either trivially forbidden (by data-to-instruction coherence) or are allowed but only the full cache synchronisation sequence provides enough guarantees to forbid it, and (§3.3) this ensures all cores will share the same consistent view of memory.

3.5 Strength of the IC Instruction

Multiple Points of Unification Cleaning the data cache, using the DC instruction, makes a write visible to instruction memory. It does this by pushing the write past the Point of Unification. However, there may be multiple Points of Unification: one for each core, where its own instruction and data memory become unified, and one for the entire system (or shareability domain) where all the caches unify. Fetching from a write implies that it has reached the closest PoU, but does not imply it has reached any others, even if the write originated from a distant core. Consider: Here Thread 0 modifies f, Thread 1 fetches the new value and performs just an IC and DSB, before signalling Thread 0 which also fetches f. That IC is not strong enough to ensure that the write is pulled into the instruction cache of Thread 0.

This is not clear in the existing prose, but the architectural intent is that it be allowed (i.e., that IC is weak in this respect). We have not so far observed it in practice. The write may have passed the Point of Unification for Thread 1, but not the shared Point of Unification for both threads. In other words, the write might reach Thread 1's instruction cache without being pushed down from Thread 0's data cache. Microarchitecturally this can be explained by *direct data*

SM.F+ic		AArch64
Initial state: 0:W0="B l1", 0:X4=f, 0:X3=x, [x]=0, 1:X4=f, 1:X2=1, 1:X3=x		
Thread 0	Thread 1	

STR W0,[X4]
LDR X2,[X3]
CBZ X2,l
l: **ISB**
BL f
MOV X1,X10
	BL f
	MOV X0,X10
	IC IVAU, X4
	DSB ISH
	STR X2,[X3]	

Allowed: 1:X0=2, 0:X2=1, 0:X1=1		

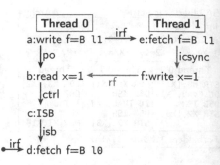

intervention (DDI), an optimisation allowing cache lines to be migrated directly from one thread's (data) cache to another. The line could be migrated from Thread 0 to Thread 1, then pushed past Thread 1's Point of Unification, making it visible to Thread 1's instruction memory without ever making it visible to Thread 0's own instruction memory. The lack of coherence between instruction and data caches would make this observable, even in multi-copy atomic machines.

Stale Fetches So far, we have only talked about fetching from two distinct writes. But theoretically there is no limit to how far back we can fetch from, with insufficient synchronization. The MP.RF+dmb+ctrl-isb test (§3.3) required the full cachesync sequence to forbid the given behaviour. Below we give a test, FOW, similar to that MP-shaped test but allowing many consumer threads to independently and simultaneously see different values in their instruction memory, even after invalidating their caches.

FOW			AArch64
Initial state: 0:W0="B l1", 0:X2=g, 0:W1="B l2", 0:X3=1, 0:X4=x, [x]=0, 1:X4=x, 2:X4=x			
Thread 0	Thread 1	Thread 2	Common

STR W0,[X2]
STR W1,[X2]
DSB ISH
IC IVAU, X2
DSB ISH
STR X3,[X4]
	LDR X0, [X4]
	CBNZ X0, la
	la: **ISB**
	BL g
	MOV X1,X10
		LDR X0, [X4]
		CBNZ X0, lb
		lb: **ISB**
		BL g
		MOV X1,X10
			g: B l0
			l2: MOV X10, #3
			RET
			l1: MOV X10, #2
			RET
			l0: MOV X10, #1
			RET

Allowed: 1:X0=1, 1:X1=2, 2:X0=1, 2:X1=1			

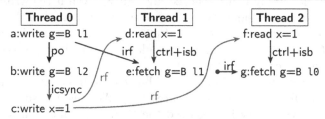

This is not clear in the existing architecture text. It is a case where the architecture design is not very constrained. On the one hand, it has not been observed, and it is thought unlikely that hardware will ever exhibit this behaviour: it would require keeping multiple writes in the coherent part of the data caches, rather than a single dirty line, which would require more complex cache coherence protocols. On the other hand, there does not seem to be any benefit to software from forbidding it. Arm therefore prefer the choice that gives a simpler and weaker model (here the two happen to coincide), to make it easier to understand and to provide more flexibility for future microarchitectural optimisations. We therefore design our models to allow the above behaviour.

3.6 Strength of the DC Instruction

Instruction Cache depth Test CoFF (§3.2) showed that fetches can see "old" writes. In principle, there is no limit to the depth of the instruction-cache hierarchy: there could be many values for a single location cached in the instruction memory for each core, even if the data cache has been cleaned. The test below illustrates this, with Thread 1 able to see all three values for g.

MP.RF+dc+ctrl-isb-isb		AArch64
Initial state: 0:W0="B l1", 0:X2=g, 0:W1="B l2", 0:X3=1, 0:X4=x, [x]=0, 1:X4=x		
Thread 0	**Thread 1**	**Common**

STR W0,[X2]
STR W1,[X2]
DSB ISH
DC CVAU,X2
DSB ISH
STR X3,[X4]
	LDR X0, [X4]
	CBNZ X0, l
	l:ISB
	BL g
	MOV X1,X10
	ISB
	BL g
	MOV X2,X10
	ISB
	BL g
	MOV X3,X10
		g: B l0
		l2:MOV X10,#3
		RET
		l1:MOV X10,#2
		RET
		l0:MOV X10,#1
		RET

Allowed: 1:X0=1, 1:X1=3, 1:X2=2, 1:X3=1		

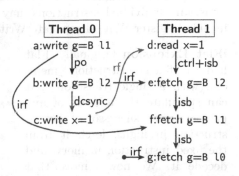

This is similar to the preceding FOW case: it is thought unlikely that hardware will exhibit this in practice, but the desire for the simpler and weaker option means the architectural intent is to allow it, and we follow that in our models.

4 An Operational Semantics for Instruction Fetch

Previous work on operational models for IBM POWER and Arm "user-mode" concurrency [46,45,22,18,19,37] has shown, surprisingly, that as far as programmer-visible behaviour is concerned, one can abstract from almost all hardware implementation details of data memory (store queues, the cache hierarchy, the cache protocol, etc.). For ARMv8-A, following their 2018 shift to a multicopy-atomic architecture, one can do so completely: the *Flat* model of [37] has a shared flat memory, with a per-thread out-of-order thread subsystem, modelling pipeline effects, responsible for all observable relaxed behaviour. For instruction-fetch, it is no longer possible to abstract completely from the data and instruction cache hierarchy, but we can still abstract from much of it.

The Flat Model is a small-step operational semantics for multi-copy atomic ARMv8-A, including the relaxed behaviours of loads and stores [37]. Its states are

abstract machine states consisting of a tree of instructions for each thread, and a flat memory subsystem shared by all threads. Each instruction in each thread corresponds to a sequence of transitions, with some guards and a potential effect on the shared memory state. The Flat model is made executable in our RMEM tool, which can exhaustively interleave transitions to enumerate all the possible behaviours. The tree of instructions for each thread models out-of-order and speculative execution explicitly. Below we show an example for a thread that is executing 10 instruction instances.
Some (grey) are finished, no longer subject to restart; others (pink) have run some but perhaps not all of their instruction semantics; in- 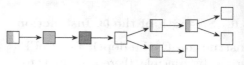 structions are not necessarily atomic. Those with multiple children are branch instructions with multiple potential successors speculated simultaneously.

For each state, the model defines the set of allowed transitions, each of which steps to a new machine state. Transitions correspond to steps of single instructions, and individual instructions may give rise to many. Example transitions include Register Write, Propagate Write to Memory, etc.

iFlat Extension Originally, Flat had a fixed instruction memory, with a single transition that can speculate the address of any program-order successor of any instruction in flight, fetch it from the fixed instruction memory, and decode it. We now remove that fixed instruction memory, so that instructions can be fetched from data writes, and add the additional structures as shown on the right. These are all of unbounded size, as is appropriate for an architecture definition.

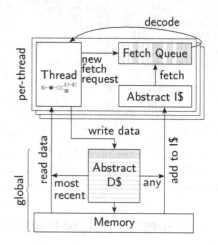

Fetch Queues (per-thread) These are ordered buffers of pre-fetched entries, waiting to be decoded and begin execution. Entries are either a fetched 32-bit opcode, or an unfetched request. The fetch queues allow the model to speculate and pre-fetch many instructions ahead of where the thread is currently executing. The model's fetch queues abstract from multiple real-hardware structures: instruction queues, line-fill buffers, loop buffers, and slots objects. We keep a close relation to this underlying microarchitecture by allowing out-of-order fetches, but we believe this is not experimentally observable on real hardware.

Abstract Instruction Cches (per-thread) These are just sets of writes. When the fetch queue requests a new entry, it gets satisfied from the instruction cache, either immediately (a *hit*) or at some later point in time (a *miss*). The nstruction cache can contain many possible writes for each location (§3.6), and t can be spontaneously updated with new writes in the system at any time ([9, §2.4.4]). To manage IC instructions, each thread keeps a list of addresses yet to be invalidated by in-flight ICs.

Data Cache (global) Above the single shared flat memory for the entire system, which sufficed for the multi-copy-atomic ARMv8-A data memory, we insert a shared buffer which is just a list of writes; abstracting from the many possible coherent data cache hierarchies. Data reads must be coherent, reading from the most recent write to the same address in the buffer, but instruction fetches are allowed to read from any such write in the buffer (§3.2).

Transitions To accommodate instruction fetch and cache maintenance, we introduce new transitions: Fetch Request, Fetch Instruction, Fetch Instruction (Unpredictable), Fetch Instruction (B.cond), Decode Instruction, Begin IC, Propagate IC to Thread, Complete IC, Perform DC, and Update Instruction Cache. We also have to modify some Flat transitions: Commit ISB, Wait for DSB, Commit DSB, Propagate Memory Write, and Satisfy Read from Memory. These transitions define the lifecycle of each instruction: a request gets issued for the fetch, then at some later point the fetch gets satisfied from the instruction cache, the instruction is then decoded (in program-order) and then handed to the existing semantics to be executed. To give a flavour, we show just one, the *Propagate IC to Thread* transition, which is responsible for invalidation of the abstract instruction caches. This is a prose rendering of the rule in our executable mathematical model, which is expressed in the typed functional subset of Lem [32].

Propagate IC to Thread An instruction i (with ID *iiid*) in state WAIT_IC *(address, state_cont)* can do the relevant invalidate for any thread *tid'*, modifying that thread's instruction cache and fetch queue, if there exists a pending entry *(iiid, address)* in that thread's *ic_writes*. Action:

1. for any entry in the fetch queue for thread *tid*, whose *program_loc* is in the same minimum-size instruction cache line as *address*, and is in FETCHED(_) state, set it to the UNFETCHED state;
2. for the instruction cache of thread *tid*, remove any write-slices which are in the same instruction cache line of minimum size as *address*.

This rule can be found under the same name in the full prose description, and in the `handle_ic_ivau` and `flat_propagate_cache_maintenance` functions in `machineDefThreadSubsystem.lem` and `machineDefFlatStorageSubsystem.lem` in the executable mathematics. Cache maintenance operations work over entire cache lines, not individual addresses. Each address is associated with at least one cache line for the data (and unified) caches, and one for the instruction caches. The cache line of minimum size is the (architected) smallest possible cache line for each of these.

Example This model correctly explains all the behaviours of §3. We illustrate this by revisiting the cache synchronization explanation of §2, which can now be re-interpreted w.r.t. our precise model, and using this to explain the thread migration case of §3.3. Given DC Xn; DSB; IC Xn; DSB we can use this model to give meaning to it (omitting uninteresting transitions): First the DC CVAU causes a **Perform DC** transition. This pushes any write that might have been in the abstract data cache into memory. Now the first DSB's **Commit DSB** can be taken, allowing **Begin IC** to happen. This creates entries for each thread, which are discharged by each **Propagate IC to Thread** (see above). Once all entries are invalidated, a **Complete IC** can happen. Now, if any thread decodes an instruction for that address, it must have been fetched from the write the DC pushed, or something coherence-after it. If the software thread performing this sequence is interrupted and migrated (by the OS) to a different hardware thread, then, so long as the OS includes the DSB to maintain the thread-local DC ordering, the DC will push the write in an identical way, since it only affects the global abstract data cache. The IC transitions can all be taken, and the sequence continues as before, just on a new hardware thread. So when the second DSB finishes, and the final **Commit DSB** transitions is taken, the effect of the full sequence will be seen system-wide even if the thread was migrated.

5   An Axiomatic Semantics for Instruction Fetch

Based on the operational model, we develop an axiomatic semantics, as an extension of the ARMv8 axiomatic reference model [15,37]. Since that does not have mixed-size support, we do not model the concurrent modification of conditional branches (§3.1), as this would require mixed-size machinery. The existing axiomatic model is a predicate on *candidate executions*, hypothetical complete executions of the given program that satisfy some basic well-formedness conditions, defining the set of *valid* executions to be those satisfying its axioms. Each candidate execution abstractly captures a particular concrete execution of the program in terms of events and relations over them. This model is expressed in the herd language [8,6,4]. The events of these executions are memory reads (the set R), memory writes (W), and memory barrier/fence events (F). The relations are: *program order* (po), capturing the sequencing of events by the same thread in the execution's control-flow unfolding; *reads-from* (rf), relating a write event w with any read event r that reads from it; the *coherence order* (co), recording the execution's sequencing of same-address writes in memory; and *read-modify-write* (rmw), capturing which load/store exclusive instructions form a successful exclusive *pair* in the execution. The derived relation *from-reads* $\mathsf{fr} = \mathsf{rf}^{-1};\mathsf{co}$ relates a read r with a write w' if r reads from a write w coherence before w'. In addition, candidate executions also have relations capturing dependencies between events: address (addr), data (data), and control dependencies (ctrl). The relation loc relates any two read/write events that are to the same memory address. The model also has relations suffixed "i" and "e": rfi/rfe, coi/coe, fri/fre. These are the restrictions of the relations rf, co, and fr, to same-thread/"internal" event pairs or different-thread/"external" event pairs. The model is defined in relational algebra. In herd, R;S stands for sequential composition of relations R and S, R^{-1} for the inverse of relation R, R|S and R&S for the union and intersection of R and S, and [A];R;[B] for the restriction of R to the domain A and range B.

Handling instruction fetch requires extending the notion of candidate execution. We add new events: an *instruction-fetch* (IF) event for each executed instruction; a DC event for each DC CVAU instruction; an IC event for each IC IVAU and IC IALLU instruction. We replace po with *fetch-program-order* (fpo) which orders the IF event of an instruction before any program-order later IF events. We add a relation *same-cache-line* (scl), relating reads, writes, fetches, DC and IC events to addresses in the same cache line. We add an acyclic transitively closed relation wco, which extends co with orderings for cache maintenance (DC or IC) events: it includes an ordering (e, e') or (e', e) for any cache maintenance event e and same-cache-line event e' if e' is a write or another cache maintenance event; where co = ([W];wco;[W]) & loc. The loc, addr, and ctrl are all extended to include DC and IC events. We add a *fetch-to-execute* relation (fe), relating an IF event to any event generated by the execution of that instruction; and an *instruction-read-from* relation (irf), which relates a write to any IF event that fetches from it. Finally, we add a boolean *constrained-unpredictable* (CU) to detect badly behaved programs. Now we derive the following relations: the standard po relation, as po = fe^{-1};fpo;fe (two events e and e' are po-related if their fetch-events are fpo-related); and *instruction-from-reads* (ifr), the analogue of fr for instruction fetches, relating a fetch to all writes coherence-after the one it fetched from: ifr = irf^{-1};co.

We then make two semantics-preserving rewrites of the existing model to make adding instruction fetches easier (described in the appendix); and make the following changes and additions to the model. The full model is shown in Figure 1, with comments pointing to the relevant locations in the model definition. For lack of space we only describe the main addition, the iseq relation, in detail (including its correspondence with the operational model of §4); for the others we give an overview and refer to the appendix for the full description.

We define the relation iseq, relating some write w to address x to an IC event completing a cache synchronisation sequence (not necessarily on a single thread): w is followed by a same-cache line DC event, which is in turn followed by a same-cache line IC event. In operational model terms, this captures traces that propagated w to memory, subsequently performed a same-cache-line DC, and then began an IC (and eagerly propagated the IC to all threads). In any state after this sequence it is guaranteed that w, or a coherence-newer same-address write, is in the instruction cache of all threads: performing the DC has cleared the abstract data cache of writes to x, and the subsequent IC has removed old instructions for location x from the instruction caches, so that any subsequent updates to the instruction caches have been with w, or co-newer writes. Adding ifr;iseq to the *observed-by* relation (obs) (4) relates an instruction fetch i to location x to an IC ic if: i fetched from a write w to x, some write w' to x is coherence-after w, and ic completes a cache synchronisation sequence (iseq) starting from w'. Then the **irreflexive ob** axiom requires that i must be ordered-before ic (because it would otherwise have fetched w').We now

```
let iseq = [W];(wco&scl);[DC];   (*1*)          | [dmb.ld]; po; [R|W]
            (wco&scl);[IC]                       | [A|Q]; po; [R|W]
                                                 | [W]; po; [dmb.st]
(* Observed-by *)                                | [dmb.st]; po; [W]
let obs = rfe | fr | wco          (*2*)          | [R|W]; po; [L]
        | irf | (ifr;iseq)        (*3,4*)        | [R|W|F|DC|IC]; po; [dsb.ish]  (*9*)
                                                 | [dsb.ish]; po; [R|W|F|DC|IC]  (*10*
(* Fetch-ordered-before *)                       | [dmb.sy]; po; [DC]            (*11*
let fob = [IF]; fpo; [IF]          (*5*)
        | [IF]; fe                 (*6*)    (* Cache-op-ordered-before *)
        | [ISB]; fe⁻¹; fpo         (*7*)    let cob = [R|W]; (po&scl); [DC]   (*12*
                                                 | [DC]; (po&scl); [DC]         (*13*
(* Dependency-ordered-before *)
let dob = addr | data                       (* Ordered-before *)
        | ctrl; [W]                         let ob = (obs|fob|dob|aob|bob|cob)+
        | (ctrl | (addr; po)); [ISB]
(*|     | [ISB]; po; [R] *)        (*8*)    (* Internal visibility requirement *)
        | addr; po; [W]                     acyclic (po-loc|fr|co|rf) as internal
        | (addr | data); rfi
                                            (* External visibility requirement *)
(* Atomic-ordered-before *)                 irreflexive ob as external
let aob = rmw
        | [range(rmw)]; rfi; [A|Q]          (* Atomic *)
                                            empty rmw & (fre; coe) as atomic
(* Barrier-ordered-before *)
let bob = [R|W]; po; [dmb.sy]               (* Constrained unpredictable *)
        | [dmb.sy]; po; [R|W]               let cff = ([W];loc;[IF]) \        (*14*)
        | [L]; po; [A]                                    ob⁻¹ \ (co;iseq;ob)
        | [R]; po; [dmb.ld]                 cff_bad cff ≡ CU                   (*15*)
```

Fig. 1. Axiomatic model

briefly overview other changes made to the axiomatic model and their intuition. We include irf in obs (3): for an instruction to be fetched from a write, the write has to have been done before. We add a relation *fetch-ordered-before* (fob) (5-7), which is included in *ordered-before*. The relation fob includes fpo and fe; including fpo (5) requires fetches to be ordered according to their position in the control-flow unfolding of the execution. and including the fe (*fetch-to-execute*) relation (6) captures the idea that an instruction must be fetched before it can execute; fetches program-order-after an ISB happen after the ISB (or else are restarted) (7). For DSB ISH instructions the edge [R|W|F|DC|IC];po;[dsb.ish] is included in ob (9): DSB ISHs are ordered with all program-order-preceding non-fetch events. Symmetrically, all non-IF events are ordered after program-order-preceding dsb.ish events (10). DCs wait for preceding dmb.sy events (11). We include the relation *cache-op-ordered-before* (cob) in ob. This relation orders DC instructions with program-order previous reads/writes and other DCs to the same cache line (12,13).

Finally, *could-fetch-from* (cff) (14) captures, for each fetch i, the writes it could have fetched from (including the one it did fetch from), which we use to define the *constrained unpredictable* axiom cff_bad (not given) (15).

5 Validation

To gain confidence in the presented models we validated the models against the Arm architectural intent, against each other, and against real hardware.

Validation against the Architecture To ensure our models correctly captured the architectural intent we engaged in detailed discussions with Arm, including the Arm chief architect. These involved inventing litmus tests (including those described in §3 and many others) and discussing what the architecture should allow in each case.

Validating against hardware To run instruction-fetch tests on hardware, we extended the litmus tool [7]. The most significant extension consists in handling code that can be modified, and thus has to be restored between experiments. To that end, code copies are executed, those copies reside in mmap'd memory with execute permission granted. Copies are made from "master" copies, in effect C functions whose contents basically consist of gcc extended inline assembly. Of course, such code has to be position independent, and explicit code addresses in test initialisation sections (such as in 0:X1=l in the test of §3.1) are specific to each copy. All the cache handling instructions used in our experiments are all allowed to execute at exception level 0 (user-mode), and therefore no additional privilege is needed to run the tests.

To automatically generate families of interesting instruction-fetch tests, we extended the diy test generation tool [3] to support instruction-fetch reads-from (irf) and instruction-fetch from-reads (ifr) edges, in both internal (same-thread) and external (inter-thread) forms, and the cachesync edge. We used this to generate 1456 tests involving those edges together with po, rf, fr, addr, ctrl, ctrlisb, and dmb.sy. diy does not currently support bare DC or IC instructions, locations which are both fetched and read from, or repeated fetches from the same location.

We then ran the diy-generated test suite on a range of hardware implementations, to collect a substantial sample of actual hardware behaviour.

Correspondence between the models We experimentally test the equivalence of the operational and axiomatic models on the above hand-written and diy-generated tests, checking that the models give the same sets of allowed final states, and that these are consistent with the hardware observations.

Making the models executable as a test oracle To make the operational model executable as a test oracle, capable of computing the set of all allowed executions of a litmus test, we must be able to *exhaustively enumerate* all possible traces. For the model as presented, doing this naively is infeasible: for each instruction it is theoretically possible to speculate any of the 2^{64} addresses as potential next address, and the interleaving of the new fetch transitions with others leads to an additional combinatorial explosion.

We address these with two new optimisations. First, we extend the fixed-point optimisation in RMEM (incrementally computing the set of possible branch targets) [37] to keep track not only of indirect branches but also the successors of every program location, and only allow speculating from this set of successors. Additionally, we track during a test which locations were both fetched and modified during the test, and eagerly take fetch and decode transitions for all other locations. As before, the search then runs until the set of branch targets *and* the set of modified program-locations reaches a fixed point. We also take some of the transitions eagerly to reduce the search space, in cases where this cannot remove behaviour: **Wait for IC**, **Complete IC**, **Fetch Request**, and **Update Instruction Cache**.

Making the axiomatic model executable as a test oracle The axiomatic model is expressed in a herd-like form, but the herd tool does not support instruction fetch and cache maintenance instructions. To make the model executable as a test oracle, we built a new tool that takes litmus tests and uses a Sail [11] definition of a fragment of the ARMv8-A ISA to generate SMT problems for the model. Using the Sail instruction semantics, we generate a Sail program that corresponds to each thread within a litmus test. The tool then partially evaluates these programs using the concrete values for addresses and registers specified in the litmus file, while allowing memory values and arbitrary addresses to remain symbolic. Using a Sail to SMT-LIB backend, these are translated into SMT definitions that include all possible behaviours of each thread as satisfiable solutions. The rules for the axiomatic model are then applied as assertions restricting the possible behaviours to just those allowed by the axiomatic model. The tool also derives the `addr` and `data` relations, using the syntactic dependencies within the instruction semantics to derive the syntactic dependencies between instructions.

For litmus tests, where we can know up-front which instructions may be modified, we would like to avoid generating IF events for instructions that cannot be modified. If we naively removed certain IF events, however, we would break the correspondence between po and fe^{-1}; fpo; fe. This can be worked around by ensuring that every modifiable instruction generates an event which appears in po, allowing fpo between the modifiable instructions to instead be derived as fe; po; fe^{-1}. Branches emit a special branch address announce event for this purpose, which is also used to derive the ctrl relation. The fpo relation can then be modified, replacing [ISB]; fe^{-1}; fpo with [ISB]; po; fe^{-1} and adding [ISB]; po. The second change ensures that all the transitive edges generated by [ISB]; fe^{-1}; fpo followed by [IF]; fe remain with fob and hence ob.

A limitation of this approach is it cannot support cases where two threads both attempt to execute the same possibly-modified instruction, as in the SM.F+ic and FOW tests.

Validation results First, to check for regressions, we ran the operational model on all the 8950 non-mixed-size tests used for developing the original Flat model (without instruction fetch or cache maintenance). The results are identical, except for 23 tests which did not terminate within two hours. We used a 160 hardware-thread POWER9 server to run the tests.

We have also run the axiomatic model on the 90 basic two-thread tests that do not use Arm release/acquire instructions (not supported by the ISA semantics used for this); the results are all as they should be. This takes around 30 minutes on 8 cores of a Xeon Gold 6140.

Then, for the key handwritten tests mentioned in this paper, together with some others (that have also been discussed with Arm), we ran them on various hardware implementations and in the operational and axiomatic models. The models' results are identical to the Arm architectural intent in all cases, except for two tests which are not currently supported by the axiomatic checker.

Test	Arm intent	op. model	ax. model	hardware obs.
CoFF	allow	=	=	42.6k/13G
CoFR	forbid	=	=	0/13G
CoRF+ctrl-isb	allow	=	=	3.02G/13G
SM	allow	=	=	25.8G/25.9G
SM+cachesync-isb	forbid	=	=	0/25.9G
MP.RF+dmb+ctrl-isb	allow	=	=	480M/6.36G
MP.RF+cachesync+ctrl-isb	forbid	=	=	0/13G
MP.FR+dmb+fpo-fe	forbid	=	=	0/13G
MP.FF+dmb+fpo	allow	=	=	447M/13G
MP.FF+cachesync+fpo	forbid	=	=	F 2.3k/13G
ISA2.F+dc+ic+ctrl-isb	forbid	=	=	0/6.98G
SM.F+ic	allow	=	unsupported	U0/12.9G
FOW	allow	=	unsupported	U0/7G
MP.RF+dc+ctrl-isb-isb	allow	=	=	U0/12.94G
MP.R.RF+addr-cachesync+dmb+ctrl-isb	forbid	=	=	0/6.97G
MP.RF+dmb+addr-cachesync	allow	=	=	U0/6.34G

[The hardware observations are the sum of testing seven devices: a Snapdragon 810 (4x Arm A53 + 4x Arm A57 cores), Tegra K1 (2x NVIDIA Denver cores), Snapdragon 820 (4x Qualcomm Kryo cores), Exynos 8895 (4x Arm A53 + 4x Samsung Mongoose 2 cores), Snapdragon 425 (4x Arm A53), Amlogic 905 (4x Arm A53 cores), and Amlogic 922X (4x Arm A73 + 2x Arm A53 cores). U: allowed but unobserved. F: forbidden but observed.]

Our testing revealed a hardware bug in a Snapdragon 820 (4 Qualcomm Kryo cores). A version of the first cross-thread synchronisation test of §3.3 but with the full cache synchronisation (MP.RF+cachesync+ctrl-isb) exhibited an illegal outcome in 84/1.1G runs (not shown in the table), which we have reported. We have also seen an anomaly for MP.FF+cachesync+fpo, currently under investigation by Arm. Apart from these, the hardware observations are all allowed by the models. As usual, specific hardware implementations are sometimes stronger.

Finally, we ran the 1456 new instruction-fetch diy tests on a variety of hardware, for around 10M iterations each, and in the operational model. The model is sound with respect to the observed hardware behaviour except for that same Snapdragon 820 device.

7   Related Work

To the best of our knowledge, no previous work establishes well-validated rigorous semantics for any systems aspects, of any current production architecture, in a realistic concurrent setting.

The closest is Raad et al.'s work on non-volatile memory, which models the required cache maintenance for persistent storage in ARMv8-A [39], as an extension to the ARMv8-A axiomatic model, and for Intel x86 [38] as an operational model, but neither are validated against hardware. In the sequential case, Myreen's JIT compiler verification [33] models x86 icache behaviour with an abstract cache that can be arbitrarily updated, cleared on a jmp. For address translation, the authoritative Arm-internal ASL model [40,41,42], and Sail model derived from it [11] cover this, and other features sufficient to boot an OS (Linux), as do the handwritten Sail models for RISC-V (Linux and FreeBSD) and MIPS/CHERI-MIPS (FreeBSD, CheriBSD), but without any cache effects. Goel et al. [21,20] describe an ACL2 model for much of x86 that covers address translation; and the Forvis [34] and RISCV-PLV [14] Haskell RISC-V ISA models are also complete enough to boot Linux. Syeda and Klein [49,50] provide an somewhat idealised model for ARMv7 address translation and TLB maintenance. Komodo [16] uses a handwritten model for a small part of ARMv7, as do Guanciale et al. [25,12]. Romanescu et al. [44,43] do discuss address translation in the concurrent setting, but with respect to idealised models. Lustig et al. [30] describe a concurrent model for address translation based on the Intel Sandy Bridge microarchitecture, combined with a synopsis of some of the relevant Linux code, but not an architectural semantics for machine-code programs.

8   Conclusion

The mainstream architectures are the most important programming languages used in practice, and their systems aspects are fundamental to the security (or lack thereof) of our computing infrastructure. We have established a robust semantics for one of those systems aspects, soundly abstracting the hardware complexities to a manageable model that captures the architectural intent. This enables future work on reasoning, model-checking, and verification for real systems code.

Acknowledgements This work would not have been possible without generous technical assistance from Arm. We thank Richard Grisenthwaite, Will Deacon, Ian Caulfield, and Dave Martin for this. We also thank Hans Boehm, Stephen Kell, Jaroslav Ševčík, Ben Titzer, and Andrew Turner, for discussions of how instruction cache maintenance is used in practice, and Alastair Reid for comments on a draft. This work was partially supported by EPSRC grant EP/K008528/1 (REMS), ERC Advanced Grant 789108 (ELVER), an ARM iCASE award, and ARM donation funding. This work is part of the CIFV project sponsored by the Defense Advanced Research Projects Agency (DARPA) and the Air Force Research Laboratory (AFRL), under contract FA8650-18-C-7809. The views, opinions, and/or findings contained in this paper are those of the authors and should not be interpreted as representing the official views or policies, either expressed or implied, of the Department of Defense or the U.S. Government.

References

1. Adir, A., Attiya, H., Shurek, G.: Information-flow models for shared memory with an application to the PowerPC architecture. IEEE Trans. Parallel Distrib. Syst. **14**(5), 502–515 (2003). https://doi.org/10.1109/TPDS.2003.1199067

2. Alglave, J., Fox, A., Ishtiaq, S., Myreen, M.O., Sarkar, S., Sewell, P., Zappa Nardelli, F.: The semantics of Power and ARM multiprocessor machine code. In: Proc. DAMP 2009 (Jan 2009)

3. Alglave, J., Maranget, L.: The diy7 tool. http://diy.inria.fr/ (2019), accessed 2019-07-08

4. Alglave, J., Maranget, L.: The herd7 tool. http://diy.inria.fr/doc/herd.html/ (2019), accessed 2019-07-08

5. Alglave, J., Maranget, L., Deplaix, K., Didier, K., Sarkar, S.: The litmus7 tool. http://diy.inria.fr/doc/litmus.html/ (2019), accessed 2019-07-08

6. Alglave, J., Maranget, L., Sarkar, S., Sewell, P.: Fences in weak memory models. In: Proc. CAV (2010)

7. Alglave, J., Maranget, L., Sarkar, S., Sewell, P.: Litmus: running tests against hardware. In: Proceedings of TACAS 2011: the 17th international conference on Tools and Algorithms for the Construction and Analysis of Systems. pp. 41–44. Springer-Verlag, Berlin, Heidelberg (2011), http://dl.acm.org/citation.cfm?id=1987389.1987395

8. Alglave, J., Maranget, L., Tautschnig, M.: Herding Cats: Modelling, Simulation, Testing, and Data Mining for Weak Memory. ACM TOPLAS **36**(2), 7:1–7:74 (Jul 2014). https://doi.org/10.1145/2627752

9. ARM Limited: ARM architecture reference manual. ARMv8, for ARMv8-A architecture profile (Oct 2018), v8.4. ARM DDI 0487D.a (ID103018)

10. Armstrong, A., Bauereiss, T., Campbell, B., Gray, S.F.J.F.K.E., Kerneis, G., Krishnaswami, N., Mundkur, P., Norton-Wright, R., Pulte, C., Reid, A., Sewell, P., Stark, I., Wassell, M.: Sail. https://www.cl.cam.ac.uk/~pes20/sail/ (2019)

11. Armstrong, A., Bauereiss, T., Campbell, B., Reid, A., Gray, K.E., Norton, R.M., Mundkur, P., Wassell, M., French, J., Pulte, C., Flur, S., Stark, I., Krishnaswami, N., Sewell, P.: ISA semantics for ARMv8-A, RISC-V, and CHERI-MIPS. In: Proc. 46th ACM SIGPLAN Symposium on Principles of Programming Languages (Jan 2019). https://doi.org/10.1145/3290384, proc. ACM Program. Lang. 3, POPL, Article 71

12. Baumann, C., Schwarz, O., Dam, M.: Compositional verification of security properties for embedded execution platforms. In: PROOFS@CHES 2017, 6th International Workshop on Security Proofs for Embedded Systems, Taipei, Taiwan, Friday September 29th, 2017. pp. 1–16 (2017), http://www.easychair.org/publications/paper/wkpS

13. Chong, N., Ishtiaq, S.: Reasoning about the ARM weakly consistent memory model. In: MSPC (2008)

14. Clester, I.J., Bourgeat, T., Wright, A., Gruetter, S., Chlipala, A.: riscv-plv risc-v isa formal specification. https://github.com/mit-plv/riscv-semantics (2019), accessed 2019-07-01

15. Deacon, W.: The ARMv8 application level memory model. https://github.com/herd/herdtools7/blob/master/herd/libdir/aarch64.cat (accessed 2019-07-01) (2016)

16. Ferraiuolo, A., Baumann, A., Hawblitzel, C., Parno, B.: Komodo: Using verification to disentangle secure-enclave hardware from software. In: Proceedings of the 26th

Symposium on Operating Systems Principles, Shanghai, China, October 28-31, 2017. pp. 287–305 (2017). https://doi.org/10.1145/3132747.3132782

17. Flur, S., French, J., Gray, K., Pulte, C., Sarkar, S., Sewell, P.: rmem. www.cl.cam.ac.uk/~pes20/rmem/ (2017)

18. Flur, S., Gray, K.E., Pulte, C., Sarkar, S., Sezgin, A., Maranget, L., Deacon, W., Sewell, P.: Modelling the ARMv8 architecture, operationally: Concurrency and ISA. In: Proceedings of POPL: the 43rd ACM SIGPLAN-SIGACT Symposium on Principles of Programming Languages (2016)

19. Flur, S., Sarkar, S., Pulte, C., Nienhuis, K., Maranget, L., Gray, K.E., Sezgin, A., Batty, M., Sewell, P.: Mixed-size concurrency: ARM, POWER, C/C++11, and SC. In: The 44st Annual ACM SIGPLAN-SIGACT Symposium on Principles of Programming Languages, Paris, France. pp. 429–442 (Jan 2017). https://doi.org/10.1145/3009837.3009839

20. Goel, S.: The x86isa books: Features, usage, and future plans. In: Proceedings 14th International Workshop on the ACL2 Theorem Prover and its Applications, Austin, Texas, USA, May 22-23, 2017. pp. 1–17 (2017). https://doi.org/10.4204/EPTCS.249.1, arXiv version: https://arxiv.org/abs/1705.01225

21. Goel, S., Hunt, W.A., Kaufmann, M., Ghosh, S.: Simulation and formal verification of x86 machine-code programs that make system calls. In: Proceedings of the 14th Conference on Formal Methods in Computer-Aided Design. pp. 18:91–18:98. FMCAD '14, FMCAD Inc, Austin, TX (2014), http://dl.acm.org/citation.cfm?id=2682923.2682944

22. Gray, K.E., Kerneis, G., Mulligan, D., Pulte, C., Sarkar, S., Sewell, P.: An integrated concurrency and core-ISA architectural envelope definition, and test oracle, for IBM POWER multiprocessors. In: Proc. MICRO-48, the 48th Annual IEEE/ACM International Symposium on Microarchitecture (Dec 2015)

23. Gu, R., Shao, Z., Chen, H., Wu, X.N., Kim, J., Sjöberg, V., Costanzo, D.: CertiKOS: An extensible architecture for building certified concurrent OS kernels. In: 12th USENIX Symposium on Operating Systems Design and Implementation, OSDI 2016, Savannah, GA, USA, November 2-4, 2016. pp. 653–669 (2016), https://www.usenix.org/conference/osdi16/technical-sessions/presentation/gu

24. Gu, R., Shao, Z., Kim, J., Wu, X.N., Koenig, J., Sjöberg, V., Chen, H., Costanzo, D., Ramananandro, T.: Certified concurrent abstraction layers. In: Proceedings of the 39th ACM SIGPLAN Conference on Programming Language Design and Implementation, PLDI 2018, Philadelphia, PA, USA, June 18-22, 2018. pp. 646–661 (2018). https://doi.org/10.1145/3192366.3192381

25. Guanciale, R., Nemati, H., Dam, M., Baumann, C.: Provably secure memory isolation for linux on ARM. Journal of Computer Security 24(6), 793–837 (2016). https://doi.org/10.3233/JCS-160558

26. Intel Corporation: Intel 64 and ia-32 architectures software developer's manual combined volumes: 1, 2a, 2b, 2c, 2d, 3a, 3b, 3c, 3d and 4. https://software.intel.com/en-us/download/intel-64-and-ia-32-architectures-sdm-combined-volumes-1-2a-2b-2c-2d-3a-3b-3c-3d-and-4, accessed 2019-06-30 (May 2019), 325462-070US

27. Klein, G., Andronick, J., Elphinstone, K., Murray, T., Sewell, T., Kolanski, R., Heiser, G.: Comprehensive formal verification of an OS microkernel. ACM Transactions on Computer Systems 32(1), 2:1–2:70 (Feb 2014). https://doi.org/10.1145/2560537

28. Kumar, R., Myreen, M.O., Norrish, M., Owens, S.: CakeML: a verified implementation of ML. In: The 41st Annual ACM SIGPLAN-SIGACT Symposium on Principles of Programming Languages, POPL '14, San Diego, CA, USA, January 20-21, 2014. pp. 179–192 (2014). https://doi.org/10.1145/2535838.2535841

29. Leroy, X.: A formally verified compiler back-end. J. Autom. Reasoning **43**(4), 363–446 (2009). https://doi.org/10.1007/s10817-009-9155-4

30. Lustig, D., Sethi, G., Martonosi, M., Bhattacharjee, A.: COATCheck: Verifying memory ordering at the hardware-OS interface. SIGOPS Oper. Syst. Rev. **50**(2), 233–247 (Mar 2016). https://doi.org/10.1145/2954680.2872399

31. Maranget, L., Sarkar, S., Sewell, P.: A tutorial introduction to the ARM and POWER relaxed memory models. Draft available from http://www.cl.cam.ac.uk/~pes20/ppc-supplemental/test7.pdf (2012)

32. Mulligan, D.P., Owens, S., Gray, K.E., Ridge, T., Sewell, P.: Lem: reusable engineering of real-world semantics. In: Proceedings of ICFP 2014: the 19th ACM SIGPLAN International Conference on Functional Programming. pp. 175–188 (2014). https://doi.org/10.1145/2628136.2628143

33. Myreen, M.O.: Verified just-in-time compiler on x86. In: Proceedings of the 37th Annual ACM SIGPLAN-SIGACT Symposium on Principles of Programming Languages. pp. 107–118. POPL '10, ACM, New York, NY, USA (2010). https://doi.org/10.1145/1706299.1706313

34. Nikhil, R.S., Sharma, N.N.: Forvis: A formal RISC-V ISA specification. https://github.com/rsnikhil/Forvis_RISCV-ISA-Spec (2019), accessed 2019-07-01

35. Owens, S., Sarkar, S., Sewell, P.: A better x86 memory model: x86-TSO. In: Proceedings of TPHOLs 2009: Theorem Proving in Higher Order Logics, LNCS 5674. pp. 391–407 (2009)

36. Pulte, C.: The Semantics of Multicopy Atomic ARMv8 and RISC-V. Ph.D. thesis, University of Cambridge (2019), https://doi.org/10.17863/CAM.39379

37. Pulte, C., Flur, S., Deacon, W., French, J., Sarkar, S., Sewell, P.: Simplifying ARM Concurrency: Multicopy-atomic Axiomatic and Operational Models for ARMv8. In: Proceedings of the 45th ACM SIGPLAN Symposium on Principles of Programming Languages (Jan 2018). https://doi.org/10.1145/3158107

38. Raad, A., Wickerson, J., Neiger, G., Vafeiadis, V.: Persistency semantics of the Intel-x86 architecture. PACMPL **4**(POPL), 11:1–11:31 (2020). https://doi.org/10.1145/3371079

39. Raad, A., Wickerson, J., Vafeiadis, V.: Weak persistency semantics from the ground up: Formalising the persistency semantics of ARMv8 and transactional models. Proc. ACM Program. Lang. **3**(OOPSLA), 135:1–135:27 (Oct 2019). https://doi.org/10.1145/3360561

40. Reid, A.: Trustworthy specifications of ARM v8-A and v8-M system level architecture. In: FMCAD 2016. pp. 161–168 (October 2016), https://alastairreid.github.io/papers/fmcad2016-trustworthy.pdf

41. Reid, A.: ARM releases machine readable architecture specification. https://alastairreid.github.io/ARM-v8a-xml-release/ (Apr 2017)

42. Reid, A., Chen, R., Deligiannis, A., Gilday, D., Hoyes, D., Keen, W., Pathirane, A., Shepherd, O., Vrabel, P., Zaidi, A.: End-to-end verification of processors with ISA-Formal. In: Chaudhuri, S., Farzan, A. (eds.) Computer Aided Verification - 28th International Conference, CAV 2016, Toronto, ON, Canada, July 17-23, 2016, Proceedings, Part II. Lecture Notes in Computer Science, vol. 9780, pp. 42–58. Springer (2016)

43. Romanescu, B., Lebeck, A., Sorin, D.J.: Address translation aware memory consistency. IEEE Micro **31**(1), 109–118 (Jan 2011). https://doi.org/10.1109/MM.2010.99

44. Romanescu, B.F., Lebeck, A.R., Sorin, D.J.: Specifying and dynamically verifying address translation-aware memory consistency. In: Proceedings of the Fifteenth Edition of ASPLOS on Architectural Support for Programming Languages and Operating Systems. pp. 323–334. ASPLOS XV, ACM, New York, NY, USA (2010). https://doi.org/10.1145/1736020.1736057

45. Sarkar, S., Memarian, K., Owens, S., Batty, M., Sewell, P., Maranget, L., Alglave, J., Williams, D.: Synchronising C/C++ and POWER. In: Proceedings of PLDI 2012, the 33rd ACM SIGPLAN conference on Programming Language Design and Implementation (Beijing). pp. 311–322 (2012). https://doi.org/10.1145/2254064.2254102

46. Sarkar, S., Sewell, P., Alglave, J., Maranget, L., Williams, D.: Understanding POWER multiprocessors. In: Proceedings of PLDI 2011: the 32nd ACM SIGPLAN conference on Programming Language Design and Implementation. pp. 175–186 (2011). https://doi.org/10.1145/1993498.1993520

47. Sarkar, S., Sewell, P., Zappa Nardelli, F., Owens, S., Ridge, T., Braibant, T., Myreen, M., Alglave, J.: The semantics of x86-CC multiprocessor machine code. In: Proceedings of POPL 2009: the 36th annual ACM SIGPLAN-SIGACT symposium on Principles of Programming Languages. pp. 379–391 (Jan 2009). https://doi.org/10.1145/1594834.1480929

48. Sewell, P., Sarkar, S., Owens, S., Zappa Nardelli, F., Myreen, M.O.: x86-TSO: A rigorous and usable programmer's model for x86 multiprocessors. Communications of the ACM **53**(7), 89–97 (Jul 2010), (Research Highlights)

49. Syeda, H., Klein, G.: Reasoning about translation lookaside buffers. In: LPAR-21, 21st International Conference on Logic for Programming, Artificial Intelligence and Reasoning, Maun, Botswana, May 7-12, 2017. pp. 490–508 (2017), http://www.easychair.org/publications/paper/340347

50. Syeda, H.T., Klein, G.: Program verification in the presence of cached address translation. In: Interactive Theorem Proving - 9th International Conference, ITP 2018, Held as Part of the Federated Logic Conference, FloC 2018, Oxford, UK, July 9-12, 2018, Proceedings. pp. 542–559 (2018). https://doi.org/10.1007/978-3-319-94821-8_32

51. Tan, Y.K., Myreen, M.O., Kumar, R., Fox, A.C.J., Owens, S., Norrish, M.: The verified CakeML compiler backend. J. Funct. Program. **29**, e2 (2019). https://doi.org/10.1017/S0956796818000229

52. Waterman, A., Asanović, K. (eds.): The RISC-V Instruction Set Manual Volume I: Unprivileged ISA (Dec 2018), document Version 20181221-Public-Review-draft. Contributors: Arvind, Krste Asanović, Rimas Avižienis, Jacob Bachmeyer, Christopher F. Batten, Allen J. Baum, Alex Bradbury, Scott Beamer, Preston Briggs, Christopher Celio, Chuanhua Chang, David Chisnall, Paul Clayton, Palmer Dabbelt, Roger Espasa, Shaked Flur, Stefan Freudenberger, Jan Gray, Michael Hamburg, John Hauser, David Horner, Bruce Hoult, Alexandre Joannou, Olof Johansson, Ben Keller, Yunsup Lee, Paul Loewenstein, Daniel Lustig, Yatin Manerkar, Luc Maranget, Margaret Martonosi, Joseph Myers, Vijayanand Nagarajan, Rishiyur Nikhil, Jonas Oberhauser, Stefan O'Rear, Albert Ou, John Ousterhout, David Patterson, Christopher Pulte, Jose Renau, Colin Schmidt, Peter Sewell, Susmit Sarkar, Michael Taylor, Wesley Terpstra, Matt Thomas, Tommy Thorn, Caroline Trippel, Ray VanDeWalker, Muralidaran Vijayaraghavan, Megan Wachs,

Andrew Waterman, Robert Watson, Derek Williams, Andrew Wright, Reinoud Zandijk, and Sizhuo Zhang

Higher-Ranked Annotation Polymorphic Dependency Analysis

Fabian Thorand and Jurriaan Hage[ORCID]

Dept. of Information and Computing Sciences, Utrecht University The Netherlands
f.thorand@gmail.com, j.hage@uu.nl

Abstract. The precision of a static analysis can be improved by increasing the context-sensitivity of the analysis. In a type-based formulation of static analysis for functional languages this can be achieved by, e.g., introducing let-polyvariance or subtyping. In this paper we go one step further by defining a higher-ranked polyvariant type system so that even properties of lambda-bound identifiers can be generalized over. We do this for dependency analysis, a generic analysis that can be instantiated to a range of different analyses that in this way all can profit.

We prove that our analysis is sound with respect to a call-by-name semantics and that it satisfies a so-called noninterference property. We provide a type reconstruction algorithm that we have proven to be terminating, and sound and complete with respect to its declarative specification. Our principled description can serve as a blueprint for making other analyses higher-ranked.

1 Introduction

The typical compiler for a statically typed functional language will perform a number of analyses for validation, optimisation, or both (e.g., strictness analysis, control-flow analysis, and binding time analysis). These analyses can be specified as a type-based static analysis so that vocabulary, implementation and concepts from the world of type systems can be reused in this setting [19,24]. In that setting the analysis properties are taken from a language of annotations which adorn the types computed for the program during type inference: the analysis is specified as an annotated type system, and the payload of the analysis corresponds to the annotations computed for a given program.

Consider for example binding-time analysis [5,7]. In this case, we have a two-value lattice of annotations containing S for static and D for dynamic (where $\bot = S \sqsubseteq D = \top$, so that whenever an expression is annotated with S, it can be soundly changed to D, because that is a strictly weaker property). An expression that is known to be static may be evaluated at compile time, because the analysis has determined that all the values that determine its outcome are in fact available at compile-time while all other expressions are annotated with D, and must be evaluated at run-time; the goal of binding-time analysis is then to (soundly) assign S to as many expressions as possible.

© The Author(s) 2020
P. Müller (Ed.): ESOP 2020, LNCS 12075, pp. 656–683, 2020.
https://doi.org/10.1007/978-3-030-44914-8_24

Static analyses may differ in precision, e.g., a monovariant binding-time analysis lacks context-sensitivity for let-bound identifiers (although some of it can be recovered with subtyping). Assuming id to be the identity function, if in the program

   let $id\ x = x$ in .. $id\ s$ .. $id\ d$ ..

the subexpression s is a statically known integer, which we denote as $s : \text{int}\langle S \rangle$, and $d : \text{int}\langle D \rangle$ a dynamic integer, then for id we arrive at $\text{int}\langle D \rangle \to \text{int}\langle D \rangle$, so that the property found for $id\ s$ is that it is a dynamic integer. Clearly, however, if the value of s is known statically then also that of $id\ s$ is! The fact that values with different properties flow to a function and we have to be (overly) pessimistic for some of these is a phenomenon sometimes called *poisoning* [28]. Context-sensitivity reduces poisoning; it can be achieved by making the analysis *polyvariant*. In that case, our type for id may become $\forall \beta.\text{int}\langle \beta \rangle \to \text{int}\langle \beta \rangle$, so that for the first call to id we may instantiate β with S and for the second choose D, essentially mimicking the polymorphic lambda-calculus at the level of annotations.

But what about a function like

   $foo = \lambda f.(f\ d, f\ s)$

in which we have two calls to a lambda-bound function argument f? Can we treat these context-sensitively as well, so that we can have the most precise types for both calls, independent of each other? The answer is: yes, we can.

Independence can be achieved by inferring for foo a type that associates with f an annotation polymorphic type,

   $\forall \beta_1.(\forall \beta_0.\text{int}\langle \beta_0 \rangle \to \text{int}\langle \beta_1\ \beta_0 \rangle)$

Here, β_0 ranges over simple annotations (such as S and D), and β_1 ranges over annotation level functions (in the terminology of this paper, these annotations are higher-sorted; see section 3). The annotation variable β_0 is a placeholder for the analysis property of the actual argument to f, while β_1 represents how that property propagates to the value returned by f. If the identity function $\forall \beta.\text{int}\langle \beta \rangle \to \text{int}\langle \beta \rangle$ is passed to foo, a pair with annotated type $\text{int}\langle D \rangle \times \text{int}\langle S \rangle$ will be returned. This is because the types of $f\ d$ and $f\ s$ can be determined independently of each other, because the choice for β_0 can be made separately for each call. The "price" we pay is that we have to know how the annotations on the values returned by f can be derived from the annotations on the arguments. This is exactly what β_1 represents.

If β_0 or β_1 would range over (annotated) types, then the underlying language itself would be higher-ranked, and inference in that case is known to be undecidable [14]. However, as we show in this paper, if they range only over annotations (even higher-sorted ones), then inference may become decidable again. Why is that? Intuitively, this is because the underlying types provide structure to the analysis inference algorithm, while a higher-ranked polymorphic type system does not have this advantage.

In which situations can we expect to benefit from higher-ranked polyvariance? Generally speaking, this is when we have functions of order 2 and higher, functions that often show up in idiomatic functional code.

Languages like Haskell do support higher-rank types [13]. Decidability is not problematic then, because the compiler expects the programmer to provide the higher-rank type signatures where necessary, and the compiler only needs to verify that the provided types are consistent: type checking *is* decidable. In our situation this is typically not acceptable: we cannot expect programmers to provide explicit control-flow [12] or binding-time information. So we have to insist on full inference of analysis information, and this paper shows how this can be done for dependency analysis [1].

Dependency analysis is in fact a family of analyses; instances include binding-time analysis, exception analysis, secure information flow analysis and static slicing. The precision of our higher-ranked polyvariant annotated type system for dependency analysis thereby carries over immediately to the instances, and metatheoretical properties we prove, like a noninterference theorem [8], need to be proven only once.

In summary, this paper offers the following *contributions*. We (1) define a higher-ranked annotation polymorphic type system for a generic dependency analysis (section 4) for a call-by-name language that takes its annotations from a simply typed lambda-calculus enriched with lattice operations (section 3). The analysis also supports polyvariant recursion [10] to improve precision for certain recursive functions. Due to the principled way in which the analysis is set-up it can serve as a blueprint for giving other analyses the same treatment. We (2) prove our system sound with respect to a call-by-name operational semantics. We also formulate and prove a noninterference theorem for our system (section 5). We (3) give a type reconstruction algorithm that is sound and complete with respect to the type system (section 6) and provide a prototype implementation (section 7). For reasons of space we omit many details that are available in a separate document [26].

2   Intuition and motivation

Before we go on to the technical details of this paper, we want to elaborate upon our intuitive description from the introduction. We do this by means of a few small examples, keeping the discussion informal. Formally discussed examples, as generated by our implementation, become big and hard to read pretty quickly; these can be found in section 7.

We start with a few examples in which binding-time analysis is the dependency analysis instance, followed by a few examples that use security flow analysis; our implementation supports both instances. We note that our implementation supports a few more language constructs than the formal specification given in this paper, giving us a bit more flexibility. Neither, however, supports polymorphism at the type level. This substantially simplifies the technicalities.

For the following example

$foo : ((\text{int} \rightarrow \text{int}) \rightarrow \text{int}) \rightarrow \text{int} \times \text{int}$
$foo = \lambda f : (\text{int} \rightarrow \text{int}) \rightarrow \text{int}.(f\ (\lambda x : \text{int}.x), f\ (\lambda x : \text{int}.0))$

our analysis can derive a higher-ranked polyvariant type for f,

$$\forall \beta_1.(\forall \beta_2.\text{int}\langle \beta_2 \rangle \rightarrow \text{int}\langle \beta_1\ \beta_2 \rangle) \rightarrow \text{int}\langle \beta_3\ \beta_2\ \beta_1 \rangle$$

where β_1 and β_2 can be instantiated independently for each of the two calls to f in foo, and β_3 is universally bound by foo and represents how the argument f uses its function argument.

Since the argument to f is itself a function, the information that flows out of, say, the first call to f can be independent of the analysis of the function that flows into the second call (and vice versa), thereby avoiding unnecessary poisoning. This means that the binding-time of, say, the second component of the pair depends only on f and the function $\lambda x : \text{int}.0$, irrespective of f also receiving $\lambda x : \text{int}.x$ as argument to compute the first component.

For the next example, let us consider security flow analysis in which we have annotations L and H that designate values (call these L-values and H-values) of low respectively high confidentiality. An important scenario where additional precision can be achieved is when analyzing Haskell code in which type classes have been desugared to dictionary-passing functional core. A function like

$$g\ x\ y = (x + y, y + y)$$

is then transformed into something like $g\ (+)\ x\ y = (x + y, y + y)$. Now, consider the case that we pass an H-value to x and an L-value to y; the operator $(+)$ produces an L-value if and only if both arguments are L-values. Without higher-ranked annotations, the annotation on the first argument to $(+)$ has to be consistent with all uses of $(+)$. Because x is an H-value, that will then also be the case for the second call to $(+)$, leading to a pair of values of which the components are both H-values. With higher-ranked annotations, we can instantiate the two instances independently, and the second component of the pair is analyzed to produce an L-value. Functions in Haskell that use type classes are extremely common.

3   The $\lambda^{\sqcup}$-calculus

An essential ingredient of our annotated type system is the language of annotations that we use to decorate our types and to represent the dependencies resulting from evaluating an expression. Indeed, the fact that annotations are in fact "programs" in a lambda calculus is what allows us to make our analysis a higher-ranked polyvariant one. For the purpose of this paper, we generalize the $\lambda^{\cup}$-calculus of [16] to the $\lambda^{\sqcup}$-calculus ($\lambda^{\sqcup}$ for short) a simply typed lambda calculus extended with a lattice structure.

The syntax of $\lambda^{\sqcup}$ is given in figure 1; from now on, we refer to its types exclusively as *sorts*. Here, κ ranges over sorts, β over annotation variables, etc.

$$\kappa \in \textbf{AnnSort} ::= \star \qquad\qquad\qquad \text{(base sort)}$$
$$\qquad | \quad \kappa_1 \Rightarrow \kappa_2 \qquad\qquad \text{(function sort)}$$
$$\beta \in \textbf{AnnVar} \qquad\qquad\qquad \text{(annotation variables)}$$
$$\xi \in \textbf{AnnTm} ::= \beta \qquad\qquad\qquad \text{(variable)}$$
$$\qquad | \quad \lambda\beta :: \kappa.\xi \qquad\qquad \text{(abstraction)}$$
$$\qquad | \quad \xi_1\,\xi_2 \qquad\qquad\quad \text{(application)}$$
$$\qquad | \quad \ell \qquad\qquad\qquad \text{(lattice value, } \ell \in \mathcal{L})$$
$$\qquad | \quad \xi_1 \sqcup \xi_2 \qquad \text{(lattice join operation)}$$

Fig. 1: The syntax of the $\lambda^\sqcup$-calculus, sorts and annotations

In order to avoid confusion with the field of (algebraic) effects, we refer to terms of $\lambda^\sqcup$ as *dependency terms* or *dependency annotations*. Terms are either of base sort $\star$, representing values in the underlying lattice $\mathcal{L}$, or of function sort $\kappa_1 \Rightarrow \kappa_2$.

On the term level, we allow arbitrary elements of the underlying lattice and taking binary joins, in addition to the usual variables, function applications and lambda abstractions. Lattice elements are assumed to be taken from a *bounded join-semilattice* $\mathcal{L}$, an algebraic structure $\langle L, \sqcup \rangle$ consisting of an underlying set L and an associative, commutative and idempotent binary operation $\sqcup$, called *join* (we usually write $\ell \in \mathcal{L}$ for $\ell \in L$), and a least element $\bot$.

The sorting rules of $\lambda^\sqcup$ are straightforward (see [26]). Values of the underlying lattice are always of sort $\star$, and the join operator is defined on arbitrary terms of the same sort:

$$\frac{\Sigma \vdash_s \xi_1 : \kappa \qquad \Sigma \vdash_s \xi_2 : \kappa}{\Sigma \vdash_s \xi_1 \sqcup \xi_2 : \kappa} \;\; [\text{S-Join}]$$

The sorting rule uses *sort environments* denoted by the letter Σ that map annotation variables β to sorts κ. We denote the set of sort environments by **SortEnv**. More precisely, a *sort environment* or *sort context* Σ is a finite list of bindings from annotation variables β to sorts κ. The empty context is written as $\emptyset$ (in code as $[]$), and the context Σ extended with the binding of the variable

$$V_\star = \mathcal{L}$$
$$V_{\kappa_1 \Rightarrow \kappa_2} = \{ f : V_{\kappa_1} \to V_{\kappa_2} \mid f \text{ mono} \}$$
$$\rho : \textbf{AnnVar} \to_{\text{fin}} \bigcup \{ V_\kappa \mid \kappa \in \textbf{AnnSort} \}$$
$$[\![\beta]\!]_\rho = \rho(\beta)$$
$$[\![\lambda\beta :: \kappa_1.\xi]\!]_\rho = \lambda v \in V_{\kappa_1}.\, [\![\xi]\!]_{\rho[\beta \mapsto v]}$$
$$[\![\xi_1\,\xi_2]\!]_\rho = [\![\xi_1]\!]_\rho \,([\![\xi_2]\!]_\rho)$$
$$[\![\ell]\!]_\rho = \ell$$
$$[\![\xi_1 \sqcup \xi_2]\!]_\rho = [\![\xi_1]\!]_\rho \sqcup [\![\xi_2]\!]_\rho$$

Fig. 2: The semantics of $\lambda^\sqcup$-calculus

β to the sort κ is written $\Sigma, \beta : \kappa$. We denote the set of annotation variables in the context Σ with $\text{dom}(\Sigma)$. When we write, $\Sigma(\beta) = \kappa$ this means that $\beta \in \text{dom}(\Sigma)$ and the rightmost occurrence of β binds it to κ. Moreover, $\Sigma \setminus B$ where $B \subseteq \textbf{AnnVar}$ denotes the context Σ where all bindings of annotation variables in B have been removed. In the remainder of this paper, we shall overload this notation for all kinds of other environments we shall be needing, including type environments, and annotated type environments.

The $\lambda^{\sqcup}$-calculus enjoys a number of properties, many of which are what one might expect; we have put these and their proofs in [26].

A *substitution* is a map from variables to terms usually denoted by the letter θ. The application of a substitution θ to a term ξ is written $\theta\xi$ and replaces all free variables in ξ that are also in the domain of θ with the corresponding terms they are mapped to. A concrete substitution replacing the variables $\beta_1, \ldots, \beta_n$ with terms $\xi_1, \ldots, \xi_n$ is written $[\xi_1/\beta_1, \ldots, \xi_n/\beta_n]$.

Assuming the usual definitions for the pointwise extension of a lattice L, and for monotone (order-preserving) functions between lattices, Figure 2 shows the denotational semantics of $\lambda^{\sqcup}$, where we employ the pointwise lifting of $\sqcup$ to functions to give semantics to the join of $\lambda^{\sqcup}$. The universe V_κ denotes the lattice that is represented by the sort κ. The base sort $\star$ represents the underlying lattice $\mathcal{L}$ and the function sort $\kappa_1 \Rightarrow \kappa_2$ represents the lattice constructed by pointwise extension of the lattice V_{κ_2} restricted to monotone functions.

The denotation function $[\![\cdot]\!]_\rho$ is parameterized with an environment ρ of the given type that provides the values of variables. The denotation of a lambda term is simply an element of the corresponding function space. Applications are therefore mapped directly to the underlying function application of the meta-theory. This is unlike the $\lambda^{\cup}$-calculus of [16] where lambda terms are mapped to singleton sets of functions and function application is defined in terms of the union of the results of individually applying each function. The crucial difference is that we have offloaded this complexity into the definition of the pointwise extension of lattices. It is therefore important to note that the join operator used in the denotation of a term $\xi_1 \sqcup \xi_2$ depends on the sort κ of this term and belongs to the lattice V_κ.

An environment $\rho : \textbf{AnnVar} \to_{\text{fin}} \bigcup \{V_\kappa \mid \kappa \in \textbf{AnnSort}\}$ and a sort environment Σ are *compatible* if $\text{dom}(\Sigma) = \text{dom}(\rho)$ and for all $\beta \in \text{dom}(\Sigma)$ we have $\rho(\beta) \in V_{\Sigma(\beta)}$. Given two dependency terms ξ_1 and ξ_2 and a sort κ such that $\Sigma \vdash_s \xi_1 : \kappa$ and $\Sigma \vdash_s \xi_2 : \kappa$, we say that ξ_2 *subsumes* ξ_1 under the environment Σ, written $\Sigma \vdash_{\text{sub}} \xi_1 \sqsubseteq \xi_2$, if for all environments ρ compatible with Σ, we have $[\![\xi_1]\!]_\rho \sqsubseteq [\![\xi_2]\!]_\rho$. They are *semantically equal* under Σ, written $\Sigma \vdash \xi_1 \equiv \xi_2$, if for all environments ρ compatible with Σ, we have $[\![\xi_1]\!]_\rho = [\![\xi_2]\!]_\rho$.

4   The declarative type system

The types and syntax of our source language are given in figure 3. The types of our source language consist of a unit type, and product, sum and function types. As mentioned earlier, let-polymorphism at the type level is not part of the

$$
\begin{array}{llr}
\tau \in \mathbf{Ty} ::= & \text{unit} & \text{(unit type)} \\
| & \tau_1 + \tau_2 & \text{(sum type)} \\
| & \tau_1 \times \tau_2 & \text{(product type)} \\
| & \tau_1 \to \tau_2 & \text{(function type)} \\
t \in \mathbf{Tm} ::= & x & \text{(variable)} \\
| & () & \text{(unit constructor)} \\
| & \lambda x : \tau.t & \text{(abstraction)} \\
| & t_1\, t_2 & \text{(application)} \\
| & (t_1, t_2) & \text{(pair constructor)} \\
| & \mathrm{proj}_i(t) & \text{(pair projections)} \\
| & \mathrm{inl}_{\tau_2}(t) \mid \mathrm{inr}_{\tau_1}(t) & \text{(sum constructors)} \\
| & \mathbf{case}\ t\ \mathbf{of}\ \{\mathrm{inl}(x) \to t_1; \mathrm{inr}(y) \to t_2\} & \text{(sum eliminator)} \\
| & \mu x : \tau.t & \text{(fixpoint)} \\
| & \mathrm{seq}\ t_1\, t_2 & \text{(forcing)} \\
| & \mathrm{ann}_\ell(t) & \text{(raise annotation level to } \ell \in \mathcal{L}) \\
\end{array}
$$

Fig. 3: The types and terms of the source language

type system. The language itself is then hardly suprising and includes variables, a unit constant, lambda abstraction, function application, projection functions for product types, sum constructors, a sum eliminator (case), fixpoints, seq for explicitly forcing evaluation in our call-by-name language, and, finally, a special operation $\mathrm{ann}_\ell(t)$ that raises the annotation level of t to ℓ. We omit the underlying type system for the source language since it consists mostly of the standard rules (see [26]). A notable exception is the rule for $\mathrm{ann}_\ell(t)$. Such an explicitly annotated term has the same underlying type as t:

$$
\frac{\Gamma \vdash t : \tau}{\Gamma \vdash \mathrm{ann}_\ell(t) : \tau} \ [\text{U-Ann}]
$$

The annotation ℓ imposed on t only becomes relevant in the annotated type system that we discuss next. In the following, we assume the usual definitions for computing the set of free term variables of a term, $\mathrm{ftv}(t)$.

The annotated type system The source language is simply a desugared variant of the functional language a programmer deals with. The target language has the same structure, but adds dependency annotations to the source syntax. These annotations are the payload of the dependency analaysis and computed by the algorithm given in section 6, so that the analysis results can be employed in the back-end of a compiler. In other words, the algorithm *elaborates* a source level term into a target term.

The syntax of the target language is shown in figure 4. *Annotated types* of the target language are denoted by $\widehat{\tau}$ and *annotated terms* are denoted by $\widehat{t}$. The annotations that we put on compound types, as well as their components are not just there for uniformity. Because of our non-strict semantics and the

$$\widehat{\tau} \in \widehat{\mathbf{Ty}} ::= \forall \beta :: \kappa.\widehat{\tau} \qquad \text{(annotation quantification)}$$
$$| \quad \widehat{\text{unit}} \qquad \text{(unit type)}$$
$$| \quad \widehat{\tau}_1\langle \xi_1 \rangle + \widehat{\tau}_2\langle \xi_2 \rangle \qquad \text{(sum type)}$$
$$| \quad \widehat{\tau}_1\langle \xi_1 \rangle \times \widehat{\tau}_2\langle \xi_2 \rangle \qquad \text{(product type)}$$
$$| \quad \widehat{\tau}_1\langle \xi_1 \rangle \rightarrow \widehat{\tau}_2\langle \xi_2 \rangle \qquad \text{(function type)}$$

$$\widehat{t} \in \widehat{\mathbf{Tm}} ::= \cdots$$
$$| \quad \lambda x : \widehat{\tau} \,\&\, \xi.\widehat{t} \qquad \text{(abstraction)}$$
$$| \quad \mu x : \widehat{\tau} \,\&\, \xi.\widehat{t} \qquad \text{(fixpoint)}$$
$$| \quad \cdots$$
$$| \quad \Lambda \beta :: \kappa.\widehat{t} \qquad \text{(dependency abstraction)}$$
$$| \quad \widehat{t}\,\langle \xi \rangle \qquad \text{(dependency application)}$$

Fig. 4: The annotated types and terms of the target language

presence of seq, we can observe the effects on a pair constructor independently of its values, so we have separate annotations to represent these.

On the type level, there is an additional construct $\forall \beta :: \kappa.\widehat{\tau}$ quantifying over an annotation variable β of sort κ. Furthermore, the recursive occurrences in the sum, product and arrow types now each carry an annotation. On the term level, the explicit type annotations of lambda expressions and fixpoints are now annotated types and also include a dependency annotation. Moreover, dependency abstraction and application have been added to reflect the quantification of dependency variables on the type level. We denote the set of free (term) variables in a target term $\widehat{t}$ by $\mathrm{ftv}(\widehat{t})$.

The formal definition of well-formedness for annotated types can be found in [26]. Informally, a type is well-formed only if all annotations are of sort $\star$ and all annotation variables that are used have previously been bound.

Below, we assume the unsurprising recursive definitions for computing the underlying terms $\lfloor \widehat{t} \rfloor$ and underlying types $\lfloor \widehat{\tau} \rfloor$ that correspond to annotated terms $\widehat{t}$ and annotated types $\widehat{\tau}$. We also straightforwardly extend the definition of free annotation variables to annotated types, and denote these by $\mathrm{fav}(\widehat{\tau})$.

Subtyping To define subtyping we need an auxiliary relation that says when two annotated types $\widehat{\tau}_1$ and $\widehat{\tau}_2$ *have the same shape*. The unsurprising formal definition is in [26], but essentially they have the same syntactic structure, and in the forall case, quantify over the same annotation variable. It can be quite easily proven that if two types have the same shape, then they have the same underlying type. This is not true the other way around: the annotated types $\forall \beta_1.\forall \beta_2.\mathrm{int}\langle \beta_1 \rangle \rightarrow \mathrm{int}\langle \beta_1 \sqcup \beta_2 \rangle$ and $\forall \beta_1.\mathrm{int}\langle \beta_1 \rangle \rightarrow \mathrm{int}\langle \beta_1 \rangle$ have the same underlying type, int $\rightarrow$ int, but do not have the same shape.

Figure 5 shows the rules defining the subtyping relation on annotated types of the same shape, that allows us to weaken the annotations on a type to a less demanding one. Intuitively, a type $\widehat{\tau}_1$ is a subtype of $\widehat{\tau}_2$ under a sort environment

$$\frac{}{\Sigma \vdash_{\text{sub}} \widehat{\tau} \leqslant \widehat{\tau}} \text{ [SUB-REFL]}$$

$$\frac{\Sigma \vdash_{\text{sub}} \widehat{\tau}_1 \leqslant \widehat{\tau}_2 \qquad \Sigma \vdash_{\text{sub}} \widehat{\tau}_2 \leqslant \widehat{\tau}_3}{\Sigma \vdash_{\text{sub}} \widehat{\tau}_1 \leqslant \widehat{\tau}_3} \text{ [SUB-TRANS]}$$

$$\frac{\Sigma, \beta :: \kappa \vdash_{\text{sub}} \widehat{\tau}_1 \leqslant \widehat{\tau}_2}{\Sigma \vdash_{\text{sub}} \forall \beta :: \kappa.\widehat{\tau}_1 \leqslant \forall \beta :: \kappa.\widehat{\tau}_2} \text{ [SUB-FORALL]}$$

$$\frac{\Sigma \vdash_{\text{sub}} \widehat{\tau}_1 \leqslant \widehat{\tau}_1' \qquad \Sigma \vdash_{\text{sub}} \widehat{\tau}_2 \leqslant \widehat{\tau}_2' \qquad \Sigma \vdash_{\text{sub}} \xi_1 \sqsubseteq \xi_1' \qquad \Sigma \vdash_{\text{sub}} \xi_2 \sqsubseteq \xi_2'}{\Sigma \vdash_{\text{sub}} \widehat{\tau}_1 \langle \xi_1 \rangle \times \widehat{\tau}_2 \langle \xi_2 \rangle \leqslant \widehat{\tau}_1' \langle \xi_1' \rangle \times \widehat{\tau}_2' \langle \xi_2' \rangle} \text{ [SUB-PROD]}$$

$$\frac{\Sigma \vdash_{\text{sub}} \widehat{\tau}_1' \leqslant \widehat{\tau}_1 \qquad \Sigma \vdash_{\text{sub}} \widehat{\tau}_2 \leqslant \widehat{\tau}_2' \qquad \Sigma \vdash_{\text{sub}} \xi_1' \sqsubseteq \xi_1 \qquad \Sigma \vdash_{\text{sub}} \xi_2 \sqsubseteq \xi_2'}{\Sigma \vdash_{\text{sub}} \widehat{\tau}_1 \langle \xi_1 \rangle \to \widehat{\tau}_2 \langle \xi_2 \rangle \leqslant \widehat{\tau}_1' \langle \xi_1' \rangle \to \widehat{\tau}_2' \langle \xi_2' \rangle} \text{ [SUB-ARR]}$$

Fig. 5: Subtyping relation ($\Sigma \vdash_{\text{sub}} \widehat{\tau}_1 \leqslant \widehat{\tau}_2$), [SUB-SUM] is like [SUB-PROD]

Σ, written $\Sigma \vdash_{\text{sub}} \widehat{\tau}_1 \leqslant \widehat{\tau}_2$, if a value of type $\widehat{\tau}_1$ can be used in places where a value of type $\widehat{\tau}_2$ is required. The subtyping relation only relates the annotations inside the types using the subsumption relation $\Sigma \vdash_{\text{sub}} \xi_1 \sqsubseteq \xi_2$ between dependency terms. Moreover, the subtyping relation implicitly demands that both types are well-formed under the environment. The [SUB-FORALL] rule requires that the quantified variable has the same name in both types. This is not a restriction, as we can simply rename the variables in one or both of the types accordingly in order to make them match and prevent unintentional capturing of previously free variables. Note that [SUB-ARR] is contravariant for argument positions. We omitted [SUB-SUM] which can be derived from [SUB-PROD] by replacing $\times$ with $+$.

The annotated type rules An *annotated type environment* $\widehat{\Gamma}$ is defined analogously to sort environments, but instead maps term variables x to pairs of an annotated type $\widehat{\tau}$ and a dependency term ξ. We extend the definition of the set of free annotation variables to annotated environments by taking the union of the free annotation variables of all annotated types and dependency terms occurring in the environment, denoted by $\text{fav}(\widehat{\Gamma})$. We denote the set of annotated type environments by **AnnTyEnv**.

We have now all the definitions in place in order to define the declarative annotated type system shown in figure 6. It consists of judgments of the form $\Sigma \mid \widehat{\Gamma} \vdash_{\text{te}} \widehat{t} : \widehat{\tau} \,\&\, \xi$ expressing that under the sort environment Σ and the annotated type environment $\widehat{\Gamma}$, the annotated term $\widehat{t}$ has the annotated type $\widehat{\tau}$ and the dependency term ξ. The dependency term in this context is also called he *dependency term* of $\widehat{t}^{\,1}$. It is implicitly assumed that every type $\widehat{\tau}$ is also well-formed under Σ, i.e. $\Sigma \vdash_{\text{wft}} \widehat{\tau}$, and that the resulting dependency annotation ξ is of sort $\star$, i.e. $\Sigma \vdash_{\text{s}} \xi : \star$.

We now discuss some of the more interesting rules of figure 6. In [T-VAR], both the annotated type and the dependency annotation are looked up in the environment. The dependency annotation of the unit value defaults to the least annotation in [T-UNIT]. While we could admit an arbitrary dependency annotation here, the same can be achieved by using the subtyping rule [T-SUB]. We employ this principle more often, e.g., in [T-ABS], and [T-PAIR]. This essentially means that the context in which such a term is used completely determines the annotation.

The rule [T-APP] may seem overly restrictive by requiring that the types and dependency annotations of the arguments match, and that the dependency annotations of the return value and the function itself are the same. However, in combination with the subtyping rule [T-SUB], this effectively does not restrict the analysis in any way. We see the same happening in other rules, such as [T-CASE] and [T-PROJ]. Note that the dependency annotation of the argument does not play a role in the resulting dependency annotation of the application. This is because we are dealing with a call by name semantics which means that the argument is not necessarily evaluated before the function call. It should be noted that this does not mean that the dependency annotations of arguments are ignored completely. If the body of a function makes use of an argument, the type system makes sure that its dependency annotation is also incorporated into the result.

When constructing a pair (rule [T-PAIR]), the dependency annotations of the components are stored in the type while the pair itself is assigned the least dependency annotation. When accessing a component of a pair (rule [T-PROJ]), we require that the dependency annotation of the pair matches the dependency annotation of the projected component. Again, this is no restriction due to the subtyping rule.

In [T-INL/INR], the argument to the injection constructor only determines the type and annotation of one component of the sum type while the other component can be chosen arbitrarily as long as the underlying type matches the annotation on the constructor. The destruction of sum types happens in a case statement that is handled by rule [T-CASE]. Again, to keep the rule simple and without loss of precision due to judicious use of rule [T-SUB], we may demand that the types of both branches match, and that additionally the dependency annotations of both branches and the scrutinee are equal.

The annotation rule [T-ANN] requires that the dependency annotation of the term being annotated is at least as large as the lattice element ℓ. In the fixpoint rule, [T-FIX], not only the types but also the dependency annotations of the term itself and the bound variables must match. Note that this rule also

---

[1] Following the literature of type and effect systems we would much like to use the term "effect" at this point, but decided to use a different term to avoid confusion with the literature on effect handlers.

$$\frac{\widehat{\varGamma}(x) = \widehat{\tau} \,\&\, \xi}{\varSigma \mid \widehat{\varGamma} \vdash_{\mathrm{te}} x : \widehat{\tau} \,\&\, \xi} \; [\text{T-Var}]$$

$$\frac{}{\varSigma \mid \widehat{\varGamma} \vdash_{\mathrm{te}} () : \widehat{\mathrm{unit}} \,\&\, \bot} \; [\text{T-Unit}]$$

$$\frac{\varSigma \mid \widehat{\varGamma}, x : \widehat{\tau}_1 \,\&\, \xi_1 \vdash_{\mathrm{te}} t : \widehat{\tau}_2 \,\&\, \xi_2}{\varSigma \mid \widehat{\varGamma} \vdash_{\mathrm{te}} \lambda x : \widehat{\tau}_1 \,\&\, \xi_1.t : \widehat{\tau}_1 \langle \xi_1 \rangle \to \tau_2 \langle \xi_2 \rangle \,\&\, \bot} \; [\text{T-Abs}]$$

$$\frac{\varSigma \mid \widehat{\varGamma} \vdash_{\mathrm{te}} t_1 : \widehat{\tau}_1 \langle \xi_1 \rangle \to \widehat{\tau}_2 \langle \xi_2 \rangle \,\&\, \xi_2 \qquad \varSigma \mid \widehat{\varGamma} \vdash_{\mathrm{te}} t_2 : \widehat{\tau}_1 \,\&\, \xi_1}{\varSigma \mid \widehat{\varGamma} \vdash_{\mathrm{te}} t_1 \; t_2 : \widehat{\tau}_2 \,\&\, \xi_2} \; [\text{T-App}]$$

$$\frac{\varSigma \mid \widehat{\varGamma} \vdash_{\mathrm{te}} t_1 : \widehat{\tau}_1 \,\&\, \xi_1 \qquad \varSigma \mid \widehat{\varGamma} \vdash_{\mathrm{te}} t_2 : \widehat{\tau}_2 \,\&\, \xi_2}{\varSigma \mid \widehat{\varGamma} \vdash_{\mathrm{te}} (t_1, t_2) : \widehat{\tau}_1 \langle \xi_1 \rangle \times \widehat{\tau}_2 \langle \xi_2 \rangle \,\&\, \bot} \; [\text{T-Pair}]$$

$$\frac{\varSigma \mid \widehat{\varGamma} \vdash_{\mathrm{te}} t : \widehat{\tau}_1 \langle \xi_1 \rangle \times \widehat{\tau}_2 \langle \xi_2 \rangle \,\&\, \xi_i}{\varSigma \mid \widehat{\varGamma} \vdash_{\mathrm{te}} \mathrm{proj}_i(t) : \widehat{\tau}_i \,\&\, \xi_i} \; [\text{T-Proj}]$$

$$\frac{\varSigma \mid \widehat{\varGamma} \vdash_{\mathrm{te}} t : \widehat{\tau}_1 \,\&\, \xi_1}{\varSigma \mid \widehat{\varGamma} \vdash_{\mathrm{te}} \mathrm{inl}_{\lfloor \widehat{\tau}_2 \rfloor}(t) : \widehat{\tau}_1 \langle \xi_1 \rangle + \widehat{\tau}_2 \langle \xi_2 \rangle \,\&\, \bot} \; [\text{T-Inl}]$$

$$\frac{\varSigma \mid \widehat{\varGamma} \vdash_{\mathrm{te}} t : \widehat{\tau}_2 \,\&\, \xi_2}{\varSigma \mid \widehat{\varGamma} \vdash_{\mathrm{te}} \mathrm{inr}_{\lfloor \widehat{\tau}_1 \rfloor}(t) : \widehat{\tau}_1 \langle \xi_1 \rangle + \widehat{\tau}_2 \langle \xi_2 \rangle \,\&\, \bot} \; [\text{T-Inr}]$$

$$\frac{\varSigma \mid \widehat{\varGamma} \vdash_{\mathrm{te}} t : \widehat{\tau}_1 \langle \xi_1 \rangle + \widehat{\tau}_2 \langle \xi_2 \rangle \,\&\, \xi \quad \begin{array}{c} \varSigma \mid \widehat{\varGamma}, x : \widehat{\tau}_1 \,\&\, \xi_1 \vdash_{\mathrm{te}} t_1 : \widehat{\tau} \,\&\, \xi \\ \varSigma \mid \widehat{\varGamma}, y : \widehat{\tau}_2 \,\&\, \xi_2 \vdash_{\mathrm{te}} t_2 : \widehat{\tau} \,\&\, \xi \end{array}}{\varSigma \mid \widehat{\varGamma} \vdash_{\mathrm{te}} \mathbf{case} \; t \; \mathbf{of} \; \{\mathrm{inl}(x) \to t_1; \mathrm{inr}(y) \to t_2\} : \widehat{\tau} \,\&\, \xi} \; [\text{T-Case}]$$

$$\frac{\varSigma \mid \widehat{\varGamma} \vdash_{\mathrm{te}} t : \widehat{\tau} \,\&\, \xi \qquad \varSigma \vdash_{\mathrm{sub}} \ell \sqsubseteq \xi}{\varSigma \mid \widehat{\varGamma} \vdash_{\mathrm{te}} \mathrm{ann}_\ell(t) : \widehat{\tau} \,\&\, \xi} \; [\text{T-Ann}]$$

$$\frac{\varSigma \mid \widehat{\varGamma}, x : \widehat{\tau} \,\&\, \xi \vdash_{\mathrm{te}} t : \widehat{\tau} \,\&\, \xi}{\varSigma \mid \widehat{\varGamma} \vdash_{\mathrm{te}} \mu x : \widehat{\tau} \,\&\, \xi.t : \widehat{\tau} \,\&\, \xi} \; [\text{T-Fix}]$$

$$\frac{\varSigma \mid \widehat{\varGamma} \vdash_{\mathrm{te}} t_1 : \widehat{\tau}_1 \,\&\, \xi \qquad \varSigma \mid \widehat{\varGamma} \vdash_{\mathrm{te}} t_2 : \widehat{\tau}_2 \,\&\, \xi}{\varSigma \mid \widehat{\varGamma} \vdash_{\mathrm{te}} \mathbf{seq} \; t_1 \; t_2 : \widehat{\tau}_2 \,\&\, \xi} \; [\text{T-Seq}]$$

$$\frac{\varSigma \mid \widehat{\varGamma} \vdash_{\mathrm{te}} t : \widehat{\tau}' \,\&\, \xi' \qquad \varSigma \vdash_{\mathrm{sub}} \widehat{\tau}' \leqslant \widehat{\tau} \qquad \varSigma \vdash_{\mathrm{sub}} \xi' \sqsubseteq \xi}{\varSigma \mid \widehat{\varGamma} \vdash_{\mathrm{te}} t : \widehat{\tau} \,\&\, \xi} \; [\text{T-Sub}]$$

$$\frac{\varSigma, \beta : \kappa \mid \widehat{\varGamma} \vdash_{\mathrm{te}} t : \widehat{\tau} \,\&\, \xi \qquad \beta \notin \mathrm{fav}(\widehat{\varGamma}) \cup \mathrm{fav}(\xi)}{\varSigma \mid \widehat{\varGamma} \vdash_{\mathrm{te}} \varLambda \beta :: \kappa.t : \forall \beta :: \kappa.\widehat{\tau} \,\&\, \xi} \; [\text{T-AnnAbs}]$$

$$\frac{\varSigma \mid \widehat{\varGamma} \vdash_{\mathrm{te}} t : \forall \beta :: \kappa.\widehat{\tau} \,\&\, \xi \qquad \varSigma \vdash_{\mathrm{s}} \xi' : \kappa}{\varSigma \mid \widehat{\varGamma} \vdash_{\mathrm{te}} t \; \langle \xi' \rangle : [\xi' / \beta]\widehat{\tau} \,\&\, \xi} \; [\text{T-AnnApp}]$$

Fig. 6: Declarative annotated type system $(\varSigma \mid \varGamma \vdash_{\mathrm{te}} \widehat{t} : \widehat{\tau} \,\&\, \xi)$

$$v' \in \mathbf{Nf}' ::= \lambda x : \hat{\tau} \,\&\, \xi.t \mid \Lambda\beta :: \kappa.t \mid () \mid \mathrm{inl}_\tau(t) \mid \mathrm{inr}_\tau(t) \mid (t_1, t_2)$$
$$v \in \mathbf{Nf} \quad ::= v' \mid \mathrm{ann}_\ell(v')$$

Fig. 7: Values in the target language

admits polyvariant recursion [23], since quantification can occur anywhere in an annotated type. Since seq t_1 t_2 forces the evaluation of its first argument, it requires that t_1's dependency annotation is part of the final result. This is justified, because the result depends on the termination behavior of t_1.

The subtyping rule [T-SUB] allows us to weaken the annotations nested inside a type through the subtyping relation (see figure 5), as well as the dependency annotations itself through the subsumption relation. The rule [T-ANNABS] introduces an annotation variable β of sort κ in the body t of the abstraction. The second premise ensures that the annotation variable does not escape its scope determined by the quantification on the type level. The annotation application rule [T-ANNAPP] allows the instantiation of an annotation variable with an arbitrary well-sorted dependency term.

5   Metatheory

In this section we develop a noninterference proof for our declarative type system, based on a small-step operational call-by-name semantics for the target language.

Figure 7 defines the values of the target language, i.e. those terms that cannot be further evaluated. Apart from a technicality related to annotations, they correspond exactly to the weak head normal forms of terms. The distinction for $\mathbf{Nf}' \subset \mathbf{Nf}$ is made to ensure that there is at most one annotation at top level.

The semantics itself is largely straightforward, except for the handling of annotations. These are moved just as far outwards as necessary in order to reach a normal form, thereby computing the least "permission" an evaluator must possess for computing a certain output. Figure 8 shows two rules: a lifting rule (for applications) and the rule for merging adjacent annotations (see the supplemental material for the others).

In the remainder of this section we state the standard *progress* and *subject reduction* theorems that ensure that our small-step semantics is compatible with

$$\frac{v' \in \mathbf{Nf}'}{(\mathrm{ann}_\ell(v'))\ t_2 \to \mathrm{ann}_\ell(v'\ t_2)}\ \text{[E-LIFTAPP]}$$

$$\frac{v' \in \mathbf{Nf}'}{\mathrm{ann}_{\ell_1}(\mathrm{ann}_{\ell_2}(v')) \to \mathrm{ann}_{\ell_1 \sqcup \ell_2}(v')}\ \text{[E-JOINANN]}$$

Fig. 8: Small-step semantics $(t \to t')$ (excerpt)

the annotated type system. The following progress theorem demonstrates that any well-typed term is in normal form, or an evaluation step can be performed.

Theorem 1 (Progress). *If* $\emptyset \mid \emptyset \vdash_{\mathsf{te}} t : \hat{\tau} \& \xi$, *then either* $t \in \mathbf{Nf}$ *or there is a* t' *such that* $t \to t'$.

The subject reduction property says that the reduction of a well-typed term results in a term of the same type.

Theorem 2 (Subject Reduction). *If* $\emptyset \mid \emptyset \vdash_{\mathsf{te}} t : \hat{\tau} \& \xi$ *and there is a* t' *such that* $t \to t'$, *then* $\emptyset \mid \emptyset \vdash_{\mathsf{te}} t' : \hat{\tau} \& \xi$.

As expected, subject reduction extends naturally to a sequence of reductions by induction on the length of the reduction sequence:

Corollary 1. *If we have* $\emptyset \mid \emptyset \vdash_{\mathsf{te}} t : \hat{\tau} \& \xi$ *and* $t \to^* v$, *then* $\emptyset \mid \emptyset \vdash_{\mathsf{te}} v : \hat{\tau} \& \xi$.

where, as usual, we write $t \to^* v$ if there is a finite sequence of terms $(t_i)_{0 \leqslant i \leqslant n}$ with $t_0 = t$ and $t_n = v \in \mathbf{Nf}$ and reductions $(t_i \to t_{i+1})_{0 \leqslant i < n}$ between them. If there is no such sequence, this is denoted by $t \Uparrow$ and t is said to *diverge*.

Finally, if a term evaluates to an annotated value, this annotation is compatible with the dependency annotation that has been assigned to the term:

Theorem 3 (Semantic Soundness). *If we have* $\emptyset \mid \emptyset \vdash_{\mathsf{te}} t : \hat{\tau} \& \xi$ *and* $t \to^*$ $\mathrm{ann}_{\ell}(v')$, *then* $\emptyset \vdash_{\mathsf{sub}} \ell \sqsubseteq \xi$.

The noninterference property An important theorem for the safety of program transformations/optimizations using the results of dependency analysis is *noninterference*. It guarantees that if there is a target term t depending on some variable x such that $\emptyset \mid x : \hat{\tau}' \& \xi' \vdash_{\mathsf{te}} t : \hat{\tau} \& \xi$ holds and the dependency annotation ξ' of the variable is not encompassed by the resulting dependency annotation ξ (i.e. $\emptyset \vdash_{\mathsf{sub}} \xi' \not\sqsubseteq \xi$), then t will always evaluate to the same normal form, regardless the value of x.

Since we are in a non-strict setting, our noninterference property only applies to the topmost constructors of values. This is because the dependency annotations derived in the annotated type system only provide information about the evaluation to weak head normal form. Nested terms might possess lower as well as higher classifications. In particular, the subterms with greater dependency annotations than their enclosing constructors prevent us from making a more general statement because those can still depend on the context whereas the top-level constructor cannot. In the noninterference theorem presented for the SLam calculus, this problem is circumvented by restricting the statement to so called *transparent* types, where the annotations of nested components are decreasing when moving further inward [9].

In the following we consider two normal forms $v_1, v_2 \in \mathbf{Nf}$ to be *similar*, denoted $v_1 \simeq v_2$, if their top level constructors (and annotations, if present) match (see the supplemental material for the unsurprising definition of $\simeq$). So, $v_1 \simeq v_2$ implies that these two values are indistinguishable without further evaluation, which is the property guaranteed by the noninterference theorem.

Theorem 4 (Noninterference). *Let t be a target term such that $\emptyset \mid x : \widehat{\tau}' \,\&\, \xi' \vdash_{\text{te}} t : \widehat{\tau} \,\&\, \xi$ and $\emptyset \vdash_{\text{sub}} \xi' \not\sqsubseteq \xi$. Let v be a value.*

If there is a t_1 with $\emptyset \mid \emptyset \vdash_{\text{te}} t_1 : \widehat{\tau}' \,\&\, \xi'$ such that $[t_1 \,/\, x]t \to^* v$, then there is a t' such that for all t_2 with $\emptyset \mid \emptyset \vdash_{\text{te}} t_2 : \widehat{\tau}' \,\&\, \xi'$ we have $[t_2 \,/\, x]t \to^* [t_2 \,/\, x]t'$ and $[t_1 \,/\, x]t' \simeq [t_2 \,/\, x]t'$.

The noninterference proofs crucially rely on the fact that the source term is well-typed, and the additional assumption $\emptyset \vdash_{\text{sub}} \xi' \not\sqsubseteq \xi$ stating that the dependency annotation of the variable in the context is not encompassed by the dependency annotation of the term being evaluated.

By introducing the restriction to transparent types, we can recover the notion of noninterference used for the SLam calculus. For example, if we have a transparent type $\widehat{\tau}_1 \langle \xi_1 \rangle \times \widehat{\tau}_2 \langle \xi_2 \rangle \,\&\, \xi$ (i.e. $\emptyset \vdash_{\text{sub}} \xi_1 \sqsubseteq \xi$ and $\emptyset \vdash_{\text{sub}} \xi_2 \sqsubseteq \xi$) and $\emptyset \vdash_{\text{sub}} \xi' \not\sqsubseteq \xi$ holds, then we also know $\emptyset \vdash_{\text{sub}} \xi' \not\sqsubseteq \xi_1$ and $\emptyset \vdash_{\text{sub}} \xi' \not\sqsubseteq \xi_2$. Otherwise, we would get $\emptyset \vdash_{\text{sub}} \xi' \sqsubseteq \xi$ by transitivity, contradicting the assumption. This means all prerequisites of the noninterference theorem are still fulfilled.

Hence, it is possible in these cases to apply the noninterference theorem to the nested (possibly unevaluated) subterms of a constructor in weak head normal form. As in the work of [1], our noninterference theorem is restricted to deal with terms depending on exactly one variable.

6 The type reconstruction algorithm

Modularity considerations When designing the type reconstruction algorithm we have two goals: it should be a conservative extension of the underlying type system, and types assigned by the analysis should be as general as possible. Concretely, a function's type must be general enough to be able to adapt to arguments with arbitrary annotations. These two goals give rise to the notion of *fully flexible* and *fully parametric* types defined by [12]. [16] calls these types *conservative* and *pattern* types respectively. Informally, an annotated type is a pattern type if it can be instantiated to any conservative type of the same shape and a conservative type is an analysis of an expression that is able to cope with any arguments it might depend on. These types are conservative in the sense that they make the least assumptions about their arguments and therefore are a conservative estimate compared to other typings with fewer degrees of freedom.

For a pattern type to be instantiable to any conservative type, we first need to make sure that all dependency annotations occurring in it can be instantiated to the corresponding dependency terms in a matching conservative type. This leads to the following definition of a *pattern* in the $\lambda^{\sqcup}$-calculus. It is based on the similar definition by [16] which in turn is a special case of a pattern in higher-order unification theory [4,21]. A $\lambda^{\sqcup}$-term is a *pattern* if it is of the form $f \, \beta_1 \, \cdots \, \beta_n$ where f is a free variable and $\beta_1, \ldots, \beta_n$ are distinct bound variables. A unification problem of the form $\forall \beta_1 \cdots \beta_n . f \, \beta_1 \cdots \beta_n = \xi$ where the left-hand side is a pattern is called *pattern unification*. A pattern unification problem $\forall \beta_1 \cdots \beta_n . f \, \beta_1 \cdots \beta_n = \xi$ has a unique most general solution, namely the substitution $[f \mapsto \lambda \beta_1 . \cdots \lambda \beta_n . \xi]$ [4].

$$\frac{\beta \notin \overline{\alpha_i}}{\overline{\alpha_i :: \kappa_{\alpha_i}} \vdash_p \widehat{\text{unit}} \& \beta \; \overline{\alpha_i} \rhd \beta :: \overline{\kappa_{\alpha_i}} \Rightarrow \star} \; [\text{P-Unit}]$$

$$\frac{\overline{\alpha_i :: \kappa_{\alpha_i}} \vdash_p \widehat{\tau_1} \& \xi_1 \rhd \overline{\beta_j :: \kappa_{\beta_j}} \qquad \overline{\alpha_i :: \kappa_{\alpha_i}} \vdash_p \widehat{\tau_2} \& \xi_2 \rhd \overline{\gamma_k :: \kappa_{\gamma_k}}}{\overline{\alpha_i :: \kappa_{\alpha_i}} \vdash_p \widehat{\tau_1}\langle\xi_1\rangle \times \widehat{\tau_2}\langle\xi_2\rangle \& \beta \; \overline{\alpha_i} \rhd \beta :: \overline{\kappa_{\alpha_i}} \Rightarrow \star, \overline{\beta_j :: \kappa_{\beta_j}}, \overline{\gamma_k :: \kappa_{\gamma_k}}} \; [\text{P-Prod}]$$

$$\frac{\emptyset \vdash_p \widehat{\tau_1} \& \xi_1 \rhd \overline{\beta_j :: \kappa_{\beta_j}} \qquad \overline{\alpha_i :: \kappa_{\alpha_i}}, \overline{\beta_j :: \kappa_{\beta_j}} \vdash_p \widehat{\tau_2} \& \xi_2 \rhd \overline{\gamma_k :: \kappa_{\gamma_k}}}{\overline{\alpha_i :: \kappa_{\alpha_i}} \vdash_p \forall \overline{\beta_j :: \kappa_{\beta_j}}.\widehat{\tau_1}\langle\xi_1\rangle \rightarrow \widehat{\tau_2}\langle\xi_2\rangle \& \beta \; \overline{\alpha_i} \rhd \beta :: \overline{\kappa_{\alpha_i}} \Rightarrow \star, \overline{\gamma_k :: \kappa_{\gamma_k}}} \; [\text{P-Arr}]$$

Fig. 9: Pattern types ($\Sigma \vdash_p \widehat{\tau} \& \xi \rhd \Sigma'$), where $\beta \notin \overline{\alpha_i}, \overline{\beta_j}, \overline{\gamma_k}$, and [P-Sum] is like [P-Prod]

The definition of a pattern is then extended to annotated types using the rules from figure 9. Our definition is more precise than the one from previous work in that it makes explicit which variables are expected to be bound and which are free. We require that all variables with different names in the definition of these rules are distinct from each other.

An annotated type and depencency pair $\widehat{\tau} \& \xi$ is a *pattern type* under the sort environment Σ if the judgment $\Sigma \vdash_p \widehat{\tau} \& \xi \rhd \Sigma'$ holds for some Σ'. We call the variables in Σ *argument variables* and the variables in Σ' *pattern variables*.

Example 1. A simple pattern type with the pattern variables $\beta :: \star \Rightarrow \star$ and $\beta' :: \star \Rightarrow \star \Rightarrow \star$ is

$$\forall \beta_1 :: \star.\widehat{\text{unit}}\langle\beta_1\rangle \rightarrow (\forall \beta_2 :: \star.\widehat{\text{unit}}\langle\beta_2\rangle \rightarrow \widehat{\text{unit}}\langle\beta' \; \beta_1 \; \beta_2\rangle)\langle\beta \; \beta_1\rangle$$

Note that since β_1 is quantified on the function arrow chain, it is passed on to the second function arrow. However, it is not propagated into the second argument. In general, annotations on the return type may depend on the annotations of all previous arguments while annotations of the arguments may not. This prevents any dependency between the annotations of arguments and guarantees that they are as permissive as possible. This is also why pattern variables in a covariant position are passed on to the next higher level while pattern variables in arguments are quantified in the enclosing function arrow. This allows the caller of a function to instantiate the dependency annotations of the parameters to the actual arguments.

As we stated earlier, a conservative function type makes the least assumptions over its arguments. Formally, this means that arguments of conservative functions are pattern types. We will later see that a pattern type can be instantiated to any conservative type of the same shape. On the other hand, non-functional conservative types are not constrained in their annotations. These characteristics are captured by the following definition based on *conservative types* [16] and *fully flexible types* [12].

An annotated type $\widehat{\tau}$ is *conservative* if

$$\frac{\beta \text{ fresh}}{\overline{\alpha_i :: \kappa_{\alpha_i}} \vdash_c \text{unit} : \widehat{\text{unit}} \;\&\; \beta \; \overline{\alpha_i} \triangleright \beta :: \overline{\kappa_{\alpha_i}} \Rightarrow \star} \; [\text{C-Unit}]$$

$$\frac{\overline{\alpha_i :: \kappa_{\alpha_i}} \vdash_c \tau_1 : \widehat{\tau}_1 \;\&\; \xi_1 \triangleright \overline{\beta_j :: \kappa_{\beta_j}} \qquad \overline{\alpha_i :: \kappa_{\alpha_i}} \vdash_c \tau_2 : \widehat{\tau}_2 \;\&\; \xi_2 \triangleright \overline{\gamma_k :: \kappa_{\gamma_k}}}{\overline{\alpha_i :: \kappa_{\alpha_i}} \vdash_c \tau_1 \times \tau_2 : \widehat{\tau}_1 \langle \xi_1 \rangle \times \widehat{\tau}_2 \langle \xi_2 \rangle \;\&\; \beta \; \overline{\alpha_i} \triangleright \beta :: \overline{\kappa_{\alpha_i}} \Rightarrow \star, \overline{\beta_j :: \kappa_{\beta_j}}, \overline{\gamma_k :: \kappa_{\gamma_k}}} \; [\text{C-Prod}]$$

$$\frac{\emptyset \vdash_c \tau_1 : \widehat{\tau}_1 \;\&\; \xi_1 \triangleright \overline{\beta_j :: \kappa_{\beta_j}} \qquad \overline{\alpha_i :: \kappa_{\alpha_i}}, \overline{\beta_j :: \kappa_{\beta_j}} \vdash_c \tau_2 : \widehat{\tau}_2 \;\&\; \xi_2 \triangleright \overline{\gamma_k :: \kappa_{\gamma_k}}}{\overline{\alpha_i :: \kappa_{\alpha_i}} \vdash_c \tau_1 \to \tau_2 : \forall \overline{\beta_j :: \kappa_{\beta_j}}.\widehat{\tau}_1 \langle \xi_1 \rangle \to \widehat{\tau}_2 \langle \xi_2 \rangle \;\&\; \beta \; \overline{\alpha_i} \triangleright \beta :: \overline{\kappa_{\alpha_i}} \Rightarrow \star, \overline{\gamma_k :: \kappa_{\gamma_k}}} \; [\text{C-Arr}]$$

Fig. 10: Type completion ($\Sigma \vdash_c \tau : \widehat{\tau} \& \xi \triangleright \Sigma'$), all β fresh, [C-Sum] is like [C-Prod]

1. $\widehat{\tau} = \widehat{\text{unit}}$, or
2. $\widehat{\tau} = \widehat{\tau}_1 \langle \xi_1 \rangle + \widehat{\tau}_2 \langle \xi_2 \rangle$ and both $\widehat{\tau}_1$ and $\widehat{\tau}_2$ are conservative, or
3. $\widehat{\tau} = \widehat{\tau}_1 \langle \xi_1 \rangle \times \widehat{\tau}_2 \langle \xi_2 \rangle$ and both $\widehat{\tau}_1$ and $\widehat{\tau}_2$ are conservative, or
4. $\widehat{\tau} = \forall \overline{\beta_j :: \kappa_j}.\widehat{\tau}_1 \langle \xi_1 \rangle \to \widehat{\tau}_2 \langle \xi_2 \rangle$ and both (a) $\emptyset \vdash_p \widehat{\tau}_1 \& \xi_1 \triangleright \overline{\beta_j :: \kappa_j}$ and (b) $\widehat{\tau}_2$ is conservative.

Moreover, an annotated type and depencency pair $\widehat{\tau} \& \xi$ is *conservative* if $\widehat{\tau}$ is *conservative* and an annotated type environment $\widehat{\Gamma}$ is *conservative* if for all $x \in \text{dom}(\widehat{\Gamma})$, $\widehat{\Gamma}(x)$ is conservative.

The following type signature for the function f is a conservative type that takes the function type from example 1 as an argument.

$$f : \forall \beta :: \star \Rightarrow \star. \forall \beta' :: \star \Rightarrow \star \Rightarrow \star. \forall \beta_3 :: \star.$$
$$(\forall \beta_1 :: \star. \widehat{\text{unit}}\langle \beta_1 \rangle \to (\forall \beta_2 :: \star. \widehat{\text{unit}}\langle \beta_2 \rangle \to \widehat{\text{unit}}\langle \beta' \; \beta_1 \; \beta_2 \rangle)\langle \beta \; \beta_1 \rangle)\langle \beta_3 \rangle$$
$$\to \widehat{\text{unit}}\langle \beta_3 \sqcup \beta \perp \sqcup \beta' \perp \ell \rangle \;\&\; \perp$$

Note that the pattern variables of the argument have been bound in the top-level function type. This allows callers of f to instantiate these patterns.

We can extend the previous definition of pattern types to the type completion relation shown in figure 10. It relates every underlying type τ with a pattern type $\widehat{\tau}$ such that $\widehat{\tau}$ erases to τ. It is defined through judgments $\Sigma \vdash_c \tau : \widehat{\tau} \& \xi \triangleright \Sigma'$ with the meaning that under the sort environment Σ, τ is completed to the annotated type $\widehat{\tau}$ and the dependency annotation ξ containing the pattern variables Σ'. The completion relation can also be interpreted as a function taking Σ and τ as arguments and returning $\widehat{\tau}$, ξ and Σ'.

Lastly, we revisit the examples from the previous sections and show how a pattern type can be mechanically derived from an underlying type.

In example 1 we presented a pattern type for the underlying type unit $\to$ unit $\to$ unit. Using the type completion relation, we can derive the pattern type,

$$(\forall \beta_1.\widehat{\text{unit}}\langle \beta_1 \rangle) \to (\forall \beta_2.\widehat{\text{unit}}\langle \beta_2 \rangle \to \widehat{\text{unit}}\langle \beta' \; \beta_1 \; \beta_2 \rangle)\langle \beta \; \beta_1 \rangle) \;\&\; \beta_3$$

without having to guess. This is because the components $\widehat{\tau}$, ξ and Σ' in a judgment $\Sigma \vdash_c \tau : \widehat{\tau} \& \xi \triangleright \Sigma'$ are uniquely determined by Σ and τ from looking at the syntax alone. The resulting pattern type contains three pattern variables, $\beta :: \star \Rightarrow \star$, $\beta' :: \star \Rightarrow \star \Rightarrow \star$ and $\beta_3 :: \star$. If the initial sort environment is empty, these are also the only free variables of the pattern type.

Based on the type completion relation we can define least type completions. These are conservative types that are subtypes of all other conservative types of the same shape. Therefore, all annotations occurring in positive positions on the top level function arrow chain must also be least. We do not need to consider arguments here because those are by definition equal up to alpha-conversion due to being pattern types. We define the *least annotation term* of sort κ as

$$\bot_\star = \bot$$
$$\bot_{\kappa_1 \Rightarrow \kappa_2} = \lambda\beta : \kappa_1.\bot_{\kappa_2}.$$

These least annotation terms correspond to the least elements of our bounded lattice for a given sort κ. This in turn leads us to the definition of the least completion of type τ (see figure 10) by substituting all free variables in the completion with the least annotation of the corresponding sort, i.e.

$$\bot_\tau = [\overline{\bot_{\kappa_i} / \beta_i}]\widehat{\tau} \text{ for } \emptyset \vdash_c \tau : \widehat{\tau} \,\&\, \xi \rhd \overline{\beta_i :: \kappa_i}.$$

The algorithm We can now move on to the type reconstruction algorithm that performs the actual analysis. At its core lies algorithm $\mathcal{R}$ shown in figure 11. The input of the algorithm is a triple $(\widehat{\Gamma}, \Sigma, t)$ consisting of a well-typed source term t, an annotated type environment $\widehat{\Gamma}$ providing the types and dependency annotations of the free term variables in t and a sort environment Σ mapping each free annotation variable in scope to its sort. It returns a triple $\widehat{t} : \widehat{\tau} \,\&\, \xi$ consisting of an elaborated term $\widehat{t}$ in the target language (that erases to the source term t), an annotated type $\widehat{\tau}$ and an dependency annotation ξ such that $\Sigma \mid \widehat{\Gamma} \vdash_{\text{te}} \widehat{t} : \widehat{\tau} \,\&\, \xi$ holds. In the definition of $\mathcal{R}$, to avoid clutter, we write Γ instead of $\widehat{\Gamma}$ because we are only dealing with one kind of type environment.

The algorithm relies on the invariant that all types in the type environment and the inferred type must be conservative. In the version of [16], all inferred dependency annotations (including those nested as annotations in types) had to be canonically ordered as well. But as it turned out that this canonically ordered form was not enough for deciding semantic equality, so we lifted this requirement. We still mark those places in the algorithm where canonicalization would have occurred with $\lfloor \cdot \rfloor$, but the actual result of this operation does not matter as long as the dependency terms remain equivalent.

The algorithm for computing the least upper bound of types ($\sqcup$ in figure 12) requires that both types are conservative, have the same shape and use the same names for bound variables. The latter can be ensured by α-conversion while the former two requirements are fulfilled by how this function is used in $\mathcal{R}$.

The restriction to conservative types allows us to ignore functions arguments because these are always required to be pattern types, which are unique up to α-equivalence. This alleviates the need for computing a corresponding greatest lower bound of types, because the algorithm only traverses covariant positions.

$\mathcal{R} : \mathbf{AnnTyEnv} \times \mathbf{SortEnv} \times \mathbf{Tm} \to \widehat{\mathbf{Tm}} \times \widehat{\mathbf{Ty}} \times \mathbf{AnnTm}$

$\mathcal{R}(\Gamma; \Sigma; x) = x : \Gamma(x)$

$\mathcal{R}(\Gamma; \Sigma; ()) = () : \widehat{\mathrm{unit}} \ \& \perp$

$\mathcal{R}(\Gamma; \Sigma; \mathrm{ann}_\ell(t)) =$
$\quad \mathbf{let}\ \widehat{t} : \widehat{\tau} \ \& \ \xi = \mathcal{R}(\Gamma; \Sigma; t)$
$\quad \mathbf{in}\ \mathrm{ann}_\ell(\widehat{t}) : \widehat{\tau} \ \& \ \lfloor \xi \sqcup \ell \rfloor_\Sigma$

$\mathcal{R}(\Gamma; \Sigma; \mathrm{seq}\ t_1\ t_2) =$
$\quad \mathbf{let}\ \widehat{t_1} : \widehat{\tau_1} \ \& \ \xi_1 = \mathcal{R}(\Gamma; \Sigma; t_1)$
$\quad\quad\ \ \widehat{t_2} : \widehat{\tau_2} \ \& \ \xi_2 = \mathcal{R}(\Gamma; \Sigma; t_2)$
$\quad \mathbf{in}\ \mathrm{seq}\ \widehat{t_1}\ \widehat{t_2} : \widehat{\tau_2} \ \& \ \lfloor \xi_1 \sqcup \xi_2 \rfloor_\Sigma$

$\mathcal{R}(\Gamma; \Sigma; (t_1, t_2)) =$
$\quad \mathbf{let}\ \widehat{t_1} : \widehat{\tau_1} \ \& \ \xi_1 = \mathcal{R}(\Gamma; \Sigma; t_1)$
$\quad\quad\ \ \widehat{t_2} : \widehat{\tau_2} \ \& \ \xi_2 = \mathcal{R}(\Gamma; \Sigma; t_2)$
$\quad \mathbf{in}\ (\widehat{t_1}, \widehat{t_2}) : \widehat{\tau_1}\langle \xi_1 \rangle \times \widehat{\tau_2}\langle \xi_2 \rangle \ \& \perp$

$\mathcal{R}(\Gamma; \Sigma; \mathrm{inl}_{\tau_2}(t)) =$
$\quad \mathbf{let}\ \widehat{t} : \widehat{\tau_1} \ \& \ \xi_1 = \mathcal{R}(\Gamma; \Sigma; t)$
$\quad \mathbf{in}\ \mathrm{inl}_{\tau_2}(\widehat{t}) : \widehat{\tau_1}\langle \xi_1 \rangle + \perp_{\tau_2}\langle \perp \rangle \ \& \perp$

$\mathcal{R}(\Gamma; \Sigma; \mathrm{inr}_{\tau_1}(t)) =$
$\quad \mathbf{let}\ \widehat{t} : \widehat{\tau_2} \ \& \ \xi_2 = \mathcal{R}(\Gamma; \Sigma; t)$
$\quad \mathbf{in}\ \mathrm{inr}_{\tau_1}(\widehat{t}) : \perp_{\tau_1}\langle \perp \rangle + \widehat{\tau_2}\langle \xi_2 \rangle \ \& \perp$

$\mathcal{R}(\Gamma; \Sigma;\ \mathbf{case}\ t_1\ \mathbf{of}\ \{\mathrm{inl}(x) \to t_2;$
$\quad\quad\quad\quad\quad\quad\quad\quad \mathrm{inr}(y) \to t_3\}) =$
$\quad \mathbf{let}\ \widehat{t_1} : \widehat{\tau}\langle \xi \rangle + \widehat{\tau'}\langle \xi' \rangle \ \& \ \xi_1 = \mathcal{R}(\Gamma; \Sigma; t_1)$
$\quad\quad\ \ \widehat{t_2} : \widehat{\tau_2} \ \& \ \xi_2 = \mathcal{R}(\Gamma, x : \widehat{\tau} \ \& \ \xi; \Sigma; t_2)$
$\quad\quad\ \ \widehat{t_3} : \widehat{\tau_3} \ \& \ \xi_3 = \mathcal{R}(\Gamma, y : \widehat{\tau'} \ \& \ \xi'; \Sigma; t_3)$
$\quad \mathbf{in}\ \mathbf{case}\ \widehat{t_1}\ \mathbf{of}\ \{\mathrm{inl}(x) \to \widehat{t_2}; \mathrm{inr}(y) \to \widehat{t_3}\}$

$\quad\quad\quad\quad\quad\quad : \lfloor \widehat{\tau_2} \sqcup \widehat{\tau_3} \rfloor_\Sigma \ \& \ \lfloor \xi_1 \sqcup \xi_2 \sqcup \xi_3 \rfloor_\Sigma$

$\mathcal{R}(\Gamma; \Sigma; \mathrm{proj}_i(t)) =$
$\quad \mathbf{let}\ \widehat{t} : \widehat{\tau_1}\langle \xi_1 \rangle \times \widehat{\tau_2}\langle \xi_2 \rangle \ \& \ \xi = \mathcal{R}(\Gamma; \Sigma; t)$
$\quad \mathbf{in}\ \mathrm{proj}_i(\widehat{t}) : \widehat{\tau_i} \ \& \ \lfloor \xi \sqcup \xi_i \rfloor_\Sigma$

$\mathcal{R}(\Gamma; \Sigma; \lambda x : \tau_1.t) =$
$\quad \mathbf{let}\ \widehat{\tau_1} \ \& \ \beta \triangleright \overline{\beta_i :: \kappa_i} = \mathcal{C}([]; \tau_1)$
$\quad\quad\ \ \Gamma' = \Gamma, x : \widehat{\tau_1} \ \& \ \beta$
$\quad\quad\ \ \Sigma' = \Sigma, \overline{\beta_i :: \kappa_i}$
$\quad\quad\ \ \widehat{t} : \widehat{\tau_2} \ \& \ \xi_2 = \mathcal{R}(\Gamma'; \Sigma'; t)$
$\quad \mathbf{in}\ \Lambda\overline{\beta_i :: \kappa_i}.\lambda x : \widehat{\tau_1} \ \& \ \beta.\widehat{t}$
$\quad\quad\quad : \forall \overline{\beta_i :: \kappa_i}.\widehat{\tau_1}\langle \beta \rangle \to \widehat{\tau_2}\langle \xi_2 \rangle \ \& \perp$

$\mathcal{R}(\Gamma; \Sigma; t_1\ t_2) =$
$\quad \mathbf{let}\ \widehat{t_1} : \widehat{\tau_1} \ \& \ \xi_1 = \mathcal{R}(\Gamma; \Sigma; t_1)$
$\quad\quad\ \ \widehat{t_2} : \widehat{\tau_2} \ \& \ \xi_2 = \mathcal{R}(\Gamma; \Sigma; t_2)$
$\quad\quad\ \ \widehat{\tau'_2}\langle \beta \rangle \to \widehat{\tau}\langle \xi \rangle \triangleright \overline{\beta_i} = \mathcal{I}(\widehat{\tau_1})$
$\quad\quad\ \ \theta = [\beta \mapsto \xi_2] \circ \mathcal{M}([]; \widehat{\tau'_2}; \widehat{\tau_2})$
$\quad \mathbf{in}\ \widehat{t_1}\ \overline{\langle \theta\beta_i \rangle}\ \widehat{t_2} : \lfloor \theta\widehat{\tau} \rfloor_\Sigma \ \& \ \lfloor \xi_1 \sqcup \theta\xi \rfloor_\Sigma$

$\mathcal{R}(\Gamma; \Sigma; \mu x : \tau.t) =$
$\quad \mathbf{do}\ i; \widehat{\tau_0} \ \& \ \xi_0 \leftarrow 0; \perp_\tau \ \& \perp$
$\quad\quad \mathbf{repeat}\ \widehat{t_{i+1}} : \widehat{\tau_{i+1}} \ \& \ \xi_{i+1}$
$\quad\quad\quad\quad\quad\quad \leftarrow \mathcal{R}(\Gamma, x : \widehat{\tau_i} \ \& \ \xi_i; \Sigma; t)$
$\quad\quad\quad\quad i \leftarrow i + 1$
$\quad\quad \mathbf{until}\quad (\widehat{\tau_{i-1}} \equiv \widehat{\tau_i} \wedge \xi_{i-1} \equiv \xi_i)$
$\quad\quad \mathbf{return}\ (\mu x : \widehat{\tau_i} \ \& \ \xi_i.\widehat{t_i}) : \widehat{\tau_i} \ \& \ \xi_i$

Fig. 11: Type reconstruction algorithm ($\mathcal{R}$)

The handling of λ-abstractions uses the type completion algorithm $\mathcal{C}$ of figure 12, that defers its work to the type completion relation defined earlier which can be interpreted in a functional way (see figure 10). The underlying type of the function argument is completed to a pattern type. The function body is analyzed in the presence of the newly introduced pattern variables. Note that this pattern type is also conservative, thereby preserving the invariant that the context only holds conservative types. The inferred annotated type of the lambda abstraction universally quantifies over all pattern variables and the quantification is reflected on the term level through annotation abstractions $\Lambda\beta :: \kappa.t$.

In order to analyze function applications, we need two more auxiliary algorithms. The first one is the instantiation procedure $\mathcal{I}$ (see figure 12) which instantiates all top-level quantifiers with fresh annotation variables. The second is the matching algorithm $\mathcal{M}$ (see figure 12) which instantiates a pattern type

$\sqcup : \widehat{\mathbf{Ty}} \times \widehat{\mathbf{Ty}} \to \widehat{\mathbf{Ty}}$

$$\begin{aligned}
&\widehat{\text{unit}} && \sqcup \widehat{\text{unit}} && = \widehat{\text{unit}} \\
&(\widehat{\tau}_1\langle\xi_1\rangle \times \widehat{\tau}_2\langle\xi_2\rangle)) && \sqcup (\widehat{\tau}_1'\langle\xi_1'\rangle \times \widehat{\tau}_2'\langle\xi_2'\rangle)) && = (\widehat{\tau}_1 \sqcup \widehat{\tau}_1')\langle\xi_1 \sqcup \xi_1'\rangle \times (\widehat{\tau}_2 \sqcup \widehat{\tau}_2')\langle\xi_2 \sqcup \xi_2'\rangle \\
&(\widehat{\tau}_1\langle\beta\rangle \to \widehat{\tau}_2\langle\xi_2\rangle)) && \sqcup (\widehat{\tau}_1\langle\beta\rangle \to \widehat{\tau}_2'\langle\xi_2'\rangle)) && = \widehat{\tau}_1\langle\beta\rangle \to (\widehat{\tau}_2 \sqcup \widehat{\tau}_2')\langle\xi_2 \sqcup \xi_2'\rangle \\
&(\forall\beta :: \kappa.\widehat{\tau}) && \sqcup (\forall\beta :: \kappa.\widehat{\tau}') && = \forall\beta :: \kappa.\widehat{\tau} \sqcup \widehat{\tau}'
\end{aligned}$$

$\mathcal{C} : \mathbf{SortEnv} \to \widehat{\mathbf{Ty}} \times \mathbf{AnnTm} \times \mathbf{SortEnv}$

$\mathcal{C}(\Sigma; \tau) = \widehat{\tau} \, \& \, \xi \rhd \overline{\beta_i :: \kappa_i}$ **where** $\Sigma \vdash_c \tau : \widehat{\tau} \, \& \, \xi \rhd \overline{\beta_i :: \kappa_i}$

$\mathcal{I} : \widehat{\mathbf{Ty}} \to \widehat{\mathbf{Ty}} \times \mathbf{SortEnv}$

$$\begin{aligned}
\mathcal{I}(\forall\beta :: \kappa.\widehat{\tau}) &= \textbf{let } \widehat{\tau}' \rhd \Sigma = \mathcal{I}(\widehat{\tau}) \textbf{ in } [\beta \mapsto \beta'](\widehat{\tau}') \rhd \beta' :: \kappa, \Sigma \textbf{ where } \beta' \text{ be fresh} \\
\mathcal{I}(\widehat{\tau}) &= \widehat{\tau} \rhd []
\end{aligned}$$

$\mathcal{M} : \mathbf{SortEnv} \times \widehat{\mathbf{Ty}} \times \widehat{\mathbf{Ty}} \to \mathbf{AnnSubst}$

$$\begin{aligned}
\mathcal{M}(\Sigma; \widehat{\text{unit}}; \widehat{\text{unit}}) &= [] \\
\mathcal{M}(\Sigma; \widehat{\tau}_1'\langle\beta \, \overline{\beta_i}\rangle \times \widehat{\tau}_2'\langle\beta' \, \overline{\beta_i}\rangle; \widehat{\tau}_1\langle\xi_1\rangle \times \widehat{\tau}_2\langle\xi_2\rangle)) &= \\
\quad [\beta \mapsto \lambda\overline{\beta_i :: \Sigma(\beta_i)}.\xi_1, \beta' \mapsto \lambda\overline{\beta_i :: \Sigma(\beta_i)}.\xi_2] &\circ \mathcal{M}(\Sigma; \widehat{\tau}_1'; \widehat{\tau}_1) \circ \mathcal{M}(\Sigma; \widehat{\tau}_2'; \widehat{\tau}_2) \\
\mathcal{M}(\Sigma; \widehat{\tau}_1\langle\beta\rangle \to \widehat{\tau}_2'\langle\beta' \, \overline{\beta_i}\rangle; \widehat{\tau}_1\langle\beta\rangle \to \widehat{\tau}_2\langle\xi\rangle)) &= \\
\quad [\beta' \mapsto \lambda\overline{\beta_i :: \Sigma(\beta_i)}.\xi] &\circ \mathcal{M}(\Sigma; \widehat{\tau}_2'; \widehat{\tau}_2) \\
\mathcal{M}(\Sigma; \forall\beta :: \kappa.\widehat{\tau}'; \forall\beta :: \kappa.\widehat{\tau}) &= \mathcal{M}(\Sigma, \beta :: \kappa; \widehat{\tau}'; \widehat{\tau})
\end{aligned}$$

Fig. 12: Least upper bound of types ($\sqcup$), completion ($\mathcal{C}$), instantiation ($\mathcal{I}$), and matching ($\mathcal{M}$). Rules for $\cdot + \cdot$ in $\sqcup$ and $\mathcal{M}$ are like those for $\cdot \times \cdot$.

with a conservative type of the same shape. It returns a substitution obtained by performing pattern unification on corresponding annotations.

Soundness and Completeness An annotated type environment $\widehat{\Gamma}$ is well-formed under an environment Σ, if $\widehat{\Gamma}$ is conservative and for all bindings $x : \widehat{\tau} \, \& \, \xi$ in $\widehat{\Gamma}$ we have $\Sigma \vdash_{\text{wft}} \widehat{\tau}$ and $\Sigma \vdash_s \xi : \star$.

In order to demonstrate the correctness of the reconstruction algorithm presented in this section we have to show that for every well-typed underlying term, it produces an analysis (i.e. annotated types and dependency annotations) that can be derived in the annotated type system (see figure 6). That is to say, algorithm $\mathcal{R}$ is sound w.r.t. the annotated type system.

Theorem 5. *Let t be a source term, Σ a sort environment and $\widehat{\Gamma}$ an annotated type environment well-formed under Σ such that $\mathcal{R}(\widehat{\Gamma}; \Sigma; t) = \widehat{t} : \widehat{\tau} \, \& \, \xi$ for some $\widehat{t}, \widehat{\tau}$ and ξ.*

Then, $\Sigma \mid \widehat{\Gamma} \vdash_{\text{te}} \widehat{t} : \widehat{\tau} \, \& \, \xi$, $\Sigma \vdash_{\text{wft}} \widehat{\tau}$, $\Sigma \vdash_s \xi : \star$ and $\widehat{\tau}$ is conservative.

The next step is to show that our analysis succeeds in deriving an annotated type and dependency annotation for any well-typed source term: it is *complete*.

The crucial part here is the termination of the fixpoint iteration. In order to show the convergence of the fixpoint iteration, we start by defining an equivalence relation on annotated type and depencency pairs.

Our type reconstruction algorithm handles polymorphic recursion through Kleene-Mycroft-iteration. Such an algorithm is based on fixpoint iteration and needs a way to decide whether two dependency terms are equal according to the denotational semantics of $\lambda^\sqcup$.

A straightforward way to decide semantic equivalence is to enumerate all possible environments and compare the denotations of the two terms in all of these (possibly after some semantics preserving normalization). This only works if the dependency lattice $\mathcal{L}$ is finite.

For some analyses, e.g., the set of all program locations in a slicing analysis, $\mathcal{L} = V_\star$ is finite but large, and deciding equality in this fashion becomes impractical. To alleviate this problem, our prototype implementation applies a partial canonicalization procedure which, while not complete, can serve as an approximation of equality: if two canonicalized dependency terms become syntactically equal, then we can be assured that they are semantically equal, but if they are not we can still apply the above procedure to the canonicalized dependency terms. We omit formal details from the paper.

We can now state our completeness results for the type reconstruction algorithm. Here, we write $\Gamma \vdash_t t : \tau$ to say that term t has type τ under the environment Γ in the underlying type system.

Theorem 6 (Completeness). *Given a source term t, a sort environment Σ, an annotated type environment $\widehat{\Gamma}$ well-formed under Σ, and an underlying type τ such that $\lfloor \widehat{\Gamma} \rfloor \vdash_t t : \tau$, then there are $\widehat{t}$, $\widehat{\tau}$ and ξ such that $\mathcal{R}(\widehat{\Gamma}; \Sigma; t) = \widehat{t} : \widehat{\tau} \& \xi$ and $\lfloor \widehat{\tau} \rfloor = \tau$, $\lfloor \widehat{t} \rfloor = t$.*

As a corollary of the foregoing theorems, our analysis is a conservative extension of the underlying type system.

Corollary 2 (Conservative Extension). *Let t be a source term, τ be a type and Γ a type environment such that $\Gamma \vdash_t t : \tau$. Then there are Σ, $\widehat{\Gamma}$, $\widehat{t}$, $\widehat{\tau}$, ξ such that $\Sigma \mid \widehat{\Gamma} \vdash_{te} \widehat{t} : \widehat{\tau} \& \xi$ with $\lfloor \widehat{t} \rfloor = t$, $\lfloor \widehat{\tau} \rfloor = \tau$ and $\lfloor \widehat{\Gamma} \rfloor = \Gamma$.*

7 Implementation and Examples

Beyond the definition of the annotated system and the development of the associated algorithm and meta-theory we also have a REPL prototype implementation of our analysis in Haskell. Compared to the annotated type system in the paper, the prototype provides support for booleans and integers, including literals and conditionals if c then t_1 else t_2 for which the type rules can be straightforwardly derived. Concrete lattice implementations are provided only for binding-time analysis and security analysis, but the reconstruction algorithm abstracts away from the choice for a particular lattice, so it is easy to add new instances. The implementation is available at http://www.staff.science.uu.nl/~hage0101/

prototype-hrp.zip. Below we walk through a few examples, taking advantage of the slightly extended source language that our implementation supports. More (detailed) examples are discussed in [26].

Construction and Elimination Whenever something is constructed, be it a product, a sum or a lambda abstraction, the outermost dependency annotation is $\bot$. This is because the analysis aims to produce the best possible and thereby least annotations for a given source program.

Consider the case of binding-time analysis, and suppose we have a variable of function type $f : \forall \beta.\text{int}\langle \beta \rangle \to \text{int}\langle \beta \rangle \& \mathbf{D}$. We can see that it preserves the annotations of its arguments, i.e. if we apply f to a static value, the return annotation is also instantiated to be static. The function itself, however, is dynamic. And therefore, the whole result of the function application must also be dynamic, because we cannot know which particular function has been assigned to f.

As elimination always introduces a dependency in the program, and this can uncover subtleties arising when functions only differ in their termination behavior. For example, compare $\lambda p : \text{int} \times \text{int}.p$ with $\lambda p : \text{int} \times \text{int}.(\text{proj}_1(p), \text{proj}_2(p))$. In a call-by-value language, these two functions would be (extensionally) equivalent. However, with non-strict evaluation, p might be a non-terminating computation. In that case, applying the former function would diverge, while the latter function at least produces the pair constructor. This is also reflected in the annotated types that are inferred. For the former, we get

$$\forall \beta_0, \beta_1, \beta_2 :: \star.(\text{int}\langle \beta_0 \rangle \times \text{int}\langle \beta_1 \rangle)\langle \beta_2 \rangle \to (\text{int}\langle \beta_0 \rangle \times \text{int}\langle \beta_1 \rangle)\langle \beta_2 \rangle \& \mathbf{S}, \text{and}$$

$$\forall \beta_0, \beta_1, \beta_2 :: \star.(\text{int}\langle \beta_0 \rangle \times \text{int}\langle \beta_1 \rangle)\langle \beta_2 \rangle \to (\text{int}\langle \beta_0 \sqcup \beta_2 \rangle \times \text{int}\langle \beta_1 \sqcup \beta_2 \rangle)\langle \mathbf{S} \rangle \& \mathbf{S}$$

for the latter. In particular, the annotation of the product in the second type signature is $\mathbf{S}$. Therefore, it can not depend on the input of the function.

Polymorphic Recursion One class of functions where the analysis benefits from polymorphic recursion are those that permute their arguments on recursive calls. Our example is a slightly modified version of an example from [5]:

$$\mu f : \text{bool} \to \text{bool} \to \text{bool}.\lambda x : \text{bool}.\lambda y : \text{bool}. \text{ if } x \text{ then } true \text{ else } f \, y \, x$$

In an analysis with monomorphic recursion, the analysis assigns the same annotation to both parameters, large enough to accommodate for both arguments. This is due to the permutation of the arguments in the else branch. An analysis with polymorphic recursion is allowed to use a different instantiation for f in that case. Our algorithm hence infers the following most general type.

$$\forall \beta_1 :: \star.\widehat{\text{bool}}\langle \beta_1 \rangle \to (\forall \beta_2 :: \star.\widehat{\text{bool}}\langle \beta_2 \rangle \to \widehat{\text{bool}}\langle \beta_1 \sqcup \beta_2 \rangle)\langle \bot \rangle \& \bot$$

We see that the result of the function indeed depends on the annotations of both arguments, as both end up in the condition of the if-expression at some

)oint. Yet, both arguments are completely unrestricted, and unrelated in their annotations. In contrast, a type system with monomorphic recursion would only admit a weaker type, possibly similar to

$$\forall \beta_1 :: \star.\widehat{\text{bool}}\langle \beta_1 \rangle \rightarrow (\widehat{\text{bool}}\langle \beta_1 \rangle \rightarrow \widehat{\text{bool}}\langle \beta_1 \rangle)\langle \bot \rangle \,\&\, \bot$$

A real world example of this kind is Euclid's algorithm for computing the greatest common divisor(see [26]).

Higher-Ranked Polyvariance This section discusses several examples for the dependency analysis instance of binding time analysis, comparing our outcomes with a let-polyvariant analysis[29].

A simple example to start with is a function that applies a function to both components of a pair[2]

$$both : (\text{int} \rightarrow \text{int}) \rightarrow \text{int} \times \text{int} \rightarrow \text{int} \times \text{int}$$
$$both = \lambda f : \text{int} \rightarrow \text{int}.\lambda p : \text{int} \times \text{int}.(f\ (\text{proj}_1(p)), f\ (\text{proj}_2(p)))$$

Suppose in the context of binding-time analysis that *both* is used to apply a statically known function to a pair whose first component is always computable at compile time, but whose second component is dynamic. For simplicity's sake, the function is the identity on integers.

$$id : \text{int} \rightarrow \text{int}$$
$$id = \lambda x : \text{int}.x$$

A non-higher-ranked analysis would assign types to *both* and *id*. The annotation on the function argument to *both* must be large enough to accommodate both components of the pair as input. When we consider the call *both id p* for some pair $p:\text{int}\langle \mathbf{S} \rangle \times \text{int}\langle \mathbf{D} \rangle \,\&\, \mathbf{S}$. Then, the whole call has the type $\text{int}\langle \mathbf{D} \rangle \times \text{int}\langle \mathbf{D} \rangle$.

Our higher-ranked analysis infers the following conservative types for *id* and *both*.

$$id : \forall \beta :: \star.\text{int}\langle \beta \rangle \rightarrow \text{int}\langle \beta \rangle \,\&\, \bot$$
$$id = \Lambda \beta :: \star.\lambda x : \text{int} \,\&\, \beta.x$$
$$both : \forall \beta_1 :: \star.\forall \beta_2 :: \star \Rightarrow \star.(\forall \beta :: \star.\text{int}\langle \beta \rangle \rightarrow \text{int}\langle \beta_2\ \beta \rangle)\langle \beta_1 \rangle$$
$$\rightarrow (\forall \beta_3, \beta_4, \beta_5 :: \star.(\text{int}\langle \beta_3 \rangle \times \text{int}\langle \beta_4 \rangle))\langle \beta_5 \rangle$$
$$\rightarrow (\text{int}\langle \beta_2\ (\beta_3 \sqcup \beta_5) \sqcup \beta_1 \rangle \times \text{int}\langle \beta_2\ (\beta_4 \sqcup \beta_5) \sqcup \beta_1 \rangle)\langle \mathbf{S} \rangle)\langle \mathbf{S} \rangle \,\&\, \mathbf{S}$$
$$both = \Lambda \beta_1 :: \star.\Lambda \beta_2 :: \star \Rightarrow \star.\lambda f : (\forall \beta :: \star.\text{int}\langle \beta \rangle \rightarrow \text{int}\langle \beta_2\ \beta \rangle).$$
$$\Lambda \beta_3 :: \star.\Lambda \beta_4 :: \star.\Lambda \beta_5 :: \star.\lambda p : \text{int}\langle \beta_3 \rangle \times \text{int}\langle \beta_4 \rangle.$$
$$(f\ \langle \beta_3 \sqcup \beta_5 \rangle\ (\text{proj}_1(p)), f\ \langle \beta_4 \sqcup \beta_5 \rangle\ (\text{proj}_2(p)))$$

In case of *both*, the function parameter f can be instantiated separately for each component because our analysis assigns it a type that universally quantifies over

---

[2] NB. *both* is a simplified instance of a traversal $\forall f.Applicative\ f \Rightarrow (Int \rightarrow f\ Int) \rightarrow (Int, Int) \rightarrow f\ (Int, Int)$, in order to fit the restrictions of the source language [6,15].

the annotation of its argument. It is evident from the type signature that the components of the resulting pair only depend on the corresponding components of the input pair, and the function and the input pair itself. They do not depend on the respective other component of the input.

If we again consider the call *both id p*, we obtain $\beta_2 = \lambda\beta :: \star.\beta$, $\beta_1 = \beta_3 = \beta_5 = \mathbf{S}$ and $\beta_4 = \mathbf{D}$ through pattern unification. Normalization of the resulting dependency terms results in the expected return type $\text{int}\langle\mathbf{S}\rangle \times \text{int}\langle\mathbf{D}\rangle$.

The generality provided by the higher-ranked analysis extends to an arbitrarily deep nesting of function arrows. The following example demonstrates this for two levels of arrows. Functions with more than two levels of arrows can arise directly in actual programs, but even more so in desugared code, e.g., when type classes in Haskell are implemented via explicit dictionary passing. Due to limitations of our source language, the examples are syntactically heavily restricted.

Consider the following function that takes a function argument which again requires a function.

$$foo : ((\text{int} \to \text{int}) \to \text{int}) \to \text{int} \times \text{int}$$
$$foo = \lambda f : (\text{int} \to \text{int}) \to \text{int}.(f\ (\lambda x : \text{int}.x), f\ (\lambda x : \text{int}.0))$$

The higher-ranked analysis infers the following type and target term (where we omitted the type in the argument of the lambda term because it essentially repeats what is already visible in the top level type signature).

$$foo : \forall\beta_4 :: \star.\forall\beta_3 :: \star \Rightarrow (\star \Rightarrow \star) \Rightarrow \star.$$
$$(\forall\beta_2 :: \star.\forall\beta_1 :: \star \Rightarrow \star.(\forall\beta_0 :: \star.\text{int}\langle\beta_0\rangle \to \text{int}\langle\beta_1\ \beta_0\rangle)\langle\beta_2\rangle$$
$$\to \text{int}\langle\beta_3\ \beta_2\ \beta_1\rangle)\langle\beta_4\rangle$$
$$\to (\text{int}\langle\beta_3\ \mathbf{S}\ (\lambda\beta_5 :: \star.\beta_5) \sqcup \beta_4\rangle \times \text{int}\langle\beta_3\ \mathbf{S}\ (\lambda\beta_6 :: \star.\mathbf{S}) \sqcup \beta_4\rangle)\langle\mathbf{S}\rangle\ \&\ \mathbf{S}$$
$$foo = \Lambda\beta_4 :: \star.\Lambda\beta_3 :: \star \Rightarrow (\star \Rightarrow \star) \Rightarrow \star.\lambda f : \cdots.$$
$$(f\ \langle\mathbf{S}\rangle\ \langle\lambda\beta_0 :: \star.\beta_0\rangle\ (\Lambda\beta_5 :: \star.\lambda x : \text{int}\ \&\ \beta_5.x)$$
$$,f\ \langle\mathbf{S}\rangle\ \langle\lambda\beta_0 :: \star.\mathbf{S}\rangle\ (\Lambda\beta_6 :: \star.\lambda x : \text{int}\ \&\ \beta_6.1))$$

Since the type of f is a pattern type, the argument to f is also a pattern type by definition. Therefore, the analysis of f depends on the analysis of the function passed to it. This gives rise to the *higher-order effect operator* β_3 [12]. Thus, f can be applied to any function with a conservative type of the right shape. As our algorithm always infers conservative types, the type of f is as general as possible. This is reflected in the body of the lambda where in both cases f is instantiated with the dependency annotation corresponding to the function passed to it. The result of this instantiation can be observed in the returned product type where β_3 is applied to the effect operators $\lambda\beta_0 :: \star.\beta_0$ and $\lambda\beta_0 :: \star.\mathbf{S}$ corresponding to the respective functions used as arguments to f.

Only when we finally apply *foo*, the resulting annotations can be evaluated.

$$bar : \forall\alpha_2 :: \star.\forall\alpha_1 :: \star \Rightarrow \star.(\forall\alpha_0 :: \star.\text{int}\langle\alpha_0\rangle \to \text{int}\langle\alpha_1\ \alpha_0\rangle)\langle\alpha_2\rangle$$
$$\to \text{int}\langle\alpha_1\ \mathbf{D} \sqcup \alpha_2\rangle\ \&\ \mathbf{S}$$
$$bar = \Lambda\alpha_2 :: \star.\Lambda\alpha_1 :: \star \Rightarrow \star.\lambda f : \cdots.f\ (\text{ann}_\mathbf{D}(0))$$

For *bar* we obtain *foo bar* : $\text{int}\langle \mathbf{D}\rangle \times \text{int}\langle \mathbf{S}\rangle$ & $\mathbf{S}$. In this case, $\beta_3 = \lambda\beta_2 ::$ $\star.\lambda\beta_1 :: \star \Rightarrow \star.\beta_1 \ \mathbf{D} \sqcup \beta_2$, because *bar* applies its argument to a value with dynamic binding time. This causes the first component of the returned pair to be deemed dynamic as well. On the other hand, in the second component *bar* is applied to a constant function. Thus, regardless of the argument's dynamic binding time, the resulting binding time is static. In a rank-1 system we would get $\text{int}\langle \mathbf{D}\rangle \times \text{int}\langle \mathbf{D}\rangle$ instead of $\text{int}\langle \mathbf{D}\rangle \times \text{int}\langle \mathbf{S}\rangle$.

8 Related Work

The basis for most type systems of functional programming languages is the Hindley-Milner type system [22]. Our algorithm R strongly resembles the well-known type inference algorithm for the Hindley-Milner type system, *Algorithm W* [3], a distinct advantage of our approach. The idea to define an annotated type system as a means to design static analyses for higher-order languages is attributed to [19]. The major technical difference compared to a let-polyvariant analysis is that our annotations form a simply typed lambda-calculus.

Full reconstruction for a higher-ranked polyvariant annotated type system was first considered by [12] in the context of a control-flow analysis. However, we found that the (constraint-based) algorithm as presented in [12] generates constraints free of cycles. Therefore, it cannot faithfully reflect the constraints necessary for the fixpoint combinator. The algorithm incorrectly concludes for the following example that only the first and third 'False' term flow into the condition x, but not the second one.

$$(fix\ (\lambda f.\ \lambda x.\ \lambda y.\ \lambda z.\text{if } x \text{ then } \textit{True} \text{ else } f\ z\ x\ y))\ \textit{False False False}$$

We reproduced this mistake with their implementation and verified that the mistake was not a simple bug in that implementation.

Close to our formulation is the (unpublished) work of [16] which deals with exception analysis, which uses a simply typed lambda-calculus with sets to represent annotations. We have chosen a more modular approach in which we offload much of the complexity of dealing with lattice values to the lattice. In [16] terms from the simply typed lambda-calculus with sets are canonicalized and then checked for alpha equivalence during Kleene-Mycroft iteration. We found however that two terms can have different canonical forms even though they are actually semantically equivalent. This causes Koot's reconstruction algorithm to diverge on a particular class of programs, because the inferred annotations continue to grow. The simplest such program we found is the following.

$$\mu f : (\text{unit} \to \text{unit}) \to \text{unit} \to \text{unit}.\lambda g : \text{unit} \to \text{unit}.\lambda x : \text{unit}.g\ (f\ g\ x)$$

Our solution is to apply canonicalization to simplify terms as much as possible, and then compare the outcomes for all possible inputs.

The Dependency Core Calculus was introduced by [1] as a unifying framework for dependency analyses. Instances include binding-time analysis (see, e.g.,

680   F. Thorand and J. Hage

[29]), exception analysis [17,16], secure information flow analysis [9] and static slicing [27]. They devised the *Dependency Core Calculus* (DCC) to which each instance of a dependency analysis can be mapped. This allowed them to compare different dependency analyses, uncover problems with existing instance analyses and to simplify proofs of noninterference [8,20]. The instance analyses in [1] were defined as a monovariant type and effect system with subtyping, for a monomorphic call-by-name language. An implicit, let-polymorphic implementation of DCC, FlowCaml, was developed by [25]. It is not higher-ranked.

The difference between DCC and our analysis is to a large extent a different focus: the DCC is a calculus defined in a way that any calculus that elaborates to DCC has the noninterference property and any other properties proven for the calculus. On the other hand, our analysis is meant to be implemented in a compiler (with the added precision), and that implementation (and its associated meta-theory) can then be reused inside the compiler for a variety of analyses. Comparable to DCC, we have proven a noninterference property for our generic higher-rank polyvariant dependency analysis, so that all its instances inherit it.

The Haskell community supports an implementation of DCC in which the (security) annotations are lifted to the Haskell type level [2]. Since the GHC compiler supports higher-rank types, the code written with this library can in fact model security flows with higher-rank. Because of the general undecidability of full reconstruction for higher-rank types [14], the programmer must however provide explicit type information. In [18], the authors introduce dependent flow types, that allows them to express a large variety of security policies. An essential difference with our work is that our approach is fully automated.

Early on in our research, we observed that the approach of [11] may lead to similar precision gains as higher-ranked annotations do. Since they deal with a different analysis, a direct comparison is impossible to make at this time.

9   Conclusion and Future Work

We have defined a higher-rank annotation polymorphic type system for a generic dependency analysis, established its soundness and provided a sound and complete reconstruction algorithm. Examples show that we can achieve higher precision than plain let-polyvariance. The analysis we have defined is for a call-by-name language. We expect the results to hold as well for a lazy language, but chose call-by-name for reduced bookkeeping in the proofs. We also believe the analysis can be adapted relatively easily to one for a call-by-value language, by letting the annotation on the argument flow into the effect of the call. However, we would need to re-examine the metatheory.

In future work we want to consider whether we can further refine the canonicalization of $\lambda^\sqcup$ terms so that syntactic equality up to alpha-equivalence can completely replace our current approach.

Acknowledgments We acknowledge the contributions of Ruud Koot in unpublished work that made this work possible.

References

1. Abadi, M., Banerjee, A., Heintze, N., Riecke, J.G.: A core calculus of dependency. In: Proceedings of the 26th ACM SIGPLAN-SIGACT symposium on Principles of programming languages - POPL '99. Association for Computing Machinery (ACM) (1999). https://doi.org/10.1145/292540.292555
2. Algehed, M., Russo, A.: Encoding dcc in haskell. In: Proceedings of the 2017 Workshop on Programming Languages and Analysis for Security. pp. 77–89. PLAS '17, ACM, New York, NY, USA (2017). https://doi.org/10.1145/3139337.3139338
3. Damas, L., Milner, R.: Principal type-schemes for functional programs. In: Proceedings of the 9th ACM SIGPLAN-SIGACT symposium on Principles of programming languages - POPL '82. Association for Computing Machinery (ACM) (1982). https://doi.org/10.1145/582153.582176
4. Dowek, G.: Handbook of automated reasoning. chap. Higher-order Unification and Matching, pp. 1009–1062. Elsevier Science Publishers B. V., Amsterdam, The Netherlands (2001), http://dl.acm.org/citation.cfm?id=778522.778525
5. Dussart, D., Henglein, F., Mossin, C.: Polymorphic recursion and subtype qualifications: Polymorphic binding-time analysis in polynomial time. In: Static Analysis, pp. 118–135. Springer Nature (1995). https://doi.org/10.1007/3-540-60360-3_36
6. Foster, J.N., Greenwald, M.B., Moore, J.T., Pierce, B.C., Schmitt, A.: Combinators for bidirectional tree transformations: A linguistic approach to the view-update problem. ACM Trans. Program. Lang. Syst. **29**(3) (May 2007). https://doi.org/10.1145/1232420.1232424
7. Glynn, K., Stuckey, P.J., Sulzmann, M., Söndergaard, H.: Boolean constraints for binding-time analysis. In: PADO '01: Proceedings of the Second Symposium on Programs as Data Objects. pp. 39–62. Springer-Verlag, London, UK (2001)
8. Goguen, J.A., Meseguer, J.: Security policies and security models. In: 1982 IEEE Symposium on Security and Privacy. pp. 11–11 (April 1982). https://doi.org/10.1109/SP.1982.10014
9. Heintze, N., Riecke, J.G.: The SLam calculus. In: Proceedings of the 25th ACM SIGPLAN-SIGACT symposium on Principles of programming languages - POPL '98. Association for Computing Machinery (ACM) (1998). https://doi.org/10.1145/268946.268976
10. Henglein, F.: Type inference with polymorphic recursion. ACM Transactions on Programming Languages and Systems **15**(2), 253–289 (4 1993). https://doi.org/10.1145/169701.169692
11. Hoffmann, J., Das, A., Weng, S.C.: Towards automatic resource bound analysis for ocaml. In: Proceedings of the 44th ACM SIGPLAN Symposium on Principles of Programming Languages. pp. 359–373. POPL 2017, ACM, New York, NY, USA (2017). https://doi.org/10.1145/3009837.3009842
12. Holdermans, S., Hage, J.: Polyvariant flow analysis with higher-ranked polymorphic types and higher-order effect operators. In: Proceedings of the 15th ACM SIGPLAN international conference on Functional programming - ICFP '10. Association for Computing Machinery (ACM) (2010). https://doi.org/10.1145/1863543.1863554
13. Jones, S.P., Vytiniotis, D., Weirich, S., Shields, M.: Practical type inference for arbitrary-rank types. Journal of Functional Programming **17**(1), 1–82 (2007). https://doi.org/http://dx.doi.org/10.1017/S0956796806006034
14. Kfoury, A., Tiuryn, J.: Type reconstruction in finite rank fragments of the second-order λ-calculus. Information and Computation **98**(2), 228–257 (6 1992). https://doi.org/10.1016/0890-5401(92)90020-g

15. Kmett, E.: The lens library (2018), http://lens.github.io/, consulted 9/7/2018
16. Koot, R.: Higher-ranked exception types (2015), https://github.com/ruudkoot/phd/tree/master/higher-ranked-exception-types, accessed 2018-03-09
17. Koot, R., Hage, J.: Type-based exception analysis for non-strict higher-order functional languages with imprecise exception semantics. In: Proceedings of the 2015 Workshop on Partial Evaluation and Program Manipulation - PEPM '15. Association for Computing Machinery (ACM) (2015). https://doi.org/10.1145/2678015.2682542
18. Lourenço, L., Caires, L.: Dependent information flow types. In: Proceedings of the 42Nd Annual ACM SIGPLAN-SIGACT Symposium on Principles of Programming Languages. pp. 317–328. POPL '15, ACM, New York, NY, USA (2015). https://doi.org/10.1145/2676726.2676994
19. Lucassen, J.M., Gifford, D.K.: Polymorphic effect systems. In: POPL '88: Proceedings of the 15th ACM SIGPLAN-SIGACT symposium on Principles of programming languages. pp. 47–57. ACM, New York, NY, USA (1988). https://doi.org/http://doi.acm.org/10.1145/73560.73564
20. McLean, J.: Security Models. Wiley Press (1994). https://doi.org/10.1002/0471028959
21. Miller, D.: A logic programming language with lambda-abstraction, function variables, and simple unification. In: Extensions of Logic Programming, pp. 253–281. Springer Nature (1991). https://doi.org/10.1007/bfb0038698
22. Milner, R.: A theory of type polymorphism in programming. Journal of Computer and System Sciences 17(3), 348–375 (12 1978). https://doi.org/10.1016/0022-0000(78)90014-4
23. Mycroft, A.: Polymorphic type schemes and recursive definitions. In: Lecture Notes in Computer Science, pp. 217–228. Springer Nature (1984). https://doi.org/10.1007/3-540-12925-1_41
24. Nielson, F., Nielson, H., Hankin, C.: Principles of Program Analysis. Springer Verlag, second printing edn. (2005)
25. Pottier, F., Simonet, V.: Information flow inference for ml. ACM Trans. Program. Lang. Syst. 25(1), 117–158 (Jan 2003). https://doi.org/10.1145/596980.596983
26. Thorand, F., Hage, J.: Addendum with proofs, definitions and examples for the esop 2020 paper, higher-ranked annotation polymorphic dependency analysis, http://www.staff.science.uu.nl/~hage0101/downloads/hrp-addendum.pdf
27. Tip, F.: A survey of program slicing techniques. Tech. rep., Amsterdam, The Netherlands, The Netherlands (1994)
28. Wansbrough, K., Jones, S.P.: Once upon a polymorphic type. In: Proceedings of the 26th ACM SIGPLAN-SIGACT symposium on Principles of programming languages - POPL '99. Association for Computing Machinery (ACM) (1999). https://doi.org/10.1145/292540.292545
29. Zhang, G.: Binding-Time Analysis: Subtyping versus Subeffecting. Msc thesis (2008), http://people.cs.uu.nl/jur/downloads/guangyuzhang-msc.pdf

ConSORT: Context- and Flow-Sensitive Ownership Refinement Types for Imperative Programs

John Toman[1], Ren Siqi[1], Kohei Suenaga[1],
Atsushi Igarashi[1], and Naoki Kobayashi[2]

[1] Kyoto University, Kyoto, Japan,
{jtoman,shiki,ksuenaga,igarashi}@fos.kuis.kyoto-u.ac.jp
[2] The University of Tokyo, Tokyo, Japan, koba@is.s.u-tokyo.ac.jp

Abstract. We present CONSORT, a type system for safety verification in the presence of mutability and aliasing. Mutability requires *strong updates* to model changing invariants during program execution, but aliasing between pointers makes it difficult to determine which invariants must be updated in response to mutation. Our type system addresses this difficulty with a novel combination of refinement types and fractional ownership types. Fractional ownership types provide flow-sensitive and precise aliasing information for reference variables. CONSORT interprets this ownership information to soundly handle strong updates of potentially aliased references. We have proved CONSORT sound and implemented a prototype, fully automated inference tool. We evaluated our tool and found it verifies non-trivial programs including data structure implementations.

Keywords: refinement types, mutable references, aliasing, strong updates, fractional ownerships, program verification, type systems

1 Introduction

Driven by the increasing power of automated theorem provers and recent high-profile software failures, fully automated program verification has seen a surge of interest in recent years [5, 10, 15, 29, 38, 66]. In particular, *refinement types* [9, 21, 24, 65], which refine base types with logical predicates, have been shown to be a practical approach for program verification that are amenable to (sometimes full) automation [47, 61, 62, 63]. Despite promising advances [26, 32, 46], the sound and precise application of refinement types (and program verification in general) in settings with mutability and aliasing (e.g., Java, Ruby, etc.) remains difficult.

One of the major challenges is how to precisely and soundly support *strong updates* for the invariants on memory cells. In a setting with mutability, a single invariant may not necessarily hold throughout the lifetime of a memory cell; while the program mutates the memory the invariant may change or evolve. To model these changes, a program verifier must support different, incompatible invariants which hold at different points during program execution. Further, precise program verification requires supporting different invariants on distinct pieces of memory.

P. Müller (Ed.): ESOP 2020, LNCS 12075, pp. 684–714, 2020.
https://doi.org/10.1007/978-3-030-44914-8_25

```
mk(n) { mkref n }

let p = mk(3) in
let q = mk(5) in
p := *p + 1;
q := *q + 1;
assert(*p = 4);
```

Fig. 1. Example demonstrating the difficulty of effecting strong updates in the presence of aliasing. The function mk is bound in the program from lines 3 to 7; its body is given within the braces.

```
1  loop(a, b) {
2    let aold = *a in
3    b := *b + 1;
4    a := *a + 1;
5    assert(*a = aold + 1);
6    if * then
7      loop(b, mkref *)
8    else
9      loop(b,a)
10 }
11 loop(mkref *, mkref *)
```

Fig. 2. Example with non-trivial aliasing behavior.

One solution is to use refinement types on the static program names (i.e., variables) which point to a memory location. This approach can model evolving invariants while tracking distinct invariants for each memory cell. For example, consider the (contrived) example in Figure 1. This program is written in an ML-like language with mutable references; references are updated with := and allocated with **mkref**. Variable p can initially be given the type $\{\nu : \mathbf{int} \mid \nu = 3\}\, \mathbf{ref}$, indicating it is a reference to the integer 3. Similarly, q can be given the type $\{\nu : \mathbf{int} \mid \nu = 5\}\, \mathbf{ref}$. We can model the mutation of p's memory on line 5 by strongly updating p's type to $\{\nu : \mathbf{int} \mid \nu = 4\}\, \mathbf{ref}$.

Unfortunately, the precise application of this technique is confounded by the existence of unrestricted aliasing. In general, updating just the type of the mutated reference is insufficient: due to aliasing, other variables may point to the mutated memory and their refinements must be updated as well. However, in the presence of conditional, *may* aliasing, it is impossible to strongly update the refinements on all possible aliases; given the static uncertainty about whether a variable points to the mutated memory, that variable's refinement may only be *weakly updated*. For example, suppose we used a simple alias analysis that imprecisely (but soundly) concluded all references allocated at the same program point *might* alias. Variables p and q share the allocation site on line 1, so on line 5 we would have to weakly update q's type to $\{\nu : \mathbf{int} \mid \nu = 4 \lor \nu = 5\}$, indicating it may hold either 4 *or* 5. Under this same imprecise aliasing assumption, we would also have to weakly update p's type on line 6, preventing the verification of the example program.

Given the precision loss associated with weak updates, it is critical that verification techniques built upon refinement types use precise aliasing information and avoid spuriously applied weak updates. Although it is relatively simple to conclude that p and q do not alias in Figure 1, consider the example in Figure 2. (In this example, * represents non-deterministic values.) Verifying this program requires proving a and b never alias at the writes on lines 3 and 4. In fact, a and b *may* point to the same memory location, but only in different invocations of loop; this pattern may confound even sophisticated symbolic alias analyses.

Additionally, a and b share an allocation site on line 7, so an approach based on the simple alias analysis described above will also fail on this example. This must-not alias proof obligation *can* be discharged with existing techniques [53, 54], but requires an expensive, on-demand, interprocedural, flow-sensitive alias analysis.

This paper presents CONSORT (CONtext Sensitive Ownership Refinement Types), a type system for the automated verification of program safety in imperative languages with mutability and aliasing. CONSORT is built upon the novel combination of refinement types and fractional ownership types [55, 56]. Fractional ownership types extend pointer types with a rational number in the range $[0, 1]$ called an *ownership*. These ownerships encapsulate the permission of the reference; only references with ownership 1 may be used for mutation. Fractional ownership types also obey the following key invariant: any references with a mutable alias must have ownership 0. Thus, any reference with non-zero ownership *cannot* be an alias of a reference with ownership 1. In other words, ownerships encode precise aliasing information in the form of *must-not* aliasing relationships.

To understand the benefit of this approach, let us return to Figure 1. As mk returns a freshly allocated reference with no aliases, its type indicates it returns a reference with ownership 1. Thus, our type system can initially give p and q types $\{\nu : \textbf{int} \mid \nu = 3\} \textbf{ref}^1$ and $\{\nu : \textbf{int} \mid \nu = 5\} \textbf{ref}^1$ respectively. The ownership 1 on the reference type constructor **ref** indicates both pointers hold "exclusive" ownership of the pointed to reference cell; from the invariant of fractional ownership types p and q must *not* alias. The types of both references can be strongly updated *without* requiring spurious weak updates. As a result, at the assertion statement on line 7, p has type $\{\nu : \textbf{int} \mid \nu = 4\} \textbf{ref}^1$ expressing the required invariant.

Our type system can also verify the example in Figure 2 *without* expensive side analyses. As a and b are both mutated, they must both have ownership 1; i.e., they cannot alias. This pre-condition is satisfied by all invocations of loop; on line 7, b has ownership 1 (from the argument type), and the newly allocated reference must also have ownership 1. Similarly, both arguments on line 9 have ownership 1 (from the assumed ownership on the argument types).

Ownerships behave linearly; they cannot be duplicated, only *split* when aliases are created. This linear behavior preserves the critical ownership invariant. For example, if we replace line 9 in Figure 2 with loop(b,b), the program becomes ill-typed; there is no way to divide b's ownership of 1 to into *two* ownerships of 1.

Ownerships also obviate updating refinement information of aliases at mutation. CONSORT ensures that only the trivial refinement ⊤ is used in reference types with ownership 0, i.e., mutably-aliased references. When memory is mutated through a reference with ownership 1, CONSORT simply updates the refinement of the mutated reference variable. From the soundness of ownership types, all aliases have ownership 0 and must therefore only contain the ⊤ refinement. Thus, the types of all aliases already soundly describe *all* possible contents.[3]

CONSORT is also *context-sensitive*, and can use different summaries of function behavior at different points in the program. For example, consider the variant

---

[3] This assumption holds only if updates do not change simple types, a condition our type-system enforces.

```
get(p) { *p }

let p = mkref 3 in
let q = mkref 5 in
p := get(p) + 1;
q := get(q) + 1;
assert(*p = 4);
assert(*q = 6);
```

Fig. 3. Example of context-sensitivity

of Figure 1 shown in Figure 3. The function **get** returns the contents of its argument, and is called on lines 5 and 6. To precisely verify this program, on line 5 **get** must be typed as a function that takes a reference to 3 and returns 3. Similarly, on line 6 **get** must be typed as a function that takes a reference to 5 and returns 5. Our type system can give **get** a function type that distinguishes between these two calling contexts and selects the appropriate summary of **get**'s behavior.

We have formalized CONSORT as a type system for a small imperative calculus and proved the system is sound: i.e., a well-typed program never encounters assertion failures during execution. We have implemented a prototype type inference tool targeting this imperative language and found it can automatically verify several non-trivial programs, including sorted lists and an array list data structure.

The rest of this paper is organized as follows. Section 2 defines the imperative language targeted by CONSORT and its semantics. Section 3 defines our type system and states our soundness theorem. Section 4 sketches our implementation's inference algorithm and its current limitations. Section 5 describes an evaluation of our prototype, Section 6 outlines related work, and Section 7 concludes.

2   Target Language

This section describes a simple imperative language with mutable references and first-order, recursive functions.

2.1   Syntax

We assume a set of *variables*, ranged over by $x, y, z, \ldots$, a set of *function names*, ranged over by f, and a set of *labels*, ranged over by $\ell_1, \ell_2, \ldots$. The grammar of the language is as follows.

$$
\begin{aligned}
d &::= f \mapsto (x_1, \ldots, x_n)\, e \\
e &::= x \mid \textbf{let}\, x = y \,\textbf{in}\, e \mid \textbf{let}\, x = n \,\textbf{in}\, e \mid \textbf{ifz}\, x \,\textbf{then}\, e_1 \,\textbf{else}\, e_2 \\
&\quad \mid\ \textbf{let}\, x = \textbf{mkref}\, y \,\textbf{in}\, e \mid \textbf{let}\, x = {*}y \,\textbf{in}\, e \mid \textbf{let}\, x = f^\ell(y_1, \ldots, y_n) \,\textbf{in}\, e \\
&\quad \mid\ x := y\,;\, e \mid \textbf{alias}(x = y)\,;\, e \mid \textbf{alias}(x = {*}y)\,;\, e \mid \textbf{assert}(\varphi)\,;\, e \mid e_1\,;\, e_2 \\
P &::= \langle \{d_1, \ldots, d_n\}, e \rangle
\end{aligned}
$$

φ stands for a formula in propositional first-order logic over variables, integers and contexts; we discuss these formulas later in Section 3.1.

Variables are introduced by function parameters or let bindings. Like ML, the variable bindings introduced by let expressions and parameters are immutable. Mutable variable declarations such as int x = 1; in C are achieved in our language with:

$$\textbf{let}\, y = 1 \,\textbf{in}(\textbf{let}\, x = \textbf{mkref}\, y \,\textbf{in} \ldots)\,.$$

As a convenience, we assume all variable names introduced with let bindings and function parameters are distinct.

Unlike ML (and like C or Java) we do not allow general expressions on the right hand side of let bindings. The simplest right hand forms are a variable y or an integer literal n. **mkref** y creates a reference cell with value y, and $*y$ accesses the contents of reference y. For simplicity, we do not include an explicit null value; an extension to support null is discussed in Section 4. Function calls must occur on the right hand side of a variable binding and take the form $f^\ell(x_1, \ldots, x_n)$, where $x_1, \ldots, x_n$ are distinct variables and ℓ is a (unique) label. These labels are used to make our type system context-sensitive as discussed in Section 3.3.

The single base case for expressions is a single variable. If the variable expression is executed in a tail position of a function, then the value of that variable is the return value of the function, otherwise the value is ignored.

The only intraprocedural control-flow operations in our language are if statements. **ifz** checks whether the condition variable x equals zero and chooses the corresponding branch. Loops can be implemented with recursive functions and we do not include them explicitly in our formalism.

Our grammar requires that side-effecting, result-free statements, **assert**(φ) **alias**$(x = y)$, **alias**$(x = *y)$ and assignment $x := y$ are followed by a continuation expression. We impose this requirement for technical reasons to ease our formal presentation; this requirement does not reduce expressiveness as dummy continuations can be inserted as needed. The **assert**(φ); e form executes e if the predicate φ holds in the current state and aborts the program otherwise. **alias**$(x = y)$; e and **alias**$(x = *y)$; e assert a must-aliasing relationship between x and y (resp. x and $*y$) and then execute e. **alias** statements are effectively *annotations* that our type system exploits to gain added precision. $x := y$; e updates the contents of the memory cell pointed to by x with the value of y. In addition to the above continuations, our language supports general sequencing with e_1; e_2.

A program is a pair $\langle D, e \rangle$, where $D = \{d_1, \ldots, d_n\}$ is a set of first-order, mutually recursive function definitions, and e is the program entry point. A function definition d maps the function name to a tuple of argument names $x_1, \ldots, x_n$ that are bound within the function body e.

Paper Syntax. In the remainder of the paper, we will write programs that are technically illegal according to our grammar, but can be easily "de-sugared" into an equivalent, valid program. For example, we will write

```
let x = mkref 4 in assert(*x = 4)
```

as syntactic sugar for:

```
let f = 4 in let x = mkref f in
let tmp = *x in assert(tmp = 4); let dummy = 0 in dummy
```

2.2   Operational Semantics

We now introduce the operational semantics for our language. We assume a finite domain of heap addresses **Addr**: we denote an arbitrary address with a.

$$\left\langle H, R, F : \vec{F}, x \right\rangle \longrightarrow_D \left\langle H, R, \vec{F}, F[x] \right\rangle$$
(R-VAR)

$$\left\langle H, R, F : \vec{F}, E[x\,;e] \right\rangle \longrightarrow_D \left\langle H, R, \vec{F}, E[e] \right\rangle$$
(R-SEQ)

$$\frac{x' \notin dom(R)}{\begin{array}{l} \left\langle H, R, \vec{F}, E[\textbf{let } x = y \textbf{ in } e] \right\rangle \\ \longrightarrow_D \left\langle H, R\{x' \mapsto R(y)\}, \vec{F}, E[[x'/x]e] \right\rangle \end{array}}$$
(R-LET)

$$\frac{x' \notin dom(R)}{\begin{array}{l} \left\langle H, R, \vec{F}, E[\textbf{let } x = n \textbf{ in } e] \right\rangle \\ \longrightarrow_D \left\langle H, R\{x' \mapsto n\}, \vec{F}, E[[x'/x]e] \right\rangle \end{array}}$$
(R-LETINT)

$$\frac{R(x) = 0}{\begin{array}{l} \left\langle H, R, \vec{F}, E[\textbf{ifz } x \textbf{ then } e_1 \textbf{ else } e_2] \right\rangle \\ \longrightarrow_D \left\langle H, R, \vec{F}, E[e_1] \right\rangle \end{array}}$$
(R-IFTRUE)

$$\frac{R(x) \neq 0}{\begin{array}{l} \left\langle H, R, \vec{F}, E[\textbf{ifz } x \textbf{ then } e_1 \textbf{ else } e_2] \right\rangle \\ \longrightarrow_D \left\langle H, R, \vec{F}, E[e_2] \right\rangle \end{array}}$$
(R-IFFALSE)

$$\frac{a \notin dom(H) \quad x' \notin dom(R)}{\begin{array}{l} \left\langle H, R, \vec{F}, E[\textbf{let } x = \textbf{mkref } y \textbf{ in } e] \right\rangle \longrightarrow_D \\ \left\langle H\{a \mapsto R(y)\}, R\{x' \mapsto a\}, \vec{F}, E[[x'/x]e] \right\rangle \end{array}}$$
(R-MKREF)

$$\frac{R(y) = a \quad H(a) = v \quad x' \notin dom(R)}{\begin{array}{l} \left\langle H, R, \vec{F}, E[\textbf{let } x = *y \textbf{ in } e] \right\rangle \longrightarrow_D \\ \left\langle H, R\{x' \mapsto v\}, \vec{F}, E[[x'/x]e] \right\rangle \end{array}}$$
(R-DEREF)

Fig. 4. Transition Rules (1).

A runtime state is represented by a configuration $\left\langle H, R, \vec{F}, e \right\rangle$, which consists of a heap, register file, stack, and currently reducing expression respectively. The register file maps variables to runtime values v, which are either integers n or addresses a. The heap maps a finite subset of addresses to runtime values. The runtime stack represents pending function calls as a sequence of return contexts, which we describe below. While the final configuration component is an expression, the rewriting rules are defined in terms of $E[e]$, which is an evaluation context E and redex e, as is standard. The grammar for evaluation contexts is defined by: $E ::= E'\,;e \mid [\,]$.

Our operational semantics is given in Figures 4 and 5. We write $dom(H)$ to indicate the domain of a function and $H\{a \mapsto v\}$ where $a \notin dom(H)$ to denote a map which takes all values in $dom(H)$ to their values in H and which additionally takes a to v. We will write $H\{a \hookleftarrow v\}$ where $a \in dom(H)$ to denote a map equivalent to H except that a takes value v. We use similar notation for $dom(R)$ and $R\{x \mapsto v\}$. We also write $\emptyset$ for the empty register file and heap. The step relation $\longrightarrow_D$ is parameterized by a set of function definitions D; a program $\langle D, e \rangle$ is executed by stepping the initial configuration $\langle \emptyset, \emptyset, \cdot, e \rangle$ according to $\longrightarrow_D$. The semantics is mostly standard; we highlight some important points below.

Return contexts F take the form $E[\textbf{let } y = [\,]^\ell \textbf{ in } e]$. A return context represents a pending function call with label ℓ, and indicates that y should be bound to the return value of the callee during the execution of e within the larger execution context E. The call stack $\vec{F}$ is a sequence of these contexts, with the first such return context representing the most recent function call. The stack grows at function calls as described by rule R-CALL. For a call $E[\textbf{let } x = f^\ell(y_1, \ldots, y_n) \textbf{ in } e]$ where f is defined as $(x_1, \ldots, x_n)e'$, the return context $E[\textbf{let } y = [\,]^\ell \textbf{ in } e]$ is

$$\frac{f \mapsto (x_1, .., x_n)e \in D}{\left\langle H, R, \vec{F}, E[\textbf{let } x = f^\ell(y_1, \ldots, y_n) \textbf{ in } e'] \right\rangle \longrightarrow_D \left\langle H, R, E[\textbf{let } x = []^\ell \textbf{ in } e'] : \vec{F}, [y_1/x_1] \cdots [y_n/x_n]e \right\rangle} \text{(R-CALL)}$$

$$\frac{R(x) = a \qquad a \in dom(H)}{\left\langle H, R, \vec{F}, E[x := y ; e] \right\rangle \longrightarrow_D \left\langle H\{a \hookleftarrow R(y)\}, R, \vec{F}, E[e] \right\rangle} \text{(R-ASSIGN)}$$

$$\frac{R(x) = R(y)}{\left\langle H, R, \vec{F}, E[\textbf{alias}(x = y) ; e] \right\rangle \longrightarrow_D \left\langle H, R, \vec{F}, E[e] \right\rangle} \text{(R-ALIAS)}$$

$$\frac{R(y) = a \qquad H(a) = R(x)}{\left\langle H, R, \vec{F}, E[\textbf{alias}(x = *y) ; e] \right\rangle \longrightarrow_D \left\langle H, R, \vec{F}, E[e] \right\rangle} \text{(R-ALIASPTR)}$$

$$\frac{R(x) \neq R(y)}{\left\langle H, R, \vec{F}, E[\textbf{alias}(x = y) ; e] \right\rangle \longrightarrow_D \textbf{AliasFail}} \text{(R-ALIASFAIL)}$$

$$\frac{R(x) \neq H(R(y))}{\left\langle H, R, \vec{F}, E[\textbf{alias}(x = *y) ; e] \right\rangle \longrightarrow_D \textbf{AliasFail}} \text{(R-ALIASPTRFAIL)}$$

$$\frac{\models [R]\varphi}{\left\langle H, R, \vec{F}, E[\textbf{assert}(\varphi) ; e] \right\rangle \longrightarrow_D \left\langle H, R, \vec{F}, E[e] \right\rangle} \text{(R-ASSERT)}$$

$$\frac{\not\models [R]\varphi}{\left\langle H, R, \vec{F}, E[\textbf{assert}(\varphi) ; e] \right\rangle \longrightarrow_D \textbf{AssertFail}} \text{(R-ASSERTFAIL)}$$

Fig. 5. Transition Rules (2).

prepended onto the stack of the input configuration. The substitution of formal arguments for parameters in e', denoted by $[y_1/x_1] \cdots [y_n/x_n]e'$, becomes the currently reducing expression in the output configuration. Function returns are handled by R-VAR. Our semantics return values by name; when the currently executing function fully reduces to a single variable x, x is substituted into the return context on the top of the stack, denoted by $E[\textbf{let } y = []^\ell \textbf{ in } e][x]$.

In the rules R-ASSERT we write $\models [R]\varphi$ to mean that the formula yielded by substituting the concrete values in R for the variables in φ is valid within some chosen logic (see Section 3.1); in R-ASSERTFAIL we write $\not\models [R]\varphi$ when the formula is *not* valid. The substitution operation $[R]\varphi$ is defined inductively as $[\emptyset]\varphi = \varphi, [R\{x \mapsto n\}]\varphi = [R][n/x]\varphi, [R\{x \mapsto a\}]\varphi = [R]\varphi$. In the case of an assertion failure, the semantics steps to a distinguished configuration **AssertFail**. The goal of our type system is to show that no execution of a well-typed program may reach this configuration. The **alias** form checks whether the two references actually alias; i.e., if the must-alias assertion provided by the programmer is correct. If not, our semantics steps to the distinguished **AliasFail** configuration. Our type system does *not* guarantee that **AliasFail** is unreachable; aliasing assertions are effectively trusted annotations that are assumed to hold.

In order to avoid duplicate variable names in our register file due to recursive functions, we refresh the bound variable x in a let expression to x'. Take expression **let** $x = y$ **in** e as an example; we substitute a fresh variable x' for x in e, then bind x' to the value of variable y. We assume this refreshing of variables preserves our assumption that all variable bindings introduced with let and function parameters are unique, i.e. x' does not overlap with variable names that occur in the program.

$$
\begin{array}{lrl}
\text{Types} & \tau ::= & \{\nu : \mathbf{int} \mid \varphi\} \mid \tau\, \mathbf{ref}^r \\
\text{Ownership} & r \in & [0,1] \\
\text{Refinements} & \varphi ::= & \varphi_1 \vee \varphi_2 \mid \neg\varphi \mid \top \\
& \mid & \phi(\widehat{v}_1, .., \widehat{v}_n) \\
& \mid & \widehat{v}_1 = \widehat{v}_2 \\
& \mid & \mathcal{CP} \\
\text{Ref. Values} & \widehat{v} ::= & x \mid n \mid \nu
\end{array}
\qquad
\begin{array}{lrl}
\text{Function Types} & \sigma ::= & \forall \lambda. \langle x_1 : \tau_1, \ldots, x_n : \tau_n \rangle \\
& & \rightarrow \langle x_1 : \tau_1', \ldots, x_n : \tau_n' \mid \tau \rangle \\
\text{Context Variables} & \lambda \in & \mathbf{CVar} \\
\text{Concrete Context} & \vec{\ell} ::= & \ell : \vec{\ell} \mid \epsilon \\
\text{Pred. Context} & \mathcal{C} ::= & \ell : \mathcal{C} \mid \lambda \mid \epsilon \\
\text{Context Query} & \mathcal{CP} ::= & \vec{\ell} \preceq \mathcal{C} \\
\text{Typing Context} & \mathcal{L} ::= & \lambda \mid \vec{\ell}
\end{array}
$$

Fig. 6. Syntax of types, refinements, and contexts.

3 Typing

We now introduce a fractional ownership refinement type system that guarantees well-typed programs do not encounter assertion failures.

3.1 Types and Contexts

The syntax of types is given in Figure 6. Our type system has two type constructors: references and integers. $\tau\, \mathbf{ref}^r$ is the type of a (non-null) reference to a value of type τ. r is an ownership which is a rational number in the range $[0, 1]$. An ownership of 0 indicates a reference that cannot be written, and for which there may exist a mutable alias. By contrast, 1 indicates a pointer with exclusive ownership that can be read and written. Reference types with ownership values between these two extremes indicate a pointer that is readable but not writable, and for which no mutable aliases exist. ConSORT ensures that these invariants hold while aliases are created and destroyed during execution.

Integers are refined with a predicate φ. The language of predicates is built using the standard logical connectives of first-order logic, with (in)equality between variables and integers, and atomic predicate symbols ϕ as the basic atoms. We include a special "value" variable ν representing the value being refined by the predicate. For simplicity, we omit the connectives $\varphi_1 \wedge \varphi_2$ and $\varphi_1 \implies \varphi_2$; they can be written as derived forms using the given connectives. We do not fix a particular theory from which ϕ are drawn, provided a sound (but not necessarily complete) decision procedure exists. $\mathcal{CP}$ are context predicates, which are used for context sensitivity as explained below.

Example 1. $\{\nu : \mathbf{int} \mid \nu > 0\}$ is the type of strictly positive integers. The type of immutable references to integers exactly equal to 3 can be expressed by $\{\nu : \mathbf{int} \mid \nu = 3\}\, \mathbf{ref}^{0.5}$.

As is standard, we denote a type environment with Γ, which is a finite map from variable names to type τ. We write $\Gamma[x : \tau]$ to denote a type environment Γ such that $\Gamma(x) = \tau$ where $x \in dom(\Gamma)$, $\Gamma, x : \tau$ to indicate the extension of Γ with the type binding $x : \tau$, and $\Gamma[x \hookleftarrow \tau]$ to indicate the type environment Γ with the binding of x updated to τ. We write the empty environment as

•. The treatment of type environments as mappings instead of sequences in a dependent type system is somewhat non-standard. The standard formulation based on ordered sequences of bindings and its corresponding well-formedness condition did not easily admit variables with mutually dependent refinements as introduced by our function types (see below). We therefore use an unordered environment and relax well-formedness to ignore variable binding order.

Function Types, Contexts, and Context Polymorphism. Our type system achieves context sensitivity by allowing function types to depend on where a function is called, i.e., the *execution context* of the function invocation. Our system represents a *concrete* execution contexts with strings of call site labels (or just "call strings"), defined by $\vec{\ell} ::= \epsilon \mid \ell : \vec{\ell}$. As is standard (e.g., [49, 50]), the string $\ell : \vec{\ell}$ abstracts an execution context where the most recent, active function call occurred at call site ℓ which itself was executed in a context abstracted by $\vec{\ell}$; ϵ is the context under which program execution begins. *Context variables*, drawn from a finite domain **CVar** and ranged over by $\lambda_1, \lambda_2, \ldots$, represent arbitrary, unknown contexts.

A function type takes the form $\forall \lambda. \langle x_1 : \tau_1, \ldots, x_n : \tau_n \rangle \to \langle x_1 : \tau_1', \ldots, x_n : \tau_n' \mid \tau \rangle$ The arguments of a function are an n-ary tuple of types τ_i. To model side-effects on arguments, the function type includes the same number of *output types* τ_i'. In addition, function types have a direct return type τ. The argument and output types are given names: refinements within the function type may refer to these names. Function types in our language are context polymorphic, expressed by universal quantification "$\forall \lambda$." over a context variable. Intuitively, this context variable represents the many different execution contexts under which a function may be called.

Argument and return types may depend on this context variable by including *context query predicates* in their refinements. A context query predicate $\mathcal{CP}$ usually takes the form $\vec{\ell} \preceq \lambda$, and is true iff $\vec{\ell}$ is a prefix of the concrete context represented by λ. Intuitively, a refinement $\vec{\ell} \preceq \lambda \implies \varphi$ states that φ holds in any concrete execution context with prefix $\vec{\ell}$, and provides no information in any other context. In full generality, a context query predicate may be of the form $\vec{\ell_1} \preceq \vec{\ell_2}$ or $\vec{\ell} \preceq \ell_1 \ldots \ell_n : \lambda$; these forms may be immediately simplified to $\top$, $\bot$ or $\vec{\ell'} \preceq \lambda$.

Example 2. The type $\{\nu : \mathbf{int} \mid (\ell_1 \preceq \lambda \implies \nu = 3) \wedge (\ell_2 \preceq \lambda \implies \nu = 5)\}$ represents an integer that is 3 if the most recent active function call site is ℓ_1, 5 if the most recent call site is ℓ_2, and is otherwise unconstrained. This type may be used for the argument of f in, e.g., $f^{\ell_1}(3) + f^{\ell_2}(5)$.

As types in our type system may contain context variables, our typing judgment (introduced below) includes a typing context $\mathcal{L}$, which is either a single context variable λ or a concrete context $\vec{\ell}$. This typing context represents the assumptions about the execution context of the term being typed. If the typing context is a context variable λ, then no assumptions are made about the execution context of the term, although types may depend upon λ with context query predicates. Accordingly, function bodies are typed under the context variable universally quantified over in the corresponding function type; i.e., no assumptions are made about the exact execution context of the function body.

As in parametric polymorphism, consistent substitution of a concrete context $\vec{\ell}$ for a context variable λ in a typing derivation yields a valid type derivation under concrete context $\vec{\ell}$.

Remark 1. The context-sensitivity scheme described here corresponds to the standard CFA approach [50] without *a priori* call-string limiting. We chose this scheme because it can be easily encoded with equality over integer variables (see Section 4), but in principle another context-sensitivity strategy could be used instead. The important feature of our type system is the inclusion of predicates over contexts, not the specific choice for these predicates.

Function type environments are denoted with Θ and are finite maps from function names (f) to function types (σ).

Well Formedness. We impose two well-formedness conditions on types: *ownership well-formedness* and *refinement well-formedness*. The ownership condition is purely syntactic: τ is ownership well-formed if $\tau = \tau' \mathbf{ref}^0$ implies $\tau' = \top_n$ for some n. $\top_i$ is the "maximal" type of a chain of i references, and is defined inductively as $\top_0 = \{\nu : \mathbf{int} \mid \top\}$, $\top_i = \top_{i-1} \mathbf{ref}^0$.

The ownership well-formedness condition ensures that aliases introduced via heap writes do not violate the invariant of ownership types *and* that refinements are consistent with updates performed through mutable aliases. Recall our ownership type invariant ensures all aliases of a mutable reference have 0 ownership. Any mutations through that mutable alias will therefore be consistent with the "no information" $\top$ refinement required by this well-formedness condition.

Refinement well-formedness, denoted $\mathcal{L} \mid \Gamma \vdash_{WF} \varphi$, ensures that free program variables in refinement φ are bound in a type environment Γ and have integer type. It also requires that for a typing context $\mathcal{L} = \lambda$, only context query predicates over λ are used (no such predicates may be used if $\mathcal{L} = \vec{\ell}$). Notice this condition forbids refinements that refer to references. Although ownership information can signal when refinements on a mutably-aliased reference must be discarded, our current formulation provides no such information for refinements that *mention* mutably-aliased references. We therefore conservatively reject such refinements at the cost of some expressiveness in our type system.

We write $\mathcal{L} \mid \Gamma \vdash_{WF} \tau$ to indicate a well-formed type where all refinements are well-formed with respect to $\mathcal{L}$ and Γ. We write $\mathcal{L} \vdash_{WF} \Gamma$ for a type environment where all types are well-formed. A function environment is well-formed (written $\vdash_{WF} \Theta$) if, for every σ in Θ, the argument, result, and output types are well-formed with respect to each other and the context variable quantified over in σ. As the formal definition of refinement well-formedness is fairly standard, we omit it for space reasons (the full definition may be found in the full version [60]).

3.2   Intraprocedural Type System

We now introduce the type system for the intraprocedural fragment of our language. Accordingly, this section focuses on the interplay of mutability and

$$\frac{}{\Theta \mid \mathcal{L} \mid \Gamma[x : \tau_1 + \tau_2] \vdash x : \tau_1 \Rightarrow \Gamma[x \leftarrow \tau_2]} \quad \text{(T-VAR)}$$

$$\frac{\Theta \mid \mathcal{L} \mid \Gamma[y \leftarrow \tau_1 \wedge_y y =_{\tau_1} x], x : (\tau_2 \wedge_x x =_{\tau_2} y) \vdash e : \tau \Rightarrow \Gamma' \qquad x \notin dom(\Gamma')}{\Theta \mid \mathcal{L} \mid \Gamma[y : \tau_1 + \tau_2] \vdash \textbf{let } x = y \textbf{ in } e : \tau \Rightarrow \Gamma'} \quad \text{(T-LET)}$$

$$\frac{\Theta \mid \mathcal{L} \mid \Gamma, x : \{\nu : \textbf{int} \mid \nu = n\} \vdash e : \tau \Rightarrow \Gamma' \qquad x \notin dom(\Gamma')}{\Theta \mid \mathcal{L} \mid \Gamma \vdash \textbf{let } x = n \textbf{ in } e : \tau \Rightarrow \Gamma'} \quad \text{(T-LETINT)}$$

$$\frac{\Theta \mid \mathcal{L} \mid \Gamma[x \leftarrow \{\nu : \textbf{int} \mid \varphi \wedge \nu = 0\}] \vdash e_1 : \tau \Rightarrow \Gamma'}{\Theta \mid \mathcal{L} \mid \Gamma[x \leftarrow \{\nu : \textbf{int} \mid \varphi \wedge \nu \neq 0\}] \vdash e_2 : \tau \Rightarrow \Gamma'}{\Theta \mid \mathcal{L} \mid \Gamma[x : \{\nu : \textbf{int} \mid \varphi\}] \vdash \textbf{ifz } x \textbf{ then } e_1 \textbf{ else } e_2 : \tau \Rightarrow \Gamma'} \quad \text{(T-IF)}$$

$$\frac{\begin{array}{c}\Theta \mid \mathcal{L} \mid \Gamma[y \leftarrow \tau_1], x : (\tau_2 \wedge_x x =_{\tau_2} y) \, \textbf{ref}^1 \vdash e : \tau \Rightarrow \Gamma' \\ x \notin dom(\Gamma')\end{array}}{\Theta \mid \mathcal{L} \mid \Gamma[y : \tau_1 + \tau_2] \vdash \textbf{let } x = \textbf{mkref } y \textbf{ in } e : \tau \Rightarrow \Gamma'} \quad \frac{\begin{array}{c}\Theta \mid \mathcal{L} \mid \Gamma \vdash e_1 : \tau' \Rightarrow \Gamma' \\ \Theta \mid \mathcal{L} \mid \Gamma' \vdash e_2 : \tau'' \Rightarrow \Gamma''\end{array}}{\Theta \mid \mathcal{L} \mid \Gamma \vdash e_1 ; e_2 : \tau'' \Rightarrow \Gamma''}$$

$$\text{(T-MKREF)} \qquad\qquad\qquad\qquad\qquad \text{(T-SEQ)}$$

$$\tau' = \begin{cases} \tau_1 \wedge_y y =_{\tau_1} x & r > 0 \\ \tau_1 & r = 0 \end{cases} \qquad\qquad \Gamma \models \varphi \qquad \epsilon \mid \Gamma \vdash_{WF} \varphi$$

$$\frac{\begin{array}{c}\Theta \mid \mathcal{L} \mid \Gamma[y \leftarrow \tau' \, \textbf{ref}^r], x : \tau_2 \vdash e : \tau \Rightarrow \Gamma' \\ x \notin dom(\Gamma')\end{array}}{\Theta \mid \mathcal{L} \mid \Gamma[y : (\tau_1 + \tau_2) \, \textbf{ref}^r] \vdash \textbf{let } x = *y \textbf{ in } e : \tau \Rightarrow \Gamma'} \qquad \frac{\Theta \mid \mathcal{L} \mid \Gamma \vdash e : \tau \Rightarrow \Gamma'}{\Theta \mid \mathcal{L} \mid \Gamma \vdash \textbf{assert}(\varphi) ; e : \tau \Rightarrow \Gamma'}$$

$$\text{(T-DEREF)} \qquad\qquad\qquad\qquad\qquad \text{(T-ASSERT)}$$

Fig. 7. Expression typing rules.

refinement types. The typing rules are given in Figures 7 and 8. A typing judgment takes the form $\Theta \mid \mathcal{L} \mid \Gamma \vdash e : \tau \Rightarrow \Gamma'$, which indicates that e is well-typed under a function type environment Θ, typing context $\mathcal{L}$, and type environment Γ, and evaluates to a value of type τ and modifies the input environment according to Γ'. Any valid typing derivation must have $\mathcal{L} \vdash_{WF} \Gamma$, $\mathcal{L} \vdash_{WF} \Gamma'$, and $\mathcal{L} \mid \Gamma' \vdash_{WF} \tau$, i.e., the input and output type environments and result type must be well-formed.

The typing rules in Figure 7 handle the relatively standard features in our language. The rule T-SEQ for sequential composition is fairly straightforward except that the output type environment for e_1 is the input type environment for e_2. T-LETINT is also straightforward; since x is bound to a constant, it is given type $\{\nu : \textbf{int} \mid \nu = n\}$ to indicate x is exactly n. The output type environment Γ' cannot mention x (expressed with $x \notin dom(\Gamma')$) to prevent x from escaping its scope. This requirement can be met by applying the subtyping rule (see below) to weaken refinements to no longer mention x. As in other refinement type systems [47], this requirement is critical for ensuring soundness.

Rule T-LET is crucial to understanding our ownership type system. The body of the let expression e is typechecked under a type environment where the type of y in Γ is linearly split into two types: τ_1 for y and τ_2 for the newly created binding x. This splitting is expressed using the $+$ operator. If y is a reference type, the split operation distributes some portion of y's ownership information to its new alias x. The split operation also distributes refinement information between the two types. For example, type $\{\nu : \textbf{int} \mid \nu > 0\} \, \textbf{ref}^1$ can be split into (1) $\{\nu : \textbf{int} \mid \nu > 0\} \, \textbf{ref}^r$ and $\{\nu : \textbf{int} \mid \nu > 0\} \, \textbf{ref}^{(1-r)}$ (for $r \in (0,1)$),

.e., two *immutable* references with non-trivial refinement information, or (2) $\{\nu : \textbf{int} \mid \nu > 0\} \textbf{ref}^1$ and $\{\nu : \textbf{int} \mid \top\} \textbf{ref}^0$, where one of the aliases is mutable and the other provides no refinement information. How a type is split depends on the usage of x and y in e. Formally, we define the type addition operator as the least commutative partial operation that satisfies the following rules:

$$\{\nu : \textbf{int} \mid \varphi_1\} + \{\nu : \textbf{int} \mid \varphi_2\} = \{\nu : \textbf{int} \mid \varphi_1 \wedge \varphi_2\} \qquad \text{(TADD-INT)}$$

$$\tau_1 \textbf{ref}^{r_1} + \tau_2 \textbf{ref}^{r_2} = (\tau_1 + \tau_2) \textbf{ref}^{r_1+r_2} \qquad \text{(TADD-REF)}$$

Viewed another way, type addition describes how to combine two types for the same value such that the combination soundly incorporates all information from the two original types. Critically, the type addition operation cannot create or destroy ownership and refinement information, only combine or divide it between types. Although not explicit in the rules, by ownership well-formedness, if the entirety of a reference's ownership is transferred to another type during a split, all refinements in the remaining type must be $\top$.

The additional bits $\wedge_y y =_{\tau_1} x$ and $\wedge_x x =_{\tau_2} y$ express equality between x and y as refinements. We use the strengthening operation $\tau \wedge_x \varphi$ and typed equality proposition $x =_\tau y$, defined respectively as:

$$\{\nu : \textbf{int} \mid \varphi\} \wedge_y \varphi' = \{\nu : \textbf{int} \mid \varphi \wedge [\nu/y] \varphi'\} \qquad (x =_{\{\nu : \textbf{int} \mid \varphi\}} y) = (x = y)$$

$$\tau \textbf{ref}^r \wedge_y \varphi' = \tau \textbf{ref}^r \qquad (x =_{\tau \textbf{ref}^r} y) = \top$$

We do not track equality between references or between the contents of aliased reference cells as doing so would violate our refinement well-formedness condition. These operations are also used in other rules that can introduce equality.

Rule T-MKREF is very similar to T-LET, except that x is given a reference type of ownership 1 pointing to τ_2, which is obtained by splitting the type of y. In T-DEREF, the content type of y is split and distributed to x. The strengthening is *conditionally* applied depending on the ownership of the dereferenced pointer, that is, if $r = 0$, τ' has to be a maximal type $\top_i$.

Our type system also tracks path information; in the T-IF rule, we update the refinement on the condition variable within the respective branches to indicate whether the variable must be zero. By requiring both branches to produce the same output type environment, we guarantee that these conflicting refinements are rectified within the type derivations of the two branches.

The type rule for assert statements has the precondition $\Gamma \models \varphi$ which is defined to be $\models [\![\Gamma]\!] \implies \varphi$, i.e., the logical formula $[\![\Gamma]\!] \implies \varphi$ is valid in the chosen theory. $[\![\Gamma]\!]$ lifts the refinements on the integer valued variables into a proposition in the logic used for verification. This denotation operation is defined as:

$$[\![\bullet]\!] = \top \qquad [\![\{\nu : \textbf{int} \mid \varphi\}]\!]_y = [y/\nu] \varphi$$

$$[\![\Gamma, x : \tau]\!] = [\![\Gamma]\!] \wedge [\![\tau]\!]_x \qquad [\![\tau' \textbf{ref}^r]\!]_y = \top$$

If the formula $[\![\Gamma]\!] \implies \varphi$ is valid, then in any context and under any valuation of program variables that satisfy the refinements in $[\![\Gamma]\!]$, the predicate φ must be true and the assertion must not fail. This intuition forms the foundation of our soundness claim (Section 3.4).

$$(\text{The shapes of } \tau' \text{ and } \tau_2 \text{ are similar})$$

$$\frac{\Theta \mid \mathcal{L} \mid \Gamma[x \leftarrow \tau_1][y \leftarrow (\tau_2 \wedge_y y =_{\tau_2} x)\,\mathbf{ref}^1] \vdash e : \tau \Rightarrow \Gamma'}{\Theta \mid \mathcal{L} \mid \Gamma[x : \tau_1 + \tau_2][y : \tau'\,\mathbf{ref}^1] \vdash y := x\,;\,e : \tau \Rightarrow \Gamma'} \quad \text{(T-ASSIGN)}$$

$$\frac{(\tau_1\,\mathbf{ref}^{r_1} + \tau_2\,\mathbf{ref}^{r_2}) \approx (\tau_1'\,\mathbf{ref}^{r_1'} + \tau_2'\,\mathbf{ref}^{r_2'})}{\Theta \mid \mathcal{L} \mid \Gamma[x \leftarrow \tau_1'\,\mathbf{ref}^{r_1'}][y \leftarrow \tau_2'\,\mathbf{ref}^{r_2'}] \vdash e : \tau \Rightarrow \Gamma'} \quad \text{(T-ALIAS)}$$
$$\overline{\Theta \mid \mathcal{L} \mid \Gamma[x : \tau_1\,\mathbf{ref}^{r_1}][y : \tau_2\,\mathbf{ref}^{r_2}] \vdash \mathbf{alias}(x = y)\,;\,e : \tau \Rightarrow \Gamma'}$$

$$\frac{(\tau_1\,\mathbf{ref}^{r_1} + \tau_2\,\mathbf{ref}^{r_2}) \approx (\tau_1'\,\mathbf{ref}^{r_1'} + \tau_2'\,\mathbf{ref}^{r_2'})}{\Theta \mid \mathcal{L} \mid \Gamma[x \leftarrow \tau_1'\,\mathbf{ref}^{r_1}][y \leftarrow (\tau_2'\,\mathbf{ref}^{r_2'})\,\mathbf{ref}^r] \vdash e : \tau \Rightarrow \Gamma'} \quad \text{(T-ALIASPTR)}$$
$$\overline{\Theta \mid \mathcal{L} \mid \Gamma[x : \tau_1\,\mathbf{ref}^{r_1}][y : (\tau_2\,\mathbf{ref}^{r_2})\,\mathbf{ref}^r] \vdash \mathbf{alias}(x = *y)\,;\,e : \tau \Rightarrow \Gamma'}$$

$$\frac{\Gamma \leq \Gamma' \quad \Theta \mid \mathcal{L} \mid \Gamma' \vdash e : \tau \Rightarrow \Gamma'' \quad \Gamma'', \tau \leq \Gamma''', \tau'}{\Theta \mid \mathcal{L} \mid \Gamma \vdash e : \tau' \Rightarrow \Gamma'''} \quad \text{(T-SUB)}$$

$$\tau_1 \approx \tau_2 \text{ iff } \bullet \vdash \tau_1 \leq \tau_2 \text{ and } \bullet \vdash \tau_2 \leq \tau_1.$$

Fig. 8. Pointer manipulation and subtyping

$$\frac{\Gamma \models \varphi_1 \implies \varphi_2}{\Gamma \vdash \{\nu : \mathbf{int} \mid \varphi_1\} \leq \{\nu : \mathbf{int} \mid \varphi_2\}} \quad \text{(S-INT)} \qquad \frac{\forall x \in dom(\Gamma').\Gamma \vdash \Gamma(x) \leq \Gamma'(x)}{\Gamma \leq \Gamma'} \quad \text{(S-TYENV)}$$

$$\frac{r_1 \geq r_2 \quad \Gamma \vdash \tau_1 \leq \tau_2}{\Gamma \vdash \tau_1\,\mathbf{ref}^{r_1} \leq \tau_2\,\mathbf{ref}^{r_2}} \quad \text{(S-REF)} \qquad \frac{\Gamma, x : \tau \leq \Gamma', x : \tau' \quad x \notin dom(\Gamma)}{\Gamma, \tau \leq \Gamma', \tau'} \quad \text{(S-RES)}$$

Fig. 9. Subtyping rules.

Destructive Updates, Aliasing, and Subtyping. We now discuss the handling of assignment, aliasing annotations, and subtyping as described in Figure 8. Although apparently unrelated, all three concern updating the refinements of (potentially) aliased reference cells.

Like the binding forms discussed above, T-ASSIGN splits the assigned value's type into two types via the type addition operator, and distributes these types between the right hand side of the assignment and the mutated reference contents. Refinement information in the fresh contents *may* be inconsistent with any previous refinement information; only the shapes must be the same. In a system with unrestricted aliasing, this typing rule would be unsound as it would admit writes that are inconsistent with refinements on aliases of the left hand side. However, the assignment rule requires that the updated reference has an ownership of 1. By the ownership type invariant, all aliases with the updated reference have 0 ownership, and by ownership well-formedness may only contain the $\top$ refinement.

Example 3. We can type the program as follows:

let x = **mkref** 5 **in**   // $x : \{\nu : \mathbf{int} \mid \nu = 5\}\,\mathbf{ref}^1$
let y = x **in**   // $x : \top_1, y : \{\nu : \mathbf{int} \mid \nu = 5\}\,\mathbf{ref}^1$
  y := 4; **assert**(*y = 4) // $x : \top_1, y : \{\nu : \mathbf{int} \mid \nu = 4\}\,\mathbf{ref}^1$

In this and later examples, we include type annotations within comments. We stress that these annotations are for expository purposes only; our tool can infer these types automatically with no manual annotations.

As described thus far, the type system is quite strict: if ownership has been completely transferred from one reference to another, the refinement information found in the original reference is effectively useless. Additionally, once a mutable pointer has been split through an assignment or let expression, there is no way to recover mutability. The typing rule for must alias assertions, T-ALIAS and T-ALIASPTR, overcomes this restriction by exploiting the must-aliasing information to "shuffle" or redistribute ownerships *and refinements* between two aliased pointers. The typing rule assigns two fresh types $\tau_1' \, \mathbf{ref}^{r_1'}$ and $\tau_2' \, \mathbf{ref}^{r_2'}$ to the two operand pointers. The choice of τ_1', r_1', τ_2', and r_2' is left open provided that the sum of the new types, $(\tau_1' \, \mathbf{ref}^{r_1'}) + (\tau_2' \, \mathbf{ref}^{r_2'})$ is equivalent (denoted $\approx$) to the sum of the original types. Formally, $\approx$ is defined as in Figure 8; it implies that any refinements in the two types must be logically equivalent and that ownerships must also be equal. This redistribution is sound precisely because the two references are assumed to alias; the total ownership for the single memory cell pointed to by both references cannot be increased by this shuffling. Further, any refinements that hold for the contents of one reference must necessarily hold for contents of the other and vice versa.

Example 4 (Shuffling ownerships and refinements). Let $\varphi_{=n}$ be $\nu = n$.

```
let x = mkref 5 in   // x : {ν : int | φ=5} ref¹
let y = x in         // x : T₁, y : {ν : int | φ=5} ref¹
  y := 4; alias(x = y) // x : {ν : int | φ=4} ref^0.5, y : {ν : int | φ=4} ref^0.5
```

The final type assignment for x and y is justified by

$$\mathsf{T}_1 + \{\nu : \mathrm{int} \mid \varphi_{=4}\} \, \mathbf{ref}^1 = \{\nu : \mathrm{int} \mid \top \wedge \varphi_{=4}\} \, \mathbf{ref}^1 \approx$$
$$\{\nu : \mathrm{int} \mid \varphi_{=4} \wedge \varphi_{=4}\} \, \mathbf{ref}^1 = \{\nu : \mathrm{int} \mid \varphi_{=4}\} \, \mathbf{ref}^{0.5} + \{\nu : \mathrm{int} \mid \varphi_{=4}\} \, \mathbf{ref}^{0.5}.$$

The aliasing rules give fine-grained control over ownership information. This flexibility allows mutation through two or more aliased references within the same scope. Provided sufficient aliasing annotations, the type system may shuffle ownerships between one or more live references, enabling and disabling mutability as required. Although the reliance on these annotations appears to decrease the practicality of our type system, we expect these aliasing annotations can be inserted by a conservative must-aliasing analysis. Further, empirical experience from our prior work [56] indicates that only a small number of annotations are required for larger programs.

Example 5 (Shuffling Mutability). Let $\varphi_{=n}$ again be $\nu = n$. The following program uses two live, aliased references to mutate the same memory location:

```
let x = mkref 0 in
let y = x in         // x : {ν : int | φ=0} ref¹, y : T₁
  x := 1; alias(x = y); // x : T₁, y : {ν : int | φ=1} ref¹
  y := 2; alias(x = y); // x : {ν : int | φ=2} ref^0.5, y : {ν : int | φ=2} ref^0.5
  assert(*x = 2)
```

$$\Theta(f) = \forall \lambda. \langle x_1 : \tau_1, \ldots, x_n : \tau_n \rangle \to \langle x_1 : \tau_1', \ldots, x_n : \tau_n' \mid \tau \rangle$$
$$\sigma_\alpha = [\ell : \mathcal{L}/\lambda] \qquad \sigma_x = [y_1/x_1] \cdots [y_n/x_n]$$
$$\cfrac{\Theta \mid \mathcal{L} \mid \Gamma[y_i \hookleftarrow \sigma_\alpha \sigma_x \tau_i'], x : \sigma_\alpha \sigma_x \tau \vdash e : \tau' \Rightarrow \Gamma' \qquad x \notin dom(\Gamma')}{\Theta \mid \mathcal{L} \mid \Gamma[y_i : \sigma_\alpha \sigma_x \tau_i] \vdash \mathbf{let}\ x = f^\ell(y_1, \ldots, y_n)\ \mathbf{in}\ e : \tau' \Rightarrow \Gamma'} \quad \text{(T-CALL)}$$

$$\cfrac{\Theta(f) = \forall \lambda. \langle x_1 : \tau_1, \ldots, x_n : \tau_n \rangle \to \langle x_1 : \tau_1', \ldots, x_n : \tau_n' \mid \tau \rangle \qquad \Theta \mid \lambda \mid x_1 : \tau_1, \ldots, x_n : \tau_n \vdash e : \tau \Rightarrow x_1 : \tau_1', \ldots, x_n : \tau_n'}{\Theta \vdash f \mapsto (x_1, .., x_n)e} \quad \text{(T-FUNDEF)}$$

$$\cfrac{\forall f \mapsto (x_1, .., x_n)e \in D.\Theta \vdash f \mapsto (x_1, .., x_n)e \qquad dom(D) = dom(\Theta)}{\Theta \vdash D} \quad \text{(T-FUNS)}$$

$$\cfrac{\Theta \vdash D \qquad \vdash_{WF} \Theta \qquad \Theta \mid \epsilon \mid \bullet \vdash e : \tau \Rightarrow \Gamma}{\vdash \langle D, e \rangle} \quad \text{(T-PROG)}$$

Fig. 10. Program typing rules

After the first aliasing statement the type system shuffles the (exclusive) mutability between x and y to enable the write to y. After the second aliasing statement the ownership in y is split with x; note that transferring all ownership from y to x would also yield a valid typing.

Finally, we describe the subtyping rule. The rules for subtyping types and environments are shown in Figure 9. For integer types, the rules require the refinement of a supertype is a logical consequence of the subtype's refinement conjoined with the lifting of Γ. The subtype rule for references is *covariant* in the type of reference contents. It is widely known that in a language with unrestricted aliasing and mutable references such a rule is unsound: after a write into the coerced pointer, reads from an alias may yield a value disallowed by the alias' type [43]. However, as in the assign case, ownership types prevent unsoundness; a write to the coerced pointer requires the pointer to have ownership 1, which guarantees any aliased pointers have the maximal type and provide no information about their contents beyond simple types.

3.3   Interprocedural Fragment and Context-Sensitivity

We now turn to a discussion of the interprocedural fragment of our language, and how our type system propagates context information. The remaining typing rules for our language are shown in Figure 10. These rules concern the typing of function calls, function bodies, and entire programs.

We first explain the T-CALL rule. The rule uses two substitution maps. σ_x translates between the parameter names used in the function type and actual argument names at the call-site. σ_α instantiates all occurrences of λ in the callee type with $\ell : \mathcal{L}$, where ℓ is the label of the call-site and $\mathcal{L}$ the typing context of the call. The types of the arguments y_i's are required to match the parameter ypes (post substitution). The body of the let binding is then checked with he argument types updated to reflect the changes in the function call (again,)ost substitution). This update is well-defined because we require all function arguments be distinct as described in Section 2.1. Intuitively, the substitution σ_α epresents incrementally refining the behavior of the callee function with partial context information. If $\mathcal{L}$ is itself a context variable λ', this substitution effectively ransforms any context prefix queries over λ in the argument/return/output ypes into a queries over $\ell : \lambda'$. In other words, while the exact concrete execution context of the callee is unknown, the context must at least begin with ℓ which can potentially rule out certain behaviors.

Rule T-FUNDEF type checks a function definition $f \mapsto (x_1, .., x_n)e$ against he function type given in Θ. As a convenience we assume that the parameter names in the function type match the formal parameters in the function definition. The rule checks that under an initial environment given by the argument types the function body produces a value of the return type and transforms the arguments according to the output types. As mentioned above, functions may be executed under many different contexts, so type checking the function body is performed under the context variable λ that occurs in the function type.

Finally, the rule for typing programs (T-PROG) checks that all function definitions are well typed under a well-formed function type environment, and that the entry point e is well typed in an empty type environment and the typing context ϵ, i.e., the initial context.

Example 6 (1-CFA). Recall the program in Figure 3 in Section 1; assume the function calls are labeled as follows:

```
p := get^{ℓ1}(p) + 1;
// ...
q := get^{ℓ2}(q) + 1;
```

Taking τ_p to be the type shown in Example 2:

$$\{\nu : \mathbf{int} \mid (\ell_1 \preceq \lambda \implies \nu = 3) \wedge (\ell_2 \preceq \lambda \implies \nu = 5)\}$$

we can give **get** the type $\forall \lambda. \langle z : \tau_p \, \mathbf{ref}^1 \rangle \to \langle z : \tau_p \, \mathbf{ref}^1 \mid \tau_p \rangle$.

Example 7 (2-CFA). To see how context information propagates across multiple calls, consider the following change to the code considered in Example 6:

```
get_real(z) { *z }
get(z) { get_real^{ℓ3}(z) }
```

The type of **get** remains as in Example 6, and taking τ to be

$$\{\nu : \mathbf{int} \mid (\ell_3 \ell_1 \preceq \lambda' \implies \nu = 3) \wedge (\ell_3 \ell_2 \preceq \lambda' \implies \nu = 5)\}$$

the type of **get_real** is: $\forall \lambda'. \langle z : \tau \, \mathbf{ref}^1 \rangle \to \langle z : \tau \, \mathbf{ref}^1 \mid \tau \rangle$.

We focus on the typing of the call to **get_real** in **get**; it is typed in context λ and a type environment where p is given type τ_p from Example 6.

Applying the substitution $[\ell_3 : \lambda/\lambda']$ to the argument type of `get_real` yields

$$\{\nu : \mathbf{int} \mid (\ell_3\,\ell_1 \preceq \ell_3 : \lambda \implies \nu = 3) \wedge (\ell_3\,\ell_2 \preceq \ell_3 : \lambda \implies \nu = 5)\}\,\mathbf{ref}^1 \approx$$
$$\{\nu : \mathbf{int} \mid (\ell_1 \preceq \lambda \implies \nu = 3) \wedge (\ell_2 \preceq \lambda \implies \nu = 5)\}\,\mathbf{ref}^1$$

which is exactly the type of p. A similar derivation applies to the return type of `get_real` and thus `get`.

3.4   Soundness

We have proven that any program that type checks according to the rules above will never experience an assertion failure. We formalize this claim with the following soundness theorem.

Theorem 1 (Soundness). *If* $\vdash \langle D, e \rangle$*, then* $\langle \emptyset, \emptyset, \cdot, e \rangle \not\longmapsto_D^* \mathbf{AssertFail}$*.*

Further, any well-typed program either diverges, halts in the configuration **AliasFail***, or halts in a configuration* $\langle H, R, \cdot, x \rangle$ *for some* H, R *and* x*, i.e., evaluation does not get stuck.*

Proof (Sketch). By standard progress and preservation lemmas; the full proof has been omitted for space reasons and can be found in the full version [60]. $\blacksquare$

4   Inference and Extensions

We now briefly describe the inference algorithm implemented in our tool CON-SORT. We sketch some implemented extensions needed to type more interesting programs and close with a discussion of current limitations of our prototype.

4.1   Inference

Our tool first runs a standard, simple type inference algorithm to generate type templates for every function parameter type, return type, and for every live variable at each program point. For a variable x of simple type $\tau_S ::= \mathbf{int} \mid \tau_S\,\mathbf{ref}$ at program point p, CONSORT generates a type template $[\![\tau_S]\!]_{x,0,p}$ as follows:

$$[\![\mathbf{int}]\!]_{x,n,p} = \{\nu : \mathbf{int} \mid \varphi_{x,n,p}(\nu; \mathbf{FV}_p)\} \quad [\![\tau_S\,\mathbf{ref}]\!]_{x,n,p} = [\![\tau_S]\!]_{x,n+1,p}\,\mathbf{ref}^{r_{x,n,p}}$$

$\varphi_{x,n,p}(\nu; \mathbf{FV}_p)$ denotes a fresh relation symbol applied to ν and the free variables of simple type **int** at program point p (denoted $\mathbf{FV}_p$). $r_{x,n,p}$ is a fresh ownership variable. For each function f, there are two synthetic program points, f^b and f^e for the beginning and end of the function respectively. At both points, CONSORT generates type template for each argument, where $\mathbf{FV}_{f^b}$ and $\mathbf{FV}_{f^e}$ are the names of integer typed parameters. At f^e, CONSORT also generates a type template for the return value. We write Γ^p to indicate the type environment at point p, where every variable is mapped to its corresponding type template. $[\![\Gamma^p]\!]$ is thus equivalent to $\bigwedge_{x \in \mathbf{FV}_p} \varphi_{x,0,p}(x; \mathbf{FV}_p)$.

When generating these type templates, our implementation also generates own-rship well-formedness constraints. Specifically, for a type template of the form $\nu : \mathbf{int} \mid \varphi_{x,n+1,p}(\nu; \mathbf{FV}_p)\} \, \mathbf{ref}^{r_{x,n,p}}$ CONSORT emits the constraint: $r_{x,n,p} = $ $\implies \varphi_{x,n+1,p}(\nu; \mathbf{FV}_p)$ and for a type template $(\tau \, \mathbf{ref}^{r_{x,n+1,p}}) \, \mathbf{ref}^{r_{x,n,p}}$ CON-SORT emits the constraint $r_{x,n,p} = 0 \implies r_{x,n+1,p} = 0$.

CONSORT then walks the program, generating constraints between relation ymbols and ownership variables according to the typing rules. These constraints ake three forms, ownership constraints, subtyping constraints, and assertion constraints. Ownership constraints are simple linear (in)equalities over ownership variables and constants, according to conditions imposed by the typing rules. For example, if variable x has the type template $\tau \, \mathbf{ref}^{r_{x,0,p}}$ for the expression $x := y \,; e$ at point p, CONSORT generates the constraint $r_{x,0,p} = 1$.

CONSORT emits subtyping constraints between the relation symbols at related program points according to the rules of the type system. For example, for he term $\mathbf{let} \, x = y \, \mathbf{in} \, e$ at program point p (where e is at program point p', and x 1as simple type $\mathbf{int} \, \mathbf{ref}$) CONSORT generates the following subtyping constraint:

$$\llbracket \Gamma^p \rrbracket \wedge \varphi_{y,1,p}(\nu; \mathbf{FV}_p) \implies \varphi_{y,1,p'}(\nu; \mathbf{FV}_{p'}) \wedge \varphi_{x,1,p'}(\nu; \mathbf{FV}_{p'})$$

in addition to the ownership constraint $r_{y,0,p} = r_{y,0,p'} + r_{x,0,p'}$.

Finally, for each $\mathbf{assert}(\varphi)$ in the program, CONSORT emits an assertion constraint of the form: $\llbracket \Gamma^p \rrbracket \implies \varphi$ which requires the refinements on integer typed variables in scope are sufficient to prove φ.

Encoding Context Sensitivity. To make inference tractable, we require the user to fix *a priori* the maximum length of prefix queries to a constant k (this choice is easily controlled with a command line parameter to our tool). We supplement the arguments in *every* predicate application with a set of integer context variables $c_1, \ldots, c_k$; these variables do not overlap with any program variables.

CONSORT uses these variables to infer context sensitive refinements as follows. Consider a function call $\mathbf{let} \, x = f^\ell(y_1, \ldots, y_n) \, \mathbf{in} \, e$ at point p where e is at point p'. CONSORT generates the following constraint for a refinement $\varphi_{y_i,n,p}(\nu, c_1, \ldots, c_k; \mathbf{FV}_p)$ which occurs in the type template of y_i:

$$\varphi_{y_i,n,p}(\nu, c_0, \ldots, c_k; \mathbf{FV}_p) \implies \sigma_x \varphi_{x_i,n,f^b}(\nu, \ell, c_0, \ldots, c_{k-1}; \mathbf{FV}_{f^b})$$
$$\sigma_x \varphi_{x_i,n,f^e}(\nu, \ell, c_0, \ldots, c_{k-1}; \mathbf{FV}_{f^e}) \implies \varphi_{y_i,n,p'}(\nu, c_0, \ldots, c_k; \mathbf{FV}_{p'})$$
$$\sigma_x = [y_1/x_1] \cdots [y_n/x_n]$$

Effectively, we have encoded $\ell_1 \ldots \ell_k \preceq \lambda$ as $\wedge_{0 < i \leq k} c_i = \ell_i$. In the above, the shift from $c_0, \ldots, c_k$ to $\ell, c_0, \ldots, c_{k-1}$ plays the role of σ_α in the T-CALL rule. The above constraint serves to determine the value of c_0 within the body of the function f. If f calls another function g, the above rule propagates this value of c_0 to c_1 within g and so on. The solver may then instantiate relation symbols with predicates that are conditional over the values of c_i.

Solving Constraints. The results of the above process are two systems of con-straints; real arithmetic constraints over ownership variables and constrained Horn clauses (CHC) over the refinement relations. Under certain assumptions about the simple types in a program, the size of the ownership and subtyping constraints will be polynomial to the size of the program. These systems are not independent; the relation constraints may mention the value of ownership variables due to the well-formedness constraints described above. The ownership constraints are first solved with Z3 [16]. These constraints are non-linear but Z3 appears particularly well-engineered to quickly find solutions for the instances generated by CONSORT. We constrain Z3 to maximize the number of non-zero ownership variables to ensure as few refinements as possible are constrained to be $\top$ by ownership well-formedness.

The values of ownership variables inferred by Z3 are then substituted into the constrained Horn clauses, and the resulting system is checked for satisfiability with an off-the-shelf CHC solver. Our implementation generates constraints in the industry standard SMT-Lib2 format [8]; any solver that accepts this format can be used as a backend for CONSORT. Our implementation currently supports Spacer [37] (part of the Z3 solver [16]), HoICE [13], and Eldarica [48] (adding a new backend requires only a handful of lines of glue code). We found that different solvers are better tuned to different problems; we also implemented *parallel mode* which runs all supported solvers in parallel, using the first available result.

4.2   Extensions

Primitive Operations. As defined in Section 2, our language can compare integers to zero and load and store them from memory, but can perform no meaningful computation over these numbers. To promote the flexibility of our type system and simplify our soundness statement, we do not fix a set of primitive operations and their static semantics. Instead, we assume any set of primitive operations used in a program are given sound function types in Θ. For example, under the assumption that $+$ has its usual semantics and the underlying logic supports $+$, we can give $+$ the type $\forall \lambda. \langle x : \top_0, y : \top_0 \rangle \to \langle x : \top_0, y : \top_0 \mid \{\nu : \mathsf{int} \mid \nu = x + y\} \rangle$. Interactions with a nondeterministic environment or unknown program inputs can then be modeled with a primitive that returns integers refined with $\top$.

Dependent Tuples. Our implementation supports types of the form: $(x_1 : \tau_1, \ldots, x_n : \tau_n)$, where x_i can appear within τ_j $(j \neq i)$ if τ_i is an integer type. For example, $(x : \{\nu : \mathsf{int} \mid \top\}, y : \{\nu : \mathsf{int} \mid \nu > x\})$ is the type of tuples whose second element is strictly greater than the first. We also extend the language with tuple constructors as a new value form, and let bindings with tuple patterns as the LHS.

The extension to type checking is relatively straightforward; the only significant extensions are to the subtyping rules. Specifically, the subtyping check for a tuple element $x_i : \tau_i$ is performed in a type environment elaborated with the types and names of other tuple elements. The extension to type inference is also straightforward; the arguments for a predicate symbol include any enclosing dependent tuple names and the environment in subtyping constraints is likewise extended.

Recursive Types. Our language also supports some unbounded heap structures via recursive reference types. To keep inference tractable, we forbid nested recursive types, multiple occurrences of the recursive type variable, and additionally

x the shape of refinements that occur within a recursive type. For recursive refinements that fit the above restriction, our approach for refinements is broadly
similar to that in [35], and we use the ownership scheme of [56] for handling
ownership. We first use simple type inference to infer the shape of the recursive
types, and automatically insert fold/unfold annotations into the source program.
As in [35], the refinements within an unfolding of a recursive type may refer to
dependent tuple names bound by the enclosing type. These recursive types can
express, e.g., the invariants of a mutable, sorted list. As in [56], recursive types
are unfolded once before assigning ownership variables; further unfoldings copy
existing ownership variables.

As in Java or C++, our language does not support sum types, and any
instantiation of a recursive type must use a null pointer. Our implementation
supports an **ifnull** construct in addition to a distinguished **null** constant. Our
implementation allows any refinement to hold for the null constant, including
$\perp$. Currently, our implementation does *not* detect null pointer dereferences, and
all soundness guarantees are made modulo freedom of null dereferences. As $[\![\Gamma]\!]$
omits refinements under reference types, null pointer refinements do not affect
the verification of programs without null pointer dereferences.

Arrays. Our implementation supports arrays of integers. Each array is given an
ownership describing the ownership of memory allocated for the entire array. The
array type contains two refinements: the first refines the length of the array itself,
and the second refines the entire array contents. The content refinement may
refer to a symbolic index variable for precise, per-index refinements. At reads
and writes to the array, CONSORT instantiates the refinement's symbolic index
variable with the concrete index used at the read/write.

As in [56], our restriction to arrays of integers stems from the difficulty of
ownership inference. Soundly handling pointer arrays requires index-wise tracking
of ownerships which significantly complicates automated inference. We leave
supporting arrays of pointers to future work.

4.3 Limitations

Our current approach is not complete; there are safe programs that will be rejected
by our type system. As mentioned in Section 3.1, our well-formedness condition
forbids refinements that refer to memory locations. As a result, CONSORT
cannot in general express, e.g., that the contents of two references are equal.
Further, due to our reliance on automated theorem provers we are restricted to
logics with sound but potentially incomplete decision procedures. CONSORT
also does not support conditional or context-sensitive ownerships, and therefore
cannot precisely handle conditional mutation or aliasing.

5 Experiments

We now present the results of preliminary experiments performed with the implementation described in Section 4. The goal of these experiments was to answer the

Table 1. Description of benchmark suite adapted from JayHorn. **Java** are programs that test Java-specific features. **Inc** are tests that cannot be handled by CONSORT, e.g., null checking, etc. **Bug** includes a "safe" program we discovered was actually incorrect

Set	Orig.	Adapted	Java	Inc	Bug
Safe	41	32	6	2	1
Unsafe	41	26	13	2	0

following questions: i) is the type system (and extensions of Section 4) expressive enough to type and verify non-trivial programs? and ii) is type inference feasible?

To answer these questions, we evaluated our prototype implementation on two sets of benchmarks.[4] The first set is adapted from JayHorn [32, 33], a verification tool for Java. This test suite contains a combination of 82 safe and unsafe programs written in Java. We chose this benchmark suite as, like CONSORT, JayHorn is concerned with the automated verification of programs in a language with mutable, aliased memory cells. Further, although some of their benchmark programs tested Java specific features, most could be adapted into our low-level language. The tests we could adapt provide a comparison with existing state-of-the-art verification techniques. A detailed breakdown of the adapted benchmark suite can be found in Table 1.

Remark 2. The original JayHorn paper includes two additional benchmark sets, Mine Pump and CBMC. Both our tool and recent JayHorn versions time out on the Mine Pump benchmark. Further, the CBMC tests were either subsumed by our own test programs, tested Java specific features, or tested program synthesis functionality. We therefore omitted both of these benchmarks from our evaluation.

The second benchmark set consists of data structure implementations and microbenchmarks written directly in our low-level imperative language. We developed this suite to test the expressive power of our type system and inference. The programs included in this suite are:

- **Array-List** Implementation of an unbounded list backed by an array.
- **Sorted-List** Implementation of a mutable, sorted list maintained with an in-place insertion sort algorithm.
- **Shuffle** Multiple live references are used to mutate the same location in program memory as in Example 5.
- **Mut-List** Implementation of general linked lists with a clear operation.
- **Array-Inv** A program which allocates a length n array and writes the value i at every index i.
- **Intro2** The motivating program shown in Figure 2 in Section 1.

---

[4] Our experiments and the CONSORT source code are available at https://www.fos.kuis.kyoto-u.ac.jp/projects/consort/.

Table 2. Comparison of CONSORT to JayHorn on the benchmark set of [32] (top) and our custom benchmark suite (bottom). *T/O* indicates a time out.

			ConSORT		JayHorn		
	Set	N. Tests	Correct	T/O	Correct	T/O	Imp.
	Safe	32	29	3	24	5	3
	Unsafe	26	26	0	19	0	7

Name	Safe?	Time(s)	Ann	JH	Name	Safe?	Time(s)	Ann	JH
Array-Inv	✓	10.07	0	T/O	Array-Inv-BUG	X	5.29	0	T/O
Array-List	✓	16.76	0	T/O	Array-List-BUG	X	1.13	0	T/O
Intro2	✓	0.08	0	T/O	Intro2-BUG	X	0.02	0	T/O
Mut-List	✓	1.45	3	T/O	Mut-List-BUG	X	0.41	3	T/O
Shuffle	✓	0.13	3	✓	Shuffle-BUG	X	0.07	3	X
Sorted-List	✓	1.90	3	T/O	Sorted-List-BUG	X	1.10	3	T/O

We introduced unsafe mutations to these programs to check our tool for unsoundness and translated these programs into Java for further comparison with JayHorn.

Our benchmarks and JayHorn's require a small number of trivially identified alias annotations. The adapted JayHorn benchmarks contain a total of 6 annotations; the most for any individual test was 3. The number of annotations required for our benchmark suite are shown in column **Ann.** of Table 2.

We first ran CONSORT on each program in our benchmark suite and ran version 0.7 of JayHorn on the corresponding Java version. We recorded the final verification result for both our tool and JayHorn. We also collected the end-to-end runtime of CONSORT for each test; we do not give a performance comparison with JayHorn given the many differences in target languages. For the JayHorn suite, we first ran our tool on the adapted version of each test program and ran JayHorn on the original Java version. We also did not collect runtime information for this set of experiments because our goal is a comparison of tool precision, not performance. All tests were run on a machine with 16 GB RAM and 4 Intel i5 CPUs at 2GHz and with a timeout of 60 seconds (the same timeout was used in [32]). We used CONSORT's parallel backend (Section 4) with Z3 version 4.8.4, HoICE version 1.8.1, and Eldarica version 2.0.1 and JayHorn's Eldarica backend.

5.1 Results

The results of our experiments are shown in Table 2. On the JayHorn benchmark suite CONSORT performs competitively with JayHorn, correctly identifying 29 of the 32 safe programs as such. For all 3 tests on which CONSORT timed out after 60 seconds, JayHorn also timed out (column *T/O*). For the unsafe programs, CONSORT correctly identified all programs as unsafe within 60 seconds; JayHorn answered UNKNOWN for 7 tests (column *Imp.*).

On our own benchmark set, CONSORT correctly verifies all safe versions of the programs within 60 seconds. For the unsafe variants, CONSORT was able to quickly and definitively determine these programs unsafe. JayHorn times out on all tests except for **Shuffle** and **ShuffleBUG** (column **JH**). We investigated the cause of time outs and discovered that after verification failed with an unbounded heap model, JayHorn attempts verification on increasingly larger bounded heaps In every case, JayHorn exceeded the 60 second timeout before reaching a pre-configured limit on the heap bound. This result suggests JayHorn struggles in the presence of per-object invariants and unbounded allocations; the only two tests JayHorn successfully analyzed contain just a single object allocation.

We do not believe this struggle is indicative of a shortcoming in JayHorn's implementation, but stems from the fundamental limitations of JayHorn's memory representation. Like many verification tools (see Section 6), JayHorn uses a single, unchanging invariant to for every object allocated at the same syntactic location; effectively, all objects allocated at the same location are assumed to alias with one another. This representation cannot, in general, handle programs with different invariants for distinct objects that evolve over time. We hypothesize other tools that adopt a similar approach will exhibit the same difficulty.

6   Related Work

The difficulty in handling programs with mutable references and aliasing has been well-studied. Like JayHorn, many approaches model the heap explicitly at verification time, approximating concrete heap locations with allocation site labels [14, 20, 32, 33, 46]; each *abstract location* is also associated with a refinement. As abstract locations summarize many concrete locations, this approach does not in general admit strong updates and flow-sensitivity; in particular, the refinement associated with an abstract location is fixed for the lifetime of the program. The techniques cited above include various workarounds for this limitation. For example, [14, 46] temporarily allows breaking these invariants through a distinguished program name as long as the abstract location is not accessed through another name. The programmer must therefore eventually bring the invariant back in sync with the summary location. As a result, these systems ultimately cannot precisely handle programs that require evolving invariants on mutable memory.

A similar approach was taken in CQual [23] by Aiken et al. [2]. They used an explicit *restrict* binding for pointers. Strong updates are permitted through pointers bound with *restrict*, but the program is forbidden from using any pointers which share an allocation site while the restrict binding is live.

A related technique used in the field of object-oriented verification is to declare object invariants at the class level and allow these invariants on object fields to be broken during a limited period of time [7, 22]. In particular, the work on Spec# [7] uses an ownership system which tracks whether object a owns object b; like CONSORT's ownership system, these ownerships contain the effects of mutation. However, Spec#'s ownership is quite strict and does not admit references to b outside of the owning object a.

Viper [30, 42] (and its related projects [31, 39]) uses access annotations (expressed as permission predicates) to explicitly transfer access/mutation permis-ions for references between static program names. Like CONSORT, permissions may be fractionally transferred, allowing temporary shared, immutable access to a mutable memory cell. However, while CONSORT automatically infers many ownership transfers, Viper requires extensive annotations for each transfer.

F*, a dependently typed dialect of ML, includes an update/select theory of heaps and requires explicit annotations summarizing the heap effects of a method [44, 57, 58]. This approach enables modular reasoning and precise specification of pre- and post-conditions with respect to the heap, but precludes full automation.

The work on rely–guarantee reference types by Gordon et al. [26, 27] uses refinement types in a language mutable references and aliasing. Their approach extends reference types with rely/guarantee predicates; the rely predicate describes possible mutations via aliases, and the guarantee predicate describes the admissible mutations through the current reference. If two references may alias, then the guarantee predicate of one reference implies the rely predicate of the other and vice versa. This invariant is maintained with a splitting operation that is similar to our + operator. Further, their type system allows strong updates to reference refinements provided the new refinements are preserved by the rely predicate. Thus, rely–guarantee refinement support multiple mutable, aliased references with non-trivial refinement information. Unfortunately this expressiveness comes at the cost of automated inference and verification; an embedding of this system into Liquid Haskell [63] described in [27] was forced to sacrifice strong updates.

Work by Degen et al. [17] introduced linear *state annotations* to Java. To effect strong updates in the presence of aliasing, like CONSORT, their system requires annotated memory locations are mutated only through a distinguished reference. Further, all aliases of this mutable reference give no information about the state of the object much like our 0 ownership pointers. However, their system cannot handle multiple, immutable aliases with non-trivial annotation information; *only* the mutable reference may have non-trivial annotation information.

The fractional ownerships in CONSORT and their counterparts in [55, 56] have a clear relation to linear type systems. Many authors have explored the use of linear type systems to reason in contexts with aliased mutable references [18, 19, 52], and in particular with the goal of supporting strong updates [1]. A closely related approach is RustHorn by Matsushita et al. [40]. Much like CONSORT, RustHorn uses CHC and linear aliasing information for the sound and—unlike CONSORT—complete verification of programs with aliasing and mutability. However, their approach depends on Rust's strict *borrowing discipline*, and cannot handle programs where multiple aliased references are used in the same lexical region. In contrast, CONSORT supports fine-grained, per-statement changes in mutability and even further control with **alias** annotations, which allows it to verify larger classes of programs.

The ownerships of CONSORT also have a connection to separation logic [45]; the separating conjunction isolates write effects to local subheaps, while CONSORT's ownership system isolates effects to local updates of pointer types. Other researchers have used separation logic to precisely support strong updates of abstract state. For example, in work by Kloos et al. [36] resources are associated with static, abstract names; each resource (represented by its static name) may be owned (and thus, mutated) by exactly one thread. Unlike CONSORT, their ownership system forbids even temporary immutable, shared ownership, or transferring ownerships at arbitrary program points. An approach proposed by Bakst and Jhala [4] uses a similar technique, combining separation logic with refinement types. Their approach gives allocated memory cells abstract names, and associates these names with refinements in an abstract heap. Like the approach of Kloos et al. and CONSORT's ownership 1 pointers, they ensure these abstract locations are distinct in all concrete heaps, enabling sound, strong updates.

The idea of using a rational number to express permissions to access a reference dates back to the type system of *fractional permissions* by Boyland [12]. His work used fractional permissions to verify race freedom of a concurrent program without a may-alias analysis. Later, Terauchi [59] proposed a type-inference algorithm that reduces typing constraints to a set of linear inequalities over rational numbers. Boyland's idea also inspired a variant of separation logic for a concurrent programming language [11] to express sharing of read permissions among several threads. Our previous work [55, 56], inspired by that in [11, 59], proposed methods for type-based verification of resource-leak freedom, in which a rational number expresses an *obligation* to deallocate certain resource, not just a permission.

The issue of context-sensitivity (sometimes called *polyvariance*) is well-studied in the field of abstract interpretation (e.g., [28, 34, 41, 50, 51], see [25] for a recent survey). Polyvariance has also been used in type systems to assign different behaviors to the same function depending on its call site [3, 6, 64]. In the area of refinement type systems, Zhu and Jagannathan developed a context-sensitive dependent type system for a functional language [67] that indexed function types by unique labels attached to call-sites. Our context-sensitivity approach was inspired by this work. In fact, we could have formalized context-polymorphism within the framework of full dependent types, but chose the current presentation for simplicity.

7   Conclusion

We presented CONSORT, a novel type system for safety verification of imperative programs with mutability and aliasing. CONSORT is built upon the novel combination of fractional ownership types and refinement types. Ownership types flow-sensitively and precisely track the existence of mutable aliases. CONSORT admits sound strong updates by discarding refinement information on mutably-aliased references as indicated by ownership types. Our type system is amenable to automatic type inference; we have implemented a prototype of this inference tool and found it can verify several non-trivial programs and outperforms a state-of-the-art program verifier. As an area of future work, we plan to investigate using fractional ownership types to soundly allow refinements that mention memory locations.

Acknowledgments The authors would like to the reviewers for their thoughtful feedback and suggestions, and Yosuke Fukuda and Alex Potanin for their feedback on early drafts. This work was supported in part by JSPS KAKENHI, grant numbers JP15H05706 and JP19H04084, and in part by the JST ERATO MMSD Project.

Bibliography

[1] Ahmed, A., Fluet, M., Morrisett, G.: L^3: a linear language with locations. Fundamenta Informaticae **77**(4), 397–449 (2007)

[2] Aiken, A., Foster, J.S., Kodumal, J., Terauchi, T.: Checking and inferring local non-aliasing. In: Conference on Programming Language Design and Implementation (PLDI). pp. 129–140 (2003). https://doi.org/10.1145/781131.781146

[3] Amtoft, T., Turbak, F.: Faithful translations between polyvariant flows and polymorphic types. In: European Symposium on Programming (ESOP). pp. 26–40. Springer (2000). https://doi.org/10.1007/3-540-46425-5_2

[4] Bakst, A., Jhala, R.: Predicate abstraction for linked data structures. In: Conference on Verification, Model Checking, and Abstract Interpretation (VMCAI). pp. 65–84. Springer Berlin Heidelberg (2016). https://doi.org/10.1007/978-3-662-49122-5_3

[5] Ball, T., Levin, V., Rajamani, S.K.: A decade of software model checking with SLAM. Communications of the ACM **54**(7), 68–76 (2011). https://doi.org/10.1145/1965724.1965743

[6] Banerjee, A.: A modular, polyvariant and type-based closure analysis. In: International Conference on Functional Programming (ICFP). pp. 1–10 (1997). https://doi.org/10.1145/258948.258951

[7] Barnett, M., Fähndrich, M., Leino, K.R.M., Müller, P., Schulte, W., Venter, H.: Specification and verification: the Spec# experience. Communications of the ACM **54**(6), 81–91 (2011). https://doi.org/10.1145/1953122.1953145

[8] Barrett, C., Fontaine, P., Tinelli, C.: The Satisfiability Modulo Theories Library (SMT-LIB). www.SMT-LIB.org (2016)

[9] Bengtson, J., Bhargavan, K., Fournet, C., Gordon, A.D., Maffeis, S.: Refinement types for secure implementations. ACM Transactions on Programming Languages and Systems (TOPLAS) **33**(2), 8:1–8:45 (2011). https://doi.org/10.1145/1890028.1890031

[10] Bhargavan, K., Bond, B., Delignat-Lavaud, A., Fournet, C., Hawblitzel, C., Hriţcu, C., Ishtiaq, S., Kohlweiss, M., Leino, R., Lorch, J., Maillard, K., Pan, J., Parno, B., Protzenko, J., Ramananandro, T., Rane, A., Rastogi, A., Swamy, N., Thompson, L., Wang, P., Zanella-Béguelin, S., Zinzindohoué, J.K.: Everest: Towards a verified, drop-in replacement of HTTPS. In: Summit on Advances in Programming Languages (SNAPL 2017). pp. 1:1–1:12. Schloss Dagstuhl-Leibniz-Zentrum fuer Informatik (2017). https://doi.org/10.4230/LIPIcs.SNAPL.2017.1

[11] Bornat, R., Calcagno, C., O'Hearn, P.W., Parkinson, M.J.: Permission accounting in separation logic. In: Symposium on Principles of Programming Languages (POPL). pp. 259–270 (2005). https://doi.org/10.1145/1040305.1040327

[12] Boyland, J.: Checking interference with fractional permissions. In: Symposion on Static Analysis (SAS). pp. 55–72. Springer (2003). https://doi.org/10.1007/3-540-44898-5_4

[13] Champion, A., Kobayashi, N., Sato, R.: HoIce: An ICE-based non-linear Horn clause solver. In: Asian Symposium on Programming Languages and Systems (APLAS). pp. 146–156. Springer (2018). https://doi.org/10.1007/978-3-030-02768-1_8

[14] Chugh, R., Herman, D., Jhala, R.: Dependent types for JavaScript. In: Conference on Object Oriented Programming Systems Languages and Applications (OOPSLA). pp. 587–606 (2012). https://doi.org/10.1145/2384616.2384659

[15] Cousot, P., Cousot, R., Feret, J., Mauborgne, L., Miné, A., Monniaux, D., Rival, X.: The ASTRÉE analyzer. In: European Symposium on Programming (ESOP). pp. 21–30. Springer (2005). https://doi.org/10.1007/978-3-540-31987-0_3

[16] De Moura, L., Bjørner, N.: Z3: An efficient SMT solver. In: Conference on Tools and Algorithms for the Construction and Analysis of Systems (TACAS). pp. 337–340. Springer (2008). https://doi.org/10.1007/978-3-540-78800-3_24

[17] Degen, M., Thiemann, P., Wehr, S.: Tracking linear and affine resources with JAVA(X). In: European Conference on Object-Oriented Programming (ECOOP). pp. 550–574. Springer (2007). https://doi.org/10.1007/978-3-540-73589-2_26

[18] DeLine, R., Fähndrich, M.: Enforcing high-level protocols in low-level software. In: Conference on Programming Language Design and Implementation (PLDI). pp. 59–69 (2001). https://doi.org/10.1145/378795.378811

[19] Fähndrich, M., DeLine, R.: Adoption and focus: Practical linear types for imperative programming. In: Conference on Programming Language Design and Implementation (PLDI). pp. 13–24 (2002). https://doi.org/10.1145/512529.512532

[20] Fink, S.J., Yahav, E., Dor, N., Ramalingam, G., Geay, E.: Effective typestate verification in the presence of aliasing. ACM Transactions on Software Engineering and Methodology (TOSEM) 17(2), 9:1–9:34 (2008). https://doi.org/10.1145/1348250.1348255

[21] Flanagan, C.: Hybrid type checking. In: Symposium on Principles of Programming Languages (POPL). pp. 245–256 (2006). https://doi.org/10.1145/1111037.1111059

[22] Flanagan, C., Leino, K.R.M., Lillibridge, M., Nelson, G., Saxe, J.B., Stata, R.: Extended static checking for Java. In: Conference on Programming Language Design and Implementation (PLDI). pp. 234–245 (2002). https://doi.org/10.1145/512529.512558

[23] Foster, J.S., Terauchi, T., Aiken, A.: Flow-sensitive type qualifiers. In: Conference on Programming Language Design and Implementation (PLDI). pp. 1–12 (2002). https://doi.org/10.1145/512529.512531

[24] Freeman, T., Pfenning, F.: Refinement types for ML. In: Conference on Programming Language Design and Implementation (PLDI). pp. 268–277 (1991). https://doi.org/10.1145/113445.113468

[25] Gilray, T., Might, M.: A survey of polyvariance in abstract interpretations. In: Symposium on Trends in Functional Programming. pp. 134–148. Springer (2013). https://doi.org/10.1007/978-3-642-45340-3_9

26] Gordon, C.S., Ernst, M.D., Grossman, D.: Rely–guarantee references for refinement types over aliased mutable data. In: Conference on Programming Language Design and Implementation (PLDI). pp. 73–84 (2013). https://doi.org/10.1145/2491956.2462160

27] Gordon, C.S., Ernst, M.D., Grossman, D., Parkinson, M.J.: Verifying invariants of lock-free data structures with rely–guarantee and refinement types. ACM Transactions on Programming Languages and Systems (TOPLAS) 39(3), 11:1–11:54 (2017). https://doi.org/10.1145/3064850

28] Hardekopf, B., Wiedermann, B., Churchill, B., Kashyap, V.: Widening for control-flow. In: Conference on Verification, Model Checking, and Abstract Interpretation (VMCAI). pp. 472–491 (2014). https://doi.org/10.1007/978-3-642-54013-4_26

29] Hawblitzel, C., Howell, J., Kapritsos, M., Lorch, J.R., Parno, B., Roberts, M.L., Setty, S., Zill, B.: IronFleet: proving practical distributed systems correct. In: Symposium on Operating Systems Principles (SOSP). pp. 1–17. ACM (2015). https://doi.org/10.1145/2815400.2815428

30] Heule, S., Kassios, I.T., Müller, P., Summers, A.J.: Verification condition generation for permission logics with abstract predicates and abstraction functions. In: European Conference on Object-Oriented Programming (ECOOP). pp. 451–476. Springer (2013). https://doi.org/10.1007/978-3-642-39038-8_19

31] Heule, S., Leino, K.R.M., Müller, P., Summers, A.J.: Abstract read permissions: Fractional permissions without the fractions. In: Conference on Verification, Model Checking, and Abstract Interpretation (VMCAI). pp. 315–334 (2013). https://doi.org/10.1007/978-3-642-35873-9_20

32] Kahsai, T., Kersten, R., Rümmer, P., Schäf, M.: Quantified heap invariants for object-oriented programs. In: Conference on Logic for Programming Artificial Intelligence and Reasoning (LPAR). pp. 368–384 (2017)

[33] Kahsai, T., Rümmer, P., Sanchez, H., Schäf, M.: JayHorn: A framework for verifying Java programs. In: Conference on Computer Aided Verification (CAV). pp. 352–358. Springer (2016). https://doi.org/10.1007/978-3-319-41528-4_19

[34] Kashyap, V., Dewey, K., Kuefner, E.A., Wagner, J., Gibbons, K., Sarracino, J., Wiedermann, B., Hardekopf, B.: JSAI: a static analysis platform for JavaScript. In: Conference on Foundations of Software Engineering (FSE). pp. 121–132 (2014). https://doi.org/10.1145/2635868.2635904

[35] Kawaguchi, M., Rondon, P., Jhala, R.: Type-based data structure verification. In: Conference on Programming Language Design and Implementation (PLDI). pp. 304–315 (2009). https://doi.org/10.1145/1542476.1542510

[36] Kloos, J., Majumdar, R., Vafeiadis, V.: Asynchronous liquid separation types. In: European Conference on Object-Oriented Programming (ECOOP). pp. 396–420. Schloss Dagstuhl-Leibniz-Zentrum fuer Informatik (2015). https://doi.org/10.4230/LIPIcs.ECOOP.2015.396

[37] Komuravelli, A., Gurfinkel, A., Chaki, S., Clarke, E.M.: Automatic abstraction in SMT-based unbounded software model checking. In: Conference on Computer Aided Verification (CAV). pp. 846–862. Springer (2013). https://doi.org/10.1007/978-3-642-39799-8_59

[38] Leino, K.R.M.: Dafny: An automatic program verifier for functional correctness. In: Conference on Logic for Programming Artificial Intelligence and Reasoning (LPAR). pp. 348–370. Springer (2010). https://doi.org/10.1007/978-3-642-17511-4_20

[39] Leino, K.R.M., Müller, P., Smans, J.: Deadlock-free channels and locks. In: European Symposium on Programming (ESOP). pp. 407–426. Springer-Verlag (2010). https://doi.org/10.1007/978-3-642-11957-6_22

[40] Matsushita, Y., Tsukada, T., Kobayashi, N.: RustHorn: CHC-based verification for Rust programs. In: European Symposium on Programming (ESOP). Springer (2020)

[41] Milanova, A., Rountev, A., Ryder, B.G.: Parameterized object sensitivity for points-to analysis for Java. ACM Transactions on Software Engineering and Methodology (TOSEM) 14(1), 1–41 (2005). https://doi.org/10.1145/1044834.1044835

[42] Müller, P., Schwerhoff, M., Summers, A.J.: Viper: A verification infrastructure for permission-based reasoning. In: Conference on Verification, Model Checking, and Abstract Interpretation (VMCAI). pp. 41–62. Springer-Verlag (2016). https://doi.org/10.1007/978-3-662-49122-5_2

[43] Pierce, B.C.: Types and programming languages. MIT press (2002)

[44] Protzenko, J., Zinzindohoué, J.K., Rastogi, A., Ramananandro, T., Wang, P., Zanella-Béguelin, S., Delignat-Lavaud, A., Hriţcu, C., Bhargavan, K., Fournet, C., Swamy, N.: Verified low-level programming embedded in F*. Proceedings of the ACM on Programming Languages 1(ICFP), 17:1–17:29 (2017). https://doi.org/10.1145/3110261

[45] Reynolds, J.C.: Separation logic: A logic for shared mutable data structures. In: Symposium on Logic in Computer Science (LICS). pp. 55–74. IEEE (2002). https://doi.org/10.1109/LICS.2002.1029817

[46] Rondon, P., Kawaguchi, M., Jhala, R.: Low-level liquid types. In: Symposium on Principles of Programming Languages (POPL). pp. 131–144 (2010). https://doi.org/10.1145/1706299.1706316

[47] Rondon, P.M., Kawaguci, M., Jhala, R.: Liquid types. In: Conference on Programming Language Design and Implementation (PLDI). pp. 159–169 (2008). https://doi.org/10.1145/1375581.1375602

[48] Rümmer, P., Hojjat, H., Kuncak, V.: Disjunctive interpolants for Horn-clause verification. In: Conference on Computer Aided Verification (CAV). pp. 347–363. Springer (2013). https://doi.org/10.1007/978-3-642-39799-8_24

[49] Sharir, M., Pnueli, A.: Two approaches to interprocedural data flow analysis. In: Muchnick, S.S., Jones, N.D. (eds.) Program Flow Analysis: Theory and Applications, chap. 7, pp. 189–223. Prentice Hall (1981)

[50] Shivers, O.: Control-flow analysis of higher-order languages. Ph.D. thesis, Carnegie Mellon University (1991)

[51] Smaragdakis, Y., Bravenboer, M., Lhoták, O.: Pick your contexts well: Understanding object-sensitivity. In: Symposium on Principles of Programming Languages (POPL). pp. 17–30 (2011). https://doi.org/10.1145/1926385.1926390

52] Smith, F., Walker, D., Morrisett, G.: Alias types. In: European Symposium on Programming (ESOP). pp. 366–381. Springer (2000). https://doi.org/10.1007/3-540-46425-5_24

53] Späth, J., Ali, K., Bodden, E.: Context-, flow-, and field-sensitive data-flow analysis using synchronized pushdown systems. Proceedings of the ACM on Programming Languages 3(POPL), 48:1–48:29 (2019). https://doi.org/10.1145/3290361

54] Späth, J., Nguyen Quang Do, L., Ali, K., Bodden, E.: Boomerang: Demand-driven flow-and context-sensitive pointer analysis for Java. In: European Conference on Object-Oriented Programming (ECOOP). pp. 22:1–22:26. Schloss Dagstuhl-Leibniz-Zentrum fuer Informatik (2016). https://doi.org/10.4230/LIPIcs.ECOOP.2016.22

55] Suenaga, K., Fukuda, R., Igarashi, A.: Type-based safe resource dealloca-tion for shared-memory concurrency. In: Conference on Object Oriented Programming Systems Languages and Applications (OOPSLA). pp. 1–20 (2012). https://doi.org/10.1145/2384616.2384618

56] Suenaga, K., Kobayashi, N.: Fractional ownerships for safe memory deal-location. In: Asian Symposium on Programming Languages and Systems (APLAS). pp. 128–143. Springer (2009). https://doi.org/10.1007/978-3-642-10672-9_11

57] Swamy, N., Hriţcu, C., Keller, C., Rastogi, A., Delignat-Lavaud, A., Forest, S., Bhargavan, K., Fournet, C., Strub, P.Y., Kohlweiss, M., Zinzindohoué, J.K., Zanella Béguelin, S.: Dependent types and multi-monadic effects in F*. In: Symposium on Principles of Programming Languages (POPL). pp. 256–270 (2016). https://doi.org/10.1145/2837614.2837655

58] Swamy, N., Weinberger, J., Schlesinger, C., Chen, J., Livshits, B.: Verifying higher-order programs with the Dijkstra monad. In: Conference on Program-ming Language Design and Implementation (PLDI). pp. 387–398 (2013). https://doi.org/10.1145/2491956.2491978

[59] Terauchi, T.: Checking race freedom via linear programming. In: Conference on Programming Language Design and Implementation (PLDI). pp. 1–10 (2008). https://doi.org/10.1145/1375581.1375583

[60] Toman, J., Siqi, R., Suenaga, K., Igarashi, A., Kobayashi, N.: Consort: Context- and flow-sensitive ownership refinement types for imperative pro-grams. https://arxiv.org/abs/2002.07770 (2020)

[61] Unno, H., Kobayashi, N.: Dependent type inference with interpolants. In: Conference on Principles and Practice of Declarative Programming (PPDP). pp. 277–288. ACM (2009). https://doi.org/10.1145/1599410.1599445

[62] Vazou, N., Rondon, P.M., Jhala, R.: Abstract refinement types. In: Euro-pean Symposium on Programming (ESOP). pp. 209–228. Springer (2013). https://doi.org/10.1007/978-3-642-37036-6_13

[63] Vazou, N., Seidel, E.L., Jhala, R., Vytiniotis, D., Peyton-Jones, S.: Refine-ment types for Haskell. In: International Conference on Functional Program-ming (ICFP). pp. 269–282 (2014). https://doi.org/10.1145/2628136.2628161

714   J. Toman et al.

[64] Wells, J.B., Dimock, A., Muller, R., Turbak, F.: A calculus with polymorphic and polyvariant flow types. Journal of Functional Programming **12**(3), 183–227 (2002). https://doi.org/10.1017/S0956796801004245

[65] Xi, H., Pfenning, F.: Dependent types in practical programming. In: Symposium on Principles of Programming Languages (POPL). pp. 214–227. ACM (1999). https://doi.org/10.1145/292540.292560

[66] Zave, P.: Using lightweight modeling to understand Chord. ACM SIGCOMM Computer Communication Review **42**(2), 49–57 (2012). https://doi.org/10.1145/2185376.2185383

[67] Zhu, H., Jagannathan, S.: Compositional and lightweight dependent type inference for ML. In: Conference on Verification, Model Checking, and Abstract Interpretation (VMCAI). pp. 295–314. Springer (2013). https://doi.org/10.1007/978-3-642-35873-9_19

Mixed Sessions

Vasco T. Vasconcelos⑩, Filipe Casal⑩, Bernardo Almeida⑩, and Andreia Mordido⑩

LASIGE, Faculdade de Ciências, Universidade de Lisboa, Lisbon, Portugal

Abstract. Session types describe patterns of interaction on communicating channels. Traditional session types include a form of choice whereby servers offer a collection of options, of which each client picks exactly one. This sort of choice constitutes a particular case of separated choice: offering on one side, selecting on the other. We introduce mixed choices in the context of session types and argue that they increase the flexibility of program development at the same time that they reduce the number of synchronisation primitives to exactly one. We present a type system incorporating subtyping and prove preservation and absence of runtime errors for well-typed processes. We further show that classical (conventional) sessions can be faithfully and tightly embedded in mixed choices. Finally, we discuss algorithmic type checking and a runtime system built on top of a conventional (choice-less) message-passing architecture.

Keywords: Type Systems · Session Types · Mixed Choice.

1 Introduction

Session types provide for describing series of continuous interactions on communication channels [16,19,43,45,49]. When used in type systems for programming languages, session type systems statically verify that programs follow protocols, and hence that they do not engage in communication mismatches.

In order to motivate mixed sessions, suppose that we want to describe a process that asks for a fixed but unbounded number of integer values from some producer. The consumer may be in two states: happy with the values received so far, or ready to ask the producer for a new value. In the former case it must notify the producer so that this may stop sending numbers. In the latter case, the client must ask the producer for another integer, after which it "goes back to the beginning". Using classical sessions, and looking from the consumer side, the communication channel can be described by a (recursive) session type T of the form

$$\oplus\{\mathsf{enough}:\mathbf{end},\ \mathsf{more}:\ ?\mathbf{int}.T\}$$

where $\oplus$ denotes internal choice (the consumer decides), the two branches in the choice are labelled with enough and more, type **end** denotes a channel on which no further interaction is possible, and ?**int** denotes the reception of an integer

P. Müller (Ed.): ESOP 2020, LNCS 12075, pp. 715–742, 2020.
https://doi.org/10.1007/978-3-030-44914-8_26

value. Reception is a prefix to a type, the continuation is T (in this case the "goes back to the beginning" part). The code for the consumer (and the producer as well) is unnecessarily complex, featuring parts that exchange messages in both directions: enough and more selections from the consumer to the producer, and int messages from the producer to the consumer. In particular, the consumer must first select option enough (outgoing) and then receive an integer (incoming).

Using mixed sessions one can *invert the direction* of the more selection and write the type of the channel (again as seen from the side of the consumer) as

$$\oplus\{\text{enough}\,!\,\textbf{unit}\,.\,\textbf{end}\,,\ \text{more}\,?\,\textbf{int}\,.\,\textsf{T}\}$$

The changes seem merely cosmetic, but label/polarity pairs (polarity is ! or ?) are now indivisible and constitute the keys of the choice type when seen as a map. The integer value is piggybacked on top of selection more. As a result, the classical session primitive operations: selection and branching (that is, internal and external choice) and communication (output and input) become one only: mixed session. The producer can be safely written as

$$\text{p (enough?z. }\textbf{0}\text{ + more!n. produce!(p, n+1))}$$

offering a choice on channel end p featuring mixed branches with labels enough? and more!, where **0** denotes the terminated process and produce(p, n+1) a recursive call to the producer. The example is further developed in Section 2.

Mixed sessions build on Vasconcelos presentation of session types which we call *classical sessions* [43], by adapting choice and input/output as needed, but keeping everything else unchanged as much as possible. The result is a language with

- a single synchronisation/communication primitive: mixed choice on a given channel that
- allows for duplicated labels in choice processes, leading to non-determinism in a pure linear setting, and
- replicated output processes arising naturally from replicated mixed choices, and that
- enjoys preservation and absence of runtime errors for typable processes, and
- provides for embedding classical sessions in a tight type and operational correspondence.

The rest of the paper is organised as follows: the next section shows mixed sessions in action; Section 3 introduces the technical development of the language, and Section 4 proves the main results (preservation and absence of runtime errors for typable processes). Then Section 5 presents the embedding and the correspondence proofs, Section 6 discusses implementation details, and Section 7 explores related work. Section 8 concludes the paper.

2   There is Room for Mixed Sessions

This section introduces the main ideas of mixed sessions via examples. We address *mixed choices*, *duplicated labels in choices*, and *unrestricted output*, in this order.

2.1   Mixed Choices

Consider the producer-consumer problem where the producer produces only in-
ofar as so requested by the consumer. Here is the code for a producer that
writes on channel end x numbers starting from n.

```
def produce (x, n) =
  lin x (enough?z. 0 +
      more!n. produce!(x, n+1)
  )
```

Syntax qx(M+N) introduces a choice between M and N on channel end x. Qualifier
q is either **un** or **lin** and controls whether the process is persistent (remains after
reduction) or is ephemeral (is consumed in the reduction process). Each branch
in a choice is composed of a label (enough or more), a polarity mark (input ?
or output !), a variable or a value (z or n), and a continuation process (after
the dot). The terminated process is represented by **0**; notation **def** introduces a
recursive process. The **def** syntax and its encoding in the base language is from
the Pict programming language [36] and taken up by Sepi [12].

A consumer that requests n integer values on channel end y can be written
as follows, where () represents the only value of type **unit**.

```
def consume (y, n) =
  if n = 0
  then lin y (enough!(). 0)
  else lin y (more?z. consume!(x, n−1))
```

Suppose that x and y are two ends of the same channel. When choices on x and
on y get together, a pair of matching label-polarities pairs is selected and a value
transmitted from the output continuation to the input continuation.

Types for the two channel ends ensure that choice synchronisation succeeds.
The type of x is **rec** a. **lin** & {enough?**unit**.end, more!int.a} where the qualifier **lin**
says that the channel end must be used in exactly one process, & denotes external
choice, and each branch is composed of a label, a polarity mark, the type of the
communication, and that of the continuation. The type **end** states that no further
interaction is possible at the channel and **rec** introduces a recursive type. The
type of y is obtained from that of x by inverting views ($\oplus$ and &) and polarities
(! and ?), yielding **rec** b. **lin** $\oplus$ {enough!**unit**.end, more?int.b}. The choice at x in the
produce process contains all branches in the type and so we select an external
choice view & for x. The choices at y contain only part of the branches, hence
the internal choice view $\oplus$. This type discipline ensures that processes do not
engage in runtime errors when trying to find a match for two choices at the two
ends of a given channel.

A few type and process abbreviations simplify coding: i) the **lin** qualifier
can be omitted, ii) the terminated process **0** together with the trailing dot can
be omitted; iii) the terminated type **end** together with the trailing dot can be
omitted; and iv) we introduce wildcards (_) in variable binding positions (in
input branches).

2.2   Duplicated Labels in Choices for Types and for Processes

Classical session types require distinct identifiers to label distinct branches. Mixed sessions relax this restriction by allowing duplicated labels whenever paired with distinct polarities. The next example describes two processes—countDown and collect—that bidirectionally exchange a fixed number of msg-labelled messages. The number of messages that flow in each direction is not fixed a priori, but instead decided by the non-deterministic operational semantics. The type that describes the channel, as seen by process countDown, is **rec** a. $\oplus$ {msg!**unit**.a, msg?**unit**.a, done!**unit**}, where one can see the msg label in two distinct branches, but with different polarities.

Process countDown features a parameter n that controls the number of messages exchanged (sent or received). The end of the interaction (when n reaches 0) is signalled by a done message.

```
countDown : (rec a.⊕{msg! unit .a, msg? unit .a, done! unit }, int)
def countDown (x, n) =
   if n = 0
   then x (done!())
   else x (msg!(). countDown!(x, n−1) +
            msg?_. countDown!(x, n−1))
```

Process collect sees the channel from the dual viewpoint, obtained by exchanging ? with ! and $\oplus$ with &. Parameter n in this case denotes the number of messages received. When done, the process writes the result on channel end r, global to the collect process.

```
collect : (rec b.&{msg! unit .b, msg? unit .b, done? unit }, int)
def collect (y, n) =
   y (msg!(). collect!(y, n+1) +
      msg?_. collect!(y, n) +
      done?_. r (result!n))
```

Mixed sessions allow for duplicated message-polarity pairs permitting a new form of non-determinism that uses exclusively linear channels. A process of the form $(\nu xy)P$ declares a channel with end points x and y to be used in process P. The process

```
(νxy)(
   x (msg!()) |
   y (msg?_. z (m!true) + msg?_. z (m!false))
)
```

featuring two linear choices may reduce to z (m!**true**) or to z (m!**false**). Non-determinism in the π-calculus without choice (that of *Functions as Processes* [27,29] for example) can only be achieved by introducing race conditions on un channels. For example, the π-calculus process

```
(νxy)(x!() | y?_.z!true | y?_.z!false))
```

educes either to (z!**true** | (νxy)y?_.z!**false**)) or to (z!**false** | (νxy)y?_.z!**true**)), leaving for the runtime the garbage collection of the inert residuals. Also note that in this case, channel y cannot remain linear.

Duplicated message-polarities in choices lead to elegant and concise code. A random number generator with a given number n of bits can be written with two processes. The first process sends n messages on channel end x. The contents of the messages are irrelevant (we use value () of type **unit**); what is important is that n more messages are sent, followed by a done message, followed by silence.

```
write : (rec a.⊕{done!unit , more!unit.a}, int)
def write (x, n) =
  if n == 0
  then x(done!())
  else x(more!(). write!(x, n−1))
```

The reader process reads the more messages in two distinct branches and interprets messages received on one branch as bit 0, and on the other as 1. Upon the reception of a done message, the accumulated random number is conveyed on channel end r, a variable global to the read process.

```
read : (rec b.&{done?unit , more?unit.b}, int)
def read (y, n) =
  y (done?_. r (result!n) +
    more?_. read!(y, 2∗n) +
    more?_. read!(y, 2∗n+1)
  )
```

Notice that mixed sessions allow duplicated label-polarity pairs in processes but not in types. This point is further discussed in Section 3. Also note that duplicated message labels could be easily added to traditional session types.

2.3   Unrestricted Output

Mixed sessions allow for replicated output processes. The original version of the π-calculus [30,31] features recursion on arbitrary processes. Subsequent versions [29] introduce replication but restricted to input processes. When compared to languages with unrestricted input only, unrestricted output allows for more concise programs and fewer message exchanges for the same effect. Here is a process (call it P) containing a pair of processes that exchange msg-labelled messages ad-aeternum,

$$(\nu xy)(\textbf{un } y \ (msg!()) \ | \ \textbf{un } x \ (msg?_-))$$

where x is of type **rec** a.**un** &{msg?**unit**.a}. The un prefix denotes replication: an un choice survives reduction. Because none of the two sub-processes features a continuation P reduces to P in one step. The behaviour of **un** y (msg!()) can be mimicked by a process without output replication, namely,

$$(\nu wz) \ w \ (\ell!()) \ | \ \textbf{un } z \ (\ell?_-. \ y \ (msg!(). \ w \ (\ell!())))$$

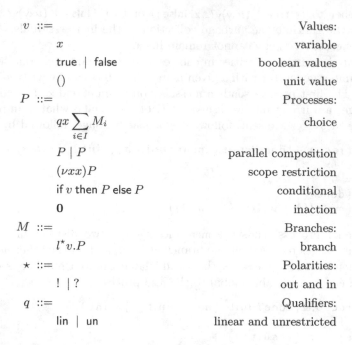

$$
\begin{array}{lll}
v & ::= & & \text{Values:} \\
& x & & \text{variable} \\
& \text{true} \mid \text{false} & & \text{boolean values} \\
& () & & \text{unit value} \\
P & ::= & & \text{Processes:} \\
& qx \sum_{i \in I} M_i & & \text{choice} \\
& P \mid P & & \text{parallel composition} \\
& (\nu xx)P & & \text{scope restriction} \\
& \text{if } v \text{ then } P \text{ else } P & & \text{conditional} \\
& \mathbf{0} & & \text{inaction} \\
M & ::= & & \text{Branches:} \\
& l^{\star} v.P & & \text{branch} \\
\star & ::= & & \text{Polarities:} \\
& ! \mid ? & & \text{out and in} \\
q & ::= & & \text{Qualifiers:} \\
& \text{lin} \mid \text{un} & & \text{linear and unrestricted}
\end{array}
$$

Fig. 1: The syntax of processes

Even if unrestricted output can be simulated with unrestricted input, the encoding requires one extra channel (wz) and an extra message exchange (on channel wz) in order to reestablish the output on channel end y.

It is a fact that unrestricted output can be added to any flavour of the π-calculus (session-typed or not). In the case of mixed sessions it arises naturally: there is only one communication primitive—choice—and this can be classified as lin or un. If an un-choice happens to behave in "output mode", then we have an un-output. It is not obvious how to design the language of mixed choices without allowing unrestricted output, while still allowing unrestricted input (which is mandatory for unbounded behaviour).

3   The Syntax and Semantics of Mixed Sessions

This section introduces the syntax and the semantics of mixed sessions. Inspired in Vasconcelos' formulation of session types for the π-calculus [43,45], mixed sessions replace input and output, selection and branching (internal and external choice), with a single construct which we call *choice*.

3.1   Syntax

Figure 1 presents the syntax of values and processes. Let x, y, z range over a (countable) set of *variables*, and let l range over a set of *labels*. Metavariable v ranges over *values*. Following the tradition of the π-calculus, set up by Milner et al. [30,31], variables are used both as placeholders for incoming values in communication and for channels. Linearity constraints, central to session types but absent in the π-calculus, dictate that the two ends of a channel must be syntactically distinguished; we use one variable for each end [43]. Different primitive values can be used. Here, we pick the boolean values (so that we may have a conditional process), and unit that plays its role in the embedding of classical session types (Section 5).

Metavariables P and Q range over processes. Choices are processes of the form $qx \sum_{i \in I} M_i$ offering a choice of M_i alternatives on channel end x. Qualifier q describes how choice behaves with respect to reduction. If q is lin, then the choice is consumed in reduction, otherwise q must be un, and in this case the choice persists after reduction. The type system in Figure 8 rejects nullary (empty) choices. There are two forms of branches: output $l^!v.P$ and input $l^?x.P$. An output branch sends value v and continues as P. An input branch receives a value and continues as P with the value replacing variable x. The type system in Figure 8 makes sure that value v in $l^!v.P$ is a variable.

The remaining process constructors are standard in the π-calculus. Processes of the form $P \mid Q$ denote the parallel composition of processes P and Q. Scope restriction $(\nu xy)P$ binds together the two channel ends x and y of a same channel in process P. The conditional process if v then P else Q behaves as process P if v is true and as process Q otherwise. Since we do not have nullary choices, we include $\mathbf{0}$—called inaction—as primitive to denote the terminated process.

3.2   Operational Semantics

The variable bindings in the language are as follows: variables x and y are bound in P, in a process of the form $(\nu xy)P$; variable x is bound in P in a choice of the form $l^?x.P$. The sets of bound and free variables, as well as substitution, $P[v/x]$, are defined accordingly. We work up to alpha-conversion and follow Barendregt's variable convention, whereby all variables in binding occurrences in any mathematical context are pairwise distinct and distinct from the free variables [2].

Figure 2 summarises the operational semantics of mixed sessions. Following the tradition of the π-calculus, a binary relation on processes—*structural congruence*—rearranges processes when preparing for reduction. Such an arrangement reduces the number of rules included in the operational semantics. Structural congruence was introduced by Milner [27,29]. It is defined as the least congruence relation closed under the axioms in Figure 2. The first three rules state that parallel composition is commutative, associative, and takes inaction as the neutral element. The fourth rule is commonly known as scope extrusion [30,31] and allows extending the scope of channel ends x, y to process Q. The side-condition

Structural congruence, $P \equiv P$

$$P \mid Q \equiv Q \mid P \qquad (P \mid Q) \mid R \equiv P \mid (Q \mid R) \qquad P \mid 0 \equiv P$$

$$(\nu xy)P \mid Q \equiv (\nu xy)(P \mid Q) \qquad (\nu xy)0 \equiv 0 \qquad (\nu wx)(\nu yz)P \equiv (\nu yz)(\nu wx)P$$

Reduction, $P \to P$

if true then P else $Q \to P$ \qquad if false then P else $Q \to Q$ \qquad [R-IfT] [R-IfF]

$$(\nu xy)(\mathsf{lin}x(M + l^! v.P + M') \mid \mathsf{lin}y(N + l^? z.Q + N') \mid R) \to (\nu xy)(P \mid Q[v/z] \mid R)$$
$$\text{[R-LinLin]}$$

$$(\nu xy)(\mathsf{lin}x(M + l^! v.P + M') \mid \mathsf{un}y(N + l^? z.Q + N') \mid R) \to \qquad \text{[R-LinUn]}$$
$$(\nu xy)(P \mid Q[v/z] \mid \mathsf{un}y(N + l^? z.Q + N') \mid R)$$

$$(\nu xy)(\mathsf{un}x(M + l^! v.P + M') \mid \mathsf{lin}y(N + l^? z.Q + N') \mid R) \to \qquad \text{[R-UnLin]}$$
$$(\nu xy)(P \mid Q[v/z] \mid \mathsf{un}x(M + l^! v.P + M') \mid R)$$

$$(\nu xy)(\mathsf{un}x(M + l^! v.P + M') \mid \mathsf{un}y(N + l^? z.Q + N') \mid R) \to \qquad \text{[R-UnUn]}$$
$$(\nu xy)(P \mid Q[v/z] \mid \mathsf{un}x(M + l^! v.P + M') \mid \mathsf{un}y(N + l^? z.Q + N') \mid R)$$

$$\frac{P \to Q}{(\nu xy)P \to (\nu xy)Q} \qquad \frac{P \to Q}{P \mid R \to Q \mid R} \qquad \frac{P \equiv P' \quad P' \to Q' \quad Q' \equiv Q}{P \to Q}$$
$$\text{[R-Res] [R-Par] [R-Struct]}$$

Fig. 2: Operational semantics

"x and y not free in Q" is redundant in face of the Barendregt convention. The fifth rule allows collecting channel bindings no longer in use, and the last rule allows for rearranging the order of channel bindings in a process.

Reduction includes six axioms, two for the destruction of boolean values (via a conditional process), and four for communication. The axioms for communication take processes of a similar nature. The scope restriction (νxy) identifies the two ends of the channel engaged in communication. Under the scope of the channel one finds three processes: the first contains an output process on channel end x, the second contains an input process on channel end y, and the third (R) is an arbitrary process that may contain other references to x and y (the witness process). Communication proceeds by identifying a pair of compatible branches, namely $l^! v.P$ and $l^? z.Q$. The result contains the continuation process P and the continuation process Q with occurrences of the bound variable z replaced by value v (together with the witness process). The four axioms differ in the treatment of the process qualifiers: lin (ephemeral) and un (persistent). Ephemeral processes are consumed in reduction, persistent processes remain in the contractum.

Choices apart, rules [R-LinLin] and [R-LinUn] are already present in the works of Milner and Vasconcelos [29,43]. Rules [R-UnLin] and [R-LinLin] are absent on the grounds of economy: replicated output can be simulated with a new channel and a replicated in input. In mixed choices these rules cannot be

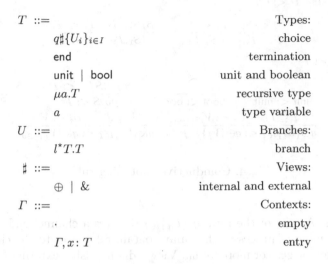

$$
\begin{array}{lll}
T ::= & & \text{Types:} \\
& q\sharp\{U_i\}_{i \in I} & \text{choice} \\
& \mathsf{end} & \text{termination} \\
& \mathsf{unit} \mid \mathsf{bool} & \text{unit and boolean} \\
& \mu a.T & \text{recursive type} \\
& a & \text{type variable} \\
U ::= & & \text{Branches:} \\
& l^* T.T & \text{branch} \\
\sharp ::= & & \text{Views:} \\
& \oplus \mid \& & \text{internal and external} \\
\Gamma ::= & & \text{Contexts:} \\
& \cdot & \text{empty} \\
& \Gamma, x : T & \text{entry}
\end{array}
$$

Fig. 3: The syntax of types

omitted for there is no distinction between input and output: choice is the only (symmetrical) communication primitive.

We have designed mixed choices in such a way that labels may be duplicated in choices; more: label-polarity pairs may be also be duplicated. This allows for non-determinism in a linear context. For example, process

$$(\nu xy)(\mathsf{lin}\, x(l^!\mathsf{true}.\mathbf{0} + l^!\mathsf{false}.\mathbf{0}) \mid \mathsf{lin}\, y(l^?z.\mathsf{lin}\, w(m^!z.\mathbf{0})))$$

reduces in one step to either $\mathsf{lin}\, w(m^!\mathsf{true}.\mathbf{0})$ or $\mathsf{lin}\, w(m^!\mathsf{false}.\mathbf{0})$.

The examples in Section 2 take advantage of a def notation, a derived process construct inspired in the SePi [12] and the Pict languages [36]. A process of the form def $x(z) = P$ in Q is understood as

$$(\nu xy)(\mathsf{un}\, y(\ell^?z.P) \mid Q))$$

and calls to the recursive procedure, of the form $x!v$, are interpreted as $\mathsf{lin}\, x(\ell^!v)$, for ℓ an arbitrarily chosen label. The derived syntax hides channel end y and simplifies the syntax of calls to the procedure. Procedures with more than one parameter require tuple passing, a notion that is not primitive to mixed sessions. Fortunately, tuple passing is easy to encode; see Vasconcelos[43].

3.3 Typing

Figure 3 summarises the syntax of types. We rely on an extra set, that of *type variables*, $a, b, \ldots$ Types describe values, including boolean and unit values, and

Branch subtyping, $U <: U$

$$\frac{S_2 <: S_1 \quad T_1 <: T_2}{l^!S_1.T_1 <: l^!S_2.T_2} \qquad \frac{S_1 <: S_2 \quad T_1 <: T_2}{l^?S_1.T_1 <: l^?S_2.T_2}$$

Subtyping, $T <: T$

$$\overline{\text{end} <: \text{end}} \qquad \overline{\text{unit} <: \text{unit}} \qquad \overline{\text{bool} <: \text{bool}} \qquad \frac{S[\mu a.S/a] <: T}{\mu a.S <: T} \qquad \frac{S <: T[\mu a.T/a]}{S <: \mu a.T}$$

$$\frac{J \subseteq I \quad U_j <: V_j}{q\oplus\{U_i\}_{i\in I} <: q\oplus\{V_j\}_{j\in J}} \qquad \frac{I \subseteq J \quad U_i <: V_i}{q\&\{U_i\}_{i\in I} <: q\&\{V_j\}_{j\in J}}$$

Fig. 4: Coinductive subtyping rules

channel ends. A type of the form $q\sharp\{U_i\}_{i\in I}$ denotes a channel end. Qualifier q states the number of processes that may contain references to the channel end: exactly one for lin, zero or more for un. View $\sharp$ distinguishes external ($\oplus$) from internal (&) choice. This distinction is not present in processes but is of paramount importance for typing purposes, as we shall see. The branches are either of output—$l^!S.T$—or of input—$l^?S.T$—nature. In either case, S denotes the object of communication and T describes the subsequent behaviour of the channel end. Type end denotes the channel end on which no more interaction is possible. Types $\mu a.T$ and a cater for recursive types.

Types are subject to a few syntactic restrictions: i) choices must have at least one branch; ii) label-polarity pairs—$l^\star$—are pairwise distinct in the branches of a choice type (unlike in processes); iii) recursive types are assumed contractive (that is, containing no subterm of the form $\mu a_1 \ldots \mu a_n.a_1$). New variables, new bindings: type variable a is bound in T in type $\mu a.T$. Again the definitions of bound and free names as well as that of substitution—$S[T/a]$—are defined accordingly.

Mixed sessions come equipped with a notion of subtyping. Figure 4 introduces the rules that allow determining whether a given type is subtype of another. The rules must be read coinductively. Base types (end, unit, bool) are subtypes to themselves. The rules for recursive types are standard. Subtyping behaves differently in presence of external or internal choice. For external choice we require the branches in the subtype to contain those in the supertype: exercising less options cannot cause difficulties on the receiving side. For internal choice we require the opposite: here offering more choices can not cause runtime errors. For branches we distinguish output from input: output is contravariant on the contents of the message, input is covariant. In either case, the continuation is covariant. Choices, input/output, and recursive types receive no different treatment than those in classical sessions [15]. We can easily show that the $<:$ relation is a preorder. Notation $S \equiv T$ abbreviates $S <: T$ and $T <: S$.

Duality is a notion central to session types. In order for channel communication to proceed smoothly, the two channel ends must be compatible: if one end says input, the other must say output; if one end says external choice, the

Polarity duality and view duality, $\sharp \perp \sharp$ and $\star \perp \star$

$$!\perp? \qquad ?\perp! \qquad\qquad \oplus\perp\& \qquad \&\perp\oplus$$

Type duality, $T \perp T$

$$\frac{}{\mathsf{end} \perp \mathsf{end}} \qquad \frac{\sharp\perp\flat \quad \star_i \perp \bullet_i \quad S_i \equiv S_i' \quad T_i \perp T_i'}{q\sharp\{l_i^\star S_i.T_i\}_{i\in I} \perp q\flat\{l_i^\bullet S_i'.T_i'\}_{i\in I}}$$

$$\frac{S[\mu a.S/a] \perp T}{\mu a.S \perp T} \qquad \frac{S \perp T[\mu a.T/a]}{S \perp \mu a.T}$$

Fig. 5: Coinductive type duality rules

un and lin predicates, $\mathsf{un}(T)$, $\mathsf{lin}(T)$

$$\mathsf{un}(\mathsf{end}) \quad \mathsf{un}(\mathsf{unit}) \quad \mathsf{un}(\mathsf{bool}) \quad \mathsf{un}(\mathsf{un}\sharp\{U_i\}) \quad \frac{\mathsf{un}(T)}{\mathsf{un}(\mu a.T)} \qquad\qquad \overline{\mathsf{lin}(T)}$$

Fig. 6: The un and lin predicates on types

other must say internal choice. In presence of recursive types, the problem of building the dual of a given type has been elusive, as works by Bernardi and Hennessy, Bono and Padovani, Lindley and Morris show [5,7,25]. Here we eschew the problem by working with a duality relation, as in Gay and Hole [15].

The rules in Figure 5 define what we mean for two types to be dual. This is the coinductive definition of Gay and Hole in rule format (and adapted to choice). Duality is defined for session types only. Type end is the dual of itself. The rule for choice types requires dual views (& is the dual of $\oplus$, and vice-versa) and dual polarities (? is the dual of !, and vice-versa). Furthermore, the objects of communications must be equivalent ($S_i \equiv S_i'$) and the continuations must be dual again ($T_i \perp T_i'$). The rules in the second line handle recursion in the exact same way as in type equivalence. As an example, we can easily show that

$$\mu a.\mathsf{lin} \oplus \{l^?\mathsf{bool.lin}\&\{m^!\mathsf{unit}.a\}\} \perp \mathsf{lin}\&\{l^!\mathsf{bool}.\mu b.\mathsf{lin}\oplus\{m^?\mathsf{unit.lin}\&\{l^!\mathsf{bool}.b\}\}\}$$

It can be shown that $\perp$ is an involution, that is, if $R \perp S$ and $S \perp T$, then $R \equiv T$.

The meaning of the un and lin predicates are defined by the rules in Figure 6. Basic types—unit, bool, end—are unrestricted; un-annotated choices are unrestricted; $\mu a.T$ is unrestricted if T is. Contractivity ensures that the predicate is total. All types are lin, meaning that both lin and non-lin types may be used in linear contexts.

Before presenting the type system, we need to introduce two notions that manipulate typing contexts. The rules in Figure 7 define the meaning of *context split* and *context update*. These two relations are taken verbatim from Vasconcelos [43]; context split is originally from Walker [48] (cf. Kobayashi et al. [22,23]). Context split is used when type checking processes with two sub-processes. In

Context split, $\Gamma = \Gamma \circ \Gamma$

$$\cdot = \cdot \circ \cdot$$

$$\frac{\Gamma_1 \circ \Gamma_2 = \Gamma \qquad \mathsf{un}(T)}{\Gamma, x \colon T = (\Gamma_1, x \colon T) \circ (\Gamma_2, x \colon T)}$$

$$\frac{\Gamma = \Gamma_1 \circ \Gamma_2}{\Gamma, x \colon \mathsf{lin}\, p = (\Gamma_1, x \colon \mathsf{lin}\, p) \circ \Gamma_2} \qquad \frac{\Gamma = \Gamma_1 \circ \Gamma_2}{\Gamma, x \colon \mathsf{lin}\, p = \Gamma_1 \circ (\Gamma_2, x \colon \mathsf{lin}\, p)}$$

Context update, $\Gamma + x \colon T = \Gamma$

$$\frac{x \colon U \notin \Gamma}{\Gamma + x \colon T = \Gamma, x \colon T} \qquad \frac{\mathsf{un}(T) \qquad T \equiv U}{(\Gamma, x \colon T) + x \colon U = (\Gamma, x \colon T)}$$

Fig. 7: Inductive context split and context update rules

this case we split the context in two, by copying unrestricted entries to both contexts and linear entries to one only. Context update is used to add to a given context an entry representing the continuation (after a choice operation) of a channel. If the variable in the entry is not in the context, then we add the entry to the context. Otherwise we require the entry to be present in the context and the type to be unrestricted.

The rules in Figure 8 introduce the typing system for mixed sessions. Here the un and lin predicates on types are pointwise extended to typing contexts. Notice that all contexts are linear and only some contexts are unrestricted. We require all instances of the axioms to be built from unrestricted contexts, thus ensuring that linear resources (channel ends) are fully consumed in typing derivations.

The typing rules for values should be straightforward: constants have their own types, the type for a variable is read from the context, and [T-Sub] is the subsumption rule, allowing a type to be replaced by a supertype.

The rules for branches—[T-Out] and [T-In]—follow those for output and input in classical session types. To type an output branch we split the context in two: one part for the value, the other for the continuation process. To type an input branch we add an entry with the bound variable x to the context under which we type the continuation process. Rule [T-In] rejects branches of the form $l^? v.P$ when v not a variable. The continuation type T is not used in neither rule; instead it is incorporated in the type for the channel in Γ (cf. rule [T-Choice] below).

The rules for inaction, parallel composition, and conditional are from Vasconcelos [43]. That for scope restriction is adapted from Gay and Hole [15]. Rule [T-Inact] follows the general pattern for axioms, requiring a un context. Rule [T-Par] splits the context in two, providing each subprocess with one part. Rule [T-If] splits the context and uses one part to type guard v. Because v is unrestricted, we know that Γ_1 contains exactly the un entries in $\Gamma_1 \circ \Gamma_2$ and that Γ_2 is equal to $\Gamma_1 \circ \Gamma_2$. Context Γ_2 is used to type *both* branches of the conditional, for only one of them will ever execute. Rule [T-Res] introduces in the typing context entries for the two channel ends, x and y, at dual types.

Typing rules for values, $\Gamma \vdash v : T$

$$\frac{\text{un}(\Gamma)}{\Gamma \vdash () : \text{unit}} \qquad \frac{\text{un}(\Gamma)}{\Gamma \vdash \text{true}, \text{false} : \text{bool}} \qquad \frac{\text{un}(\Gamma_1, \Gamma_2)}{\Gamma_1, x : T, \Gamma_2 \vdash x : T} \qquad \frac{\Gamma \vdash v : S \quad S <: T}{\Gamma \vdash v : T}$$

$$\text{[T-Unit]} \ \text{[T-True]} \ \text{[T-False]} \ \text{[T-Var]} \ \text{[T-Sub]}$$

Typing rules for branches, $\Gamma \vdash M : U$

$$\frac{\Gamma_1 \vdash v : S \quad \Gamma_2 \vdash P}{\Gamma_1 \circ \Gamma_2 \vdash l^! v.P : l^! S.T} \qquad \frac{\Gamma, x : S \vdash P}{\Gamma \vdash l^? x.P : l^? S.T} \qquad \text{[T-Out]} \ \text{[T-In]}$$

Typing rules for processes, $\Gamma \vdash P$

$$\frac{\text{un}(\Gamma)}{\Gamma \vdash \mathbf{0}} \qquad \frac{\Gamma_1 \vdash P \quad \Gamma_2 \vdash Q}{\Gamma_1 \circ \Gamma_2 \vdash P \mid Q} \qquad \text{[T-Inact]} \ \text{[T-Par]}$$

$$\frac{\Gamma_1 \vdash v : \text{bool} \quad \Gamma_2 \vdash P \quad \Gamma_2 \vdash Q}{\Gamma_1 \circ \Gamma_2 \vdash \text{if } v \text{ then } P \text{ else } Q} \qquad \frac{\Gamma, x : S, y : T \vdash P \quad S \perp T}{\Gamma \vdash (\nu xy)P} \qquad \text{[T-If]} \ \text{[T-Res]}$$

$$\frac{q_1(\Gamma_1 \circ \Gamma_2) \quad \Gamma_1 \vdash x : q_2 \sharp \{l_i^\star S_i.T_i\}_{i \in I} \quad \Gamma_2 + x : T_j \vdash l_j^\star v_j.P_j : l_j^\star S_j.T_j \quad \{l_j^\star\}_{j \in J} = \{l_i^\star\}_{i \in I}}{\Gamma_1 \circ \Gamma_2 \vdash q_1 x \sum_{j \in J} l_j^\star v_j.P_j}$$

$$\text{[T-Choice]}$$

Fig. 8: Inductive typing rules

The rule for choice is new. The incoming context is split in two: one for the subject x of the choice, the other for the various branches in the choice. The qualifier of the process, q_1, dictates the nature of the incoming context: un or lin. This allows for a linear choice to contain channels of an arbitrary nature, but limits unrestricted choices to unrestricted channels only (for one cannot predict how many times such choices will be exercised). The second premise extracts a type $q_2 \sharp \{l_i^\star S_i.T_i\}$ for x. The third premise types each branch: type S_j is used to type values v_j in the branches and each type T_j is used to type the corresponding continuation. The rule updates context Γ_2 with the continuation type of x: if q_2 is lin, then x is not in Γ_2 and the update operation simply adds the entry to the context. If, on the other hand, q_2 is un, then x is in Γ_2 and the context update operation (together with rule [T-Sub]) insists that type T_j is a subtype of $\text{un}\sharp\{l_j^\star S_j.T_j\}$, meaning that T_j is a recursive type.

The last premise to rule [T-Choice] insists that the set of labels in the choice type coincides with that in the choice process. That does not mean that the label-polarity pairs are in a one-to-one correspondence: label-polarity pairs are pairwise distinct in types (see the syntactic restrictions in Section 3.3), but not in processes. For example, process $\text{lin} x(l^? y.\mathbf{0} + l^? z.\mathbf{0})$ can be typed against context $x : \text{lin} \oplus \{l^? \text{bool.end}\}$. From the fact that the two sets must coincide does not follow that the label-polarity pairs type in the context must coincide with those in the process. Taking advantage of subtyping, the above process can still be typed against context $x : \text{lin} \oplus \{l^? \text{bool.end}, m^! \text{unit.end}\}$ because $\text{lin} \oplus \{l^? \text{bool.end}, m^! \text{unit.end}\} <: \text{lin} \oplus \{l^? \text{bool.end}\}$. The opposite phenomenon happens with external choice, where one may remove branches by virtue of subtyping.

We complete this section by discussing examples that illustrate options taken in the typing system (we postpone the formal justification to Section 4). Suppose we allow empty choices in the syntax of types. Then the process

$$(\nu xy)(x() \mid y())$$

would be typable by taking $x\colon \oplus(), y\colon \&()$, yet the process would not reduce. We could add an extra reduction rule for the effect

$$(\nu xy)(x() \mid y() \mid R) \to (\nu xy)R$$

which would satisfy preservation (Theorem 2). We decided not to include it in our reduction rules as we did not want the extra complexity. Including the rule also does not bring any apparent benefit.

The syntax of processes places no restrictions on the label-polarity pairs in choices; yet that of types does. What if we relax the restriction that label-polarities pairs in choice types must be pairwise distinct? Then process

$$(\nu xy)(x(l^!\mathsf{true} + l^!()) \mid y(l^?z.\mathsf{if}\ z\ \mathsf{then}\ \mathbf{0}\ \mathsf{else}\ \mathbf{0}))$$

could be typed under context $x\colon \&\{l^!\mathsf{bool}, l^!\mathsf{unit}\}, y\colon \oplus\{l^?\mathsf{bool}, l^?\mathsf{unit}\}$, yet the process might reduce to if $()$ then $\mathbf{0}$ else $\mathbf{0}$ which is a runtime error.

4 Well-typed Mixed Sessions Do Not Lead to Runtime Errors

This section introduces the main results of mixed choices: absence of runtime errors and preservation, both for well-typed processes.

We say that a process is a *runtime error* if it is structurally congruent to:

− a process of the form

$$(\nu x_1 y_1)\dots(\nu x_n y_n)(\nu xy)(qx \sum_{i \in I} l_i^\star v_i.P_i \mid q'y \sum_{j \in J} l_j^\star w_j.Q_j \mid R)$$

where $\{l_i^\bullet\}_{i \in I} \cap \{l_j^\star\}_{j \in J} = \emptyset$ with each $\bullet_i$ is obtained by dualising $\star_i$, or
− a process of the form $qz(M + l^?v.P + N)$ and v is not a variable, or
− a process of the form if v then P else Q and v is neither true nor false.

Examples of processes which are runtime errors include:

$$(\nu xy)(\mathsf{lin}x(l^!\mathsf{true}.\mathbf{0}) \mid \mathsf{lin}y(l^!\mathsf{true}.\mathbf{0}))$$
$$(\nu xy)(\mathsf{un}x(l^!\mathsf{true}.\mathbf{0}) \mid \mathsf{lin}y(m^?z.\mathbf{0}))$$
$$\mathsf{un}x(l^?\mathsf{false}.\mathbf{0})$$
$$\mathsf{if}\ ()\ \mathsf{then}\ \mathbf{0}\ \mathsf{else}\ \mathbf{0}$$

Notice that processes of the form $(\nu xy)\mathsf{lin}x\sum_{i\in I}M_i$ cannot be classified as runtime errors for they may be typed. Just think of $(\nu xy)\mathsf{lin}x(l^?z.\mathsf{lin}y(l^!\mathsf{true}.\mathbf{0}))$, typable under the empty context. Unlike the interpretations of session types in linear logic by Caires, Pfenning and Wadler [8,14,46,47], typable mixed session processes can easily deadlock. Similarly, processes with more than one lin-choice on the same channel end can be typed. For example process $\mathsf{lin}x(l^!\mathsf{true}.\mathbf{0})\mid$ $\mathsf{lin}x(l^?z.\mathbf{0}))$ can be typed under context $x\colon \mu a.\mathsf{un}\oplus\{l^!\mathsf{unit}.a,l^?\mathsf{bool}.a\}$. Recall the relationship between qualifiers in processes q_1 and those in types q_2 in the discussion of the rules for choice in Section 3.

Theorem 1 (Well-typed processes are not runtime errors). *If $\cdot\vdash P$, then P is not a runtime error.*

Proof. In view of a contradiction, assume that $\cdot\vdash P$ and that P is

$$(\nu x_1y_1)\dots(\nu x_ny_n)(q_1x_n\sum_{i\in I}l_i^\star v_i.P_i\mid q_2y_n\sum_{j\in J}l_j^\star w_j.Q_j\mid R)$$

and $\{l_i^\bullet\}_{i\in I}\cap\{l_j^\star\}_{j\in J}=\emptyset$ with $\star_i\bot\bullet_i$. From the typing derivation for P, using [T-PAR] and [T-RES], we obtain a context $\Gamma=\Gamma_1\circ\Gamma_2\circ\Gamma_3=$ $x_1\colon T_1,y_1\colon S_1,\dots,x_n\colon T_n,y_n\colon S_n$, $T_i\bot S_i$ for all $i=1,\dots,n$ and that $\Gamma_1\vdash$ $q_1x_n\sum_{i\in I}l_i^\star v_i.P_i$ and $\Gamma_2\vdash q_2y_n\sum_{j\in J}l_j^\star w_j.Q_j$ and $\Gamma_3\vdash R$. Without loss of generality, due to the fact that x_n and y_n have dual types and from the premises of rule [T-CHOICE], assume that $\Gamma_1'\vdash x_n\colon q_1'\&\{l_k^\star T_k'.T_k''\}_{k\in K}$ and $\Gamma_2'\vdash y_n\colon q_2'\oplus\{l_k^\star S_k'.S_k''\}_{k\in K}$, $\{l_i^\star\}_{i\in I}=\{l_k^\star\}_{k\in K}$ and $\{l_j^\star\}_{j\in J}\subseteq\{l_k^\bullet\}_{k\in K}$, with $\star_k\bot\bullet_k$. This also implies that $\{l_i^\bullet\}_{i\in I}=\{l_k^\bullet\}_{k\in K}$. Thus, a label $l_j^\star$ from $q_2y_n\sum_{j\in J}l_j^\star w_j.Q_j$ belongs to the set of labels $\{l_i^\star\}_{i\in I}\colon l_j^\star\in\{l_k^\star\}_{k\in K}=\{l_i^\star\}_{i\in I}$, contradicting $\{l_i^\bullet\}_{i\in I}\cap\{l_j^\star\}_{j\in J}=\emptyset$ with $\star_i\bot\bullet_i$

When P is $qz(M+l^?v.P+N)$ and v is not a variable, the contradiction is with rule [T-OUT], which can only be applied when the value v is a variable.

When P is if v then P else Q and v is not a boolean value, the contradiction immediately arises with rule [T-IF]. □

In order to prepare for the preservation result we introduce a few lemmas.

Lemma 1 (Unrestricted weakening). *If $\Gamma\vdash P$ and $\mathsf{un}(T)$, then $\Gamma,x\colon T\vdash P$.*

Proof. The proof goes by mutual induction on the rules for branches and processes, but we first need to show the result for the value typing rules. We need to show that if $\Gamma\vdash v\colon S$ and $\mathsf{un}(R)$ then $\Gamma,x\colon R\vdash v\colon S$. This follows by a simple case inspection of the rules [T-UNIT], [T-TRUE],[T-FALSE],[T-VAR] taking into consideration that $\mathsf{un}(R)$. For the rule [T-SUB], use the induction hypothesis to obtain $\Gamma,x\colon R\vdash v\colon S$ and conclude, using [T-SUB], that $\Gamma,x\colon R\vdash v\colon T$.

For the branch and processes typing rules we detail the proof when the last rule is [T-OUT]. Using the result for typing values, we obtain $\Gamma_1,x\colon R\vdash v\colon S$, and the induction hypothesis for processes leads to $\Gamma_2,x\colon R\vdash P$. Using the un context split property, taking into account that $\mathsf{un}(R)$, we conclude that $\Gamma_1\circ\Gamma_2,x\colon R\vdash l^!v.P\colon l^!S.T$.

For the processes rule [T-INACT], the result is a simple consequence of un(T). For the other rules, the result follows by induction hypothesis in processes and branches rules, as well as using the value typing result. We detail the proof for rule [T-IF]. Using the typing values result, we know that $\Gamma_1, x \colon T \vdash x \colon$ bool. By induction hypothesis we also obtain that $\Gamma_2, x \colon T \vdash P$ and $\Gamma_2, x \colon T \vdash Q$. Using the un context split property, we conclude $\Gamma_1 \circ \Gamma_2, x \colon T \vdash$ if v then P else Q.   □

Lemma 2 (Preservation for $\equiv$). *If $\Gamma \vdash P$ and $P \equiv Q$, then $\Gamma \vdash Q$.*

Proof. As in Vasconcelos [43, Lemma 7.4] since we share the structural congruence axioms.   □

Lemma 3 (Substitution). *If $\Gamma_1 \vdash v \colon T$ and $\Gamma_2, x \colon T \vdash P$ and $\Gamma = \Gamma_1 \circ \Gamma_2$, then $\Gamma \vdash P[v/x]$.*

Proof. The proof follows by mutual induction on the rules for processes and branches.   □

Theorem 2 (Preservation). *If $\Gamma \vdash P$ and $P \to Q$, then $\Gamma \vdash Q$.*

Proof. The proof is by rule induction on the reduction, making use of the weakening, substitution lemmas, and preservation for structural congruence. We sketch the cases for [R-LINLIN] and [R-LINUN].

When reduction ends with rule [R-LINLIN], we know that rule [T-RES] introduces $x \colon X, y \colon Y$ with $X \perp Y$ in the context Γ. From there, with applications of [T-PAR] and [T-CHOICE], $\Gamma = \Gamma_1 \circ \Gamma_2 \circ \Gamma_3$ and $\Gamma_1 \vdash \text{lin}\, x(M + l^l v.P + M')$, $\Gamma_2 \vdash \text{lin}\, y(N + l^? z.Q + N')$, $\Gamma_3 \vdash R$. Furthermore, $\Gamma_1 = \Gamma_1' \circ \Gamma_1''$ and $\text{lin}(\Gamma_1)$, $\Gamma_1' \vdash x \colon \text{lin} \oplus \{M, l^l S.T, M'\}$ and $\Gamma_1'', x \colon T \vdash l^l v.P \colon l^l S.T$. From the [T-OUT] rule, $\Gamma_v \vdash v \colon S$ and $\Gamma_4 \vdash P$. For the y side, $\Gamma_2' \vdash y \colon \text{lin}\&\{N, l^? U.V, N'\}$ and $\Gamma_2'', y \colon Y \vdash l^? z.Q \colon l^? U.V$. From the [T-IN] rule, $\Gamma_z, y \colon V, z \colon U \vdash Q$. We also have that $S \equiv U$ from the duality of x and y. Using the substitution Lemma 3, $\Gamma_z, y \colon V, \Gamma_v \vdash Q[v/z]$. Using [T-PAR] with the remaining contexts and [T-RES] types the conclusion of [R-LINLIN].

When reduction ends with rule [R-LINUN], we know that rule [T-RES] introduces $x \colon X, y \colon Y$ with $X \perp Y$ in the context Γ. From there, with applications of [T-PAR] and [T-CHOICE], $\Gamma = \Gamma_1 \circ \Gamma_2 \circ \Gamma_3$ and $\Gamma_1 \vdash \text{lin}\, x(M + l^l v.P + M')$, $\Gamma_2 \vdash \text{un}\, y(N + l^? z.Q + N')$, $\Gamma_3 \vdash R$. Furthermore, $\Gamma_1 = \Gamma_1' \circ \Gamma_1''$ and $\text{lin}(\Gamma_1)$, $\Gamma_1' \vdash x \colon \text{un} \oplus \{M, l^l S.T, M'\}$. Here x is un since x and y are dual. We also have $\Gamma_1'', x \colon T \vdash l^l v.P \colon l^l S.T$, from which follows $\Gamma_4 \vdash v \colon S$ and $\Gamma_5 \vdash P$ from rule [T-OUT]. For the y side, $\Gamma_2' \vdash y \colon \text{un}\&\{N, l^? U.V, N'\}$ and $\Gamma_2'', y \colon Y \vdash l^? z.Q \colon l^? U.V$ which has $\Gamma_6, y \colon V, z \colon U \vdash Q$ from [T-IN].

Types S and U are equivalent due to the duality of x, y and so $\Gamma_6, y \colon V, z \colon S \vdash Q$. Using the substitution Lemma 3, $\Gamma_6 \circ \Gamma_4, y \colon V \vdash Q[v/z]$. From Γ_5 we also type the process P. Using [T-PAR] with the remaining contexts and [T-RES], types the conclusion of [R-UNLIN].   □

5   Classical Sessions Were Mixed All Along

This section introduces the syntax and semantics of classical session types and shows that the language of classical sessions can be embedded in that of mixed sessions.

The syntax and semantics of classical session types are in Figure 9; we follow Vasconcelos [43]. The syntax and the rules for the various judgements extend those of Figures 1 to 8, where we remove choice both from grammar productions (for processes and types) and from the various judgements (operational semantics, subtyping, duality, and typing). On what concerns the syntax of processes, the choice construct of Figure 1 is replaced by new process constructors: output, linear (lin) and replicated (un) input, selection (internal choice) and branching (external choice). The four reduction axioms in Figure 2 that pertain to choice ([R-LinLin], [R-LinUn], [R-UnLin], [R-UnUn]) are replaced by the three axioms in Figure 9. Rule [R-LinCom] describes the output against ephemeral-input interaction, rule [R-UnCom] the output against replicated-input interaction, and rule [R-Case] selects a label in the menu at the other channel end.

The syntax of types features new constructs—linear or unrestricted input and output, and linear or unrestricted external and internal choice—replacing the choice construct in Figure 3. The subtyping rules for the new type constructors are taken from Gay and Hole [15]. Type duality is such that the objects of communication must be equivalent and the continuations (both in communication and choice) must be dual again. We omit the dual rules for $q!S.S' \perp q?T.T'$ and $q\&\{l_i: S_i\}_{i\in I} \perp q\oplus\{l_i: T_i\}_{i\in I}$. The new duality rules are adapted from the coinductive definition of Gay and Hole [15]. The un predicate on types insists on the idea that un-annotated types are unrestricted: $\mathsf{un}(\mathsf{un} \star S.T)$ and $\mathsf{un}(\mathsf{un}\sharp\{l_i: T_i\})$. The typing rule for choice in Figure 8 is replaced by the four rules in Figure 9; these are taken verbatim from Vasconcelos [43].

The embedding of classical session types in mixed sessions is defined in Figure 10. It consists of two maps, one for processes, the other for types. These maps act as homomorphisms on all process and type constructors not explicitly shown. For example $[\![P \mid Q]\!] = [\![P]\!] \mid [\![Q]\!]$. We distinguish one label, msg, and use it to encode input and output (both processes and types). Input and output processes are encoded in choices with one only msg-labelled branch. The output process is qualified as lin (it does not survive reduction) and the input process reads its qualifier q from the incoming process. Choice processes in classical sessions are encoded in choices in mixed sessions. The value transmitted on the mixed session is irrelevant: we pick () of type unit for the output side, and a fresh variable y_i on the input side. Both types are linear.

Input and output types are translated in choice types. For output we *arbitrarily* pick an external choice ($\oplus$), and conversely for the input. The label in the only branch is msg in order to match our pick for processes, and the qualifier is read from the incoming type. For classical choices, we read the qualifier and the view from the incoming type. The type of the communication in the branches of the mixed choice is unit, again so that it matches our pick for processes.

Typing correspondence says that the embedding preserves typability.

Classical syntactic forms

$$
\begin{array}{ll}
P ::= \dots & \text{Processes:} \\
\quad x!v.P & \text{output} \\
\quad qx?x.P & \text{input} \\
\quad x \lhd l.P & \text{selection} \\
\quad x \rhd \{l_i : P_i\}_{i \in I} & \text{branching} \\
T ::= \dots & \text{Types:} \\
\quad q \star T.T & \text{communication} \\
\quad q \sharp \{l_i : T_i\}_{i \in I} & \text{choice}
\end{array}
$$

Classical reduction rules, $P \to P$, (plus [R-RES] [R-PAR] [R-STRUCT] from Figure 2)

$$(\nu xy)(x!v.P \mid \lin y?z.Q \mid R) \to (\nu xy)(P \mid Q[v/z] \mid R) \qquad \text{[R-LINCOM]}$$

$$(\nu xy)(x!v.P \mid \un y?z.Q \mid R) \to (\nu xy)(P \mid Q[v/z] \mid \un y?z.Q \mid R) \qquad \text{[R-UNCOM]}$$

$$\frac{j \in I}{(\nu xy)(x \lhd l_j.P \mid y \rhd \{l_i : Q_i\}_{i \in I} \mid R) \to (\nu xy)(P \mid Q_j \mid R)} \qquad \text{[R-CASE]}$$

Classical subtyping rules, $T <: T$

$$\frac{T <: S \qquad S' <: T'}{q!S.S' <: q!T.T'} \qquad \frac{S <: T \qquad S' <: T'}{q?S.S' <: q?T.T'}$$

$$\frac{J \subseteq I \qquad S_j <: T_j}{q \oplus \{l_i : S_i\}_{i \in I} <: q \oplus \{l_j : T_j\}_{j \in J}} \qquad \frac{I \subseteq J \qquad S_i <: T_i}{q \& \{l_i : S_i\}_{i \in I} <: q \& \{l_j : T_j\}_{j \in J}}$$

Classical type duality rules, $T \perp T$

$$\frac{S \equiv T \qquad S' \perp T'}{q?S.S' \perp q!T.T'} \qquad \frac{S_i \perp T_i}{q \oplus \{l_i : S_i\}_{i \in I} \perp q \& \{l_i : T_i\}_{i \in I}}$$

Classical typing rules, $\Gamma \vdash P$

$$\frac{\Gamma_1 \vdash x : q!T.U \qquad \Gamma_2 \vdash v : T \qquad \Gamma_3 + x : U \vdash P}{\Gamma_1 \circ \Gamma_2 \circ \Gamma_3 \vdash x!v.P} \qquad \text{[T-TOUT]}$$

$$\frac{q_1(\Gamma_1 \circ \Gamma_2) \qquad \Gamma_1 \vdash x : q_2?T.U \qquad (\Gamma_2 + x : U), y : T \vdash P}{\Gamma_1 \circ \Gamma_2 \vdash q_1 x?y.P} \qquad \text{[T-TIN]}$$

$$\frac{\Gamma_1 \vdash x : q \& \{l_i : T_i\}_{i \in I} \qquad \Gamma_2 + x : T_i \vdash P_i \qquad \forall i \in I}{\Gamma_1 \circ \Gamma_2 \vdash x \rhd \{l_i : P_i\}_{i \in I}} \qquad \text{[T-BRANCH]}$$

$$\frac{\Gamma_1 \vdash x : q \oplus \{l_i : T_i\}_{i \in I} \qquad \Gamma_2 + x : T_j \vdash P \qquad j \in I}{\Gamma_1 \circ \Gamma_2 \vdash x \lhd l_j.P} \qquad \text{[T-SEL]}$$

Fig. 9: Classical session types

Theorem 3 (Typing correspondence).

1. *If* $\Gamma \vdash v : T$, *then* $[\![\Gamma]\!] \vdash v : [\![T]\!]$.
2. *If* $\Gamma \vdash P$, *then* $[\![\Gamma]\!] \vdash [\![P]\!]$.

Process translation

$$[\![x!v.P]\!] = \mathsf{lin}\,x\{\mathsf{msg}^!v.[\![P]\!]\}$$

$$[\![qx?y.P]\!] = q\,x\{\mathsf{msg}^?y.[\![P]\!]\}$$

$$[\![x \vartriangleleft l.P]\!] = \mathsf{lin}\,x\{l^!().[\![P]\!]\}$$

$$[\![x \vartriangleright \{l_i\colon P_i\}_{i\in I}]\!] = \mathsf{lin}\,x\{l_i^?y_i.[\![P_i]\!]\}_{i\in I} \quad (y_i \notin \mathrm{fv}(P_i))$$

(Homomorphic for $\mathbf{0}$, $P \mid Q$, $(\nu xy)P$, and if v then P else Q)

Type translation

$$[\![q!S.T]\!] = q\oplus\{\mathsf{msg}^![\![S]\!].[\![T]\!]\}$$

$$[\![q?S.T]\!] = q\&\{\mathsf{msg}^?[\![S]\!].[\![T]\!]\}$$

$$[\![q\oplus\{l_i\colon T_i\}_{i\in I}]\!] = q\oplus\{l_i^!\mathsf{unit}.[\![T_i]\!]\}_{i\in I}$$

$$[\![q\&\{l_i\colon T_i\}_{i\in I}]\!] = q\&\{l_i^?\mathsf{unit}.[\![T_i]\!]\}_{i\in I}$$

(Homomorphic for end, unit, bool, $\mu a.T$, and a)

Fig. 10: Embedding classical session types

Proof. 1. A straightforward rule induction on the hypothesis.

2. By rule induction on the hypothesis. We sketch a few cases.

When the derivation ends with [T-TIN], we use item 1., induction, the fact that $q_1(\Gamma_1 \circ \Gamma_2)$ implies $q_1[\![\Gamma_1 \cdot \Gamma_2]\!]$, and that $(\Gamma_2 + x\colon T), y\colon T = (\Gamma_1, y\colon T)+x\colon S$ because x and y are distinct variables.

When the derivation ends with [T-BRANCH], we obtain $(\Gamma_2 + x\colon T_i), y_i\colon \mathsf{unit} \vdash [\![P_i]\!]$ from the induction hypothesis $\Gamma_2 + x\colon T_i \vdash [\![P_i]\!]$ using weakening (Lemma 1). $\qquad\square$

We complete this section by proving that the classical-mixed translation meets Gorla's good encoding criteria [17]. The five criteria proposed by Gorla ensure that the encoding is meaningful. There are two syntactical and three semantics-related criteria.

Let $\mathcal{C}$ range over classical processes and $\mathcal{M}$ range over mixed choice processes. The map $[\![\cdot]\!] : \mathcal{C} \to \mathcal{M}$ described in Figure 10 is a translation from classical processes to mixed choice processes. To be in line with the criteria, we add the process $\checkmark$ representing a successfully terminating process to the syntax of both the source and the target languages. We denote by $\Rightarrow$ the reflexive and transitive closure of the reduction relations, $\to$, in both the source and target languages. Sometimes we use subscript $\mathcal{M}$ to denote the reduction of mixed choice processes and the subscript $\mathcal{C}$ for the reduction of classical processes, even though it should be clear from context.

We say that a process P does not reduce, $P \nrightarrow$, when it cannot make any reduction step. We say that a process *diverges*, $P \to^\omega$, when P can do an infinite number of reductions. On the other hand, a process is *successful*, $P \Downarrow$, if P reduces to a process in parallel with a success $\checkmark$, that is, $P \Rightarrow P' \mid \checkmark$. Gorla's criteria view calculi as triples $\langle \mathcal{P}, \rightarrow, \asymp \rangle$, where $\mathcal{P}$ is a set of processes, $\rightarrow$ a reduction relation (the operational semantics), and $\asymp$ is a behavioral equivalence on processes.

The behavioral equivalence $\asymp$ for mixed sessions we use coincides with structural congruence $\equiv$.

The first criterion states that the translation is compositional. For this purpose, we define a context $\mathcal{C}(\_1; \ldots; \_k)$ as a classical process with k holes.

Theorem 4 (Compositionality). *The translation* $[\![\cdot]\!] : \mathcal{C} \longrightarrow \mathcal{M}$ *is compositional, i.e., for every k-ary operator* op *of $\mathcal{M}$ and for every subset N of channel ends, there exists a k-ary context* $\mathcal{C}^N_{\mathrm{op}}(\_1; \ldots; \_k)$ *such that for all $P_1, \ldots, P_k$ with* $\cup_{i=1}^k \mathrm{fv}(P_i) = N$ *and* $[\![\mathrm{op}(P_1, \ldots, P_k)]\!] = \mathcal{C}^N_{\mathrm{op}}([\![P_1]\!]; \ldots; [\![P_k]\!])$.

Proof. The translation of a process is defined in terms of the translation of their subterms, see Figure 10. $\square$

Following the ideas from Peters et al. [34], the translation from mixed to classical sessions can be enriched with a *renaming policy* $\varphi_{[\![\ ]\!]}$, representing a map from channel ends to sequences of channel ends. The following theorem states that the proposed translation is name invariant.

Theorem 5 (Name invariance). *The translation* $[\![\cdot]\!] : \mathcal{C} \longrightarrow \mathcal{M}$ *is name invariant, i.e., for every classical process P and substitution σ,*

$$[\![P\sigma]\!] \begin{cases} = [\![P]\!]\sigma' \text{ if } \sigma \text{ is injective} \\ \asymp [\![P]\!]\sigma' \text{ otherwise} \end{cases}$$

where σ' is such that $\varphi_{[\![\ ]\!]}(\sigma(x)) = \sigma'(\varphi_{[\![\ ]\!]}(x))$, for every channel end x.

Proof. The translation transforms each channel end (x, in Figure 10) into itself. Thus, any substitution is preserved. See Figure 10. $\square$

Operational correspondence states that the embedding preserves and reflects reduction. In our case the embedding is quite tight: one reduction step in classical sessions corresponds to one reduction step in mixed sessions. There is no runtime penalty in running classical sessions on a mixed sessions machine. Further notice that we do not rely on any equivalence relation on mixed sessions to establish the result: mixed-sessions images leave no "junk" in the process of simulating classical sessions.

Theorem 6 (Operational correspondence). *Let P, P' be classical sessions processes and Q a mixed sessions process.*

1. *If $P \rightarrow P'$, then $[\![P]\!] \rightarrow [\![P']\!]$.*
2. *If $[\![P]\!] \rightarrow Q$, then $P \rightarrow P'$ and $[\![P']\!] = Q$, for some P'.*

Proof. Straightforward rule induction on the hypotheses, relying on the fact that $[\![P]\!][v/x] = [\![P[v/x]]\!]$ and $x_i \notin \mathrm{fv}(P_i)$ in the translation of $x \triangleright \{l_i: P_i\}_{i \in I}$. $\square$

The following theorems concern the finite and infinite behavior of classical session processes and their corresponding translations.

Theorem 7 (Divergence Reflection). *The translation* $[\![\cdot]\!] : \mathcal{C} \longrightarrow \mathcal{M}$ *reflects divergence, i.e., if* $[\![P]\!] \rightarrow^{\omega}_{\mathcal{M}}$ *then* $P \rightarrow^{\omega}_{\mathcal{C}}$ *for every process* $P \in \mathcal{C}$.

Proof. Corollary of Theorem 6. □

Theorem 8 (Success Sensitivity). *The translation* $[\![\cdot]\!] : \mathcal{C} \longrightarrow \mathcal{M}$ *is success sensitive, i.e.,* $P \Downarrow_{\mathcal{C}}$ *iff* $[\![P]\!] \Downarrow_{\mathcal{M}}$, *for every process* $P \in \mathcal{C}$.

Proof. Corollary of Theorem 6. □

6   What is in the Way of a Compiler?

This section discusses algorithmic type checking and the implementation of choice in message passing architectures.

We start with type checking and then move to the runtime system. Gay and Hole present an algorithmic subtyping system for classical sessions [15]. Algorithmic subtyping for mixed sessions can be obtained by adapting the rules in Figure 4 along the lines of Gay and Hole. [T-SUB] is the only non syntax-directed rule in Figure 8.We delete this rule and distribute subtype checking among all rules that use, in their premises, sequents $\Gamma \vdash v \colon T$, as usual. Most of the rules include a non-deterministic context split operation. Take rule [T-PAR], for example. Rather than guessing the right split, we take the incoming context and give it all to process P, later reclaiming the unused part. This outgoing context is then passed to process Q. The outgoing context of the parallel composition $P \mid Q$ is that of Q. See, e.g., Vasconcelos or Walker for details [43,48]. Rule [T-RES] requires guessing the type of the two channel ends, so that one is dual to the other. Rather than guessing the type of channel end x, we require the help of the programmer by working with an explicitly typed syntax—$(\nu xy : T)P$—as in Franco and Vasconcelos [12,43], where T refers to the type of channel end x. For the type of channel end y, rather than guessing, we build it from type T; cf. [4,5,7,25].

Running mixed sessions on a message passing architecture need not be an expensive operation. Take one of the communication axioms in Figure 2. We set up a broker process that receives the label-polarity pairs of both processes ($\{l_i^{\star}\}_{i \in I}$ and $\{l_j^{\star}\}_{j \in J}$), decides on a matching pair (guaranteed to exist for typed processes), and communicates the result back to the two processes. The processes then exchange the appropriate value, and proceed. If the broker is an independent process, then we exchange five messages per choice synchronisation. This *basic broker* is instantiated for two processes $P \triangleq \text{lin } x(l_1^? z.P_1 + l_2^! v_2.P_1 + l_3^! v_3.P_3)$ and $Q \triangleq \text{lin } y(l_1^! v_1.Q_1 + l_3^? w.Q_3)$ in Figure 11a.

We can do better by piggybacking the values in the output choices together with the label-polarities pairs. The broker passes its decision to the input side in the form of a triple label-polarity-value, yielding one less message exchanged, as showcased in Figure 11b.

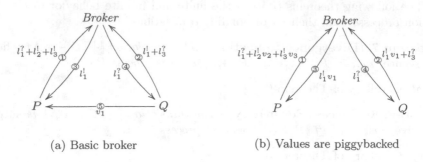

(a) Basic broker   (b) Values are piggybacked

Fig. 11: Broker is an independent process

(a) P is the broker   (b) Q is the broker

Fig. 12: Broker is P or Q

Finally, we observe that the broker need not be an independent process; it can ɔcated at one of the choice processes. This reduces the number of messages to two messages in the general case, as described in Figures 12a and 12b either P is the broker or Q is the broker. Even if the value was already s⸱ Q in the case that P is the broker, P must still let Q know which choice wa⸱   n, so that Q may proceed with the appropriate branch.

H⸱   ⸱r, in particular cases one message may be enough. Take, for instance a proc⸱   ⸱ ≜ un $x(l_1^! v_1.P' + l_2^! v_2.P')$. Independently of which branch is taken, the proc⸱   ɔroceeds as P'. Thus, if the broker is located in a process Q, then P needs n⸱   be informed of the selected choice. The same is true for classical sessions whɛ   selection is a mixed-out choice of a single branch.

There are vo other aspects that one should discuss when implementing mixed sessions n a message passing architecture other than the number of messages exchang̜ ɔd.

The first is related the type of broker used and to which values are revealed in a choice to the other party. In the case of the basic broker, only the chosen option value is revealed, and never to the broker itself. However, when we piggyback the values in the second type of broker, all values in the choice branches are revealed to the broker, even if they are not used in the end. This is even more striking in the case where one of the processes is the broker—the other party has access to all the possible values, independently of the choice that is taken.

The second aspect is also related to the values themselves which, in order to be presented in the choice, values must be computed *a priori*, even if they are not used in the choice.

When dealing with the privacy of the values, we can choose which type of broker to use depending on how much we want to reveal to the other party. However, to prevent computing before a branch is chosen, one should instead use classical sessions.

7   Related Work

The origin of choice Free (completely unrestricted) choice is central to process algebras, including BPA and CCS [3,26]. Here we usually find processes of the form $P + Q$, where P and Q are arbitrary process. Free choice is also present in the very first proposal of the π-calculus [30,31], even if Milner later uses guarded choice [28]. Sangiorgi and Walker's book builds on the pi-calculus with guarded (mixed) choice [38]. Guarded choices in all preceding proposals operate on possibly distinct channels—$x!\text{true}.P + y?z.Q$— whereas choices on mixed sessions run on a common channel—$x(l!\text{true}.P + m?y.Q)$. Kouzapas and Yoshida introduce the notion of mixed session in the context of multiparty session types [24]. Multiparty session types are projected into binary session types, hence the authors also consider mixed choices for binary sessions. This language is not as concise as the one we present, probably because it is designed so as to match projection from multiparty types.

Labelled-choices were embedded in the theory of session types by Honda et al. [18,19,41], where one finds primitives for value passing—$x!\text{true}.P$ and $x?y.Q$—and, separately, for choice in the form of labelled selection—$x \lhd l.P$— and branching—$x \rhd \{l_i : P_i\}_{i \in I}$—see Section 5. Coalescing label selection with output and branching with input was proposed by Vasconcelos [44] (and later used by Sangiorgi [37]) as a means to describe concurrent objects. Demangeon and Honda use a similar language to study embeddings of calculi for functions and for session-based communication [9]. All these languages offer only separated (unmixed) choices and only on the input side.

Mixed choices in the Singularity operating system Concrete syntax apart, the language of linear mixed choices is quite similar to that of channel contracts in Sing# [10]. Rather than explicit recursive types, Sing# contracts uses named states (akin to typestates [40]), providing for more legible contracts. In Sing#, each state in a contract corresponds to a mixed session $\text{lin\&}\{l_i^\star S_i.T_i\}$ (contracts are always written from the consumer side) where each l_i denotes a message tag, $\star$ the message direction (! or ?), S_i the type of the value in the message, and T_i the next state.

Stengel and Bultan showed that processes that follow Sing# contracts can engage in communication errors [39]. They further provide a realizability condition for contracts that essentially rules out mixed choices. Bono and Padovani present a calculus and a type system that models Sing# [6,7]. The type system ensures that well-typed processes are exempt from communication errors, but the language of types excludes mixed-choices. So it seems that Sing#-like languages only function properly under separated choice, yet our work survives under mixed choices. Contradiction? No! Sing# features asynchronous (or buffered) semantics whereas mixed sessions run under synchronous semantics. The operational semantics makes all the difference in this case.

Synchronicity, asynchronicity, and choice Pierce and Turner identified the problem: "In an asynchronous language guarded choice should be restricted still further since an asynchronous output in a choice is sensitive to buffering" [36] and Peters et al. state that "a discussion on synchrony versus asynchrony cannot be separated from a discussion on choice" [34,35]. Based on classical sessions, mixed sessions are naturally synchronous. The naive introduction of an asynchronous semantics would ruin the main results of the language (see Section 4). Asynchronous semantics are known to be compatible with classical sessions; see Honda et al. [20,21] for multiparty asynchronous session types and Fowler et al. [11] and Gay and Vasconcelos [16] for two examples of functional languages with session types and asynchronous semantics. So one can ask whether a language can be designed where mixed-choices are handled synchronously and separated-choices asynchronously, a type-guided operational semantics with by-default asynchronous semantics, reverting to a synchronous semantics when in presence of mixed-choices.

Separation results P ˋamidessi shows that the π-calculus with mixed choice is more expressive tha ` subset with separated choice [32]. Gorla provides a simpler proof [17] ´   ˋame result and Peters and Nestmann analyse the problem from the per.   of breaking initial symmetries in separated-choice processes [33]. Unlike the   ulus with separated choices, mixed choices operate on the same channel an.   ˋuided by types. It would be interesting to look into separation results for clas.   sessions and mixed sessions. Are mixed sessions more expressive than classiˋ   ˋssion under some widely accepted criteria (those of Gorla [17], for example)?

The origin of mixed sessions Mixed sessionˋ ˋawned on us when looking into an algorithm to decide the equivalence of conte.ˋt-free session types [1,42]. The algorithm translates types into (simple) context-free grammars. The decision procedure runs on arbitrary simple grammars: the right-hand sides of grammar productions may start with a label-output or a label-input pair for the same non-terminal symbol at the left of the production. We then decided to explore mixed sessions and picked the simplest possible language for the effect: the π-calculus. It would be interesting to look into mixed context-free session types, given that decidability of type equivalence is guaranteed.

8   Conclusion

We introduce mixed sessions: session types with mixed choice. Classical session types feature separated choice; in fact all the proposals in the literature we are aware of provide for choice on the input side only, even if we can easily think of choice on the output side. Mixed sessions increase flexibility in programming and are easily realisable in conventional message passing architectures.

Mixed choices come with a type system featuring subtyping. Typability is preserved by reduction. Furthermore well-typed programs are exempt from run-time errors. We provide suggestions on how to derive a type checking procedure, even if we do not formalise it. Classical session types are a particular case of mixed sessions: we provide for an encoding and show typing and operational correspondences.

We leave open the problem of looking into a *typed* separation result (or a proof of inseparability) between classical sessions and mixed sessions. An interesting avenue for further development includes looking for a hybrid type-guided semantics, asynchronous by default, that reverts to synchronous when in presence of an output choice.

Acknowledgements We thank Simon Gay, Uwe Nestmann, Kirstin Peters, and Peter Thiemann for comments and discussions. This work was supported by FCT through the LASIGE Research Unit, ref. UIDB/00408/2020, and by Cost Action CA15123 EUTypes.

References

1. Almeida, B., Mordido, A., Vasconcelos, V.T.: Checking the equivalence of context-free session types. In: Tools and Algorithms for the Construction and Analysis of Systems - 26th International Conference, TACAS 2020. Lecture Notes in Computer Science, Springer (2020)
2. Barendregt, H.P.: The lambda calculus - its syntax and semantics, Studies in logic and the foundations of mathematics, vol. 103. North-Holland (1985)
3. Bergstra, J.A., Klop, J.W.: Process theory based on bisimulation semantics. In: Linear Time, Branching Time and Partial Order in Logics and Models for Concurrency. Lecture Notes in Computer Science, vol. 354, pp. 50–122. Springer (1988). https://doi.org/10.1007/BFb0013021
4. Bernardi, G., Dardha, O., Gay, S.J., Kouzapas, D.: On duality relations for session types. In: Trustworthy Global Computing. Lecture Notes in Computer Science, vol. 8902, pp. 51–66. Springer (2014). https://doi.org/10.1007/978-3-662-45917-1_4
5. Bernardi, G., Hennessy, M.: Using higher-order contracts to model session types. Logical Methods in Computer Science **12**(2) (2016). https://doi.org/10.2168/LMCS-12(2:10)2016
6. Bono, V., Messa, C., Padovani, L.: Typing copyless message passing. In: Programming Languages and Systems. Lecture Notes in Computer Science, vol. 6602, pp. 57–76. Springer (2011). https://doi.org/10.1007/978-3-642-19718-5_4

7. Bono, V., Padovani, L.: Typing copyless message passing. Logical Methods in Computer Science **8**(1) (2012). https://doi.org/10.2168/LMCS-8(1:17)2012
8. Caires, L., Pfenning, F., Toninho, B.: Linear logic propositions as session types. Mathematical Structures in Computer Science **26**(3), 367–423 (2016). https://doi.org/10.1017/S0960129514000218
9. Demangeon, R., Honda, K.: Full abstraction in a subtyped pi-calculus with linear types. In: CONCUR 2011 - Concurrency Theory. Lecture Notes in Computer Science, vol. 6901, pp. 280–296. Springer (2011). https://doi.org/10.1007/978-3-642-23217-6_19
10. Fähndrich, M., Aiken, M., Hawblitzel, C., Hodson, O., Hunt, G.C., Larus, J.R., Levi, S.: Language support for fast and reliable message-based communication in singularity OS. In: Proceedings of the 2006 EuroSys Conference. pp. 177–190. ACM (2006). https://doi.org/10.1145/1217935.1217953
11. Fowler, S., Lindley, S., Morris, J.G., Decova, S.: Exceptional asynchronous session types: session types without tiers. PACMPL **3**(POPL), 28:1–28:29 (2019). https://doi.org/10.1145/3290341
12. Franco, J., Vasconcelos, V.T.: A concurrent programming language with refined session types. In: Software Engineering and Formal Methods. Lecture Notes in Computer Science, vol. 8368, pp. 15–28. Springer (2013). https://doi.org/10.1007/978-3-319-05032-4_2
13. Garrigue, J., Keller, G., Sumii, E. (eds.): Proceedings of the 21st ACM SIGPLAN International Conference on Functional Programming, ICFP 2016, Nara, Japan, September 18-22, 2016. ACM (2016). https://doi.org/10.1145/2951913
14. Gastin, P., Laroussinie, F. (eds.): CONCUR 2010 - Concurrency Theory, 21th International Conference, CONCUR 2010, Paris, France, August 31-September 3, 2010. Proceedings, Lecture Notes in Computer Science, vol. 6269. Springer (2010). https://doi.org/10.1007/978-3-642-15375-4
15. Gay, S.J., Hole, M.: Subtyping for session types in the pi calculus. Acta Inf. **42**(2-3), 191–225 (2005). https://doi.org/10.1007/s00236-005-0177-z
16. Gay, S.J., Vasconcelos, V.T.: Linear type theory for asynchronous session types. J. Funct. Program. **20**(1), 19–50 (2010). https://doi.org/10.1017/S0956796809990268
17. Gorla, D.: Towards a unified approach to encodability and separation results for process calculi. Inf. Comput. **208**(9), 1031–1053 (2010). https://doi.org/10.1016/j.ic.2010.05.002
18. Honda, K.: Types for dyadic interaction. In: CONCUR '93, 4th International Conference on Concurrency Theory. Lecture Notes in Computer Science, vol. 715, pp. 509–523. Springer (1993). https://doi.org/10.1007/3-540-57208-2_35
19. Honda, K., Vasconcelos, V.T., Kubo, M.: Language primitives and type discipline for structured communication-based programming. In: Programming Languages and Systems. Lecture Notes in Computer Science, vol. 1381, pp. 122–138. Springer (1998). https://doi.org/10.1007/BFb0053567
20. Honda, K., Yoshida, N., Carbone, M.: Multiparty asynchronous session types. In: Proceedings of the 35th ACM SIGPLAN-SIGACT Symposium on Principles of Programming Languages. pp. 273–284. ACM (2008). https://doi.org/10.1145/1328438.1328472
21. Honda, K., Yoshida, N., Carbone, M.: Multiparty asynchronous session types. J. ACM **63**(1), 9:1–9:67 (2016). https://doi.org/10.1145/2827695
22. Kobayashi, N., Pierce, B.C., Turner, D.N.: Linearity and the pi-calculus. In: Conference Record of POPL'96. pp. 358–371. ACM Press (1996). https://doi.org/10.1145/237721.237804

23. Kobayashi, N., Pierce, B.C., Turner, D.N.: Linearity and the pi-calculus. ACM Trans. Program. Lang. Syst. **21**(5), 914–947 (1999). https://doi.org/10.1145/330249.330251
24. Kouzapas, D., Yoshida, N.: Mixed-choice multiparty session types (2020), unpublished
25. Lindley, S., Morris, J.G.: Talking bananas: structural recursion for session types. In: Garrigue et al. [13], pp. 434–447. https://doi.org/10.1145/2951913.2951921
26. Milner, R.: A Calculus of Communicating Systems, Lecture Notes in Computer Science, vol. 92. Springer (1980). https://doi.org/10.1007/3-540-10235-3
27. Milner, R.: Functions as processes. In: Automata, Languages and Programming. Lecture Notes in Computer Science, vol. 443, pp. 167–180. Springer (1990). https://doi.org/10.1007/BFb0032030
28. Milner, R.: The polyadic pi-calculus: A tutorial. ECS-LFCS 91–180, Lab oratory for Foundations of Computer Science, Department of Computer Science, University of Edinburgh (1991), this report was published in F. L. Hamer, W. Brauer and H. Schwichtenberg, editors, Logic and Algebra of Specification. Springer-Verlag, 1993
29. Milner, R.: Functions as processes. Mathematical Structures in Computer Science **2**(2), 119–141 (1992). https://doi.org/10.1017/S0960129500001407
30. Milner, R., Parrow, J., Walker, D.: A calculus of mobile processes, I. Inf. Comput. **100**(1), 1–40 (1992). https://doi.org/10.1016/0890-5401(92)90008-4
31. Milner, R., Parrow, J., Walker, D.: A calculus of mobile processes, II. Inf. Comput. **100**(1), 41–77 (1992). https://doi.org/10.1016/0890-5401(92)90009-5
32. Palamidessi, C.: Comparing the expressive power of the synchronous and asynchronous pi-calculi. Mathematical Structures in Computer Science **13**(5), 685–719 (2003). https://doi.org/10.1017/S0960129503004043
33. Peters, K., Nestmann, U.: Breaking symmetries. Mathematical Structures in Computer Science **26**(6), 1054–1106 (2016). https://doi.org/10.1017/S0960129514000346
34. Peters, K., Schicke, J., Nestmann, U.: Synchrony vs causality in the asynchronous pi-calculus. In: Proceedings 18th International Workshop on Expressiveness in Concurrency. EPTCS, vol. 64, pp. 89–103 (2011). https://doi.org/10.4204/EPTCS.64.7
35. Peters, K., Schicke-Uffmann, J., Goltz, U., Nestmann, U.: Synchrony versus causality in distributed systems. Mathematical Structures in Computer Science **26**(8), 1459–1498 (2016). https://doi.org/10.1017/S0960129514000644
36. Pierce, B.C., Turner, D.N.: Pict: a programming language based on the pi-calculus. In: Proof, Language, and Interaction, Essays in Honour of Robin Milner. pp. 455–494. The MIT Press (2000)
37. Sangiorgi, D.: An interpretation of typed objects into typed pi-calculus. Inf. Comput. **143**(1), 34–73 (1998). https://doi.org/10.1006/inco.1998.2711
38. Sangiorgi, D., Walker, D.: The Pi-Calculus - a theory of mobile processes. Cambridge University Press (2001)
39. Stengel, Z., Bultan, T.: Analyzing singularity channel contracts. In: Proceedings of the Eighteenth International Symposium on Software Testing and Analysis. pp. 13–24. ACM (2009). https://doi.org/10.1145/1572272.1572275
40. Strom, R.E., Yemini, S.: Typestate: A programming language concept for enhancing software reliability. IEEE Trans. Software Eng. **12**(1), 157–171 (1986). https://doi.org/10.1109/TSE.1986.6312929
41. Takeuchi, K., Honda, K., Kubo, M.: An interaction-based language and its typing system. In: PARLE '94: Parallel Architectures and Languages Europe. Lecture Notes in Computer Science, vol. 817, pp. 398–413. Springer (1994). https://doi.org/10.1007/3-540-58184-7_118

42. Thiemann, P., Vasconcelos, V.T.: Context-free session types. In: Garrigue et al. [13], pp. 462–475. https://doi.org/10.1145/2951913.2951926
43. Vasconcelos, V.T.: Fundamentals of session types. Inf. Comput. **217**, 52–70 (2012). https://doi.org/10.1016/j.ic.2012.05.002
44. Vasconcelos, V.T.: Typed concurrent objects. In: Object-Oriented Programming. Lecture Notes in Computer Science, vol. 821, pp. 100–117. Springer (1994). https://doi.org/10.1007/BFb0052178
45. Vasconcelos, V.T.: Fundamentals of session types. In: Formal Methods for Web Services. Lecture Notes in Computer Science, vol. 5569, pp. 158–186. Springer (2009). https://doi.org/10.1007/978-3-642-01918-0_4
46. Wadler, P.: Propositions as sessions. In: ACM SIGPLAN International Conference on Functional Programming. pp. 273–286. ACM (2012). https://doi.org/10.1145/2364527.2364568
47. Wadler, P.: Propositions as sessions. J. Funct. Program. **24**(2-3), 384–418 (2014). https://doi.org/10.1017/S095679681400001X
48. Waker, D.: Advanced Topics in Types and Programming Languages, chap. Substructural Type Systems. The MIT Press (2005)
49. Yoshida, N., Vasconcelos, V.T.: Language primitives and type discipline for structured communication-based programming revisited: Two systems for higher-order session communication. Electr. Notes Theor. Comput. Sci. **171**(4), 73–93 (2007). https://doi.org/10.1016/j.entcs.2007.02.056

Higher-Order Spreadsheets with Spilled Arrays

Jack Williams[1] , Nima Joharizadeh[2] , Andrew D. Gordon[1,3] , and
Advait Sarkar[1,4]

[1] Microsoft Research, Cambridge, UK
{t-jowil,adg,advait}@microsoft.com
[2] University of California, Davis, USA
johari@ucdavis.edu
[3] University of Edinburgh, Edinburgh, UK
[4] University of Cambridge, Cambridge, UK

Abstract. We develop a theory for two recently-proposed spreadsheet mechanisms: *gridlets* allow for abstraction and reuse in spreadsheets, and build on *spilled arrays*, where an array value spills out of one cell into nearby cells. We present the first formal calculus of spreadsheets with spilled arrays. Since spilled arrays may collide, the semantics of spilling is an iterative process to determine which arrays spill successfully and which do not. Our first theorem is that this process converges deterministically. To model gridlets, we propose the *grid calculus*, a higher-order extension of our calculus of spilled arrays with primitives to treat spreadsheets as values. We define a semantics of gridlets as formulas in the grid calculus. Our second theorem shows the correctness of a remarkably direct encoding of the Abadi and Cardelli object calculus into the grid calculus. This result is the first rigorous analogy between spreadsheets and objects; it substantiates the intuition that gridlets are an object-oriented counterpart to functional programming extensions to spreadsheets, such as sheet-defined functions.

1 Introduction

Many spreadsheets contain repeated regions that share the same formatting and formulas, perhaps with minor variations. The typical method for generating each variation is to apply the operations *copy-paste-modify*. That is, the user copies the region they intend to repeat, pastes it into a new location, and makes local modifications to the newly pasted region such as altering data values, formatting, or formulas. A common problem associated with *copy-paste-modify* is that updates to a source region will not propagate to a modified copy. A user must modify each copy manually—a process that is tedious and error-prone.

Gridlets [12] are a high-level abstraction for re-use in spreadsheets based on the principle of *live copy-paste-modify*: a pasted region of a spreadsheet can be locally modified without severing the link to the source region. Changes to the source region propagate to the copy.

© The Author(s) 2020
P. Müller (Ed.): ESOP 2020, LNCS 12075, pp. 743–769, 2020.
https://doi.org/10.1007/978-3-030-44914-8_27

The *central idea of this paper* is that we can implement gridlets using a formula operator G. If a cell a contains the formula

$$G(r, a_1, F_1, \ldots, a_n, F_n)$$

then the behaviour is to copy range r, modify cells a_i with formulas F_i, and paste the computed array in cell a where its elements may be displayed in the cells below and to the right.

Consider the following example:

	A	B	C
1	*"Edge"*	*"Len."*	
2	*"a"*	3	= B2^2
3	*"b"*	4	= B3^2
4	*"c"*	= SQRT(C4)	= C2 + C3

	A	B	C
1	*"Edge"*	*"Len."*	
2	*"a"*	3	9
3	*"b"*	4	16
4	*"c"*	5	25

Source sheet   Evaluated sheet

The table computes and displays a Pythagorean triple, with intermediate calculation spread across many cells. To reuse the table a user creates a gridlet by inserting[5] a G formula in cell A6 as follows.

	A	B	C
	⋮	⋮	⋮
6	= G(A1:C4, B2, 7, B3, 24)		
7			
8			
9			

	A	B	C
	⋮	⋮	⋮
6	*"Edge"*	*"Len."*	
7	*"a"*	7	49
8	*"b"*	24	576
9	*"c"*	25	625

Source sheet   Evaluated sheet

The formula in A6 is interpreted as: *compute the source range* A1:C4 *with* B2 *bound to* 7, *and* B3 *bound to* 24. The result of the formula is an array corresponding to the computed range which then displays in the grid, emulating a *paste* action. A consequence of this design is that this single formula controls the content of a range of cells, below and to the right; we say that it *spills* into these cells.

Our overall goal is to explain the semantics of the gridlet operator G using array spilling. Spilling is not new in spreadsheets: both Microsoft Excel and Google Sheets allow a cell to contain a formula that computes an array, and whose computed value then spills into vacant cells below and to the right. While there is a practical precedent for spilling in spreadsheets, there is no corresponding formal precedent from which to derive a semantics for G. This paper therefore proceeds in two parts.

---

[5] The user may enter this formula either directly, or indirectly via some grid-based interface [12]; details of the user experience are beyond the scope of this paper.

First, we make sense of array spilling and its subtleties. Two formulas spilling into the same cell, or colliding, is one problem. Another problem is a formula spilling into an area on which it depends, triggering a *spill cycle*. Both problems make preserving determinism and acyclicity of spreadsheet evaluation a challenge. We give a semantics of spilling that exploits iteration to determine which arrays spill successfully, and which do not. Our solution ensures that there is at most one array that spills into any address, and that the iteration converges.

Second, we develop three new spreadsheet primitives that implement G when paired with spilled arrays. We present a higher-order spreadsheet calculus, the *grid calculus*, that admits sheets as first-class values and provides operations that manipulate sheet-values. Previous work has drawn connections between spreadsheets and object-oriented programming [5,8,9,15,17], but we give the first direct correspondence by showing that the Abadi and Cardelli object calculus [1] can be embedded in the grid calculus. Our translation constitutes a precise analogy between objects and sheets, and between methods and cells.

In our semantics for gridlets, we make three distinct technical contributions:

- We develop the *spill calculus*, the first formalisation of spilled arrays for spreadsheets. Our first theorem is that the iterative process of spilling we present converges deterministically (Section 4). Our formal analysis of spilled arrays, a feature now available in commercial spreadsheet systems, is a substantial contribution of this work, independent of our gridlet semantics.
- We develop the *grid calculus*, an extension of the spill calculus with three higher-order operators: GRID, VIEW, and UPDATE. These correspond to *copy*, *paste*, and *modify*, and suffice to encode the operator G (Section 5).
- In the course of developing the grid calculus, we realised a close connection between gridlets and object-oriented programming. We make this precise by encoding the Abadi and Cardelli object calculus into the grid calculus. Our second theorem shows the correctness of this encoding (Section 6).

2   Challenges of Spilling

In this section we describe the challenges of implementing spilled arrays. We describe core design principles for spreadsheet implementations and then illustrate how spilled arrays challenge these principles.

2.1   Design Principles for Spreadsheet Evaluation

Spreadsheet implementations rely on the following two properties to be predictable and efficient.

Determinism Evaluation should produce identical output given identical input; this property is exploited for efficient recalculation.

Acyclicity Evaluation should not be self-referential. The dependency graph of a spreadsheet should form a directed acyclic graph and no cell should depend on its own value. Creating self-referential formulas cannot be prevented, but violations of acyclicity should be observable and not cause divergence.

Both properties are satisfied by standard spreadsheet implementations, if we exclude a few nondeterministic worksheet functions such as RAND. Throughout this work we consider only deterministic worksheet functions. Given this assumption, spreadsheet formulas constitute a purely functional language, and so evaluation is deterministic. Cell evaluation tracks a *calculating* state for every cell and raises a circularity violation for any cell that depends on its own value.

Spilled arrays pose a challenge for preserving determinism and acyclicity which we illustrate with examples. For the remainder of our technical developments we drop the leading = from formulas. We begin with core terminology.

Arrays Spreadsheet arrays are finite two-dimensional matrices that use *one-based* indexing and are non-empty. We denote an (m, n) array literal as

$$\{V_{1,1}, \ldots, V_{1,n}; \ldots; V_{m,1}, \ldots, V_{m,n}\}$$

where (,) delimits the n columns and (;) delimits the m rows. We use V to range over values, which are described in Section 3.

Spilling Address a_r (i, j)-spills into address a_t iff the value of a_r is an (m, n) array and a_t is $i - 1$ rows below and $j - 1$ columns right of a_r, where $i \in 1..m$ and $j \in 1..n$. In particular, a_r (1,1)-spills into itself.

Roots, targets, & areas If a_r (i, j)-spills into address a_t we call a_r the *spill root* and a_t a *spill target*. The *spill area* of a_r is the set of its spill targets. The value of a_t is element (i, j) of the array that is the value of a_r.

Consider the following example:

	A	B
1	{10, 20}	
2		

	A	B
1	10	20
2		

Source Sheet   Evaluated Sheet

Address A1 evaluates to a $(1, 2)$ array and is a spill root with spill area $\{A1, B1\}$. Address A1 $(1, 1)$-spills into A1, and $(1, 2)$-spills into B1.

2.2   Spill Collisions

Spill collisions can be *static* or *dynamic*, and may interfere with determinism.

Static Collision Every cell in a spill area should be *blank* except for the spill root; a blank cell has no formula. A static collision occurs when a spill root spills into another non-blank cell, and we say the non-blank cell is an *obstruction*. The choice to read the value from the obstruction or the spilled value violates determinism. We adopt a simple mechanism used by Excel and Sheets to resolve static spill collisions: the root evaluates to an error value, not an array, and spills nowhere. The ambiguity between reading the obstructing cell's value and the root's spilled value is resolved by preventing the root from spilling—we always read the value from the obstructing cell. Consider the following example:

	A	B
1	{10, 20}	40
2		B1 + 2

	A	B
1	ERR	40
2		42

Source Sheet   Evaluated Sheet

The address B1 obstructs spill root A1 and consequently address A1 evaluates to an error value, address B1 evaluates to 40, and address B2 evaluates to 42.

Dynamic Collisions A dynamic collision occurs when a blank cell is a spill target for two distinct spill roots. Dynamic collisions can be resolved in different ways.

- The conservative approach is to say no colliding spill root spills and each root evaluates to an error.
- The liberal approach is to say that every colliding spill root spills. This approach can be non-deterministic because the spill target obtains its value by choosing one of the multiple colliding spill roots. Google Sheets takes the liberal approach.
- An intermediate approach enforces what we call the *single-spill policy*. One root from the set of colliding roots is permitted to spill and the rest evaluate to an error. This approach can be non-deterministic because there is a choice of which root is permitted to spill. Excel takes the single-spill approach.

Consider the following example that uses the single-spill approach:

	A	B
1	B2	{3; 4}
2	{1, 2}	

	A	B
1	2	ERR
2	1	2

	A	B
1	4	3
2	ERR	4

Source Sheet   Root A2 wins   Root B1 wins

Addresses A2 and B1 are spill roots: the former evaluates to an array of size $(1, 2)$ while the latter evaluates to an array of size $(2, 1)$. The value of address A1 depends on which address from the colliding spill roots A2 and B1 are permitted to spill. Arbitrarily selecting which root is permitted to spill violates deterministic evaluation. Sheets and Excel resolve collisions using an ordering that prefers newer formulas. While consecutive evaluations of the same spreadsheet will produce the same result, two syntactically identical spreadsheets constructed in different ways can produce different results. In Section 4 we give a deterministic semantics for spilling that uses a total ordering on addresses to select a single root from a set of colliding roots.

2.3   Spill Cycles

A *spill cycle* occurs when the value of a spill root depends on an address in its spill area. Spill cycles violate acyclicity and subtly differ from cell cycles. A cell cycle occurs when the value of a formula in a cell depends on the value of the cell itself. We know that it is never legal for a cell to read its own value and therefore it is possible to eagerly detect cell cycles during evaluation of a cell. In contrast, a spill cycle only occurs if the cell evaluates to an array that is spilled into a range the cell depends on, so it is not possible to detect the cycle until the cell has been evaluated.

We can thus proactively detect cell cycles, but only retroactively detect spill cycles. To see why, let us consider the following example, wherein we assume the definition of a conditional operator IF that is lazy in the second and third arguments, and the function INC that maps over an array and increments every number and converts ϵ to 0, where ϵ is the value read from a blank cell.

	A	B
1	42	IF(A1 = 42, SUM(B2:B3), INC(B2:B3))
2		
3		

The evaluation of address B1 returns the sum of the range B2:B3. While the value of B1 depends on the values in the range B2:B3, the sum returns a scalar and therefore no spilling is required.

Consider the case where the value in A1 is changed to 43. The address B1 will evaluate the formula INC(B2:B3), first by dereferencing the range B2:B3 to yield $\{\epsilon; \epsilon\}$, and then by applying INC to yield $\{0; 0\}$. The array $\{0; 0\}$ will attempt to spill into the range B1:B2—a range just read from by the formula. The attempt to spill will induce a spill cycle; there is no consistent value that can be assigned to the addresses B1, B2, and B3.

In Section 4 we give a semantics for spilling that uses dynamic dependency tracking to ensure that no spill root depends on its own spill area.

3   Core Calculus for Spreadsheets

In this section we present a core calculus for spreadsheets that serves as the foundation of our technical developments.

3.1   Syntax

Figure 1 presents the syntax of the core calculus. Let a and b range over A1-style addresses, written Nm, composed from a column name N and row index m. A column name is a base-26 numeral written using the symbols A..Z. A row index is a decimal numeral written as usual. Let m and n range over positive natural numbers which we typically use to denote row or array indices. We assume a locale in which rows are numbered from top to bottom, and columns from left to right, so that A1 is the top-left cell of the sheet. We use the terms *address* and *cell* interchangeably. Let r range over *ranges* that are pairs of addresses that denote a rectangular region of a grid. Modern spreadsheet systems do not restrict which

A1-style column name	N	$::= A \mid \ldots \mid Z \mid AA \mid AB \mid \ldots$	
	$m, n \in$	$\mathbb{N}_1$	
Address	a, b	$::= Nm$	
Range	r	$::= a_1 : a_2$	
Value	V	$::= \epsilon \mid c \mid \mathsf{ERR} \mid \{V_{i,j}{}^{i \in 1..m, j \in 1..n}\}$	
Formula	F	$::= V \mid r \mid f(F_1, \ldots, F_n)$	(f function name)
Sheet	$\mathcal{S}$	$::= [a_i \mapsto F_i{}^{i \in 1..n}]$	(a_i distinct and no $F_i = \epsilon$)
Grid	γ	$::= [a_i \mapsto V_i{}^{i \in 1..n}]$	(a_i distinct)

Fig. 1. Syntax for Core Calculus

corners of a rectangle are denoted by a range but will automatically normalise the range to represent the top-left and bottom-right corners. We implicitly assume that all ranges are written in the normalised form such that range B1:A2 does not occur; instead, the range is denoted A1:B2.

A value V is either the blank value ϵ, a constant c, an error ERR, or a two-dimensional array $\{V_{i,j}{}^{i \in 1..m, j \in 1..n}\}$. We write $\{V_{i,j}{}^{i \in 1..m, j \in 1..n}\}$ as short for array literal $\{V_{1,1}, \ldots, V_{1,n}; \ldots; V_{m,1}, \ldots, V_{m,n}\}$.

Let F range over formulas. A formula is either a value V, a range r, or a function application $f(F_1, \ldots, F_n)$, where f ranges over names of pre-defined worksheet functions such as SUM or $\mathsf{PRODUCT}$.

Let $\mathcal{S}$ range over sheets, where a sheet is a partial function from addresses to formulas that has finite domain. We write $[]$ to denote the empty map, and we write $\mathcal{S}[a \mapsto F]$ to denote the extension of $\mathcal{S}$ to map address a to formula F, potentially shadowing an existing mapping. We do not model the maximum numbers of rows or columns imposed by some implementations. Each finite $\mathcal{S}$ represents an unbounded sheet that is almost everywhere blank: we say a cell a is blank to mean that a is not in the domain of $\mathcal{S}$.

Let γ range over grids, where a grid is a partial function from addresses to values that has finite domain. A grid can be viewed as a function that assigns values to addresses, obtained by evaluating a sheet.

3.2 Operational Semantics

Figure 2 presents the operational semantics of the core calculus. Auxiliary definitions are present at the top of Figure 2.

Formula Evaluation The relation $\mathcal{S} \vdash F \Downarrow V$ means that in sheet $\mathcal{S}$, formula F evaluates to value V. A value V evaluates to itself. A function application $f(F_1, \ldots, F_n)$ evaluates to V if the result of applying $[\![f]\!]$ to evaluated arguments is V, where $[\![f]\!]$ is the underlying semantics of f, a total function on values. A single cell range $a:a$ evaluates to V if address a dereferences to V. A multiple cell range $a_1:a_2$ evaluates to an array of the same dimensions, where each value in the array is obtained by dereferencing the corresponding single cell within the range. We write $\mathsf{size}(a_1:a_2)$ to denote the operation that returns the dimensions

$$\text{size}(N_1 m_1 : N_2 m_2) = (m_2 - m_1 + 1, N_2 - N_1 + 1)$$
$$Nm + (i, j) \qquad = (N + j - 1)(m + i - 1)$$

> Formula evaluation: $\mathcal{S} \vdash F \Downarrow V$

$$\frac{}{\mathcal{S} \vdash V \Downarrow V} \qquad \frac{\mathcal{S} \vdash F_i \Downarrow V_i \quad [\![f]\!](V_1, \ldots, V_n) = V}{\mathcal{S} \vdash f(F_1, \ldots, F_n) \Downarrow V} \qquad \frac{\mathcal{S} \vdash a \,!\, V}{\mathcal{S} \vdash a{:}a \Downarrow V}$$

$$\frac{a_1 \neq a_2 \quad \text{size}(a_1{:}a_2) = (m, n) \quad \forall i \in 1..m, j \in 1..n. \; \mathcal{S} \vdash (a_1 + (i, j)) \,!\, V_{i,j}}{\mathcal{S} \vdash a_1{:}a_2 \Downarrow \{V_{i,j}{}^{i \in 1..m, j \in 1..n}\}}$$

> Address dereferencing: $\mathcal{S} \vdash a \,!\, V$

$$\frac{\mathcal{S}(a) = F \quad \mathcal{S} \vdash F \Downarrow V}{\mathcal{S} \vdash a \,!\, V} \qquad \qquad \frac{a \notin \text{dom}(\mathcal{S})}{\mathcal{S} \vdash a \,!\, \epsilon}$$

> Sheet evaluation: $\mathcal{S} \Downarrow \gamma$

$$\mathcal{S} \Downarrow \gamma \stackrel{\text{def}}{=} \forall a \in \text{dom}(\mathcal{S}). \; \mathcal{S} \vdash a \,!\, \gamma(a)$$

Fig. 2. Operational Semantics for Core Calculus

---

of a range written (m, n), where m is the number of rows, and n is the number of columns. We write $a + (i, j)$ to denote the address offset to the right and below a by $i - 1$ rows and $j - 1$ columns. For example, $a + (1, 1)$ maps to a, and $a + (1, 2)$ maps to the address immediately to the right of a. Both $\text{size}(a_1{:}a_2)$ and $a + (i, j)$ are defined in Figure 2.

Address Dereferencing The relation $\mathcal{S} \vdash a \,!\, V$ means that in sheet $\mathcal{S}$, address a dereferences to V. If address a maps to formula F in sheet $\mathcal{S}$, then dereferencing a returns V when F evaluates to V. If address a is not in the domain of $\mathcal{S}$ then dereference a returns the blank value ϵ. We make range evaluation and address dereferencing distinct relations to aid our presentation in Section 4.

Sheet Evaluation The relation $\mathcal{S} \Downarrow \gamma$ means that sheet $\mathcal{S}$ evaluates to grid γ and the relation is defined by point-wise dereferencing of every address in the sheet. Recall the spreadsheet design principles of determinism and acyclicity from Section 2.1. The relations of our semantics are partial functions (as stated in Appendix A of the extended version [21]). As for acyclicity, if there is a cycle where $\mathcal{S}(a) = F$ and evaluation of formula F must dereference cell a, then we cannot derive $\mathcal{S} \vdash F \Downarrow V$ for any V. Although our calculus could be modified to model a detection mechanism for cell cycles, we omit any such mechanism for the sake of simplicity.

Formula	$F ::= \cdots \mid a\#$ (postfix operator)	
Dependency set	$\mathcal{D} ::= \{a_1, \ldots, a_n\}$	
Grid	$\gamma ::= [a_i \mapsto (V_i^{\#}, V_i^{!}, \mathcal{D}_i)^{i \in 1..n}]$	(a_i distinct)
Spill permit	$p ::= \checkmark \mid \times$	
Spill oracle	$\omega ::= [a_i \mapsto (m_i, n_i, p_i)^{i \in 1..n}]$	(a_i distinct)

Fig. 3. Syntax for Spill Calculus (Extends and modifies Figure 1)

---

4   Spill Calculus: Core Calculus with Spilled Arrays

The spill calculus, presented in this section, is the first formalism to explain the semantics of arrays that spill out of cells in spreadsheets. The spill calculus and its convergence, Theorem 1, is our first main technical contribution.

4.1   Syntax

Figure 3 presents the extensions and modifications to the syntax of Figure 1; we omit syntax classes that remain unchanged.

Let F range over formulas, extended to include the postfix root operator $a\#$. The root operator $a\#$ evaluates to an array if address a is a *spill root*. Accessing an array via the root operator instead of a fixed-size range is more robust to future edits. For example, consider the sheet $[A1 \mapsto F, B1 \mapsto \text{SUM}(A1:A10)]$ where formula F evaluates to a $(10, 1)$ array. If the user modifies F such that the formula evaluates to an array of size $(11, 1)$ then the summation in B1 still applies only to the first ten elements that spill from A1, even if the user intends to sum the whole array. The root operator allows a more robust formulation: $[A1 \mapsto F, B1 \mapsto \text{SUM}(A1\#)]$. The summation in B1 applies to the entire array that spills from A1, regardless of its size. Section 4.3 shows the full semantics of the root operator.

Let $\mathcal{D}$ range over dependency sets, which denote a set of addresses that a formula bound to an address depends on.

Let γ range over grids, which now map addresses to tuples of the form $(V^{\#}, V^{!}, \mathcal{D})$. If $\gamma(a) = (V^{\#}, V^{!}, \mathcal{D})$ then $V^{\#}$ is the pre-spill value obtained by applying the root operator $\#$ to a, while $V^{!}$ is the post-spill value obtained by evaluating a, and $\mathcal{D}$ is the dependency set required to dereference a. Each dereferenced address has both a pre-spill and post-spill value, even if the cell content does not spill. If the pre-spill value is not an array, it cannot spill, and the post-spill value equals the pre-spill value.

Let p range over spill permits, where $\checkmark$ denotes that a root is permitted to spill and $\times$ denotes that it is not.

Let ω range over spill oracles, which map addresses to tuples of the form (m, n, p). A spill oracle governs how arrays spill in a sheet.

- If $\omega(a) = (m, n, p)$ we expect a to be a spill root for an (m, n) array:
    - If $p = \checkmark$ the contents of a can spill with no obstruction.

$$\text{Let } \mathcal{S} \stackrel{\text{def}}{=} [\text{A1} \mapsto \{7;8\}, \text{B1} \mapsto \text{IF}(\text{A2} = 8, \{9;10\}, 100)]$$

	A	B
1	$\{7;8\}$	100
2		

Round 1: $\omega_1 = []$

	A	B
1	7	$\{9;10\}$
2	8	

Round 2:
$\omega_2 = [\text{A1} \mapsto (2,1,\checkmark)]$

	A	B
1	7	9
2	8	10

Round 3: $\omega_3 = [\text{A1} \mapsto$
$(2,1,\checkmark), \text{B1} \mapsto (2,1,\checkmark)]$

Fig. 4. Example Spill Iteration

– If $p = \times$ then a cannot spill because either a formula obstructs the spill area, or another spill root will spill into the area.

Oracles track the size of each spilled array so we can find the spill root a of any spill target, and hence obtain the value for a spill target by dereferencing a.

4.2 Spill Oracles and Iteration

As discussed in Section 2.2, spill collisions have the potential to introduce non-determinism if not handled appropriately. Our solution is to evaluate a sheet in a series of rounds, each determined by a *spill oracle*. Given a sheet, a grid is induced by evaluating the sheet and using the oracle to deterministically predict how each root spills. A discrepancy could be a new spill root the oracle missed, or an existing spill root with dimensions differing from the oracle. If any discrepancies are found we compute a new oracle, and start a new round. Iteration halts when the oracle is *consistent* with the induced grid. The notion of a consistent oracle is defined in Section 4.4. We can view the iteration as a sequence of n oracles where only the final oracle is consistent:

$$[] = \omega_1 \longrightarrow \omega_2 \longrightarrow \cdots \longrightarrow \omega_n \text{ and } \omega_n \text{ is consistent}$$

Consider the example in Figure 4. At the top we show the bindings of the sheet; at the bottom we show the oracle and induced grid for each round of spilling.

We define the initial spill oracle as $\omega_1 = []$ and in the first round the oracle is empty. An empty oracle anticipates no spill roots and therefore no roots are permitted to spill. The array in A1 remains collapsed and B1 evaluates using the false branch. Once the sheet has been fully evaluated we determine that ω_1 was not a consistent prediction because there is an array in A1 with no corresponding entry in ω_1. We compute a new oracle that determines that A1 is allowed to spill because the area is blank. We define the new oracle as $\omega_2 = [\text{A1} \mapsto (2,1,\checkmark)]$.

In the second round the root A1 is permitted to spill by the oracle and as a consequence B1 now evaluates to the array $\{9;10\}$—this array is not anticipated by the oracle and remains collapsed. Once the sheet has been fully evaluated we determine that ω_2 was not a consistent prediction because there is an array in

B1 with no corresponding entry in ω_2. We compute a new oracle that determines that B1 is allowed to spill because the area is blank in the grid induced by ω_2. We define the third oracle as $\omega_3 = [A1 \mapsto (2,1,\checkmark), B1 \mapsto (2,1,\checkmark)]$.

In the third and final round the root A1 is permitted to spill by the oracle and B1 evaluates to the array $\{9;10\}$. This time the oracle anticipates the root in B1 and permits the array to spill. Once the sheet has been fully evaluated we determine that ω_3 is a consistent prediction because the spill roots A1 and B1 are contained in the oracle. The iteration is the sequence of three oracles:

$$[] \longrightarrow [A1 \mapsto (2,1,\checkmark)] \longrightarrow [A1 \mapsto (2,1,\checkmark), B1 \mapsto (2,1,\checkmark)]$$

Spill Rejection Spill oracles explicitly track the anticipated size of the array to ensure that spill rejections based on incorrect dimensions can be corrected. Consider the following example:

	A	B	C
1		IF(C2 = 2, $\{10; 20\}$, $\{10; 20; 30\}$)	$\{1; 2\}$
2			
3	$\{1,2,3\}$		

After the first round using an empty spill oracle there are three spill roots: A3 $= \{1,2,3\}$, B1 $= \{10;20;30\}$, and C1 $= \{1;2\}$. There is sufficient space to spill C1 but only space to spill one of A3 and B1; the decision is resolved using the total ordering on addresses. Suppose that we allow A3 to spill such that the new oracle is: $[A3 \mapsto (1,3,\checkmark), B1 \mapsto (3,1,\times), C1 \mapsto (2,1,\checkmark)]$.

After the second round we find that address B1 returns an array of a smaller size because the root C1 spills into C2. Previously we thought B1 was too big to spill but with the new oracle we find there is now sufficient room; by explicitly recording the anticipated size it is possible to identify cases that require further refinement. We compute the new oracle $[A3 \mapsto (1,3,\checkmark), B1 \mapsto (2,1,\checkmark), C1 \mapsto (2,1,\checkmark)]$ that is consistent.

An interesting limitation arises if the total ordering places B1 before A3, which we discuss in Section 4.6.

4.3   Operational Semantics

Figure 5 presents the operational semantics for the spill calculus. The key additions to the relations for formula evaluation and address dereferencing are an oracle ω that is part of the context, and a dependency set $\mathcal{D}$ that is part of the output. We discuss each relation in turn and focus on the extensions and modifications from Figure 2. Auxiliary definitions are present at the top of Figure 5.

Formula Evaluation: $\mathcal{S}, \omega \vdash F \Downarrow V, \mathcal{D}$ The spill oracle ω is not inspected by the relation but is threaded through the definition. Dependency set $\mathcal{D}$ denotes the transitive dependencies required to evaluate F. Evaluating a value or function application is as before, except we additionally compute the dependencies of the

$\text{owners}(\omega, a) = \{(a_r, i, j) \mid \omega(a_r) = (m, n, \checkmark) \text{ and } a_r + (i, j) = a \text{ and } (i, j) \le (m, n)\}$

$\text{area}(a, m, n) = \{a + (i, j) \mid \forall i \in 1..m, \forall j \in 1..n\}$

$\text{size}(V) \quad = \begin{cases} (m, n) & \text{if } V = \{V_{i,j}^{\,i \in 1..m, j \in 1..n}\} \\ \bot & \text{otherwise} \end{cases}$

$$\boxed{\text{Formula evaluation: } \mathcal{S}, \omega \vdash F \Downarrow V, \mathcal{D}}$$

$$\frac{}{\mathcal{S}, \omega \vdash V \Downarrow V, \varnothing} \qquad \frac{\mathcal{S}, \omega \vdash F_i \Downarrow V_i, \mathcal{D}_i \qquad [\![f]\!](V_1, \ldots, V_n) = V}{\mathcal{S}, \omega \vdash f(F_1, \ldots, F_n) \Downarrow V, \bigcup_{i=1}^{n} \mathcal{D}_i}$$

$$\frac{\mathcal{S}, \omega \vdash a \,!\, V^{\#}, V^{!}, \mathcal{D}}{\mathcal{S}, \omega \vdash a\# \Downarrow V^{\#}, \mathcal{D} \cup \{a\}} \qquad \frac{\mathcal{S}, \omega \vdash a \,!\, V^{\#}, V^{!}, \mathcal{D}}{\mathcal{S}, \omega \vdash a{:}a \Downarrow V^{!}, \mathcal{D} \cup \{a\}}$$

$$\frac{a_1 \ne a_2 \qquad}{\text{size}(a_1{:}a_2) = (m, n) \qquad \forall i \in 1..m, j \in 1..n. \;\; \mathcal{S}, \omega \vdash a_1 + (i, j) \,!\, V_{i,j}^{\#}, V_{i,j}^{!}, \mathcal{D}_{i,j}}$$

$$\frac{}{\mathcal{S}, \omega \vdash a_1{:}a_2 \Downarrow \{V_{i,j}^{!\,i \in 1..m, j \in 1..n}\}, \bigcup_{i,j=1,1}^{m,n} \mathcal{D}_{i,j} \cup \{a_1 + (i, j)\}}$$

$$\boxed{\text{Address dereferencing: } \mathcal{S}, \omega \vdash a \,!\, V^{\#}, V^{!}, \mathcal{D}}$$

$$\frac{\text{owners}(\omega, a) = \varnothing \qquad a \notin \text{dom}(\omega) \qquad \mathcal{S}(a) = F \qquad \mathcal{S}, \omega \vdash F \Downarrow V, \mathcal{D}}{\mathcal{S}, \omega \vdash a \,!\, V, V, \mathcal{D}} \quad (1)$$

$$\frac{\text{owners}(\omega, a) = \varnothing \qquad a \notin \text{dom}(\omega) \qquad a \notin \text{dom}(\mathcal{S})}{\mathcal{S}, \omega \vdash a \,!\, \epsilon, \epsilon, \varnothing} \quad (2)$$

$$\frac{\text{owners}(\omega, a) = \varnothing \qquad \omega(a) = (m, n, \times) \qquad \mathcal{S}(a) = F \qquad \mathcal{S}, \omega \vdash F \Downarrow V, \mathcal{D}}{\mathcal{S}, \omega \vdash a \,!\, V, \text{ERR}, \mathcal{D}} \quad (3)$$

$$\frac{\begin{array}{c} (a_r, i, j) \in \text{owners}(\omega, a) \qquad \omega(a_r) = (m, n, \checkmark) \qquad \mathcal{S}(a_r) = F \\ \mathcal{S}, \omega \backslash a_r \vdash F \Downarrow V, \mathcal{D} \qquad \text{size}(V) = (m, n) \qquad \text{area}(a_r, m, n) \cap \mathcal{D} = \varnothing \end{array}}{\mathcal{S}, \omega \vdash a \,!\, (a = a_r \,?\, V : \epsilon), V_{i,j}, \mathcal{D}} \quad (4)$$

$$\frac{\begin{array}{c} (a_r, i, j) \in \text{owners}(\omega, a) \\ \omega(a_r) = (m, n, \checkmark) \qquad \mathcal{S}(a_r) = F \qquad \mathcal{S}, \omega \backslash a_r \vdash F \Downarrow V, \mathcal{D} \qquad \text{size}(V) \ne (m, n) \end{array}}{\mathcal{S}, \omega \vdash a \,!\, (a = a_r \,?\, V : \epsilon), (a = a_r \,?\, V : \epsilon), (a = a_r \,?\, \mathcal{D} : \varnothing)} \quad (5)$$

$$\boxed{\text{Sheet evaluation: } \mathcal{S}, \omega \Downarrow \gamma}$$

$$\mathcal{S}, \omega \Downarrow \gamma \stackrel{\text{def}}{=} \forall a \in \text{dom}(\mathcal{S}). \; \mathcal{S}, \omega \vdash a \,!\, \gamma(a)$$

Fig. 5. Operational Semantics for Spill Calculus

formula. The dependency set required to evaluate a value is $\varnothing$. The dependency set required to evaluate a function application is the union of the dependencies of the arguments. Evaluating a root operation $a\#$ dereferences a and returns the pre-spill value $V^{\#}$. The dependency set required to evaluate a root operation $a\#$ is the dependency set required to dereference a and the address a itself. Evaluating a single cell range $a{:}a$ dereferences a and returns the post-spill value $V^{!}$. The dependency set required to evaluate a single cell range $a{:}a$ is the dependency set required to dereference a and the address a itself. Evaluating a multiple cell range $a_1{:}a_2$ returns an array of the same dimensions, where each value in the array is obtained by dereferencing the corresponding single cell and extracting the post-spill value. The dependency set required to evaluate a multiple cell range is the dependency set required to dereference every address in the range, and the range itself.

Address dereferencing The relation $\mathcal{S}, \omega \vdash a\,!\,V^{\#}, V^{!}, \mathcal{D}$ means that in sheet $\mathcal{S}$ with oracle ω, address a dereferences to pre-spill value $V^{\#}$ and post-spill value $V^{!}$, and depends upon the addresses in $\mathcal{D}$. Five rules govern address dereferencing, based on spill oracle ω and *owners* set $\mathsf{owners}(\omega, a)$.

The set $\mathsf{owners}(\omega, a)$ is key to the operational semantics and denotes the set of owners for address a. If a tuple (a_r, i, j) is in the set $\mathsf{owners}(\omega, a)$, we say a_r *owns* a, meaning that a_r is a spill root that we expect to spill into address a, and that a is offset from a_r by $i-1$ rows and $j-1$ columns. Hence, to dereference a we must first compute the root a_r and extract the $(i,j)^{th}$ spilled value from the root array. Our definition allows an address to own itself, denoted $(a, 1, 1) \in \mathsf{owners}(\omega, a)$, and does not preclude an address having multiple owners, violating the *single-spill policy*. We enforce the single-spill policy in our technical results using an additional well-formedness condition on oracles, defined in Section 4.5.

Rule (1) applies when the address has no owner, the address is not a spill root, and the address has a formula binding in $\mathcal{S}$. The pre-spill and post-spill values are the value obtained by evaluating the bound formula.

Rule (2) applies when the address has no owner, the address is not a spill root, and the address has no formula binding in $\mathcal{S}$. The pre-spill and post-spill values are the blank value ϵ and the dependency set is empty. Rules (1) and (2) correspond to the address dereferencing behaviour described in the core calculus (Section 3) which is lifted to the new relation.

Rule (3) rule applies when the address is a spill root and the root is not permitted to spill. The pre-spill value is the value obtained by evaluating the bound formula; the post-spill value is an error value. If the address has no bound formula then the relation is undefined.

Rules (4) and (5) apply when an address with an *owner* is dereferenced. The owner a_r is omitted from the spill oracle before evaluating the associated formula, denoted by $\mathcal{S}, \omega \backslash a_r \vdash F \Downarrow V, \mathcal{D}$. This prevents cycles when the oracle incorrectly expects the root to spill, but the root does not, and instead depends on the expected spill area. For example, B1 = SUM(B2:B3) and $\omega = [\text{B1} \mapsto (3, 1, \checkmark)]$. The address B1 owns B2 according to ω, therefore dereferencing address B2 requires dereferencing B1, which in-turn depends on B2. If we did not remove

B1 from ω when evaluating the formula bound to B1 we would create a cycle. We remove B1 from ω so that when formula SUM(B2:B3) dereferences B2 a blank value is returned. Genuine spill cycles are detected post-dereferencing using the dependency set.

Rule (4) applies when the address has an owner and the formula bound to the owner evaluates to an array of the expected size according to ω. This rule is only defined when the intersection of the spill root's dependencies and its spill area is empty, preventing spill cycles. The pre-spill value is obtained using the conditional operator $a = a_r ? V : \epsilon$. When the dereferenced cell is the root then the value is the root array, otherwise the value is blank. The post-spill value is obtained by indexing into the root array at the $(i, j)^{th}$ position.

Rule (5) applies when the address has an owner and the formula bound to the owner *does not* evaluate to an array of the expected size according to ω. In this case there is no attempt to spill as the oracle is incorrect. When the dereferenced address is the root then the pre-spill and post-spill values are obtained from the formula, otherwise the pre-spill and post-spill values are blank.

Sheet evaluation: $S, \omega \Downarrow \gamma$ Sheet evaluation in the spill calculus accepts a spill oracle, but is otherwise unchanged from sheet evaluation in the core calculus. The computed grid only contains the value of addresses with a bound formula, and does not include the value of any blank cells that are in a spill area. In contrast, a spreadsheet application would display the value for all addresses, including those within a spill area. Obtaining this view can be done by dereferencing every address in the viewport using the sheet and oracle.

4.4   Oracle Refinement

We have shown how to compute a grid given a sheet and oracle, but we have not considered the accuracy of the predictions provided by the oracle. In Section 4.2 we informally describe an iterative process to refine an oracle from a computed grid; in this section we give the precise semantics of oracle refinement. Figure 6 presents the full definition of oracle refinement.

Consistency The relation $\gamma \models \omega$ states that grid γ is consistent with oracle ω. A grid is consistent if every address is consistent, written $\gamma \models_a \omega$. An address a is consistent in γ and ω if, and only if, the grid and oracle agree on the size of the value at address a. Consistency tells us that the oracle has correctly predicted the location and size of every spill root in the grid, and has not predicted any spurious roots.

Refinement The function refine(S, ω, γ) takes an inconsistent oracle and returns a new oracle that is refined using the computed grid. The function is defined as follows. First, start with subset ω_{ok} of ω that is consistent with γ. Second, collect the remaining unresolved spill roots in γ, denoted γ_r. Finally, recursively select the smallest address in γ_r according to a total order on addresses, determining whether the root is permitted to spill and adding the permit to the accumulating

$$\gamma \models_a \omega \overset{\text{def}}{=} \forall m, n, p.\ (\omega(a) = (m, n, p)) \Leftrightarrow$$
$$\exists V^{\#}, V^!, \mathcal{D}.\ (\gamma(a) = (V^{\#}, V^!, \mathcal{D}) \wedge \text{size}(V^{\#}) = (m, n))$$
$$\gamma \models \omega \overset{\text{def}}{=} \forall a.\ \gamma \models_a \omega$$

$\text{refine}(\mathcal{S}, \omega, \gamma) = \text{decide}(\mathcal{S}, \omega_{\text{ok}}, \gamma_r)$ where

$$\omega_{\text{ok}} = \{a \mapsto (m, n, p) \in \omega \mid \gamma \models_a \omega\}$$
$$\gamma_r = \{a \mapsto (V^{\#}, V^!, \mathcal{D}) \in \gamma \mid \exists m, n.\ \text{size}(V^{\#}) = (m, n) \text{ and } a \notin \text{dom}(\omega_{\text{ok}})\}$$

$\text{decide}(\mathcal{S}, \omega, []) = \omega$
$\text{decide}(\mathcal{S}, \omega, \gamma[a \mapsto (V^{\#}, V^!, \mathcal{D})]) = \text{decide}(\mathcal{S}, \omega[a \mapsto (m, n, p)], \gamma)$
where a is the least element in $\text{dom}(\gamma)$ and $\text{size}(V^{\#}) = (m, n)$

$$p = \begin{cases} \checkmark & \text{if } \forall a_t \in \text{area}(a, m, n).\ a \neq a_t \Rightarrow a_t \notin \text{dom}(\mathcal{S}) \text{ and } \text{owners}(\omega, a_t) = \varnothing \\ \times & \text{otherwise} \end{cases}$$

$\boxed{\text{Spill iteration: } \omega \longrightarrow_S \omega'}$ $\qquad\qquad$ $\boxed{\text{Final oracle: } \mathcal{S} \vdash \omega \text{ final}}$

$$\frac{\mathcal{S}, \omega \Downarrow \gamma \qquad \gamma \not\models \omega \qquad \text{refine}(\mathcal{S}, \omega, \gamma) = \omega'}{\omega \longrightarrow_S \omega'} \qquad\qquad \frac{\mathcal{S}, \omega \Downarrow \gamma \qquad \gamma \models \omega}{\mathcal{S} \vdash \omega \text{ final}}$$

$\boxed{\text{Final sheet evaluation: } \mathcal{S} \Downarrow \gamma}$

$$\mathcal{S} \Downarrow \gamma \overset{\text{def}}{=} [] \longrightarrow_S^* \omega \text{ and } \mathcal{S} \vdash \omega \text{ final and } \mathcal{S}, \omega \Downarrow \gamma$$

Fig. 6. Oracle Refinement

---

oracle. A root is permitted to spill if the potential spill area is blank (excluding the root itself) and each address in the spill area has no owner, thereby preserving the single-spill policy.

Spill iteration The relation $\omega \longrightarrow_S \omega'$ denotes a single iteration of oracle refinement. When a computed grid is not consistent with the spill oracle that induced it, written $\gamma \not\models \omega$, a new oracle is produced using function $\text{refine}(\mathcal{S}, \omega, \gamma)$. We write $\longrightarrow_S^*$ for the reflexive and transitive closure of $\longrightarrow_S$.

Final oracle The relation $\mathcal{S} \vdash \omega$ final states that oracle ω is final for sheet $\mathcal{S}$, and is valid when the grid induced by ω is consistent with ω.

Final sheet evaluation The relation $\mathcal{S} \Downarrow \gamma$ denotes the evaluation of sheet $\mathcal{S}$ to grid γ which implicitly refines an oracle to a final state. The process starts with an empty oracle $[]$ and iterates until a final oracle is found.

4.5   Technical Results

This section presents the main technical result of the spill calculus: that iteration of oracle refinement converges for well-behaved sheets. We begin with preliminary definitions and results.

To avoid ambiguous evaluation every spill area must be disjoint and unobstructed; an oracle is *well-formed* if it predicts non-blank spill roots, and predicts disjoint and unobstructed spill areas, defined below:

Definition 1 (Well-formed oracle).   *We write $S \vdash \omega$ wf if oracle ω is well-formed for sheet S. An oracle ω is well-formed if for all addresses a the following conditions are satisfied:*

1. *If $a \notin \mathrm{dom}(S)$ then $a \notin \mathrm{dom}(\omega)$.*
2. *$|\mathsf{owners}(\omega, a)| \leq 1$.*
3. *If $(a_r, i, j) \in \mathsf{owners}(\omega, a)$ and $a \neq a_r$ then $a \notin \mathrm{dom}(S)$.*

The definition of oracle refinement in Figure 6 preserves well-formedness.

Lemma 1.   *If $S \vdash \omega$ wf and $S, \omega \Downarrow \gamma$ then $S \vdash \mathsf{refine}(S, \omega, \gamma)$ wf.*

Producing well-formed oracles alone is insufficient to guarantee convergence. Oracle refinement would never reach a consistent state if the predicted spill areas were incorrectly sized.

The definition of oracle refinement in Figure 6 predicts spill areas that are correctly sized with respect to the current grid.

Lemma 2.   *If $S \vdash \omega$ wf and $S, \omega \Downarrow \gamma$ then $\gamma \models \mathsf{refine}(S, \omega, \gamma)$.*

Predicting correctly sized spill areas is also insufficient to guarantee convergence. Oracle refinement would never reach a consistent state if it oscillates between permitting and rejecting the same root to spill. Consider the sheet:

$$\text{Let } S \overset{\text{def}}{=} [\text{A1} \mapsto \{1; 2\}, \text{B1} \mapsto \text{IF}(\text{A2} = 2, \{3; 4\}, 0)]$$

Spill iteration would continue indefinitely if refinement cycled between the following two well-formed and correctly sized oracles:

$$[\text{A1} \mapsto (2, 1, \checkmark)] \longrightarrow [\text{A1} \mapsto (2, 1, \times), \text{B1} \mapsto (2, 1, \checkmark)] \longrightarrow \cdots$$

To avoid oscillating spill iteration the process of oracle refinement should be *permit preserving*, defined below:

Definition 2 (Permit preserving extension).   *We write $\gamma \vdash \omega \lesssim \omega'$ if oracle ω' is a permit preserving extension of ω in context γ. Defined as:*

$$\gamma \vdash \omega \lesssim \omega' \overset{\text{def}}{=} \forall a, m, n, p. \ (\gamma \models_a \omega \land \omega(a) = (m, n, p)) \Rightarrow \omega'(a) = (m, n, p)$$

The definition of oracle refinement in Figure 6 is permit preserving.

Lemma 3. *If* $\mathcal{S} \vdash \omega$ wf *and* $\mathcal{S}, \omega \Downarrow \gamma$ *then* $\gamma \vdash \omega \lesssim \mathsf{refine}(\mathcal{S}, \omega, \gamma)$.

Spill iteration should be a converging iteration but this cannot be guaranteed in general; at any given step in the iteration a sheet can fail to evaluate to a grid. This can happen because the sheet contains a cell cycle, spill cycle, or diverging grid calculus term. Instead, we only expect that if the sheet is free from these divergent scenarios then spill iteration must converge. To allow us to dissect different forms of divergence and focus on spill iteration we only consider *acyclic* sheets, defined below:

Definition 3 (Acyclic). *A sheet $\mathcal{S}$ is acyclic if for all ω such that $\mathcal{S} \vdash \omega$ wf, there exists some γ such that $\mathcal{S}, \omega \Downarrow \gamma$.*

For instance, none of the following sheets are acyclic: $[\mathrm{A1} \mapsto \mathrm{A1}]$ has a cell cycle, $[\mathrm{A1} \mapsto \mathrm{B1:C1}]$ has a spill cycle, and $[\mathrm{A1} \mapsto \Omega]$ has a formula Ω that diverges. Divergent terms are not encodable in the spill calculus but are encodable in the grid calculus, as we show in Section 6.1. An alternative approach would be to explicitly model divergence in our semantics of sheet evaluation and show that iteration converges or the sheet diverges. We choose not to pursue this approach to improve the clarity of our operational semantics, but note that our semantics can be extended to model cycles.

For any acyclic sheet, spill iteration will converge to a final spill oracle.

Theorem 1 (Convergence). *For all acyclic $\mathcal{S}$ and ω such that $\mathcal{S} \vdash \omega$ wf, there exists an oracle ω' such that $\omega \longrightarrow_{\mathcal{S}}^* \omega'$ and $\mathcal{S} \vdash \omega'$ final.*

Proof. (Sketch—see Appendix B of the extended version [21] for the full proof.) The value of any address with a binding is a function of its dependencies and the oracle prediction for that address. We inductively define an address as *fixed* if the oracle prediction is consistent for the address, and every address in the spill-dependency set (defined in [21]) is fixed. Lemma 3 states that correct predictions are always preserved, therefore a fixed address remains fixed through iteration and its value remains invariant. The dependency graph of the sheet is acyclic therefore if there is a non-fixed address then there must be a non-fixed address with no dependencies but an inconsistent oracle prediction—we call this a *non-fixed source*. Lemma 2 states that every new oracle correctly predicts the size with respect to the previous grid, therefore any non-fixed sources will be fixed in the new oracle. We conclude by observing that the number of fixed addresses in the sheet strictly increases at each step, and when every address is fixed the oracle is final.

4.6   Limitations and Differences with Real Systems

Permit preservation requires that if the size of an array does not change then the permit (which may be $\times$) is preserved—this property is crucial for our proof of convergence.

Real spreadsheet systems such as Sheets and Excel do not guarantee permit preservation. A root a that is prevented from spilling using a permit $\times$ can later be permitted to spill, even if the size of the associated array does not change. This particular interaction arises when a root that was previously preventing a from spilling changes dimension, freeing a previously occupied spill area. Permitting roots to spill into newly freed regions of the grid is desirable from a user perspective because it reflects the visual aspect of spreadsheet programming where an array will spill into any unoccupied cells.

A limitation of our formalism, if implemented directly, is that there exist some spreadsheets that when evaluated will prevent an array from spilling, despite the potential spill area being blank. Consider the sheet:

$$[A3 \mapsto \{1, 2, 3\}, C1 \mapsto \mathsf{IF}(\mathsf{ISERROR}(A3), 0, \{4; 5; 6\})]$$

When the total ordering used by oracle refinement orders A3 before C1 then the behaviour is as expected: A3 spills to the right and C1 evaluates to an error value. When the total ordering used by oracle refinement orders C1 before A3 then the behaviour appears peculiar: A3 evaluates to an error value and C1 evaluates to 0. The root A3 is prevented from spilling despite there appearing room in the grid! The issue is that the array in A3 never changes size, therefore the permit × assigned to the root is preserved, despite root C1 relinquishing the spill area on subsequent spill iterations.

The fundamental problem is one of constraint satisfaction. We would like to find a well-formed oracle that maximizes the number of roots that can spill in a deterministic manner. The total order on addresses ensures determinism but restricts the solution space. Our approach could be modified to deterministically permute the ordering until an optimal solution is found, however such a method would be prohibitively expensive.

Both Sheets and Excel find the best solution to our example sheet. We expect their implementations do not permute a total order on addresses, but implement a more efficient algorithm that runs for a bounded time. Finding a more efficient algorithm that is guaranteed to terminate remains an open challenge.

The limitation we present in our formalism only arises when a spreadsheet includes dynamic spill collisions and conditional spilling. We anticipate that this is a rare use case for spilled arrays, and does not arise when using spilled arrays to implement gridlets for live copy-paste-modify.

5 Grid Calculus: Spill Calculus with Sheets as Values

In this section we present the grid calculus: a higher-order spreadsheet calculus with sheets as values. The grid calculus extends the spill calculus of Section 4.

5.1 Extending Spreadsheets with Gridlets

The gridlet concept [12] has been proposed but not implemented. Our observation is that spilling a range reference acts much like copy-paste, but lacks local modification. We propose to implement gridlets using spilled arrays, by extending the spill calculus with primitives that implement first-class grid modification.

	A	B	C
1	"Edge"	"Len."	
2	"a"	3	B2^2
3	"b"	4	B3^2
4	"c"	SQRT(C4)	C2 + C3
	$\vdots$	$\vdots$	$\vdots$

	A	B	C
	$\vdots$	$\vdots$	$\vdots$
6	G(A1:C4, B2, 7, B3, 24)		
7			
8			
9			

Source range A1:C4   Gridlet invocation in A6

Revisiting the example from the introduction, there are four key interactions happening in the invocation of a gridlet.

First, select the content in the grid that is to be modified.
Second, apply the selected modifications or updates.
Third, calculate the grid using the modified content.
Fourth and finally, project the calculated content into the grid.

Spreadsheets with spilled arrays support the final step but lack the capabilities to support the first three. We add these capabilities using four new constructs.

First-class sheet values $\langle S \rangle$.
Operator GRID that evaluates to the current sheet.
Operator UPDATE that binds a formula in a sheet-value.
Operator VIEW that evaluates a given range in a sheet-value to an array.

Using these constructs we can implement gridlets, for example:

$$G(A1:C4, B2, 7, B3, 24) \overset{\text{def}}{=}$$
$$VIEW(UPDATE(UPDATE(GRID, B2, 7), B3, 24), A1:C4)$$

Formatting is a core feature of Gridlets, but we omit formatting from the grid calculus for clarity, on the basis that it would be a straightforward addition. We now describe the details of the grid calculus.

5.2   Syntax and Operational Semantics

Figure 7 presents the syntax and operational semantics for the grid calculus. The grid calculus does not require modification of existing rules; we only add formula evaluation rules for the new constructs, and evaluation relations for *views*.

Syntax Let x range over formula identifiers. Let F range over formulas which may additionally be identifiers x, $LET(x, F_1, F_2)$ which binds the result of evaluating F_1 to x in F_2, GRID which captures the current sheet, $UPDATE(F_1, a, F_2)$ which updates a formula binding in a sheet-value, and $VIEW(F, r)$ which extracts a dereferenced range from a sheet-value. Let V range over values which may additionally be a sheet-value $\langle S \rangle$. Let $\mathcal{V}$ range over views; a view is a sheet with a range, denoted $\langle S, r \rangle$. A view range r delimits the addresses to be computed in sheet S.

Identifier $x \in$ IDENT
Formula $F ::= \cdots \mid x \mid \mathsf{LET}(x, F_1, F_2) \mid \mathsf{GRID} \mid \mathsf{UPDATE}(F_1, a, F_2) \mid \mathsf{VIEW}(F, r)$
Value $V ::= \cdots \mid \langle S \rangle$
View $\mathcal{V} ::= (S, r)$

$$\boxed{\text{Formula evaluation: } S, \omega \vdash F \Downarrow V, \mathcal{D}}$$

$$\frac{S, \omega \vdash F_1 \Downarrow V_1, \mathcal{D}_1 \quad S, \omega \vdash F_2[x := V_1] \Downarrow V_2, \mathcal{D}_2}{S, \omega \vdash \mathsf{LET}(x, F_1, F_2) \Downarrow V_2, \mathcal{D}_1 \cup \mathcal{D}_2} \qquad \frac{}{S, \omega \vdash \mathsf{GRID} \Downarrow \langle S \rangle, \varnothing}$$

$$\frac{S, \omega \vdash F_1 \Downarrow \langle S_1 \rangle, \mathcal{D}}{S, \omega \vdash \mathsf{UPDATE}(F_1, a, F_2) \Downarrow \langle S_1[a \mapsto F_2] \rangle, \mathcal{D}_1} \qquad \frac{S, \omega \vdash F \Downarrow \langle S_1 \rangle, \mathcal{D} \quad (S_1, r) \Downarrow V}{S, \omega \vdash \mathsf{VIEW}(F, r) \Downarrow V, \mathcal{D}}$$

$$\boxed{\text{View evaluation: } \mathcal{V}, \omega \Downarrow \gamma}$$

$$(S, r), \omega \Downarrow \gamma \overset{\text{def}}{=} \forall a \in \mathrm{dom}(S) \cap \mathrm{area}(r). \; S, \omega \vdash a \, ! \, \gamma(a)$$

$$\boxed{\text{Spill iteration: } \omega \longrightarrow_{\mathcal{V}} \omega'} \qquad\qquad \boxed{\text{Final oracle: } \mathcal{V} \vdash \omega \text{ final}}$$

$$\frac{(S, r), \omega \Downarrow \gamma \quad \gamma \not\models \omega \quad \mathrm{refine}(S, \omega, \gamma) = \omega'}{\omega \longrightarrow_{(S,r)} \omega'} \qquad \frac{\mathcal{V}, \omega \Downarrow \gamma \quad \gamma \models \omega}{\mathcal{V} \vdash \omega \text{ final}}$$

$$\boxed{\text{Final view evaluation: } \mathcal{V} \Downarrow V}$$

$$(S, r) \Downarrow V \overset{\text{def}}{=} [] \longrightarrow^*_{(S,r)} \omega \text{ and } (S, r) \vdash \omega \text{ final and } S, \omega \vdash r \Downarrow V, \mathcal{D}$$

Fig. 7. Syntax and Operational Semantics for Grid Calculus (Extends Figures 3—6)

Formula evaluation: $S, \omega \vdash F \Downarrow V, \mathcal{D}$ A formula $\mathsf{LET}(x, F_1, F_2)$ evaluates in the standard way. A formula GRID evaluates to a sheet-value that captures the current sheet. A formula $\mathsf{UPDATE}(F_1, a, F_2)$ updates a formula binding in a sheet-value. If evaluating formula F_1 produces sheet-value $\langle S_1 \rangle$ then $\mathsf{UPDATE}(F_1, a, F_2)$ evaluates to the sheet-value where a is bound to F_2 in S_1, denoted $\langle S_1[a \mapsto F_2] \rangle$. A formula $\mathsf{VIEW}(F, r)$ evaluates a sheet-value and extracts a range. If evaluating formula F produces sheet-value $\langle S_1 \rangle$ then $\mathsf{VIEW}(F, r)$ evaluates to the value obtained by evaluating view (S_1, r). View evaluation is defined in Figure 7 and we describe the semantics at the end of the section. Here we address a subtle property of VIEW; evaluating a view (S, r) adds no dependencies to the containing formula. Dependency tracking in our semantics is used to prevent spill cycles and captures dependence between *values* of addresses: the value of a spill root should not depend on the value of an address in the spill area. In contrast, sheet-values depend on the *formula* of an address in the containing sheet, but not the value of an address in the containing sheet. For example:

$$\text{Let } \mathcal{S} \stackrel{\text{def}}{=} [\text{A1} \mapsto \text{VIEW}(\text{UPDATE}(\text{GRID}, \text{A1}, 10), \text{A2}), \text{A2} \mapsto \text{A1}]$$

Sheet $\mathcal{S}$ evaluates to grid $[\text{A1} \mapsto 10, \text{A2} \mapsto 10]$. What are the dependencies of each address? The value of A2 in the grid depends on the value of A1 in the grid. In contrast, the value of A1 in the grid does not depend on the value of A2 in the grid. This is because evaluating the formula in A1 constructs a private grid from which the value of A2 is obtained. However, A1 does depend on the formula f A2 in the containing grid. Our semantics only considers value dependence, therefore the dependency set of A1 is $\varnothing$—the address has no dependence on values in the containing grid.

Formula dependence is vital for efficient recalculation, though we do not model that in our semantics and only use dependency tracking to prevent spill cycles. If an address depends on the value of another address bound in a sheet, then it also depends on the formula of that address. The converse is not true in the presence of sheet-values.

View evaluation: $\mathcal{V}, \omega \Downarrow \gamma$ Evaluation of view $(\mathcal{S}, r)$ with oracle ω is defined in a similar manner as evaluation of sheets, however the induced grid γ is limited to the sheet bindings that intersect the range r. There are two key consequences that arise from limiting the induced grid. First, we only evaluate the bindings in $\mathcal{S}$ required to evaluate the bindings in r. Second, only roots that are within range r are permitted to spill; any root that is outside r remains as an address containing a collapsed array. There is a difference between an address that holds a collapsed array and a root that is prevented from spilling an array by permit $\times$. The former has a pre-spill and post-spill value that is an array; the latter has a pre-spill value that is an array and a post-spill value that is an error.

Spill iteration: $\omega \longrightarrow_{\mathcal{V}} \omega'$ The definition of spill iteration for views is the same as spill iteration for sheets, except that we use view evaluation rather than sheet evaluation.

Final oracle: $\mathcal{V} \vdash \omega$ *final* The definition of a final oracle for views is the same as a final oracle for sheets, except that we use view evaluation rather than sheet evaluation.

Final view evaluation: $\mathcal{V} \Downarrow V$ Evaluating a view $(\mathcal{S}, r)$ computes a final oracle for the view and then evaluates range r in the context of sheet $\mathcal{S}$. Final view evaluation will evaluate range r, rather than extracting values from an induced grid, because viewing a range should sample all values in the range—including blank cells. If we extract values from the induced grid we can only obtain the values for addresses with a binding in r.

5.3   Formulas for Gridlets

We can encode the G operator using primitives from the grid calculus.

$$\llbracket G(r, a_1, V_1, \ldots, a_n, V_n) \rrbracket = \mathsf{VIEW}(\llbracket (a_1, V_1, \ldots, a_n, V_n) \rrbracket, r)$$
$$\llbracket (a_1, V_1) \rrbracket = \mathsf{UPDATE}(\mathsf{GRID}, a_1, V_1)$$
$$\llbracket (a_1, V_1, \ldots, a_{n+1}, V_{n+1}) \rrbracket = \mathsf{UPDATE}(\llbracket (a_1, V_1, \ldots, a_n, V_n) \rrbracket, a_{n+1}, V_{n+1})$$

The G operator translates to the VIEW operator, and any bindings translate to a sequence of UPDATE operations. The initial sheet-value is obtained from the context using the GRID operator.

The translation illustrates that G is not higher-order because every application returns the value obtained by evaluating a view on a sheet-value. A language that only provides G does not permit sheet-values to escape and be manipulated by formulas. This is acceptable when emulating copy-paste because a copy is always taken with respect to the top-level sheet, however this does limit the usefulness of G as an implementation construct. This limitation motivates the design of the grid calculus; as we show in the next section, the grid calculus is capable of encoding other language features.

6   Encoding Objects, Lambdas, and Functions

In this section we give three encodings that target the grid calculus: objects, lambdas, and sheet-defined functions.

6.1   Encoding the Abadi and Cardelli Object Calculus

We introduce the grid calculus to implement gridlets and the concept of live copy-paste. Perhaps surprisingly, the grid calculus can encode object-oriented programming, in particular the untyped object calculus of Abadi and Cardelli [1]. Their calculus is a tiny object-based programming language, akin to a prototype-based language such as Self [6], but capable of representing class-based object-oriented programming via encodings.

We draw a precise analogy between spreadsheets and objects. A sheet is like an object. A cell is like a method name. A formula in a cell is like a method implementation. The GRID operator is like the this keyword. Formula update is like method update.

We assume an isomorphism between method names ℓ and cell addresses a and use ℓ in both the object calculus and grid calculus. We define the translation of object calculus terms to grid calculus formulas, denoted $\llbracket b \rrbracket$, as follows:

$$\llbracket x \rrbracket = x$$
$$\llbracket [\ell_i = \varsigma(x_i)b_i{}^{i \in 0..n}] \rrbracket = \langle [\ell_i \mapsto \llbracket \varsigma(x_i)b_i \rrbracket^{i \in 0..n}] \rangle$$
$$\llbracket b.\ell \rrbracket = \mathsf{VIEW}(\llbracket b \rrbracket, \ell)$$
$$\llbracket b_1.\ell \Leftarrow \varsigma(x)b_2 \rrbracket = \mathsf{UPDATE}(\llbracket b_1 \rrbracket, \ell, \llbracket \varsigma(x)b_2 \rrbracket)$$
$$\llbracket \varsigma(x)b \rrbracket = \mathsf{LET}(x, \mathsf{GRID}, \llbracket b \rrbracket)$$

The translation makes our analogy concrete. We use the LET formula to lexically capture *self* identifiers. The grid calculus allows the construction of diverging formulas, as discussed in Section 4.5. We demonstrate this using a diverging object calculus term.

$$\Omega = [\![[A1 = \varsigma(x)x.A1].A1]\!] = \mathsf{VIEW}(\langle [A1 \mapsto \mathsf{LET}(x, \mathsf{GRID}, \mathsf{VIEW}(x, A1))] \rangle, A1)$$

The operational semantics are preserved by the translation. We assume a big-step relation for object calculus terms, denoted $b \Downarrow o$. The proof is in Appendix $\mathcal{J}$ of the extended version [21].

heorem 2. *If b is a closed and $b \Downarrow o$ then $[], [] \vdash [\![b]\!] \Downarrow [\![o]\!], \varnothing$.*

6.2 Encoding the Lambda Calculus

We give an encoding of the lambda calculus that is inspired by the object calculus embedding of the lambda calculus. We use ARG1 to hold the argument and VAL1 to hold the result of a lambda. In spreadsheet languages both ARG1 and VAL1 are legal cell addresses; for example, address ARG1 denotes the cell at column 1151 and row 1.

$$[\![x]\!] = x$$
$$[\![\lambda x.M]\!] = \mathsf{UPDATE}(\mathsf{GRID}, \mathsf{VAL1}, \mathsf{LET}(x, \mathsf{VIEW}(\mathsf{GRID}, \mathsf{ARG1}), [\![M]\!]))$$
$$[\![M\,N]\!] = \mathsf{VIFW}(\mathsf{UPDATE}([\![M]\!], \mathsf{ARG1}, [\![N]\!]), \mathsf{VAL1})$$

6.3 Encoding Sheet-Defined Functions

A sheet-defined function [14, 17, 19, 20] is a mechanism for a user to author a function using a region of a spreadsheet. We can model a sheet-defined function f as a triple $(\mathcal{S}, (a_0, \ldots, a_n), r)$ that consists of the moat or sheet-bindings for the function, the addresses from the moat that denote arguments, and the range from the moat that denotes the result. The application $f(V_0, \ldots, V_n)$ can be encoded in the grid calculus as follows, where $f = (\mathcal{S}, (a_0, \ldots, a_n), r)$:

$$[\![f(V_0, \ldots, V_n)]\!] = \mathsf{VIEW}([\![(V_0, \ldots, V_n)]\!], r)$$
$$[\![()]\!] = \langle \mathcal{S} \rangle$$
$$[\![(V_0, \ldots, V_{n'+1})]\!] = \mathsf{UPDATE}([\![(V_0, \ldots, V_{n'})]\!], a_{n'+1}, V_{n'+1})$$

7 Related Work

Formal Semantics of Spreadsheets. Our core calculus is similar to previous formalisms for spreadsheets, Several previous works [3, 7, 14, 19] offer formal semantics for spreadsheet fragments. Mokhov et al. [16] capture the logic of recalculating dependent cells. Finally, Bock et al. [4] provide a cost semantics for evaluation of spreadsheet formulas.

Spilling. Major spreadsheet implementations like Sheets [6] and Excel [7] implement spilled arrays [11], but do not document details of the implementation. In [17], authors propose a spilling-like mechanism that allows matrix values in cells to spread across a predefined range—this is closely related to *"Ctrl+Shift+Enter"* *formulas* [8] in Excel. The proposal in [17] is significantly simpler than spilled arrays because the dimension of the spilled area is fixed and declared ahead of time. Sarkar et al. [18] note that spilled arrays violate Kay's *value principle* [13] because a user is unable to edit constituent cells, except for the spill root.

Extending the Spreadsheet Paradigm. Clack and Braine [8] propose a spreadsheet based on a combination of functional and object-oriented programming. Their integration is different from our analogy: in their system, a class is a collection of parameterised worksheets, and a parameterised worksheet corresponds to a method. In gridlets, the grid corresponds to an object and cells on the grid correspond to methods of the object.

Similarity Inheritance in Forms/3. Forms/3 [5] is a visual programming language that borrows the key concept of cell from spreadsheets. Instead of a tabular sheet, cells in Forms/3 are arranged on a *form*: a canvas with no structure. Forms/3 explored an abstraction model called "similarity inheritance" through which a form may borrow cells from another form and optionally modify attributes of certain cells. This resembles substitution in gridlets, however reusing a portion of the tabular grid and spilling into adjacent cells are primary to gridlets, whereas such notions are absent from Forms/3.

Sheet-defined Functions. Sheet-defined functions [17] (SDFs) allow the user to reuse logic defined using formulas in the grid. The user nominates input cells, an output cell, and gives the function a name. When the function is called, a virtual copy of the workbook is instantiated. Arguments to the function are placed in the input cells, the virtual workbook is calculated, and the result from the output cell is returned.

Elastic SDFs [14] generalize SDFs to handle input arrays of arbitrary size. In [4], the authors provide a precise semantics for SDFs, closures and array formulas, but not for spilling. Gridlets are more general than SDFs as each Gridlet invocation can have a unique set of local substitutions, whereas all calls to an SDF share the same arguments, giving greater flexibility to the user.

Error prevention and Error detection. Abraham and Erwig propose type systems for error detection [3] and automatic model inference [2]. Abraham and Erwig [3] provide an operational semantics for sheets that is similar to the core calculus in Section 3, but they do not give a semantics for spilled arrays.

Gencel [10] is a typed "template language" that describes the layout of a desired worksheet along with a set of customized update operations that are specific

---

[6] https://support.google.com/docs/answer/6208276?hl=en

[7] https://aka.ms/excel-dynamic-arrays

[8] https://aka.ms/excel-cse-formulas

to the particular template. The type system guarantees that the restricted set of update operations keeps the desired worksheet free from omission, reference, and type errors.

Cheng and Rival [7] use abstract interpretation to detect formula errors due to mismatch in type. Their technique also incorporates analysis of associated programs, such as VBA scripts, along with formulas on the grid.

8   Conclusion

Repetition is common in programming—spreadsheets are no different. The distinguishing property of spreadsheets is that reuse includes formatting and layout, and is not limited to formula logic. Gridlets [12] are a high-level re-use abstraction for spreadsheets. In this work we give the first semantics of gridlets as a formula. Our approach comes in two stages.

First, we make sense of spilled arrays, a feature that is available in major spreadsheet implementations but not previously formalised. The concept is simple and belies the many subtleties involved in implementing spilled arrays. We present the spill calculus as a concise description of spilling in spreadsheets.

Second, we extend the spill calculus with the tools to implement gridlets. The grid calculus introduces the concept of first-class sheet values, and describes the semantics of three higher-order operators that emulate *copy-paste-modify*. The composition of these operators gives the semantics for gridlet operator G.

Spreadsheet programming bears a resemblance to object-oriented programming, alluded to often in the literature. We show that the resemblance runs deep by giving an encoding of the object calculus into the grid calculus, with a direct parallel between objects and sheets.

Acknowledgements

Thank you to the Microsoft Excel team for hosting the second author during his research internship at Microsoft's Redmond campus. Thank you to Tony Hoare, Simon Peyton Jones, Ben Zorn, and members of the Microsoft Excel team for their feedback and assistance with this work.

Cambridge, UK, and Davis, California, USA
Spreadsheet Day, October 17, 2019

References

1. Abadi, M., Cardelli, L.: A Theory of Objects. Monographs in Computer Science, Springer (1996)
2. Abraham, R., Erwig, M.: Inferring templates from spreadsheets. In: Proceedings of the 28th International Conference on Software Engineering. pp. 182–191. ICSE '06, ACM, New York, NY, USA (2006)
3. Abraham, R., Erwig, M.: Type inference for spreadsheets. In: Proceedings of the 8th ACM SIGPLAN International Conference on Principles and Practice of Declarative Programming. pp. 73–84. PPDP '06, ACM, New York, NY, USA (2006)
4. Bock, A.A., Bøgholm, T., Sestoft, P., Thomsen, B., Thomsen, L.L.: Concrete and abstract cost semantics for spreadsheets. Tech. Rep. TR–2008–203, IT University of Copenhagen (2018)
5. Burnett, M., Atwood, J., Djang, R.W., Reichwein, J., Gottfried, H., Yang, S.: Forms/3: A first-order visual language to explore the boundaries of the spreadsheet paradigm. Journal of functional programming 11(2), 155–206 (2001)
6. Chambers, C., Ungar, D.M.: Customization: Optimizing compiler technology for self, A dynamically-typed object-oriented programming language. In: PLDI. pp. 146–160. ACM (1989)
7. Cheng, T., Rival, X.: Static analysis of spreadsheet applications for type-unsafe operations detection. In: Vitek, J. (ed.) Programming Languages and Systems. pp. 26–52. Springer Berlin Heidelberg, Berlin, Heidelberg (2015)
8. Clack, C., Braine, L.: Object-oriented functional spreadsheets. In: 10th Glasgow Workshop on Functional Programming. pp. 1–12 (1997)
9. Djang, R.W., Burnett, M.M.: Similarity inheritance: a new model of inheritance for spreadsheet vpls. In: Proceedings. 1998 IEEE Symposium on Visual Languages (Cat. No. 98TB100254). pp. 134–141. IEEE (1998)
10. Erwig, M., Abraham, R., Cooperstein, I., Kollmansberger, S.: Automatic generation and maintenance of correct spreadsheets. In: Proceedings of the 27th international conference on Software engineering. pp. 136–145. ACM (2005)
11. Jelen, B.: Excel Dynamic Arrays Straight to the Point. Holy Macro! Books (2018), see also https://blog-insider.office.com/2019/06/13/dynamic-arrays-and-new-functions-in-excel/
12. Joharizadeh, N., Sarkar, A., Gordon, A.D., Williams, J.: Gridlets: Reusing spreadsheet grids. In: Extended Abstracts of the 2020 CHI Conference on Human Factors in Computing Systems. CHI EA '20, ACM, New York, NY, USA (2020). https://doi.org/10.1145/3334480.3382806, http://doi.acm.org/10.1145/3334480.3382806
13. Kay, A.: Computer software. Scientific American 251(3), 52–59 (1984), http://www.jstor.org/stable/24920344
14. McCutchen, M., Borghouts, J., Gordon, A.D., Peyton Jones, S., Sarkar, A.: Elastic sheet-defined functions: Generalising spreadsheet functions to variable-size input arrays (2019), unpublished manuscript available at https://aka.ms/calcintel
15. McCutchen, M., Itzhaky, S., Jackson, D.: Object spreadsheets: A new computational model for end-user development of data-centric web applications. In: Proceedings of the 2016 ACM International Symposium on New Ideas, New Paradigms, and Reflections on Programming and Software. pp. 112–127. Onward! 2016, ACM, New York, NY, USA (2016)
16. Mokhov, A., Mitchell, N., Peyton Jones, S.: Build systems à la carte. PACMPL 2(ICFP), 79:1–79:29 (2018)

17. Peyton Jones, S.L., Blackwell, A.F., Burnett, M.M.: A user-centred approach to functions in Excel. In: ICFP. pp. 165–176. ACM (2003)
18. Sarkar, A., Gordon, A.D., Jones, S.P., Toronto, N.: Calculation view: multiple-representation editing in spreadsheets. In: 2018 IEEE Symposium on Visual Languages and Human-Centric Computing (VL/HCC). pp. 85–93 (Oct 2018). https://doi.org/10.1109/VLHCC.2018.8506584
19. Sestoft, P.: Implementing function spreadsheets. In: Proceedings of the 4th international workshop on End-user software engineering. pp. 91–94. ACM (2008)
20. Sestoft, P., Sørensen, J.Z.: Sheet-defined functions: Implementation and initial evaluation. In: Dittrich, Y., Burnett, M., Mørch, A., Redmiles, D. (eds.) End-User Development. pp. 88–103. Springer Berlin Heidelberg, Berlin, Heidelberg (2013)
21. Williams, J., Joharizadeh, N., Gordon, A.D., Sarkar, A.: Higher-order spreadsheets with spilled arrays (with appendices). Tech. rep., Microsoft Research (2020), https://aka.ms/calcintel

Author Index

Printed in the United States
by Baker & Taylor Publisher Services